CW00933180

Palgrave Handbooks in the Philosophy of Law

Series Editor
Matthew C. Altman
Philosophy & Religious Studies
Central Washington University
Ellensburg, WA, USA

Palgrave Handbooks in the Philosophy of Law is a series of authoritative, contributed volumes covering every major topic in the philosophy of law. Each volume in the series comprehensively explores the full range of scholarly positions and debates, provides key historical background, and engages contemporary social issues. Providing unequaled depth of coverage, this groundbreaking series will help define the subject for years to come.

Matthew C. Altman
Editor

The Palgrave Handbook on the Philosophy of Punishment

palgrave
macmillan

Editor
Matthew C. Altman
Philosophy & Religious Studies
Central Washington University
ELLENSBURG, WA, USA

ISSN 2730-9169 ISSN 2730-9177 (electronic)
Palgrave Handbooks in the Philosophy of Law
ISBN 978-3-031-11873-9 ISBN 978-3-031-11874-6 (eBook)
https://doi.org/10.1007/978-3-031-11874-6

© The Editor(s) (if applicable) and The Author(s), under exclusive licence to Springer Nature Switzerland AG 2023
This work is subject to copyright. All rights are solely and exclusively licensed by the Publisher, whether the whole or part of the material is concerned, specifically the rights of translation, reprinting, reuse of illustrations, recitation, broadcasting, reproduction on microfilms or in any other physical way, and transmission or information storage and retrieval, electronic adaptation, computer software, or by similar or dissimilar methodology now known or hereafter developed.
The use of general descriptive names, registered names, trademarks, service marks, etc. in this publication does not imply, even in the absence of a specific statement, that such names are exempt from the relevant protective laws and regulations and therefore free for general use.
The publisher, the authors, and the editors are safe to assume that the advice and information in this book are believed to be true and accurate at the date of publication. Neither the publisher nor the authors or the editors give a warranty, expressed or implied, with respect to the material contained herein or for any errors or omissions that may have been made. The publisher remains neutral with regard to jurisdictional claims in published maps and institutional affiliations.

Cover illustration: Library of Congress, Prints & Photographs Division, photograph by Carol M. Highsmith [reproduction number, e.g., LC-USZ62-123456]

This Palgrave Macmillan imprint is published by the registered company Springer Nature Switzerland AG.
The registered company address is: Gewerbestrasse 11, 6330 Cham, Switzerland

Series Editor's Preface

Philosophy of law emerged as a distinct subdiscipline only a few hundred years ago, yet today it is one of the most vibrant and important fields of philosophical inquiry. For one thing, philosophy of law is deeply interdisciplinary, lying at the intersection of the humanities and the sciences. General jurisprudence, which investigates the nature of law and its normativity, incorporates social and political philosophy, history, morality, and religion. The theory of punishment not only involves ethics but also political science, criminology, economics, and statistics. And the study of criminal liability includes neuroscience alongside philosophical discussions of agency and free will. As academia begins to challenge traditional divisions of intellectual labor, philosophy of law stands as a testament to the value of crossing disciplinary boundaries.

Furthermore, legal philosophy is relevant to some of our most pressing social concerns. A spotlight on the use of force by police has made us ask what justifies it and the extent of officers' legal liability, as well as whether policing and criminal justice are used to oppress marginalized communities. Feminist and critical race theorists have challenged the universality of legal norms and identified the ways that they have been influenced by sexist, heterosexist, classist, and racist assumptions. During the coronavirus pandemic, stay-at-home and social distancing orders as well as mask and vaccine mandates laid bare tensions between individual rights and public safety. The surge of refugees from Syria, Venezuela, Afghanistan, Ukraine, and elsewhere has tested the capacity of international law to solve global problems. Under the circumstances, philosophers of law are actively involved not only in clarifying the issues but also in guiding real-world decisions. Indeed, philosophers are helping to form public policies—as members of presidential and parliamentary commissions, for example—now more than ever before.

To contribute to these ongoing conversations, the volumes in the *Palgrave Handbooks in the Philosophy of Law* series provide surveys of the major topics in philosophy of law, with a breadth and depth of coverage that distinguishes them from other collections. Chapters have been specially commissioned for this series, and they are written by both established and emerging scholars from all over the world. Contributors not only provide overviews of their subject matter but also explore the cutting edge of the discipline by advancing original theses. These handbooks thus give students a natural starting point from which to begin their work in the field, and they serve as a resource for advanced scholars to engage in meaningful discussions about the theoretical and practical issues surrounding general jurisprudence, rights, punishment, constitutional interpretation, criminal liability, international law, feminist legal philosophy, and more.

In short, the *Palgrave Handbooks in the Philosophy of Law* series has comprehensiveness, accessibility, depth, and philosophical rigor as its overriding goals. These are challenging aims, to be sure, especially when held simultaneously, but that is the task that the excellent scholars who are editing and contributing to these volumes have set for themselves.

Ellensburg, WA, USA

Matthew C. Altman

Preface

In every country in the world, governments purposely inflict suffering on their own citizens in response to supposed wrongdoing. Within this common practice, there is endless variation. There are worse prison conditions at Camp 22 in North Korea than at Pentonville Prison in England, which is worse than Halden Prison in Norway. Most of the developed world has abolished the death penalty, but Japan executes about five people a year, and China executes thousands. Iran sometimes cuts off the hands of thieves who are guilty of stealing; in the United States, such "cruel and unusual punishment" is constitutionally prohibited. Recreational drugs are legal in some places, decriminalized in others, and severely punished elsewhere. In Portugal, drug possession gets you a hearing before a local commission to discuss treatment options; in Singapore, you can be hanged. There is penal diversity even within countries. For example, the United States is actually comprised of fifty-one separate criminal justice systems (fifty states plus the federal government), more if we include tribal courts and the military. In Oregon, "physician-assisted dying" is regulated and legally permitted; in Missouri, assisting someone in "the commission of self-murder" is voluntary manslaughter, a felony.

The reasons to punish that are codified in different countries' criminal laws also vary considerably. Courts and legislatures say that offenders deserve to suffer, that they should be rehabilitated so they can reenter society, and that punishment should deter crime—principles that can come into conflict but are often held simultaneously. Penal institutions are not systematically devised by one body with a coherent set of practical commitments; rather, they are the result of diverse social influences over long histories, meaning that retribution, deterrence, rehabilitation, denunciation, incapacitation, and restoration may all inform the myriad parts of a given system in different ways. And the importance of these principles can ebb and flow over time. For example, in the U.S., rehabilitation as an aim fell into disfavor in the 1970s, replaced by an emphasis on retribution. The effort to give offenders hard treatment because they deserve it has been a precipitating cause of mass incarceration.

Historians can plot trends in how we punish and social scientists can measure its effects on offenders and communities, but philosophers are uniquely equipped to address the normative issues that underlie criminal justice practices. Legal punishment raises many important philosophical questions, including:

- Does the commission of a crime render something right—purposely harming someone—that would otherwise be wrong, or is even justified punishment always the lesser of two evils?
- Does the justification of punishment depend on how it functions in specific legal, political, and social institutions? How do we evaluate institutional actors such as police, prosecutors, judges, and legislators?
- How do we determine the appropriate kind and amount of punishment?
- Do recent advances in neuroscience undermine legal traditions that include folk psychological claims about an offender's state of mind?
- What obligations does society have to its criminals, and are there special obligations to juvenile offenders or members of disadvantaged groups?
- Should there be limits on what society can do to its criminals? Is the death penalty or punitive torture ever appropriate?
- Is punishment inherently wrong—intentionally harmful, barbaric, socially destructive, or ineffective in helping victims—such that it ought to be replaced with something else?

The Palgrave Handbook on the Philosophy of Punishment addresses all these difficult questions and more. It includes thirty-five newly commissioned chapters by some of the most accomplished scholars in the field. Contributors provide accessible introductions to the topics and defend their own positions, in the process confronting some of the most challenging social issues of our time. Thus, the book is an important resource both for students with an interest in punishment theory and for established researchers who want to participate in contemporary debates.

Because punishment is so ubiquitous, we often uncritically assume that it is justified and that existing practices—whatever they may be—are correct, despite the moral risk that we will treat our fellow citizens unjustly. We need philosophers, with their unique ability to scrutinize our theoretical assumptions, to join political scientists, criminologists, and legal scholars, so that together they can generate a thoroughgoing, critical interrogation of the institutions of criminal justice.

Ellensburg, WA, USA Matthew C. Altman

Contents

Notes on Contributors

Craig K. Agule is an Assistant Professor of Philosophy at Rutgers University—Camden. He works on the philosophy of law and moral psychology, focusing particularly on questions of moral and legal responsibility and the ethics of blame and punishment.

Matthew C. Altman is Professor of Philosophy at Central Washington University. He has authored, coauthored, and edited several books on Kant and German philosophy. His most recent monograph is *A Theory of Legal Punishment: Deterrence, Retribution, and the Aims of the State* (2021). In addition to editing this volume, he is series editor of *Palgrave Handbooks in the Philosophy of Law*. He has also published numerous articles on applied ethics, philosophy of law, and the history of philosophy.

Peter Brian Barry is the Finkbeiner Endowed Professor in Ethics and Professor of Philosophy at Saginaw Valley State University. He is the author of *Evil and Moral Psychology* (2012), *The Fiction of Evil* (2016), and *The Ethics of George Orwell* (2023). His interests are in ethics (broadly construed), social and political philosophy, and philosophy of law.

Christopher Bennett is Professor of Philosophy at the University of Sheffield. He is the author of *The Apology Ritual: A Philosophical Theory of Punishment* (2008), as well as numerous articles on topics in moral, political, and legal philosophy; philosophy of action and emotion; and history of philosophy. Recent publications include "The Alteration Thesis: Forgiveness as a Normative Power," *Philosophy & Public Affairs* (2018); "The Authority of Moral Oversight: On the Legitimacy of Criminal Law," *Legal Theory* (2019); "The Problem of

Expressive Action," *Philosophy* (2021); and "How and Why to Express the Emotions: A Taxonomy with Historical Illustrations," *Metaphilosophy* (2021).

Colleen M. Berryessa is an Assistant Professor at the Rutgers University School of Criminal Justice. Her research, utilizing both qualitative and quantitative methods, considers how psychological processes, perceptions, attitudes, and social contexts affect the criminal justice system, particularly related to courts, sentencing, and punishment. She received her Ph.D. in Criminology from the University of Pennsylvania and her B.A. in Government and Mind, Brain, and Behavior from Harvard University.

John D. Bessler is Professor of Law at the University of Baltimore. His 2014 book about the Italian philosopher Cesare Beccaria, *The Birth of American Law: An Italian Philosopher and the American Revolution*, won the Scribes Book Award, an annual award given out since 1961 for "the best work of legal scholarship published during the previous year." He has also taught law at Georgetown University, the University of Minnesota, the George Washington University, Rutgers, and the University of Aberdeen in Scotland. In 2018, he received a University System of Maryland Board of Regents' Faculty Award for his scholarship.

Thom Brooks is Professor of Law and Government at Durham University, where he served as Dean of the Law School from 2016 to 2021. His books include *Rawls's Political Liberalism* (with Martha C. Nussbaum) (2015); *The Oxford Handbook of Global Justice* (2019); *Punishment: A Critical Introduction*, 2nd ed. (2021); and *The Trust Factor* (2022).

Gregg D. Caruso is Professor of Philosophy at SUNY Corning, Visiting Fellow at the New College of the Humanities (NCH London), and Honorary Professor of Philosophy at Macquarie University. His research focuses on free will, moral responsibility, punishment, philosophy of law, jurisprudence, social and political philosophy, moral philosophy, philosophy of mind, moral psychology, and neurolaw. His books include *Rejecting Retributivism: Free Will, Punishment, and Criminal Justice* (2021), *Just Deserts: Debating Free Will* (with Daniel C. Dennett, 2021), and *Free Will and Consciousness: A Determinist Account of the Illusion of Free Will* (2012).

Vincent Chiao is the Tyler Haynes Professor at the University of Richmond School of Law and the Jepson School of Leadership. He writes on the intersection of political philosophy, legal theory and public law, with a particular emphasis on criminal justice.

Leora Dahan Katz is an Assistant Professor at the Hebrew University of Jerusalem Faculty of Law. Her primary areas of research include the philosophy of law, normative ethics, and criminal law theory, with special focus on the philosophy of punishment, blame, and retribution.

Michael Davis is Senior Fellow at the Center for the Study of Ethics in the Professions and Emeritus Professor of Philosophy, Illinois Institute of Technology. Among his recent publications are: *Engineering as a Global Profession* (2021); *Codes of Ethics and Ethical Guidelines: Emerging Technologies, Changing Fields* (edited, with Kelly Laas and Elisabeth Hildt, 2022); and "Ethical Issues in the Global Arms Industry: A Role for Engineers," in *Ethical Dilemmas in the Global Defense Industry* (2021).

Göran Duus-Otterström is Professor of Political Science at the University of Gothenburg. His research interests include the justification of punishment and the relationship between political obligation and the state's right to coerce citizens. His work on punishment has primarily been devoted to exploring various puzzles facing retributivism, but he has also written on fair play as a justification of both punishment and political obligation. He has published articles in such journals as *Law and Philosophy* and *Criminal Law and Philosophy.*

Benjamin Ewing is Assistant Professor at Queen's University Faculty of Law in Kingston, Ontario, Canada, where he teaches criminal law, criminal procedure, and criminal law theory. He is the author or coauthor of multiple book chapters in edited volumes as well as articles published in the *Yale Law Journal*, *Law and Philosophy*, the *American Journal of Criminal Law*, *Criminal Law and Philosophy*, the *Journal of Tort Law*, and the *Canadian Journal of Law & Jurisprudence*.

Edward Feser is Professor of Philosophy at Pasadena City College in Pasadena, California. He is the author of many academic articles and books, including *Aquinas* (2009), *By Man Shall His Blood Be Shed: A Catholic Defense of Capital Punishment* (with Joseph M. Bessette, 2017), and *Aristotle's Revenge: The Metaphysical Foundations of Physical and Biological Science* (2019).

Chad Flanders is a professor of law and philosophy (by courtesy) at Saint Louis University. He received his M.A. and Ph.D. in philosophy from the University of Chicago and his J.D. from Yale Law School. Flanders teaches and writes in the areas of the philosophy of law, law and religion, and criminal law, and he is the editor of *The New Philosophy of Criminal Law* (with Zachary Hoskins, 2016) and *The Rise of Corporate Religious Liberty* (with Micah

Schwartzman and Zoë Robinson, 2016). He is licensed to practice law in Alaska and Missouri.

Farah Focquaert is part of the Department of Philosophy and Moral Sciences at Ghent University. She is a Research Fellow at the Research Foundation—Flanders, a member of the Moral Brain research group, and one of the directors of the Justice Without Retribution Network. Her current research, situated in the field of neuroethics, focuses on the philosophical and ethical issues surrounding neuromodulation research and treatment for psychiatric conditions, examining questions related to personal identity, the mind-body problem, and criminal behavior.

Nathan Hanna is Associate Professor of Philosophy at Drexel University. He specializes in ethics and philosophy of law. His work focuses primarily on the ethics of legal punishment and on related issues such as the nature of moral desert, harm, and moral responsibility. He has also written on topics in epistemology, metaethics, and political philosophy.

Douglas Husak is a Distinguished Professor of Philosophy at Rutgers University in New Brunswick, New Jersey. He holds both a Ph.D. and a J.D. and is the former Editor-in-Chief of both *Law and Philosophy* and *Criminal Law and Philosophy*. He is the author of numerous books and articles about the philosophy of criminal law.

Whitley Kaufman is Professor in the Philosophy Department at the University of Massachusetts Lowell. His areas of research include ethics, the philosophy of law, philosophy of religion, and philosophy of literature. His books include *Justified Killing: The Paradox of Self-Defense* (2008), *Honor and Revenge: A Theory of Punishment* (2012), *Human Nature and the Limits of Darwinism* (2016), and *Seinfeld and the Comic Vision* (2021). He has also published numerous articles in ethics, philosophy of religion, and philosophy of humor and comedy.

Stephen Kershnar is a distinguished teaching professor in the philosophy department at the State University of New York at Fredonia and an attorney. He focuses on applied ethics and political philosophy. Kershnar has written more than one hundred articles and book chapters on such diverse topics as affirmative action, capitalism, equal opportunity, hell, pornography, punishment, reparations for slavery, sexual fantasies, slavery, and torture. He is the author of ten books, including *Desert Collapses: Why No One Deserves Anything* (2021), *Total Collapse: The Case Against Morality and Responsibility* (2018), and *Abortion, Hell, and Shooting Abortion-Doctors: Does the Pro-Life Worldview*

Make Sense? (2017). He graduated from Cornell University and the University of Pennsylvania School of Law.

John Kleinig is Emeritus Professor of Philosophy in the Department of Criminal Justice, John Jay College of Criminal Justice, and in the Ph.D. Program in Philosophy, CUNY Graduate Center. From 1987 to 2011, he was Director of the Institute for Criminal Justice Ethics, CUNY, and editor of the journal *Criminal Justice Ethics*. He is the author/editor of twenty-three books, most recently *Loyalty and Loyalties: The Contours of a Problematic Virtue* (2014), *The Ethics of Patriotism: A Debate* (with Simon Keller and Igor Primoratz, 2015), and *Ends and Means in Policing* (2019).

Hsin-Wen Lee is Assistant Professor of Philosophy at the University of Delaware. Her areas of specialization include political philosophy and philosophy of law. Her research interests include nationalism and the philosophy of criminal punishment. She is currently completing a book-length manuscript on criminal punishment and the protection of rights.

Margaret Martin is an Associate Professor at the Faculty of Law at Western University, in Canada. She holds a Ph.D. from the Faculty of Law at the University of Cambridge. She has held fellowships at the University of Toronto and at Corpus Christie College at the University of Cambridge. Her monograph, *Judging Positivism*, was published in 2014. She writes on topics in legal philosophy, criminal theory, and the history of political thought. Martin is coeditor of the *Canadian Journal of Law and Jurisprudence* in addition to being on the editorial board of *Jurisprudence* and the *American Journal for Jurisprudence*.

Matt Matravers is Professor of Law and Director of the Morrell Centre for Legal and Political Philosophy at the University of York. He is the author of two monographs, *Justice and Punishment* (2000) and *Responsibility and Justice* (2007), and of numerous papers in legal and political philosophy. In addition, he has edited seven volumes, the latest of which is *The Criminal Law's Person* (2022). He has held visiting appointments at Yale University and the University of Minnesota, and is currently Visiting Fellow at the Institute of Criminology and Visiting Professorial Fellow at Fitzwilliam College, both at the University of Cambridge.

Phillip Montague is Professor Emeritus in the Department of Philosophy at Western Washington University. He has published books and articles in ethical theory, applied ethics, social philosophy, political philosophy, and aesthetics, and he has participated in conferences and seminars in those areas as well as in the philosophy of law.

Clark M. Neily III is senior vice president for legal studies at the Cato Institute. His areas of interest include constitutional law, judicial engagement, coercive plea bargaining, police accountability, and gun rights. Neily served as co-counsel in *District of Columbia v. Heller* (2008), in which the Supreme Court held that the Second Amendment protects an individual right to own a gun. Neily received his undergraduate and law degrees from the University of Texas at Austin, and he is the author of *Terms of Engagement: How Our Courts Should Enforce the Constitution's Promise of Limited Government* (2013).

Katrina L. Sifferd is Professor and Chair of Philosophy at Elmhurst University, where she holds the Genevieve Staudt Endowed Chair. She holds a Ph.D. in philosophy from the University of London, King's College. Before becoming a philosopher, she earned a Juris Doctorate and worked as a senior research analyst on criminal justice projects for the National Institute of Justice. She is the author of numerous articles and book chapters on criminal responsibility, folk psychology and law, and punishment. In 2018, she and her colleagues William Hirstein and Tyler Fagan published a monograph titled *Responsible Brains: Neuroscience and Human Culpability*. She currently serves as Co-Editor-in-Chief of the journal *Neuroethics*.

Chris W. Surprenant is Professor of Ethics, Strategy, and Public Policy at the University of New Orleans, where he directs UNO's University Honors Program and UNO's Urban Entrepreneurship and Policy Institute.

Benjamin Vilhauer is Professor of Philosophy at The City College and Graduate Center of the City University of New York. He works on contemporary free will theory and Kant's theory of freedom, along with related issues in the philosophy of punishment and moral psychology. His current project is a non-retributive reconstruction of Kant's theory of freedom.

Lode Walgrave is Emeritus Professor in Criminology at the University Leuven, where he focused on youth criminology and on restorative justice. He received the ESC European Criminology Award in 2008 and the Bianchi Prize for Restorative Justice in 2019. He has given numerous keynotes, guest lectures, and conferences worldwide. He was chair of the International Network for Research on Restorative Justice and of the International Association of Criminology of Youth. Currently, he is associate editor of *The International Journal of Restorative Justice*. He has published more than 400 titles in Dutch (his mother tongue), English, and French, and his work has been translated into Chinese, German, Portuguese, Russian, and Spanish.

Bruce N. Waller is an emeritus professor at Youngstown State University. He is the author of several books, including *Against Moral Responsibility* (2011), *The Stubborn System of Moral Responsibility* (2015), and most recently *Free Will, Moral Responsibility, and the Desire to Be a God* (2020). His CV, reviews of his books, and copies of his published articles can be found at BruceNWaller.com.

Isaac Wiegman is a Lecturer of Philosophy at Texas State University in San Marcos, Texas. His work investigates how evolution has shaped the human mind and the normative implications of that shaping. This work has expanded out from the evolution of emotions like anger and disgust to the origins of virtue, vice, and desert.

Javier Wilenmann is Associate Professor and Director of Centro de Investigación en Derecho y Sociedad at the Faculty of Law of the Universidad Adolfo Ibáñez. His main areas of work relate to the organizational dynamics of criminal justice.

Amelia M. Wirts is an Assistant Professor of Philosophy at the University of Washington. She works in philosophy of punishment, social/political philosophy, feminist theories of oppression, and philosophy of race. In addition to getting a Ph.D. in philosophy, she graduated from Boston College Law School and clerked for the United States Court of Appeals for the Tenth Circuit. Her legal education and training focused on anti-discrimination law, particularly race, sex, and disability-based employment discrimination claims.

Bill Wringe is Associate Professor of Philosophy at Bilkent University. His research interests include the philosophy of punishment, collective obligations, and the philosophy of emotion. He is the author of *An Expressive Theory of Punishment* (2016) and of several papers on "non-paradigmatic" forms of punishment—punishment by authorities other than the state, using non-standard means, or inflicted on offenders who are not fully responsible individual citizens. His most recent paper on this topic (coauthored with Helen Brown Coverdale) appears in *Philosophy Compass*.

Sandy Xie is a Ph.D. student in Criminal Justice at Rutgers University. Her main areas of research interest include neurocriminology, neuroethics, and neuroscience in the criminal justice system, as well as law and culpability, mental health, and overall perceptions of crime and punishment. She received her B.A in Criminology with minors in Sociology and Neuroscience from the

Pennsylvania State University and her M.S. in Criminology from the University of Pennsylvania.

Benjamin S. Yost is Professor of Philosophy, Adjunct at Cornell University. His work focuses on the philosophy of punishment, in particular the moral questions surrounding the death penalty and the punishment of the disadvantaged. He also has a lively interest in Kant's practical philosophy. Yost's book, *Against Capital Punishment*, was published in 2019. He recently coedited *The Movement for Black Lives: Philosophical Perspectives* (2021). Other published work appears in journals such as *Criminal Law and Philosophy*, *Utilitas*, *Journal of the American Philosophical Association*, *Kantian Review*, and *Continental Philosophy Review*.

Leo Zaibert is Andreas von Hirsch Professor of Penal Theory and Ethics at Cambridge University. He is the author of over one hundred publications and has been the recipient of numerous fellowships and invited professorships. Most of his research is centered around our responses to (perceived) wrongdoing, with special emphasis on blame, punishment, and forgiveness. His latest book, *Rethinking Punishment*, came out in 2018.

1

Introduction: Punishment, Its Meaning and Justification

Matthew C. Altman

Punishment would be unnecessary in a society of one. People are punished because they transgress legal boundaries that are established to facilitate communal living. It would be unnecessary in a group of nonrational animals. No one would have the standing to impose the law, and no one could be held accountable for wrongdoing. It would also be unnecessary if we were perfectly virtuous. There would be no wrong in need of deterrence, and no one would deserve to suffer. Therefore, punishment reflects fundamental commitments about what it means to be a responsible, imperfect, intersubjective being. It also reveals that we expect (or hope) to inhabit a basically secure and orderly world, in which people are protected from random violence and loss. At its best, punishment not only promotes our well-being but also protects our freedom, although how it does so is a matter of debate—perhaps by deterring antisocial behavior, treating offenders as blameworthy agents, reinforcing shared norms, or teaching them how to control their impulses and act morally. But punishment can also be used tyrannically—to enforce unjust laws, or to train people to follow orders and be "good citizens."

Because of the power, promise, and risks of punishment, its potential value and potential harms, it is one of the main topics in the philosophy of law. Among other things, philosophers examine what legal punishment is and how it is justified (if it is justified at all), whether it can be evaluated separately

M. C. Altman (✉)
Central Washington University, Ellensburg, WA, USA
e-mail: matthew.altman@cwu.edu

© The Author(s), under exclusive license to Springer Nature Switzerland AG 2023

M. C. Altman (ed.), *The Palgrave Handbook on the Philosophy of Punishment*, Palgrave Handbooks in the Philosophy of Law, https://doi.org/10.1007/978-3-031-11874-6_1

from the state's authority and its political function, and whether alternatives to punishment are morally preferable. They consider which assumptions regarding freedom are foundational to the criminal law, and whether the possibility of determinism changes whom we punish and how. And they apply punishment theory to pressing social issues such as mass incarceration and the death penalty.

1 What Is Legal Punishment?

Philosophical accounts of punishment typically focus on legal punishment as a social practice that is distinct from less formal kinds of punishment at home, at school, and in the workplace. They have elements in common, of course. For example, they all involve the imposition of a burden, deprivation, or suffering; an authority who imposes it; and a rule violation or wrongdoing that warrants it. A teacher scolding a student for disrupting class is similar to a boss docking the pay of an employee who is repeatedly late for work, which is similar to a judge sentencing a defendant to prison after they are found guilty of assault. But there are notable differences. For example, the association between a person and the state is not natural, like the parent-child relationship, but it is also not merely a contractual agreement that one can take or leave at will, like the employer-employee relationship. Outside of authoritarian systems, citizens consent to abide by the laws of their country, but their country is also crucial to their identity and shapes them from their infancy. Socrates said that the state is like a parent to whom we owe obedience—even as he awaited his execution (Plato 1961).

For some philosophers, it is crucial to recognize what all forms of punishment have in common to understand what justifies legal punishment in particular. For example, Leo Zaibert says that what essentially defines punishment is the fact that, in all cases, it is a response to blameworthiness. He then claims that punishing someone because they are blameworthy is an intrinsic good (2006, 181–216). For other philosophers, recognizing the differences between parental, divine, and legal punishment reveals what is distinctive about it. For example, I have argued that, unlike those other punitive practices, the purpose of punishment as a legal institution is to preserve the public order and promote the common good (Altman 2021, esp. 41–53; see also McCloskey 1962; McPherson 1967, 23).

Most philosophers, however, largely ignore punishment in non-legal contexts, and their working definition of punishment reflects that focus. In the 1950s, Antony Flew (1954), Stanley Benn (1958), and H. L. A. Hart (1960) all devised what was later dubbed the "standard definition" (or the "Flew-Benn-Hart definition") of punishment. Hart says that legal punishment typically includes five elements:

1. It must involve pain or other consequences normally considered unpleasant.
2. It must be for an offence against legal rules.
3. It must be of an actual or supposed offender for his offence.
4. It must be intentionally administered by human beings other than the offender.
5. It must be imposed and administered by an authority constituted by a legal system against which the offence is committed. (1960, 4)

So, when a legal authority imposes some burden on a wrongdoer because they committed a crime, that is punishment—at least according to the standard definition.

This raises several questions that have been discussed in the secondary literature. For example, must the state *intend* to inflict pain on offenders, as if there is some value to pain apart from any further purpose? Is that the proper role of the state? Is it not punishment if it ultimately benefits the offender? Can innocents ever be deliberately punished (e.g., framed for crimes they did not commit), or is that ruled out by definition because they are not "actual or supposed offender[s]"? Must a legal rule be promulgated and acknowledged in order for its enforcement to be punishment, as opposed to a mere use of force by those in power?

The standard definition is supposed to be justificatorily neutral—that is, it does not assume that punishment is justified or, if it is, that it is justified by a particular theory. Philosophers typically distinguish the definition of a practice from its justification—the former of which is descriptive ("is") and the latter of which is evaluative ("ought"). But this commonplace distinction has been challenged when it comes to punishment. For example, Thomas McPherson (1967) claims that punishment is such a value-laden concept that, if we exclude its justification from the definition, then we would not adequately account for what punishment is. On this view, to say that someone in prison is being punished is already to give a kind of justification. Although the infliction of harm must be justified, McPherson says, construing it as punishment assumes that it is deserved or serves some other valued purpose. Similarly, Douglas Husak says that suffering can only count as punishment if the authority that inflicts it has a "*punitive intention*" (2000, 963). But we can only know whether the intention is punitive if we know what the authority is trying to accomplish by means of the sanction. Therefore, legal punishment cannot be defined by its structure; it is identified by its function: "We can only recognize a sanction as a punishment if we know what punishment is for" (Husak 2000, 963–64). On this view, the definition must include some theoretical commitment to what punishment is trying to accomplish or why we inflict it, making punishment in a sense "self-justifying" (McPherson 1967, 26). There is still room for evaluation, of course—no one is saying that all punishments are good or equally good—but the question of which punishment is better or worse is not distinct from the question of which action is properly construed *as* punishment rather than, say, an act of aggression or an abuse of power.

There have been other challenges to the standard definition of punishment, most notably from Joel Feinberg (1965), who says that it is at least incomplete. He argues that the Flew-Benn-Hart definition misses the fact that punishment also has a condemnatory social function. What distinguishes punishments from other harms—dying of cancer versus being executed by the state, for example—is essentially the expression of disapproval that punishments are supposed to convey. A parking ticket, although it is an unpleasant consequence imposed by the legal authority, and although it may deter the driver from parking illegally in the future, is not symbolically significant. It is a correction, not a condemnation, a mere penalty rather than a punishment. By contrast, the community's responses to theft, assault, arson, rape, and murder involve judgments that the offenders are blameworthy and that they acted wrongly. Both incarceration and the stigma that offenders face upon release—such as discrimination by potential employers, loss of voting rights, and ineligibility for public benefits—are "conventional symbols of public reprobation" (Feinberg 1965, 402). Feinberg lists four symbolic functions that the law may serve in condemning criminal actions by means of punishment: the state may use punishment to disavow the criminal act by holding the offender responsible (rather than claiming responsibility itself); it may go on record against the offense insofar as punishment announces that the action is wrong ("symbolic nonacquiescence"); it may vindicate a law that is on the books by affirming what it means and enforcing it; or it may absolve others of blame who were previously suspected (1965, 404–8). Adding the expressive function of punishment to the standard definition looks something like this: when a legal authority imposes some burden on a wrongdoer *and reproves them* because they committed a crime, that is punishment. Although this is a definitional claim, it follows that any attempted justification of punishment must not only give reasons to impose hard treatment but must also account for its expressive function in censuring offenders or disapproving of wrongdoing—if, of course, Feinberg is correct.

Another longstanding debate in the secondary literature concerns the intention behind punishment. The idea that punishment must "*involve* pain or other consequences normally *considered* unpleasant" is ambiguous. Some theorists insist that the authority must intend to make the guilty person suffer, a claim that is crucial to the arguments against punishment from David Boonin and Nathan Hanna. They both contend that an agent can only punish another agent if they are trying to harm them (Boonin 2008, 6–21; Hanna 2008, 125–28, 2009, 329–31). So, if we can accomplish the purposes of punishment, whatever they are, without causing harm, then it is morally incumbent on us to abolish punishment. As an alternative, Boonin proposes pure victim restitution (2008, 215–75); Hanna suggests non-punitive measures such as having the offender compensate the state and crime victims, probation, and confinement (for the purpose of incapacitation) (2009, 335–36). In contrast to this interpretation, other theorists, most notably Bill Wringe (2013), claim that punishment need not intend to cause suffering. On his view (following Feinberg), the purpose of punishment is to denounce wrongful actions or to communicate to the public its commitment to shared norms of behavior. Although "burdensome treatment" is typically unpleasant for offenders, the intention is expressive, not punitive. Wringe concludes that, although our existing systems of punishment may be in need of reform, punishment itself should not be abolished. It can be justified.

2 How Is Punishment Justified?

Historically, forms of punishment include death (execution), deprivation (e.g., imprisonment, probation, exile), pain (e.g., punitive torture, flogging, caning), shame (e.g., stocks, branding, "scarlet letters"), or other burdens (e.g., forced labor, monetary fines, restitution). Doing these things to people would be wrong in just about any other context, but all supposedly civilized countries do some of these things to criminals every day. Philosophers disagree about whether and which of these commonly accepted practices are morally right, merely permissible, or wrong, and about how we would justify (or try to justify) them.

For most of human history, punishment practices have been used as a method of social control and a way to dominate one's enemies, both inside and outside the community. Friedrich Nietzsche famously described punishment as a way to sublimate our primitive instincts so that the pleasure we take in harming others can be validated: the idea that we inflict suffering on evil people because they deserve it is a contrivance (1967, II:4–6 [pp. 62–67]). Although they were eventually codified, institutions of legal punishment arose out of social customs and traditional practices rather than being founded on philosophical principle. Therefore, Antony Duff says, "It would clearly be absurd to try to explain any existing penal system, whose historical development reflects an unsystematic diversity of competing influences, in terms of some unitary set of coherent values and purposes" (1986, 5). Most countries are not committed, explicitly or implicitly, to one theoretically homogenous system of criminal justice. Instead, they combine many rationales simultaneously and not always consistently, including deterrence, incapacitation, rehabilitation, retribution, and restoration.

In spite of their non-ideal origins, philosophers have been evaluating systems of legal punishment and inquiring into their justification at least since the time of Socrates. And two theories—or, rather, two classes of theories—have largely dominated the field: consequentialism and retributivism. This distinction parallels a key distinction in normative ethics between utilitarianism and deontological ethics: the former judges the rightness of actions based on whether they maximize happiness, and the latter judges the rightness of principles of acting based on whether they fulfill our duties. According to utilitarianism, happiness is an end in itself (Mill 2001, 7); according to deontological ethics, happiness is only good if someone is worthy of happiness (Kant 1996a, 4:393 [p. 49]). Similarly, in punishment theory, consequentialists believe that the suffering of offenders is intrinsically bad and can be worth it only if it produces the most net benefit compared to the alternatives. In other words, the harm done to the guilty is only instrumentally good, if it is good at all (Bentham 1970, ch. XIII, §2 [p. 158]). By contrast, retributivists believe that the suffering of offenders is intrinsically good. Making them suffer to achieve some social purpose would be to demean them, treating them merely as means to an end (Kant 1996b, 6:331 [p. 473]). It is no coincidence that Jeremy Bentham, an originator of utilitarianism, defended a consequentialist theory of punishment, and Immanuel Kant, an originator of deontological ethics, was committed to retributivism.

Consequentialism is thus forward-looking in the sense that it justifies punishment in terms of the benefits that it produces. For example, Cesare Beccaria writes:

> the purpose of punishment is not that of tormenting or afflicting any sentient creature, nor of undoing a crime already committed. … The purpose, therefore,

> is nothing other than to prevent the offender from doing fresh harm to his fellows and to deter others from doing likewise. (1995, 31)

Different consequentialist theories are defined by what end state they are trying to maximize, such as happiness (utilitarianism), rights-protection, or harm-reduction. To achieve these ends, the state may threaten potential criminals with punishment if they break the law (general deterrence), impose hard treatment on actual offenders to discourage them from recidivating (specific deterrence), restrain criminals to physically prevent them from committing other crimes (incapacitation), or improve an offender's character and prospects (with drug treatment, counseling, education, job training, etc.) so that they do not want or have the need to reoffend (rehabilitation).

Consequentialists look to social scientific research so they can compare the relative effectiveness of different punishment strategies at maximizing the good. Consequentialism would justify capital punishment, for example, only if it reduces violent crime more than alternatives such as life in prison, and if it is comparatively better than lower-cost alternatives such as increased policing or increased spending on public education. Both Bentham and Beccaria appealed to utilitarian principles to argue against contemporary penological practices that they claimed were causes of useless suffering: Bentham argued for prison reform (1970, esp. chs. XII–XV [pp. 143–86]), and Beccaria argued against the death penalty (1995, 66–72).

In contrast to consequentialism, retributivism is backward-looking in the sense that it justifies punishment with reference to what offenders have done. Paradigmatically, retributivists think that wrongdoers should be punished because they deserve to suffer. As Kant puts it,

> *Punishment by a court* ... can never be inflicted merely as a means to promote some other good for the criminal himself or for civil society. It must always be inflicted upon him only *because he has committed a crime*. (1996b, 6:331 [p. 473])

There are many varieties of retributivism, depending on how we conceive of the basis of this desert claim. To take only a few examples, criminals may deserve to be punished because they incurred a debt to society (repayment theory) or took unfair advantage of the system (fair play theory), such that punishment would annul the wrong (annulment theory) or publicly condemn it (denunciation theory) (Cottingham 1979; Walker 1999). What all these theories share is the claim that there is value in punishing the guilty regardless of the costs and benefits.

Retributivists also disagree about what desert claims entail regarding punishment. Specifically, they disagree about the strength of the desert claim: whether it is an absolute duty, a pro tanto obligation (that is, an obligation that must be weighed against other, conflicting obligations), or merely a necessary but insufficient condition for warranting punishment.

1. For the positive or bold retributivist, guilt is necessary and sufficient to justify punishment.
    (a) For the extreme or maximalist retributivist, punishment is morally obligatory, regardless of the costs and benefits.
    (b) For the moderate or minimalist retributivist, punishment is morally permissible, even in the absence of other reasons to punish.
2. For the negative, weak, or modest retributivist, guilt is only necessary for punishment. To justify it, there must also be some other, positive reason to punish, such as promoting the common good.

Kant is usually considered an extreme retributivist, but it is not a widely held position. Most self-described retributivists hold the moderate position. They believe that desert is a good enough reason to punish someone on its own but that, in some cases, we should not give the guilty what they deserve if refraining would promote other important goods. For example, Larry Alexander and Kimberly Kessler Ferzan claim that retributivism places a side-constraint on punishment—innocents cannot be punished, and the guilty cannot be punished more than they deserve—but that there is a plurality of values that punishment could produce: retributive justice is one of them, but societal welfare, distributive justice, and corrective justice are others (2009, esp. 7–10). Any of these other valued ends may moderate our commitment to retribution.

Retributivists also support proportionality in sentencing. On the retributivist view, only the guilty ought to be punished, and the punishment ought somehow to "fit" the crime—with the severity of punishment matching the degree of blame, the seriousness of the wrong, or the amount of harm caused. Kant is a proponent of *lex talionis* (the law of retaliation), according to which the punishment must be equivalent to the crime (1996b, 6:332 [p. 473]), but others believe that proportionality is sufficient, with worse crimes warranting worse punishments. So, on the former interpretation (equality retributivism), murderers must be executed to achieve justice, regardless of whether there is any benefit for the community (Kant 1996b, 6:333 [p. 474]). On another interpretation (proportional retributivism), it would be sufficient to give the worst criminal the worst punishment on a scale (the high-end "anchor point"), even if life in prison without parole were the worst punishment we choose to assign (Nathanson 2001, 72–77).

As complicated as this taxonomy is—consequentialism and retributivism have many variations, as we have seen—it actually oversimplifies things. There are also mixed views that attempt to bring consequentialism and retributivism together in one overarching framework. And there are other theories of punishment that do not fit neatly into one side or the other, such as expressivism and communication theory, societal self-defense theory, rights-forfeiture theory, and restoration theory, among others. Sometimes these theories are versions of consequentialism or retributivism, and different philosophers who seem to be defending the same position end up on different sides of the divide. For example, some theorists claim that the expression of social disapproval is justified insofar as it has a deterrent effect on future crimes (Andenaes 1974, 110–28; see also Braithwaite and Pettit 1990), while others claim that punishment is a kind of secular penance owed to the state that is good in itself (Duff 1986, ch. 9). Other theories do not seem to be either retributivist or consequentialist. For example, Jean Hampton's (1984) moral education theory attempts to confer a benefit on the offender: moral improvement of their character. This is not a deserved harm, nor is it done instrumentally to maximize some outcome (unless virtue is an "outcome"), so it is neither retributivist nor consequentialist (at least not uncontroversially so).

The lines are further blurred by theorists who believe that giving people what they deserve is a crucial element in deterring crime. For example, Paul Robinson and John Darley (1997) claim that the threat of punishment will only effectively deter criminal behavior if it aligns with the community's shared moral commitments, including the belief in degrees of moral blameworthiness. Giving someone what they deserve serves a "psychological function" because it reinforces our shared values, thus increasing people's respect for the law's moral authority. For these theorists and others, criminal justice is forward-looking only when it is backward-looking.

In light of these complications, other taxonomies have been proposed. For example, Michael Davis (2009) says that retributivism can be construed as forward-looking and consequentialism can be construed as backward-looking, depending on how they are interpreted. Retributivists may punish offenders in order to restore a relation of equality between offender and victim, annul the crime, or negate the offender's advantage—all of which are consequences. In other words, retribution itself may be a good that we ought to maximize. And even consequentialists believe that there must be some relationship between punishment and crime, lest they risk unjustly punishing the innocent or not really supporting a system of *criminal* law. As an alternative to the consequentialist/retributivist distinction, Davis classifies theories as either empirical/externalist or conceptual/internalist. On the former set of views, the rightness of a punishment depends on empirical considerations, such as its deterrent effect, that are true of our world specifically. On the latter set of views, the rightness of a punishment depends on how the crime and punishment are conceptually related, such as the offender's guilt serving as a reason to impose hard treatment, which is true in worlds even radically different from our own (M. Davis 2009, 80–83).

The question of justification is further complicated by the fact that there are at least three justificatory domains. Hart usefully distinguishes the "general justifying aim" of punishment from its "distribution," with the latter subdivided into questions concerning its "title" and "amount" (1960, 4, 8–9):

1. General justifying aim: What is the institution of punishment trying to achieve? What social obligation does it fulfill, or what good does the system produce on the whole?
2. Distribution
   (a) Title: Whom should we punish? What is our standard of criminal liability or guilt? Is it ever right to punish the innocent?
   (b) Amount: How much should an offender be punished? For example, should the severity of a punishment be determined by how much good will be produced or should it be proportional to the seriousness of the crime?

The different justifications of punishment that I have mentioned (and others I have not) may answer all three questions or only some of them. Some mixed theorists take this distinction to be crucial insofar as they attribute different rationales to different branches of government. For example, John Rawls (1955) says that the legislature should be guided by consequentialist considerations when it forms criminal laws and statutory penalties, and judges should appeal to retribution when reaching verdicts and sentencing individual offenders (see also Hart 1960; Altman 2021).

The fact that legal punishment must be situated in an institutional structure has led some philosophers to abandon the terms of the traditional debate and develop a political conception of the criminal law. Proponents of the so-called "political turn" reject the idea that legal punishment is just another branch of applied interpersonal ethics. Historically, they say, criminal law was not designed to protect individual rights against theft and violence, but to preserve the state. It may be an instrument of public policy, on par with education and healthcare, to foster social cooperation (Chiao 2019) and secure civil order (Farmer 2016); or it may be constitutive of the civil order itself by securing a system of cooperation for mutual advantage (Matravers 2000) or defining and preserving our intrinsically valuable roles within a constitutional system (Thorburn 2011, 2012). To evaluate punishment, then, we must evaluate the state's authority and the function punishment serves in furthering its aims, such as a liberal commitment to freedom and equality. Punishment can only be justified insofar as it supports a just political community.

Some critics have challenged the idea that legal punishment is even intended to promote justice, control crime, or hold individual wrongdoers accountable. Instead, punishment is an instrument of "criminal oppression" that excludes stigmatized members of the community, especially racial and ethnic minorities, the poor, and immigrants, from full participation in social and political institutions (Wirts 2020). On this view, the criminal law maintains race- and class-based, and often nativist, hierarchies, with Black people construed as uncontrollable criminals and potential criminals (A. Davis 2003; Altman and Coe 2022), the urban poor labeled as a violent threat (Reiman and Leighton 2020), and immigrants portrayed as predators (or, at best, economic burdens) who are opposed to "law and order" (Platt 2021). All of them are subject to harsh penalties for individual street crimes, including nonviolent drug offenses, while white-collar criminals are rarely punished for what are often more destructive corporate crimes. The result has been a dramatic increase in the incarceration rate, with poor Blacks and Latinos overrepresented in prison and subject to other forms of state control (such as parole and probation). Michelle Alexander (2020) has famously called mass incarceration a caste system, mostly along racial lines: "the New Jim Crow." The policies that have led to mass incarceration have had little effect on crime rates. These critics claim that talking about deterrence and retribution covers over the criminal justice system's lack of basic fairness, and it distracts us from the state's complicity in not addressing criminogenic conditions.

This kind of critique is indicative of a broader concern that punishment cannot be justified. As I mentioned earlier, philosophers such as Boonin and Hanna have claimed that the intent to harm is too morally problematic to save. Others have said that we cannot establish liability conditions with enough reasonable assurance to overcome the moral risk, or that the concept of free will makes so little sense that it cannot be used to ground desert claims. So-called abolitionists insist that we ought to adopt alternatives to punishment, such as prevention, victim restitution, or incapacitation of dangerous criminals to protect the innocent. Which side has the better argument—abolitionism or one of the many proposed justifications of punishment—is a matter of contention among philosophers. The outcome of this debate will have implications for existing punishment practices, including the death penalty and incarceration (who is incarcerated, for how long, and under what conditions), rehabilitation programs and other efforts to reintegrate offenders into the community, and the participation of crime victims in the criminal justice process.

3 Summary of Chapters

Clearly, an examination of legal punishment poses a number of complex philosophical questions. In order to address them, the chapters that follow bring together many of the most important punishment theorists working today. The book begins with Part I, a brief but comprehensive philosophic history of punishment. In chapter 2, John D. Bessler gives an overview of historical trends in punishment from ancient times to the nineteenth century, covering the transition from the divine right of kings to the rule of law and equal treatment under the law; the shift from religious justifications for punishment to secular rationales, such as proportionality and parsimony; and the switch from "bloody" punishments to the penitentiary system. Margaret Martin focuses on legal positivism in chapter 3, examining the Hobbesian assumptions in Hart's conception of criminal law. She claims that, where the two diverge, particularly on punishment, Hart's theory suffers. He, unlike Hobbes, cannot invoke the "sovereign" and the "state" as legal fictions, which creates an irreconcilable tension between the utilitarian aim of punishment as an institution and the retributivist aim of specific punishments. In chapter 4, Amelia Wirts covers historical trends in the justification of punishment in the twentieth and twenty-first centuries. She claims that the rehabilitative model, retributivism, and the social critical view are grounded in different conceptions of the cause of crime—respectively, illness caused by social circumstances, personal immorality, or social injustice—and she makes a case for the social critical view.

Parts II and III turn our attention to justifications of punishment, first by focusing on the traditional opposition between retributivism and consequentialism. In chapter 5, Leora Dahan Katz enumerates the core claims of retributivism and identifies some common objections: that assigning intrinsic value to suffering is morally repugnant, that desert is not a conclusive reason to do anything, that the state does not have the authority to impose it, and that we cannot know what offenders deserve. She then defends a relational conception of retribution, the response-retributive theory, which answers these challenges. Isaac Wiegman questions both the motivation and justification for retribution in chapter 6. He argues that the retributive impulse is bound up with emotions such as anger and vengefulness, and that the resulting disposition to punish has its evolutionary roots in sustaining cooperation in large populations. He concludes that punishment is not non-instrumentally good or right, as the retributivist contends, but it can have instrumental value for maintaining shared values.

In chapter 7, Hsin-Wen Lee evaluates several consequentialist theories of punishment, including general and specific deterrence theories, and she defends rights-protection theory as the best alternative. On this view, the fact that we have the rights to life, liberty, and property entails that we have the right to defend them, including by means of punishment. Christopher Bennett surveys some of the main criticisms of consequentialism in chapter 8: it could justify punishing innocent people, it allows us to treat offenders as mere means, it fails to respect them as moral agents, and it takes an objective attitude toward human relations. He concludes that these objections only apply to one form of consequentialism, but avoiding them comes at the cost of losing the theory's distinctive moral vision.

I defend a mixed theory of punishment in chapter 9, arguing that the community has both backward-looking expressive obligations, lest we trivialize wrongdoing, and forward-looking obligations to further the aims of the state and promote the common good. On the two-tiered model, punishment policies at the institutional level are justified by their support of a just legal arrangement, while punishment in the criminal courts is given to offenders based on what they deserve. In chapter 10, Leo Zaibert questions whether mixed theories can overcome a fundamental axiological difference between utilitarianism and retributivism: on the former view, suffering is intrinsically bad (even if it may be a necessary evil), while on the latter view, deserved suffering is intrinsically good. In addition, any viable form of pluralism would engage a variety of other values, beyond what is good for utilitarians and retributivists, both within and outside of the legal realm.

Part III surveys a selection of justificatory approaches that do not fit neatly into the traditional dichotomy between consequentialism and retributivism. Bill Wringe distinguishes definitional and justificatory versions of expressivism in chapter 11, and he assesses some traditional expressivist justifications (from Jean Hampton and Antony Duff) that focus on what is communicated to victims or offenders. As an alternative, Wringe proposes a denunciatory view according to which punishment expresses a condemnatory message to society at large about the wrongness of crimes. In chapter 12, Phillip Montague looks at what justifies harming someone in cases of self-defense against culpable offenders, and he extends that reasoning to justify punishment as a joint action to defend society as a whole. On his view, punishment is required by distributive justice, not backward-looking retributive justice. In chapter 13, Göran Duus-Otterström covers fair play theory, which says that punishment corrects offenders' unfair advantage over those who follow the law. He defends the theory against a common objection: that the theory is incomplete because some crimes produce no benefit for the offender that is in need of correction. Finally, in chapter 14, Whitley Kaufman discusses the rights-forfeiture theory, which says that offenders forfeit their right against being harmed and thus can justifiably be punished for their wrongdoings. Kaufman criticizes the theory, claiming that it cannot explain what rights are forfeited or what that entails, so it amounts to little more than a claim about the permissibility of punishment without an explanation of why.

Part IV considers punishment in the context of the state and criminal law. In chapter 15, Matt Matravers explains the political turn in punishment theory, according to which state punishment, unlike other forms of punishment, serves a distinct legal or political function, which is crucial to understanding its value. He claims that state punishment is not justified by retributivism or consequentialism; rather, it is constitutive of the civil order, specifically a liberal political community in which we regulate our behavior for mutual advantage. In chapter 16, Javier Wilenmann and Vincent Chiao explain why a broad commitment to retributivism has led to a neglect of policing as an object of philosophical scrutiny. Policing becomes important if we expand our narrow focus on punishment to consider criminal justice in the broader context of social welfare policy. From this perspective, they investigate and evaluate the reasoning behind calls to abolish the police. In chapter 17, Clark M. Neily III and Chris W. Surprenant describe the role of prosecutors in the United States, focusing on plea bargaining and disincentives to go to trial. Because this leads to widespread disfunction and unjust outcomes—especially the conviction of innocents (overcriminalization) and imprisonment for minor offenses (overcharging)—they argue that we should greatly reduce or eliminate plea bargaining and replace it with a system in which the jury chooses between an option presented by the prosecution and one proposed by the defense—like the practice in ancient Greece.

The two contributors in Part V, Stephen Kershnar and Douglas Husak, address proportionality and sentencing. In chapter 18, Kershnar argues that proportionality cannot be justified because there is no adequate mathematical relation between the seriousness of a wrongdoing and the severity of a punishment. This calls into question non-consequentialist justifications of punishment that warrant it based on past actions. Husak argues for what he calls sentencing pluralism in chapter 19. He claims that there are diverse goals of a sentencing scheme—promoting justice, increasing public safety, and using resources efficiently, among others—for which we must consult different disciplines. Furthermore, what an offender deserves cannot be settled using only a proportionality calculus; we confront several irresolvable problems in trying to devise and apply such a scheme.

Assigning desert seems to depend on holding someone personally responsible, yet what makes someone an agent who can be criminally liable for an offense is a complex philosophical and legal issue. Longstanding doubts about the plausibility of free will and recent discoveries in neuroscience have challenged traditional conceptions of intentionality and guilt that are embedded in the criminal law. Part VI shows the contours of this debate and its implications for punishment theory. In chapter 20, Sandy Xie, Colleen M. Berryessa, and Farah Focquaert examine research on how neural networks contribute to moral decision-making, investigate how neuromorality may affect perceptions of moral responsibility in criminal sentencing, and consider its implications for utilitarian and retributivist justifications of punishment. In chapter 21, Bruce N. Waller argues that punishment is never deserved because no one is morally responsible, so it is unjust even when we inflict it for the purposes of deterrence and restraint. He says that we try to cover this up with a groundless belief in a just world, but what we ought to do is acknowledge the injustice and try to reduce it. Gregg Caruso presents six distinct arguments against retributivism in chapter 22, including the claim that we are probably not morally responsible in a way that would justify it (free will skepticism) and that our belief in responsibility is too weakly supported to overcome the moral risk of making people suffer for their wrongs. As an alternative, he proposes the public health-quarantine model: to defend ourselves, we ought to incapacitate criminals using the minimum harm required.

The last two chapters in Part VI attempt to defend legal punishment despite the challenges of neuroscience and free will skepticism. Katrina L. Sifferd claims in chapter 23 that we are capable of moral and legal responsibility, even if we are determined, because of our capacity for reasons-responsiveness and mental causation. Thus, we can in some cases deserve punishment as an expressive form of blame on behalf of the community. In chapter 24, Benjamin Vilhauer draws on Kant to justify punishment from a modified Rawlsian original position: if, in the original position, we do not know whether we will be an offender or a victim, how would we consent to be treated if we value people's humanity and we adopt others' ends as our own? Vilhauer claims that we would try to avoid punishment but would accept humane punishment if it was necessary to deter and incapacitate violent offenders.

Challenges and alternatives to punishment are considered in Parts VII (on abolitionism) and VIII (on forgiveness and restoration). Nathan Hanna argues for abolitionism in chapter 25: we could only justify punishment if we were sure enough that an accused offender acted illegally, freely, and culpably (among other things) to avoid wrongly harming them. Given the uncertainly around these issues, it is better to risk not punishing someone who deserves it than to risk punishing someone who does not deserve it. Michael Davis responds to the abolitionist challenge in chapter 26. He says that deterrence and retribution could not warrant doing away with punishment, that incapacitation is an incomplete alternative, and that reform theories, which would lead to the abolition of punishment, are inconsistent with historical practice and cannot address all classes of crime. Therefore, abolishing punishment for all crimes cannot be justified.

In chapter 27, John Kleinig addresses the question of whether forgiveness is ever compatible with punishment or whether it cancels whatever punishment is due. He concludes that, although forgiveness is the foreswearing of resentment, it does not necessarily entail that punishment should be withdrawn. Lode Walgrave explains the intellectual history of restorative justice in chapter 28, and he contrasts it with traditional views of punishment such as retributivism and instrumentalism. As an alternative to punishment, he defends a "consequential" approach to restorative justice, which aims to repair social life and further the process of civilization. Although he sees the value of restorative approaches, Thom Brooks argues in chapter 29 that they should be embedded into existing punishment practices. Doing so would achieve the restoration of rights infringed or threatened by crime while allowing for a wider available range of options in the restorative contract, including forms of hard treatment. Punitive restoration would, he says, support victims, reduce reoffending, and lower costs; it would be applicable to both serious and minor crimes; and it would gain broad public support.

Part IX applies the philosophy of punishment to several important ethical and legal issues concerning the treatment of offenders. It begins with two chapters on the risk of unjustly imposing punishment on less culpable offenders or those who face criminogenic disadvantage. In chapter 30, Benjamin Ewing investigates what many people believe is the most important social justice issue of our time: mass incarceration. Situating himself in relation to others who have addressed this issue, he argues that traditional justifications of punishment cannot account for its injustice. He claims instead that mass incarceration is a problem of distributive injustice, specifically how to fairly allocate security against both crime and punishment. Craig K. Agule turns our attention to juvenile justice in chapter 31. He rejects the idea that children are less culpable because of their immaturity, claiming instead that we should think about who is doing the blaming. The adult-dominated criminal justice system has its own threshold of capable agency that kids often fall short of. In light of this, Agule defends an institutional age proxy for partial competence.

The last four chapters of the book consider kinds of punishment and whether there are limits to how we can treat wrongdoers. In chapter 32, Peter Brian Barry says that, although there is a plausible retributivist argument for punitive torture, it could never be justified in practice because it risks treating offenders disproportionately and risks a slippery slope where the undeserving are harmed. Since the strongest argument for punitive torture fails, and the consequentialist argument fails for similar reasons, we should not legalize punitive torture. In chapters 33 and 34, Edward Feser and Benjamin S. Yost argue for and against capital punishment, respectively. Feser draws on natural law theory to make the retributivist case that some crimes are so bad that only death is morally appropriate. Yost says that the risk of accidental overpunishment, coupled with the fact that we cannot remedy a wrongful execution, entails that we should err on the side of leniency and not execute anyone, even those who seem to deserve it. And in chapter 35, Chad Flanders examines the prohibition on "cruel and unusual" punishment in the Eighth Amendment to the U.S. Constitution. He surveys the theoretical frameworks used to interpret that clause and how it is currently understood in light of Supreme Court precedent, and he considers whether imprisonment and punishment in general could be deemed cruel.

4 Conclusion

Punishment has been the focus of an extensive scholarship, and it is at the center of a number of philosophical debates regarding the justification of state-sanctioned harm, the function of the government, the use of social scientific data, the role of forgiveness, and the concepts of moral responsibility and legal liability, among other topics. Many of our collective obligations relate to punishment in one way or another. This volume testifies to the vibrancy and relevance of this field in the philosophy of law. It provides a snapshot of the current state of the discipline and establishes fertile ground for future research.[1]

[1] I am grateful to Cynthia Coe and Christopher Bennett for helpful comments on earlier drafts.

References

Alexander, Larry, and Kimberly Kessler Ferzan. 2009. *Crime and Culpability: A Theory of Criminal Law*. Cambridge: Cambridge University Press.

Alexander, Michelle. 2020. *The New Jim Crow: Mass Incarceration in the Age of Colorblindness*. 10th anniversary ed. New York: New Press.

Altman, Matthew C. 2021. *A Theory of Legal Punishment: Deterrence, Retribution, and the Aims of the State*. London: Routledge.

Altman, Matthew C., and Cynthia D. Coe. 2022. "Punishment Theory, Mass Incarceration, and the Overdetermination of Racialized Justice." *Criminal Law and Philosophy* 16, no. 3 (October): 631–49.

Andenaes, Johannes. 1974. *Punishment and Deterrence*. Ann Arbor, MI: University of Michigan Press.

Beccaria, Cesare. 1995. *On Crimes and Punishments and Other Writings*. Translated by Richard Davies, Virginia Cox, and Richard Bellamy. Edited by Richard Bellamy. Cambridge: Cambridge University Press.

Benn, S. I. 1958. "An Approach to the Problems of Punishment." *Philosophy* 33, no. 127 (October): 325–41.

Bentham, Jeremy. 1970. *An Introduction to the Principles of Morals and Legislation*. Edited by J. H. Burns and H. L. A. Hart. Oxford: Clarendon.

Boonin, David. 2008. *The Problem of Punishment*. Cambridge: Cambridge University Press.

Braithwaite, John, and Philip Pettit. 1990. *Not Just Deserts: A Republican Theory of Criminal Justice*. Oxford: Clarendon.

Chiao, Vincent. 2019. *Criminal Law in the Age of the Administrative State*. Oxford: Oxford University Press.

Cottingham, John. 1979. "Varieties of Retribution." *Philosophical Quarterly* 29, no. 116 (July): 238–46.

Davis, Angela Y. 2003. *Are Prisons Obsolete?* New York: Seven Stories.

Davis, Michael. 2009. "Punishment Theory's Golden Half Century: A Survey of Developments from (about) 1957 to 2007." *Journal of Ethics* 13, no. 1 (January): 73–100.

Duff, R. A. 1986. *Trials and Punishments*. Cambridge: Cambridge University Press.

Farmer, Lindsay. 2016. *Making the Modern Criminal Law: Criminalization and Civil Order*. Oxford: Oxford University Press.

Feinberg, Joel. 1965. "The Expressive Function of Punishment." *Monist* 49, no. 3 (July): 397–423.

Flew, Antony. 1954. "The Justification of Punishment." *Philosophy* 29, no. 111 (October): 291–307.

Hampton, Jean. 1984. "The Moral Education Theory of Punishment." *Philosophy & Public Affairs* 13, no. 3 (Summer): 208–38.

Hanna, Nathan. 2008. "Say What? A Critique of Expressive Retributivism." *Law and Philosophy* 27, no. 2 (March): 123–50.
———. 2009. "Liberalism and the General Justifiability of Punishment." *Philosophical Studies* 145, no. 3 (September): 325–49.
Hart, H. L. A. 1960. "Prolegomenon to the Principles of Punishment." *Proceedings of the Aristotelian Society* 60, no. 1 (June): 1–26.
Husak, Douglas N. 2000. "Retribution in Criminal Theory." *San Diego Law Review* 37, no. 4: 959–86.
Kant, Immanuel. 1996a. *Groundwork of the Metaphysics of Morals*. In *Practical Philosophy*, translated and edited by Mary J. Gregor, 41–108. Cambridge: Cambridge University Press.
———. 1996b. *The Metaphysics of Morals*. In *Practical Philosophy*, translated and edited by Mary J. Gregor, 363–602. Cambridge: Cambridge University Press.
Matravers, Matt. 2000. *Justice and Punishment: The Rationale of Coercion*. Oxford: Oxford University Press.
McCloskey, H. J. 1962. "The Complexity of the Concepts of Punishment." *Philosophy* 37, no. 142 (October): 307–25.
McPherson, Thomas. 1967. "Punishment: Definition and Justification." *Analysis* 28, no. 1 (October): 21–27.
Mill, John Stuart. 2001. *Utilitarianism*. 2nd ed. Edited by George Sher. Indianapolis, IN: Hackett.
Nathanson, Stephen. 2001. *An Eye for an Eye: The Immorality of Punishing by Death*. 2nd ed. Lanham, MD: Rowman & Littlefield.
Nietzsche, Friedrich. 1967. *On the Genealogy of Morals*. Translated by Walter Kaufmann and R. J. Hollingdale. New York: Vintage.
Plato. 1961. *Crito*. In *The Collected Dialogues of Plato*, edited by Edith Hamilton and Huntington Cairns, 27–39. Princeton, NJ: Princeton University Press.
Platt, Joel. 2021. "(Cr)immigration, Race and Belonging: Why We Must Conceptualize Immigration Detention as Punishment?" *Journal of Identity and Migration Studies* 15, no. 1: 2–28.
Rawls, John. 1955. "Two Concepts of Rules." *Philosophical Review* 64, no. 1 (January): 3–32.
Reiman, Jeffrey, and Paul Leighton. 2020. *The Rich Get Richer and the Poor Get Prison: Thinking Critically about Class and Criminal Justice*. New York: Routledge.
Robinson, Paul H., and John M. Darley. 1997. "The Utility of Desert." *Northwestern University Law Review* 91, no. 2 (Winter): 453–99.
Thorburn, Malcolm. 2011. "Criminal Law as Public Law." In *Philosophical Foundations of Criminal Law*, edited by R. A. Duff and Stuart P. Green, 21–43. Oxford: Oxford University Press.
———. 2012. "Constitutionalism and the Limits of the Criminal Law." In *The Structures of the Criminal Law*, edited by R. A. Duff, Lindsay Farmer, S. E. Marshall, Massimo Renzo, and Victor Tadros, 85–105. Oxford: Oxford University Press.

Walker, Nigel. 1999. "Even More Varieties of Retribution." *Philosophy* 74, no. 4 (October): 595–605.
Wirts, Amelia. 2020. "Criminal Oppression: A Non-Ideal Theory of Criminal Law and Punishment." Ph.D. diss., Boston College, 2020. https://dlib.bc.edu/islandora/object/bc-ir:108954/datastream/PDF/view.
Wringe, Bill. 2013. "Must Punishment Be Intended to Cause Suffering?" *Ethical Theory and Moral Practice* 16, no. 4 (August): 863–77.
Zaibert, Leo. 2006. *Punishment and Retribution*. Aldershot, UK: Ashgate.

Part I

Philosophic History of Punishment Theory

2

The Philosophy of Punishment and the Arc of Penal Reform: From Ancient Lawgivers to the Renaissance and the Enlightenment, and through the Nineteenth Century

John D. Bessler

1 Ancient Lawgivers and Philosophers: From Urukagina and the Code of Hammurabi to Draco and Plato

The earliest legal systems and law codes regulated morality, subordinated minorities and women, and authorized amercements, fines, banishment, grotesque corporal punishments, and death sentences to punish crime and as forms of social control. A Sumerian inscription of Urukagina (circa 2380 to 2360 BCE), the ruler of the Mesopotamian city-state of Lagesh, recited that thieves and women who committed adultery or took two husbands would be stoned to death and that "if a woman speaks … disrespectfully to a man, that woman's mouth is crushed with a fired brick"; the Code of Ur-Nammu (circa 2100 to 2050 BCE) of Mesopotamia, or modern-day Iraq, punished murder, rape, robbery, and adultery with death; and the Babylonian Code of Hammurabi (circa 1780 BCE), engraved on an eight-foot-high stone slab now displayed at the Musée du Louvre, made twenty-five crimes punishable by death. One provision of Hammurabi's Code allowed a husband to drown an adulterous wife while another stated that, "if a man's wife, for the sake of

J. D. Bessler (✉)
University of Baltimore, Baltimore, MD, USA
e-mail: jbessler@ubalt.edu

© The Author(s), under exclusive license to Springer Nature Switzerland AG 2023

M. C. Altman (ed.), *The Palgrave Handbook on the Philosophy of Punishment*, Palgrave Handbooks in the Philosophy of Law, https://doi.org/10.1007/978-3-031-11874-6_2

another, has caused her husband to be killed, that woman shall be impaled." Fifteen laws of the Old Hittite Kingdom (circa 1600 to 1400 BCE) likewise made various acts, including incest, theft, and sorcery, punishable by death, with an Anglo-Saxon king, Ethelbert, mandating an intricate system of payments for criminal acts (*wergild* for injuries resulting in death, *bot* for non-lethal injuries, and *wite* for payment to those overseeing the compensation scheme) (Good 1967, 957–64; Wink and Wink 1993, 350; Barmash 2020, 19–34).

Punishment has been defined as "the infliction by state authority of a consequence normally regarded as an evil (for example, death or imprisonment) on an individual found to be legally guilty of a crime" (Murphy and Coleman 1990, 117). While societal custom or a specific law often dictated an offender's punishment (e.g., bribery was punished in Rome by ten years of exile after Cicero sponsored a law to that effect) or death at the state's hands, Draco is now remembered as the first Athenian lawgiver to whom a specific set of laws is attributed. As the first written constitution of Athens (circa 622/621 BCE), Draco's code replaced oral laws reflecting customary practices, making both the most serious and lower-level offenses punishable by death. "In its employment of the penalty of death for a wide range of offenses, even for offenses as minor as petty theft," M. Stuart Madden has observed, "Draco's code … was extraordinarily harsh by today's standards," with the modern-day expression "Draconian" still put to use (2006, 886). The fourth-century BCE orator Demades went so far as to say that "Draco's laws were written in blood," with Solon (circa 630–560 BCE)—the Athenian statesman who allowed any citizen to initiate a public prosecution against a wrongdoer (Carugati et al. 2015, 298)—repealing almost all of Draco's code in 594 BCE, making only treason and murder punishable by death (Hyde 1918, 328; Carawan 1998, 2). Under the Twelve Tables of Roman law, crimes such as arson and the nocturnal theft of crops were punishable by death (Wolff 1951, 53), and in ancient Rome, the enslaved were regarded as property instead of human beings, with the concept of *dominium* giving owners unlimited power. This meant that "a master could do what he liked with his slave, over whom he had the power of life and death" (Borkowski 1994, 84).

For centuries, many societies operated without written laws or well-organized legal systems, and the law was "largely a matter of social custom" (Mather 2002, 324). According to Henry Mather, "even the written law codes were primitive," and such codes "consisted largely of penalties for various forms of violence" (324). Mather points to the written codes of Lombard kings promulgated from 643 to 755 CE, including the code issued by King Rothair (or Rothari) in 643 CE: "Titles 1 through 152 and titles 277 through

358 prescribe in gory detail penalties for offenses we would characterize as crimes or torts" (324). Mather describes specific code provisions: "Title 48, for example, sets the penalty for gouging out a freeman's eye, while title 50 prescribes a different penalty for cutting off a freeman's lip. The penalty for cutting off a freeman's index finger (title 64) is sixteen solidi, whereas the penalty for cutting off a freeman's middle finder (title 65) is only five solidi" (324). Noting that legal systems have existed around the world throughout the past five thousand years, one prominent legal scholar—taking stock of the law's long, often torturous history—had this to say: "For most of this five-thousand-year history, laws and legal systems have mostly been tools of social control used by those in power to dominate their opponents" (Bassiouni 2010, 274).

Laws and punishments were tailored to fit then-existing societal beliefs. In *The Republic*, Plato wrote that "each ruling group sets down laws for its own advantage; a democracy sets down democratic laws; a tyranny, tyrannic laws," with any "breaker of the law" and "doer of unjust deeds" punished for violations (1991, 338d–339a [p. 16]). Assuming the persona of Protagoras, Plato described an ancient ideal of the law's purpose:

> In punishing wrongdoers, no one concentrates on the fact that a man has done wrong in the past, or punishes him on that account, unless taking blind vengeance like a beast. No, punishment is not inflicted by a rational man for the sake of the crime that has been committed—after all one cannot undo what is past—but for the sake of the future, to prevent either the same man or, by the spectacle of his punishment, someone else, from doing wrong again. (1961, 324a–b [p. 321])

R. F. Stalley notes of Plato's Socratic dialogue, "Protagoras allows that cities may, by penalties of death or exile, rid themselves of those evil characters who are incapable of acquiring justice" (1983, 140). In that dialogue, corporal punishments are regularly inflicted on enslaved persons and foreigners, with capital punishment imposed for an array of offenses, including premeditated murder, wounding a relative with intent to kill, acts of impiety, atheism, theft, harboring exiles, taking bribes, waging private war, and obstructing justice (Stalley 1983, 137, 139). In Book 9 of *The Laws*, Plato—speaking in an Athenian's voice—discussed "the principles on which we are arranging our laws" (2016, 853a [p. 324]):

> For him who obeys, the law should be passed over in silence; for him who does not obey, … we must intone, in a loud voice: '*Anyone caught robbing a temple, if*

> *he is a slave or foreigner, shall be branded on the face and hands to show what he has come to; he shall be whipped—however many strokes the court decides—and expelled naked from the country, beyond its borders. Perhaps after this punishment he will become a better person, having learnt self-control.'* After all, no punishment imposed by the law is imposed with an evil intention; it has, broadly speaking, one of two effects: it makes the one who is punished either a better person, or a less evil one. (854c–e [p. 326])

Because of the advantage of their prior education, citizens "caught doing something of this kind" were regarded as "already incurable" and might be put to death (854e [p. 326]).

Punishment practices have long pedigrees, whether in ancient Mesopotamia, Rome, Greece, or elsewhere. In his *Laws*, Plato asserts that the purpose of punishment is

> not as a penalty for his wrong-doing—after all, what has been done is never going to be undone—but so that, for the future, he himself and those who see him being punished may either be filled with hatred for his unjust behaviour, or at any rate more or less recover from this affliction.
>
> For all those reasons, and with all those aims in view, our laws, like a good archer, must take careful aim—concentrating on the magnitude of the punishment in any particular case, and above all on what is deserved. (2016, 934a–b [pp. 428–29])

In the sixth century BCE, one Greek lawgiver, Charondas, reportedly took his laws so seriously that he took his own life after violating one. As a popular history of Greek civilization reports:

> Charondas, according to a typically Greek tale, forbade the citizens to enter the assembly while armed. One day, however, he himself came to the public meeting forgetfully wearing his sword. When a voter reproached him for breaking his own law he answered, "I will rather confirm it," and slew himself. (Durant 1966, 170)

Before plunging his sword into his breast, Charondas is said to have invoked Zeus, the Greek god.

A number of ancient philosophers wrote about justice and punishment, with laws often associated with the commands—or the prevailing interpretations—of religious texts. It was Plutarch's saying, the Dutch jurist and diplomat Hugo Grotius pointed out, that "*Justice is the Attendant of God to take Vengeance of those who transgress the divine Law, which all Men naturally have*

Recourse to against all Men as their Fellow Citizens" (1715, 438). As Grotius observed of ancient times, Hierax described "Justice" as "*the Exaction of Punishment on those who have first offended*"; Hierocles called "Punishment" the "*Medicine of Wickedness*"; and Plato emphasized, "*neither God nor Man ever said this, that he, who hath done wrong, doth not deserve to suffer for it*" (438) "But what we have said of *Punishment*," Grotius added, "must necessarily be the consequence of some Crime or Demerit, as St. Austin has observed, *All Punishment, if it be just, must be the Punishment of some Crime*; which is true even of those Punishments that are inflicted by *God* himself ..." (438). Readers of Grotius thus encountered this idea: a person "ought to *deserve* Punishment" (440). As one scholar, examining the state's ultimate sanction and alluding to human sacrifices, explains of executions and what warranted them in ancient times:

> The death penalty originated as a way to "placate the gods," and evolved as a punishment toward an individual. In the time of Moses in the Bible, the death penalty was inflicted for crimes ranging from murder to gathering sticks on the Sabbath. (Mayer 2007, 728n8)

The history of punishment involves both the public administration of monarchical or state power and, depending on the time period and specific locale, decentralized law enforcement through private prosecution (Bessler 2022, 3–4). In the year 1000 CE in the Icelandic Republic, or Free State, the laws—inherited from Germanic tribes—were customary in nature and were applied by a Folkmeet, called the *Althing*—the name of Iceland's Parliament or "general assembly." The world's oldest functioning legislature (established in 930 CE), the *Althing* met every summer northeast of Reykjavik. Once a year, all of Iceland's freemen gathered at Thingvillir to perform legislative and adjudicative functions and, as necessary, to amend the customary laws (Anderson 1991, 3–4). "Primitive legal systems," one political scientist explains, "are characterized by decentralized police function" and "customary law" passed down from one generation to the next (2). Drawing upon the Icelandic example, he explains how that ancient legal system operated:

> Everyone participated in enforcing the law. When the court sat and adjudged that a crime had been committed—normally a crime against property (theft or robbery) or a crime against the person (violence, including murder)—a punishment would be declared. (4)

Punishments, he notes, pointing out the equivalent ancient English terminology,

> consisted either of a fine (in England, the *Wergild*, which varied according to the rank of the victim) or banishment, termed outlawry, which meant that the person who had been convicted was outside the protection of the law and anyone could kill him. (4–5)

In effect, "all weapon-bearing Icelanders were policemen" (5).

Every society has witnessed violence and state-sanctioned killing. While Niccolò Machiavelli, in his *Il Principe* (*The Prince*) (1532), lauded the use of cruelty, fear, and brutal public executions to terrify the populace "by a dread of punishment" (2003, 25, 55), the English legal system and its own gruesome "Bloody Code"—predicated on customary practices and the common law and making scores of crimes punishable by death—had public and private aspects to it. The English attorney general, known first as the "King's Attorney," came into existence in the fifteenth century, though before the thirteenth century England's king appointed "special attorneys" (judges used the terms *attornatus regis* and *sequitur pro rege* when referring to those appearing on the king's behalf) to prosecute criminal cases of interest to the monarch. The duties of England's attorney general included "investigating homicides to hear and determine what pertained to the Crown" and "to prosecute serious criminal cases" (Dahlquist 2000, 749–52), although private prosecutions—initiated through *appeals* by crime victims or their relatives—were, by far, the predominant method of prosecuting English offenders (Bessler 2022, 18–19). Grand juries were convened as prerequisites to criminal charges and to prevent "false and malicious accusations" or those seeking to gratify "private revenge" (Forsyth and Morgan 1994, 178–79), but the common law allowed persons to be "tried, convicted, and executed" on "appeals of murder"—prosecutions initiated by the victim's spouse or heir (LaFave et al. 2015, §15.1[c]). England's first Director of Public Prosecutions was not appointed until 1879, and the country's Crown Prosecution Service was not created until 1986. Scotland, by contrast, developed a tradition of public prosecution—a system led by its Lord Advocate—centuries earlier than England (Bessler 2022, 104–5). James Moncreiff, one Lord Advocate, gave this testimony in the 1850s about the Scottish approach:

> The system proceeds upon the principle that it is the duty of the State to detect crime, apprehend offenders, and punish them, and that independently of the interest of a private party. The Scotch system acknowledges the right of a private

> party to prosecute; but the duty of the public prosecutor is altogether irrespective of that. (Barrie and Broomhall 2014, 57)

Societies embracing public prosecution systems sought to make prosecutorial decisions more disinterested—and less vengeful—in nature.

2 The Bible and the Punishment of Sin: God's Law and the Divine Right of Kings

In prior centuries, the administration of the criminal law—with continental European states resorting to judicial torture to exact confessions or to implicate accomplices (Bessler 2017, 9)—was tied to the whims of monarchs, the interpretation of biblical verses, the desire to punish sinners and secure repentance, and efforts to deter treason and other acts of disloyalty or criminality (Rutherfurd 1645, 176–77). Decapitated heads were frequently publicly displayed on spikes (Larson 2014, 91–92, 155–56), and the Puritans—seeing sin as a manifestation of evil—looked to scriptural passages in setting up their criminal codes, seeking confessions and making use of public apologies and expressions of guilt or remorse to enforce a strict moral order (Gerber 2015, 167–70). As for the goal of deterrence, Michel de Montaigne, a philosopher of the French Renaissance, once asserted: "It is a custom of our justice to punish some as a warning to others" (1991, III.8 [p. 1044]). Paraphrasing Plato, Montaigne contended:

> For to punish them for *having done* wrong would, as Plato says, be stupid: what is done cannot be undone. The intention is to stop them from repeating the same mistake or to make others avoid their error. We do not improve the man we hang: we improve others by him. (1991, III.8 [p. 1044])

"I once heard a prince, a very great general, maintain that a soldier should not be condemned to death for cowardice," Montaigne wrote of one context, observing of the then-prevailing wartime tradition: "in ancient times the laws of Rome condemned deserters to death" (1991, I.16 [p. 75]). While corporal punishments and death sentences were frequently meted out, if indiscriminately and discriminatorily, torture was often used selectively against traitors, enslaved persons, heretics, and those suspected of witchcraft. "Honorable persons and aristocrats, usually, though not always, enjoyed the privilege to be exempt from the painful question"—the terminology used for judicial torture (Frankenberg 2008, 409).

Many acts of cruelty and torture have occurred throughout world history, and they can be found in pre-trial custodial interrogations and post-trial punishment practices alike through the centuries. Montaigne once wrote: "I fear that Nature herself has attached to Man something which goads him on towards inhumanity" (1991, II.11 [p. 485]). Montaigne said elsewhere:

> In truth it is reasonable that we should make a great difference between defects due to our weakness and those due to our wickedness. In the latter we deliberately brace ourselves against reason's rules, which are imprinted on us by Nature; in the former it seems we can call Nature herself as a defence-witness for having left us so weak and imperfect. That is why a great many people believe that we can only be punished for deeds done against our conscience: on that rule is partly based the opinion of those who condemn the capital punishment of heretics and misbelievers as well as the opinion that a barrister or a judge cannot be arraigned if they fail in their duty merely from ignorance.
>
> Where cowardice is concerned the usual way is, certainly, to punish it by disgrace and ignominy. It is said that this rule was first introduced by Charondas the lawgiver, and that before his time the laws of Greece condemned to death those who had fled from battle, whereas he ordered that they be made merely to sit for three days in the market-place dressed as women. (I.16 [p. 75])

Offering a maxim, "'*Suffundere malis hominis sanguinem quam effundere*' [Make the blood of a bad man blush not gush]," Montaigne reported that Charondas "hoped he could still make use of [deserters] once he had restored their courage by this disgrace" (I.16 [p. 75]).

Prominent religious figures, such as theologian John Calvin, routinely invoked God's law, and they saw magistrates, in inflicting punishments, as executing God's judgments (Stevenson 2004, 178). Judges and magistrates—seen as ministers or "vicars" of God—frequently resorted to the ancient doctrine of *lex talionis*, traditionally expressed as an "eye for an eye." In the Code of Hammurabi, provisions such as these reflected that ancient philosophy of punishment: "If a son strike his father, they shall cut off his fingers"; "If a man destroy the eye of another man, they shall destroy his eye"; "If one break a man's bone, they shall break his bone" (Harper 1999, 73). Societies punished religious offenses (Perrinchief 1663, 27–29) and injuries done to "Divine Law" and "the divine Majesty" (Servita 1655, 75; Woodhead 1688, 66), with death sentences and corporal punishments handed out as part of "God's justice" (Monro 1637, 44). In 1652, one "Reverend Authour" wrote that "the suffering of punishment extorts the Confession of sin"; that "the punishment in generall bringeth sin to minde, which else would be forgotten"; and that God's justice, "in the punishing of sin visibly, is one of the strongest motives to make an Atheist confesse there is a God" (Mede 1652, 194). Centuries ago, executions were almost uniformly carried out publicly, with large, often unruly crowds gathering to witness them (Friedland 2014, 119–23; Elkins 2019, 113). At such spectacles, ministers sought to have the condemned repent on the gallows as a warning to others to avoid sin:

> In Protestant, Georgian England, the "purificatory liturgy" was performed on the day before the execution, followed by a processional on execution day in which the parson and the offender performed a "carefully stage-managed theatre of guilt" displaying "exhortation, confession and repentance before an awed and approving crowd." (Long 2015, 7–8)

Be it in seventeenth-century England or early America, the procession to the gallows, the condemned's last words, and the minister's sermon to the execution-day crowd sought to promote "civil and religious order" and "what the social elite of the period deemed to be positive values" (Santamarina 1992, 101). Ministers denounced offenders' crimes from the pulpit, took notice of exactly how the condemned had arrived at their fate, and sought to use executions to warn others against wickedness (Madow 1995, 505n187).

In bygone eras, prevailing societal attitudes determined the mode of inflicting punishment, with lay brothers in places such as Florence and Rome attending to the condemned's spiritual needs on the eve of an execution (Olson 2006–7, 113). One source—in line with others discussing Scandinavian penal codes (von Bar 1916, 295–96; Orfield 2002, 280)—notes that, in the seventeenth century,

> the dominant principles of punishments were said to be: 1. *lex talionis* is the highest justice according to the Law of God; 2. the legislator shall endeavor to frighten prospective criminals by the most severe penalties; and 3. the legislator shall seek to appease the Deity by the most severe penalties. (Hornum 1972, 70)

In 1658, one self-described "Minister of the Gospel," observed:

> God hath given in charge, to Magistrates, his vice-gerents for to punish. They are *revengers to execute wrath upon them that do evil*, Rom. 13.4. They are *sent of God for the punishment of evil doers*, 1 Pet. 2.14. They have no commission to spare, upon supposal of any interest, in God or grace, when they are found in any acts that are wicked. What they do, God does, they acting by his command, and by vertue of his commission. (Blake 1658, 81)

The theologian Jonathan Edwards took specific note of the close "connexion" between "the sin and the punishment," observing, "the sin necessarily inferring the punishment, and the punishment being the clear evidence and proof of the Sin" (1698, 41).

Puritans in England and New England steadfastly believed that divine law served as the basis for all law, and their legal codes reflected that reality. The Massachusetts "Body of Liberties," adopted in 1641 after a committee had been appointed in 1636 to "make a draught of lawes agreeable to the word of God," contained twelve capital offenses and authorized the imposition of up to forty lashes (Cahn 1989, 116n55; Miethe and Lu 2005, 87). A number of identified offenses—including adultery and bestiality, blasphemy and witchcraft, and murder and rebellion—were punishable by death, with eleven of the twelve listed offenses (as in Connecticut's similar 1642 colonial code) expressly citing Bible passages as authority for the imposition of that punishment. The Body of Liberties, written by Nathaniel Ward, a pastor and a lawyer, relied heavily on the Old Testament, with one provision—citing Deuteronomy and Exodus as authority—providing that "if any man after legall conviction shall have or worship any other god, but the lord god, he shall be put to death" (Ward 1998, 83).

Although religious justifications for punishments continued throughout the seventeenth and eighteenth centuries, England's Glorious Revolution (1688–1689), America's Revolutionary War (1775–1783), and the French Revolution (1789–1799) ultimately put constraints on monarchical power, with the doctrine of separation of church and state later used in Western societies to challenge laws predicated on religious tenets (Levy 1993, 400–423). In his revolutionary pamphlet, *Common Sense* (1776), Thomas Paine referred to what people in the modern era call the Rule of Law: "In America THE LAW IS KING. For as in absolute governments the King is law, so in free countries the law *ought* to be King; and there ought to be no other" (29).

The topic of a sovereign's power to punish has long been the subject of debate and discussion. For example, in *The Prince*, Machiavelli described Cesare Borgia's execution of his former henchman, the ruthless Remirro de Orco. Borgia had appointed de Orco to pacify a territory but then had him killed to curry favor and out of concern that the occupied city of Cesena might rebel against de Orco's cruelty. "One morning," Machiavelli wrote, "Remirro's body was found cut in two pieces on the piazza at Cesena, with a block of wood and a bloody knife beside it. The brutality of the spectacle kept the people of the Romagna at once appeased and stupefied" (2003, 25). Based on Livy's *History of Rome* in which the consul Lucius Junius Brutus supervises the execution of his own sons for plotting against exiled Tarquin kings, Machiavelli instructs: "there is no remedy more powerful, nor more valid, more secure, and more necessary, than to kill the sons of Brutus" (1996, 45; see also Biagini 2009–10, 44–45, 53). Centuries later, Rousseau—the social contract theorist—asserted that the sovereign has the right to "put to death, even as an example, only someone who cannot be preserved without danger" (1988, 36). But the Italian philosopher Cesare Beccaria—taking a different approach while applying Rousseau's theory—posited that humans, in forming a social contract with the state, do not confer upon the sovereign the right to deprive them of their own lives. Beccaria observed of the social compact:

> It was necessity which compelled men to give up a part of their freedom; and it is therefore certain that none wished to surrender to the public repository more than the smallest possible portion consistent with persuading others to defend him. The sum of these smallest possible portions constitutes the right to punish; everything more than that is no longer justice, but an abuse; it is a matter of fact not of right. (1995, 11)

Beccaria's ideas kickstarted a global conversation about capital punishment that continues to this day.

Before the Enlightenment and the rise of secular justifications for punishment (e.g., deterrence) offered by thinkers such as Beccaria, whose 1764 book, *Dei delitti e delle pene* (*On Crimes and Punishments*), became a must-read among intellectuals and revolutionaries (Bessler 2018b, 2019c), religion and punishment went hand in hand. For example, on October 8, 1699, at the Parish Church of St. Nicholas, Nathanael Ellison, the Vicar of Newcastle, preached an entire sermon about the obligation of magistrates to punish vice. In his sermon, delivered before the mayor, aldermen, and sheriff of the Town and County of Newcastle upon Tyne, Ellison argued that magistrates not only possess the power but the obligation "to Punish Vice, and *Execute Sentence upon every evil Work*" (1700, 2). In speaking to those in power, he pointed out that

> God has invested and intrusted you with this *Power* and Authority [to punish vice], and also has laid an *Indispensable Obligation* upon you, to Correct and Punish Delinquents. … This Trust … is reposed in you by God, the King, and your Country. … Supreme Magistrates *are* God's Ministers … accountable to God, their King and their Country for the Discharge *of that Trust* reposed in them. (3, 12, 13)

Ellison says that they would betray their "*sacred Oath*" if they neglected their duties (13). "*Let the Great as well as the Small*, your nearest Relations within your own Gate, as well as the Stranger, feel the Severity of the law, in case they deserve it," Ellison said. Punishment, he observed, was necessary "*to the maintenance of true Religion and Vertue*" (31). "The Punishing of Criminals is what is very disagreeable to all good Tempers," he offered, adding that "our *English Nation* … perhaps is the most Merciful and Compassionate in the World" (3). But Ellison concluded that "the salutary Execution of Penal Laws" is "*absolutely necessary* to the support of Religion and Government, and the Preservation of good Manners" (4). "'Twas Plato's Opinion, That neither God nor Man would say it was any Injustice to Punish Criminals," Ellison stated (5), quoting the biblical verse, "*Whoso sheddeth Man's Blood, by Man shall his Blood be shed*" (Genesis 9:6) (6). "There's little question then to be made, but that all Supreme and Subordinate Magistrates have a Power to coerce and punish Criminals" (11), Ellison preached, stressing:

> 'Tis well if those that are in Authority would consider, that this Power of theirs is not so much a *Privilege and Royalty*, which they may use at Pleasure, as 'tis a *Duty incumbent* upon them, which they are *oblig'd to* under the severest Penalties. (12)

In that era, religious justifications for draconian punishments were extremely common.

3 From the Renaissance to the Enlightenment and Beyond: Reconceptualizing Punishment in the Age of Beccaria and in the Nineteenth Century

As history shows, punishment practices of nations and states gradually changed over time: "From the Renaissance to the Enlightenment, generations of influential thinkers expressed growing concern about torture and excessive punishments, such as Erasmus, Montaigne, Montesquieu, Joseph von Sonnenfels, and John Howard" (Jouet 2021, 154). To be sure, punishment practices had deep, highly religious roots. "Many philosophers of the Renaissance and Reformation believed capital punishment was a just and acceptable form of punishment," Liam Denney notes, emphasizing that the Catholic Church "accepted the legitimacy of capital punishment from 1566 until Vatican II" (2000, 806). But in his influential treatise, *The Spirit of the Laws* (1748), Montesquieu not only discussed the importance of separation of powers to prevent governmental abuse but questioned the need for executions for certain offenses and declared torture to be "not necessary," laying down this important maxim: "Every penalty that does not derive from necessity is tyrannical" (1989, 92, 316; see also Bessler 2019a, 22–23). It was Beccaria's book—inspired by Montesquieu, Voltaire, and other Enlightenment writers; at first published anonymously because of a fear of persecution and the Inquisition; and widely read by eighteenth- and nineteenth-century jurists and lawmakers—that proved especially influential throughout Europe and the Americas in shaping criminal justice reform (Bessler 2014a). The ideas in *On Crimes and Punishments* fueled the abolition of torture and led to the death penalty's abolition in Tuscany (1786) and Austria (1787), and to the curtailment of capital punishment in places such as Pennsylvania in the 1780s and 1790s, with Beccaria's slender treatise inspiring many penal reformers throughout the world (Bessler 2014a, 2014b, 2018a). Voltaire believed punishments were too constrained by ancient traditions, and he criticized the *Ordonnance Criminelle* of 1670 that had stiffened criminal penalties and allowed for the frequent mutilation and execution of offenders. Voltaire expressed particular outrage at the execution of innocent people, decried the state's routine use of harsh punishments, and offered this advice: "The punishment of criminals should be useful. A hanged man is good for nothing, and a man condemned to public labour still serves the fatherland and is a living lesson" (1972, 289).

Beccaria's treatise, praised by Voltaire and translated into French, English, and an array of other languages, called for proportionality between crimes and punishments, opposed torture and runaway judicial discretion, and argued for the death penalty's abolition (Beccaria 1995; Bessler 2018b, 80–88). William Blackstone, in the fourth volume of his *Commentaries on the Laws of England* (1769), called Beccaria "an ingenious writer, who seems to have well studied the springs of human action, that crimes are more effectively prevented by the certainty, than by the severity of punishment" (1979, 4:17). Although Blackstone himself remained supportive of corporal punishments (e.g., nose and ear cutting) and executions for certain categories of offenders, he—in line with Montesquieu, Voltaire and Beccaria—concluded that it was "absurd and impolitic to apply the same punishment to crimes of different magnitude" (1979, 4:17; see also Bessler 2009). Seventeenth-century Quakers such as George Fox and John Bellers had opposed executions, with the latter writing a whole essay titled "Some Reasons against putting of Fellons to Death" (Clarke 1987, 102–3).

Such advocacy bore some fruit even before Montesquieu and Beccaria rose to fame. An assembly of freeholders convened by William Penn—the Quaker founder of the colony of Pennsylvania—restricted the death penalty's use to treason and murder in the "Great Law" of 1682, though that law still provided that adulterers would be publicly whipped and imprisoned for up to a year and made sodomy and incest punishable by forfeiture of assets and a term of imprisonment (Warden and Lennard 2018, 202). The Quaker-inspired death penalty reform remained in place for a time, but Penn's scheme of punishment was abruptly revoked after his death in 1718 by Queen Anne, with the then much harsher English system of criminal justice imposed upon the colony (Bessler 2014a).

During the medieval and early Renaissance periods and in seventeenth-century England, exorbitant fines and forfeitures and, all too frequently, death sentences were the product of state trials or criminal convictions. Kurt Denk writes of those now centuries-old views:

> Second- and third-century theologians harmonized biblical warrants for the death penalty with endorsements of the state's right to impose it. … Positivist affirmations of capital punishment found intellectual support in Saint Thomas Aquinas (1225–1274), whose Summa Theologica affirmed exceptions to the Decalogue's prohibition against killing—capital sentences among them—on the premise of authority's duty to defend the common good. By the late medieval period, church-state collusion in capital punishment was settled in both theory and practice. (2012, 372, 373)

But the Renaissance saw some pushback against the absolute power of royals. As Keyishian notes of Edward Coke, who drew upon thirteenth-century jurist Henry de Bracton's *De legibus et consuetudinibus Angliae* (*On the Laws and Customs of England*):

> Edward Coke, in his constitutional battles with James I over the issue of the supremacy of Common Law versus the royal prerogative, often cited Bracton's centuries-old endorsement of his own position—that "nothing is more fitting for a sovereign than to live by the laws, nor is there any greater sovereignty than to govern according to law … for the law makes him king." (2008, 446)

It would take considerable time, though, before revolutionaries toppled monarchies and set up representative democracies.

As the Renaissance gave way to the Enlightenment, the subject of punishment was studied with even greater care and attention, with a wide array of intellectuals taking up that subject in their writings (Heineccius 1741, 159–65; Burlamaqui 1752, 65–66, 121, 182–202). Samuel von Pufendorf devoted a whole chapter *Of the Law of Nature and Nations* (1729) to "the Power of the Sovereign over the Lives of the Subject, in Defence of the Commonwealth" (757–98). Daniel Defoe observed: "Punishments are … absolutely necessary for the Security, Preservation, Ease and Happiness of Mankind" (1712, 5). And Thomas Hobbes wrote in *Leviathan*:

> A PUNISHMENT *is an Evil inflicted by publique Authority, on him that hath done, or omitted that which is Judged by the same Authority to be a Transgression of the Law; to the end that the will of men may thereby the better be disposed to obedience.* (1651, II.xxviii.1 [pp. 152–53])

Shortly after the execution of King Charles I in 1649 and before the short-lived establishment of the Commonwealth of England, Scotland, and Ireland by Oliver Cromwell, Hobbes emphasized: "Punishment is a known consequence of the violation of the Laws in every Common-wealth; which punishment, if it be determined already by Law, he is subject to that; if not, then is he subject to Arbitrary punishment" (1651, II.xxvii.7 [pp. 161–62]). The Magna Carta (1215) itself had previously guaranteed English subjects certain procedural rights in criminal cases, including the right to a trial by jury before the administration of any punishment. As one clause of the Magna Carta read:

> No free man is to be taken or imprisoned or disseised or outlawed or exiled or in any way ruined, nor will we go or send against him, except by the lawful judgement of his peers or by the law of the land. (Holt 2015, 389)

The Magna Carta—lauded for centuries to come as a foundational legal document—represented a crucial step forward toward curtailing arbitrary monarchical power.

The principle of legality, formulated in Latin as *nullum crimen sine lege, nulla poena sine lege* ("no crime without law, nor punishment without law"), became firmly entrenched as a result of the Enlightenment, expressing the notion that conduct cannot be subject to a legal rule without adequate notice that the rule applied at the time of the conduct in question (Colangelo 2012, 71). As Hobbes observed of the importance of notice of the law's requirements—a principle that dictates the prohibition of *ex post facto* punishments (a prohibition expressly found in the U.S. Constitution)—in the context of England's common law system grounded in English custom:

> When a penalty, is either annexed to the Crime in the Law it self, or hath been usually inflicted in the like cases; there the Delinquent is Excused from a greater penalty. For the punishment foreknown, if not great enough to deterre men from the action, is an invitement to it: because when men compare the benefit of their Injustice, with the harm of their punishment, by necessity of Nature they choose that which appeareth best for themselves: and therefore when they are punished more than the Law had formerly determined, or more than others were punished for the same Crime; it is the Law that tempted, and deceiveth them.
>
> No Law, made after a Fact done, can make it a Crime. (1651, II.xxvii.8–9 [p. 153])

By requiring that people have proper notice of the law's requirements before being put on trial and punished for their conduct, the law took another important step forward toward eliminating arbitrary punishments.

Although England had a long history of private prosecution by victims of crime and their family members (Bessler 2022, 3–105), Hobbes inferred from "the definition of Punishment" he laid out that "neither private revenges, nor injuries of private men, can properly be stiled Punishment; because they proceed not from publique Authority" (1651, II.xxviii.3 [p. 162]). Among the many observations Hobbes made on the subject of punishment (with some penalties identified by Parliament and others left to the discretion of English judges):

> If a Punishment be determined and prescribed in the Law itself, and after the crime committed, there be a greater Punishment inflicted, the excess is not Punishment but an act of hostility. For seeing the aim of Punishment is not a revenge, but terrour; and the terrour of a great Punishment unknown, is taken away by the declaration of a less, the unexpected addition is no part of the Punishment.
>
> But where there is no Punishment at all determined by the Law, there whatsoever is inflicted, hath the nature of Punishment. For he that goes about the violation of a Law, wherein no penalty is determined, expecteth an indeterminate, that is to say, an arbitrary Punishment. (1651, II.xxviii.10 [pp. 162–63])

Reining in the law's arbitrariness—as well as the cruelty and severity of punishments—became a major goal of Enlightenment-era penal reformers.

Hobbes broke punishments into two categories: "*Divine*" and "*Humane*," the latter of which are "inflicted by the Commandment of Man" (1651, II.xxviii.14–15 [p. 163]). Hobbes wrote of the "Kingdom of God" and the "Laws of God" (II.xxxi.1 [p. 186]), and he referred to "either *Corporal*, or *Pecuniary*, or *Ignominy*, or *Imprisonment*, or *Exile*, or mixt of these" (II.

xxviii.15 [p. 163]). Hobbes described corporal punishments as those "inflicted on the body directly," and he observed that "some be *Capital*, some *Less* than *Capital*" (II.xxviii.16–17 [p. 163]). As Hobbes explained of the division of those categories of bodily punishments:

> Capital, is the Infliction of Death; and that either simply, or with torment. Less than Capital, are Stripes, Wounds, Chains, and any other corporal Pain, not in its own nature mortal. … Where a Law exacteth a Pecuniary mulct, of them that take the name of God in vain, the payment of the mulct, is not the price of a dispensation to sweare, but the Punishment of the transgression of a Law undispensable. (II.xxviii.17–18 [pp. 163–64])

More than a century later, in 1777, Thomas Jefferson would methodically divide crimes into three categories: (1) capital offenses or—in his words—"Crimes whose punishment Extends to *Life*"; (2) "Crimes whose punishment goes to *Limb*," such as castration for rapists; and (3) "Crimes punishable by *Labor*" (1903–4, 2:202; see also Bessler 2013, 428).

As penal reformers agitated for change, Enlightenment and nineteenth-century thought eventually brought massive changes to the law and punishment practices. As a result of the Glorious Revolution of 1688, the English Parliament adopted the English Bill of Rights (1689) that put legal limits on punishments. In particular, the English Bill of Rights proclaimed in these hortatory words: "That excessive Baile ought not to be required nor excessive Fines imposed nor cruell and unusuall Punishments inflicted." Some of the grievances that were reported in the lead up to that landmark set of legal protections later provided a model for America's revolutionary state constitutions and for the language in the U.S. Constitution's Eighth Amendment: "extravagant bail," "the requiring excessive bail of persons committed in criminal cases," "excessive fines have been imposed," "illegal and cruel punishments inflicted," and "imposing excessive fines and illegal punishments" (see Bessler 2012; 2019b, 1000–1001, 1007–8). At that time, hanging was "the usual Punishment" in England for "High Treason, Petty Treason, or Felony." A traitor "to the King and Government" faced a particularly horrific fate—"to be drawn upon a Hurdle or Sledge to the Gallows, and there to be hanged by the Neck," to be "cut down alive," to have his entrails "pulled out of his Belly and burnt before his Face, his Head cut off, his Body divided into four Parts, and both the Head and Body hung up or impaled where the King shall command" (Miege 1691, 125).

Shortly after the Glorious Revolution, the English philosopher and physician John Locke also wrote about punishment. In *A Second Letter Concerning Toleration* (1690a), Locke wrote:

> All Punishment is some evil, some inconvenience, some suffering; by taking away or abridging some good thing, which he who is punished has otherwise a right to. Now to justifie the bringing any such evil upon any man, two things are requisite. First, That he who does it has Commission and Power so to do. Secondly, That it be directly useful for the procuring some greater good. Whatever Punishment one man uses to another, without these two conditions, whatever he may pretend, proves an injury and injustice, and so of right ought to have been left alone. (47)

Locke saw the "Usefulness" of a punishment as making it "just," with Locke writing that a "useless Punishment be unlawful from any hand; yet useful Punishment from every hand is not lawful" (1690a, 47). Still, in his *Second Treatise of Government* (1690b), Locke interspersed biblical statements—"*who so sheddeth Mans Blood, by Man shall his Blood be shed*"—with secular justifications for punishment, writing that "each transgression, may be punished to that Degree, and with so much Severity, as will suffice to make it an ill bargain to the Offender, give him Cause to repent, and terrifie others from doing the like" (§§11–12 [p. 229]).

One major motivation for punishment—the notion of deterrence—thus appears in Locke's writings, with the concept of punishments serving as an example to discourage crime invoked by many others, including Pufendorf and, later, Beccaria and one of his biggest disciples, the English philosopher and utilitarian Jeremy Bentham. For example, Pufendorf wrote in 1698:

> The *Genuine end of Punishments in a State* is, the Prevention of wrongs and injuries: which then has its effect, when he who does the Injury is amended, or for the future incapacitated to do more, or others taking Example from his Sufferings are deter'd from like Practices. Or, to express it an other way; That which is to be considered in the business of Punishments, is the *Good*, either of the Offender, or the Party offended, or generally of All. (300)

Pufendorf asserted that "*he who Evil does should Evil suffer*. Yet in the course of Humane Punishments, we are not solely to regard the quality of the Crime, but likewise to have an Eye upon *the Benefit of the Punishment*" (302). As Pufendorf put it of punishment (also noting it would be "over-severe in Laws, to punish the most minute Lapses in the actions of men" because "in the condition of our Natures the greatest attention cannot prevent them" [304]):

> By no means executing it on purpose to feed the fancy of the party injured, or to give him pleasure in the pains and sufferings of his Adversary: Because such kind of Pleasure is absolutely inhumane, as well as contrary to the disposition of a good fellow-Subject. (302)

The aspiration to curtail cruel punishments—as expressed in the English Bill of Rights and later in revolutionary constitutions and the U.S. Constitution's Eighth Amendment—became a major theme of Enlightenment criminal justice reform.

Eighteenth- and nineteenth-century philosophers articulated very different rationales for punishment, with criminal-law theorists falling into a utilitarian camp, a retributivist camp, or some blend of the two. Echoing Beccaria, Bentham wrote:

> The general object which all laws have, or ought to have, in common, is to augment total happiness of the community; and therefore, in the first place, to exclude, as far as may be, every thing that tends to subtract from that happiness: in other words, to exclude mischief.
>
> But all punishment is mischief: all punishment in itself is evil. Upon the principle of utility, if it ought at all to be admitted, it ought only to be admitted in as far as it promises to exclude some greater evil. (1789, ch. XIII, §§1–2 [p. 166])

In contrast, the German philosophers Immanuel Kant and Georg Wilhelm Friedrich Hegel promoted and heavily influenced the concept of retributivism, which concerns an offender's blameworthiness or "just deserts"—an idea tied to ancient Judeo-Christian texts articulating the "*law of retribution*" or *lex talionis* (Kant 1996, 6:332, 363 [pp. 473, 497]; Hegel 1991, §§101, 218 [pp. 127, 251]). Punishment, Kant asserted, "must always be inflicted" on an offender "only *because he has committed a crime*" and not "merely as a means to the purposes of another" (1996, 6:331 [p. 473]). Calling punishment "a categorical imperative," or duty, Kant dismissed Beccaria's critique of capital punishment as "sophistry," and in explaining the concept of *lex talionis*, said "what is done to him [the offender] in accordance with penal law is what he has perpetrated on others" (Kant 1996, 6:331, 335, 365 [pp. 473, 476, 498]). Hegel saw both crime and punishment as coercive and "*contrary to right*," and he said that the *lex talionis* concept could be reduced to "an absurdity" (i.e., "theft as retribution for theft, robbery for robbery, an eye for an eye, and a tooth for a tooth, so that one can even imagine the miscreant as one-eyed or toothless") (1991, §§92, 101 [pp. 120, 128]). Nonetheless, he expressed the view that, because punishment follows crime, "*coercion is cancelled* [*aufgehoben*] *by coercion*; it [punishment] is therefore not only conditionally right but necessary—namely as a *second* coercion which cancels an initial coercion" (§93 [p. 120]). Believing punishment negates crime, Hegel expressed the view—in what has been described as his "annulment theory"—that punishment is "the negation of the negation" and that "*what the criminal has done should also happen to him*" with some sort of equivalence (§97, 101, 104 [pp. 123, 127, 131]; see also Christopher 2002, 860n79; Dubber 1994, 1578–83).

Retributivists "do not look forward, so much as back—back 'to the seriousness and harmfulness of the offense that has been committed and to the moral blameworthiness of the offender'" (Pauley 1994, 97). Those ascribing to utilitarianism, however, take a more forward-looking approach after a crime's commission, seeking to deter future wrongdoing (by the offender and others) and to facilitate an offender's rehabilitation. Beccaria, who once made use of algebra in an effort to articulate the optimal punishment for smuggling, himself laid the foundation for deterrence theory while seeking to protect liberty and a person's humanity in the criminal justice process (Christopher 2002, 925). As Beccaria declared: "There is no freedom when the laws permit a man in some cases to cease to be a *person* and to become a *thing*" (1995, 50). As Keith Hylton emphasizes:

> Utilitarianism and the theory of punishment again coalesced in the hands of Bentham in the late 1770s. Bentham adopted Beccaria's formula that the penalty should be set at a level that eliminates gain on the part of the offender. Bentham's major practical innovation was the introduction of marginal deterrence concerns—that a very harsh punishment would not discourage the offender from committing a more harmful act which carried the same, or only slightly harsher, punishment. (1998, 426)

Debates over retributivism versus utilitarianism continue unabated, though the rise of civil and dignity rights and international human rights law have fundamentally altered the criminal justice landscape beyond the issue of deterrence conceptualized centuries ago.

The eighteenth and nineteenth centuries ushered in a period of transition from "sanguinary" or "bloody" laws and punishments to the "penitentiary" system (Willis 2005, 177, 187; Bessler 2014a). Prisons were constructed in various American states and in Europe, with America's first penitentiary, the Walnut Street Prison, opening in Philadelphia in 1790. New York City's Newgate Prison emerged in 1796; by 1810, nine American states had built penitentiaries; the State of New York authorized the construction of the

Auburn State Prison in 1816; and Pennsylvania's legislature authorized the construction of the Western State Penitentiary near Pittsburgh and the Eastern State Penitentiary in Philadelphia in 1818 and 1821, respectively. Across the Atlantic, Bentham designed and proposed a plan for a circular prison, publishing his ideas in *Panopticon, or The Inspection House* (1791), though it took considerable time—decades, actually—before experimentation with Bentham's ideas occurred in England. The penitentiaries that got built, though, allowed for the use of terms of imprisonment in lieu of executions, led to hard labor and harsh solitary confinement regimes, and attracted significant public attention after their construction (Foucault 1995, 203–7; Rubin 2015, 377–79). From 1831 to 1832, Alexis de Tocqueville—the French political thinker, famous for his two-volume *Democracy in America* (1835, 1840)—even traveled to America with Gustave de Beaumont for the express purpose of studying America's prisons (Beaumont and de Tocqueville 2018, xv). Their book, *On the Penitentiary System in the United States and Its Application to France* (1833), was "the product of their official investigation on behalf of the French government, designed to elucidate whether one of two primary American penitentiary systems (Philadelphia or Auburn) could be implemented to successfully reform French prisons" (Phillips 1998, 110).

In time, the embrace of the penitentiary system, along with waves of anti-gallows agitation that sought to rehabilitate instead of exterminate offenders, led to the abolition of capital punishment in places such as Michigan (1846), Rhode Island (1852), and Wisconsin (1853), and to less use of the death penalty (at least for certain categories of offenders) and other bodily punishments (Fisher 1995, 1236–40). Back in 1793, Massachusetts governor John Hancock had openly called for an end to "the infamous punishments of cropping and branding, as well as that of the Public Whipping Post," which he called "an indignity to human nature" ([1793] 1996, 417). Much reform had ensued, though prison officials continued to resort to corporal punishments to discipline prisoners in some locales. In 1840, in *Democracy in America*, de Tocqueville remarked on the "mildness" of America's criminal justice system, observing that, "whereas the English seem to want to preserve carefully the bloody traces of the Middle Ages in their penal legislation, the Americans have almost made the death penalty disappear from their codes" (2000, 538; see also Steiker 2002, 98–99). According to Meghan Ryan, "Beginning in the late eighteenth and early nineteenth centuries, consequentialist theories of punishment—rehabilitation, deterrence, and incapacitation—challenged retribution's position as the primary justification for punishment in the legal and philosophical landscapes" (2012, 1055–56).

Even the English "Bloody Code"—the draconian English system of criminal law in the eighteenth and early nineteenth centuries, when scores of felonies were punishable by death—eventually gave way to a more humane system. In explaining the gradual transition that occurred across the world in terms of punishment practices, Michael Madow notes that England's Parliament abolished branding in 1779 via the same act that authorized the construction of penitentiaries; Massachusetts abolished branding, the pillory, and whipping in the 1804–1805 legislative session; and France abolished branding in 1832 (1995, 491–92). In England, the pillory—notoriously used against various offenders (Bessler 2019b, 1013, 1021–27, 1042)—was also abolished as societal sensibilities about criminals and the infliction of pain and suffering changed. Taking note of the societal change, Madow writes:

> By 1850 or thereabouts, such practices as branding, whipping, the pillory, the public exposure of corpses, and punitive public dissection, had been abolished or sharply curtailed, and "reformative" imprisonment had been installed as the punishment of first resort for most crimes. In the same period, capital punishment was confined to a few very grave crimes, and a variety of measures were adopted to reduce its public visibility and "spectacular" character. (1995, 491–92)

The abolition of corporal punishments and the curtailment of executions ushered in a decidedly new approach to crime and punishment.

Ultimately, Enlightenment and nineteenth-century thinkers put an end to the *ancien régime*—though vestiges of it, including the death penalty and state-sanctioned corporal punishments in some societies (e.g., Saudi Arabia), still linger in modern life. In his *Enquiry How Far the Punishment of Death Is Necessary in Pennsylvania* (1793), William Bradford Jr. tellingly declared that Montesquieu and Beccaria had "led the way" and that many of their

> principles … have obtained the force of axioms, and are no longer considered as the subjects either of doubt or demonstration. "*That the prevention [o]f crimes is the sole end of punishment*," is one of these: and it is another, "*That every punishment which is not absolutely necessary for that purpose is a cruel and tyrannical act*." To these may be added a third, (calculated to limit the first) which is, "*That every penalty should be proportioned to the offence*." (1793, 3; see also Bessler 2019a, 97–98)

In the 1820s, as part of an autobiographical sketch, Thomas Jefferson recalled his own work to revise and reform Virginia's criminal law in the 1770s, explaining that "Beccaria, and other writers on crimes and punishments, had satisfied the reasonable world of the unrightfulness and inefficacy of the punishment of crimes by death" (Jefferson 1903–4, 1:67). Jefferson and other American founders forever marred their reputations by failing to emancipate the enslaved—and by authorizing horrific corporal punishments and executions (Steiker and Steiker 2015, 245–46). Enlightenment thinkers, in fact, under-conceptualized torture, totally neglecting, for instance, the psychological torture inherent in death sentences (Bessler 2017, 2019d). By failing to classify barbarous corporal punishments and death sentences (the latter involving the systematic use of state-sponsored death threats) as torturous punishments, they left that task to future penal reformers, even though much criminal law reform occurred over the course of the Enlightenment and into the nineteenth century (Bessler 2013, 2019d). Indeed, in the wake of America's bloody Civil War (1861–1865), the principle of equality—long invoked by revolutionaries and lawmakers—came into better focus and was put into binding legal provisions as nations, one by one, outlawed slavery. In 1866, for instance, the United States Congress passed its first Civil Rights Act, requiring that citizens "of every race and color, without regard to any previous condition of slavery or involuntary servitude," be subjected "to like punishment, pains, and penalties" (14 Stat. 27–30).

4 Conclusion

A few major themes emerge as one examines the transition from the *ancien régime* to the beginnings of modernity that the Enlightenment and the nineteenth century brought into existence. First, unwritten laws or customs—often providing for barbarous punishments that were publicly inflicted and used in a highly discriminatory fashion—gradually transitioned to codified legal codes that, in time and on their face, required equality of treatment and a more even-handed administration of the law (Bessler 2014a, 2016). The ratification of the U.S. Constitution's Fourteenth Amendment in 1868 came just three years after the Thirteenth Amendment's abolition of slavery and involuntary servitude "except as a punishment for crime" in 1865. The Fourteenth Amendment required "equal protection of the laws," and—in time—was interpreted to incorporate against American states the protections of the U.S. Bill of Rights, including the Eighth Amendment's all-important proscriptions on "excessive bail," "excessive fines," and "cruel and unusual punishments" (see Bessler 2012, 304–7; 2020, 24; see also Epps 2013). Second, and relatedly, as the proportionality and parsimony principles emphasized by Montesquieu, Beccaria, and others grew deeper roots, with Beccaria calling for a scale of crimes and a corresponding scale of punishments, and for *absolute necessity* to dictate the level of an offender's punishment (with *certainty* and *uniformity* to replace *severity* and *arbitrariness*), societies gradually began to abandon or discontinue torturous cruelty and the use of executions, maiming, and other corporal punishments (Bessler 2013, 2014a, 2018a).

Finally, from the Renaissance to the Enlightenment to the nineteenth century, societies reconceived of the underpinnings and justifications for punishment. They shifted away from the "divine right of kings" and principally religious justifications for punishment to an administration of justice premised on the Rule of Law, secular rationales, the protection of liberty and human rights (including the rights of the accused and those confined within prisons), and the value of non-discrimination, though the law—as history clearly shows—was nonetheless frequently abused or applied in a highly discriminatory fashion, with even more fights to come (e.g., against racial segregation and post-Reconstruction Jim Crow laws) in the twentieth century. "In the years following the Civil War," Kevin Barry and Bharat Malkani write of America's nineteenth-century legal landscape, "slave codes gave way to 'Black Codes,' which reinstated a dual system of criminal justice based explicitly on race, with the death penalty at its center" (2017, 191). Despite the failings of the Enlightenment and eighteenth- and nineteenth-century lawmakers to achieve the promise of true equality, material progress was achieved through concerted struggle. Although *de jure* and *de facto* racial and gender discrimination stubbornly persisted in so many locales around the globe, the law's overarching North Star—though still at a great distance, with John Adams, the penman of the Massachusetts Constitution of 1780, promising in that constitution's thirtieth article "a government of laws and not of men"—had at least been alluringly sighted in the dark night sky: the protection of fundamental and universal human rights, including the right to equality of treatment and the right to be free from discrimination, torture, and other forms of cruelty.

References

Anderson, Stanley. 1991. "Human Rights and the Structure of International Law." *New York Law School Journal of International and Comparative Law* 12, nos. 1–2: 1–28.

Barmash, Pamela. 2020. *The Laws of Hammurabi: At the Confluence of Royal and Scribal Traditions*. Oxford: Oxford University Press.

Barrie, David G., and Susan Broomhall. 2014. *Police Courts in Nineteenth-Century Scotland: Magistrates, Media and the Masses*. Surrey, UK: Ashgate.

Barry, Kevin, and Bharat Malkani. 2017. "The Death Penalty's Darkside: A Response to Phyllis Goldfarb's *Matters of Strata: Race, Gender, and Class Structures in Capital Cases*." *Washington and Lee Law Review Online* 74, no. 1: 184–214.

Bassiouni, M. Cherif. 2010. "Perspectives on International Criminal Justice." *Virginia Journal of International Law* 50, no. 2 (Winter): 269–324.

Beaumont, Gustave de, and Alexis de Tocqueville. 2018. *On the Penitentiary System in the United States and Its Application to France: The Complete Text*. Translated by Emily Katherine Ferkaluk. Cham, Switzerland: Palgrave Macmillan.

Beccaria, Cesare. 1995. *On Crimes and Punishments and Other Writings*. Translated by Richard Davies, Virginia Cox, and Richard Bellamy. Edited by Richard Bellamy. Cambridge: Cambridge University Press.

Bentham, Jeremy. 1789. *An Introduction to the Principles of Morals and Legislation*. London: T. Payne, and Son.

Bessler, John D. 2009. "Revisiting Beccaria's Vision: The Enlightenment, America's Death Penalty, and the Abolition Movement." *Northwestern Journal of Law and Social Policy* 4, no. 2 (Fall): 195–328.

———. 2012. *Cruel and Unusual: The American Death Penalty and the Founders' Eighth Amendment*. Boston, MA: Northeastern University Press.

———. 2013. "The Anomaly of Executions: The Cruel and Unusual Punishments Clause in the 21st Century." *British Journal of American Legal Studies* 2, no. 2 (Fall): 297–451.

———. 2014a. *The Birth of American Law: An Italian Philosopher and the American Revolution*. Durham, NC: Carolina Academic Press.

———. 2014b. "Foreword: The Death Penalty in Decline: From Colonial America to the Present." *Criminal Law Bulletin* 50, no. 2 (March-April): 245–62.

———. 2016. "The Inequality of America's Death Penalty: A Crossroads for Capital Punishment at the Intersection of the Eighth and Fourteenth Amendments." *Washington and Lee Law Review Online* 73: 487–571.

———. 2017. *The Death Penalty as Torture: From the Dark Ages to Abolition*. Durham, NC: Carolina Academic Press.

———. 2018a. "The Abolitionist Movement Comes of Age: From Capital Punishment as a Lawful Sanction to a Peremptory, International Law Norm Barring Executions." *Montana Law Review* 79, no. 1 (Winter): 7–48.

———. 2018b. *The Celebrated Marquis: An Italian Noble and the Making of the Modern World*. Durham, NC: Carolina Academic Press.

———. 2019a. *The Baron and the Marquis: Liberty, Tyranny, and the Enlightenment Maxim That Can Remake American Criminal Justice*. Durham, NC: Carolina Academic Press.

———. 2019b. "A Century in the Making: The Glorious Revolution, the American Revolution, and the Origins of the U.S. Constitution's Eighth Amendment." *William & Mary Bill of Rights Journal* 27, no. 4 (May): 989–1078.

———. 2019c. "The Marquis Beccaria: An Italian Penal Reformer's Meteoric Rise in the British Isles in the Transatlantic Republic of Letters." *Diciottesimo Secolo* 4: 107–20.

———. 2019d. "Taking Psychological Torture Seriously: The Torturous Nature of Credible Death Threats and the Collateral Consequences for Capital Punishment." *Northeastern University Law Review* 11, no. 1: 1–97.

———. 2020. "From the Founding to the Present: An Overview of Legal Thought and the Eighth Amendment's Evolution." In *The Eighth Amendment and Its Future in a New Age of Punishment*, edited by Meghan J. Ryan and William W. Berry III, 11–26. Cambridge: Cambridge University Press

———. 2022. *Private Prosecution in America: Its Origins, History, and Unconstitutionality in the Twenty-First Century*. Durham, NC: Carolina Academic Press.

Biagini, Theodore J. 2009–10. "Machiavelli and His Influence on Modern International Law: Victory Goes to the Swift, the Strong, and Sometimes, the Ruthless." *Lincoln Law Review* 37: 1–85.

Blackstone, William. 1979. *Commentaries on the Laws of England: A Facsimile of the First Edition of 1765–1769*. Chicago: University of Chicago Press.

Blake, Thomas. 1658. *Vindiciæ Foederis; or, A Treatise of the Covenant of God Entered with Man-Kinde, in the Several Kindes and Degrees of It*. 2nd ed. London: Abel Roper.

Borkowski, Andrew. 1994. *Textbook on Roman Law*. London: Blackstone.

Bradford, William Jr. 1793. *An Enquiry How Far the Punishment of Death Is Necessary in Pennsylvania*. Philadelphia: T. Dobson.

Burlamaqui, Jean Jacques. 1752. *The Principles of Politic Law: Being A Sequel to the Principles of Natural Law*. Translated by Thomas Nugent. London: J. Nourse.

Cahn, Mark D. 1989. "Punishment, Discretion, and the Codification of Prescribed Penalties in Colonial Massachusetts." *American Journal of Legal History* 33, no. 2 (April): 107–36.

Carawan, Edwin. 1998. *Rhetoric and the Law of Draco*. Oxford: Clarendon.

Carugati, Federica, Gillian K. Hadfield, and Barry R. Weingast. 2015. "Building Legal Order in Ancient Athens." *Journal of Legal Analysis* 7, no. 2 (Winter): 291–324.

Christopher, Russell L. 2002. "Deterring Retributivism: The Injustice of 'Just' Punishment." *Northwestern University Law Review* 96, no. 3 (Spring): 843–976.

Colangelo, Anthony J. 2012. "Spatial Legality." *Northwestern University Law Review* 107, no. 1 (Fall): 69–125.

Clarke, George, ed. 1987. *John Bellers: His Life, Times and Writings*. London: Routledge & Kegan Paul.

Dahlquist, David Edward. 2000. "Inherent Conflict: A Case against the Use of Contingency Fees by Special Assistants in Quasi-Governmental Prosecutorial Roles." *DePaul Law Review* 50, no. 2 (Winter): 743–98.

Defoe, Daniel. 1712. *No Punishment No Government: And No Danger Even in the Worst Designs*. London: Booksellers of London and Westminster.

Denk, Kurt M. 2012. "Jurisprudence That Necessarily Embodies Moral Judgment: The Eighth Amendment, Catholic Teaching, and Death Penalty Discourse." *Notre Dame Law Review* 88, no. 1: 323–93.

Denney, Liam P. 2000. Review of *The Abolition of the Death Penalty in International Law*, by William A. Schabas. *Suffolk Transnational Law Review* 23: 803–14.

Dubber, Markus Dirk. 1994. "Rediscovering Hegel's Theory of Crime and Punishment." *Michigan Law Review* 92, no. 6 (May): 1577–1621.

Durant, Will. 1966. *The Life of Greece: A History of Greek Government, Industry, Manners, Morals, Religion, Philosophy, Science, Literature and Art from the Earliest Times to the Roman Conquest*. New York: Simon and Schuster.

Edwards, Jonathan. 1698. *A Preservative against Socinianism*. Pt. 2. 2nd ed. Oxon, UK: Clements.

Elkins, Nathan T. 2019. *A Monument to Dynasty and Death: The Story of Rome's Colosseum and the Emperors Who Built It*. Baltimore: Johns Hopkins University Press.

Ellison, Nathanael. 1700. *The Magistrates Obligation to Punishment to Punish VICE: A Sermon Preach'd before The Right Worshipful the Mayor, Aldermen, Sheriff, &c. of the Town and County of Newcastle upon Tyne*. London: W. B. (for Richard Randell).

Epps, Garrett. 2013. *Democracy Reborn: The Fourteenth Amendment and the Fight for Equal Rights in Post-Civil War America*. New York: Holt.

Fisher, George. 1995. "The Birth of the Prison Retold." *Yale Law Journal* 104, no. 6 (April): 1235–1324.

Forsyth, William, and James Appleton Morgan. 1994. *History of Trial by Jury*. 2nd ed. Union, NJ: Lawbook Exchange.

Foucault, Michel. 1995. *Discipline and Punish: The Birth of the Prison*. Translated by Alan Sheridan. New York: Vintage.

Frankenberg, Günter. 2008. "Torture and Taboo: An Essay Comparing Paradigms of Organized Cruelty." *American Journal of Comparative Law* 56, no. 2 (Spring): 403–22.

Friedland, Paul. 2014. *Seeing Justice Done: The Age of Spectacular Capital Punishment in France*. Oxford: Oxford University Press.

Gerber, Scott D. 2015. "Law and Religion in Colonial Connecticut." *American Journal of Legal History* 55, no. 2 (April): 149–93.

Good, Edwin M. 1967. "Capital Punishment and Its Alternatives in Ancient Near Eastern Law." *Stanford Law Review* 19, no. 5 (May): 947–77.

Grotius, Hugo. 1715. *On the Rights of War and Peace, in Three Volumes; in Which Are Explain'd the Laws and Claims of Nature and Nations, and the Principal Points That Relate Either to Publick Government, or the Conduct of Private Life*. London: D. Brown, T. Ward and W. Meares.

Hancock, John. [1793] 1996. Speech to the General Court, January 30, 1793. In *John Hancock's Life and Speeches: A Personalized Vision of the American Revolution, 1763–1793*, by Paul D. Brandes, 414–21. Lanham, MD: Scarecrow.

Harper, Robert Francis. 1999. *The Code of Hammurabi King of Babylon about 2250 B.C.* Union, NJ: Lawbook Exchange.

Hegel, G. W. F. 1991. *Elements of the Philosophy of Right*. Translated by H. B. Nisbet. Edited by Allen W. Wood. Cambridge: Cambridge University Press.

Heineccius, Johann Gottlieb. 1741. *A Methodical System of Universal Law: Or, the Laws of Nature and Nations Deduced from Certain Principles, and Applied to Proper Cases*. Translated by George Turnbull. London: J. Noon.

Hobbes, Thomas. 1651. *Leviathan, or, The Matter, Form, and Power of a Commonwealth Ecclesiastical and Civil*. London: Andrew Crooke.

Holt, J. C. 2015. *Magna Carta*. 3rd ed. Cambridge: Cambridge University Press.

Hornum, Finn. 1972. "The Executioner: His Role and Status in Scandinavian Society." In *Selected Readings for Introductory Sociology*, edited by Charles H. Ainsworth, 67–79. New York: MSS Information Corporation.

Hyde, Walter Woodburn. 1918. "The Homicide Courts of Ancient Athens." *University of Pennsylvania Law Review* 66, nos. 7–8: 319–62.

Hylton, Keith N. 1998. "Punitive Damages and the Economic Theory of Penalties." *Georgetown Law Journal* 87: 421–71.

Jefferson, Thomas. 1903–4. *The Writings of Thomas Jefferson*. 20 vols. Edited by Albert Ellery Bergh and Andrew A. Lipscomb. Washington, DC: Thomas Jefferson Memorial Association.

Jouet, Mugambi. 2021. "Revolutionary Criminal Punishments: Treason, Mercy, and the American Revolution." *American Journal of Legal History* 61, no. 2 (June): 139–76.

Kant, Immanuel. 1996. *The Metaphysics of Morals*. In *Practical Philosophy*, translated and edited by Mary J. Gregor, 363–602. Cambridge: Cambridge University Press.

Keyishian, Harry. 2008. "Henry de Bracton, Renaissance Punishment Theory, and Shakespearean Closure." *Law and Literature* 20, no. 3 (Fall): 444–58.

LaFave, Wayne R., Jerold H. Israel, Nancy J. King, and Orin S Kerr. 2015. *Criminal Procedure*. 7 vols. 4th ed. New York: Thomson Reuters.

Larson, Frances. 2014. *Severed: A History of Heads Lost and Heads Found*. London: Granta.

Levy, Leonard W. 1993. *Blasphemy: Verbal Offense against the Sacred, from Moses to Salman Rushdie*. Chapel Hill, NC: University of North Carolina Press.

Locke, John. 1690a. *A Second Letter Concerning Toleration*. London: Awnsham Churchill.

———. 1690b. *Two Treatises of Government*. London: Awnsham Churchill.

Long, Walter C. 2015. "The Constitutionality and Ethics of Execution-Day Prison Chaplaincy." *Texas Journal on Civil Liberties & Civil Rights* 21, no. 1 (Fall): 1–33.

Machiavelli, Niccolò. 1996. *Discourses on Livy*. Translated by Harvey C. Mansfield and Nathan Tarcov. Chicago: University of Chicago Press.

———. 2003. *The Prince*. Translated by George Bull. London: Penguin.

Madden, M. Stuart. 2006. "The Græco-Roman Antecedents of Modern Tort Law." *Brandeis Law Journal* 44, no. 4: 865–910.

Madow, Michael. 1995. "Forbidden Spectacle: Executions, the Public and the Press in Nineteenth Century New York." *Buffalo Law Review* 43, no. 2 (Fall): 461–562.

Mather, Henry. 2002. "The Medieval Revival of Roman Law: Implications for Contemporary Legal Education." *Catholic Lawyer* 41, no. 4 (Spring): 323–62.
Mayer, Gregg. 2007. "The Poet and Death: Literary Reflections on Capital Punishment through the Sonnets of William Wordsworth." *Saint John's Journal of Legal Commentary* 21, no. 3 (Spring/Summer): 727–65.
Mede, Joseph. 1652. *Discourses on Sundry Texts of Scripture*. London: J. F. (for John Clark).
Miege, Guy. 1691. *The New State of England under Their Majesties K. William and Q. Mary*. London: H. C. (for Jonathan Robinson).
Miethe, Terance D., and Hong Lu. 2005. *Punishment: A Comparative Historical Perspective*. Cambridge: Cambridge University Press.
Monro, Robert. 1637. *Monro: His Expedition with the Worthy Scots Regiment (Called Mac-Keyes Regiment) Levied in August 1626*. London: William Jones.
Montaigne, Michel de. 1991. *The Complete Essays*. Translated by M. A. Screech. London: Penguin.
Montesquieu, Charles de Secondat baron de. 1989. *The Spirit of the Laws*. Translated by Anne M. Cohler, Basia Carolyn Miller, and Harold Samuel Stone. Cambridge: Cambridge University Press.
Murphy, Jeffrie G., and Jules L. Coleman. 1990. *Philosophy of Law: An Introduction to Jurisprudence*. 2nd ed. Boulder, CO: Westview.
Olson, Trisha. 2006–7. "The Medieval Blood Sanction and the Divine Beneficence of Pain: 1100–1450." *Journal of Law and Religion* 22, no. 1: 63–130.
Orfield, Lester Bernhardt. 2002. *The Growth of Scandinavian Law*. Union, NJ: Lawbook Exchange.
Paine, Thomas. 1776. *Common Sense*. Philadelphia: J. Almon.
Pauley, Matthew A. 1994. "The Jurisprudence of Crime and Punishment from Plato to Hegel." *American Journal of Jurisprudence* 39, no. 1: 97–152.
Perrinchief, Richard. 1663. *Samaritanism: Or, A Treatise of Comprehending, Compounding, and Tolerating Several Religions in One Church, Demonstrating, the Equity and Necessity of the Act, and Late Vote of Parliament against Non-Conformists*. London: Robert Clavel.
Phillips, Jim. 1998. Review of *Qualities of Mercy: Justice, Punishment, and Discretion*, edited by Carolyn Strange. *American Journal of Legal History* 42, no. 1 (January): 109–111.
Plato. 1961. "Protagoras." In *The Collected Dialogues of Plato*, edited by Edith Hamilton and Huntington Cairns, 308–52. Princeton, NJ: Princeton University Press.
———. 1991. *The Republic of Plato*. Translated by Allan Bloom. 2nd ed. New York: Basic.
———. 2016. *The Laws*. Translated by Tom Griffith. Edited by Malcolm Schofield. Cambridge: Cambridge University Press.
Pufendorf, Samuel. 1698. *The Whole Duty of Man According to the Law of Nature*. 2nd ed. London: Benjamin Motte (for Charles Harper).

———. 1729. *Of the Law of Nature and Nations*. 4th ed. London: J. Walthoe et al.
Rousseau, Jean-Jacques. 1988. *On the Social Contract*. Translated and edited by Donald A. Cress. Indianapolis, IN: Hackett.
Rubin, Ashley T. 2015. "A Neo-Institutional Account of Prison Diffusion." *Law & Society Review* 49, no. 2 (June): 365–99.
Rutherfurd, Samuel. 1645. *The Tryal & Triumph of Faith: Or, An Exposition of the History of Christs Dispossessing of the Daughter of the Woman of Canaan*. London: John Field.
Ryan, Meghan J. 2012. "Proximate Retribution." *Houston Law Review* 48, no. 5 (Winter): 104–6.
Santamarina, Gil. 1992. "The Case for Televised Executions." *Cardozo Arts & Entertainment Law Journal* 11: 101–43.
Servita, Paul. 1655. *The History of the Inquisition*. London: Humphrey Moseley.
Stalley, R. F. 1983. *An Introduction to Plato's Laws*. Indianapolis, IN: Hackett.
Steiker, Carol S. 2002. "Capital Punishment and American Exceptionalism." *Oregon Law Review* 81, no. 1 (Spring): 97–130.
Steiker, Carol S., and Jordan M. Steiker. 2015. "The American Death Penalty and the (In)Visibility of Race." *University of Chicago Law Review* 82, no. 1 (Winter): 243–94.
Stevenson, William R. Jr. 2004. "Calvin and Political Issues." In *The Cambridge Companion to John Calvin*, edited by Donald K. McKim, 173–87. Cambridge: Cambridge University Press.
Tocqueville, Alexis de. 2000. *Democracy in America*. Translated and edited by Harvey C. Mansfield and Delba Winthrop. Chicago: University of Chicago Press.
Voltaire. 1972. *Philosophical Dictionary*. Translated and edited by Theodore Besterman. New York: Penguin.
von Bar, Car Ludwig. 1916. *A History of Continental Criminal Law*. Translated by Thomas S. Bell. Boston: Little, Brown, and Co.
Ward, Nathaniel. 1998. "The Massachusetts Body of Liberties." In *Colonial Origins of the American Constitution: A Documentary History*, edited by Donald S. Lutz, 70–87. Indianapolis, IN: Liberty Fund.
Warden, Rob, and Daniel Lennard. 2018. "Death in America under Color of Law: Our Long, Inglorious Experience with Capital Punishment." *Northwestern Journal of Law and Social Policy* 13, no. 4: 194–306.
Willis, James J. 2005. "Transportation versus Imprisonment in Eighteenth- and Nineteenth-Century Britain: Penal Power, Liberty, and the State." *Law and Society Review* 39, no. 1 (March): 171–210.
Wink, Stephen P., and Walter Wink. 1993. "Domination, Justice and the Cult of Violence." *Saint Louis University Law Journal* 38, no. 2: 341–78.
Wolff, Hans Julius. 1951. *Roman Law: An Historical Introduction*. Norman, OK: University of Oklahoma Press.
Woodhead, Abraham. 1688. *The Second Treatise Containing a Discourse of the Succession of Clergy*. Oxford: O. Walker.

3

Hobbes versus Hart: Reflections on Legal Positivism and the Point of Punishment

Margaret Martin

It is often believed that H. L. A. Hart dons two hats. He is a criminal theorist when he writes about criminal responsibility, and he is a legal positivist when he explores questions about law in general. His narrow vision of legal theory, which involves substantive and methodological constraints, means that theories that fail to adhere to these constraints are outside of the domain of jurisprudence. From a methodological perspective, Hart maintains that jurisprudence is a non-normative enterprise that seeks to make sense of our shared concept of law by engaging in what he calls "descriptive sociology" (1997, vi).[1] Instead of grounding one's theory of law in a contestable conception of human nature, legal philosophers must become careful observers of law as it exists. According to Hart, the legal philosopher is tasked with separating the *necessary* elements of law that are shared by all existing legal systems from the *contingent* ones. Only elements deemed "necessary" qualify for inclusion in the concept of law that emerges from this process. Hart identifies two conditions that are "necessary and sufficient for the existence of a legal system": (1) the union of primary and secondary rules, including a rule of recognition; and (2) obedience by most of the population. Hart adds that they may obey "from any motive whatsoever," including fear (1997, 116).

[1] Hart's methodology changes over time (see Martin 2021). In this chapter, I focus on the method used in *The Concept of Law* and not the Postscript that was eventually added to the text.

M. Martin (✉)
Western University, London, ON, Canada
e-mail: mmart2@uwo.ca

© The Author(s), under exclusive license to Springer Nature Switzerland AG 2023

M. C. Altman (ed.), *The Palgrave Handbook on the Philosophy of Punishment*, Palgrave Handbooks in the Philosophy of Law, https://doi.org/10.1007/978-3-031-11874-6_3

This new approach, which famously keeps what law *is* separated from what it *ought* to be, is introduced in the hopes of escaping from the value-laden debates engaged in by philosophers in the tradition. To begin with a contestable account of human nature means that the debate about the nature of law can never escape from the intractable disagreements about the nature of the human condition more generally. Progress in the field is only possible if one can focus on what law *is*. In other words, the promise contained in *The Concept of Law* is that of a new beginning.

In what follows, I call into question this approach. I will argue that there is more continuity in legal positivist thought than is often assumed. A number of Hart's foundational assumptions are Hobbesian. Once this becomes apparent, the sharp dividing line between legal philosophy and other kinds of philosophy (including criminal theory) ceases to hold. This becomes clearer when their respective accounts of punishment are explored. I will argue that Hobbes's complex account is preferable to Hart's because the relationship between theses can be discerned. Hart's account, on the other hand, is incomplete and potentially incoherent. It is unclear if the elements of his "mixed" account can coexist as he supposes. It is also unclear whether Hart's central claims in *Punishment and Responsibility* can coexist alongside *The Concept of Law*. I will begin by exploring how juridical ideas permeate Hobbes's theory, which sets the stage for a discussion of punishment.

1 Hobbes's War: A Juridical Idea?

To understand the nature of Hobbesian civil society, the role of positive law within it, and his account of punishment, it is imperative to begin in his state of nature. Hobbes needs a war of all against all in order to generate peace. War, however, is not a given but an intellectual achievement. This has implications for all aspects of his account.

Hobbes begins by assuming that humans are isolated individuals with insatiable appetites and an overriding fear of death. He then tells us that goods are scarce. These assumptions alone seem to be sufficient to trigger a war. But war proves elusive. Hobbes needs an additional assumption—he needs equality. Hobbes argues that individuals in the state of nature enjoy equality of the "faculties of body and mind" (1994, I.xiii.1 [p. 74]). Hobbes excludes women and children from the state of nature, leaving only men primed for battle. He must do so because otherwise the weak will be incentivized to submit to the strong for the sake of self-preservation. Domination and hierarchy would quickly emerge as the natural state of humankind. Notice that even with the assumption of equality of strength and intelligence, Hobbes's war has not yet taken hold.

The fear of losing a battle against an equally able opponent means the risk to life and limb remains high. Thus, it will still be rational to submit to one's opponent in many instances, and domination, once again, becomes inevitable. Hobbes spies the problem and provides the needed solution: the state of nature, he argues, is marked by "equality of hope" (1994, I.xiii.3 [p. 75]). All parties *believe* they can win a given battle and consequently, when they seek the same object, they "endeavour to destroy or subdue one another" (I.xiii.3 [p. 75]). Ego is the final ingredient required to generate the famous war of all against all. Men in a state of nature "have no pleasure, but on the contrary a great deal of grief, in keeping company where there is no power able to overawe them all" (I.xiii.5 [p. 75]). Notice, also, that the presumption of equality is necessary to create the preconditions for the social contract. If the state of nature had been defined by hierarchy, individuals at the top would have no reason to submit to the sovereign, while those at the bottom would not have the power to make this choice.

If we reflect on the nature of contract law, the extent to which Hobbes's account is driven by the needs of this particular legal mechanism is revealed. Contract law, as lawyers know, presupposes the equality of the contracting parties. It is an abstract, empty idea of equality that animates the practice (Simmonds 1985). Thus, it is not a coincidence that in Hobbes's state of nature we find precisely this kind of empty equality. Individuals are empty placeholders. All individuating characteristics have been excluded: humans are comprised of appetite, will, and reason. The will allows an individual to consent to the contract, and reason enables him to see the need to do so. The individuals' appetites create the conditions that render life in this natural state unbearable. In sum, the condition of abstract, empty equality is needed for the contract to be possible, while war is necessary to incentivize its creation. When viewed from this perspective, we can see the juridical underpinnings of Hobbes's state of nature.[2]

While there are complexities involved in the movement from the state of nature to the civil society, the key idea is that everyone in the state of nature can see that it is rational to lay down their rights to all things to an individual

[2] One of the implications of this analysis is that we cannot know if Hobbes really thinks humans are like this or whether he simply needs to present them in this way given the demands of contract law.

who is outside of the social contract.[3] Once civil society is established, the importance of positive law cannot be overstated.

With the arrival of positive law comes justice, which is defined as keeping one's covenants (Hobbes 1994, I.xv.2 [p. 89]).[4] It is unjust to break your contracts, and it is just to keep them. Law becomes the measure of things. In addition, positive law is what allows social bonds to be forged and progress to take hold (I.xiii.9 [p. 76]). A system of posited norms issued by a single source is meant to displace old hierarchies of power along with familiar sources of legal authority. For instance, Hobbes rejects the idea of the common law as the "'artificial perfection of reason, gotten by long study, observation, and experience,'" which he attributes to Sir Edward Coke (II.xxvi.11 [p. 176]). Instead, he insists that it is equally possible that "long study" may confirm errors in the law and lead judges and lawyers to build "on false grounds," adding that "the more they build the greater is the ruin" (I.xxvi.11 [p. 176]). The tradition we inherit should be replaced by the one we fashion ourselves. Here Hobbes positions himself against the veneration of custom and the inherited system of power, which he views as arbitrary.

A system of positive law is preferable to the common law for yet another reason: the common law also poses a threat to the law's unifying role by splintering authority. If we have one ruler, "there cannot easily arise any contradiction in the laws" (Hobbes 1994, I.xxvi.11 [p. 176]). Hobbes needs the law to be public, clear, prospective, and free of contradictions in order for the law to function as he envisions.[5] Given that the sovereign is issuing legal directives into the void, Hobbes also assumes that clearly articulated rules are the sole unifying source for an otherwise disparate populace. While the threat of coercion is an essential part of the theory, it will be of little use if citizens cannot understand what is expected of them.

From the perspective of the newly created civil society, it may seem as if the content of the law is beholden to the whims of the sovereign. While, in a sense, this is true, the logic of the system demands that certain kinds of laws are enacted. The familiar Hartian distinction between necessary elements and contingent ones is found in Hobbes. The necessary elements of the legal system amount to the terms of the social contract made manifest. As noted above, contract law is a necessary feature of civil society. But so, too, are the

[3] Hobbes's second law of nature is as follows: "*that a man be willing, when others are so too, as far-forth as for peace and defence of himself he shall think it necessary, to lay down this right to all things, and be contented with so much liberty against other men, as he would allow other men against himself*" (1994, I.xiv.5 [p. 80]).

[4] "Where there is no common power, there is no law; where no law, no injustice" (Hobbes 1994, I.xiii.13 [p. 78]).

[5] For an interpretation of Hobbes that emphasizes this aspect of his theory, see Dyzenhaus (2001).

laws that protect bodily integrity and property. These areas of law are essential to the commonwealth, but they are also essential to the personal identity of its citizens.

By exploring Hobbes's conception of property, it becomes apparent that it is constitutive of individuals in civil society. At first glance, it is tempting to think of property as something external to us. C. B. MacPherson (1975) argues that the conception of property found in *Leviathan* is more radical than readers grasp. In part, this is because Hobbes is committed to the view that we own "ourselves." Who we are is inseparable from the law that governs us. We are barely recognizable as human outside of the law. In *De Cive*, Hobbes argues that "Man is a wolf to Man" (1998, 3).

MacPherson points out that, historically, "different people might have different rights in the same piece of land, and by law or manorial custom, many of those rights were not fully disposable by the current owner of them either by sale or bequest" (1975, 93). Hence the "property he had was obviously the right in the land, not the land itself" (93). Conversely, Hobbes considers property to be a matter of *exclusive* possession. This was a novel development at the time. According to MacPherson, one of the implications of this point is that the distinction between "right" and "thing" becomes blurred. Hobbes's new account of property both animates and normalizes the burgeoning market society. In *Leviathan*, Hobbes treats exchange through contract law as the lifeblood of his "Artificial Man": "for natural blood is in like manner made of the fruits of the earth, and circulating, nourisheth by the way every member of the body of man" (1994, II.xxiv.11 [p. 164]).

Criminal laws are also necessary, particularly those that protect bodily integrity and property. Hobbes's account of crime is also borne out of his conception of human nature. Hobbes explains that "the source of every crime is some defect of the understanding, or some error in reasoning, or some sudden force of the passions" (1994, II.xxvii.4 [p. 191]). This is consistent with the logic of his system: the state is created to scare us into cooperating. We consent to be ruled—to give up all our rights—in exchange for security. To risk punishment is irrational because it is contrary to our act of consent and because we are fearful creatures. Notice that the source of crime, on this view, is the citizen who chooses to break the law and not those who are the power-wielders. Law is presented as a static set of posited rules that agents can choose to follow or breach.

If we translate Hobbes's account of the criminal law into contemporary terms, we can see that Hobbes unites utilitarian and retributivist elements into a single account. For Hobbes, criminal law is underpinned by a general utilitarian argument: peace and order are preferable to war and disorder. Once the law is established, the general aim is to deter: rational actors will want to avoid sanctions and, therefore, will (ideally) be motivated to obey the law. Obedience through fear is Hobbes's recipe. Significantly, there is also a clear retributivist element in Hobbes's account. Given that the state exists to protect bodily integrity and property (in that order), Hobbes maintains that the innocent should not be punished (1994, II.xxviii.22 [p. 208]). If the innocent were to be punished regularly, the state of nature would begin to look more attractive than civil society—at least power is symmetrical in the state of nature.

Observe, also, that the conception of human beings as choosing agents is preserved once the state is formed. Positive law tugs at our deep-seated fear of punishment *and* our capacity for rational action in equal measure. At the center of Hobbes's conception of the criminal law (and law more generally) is the idea of the individual as choosing agent. The idea of equality is now presented as a juridical ideal, even if the ideal is tempered by the fact that the sovereign may give us few freedoms. Everyone, save the sovereign, stands in the same relationship with the state and with each other. When it comes to Hobbes's account of punishment, it is essential to see that the social contract produces artificial persons (i.e., legal fictions) and that the lives of actual people are transformed by the introduction of these new legal ideas.

2 Hobbes on Punishment

A puzzle has been identified at the heart of Hobbes's theory of punishment in *Leviathan*, which centers on the relationship between two claims: the sovereign has the right to punish, and individuals have the right to resist punishment (Yates 2014). Hobbes is clear that "covenants not to defend a man's own body are void" (1994, II.xxi.11 [p. 141]). This is so, Hobbes argues, even if the punishment being meted out is deserved. Given the seemingly difficult relationship between these two propositions, which commentators have labelled an "antimony," it is often argued that the sovereign's right to punish is explained by the fact that the sovereign remains in the state of nature (Yates 2014).[6] This interpretation of Hobbes seems to gain some support from chapter twenty-eight of *Leviathan*:

> For the subjects did not give the sovereign that right, but only (in laying down theirs) strengthened him to use his own as he should think fit, for the preservation

[6] Yates rejects the traditional view, but he sets it out beautifully (see 2014, 234–38).

> of them all; so that it was not given, but left to him, and to him only, and (excepting the limits set him by natural law) as entire as in the condition of mere nature, and of war of every one against his neighbour. (1994, II.xxviii.2 [p. 204])

Is it the case that the sovereign's natural power is merely strengthened, or does the amplification of this power involve a change in degree *and* kind? In my view, the second possibility is the correct one. While the sovereign's right to punish is parasitic on his right to violence in the state of nature, the social contract is the source of his ability to "punish" rather than to harm or harass. To see this point and to dissolve the apparent antinomy, Quentin Skinner's idea of representation proves invaluable.

Skinner asks the following question: who does the sovereign answer to? He argues that Hobbes flatly rejects one standard reply: "the people." Hobbes dismisses the idea that "the people" are a unity in a pre-political sense: "One of [Hobbes's] underlying purposes in presenting his celebrated picture of man's life in the state of nature as nasty, brutish and short is to insist that the image of the people as a united body makes no sense" (Skinner 2009, 342). Instead, Skinner maintains that Hobbes's sovereign must answer to the "state." The state is an *idea* that represents the artificial unity of the people *after* the social contract is created (Skinner 2009, 346). The state does not represent the aggregate interests of the citizens at any one time; instead, the interests are determined by the terms of the social contract. Notice that the role of positive law is, once again, fundamental to Hobbes's account: positive law is responsible for creating the artificial unity of the state and for mediating the relationship between the sovereign and the citizens.

The artificial unity of the state relies on the existence of the citizens, but it is fundamentally different from them. In Skinner's words, it represents them. The state is best understood as a fictional or artificial person. Hobbes is careful to include the idea of an artificial person within his definition of "person":

> A person is he *whose words or actions are considered either as his own, or as representing the words or actions of another man, or of any other thing to whom they are attributed, whether truly or by fiction*. When they are considered as his own, then is he called a *natural person*; and when they are considered as representing the words and actions of another, then is he a *feigned* or *artificial person*. (1994, I.xvi.1–2 [p. 101])

Skinner adds that it would be erroneous "to infer from the fictional character of the state that it cannot act as an agent in the real world" (2018, 359). Consider his example: public debt. The debt does not attach to government officials, nor has it been incurred by an aggregate of citizens. Instead, Skinner argues, it attaches to the artificial person of the state (2018, 367).

The state is distinct from the citizens that populate it, yet it depends on them for its existence. The same holds for the sovereign. The idea of the sovereign (as an artificial person) is distinct from the person who occupies the position at any given time. Laurens van Apeldoorn draws attention to the fact that a new argument appears in *Leviathan* that is absent in Hobbes's earlier works, namely the idea that individuals alienate their rights *in addition* to establishing an authorized representative (2020, 50). He notes that Hobbes is clear that the sovereign

> representeth two persons, or (as the more common phrase is) has two capacities, one natural and another politic (as a monarch hath the person not only of the commonwealth, but also of a man; and a sovereign assembly hath the person not only of the commonwealth, but also of the assembly). (1994, II.xxiii.2 [pp. 155–56])

The sovereign is *both* "person" and "artificial person." I agree with Apeldoorn that the capacities are distinct yet indivisible: the existence of the role is itself parasitic on the existence of the person of the sovereign, who, by definition, retains his natural right to violence. Apeldoorn turns to history to support this interpretation: "This view, which in the turmoil of the civil war became associated with the supporters of Charles I, admitted that the monarch has distinct bodies or capacities, but stressed that they are inseparable" (2020, 53). This idea would not have been foreign to Hobbes, thereby lending plausibility to this interpretation of the idea of sovereignty.

My position differs from Skinner's insofar as he locates sovereignty solely in the seat of the sovereign (i.e., the idea of the state) (2018, 367). Nevertheless, Skinner's analysis remains indispensable to the overarching picture of punishment. We can only consider what the *person* of the sovereign adds to the picture once we grasp the nature of obligations that the sovereign has vis-à-vis the fictional person of the state. When Skinner fleshes out what the sovereign owes the state, the nature of the ideal that is embodied in the artificial person of the state becomes visible. According to Skinner, the sovereign's job is to protect the "life and health" of this artificial person through time, which means he must serve the common good of the people (2009, 348). As argued in the prior section, the terms of the social contract dictate the content of the common good: laws that protect bodily integrity and property, in addition to contract law, are necessary elements of the state. Furthermore, Hobbes is clear that "punishment" must take place in accordance with preexisting law:

> A PUNISHMENT *is an evil inflicted by public authority on him that hath done or omitted that which is judged by the same authority to be a transgression of the law, to the end that the will of men may thereby the better be disposed to obedience.* (1994, II.xxviii.1 [p. 203])

Hobbes adds that an "evil inflicted by public authority without precedent public condemnation is not to be styled by the name of punishment" precisely "because the fact for which a man is punished ought first to be judged by public authority to be a transgression of the law" (II.xxviii.5 [p. 204]). In other words, the possibility of punishment, understood as the legitimate (authorized) use of violence, is different from the mere infliction of harm (or "evil"). Critics who argue that the right to punish is pre-political in nature must assume that Hobbes's definition of punishment is erroneous. Surely this must be the path of last resort.

When Hobbes's account of punishment is conceptualized as a legal relationship between the state and the sovereign (understood in isolation from the person of the sovereign), the theory is idealistic and far removed from the dark image of society that has brought Hobbes considerable fame. The discussion thus far has focused on what *should* happen given what has been authorized by the social contract. In other words, the rights and obligations are suspended in time in the respective legal fictions of "state" and "sovereign." As mentioned, these ideas cannot exist apart from the people whose interests are represented (the citizens) or the person who holds the office of the sovereign at any moment in time. When real people enter the picture, the scene Hobbes constructs becomes dark once again and markedly more complex. The sovereign, of course, remains in the state of nature; consequently, the social contract is a risky endeavor.

Precisely because the person of the sovereign remains in the state of nature, he will continue to pursue everything he desires, likely with great success. It follows from Hobbes's definition of punishment that when the sovereign is acting in his personal capacity, he is inflicting harm. The problem citizens face is not simply that of a single rogue ruler taking what he likes. Skinner draws attention to the basic fact that the centralization of power means "that the outcome could easily be destructive of the very interests they are instituted to promote" (2018, 383). Wicked laws may be enacted, and state-sanctioned extra-legal violence may become commonplace. Crucially, the gap between the ideal exercise of power and its actual exercise is not supposed to be patrolled by the citizens.[7] The contracting parties have assumed the risk.

[7] This view is also present in Plato's *Crito* (see Martin 2020b).

When Hobbes turns his mind to the role of the subjects in the commonwealth, he is clear that they have alienated their wills. Out of a plurality of wills, emerges one (Hobbes 1994, II.xviii.3 [pp. 110–11]). Once this transformation takes place, every subject must "own and acknowledge himself to be the author of whatsoever he that so beareth their person shall act" (II. xvii.13 [p. 109]). If individuals act against the sovereign, they are authors of their own punishment (II.xviii.3 [p. 111]). The distinction between the person of the sovereign and his role disappears, and this is not an accident. While we are not wedded to the perspective of the citizen, the point is that the social contract realizes a vision of sovereignty that includes *both* capacities of the sovereign. His natural power has been amplified *and* changed. In short, given that the act of submission is near-absolute, the practical realities of sovereign power cannot be separated from its ideal instantiation. Both are needed to grasp the idea of sovereignty, but they remain indivisible.

What, then, do we make of the other half of the seeming antimony—namely, the right to self-defense that individuals retain throughout their lives, regardless of whether they are in the state of nature or civil society? On this point, I agree with Arthur Yates that it is *not* a right held against the sovereign (2014, 241); instead, it is a part of Hobbes's conception of human nature that it is held against everyone. The right to resist is not found in the terms of the social contract, which is articulated in conditional terms: *if* anyone breaks the law, *then* the sovereign is authorized to punish them. Rather, the right to self-defense is akin to the sovereign's appetites: both are remnants of the state of nature. They are ineradicable features of human nature that do not play a part in the juridical relationships established by the social contract. As a merely practical matter, the sovereign can anticipate that individuals will resist, but the risk is easily managed insofar as he is sufficiently powerful.

3 Hart, Hobbes, and the Minimum Content of Natural Law

The points of commonality between Hobbes's and Hart's accounts of punishment are many, but Hart's Hobbesian assumptions are not limited to his work in criminal theory. By exploring Hart's discussion of Hobbes in *The Concept of Law*, the problems with Hart's method are revealed while indicating the presence of a surprising degree of unity in legal positivist thought.

Curiously, Hart treats Hobbes's deeply philosophical, contestable account of the human condition as a set of mundane observations about life under law. Hart interprets Hobbes as if Hobbes is merely describing the world we live in, when Hobbes is advocating for a new radical vision of politics. Hart's faith in the descriptive method is on display in this discussion.

Like Hobbes before him, Hart rejects the teleological view of nature: teleological thinking appeals to contestable values that are difficult to defend as the "proper end" of man (Hart 1997, 189). Following Hobbes, Hart prefers to lower his sights and focus on "the modest aim of survival" (191). Hart insists that this aim is indisputable. Otherwise, there would be "no association of individuals" that would lead us to entertain the ideas at issue (191). Language also indicates that we have this shared commitment. Words like "danger, safety, harm and benefit" presuppose our commitment to survival (192). The assumption that consensus ought to guide our theoretical analysis is not one that Hobbes shares. Hobbes wants to convince people to think in terms of survival, but he does not presuppose that they already do. Hart has fundamentally misunderstood Hobbes's project. This becomes clearer still when we turn to Hart's discussion of equality.

Hart repeats Hobbes's claim that humans are fundamentally equal, but he fails to mention that Hobbes puts forward this thesis in the context of his state of nature. Instead, Hart claims that human society is marked by a state of "approximate equality": no single individual can "dominate or subdue" another for "more than a short period" of time without cooperation (1997, 195). Hart then insists that this "fact of approximate equality, more than any other, makes obvious the necessity of a system of mutual forbearance and compromise which is the base of both legal and moral obligation" (195). He adds that such a system may be "irksome at times," but it is "less nasty, less brutish, and less short than unrestrained aggression for beings thus approximately equal" (195).

Hart has repackaged Hobbes's highly contestable account of human beings in the state of nature as a set of discrete observations about his own society. But Hart is wrong. Domination of the kind Hart rules out is always possible. For instance, it is easy for any adult to dominate any child, but we rarely observe domination of this kind because it is prohibited by law. At best, equality is a juridical idea about the legal relationship between people. Hart's misreading of Hobbes tempts his readers into believing that a wide array of ideas have the status of uncontestable observations. One wonders if Hart's faith in his descriptive method leads him to assert other claims that stand in need of defense. For instance, Hart adopts a Hobbesian view of the manner in which law guides conduct. He mentions this view in passing as if it is an uncontroversial fact that law guides conduct with remarkable ease: "If it were not possible to communicate general standards of conduct, which multitudes of individuals could understand, without further direction, as requiring from them certain conduct when occasion arose, nothing that we now recognize as law could exist" (1997, 121). Hart has rejected, without argument, the possibility that law relies on preexisting social norms and practices to guide law's subjects (see Simmonds 2006). Hart also fails to defend his account of the critical role language plays in his understanding of law's guidance function.[8] His assumptions about how law guides conduct are distinctively Hobbesian, but this link is rarely explored because Hart does not invoke the idea of a sovereign holding a sword. To see the depth of Hart's commitment to Hobbesian assumptions, it is useful to explore his discussion of the minimum content of natural law in more detail.

Hart insists that all existing legal systems have a minimum content of natural law. Every legal system includes laws prohibiting basic offenses such as murder, theft, and rape (1997, 291). To ensure that he is not mistaken for a natural law theorist, Hart reminds readers that these basic protections can exist alongside great inequality (so law as it *is* remains distinct from law as it *ought* to be, or so he claims). Hart maintains that while legal regimes can "offer some of its members a system of mutual forbearances, it need not, unfortunately, offer them to all" (201). He cites Apartheid South Africa, Nazi Germany, and slave-owning societies as three examples (200). Governments use force unevenly, and this has implications.

Hart explains that, in any established legal regime, officials can wield coercive power in one of two ways. First, it can be harnessed to compel those who willingly disobey the system's norms to align themselves with the law or face punishment. Hart calls these individuals "malefactors" (1997, 201). Alternatively, coercive power can be weaponized against a group (large or small) that occupies a position of "permanent inferiority" in relation to a "master group" (201). Not only are members of these oppressed groups denied the legal protections that others enjoy, but, Hart argues, the state often targets them (201). He identifies these individuals as law's "victims" (201). Victims do not view the law as a set of reasons for action but only care about the law because they wish to avoid sanctions. Gerald Postema explains that these norms reach Hart's victims as a set of arbitrary dictates (1998, 340).

In other words, legal norms offer us reasons for action *if and only if* basic protections are secured. Malefactors are given basic legal protections, but they fail to recognize the reason-giving nature of law. Conversely, victims rightly recognize that the law does not bind them (see Martin 2020a, 205–11). Herein lies Hart's version of a *social contract* argument: those who enjoy law's

[8] Fuller discusses this point in detail (1958, 661–69).

basic protections should recognize its reason-giving nature; those who do not, *should* not.

While Hartians will argue that this discussion is peripheral to Hart's project, it is far from clear that it is. The challenge for Hart, which I will only outline here, is that his central figure (whom I shall call the committed participant) is not a member of the victim class. Committed participants adopt what Hart calls the "critical reflective attitude," whereby they internalize the standards of behavior embodied in the law (1997, 89). Hart famously insists that legal philosophers must take the participants' perspective seriously if they are to make sense of law. This is presented merely as an observation, but it requires a judgment of importance, which is normative (Postema 1998, 331). Once victims are placed beside committed participants, the nature of this judgment is apparent. Hart's committed participants are not members of the victim class. They enjoy the benefits law provides, and, in turn, they recognize the law's reason-giving authority by internalizing the law (the law becomes a part of them). The committed participant is the incarnation of an account of law's authority (albeit one that is insufficiently developed or defended). Hart is not making a "neutral" choice here. He is offering a normative judgment about how one *ought* to treat the law given one's position vis-a-vis the state (see Martin 2020a, 207–11). In sum, Hart offers a normative account of authority that takes the form of a social contract. It is hard to sustain Hart's claim that we can analyze concepts without introducing normative arguments or assumptions. Hart is closer to Hobbes than many assume.

4 Hart's *Punishment and Responsibility*: An Incomplete Account?

In *Punishment and Responsibility*, Hart collects the essays he wrote in criminal theory over the span of a decade. There is much of value in this work, and my comments will not capture the breadth or depth of analysis found in his work. By focusing on his account of the criminal law as a "choosing" system, Hart's Hobbesian assumptions come into view, alongside points of friction with *The Concept of Law*. While Hobbes's account is controversial, Hart's remains incomplete.

In this work, Hart offers what he calls a "mixed theory" of punishment (Gardner 2008, xxviii). He aims to uncover an intellectual space between retributivism and utilitarianism. Against the utilitarian, Hart argues that the need to establish individual responsibility should not be sacrificed to achieve another goal, such as deterrence. Against the retributivist, Hart contends that the idea of a pre-political moral wrong is unhelpful. But Hart retains the retributivists' commitment to the autonomous choosing agent. This is a strategy Hart has employed before. He is, once again, locating a "conceptual" space between intellectual competitors.[9] In so doing, he aims to dispel confusion. I will suggest that, at times, what Hart calls "confusion" is simply a debate that involves different first principles.

In the opening chapter, "Prolegomenon to the Principles of Punishment," Hart maintains that "much confusing shadow-fighting between utilitarians and their opponents" can be avoided if we ask additional questions and offer more complex answers to the questions posed (2008, 9). For instance, Hart insists that criminal theorists should not simply inquire into the purpose of punishment; instead, they must attend to a distinct set of questions: "What justifies the general practice of punishment? To whom may punishment be applied? How severely may we punish?" (2008, 3). The first two questions are particularly informative for our purposes.

Hart's answer to the first question involves identifying the "General Justifying Aim" of criminal punishment: punishment is meant to deter the general populace from engaging in prohibited behavior (2008, 4). Thus, the point of punishment is a utilitarian one. However, Hart is adamant that only those who intentionally break the law should be punished.[10] In reference to the second question—"To whom may punishment be applied?"—Hart offers a simple answer: "an offender for an offence" (2008, 9). Guilt must be established in the manner that retributivists establish it. In other words, the two questions dovetail beautifully with the theses he is forwarding. What Hart identifies as "confusion" may be nothing more than a typical philosophical disagreement.

Consider his main charge against utilitarianism. Hart insists that the idea of *mens rea* must be preserved in all (or at least most) cases. Legal systems do not simply involve the use of force to achieve a given end. Instead, they are fundamentally about the agency of individuals who are governed by law:

> We must cease, therefore, to regard the law simply as a system of stimuli goading the individual by its threats into conformity. Instead, I shall suggest a mercantile analogy. Consider the law not as a system of stimuli but as what might be termed a *choosing system*, in which individuals can find out, in general terms at

[9] In *The Concept of Law* (1997), Hart aims to locate a space between natural law and legal realism.

[10] Hart does not argue that punishment is therefore justified. Rather, as Gardner (2008) points out, Hart views punishment as problematic.

> least, the costs they have to pay if they act in certain ways. This done, let us ask what value this system would have in social life and why we should regret its absence. (Hart 2008, 44)

The law treats individuals as autonomous agents. It does so by laying out the consequences for a given set of actions; citizens must then choose how to act. It can only achieve this end if the criminal law includes excusing conditions. The inclusion of such conditions gives the individual the "power at any time to predict the likelihood that the sanctions of the criminal law will be applied to him" (Hart 2008, 47). The individual is portrayed as a utility-maximizer who wishes to avoid sanctions. Here Hart is closer to Hobbes than he is to the views expressed in *The Concept of Law*.

This predictive account of law is one that Hart rejects in *The Concept of Law*: only Oliver Wendell Holmes's (1897) proverbial "badman" adopts this posture toward the law. Now the "badman" is the *everyman*. Hart's quintessential subject is a self-interested agent who constantly makes utilitarian calculations: the individual "can weigh the cost to him of obeying the law—and of sacrificing some satisfaction in order to obey—against obtaining that satisfaction at the cost of paying 'the penalty'" (Hart 2008, 44). Hart's account of agency is Hobbesian. Once individuals choose to disobey, they can expect to be met with punishment. Hart explains that "by adopting this system of attaching excusing conditions we provide that, if the sanctions of the criminal law are applied, the pains of punishment will for each individual represent the price of some satisfaction obtained from breach of law" (47). According to this view, individuals bring punishment upon themselves: they are the author of their own punishment because they have chosen to disobey.

Like Hobbes, Hart identifies the individual choosing agent as the source of criminality. It does not stem from the more powerful party in the relationship, namely the state. And like Hobbes, Hart combines a utilitarian justification with a retributivist one, although the unifying idea (the social contract) is not offered. Instead, Hart tethers his account to the status quo. He wants to explain criminal law as he finds it. Hart appeals to an imaginary world to shore up the conclusions he wishes to draw in the real one.

To secure the centrality of the idea of choice without appealing to a pre-political idea of moral wrong, Hart introduces an "experiment of imagining" (2008, 45). He asks readers to think of "a system where no mental conditions would be recognized as invalidating such transactions and the consequent loss of control over the future that the individual would suffer" (2008, 45). In other words, this fictional system does not include justifications or excuses. It is an imaginary system where all criminal offenses are strict liability offenses.

By carrying out this thought experiment, readers are invited to conclude that the existence of excusing conditions is both familiar to us (it is at the center of our law) and that they *should* be part of our system. Hart is attempting to secure both conclusions in the reader's mind *without making a moral argument.* As Richard A. Wasserstrom points out, this argument fails to explain why the retributivist has erred by relying on a pre-political moral wrong (1967, 104). Hart also fails to accommodate familiar elements of the criminal law, like negligence, within this sharp dichotomy that structures his thought experiment and his argument more generally (Wasserstrom 1967, 102). The appeal to an imaginary world does not do the needed intellectual work.

For Hart's next attempt to address the retributivist's challenge, he divides the retributivist's question about the purpose of punishment into two. His aim, once again, is to dispel confusion. Hart insists that the first question that must be posed is "a general question about the moral value of the laws," namely, "will enforcing them produce more good than evil?" (2008, 39). To answer this first question, Hart turns to a Hobbesian worldview:

> We would all agree that unless a legal system was as a whole morally defensible, so that its existence was better than the chaos of its collapse, and more good than evil was secured by maintaining and enforcing laws in general, these laws should not be enforced, and no one should be punished for breaking them. (2008, 39)

In other words, *if the system in question is morally preferable to chaos, then judges should apply the laws of the system* and people should be punished for breaking them. This moral baseline is Hobbesian. Hart has set the bar low.

Once we determine that it is morally permissible to enforce the law, Hart prompts us to ask a second question: is it morally permissible to punish an individual for breaking a given legal norm, or is an excuse available? In other words, did the accused *intentionally* violate the law? Hart responds by repeating his main claim: the accused must intentionally break the law to be held criminally responsible. Hart has simply restated the problem in terms that suit him without offering a reason for rejecting the retributivist's idea of pre-political moral rights. Hart has defined away the debate while propping up his own theory. Further, Hart's failure to address the retributivist's point in a convincing fashion means that he has notnaged to shore up his claim about the importance of the mental element for criminal liability. It is still unclear how he can protect this element from utilitarian calculations that threaten to sacrifice it (in general or on occasion) to some conception of the common good, like deterrence. This problem is underscored once we canvass Hart's general views about the legitimacy of punishment.

Hart continually repeats his view that the innocent should not be punished, but what about the guilty? As John Gardner notes, Hart aligns himself with Jeremy Bentham when he addresses the question of punishing individuals for wrongs that have already been committed: "For [Hart] the suffering of the punished wrongdoer, be he ever so guilty, is always a cost and never a benefit of the criminal justice system" (Gardner 2008, xiv). While much can be said about this position, it is unclear if it can live alongside Hart's retributivist thesis. If Hart's overarching view of punishment is utilitarian, how does he secure a place for the mental element? Gardner remains unpersuaded by Hart's attempts to do so (2008, xiv–vi). I will explore the problem in a different way.

One potential escape route has been taken already by Hobbes. In Hobbes, it is clear how the retributivist elements are united with the utilitarian ones. The source of this unity is, of course, the social contract. Recall that the plausibility of Hobbes's account turns on the manner in which the artificial person of the state embodies the requirements of the contract. Once Hart becomes a Benthamite utilitarian, both the legal fiction of the state and the idea of the social contract are deemed irrelevant (see Skinner 2018, 374). It is unlikely, therefore, that Hart can find a way to make the elements of his mixed account cohere.

It is nevertheless worth asking whether Hobbes can secure his retributivist thesis without appealing to a moralized understanding of the state of nature. In other words, is Hobbes on solid philosophical footing when he treats the individual moral agent as worthy of legal protections? His answer, of course, is that law is introduced to help ensure our survival. But why is survival a value? One answer might come from Hobbes's conception of human nature: humans are matter in motion, and they want to keep moving (in accordance with the laws of physics) (1994, I.ii.1–2 [pp. 7–8]). But recall that, in *Leviathan*, the physical world is conceived of as a cold and indifferent realm of causality devoid of inherent value. The universe is indifferent to the survival of anything; only human beings themselves care about self-preservation. Thus, the only move Hobbes can make is to turn to the subjective desires of the members of the state of nature. Through the idea of a social contract, Hobbes has quietly adopted the participant's perspective. Once we see this, another question arises: why prioritize the subjective desires of imagined people over the subjective desires of actual people? Hobbes has a well-known answer: peace. But now we are back to the beginning of what has revealed itself to be a circle.

Retributivists know, I suspect, that they need to presuppose (or argue for) the existence of a moral universal. They must do this to shore up their thesis about the value of the individual self. Given the deep divide that is now apparent between Hobbesian positivism and a retributivist worldview, it is unlikely that Hart can successfully wed retributivism with Benthamite utilitarianism.

5 Concluding Remarks: Revisiting the Positivist Puzzle

Hart's decision to place the idea of choice at the center of his account comes with an additional complication. Gardner rightly explains that Hart is committed to an understanding of the ideal of the rule of law: laws must be prospective, public, clear, and consistent to provide individuals with choices (2008, xxxvi). These features of the rule of law assume that the law's subjects enjoy a degree of freedom (even if, in some cases, the sphere of freedom is "vanishingly small") (Gardner 2008, xxxviii). Hart's reliance on the ideal of the rule of law in his account of punishment raises an essential question about how Hart conceives of legal philosophy in *The Concept of Law*: does it make sense to think about criminal law as inextricably bound up with the idea of the rule of law, but then to insist that "law in general" can be grasped without reliance on this ideal? Is it possible to rise so high above the clouds that the particular features of the criminal law are no longer visible, and instead, we see only the broad contours of "law in general"? I propose that, in the process of abstraction, critical ideas are lost, and consequently, the nature of law is obscured, not clarified.

Hart's account must also answer to history. The problem with Hart's single-minded focus on the idea of choice, Nicola Lacey argues, is that it inadvertently idealizes a very narrow vision of criminal law (2016, 177–78). Hart overlooks vital institutions and practices crucial to the criminal justice systems, "from legislation *via* prosecution to punishment" (183). In addition, Hart's narrow focus prevents him from attending to the variables that must hold for any system to retain the centrality of the *mens rea* element through time. For instance, Lacey is correct that the trial is where the idea of choice is relevant. The problem she identifies is a practical reality in many jurisdictions: a trial is now considered an "expensive luxury"; plea bargaining is the norm (185). This means that prosecutors wield significant power, as do police officers. Their choices determine who is deemed a "criminal" as much, if not more, than the choices made by individuals (183–84; see also Karakatsanis

2019). Lacey warns that, insofar as debates in criminal theory circles stay focused on narrow theoretical issues like criminal intent, theorists inadvertently preserve existing power structures by failing to attend to how actual practices have strayed from the ideals under consideration.

Hart's conceptual approach renders his account more vulnerable to this kind of criticism than Hobbes's political account of law and the state, but Hobbes is still offering a "universal" answer to the question of political obligation that may render it unresponsive to current political realities. John Dunn muses that "in sedate and prosperous modern polities, the problem of political obligation retains little urgency"; however, where "their calm rhythms are disturbed, and their prosperity actively threatened their plurality soon shows a less bland face" (1996, 87). If the unity of society turns on the ability of everyone to see themselves in a particular way, then there is the possibility that disunity can emerge in the form of "a war of each theory against every other theory" (87). Hobbes is correct that the state of war may be best defined as a perpetual state of insecurity and not of actual battles (1994, I.xiii.8 [p. 76]). But Hobbes is wrong to presuppose that it is a state of being that exists outside of the state or following its breakdown. Hart's discussion of the victim, canvassed above, illustrates that the state can be the cause of the very conditions Hobbes looks to the state to solve.

Michael Oakeshott suggests that Hobbes's vision of the nature of philosophy "is like the music that gives meaning to the movement of dancers, or the law of evidence that gives coherence to the practice of a court" (1946, 10). Hart's account of the nature of legal philosophy serves a similar role in *The Concept of Law*. While Hobbes offers a new "scientific" approach to philosophy, it is Hart, not Hobbes, whose method, if successful, would allow legal philosophers to break from the history of philosophy. Upon closer inspection, what we find in Hart is not a new start but the rearranging of the familiar pieces of an old positivist puzzle.

Hobbes aims to generate political consensus in civil society by calling for the establishment of the centralization of power in a single person. Politics in the real world must lower its sights and focus only on survival, which is the only value around which political consensus can be generated. Hobbes's aim is peace in the world. Hart has the same leaping-off point as Hobbes, namely the importance of survival. But Hart lands in a radically different place. Peace and its corollary, a functioning legal order, are presupposed at the outset of his reflections. Hart does not seek to generate consensus among citizens; instead, he aims to generate consensus among legal philosophers. This shift has implications.

As mentioned, Hobbes's break from history is intentional. He aimes to refashion society to secure peace in his time. Hobbes's state of nature acts as a blank slate, cut off from history. Hobbes is the artist (or the scientist) who constructs the scene and molds the individuals who will populate this imagined space. The individuals in the state of nature are defined by a basic set of properties that capture their humanity as he envisions it. All individuating features are omitted. Once civil society is created by a single act of contract, the sharp distinctions are reconfigured within the state. Recall that individuals who began with no rights are then given *exclusive* rights over their property and their person. A new set of rights and duties emerge that are legally determined. Hobbes's account intentionally displaces the more complex account of property typified in feudal relations (see Fink 1981).

These elements find their way into Hart's account, but in a novel way. Hart, in his capacity as philosopher, occupies the blank slate. Hart does not attempt to break from history; instead, he aims to conceptualize law as he finds it during his lifetime. It is not history but the history of philosophy from which Hart aims to make a clean break. Instead of identifying basic features of human nature that could serve as the foundation of a new vision of political society, Hart identifies the necessary elements of existing legal systems with the aim of securing agreement among philosophers. Recall also that, in Hobbes's account, individuals become the locus of rights that give them exclusive possession of property. Crucially, in Hart's account, legal philosophy takes the form of an *exclusive* domain, displacing a more permissive understanding of the discipline that preceded it. All propositions about the nature of law that do not meet his methodological requirements are excluded from the domain of general jurisprudence as he conceives of it. We can have debates about what law ought to be, of course, but they presuppose agreement about what law is.

Significantly, Hobbes's version of a clean slate—his state of nature—is a fiction that allows him to make a political point. But it is a fiction nonetheless. This suggests that Hart's foundational assumption—that legal theory can begin anew—is itself a fiction. Perhaps there are no new beginnings but only a reconsideration of important questions in time. When the questions posed pertain to the use of force by the state, a sense of urgency accompanies this task.

References

Dunn, John. 1996. *The History of Political Theory and Other Essays.* Cambridge: Cambridge University Press.

Dyzenhaus, David. 2001. "Hobbes and the Legitimacy of Law." *Law and Philosophy* 20, no. 5 (September): 461–98.

Fink, Hans. 1981. *Social Philosophy*. London: Routledge.

Fuller, Lon L. 1958. "Positivism and Fidelity to Law: A Reply to Professor Hart." *Harvard Law Review* 71, no. 4 (February): 630–72.

Gardner, John. 2008. Introduction to *Punishment and Responsibility*, by H. L. A. Hart, 2nd ed., xiii-liii. Oxford: Oxford University Press.

Hart, H. L. A. 1997. *The Concept of Law*. 2nd ed. Oxford: Clarendon.

———. 2008. *Punishment and Responsibility: Essays in the Philosophy of Law*. 2nd ed. Oxford: Oxford University Press.

Hobbes, Thomas. 1994. *Leviathan*. Edited by Edwin Curley. Indianapolis, IN: Hackett.

———. 1998. *On the Citizen*. Edited and translated by Richard Tuck and Michael Silverthorne. Cambridge: Cambridge University Press.

Holmes, Oliver Wendell, Jr. 1897. "The Path of Law." *Harvard Law Review* 10, no. 8 (March 25): 457–78.

Karakatsanis, Alec. 2019. "The Punishment Bureaucracy: How to Think about 'Criminal Justice Reform.'" *Yale Law Journal Forum* 128 (March 28): 848–906.

Lacey, Nicola. 2016. *In Search of Criminal Responsibility: Ideas, Interests, and Institutions*. Oxford: Oxford University Press.

MacPherson, C. B. 1975. "Liberalism and the Political Theory of Property." In *Domination*, edited by Alkis Kontos, 89–100. Toronto: University of Toronto Press.

Martin, Margaret. 2020a. "Postema on Hart: The Illusion of Value-Neutrality." In *Philosophy of Law as an Integral Part of Philosophy: Essays on the Jurisprudence of Gerald J. Postema*, edited by Thomas Bustamante and Thiago Lopes Decat, 193–211. Oxford: Hart.

———. 2020b. "Persuade or Obey: *Crito* and the Preconditions for Justice." In *Contemporary Perspectives on Legal Obligations*, edited by Stefano Bertea, 153–72. Abingdon, UK: Routledge.

———. 2021. "Method Matters: Non-Normative Jurisprudence and the Re-Mystification of the Law." In *Elucidating the Concept of Law: Contemporary Disputes*, edited by Jorge Luis, Fabra-Zamora and Gonzalo Villa, 53–72. New York: Springer.

Oakeshott, Michael. 1946. Introduction to *Leviathan: Or, The Matter, Forme and Power of a Commonwealth, Ecclesiasticall and Civil*, by Thomas Hobbes, edited by Michael Oakeshott, vii–lxvi. Oxford: Basil Blackwell.

Postema, Gerald J. 1998. "Jurisprudence as Practical Philosophy." *Legal Theory* 4, no. 3 (September): 329–57.

Simmonds, Nigel. 1985. "Pashukanis and Liberal Jurisprudence." *Journal of Law and Society* 12, no. 2 (Summer): 135–51.
———. 2006. *Law as a Moral Idea*. Oxford: Oxford University Press.
Skinner, Quentin. 2009. "A Genealogy of the Modern State." *Proceedings of the British Academy* 162: 325–70.
van Apeldoorn, Laurens. 2020. "On the Person and Office of the Sovereign in Hobbes' *Leviathan*." *British Journal for the History of Philosophy* 28, no. 1: 49–68.
Wasserstrom, Richard A. 1967. "H. L. A. Hart and the Doctrines of *Mens Rea* and Criminal Responsibility." *University of Chicago Law Review* 35, no. 1 (Autumn): 92–126.
Yates, Arthur. 2014. "The Right to Punish in Thomas Hobbes's *Leviathan*." *Journal of the History of Philosophy*, 52, no. 2 (April) 2014, pp. 233–254.
———. 2018. *From Humanism to Hobbes: Studies in Rhetoric and Politics*. Cambridge: Cambridge University Press.

4

Is Crime Caused by Illness, Immorality, or Injustice? Theories of Punishment in the Twentieth and Early Twenty-First Centuries

Amelia M. Wirts

In the twenty-first century in the United States, discussions of punishment often raise critical questions about mass incarceration, racial and class disparities in the criminal justice system, mental health crises among incarcerated and poor communities, and the moral legitimacy of policing and incarceration. These popular discussions implicate philosophical questions that are perennial. Is the purpose of punishment to bring about social benefits such as reducing crime, rehabilitating those who commit crimes, and protecting the public from threats to safety? Those who think that crime primarily occurs because those who commit crimes lack mental health treatment or the right incentives to follow the law will likely take this *utilitarian* view of punishment. Or, is punishment always the right response to crime, regardless of whether punishment brings about any social benefits? Those who think that crime is a moral problem that stems from the moral failings of individuals as agents will likely take this *retributivist* view of punishment. For retributivists, we punish because imposing hardship on those who commit crimes is simply the right thing to do. These two approaches to thinking about the causes of crime and the proper punitive responses animated debates in punishment theory in the twentieth century.

A. M. Wirts (✉)
University of Washington, Seattle, WA, USA
e-mail: amwirts@uw.edu

© The Author(s), under exclusive license to Springer Nature Switzerland AG 2023

M. C. Altman (ed.), *The Palgrave Handbook on the Philosophy of Punishment*, Palgrave Handbooks in the Philosophy of Law, https://doi.org/10.1007/978-3-031-11874-6_4

In the early twentieth century, punishment theory was dominated by the rehabilitative ideal. This particular strand of utilitarianism presented much like a medical model of crime. Crime was like an illness, and punishment was best understood as treatment for the person who committed a crime. Punishment helped the person recover from the illness of criminality by offering mental health care, treatment for addiction, job training, or other social services.

In the 1970s, the consensus was that the rehabilitative model failed. This may have been fueled by increasing empirical evidence that rehabilitation did not actually help people commit fewer crimes, or by rising crime rates, or both. In its wake, philosophers took up retributivist justifications of punishment. Retributivists railed against the view that criminals were ill, arguing that this undermined the agency of those who committed crimes. The rehabilitative model, they argued, misunderstood the problem of crime. It was a moral problem, not a health problem.

Utilitarian and retributivist approaches to theorizing crime and punishment have dominated philosophy of punishment since the beginning of the twentieth century (Feinberg 2008). But there was also another view of crime that motivated social movements against police brutality and prisons during that time, even if it was more rarely discussed in philosophy journals or law schools. On this view, crime was a consequence of an unjust social structure, not of psychological or moral deficiencies of individuals. The *social critical* view of crime entailed that punishment cannot address the underlying issues of crime because punishment can only address the individual, not the society. While the classical debates in philosophy of punishment were framed around what can justify punishment practices, both these theories relied, implicitly or explicitly, on the idea that crime stems from defects in the individual person. In contrast, social critics of punishment have instead argued that crime stems from moral defects in society itself, including racism, poverty, and ablism.

Increasingly, the social critical view has come to animate public protests and popular discourse about policing and mass incarceration, especially since 2020. Social critics continue to argue that the practice of punishment cannot address the problem of crime because punishments, by their nature, address individuals. For example, Angela Davis (2003) has consistently argued that crime is an excuse to maintain anti-Black racial hierarchies, not to keep society safe. She also argues that the way to address crimes is to understand them as effects of social injustice rather than individual moral failings or disorders.

This chapter makes the case that, since 1900, debates about the justification of punishment have also been debates about the cause of crime. In part one, I explain how the rehabilitative ideal of punishment viewed mental illness and dysfunction in individuals as the cause of crime. Since rehabilitative models found social and mental defects in the individual as causes of crime, they treated crime with mental health care and social training. In section 2, I argue that mixed models of punishment criticized the rehabilitative view that most people who commit crimes lack agency, but mixed models still maintained the view that mental illnesses and other circumstances could radically undermine a person's agency. H. L. A. Hart's criticisms of rehabilitation presaged those of the retributivists. In section 3, I argue that retributivism was best understood as identifying the immorality of human agents as the source of crime, which dovetailed well with the "tough-on-crime" political milieu of the 1980s and 1990s that produced mass incarceration. The only legitimate response to crime was a kind of punishment that addressed the moral failings of the person. In section 4, I briefly offer an alternative to both retributivism and rehabilitation, which both found deficiencies in individuals to be the cause of crime. Following Davis, I suggest that crime is best understood as a product of an unjust society, not faulty human beings. Thus, punishment, which is only aimed at individuals, cannot address the deeper causes of crime. But, since this view tends to emphasize rebuilding social services, it must take the lessons learned by the critiques of rehabilitation and resist the tendency to reduce human beings to recipients of those social services.

1 The Early Twentieth Century: The Reign of Rehabilitation and Incapacitation

In the first half of the twentieth century, philosophers, criminologists, and legal institutions emphasized rehabilitation and incapacitation (von Hirsch 1985; M. Davis 1990, 2009). According to legal scholar Francis Allen:

> The rehabilitative ideal is the notion that a primary purpose of penal treatment is to effect changes in the characters, attitudes, and behavior of convicted offenders, so as to strengthen the social defense against unwanted behavior, but also to contribute to the welfare and satisfactions of offenders. (1981, 2)

Rehabilitation, then, relied on a broadly utilitarian justification because punishment on this account produces good results for individual people who have committed crimes and for society by reducing crime. Based on this idea, novel punishment practices emerged because of a focus on improving the person who committed the crime instead of merely causing them suffering. These new practices included (1) pre-sentencing reports and diagnoses, (2) sentences that were longer and indeterminate because they were defined by treatment goals, (3) probation and parole that allowed for court control even beyond physical custody, and (4) special attention paid to youth who had committed crimes because they were thought to more responsive to rehabilitation than adults (Bailey 2019, 3).[1]

The rehabilitative ideal depended on at least two assumptions. First, it depicted "crime as a social problem that manifested itself in individual acts; individuals became delinquent because they were deprived of education, family socialization, or treatment for their abnormal psychology" (Bailey 2019, 4). Second, it depended on the idea that treatment efforts could change "habits and values of individuals" (4). These assumptions painted a picture of individuals who committed crimes as at the mercy of social circumstances and ultimately dependent on the state's penological responses. While rehabilitation did recognize that crime was connected to poverty and lack of education or social support, rehabilitation sought to treat individuals, not to change the underlying inequalities that produce poverty, lack of education, and unstable social settings. On this medical model, the person who committed a crime was ill, and rehabilitative tools were like medical treatments. Moreover, just as blame was an inappropriate response to illness, blaming those who committed crimes was not appropriate under the rehabilitative model. Instead of evaluating the moral character of a person who committed a crime, the rehabilitative ideal recommended evaluations of mental health, addiction, education, and social training. Punishments came in the form of compulsory mental health treatment, job training, and addiction counseling.

To many readers, this view will sound preferable to the realities of the 2020s, which include mass incarceration, abysmal prison conditions, and heavy stigmatization of those convicted of crimes in the United States (not to mention police brutality). And, in many ways, it was. Professionals in the criminal justice system saw themselves as social workers, and those who were poor or mentally ill were not blamed for the actions that they likely could not have avoided carrying out. But there remained a darker side to this medical model of the cause of crime. Even though they received social services, the individuals convicted of crimes on a rehabilitative model were seen as

---

[1] While Victor Bailey (2019) describes the rehabilitative ideal in his book, he also critiques the standard story that the rehabilitative ideal was as dominant in the early twentieth century.

defective in some way, be it in terms of mental health, education, or training. While they were not morally blamed, as those convicted of crimes are in the current mainstream view, they were seen as pitiful, in need of rescue by their benevolent betters, and unable to manage their own lives. This was why critics of the rehabilitative ideal argued that it denied the agency of those who committed crimes, treating them as passive participants in their own rehabilitation rather than as responsible individuals.

An even bleaker result of the denial of agency was the concern that some people could not be rehabilitated at all. Indeed, just as rehabilitative sciences were developing, so were programs designed to predict who would continue to commit crimes regardless of treatment. Most criminal sentences were indeterminate, so that one would only be released when they were shown to be recovered. Of course, this meant that many people were simply never released from rehabilitative treatment at all. In cases where rehabilitation was impossible, incapacitation through indefinite incarceration was used as a means of protecting the community (von Hirsch 1985, 5).[2]

2 The Mid-Twentieth Century: Mixed Theories and the Struggle between Medical and Moral Explanations of Crime

Before rehabilitation was completely eclipsed by retribution in the 1970s, philosophers of law were already anxious about the implications of the rehabilitative ideal for concepts of human freedom. These thinkers were still fundamentally concerned with the necessity of punishment for upholding social values like the rule of law and general deterrence, but they were concerned that, without a strict rule in place to ensure that only those who culpably committed crimes be punished, the rehabilitation model would spread past the criminal justice system and become a project of pure social hygiene. Why wait for a person to commit a crime if social scientists could predict that people with certain mental illnesses or social backgrounds were bound to offend—especially if the "punishments" were viewed as treatments designed to cure the person, not to cause suffering? To avoid such implications, so-called "mixed theories" of punishment used utilitarian arguments to justify

[2] Though rehabilitation is not very common penal practice today, it does undergird the civil commitment system in the United States. Indeterminate or permanent incapacitation lives on through this practice, where people who are not convicted due to mental illness or those with some kinds of disorders who are committed without ever committing a crime are incapacitated in "hospitals." See, for example, Hamilton-Smith (2018).

the institution of punishment (usually arguing for the idea that punishment is a necessary deterrent to prevent crime) and retributivist arguments to justify the application of punishment, but only for individuals who are both guilty and morally culpable for committing crimes.[3] The elaboration of Hart's mixed model was a microcosm of the debate between rehabilitation theorists and retribution theorists.

Elaborating the foundations of his mixed model theory about punishment in his Presidential Address to the Aristotelian Society, Hart explained his major concern about theories of punishment that did not take human freedom seriously (2008, 1–27). He divided the justification of punishment into three related questions: (1) "What justifies a general practice of punishment?" (2) "To whom may punishment be applied?" and (3) "How severely may we punish?" (2008, 3). Most theorists, he argued, had tried to answer all three questions with the same theory. But, he argued, one could give a retributivist answer to the second question while still maintaining a utilitarian answer to the first. Importantly, he insisted that there is no utilitarian principle that limited punishment to the guilty, so if one was to be committed to only punishing the guilty, they needed a retributivist theory to answer the second question of punishment. Hart argued that we could accept a guilt requirement in the distribution of punishment, in essence taking the retributivist response to the answer of who gets punished, without being committed to a retributivist answer of why we punish in the first place. Later, the view that guilt was a necessary but not sufficient requirement for punishment would be termed "negative retributivism."

Some utilitarians responded to the criticism that utilitarianism would permit the punishment of innocent people by arguing that, by definition, punishment was the application of suffering in response to the commission of crime, not just any application of suffering. Hart dismissed this argument as a "definitional stop" (2008, 5). The definition stopped us from inquiring into the heart of this criticism: "Why do we prefer [a system of punishing the guilty] to other forms of social hygiene which we might employ to prevent anti-social behavior …?" (6). In other words, if we were going to force some people to be treated for mental illness, addiction, or other "anti-social" tendencies, why wait for them to commit a crime? If the only thing we were after

[3] In the 1950s, John Rawls and H. L. A. Hart both advanced mixed theories of punishment that drew both on utilitarian justifications for punishment and on some retributivist tenets. In 1955, Rawls introduced his approach to punishment in his famous "Two Concepts of Rules." There, Rawls argued that, while the practice of punishment itself was justified by appealing to utilitarian principles, the actual application of the practice through rule to any particular person was justified by the retributive principle of guilt (1955, 4–7).

was reducing crime, as utilitarians suggested, we should have given people rehabilitative treatment as soon as they showed signs that they *might* commit crimes.

Far from being an abstract debate about how definitions work, the definitional stop critique was motivated by highly practical concerns. Hart was worried about proposals by criminologists of his day, led by Lady Barbara Wootton, to use the criminal legal system as a system of social hygiene. Wootton argued that criminal courts could not tell if someone who committed a crime had done so truly voluntarily (Hart 2008, 178–81). She made this argument after a thorough study of how the English courts had made determinations about who had "diminished capacities" and were thus subjected to lesser punishments. She showed that courts either made a circular claim that a person did not have the capacity to follow the law because they regularly committed crimes, or courts simply claimed that having certain categories of mental illness meant that a person had diminished capacity. There was no evidence that directly connected the mental illness with an incapacity to conform oneself to the law. She argued that, while we can make general claims that some kinds of mental illness seemed to occur more often in people who committed crimes, we did not have sufficient evidence that the mental illness was the cause of the crime in any individual case. But, she argued, that did not matter if the best response to all criminal behavior was mental health treatment or other rehabilitative responses. The capacity of the individual was not relevant for determining what kind treatment they needed as "punishment."

Hart found this conclusion troubling because he insisted that we should not punish people who could not have acted differently, even if the punishment itself was rehabilitative. He argued that punishment should track moral blameworthiness as much as possible. In order to be held morally blameworthy for committing a bad act, a person must have had what he called "capacity-responsibility." Hart defined capacity-responsibility thusly:

> "He is responsible for his actions" is used to assert that a person has certain normal capacities. … The capacities in question are those of understanding, reasoning, and control of conduct: the ability to understand what conduct legal rules or morality require, to deliberate and reach decisions concerning these requirements, and to conform to decisions when made. (2008, 227)

A person was only responsible in a moral sense if they could have understood what they were doing (e.g., they were not hallucinating), if they could have decided about a plan of action (e.g., they did not have mental illnesses that impair planning), and if they could have carried out that plan (e.g., they were not operating under a compulsive disorder). If a person could not have understood a moral rule or was unable to make themselves conform to it, then they could not have been morally responsible. While not every legal system limited criminal liability to those with capacity-responsibility, Hart argued that it was unjust to punish someone without a procedure in place to make sure that they had had capacity-responsibility (2008, 227–30). If Wootton was right that courts could not have actually determined if any particular person who had committed a crime could have acted otherwise, that fact undermined traditional retributivism and Hart's own mixed theory that relied on individual guilt as a necessary condition for legitimate punishment.

Hart insisted that, even in the face of Wootton's evidence that courts did not have the means to determine if a person committed a crime as a result of mental illness, the legal system should not have abandoned the question of whether or not a person could have avoided committing a crime. In the face of uncertainty about whether or not we could have really known if other people were acting with full capacity-responsibility, Hart called for a different approach to thinking about responsibility based on social practices that prioritize human freedom (2008, 181).

For Hart, Wootton's position was not tenable because failing to take the capacity-responsibility of the person who committed a crime into account was at odds with every other aspect of social life. Hart argued that, even if we had some reason to believe that there were times when people, due to mental illness, could not have acted otherwise, we should have assumed, as a general rule, that others did act volitionally:

> Human society is a society of persons; and persons do not view themselves or each other merely as so many bodies moving in ways which are sometimes harmful and have to be prevented or altered. Instead persons interpret each other's movements as manifestations of intention and choices, and these subjective factors are often more important to their social relations than the movements by which they are manifested or their effects. (2008, 182)

No matter how much scientific evidence we may have had that other people's actions were produced by a chemical deficiency, disorder, or other source, Hart argued that we, as human beings, still interpreted the actions of others through the lens of intentionality. It mattered to us, he argued, whether our neighbor accidentally elbowed us in the face or purposefully did so, even if both actions cause a bloody nose.

Thus, Hart insisted that legal systems should have endeavored to determine if a person who committed a crime had capacity-responsibility at the time. In general, we should have assumed that people did have control over their actions, meaning that they had capacity-responsibility. Only when there was positive evidence that a person did not have capacity-responsibility at the time of the crime should we have reduced their legal liability for that crime.

While Hart argued that Wootton went too far in rejecting the idea that people were morally responsible for the crimes they committed, he bemoaned the reality that most criminal legal systems had not done enough to prevent those with diminished capacity-responsibility from being punished. For example, Hart discussed the M'Naghten Rule, a test to determine if someone was mentally incapacitated in a way that undermined their criminal liability even though they committed a criminal act. This "insanity" test was articulated after Daniel M'Naghten killed the secretary to the prime minister of England in 1843, believing him to be the actual prime minister. M'Naghten believed that the Tories were conspiring to kill him, and his lawyer successfully argued to a jury that he should be found not guilty by reason of insanity. When popular outrage at the not guilty verdict erupted, a new rule, now called the M'Naghten rule, was articulated delineating a relatively narrow criterion for criminal insanity:

> All defendants are presumed to be sane unless they can prove that—at the time of committing the criminal act—the defendant's state of mind caused them to (1) not know what they were doing when they committed said act, or (2) that they knew what they were doing, but did not know that it was wrong. (Legal Information Institute 2022b, "M'Naghten Rule")

This test allowed for a person who had a *cognitive* failing due to mental illness to avoid criminal responsibility. For example, if a person had killed someone while under a delusion that the victim was a violent extraterrestrial bent on destroying humankind, the killer would have been found "not guilty by reason of insanity." However, if a person knew fully well what they were doing but were unable to stop themselves because of a compulsive disorder, they would not have counted as "insane" under the M'Naghten test. This means that a *volitional* failing was not enough to qualify a person as "not guilty by reason of insanity."

During the 1950s and 1960s, some states in the U.S. adopted new tests to remedy this apparent mismatch, most notably the test developed by the American Legal Institute as a part of its project to update and standardize American criminal law through the creation of the Model Penal Code (MPC), the first version of which was published in 1962. Under the MPC test,

> an individual is not liable for criminal offenses if, when he or she committed the crime or crimes, the individual suffered from a mental disease or defect that resulted in the individual lacking the substantial capacity [1] to appreciate the wrongfulness of his or her actions or [2] to conform his or her actions to requirements under the law. (Legal Information Institute 2022a, "Model Penal Code Insanity Defense")

While the first clause was meant to capture the essence of the *cognitive* criterion spelled out in the M'Naghten test, the second clause was meant to offer a *volitional* criterion that would cover instances where a person's mental illness impaired their ability to control their actions but did not impair their ability to comprehend the situation or its normative requirements. The MPC test and other similar tests that included something like the volitional element, such as the Durham test and the irresistible impulse test, were widely adopted in the United States starting in the 1960s. Meanwhile, in the U.K., the Homicide Act of 1957 (5 & 6 Eliz. 2 Ch. 11) did not amend the M'Naghten Rule but instead added a partial defense of diminished responsibility, which mitigated a murder charge to manslaughter.[4] Hart favored the expansion of insanity tests, noting that many European codes included both cognitive and volitional prongs. In contrast, he considered the Homicide Act's provision "both meagre and half-hearted" (2008, 193).

Hart's opponent, Wootton, would have argued that none of these tests could have accurately determined who had capacity-responsibility, and even if they could have, they were not necessary (Hart 2008, 178). But Hart insisted that punishment was only appropriate when a person had both the capacity and a fair opportunity to avoid committing a crime. Although tests for diminished capacity and insanity may have been imperfect, they were still preferable to abandoning the question of capacity-responsibility for crime completely. With this move, Hart was attempting to walk a fine line. On the one hand, he argued that it mattered to us deeply in our daily lives whether or not others acted with intention, which seemed to indicate that we cared if someone could have acted differently when they did something harmful. But social

[4] The Royal Commission on Capital Punishment that convened from 1949 to 1953 officially recommended that the M'Naghten Rule be amended along similar lines as the MPC test. The Commission recommended the following language: "The jury must be satisfied that, at the time of committing the act, the accused, as a result of disease of the mind (or mental deficiency) (a) did not know the nature and quality of the act or (b) did not know that it was wrong or (c) was incapable of preventing himself from committing it" (Royal Commission on Capital Punishment 1953, 111). To count as diminished responsibility under the Homicide Act of 1957, a criminal defendant must show that they were "suffering from such abnormality of mind (whether arising from a condition of arrested or retarded development of mind or any inherent causes responsibility, or induced by disease or injury) as substantially impaired [their] mental responsibility" (Homicide Act of 1957 [5 & 6 Eliz. 2 Ch. 11], Pt. 1, sec. 2).

science research seemed to suggest that we could not know if an act was truly voluntary or not (if any act was every truly voluntary). So, we would have to rely on our social conventions to tell us whether acts were done purposefully or not. We could observe the actions of others for telltale signs that bodily movements were involuntary—a tick, a startle, or other indication of accidental movement—or that the person's actions looked purposeful. We asked people why they did certain actions and evaluated their credibility when they answered. And the criminal law also properly relied on these standards, allowing inferences of capacity based on commonsense reasoning.

Hart wrestled with how to address the question of determining who had a meaningful ability to act otherwise when they committed a crime. His rejection of Wootton's position entailed a rejection of the rehabilitative ideal's model that crime was caused by mental problems or other types of social defects. The only crimes that we were justified in punishing were those that arose out of an individual's agency, so we needed robust tests for legal insanity. But Hart also asserted that, outside the rare times these tests captured, most people had capacity-responsibility most of the time.

3 The 1970s: The Rise of Retributivism and the Moral Description of Crime

While Hart had already raised alarms about rehabilitation's implications for the domain of human freedom in the late 1950s and 1960s, it was not until the 1970s that retributivism replaced the rehabilitative ideal as the dominant theory of punishment. In this "golden half-century" of punishment theory starting in 1957,[5] most punishment theories focused on justifying punishment by appealing to the concept of punishment itself, not on empirical facts about what punishment could achieve (M. Davis 2009). But the myriad of theories that developed under the moniker of "retributivism" were so diverse that the term failed to capture the meaning of all these different theories. Basically, any account that did not rely primarily on empirically measurable social outcomes tended to fall under this label.[6] I cannot give an account of each of these wide varieties of retributivism here, so I will focus on three theorists that illustrate the retributivist assumption that crime is primarily a moral

[5] Michael Davis (2009) traced the beginning of the rise of retributivism all the way back to 1957, while von Hirsch (1985, 9) argued that 1971 was when serious retributivist theory took root.

[6] Michael Davis helpfully argued that we should shed the utilitarian/retributivist distinction and replace it with an empirical/conceptual conception (2009, 89).

problem. These three theories highlight important shared values with the "law and order" movement that many scholars of incarceration link to mass incarceration.

While there were likely many causes of its decline, empirical evidence that the penal practices meant to rehabilitate did not in fact produce the intended results of reducing recidivism fueled many critiques of rehabilitative models (Alschuler 2003, 9). Andrew von Hirsch summarized: "The results were disappointing, indeed. Although many offenders seemed to show improvement (that is, did not return to crime), this tended to occur as much among untreated as among treated individuals—the treatment as such had little perceptible influence" (1985, 4).[7] Moreover, between 1960 and 1980, crime rates rose suddenly and quickly. Property crime rates rose by 200 percent and violent crime rates rose by about 250 percent (Pfaff 2017, 3).

Deterrence, a different utilitarian ideal of punishment, briefly took center stage for punishment theorists. In the 1970s, as rehabilitation theories declined, von Hirsch argued that general deterrence took on an outsized role in punishment, particularly as philosophers and jurists appealed to law and economics modeling (von Hirsch 1985, 7–9). While still aiming to reduce crime overall, this approach instead viewed those who might commit crimes as rational agents who would take harsher penalties into account. Just as with rehabilitation, the role of incapacitation paired nicely with the aim of general deterrence, as some criminologists thought that much violent crime was perpetrated by a handful of repeat offenders. Thus, long prison sentences had the double effect of taking repeat offenders off the streets and sending a strong deterrent message to those members of society who would respond to rational incentives (von Hirsch 1985, 7–9).

According to von Hirsch, deterrence fit the new "law and order" attitude that was emerging in the 1970s in the United States (von Hirsch 1985, 9). Indeed, the 1970s marked the point when the incarceration rate in the U.S. broke from historically stable rates, slowly increasing as the decade went on. At the beginning of the 1970s, the rate of incarceration was in line with what it had been since the mid-1800s and broadly consistent with the incarceration rates of the U.K. and European countries (Pfaff 2017, 1). During the 1970s, scholars tended to think that the incarceration rate would either radically decrease from its already low rate because of continuous prison reformation projects (Rothman 1990, 295) or remain steady indefinitely because states would adjust policies to maintain relatively consistent incarceration

[7] For more information on the decline of the rehabilitative ideal, see Secherest et al. (1979), Allen (1981), and Bailey (2019).

rates (Blumstein and Moitra 1979, 376). But both would soon be proven wrong. To highlight the contrast, at a low water mark, in 1972, fewer than 200,000 people were incarcerated in state and federal facilities, but that number jumped to 1.56 million in 2014, not including county jails (Pfaff 2017, 2).

It is impossible to draw causal connections one way or the other between philosophers and policymakers, but there are certainly affinities between some theories and the public policies that led to mass incarceration. Von Hirsch may have been correct to note that the deterrence theorists he highlighted seemed to align with the growing "law and order" mentality in the United States. But retributivist models shared a distinctive emphasis on individual moral responsibility with the "tough-on-crime" political rhetoric of the 1980s and 1990s, the same decades that saw huge increases in incarceration rates. By that point, retributivist theories, particularly those focusing on moral desert, had established predominance in philosophy of punishment.

At first, it seemed that retributivist theories were actually meant to be kinder, more balanced approaches to punishment. In contrast to deterrence, desert-based theories of punishment held that the central purpose and justification of punishment was to give those who had committed crimes what they deserve. The severity of punishment (particularly the length of a prison sentence) was meant to match the severity of the crime committed. Sentences were not to be designed to rehabilitate the person who committed the crime or deter others from committing the same crime. In the face of sentences that were indeterminate (rehabilitative) or excessively long (deterrence-based), von Hirsch argued that the desert-based models were introduced as justice-centric interventions to limit extreme or indeterminate sentences (von Hirsch 1985, 11).

Moreover, as Hart's arguments against Wootton emphasized, retributivism entailed a deep respect for the agency of individual human beings. While there may be real cases in which mental illness or other problems prevented people from acting freely, retributivists were wary of granting too many exceptions to the rule that people were agents who were responsible and blameworthy for criminal actions. For many retributivists, moral desert and strong blaming practices went hand in hand.

But, just as rehabilitation had a dark side, moralistic retributivism also had pernicious views of individuals who commit crimes. One of the most moralistic versions of retributivism that arose in response to the rehabilitative ideal was Michael S. Moore's theory. In an essay first published in 1987, he explained, "Retributivism is a very straightforward theory of punishment: We are justified in punishing because and only because offenders deserve it" (2010, 181). For Moore, guilt was sufficient on its own sufficient to justify punishment. To defend the idea that guilt was sufficient for warranted punishment, Moore argued that we should pay attention to our intuitions when we hear about the commission of heinous crimes. To motivate this argument, he quoted at length from a 1981 editorial by Mike Royko, a long-time columnist for the *Chicago Times*.[8] In the column, Royko explained his outrage at anti-death penalty advocates who sang "We Shall Overcome" outside a prison that held murderer Steven Judy. Royko could not sympathize with the protestors because he had met living relatives of a number of murder victims, including Judy's victim. Royko detailed many other violent and shocking crimes alongside empathetic portrayals of victims and their families (Royko 1981).

This newspaper column was the start of Moore's argument. Moore continued, arguing that most people would have the immediate intuition that the people who committed the crimes that Royko describes should be punished (and harshly). That immediate intuition was an important source of knowledge about what punishment was deserved. But, Moore said, most people would then correct their initial response by adding that the reason to punish was to deter, rehabilitate, or incapacitate. This invalidation of the retributivist intuition was where people went wrong. Moore asserted that the emotions that attend retributivism were not misleading. These emotions gave us helpful information to form our moral judgments.

In another appeal to intuitions, Moore again turned to an example of a real, heinous crime to motivate his argument. This time, he asked readers about their intuitions about a jilted boyfriend, Herrin, who murdered his girlfriend, Garland, with a hammer (2010, 213). Moore argued that we should all agree that we could see ourselves ending up making a horrible mistake with brutal consequences, just like Herrin. A failure to understand this truth could only

[8] Royko's disdain for criminals also took on racial tones in his 1993 article contrasting Rodney King to Barbara Meller Jensen, a German woman who was murdered when she got lost and ended up in a "low-income, high-crime area" (Royko 1993). He went on to complain that King's beating got too much attention, while Jensen's murder was quickly forgotten:

> Despite his troubles, Rodney King is a lucky guy. He is a criminal by trade, having served time for armed robbery. He was beaten after driving drunk and being chased at dangerously high speeds, putting innocent motorists at risk. He was a social menace. In contrast, Mrs. Jensen was a law-abiding, useful person: a therapist for handicapped children. She had gone to Florida because her husband, a biologist, needed solitude to complete a book. She wasn't a threat to anyone. (Royko 1993)

Of course, one cannot impute every view that Royko articulated in his decades as a well-loved columnist to Moore just because Moore quoted him at length in one paper in 1988. But the sentiment of these two columns is consistent. Those who commit crimes deserve harsh punishments, not our sympathy. Because we care about the victims of crimes, we are justified in retributive feelings, and the institutions of the state should carry out punishments in accordance with these retributive feelings.

be attributed to those people who have made a deep "we-they" distinction between themselves and those who commit crimes. Knowing that anyone was capable of violence in the right circumstances, he followed up:

> Then ask yourself: What would you feel like if it was you who had intentionally smashed open the skull of a 23-year-old woman with a claw hammer while she was asleep, a woman whose fatal defect was a desire to free herself from your too clinging embrace? My own response, I hope, would be that I would feel guilty unto death. I couldn't imagine any suffering that could be imposed upon me that would be unfair because it exceeded what I deserved. (Moore 2010, 213)

At first, he invited the reader to feel the pain of having killed another person. Intuition told readers what murderers deserve, which they could trust because it was what they would ask for if they committed such a crime.

Next, Moore described Herrin's interview with a psychiatrist in which Herrin asserted that his eight-year sentence was too long, and that he should have been let out after two years, considering his personal circumstances, including no history of prior crimes. To those who would have argued that guilt was an unhelpful or even destructive emotion, Moore responded that feeling guilty and wanting punishment were a much better alternative than Herrin's "shallow, easily obtained self-absolution" (2010, 214). Moore was not arguing for a rehabilitative aim. He did not think Herrin should be punished in order to induce a proper sense of guilt. Instead, Moore deplored the lack of blame and personal responsibility that Herrin's comments exhibited. The fact that we would all presumably feel that no punishment was too great for us if we were in Herrin's shoes was itself reliable evidence for us make judgments about what appropriate punishment was for others.

Moore insisted on the value of individual responsibility, rejecting Herrin's view that his background circumstances made him less culpable. A refusal to consider factors that might undermine the capacity of an individual to make better choices was paradigmatic of the "law and order" era. In a reversal of the 1960s legal movement to broaden the category of "insanity," in the 1980s, there was a massive movement in the United States to return to the more restrictive M'Naghten test. Again, an assassination attempt motivated the narrowing of the insanity defense. John Hinkley, who had attempted to assassinate President Ronald Reagan, was found "not guilty by reason of insanity" in federal court, which used the broader MPC test. Following public outcry, U.S. Congress responded to Hinkley's verdict by changing federal law, returning to the narrower M'Naghten formulation of "insanity." Most states quickly did the same, and five states even passed legislation to abolish the insanity defense altogether (Morse 2021, 2–3). The narrowing of excuses for crimes was an essential feature of both of Moore's retributivism and the 1980s "law and order" movement.

This attitude was also seen in the rhetoric of politicians. While Republican leaders had often been associated with the tough-on-crime attitudes and rhetoric, many Democratic leaders in the 1990s expressed the same sentiments. Take current President Joe Biden as an example. When Biden was a senator in the 1990s, he was known for being tough on crime. When proposing stringent new crime bills, he talked about "predators on our streets" in a speech in 1993. In 1994, he lauded Nixon's criminal justice policies: "Every time Richard Nixon, when he was running in 1972, would say, 'Law and order,' the Democratic match or response was, 'Law and order with justice'—whatever that meant. And I would say, 'Lock the S.O.B.s up.'" And like Moore, he had no patience for hearing about the social backgrounds of those who commit crimes: "It doesn't matter whether or not they're the victims of society. I don't want to ask, 'What made them do this?' They must be taken off the street," Biden said in 1993 (Stolberg and Herndon 2019).

While Moore's retributivism was especially stark in its emphasis on heinous crimes, strong moral condemnation of any person who committed a crime, and limiting excuses, other retributivists drew similar conclusions by emphasizing the moral nature of criminal wrongs. Jean Hampton (1992) used an expressive retributivism that also encompassed a moral education view to argue that criminal punishments were the best moral responses to sexist and racist crimes. Both her retributivism and her moral education justifications came out of what she saw as the expressive capacities of criminal acts and punishments. She argued that when a person committed a crime, they expressed the idea that they were more important that victims or society at large (1666). The act itself communicated this message by diminishing the victim. This was true of the most heinous crimes. Hampton used the example of a particularly violent anti-Black hate crime in which a White farmer tortured, killed, and mutilated five Black farm hands, a man and his four sons, in response to some minor slight (1675). But it also can be true of the most minor infraction. Hampton used the example of a person who snuck a book out of the university library without checking it out (1680). This person's act announced that they thought their own unfettered access to the book was more important than that of the other members of the university.

For Hampton, punishment was necessary to right these diminishing wrongs. It sent a message that the person who committed the crime was not above the law, and that they were not more valuable than their victim or the community. Because of its capacity to communicate this moral message,

Hampton also thought that punishment could morally educate the person who had committed the crime. But Hampton insisted on a sharp distinction between rehabilitation and moral education: "Apart from any literacy problems, occupational problems, or mental problems, this view [moral education] holds that those who are guilty of a criminal offense have a moral problem" (1998, 40). Punishment sent a moral message that the convicted person could chose to accept or not. It did not, as with rehabilitation, act on a passive patient who had no real agency in their own crimes or their potential redemption.

While Hampton often expressed skepticism about the role of incarceration in punishment in North America, she also argued in favor of limiting a criminal's right to vote based on her emphasis on crime's moral wrongs to victims. She argued that allowing White men who had committed anti-Black hate crimes to vote would communicate the idea that these men are still members of the political community, even if they expressly denied a political value of the equality of all members of the community regardless of race. Likewise, Hampton argued that those who committed violence against women expressed the view that women are less valuable members of society:

> To hand the levers of political power over to someone whose behavior manifests an intention to accomplish the subordination of women to men undermines not only the democratic value of equality but also the status and safety of women in that society. (1998, 42)

Because crimes sent messages about the value of their victims, failing to punish crimes sent a message that the government (and the political community it represented) did not care about women's well-being either.

Hampton's view of criminal punishment as a tool to fight women's oppression was also consistent with the spirit of the tough-on-crime 1990s. Beth R. Richie argued that the women's anti-violence movement split in the 1980s, as some feminists pragmatically chose to align themselves with the "law and order" movement (2012, 84–86). Framing violence against women as a criminal justice issue (rather than a more widespread social issue), these groups secured resources and had a large impact on legislation. The most well-known and significant piece of this legislation was the Violence Against Women Act, first passed in 1994, which foremost provided criminal justice tools for fighting violence against women, and also added funding for shelters and other victims' services. It is less well-known, however, that it was passed as part of the now infamous Omnibus Crime Bill (Pub.L. 103–322), which, among other things, created sixty new federal capital crimes, ended Pell Grants for prisoners, and provided extensive funding for new prisons and police programs (Richie 2012, 84–86). Hampton's feminist, expressivist retributivism aligned with some feminists' attempts to use the criminal law's power to condemn as a tool to fight gender-based violence. As Richie noted, this strategy was ultimately only successful for middle class, White, heterosexual women (2012, 1–4).

Another moralistic retributivist, Herbert Morris (1968), argued for the right to be punished as a recognition of one's capacity as an agent, offering an argument similar to Moore's. Like Moore, Morris imagined that if he were the one who had committed a heinous crime, he would accept any punishment, so we should want that for others. To make this point, he argued that, if we saw ourselves as potential or actual criminal wrongdoers, we would want a system of punishment that would allow us redemption. Speaking of the person who committed a crime, Morris wrote, "Further, the evil … that he has done himself by his wrongdoing is a moral evil greater than he has done others. His soul is in jeopardy as his victim's is not" (1981, 267). In a softer tone than Moore, Morris argued that, "but for the grace of God," we could all commit crimes that we ourselves abhor. We would have all wanted a path to redemption and reconciliation, so we should have wanted that for others. Punishment offered this path.

Morris proposed a softer version of retributivism than Moore, but his conclusion was the same. Individuals who committed crimes had deep moral problems that only punishment could address. We should have punished these individuals regardless of whether that punishment reduced crime or helped anyone. Of course, we cannot draw a causal connection between retributivist theorists such as Morris, Hampton, or even Moore and mass incarceration or the increasingly obvious injustices of the American criminal legal system. But they shared a certain spirit: the idea of moral responsibility for crime, the blameworthiness of the person who committed it, and the dismissal of factors that might mitigate culpability. Retributivism was the dominant theory of punishment in the 1980s and 1990s, when incarceration saw its sharpest increases, new tough-on-crime legislation passed, and legal defenses shrunk.

In contrast to the more explicitly moralistic desert-based theories, another type of retributivist theory, the "benefits and burdens" theory (also called the "fair play" theory) situated criminal punishment in the context of a larger social-political system.[9] Roughly speaking, those who endorsed this view recognized that society was a cooperative endeavor and that laws were required

[9] Other benefits and burdens theories included Morris (1968), Murphy (1973), and Sher (1987).

to maintain this cooperation. Because members got the benefits of the laws—that is, society ran smoothly enough for them to live comfortably within it—each member was required to take their fair share of the burdens. Those burdens included following the law. When a person broke the law, they took unfair advantage of this balance, and punishment was necessary to reset the just distribution. This may have had the ring of deterrence to it, but for benefits and burdens theorists, resetting the balance was a moral response to crime, not an instrumental one.

On Richard Dagger's (1993) version of a benefits and burdens argument, a system of punishment secured social cooperation by deterring would-be rule-breakers and assuring those who want to follow the rules that they will not be taken advantage of. This system of benefits and burdens created obligations for each person to follow the law:

> Criminals act unfairly when they take advantage of the opportunities the legal order affords them without contributing to the preservation of that order. In doing so, they upset the balance between benefits and burdens at the heart of the notion of justice. (Dagger 1993, 476)

Thus, each crime committed was morally wrong not just if the act itself was morally wrong outside the law (murder, assault), but it was also wrong because it violated a moral obligation to support the system of social cooperation. Moreover, this meant that in committing a crime, one did not just break a moral duty to a specific victim, if there was one, but also to every member of society.

One interesting upshot of the benefits and burdens version of retributivism was that deep injustice in the system of social cooperation undermined the justification of punishment: "And this means that punishment is justified only when there is a just balance of benefits and burdens to begin with—when the social order is just, or reasonably so" (Dagger 1993, 177). We could not blame a person for upsetting a fairly balanced set of benefits and burdens if there was not a fair equilibrium to start with. With this in mind, Jeffrey Reiman argued, "Since the obligation to obey the law is a function of the benefits one receives, it follows that many disadvantaged criminals are not violating their moral obligations to obey the law" (2007, 7–8). Thus, in the United States and other similar political communities, many people who have committed crimes were not morally obligated to follow the law itself and did not merit state-based punishment (although they may still have been morally obligated, to, say, avoid assault or murder).

This version of retributivism was a vast improvement on desert-based theories in light of the concerns that continue to plague the American criminal legal system in the 2020s. Benefits and burdens theories left room for thinking about how background injustices affected the obligations that members of a society had toward one another. They raised questions about the legitimacy of punishing oppressed groups, including those living in poor Black neighborhoods that were especially impacted by crime, violent policing, and incarceration.[10] But, at the same time, they shared much with retributivism's more classic version. Even if a person should not have been punished because of background injustice, the framework was still about individual obligations to follow the law and whether those obligations applied.

4 Concluding Remarks on the Social Critical View of Crime

Throughout the twentieth and twenty-first centuries in the United States, social critics of punishment have led social movements, sometimes within prisons themselves (Adelsberg et al. 2015). Angela Davis, a trained philosopher and social movement leader, has long been a part of anti-prison movements. In her abolitionist text, she asks "why 'criminals' have been constituted as a class, and indeed a class of human beings undeserving of the civil and human rights accorded to others" (2003, 112). The social critical view of crime is that it is caused by deep injustices in the basic structure of society, including racial and gender oppression, poverty and inequality, and ablism. Viewing crime as primarily a result of structural injustice means that dealing with crime through individual punishments cannot address the problem of crime either practically or morally. Criminal law functions to maintain group-based oppressions, regardless of the intentions of individuals who carry out the tasks of the criminal justice system. In the United States, Black Americans, especially those descended from enslaved people, were (and continue to be) particularly targeted by the criminal law (Alexander 2012). Moreover, the vast majority of people of all races who end up being incarcerated were (and continue to be) extremely poor.

Whereas the Black Lives Matter protests starting in 2014 often included calls for particular officers to be arrested and convicted, in 2020, many Black Lives Matter protesters started to demand that police departments be

[10] For a nuanced discussion of the legitimacy of punishing poor Black people in the United States, see Shelby (2016).

defunded, appealing to similar themes from prison abolitionists like Davis. Protestors called for a shift in funding from police to education, healthcare, housing, and other public services. At first glance, the contemporary calls for ending policing and incarceration are similar to the old rehabilitative model. Like the rehabilitative model, the social critical view sees social and political problems rather than moral problems as the root of crime. It also emphasizes the value of social services and recognizes that those who live in poverty have many more reasons to commit crimes than those with financial stability.

But the social critical view is fundamentally different than the rehabilitative model because it does not focus on compelling those who have committed crimes to accept services such as mental health care, job training, and addiction treatment. Rather than addressing crime by treating those who committed crimes as patients receiving care from benevolent experts, the social critical model emphasizes the active involvement of communities that have been excluded from political life and most impacted by crime and punishment. The state is complicit in the harms that crime causes because it contributes to income inequality, racial disparities, and lack of access to health care and income. In addition to increasing mental health care and substance abuse treatment access, as was typical of rehabilitation, social critics call for addressing crime at its root. This means fighting poverty though measures such as stronger progressive taxation, welfare, or universal basic income; providing free higher education and job training; and investing in infrastructure in Black, Indigenous, and Latinx communities. As social movements and policy makers move into the next decade of addressing crime and punishment, the social critical view of crime is a powerful philosophical approach to thinking about punishment and justice. Present-day activists and theorists who justly demand the return of vital social services, which were dismantled with the rehabilitative ideal, should do so while being wary of repeating the mistakes of the rehabilitative model. But we should not understand the social critical view or abolition and defunding movements as merely demanding more social services.

References

Adelsberg, Geoffrey, Lisa Guenther, and Scott Zeman. 2015. *Death and Other Penalties: Philosophy in a Time of Mass Incarceration*. New York: Fordham University Press.

Alexander, Michelle. 2012. *The New Jim Crow: Mass Incarceration in the Age of Colorblindness*. Rev. ed. New York: New Press.

Allen, Francis A. 1981. *The Decline of the Rehabilitative Ideal: Penal Policy and Social Purpose*. New Haven, CT: Yale University Press.
Alschuler, Albert W. 2003. "The Changing Purposes of Criminal Punishment: A Retrospective on the Past Century and Some Thoughts about the Next." *University of Chicago Law Review* 70, no. 1 (Winter): 1–22.
Bailey, Victor. 2019. *The Rise and Fall of the Rehabilitative Ideal, 1895–1970*. Abingdon, UK: Routledge.
Blumstein, Alfred, and Soumyo Moitra. 1979. "An Analysis of the Time Series of the Imprisonment Rate in the States of the United States: A Further Test of the Stability of Punishment Hypothesis." *Journal of Criminal Law & Criminology* 70, no. 3 (Autumn): 376–90.
Dagger, Richard. 1993. "Playing Fair with Punishment." *Ethics* 103, no. 3 (April): 473–88.
Davis, Angela Y. 2003. *Are Prisons Obsolete?* New York: Seven Stories.
Davis, Michael. 1990. "Recent Work in Punishment Theory." *Public Affairs Quarterly* 4, no. 3 (July): 217–32.
———. 2009. "Punishment Theory's Golden Half Century: A Survey of Developments from (about) 1957 to 2007." *Journal of Ethics* 13, no. 1 (January): 73–100.
Feinberg, Joel. 2008. "The Classic Debate." In *Philosophy of Law*, 8th ed., edited by Joel Feinberg and Jules Colman, 625–29. Belmont, CA: Wadsworth.
Hamilton-Smith, Guy. 2018. "The Endless Punishment of Civil Commitment." *Appeal*, September 4. https://theappeal.org/the-endless-punishment-of-civil-commitment/.
Hampton, Jean. 1992. "Correcting Harms versus Righting Wrongs: The Goal of Retribution." *UCLA Law Review* 39, no. 6 (August): 1659–702.
———. 1998. "Punishment, Feminism, and Political Identity: A Case Study in the Expressive Meaning of the Law." *Canadian Journal of Law and Jurisprudence* 11, no. 1 (January): 23–45.
Hart, H. L. A. 2008. *Punishment and Responsibility: Essays in the Philosophy of Law*. 2nd ed. Oxford: Oxford University Press.
Legal Information Institute. 2022a. "Model Penal Code Insanity Defense." *Wex Legal Dictionary*. Cornell Law School. Accessed April 6. https://www.law.cornell.edu/wex/model_penal_code_insanity_defense.
———. 2022b. "M'Naghten Rule." *Wex Legal Dictionary*. Cornell Law School. Accessed April 6. https://www.law.cornell.edu/wex/m%27naghten_rule.
Moore, Michael S. 2010. "The Moral Worth of Retribution." In *Responsibility, Character, and the Emotions: New Essays in Moral Psychology*, edited by Ferdinand Schoeman, 179–219. Cambridge: Cambridge University Press.
Morris, Herbert. 1968. "Persons and Punishment." *Monist* 52, no. 4 (October): 475–501.
———. 1981. "A Paternalistic Theory of Punishment." *American Philosophical Quarterly* 18, no. 4 (October): 263–71.

Morse, Stephen J. 2021. "Before and after Hinckley: Legal Insanity in the United States." *Faculty Scholarship at Penn Law*. 2252. https://scholarship.law.upenn.edu/faculty_scholarship/2252.

Murphy, Jeffrie G. 1973. "Marxism and Retribution." *Philosophy & Public Affairs* 2, no. 3 (Spring): 217–43.

Pfaff, John F. 2017. *Locked In: The True Causes of Mass Incarceration—and How to Achieve Real Reform*. New York: Basic.

Rawls, John. 1955. "Two Concepts of Rules." *Philosophical Review* 64, no. 1 (January): 3–32.

Reiman, Jeffrey. 2007. "The Moral Ambivalence of Crime in an Unjust Society." *Criminal Justice Ethics* 26, no. 2 (Summer/Fall): 3–15.

Richie, Beth E. 2012. *Arrested Justice. Arrested Justice: Black Women, Violence, and America's Prison Nation*. New York: New York University Press.

Royko, Mike. 1981. "Nothing Gained by Killing a Killer? Oh Yes, There Is." *Los Angeles Times*, March 13.

———. 1993. "Rodney King and a Double Standard." *Chicago Daily Tribune*, April 6. https://www.chicagotribune.com/news/ct-xpm-1993-04-07-9304070056-story.html.

Rothman, David J. 1990. *The Discovery of the Asylum: Social Order and Disorder in the New Republic*. Rev. ed. Boston: Little, Brown.

Royal Commission on Capital Punishment. 1953. *Royal Commission on Capital Punishment, 1949–1953: Report*. London: H. M. Stationery Office.

Sechrest, Lee, Susan O. White, and Elizabeth D. Brown, eds. 1979. *The Rehabilitation of Criminal Offenders: Problems and Prospects*. Washington, DC: National Academy of Sciences.

Shelby, Tommie. 2016. "Punishment." In *Dark Ghettos: Injustice, Dissent, and Reform*, 228–51. Cambridge, MA: Belknap.

Sher, George. 1987. *Desert*. Princeton, NJ: Princeton University Press.

Stolberg, Sheryl Gay, and Astead W. Herndon. 2019. "Lock the S.O.B.'s Up: Joe Biden and the Era of Mass Incarceration." *New York Times*, June 25. https://www.nytimes.com/2019/06/25/us/joe-biden-crime-laws.html.

von Hirsch, Andrew. 1985. *Past or Future Crimes: Deservedness and Dangerousness in the Sentencing of Criminals*. New Brunswick, NJ: Rutgers University Press.

Part II

Retributivism, Consequentialism, and Mixed Theories

5

Relational Conceptions of Retribution

Leora Dahan Katz

1 Introduction

Retributive theory refers to a set of views of punishment, central to which is the claim that punishment is justified by the desert of the offender.[1] On retributive views, those who engage in culpable wrongdoing are understood to deserve some negative, burdensome response to their wrong, while one's desert is taken to justify the imposition of such punitive response, that is, to render punishment permissible, and on positive retributive views, right or good. Retributive views are generally contrasted with consequentialist justifications that take punishment to be an evil, justified as a necessary means toward the attainment of (non-retributive) ends such as deterrence, rehabilitation, incapacitation, and other goods.[2] Retributive views, on the other hand, are those that take punishment to be justified by the act in question and the desert of the offender, with no further consequences necessary to account for the rightness or goodness of punishment.

[1] Desert is the central notion common to most retributive theories, though not all center on desert. For example, Herbert Morris's (1968) fairness-based retributivism does not refer to "desert" (though arguably such views may still be understood as a way of cashing out a particular conception of desert that justifies punishment).

[2] For an elaboration on consequentialist versus non-consequentialist versions of retributivism (the former of which aim to promote a retributive good), see Berman (2011).

L. Dahan Katz (✉)
Hebrew University of Jerusalem, Jerusalem, Israel
e-mail: leora.dahankatz@mail.huji.ac.il

© The Author(s), under exclusive license to Springer Nature Switzerland AG 2023

M. C. Altman (ed.), *The Palgrave Handbook on the Philosophy of Punishment*, Palgrave Handbooks in the Philosophy of Law, https://doi.org/10.1007/978-3-031-11874-6_5

On most varieties of retributivism, what justifies punishment is non-relational, that is, does not depend on facts about the relations between the parties to punishment. Rather, it depends primarily on facts about the act of wrongdoing and the offender. On the retributive approach I defend here, the relations between the punisher and punishee play a central role in the justification of punishment and in the conception of desert upon which such justification relies. I begin in sections 2 and 3 by making some general clarifications about retributive theory and central objections raised against it, which are alleged to provide sufficient reason to reject retributivism as a viable theory of punishment. Next I develop the retributive line of thought I take to be most promising—relational conceptions of retribution—and elucidate what they offer in the way of advancing the retributive project (section 4). Section 5 then demonstrates that the objections raised against retributivism provide no reason to reject relational views. Such conceptions, however, raise their own concerns, which section 6 turns to address. Finally, section 7 briefly reflects on the kinship between such accounts and P. F. Strawson's work on moral responsibility practices, highlighting that which is drawn from Strawson's work, while elucidating the aspects of his thought that need not be taken on in the move from non-relational to relational retributive views. Together, I take these to offer a broad view of why retributivists and critics alike have reason to view relational conceptions of retribution as offering a promising path toward the justification of punishment.

2 Central Objections

Retributivism has been subject to a wide variety of criticisms that claim to defeat it as a viable theory of punishment. Primary among these, though outside the scope of interest in this chapter, has been the free will or moral responsibility skepticism objection to retributive theory (see Caruso's and Vilhauer's chapters in this volume). Per this objection, the retributive justification of punishment relies on the assumption that persons can be robustly morally responsible for their actions, where this requires subscribing to certain metaphysical commitments, such as the existence of free will or an adequate combatibilist alternative. Yet persons do not have the capacities necessary for such responsibility, so they can never be responsible or deserving in the relevant sense (Pereboom 2013). Thus retributivism fails as a justification of punishment.

I will not have much to say about this objection other than to agree that robust moral responsibility must be possible for retributive justification to succeed (though it need not rely on libertarian free will).[3] Yet as I think this is a problem for all viable forms of retributivism, I will set this objection aside. Instead, I will focus on central worries that threaten to relegate retributivism to the wastebasket of punishment theory even if we accept that persons can be morally responsible in the relevant sense.

2.1 Repugnancy

An oft-repeated allegation against retributivism charges that retributive theory attributes positive moral valence to human suffering, and as such is an objectionable theory on any plausible moral view (see, e.g., Honderich 1970; Narveson 1974, 192; Golash 2005; Tadros 2011; Scanlon 2013). Per this objection, retributive theory takes human suffering to be *good* or valuable, while such ascription of value is "morally repugnant" (Scanlon 2013, 102). To avoid such "barbarism" (Tadros 2011, 63), critics argue, retributive theory must be rejected in favor of a theory of punishment that takes human suffering to be at most *instrumentally* valuable, as is the case, for example, on utilitarian and other non-retributive theories of punishment that take suffering to be a necessary evil rather than a welcome event to be celebrated.

2.2 Conclusiveness

A second central objection alleges that, even if it is conceded that it is good for persons to "get what they deserve," this is still insufficient to provide a justification for punishment; for conceding that something is good does not suffice to offer conclusive grounds for bringing it about. This objection can be parsed into a number of arguments. First, it is not even clear that valuable states of affairs always generate reasons to bring them about. They certainly do not all generate conclusive reasons to bring them about. By way of illustration, it is often highlighted that we do not think we have (conclusive) reasons to guarantee that people receive their positive deserts. Thus a challenge is raised to explain what is special about punishment or ill-desert such that it uniquely generates conclusive reasons in favor of manufacturing this specific end state of affairs (e.g., Dolinko 1991, 1992; Golash 2005, 80; see also Davis 1972).[4]

[3] I refer here to responsibility in the accountability sense of the term. See Watson (1996) and Shoemaker (2015).

[4] In his analysis of desert, George Sher comments that, in many cases, desert claims "do not imply anything about what particular persons ought to do," while retributive desert claims are exceptional in this way (1987, 5).

Second, even if reasons are generated, not all means toward a desirable end are necessarily justified or permissible. Again, by way of illustration, critics point out that, even if an undeserving individual has access to or rights over goods they do not deserve, this does not make it permissible for others to forcibly remove the goods from their possession and transfer them to a deserving individual, even if the value or justice of desert might ultimately be served by this removal (Dolinko 1991, 544; 1997, 522–27).

2.3 Authority (of the State)

Relatedly, considering the political features of criminal punishment, critics argue that claims about the moral force of desert do not demonstrate *who* ought to punish, and they fail to show that the state has the *authority* to punish and to give offenders their "just" deserts. That is, they fail to offer an answer to the question: "even if [wrongdoers] deserve to suffer, or to be burdened in some distinctive way, why should it be for the state to inflict that suffering or that burden on them?" (Hoskins and Duff 2021; see also Dolinko 1991, 1992). Further argument is necessary to establish that there is any particular agent who ought to impose valuable punishment (see, e.g., Kleinig 1973, 71; Árdal 1984, 243), while in the case of criminal punishment, this would seem to require an argument in support of the state as the earthly arbiter of moral desert. Thus, many scholars who focus on the political rather than moral question of punishment object that retributivism (as well as utilitarian theories) fails to establish the permissibility or legitimacy of state punishment.

2.4 Epistemic-Indeterminacy Objection

Finally, even if retributivism is able to abstractly defend the relevant claims—that it is valuable that wrongdoers receive their deserts or that wrongdoers ought to be treated in the ways countenanced by punishment, and that the state has the authority punish—retributivism remains plagued by the problem of epistemic opaqueness: the insurmountable challenge of identifying what it is that wrongdoers deserve. The concept of desert presumes a relation of fittingness between some act of culpable wrongdoing and some burden to be imposed on the offender. But, critics allege, retributivism does not have the resources to offer guidance on the question of how to identify or determine such deserts. Though many are prepared to concede that retributivism can offer well-defended arguments with respect to matters of ordinal proportionality—that is, the question of where along the scale of punishments the deserved punishment of a wrongdoer will fall *relative* to other cases—it cannot offer guidance with respect to the question of determinate deserts (more than to offer an intuitionist assertion that there is an intrinsic relation between a particular wrong and particular punishment). As one critic puts it, "I don't believe that we can ever know this. My suspicion is that we are in the dark on this matter because there is no determinate kind or amount of suffering that a criminal morally deserves" (Shafer-Landau 2000, 191). Though retributivism might appeal to an institutional solution to this problem, for example, by adopting legislated or otherwise institutionally determined deserts produced by decision procedures that clearly define what a wrongdoer deserves under any specified set of conditions, this solution would seem to undermine the very appeal of retributive theory, as it renders desert a *product* rather than *ground* of a well-designed practice of punishment. Thus, lacking epistemic access to our just deserts, even if retributivism is a theoretically viable theory of punishment, it fails as a justification of any particular punishments.

The above presents a broad view of central criticisms taken by many to undermine retributive theory. While these are serious charges, their force and success in fact depend on which conceptions of retributivism and desert we adopt.[5] It is thus worth clarifying some central distinctions within retributive theory. This will further help pave the path toward the most promising retributivist account, which, I believe, there is not only freestanding reason to endorse, but which further avoids these purported objections to retributive theory.

3 Important Clarifications

First, retributivism might center on a claim that is either axiological (i.e., a matter of value) or deontic. Axiological retributivism generally alleges that it is *intrinsically good* that offenders get what they deserve (suffer on account of their wrongdoing or some parallel formulation).[6] By contrast, on deontic versions of retributivism, the justification of punishment need not rely on a claim about the goodness of punishment or suffering. Rather, punishment is taken

[5] For example, some retributive views reject the repugnancy of the goodness of suffering (Murphy 2016; Zaibert 2018), while others avoid relying upon the intrinsic goodness claim, muting concerns about repugnancy. Fair-play accounts (Morris 1968; Dagger 1993) respond well to the challenge of authority, while conventionalist accounts provide a solution to the indeterminacy challenge.

[6] This axiological claim is often taken to have deontic implications (e.g., Moore 1997), but the justification of punishment is ultimately dependent on claims about value.

to be right or just, a matter of duty, while the burdensomeness or suffering involved in punishment is taken to be constitutive of the right (independent of whether it is also good).

Deontic retributive claims can also come in different stripes, notably pro tanto retributivism, according to which there is a pro tanto duty to impose retributive punishment (White 2011; Husak 2012), and all-things-considered retributivism. On the former, while we have a duty to impose retributive punishment, this duty can be defeated by overriding reasons not to punish; on the latter, presumably not. While retributivism is often painted by critics in this latter light, as a view that contends that those who deserve punishment *must* be punished regardless of other moral considerations or of the consequences of punishment (see, e.g., Nino 1996; Scanlon 1999; Chiao 2019), I doubt any retributivist has ever held this view. Retributivists are more realistically understood as disagreeing about just how strong the duty or weight of the reasons in favor of punishment are (or how much value there is in punishment), with weaker retributivism allowing retributive reasons to be defeated more easily and stronger retributivism alleging that countervailing considerations must be quite weighty before retributive punishment is to be permissibly sacrificed in the face of other concerns.[7]

Furthermore, retributivists are divided on the question of just what it is that culpable wrongdoers deserve. Joel Feinberg (1970) famously analyzed desert as a triadic relation involving a desert subject (the wrongdoer), a desert basis (that in virtue of which we are deserving—in the case of punishment, culpable wrongdoing), and a desert object (that which the subject deserves in virtue of the desert basis).[8] The retributive desert object is generally thought to be suffering: what offenders deserve is to *suffer*, often meaning to experience a quantum of pain, in proportion to their culpable wrong. This aspect of retributive thought has led to much resistance among critics, primarily when it, together with the above axiological claim, are taken to be the necessary commitments of a retributive view, resulting in the conjoint claim that the suffering of persons—albeit of the deserving—is intrinsically good. Yet once again, while many critics (and friends) assume that retributivism must be

[7] For a weaker retributive view, see Husak (2012). For a stronger view, see Murphy (2016) (though Murphy has other reservations about retribution). Even Kant, taken by many to be the paradigm all-things-considered retributivist (though it is debatable whether he was a strict retributivist at all, see, e.g., Byrd 1989 and Hill 1999), explicitly argues against imposing deserved punishment in specified cases (1996, 6:334 [p. 475]).

[8] Feinberg coined the term "desert object," while Berman (2011) has coined and elaborated on the desert subject and basis.

beholden to this desert object (e.g., Scanlon 2013), this is not the case.[9] Some have endorsed it (e.g., Davis 1972; Alexander 2018; Zaibert 2018), while others have focused on alternatives, including that what one deserves is the humbling of one's will (Fingarette 1977), that one's life go less well (Berman 2013), loss of liberty (Markel and Flanders 2010), or paternalistic interference.[10] Jeffrie Murphy has proposed, on the one hand, that the retributive desert object is in fact suffering, but that suffering in this context is wrongly understood as intrinsically related to pain. It is rather to be identified with the original meaning of the word: "to *endure* something that is not within the control of one's own will" (2016, 33). All these alternatives distance retributivism from the claims that underlie the charge of repugnancy and the association of retributivism with the glorification of suffering.

A further proposal, evident in many formulations of retributivism, asserts that what one deserves is *to be punished*. This may seem a circular claim, yet the meaning of this alternative might be understood from a central motivation for replacing "suffering" with "punishment." Consider the following: if a murderer gets into a car accident and suffers serious bodily injuries, have they gotten what they deserved? On the one hand, they may have experienced a quantum of pain proportionate to the culpable wrong (or, for that matter, been forced to endure that which is outside of their will, or had their life go less well to the relevant extent, etc.). Yet there appears to be something lacking in this case of inadvertent or arbitrary correspondence between the unwelcome fate suffered by the agent and that which they deserve to experience as a consequence of their wrong, which I suggest is this: the fate suffered bears no relation-of-intention to the relevant wrong.[11] An indication that such an event is taken to be inadequate (even if not irrelevant) is that legal systems do not even attempt to assess the wrongdoer's general state of well-being before determining what apt punishment might be. This helps clarify the idea that is defended in proposing that it is punishment rather than suffering per se that is the retributive desert object: when one engages in a culpable wrong, one deserves the *imposition*, rather than the befalling, of some unwelcome response *for the reason* that one has culpably wronged, and by implication, *by another agent*, engaged in addressing the wrong.[12]

---

[9] This means that a successful criticism of retributivism that relies on such assumptions is highly limited in its applicability, relevant only to a narrow set of retributive views rather than to retributivism as such.

[10] For a discussion of these options (without endorsing a retributive view), see Radzik (2017).

[11] I set aside here the interpretative move that would make this a case of divine justice.

[12] Central definitions of punishment presume that for a burden or deprivation to count as punishment it must be imposed by others *for* the wrong, and *by an authority*. See, e.g., Flew (1954), Hart (1960), and Gardner (2007).

This brings us closer to the retributive conception that will be of interest in the remainder of this chapter. It introduces the significance of desert and retribution as *inter-agential* or *reactive*, though it does not yet make explicit the features of desert I take to be central to a successful retributive justification of punishment. In this chapter, I defend what might be called *relational conceptions* of desert and retribution, which do more than require that the suffering, burdens, or deprivations visited on the wrongdoer be imposed by another agent for their wrong. They insist further that the grounds of such imposition lie in the very relations between the parties to punishment, adopting a conception of desert that is neither absolute nor freestanding, but determined, inter alia, by the nature and details of such relations themselves. Such relational conceptions have been defended by, for example, Antony Duff (2001, 2006, 2013) in his communicative theory of punishment,[13] Adil Ahmad Haque (2005) in his victim-centered theory, and in my response-retributive theory of punishment (Dahan Katz 2021). I intend the following to both advance such retributivist conceptions and to provide further support for the justification of punishment I have defended elsewhere.

4 From Deserving Punishment to a Relational Conception of Retribution

From a standard retributivist standpoint, the focus of punishment and its justification lies squarely on the offender. To ascertain whether a wrongdoer is the appropriate target of punishment, we look to the nature of the action performed by the agent, the wrong, as well the level of the agent's culpability. These are taken to be the central determinants relevant not only to the broad question of the justification of punishment, but also to whether a particular agent should be punished, and the extent to which they should be punished. This is often contrasted with the standard utilitarian standpoint, which focuses on the consequences of punishment for its justification and determination.

The relational standpoint offers a modification of the traditional retributive view. It maintains the relevance of the elements of wrongfulness and culpability, yet expands our perspective: it proposes that the justification of punishment relies not only on facts about offenders and their actions, but also on the

[13] Duff relies on penal desert in his communicative theory of punishment. For more on the retributive dimensions of his view, see, e.g., Duff (2011). Duff goes a step farther and takes the view that *responsibility* is relational. For more on his view of "responsibility as answerability," see Duff (2013). In contrast to Duff, I take "basic responsibility" to be non-relational and specifiable in terms that do not require appeal to another (actual or hypothetical) party.

punishment relation, that is, the relations between the parties to punishment, primarily the punisher and the punishee. While the relations with the victim can play a further role, I leave their role in punishment theory aside for now.[14] Instead, I concentrate on expanding our view from an exclusive focus on the wrongdoer and their independently determined deserts to one that understands the wrongdoer as one party in a more complex punishment relation that plays a crucial role in punishment's justification.

Per relational conceptions, the state is not merely an instrument for realizing an impersonal good or value, or for realizing an impersonal form of justice that could in principle have been realized by some other agent acting to promote the relevant value or on the relevant reasons. This is the case, for example, on any view that takes the realization of retributive value or justice to be a matter of ensuring that a wrongdoer "gets their due," where this would entail that the wrongdoer suffers or is subjected to some to-be-specified quantum of pain, deprivation, setback, or other target burden appropriate to their culpable, wrongful action. That wrongdoers "get what they deserve" in this punisher-independent sense does not, on the relational view, serve as the primary justification for state punishment, or for that matter, for punishment at the hands of any agent.[15] Rather, the punisher is understood to stand in specific relations vis-à-vis the wrongdoer that call for *the particular punishing agent* to act, or rather *react*, not only in virtue of what the wrongdoer has done, but also in virtue of the relations that exist between the parties, which call upon the punisher to react retributively to the wrong.

Such relational reasons are on display when one has a duty, for example, to care for a child *because* one is the child's parent, or to encourage an athlete *because* one is their coach. There may be non-relational, impersonal reasons to care for the child—for example, because human well-being is valuable and one is in a position to promote the child's well-being. Yet relational reasons are those that arise by virtue of the relations between the parties (the existence of which may be explained on relational or non-relational grounds [see Gardner 2011; Duff 2013]), are not applicable to all, and have distinctive content owing to their grounds.

[14] For a relational view that takes the relations with the victim to be the central punishment relation, see Haque (2005). See also Dahan Katz (2022).

[15] This is not to deny that such events have value, or to claim that they are irrelevant to the evaluation of actions and states of affairs. For example, we might think that, in the absence of human respondents, there still is some measure of burdening that the wrongdoer ought to experience. It is only to deny that such value provides the best grounds for the justification for *imposing* punishment on wrongdoers (among others, due to the concerns raised by critics addressed in section 2).

In a similar vein, per the defended approach, the justification of punishment emerges from an agent's relational duty to respond retributively to another's wrong. No other agent can fulfill this responsibility. This is not merely because others lack the authority to punish. State authority might be conceived such that the state is the only agent in the position to punish—for example, because it retains a legitimate monopoly on violence, where certain acts of punishment require visiting violence upon wrongdoers that no other agent may permissibly inflict. While the state may be the best (or only) agent in a position to bring about some morally valuable or just state of affairs, such as having wrongdoers' lives reflect their deserts, such value may still be fully determined by facts that are independent of the punisher or punishing relation. By contrast, on relational conceptions of retribution, the punitive response of the punishing agent is called for *on account of the relations between the parties.*[16] They are a constitutive element of the story that makes punishment appropriate, where each particular relational account will offer a defense of why relations at all, and the particular relation in question—in the context of criminal punishment, the political relation between the state and those bound by law[17]—ground retributive reasons to punish under specified circumstances.[18]

Consider a sample relational conception. On the response-retributive view I have defended, agents who stand in relations with the wrongdoer, that bring the wrongdoing within the purview of the relations, have a duty to reject the devaluation inherent in the culpable wrong. This might be the case within private relations, such as when one's spouse is called upon to react to hurtful comments or actions their spouse intentionally directs at others; or within institutional relations, where one's employer might be called upon to react to

[16] Per Duff (2013), such relational reasons are grounded in the value of the relations (taking a Strawsonian route; see section 7). Gardner (2011) denies that one's responsibility to the state is (necessarily) robustly relational in this way, as proposed by Duff. Yet he has in mind responsibility in the general sense of answerability to the state, not exclusively in the context of punishment (though he does specifically doubt the relevance of relational reasons for the grounding of agents' responsibility to criminal courts [Duff 2011, 92]), and in any event he broadly rejects retributive punishment altogether (Gardner 2007, ch. 11). Thus, Gardner cannot be read as rejecting the relational grounds of *retributive* punishment, and his disagreement with Duff on this point does not offer any direct objection to the relational retributive thesis that I propose.

[17] But see Duff (2018), who takes the relevant relation to be that between the state and its *citizens* (and among citizens as members of the liberal moral community). On my view, this is to privilege citizenship (even in the broad sense intended by Duff) in ways that are both objectionable and unwarranted. Further, on my suggested account, there is no puzzle about the justification of punishing non-citizens, non-residents, and "guests."

[18] The above highlights that criminal punishment is just one of a number of inter-agential punitive practices that might be called for on a relational view, where each relation might require a dissociative reaction to wrongdoing and for punishment.

one employee's harassment of another employee in the workplace; or within political relations, where the state is called upon to react to a wrong that consists in a breach of the peace. On this view, what wrongdoers deserve is to be treated in ways that allow relevantly related others to reject and dissociate from the devaluative conception of the worth of others inherent in the wrong, including by imposing whatever negative, burdensome reaction is required for such a dissociative reaction (as determined, inter alia, by the details of the relations between the parties) (Dahan Katz 2021).[19] Importantly, on such a view, the identity of the punisher matters to the determination *that* one ought to punish, and to the determination of *what* the punishee deserves, which may involve blame, censure, further deprivations, or the imposition of mild and even heavy burdens on the wrongdoer.[20]

This contrasts with non-relational views in which the involvement of any particular punisher can be called into question, while the determination of what one deserves is broadly divorced from facts specific to the situation at hand. To highlight the way that this differs from non-relational conceptions of retribution, consider, for example, the traditional view defended by Larry Alexander, who writes that "punishment should be measured by the ill-desert of the offender. … What one deserves for one's wrongdoing … is invariant through time and space," while "a wrongdoer can experience [deserved] suffering without anyone's imposing it on him" (2018, 178, 179, 181).[21] Note first that the justification of punishment is mounted here in non-relational terms, where the ground of such justification lies in the achievement of a target relation between the wrongdoer's well-being and their moral status (as determined by their desert), while the value realized by retributive punishment might in principle be realized by any agent or by no agent at all. Further, one's desert is devoid of any reference to relational facts. It is rather "invariant through space and time": the quantum of suffering that a wrongdoer deserves to experience is fully determined by the agent's culpable actions (though the particular form it will take may vary). This contrasts with a further dimension of a relational retributive theory, which understands retributive desert itself to be relational, that is, determined in part by facts about the relations between

[19] Compare this to Duff's view, according to which an agent deserves "to be called to account by those who[se] business that wrong is, to suffer the forceful communication of the censure that they have the standing to administer, and to be required to make appropriate moral reparation to them" (2013, 205).

[20] Punishment thus need not involve a violation of rights or "hard treatment," though it must involve a negative burden deliberately imposed. See Hampton (1992a, 1694–95).

[21] See also the views defended by Moore (1997), Zaibert (2006), Berman (2013), and Murphy (2016). Berman (2008) points to the option of a relational conception of retribution, recognizing the potential of developing such an account. In his defense of his "life going less well" conception, however, he appears to reject this option.

the parties. What is it that culpable wrongdoers deserve? On non-relational conceptions of desert, this can be specified without reference to the relations and can, for example, consist in a singular, pre-institutional quantum of punishment that it would be fitting that the wrongdoer suffer, as in the case of Alexander's defense of retribution. By contrast, on a relational conception, the answer to this question is tacked to the specific punisher, considering features of the relations that exist between the two parties. (The treatment warranted by relations with a spouse or a personal friend will differ from those warranted by the political relation, though all may be called upon to retributively react to the relevant wrong and respond in negative, burdensome ways that allow them to dissociate from the devaluative wrong).

Such traditional views are especially vulnerable to the objections to retributivism referenced above (though not necessarily without resources to respond). This is because on such views, there is no non-contingent value in the state's intervening to give wrongdoers what they deserve, even if there are good reasons for the state to intervene. This leaves the justification of *state* punishment "up in the air." Allowing that others can in principle realize the relevant value means further that if one has already been subjected to the relevant suffering or punishment, this undermines the permissibility of state punishment. We thus *must* be interested in what others have imposed upon the wrongdoer, or how their life has otherwise gone, if we are to have legitimate practices of punishment. Yet it seems an unintuitive requirement to hang the pro tanto justifiability of any form of punitive reaction on such inquiry. Such approaches also seem a weak justification of an institution that does not take the question of what goes on with the wrongdoer irrespective of its punitive intervention to be relevant to the permissibility of punishing.[22] Further, epistemic concerns about how to identify one's deserts are starkest in the context of such views.

Still, such approaches might be too far from the defended conception to provide a useful contrast, and one that particularly highlights the contribution that relationality makes to punishment's justification. I will thus focus on a contrast case that I take to be a particularly well-developed though still wanting version of retributivism: Jean Hampton's influential defense of expressive retributivism. The contrast will be used to demonstrate that, although the view does take punishment to be reactive and inter-agential, it nonetheless goes awry in failing to offer a relational account, and to show the progress that can be made by adopting a relational conception.

On Hampton's account (1991, 1992a, 1992b), when offenders engage in criminal wrongdoing, they send a message about the relative (lesser) worth of

[22] Though facts of this nature may impact prosecutorial and judicial decision-making. See section 6.

their victims. The account proposes that wrongdoers deserve to be subject to the hard treatment that serves as an emphatic repudiation of this message of disrespect, a counter-message intended as evidence of the victim's equal moral worth. In the absence of punishment, the wrongful message would be allowed to stand unchallenged, while state punishment "strikes back" at the offender, countering the evidence of the offender's superiority, thus annulling the wrongdoer's message of disrespect and vindicating the victim's equal moral worth.

There is much to be valued in Hampton's account that I cannot do justice to here, but one thing is certainly unclear about the path she provides to punishment's justification. In committing a crime, it is the offender who offers a demeaning message about the victim's inferiority (or, on a more substantive interpretation of this expressive element, who actively disrespects the victim's value), not the state. So, the emphatic message sent by the state (offering its own view of the victim's equal status) appears irrelevant if what is of interest is the annulment of the *wrongdoer's* message, the content of which was never expressed or affirmed by the state to begin with. The offender has not changed that message (unless they repent) (see Hampton 1991).[23] So how can a message by an external party make the relevant difference? How does state punishment "annul" the wrongdoer's message of disrespect, as Hampton thought it did? And what justifies the intervention of *the state* in this regard? If persons have equal moral worth irrespective of how they are treated by others (as on a Kantian view), the wrongdoer's act should be neither here nor there in terms of providing evidence of the victim's lower status or the capacity to damage the victim's worth. If, on the other hand, crime does provide evidence of one's lower status, one would think that it is the *victim* who would have to retaliate for such evidence to be refuted, demonstrating her non-inferiority relative to the offender (as is in fact recognized by Hampton's intuition-pumping example of a bullied child who "strikes back" to "counter with punishment" the demeaning message sent by his aggressor [1991, 397–98]). In a telling moment, Hampton writes that the message carried by retributive punishment is: "'What you did to her, *she* can do to you …' In this way, the demeaning message implicit in his action is denied" (1992b, 19).[24] Yet this attempt seems to misfire, as the victim is not an active agent involved in punishment. Criminal punishment is rather at the hands of a third party, the state, which may intend to vindicate the victim. However, in usurping the role of the

[23] See also Murphy (2012, ch. 6) on why repentance reduces penal desert on such a view for this very reason.

[24] Italics in the original. The use of the feminine pronoun in this context is not arbitrary, given Hampton's feminist perspective on punishment and on the political.

retaliating victim and acting to voice a counter-message of equality (largely independent of the victim's involvement or preferences), the state not only leaves the offender's objectionable conception intact but also seems to reaffirm the helplessness and passivity of the victim herself, who is left out of the retributive-expressive interaction over the determination of her value—a subject whose worth is to be negotiated through the actions of others. So there is a puzzle about how punishment works to achieve the very aims that are supposed to justify it on Hampton's account (cf. Dolinko 1991, 553).

On my view, there are two elements that are missing here. The first highlights the substantiveness of the disrespect involved in failing to punish, rather than the expressive character of the exchanges between the parties—a matter I have elaborated on elsewhere and will not develop here (Dahan Katz 2021).[25] More to the concern of this chapter, the account fails to recognize the relational grounding of the retributive response, and in doing so misses crucial elements that could otherwise strengthen the Hamptonian proposal. What is missing is the link between the offender's wrongdoing and the status of the state's omissions, which is generated by the *preexisting relations* between the parties to punishment. Consider again the substantive version of Hampton's view: The wrongdoer not only sends a message to the victim, but actively disrespects and devalues the victim. This may have no impact on the duties of those who are sufficiently distant from the wrongdoer and the wrongdoer's action, such that the lack of involvement remains morally neutral (and even laudable or required).[26] By contrast, those whose omission can properly be described as "standing by" in the face of the culpable wrong—because they already stand in relations with the wrongdoer that render the wrong within the preview of the relations—*are* morally implicated by what has transpired. They are rendered potentially acquiescent bystanders who, if they fail to react in a way that rejects the wrong (or rejects the message of inferiority implicit in the wrong), commit an omission that amounts itself to an act of disrespect toward the victim (or relevant value), with its own independent moral meaning.[27] Silence in the face of such relationally relevant wrongdoing is indicative (and can be constitutive) of the state's insufficient regard for the victim, whose original subjection to demeaning treatment fails to move the state to action,

---

[25] Hampton herself at times writes in a more substantive vein, and at others, in the expressive.

[26] Though they may yet have reasons to hold certain evaluative beliefs about what has transpired, or to adopt a particular attitude toward the event and parties involved.

[27] See Kant (1996, 6:333 [p. 474]) on the complicity involved in failing to respond—though I would not explain the failure as one that involves complicity in the wrong, but rather one that involves an *independent* wrong. See also Altman's chapter in this volume.

despite the relational reasons it has to respond to the wrong.[28] In other words, the right relational context renders certain actions of those with whom the state stands in specified relations[29] morally relevant, such that, under the appropriate conditions, they demand a retributive reaction, in the absence of which the state's omission becomes meaningful and *wrongful* (unless adequately justified by countervailing reasons to refrain).

With this relational foundation in view, we can now revise the Hamptonian account to produce a stronger justification of punishment: It is not that the message *of the wrongdoer* remains intact until the state acts. It is that the state's omission in the face of the wrongdoer's wrong becomes itself meaningful—indicative or constitutive of a willingness to stand by as others disrespect the victim, where this willingness is morally meaningful and itself *independently disrespectful* of the victim and values at stake. The action of the state thus is not (primarily, if at all) a further piece of evidence as to the worth or status of the victim. The victim has equal worth regardless, insofar as such worth is fully determined by one's status as a person. Nor is it an act that annuls the offender's message, which, sadly, stands insofar as the offender does not disavow the action (though its bearing on the life and status of the victim can, one hopes, be marginalized through punishment). It is rather constitutive of the state's refusal to disrespect the victim (or relevant value), as demanded by the position of the state vis-à-vis the offender and their wrong (barring countervailing reasons to refrain). Were the state in no way related to the offender, such demand would not arise, as it is the relations between the parties that generate the moral meaning of the omission as wrongful (which might otherwise have been morally neutral), grounding the duty to retributively react.

Considering this analysis, we can now identify the significance of the relational foundation of retributive punishment: it is not merely that the wrongdoer must be subjected to retribution, nor that a retributive burden (or message) must be intentionally directed at the wrongdoer. Rather, it is the *punisher in question* who must retributively respond. It is the punishing agent's relations with the wrongdoer that make the punisher distinctively vulnerable to be morally implicated by the wrong, calling on the agent to react retributively—to take the right stance toward the wrong and toward the wrongdoer as the author of the culpable wrong, by directing such a negative and

---

[28] Why the reaction required must be punitive rather than non-punitive is a separate question that can be filled in with the details of Hampton's own account or with the kindred response-retributive account I have defended.

[29] See note 17.

burdensome response at the wrongdoer as might be required.[30] Relational views thus anchor the practice of punishment, tethering punishment to the actions and agents involved in a way that relieves many of the concerns thought to plague retributive theory as such. It solidifies the role of the punisher in retributive punishment—whose intervention is neither arbitrary nor contingent—pointing to why *this* agent must intervene and what goes independently wrong if it does not.

Of course, to offer a concrete justification of state punishment, we need to fill in an account of the political relation that demonstrates why such reasons to retributively respond and punish arise in the political context. We need a political theory of the state that renders a specifiable subset of wrongdoings relevant to the state, demanding its response,[31] and one that accounts for the punitive character of the proper response to such wrongs.[32] My aim here has not been to offer such an account, but to identify features and advantages of any such (successful) proposal.[33]

[30] The punishing agent's relation to the victim may have further implications here. See note 14.

[31] There is no single answer to the question of the nature of the political relations and scope of "relevant wrongs" it will be called upon to respond to. Like personal relations that might be shaped intentionally, independently of the will of the parties or by evolution of involvement, the political relation—and the question of what it ought to respond to—is sensitive to a variety of features, such that states can be designed to be more "involved" or less "involved" in the lives of those bound by law, generating different contours of wrongs that it is called upon to reject. We can of course have (extrinsic) reasons to shape or not to shape the political relation in a certain way. (That is, one theory may be better than another on any number of grounds, including how just or unjust the resulting political arrangement will be. This is rehearsed in debates in political theory about the proper contours of the state—for example, the libertarian, liberal, and others arguing over how the political relation *should* be shaped and what the level of involvement in the lives of those bound by law should be). Still, the shape the state takes in relations to those bound by law—the factual relations—*will* determine when state inaction can be taken to be meaningful and problematic (given the state's level of involvement in other aspects of life).

[32] Such an account will further have to explain why the state can legitimately respond in ways that are not merely intentionally burdensome, or broadly retributive, but further violative of rights.

[33] Briefly, I would suggest that it is the authority of law over other domains of the lives of those bound by law that generate reasons for the state to respond retributively to public wrongdoing and that justify state punishment. Consider, by comparison, a schoolteacher who takes educational responsibility over a class of children. The teacher cannot ignore or remain neutral in the face of attacks or bullying that goes on within the classroom; they cannot claim that the only sphere they are required to address is formal educational. Similarly, the authority of the state over the lives of those bound by law renders the state responsible for addressing wrongful interactions that occur between agents that are appropriately understood to be public. It too cannot remain neutral in the face of wrongs performed in the public domain without this omission becoming morally and politically meaningful.

5 Advantages: Overcoming Objections

We are now in a position to reflect on how relational conceptions avoid the central worries raised against retributive theories of punishment. First, such conceptions need not rely on a claim about the intrinsic goodness of suffering. None of the relational conceptions addressed herein endorse this claim. This does not mean that retributive views that do endorse the claim should be rejected, but rather that the charge of repugnancy fails as an objection to relational retributive views.

Furthermore, such views are not vulnerable to charges that aim to challenge the gap between the value underlying retributive punishment and the justification of imposing such punishment. The justification of punishment they offer does not derive from the value or justice of some target state of affairs (e.g., wherein the deserving receive their due), but is rather grounded in agent-specific reasons and the duty to punish. Therefore, the question of why desert gives anyone at all, and particularly the state, reasons or the authority to act dissipates. The liberal-political question of why imposing one's deserts is the business of the state turns out to be a nonstarter if punishment is relationally (rather than impersonally) deserved, and required for the state to avoid doing wrong.

Finally, worries about epistemic access to determinate deserts are substantially softened on relational accounts given that the punishment deserved is in large part determined by empirical facts about the relations themselves. Not appealing to pre-institutionally determined deserts (e.g., quanta of suffering or diminutions in well-being), they thus provide guidance on what empirical features of the world are relevant to the determination of wrongdoers' deserts.[34]

6 New Objections

Recognizing the relationality that underlies retributive punishment might nonetheless raise new worries. On a relational view, wrongdoing potentially generates not a single desert claim but rather a series of independently

[34] It warrants mentioning that fair play theories (Morris 1968; Dagger 1993) also fair well with respect to the epistemic indeterminacy objection. However, they are notorious for suffering from other devastating flaws, primarily their characterization of the wrongfulness for which punishment is imposed as a matter of freeriding or taking unfair advantages over others, while failing to address what is fundamentally wrong with core forms of wrongdoing (e.g., murder, rape). On this score, relational views not only avoid these flaws, but offer a far improved modification of the standard view. For a response to the no-benefit objection to fair play theories, see Duus-Otterström's chapter in this volume.

grounded deserts, each emerging from relations of others with the wrongdoer. Each relevant relation can be an independent source of desert claims and reasons to punish, which are not vitiated by the reasons others have to react retributively, as opposed to singular conceptions of desert wherein the meting out of *the* deserved punishment exhausts the range of behavior justified by retributive justification.

The result—a proliferation of reasons to retributively respond to the wrong, and potentially of justified punishments—may at first appear draconian. Yet it need not be. First, the proliferation of reasons and pro tanto duties to respond negatively to wrongdoing does not mean that the imposition of punishment by some agents (and its effects on the wrongdoer's well-being) is irrelevant to the all-things-considered justifiability of imposing further deserved treatment upon the wrongdoer. There is no inconsistency in embracing a relational conception of desert according to which there is, in the first place, reason and a duty to respond retributively to wrongdoing and punish where appropriate, which generates a multiplicity of reasons in favor of punishing that apply to different agents, each of whom has a duty to respond; while also affirming that the impact of deserved punishment as imposed by some agents upon the wrongdoer may change the moral stakes for the imposition of further deserved punishments at the hands of others, modifying what others have all-things-considered reason to do.[35] Opinions can diverge as to whether (and the extent to which) such factors implicate the propriety of punishment, yet this remains a possibility.

Further, it in fact seems intuitively plausible that such various punishment practices should coexist. Imagine a particular case of a wrongdoer who has physically attacked a victim. That the wrongdoer is punished by their spouse or friend does not appear even intuitively to vitiate the pro tanto reason that others, such as the state, have to punish the wrongdoer. One might worry that endorsing a relational rather than non-relational basis for retributive punishment means that the more meaningful relations we are involved in and the more institutions and communities we are members of, the more vulnerable we are to punishment and to greater suffering for our wrongs. Yet I take this to be feature rather than a drawback of such accounts. Interpersonal relations make a difference to our liability to blame and punishment. Being in relations with others comes with benefits but also burdens, including the burden of retributive punishment—both the liability to bear punishment as well as the burden of being required to impose it. While one might escape punitive

[35] This is to reject any claim to the all-things-considered sufficiency of desert for the justification of punishment.

behaviors by severing all ties with others, this is far from a desirable path. In a Strawsonian vein, much of what makes our lives valuable is impossible without rendering ourselves vulnerable to the negative reactions of others, while any attempt to rid ourselves of such "negativity" is bound to be a superficializing enterprise. While we should of course eradicate suffering, burdens, and negativity that are unjust, arbitrary, and without value, we should take care not to "throw the baby with the bathwater" and object unreflectively to anything that would introduce (more) liability to suffering into our lives.

7 Relationality and Strawsonian Thought: A Postscript

No such relational account can be developed without a nod of recognition to Strawson and his work on responsibility practices, of which blame and punishment form a central part. I thus conclude with a brief reflection on what aspects of Strawsonian thought pervade the account defended here, and where the account "gets off the Strawsonian boat."

The thought that punitive practices are not about what a single agent should be subjected to, but about the interpersonal interactions that occur in the context of morally significant relations, owes much to Strawson. The Strawsonian perspective highlights the significance of the relations within which such practices are situated as well as the intrinsic connections between the two. While Strawson is particularly interested in responsibility practices that involve the (emotive) reactive attitudes, he takes punishment, like blame, to be on a continuum with these. This is a further feature of Strawson's thought that sits well with the relational account, which takes responses to wrongdoing to be required because of the relations between the parties and the relevance of the wrong within the relations. Such relations are bound to render relevant a wide variety of wrongdoing. They are also bound to vary widely with respect to the modes of reaction that might legitimately be engaged in between the parties. In light of this, viewing responses that involve attitudes, emotions, expressive and condemnatory behavior, and punitive responses, as all of a piece (though not lacking morally significant distinctions) and all part of our responsibility practices is helpful in allowing us to see that these may all be appropriate reactions to relevant wrongdoing,[36] while punishment does

[36] Strawson (1962) of course does not restrict his view to the negative evaluative side of our responsibility practices and equally addresses positive evaluative attitudes (such as praise and gratitude), yet these are beyond the scope of our inquiry.

not stand apart in its construction or basic justification (see Watson 1996; Wallace 2011).[37] It rather emerges from normative grounds common to all such (unwelcome) interactions between agents. All involve taking the right attitude, or what might be thought of as a *reactive stance*, to another's wrongdoing through such intrinsically unpleasant responses.[38]

Further, on such Strawsonian accounts, our accountability practices, including inter-agential blame and punishment, while negative and burdensome, are integral parts of valuable, healthy relations, which would themselves be distorted in the absence of such responses. Their negativity and burdensomeness are thus not necessarily to their discredit but are organic features of inter-agential interactions that do not descend into what Strawson terms "the objective attitude." That is, they do not treat persons as objects to be managed or dealt with (as in classic utilitarian approaches to punishment), but rather adopt an attitude that regards others as to-be-engaged-with agents.

But while Strawson grounded the justification of such practices in the value of the relations themselves, the account I have proposed does not follow him down this path. Rather, I suggest—to perhaps return to the metaphysical commitments he and others sought to avoid—that our reactive attitudes and behaviors are called for by our *nonrelational* foundational moral duties—namely, to respect the worth of others—which are *triggered* by the relations we have with others when they engage in relevant wrongs (cf. Duff 2013). We have duties to respect the moral worth of others *independent* of our relations and not just in virtue of the constitutive practices of valuable relations, though this does not mean they are morally inert or morally irrelevant to how we should interact with one another. Rather, I have suggested that the content of our non-relational duties is modified by our being in relations with others (a fact not accorded significance within traditional retributive views in the context of punishment), rendering, inter alia, otherwise innocent omissions morally meaningful and potentially wrongful, which would not have been the case but for said relations. Relations thus play a crucial role in the justification of retributive responses, though they do not provide independent foundational grounds from which the justification of our accountability practices emerge.

[37] Many Strawsonians do not follow Strawson here, positing a categorical divide between the blame and punishment. See, e.g., Scanlon (2009).

[38] Though, in the context of the state, talk of emotive reactive attitudes might be out of place, given that non-natural agents such as the state do not react emotively in the way natural to persons, institutions nonetheless can be understood to take up reactive stances to the actions of others, expressed in their deliberations, decisions, and actions, including their practices of punishment.

References

Alexander, Larry. 2018. "Retributive Justice." In *The Oxford Handbook of Distributive Justice*, edited by Serena Olsaretti, 177–94. Oxford: Oxford University Press.

Árdal, Páll S. 1984. "Does Anyone Ever Deserve to Suffer." *Queen's Quarterly* 91, no. 2 (Summer): 241–57.

Berman, Mitchell N. 2008. "Punishment and Justification." *Ethics* 118, no. 2 (January): 258–90.

———. 2011. "Two Kinds of Retributivism." In *Philosophical Foundations of Criminal Law*, edited by R. A. Duff and Stuart P. Green, 433–57. Oxford: Oxford University Press.

———. 2013. "Rehabilitating Retributivism." *Law and Philosophy* 32, no. 1 (January): 83–108.

Byrd, B. Sharon. 1989. "Kant's Theory of Punishment: Deterrence in Its Threat, Retribution in Its Execution." *Law and Philosophy* 8, no. 2 (August): 151–200.

Chiao, Vincent. 2019. *Criminal Law in the Age of the Administrative State*. Oxford: Oxford University Press.

Dahan Katz, Leora. 2021. "Response Retributivism: Defending the Duty to Punish." *Law and Philosophy* 40, no. 6 (December): 585–615.

———. 2022. "How Victims Matter: Rethinking the Significance of the Victim in Criminal Theory." *University of Toronto Law Journal*. https://doi.org/10.3138/utlj.2021-0091.

Dagger, Richard. 1993. "Playing Fair with Punishment." *Ethics* 103, no. 3 (April): 473–88.

Davis, Lawrence H. 1972. "They Deserve to Suffer." *Analysis* 32, no. 4 (March): 136–40.

Dolinko, David. 1991. "Some Thoughts about Retributivism." *Ethics* 101, no. 3 (April): 537–59.

———. 1992. "Three Mistakes of Retributivism." *UCLA Law Review* 39, no. 6 (August): 1623–58.

———. 1997. "Retributivism, Consequentialism, and the Intrinsic Goodness of Punishment." *Law and Philosophy* 16, no. 5 (September): 507–28.

Duff, R. A. 2001. *Punishment, Communication, and Community*. Oxford: Oxford University Press.

———. 2006. "Answering for Crime." *Proceedings of the Aristotelian Society* 106, no. 1 (June): 87–113.

———. 2011. "Retrieving Retributivism." In *Retributivism: Essays on Theory and Policy*, edited by Mark D. White, 3–24. New York: Oxford University Press.

———. 2013. "Relational Reasons and the Criminal Law." In *Oxford Studies in Philosophy of Law*, vol. 2, edited by Leslie Green and Brian Leiter, 175–208. Oxford: Oxford University Press.

———. 2018. *The Realm of Criminal Law*. Oxford: Oxford University Press.

Feinberg, Joel. 1970. *Doing & Deserving; Essays in the Theory of Responsibility*. Princeton, NJ: Princeton University Press.

Fingarette, Herbert. 1977. "Punishment and Suffering." *Proceedings and Addresses of the American Philosophical Association* 50, no. 6 (August): 499–525.

Flew, Antony. 1954. "The Justification of Punishment." *Philosophy* 29, no. 111 (October): 291–307.

Gardner, John. 2007. *Offences and Defences: Selected Essays in the Philosophy of Criminal Law*. Oxford: Oxford University Press.

———. 2011. "Relations of Responsibility." In *Crime, Punishment, and Responsibility: The Jurisprudence of Antony Duff,* edited by Rowan Cruft, Matthew H. Kramer, and Mark R. Reiff, 87–102. Oxford: Oxford University Press.

Golash, Deirdre. 2005. *The Case against Punishment: Retribution, Crime Prevention, and the Law*. New York: New York University Press.

Hampton, Jean. 1991. "A New Theory of Retribution." In *Liability and Responsibility: Essays in Law and Morals*, edited by R. G. Frey and Christopher W. Morris, 377–414. Cambridge: Cambridge University Press.

———. 1992a. "Correcting Harms versus Righting Wrongs: The Goal of Retribution." *UCLA Law Review* 39, no. 6 (August): 1659–702.

———. 1992b. "An Expressive Theory of Retribution." In *Retributivism and Its Critics*, edited by Wesley Cragg, 1–25. Stuttgart: Steiner.

Hart, H. L. A. 1960. "Prolegomenon to the Principles of Punishment." *Proceedings of the Aristotelian Society* 60, no. 1 (June): 1–26.

Haque, Adil Ahmad. 2005. "Group Violence and Group Vengeance: Toward a Retributivist Theory of International Criminal Law." *Buffalo Criminal Law Review* 9, no. 1 (April): 273–328.

Hill, Thomas E., Jr. 1999. "Kant on Wrongdoing, Desert, and Punishment." *Law and Philosophy* 18, no. 4 (July): 407–41.

Honderich, Ted. 1970. *Punishment: The Supposed Justifications*. New York: Harcourt, Brace & World.

Hoskins, Zachary, and Antony Duff. 2021. "Legal Punishment." *Stanford Encyclopedia of Philosophy* (Winter 2021 edition), edited by Edward N. Zalta. https://plato.stanford.edu/archives/win2021/entries/legal-punishment/.

Husak, Douglas. 2012. "Retributivism *In Extremis*." *Law and Philosophy* 32, no. 1 (January): 3–31.

Kant, Immanuel. 1996. *The Metaphysics of Morals*. In *Practical Philosophy*, translated and edited by Mary J. Gregor, 363–602. Cambridge: Cambridge University Press.

Kleinig, John. 1973. *Punishment and Desert*. The Hague: Nijhoff.

Moore, Michael S. 1997. *Placing Blame: A General Theory of the Criminal Law*. Oxford: Oxford University Press.

Markel, Dan, and Chad Flanders. 2010. "Bentham on Stilts: The Bare Relevance of Subjectivity to Retributive Justice." *California Law Review* 98, no. 3 (June): 907–88.

Morris, Herbert. 1968. "Persons and Punishment." *Monist* 52, no. 4 (October): 475–501.

Murphy, Jeffrie G. 2012. *Punishment and the Moral Emotions: Essays in Law, Morality, and Religion*. Oxford: Oxford University Press.

———. 2016. "Last Words on Retribution." In *The Routledge Handbook of Criminal Justice Ethics*, edited by Jonathan Jacobs and Jonathan Jackson, 28–41. Abingdon, UK: Routledge.

Narveson, Jan. 1974. "Three *Analysis* Retributivists." *Analysis* 34, no. 6 (June): 185–93.

Nino, Carlos Santiago. 1996. *Radical Evil on Trial.* New Haven, CT: Yale University Press.

Pereboom, Derk. 2013. "Free Will Skepticism and Criminal Punishment." In *The Future of Punishment*, edited by Thomas A. Nadelhoffer, 49–78. Oxford: Oxford University Press.

Radzik, Linda. 2017. "Desert of What? On Murphy's Reluctant Retributivism." *Criminal Law and Philosophy* 11, no. 1 (March): 161–73.

Scanlon, T. M. 1999. "Punishment and the Rule of Law." In *Deliberative Democracy and Human Rights*, edited by Harold Hongju Koh and Ronald C. Slye, 257–71. New Haven, CT: Yale University Press.

———. 2009. *Moral Dimensions: Permissibility, Meaning, Blame.* Cambridge, MA: Harvard University Press.

———. 2013. "Giving Desert Its Due." *Philosophical Explorations* 16, no. 2: 101–16.

Shafer-Landau, Russ. 2000. "Retributivism and Desert." *Pacific Philosophical Quarterly* 81, no. 2 (June): 189–214.

Sher, George. 1987. *Desert.* Princeton, NJ: Princeton University Press.

Shoemaker, David. 2015. *Responsibility from the Margins.* Oxford: Oxford University Press.

Strawson, P. F. 1962. "Freedom and Resentment." *Proceedings of the British Academy* 48: 1–25.

Tadros, Victor. 2011. *The Ends of Harm: The Moral Foundations of Criminal Law.* Oxford: Oxford University Press.

Watson, Gary. 1996. "Two Faces of Responsibility." In *Agency and Answerability: Selected Essays*, 260–88. Oxford: Clarendon.

Wallace, R. Jay. 2011. "Dispassionate Opprobrium: On Blame and the Reactive Sentiments." In *Reasons and Recognition: Essays on the Philosophy of T. M. Scanlon*, edited by R. Jay Wallace, Rahul Kumar, and Samuel Freeman, 348-72. Oxford: Oxford University Press.

White, Mark D. 2011. "*Pro Tanto* Retributivism: Judgment and the Balance of Principles in Criminal Justice." In *Retributivism: Essays on Theory and Policy*, edited by Mark D. White, 129–45. Oxford: Oxford University Press.

Zaibert, Leo. 2006. *Punishment and Retribution.* Aldershot, UK: Ashgate.

———. 2018. *Rethinking Punishment.* Cambridge: Cambridge University Press.

6

Doubts about Retribution: Is Punishment Non-Instrumentally Good or Right?

Isaac Wiegman

It is not much of an oversimplification to say that retribution involves repaying past wrongdoing to the wrongdoer. As I understand it, retribution describes most acts of punishment as well as their justification and motivation. That is, when people and institutions punish, they usually take themselves to be repaying the wrongdoer (giving them their "just deserts"); they are motivated by some pro-attitude[1] toward repayment; and they consider each action of punishment to be justified (in part) by the fact that it repays the wrong done. Moreover, all these dimensions of retribution are unified by the presumption that acts of punishment are non-instrumentally good or right or fitting. In other words, punishment need not be organized to accomplish some good outcome (separate from the act itself or its relationship to past wrongdoing) in order to have moral worth of some kind. As I see it, there is growing doubt among philosophers that punishment is good in itself, doubts that I welcome and for which I have given my own arguments (Wiegman

[1] A pro-attitude is just a catch-all for mental states that favor action. The category could include pleasures, desires, urges, impulses, and perhaps even evaluative judgments. I see little reason for any more precise distinction among these various attitudes in what follows.

I. Wiegman (✉)
Texas State University, San Marcos, TX, USA
e-mail: isaac.wiegman@txstate.edu

© The Author(s), under exclusive license to Springer Nature Switzerland AG 2023
M. C. Altman (ed.), *The Palgrave Handbook on the Philosophy of Punishment*, Palgrave Handbooks in the Philosophy of Law, https://doi.org/10.1007/978-3-031-11874-6_6

2016, 2017, 2020). However, the goodness of punishment is one thing and the rightness of punishment is another. As I explain below, it can make sense to think that punishment is the right thing to do without thinking that it is good for anyone and without thinking that it makes the world a better place in any sense. So, after setting out my own reasons for doubting that punishment is good in itself, I extend those arguments to undercut the claim that it is right in itself. All the evidence for thinking that punishment is right in and of itself can be better explained by the view that punishment is right in relation to present and future goods and future-regarding duties rather than past wrongs.

1 What Is Retribution?

First, I want to say what I mean by "retribution." As I said above, the word describes actions, as well as their justification and motivation, but were I to *define* it, I would say that retribution is a *phenomenon* of action, motivation, and justification. Moreover, that phenomenon is worth naming because it draws together instances of action (etc.) that share a common cause. Compare: we use the word "water" to describe numerous and diverse phenomena, and these phenomena are worth naming because they draw together instances that share a common cause, namely the chemical compound H_2O. However, we had the name long before we had a good understanding of the underlying cause. I want to suggest that the same is true for retribution: we have long had a name for the phenomenon, even though we are still uncovering the underlying psychological causes of it.

To circumscribe the phenomenon, it is worth contrasting retribution with consequentialist justifications for punishment. In general, a consequentialist evaluation of action (as right or wrong) "depends only on [the action's] consequences (as opposed to the circumstances or the intrinsic nature of the act or anything that happens before the act)" (Sinnott-Armstrong 2003). In other words, a consequentialist justification for punishment will refer to the likelihood that punishment will bring about good outcomes. The good outcomes that justify punishment might vary (e.g., incapacitation or rehabilitation of the offender, deterrence of crime) along with the metric by which outcomes are evaluated (e.g., pleasure, pain, satisfied preferences, or even virtue and vice). Insofar as punishment brings about a better outcome than alternatives (as determined by the value assigned to the outcome), there is a reason to punish. From a psychological perspective, people are moved by consequentialist reasons when their actions are instrumental for bringing about good outcomes.

Retribution is helpfully defined in opposition to consequentialism:[2] Consequentialism says punishment has worth *only because of* its consequences. Retribution, on the other hand says punishment has some positive worth *aside from* its consequences. The forward-looking focus of consequentialism (on future outcomes) contrasts with the backward-looking focus of retributivism: giving the offender the punishment that fits the crime. This sense of fittingness or appropriateness is usually understood in terms of desert.[3]

Such justifications for punishment have considerable intuitive appeal (as I demonstrate below), and they factor strongly into arguments (popular or otherwise) for harsh punishments such as the death penalty (Berns 1980; Moore 1997; Pojman 1997). These arguments seem compelling to many in large part because retribution is intuitive. In other words, the death penalty seems appropriate to many people because, intuitively, it seems good or right to impose it even if the murderer's death does not leave anyone better off.[4]

Intuitions like this are underpinned by a real psychological motive, one that leads agents to choose punishment over a range of alternatives even when there are few good outcomes for punishing. Despite being intuitive, this motive to punish is deeply mysterious on closer inspection: "it appears to be a mysterious piece of moral alchemy in which the combination of the two evils of moral wickedness and suffering are transmuted into good" (Hart 2008, 234–35). Part of H. L. A. Hart's mystery lies in the assumption that suffering is what retributive punishment aims at, that suffering is the object of desert (i.e., what a person deserves for wrongdoing). Nevertheless, even if one assumes that offenders deserve something else (e.g., hard treatment or censure) for their wrongdoing, intractable questions remain: Why are humans motivated to punish even apart from the good consequences that punishment can bring about? Is there any good reason to invest in reacting to the past, when it is so often more advantageous to let bygones be bygones?

Philosophers have offered several answers to these questions. Some are based on rectifying the advantages that people gain from acting wrongly,

[2] I have argued that there are deep reasons for this opposition, deriving from distinct neural systems for behavior selection (Wiegman 2020).

[3] When desert is considered basic (in roughly Gregg Caruso's sense—see his chapter in this volume), the fittingness or appropriateness of a punishment response is entirely determined by looking back at the nature of the offense and the culpability of the wrongdoer. On the other hand, non-basic conceptions of desert mark out what someone deserves by looking forward at how the wrongdoer might be reformed, at how others might be protected from harm, and so on. Dahan Katz offers a modified conception of desert on which one's just deserts are determined in part by their relations with others rather than being determined only by the nature of the offense (see her chapter in this volume). This conception of desert is also a form of basic desert, since it is not determined by forward-looking considerations.

[4] Some of my own work aims to explain why these justifications are intuitive in order to explain them away (e.g., Wiegman 2017, 2020).

advantages that are not deserved (Morris 1968). Others are based on communicating censure or moral condemnation for wrongdoing, whether or not this communication has a good outcome (e.g., Duff 2001). Still others focus on vindicating the moral status of victims, which is compromised by wrongdoing (Hampton 1992). This vindication is thought of as an appropriate response to wrongdoing, independently of whether it brings about any future benefits.

Nevertheless, as a psychological phenomenon, retributive motives do not depend on any of these justifications. The motives themselves preexist any attempts by philosophers to justify them or make them intelligible (see, e.g., Daly and Wilson 1988, ch. 10). Moreover, there remains a strong feeling that wrongdoers deserve to be punished whether or not one accepts any of these justifications. For my purposes, the point is twofold. There is an interesting phenomenon to explain and a psychological motive to evaluate even aside from the patterns of reasoning that philosophers use to support retributive reasons to punish.

From a psychological perspective, the most straightforward way to characterize the motive is not the patterns of reasoning that support it, but rather the patterns of action for which it is responsible. If one is moved by retributive motives, then there are cases in which one would punish, or report that punishment is fitting, even though one knows that punishment would not bring about any future benefit. Moreover, retributive motives explain this pattern, because they place value on punishment as appropriate, fitting, or deserved (however these notions happen to be fleshed out or rationally supported) in response to past wrongdoing (rather than because of its future consequences). As such, they motivate punishment in accordance with the following principle:

> R—The [moral worth] … of an act of punishment is not (or not only) derived from the consequences of the act. (Wiegman 2017, 202)

In sum, the psychological entity that I am interested in explaining and evaluating is the retributive motive. It is a motive to punish in response to wrongdoing. It is best captured by the pattern of actions it produces: punishment when it will obtain no future benefit. It produces those patterns of action because people find punishment fitting (in some sense) as a response to past wrongdoing (where fittingness is understood independently of the consequences that punishment brings about). Moreover, retributivism's focus on the past is often understood in terms of desert.

1.1 The Phenomena of Punishment and Retribution

Fortunately, there is a wealth of studies in psychology and in behavioral economics relevant to retributive motives for punishment. Here I review some of this work. Importantly, this work suggests that anger influences many peoples' judgments and actions concerning punishment, and it may be responsible for the retributive bent of those judgments. Nevertheless, people also tend to make dispassionate judgments that retribution is fitting, and explaining this requires some conjecture above and beyond existing psychological evidence.

1.1.1 The Influence of Anger on Retributive Punishment

One fairly direct source of evidence about the influence of anger comes from experiments on the ultimatum game (UG). In this game, one player, the proposer, receives a sum of money and is instructed to choose how much of it to share with another player, the receiver. The receiver then has the option of accepting or rejecting the offer. If the receiver accepts, then both players get the portion of money assigned by the proposer. If the receiver rejects, then neither player gets any money. Prima facie, peoples' performance on one-shot UGs looks retributive. Low offers (e.g., \$2 out of \$10) are frequently rejected, even when people are playing with real money. Thus, receivers frequently impose costs on proposers, even though (due to fact that the interaction is not repeated) there *appears* to be no visible benefit. This is just what we might predict if receivers have a retributive motive for rejecting low offers.

Of course, we must consider the possibility that these appearances are misleading. Perhaps receivers want to enforce fairness norms that might benefit many people in the long run. Likewise, it is unclear whether the receiver interprets the proposer's behavior as wrongdoing. Fortunately, there is an abundance of data on the UG to resolve these ambiguities. Receivers do judge low offers to be unfair (Pillutla and Murnighan 1996), and as such, this is good reason to suppose that they believe the proposer acted wrongly (by acting unfairly). While their unfairness ratings tend to correlate strongly with rejections, unfairness ratings do not entirely explain rejections. For instance, rejections of unfair offers are correlated with activation of the anterior insula (as measured by changes in blood oxygen levels detected via fMRI), an area of the brain associated with anger and disgust (Sanfey et al. 2003). Additionally, UG participants more frequently reject low offers if anger is induced (e.g., by journaling about an angering event in their past) prior to playing the UG (Srivastava et al. 2009). In some of these anger induction experiments, participants are alerted to their emotional state and instructed to make sure that induced anger does not influence their performance on the UG. In these experiments, the rejection of unfair offers goes down even though their judgments of unfairness remain relatively constant. So, anger seems to motivate rejections of low offers over and above the mere judgment that low offers are unfair.[5]

Of course, these results still only deal with incidental anger. In another study (Fabiansson and Denson 2012), participants were angered by a confederate who criticized a speech that they had just given. These participants then participated in several one-shot, computerized UGs with the speech counterpart and two other players (the offers in the game were surreptitiously automated, and a photograph of the "other player" was shown during play). Participants were more likely to reject unfair offers from the person who criticized their speech than from the two other fictitious players. The difference in rejection rate is not easily explained without referring to anger directed at the speech counterpart, nor is it easily explained by referring to any future outcome that participants hoped to bring about.[6] Rather, the clearest explanation is that participants were angry at the speech counterpart, and this anger made them more likely to reject offers from the speech counterpart, regardless of whether this would bring about a future benefit.

In sum, these and many other studies suggest that anger motivates punitive reactions to perceived wrongdoing that are not instrumental for any obvious outcome. This corresponds closely with the definition of retributive motives above, suggesting that anger is a retributive motive.

1.1.2 Objection: Retribution Is Distinct from Revenge

At this point, some will object that, due to the influence of anger, this behavior in the UG is more like revenge than retribution, concepts which many philosophers keep separate. According to Robert Nozick, "Revenge involves a particular emotional tone, pleasure at the suffering of another, while retribution either need involve no emotional tone or involves another one, namely pleasure at justice being done" (1981, 367). Nevertheless, as Leo Zaibert (2006) argues in detail, this supposed difference between punishment and

---

[5] Moreover, it is not just the negative valence of anger that influences rejection. When sadness is induced and participants are instructed to ignore their sadness, their rejection of low offers does not diminish (Srivastava et al. 2009).

[6] It is not inconceivable that participants wanted to deter the speech counterpart from insulting others, but to me it seems much more likely that the motive was retributive.

revenge is not only sorely under-defended, but also highly implausible. To see the implausibility, one need only imagine the archetypal *Godfather* Don calling in a hit on someone who has just left his office. We can imagine him having exactly the degree of emotional detachment as a judge pronouncing the death sentence on a convicted murderer. This does not make the hit an act of retribution rather than revenge. (To the mafioso, it may be understood as both!) By contrast, we can easily imagine a judge sentencing a criminal with all the fury of a McCoy avenging themselves on a Hatfield. In this case, one need not think that the judge is *really* acting as an avenger rather than a punisher.

More importantly, it is empirically false that retribution has no emotional tone, nor is there any reason to believe that retribution is accompanied only by "pleasure at justice being done." C. Daniel Batson's work on moral outrage casts some doubt on the latter idea (Batson et al. 2007; Batson et al. 2009), though I have not the space here to review it.

On the other hand, some kind of emotional tone can be observed even when participants in a psychological study are asked to determine punishments impartially after reading vignettes of wrongdoing. In studies like these, there is a high association between reports of anger or moral outrage at an offense and the severity of punishments (Carlsmith et al. 2002; Baron and Ritov 2011). Moreover, in one experiment, the degree of activation in brain regions associated with emotion (e.g., the amygdala) varied in proportion to the severity of punishment that subjects assign in response to vignettes describing criminal behavior (Buckholtz et al. 2008). This suggests that some emotional processing influences punishment judgments even when those judgments are made from an impartial standpoint.

Other examples of impartial punishment appear in studies of the dictator game (DG), a modified version of the UG. In this version of the game, the receiver passively receives the offer of the proposer (the "dictator") and has no option to accept or reject it. Nevertheless, when a third party is added to this scenario and given the option of deducting points from the dictator at a cost to the third party themselves (e.g., Fehr and Fischbacher 2004), we can observe actions that fit more readily into the phenomenon of retribution than revenge. This is because costs are imposed in response to an action that is judged unfair *from an impartial standpoint*. However, even in this case, the third party reports anger in response to the dictator's offer. Moreover, reported anger predicts punishment and mediates the influence of retributive justifications, such as the dictator's culpability for low offers (Nelissen and Zeelenberg 2009). The point is that reports of outrage and anger do not just accompany *judgments* that someone deserves punishment, nor do they only accompany punishment behaviors that resemble *revenge* (as in the UG), but they also accompany behaviors that are imposed from an impartial perspective (and sometimes at a cost to the punisher). Henceforth, I will call these behaviors *impersonal punishment*, as opposed to the more personal form of punishment observed in the UG.[7]

There probably are interesting psychological differences between impersonal and personal punishment. Nevertheless, the difference between these phenomena is not that one of them lacks any influence from anger. Rather, the difference more likely resides in the *nature* of the influence that anger exerts over these distinct phenomena. To see this, let us first put on the table some differences and similarities between impersonal punishment and personal punishment (for instance, in the UG), and then I will offer a conjecture that explains similarities and differences alike. Differences first: In one experiment, Mascha van t' Wout et al. (2006) found that when their participants played the UG (as the receiver and ostensibly against other humans) their skin conductance activity (a measure of affective response) was higher for lower offers and was correlated with rejections. However, when people were told to play the UG against a computer program, neither relationship was observed. Similarly, Claudia Civai et al. (2010) had participants play the UG (also as the receiver) both for their own monetary gain (the *myself* condition) and then for the benefit of a third party (the *third-party* condition). While rejection rates were very similar between the two tasks, rejection of offers was only accompanied by differences in skin conductance in the *myself* condition. No significant difference was found between rejection and acceptance of offers in the *third-party* condition, presumably because low offers did not affect the participant's payout.

Other studies suggest that, regardless of what participants report, anger and outrage may not be *experienced* in conjunction with impersonal punishment. For instance, psychologists have yet to identify any cases in which outrage is elicited by the fact that someone violated a moral norm, as opposed to the fact that the violation harmed the subject or someone they care about (Batson et al. 2007; Batson et al. 2009). At the very least, the difference in skin conductance between personal and impersonal punishment suggests that emotional arousal is lower for impersonal punishment. This might tempt someone to think that personal and impersonal punishment are distinct phenomena and that only impersonal punishment is influenced by anger. But this does not cohere well with the data presented above. If anger does not influence

[7] Usually, this kind of punishment is referred to as "third-party punishment."

impersonal punishment in some way, then it is difficult to explain, for instance, why reported anger would predict punishment, even in the dictator game.

Moreover, there are interesting neurological and genetic connections between the phenomena of impersonal punishment and personal punishment that should be accounted for. For instance, Alexander Strobel et al. (2011) analyzed brain activation of participants who engaged in both an impersonal punishment task (as a third party in the DG) and in a personal punishment task (similar to the UG). Activation in the nucleus accumbens and nucleus caudatus (brain regions associated with reward) differed significantly depending on whether the participant punished or not (as did other brain regions associated with emotion, e.g., the amygdala). Moreover, the difference was observed in both the impersonal and personal punishment tasks (though there was a difference in the magnitude of activation between personal and impersonal punishment). This suggests that the motivation to punish may have some deep similarities across impersonal and personal punishment.

Strobel et al. (2011) also found genotype-specific differences in brain activation based on the contrast between punishment and non-punishment (across the impersonal and personal punishment tasks). That is, a specific allele for a gene controlling dopamine turnover predicted the difference in activation in several regions (including the nucleus accumbens and the amygdala) between punishment and non-punishment, regardless of whether punishment was impersonal or personal. Without a far better understanding of the neuroscience of anger and punishment, few firm conclusions can be drawn from a study like this. However, some conjecture may be warranted in conjunction with some armchair observations about anger: it is likely to influence the *development* of impersonal punishment, even if it is not manifested or experienced prior to impersonal judgments or punishments.

Specifically, anger influences the development of certain *response-dependent* concepts, and if so, it is also likely to influence judgments concerning punishment. Response-dependent concepts are ones that include objects or states of affairs that elicit specific kinds of responses. For instance, concepts such as SCARY or FEARSOME intend *that which elicits fear*, whereas a concept such as OUTRAGEOUS intends (roughly) *that which elicits anger*. Philosophers have long discussed the existence and metaphysics of response-dependent categories and debated about their role in moral evaluation (e.g., Gibbard 1992; Prinz 2007), but for my purposes, there are three specific things to notice about these concepts. First, such categories could not develop were it not for experiences and observations of specific emotions. That is, the experience of anger (in oneself or in others) is necessary for someone to understand the category of the OUTRAGEOUS. Second, one can judge that a response-dependent concept applies to a situation without feeling any emotion. For example, when considering a moral offense (as in some of the studies above), one could judge that the offense was more or less outrageous, without experiencing any feelings of outrage or anger. Third, whereas the concept of the OUTRAGEOUS focuses on the appropriateness of anger, other response-dependent concepts focus on the appropriateness of anger's action-tendency. Concepts such as BLAMEWORTHY or REPREHENSIBLE refer to those things for which blame and punishment are appropriate responses. And insofar as anger motivates blame and punishment, there will inevitably be conceptual links between the OUTRAGEOUS and the BLAMEWORTHY. In other words, this explains why response-dependent categories would come to have a certain logic: it is easy to see how one could come to think of outrageous actions as *those toward which blame, punishment, and retaliation is appropriate* (cf. Wiegman and Fischer 2022, 1001–2). If so, then we can imagine someone engaging in impersonal punishment because they judge impartially that an action is morally outrageous and because they judge that punishment is an appropriate response to morally outrageous action. If people make intuitive judgments in this way, then this sense of appropriateness could easily be rationalized as desert. Call this the *logic of blame hypothesis*.

Moreover, this would explain why self-reports of outrage and anger often accompany impersonal punishment even though we have reason to believe that such actions are not accompanied by affective arousal (as indicated by the skin conductance response, for instance). Finally, it is a mechanism by which retributive motives (and the accompanying notions of appropriateness and desert) can be extended from the personal domain (as in the UG) to the impersonal domain (as in responses to questionnaire studies and punishment in other economic games).

Little evidence has been collected that would confirm or disconfirm the logic of blame hypothesis. Moreover, it is unclear which competing hypotheses might also explain the data. There is however some indirect evidence that childhood experiences with anger influence punitive judgments later in life. For instance, children whose parents practiced corporal punishment are more likely to affirm the death penalty as adults, and this effect is mediated by trait anger, a measure of one's tendency to get angry (Milburn et al. 1995; Milburn et al. 2014). This effect falls short of directly confirming my hypothesis about the development of the category of outrageousness, but it does suggest that a child's development influences their affective responses in a way that may also influence their punitive judgments. In any case, my hypothesis has a good deal of initial plausibility, and I will adopt it in what follows as a working hypothesis.

2 Is Punishment Good in Itself?

So far, what we have is a psychological characterization of the retributive motive in terms of how it actually functions in some human beings: The motive is deeply influenced by occurrent anger and likely over the course of development, as well. While punishment intuitions are also shaped by processes of giving and responding to reasons, the influence of anger seems to account more fully for our tendency to view punishment as intrinsically good, that is, good independently of punishments' outcomes. The tendency to view it as such precedes any subsequent attempts to explain the motivation in terms of other moral or prudential reasons.[8] Nevertheless, this is not yet a reason to deny that punishment might be good in itself. Perhaps anger is a faculty that reliably tracks the intrinsic value of punishment.

For the sake of argument, suppose that it is a reliable indicator of the intrinsic value of punishment. It would follow that there is a non-accidental correlation between retributive sentiments and impulses (to seek repayment of wrongs as an end in itself) and the intrinsic value of punishment. This means that the correlation must be supported by some dependency relation that makes the correlation non-accidental. Specifically, without some causal or constitutive dependency between retributive sentiments and the intrinsic value of punishment, any correlation between the two would be spurious. To see this, consider several very tight correlations observed by data scientists (Van Cauwenberge 2016). From 1999 until 2009, there were strong correlations between the following four pairs of variables:

(a) U.S. spending on science and technology on the one hand and suicides by hanging on the other.
(b) The number of movies with Nicholas Cage on the one hand and drowning deaths in swimming pools on the other.
(c) The consumption of margarine per capita on the one hand and the divorce rate in Maine on the other.
(d) The revenue generated by arcades on the one hand and the number of doctoral degrees awarded in computer science on the other.

These correlations are obviously spurious because, given what we know about the world, we have no reason to believe that there is any real

[8] By all accounts, first came the impulse to avenge, then came norms for exacting revenge or demanding blood money. Then came centrally governed norms to restrain these impulses, but not to substantially alter them. Daly and Wilson (1988, ch. 10) detail this progression in the English legal tradition.

dependency between these variables. See for yourself: Is there any reason to believe that the divorce rate in Maine depends on the per capita consumption of margarine, or vice versa? Is there any a common cause of both variables? In each of the four cases, the answer is a clear "no." We can know that these correlations are spurious because we know that there is no plausible dependency between each pair of variables. Lacking any obvious dependency relation, no reasonable person would expect these pairs of variables to correlate before 1999 or after 2009. Consequently, we also know that spending on science and technology is not a good *indicator* of suicides (and so on for all the other pairs of variables).

Given our best understanding of the origins of the retributive motive, neither is it an indicator of the intrinsic value of punishment, because neither is there any dependency relation between the two. And because our retributive intuitions and impulses are the only real reason to believe that it has intrinsic value, this is my reason for doubting that punishment can be good in itself. To see this, consider a thought experiment:

> Suppose that Geppetto is designing the psychology of a cyborg that he calls Pinocchio. Geppetto wants to make Pinocchio very realistic, and his aesthetic sensibilities favor a slightly scrawny boy. He foresees that this design preference will result in real boys picking on Pinocchio. Thus, he programs into Pinocchio a strong drive to resist bullies. He reasons that the policy of resisting bullies, even in cases where immediate consequences militate against doing so, will lead Pinocchio to suffer less from bullies in the long run. Bullies will realize that it is less costly to pick on other scrawny boys who are less scrappy, and they will bother Pinocchio less as a result. Geppetto wants Pinocchio to have the capacity for [forethought], but Geppetto cannot guarantee that Pinocchio will consistently anticipate the long-term value of resisting bullies. Therefore, Geppetto designs Pinocchio with a drive to resist bullies that is not derived from the immediate prospective value of doing so. This drive gives Pinocchio an urge to react to the provocations of bullies rather than only to respond to the immediate prospects (largely negative) of doing so. To Pinocchio, the urge to resist is there whether or not it will result in a good outcome, thus to him, the urge does not seem to derive from the anticipated outcome of resisting (nor from the anticipated outcome of a policy of resisting). Once Geppetto completes his design, Pinocchio will tend to act and judge in accordance with the principle that resisting bullies has value not derived from its consequences or [intrinsic] value. He might even discover that his intuitions about resisting bullies support the following principle and come to consciously believe it.
>
> B—The value of an act of resistance toward bullies is not (or not only) derived from its consequences (or from the consequences of the policy of resisting).

> … If someone were to tell Pinocchio of Geppetto's design choices, he should no longer believe B. [Rather,] he should conclude that his inclinations to resist bullies are not good evidence for B. Since Pinocchio's inclinations to resist bullies are disconnected from any source of value that resistance might have aside from its consequences, he has an undercutting defeater for those intuitions. Therefore, Pinocchio should not believe B on the basis of his intuitions. (Wiegman 2017, 205–6)

In this example, Pinocchio's belief that B gets debunked because of two things: First, his belief is solely based on his impulse to resist bullies. Second, Geppetto's influence reveals that this impulse is disconnected from any intrinsic value that resistance might have. In the terms I used above, even if there were a correlation between Pinocchio's urge to resist on the one hand and some intrinsic value of resisting on the other, that correlation would be spurious. Geppetto's influence would have broken or distorted any dependency relation between the two. This is because Geppetto's influence is based entirely on the *instrumental* value of resistance, and there is no dependency relation between the instrumental value of a thing and its intrinsic value. By definition, if something is intrinsically valuable, then it need not be instrumentally valuable, and vice versa. That is why Pinocchio should no longer believe B.

Given the most plausible hypotheses concerning the origins of anger and retributive punishment, these impulses have a very similar function to Pinocchio's impulse to resist bullies. That is, they evolved as a way of motivating behaviors of confrontation and retaliation that have long-term benefits in the face of immediate costs (Frank 1988; Wiegman 2019; see also, e.g., Boyd et al. 2003). For instance, in the long run a motivation to retaliate against perceived wrongs can foster a reputation that deters offenses by making the threat of reprisal more credible. Alternatively, a cooperative group that punishes cheaters, bullies, and free riders is more stable and immune to exploitation. Moreover, retributive motives achieve these effects by making organisms value payback in its various guises (retaliation, redirected aggression, revenge, and retribution) as an end in itself. Recall that our angry impulses give rise to our own tendency to believe in the retributive principle R, that the value of an act of punishment is not derived from its consequences. If so, the influence of evolution on this belief is just like Geppetto's influence on Pinocchio's belief in the principle of resistance (B). It follows that our own belief in the intrinsic value of retribution is likewise undercut. This is an evolutionary debunking argument: Even if there were a correlation between our retributive impulses and the intrinsic value of punishment, the influence of evolution breaks any dependency relation between the two because it selected these impulses for their instrumental value. Any correlation between anger (or judgments of outrageousness) and the intrinsic value of punishment would be spurious. Thus, we have no good reason to believe that punishment is intrinsically good.

3 Is Punishment Right in Itself?

Thus far, my argument has been that we have no good reason to think that punishment is good in itself. Now I want to undercut the belief that punishment is in itself a right or appropriate response. This argument is possible because our judgments about what is appropriate are plausibly connected to the very same evolved motivations and likely contributed to the survival of ancient humans to a similar extent.

However, the argument will not be comprehensible without a brief explanation of the distinction between goodness and rightness: When an action falls on the wrong side of what is morally right, then the agent of the action is subject to some form of social sanction; blame, criticism, or punishment are among the possibilities. Not so with GOOD/BAD or anything on that scale. An action (say, giving millions to charity) can be very good without being required, and a choice can have a worse outcome than the alternatives, while also being required. For example, suppose you are a surgeon caring for five transplant patients who all need different organs and who could not be more deserving of another lease on life. Moreover, you know that they all happen to be a match with another of your patients who happens to be a misanthropic loner. The world would certainly be a better place if you killed the misanthrope and harvested the person's organs for the five. Even so, you are required not to do so. In effect, you are morally required to choose the option with the worse outcome (letting the misanthrope live and the five patients die). This requirement can also be captured with the language of duty: you have a duty not to kill your patient, and that duty requires you not take the action that would otherwise produce the better outcome. So, it is pretty clear that what is good and what is right can come apart, such that it is often right to choose the action with a worse outcome.

3.1 Reasons to Doubt that Punishment Is Right in Itself

And that is how some philosophers think about retribution: the suffering or hard treatment resulting from punishment is actually a bad thing and is never good in itself, yet punishment is still right (i.e., permitted or required). This idea is not foreign. After all, parents and judges alike can appreciate that punishment may give little pleasure or satisfaction to anyone but that it is necessary and fitting all the same. On this kind of view, punishment is a duty, and sometimes duty trumps the greater good (as in the transplant case above).

This view finds some support in how we think about wrongdoing more generally. As Leora Dahan Katz argues (2021, and her chapter in this volume), we not only have primary duties to avoid harming people and their property, but we also have secondary duties to respond appropriately when others violate these duties. Consider an example:

> A wrongdoer attacks and robs a victim. Suppose that the event occurs just as the wrongdoer's spouse arrives to pick the wrongdoer up for their evening plans, and upon learning of what has transpired, the spouse simply continues to dinner as usual; or, if you will, approaches the victim to ensure he is not hurt, but otherwise does not relate to the wrong. The wrongdoer's taking of his own interest in financial gain to be weightier than his victim's interest in security and bodily integrity is what might be thought of as devaluative, that is, defective in its undervaluation of the interests and worth of others. But what of the spouse? If one shares the sense that the spouse's response is inadequate and criticizable, this may be because one subscribes to the … thought that … we have duties to respond meaningfully to wrongdoing. And that when we fail to do so, this is a wrong in and of itself. (Dahan Katz 2021, 592)

If we suppose with Dahan Katz that we have a basic duty to respect the moral worth of each person, then we have primary duties not to act like the wrongdoer in Dahan Katz's example. But the example also suggests that respect for persons involves secondary duties to respond to the abrogation of primary duties:

> others who are in an appropriate relationship with the wrongdoer have a pro tanto duty [i.e., a duty that can be overruled by other considerations] to respond in ways that constitute meaningful dissociation from the devaluation inherent in the action of the wrongdoer. Respondents are called upon to reject the devaluation inherent in the wrong and align themselves against such devaluation. (Dahan Katz 2021, 593)

On Dahan Katz's view, continuing on to dinner with the wrongdoer would be inappropriate for the spouse because it would be a failure to respect the worth of the victim. Moreover, one cannot reject the devaluation of the victim merely by trying to reform the wrongdoer or by trying to help the victim. The duty to respond is directed at the wrongdoer, and meaningful dissociation from the wrong done requires some kind of negative response to the wrongdoer. In sum, Dahan Katz thinks there is a duty to punish and that the duty is directed at the wrongdoer and based on the inappropriateness of continuing ordinary relations with the wrongdoer given their failure to respect the worth of the victim. The duty to dissociate via punishment is thus an act of respect for the victim's worth, an action that is good in itself.

I think Dahan Katz is right that there is a duty to respond to wrongdoing but wrong that this kind of duty is good in itself. She understands this duty in terms of "the ethics of appropriate response," and this is part and parcel of what it means for actions to be good in themselves: an action can be fitting or appropriate even if it is not an effective way of accomplishing anything outside of the action itself. But is it possible that our intuitions about "appropriate responses" are tailored for an effective outcome? Consider: What is the purpose of dissociation? What is its reason for being? In Dahan Katz's example of the spouse of the transgressor, I would agree that the spouse should not continue ordinary relations with the transgressor. But I have doubts about her explanation why. She thinks that continuing ordinary relations would be inappropriate because it disrespects the worth of the victim or fails to respect it by responding to the wrongdoer. This suggests that one should respond to the wrongdoer as an act of respect even if it does nothing to change the wrongdoer's moral compass. But imagine someone whose only repertoire for dissociation is a set of behaviors that would exacerbate the shame of the offender and thus make them more likely to reoffend and less likely to accept responsibility and change their future behavior. Should we really say that it is this respondent's duty to invoke shame when one of their relations commits a serious offense? Should we say that someone acts wrongly if they restrain the respondent from performing this "duty" in the only way they know how? My feeling is that the better dissociative responses are the ones that urge the offender toward reform. But this suggests that the duty to respond is governed by a purpose of changing the offender's future reasons for acting or reorienting them to the worth of the victim, rather than merely dissociating from the wrong she has done. In that case, it is not good in itself. Instead, it is good as a method for accomplishing something.

But this is not entirely satisfying as a response. This is because I share Dahan Katz's sense that it is appropriate to disassociate from wrongdoing (and inappropriate not to do so), and the sense of appropriateness does not intuitively depend on efficacy. So, it is not sufficient to merely reframe these intuitions with an alternative explanation of why we should respond. I would rather come away with a deeper understanding of the origins of these judgments of appropriateness. I would rather find a better understanding of them; a way to place them in relation to other judgments about what is good and right.

3.2 Debunking the Judgment that Punishment Is Appropriate

And this is where another iteration of the evolutionary debunking argument comes into play. Evolutionary explanations of human behavior invoke punishment as critical for explaining the scale and scope of cooperation. Dispositions to dissociate from wrongdoing and dispositions to punish as an end in itself exist because they allow humans to sustain cooperation in large populations where reputation cannot be tracked. But if our dispositions came into existence because they are instrumental for some outcome (i.e., the maintenance of cooperation), then the dispositions themselves can give us no reason to believe that punishment is intrinsically good. In other words, punishment often seems an appropriate response to wrongdoing, and its appropriateness seems basic, that is, not definable in terms of the outcomes of punishment. Nevertheless, evolutionary explanations of punishment show these appearances to be deceiving.

Like the debunking argument above, this one is analogous to the Pinocchio thought-experiment. There, the analogy was something like the following:

1. Pinocchio's impulse to resist bullies : Pinocchio's belief in B (resisting bullies is intrinsically good) :: our impulse to punish : our belief in R (punishing offenders is intrinsically good)

Just as Pinocchio's impulse is explained by Geppetto's influence, our impulse to punish is explained by evolution's influence. Moreover, the purposes of Geppetto and of the evolutionary process have a similar role: they show that the impulse exists as instrumental for some outcome. This in turn, shows that the impulse cannot indicate that punishment's value is non-instrumental. To address a relational retributive view like Dahan Katz's, the analogy has to shift: The impulse to punish is slightly different. It is more that we judge it wrong to associate with the offender in ways that continue to benefit them. Moreover, the resulting belief is also slightly different:

> A—The (pro tanto) appropriateness of a dissociative response (including punishment) depends only on the nature of the wrong, the culpability of the

offender, and one's relation to the offender (rather than depending on any forward-looking outcome or purpose).

For the argument to work in the same way, we need to know why the dissociative response seems fitting or appropriate to us, and we need an explanation for its existence that appeals to some forward-looking outcome or purpose.

Evolutionary accounts of cooperation and punishment give us exactly that. We already have the beginning of an explanation for why dissociative responses would seem fitting or appropriate. The work reviewed above (in section 1.1.1) from psychology and behavioral economics involved angry, retributive responses that involved inflicting harm and withholding benefits alike, which are precisely the kind of responses that Dahan Katz deems dissociative. Moreover, we have a clear story about how anger is likely to influence beliefs about the appropriateness of these action-tendencies (in section 1.1.2). What evolutionary explanations add is a compelling ultimate explanation of why punishment is viewed as pro tanto appropriate independently of any forward-looking purpose or outcome, and they specify why it must be viewed in this way in order to accomplish certain ends (i.e., relative advantages of survival and reproduction via the maintenance of cooperation).

To understand these explanations, we need a brief overview of prior work on evolutionary explanations of cooperation and what newer explanations add. Kin selection explains why genetically related individuals would cooperate (Hamilton 1964). People who are genetically related have overlapping interests in the game of getting copies of their genes into the next generation. So, it benefits kin to cooperate with one another. Reciprocal altruism explains why frequent consociates would cooperate (Trivers 1971): "I'll scratch your back if you scratch mine" works if individuals interact frequently because the benefits of future interactions outweigh the immediate advantages of freeriding on the counterpart's good will (accepting a back-scratching without reciprocating).

Nevertheless, human cooperation extends far beyond individuals who are genetically related and who interact frequently. Other theories of cooperation fill in this gap. Theories of indirect reciprocity explain why people cooperate even when they do not interact frequently (Nowak and Sigmund 2005). If reputation can be tracked (say, via gossip), a good turn in one person's favor can be rewarded by another: "I'll scratch your back if you've scratched someone else's" works if we can track free riders (who refuse to scratch others' backs) and then refuse to scratch the backs of free riders. What is important about an evolved strategy like this is that its success cannot depend on an individual's awareness of the purpose of the strategy. The strategy will not be as effective if people have to spend time learning that they should not cooperate with free riders (i.e., those with a reputation for refusing to scratch backs).[9] So, on these explanations of cooperation, refusing to cooperate with free riders must have non-instrumental value (for a more detailed argument like this, see Wiegman 2019, 1107–8). Thus, these evolutionary models offer the beginning of an explanation of why we would view dissociation from wrongdoing as intrinsically appropriate. Nevertheless, they do not yet explain why we would judge it inappropriate and wrong not to disassociate. That is, if I scratch the back of someone who has a reputation for not scratching anyone else's back, that will not necessarily lead others to exclude me from future back scratching. Nevertheless, in Dahan Katz's example, if the spouse of the thief continues ordinary relations in which she offers continued benefits to the wrongdoer, she is seen as acting wrongly. In other words, theories of indirect reciprocity do not explain why we feel the intuitive pull to enforce secondary duties (e.g., by criticizing or punishing the spouse of the thief who continues ordinary relations).

Other theories of cooperation fill this gap and other gaps: humans cooperate even in large cities where reputation cannot be tracked. Moreover, these forms of cooperation are obviously vulnerable to exploitation by free riders (e.g., con men thrive where their reputations cannot keep up with them). So, how is it that these risky forms of cooperation could be beneficial and stable against such free riding? Theories of *strong reciprocity* explain how cooperation can exist in very large groups where reputation cannot be tracked (Gintis 2000; Gintis et al. 2008). First, there are clear benefits to living in larger cooperative groups, but to secure these benefits, groups need to solve two problems. One problem is that of first-order free riding, in which free riders exploit the cooperative tendencies of others in the group. Another is the problem of second-order free riding, in which otherwise cooperative individuals refuse to cooperate in the punishment of free riders. Even though such individuals are baseline cooperative, they are still refusing to bear the cost of punishing first-order free riders and thereby receive the benefits of cooperation without bearing any costs. They are second-order free riders. On models of strong reciprocity, cooperation in very large groups can be stable once almost everyone takes on the strategy of cooperating, punishing free riders, punishing those who do not punish free riders, and also punishing those who do not

[9] Or at least, game theoretical models explain how these strategies could arise without any such awareness.

punish those who do not punish free riders, and so on. So, these models also do a better job of explaining why we would intuitively believe that we have secondary duties to dissociate from wrongdoing, and why we tend to think those secondary duties are likewise enforceable.

Thus, we have the beginning of an explanation that would debunk our belief in retributive principle A. These evolutionary theories explain why we would believe (or have dispositions in line with the belief) that dissociative responses are intrinsically appropriate, and they explain this in terms of the instrumental value of this belief (or disposition). Again, the influence of evolution is like Geppetto's influence, breaking any clear dependency between our punitive dispositions and the retributive beliefs that they inculcate.

4 Conclusion: Putting Punishment in Its Place

I have argued that punishment is not intrinsically good or intrinsically right. It makes sense that we feel and sometimes even believe it to be good and right as an end in itself. Yet, when we look at the origins of these feelings and beliefs, we see that they are instrumental for various purposes (e.g., self-protection and a cooperative social order). So, these feelings and beliefs cannot be a good reason to believe in the intrinsic worth of punishment.

So, what if anything makes punishment good or right? While I have been arguing against Dahan Katz's view, it is worth discussing because it is close to the mark. The evolutionary picture I have painted suggests to me that our intuitions are skewed, not that they are fundamentally incorrect. Our intuitions about what is appropriate evolved in service of the survival of individuals and large cultural groups in our ancestral past. I would add that they were (and are) critical for securing certain goods and for respecting certain values that are essential for beings like us to survive and flourish. While I have argued that this speaks against the view that punishment is good or right in itself, it does not rule out the view that punishment is right in relation to certain goods or purposes. So far as I have described it, the motivations and judgments surrounding punishment are an ideal way to help individuals converge on and maintain shared values by correcting those who fail to satisfactorily promote and respect them. On this revised relational view (which I cannot fully defend here), punishment should be thought of as a way of urging others to change their reasons for acting, their valuation and respect for others, and their ways of relating to others (both habitual and otherwise). And it is likely to be justified when it is organized to do so effectively. This view must be relational because it is mainly by virtue of relationships that we are able to urge anyone toward what is good and right. This is a stark contrast with the ethics of appropriate response, where an action need not be effective to be appropriate. Whereas our intuitions about appropriateness may be vindicated on this view, they are not vindicated as appropriate responses per se but only as (fallible) indicators of effectiveness at maintaining shared values and public standards.

References

Baron, Jonathan, and Ilana Ritov. 2011. "The Role of Probability of Detection in Judgments of Punishment." *SSRN Electronic Journal* 1, no. 2 (January): 553–90.

Batson, C. Daniel, Mary C. Chao, and Jeffery M. Givens. 2009. "Pursuing Moral Outrage: Anger at Torture." *Journal of Experimental Social Psychology* 45, no. 1 (January): 155–60.

Batson, C. Daniel, Christopher L. Kennedy, Lesley-Anne Nord, E. L. Stocks, D'Yani A. Fleming, Christian M. Marzette, David A. Lishner, Robin E. Hayes, Leah M. Kolchinsky, and Tricia Zerger. 2007. "Anger at Unfairness: Is It Moral Outrage?" *European Journal of Social Psychology* 37, no. 6 (November/December): 1272–85.

Berns, Walter. 1980. "Defending the Death Penalty." *Crime & Delinquency* 26, no. 4 (October): 503–11.

Boyd, Robert, Herbert Gintis, Samuel Bowles, and Peter J. Richerson. 2003. "The Evolution of Altruistic Punishment." *Proceedings of the National Academy of Sciences* 100, no. 6 (March 11): 3531–35.

Buckholtz, Joshua W., Christopher L. Asplund, Paul E. Dux, David H. Zald, John C. Gore, Owen D. Jones, and René Marois. 2008. "The Neural Correlates of Third-Party Punishment." *Neuron* 60, no. 5 (December 10): 930–40.

Carlsmith, Kevin M., John M. Darley, and Paul H. Robinson. 2002. "Why Do We Punish? Deterrence and Just Deserts as Motives for Punishment." *Journal of Personality and Social Psychology* 83, no. 2 (August): 284–99.

Civai, Claudia, Corrado Corradi-Dell'Acqua, Matthias Gamer, and Raffaella I. Rumiati. 2010. "Are Irrational Reactions to Unfairness Truly Emotionally-Driven? Dissociated Behavioural and Emotional Responses in the Ultimatum Game Task." *Cognition* 114, no. 1 (January): 89–95.

Dahan Katz, Leora. 2021. "Response Retributivism: Defending the Duty to Punish." *Law and Philosophy* 40, no. 6 (December): 585–615.

Daly, Martin, and Margo Wilson. 1988. *Homicide*. New Brunswick, NJ: Transaction.

Duff, R. A. 2001. *Punishment, Communication, and Community*. Oxford: Oxford University Press.

Fabiansson, Emma C., and Thomas F. Denson. 2012. "The Effects of Intrapersonal Anger and Its Regulation in Economic Bargaining." *PloS One* 7, no. 12: e51595.

Fehr, Ernst, and Urs Fischbacher. 2004. "Third-Party Punishment and Social Norms." *Evolution and Human Behavior* 25, no. 2 (March): 63–87.

Frank, Robert H. 1988. *Passions within Reason: The Strategic Role of the Emotions*. New York: Norton.

Gibbard, Alan. 1992. *Wise Choices, Apt Feelings: A Theory of Normative Judgment*. Cambridge, MA: Harvard University Press.

Gintis, Herbert. 2000. "Strong Reciprocity and Human Sociality." *Journal of Theoretical Biology* 206, no. 2 (September 21): 169–79.

Gintis, Herbert, Joseph Henrich, Samuel Bowles, Robert Boyd, and Ernst Fehr. 2008. "Strong Reciprocity and the Roots of Human Morality." *Social Justice Research* 21, no. 2 (June): 241–53.

Hamilton, W. D. 1964. "The Genetical Evolution of Social Behavior. I." *Journal of Theoretical Biology* 7, no. 1 (July): 1–16.

Hampton, Jean. 1992. "An Expressive Theory of Retribution." In *Retributivism and Its Critics*, edited by Wesley Cragg, 1–25. Stuttgart: Steiner.

Hart, H. L. A. 2008. *Punishment and Responsibility: Essays in the Philosophy of Law*. 2nd ed. Oxford: Oxford University Press.

Milburn, Michael A., S. D. Conrad, Fabio Sala, and Sheryl Carberry. 1995. "Childhood Punishment, Denial, and Political Attitudes." *Political Psychology* 16, no. 3 (September): 447–78.

Milburn, Michael A., Miho Niwa, and Marcus D. Patterson. 2014. "Authoritarianism, Anger, and Hostile Attribution Bias: A Test of Affect Displacement." *Political Psychology* 35, no. 2 (April): 225–43.

Moore, Michael S. 1997. *Placing Blame: A General Theory of the Criminal Law*. Oxford: Oxford University Press.

Morris, Herbert. 1968. "Persons and Punishment." *Monist* 52, no. 4 (October): 475–501.

Nelissen, Rob M. A., and Marcel Zeelenberg. 2009. "Moral Emotions as Determinants of Third-Party Punishment: Anger, Guilt, and the Functions of Altruistic Sanctions." *Judgment and Decision Making* 4, no. 7 (December): 543–53.

Nowak, Martin A., and Karl Sigmund. 2005. "Evolution of Indirect Reciprocity." *Nature* 437, no. 7063 (October 27): 1291–98.

Nozick, Robert. 1981. *Philosophical Explanations*. Cambridge, MA: Belknap.

Pillutla, Madan M., and J. Keith Murnighan. 1996. "Unfairness, Anger, and Spite." *Organizational Behavior and Human Decision Processes* 68, no. 3 (December): 208–24.

Pojman, Louis P. 1997. "In Defense of the Death Penalty." *International Journal of Applied Philosophy* 11, no. 2 (Winter/Spring): 11–16.

Prinz, Jesse J. 2007. *The Emotional Construction of Morals*. Oxford: Oxford University Press.

Sanfey, Alan G., James K. Rilling, Jessica A. Aronson, Leigh E. Nystrom, and Jonathan D. Cohen. 2003. "The Neural Basis of Economic Decision-Making in the Ultimatum Game." *Science* 300, no. 5626 (June 13): 1755–58.

Sinnott-Armstrong, Walter. 2003. "Consequentialism." *Stanford Encyclopedia of Philosophy* (Fall 2021 edition), edited by Edward N. Zalta. https://plato.stanford.edu/entries/consequentialism/.
Srivastava, Joydeep, Francine Espinoza, and Alexander Fedorikhin. 2009. "Coupling and Decoupling of Unfairness and Anger in Ultimatum Bargaining." *Behavioral Decision Making* 22, no. 5 (December): 475–89.
Strobel, Alexander, Jan Zimmermann, Anja Schmitz, Martin Reuter, Stefanie Lis, Sabine Windmann, and Peter Kirsch. 2011. "Beyond Revenge: Neural and Genetic Bases of Altruistic Punishment." *NeuroImage* 54, no. 1 (January 1): 671–80.
Trivers, Robert L. 1971. "The Evolution of Reciprocal Altruism." *Quarterly Review of Biology* 46, no. 1 (March): 35–57.
Van Cauwenberge, Laetitia. 2016. "Spurious Correlations: 15 Examples." *Data Science Central.* https://www.datasciencecentral.com/spurious-correlations-15-examples/.
van t' Wout, Mascha, René S. Kahn, Alan G. Sanfey, and André Aleman. 2006. "Affective State and Decision-Making in the Ultimatum Game." *Experimental Brain Research* 169, no. 4 (March): 564–68.
Wiegman, Isaac. 2016. "Divine Retribution in Evolutionary Perspective." In *In Spirit and Truth: Philosophical Reflection on Liturgy and Worship*, edited by William Curtis Holtzen and Matthew Nelson Hill, 181–202. Claremont, CA: Claremont School of Theology Press.
———. 2017. "The Evolution of Retribution: Intuitions Undermined." *Pacific Philosophical Quarterly* 98, no. 2 (June): 193–218.
———. 2019. "Payback without Bookkeeping: The Origins of Revenge and Retaliation." *Philosophical Psychology* 32, no. 7: 1100–1128.
———. 2020. "The Reactive Roots of Retribution: Normative Implications of the Neuroscience of Punishment." In *Does Neuroscience Have Normative Implications?* edited by Geoffrey S. Holtzman and Elizabeth Hildt, 111–36. Cham, Switzerland: Springer.
Wiegman, Isaac, and Bob Fischer. 2022. "Disgust and the Logic of Contamination: Biology, Culture, and the Evolution of Norm (Over)Compliance." *Mind and Language* 37, no. 5 (November): 993–1010.
Zaibert, Leo. 2006. "Punishment and Revenge." *Law and Philosophy* 25, no. 1 (January): 81–118.

7

Consequentialist Theories of Punishment

Hsin-Wen Lee

In this chapter, I consider contemporary consequentialist theories of punishment. Consequentialist theories look to the consequences of punishment to justify the institution of criminal punishment. Two types of theories fall into this category: teleology and aggregationism. I argue that teleology is implausible because it is based on a problematic assumption about the ultimate, final value of criminal punishment. Aggregationism is a more reasonable alternative. It holds that punishment is morally justified because it is an institution that helps society to aggregate important moral values. Several theories fall into this category, including general deterrence theories, specific deterrence theories, and preventionism. I argue that the policies supported by general deterrence theories fail to serve the aim of crime deterrence, and policies recommended by preventionism do not serve the aim of crime prevention. Erin Kelly's specific deterrence theory, namely just harm reduction, also fails to serve the purpose of specific deterrence. Only my rights-protection theory supports an institution of punishment that is designed to deter crime.

H.-W. Lee (✉)
University of Delaware, Newark, DE, USA
e-mail: hwl@udel.edu

© The Author(s), under exclusive license to Springer Nature Switzerland AG 2023
M. C. Altman (ed.), *The Palgrave Handbook on the Philosophy of Punishment*, Palgrave Handbooks in the Philosophy of Law, https://doi.org/10.1007/978-3-031-11874-6_7

1 Consequentialist and Deontological Theories of Punishment

Deontology holds that the moral value of an action is determined by the qualities inherent in the action. For example, lying is inherently wrong, and the wrongness lies in the action itself—e.g., the principle behind it cannot become a universal law or the act fails to respect people—not in factors external to it—e.g., bringing about negative short-term or long-term consequences. In contrast, consequentialism holds that an action's moral value is determined by its consequences. Thus, the moral value of lying can be positive or negative, depending on its consequences.

Similarly, to evaluate the moral value of punishment, deontology requires that we examine the qualities inherent in the acts of punishment, while consequentialism demands that we consider the consequences of punishment. Deontological theories of punishment—retributivism (Kleinig 1973; Moore 1997), desert theory (Kershnar 2000; von Hirsch 2017), expressivism (Feinberg 1965), communicative theory (Duff 2001), and so on—hold that punishment is morally justified when an offender commits a crime without any excuse or justification. Accordingly, the morally correct response to such criminal wrongdoing is to express blame through the imposition of proportionate punishment (Strawson 1962). An important feature of deontological theories of punishment is that they are *backward-looking*: to justify the imposition of punishment, deontological theories look to past wrongdoing to support the moral adequacy of punishment.

In contrast, a consequentialist theory of punishment is *forward-looking*; it holds that the institution of punishment can be morally justified because of the good consequences it is expected to bring about in the future. For instance, punishment discourages criminal offenses and thereby leads to the good consequence of crime deterrence, reduction, or prevention. Different forms of punishment may bring about different costs and benefits. A fine costs an offender money, but this is good because it teaches them a lesson and brings monetary profit to society. Community service takes time and physical labor from the offender but offers valuable service to the community. Imprisonment deprives an offender of some of their most essential liberties; however, it also incapacitates the offender so that they are no longer at liberty to commit more crimes in the community. The death penalty takes an offender's life away and thus they cannot commit a crime again. Punishment also sends actual and potential offenders a message about the price of criminal wrongdoing: if one commits the same crime, then they will receive the same punishment as the wrongdoer. Further, some forms of punishment may serve to rehabilitate and even morally reform convicted offenders. When offenders receive the education, psychological or psychiatric treatment, or job training that they need to lead a normal life, they are less likely to commit crimes again in the future. If they morally reform and learn to obey the law, they are more likely to respect the rights of others and less likely to commit crimes again in the future. Consequentialist theories appeal to these good consequences to justify the institution of punishment.

2 Consequentialist Theory of Punishment: Teleology or Aggregationism?

Next, I will consider two different types of consequentialism: teleology and aggregationism. According to teleology, there is only one thing or one state of affairs that possesses the ultimate moral value, namely, the *telos*. The telos is our final end or ultimate objective; it tells us how we can evaluate the moral values of different actions. The moral value of an action depends on its contribution to the telos. For two actions, X and Y, if X helps to bring about the telos more quickly or more effectively than does Y, then X has a higher moral value than Y. Without such an instrumental contribution, actions themselves are not valuable. In other words, the only way actions can have moral value is by making an instrumental contribution to bringing about the ultimate good.

While teleology assumes that there is only one state of affairs that is ultimately valuable, aggregationism does not make this assumption. Instead, it maintains that the right course of action is the one that will help to aggregate the highest values. Thus, the best consequence depends on the value system one believes in and the possibility of value maximization. For the value system, one can be a value monist or a value pluralist. Monists believe that there is only one type of intrinsic value, and we ought to act in ways that will maximize the aggregated, total value at the end. For example, Jeremy Bentham (1970) believes that there is only one intrinsic value, pleasure, and only one intrinsic evil, pain. The right action is the one that leads to the highest balance of pleasure over pain. On the other hand, a value pluralist believes that there can be different types of intrinsic values. For instance, John Stuart Mill (2011) believes that there can be higher and lower pleasures; that is, values can be ranked. Accordingly, we may rank the moral values of different actions by considering which pleasures they generate in the end. So long as an action brings about the highest possible aggregated moral value, it is the right action;

if an action does not do that, then it is wrong. The possibility of value maximization depends on several factors, including the feasibility of different plans, the possibility of coordination among different people, and the current conditions of things and people (e.g., individual preferences). Thus, whether an action is the right one depends on the highest moral value it can possibly generate.

Accordingly, when one speaks of "a consequentialist theory of punishment," one may have in mind either a teleological or an aggregationist theory of punishment. Presumably, a teleological theory of punishment is a theory that takes the punishment of criminal offenders to be the ultimate good. We are to evaluate the moral values of laws and policies by examining their contribution to this final purpose. The view is implausible because, to achieve the ultimately good state of affairs, some crime must be committed first. Without a criminal offense, it is impossible to achieve the telos. I am not aware of any philosopher who defends this view.

There is another closely related view about punishment. Some philosophers argue that it is inherently morally good that offenders are punished (Kleinig 1973, 67; Moore 1997, 157). Accordingly, when offenders commit crimes, they ought to be punished, unless there are countervailing reasons not to do so. This view does not assume that the punishment of offenders is the ultimate good; neither does it require that any crime be committed. All it demands is that we punish offenders when they commit crimes. According to this view, the value of punishment lies in itself and not its consequences. Thus, it is a deontological theory of punishment rather than a consequentialist one. It suggests only that we have a *prima facie* duty to punish those who commit crimes. In determining the moral value of punishment, the theory looks to the past (backward-looking), and not to the future (forward-looking). It does not specify the ultimately good state of affairs; nor does it require that we aggregate any particular value. It only tells us the kind of duty we have. Therefore, it seems that the teleological theory of punishment is implausible.

So, how should we evaluate the consequences of punishment? How do we know whether and how punishment brings about good consequences? In the literature, several different theories of punishment are categorized as consequentialist: general deterrence theories, specific deterrence theories, and preventionism. General deterrence theories hold that punishment is justified because it helps to deter potential offenders. Specific deterrence theories hold that punishment is justified because it helps to deter specific offenders, namely, convicted criminals themselves. Preventionism holds that extended punishment can be morally justified because it helps to prevent crime; that is, the good consequence of having the institution of punishment is that crimes will be deterred or prevented.

In the following sections, I will consider four general deterrence theories, two specific deterrence theories, and preventionism. I will argue that punishment does not help to achieve the consequences that preventionism intends, and that general deterrence theories fail to take effective measures to deter crime. Only one specific deterrence theory makes a genuine effort to deter crime: my rights-protection theory.

3 General Deterrence Theories

General deterrence theories of punishment hold that the institution of punishment is morally justified because it deters potential criminal offenses. The moral value of punishment is not intrinsic but instrumental; its value is in its contribution to the aim of crime deterrence. Having the institution of punishment means having an institution that will punish offenders whenever crimes are committed. Knowing that the institution of punishment is legally valid and effective, people know that there is an institution that will punish them if they commit crimes. Given that most people do not want to be punished, they will avoid committing crimes so that they will not be punished. In other words, having the institution of punishment gives people a prudential reason not to commit crimes, thereby deterring criminal offenses.

3.1 Quinn: Automatic Retaliation Device

Warren Quinn defends a general deterrence theory of punishment. According to Quinn, punishment is morally justified because we have a right to defend ourselves against aggressions. To protect ourselves against possible aggressions, we may threaten to punish those who harm us. The right of self-defense entails a right to threaten to punish those who will harm us. Accordingly, we also have the right to punish offenders. While many believe that we have a right to threaten to punish because we have the right to punish, Quinn argues that we have a right to punish because we have a right to threaten (1985, 336–37). The right of self-defense justifies the right to threaten to punish, and the right to threaten to punish justifies the right to punish.

In a similar manner, we have a right to activate an automatic retaliation machine (Quinn 1985, 337). The automatic retaliation machine that Quinn has in mind automatically identifies criminal wrongdoers and imposes on them the threatened punishment. Because people do not want to be punished, activating such a device will deter crime and protect society. Accordingly, our right of self-defense gives us a right to activate the machine to punish actual offenders in self-defense. If our right of self-defense gives us a right to activate such a machine, then it equally gives us the right to create the institution of punishment, which serves the same function and purpose.

While it may seem clear that we may activate an automatic retaliation machine to defend ourselves, it is less clear what kind of punishment program should be enforced by such a machine. First, from the point of view of crime deterrence, the threat of a disproportionate punishment may be more effective than the threat of proportionate punishment. Does this mean that we may threaten to impose disproportionate punishments on offenders, and does it also mean that we may actually impose the threatened disproportionate punishments on them (Alexander 1980; Tadros 2011, 269)? In the literature, proportionate punishment is a standard requirement; however, there seems to be some tension between Quinn's view and this requirement.

Second, proportionate or not, regardless of the amount of punishment threatened, we may wonder whether implementing the threatened punishment really serves to deter crime. The fact that a crime is committed is evidence that the threatened punishment failed to deter at least that crime. Because the threat of punishment happens before crimes are committed, there can be a discrepancy between what was threatened for self-defense and what becomes necessary for future self-defense. Carrying out the threatened punishment does not necessarily serve to deter future crimes (Farrell 1989; Ellis 2003, 339). If one is serious about crime deterrence, one will not insist on carrying out the threatened punishment but would be willing to adjust the form and amount of punishment according to the need for future crime deterrence. Thus, it is not clear whether Quinn's argument supports punitive policies that genuinely aim to deter.

3.2 Montague: Principle of Distributive Justice

Philip Montague suggests that, when offenders commit crimes, they force us to make a choice between allowing ourselves to be harmed and defending ourselves against their attack (1995, 40). No one has a duty to be harmed unless one was responsible for the harm created. Crime victims have the right to act in ways that would protect themselves from the harm created by their aggressors. Further, they are allowed to redistribute the harm that would befall them back to their aggressors. Because the harm was caused by the aggressors themselves, they cannot complain that the harm imposed on them is unjust. This is simply a matter of distributive justice. Montague calls the principle that allows us to redistribute the harm back to the aggressor *Principle J* (42). He believes that the same principle of distributive justice allows us to create the institution of criminal punishment, which allows us to redistribute the harm offenders created back to the offenders themselves. Because the institution of punishment is created to defend ourselves against unwanted harm, it is a form of self-defense and is subject to commonly accepted constraints of self-defense, including proportionality, minimization, and side effects (45–46).

While the principle of distributive justice that Montague defends is clearly plausible, it is less clear how this principle can be used to morally justify the institution of criminal punishment. First, the institution of punishment is primarily about the offender, not the victim; however, Principle J is primarily about the victim, not the offender. The principle supports the right of victims to defend themselves against the harm that was created by their aggressors. That is, the principle seeks to defend victims against unjustified aggression. However, it is not clear whether and how the institution of criminal punishment helps to serve this purpose. To begin with, punishment happens after a crime is committed and the harm has already been imposed on the victim. Thus, it is not clear how punishment helps to defend the victim against aggression. Further, typical cases of punishment—monetary fines, community service, imprisonment, the death penalty—are not designed to protect victims' rights or enhance their well-being. Depending on the conception of punishment to which one subscribes, punishment may be designed to give offenders what they deserve or to send potential offenders a warning message. It is not clear how such an institution helps to protect the victim against aggression and achieve distributive justice. Instead of punishing the offender, perhaps distributive justice should require that we make sure that the losses of victims are compensated for. Still, even when we take effective measures to protect victims and make up for their losses, it does not seem that we run out of reasons to punish offenders.

3.3 Farrell: Weak Retributivism

Daniel Farrell embraces the principle of distributive justice that Montague proposes. He argues that Principle J is more fundamental than the principle of self-defense. Based on this assumption, he further develops a general deterrence theory of punishment. When offenders commit crimes, they force us to make a choice between allowing victims to be harmed and harming the wrongdoers (Farrell 1985, 374). We are justified in choosing the latter.

Further, when offenders commit crimes, we normally feel that they should be held accountable for only the harms they create and no more. Thus, adequate punishment is determined primarily by the harms that the offender creates. However, according to Farrell's account, when an offender commits a crime, the harms they create are not limited to the ones that they actually cause with their offense. For instance, an offense may make the victim weaker and less able to defend themselves against later attacks by others, or the offense may expose the victim's weakness to other potential attackers, thereby making the victim more vulnerable than before. Thus, an offender is accountable not only for the harms they directly create with their offense, but also for the additional risk and danger that their offense indirectly brings about to the victim (1985, 383–84). Accordingly, Principle J would allow us to impose additional harm on the offender when doing so is necessary for self-protection. In short, distributive justice allows us to punish wrongdoers more than they harm us. Farrell calls this view *weak retributivism*. Farrell suggests, "wrongdoers may be punished beyond what is necessary to keep them from doing wrong again—if so punishing them can plausibly be said to be likely to deter others from doing wrong themselves" (1985, 368).

While Farrell's argument seems plausible, it is not clear why self-defense would require that offenders be punished more than is necessary. First, it is not clear how punishing an offender more would help to deter other potential offenders from committing similar crimes. People are situated differently; they have different beliefs about facts and values. Accordingly, the same punishment may not serve to deter all of them. For various reasons, potential offenders may not be deterred even by an actual case of severe punishment. For instance, one may be confident that one will not be caught—because one is very careful about one's criminal activities, or because one is a member of law enforcement and has some control over the criminal justice procedure, or one may lack the mental capacity to comprehend how this particular punishment gives one a reason not to commit a crime, or one may commit a crime because one is overwhelmed by strong emotion, temporarily fails to consider one's reasons properly, and loses control of one's actions (Lee 2017). Under those circumstances, one cannot be deterred. Consequently, punishing someone to deter someone else is an inherently shaky undertaking. Because the target audience is not homogeneous, one cannot be sure how the different audiences will perceive the reason provided.

Second, because Farrell's argument is based on Montague's principle of distributive justice, it encounters the same problem. Distributive justice in forced choice situations focuses primarily on the protection of victims rather than on the punishment of wrongdoers. The principle provides moral support for policies that favor victim compensation; however, it is unclear what it entails about punishing offenders.

3.4 Tadros: An Enforceable Duty to Protect

Victor Tadros argues that, from the duty not to cause harm to others, we may derive a duty to protect one's victims, which in turn supports an offender's duty to be punished. People have rights against being harmed, and we have a duty not to harm others. If one harms another person, one violates one's duty not to harm others. When this happens, the duty not to harm generates a duty to protect one's victims from the harms one caused (Tadros 2011, 3–4).

According to Tadros, this duty to protect is enforceable and grounds our right to punish offenders. When offenders commit crimes, they incur a duty to protect their victims. How can they fulfill this duty? Tadros believes that they can fulfill this duty by being punished. When offenders are punished, their punishment sends a warning message to potential offenders in the community and deters them from committing more crimes, thereby protecting their victims.

Tadros's argument suffers from the same problem as other general deterrence theories—namely, the punishment of convicted offenders does not necessarily serve the purpose of crime deterrence. To be clear, punishment of offenders may deter at least some people—those who, upon learning about the punishment, are concerned about the consequence of punishment. However, offenders are different, and seeing that someone is punished does not give everyone a reason against committing an offense. I mentioned this point briefly in the last subsection and will consider it in more detail when I discuss my rights-protection theory in section 4.2.

3.5 On General Deterrence

Before moving on to specific deterrence theories, I should describe how the four general deterrence theories of punishment respond to some common objections.

In the literature, many people consider consequentialist theories of punishment to be implausible because they are associated with problematic moral judgments. First, consequentialist theories look to the consequences of an action to determine its moral value; accordingly, as long as the consequences are good, we may punish innocent persons or impose disproportionate punishment on offenders (McCloskey 1965). Further, consequentialist theories allow us to use persons as mere means. General deterrence theories require that we punish actual offenders for the sake of warning potential offenders, and this clearly uses convicted offenders as mere means. Most people are appalled by these ideas and thus believe that we must reject consequentialist theories of punishment.

3.5.1 Punishing Innocent Persons

It does not seem that any of the general deterrence theories considered here support the punishment of innocent persons. Quinn's automatic retaliation device is activated by actual criminal offenses only; innocent persons cannot active this device and thus will not be punished. Montague's principle of distributive justice would require that we redistribute the harm back to the aggressor only; because we cannot "redistribute" the harm back to innocent persons, his argument would not support the punishment of innocent persons either. Because both Farrell's weak retributivism and Tadros's enforceable duty view appeal to Montague's Principle J, neither of them would support the punishment of innocent persons either.

3.5.2 Proportionate Punishment

Except for Farrell's weak retributivism, which explicitly endorses additional, disproportionate punishment, all general deterrence theories of punishment considered here require that punishment be proportionate. In Quinn's theory, the automatic retaliation device is programmed for self-defense; thus, the same principles and requirements that govern measures of self-defense also apply to this self-defensive device. The principle of proportionality is a standard requirement in self-defense. Thus, Quinn's theory has no problem accommodating the principle of proportionality.

Montague's principle of distributive justice would also support proportionate punishment. The amount of harm we may permissibly impose on an offender is the amount of harm that they imposed on their victims. We are allowed only to redistribute the harm that the offender created back to them, and we are not allowed to create additional harm. Thus, punishment must be proportionate to the crime committed.

Tadros argues that the amount of punishment that an offender ought to receive is determined by the duty that they have to protect their victims against their attack. This duty is in turn determined by the amount of harm they created by their offense. Offenders are to be punished so as to send a warning message to potential offenders. Accordingly, punishment must be proportionate to the crime committed.

On the other hand, Farrell's weak retributivism allows us to punish offenders more than is required to deter their offenses. This is because the harms generated by an offense are not limited to the harms created directly by the offense, but also the harms that are indirectly caused by it. Does this entail that we may impose a disproportionately severe punishment on an offender? Farrell says yes, we may punish offenders more severely than their crimes. Disproportionate punishment can be morally justified.

3.5.3 Using Persons as Mere Means

In Quinn's theory, although the institution of punishment is created to deter criminal offenses, punishment is not implemented until some offender actually commits a crime. Punishment is imposed on actual offenders because they ignore the threat of punishment, commit crimes, and activate the automatic retaliation process. Thus, their punishment is the result of their criminal wrongdoing and is not meant to teach anyone else a lesson. Offenders are punished because they activate the device. They are not used as mere means (Ellis 2003).

In both Montague's and Farrell's theories, the aim of punishment is to redistribute the harm back to the offender. Neither would require offenders to be punished for reasons other than their own offenses. Accordingly, when punished, offenders are not treated as mere means.

On the other hand, Tadros argues that offenders can be used as mere means. Normally, we should not use people as mere means; he calls this *the means principle*. However, wrongdoers may be used as means to protect their victims against the harms that they created (Tadros 2011, 193). This is because they violate their duty not to harm people and thereby acquire a duty to protect their victims. Further, if two offenders cannot protect their own victims against the harms that they created but are in positions that allow each of them to protect the other's victim, then Tadros argues that they have a duty to protect the other's victim, so long as their duties are similar in kind and stringency (275).

4 Specific Deterrence Theories

A specific deterrence theory holds that punishment can be morally justified because punishment deters specific offenders from committing crimes. According to Erin Kelly, "Specific deterrence involves the application of sanctions to a particular person to induce that person to refrain from engaging in harmful behavior. It is contrasted with general deterrence, in which we harm a person in order to deter another" (2018, 126). In other words, the intended audiences are different for general and specific deterrence theories. By punishing offenders, general deterrence theories intend to deter people other than the offenders, while specific deterrence theories aim to deter the offenders themselves.

In the contemporary literature, only two philosophers support a specific deterrence theory: Kelly and me.

4.1 Kelly: Just Harm Reduction

The fundamental moral principle that guides Kelly's account is *fairness*. According to Kelly, the institution of criminal punishment is created to guide people's conduct. Criminal offenses are behaviors that people have no right to engage in; thus, attaching punishment to criminal offenses does not impose any unfair burden on people. Further, a competent adult enjoys fair opportunities not to commit a crime; if not, they would be excused and not be punished. One can avoid punishment simply by not committing any crimes (Kelly 2018, 135). The threat of punishment gives people a rational incentive not to commit crimes; thus, criminal punishment contributes to the aim of harm reduction. If one chooses to commit a crime, then the threatened punishment will be imposed on them. The institution of punishment, accordingly, is designed to convince everyone not to commit crimes. Punishment is imposed on actual offenders only.

An interesting feature of Kelly's account is that, while she appeals to a specific deterrence theory to justify the institution of punishment, she adopts a general deterrence theory to select punishment policies. One might think that the specific deterrence theory of punishment would require that we make sentencing decisions by considering how effectively a form of punishment deters offenders. Because convicted offenders are different, presumably, the correct punishment for them would also be different. Further, because different offenders can be deterred by different types of punishment, the specific deterrence theory cannot support a system of standardized punishment for all offenders who commit the same type of crime.

However, this is not how Kelly thinks about sentencing policies. The principle that guides her account is fairness, and fairness requires that offenders who commit the same type of crime receive the same type of punishment. According to Kelly,

> Reasonable opportunity generalizes across persons. Fairness requires us to evaluate and respond to individual infractions with standards that extend to relevantly similar cases. We should treat like cases alike, or at least with reasonable similarity. … Both positivist and non-positivist legal philosophers have recognized this principle. H. L. A. Hart refers to it as part of the minimum moral content of law, and Ronald Dworkin calls it a matter of integrity in the law. (2018, 135)

How much punishment should be imposed on offenders, then? The amount of punishment is to be determined by the deterrence value of punishment, and the deterrence value of a form of punishment is determined by its *general* deterrence value, not by its impact on individual convicted offenders. That is, we calculate the deterrence value of punishment by considering how it deters *an average offender* (Kelly 2018, 136). According to Kelly, "in calculating our threats to deter people from reoffending we are, in effect, calculating the general deterrence value of the punishment" (137). After calculating how much punishment is needed to deter people from committing a particular type of crime, we may impose the estimated punishment so as to deter people from committing the same crime. Thus, according to Kelly's account, the justification for punishment is specific deterrence, but the effect is general deterrence.

Although Kelly appeals to a specific deterrence theory, her fairness view supports punishment policies that are based on a general deterrence theory. This is an interesting feature of her theory, but also a problematic one. Her argument assumes that the same standardized punishment should be used to deter different criminal offenders. However, because different criminal offenders commit the same crime for different reasons, it is not clear how imposing the same punishment on them, which is designed to deter "an average offender," can deter all of them. Some offenders commit crimes because they have false beliefs about facts or values. To deter them, we must help them to acquire true beliefs; otherwise, there is no reason to expect that they will not commit a crime again. Others have problems controlling their emotions, desires, or conduct. To deter them, we must help them to control themselves; without such efforts, they are likely to commit crimes again, given their personality traits and tendencies. Still others lack the capacity to understand the impact of their actions, including the possibility that they will be punished. To deter them, we must help them to explore possible options and solutions (Lee 2017). Accordingly, to deter individual offenders from committing crimes, we must examine the reason why they committed crimes in the first place and then learn how to prevent them from committing crimes again in the future. This requires that we invest some time to learn the background of individual offenders—their beliefs and values, whether they can be persuaded into changing their beliefs and lifestyles, and how we may help them to lead a life that is crime-free. The punishment policy that Kelly proposes—to impose punishment according to their deterrence impact on an average offender—does not support the aim of specific deterrence because it fails to address individual offenders.

4.2 Lee: The Rights-Protection Theory

I defend a societal self-defense theory of punishment, the rights-protection theory (Lee 2018). According to this theory, the fact that we have certain core rights (to life, liberty, and property) entails that we also have derived rights to take measures to protect these core rights. That is, the fact that we have rights at all gives us a further right to defend these rights. We may take self-defensive measures against encroachment upon our rights; otherwise, our rights would be empty. This right of self-defense in turn gives us a right to create the institution of criminal punishment to sanction those who violate our rights. The institution of criminal punishment is one of the measures that we can take to protect our core rights. Because the right to punish is derived from the right of self-defense, which in turn is derived from our core rights, the same constraints that apply to the right of self-defense also apply to criminal punishment.

My rights-protection theory takes the protection of our core rights to be the fundamental value that provides the ultimate moral justification for the institution of criminal punishment. Therefore, in selecting punishment policies or designing the institution of punishment, we must make sure that the policies and institutions will not undermine the fundamental value of rights-protection; further, we must prioritize those policies and institutions that serve to protect rights. In other words, the aim of rights-protection both justifies and constrains the institution of punishment.

Because the institution of punishment is created to serve the aim of rights-protection, we ought to prioritize punishment policies that contribute to this purpose. If a punishment policy or decision is likely to undermine this aim, then we ought to adopt some alternative measures to ensure that punishment does not undermine its justifying aim. This means that if forms of punishment are more likely to reduce crime and recidivism rates—e.g., job-training programs, drug-rehabilitation programs, psychological or psychiatric treatments—then we ought to adopt these forms of punishment, as they help to protect citizens' rights. On the other hand, if a form of punishment is likely to increase crime or recidivism rates, then we ought to use it only as a last resort. For instance, empirical studies show that imprisonment tends to have a prisonization effect, which in turn makes recidivism more likely, so we should not adopt imprisonment as the default form of punishment and should use it only when it is necessary.

Further, the constraints on the right of self-defense apply equally to the institution of criminal punishment. Commonly accepted constraints on the right of self-defense include discrimination, proportionality, and necessity. Very briefly, discrimination requires that we punish the actual offender and no one else. Proportionality requires that, in defending ourselves against an offense, other things being equal, we adopt self-defensive measures that are proportionate to the harm created by the offense. Necessity requires that the measures that we adopt to defend ourselves be causally connected to the ending of the aggression. Although I do not have the space to defend it here, I would also argue that there is a fourth constraint, which I call minimum rationality. Minimum rationality requires that the self-defensive measures we adopt not undermine our aim of rights-protection. That is, in punishing to protect our rights, we should not end up harming the rights we intend to protect.

Specific deterrence requires that we consider how the punishment of an offender increases or decreases their chance of recidivism. This requires that we analyze the type of offender one is and consider how to come up with an individualized plan to help the offender lead a normal, crime-free life in the community. The imposition of proportionate harm on offenders does not necessarily contribute to this aim and is not an essential aspect of punishment.

4.3 On Specific Deterrence

Before moving on, I will consider briefly how the two specific deterrence theories respond to common objections to consequentialist theories of punishment. Because specific deterrence theories of punishment aim to deter actual criminal offenders, punishment is not imposed for the sake of deterring other potential offenders, but for the actual offenders themselves.

Thus, specific deterrence does not use offenders as mere means. Neither does the specific theory require the punishment of innocent persons, because punishment of innocent persons does not help to deter the actual offenders.

Do specific deterrence theories support disproportionate punishment? Kelly specifically argues that sentencing policies must address an average offender. Thus, her theory requires proportionate punishment. My theory, on the other hand, sees proportionate punishment policies as having expressivist value, but not ultimate value. That is, punishment ought to be proportionate because we want to express equal condemnation of the same types of offenses. However, I do not believe that this requires that offenders who commit the same type of crimes must receive the same punishment or be treated in the same way. The aim of specific crime deterrence is to deter individual offenders, not an average offender. If the same punishment deters one offender but not the other, there is no need to insist that they be punished in the same way. If the same punishment does not deter one of them, we must seek alternative forms of punishment. For instance, if a monetary fine deters one offender but not the other, then we must seek alternative forms of punishment, such as community service or short-term imprisonment.

Further, if statistical evidence shows that a form of punishment leads to a higher recidivism rate, then, although my theory would not reject this particular form of punishment outright, it would regard it as the last resort, not the first or the standard resort, of punishment. For instance, if there is a serious negative impact of imprisonment, as studies consistently show, then we ought no longer to use imprisonment as the standard form of punishment and ought to use it only as a last resort for punishing violent offenders. This means that, even if we were to insist on proportionate punishment, we must adopt other alternative forms of punishment that could deliver proportionate punishment, such as open prisons, community service, and so on.

5 Preventionism

Many people believe that it is more important to prevent crime than to punish offenders (Ashworth and Zedner 2014, 29). Instead of waiting for crimes to happen and then punishing offenders, we should take active steps to prevent crimes from being committed. In the literature, preventionism refers to a specific view about punishment that sees additional punishment as justified because it serves to prevent offenders from committing crimes.[1] This view is different from deterrence theories of punishment, which hold that the institution of criminal punishment is morally justified because having such an institution helps to deter criminal offenses. Preventionism holds that, if we know that some offenders are dangerous—for instance, they are repeat offenders who are likely to commit crimes again—then the court may impose sentences on them that are longer than the ones they would have received if they were not likely to reoffend. According to Frederick Schauer, "Preventive detention ... involves punishing people for the harmful acts in which they might engage rather than for the harmful acts in which they have already engaged" (2013, 3). Consequentialists and deontologists alike generally believe that punishment must be proportionate to the crime committed. Thus, if a punishment is more severe than the crime committed, then it is disproportionate and cannot be right. However, according to preventionism, a longer sentence can be morally justified if the extended sentence serves to prevent the offender from committing more crimes. Under this view, a longer sentence can be morally justified because it serves to incapacitate the offender, thereby preventing them from committing additional crimes.

Notice that this view says nothing about the punishment of non-recidivist offenders who are not likely to reoffend. It tries to justify extended sentences for recidivists only. Thus, the theory may be combined with a retributive or a deterrence theory of punishment; they would provide us with instructions on how to punish offenders who are not likely to reoffend. Preventionism is primarily concerned with the punishment of dangerous and repeat offenders.

However, because offenders have yet to commit the crime that we suspect that they would, many punishment theorists are concerned with the moral soundness of preventionism. Punishment is justified for its expected preventive effect. However, there are reasons to doubt that a longer sentence serves its intended purpose. First, this argument assumes that the offender will commit a crime again, and thus that they need to be prevented from doing so. However, it is not clear how this belief is justified. During an ideal trial, one sees the evidence for an offender's crime; however, it is not clear if the evidence can provide a good reason for believing that they will commit a crime

[1] For example, Bernard Harcourt suggests that, according to consequentialism, "punishment was a central part of prevention: it was, for instance, fully justified to lengthen a sentence (to punish more) for someone who recidivated because the recidivist carried a higher likelihood of reoffending" (2013, 258). Similarly, Kevin Arthur says that "detention designed to protect society from predicted but unconsummated offenses does not increase the likelihood of a fair trial. Accordingly, such detention is not simply regulatory" (1987, 403–4), and "a restraint on liberty such as preventive detention is regulatory rather than punitive only if it serves a 'legitimate and compelling' state purpose. The [U.S. Supreme] Court decided that crime prevention was such a purpose" (396).

again in the future. If the evidence is sufficient to support the belief that they will commit a crime, then, very likely, the court may punish the offender for an inchoate crime—attempt, solicitation, and conspiracy. If the evidence is not sufficient to support the belief, then it is not clear why we can assume that they need to be prevented from doing so. Preventionists are likely to refer to an offender's past recidivism to support the belief in their future reoffense. This would essentially be a type of inductive argument. Accordingly, the truth of the premise does not guarantee the truth of its conclusion. After all, it is possible that some incident happens to the offender before they have a chance to commit another crime. For instance, they might convert to a new religion that makes them no longer interested in their earlier criminal career. Or they might become the parent of a newborn baby and suddenly realize that they need to have an honorable career or be on the morally right path. Or some accident might happen to them that deprives them of essential skills to commit crimes. For instance, a thief may no longer be able to steal because they are in a car accident, become crippled, and can no longer run as fast as they used to.

Further, some punishment theorists are concerned that giving an offender a longer custodial sentence means that they will receive more punishment than they deserve, or more than what is proportionate to the crime they committed (Ashworth and Zedner 2014, 151). The amount of punishment should be determined by the seriousness of the crime. However, preventionism allows preventive considerations to play a role in determining offenders' sentences, which seems unjustified.

In addition, it is not clear why we should believe that simply having a longer sentence will prevent an offender from committing crimes again. First, it is important to acknowledge that custodial sentences do incapacitate offenders. So long as an offender stays in prison, they cannot commit crimes that would harm the community (though they can still act in ways that harm other inmates or correctional officers). Thus, the community is safer and people's rights are protected during the time of their extended stay. However, unless the offender will stay in prison until their death, there will be a day when they are out of prison. If they never change their mind, then having a longer sentence prevents them from committing crimes only during the period of time when they are in prison; they can still commit crimes after they get out. That is, an extended sentence serves only to delay crime, not to stop crime.

Second, if we really care about preventing crime, we must consider how a longer sentence affects crime prevention. First, there is a risk that an offender will be subject to more bad influences in prison. While staying in prison, one must learn to live with other inmates and acclimate oneself to prison culture.

Depending on what other inmates are like, one may make friends with some of them and then learn about committing crimes more effectively. This is problematic if we are concerned with crime prevention. Second, having a longer sentence effectively means that it will be more difficult for the offender to reenter society. They lose contact with friends and family; they are less familiar with how to live in the community; and, after serving time in prison, it becomes more difficult for ex-inmates to find housing, jobs, and a support system. Longer custodial sentences effectively mean that their lives outside prison will be more difficult, not to mention that having a criminal record already makes one's life more difficult. If their reentry back into the community is difficult, then they may be motivated to go back to their old ways and commit crimes again. This is, again, quite bad at preventing crime.

In other words, simply having a longer sentence does not necessarily prevent an offender from committing additional crimes. So, what steps should the criminal justice system take to ensure that offenders are not likely to commit crimes again in the future? Elsewhere I argue that there are different types of offenders and that different strategies must be employed to deter them (Lee 2017). For example, some offenders are not concerned about the consequences of their actions because they lack proper education or financial support. To prevent them from committing crimes again, it is important to make sure that they understand the impact and significance of their actions and that they have the opportunity to earn an adequate income. Other offenders may require education, training, or treatment. There is no perfect way to ensure that offenders will not commit crimes; education, training, and treatment programs may or may not help. Nevertheless, simply putting offenders in prison for a longer period of time can only deter those who strongly dislike prison. It may not deter those who do not care or cannot care.

6 Conclusion

Consequences matter in consequentialist theories of punishment. In general deterrence theories, the aim of punishment is to deter potential offenders. While most forms of punishment do deter most people most of the time—people who can think rationally about the consequences of their actions and are afraid of being punished—punishment cannot deter all possible types of potential offenders. Preventionism aims to prevent repeat offenders from committing crimes again. However, without any attempt at rehabilitating and reforming them, extended punishment does not help to prevent repeat offenders from committing crimes; extended punishment serves only to postpone them. Specific deterrence aims to deter convicted offenders. To accomplish this, punishment must be designed to persuade them not to commit crimes again. Proportionate sentencing policies are not designed to serve this purpose. To deter convicted offenders, individualized rehabilitation plans must be adopted.

References

Alexander, Lawrence. 1980. "The Doomsday Machine: Proportionality, Punishment and Prevention." *Monist* 63, no. 2 (April): 199–227.

Arthur, Kevin F. 1987. "Preventive Detention: Liberty in the Balance." *Maryland Law Review* 46, no. 2: 378–407.

Ashworth, Andrew, and Lucia Zedner. 2014. *Preventive Justice*. Oxford: Oxford University Press.

Bentham, Jeremy. 1970. *An Introduction to the Principles of Morals and Legislation*. Edited by J. H. Burns and H. L. A. Hart. Oxford: Clarendon.

Duff, R. A. 2001. *Punishment, Communication, and Community*. Oxford: Oxford University Press.

Ellis, Anthony. 2003. "A Deterrence Theory of Punishment." *Philosophical Quarterly* 53, no. 212 (July): 337–51.

Farrell, Daniel M. 1985. "The Justification of General Deterrence." *Philosophical Review* 94, no. 3 (July): 367–94.

———. 1989. "On Threats and Punishments." *Social Theory and Practice* 15, no. 2 (Summer): 125–54.

Feinberg, Joel. 1965. "The Expressive Function of Punishment." *Monist* 49, no. 3 (July): 397–423.

Harcourt, Bernard E. 2013. "Punitive Preventive Justice: A Critique." In *Prevention and the Limits of the Criminal Law*, edited by Andrew Ashworth, Lucia Zedner, and Patrick Tomlin, 252–72. Oxford: Oxford University Press.

Kelly, Erin I. 2018. *The Limits of Blame: Rethinking Punishment and Responsibility*. Cambridge, MA: Harvard University Press.

Kershnar, Stephen. 2000. "A Defense of Retributivism." *International Journal of Applied Philosophy* 14, no. 1 (Spring): 97–111.

Kleinig, John. 1973. *Punishment and Desert*. The Hague: Nijhoff.

Lee, Hsin-Wen. 2017. "Taking Deterrence Seriously: The Wide-Scope Deterrence Theory of Punishment." *Criminal Justice Ethics* 36, no. 1 (April): 2–24.

———. 2018. "A New Societal Self-Defense Theory of Punishment—The Rights-Protection Theory." *Philosophia—Philosophical Quarterly of Israel* 46, no. 2 (June): 337–53.

McCloskey, H. J. 1965. "A Non-Utilitarian Approach to Punishment." *Inquiry* 8, nos. 1–4: 239–55.

Mill, John Stuart. 2011. *Utilitarianism*. 2nd ed. Edited by George Sher. Indianapolis, IN: Hackett.

Montague, Phillip. 1995. *Punishment as Societal-Defense*. Lanham, MD: Rowman & Littlefield.

Moore, Michael S. 1997. *Placing Blame: A General Theory of the Criminal Law*. Oxford: Oxford University Press.

Quinn, Warren. 1985. "The Right to Threaten and the Right to Punish." *Philosophy & Public Affairs* 14, no. 4 (Autumn): 327–73.

Schauer, Frederick. 2013. "The Ubiquity of Prevention." In *Prevention and the Limits of the Criminal Law: Principles and Policies*, edited by Andrew Ashworth, Lucia Zedner, and Patrick Tomlin, 10–22. Oxford: Oxford University Press.

Strawson, P. F. 1962. "Freedom and Resentment." *Proceedings of the British Academy* 48: 1–25.

Tadros, Victor. 2011. *The Ends of Harm: The Moral Foundations of Criminal Law*. Oxford: Oxford University Press.

von Hirsch, Andreas. 2017. *Deserved Criminal Sentences: An Overview*. London: Bloomsbury.

8

Rethinking Four Criticisms of Consequentialist Theories of Punishment

Christopher Bennett

1 Introduction

Consequentialist theories represent one major approach to the question of whether punishment can be justified. Punishment, unlike social justice or world peace, is not a straightforwardly justifiable and choiceworthy goal. Punishment involves the intentional imposition of types of treatment that tend to cause significant suffering, harm, or deprivation. There is a question as to whether, or under what conditions, there is sufficient justification for such a practice. The consequentialist answer to this question is that, if punishment of wrongdoing is justifiable, it is only because of the beneficial consequences that it brings about. It is compatible with a consequentialist approach, of course, that punishment is never justifiable.

This chapter discusses some key features and criticisms of consequentialist theories of punishment, and it looks at whether consequentialism has the resources to respond adequately to those criticisms. I argue that some common criticisms of consequentialist theories of punishment are better thought of as criticisms of a specific form of consequentialism rather than consequentialism as such. The question of whether the whole consequentialist approach

C. Bennett (✉)
University of Sheffield, Sheffield, UK
e-mail: c.bennett@sheffield.ac.uk

© The Author(s), under exclusive license to Springer Nature Switzerland AG 2023
M. C. Altman (ed.), *The Palgrave Handbook on the Philosophy of Punishment*, Palgrave Handbooks in the Philosophy of Law, https://doi.org/10.1007/978-3-031-11874-6_8

is problematic is much more complex. While I do not try in this chapter to resolve that latter question, I look at some considerations that bear on it.

Throughout, the orientation will be toward general principles rather than in-depth analysis of particular authors. I am interested in delineating the *shape* of the consequentialist approach and the fact that a theory with that shape will inevitably attract certain criticisms as well as having certain advantages. I will focus on four interconnected criticisms that are current in the literature on philosophy of punishment. The first criticism says that consequentialist theories wrongfully treat it as permissible to punish an innocent person if doing so will lead to optimal consequences. The second criticism says that consequentialist theories allow the treatment of offenders (and others) as mere means. The third criticism says that consequentialist theories fail to respect offenders as moral agents. The fourth criticism says that consequentialist theories recommend responses to wrongdoing that ignore or displace other valuable responses to wrongdoing, or other valuable forms of human relation.

The chapter will proceed as follows. In part 2, I introduce consequentialism as a general theory, looking at its defining features and variants. In part 3, I look at consequentialist theories of punishment specifically. In part 4, I introduce the four criticisms, and in part 5, I look at responses that consequentialists can make to these criticisms. Part 6 assesses the prospects for non-consequentialist criticisms in the light of these responses. The conclusion introduces a final important consideration.

2 Consequentialism in General

Consequentialism is an all-purpose theory of justification.[1] It can be used for the evaluation of acts, activities, practices, ways of life, rules, habits, and institutions. It can even be extended to the evaluation of outlooks, emotions, and beliefs. The consequentialist approach to justification takes into account the *consequences* (or *outcomes* or *resulting states of affairs*) produced by those acts, practices, institutions, etc., and nothing more. Consequentialism is motivated by the intuition that we should assess things from the perspective of how the world can be made better (or how it can be made the best it can be). Roughly, if the consequences are as beneficial as can feasibly be (call this outcome *optimal*), then the object of evaluation—for example, the action, practice, or

[1] For good discussions of consequentialism, see Smart and Williams (1973), Scheffler (1982), Pettit (1991), and Sinnott-Armstrong (2019).

institution—is *right*; but if the object of evaluation has consequences that are not as good as they could have been (call this outcome *suboptimal*), then it is *wrong*. The consequentialist procedure for justification is thus to compare the range of available alternatives and to rank them by the overall goodness of their consequences. Nothing else is relevant. This last point is important. While many normative theories give *some* role to the consequences, what is distinctive about consequentialism is that it *only* takes consequences into account.

We can highlight two rival approaches to consequentialism: *deontological* accounts and *relational* accounts. The deontological position treats the idea of law or requirement as morally basic. On this view, certain actions are morally required or prohibited (as if by law), on grounds independent of resulting consequences. Meanwhile the relational theorist treats certain relational claims as basic and holds that certain actions, or forms of treatment, are in themselves incompatible with such claims (Wallace 2019). Both of these alternatives seek to explain how there could be a valid standard of evaluation (that is, of justification, of choiceworthiness or good reason, of moral obligation or prohibition) other than "brings about the best overall consequences." For instance, on these views, actions such as the purposeful killing of the innocent, torture, or sexual violence might be held to be wrongful and not-to-done on the basis of the relevant deontological standards or relational claims—and thus wrongful independently of any good (or bad) consequences that might come from performing them. The wrongful nature of such acts, on this view, preempts consideration of the consequences and renders any such calculation redundant, taking them "off the table" before any survey of costs and benefits of available alternatives begins (Williams 1973; Nozick 1974).[2] What takes these options off the table, according to the non-consequentialist approach, is some designation of certain actions or forms of treatment as in principle impermissible. It is a weakness of consequentialism, according to proponents of these rival views, that it holds *any* option to be in principle available, subject to the result of an assessment of overall good. The consequentialist might end up recommending killing the innocent, torture, or the use of sexual violence if the consequences of doing so were sufficiently good. Because consequentialism holds that nothing matters to moral assessment other than consequences, it rules out nothing in advance of an assessment of those consequences. (The consequentialist, for their part, will retort that it

[2] For a list of examples, see, e.g., Walen (2016).

would be irrational to rule anything out in advance of an assessment of the resulting costs and benefits.)

If that is the basic idea, one thing a more developed consequentialist theory requires is a theory of what good and bad consequences are. Otherwise put, we need an *axiology*: a theory of final ends, or of intrinsic value—for short, a theory of the good. Unless we know what we should be aiming for—and avoiding—our consequentialist theory will not get off the ground. Furthermore, the consequentialist will need a theory of the good that is in some sense quantifiable. Our understanding of good consequences needs to function as a metric through which we can reach an evaluation of which course of action (etc.) would be best. As part of this theory of the good, a consequentialist theory would also need to decide on scope. This is the question whether the goods that are relevant are limited to those of a particular person (unlikely) or of a particular group, or of a particular location (spatial, temporal, etc.); or whether indeed the scope is unlimited.

Second, a consequentialist theory needs to decide what the right level of evaluation is. For instance, if we look at the consequences of an *individual act* of keeping one's promise, we might find, in a given situation, that those consequences would be bad, or at least suboptimal. But if we look at the consequences of the *overall rule, practice, or social habit of promising*, it might turn out that a society with such a practice is better off than one that does not (Rawls 1955). Until it non-arbitrarily specifies which level is relevant, a consequentialist theory provides conflicting answers to the agent who wants to know whether to keep their promise.

Third, a consequentialist theory needs to decide whether what determines rightness is the expected or the actual consequences. Is an action right if it was the option with the greatest probability of bringing about good consequences? Or is it only right if it actually does bring about the best available consequences? Some theorists answer that taking the option with the best expected consequences shows one to be a good consequentialist *agent*, but that one's *action* was only right if it had actually good consequences.

Fourth, a consequentialist theory has to decide whether rightness requires the *maximization* of the good, or whether there is some amount less than the maximum that would be *sufficient*. If we should optimize then there is likely to be only one right option in any situation; whereas if we need only reach some threshold of adequacy, a range of options may be right.[3]

[3] For the claim that consequentialism should adopt "satisficing" rather than maximizing, see Slote and Pettit (1984).

A well-known consequentialist theory is utilitarianism. Indeed, utilitarianism was historically the first consequentialist theory to be developed, and the interest in consequentialism per se arose as its defenders sought to preserve what seemed to them correct within that view against objections. According to utilitarianism, rightness depends on whether the object of evaluation brings about the greatest possible balance of happiness over unhappiness of available alternatives. Utilitarianism thus answers our first question by specifying that the relevant good consequences are welfare or happiness. It assumes that happiness is quantifiable (as with Bentham's "felicific calculus," for instance). And it appears to treat the relevant pool of happiness as unlimited, in the sense that it is not only human happiness, but happiness in the world more generally that is at issue. It answers the fourth question by specifying that we should maximize the good. Utilitarians thus hold that no action other than the optimal one is right. In answer to the second question, there are different varieties of utilitarianism: act-utilitarianism, rule-utilitarianism, character- or motive-utilitarianism, and utilitarianism applied to whole lives, for instance. In answer to the third question, utilitarianism has variations that employ expected utility and variations that employ actual utility. From this brief survey, we can see that (a) utilitarianism is not the only possible form of consequentialism, and (b) there may be reasons to adopt a non-utilitarian form of consequentialism.

One criticism of utilitarianism is that happiness is not the only value, and hence not the only valuable consequence. Someone might well accept the consequentialist intuition that making the world the best it can be is the only thing relevant to evaluation, but think that, in addition to happiness, knowledge, art, biodiversity, friendship, religion, justice, and so on are also good. The utilitarian might agree that these things are good but say that they are only good because they make us happy, or make our lives go better. Whether this is plausible will depend on what happiness is—whether only pleasure or something broader. However, for many people, knowledge, friendship, justice, and so on can have value independently of being an ingredient in happiness. A work of art might be valuable, and in some sense the world might be better for containing that work, even if no one can access it to be made happier by it. Consequentialist theories can thus be monistic and claim that there is only one fundamental good—though they need not claim that this is happiness—or they could be pluralistic. If a consequentialist theory is pluralistic, then it would need to specify an ordering of goods in order to avoid irresolvable conflicts in situations in which a multiplicity of goods could be produced.

Before proceeding, we can now recapitulate the structure of consequentialism. Let X be some action/practice/institution. Let Y be "the good"—where this may be monistic or pluralistic. To assess X, according to consequentialism, we just have to find out to what extent X leads to Y (minus any bad consequences). Nothing else matters. That is, if we compare X with alternatives (A, B, C, etc.), the only reason to prefer X over those alternatives is that it produces more overall good.

3 What Is a Consequentialist Theory of Punishment?

What does consequentialism recommend when applied to punishment? A consequentialist theory would be abolitionist if it were to show that punishment would never bring about sufficient good to be justifiable. An abolitionist theory might argue for this conclusion relative to different levels of evaluation: for instance, it might argue that no *individual act* of punishment could ever bring about sufficient good, or that no *rule* or *practice* or *institution* could. It might argue specifically that *state* punishment can never bring about sufficient good, but that more informal forms of punishment (e.g., in the context of the family) might do so.

How would consequentialism go about evaluating punishment? A consequentialist argument for or against punishment will be partially empirical because it will be based in part on working out which alternatives are in fact available and what consequences will actually result from taking each of those alternatives. This will involve understanding the causal pathways that lead from an individual action, or a practice of so acting, to the production of consequences, and the ways in which those consequences might be more or less likely to be produced given certain other causal factors being in play. It will also involve the measurement—perhaps as an estimate—of the good to be obtained under each of the alternatives.

One strength of the consequentialist approach is therefore that it calls for an evidence-based process for evaluating punishments that is sensitive to the different contexts in which punishment is being used. It also requires us to assess non-punitive alternatives such as rehabilitation, education, accommodation, or shaming as alternative ways of bringing about the desired outcomes. Such an approach would also look at factors such as (a) whether the good brought about by punishment is accompanied by other negative side effects that affect the overall evaluation of consequences, and (b) how probable it is that intervening events or factors might prevent that good from being realized.

This is not to say that the consequentialist evaluation of punishment is purely empirical and free from the complexities of moral argument. The evaluation will also require non-empirical reasoning to specify what the good is (and if the good is plural, how the different goods should be ordered), what the right level of evaluation is, what the right notion of "consequence" is, and so on. These issues cannot be settled by empirical evidence but are rather part of the theoretical or principled framework that directs or orients our empirical inquiries.

The term "consequentialist theory of punishment" is often used to denote the view that evaluates punishment as an instrumental means to something like the reduction of harm (Duff 1986; Wood 2010).[4] Such harm-reduction theories of punishment are often characterized as "forward-looking." The future benefits, on such views, are usually seen in terms of an increase in safety or security or well-being of members of a society, and thus a decline in the amount of crime and in particular the harm it causes. In such discussions, these views are then contrasted with retributivist "backward-looking" views that appeal, not to contingent future benefits of punishment, but to its inherent appropriateness as a matter of justice or desert. Punishment is thus thought, by such instrumental theories, to be justified only if it has a protective, preventative function—specifically, that it will deter, incapacitate, or reform and rehabilitate actual or potential offenders, decreasing risks of harm and leaving society better off as a result.

So understood, harm-reduction and consequentialist approaches share a commitment to the idea that punishment is justified only if it produces some good. However, this is not to say that harm-reduction theories are identical to consequentialist theories or that retributivist theories must be non-consequentialist (Berman 2010). First, not all harm-reduction theories are consequentialist. To see this point, we can consider the "societal-defense" theory (Montague 1983; Farrell 1985; see also Tadros 2011). This theory models the permissibility of punishment on the permissibility of self- or other-defense. It argues that, if strictly necessary, it can be justifiable to use force to defend an innocent victim of aggression, because, unlike the victim, the aggressor is *responsible* for having created a situation in which at least one party must bear some harm. Punishment, according to this theory, is justified on similar grounds, because it protects innocent victims against aggressors by the threat and the imposition of deterrent punishment on those who are responsible for creating a situation in which either innocents will be harmed or aggressors will be punished. The societal-defense theory is a harm-reduction

[4] I have also used such terminology in the past.

theory because it argues that punishment is justified only if it brings about the benefits of deterring aggressors. However, it is not necessarily a consequentialist theory—and, indeed, its major proponents defend it as a non-consequentialist theory. This is because the societal-defense theory can hold that using force against an innocent is impermissible no matter what good consequences would come from doing so, and that the use of force against the aggressor is permissible *only* because of their forfeiture of rights against punishment through voluntary engagement in moral wrongdoing directed against the victim. Understood in this way, the societal-defense view could be a non-consequentialist harm-reduction theory of punishment.

Second, consequentialist theories need not be non-retributive. To see this, recall that, unlike utilitarianism, consequentialist theories are not wedded to the idea that the good consists in happiness or welfare. As we saw, consequentialists can agree with those critics of utilitarianism who say that happiness is too narrow to capture all the inherently good consequences that we should aim to produce. It is possible, in particular on a pluralistic form of consequentialism, that one of the good consequences a theory might recognize is what Kant called the "highest good"—the situation in which happiness aligns most perfectly with virtue, and unhappiness with vice. Yet this position would be a retributive one, since it would regard these alignments as non-instrumentally good (for examples, see Feldman 1995; Kagan 2012).

The discussion in this section has proceeded at a very general level. But this is with good reason. Applied to punishment, we can see that, beyond simply looking at whether punishment brings about good consequences, it is impossible to specify what a consequentialist theory of punishment would say without taking a particular position on a range of further questions. To produce an informative consequentialist theory, one would need to specify what the relevant good (and bad) consequences are, such that we can investigate whether and how, and the extent to which punishment brings about those consequences. It will need to specify whether we are to evaluate the consequences of individual acts of punishment, a social practice of punishment, social attitudes about punishment, or a formal institution of punishment. It will need to decide whether evaluations of expected consequences are sufficient, and if so, which levels of probability, risk, and opportunity are relevant to such evaluation. And it will need to decide whether punishment can be justified only if it is optimal or whether it could be justified as long as it produces some sufficient amount of good. Furthermore, it goes without saying that a consequentialist theory of punishment will need to settle on these positions for good rather than morally arbitrary reasons, and thus that the positions taken should not be ad hoc. A consequentialist theory would be abolitionist if its theory of the good is such that punishment fails to contribute optimally to the production of that good. It would conclude that punishment is right if there is good empirical evidence that punishment does help to produce the relevant good (better than any alternative and without sufficiently serious negative side effects). But this will all depend on how the consequentialist theory is further specified. The mere fact that it is a consequentialist theory does not settle these further specifications. A survey of all the possibilities for consequentialist theories and their comparative advantages and disadvantages is far beyond the scope of this chapter.

4 Four Objections to the Consequentialist Approach to Punishment

The level of indeterminacy with which we are left makes it difficult to make a general assessment of consequentialist theories of punishment. Nevertheless, the possibility remains that there are some objections to consequentialist theories of punishment simply by virtue of those very basic commitments that make those theories consequentialist. As I said in the introduction, I will be looking at four such candidate criticisms that are current in the literature on philosophy of punishment.

The first criticism says that consequentialist theories allow for the punishment of the innocent. Yet, the criticism assumes, the punishment of the innocent is always unjustifiable. Therefore, the criticism concludes that consequentialist theories are unacceptable. The argument for the first premise often proceeds by illustration. Imagine a situation in which a mob seeks vengeance against a perceived wrongdoer, X, for a perceived wrong. If nothing is done to satisfy the mob, it is highly likely to wreak havoc, causing significant loss of life and property. The chief of police is aware that the person who is the object of the mob's wrath is innocent. As it happens, however, it is possible for the chief of police to frame X in such a way that only the chief and X will know that X has been framed. The chief can destroy any evidence of the framing, so it will never come to light and harm the credibility of the justice system. Looking only at the consequences of the alternatives, it seems as though the police chief should weigh up how bad it would be if the mob were not pacified (very bad indeed if it is likely to involve multiple deaths) against how bad it would be for the innocent X to be framed and punished (very bad for X, but not so bad as the loss of life).

This consequentialist verdict has been widely taken to be deeply counterintuitive and unacceptable. While many people may nod along to the thought that there is some sense in which being punished for something one did not do is not so bad as the loss of life, there remains the thought that poor X has not done anything to bring this on themselves. To develop this intuitive view, we might say that we tend to take it that people have a right to be left alone, at least in regard to punishment, unless they commit some wrongdoing whereby that right is forfeited (Wellman 2012). Until such time as an agent commits some significant wrong, each agent has a right against punishment that functions decisively to take the option of punishing them off the table (Husak 2007). The right functions, as it were, as a protection against punishment that can only be lost by the specific action of committing wrongdoing. The consequentialist, so the charge goes, cannot accommodate such rights against punishment. While the consequentialist might bite the bullet and argue that punishment of the innocent can be justified, this would add fuel to the concern that consequentialist theories like utilitarianism neglect the individual in their concern for overall impersonal good.

The second criticism is that consequentialism allows people to be treated as mere means (Duff 1986; Tadros 2011). This is related to the previous criticism. It might be said that punishing an innocent person is a prime case of treating a person as a mere means. The innocent X is used in a certain way to avoid the terrible outcome of the mob rioting, where that involves subjecting X to framing and punishment. The emphasis on being treated as a *mere* means is important. There is in general nothing wrong with using a person for all sorts of ends: using the shopkeeper to get yourself the ingredients for dinner, using the bus driver to get you to work, using another person's body for sexual pleasure, and so on. The problem comes when someone is treated as a *mere* means, as this involves that person being treated as if their *only* value or significance stems from the use that can be made of them in bringing about the desired outcome. To put it another way, the problem comes when a person is treated as having only instrumental or use-value as opposed to intrinsic value. In this sense, X is treated as expendable, as a being whose loss can be substituted or compensated for by gains elsewhere, rather than as something irreplaceable. To treat someone as irreplaceable involves, among other things, treating them as having a decisive right against punishment that can only be forfeited by voluntary wrongdoing. To properly value persons is to recognize certain constraints on the way persons are to be treated. This could be thought of as an interpretation of John Rawls's (1971) claim that utilitarianism neglects the separateness of persons: that these constraints arise because each person is to be treated as valuable in their own right, and thus, as it were, given separate consideration.

The third criticism says that consequentialism fails to respect offenders (and others) as moral agents. This again is connected to the previous points, and in particular the charge that consequentialism does not recognize rights against punishment, or the special significance of wrongdoing as the forfeiture of such a right. One way of developing this criticism would be to say that consequentialism does not recognize the importance of the distinction between guilt and innocence. This alleged feature of the consequentialist approach gives rise to the criticism that the consequentialist wrongly thinks that the innocent may be punished in the same way as the guilty; fails to give proper weight to the moral nature of crime; fails to recognize the difference in significance between those harms that are wrongs and those harms that are not wrongs; and fails to give proper respect to the offender as an agent who has normative competence to take responsibility for acting rightly. We could again treat this point as having two premises: the first premise points out that consequentialism gives no special place to the moral nature of crime and the moral capacities of the offender, and then the second premiss claims that a failure to give a special place to these considerations is unacceptable. The conclusion is drawn that the consequentialist account is unacceptable.

For instance, P. F. Strawson (1962) draws attention to the fact that we react quite differently to a harmful act, such as someone standing on one's hand, depending on whether we view that act as having been intentional or accidental (see also Darwall 2006). Both acts may be the same in terms of the harm they cause, but the presence or absence of intention accounts for the difference. Followers of Strawson have argued that this shows that bad "quality of will" is to be responded to non-instrumentally. Yet this conclusion, according to this third criticism, is incompatible with the consequentialist approach, which sees all such responses as justifiable only in terms of whether they lead to those states of affairs designated as the good. If the consequentialist approach does not give special importance to responses that target the moral nature of wrongdoing, the criticism might proceed, it likewise does not give special importance to the moral capacities of persons. Yet, the criticism claims, moral agency is one of the valuable capacities that ground the distinctive value of human beings (and any other creatures that possess it). This moral agency calls for a distinctive kind of recognition or treatment, one that does justice to the identity of the person as a moral agent. So, a failure to take seriously the moral nature of the crime is not simply an impersonal wrong, and it does not simply let down the victim; it also wrongs the offender, who is not given a kind of respect that is their due.[5]

The fourth criticism also picks up a theme in Strawson's work. Strawson was interested in what he called "reactive attitudes"—reactive in the sense that they are attitudes to the attitudes of others (Strawson 1962). Reactive attitudes are such things as resentment and indignation, but also love and forgiveness (if forgiveness is an attitude). These attitudes, Strawson thinks, are a central part of our accountability practices. He clearly thinks that reactive attitudes are related to punishment, though they extend significantly beyond punishment. The reactive attitudes are partly constitutive of our accountability practices, which Strawson thinks of as exhibiting a non-instrumental concern with others' quality of will.[6] Central to Strawson's vindication of these reactive attitudes is an argument that they are partly constitutive of a certain valuable mode of interpersonal relations—the "participant" stance—in which people care non-instrumentally about the quality of the relationships they have with others and the quality of will others adopt to them.

Strawson contrasts this participant stance with what he calls the "objective attitude" (1962, 194). In the objective attitude, it is not a person's identity as a responsible moral agent that is foregrounded in determining how they are to be treated. Rather, people are to be treated in whatever way best brings about the desired modification of their behavior, and the approach we take to a person is governed only by instrumental considerations. Strawson's claim was that if we abandoned the participant stance and our interpersonal dealings were governed only by the objective attitude, human life would be seriously impoverished.

In his portrayal of the objective attitude, Strawson seems to have had in mind the insistence of consequentialist or specifically utilitarian approaches that only instrumental considerations count toward justification. Strawson was pointing out that there is immense value to human life in the fact that we engage in non-consequentialist reasoning about our relations with one another, and that we do not let consequentialist considerations govern our dealings. Here the concern is that the objective attitude overlooks and/or displaces alternative ways of responding to wrongdoing that have value in themselves, and that value would be lost if the consequentialist approach were adopted.

[5] For some discussion and reconstruction of this Strawsonian approach, see Bennett (2008, ch. 3).

[6] It is also possible that there are reactive attitudes directed to one's own quality of will, or that of one's past self.

5 Lines of Consequentialist Response

Do these criticisms point to serious weaknesses in the consequentialist approach to punishment? These criticisms might be good objections to a utilitarian form of consequentialism. Utilitarianism holds that seeking to bring about a significant reduction in future harm, or a correlative increase in welfare, is the only response that matters in response to wrongdoing; and it takes it that such a reduction can be sufficient to make an action (or practice, institution, etc.) right, no matter whether the agent it is imposed on is guilty or innocent. However, as we have seen, there are non-utilitarian forms of consequentialism. So, are these good criticisms of consequentialism in general? Let us consider a number of strategies that are open to the consequentialist by way of response. In doing so, we will be drawing on the survey of resources available to consequentialism that we conducted in parts 2 and 3.

5.1 Catholicism about the Good

This is "catholicism" with a lower-case 'c.' By this I mean that the consequentialist can have as broad a view of the good as seems to be justified by whatever evidence we have in such matters. As we noted, while utilitarianism is a form of consequentialism for which only happiness is good, other forms of consequentialism might be more catholic. Thus, if it seems that one or other set of the criticisms noted above is successful, and that it points out the inadequacy of that utilitarian approach, the answer might be to broaden our conception of the good rather than abandoning consequentialism.

Let us suppose, for instance, that we are persuaded by the considerations above that it is genuinely problematic that utilitarianism seems to have no fundamental role for the distinction between guilt and innocence. In response, it might be argued that, rather than showing that consequentialism is flawed, this only shows that our axiology should include something like retributive justice or desert. That is, perhaps we should recognize that it is an intrinsically good state of affairs when those who are good are rewarded with happiness and those who are bad are punished with unhappiness. A corollary might then be recognizing that it is an intrinsically bad state of affairs when the opposite happens, and thus when the bad profit from their wrongdoing while the innocent suffer through it. Another possibility is that, if we are persuaded that consequentialism overlooks the intrinsic importance of rights, moral agency, or individuality, we should amend our axiology to include the idea that it is an intrinsically valuable state of affairs when people have their rights, dignity as a moral agent, or individual value recognized. This is a possibility recognized by Robert Nozick in his reflections on a "utilitarianism of rights" (1974, 28).

Similarly, if we are persuaded by Strawson that human life would be impoverished if people took seriously only the goal of promoting happiness and reducing harm—that is, if the pursuit of this goal excluded the possibility of a valuable sort of interpersonal relationship—then again the correct answer to this criticism might be that this shows, not that we should abandon consequentialism, but that we should revise our understanding of the goods we seek to promote. We might, for instance, think that the state of affairs in which human beings have the kinds of relationships that Strawson depicts is precisely one of the things that is intrinsically valuable and that we should seek to bring about. This catholicism about the good allows the consequentialist to argue that the critic seems to be pointing to ways in which life would be impoverished if everyone adopted the utilitarian view, and then to resist the criticism by agreeing that ends other than happiness are (also) intrinsically important.

5.2 Going Indirect

Another approach that the consequentialist might take is to argue that the good consequentialist agent appeals to consequentialism only *indirectly* in their decision-making about how to act. To see the point here, we need to distinguish two ways in which consequentialism can be understood (Bales 1971). As I introduced it above, consequentialism can be understood as a criterion of evaluation. It tells us whether the institutions we have, or the actions we have performed, are the right ones to have. According to the consequentialist, they are the right ones only if they bring about (or maximize) the good. Thus, as a *criterion of rightness*, consequentialism says: an act/practice/institution is right only if it brings about (or maximizes) the good. However, plausibly, this is not the only thing that we might want from a normative theory. Another role that consequentialism could play is as a *decision procedure*. A decision procedure is what we need when we are faced with a situation that calls for a decision, and we are unsure what to do for the best. The decision procedure would be a rule that we could consult. If consequentialism is a decision procedure, then it says: always act so as to bring about the good. From these two statements, we can see the difference between the approaches. The criterion of rightness tells us what is right but does not tell us what to do; we would have to supplement the criterion of rightness in order to have a rule for action. The decision procedure interpretation does tell us what to do.

Now this distinction might seem a bit obscure, even pointless. Isn't the obvious way to get a decision procedure from the criterion of rightness just to frame it as the decision procedure interpretation does? If this was the case, then the distinction would indeed be unimportant. However, consequentialists have come to think that this distinction is very important, and that is precisely because they (or at least some of them) have come to think that the right way to get a decision procedure from the criterion of rightness is not to state it in the way the decision procedure interpretation does. Why? Well, this is because these consequentialists agree with some of their critics in concluding that human life would be impoverished in various ways if people were always and only motivated by a concern to produce the most overall good that they could. To point to just one problem, people who were always attempting to follow the rule "always act so as to do the most good" would forever be calculating before they act. As Strawson points out, this calculating "objective attitude," if universalized, does not look to be compatible with the kind of relations that many of us would wish to have with other human beings.

However, the indirect consequentialist can argue, in that case we have an example of a situation in which following the decision procedure leads to a loss of the good. And if following the decision procedure leads to a loss of the good, then, according to consequentialism, it surely cannot be right to adopt it (Railton 1984). To avoid the conclusion that consequentialism is self-contradictory (recommending both that we do and do not act always to maximize the good), the consequentialist can remain neutral on the question of which decision procedure to adopt. This is not to say that consequentialism can do away with a decision procedure. Of course, people need to know how to act. But the consequentialist should agree that it is in part an empirical question the following of which rule of action (in which set of circumstances, or which kind of society, etc.) will produce the most overall good. The choice of decision procedure is itself one of the things that we should submit to consequentialist evaluation, just as with any other action. The crucial thing is that the consequentialist can a) agree with Strawson that interpersonal relations characterized by the reactive attitudes are intrinsically valuable; and b) deny that consequentialists are committed to the calculating "objective attitude."

5.3 Turning the Criticism Around

We can now bring out a point that has been implicit in the previous two lines of consequentialist defense. This is that the consequentialist can seek to argue that at least some of the influential criticisms that have been made of consequentialism turn out themselves to reveal the validity of some version of consequentialism. Such criticisms, it can be said, are thus better understood as criticisms of one version of consequentialism from the perspective of another version of consequentialism. For instance, it might be said that the criticism about punishing the innocent, if valid, simply shows the intrinsic value of retributive justice and desert. The criticism about people being treated as mere means, if valid, simply shows the intrinsic value of a state of affairs in which people relate to one another as having something more than merely use-value, and the impoverishment of human relations that are based solely on use. The criticism about moral agency, if valid, shows the intrinsic value of a state of affairs in which people give one another's moral competences a high degree of importance. The criticisms put forward by Strawson show the intrinsic value of a state of affairs in which people have relationships and they care about one another's quality of will, and acts are taken seriously for the quality of will they express.

There are other important versions of the same move. For instance, consequentialism has been criticized for its totalizing quality, and it has been argued that its neglect of individuals is tied up with this totalizing, aggregative approach. Because it is concerned with overall consequences (either in a limited or unlimited sense), consequentialism has appeared to some to have no room for the value of the individual, considered qua individual. Rawls (1971) famously expressed this thought in relation to utilitarianism by saying that it did not recognize the "separateness of individuals." Thus the criticism has been put forward that this concern with overall consequences might, for instance, lead us to sacrifice the rights or interests of a particular individual, or some minority, if mistreating those parties were the way to bring about the optimal outcome. For instance, maybe society would produce the greatest amount of happiness, knowledge, and aesthetic attainment if a small minority were enslaved and made to serve the majority through menial tasks. The lesson Rawls draws from this is that, rather than simply having a concern with maximizing the overall amount of good (or as with utilitarianism, the overall amount of happiness), morality requires us to think about the *distribution* of those consequences, such as some notion of fair shares, or fair opportunity.

However, it is unclear whether this is really a good criticism of consequentialism as such, even if it is a good criticism of utilitarianism. After all, the fair distribution of benefits (and burdens) or social cooperation picks out a certain state of affairs, something entirely compatible with the consequentialist way of thinking. Thus, what Rawls seems to be saying is that the state of affairs in which there is a fair distribution of benefits is a better one than one in which the total amount of benefit is greater but the distribution unfair. Rawls's point may be better understood as an argument that the optimal consequence at which we should be aiming is not simply that in which there is the greatest amount of good, but rather one in which that good is distributing in a certain way—that is, in the way specified by Rawls's principles of justice (Nozick 1974). Whatever the accuracy of Rawls's criticism, both sides of the argument seem to accept that it is an end-state (or a state of affairs, an outcome) that we ought to be guided by, and the question is only which outcome is most desirable. This apparent criticism of consequentialism can thus be turned around and claimed to reveal the truth of consequentialism.

6 Assessing the Debate

So, should the critics of consequentialism be impressed by these responses? It might seem that these lines of consequentialist response give the critics much of what they were concerned about. Nevertheless, we should bear in mind that there are many variants of consequentialism, as we noted in part 2, and that the consequentialist responses that we have just been canvassing may not be available to all of them. Furthermore, it may be that the version of consequentialism that is most plausible in terms of responding to these criticisms is not the most plausible overall: perhaps, for instance, it would be subject to other failings by virtue of the features that make it able to respond to these criticisms; or perhaps it would fail to be true to the spirit, or basic commitments, of consequentialism.

One potential problem is that the responses that we have outlined above, on behalf of the consequentialist, are entirely provisional. For instance, we have imagined that the consequentialist might be able to acknowledge the distinction between guilt and innocence if they incorporate a commitment to retributive justice or desert into their axiology. However, does this mean that, practically speaking, a consequentialist theory would never judge it right to punish the innocent? Not so fast. Unlike the deontological and relational theorist opponents introduced at the start, the consequentialist takes no options off the table in advance. They keep open the option to punish the innocent if, in some situation, it is optimal to do so. The best that the consequentialist can offer, in response to the "punishing the innocent" criticism, is the claim that punishing the innocent is highly unlikely to be optimal. But this would need to be worked through. Whether punishing the innocent is sub-optimal will depend on: a) what other intrinsic values should be recognized in our axiology; b) which of these intrinsic values are at play in the situation at hand, and whether their satisfaction conflicts with the satisfaction of the demands of retributive justice; and c) how the intrinsic values are to be weighted in the situation. It is at least possible that things would so fall out, in a particular situation, that the act or rule or practice of framing the innocent is the right one. It is a feature of consequentialism that it takes nothing off the table in advance of the calculation of trade-offs and the costs and benefits of different options. What is right depends entirely on the context.

For many, this is an unacceptable conclusion. Like the deontologists and relational theorists, many people think that certain actions, or more broadly certain ways of treating persons, represent a line in the sand, not to be crossed. One way of putting this might be to say that the correct way to value human beings is to respect them, where this means precisely to exclude certain ways in which we can treat them, or certain options involving them. For instance, one interpretation of Kant's view is that rational agency has an intrinsic value such that it must be respected, where respect means that rational agents are never to be treated as a mere means. The view here is something like the idea that a moral tie exists between each rational agent and any other, whereby certain options are excluded *a priori*. This is what Kant calls the Kingdom of Ends. The Kingdom of Ends, on the non-consequentialist view, is not simply an intrinsically valuable state of affairs in which people respect one another; it is a constraint on the agency of each member as a result of the intrinsic value of the rational agency of each member. While the precise way to articulate the nature of these constraints is debated (see, e.g., Kamm 2007; Øverland 2014; Walen 2016), it is a commitment to the existence of such constraints that is one of the distinguishing features of non-consequentialism.

The consequentialist will insist that theirs is the correct position. The non-consequentialist insistence on moral constraints has well-known problems. For instance, can we not imagine cases in which the consequences of not punishing an innocent person would be so catastrophic that almost everyone would agree that punishing the innocent was the thing to do? And if so, does that not show the correctness of the consequentialist position that everything should be left on the table? Furthermore, there could be cases in which a failure to punish one innocent person would lead to more innocent people being punished. Would it not be self-defeating for someone committed to the wrongness of punishing the innocent to refuse to recognize that the right thing to do in such a situation would be to punish one innocent person in order to prevent a greater number of such violations? In response, the non-consequentialist can insist that the nature of moral prohibitions is not simply a matter of looking at things from an impartial or "agent-neutral" perspective, and minimizing the number of wrongs that occur in the world. Such prohibitions, it might be said, derive from the irreplaceability of each rational agent and, as with the Kantian view sketched above, are constraints on the agency of each agent in relation to each agent. If the way in which rational agents are valuable is such as to issue in a moral demand that they always be treated as irreplaceable, then the punishment of one innocent person can never be compensated for by the prevention of such violations elsewhere. Morality, on this non-consequentialist view, puts us each in mutual relation and demands that in all our actions we treat each other person with the required respect.

So, can the non-consequentialist simply wash their hands of the terrible consequences that might come of complying with these moral constraints? Should non-consequentialists agree that it would never be the thing to do to violate these constraints? Surely this also seems unacceptable, and the consequentialist might get on top of the argument again by claiming that their view rightly tells us to take the least bad option in such very difficult situations. However, this reveals a further important feature of consequentialism. What the non-consequentialist can do at this point is to refuse to agree that either option is right, and to insist that whatever one does in such a situation is wrong. For the non-consequentialist, some options are morally unthinkable, and it is a kind of moral disaster to be placed in a situation in which one has to deal with them (Williams 1973; Gaita 1999). Therefore, the non-consequentialist can recognize moral dilemma situations in which whatever one does is wrong. By contrast, the consequentialist is committed to there being no moral dilemmas, there being nothing that is genuinely morally unthinkable, and the least bad option always being the right one. Which side of the debate has it right I now leave to the reader to decide, but I hope to have given some sense of how the debates in this area proceed.[7]

A final point to bear in mind is that the criticisms that we have considered in this chapter do not exhaust the problems that have been laid at the door of consequentialism. For instance, a consequentialist theory needs to explain

[7] There are further moves in the debate, for instance, where the consequentialist may try to argue that even the idea of agent-relative constraints can be accommodated in a form of consequentialism. However, this may lead to the charge that the term "consequentialism" is no longer being used for a distinctive normative approach. For an attempt to define consequentialism in the face of this "consequentializing" move, see Brown (2011).

how we compare the consequences of the alternatives open to us and assess which is most beneficial. At some level, therefore, consequentialism is committed to the importance of measurement, or at least the rational comparison of options. And it is committed to this being possible and acceptable in all situations that we want to evaluate, and presumably also in quite a fine-grained way. But is this possible? This point has a number of aspects. A consequentialist theory's understanding of good consequences needs to function as a metric through which we can reach an evaluation of which course of action/practice/institution would be best. But can (all) goods be measured in the way that this would require? It might have appeared plausible to Bentham that pleasure could be measured, since pleasure, he assumed, was ultimately a simple mental state. But the more catholic or pluralistic we are about the good, the more complex such measurement becomes—and perhaps, the more difficult it becomes to see how it might be possible to say that a loss in one type of good is worth it given the gains in another.

For instance, assume for a moment that both retributive justice and fair equality of opportunity are intrinsically valuable. Say we are also in a social situation in which, because of the foreseeable effect of our punitive practices on already socially excluded communities, our pursuit of retributive justice is detrimental to fair equality of opportunity. The consequentialist approach assumes that there is an answer to this question—that there are no unanswerable moral dilemmas in which whatever one does is wrong. It is simply a question, for the consequentialist, of thinking through the trade-offs sufficiently carefully and thoroughly. But how do we determine what the answer is? What does deliberation or calculation about such a question even look like? Even if such value trade-offs could *in principle* be measured, are *we* realistically able to measure them? Since acts continue to have effects indefinitely into the future, is the idea of a "consequence" simply too open-ended to say with any precision whether the consequences were good or bad (Lenman 2000)? And given that the "goods" we should be aiming to bring about may be neither unitary nor simple, how do we rank, for example, peace against justice—or the particular kind of peace that we might be able to bring about in a given situation against the particular kind of justice—in order to provide an overall justification for prioritizing one over the other? The consequentialist appears to be committed to there being intelligible answers to these questions, but whether that is plausible is, again, a question I leave to the reader for further investigation.

7 Conclusion

In this chapter, I have reviewed four interrelated criticisms that have been put forward against consequentialist theories of punishment. I have shown the complexity of consequentialism and the range of resources available to theories that share a fundamentally consequentialist structure. On the basis of this survey of consequentialist possibilities, I have concluded that the criticisms in question could plausibly be thought of as criticisms of one type of consequentialism rather than criticisms of consequentialist approaches as such. Nevertheless, this line of defense is not the end of the matter. As we have seen, there is something in the deontological and relational views that is hard to capture on the agent-neutral consequentialist view. Whether what is not captured is morally important is not something I have attempted to give a final verdict on here.

Our discussion might give rise to a concern that there is no longer anything important at stake in the debate over consequentialism. What we have seen, in effect, is that consequentialism can be expanded to accommodate many of the objections that have been made of utilitarianism. There are important questions about what our axiology ought to be, and about priorities among values, and so on, but these are settled within a consequentialist (or non-consequentialist) theory and are not part of the substance of the debate between consequentialism and its opponents. The effect of this might appear to be that consequentialism no longer represents a distinctive and clearly defined alternative moral vision. Whereas utilitarianism, at least in its early days, clearly put forward a distinctive moral approach that one might be for or against, consequentialism now looks so capacious that the difference between consequentialism and non-consequentialism might appear of much less significance than the differences among particular versions of consequentialism.

Nevertheless, the claim that only consequences matter to moral evaluation *is* highly ambitious, at least in one respect. There are clearly many non-consequentialist moral possibilities that the consequentialist view rules out. And a claim like Philip Pettit's, that the correct response to any value is to seek to promote it, rules out the possibility that the correct response to some values is to respect them, to appreciate them, or simply to acknowledge and bear witness to them. Seen in this way, consequentialism asserts an ambitious generalization. And this raises a final question for our consideration: what grounds does the consequentialist have for thinking that this generalization would be true? By this, I do not mean what normative arguments might a theorist offer for their particular version of consequentialism. My concern is rather at a more abstract level: how compatible is the claim that only consequences matter with what we know about the nature of moral reality and moral epistemology? The utilitarian had a clear answer to this question, but the shift from utilitarianism to consequentialism means that this answer is no longer available.

Utilitarians could claim that their view is likely to be correct since it is securely grounded in tangible effects on welfare. Claims about welfare, they could argue, are claims about real properties in the world and on which we have a good cognitive grip. Welfare clearly matters; it could be claimed to be self-evidently valuable. Welfare can be tested and measured. Welfare could be seen as a universal human concern, providing a way of evaluating diverse cultural practices. The utilitarian could claim their view to be on a firmer ontological and epistemological foundation than claims about relationships, dignity, and rights. Such claims, they could say, simply reflect our emotions, or socially constructed practices and conventions. They are merely matters of intuition, and intuition, by comparison with tangible measurements of welfare, is not to be trusted. While many will doubt that this utilitarian story is plausible, it does at least explain why it could be reasonable to believe that only consequences for welfare matter.

With the move away from utilitarianism, however, consequentialist theories can no longer deploy such a story. Non-utilitarian consequentialists assert the validity of values other than welfare—such as retributive justice. But unlike welfare, these values cannot be claimed to matter self-evidently. Like their non-consequentialist opponents, non-utilitarian consequentialists must appeal to intuition to defend their views about these "intangible" values. (Furthermore, it is surely intuition that underpins Pettit's claim that value is always only to be promoted.) As a result, consequentialists are in the same position as everyone else, trying to assess, by our best available methods, which intuitions are misleading and which are valid. And this raises the question why, if we no longer have the utilitarian story, we should expect the result that only consequences matter. Once we are no longer thinking of "consequences" as especially tangible in the way that welfare might be thought to be, it is unclear why, of all the things that might be morally relevant, it is only consequences that are. There is not an obvious reason why consequences as such should have any such special status. An important question to ask about consequentialism is thus whether it has any explanation about why we should expect its ambitious generalization to hold. While there is not space here to explore that question in any depth, we might conclude that a more reasonable approach is to remain open-minded on this question, and to see where the progress of moral inquiry takes us.[8]

References

Bales, R. Eugene. 1971. "Act-Utilitarianism: Account of Right-Making Characteristics or Decision-Making Procedure?" *American Philosophical Quarterly* 8, no. 3 (July): 257–65.

Bennett, Christopher. 2008. *The Apology Ritual: A Philosophical Theory of Punishment.* Cambridge, MA: Cambridge University Press.

Berman, Mitchell N. 2010. "Two Kinds of Retributivism." In *Philosophical Foundations of Criminal Law*, edited by R. A. Duff and Stuart Green, 433–57. Oxford: Oxford University Press.

Brown, Campbell. 2011. "Consequentialize This." *Ethics* 121, no. 4 (July): 749–71.

Darwall, Stephen. 2006. *The Second-Person Standpoint: Morality, Respect, and Accountability*. Cambridge, MA: Harvard University Press.

Duff, R. A. 1986. *Trials and Punishments*. Cambridge: Cambridge University Press.

Farrell, Daniel M. 1985. "The Justification of General Deterrence." *Philosophical Review* 94, no. 3 (July): 367–94.

Feldman, Fred. 1995. "Adjusting Utility for Justice: A Consequentialist Reply to the Objection from Justice." *Philosophy and Phenomenological Research* 55, no. 3 (September): 567–85.

Gaita, Raimond. 1999. *A Common Humanity: Thinking about Love and Truth and Justice*. Abingdon, UK: Routledge.

Husak, Douglas. 2007. *Overcriminalization: The Limits of the Criminal Law*. Oxford: Oxford University Press.

Kagan, Shelly. 2012. *The Geometry of Desert*. Oxford: Oxford University Press.

Kamm, F. M. 2007. *Intricate Ethics: Rights, Responsibilities, and Permissible Harm.* Oxford: Oxford University Press.

Lenman, James. 2000. "Consequentialism and Cluelessness." *Philosophy & Public Affairs* 29, no. 4 (Autumn): 342–70.

Montague, Phillip. 1983. "Punishment and Societal Defense." *Criminal Justice Ethics* 2, no. 1: 30–36.

Nozick, Robert. 1974. *Anarchy, State, and Utopia*. New York: Basic.

Øverland, Gerhard. 2014. "Moral Obstacles: An Alternative to the Doctrine of Double Effect." *Ethics* 124, no. 3 (April): 481–506.

Pettit, Philip. 1991. "Consequentialism." In *A Companion to Ethics*, edited by Peter Singer, 230–40. Oxford: Blackwell.

[8] For helpful comments on a previous version, I am grateful to Sebastian Pineda Herrera.

Railton, Peter. 1984. "Alienation, Consequentialism and the Demands of Morality." *Philosophy & Public Affairs* 13, no. 2 (Spring): 134–71.

Rawls, John. 1955. "Two Concepts of Rules." *Philosophical Review* 64, no. 1 (January): 3–32.

———. 1971. *A Theory of Justice*. Cambridge, MA: Belknap.

Scheffler, Samuel. 1982. *The Rejection of Consequentialism: A Philosophical Investigation of the Considerations Underlying Rival Moral Conceptions*. Oxford: Clarendon.

Sinnott-Armstrong, Walter. 2019. "Consequentialism." *Stanford Encyclopedia of Philosophy* (Fall 2021 edition), edited by Edward N. Zalta. https://plato.stanford.edu/archives/fall2021/entries/consequentialism/.

Slote, Michael, and Philip Pettit. 1984. "Satisficing Consequentialism." *Proceedings of the Aristotelian Society* 58: 139–76.

Smart, J. J. C., and Bernard Williams. 1973. *Utilitarianism: For and Against*. Cambridge: Cambridge University Press.

Strawson, P. F. 1962. "Freedom and Resentment." *Proceedings of the British Academy* 48: 1–25.

Tadros, Victor. 2011. *The Ends of Harm*. Oxford: Oxford University Press.

Walen, Alec. 2016. "The Restricting Claims Principle Revisited: Grounding the Means Principle on the Agent-Patient Divide." *Law and Philosophy* 35, no. 2 (April): 211–47.

Wallace, R. Jay. 2019. *The Moral Nexus*. Princeton, NJ: Princeton University Press.

Wellman, Christopher Heath. 2012. "The Rights Forfeiture Theory of Punishment." *Ethics* 122, no. 2 (January): 371–93.

Williams, Bernard. 1973. "A Critique of Utilitarianism." In *Utilitarianism: For and Against*, by J. J. C. Smart and Bernard Williams, 75–150. Cambridge: Cambridge University Press.

Wood, David. 2010. "Punishment: Consequentialism." *Philosophy Compass* 5, no. 6 (June): 455–69.

9

In Defense of a Mixed Theory of Punishment

Matthew C. Altman

The debate over how to justify legal punishment has been dominated by two theories: consequentialism, represented historically by Cesare Beccaria and Jeremy Bentham; and retributivism, represented historically by Immanuel Kant and G. W. F. Hegel. Despite the existence of other approaches, most philosophers still presuppose either that punishment must deter and rehabilitate criminals and potential criminals in order to protect society or that it should give criminals what they deserve, either in addition to or regardless of its social utility. Although these aims seem to be mutually exclusive, H. L. A. Hart explained how the two theories can be incorporated into the same legal system, if only we distinguish the "*General Justifying Aim*" of punishment as an institution from its "*Distribution*" to specific criminals (2008, 3–4). If neither consequentialism nor retributivism is sufficient on its own, then Hart's distinction provides the path forward to formulate a mixed or hybrid theory that draws on the strengths of both views while avoiding their pitfalls, such as punishing innocents (a problem with consequentialism) and inflicting useless suffering on those who deserve it (a problem with retributivism).

In a recent monograph (Altman 2021), I argued that criminal laws and statutory penalties are (or ought to be) justified on consequentialist grounds.

M. C. Altman (✉)
Central Washington University, Ellensburg, WA, USA
e-mail: matthew.altman@cwu.edu

© The Author(s), under exclusive license to Springer Nature Switzerland AG 2023

M. C. Altman (ed.), *The Palgrave Handbook on the Philosophy of Punishment*, Palgrave Handbooks in the Philosophy of Law, https://doi.org/10.1007/978-3-031-11874-6_9

They should be created and enforced to further the aims of the state and preserve the public order through general and specific deterrence, rehabilitation, and incapacitation. For example, in a liberal state, where the purpose of government is to protect people's rights, the law should deter people from violating others' rights and it should be enforced to make the threat credible—a consequentialism of rights. By contrast, the criminal judiciary should be retributivist. In determining whether the defendant committed the crime (*actus reus*) and did it intentionally or knowingly (*mens rea*), judges and juries should not be concerned with whether the punishment would deter others or reform the criminal. The defendant is punished if and only if they are (believed to be) guilty, and in proportion to their degree of guilt. By giving individual offenders what they deserve, criminal courts express the community's justified feeling of resentment at having been wronged.

The correct theory of legal punishment should thus be mixed, with the institution of punishment—statutory offenses and penalties—warranted by its costs and benefits, and the distribution of punishment—who is punished and how much—warranted by what offenders deserve. I call this the two-tiered model of punishment because two theories—consequentialism and retributivism—are plugged into an organizing structure that tracks, respectively, the guiding principles of the legislature and the criminal judiciary (Fig. 9.1). The legislature acts rightly if it effectively advances the state's aims and if the state's aims are just. Criminological research into the effectiveness of punishment and other correctional practices gives us a standard against

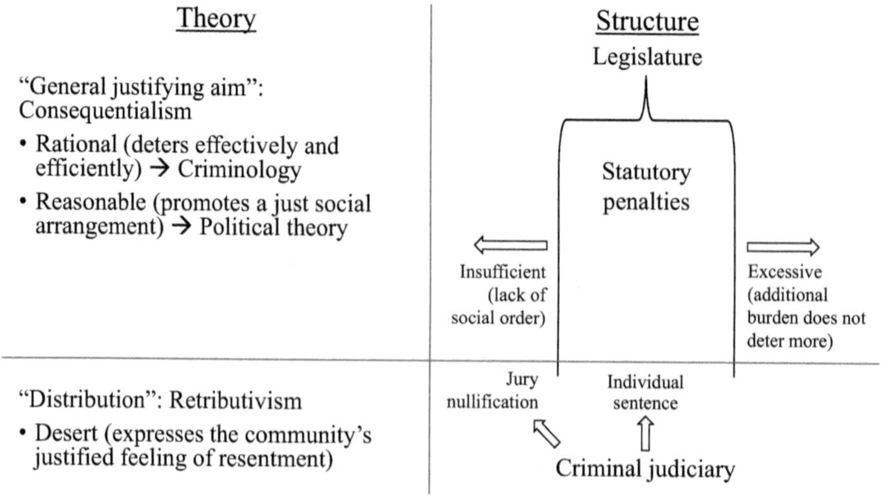

Fig. 9.1 The two-tiered model of punishment

which to judge whether such policies are rational. If political theory can provide insight into which social arrangement is just (or more just than the live alternatives), then the legislature's pursuit of that aim by means of punishment is also reasonable. If a just government protects the rights of its citizens, for example, punishment under the criminal law would be justified insofar as it protects people's rights and does so with the least amount of harm. By contrast, in criminal courts, verdicts and sentences are justified by retribution—that is, if our resentment is justified (i.e., the accused is guilty) and the imposed burdens are proportional to the strength of the resentment, which is correlated with the gravity of the criminal conduct (i.e., the punishment is deserved). Punishment options are not available to judges and juries if they impose excessive harm or burdens on offenders—that is, if they go unreasonably beyond what advances the just social order.[1]

Justifying my specific version of a mixed theory requires separate arguments for consequentialism and retributivism as well as an argument for why the two theories should be arranged along the lines of a traditional separation of powers. In *A Theory of Legal Punishment* (2021), I defended both consequentialism (41–53) and expressive retributivism (67–83), and I supported the two-tiered model with three different arguments: an epistemic argument (121–31), a compatibilist argument (132–42), and a moral argument (143–53). I do not attempt full-scale defenses of consequentialism and expressive retributivism in this chapter, nor do I repeat these three arguments. Instead, I give three additional arguments:

1. Consequentialism is insufficient on its own because it cannot capture the condemnatory function of the law as an expression of the community's resentment.
2. Retributivism is insufficient on its own because any plausible legal arrangement must be committed to some non-retributivist values.
3. Using retributivist reasoning for criminal lawmaking and consequentialist reasoning for criminal judgments and sentencing—the opposite of the two-tiered model—leads to absurd conclusions.

The first two arguments jointly demonstrate the need for a pluralistic view of legal punishment, and the third argument shows why the actions of the legislature and the criminal judiciary cannot be justified in the same way. The three arguments thus function interdependently; in isolation, none of them

---

[1] For a discussion of jury nullification as it functions in the two-tiered model, see Altman (2021, 199–200, 208–9).

would justify my mixed theory. While the first and second arguments taken individually seem to argue, respectively, for retributivism and consequentialism, taken together they justify the claim that both approaches must be incorporated into any complete theory of punishment. The third argument then entails that both theories inform different functions of the state, along the lines of the two-tiered model, with the general aim of punishment justified by its consequences and its distribution justified by what offenders deserve.

1 Argument #1: Backward-Looking Expressive Obligations

Many people are familiar with the dichotomy in normative ethics between consequentialist ethics and deontological ethics, typified by John Stuart Mill's utilitarianism and Immanuel Kant's duty-based theory. For Mill, we are bound by the principle of utility, which enjoins us to choose the action or policy that produces the most amount of pleasure, happiness, or satisfaction of preferences, or the least amount of pain, unhappiness, or dissatisfaction. The theory is forward-looking in the sense that only the outcome produced by an action or rule matters for assessing its morality. Thus, I should keep my promises because it will make people more likely to trust me in the future or because if we all keep promises, as a rule, then there will be stronger social cooperation—both of which are better states of affairs than the alternatives. By contrast, for Kant, the moral duties derived from the categorical imperative are right in themselves; a good will is intrinsically good. Kant evaluates the maxim, or principle of acting, rather than the action itself or what is produced as a result. In that sense, it is not forward-looking. For Kant, lying is wrong because, if I lie, I make an exception of myself by expecting everyone else generally to tell the truth, so that I am believed. When universalized, such a maxim is inconsistent and irrational. Some of our duties, such as the duty of fidelity, depend on a commitment that I made in the past: I ought to keep a promise because it is a moral duty to fulfill the obligation that I have taken on by making the promise (cf. Ross 2002, 21). For the Kantian deontological ethicist, the consequences of keeping the promise are morally irrelevant.

A similar dichotomy exists in the philosophy of law between consequentialism and retributivism. There are many versions of consequentialism, but all of them focus on the future: a utilitarian theory has the state punish people in order to maximize happiness, a consequentialism of rights punishes people in order to maximize rights protections, and a societal safety-valve theory punishes people in order to avoid blood feuds and other socially destructive forms of vigilante justice. This class of theories is forward-looking in the sense that they value reducing the harm caused by crime by deterring potential criminals (general deterrence) and deterring, reforming, or physically restraining actual criminals (specific deterrence, rehabilitation, and incapacitation, respectively). If punishing someone creates no benefit, for either the community or the wrongdoer, then it causes gratuitous suffering and would thus be wrong. For example, the fact that the death penalty does not deter more than life in prison and that the vast amounts of money spent on capital trials could be allocated to more effective crime-prevention efforts are good reasons to abolish capital punishment, even if we think that murderers deserve to die.

In the case of legal punishment at least, there are reasons to believe that forward-looking concerns do not exhaust our obligations—that is, that some of our collective obligations arise because of what the offender did, and our proper response to what they did, rather than focusing exclusively on what will be accomplished as a result of the punishment. On my view, retribution is justified as an expression of resentment on the part of the community, and that expression has intrinsic value that is distinct from the aims of forward-looking deterrence. If such a response is morally justified, regardless of its effects on the crime rate, then expressive retributivism has at least some justificatory role to play in legal punishment.

Suffering can have moral value apart from its consequences. Specifically, legal punishment, as a kind of burden or deprivation, is one way of holding people to account for wrongdoing. Consider the following: Imagine that someone committed a series of assaults from which the victims continue to suffer the effects. The offender is held in solitary confinement and will die before they are released, so they pose no further threat to anyone and they do not need to be rehabilitated (at least not to protect the community). The public is uninterested in the case, and the victims just want to put the incidents behind them, so there is nothing the offender can do to make amends. In short, neither incapacitation, specific deterrence, nor general deterrence will be improved as a result of how the criminal *feels*. Under these circumstances, there would be nothing wrong, on the utilitarian view, with giving the convict a pill that alters their emotional response to the thought of what they did so that they feel no guilt or remorse. Such a "moral sedative" would be justified on consequentialist grounds because it would lessen overall suffering. Yet, most of us think that the offender ought to feel guilty, lest we—by numbing their moral emotions—trivialize the crimes.[2] As Antony Duff (2001) puts it,

[2] I have borrowed this example, including some specific phrases, from Vilhauer (2022).

offenders deserve censure for their wrongdoings, and they ought to suffer the pain of remorse. Punishment, and specifically hard treatment, should communicate this to the offender.

Many philosophers dismiss this desire for offenders to suffer for its own sake as morally insignificant, illegitimate, or even barbaric. Friedrich Nietzsche describes retribution as a primitive urge to lash out at those who harm us (1967, II, 5–6 [pp. 64–67]). Bruce Waller says that the foundation of the belief in retribution is the "strike-back desire" that has its roots in nonhuman animalistic impulses, which were absorbed by early human cultures and passed down to us (2018, 41–52; see also Wiegman's chapter in this volume). And Martha Nussbaum characterizes it as a kind of "magical thinking" by which we believe that suffering will somehow undo the wrong and balance the scales of justice (2015, 48).

Contrary to their characterizations, however, the expressive function of punishment serves a moral purpose that is distinct from the desire for revenge. Joel Feinberg lists several functions of punishment that are accomplished only through the legal process, including symbolically disavowing the criminal act and recognizing it as wrong; reaffirming the force of the law; and absolving other, innocent people of blame (1970, 101–5). Punishment also supports the victim by accepting their account of the crime and validating their sense of resentment at having been wronged. The state is reinforcing the idea that people are equal under the law by condemning the disrespect that the criminal showed to the victim; punishment tries to correct the victim's degraded status (Hampton 1988). To be sure, society's condemnation of criminal acts may also have a deterrent effect, insofar as potential criminals want to avoid social disapproval (Andenaes 1974, 110–28; Braithwaite and Pettit 1990), but the retributive functions of punishment are distinct and morally significant. They are retributive insofar as they have a backward-looking focus: it is important to express resentment because the offender did something wrong and they ought to be held accountable. It is good for its own sake, not because it will achieve some positive outcome.

Unlike some forms of retributivism, in which the suffering of offenders is good in itself, the value of suffering is more complicated under expressivism. Duff (2001), for example, does not simply want the wrongdoer to suffer. The kind of suffering he wants them to experience is guilt (see also Bennett 2008). On this view, someone who understands that what they did was wrong and feels bad about it while otherwise living well is better than someone who feels no remorse but is suffering intensely—which is why Duff (2003) has endorsed restorative practices as an alternative form of punishment, at least in some cases. There is value in the recognition of wrongdoing found in guilt rather than in suffering per se. On my view, however, punishment serves an expressive function that goes beyond communicating disapproval to and instilling guilt in offenders. As Feinberg says, punishment can disavow the criminal act and reaffirm the force of the law, both of which are more generalized forms of expression. And denouncing lawbreaking may be better accomplished though hard treatment.[3] For the expressive retributivist, imprisonment can serve a larger social function. It can validate the community's collective feeling of resentment at having been wronged, regardless of what the offender feels.

Indeed, we are obligated to condemn wrong actions even when such expressions will have little effect—on either society as a whole or the wrongdoer in particular. For example, imagine that you are visiting an older relative when they make an ignorant, racist comment. Nothing you say will change their offensive views, which have sedimented over many years. And there is no one else there for whom you need to signal your personal virtue. Still, if you say nothing in response and simply go on as if nothing has happened, you may feel like something important has been left undone. When a wrong and morally problematic view is expressed, it sort of hangs in the air, in need of rebuttal. You may feel guilty for some reason—not because you agree with the claim, but because you feel complicit if you do not explicitly reject it, as if you have tacitly approved of what they said.

Similarly, imagine someone whose house is occupied by Nazi soldiers during World War II. A single person lives there, and they are confronted by several angry and committed Nazis who hold the person at gunpoint. Although the person detests Nazism, they can pacify the soldiers and save their own life if they vociferously express a strident commitment to Nazi ideology. If they condemn the movement or remain silent, they will be shot without a second thought—and no one else would be aware of what happened, one way or another. To be sure, few people would blame the person for lying to avoid death. If they express support for the soldiers' cause, it will not convert anyone to Nazism or bolster the German war effort. Still, someone who does this may feel guilty in retrospect. And if, instead, they give a passionate speech defending the value of all human life and denouncing the Nazis' repulsive views, only to be killed on the spot, we would think that the person acted heroically in standing up to the oppressors, even if it does not spark a rebellion or inspire others. In fact, it may be even more laudable because of its futility. There is no instrumental good to be achieved; the person is simply being true to their right beliefs.

[3] This is not to say that the expression of resentment *must* involve hard treatment. For my own defense of restorative practices, see Altman (2021, 238–53).

The point of these two examples is that some wrong actions place a demand on us to condemn them. Correspondingly, public wrongs require an expressive or denunciatory response on the part of the community. The state has an obligation to its members not only to protect them but to affirm the shared values that are codified in the criminal law. Unlike civil violations, criminal acts disrupt the basic conditions that allow the community to maintain itself—what Duff (2018) calls public wrongs that impinge on the polity's civil order. Thus, criminal offenders violate their duties to the community as a whole, not just to individual victims, which is one reason why they are punished through the formal legal process. If the state refuses to punish them or does not subject them to the real possibility of punishment, it would not be supporting its own values, nor would it be aligning itself with victims over wrongdoers. Consider the cases of lynching in the United States where the crimes were not investigated, the offenders were not charged, or they were given a sham trial for which a not guilty verdict (by an all-white jury) was preordained. The fact that lynching was not deterred is only one of the problems with this. It also rendered murder statutes meaningless (as long as a Black man was lynched by a white mob for some supposed offense), it communicated to Black Americans their inferior position under the law, and it made the state complicit in the wrongdoings after the fact.[4]

This notion of complicity is the moral intuition behind Kant's famous *Blutschuld* passage in the *Metaphysics of Morals*, where he imagines a community that, without any need to use punishment to maintain itself, simply ignores what an offender deserves:

> Even if a civil society were to be dissolved by the consent of all its members (e.g., if a people inhabiting an island decided to separate and disperse throughout the world), the last murderer remaining in prison would first have to be executed, so that each has done to him what his deeds deserve and blood guilt [*Blutschuld*] does not cling to the people for not having insisted upon this punishment; for otherwise the people can be regarded as collaborators [or participants, *Teilnehmer*] in this public violation of justice. (Kant 1996, 6:333 [p. 474])

[4] Steven Swartzer (2019) claims that the criminal legal system in the U.S. expresses anti-Black racist sentiments through its policing and incarceration, and he uses that point to criticize communication theories of punishment, including expressivism. I agree with Swartzer's concerns about desert claims being motivated by racial bias (see Altman and Coe 2022). However, on my view the feeling of resentment is a reactive attitude with cognitive content, so it is open to critique and correction. Thus we can judge whether our resentment is well-founded or biased, and, in the context of our legal institutions, whether it is conducive to justice or injustice. See Altman (2021, 59–61, 67–83, 204–5).

There are compelling challenges to Kant's justification of the death penalty (e.g., Altman 2014, 117–38), and he may overstate his case when he describes the people as "collaborators." Still, he correctly reminds us that legal punishment serves purposes other than the preservation of society. For Kant, it fulfills the *lex talionis* (the law of retaliation). On my view, it collectively expresses justified resentment toward wrongdoing and blames the offender for the act, thus accomplishing the non-consequentialist aims of the criminal law that Feinberg and I have recognized. The state signals to criminals that they have done wrong, that their victims are justified in feeling wronged, and that we support the rules that are designed to promote a just social arrangement.

Another example will demonstrate the kernel of truth in Kant's hypothetical. Imagine that a woman is raped, and she is a member of a neglected, disadvantaged, or oppressed group; the rape occurred in a region of the country with less aggressive law enforcement; and, for one reason or another, the community as a whole is uninterested in pursuing the case and prosecuting the offender.[5] Rape victims often experience a bundle of conflicting emotions, including anger toward the perpetrator, a sense of guilt or shame, and isolation from their peers. They may act in ways that even they do not understand. As Naomi Scheman (1993) says, we tend to think that emotions are simply there, fully formed, to be discovered in the mind. But, for any given emotion, there is no one identifiable feeling, belief, or pattern of behavior. Under the circumstances, society can provide meaning to an experience by likening it to other, similar cases—in effect making the victim's response into resentment by telling her, the offender, and the rest of society that the victim's account of the event is correct, the action is wrong, and the offender is to blame. In this case, if the state does not punish the perpetrator, either because no charges are brought or because a jury acquits them, the rape victim may doubt her own version of the event or feel like she brought the assault on herself. She may feel revictimized, like her fellow citizens are excusing or even condoning the action and are thus, as Kant says, "collaborators in this public violation of justice."[6] As an expression of resentment on behalf of the community, punishment validates the law. Insofar as the resentment is justified, punishment is justified pro tanto, even apart from its deterrent effect.

---

[5] In explaining and defending her own feminist approach to expressive retributivism, Jean Hampton regularly appeals to cases of rape and other forms of sexual violence. See, for example, Hampton (1992, 1998).

[6] A real-world example of this is that, in the U.S., non-Native perpetrators of sexual assault against Native American women on tribal lands were for many years not prosecuted, leaving Native women with a sense that their own country had abandoned them. This was (partially) addressed only in 2013 with the extension of the Violence Against Women Act.

2 Argument #2: The Costs of Giving People What They Deserve

Although all forms of retributivism include the claim that justified punishment is deserved (Altman 2021, 2–3n2), it is, like consequentialism, not one theory but a class of related theories. The different justifications of retributivism have been enumerated by John Cottingham (1979) and Nigel Walker (1999), and they include repayment theory, fair play theory, annulment theory, and more. In addition to these "varieties of retributivism," there are also different ways of understanding the normative force of desert claims. When the retributivist says that punishing the guilty is intrinsically valuable, they could mean any one of three things:

1. Weak retributivism: Desert is necessary to justify punishment. Only someone who has done wrong is eligible for punishment, but desert alone cannot justify punishing them.
2. Moderate retributivism: Desert is necessary and sufficient to justify punishment, and we *may* punish those who deserve it just because they deserve it. There is some intrinsic value in punishing the guilty, but there may be other, more important reasons not to punish them.
3. Extreme retributivism: Desert is necessary and sufficient to justify punishment, and we *must* punish those who deserve it. Desert is the primary or only good reason to punish the guilty, and it is important enough that it cannot be outweighed by other, competing goods. (Alexander 1980)

Because desert is necessary under all these formulations, retributivists claim that it is impermissible to punish the innocent or to punish the guilty more than they deserve in order to deter would-be offenders. However, only one of these three views—extreme retributivism—ignores consequences entirely when justifying punishment for the guilty. Kant's *Blutschuld* passage encapsulates this view: even if there is no non-retributivist reason to punish, or there are good reasons not to, we must do what justice demands.

Weak retributivism and moderate retributivism are not axiologically monistic—that is, they leave room for other things we value to play a role in punishment decisions. Weak retributivists believe that someone who has committed a wrong has only made themselves eligible for punishment by relinquishing their right not to be punished. Even though punishment is permissible in such a case, there must be some positive reason, such as deterrence, to impose hard treatment on the offender. Therefore, weak retributivism is a mixed theory, requiring both retributivist and (typically) consequentialist justifications; indeed, it is sometimes called "side-constrained consequentialism." Moderate retributivists say that punishing the guilty may be justified even if it has some negative consequences or not punishing them would have some positive consequences. But if there were significant enough negative consequences, punishment—or punishment proportional to the offender's guilt—may not be justified, all things considered. That is, desert provides a strong positive reason to punish, but it may not be a compelling enough reason because of other obligations. For example, if executions increase crime through a "brutalization effect," then there is a compelling reason not to execute murderers (and imprison them instead) even if they deserve the ultimate punishment. Therefore, moderate retributivism is also a mixed theory insofar as it gives weight in our punishment decisions to both retribution and non-retributivist aims; retribution may be an overriding obligation in any given case but not in every case.

Only extreme retributivism rejects any tincture of consequentialism in justifying the intentional infliction of hard treatment in response to wrongdoing. Good consequences may occur, but they are incidental side effects rather than positive reasons to punish, lest we treat the person merely as an instrument to achieve some social purpose. It is enough that the person deserves to suffer—and they *must* suffer. Although such a view would make sense for God in the afterlife, the theory does not make sense when it comes to legal punishment. And if we reject extreme retributivism, then any alternative form of retributivism may be only one part of a mixed theory along with consequentialism.

Douglas Husak (2000) explains why retribution is not a strong enough reason on its own to justify legal punishment. The criminal law is part of the political structure of the state, and punishment must be evaluated in the context of the state's proper functioning. Husak imagines a state that has not yet established a criminal justice system. Even if this newly formed government recognizes the value of giving people what they deserve, it must also consider the drawbacks, including:

1. the great financial cost to taxpayers and the allocation of limited funds that could be spent elsewhere (on education, healthcare, and other enhancements of public welfare);[7]

---

[7] In the United States in 2016, the cost of federal, state, and local corrections was about $88.5 billion for the year, an over fivefold increase in real dollars since 1980 ($17 billion). If police and court costs are also included, the direct cost was $295.6 billion (Hyland 2019, Table 1). The growth in spending on prisons has far outpaced the growth of spending in other areas, and it has led to "a diversion of public resources from social institutions providing education, child care, food, and housing for primarily inner-city poor women and children to penal institutions that confine primarily inner-city poor men" (Comfort 2007, 285). Ellwood and Guetzkow (2009) found that for every 1 percent of the state budget that was diverted to corrections, there was a corresponding decrease of about 1.7 percent spent on welfare.

2. the inevitability of error, including accidentally punishing the innocent, disproportionately punishing the guilty, and improperly criminalizing permissible behavior; and
3. the likelihood that the legal authority will be abused and will inflict harm on its citizens unjustly. (996–1000; see also Husak 2008, 203–6; and his chapter in this volume)

Husak doubts whether the intrinsic value of giving offenders what they deserve is "*sufficiently* valuable to offset these three drawbacks of punishment and thus penal institutions that serve this retributivist objective" (998). If these are not enough, there are additional drawbacks not mentioned by Husak, specifically related to imprisonment, that also add to the cost:

4. collateral costs to innocents, such as decreased educational attainment for children of incarcerated parents (Nichols and Loper 2012) and financial hardships for families (Geller et al. 2006); and
5. crime-causing (criminogenic) effects, including increased recidivism among the incarcerated (Song and Lieb 1993); higher levels of aggression and criminality among children of prisoners (Loeber and Stouthamer-Loeber 1986); and, when large numbers of offenders are removed from particular communities, weakened informal mechanisms of social control (Rose and Clear 1998; see also Pritikin 2008).

Under the circumstances, even if it is important to punish the guilty simply because of their guilt, we would not think it unreasonable if the citizens of this new state refused to establish the institution for that purpose alone and instead considered how it fits among their other priorities, and how best to accomplish them (see Lippke 2019). In this way, Husak (2000) says, retributive justice is "holistic." When forming the criminal law, people would want to know first how these drawbacks will be mitigated. If they cannot be, or they cannot be sufficiently mitigated, then there are reasons to diverge from what is dictated by retribution.

A legislature that inflicts suffering on the guilty for its own sake, regardless of its social costs, would be misunderstanding its job. Legislators are not Anubis in the underworld, weighing a person's heart on a scale. They are tasked with preserving the social order and advancing the common good. In a liberal system, the state's purpose is well-defined: to secure our rights. And protecting people's rights may be achieved more efficiently and effectively with policies that do not always give people precisely what they deserve. For example, even if we, like Kant, believe that execution is the deserved punishment for murder, the exorbitant cost of capital trials versus non-capital trials, the irreparable harm done to the wrongly executed, and its potential brutalizing effects should make us reject capital punishment, instead funneling our limited funds into social programs such as public education, which not only benefits people directly and respects their rights—in this case, the right to education—but also has a substantial downward effect on the crime rate (Lochner and Moretti 2004).

We seem to be pluralists in just about every other area of our lives. We value various things—happiness, rights, virtue, health, relationships, knowledge, and so on—and none of the things we value give us conclusive reasons to pursue them, come what may. Maximizing happiness sounds good until it would require us to cut up a healthy loner and distribute the person's organs to five people who need transplants (Thomson 1985). The duty not to lie sounds reasonable until we are confronted by a murderer at the door (Bok 1978). One kind of good may be overridden by another kind of good, especially when it comes to public policy decisions, which are often even more complex than interpersonal relationships. The extreme retributivist would have to produce some argument for why desert is so powerful a reason-generating force—different from almost every other good—that it produces an absolutely constraining duty. As Feinberg says, even if desert gives us a reason to treat someone in accordance with that desert, it is "not always a conclusive reason" because "considerations irrelevant to his desert can have overriding cogency in establishing how he ought to be treated on balance" (1970, 60; see also Dolinko 1991). If we believe that people should get what they deserve but we are not retributivists come what may, then we are committed to some kind of mixed theory.

As Leora Dahan Katz says (in her chapter in this volume), it is probably the case that no retributivist has ever held the extreme position. Instead, they disagree about how much weight desert has, or how strong the resulting duty to punish is, so that it can be overridden more or less easily by other considerations. Two examples will suffice to illustrate this point: Michael Moore and Immanuel Kant, both of whom seem to be committed to the extreme version but in fact have more pluralistic commitments. Moore (1997) says that "we are justified in punishing because and only because offenders deserve it," which "gives society the *duty* to punish" (91); otherwise, it would be using offenders merely as means to achieve socially desirable ends (87). However, he also says that we only have a pro tanto obligation to punish the guilty (189–229, 403–19) and that torturing or killing an innocent person may be justified to avert catastrophic consequences (719–26).[8] If we could subject the innocent to such undeserved treatment, presumably it would be even easier to justify not punishing the guilty, or not punishing them as much as they deserve, because of the financial costs, the risks of wrongful conviction, or the possibility of abuse.

Kant is also usually characterized as an extreme retributivist.[9] He states his position clearly in the *Metaphysics of Morals*:

> *Punishment by a court* ... can never be inflicted merely as a means to promote some other good for the criminal himself or for civil society. It must always be inflicted upon him only *because he has committed a crime*. (1996, 6:331 [p. 473])

Kant describes our obligation to execute a murder as "the categorical imperative of penal justice," which admits of no exception (1996, 6:336 [p. 477]). However, he also says that, if the sheer number of executions would lead to the dissolution of the state, the sovereign should reduce the severity of the punishments (through an act of clemency) in order to preserve it—for example, by deporting accomplices instead of killing them (1996, 6:334 [p. 475]). Furthermore, in notes from his lectures on ethics, Kant distinguishes the function of a criminal trial (the distribution of punishment)—where, as we saw, he says that punishment depends only on guilt—from the function of the government in establishing punishment an institution (its general justifying aim):

> All the punishments of princes and governments are pragmatic, the purpose being either to correct or to present an example to others. Authority punishes, not because a crime has been committed, but so that it shall not be committed. (1997, 27:286 [p. 769])

Although courts are morally obligated to punish the guilty, the government's legal obligations are more complicated and indeed axiologically pluralistic. The state must maintain itself in order to promote a rightful condition—that is, so it can protect its citizens' freedom, equality, and independence (Kant 1996, 6:314 [pp. 457–58]). If proportional punishment is inimical to this

---

[8] Other prominent retributivists who claim that desert gives us only a pro tanto reason to punish include Douglas Husak, who talks about "external constraints" on deserved punishments that are derived from political theory (2008, 120–32); and Leo Zaibert, who defends the "axiological" view that it is intrinsically good to punish the deserving but rejects the "deontic" view that we necessarily ought to punish them (2018, esp. 14–20).

[9] Indeed, Larry Alexander and Kimberly Kessler Ferzan call the extreme position "Kantian retributivism" (2009, 7). See also Dolinko (1991, 543).

aim, it must be moderated. In light of these considerations, many contemporary Kant scholars classify him as a mixed theorist (e.g., Byrd 1989; Tunick 1996; Brooks 2003; Vilhauer 2017).

In short, the most common and justifiable forms of retributivism recognize the existence of other values that supplement or compete with the more or less weighty obligation to give offenders what they deserve. In the legal context, retribution can at most provide only a pro tanto reason to punish because we must consider how it fits with society's other valued ends, all things considered (Feinberg 1970, 60). If any of those other values concern or have implications for the treatment of offenders or their victims—such as deterrence (or other forms of prevention), rehabilitation, or restoration—then, at least at the institutional level, retribution is not sufficient to justify legal punishment.

This conclusion, coupled with the conclusion of Argument #1—that expressive retribution has value and ought to be promoted—yields a mixed theory of punishment. Punishment is justified both by what the offender deserves and by its consequences for the political community, including its deterrent effects. These two theoretical approaches may lead to contradictory conclusions, however; a punishment could be right or permissible under one justificatory scheme and wrong under the other. The next question, then, is how the two approaches can function together in one legal system.

3 Argument #3: *Reductio ad absurdum* Argument for the Two-Tiered Model

According to the two-tiered model, punishment policies at the institutional level are justified by their consequences. The legislature compares expected outcomes of potential criminal statutes and chooses the ones that most effectively support a just legal arrangement—much like a utilitarian calculus, although the end need not be happiness. In a liberal system, for example, the purpose of punishment is to maximize the protection of rights. This is achieved through general and specific deterrence, rehabilitation, and incapacitation.

By contrast, punishment in the criminal courts is given to offenders based on what they deserve. Individual defendants are found guilty and sentenced only if they are determined to be guilty based on the evidence—that is, if they are found to have intentionally, recklessly, or carelessly (depending on standard of liability set out in the statute) committed the crime. The very definition of the crime (as manslaughter or murder, for instance) often depends on the intent of the criminal. Since the law cannot deter intent, only behavior—what Kant calls outer freedom rather than inner freedom (1996, 6:230–31, 396 [pp. 387–88, 526])—that is a backward-looking way of determining the appropriate punishment, proportional to what they deserve. The kind and severity of punishment is determined based on the offender's degree of guilt, and it is justified as an expression of the community's collective sense of resentment at the offender for violating the shared norms that make law-governed society possible.

For most people, I imagine that this way of organizing criminal justice is intuitively correct. According to the two-tiered model, legislative decisions should be informed by the best social scientific research to determine what most effectively deters wrongdoers—and, in fact, this is what many legislatures do. For example, in 1984 the United States Congress established the U.S. Sentencing Commission and tasked it with creating federal sentencing guidelines. The main purpose of the commission is not only to make judicial sentencing decisions less arbitrary and more consistently proportional to the crime but also to analyze criminological research to develop "effective and efficient crime policy"—that is, to recommend the "form and severity of punishment" that best promotes public safety given the limited correctional resources available (United States Sentencing Commission 2021).

In criminal courts, judges and juries consider the evidence against individual defendants and whether it proves beyond a reasonable doubt that they are guilty. A defendant's guilt is both necessary and sufficient to justify the verdict. The judge then assesses the degree of their guilt, based on aggravating and mitigating factors that enhance or diminish it, to determine what punishment they should receive within the statutory sentencing range. For example, if the victim is especially vulnerable, then we think that the offense is worse and that the offender deserves a harsher punishment than if the victim is an adult capable of defending themselves, even if the crime in each case is the same. The harshness of the penalty is matched to the seriousness of the crime, and the seriousness of the crime depends on the harm caused and the culpability of the offender.

As I mentioned earlier, I gave three arguments for the two-tiered model in *A Theory of Legal Punishment* (Altman 2021, 119–53). In this chapter, having demonstrated that we must value both crime reduction and retribution, I now consider an alternative way to accommodate mixed justifications, and I argue for its implausibility. Specifically, if public policy decisions regarding punishment were justified on retributivist grounds and individual criminal cases were decided based on consequences, it would have absurd implications.

Imagine a judge and jury in a criminal trial who are concerned with the consequences of their verdict rather than the actual guilt of the accused. The defendant's guilt may be relevant—if it is predictive of future behavior, for example—but it need not be. This is a traditional objection to consequentialist theories of punishment: they allow for the punishment of innocents (e.g., Anscombe 1958, 15–17).[10] If the defendant were an otherwise bad (or unpopular!) person, that would be important, whether or not they committed the crime of which they are accused—say, a drug dealer who is accused of a murder that it becomes apparent they did not commit. Contrary to current rules, prior bad acts would be admissible as evidence of the defendant's character, even if they have no probative value for the case at hand, since guilt now is understood more broadly to include not (or not only) whether the defendant is guilty of the crime charged but whether they are a bad person. That is because bad people (such as drug dealers) pose more of a threat to a just social order, and incapacitating them may be beneficial overall regardless of whether they committed this particular crime.

For utilitarian judges and juries, the amount of public outrage caused by a conviction or acquittal would also be important. They would have to consider the public's feelings about the defendant and the victims—whether sympathetic, neutral, or hostile—and how they would likely respond to a conviction or acquittal—with riots, indifference, or celebration. The best judges and juries would make fine-grained distinctions regarding public perceptions, such as the strength of people's feelings, the likelihood of their acting on those feelings, and whether those who are sympathetic to the defendant are more or less politically powerful than those who are hostile to them. Instead of asking to examine the evidence and the trial transcripts, perhaps they would request that a series of polls be conducted or focus groups convened. The defendant's likelihood of being convicted would depend in part on how much publicity the trial is getting, the persuasiveness of the different news outlets, and which demographic is being targeted, because different demographics have different levels of political and social influence. In such circumstances, racially biased outcomes would not only be likely but may also be justified—provided that the biases are shared by enough of the general population. If the public would be satisfied only with disproportionately severe punishments, the fact that they are undeserved hardly matters.[11]

---

[10] See Altman (2021, 124n2) for a list of other authors who raise this objection.

[11] Many people object to the election of local prosecutors and judges because, when they are chosen by popular vote, they are more likely to reflect the community's biases, including its sometimes arbitrary and illegitimate anger, rather than giving offenders what they deserve. In fact, trial judges are more likely to impose steeper sentences (Berry 2015) and state appeals court judges are more likely to affirm death sentences (Canes-Wrone et al. 2014) when they are up for re-election.

In death penalty cases, the jury would have to sort through the hundreds of studies that examine whether executions have a deterrent effect, and they would have to evaluate the different studies and decide which conclusion to reach (Altman 2021, 130–31). Or perhaps they would call on a series of experts during the penalty phase—not to attest to the victims' suffering or the defendant's mental state, but to help them determine whether this particular execution would deter other potential murderers. Psychiatrists would be replaced by criminologists and economists as the expert witnesses who are called to testify. Depending on the studies the judge and jury accept, the decision could be even more complicated. For example, an econometric study by Joanna Shepherd (2005) found that deterrence rates vary among states because the death penalty does not have a deterrent effect until it reaches a threshold of nine executions annually. Fewer than nine executions do not deter and may in fact increase the murder rate through a brutalization effect, while nine or more executions do deter. If these results can be trusted—the jury would have to evaluate Shepherd's methodology, too—the jury would have to survey the results of other capital trials that year. Would sentencing this defendant to death push the state over the threshold? If not, the jury would have to think about whether this execution would add to a brutalization effect or not, which would depend on how many more murder trials will occur that year, how likely it is that other defendants will be convicted, how likely it is that the other juries will give them the death penalty, and so on. If two capital cases are going on at once and there have already been seven executions this year, what should the two juries do? One jury should sentence the defendant to death only if the other one also does, because only that would result in reaching the threshold; otherwise, an execution would increase the murder rate.

Correlatively, if a legislature appealed to retribution to justify the institution of punishment, it would create very different criminal statutes and corresponding penalties. Retributivists typically establish appropriate penalties by pairing up crimes and punishments on a scale of proportionality that matches the seriousness of a crime with the severity of a punishment (e.g., Davis 1992, 77–83). On this view, research on the deterrent effects, cost, and rehabilitative effects of punishment would be irrelevant, even if they could provide action-guiding data on how best to advance the common good. If it were conclusively demonstrated that the death penalty does not deter, or even has a brutalization effect, the legislature would have to prioritize killing killers (assuming that they deserve it), directing its limited funds to much more costly capital trials, even if they could save more potential victims by not executing them and instead funding more effective crime prevention efforts such as an increased police presence and community policing (Chalfin and McCrary 2013; Mello 2019), drug treatment (Bondurant et al. 2016), and rehabilitation programs (Gendreau et al. 2006; Cullen and Gendreau 2012). The government would abandon its purpose of preserving the public order—for example, protecting citizens' basic rights—in order to take on the godlike role of, in Kant's words, administering justice based on people's "*inner wickedness*" (1996, 6:333 [p. 474]). If retribution is our only or overriding obligation when it comes to criminal law, then we would not only be obligated to punish the guilty when the state is dissolved, as Kant says (1996, 6:333 [p. 474]), but, contrary to Kant's seemingly mixed view, we may also be obligated to do so if it causes the state's dissolution. After all, we must punish the guilty in proportion to their guilt, and consequences are irrelevant. *Fiat iustitia et pereat mundus.* As we saw earlier, anything short of this extreme position must be committed to a plurality of values, which amounts to a mixed view.

Of course, this *reductio ad absurdum* argument alone does not entail that the two-tiered model is correct. For example, one could argue, as John Rawls does in "Two Concepts of Rules" (1955), that the retributivist justification of individual criminal judgments is ultimately based on consequentialist grounds. Contrary to the two-tiered model, such a position is axiologically monistic. For Rawls, retribution has no intrinsic value. It is justified in the courts because, when carried out collectively by judges as a practice, it maximizes happiness. If the practice of punishment is justified by the principle of utility, then particular punishments that follow the practice are justified, provided that judges correctly adhere to the rules. Ignoring what someone deserves in an effort to promote some social good would be a different practice that would only be available to judges under a different institution, what Rawls dubs "telishment" (1955, 11–12).

There are problems with this mixed approach that do not plague the two-tiered model. Rawls says that, if a judge punished the innocent, they would no longer be acting as a judge and would no longer be engaging in the practice of punishment. But the act-utilitarian would in this case simply ask why the judge ought to act like a judge and ought not to engage in this individual act of telishment. If the judge finds the innocent person not guilty and lets loose a wave of fear and violence, it would hardly be sufficient for the judge to say that they are just doing their job or that people should talk to their legislators. After all, the judge has obligations just like any other moral agent, so their decision needs to be justified and not just explained.

Even rule-utilitarianism, which would seem to support Rawls's view, would not support his practice conception of rules. Following a practice that typically maximizes utility, even when making an exception to the practice or following another practice (such as telishment) would maximize utility, amounts to what J. J. C. Smart calls a kind of "rule worship" rather than utilitarianism (1956, 107). Alternatively, we could devise a rule that allows for such exceptions—including an exception for punishing the innocent when the risk would be low and the positive consequences would be great—a practice that maximizes utility but clearly diverges from retributivism.

An axiologically monistic theory acknowledges only one kind of value: retributivism is committed to the intrinsic value of desert, and consequentialism is committed to the usefulness of punishment in producing some end. If they also accept the different roles of the legislature and the judiciary, in accordance with our considered intuitions, then any such theory puts those people in awkward positions as practical reasoners. On Rawls's view, judges presumably know the utilitarian purpose of the law as an institution, and they also know that their actions (i.e., their verdicts and sentencing) ought to further this aim. Saying that judges must follow a retributivist practice even in cases where not following the practice would maximize utility "seems to introduce a kind of moral schizophrenia" (Matravers 2000, 21). It makes more sense for judges to be driven by retributivism if it, rather than utilitarianism, actually and ultimately justifies their actions. All of this is to say that, if the legislature and the criminal judiciary justify and ought to justify their actions differently, a simpler explanation of such practices is that a mixed theory of punishment is true.

According to the two-tiered model, the distribution of punishment is justified separately as an expression of resentment on behalf of the community, which places distinct moral demands on judges in a way that Rawls's practice conception of rules does not. In contrast to Rawls's view, the two-tiered model explains what is wrong with punishing the innocent: not that judges would be following the wrong practice, but that the expression of resentment is unjustified and the punishment undeserved. That the judge would not be acting like a judge mischaracterizes what is going wrong. A separate, retributivist principle, distinct from the legislature's consequentialism, ought to guide the criminal judiciary.

4 Conclusion

The two main theories of punishment, consequentialism and retributivism, are subject to some longstanding objections. For consequentialism, the main worry is that people are instrumentalized rather than respected as responsible agents, so they could be used to achieve socially desirable ends, regardless of whether they are guilty. For retributivism, its practical implications are morally problematic: among other things, it leads to overincarceration, without any concern for its social and economic costs or its effectiveness at rehabilitation. Each theory solves that problem for the other: retributivists respect people's right to be punished and refuse to punish the innocent, and consequentialists seek to reduce overall harm through effective crime prevention instead of hard treatment for its own sake. As I show in this chapter, expressive retributivism also captures our backward-looking obligations to condemn wrong actions, affirm the rule of law, and side with victims. Consequentialism provides positive reasons to punish when we adopt any but the most extreme form of retributivism—that is, when we may punish the guilty because they deserve it, but only when it advances important social aims. Both theories have significant things to say about punishment, and we lose something of value when we reject one in favor of the other. We ought to incorporate them both into a mixed theory.[12]

References

Alexander, Larry, and Kimberly Kessler Ferzan. 2009. *Crime and Culpability: A Theory of Criminal Law*. Cambridge: Cambridge University Press.

Alexander, Lawrence. 1980. "The Doomsday Machine: Proportionality, Punishment and Prevention." *Monist* 63, no. 2 (April): 199–227.

Altman, Matthew C. 2014. *Kant and Applied Ethics: The Uses and Limits of Kant's Practical Philosophy*. Malden, MA: Wiley Blackwell.

———. 2021. *A Theory of Legal Punishment: Deterrence, Retribution, and the Aims of the State*. London: Routledge.

Altman, Matthew C., and Cynthia D. Coe. 2022. "Punishment Theory, Mass Incarceration, and the Overdetermination of Racialized Justice." *Criminal Law and Philosophy* 16, no. 3 (October): 631–49.

Andenaes, Johannes. 1974. *Punishment and Deterrence*. Ann Arbor, MI: University of Michigan Press.

Anscombe, Elizabeth. 1958. "Modern Moral Philosophy." *Philosophy* 33, no. 124 (January): 1–19.

Bennett, Christopher. 2008. *The Apology Ritual: A Philosophical Theory of Punishment*. Cambridge: Cambridge University Press.

[12] Part of this paper was presented at the Northwest Philosophy Conference in November 2021. I would like to thank the conference organizers and participants, especially Amelia Wirts, for their notes and suggestions. I am also indebted to Cynthia Coe and Jason Byas for reading early drafts and suggesting promising directions for this chapter.

Berry, Kate. 2015. *How Judicial Elections Impact Criminal Cases*. New York: Brennan Center for Justice. https://www.brennancenter.org/sites/default/files/publications/How_Judicial_Elections_Impact_Criminal_Cases.pdf.

Bok, Sissela. 1978. *Lying: Moral Choice in Public and Private Life*. New York: Vintage.

Bondurant, Samuel R., Jason M. Lindo, and Isaac D. Swensen. 2016. "Substance Abuse Treatment Centers and Local Crime." NBER Working Paper No. 22610, September. https://www.nber.org/papers/w22610.pdf.

Braithwaite, John, and Philip Pettit. 1990. *Not Just Deserts: A Republican Theory of Criminal Justice*. Oxford: Clarendon.

Brooks, Thom. 2003: "Kant's Theory of Punishment." *Utilitas* 15, no. 2 (July): 206–24.

Byrd, B. Sharon. 1989. "Kant's Theory of Punishment: Deterrence in Its Threat, Retribution in Its Execution." *Law and Philosophy* 8, no. 2 (February): 151–200.

Canes-Wrone, Brandice, Tom S. Clark, and Jason P. Kelly. 2014. "Judicial Selection and Death Penalty Decisions." *American Political Science Review* 108, no. 1 (February): 23–39.

Chalfin, Aaron, and Justin McCrary. 2013. "The Effect of Police on Crime: New Evidence from U.S. Cities, 1960–2010." NBER Working Paper No. 18815, February. https://www.nber.org/papers/w18815.pdf.

Comfort, Megan. 2007. "Punishment beyond the Legal Offender." *Annual Review of Law and Social Science* 3: 271–96.

Cottingham, John. 1979. "Varieties of Retribution." *Philosophical Quarterly* 29, no. 116 (July): 238–46.

Cullen, Francis T., and Paul Gendreau. 2012. "Assessing Correctional Rehabilitation: Policy, Practice, and Prospects." In *Policies, Processes, and Decisions of the Criminal Justice System*, vol. 3 of *Criminal Justice 2000*, edited by Julie Horney, 109–75. Washington, DC: National Institute of Justice.

Davis, Michael. 1992. *To Make the Punishment Fit the Crime: Essays in the Theory of Criminal Justice*. Boulder, CO: Westview.

Dolinko, David. 1991. "Some Thoughts about Retributivism." *Ethics* 101, no. 3 (April): 537–59.

Duff, R. A. 2001. *Punishment, Communication, and Community*. Oxford: Oxford University Press.

———. 2003. "Restoration and Retribution." In *Restorative Justice and Criminal Justice: Competing or Reconcilable Paradigms?* edited by Andrew von Hirsch, Julian Roberts, Anthony E. Bottoms, Kent Roach, and Mara Schiff, 43–59. Oxford: Hart.

———. 2018. *The Realm of Criminal Law*. Oxford: Oxford University Press.

Ellwood, John W., and Joshua Guetzkow. 2009. "Footing the Bill: Causes and Budgetary Consequences of State Spending on Corrections." In *Do Prisons Make Us Safer? The Benefits and Costs of the Prison Boom*, edited by Steven Raphael and Michael A. Stoll, 207–38. New York: Russell Sage Foundation.

Feinberg, Joel. 1970. *Doing & Deserving: Essays in the Theory of Responsibility*. Princeton, NJ: Princeton University Press.

Geller, Amanda, Irwin Garfinkel, and Bruce Western. 2006. "The Effects of Incarceration on Employment and Wages: An Analysis of the Fragile Families Survey." Working Paper #2006-01-FF, Center for Research on Child Wellbeing, January, revised August. http://citeseerx.ist.psu.edu/viewdoc/download?doi=10.1.1.517.388&rep=rep1&type=pdf.

Gendreau, Paul, Paula Smith, and Sheila A. French. 2006. "The Theory of Effective Correctional Intervention: Empirical Status and Future Directions." In *Taking Stock: The Status of Criminological Theory*, edited by Francis T. Cullen, John Paul Wright, and Kristie R. Blevins, 419–46. New Brunswick, NJ: Transaction.

Hampton, Jean. 1988. "The Retributive Idea." In *Forgiveness and Mercy*, edited by Jeffrie G. Murphy and Jean Hampton, 111–61. Cambridge: Cambridge University Press.

———. 1992. "Correcting Harms versus Righting Wrongs: The Goal of Retribution." *UCLA Law Review* 39, no. 6 (August): 1659–702.

———. 1998. "Punishment, Feminism, and Political Identity: A Case Study in the Expressive Meaning of the Law." *Canadian Journal of Law and Jurisprudence* 11, no. 1 (January): 23–45.

Hart, H. L. A. 2008. "Prolegomenon to the Principles of Punishment." In *Punishment and Responsibility: Essays in the Philosophy of Law*, 1–27. 2nd ed. Oxford: Oxford University Press.

Husak, Douglas. 2000. "Holistic Retributivism." *California Law Review* 88, no. 3 (May): 991–1000.

———. 2008. *Overcriminalization: The Limits of the Criminal Law*. Oxford: Oxford University Press.

Hyland, Shelley S. 2019. "Justice Expenditure and Employment Extracts, 2016—Preliminary." Bureau of Justice Statistics, Office of Justice Programs, U.S. Department of Justice, November 7. https://www.bjs.gov/index.cfm?ty=pbdetail&iid=6728.

Kant, Immanuel. 1996. *The Metaphysics of Morals*. In *Practical Philosophy*, translated and edited by Mary J. Gregor, 363–602. Cambridge: Cambridge University Press.

———. 1997. *Lectures on Ethics*. Translated by Peter Heath. Edited by Peter Heath and J. B. Schneewind. Cambridge: Cambridge University Press.

Lippke, Richard L. 2019. "The Nature of Retributive Justice and Its Demands on the State." *Law and Philosophy* 38, no. 1 (February): 53–77.

Lochner, Lance, and Enrico Moretti. 2004. "The Effect of Education on Crime: Evidence from Prison Inmates, Arrests, and Self-Reports." *American Economic Review* 94, no. 1 (March): 155–89.

Loeber, Rolf, and Magda Stouthamer-Loeber. 1986. "Family Factors as Correlates and Predictors of Juvenile Conduct Problems and Delinquency." In *Crime and Justice: A Review of Research*, vol. 7, edited by Michael Tonry and Norval Morris, 29–149. Chicago: University of Chicago Press.

Matravers, Matt. 2000. *Justice and Punishment: The Rationale of Coercion*. Oxford: Oxford University Press.
Mello, Steven. 2019. "More COPS, Less Crime." *Journal of Public Economics* 172 (April): 174–200.
Moore, Michael S. 1997. *Placing Blame: A General Theory of the Criminal Law*. Oxford: Oxford University Press.
Nichols, Emily Bever, and Ann Booker Loper. 2012. "Incarceration in the Household: Academic Outcomes of Adolescents with an Incarcerated Household Member." *Journal of Youth and Adolescence* 41, no. 11 (November): 1455–71.
Nietzsche, Friedrich. 1967. *On the Genealogy of Morals*. Translated by Walter Kaufmann and R. J. Hollingdale. New York: Vintage.
Nussbaum, Martha C. 2015. "Transitional Anger." *Journal of the American Philosophical Association* 1, no. 1 (Spring): 41–56.
Pritikin, Martin H. 2008. "Is Prison Increasing Crime?" *Wisconsin Law Review* 6: 1049–1108.
Rawls, John. 1955. "Two Concepts of Rules." *Philosophical Review* 64, no. 1 (January): 3–32.
Rose, Dina R., and Todd R. Clear. 1998. "Incarceration, Social Capital, and Crime: Implications for Social Disorganization Theory." *Criminology* 36, no. 3 (August): 441–80.
Ross, W. D. 2002. *The Right and the Good*. Edited by Philip Stratton-Lake. Oxford: Clarendon.
Scheman, Naomi. 1993. "Anger and the Politics of Naming." In *Engenderings: Constructions of Knowledge, Authority, and Privilege*, 22–35. New York: Routledge.
Shepherd, Joanna M. 2005. "Deterrence versus Brutalization: Capital Punishment's Differing Impacts among States." *Michigan Law Review* 104, no. 2 (November): 203–55.
Smart, J. J. C. 1956. "Extreme and Restricted Utilitarianism." *Philosophical Quarterly* 6, no. 25 (October): 344–54.
Song, Lin, and Roxanne Lieb. 1993. "Recidivism: The Effect of Incarceration and Length of Time Served." Washington State Institute for Public Policy (Olympia, Washington), September. http://www.wsipp.wa.gov/rptfiles/IncarcRecid.pdf.
Swartzer, Steven. 2019. "Race, Ideology, and the Communicative Theory of Punishment." *Philosophers' Imprint* 19, no. 53 (December): 1–22.
Thomson, Judith Jarvis. 1985. "The Trolley Problem." *Yale Law Journal* 94, no. 6 (May): 1395–1415.
Tunick, Mark. 1996. "Is Kant a Retributivist?" *History of Political Thought* 17, no. 1 (Spring): 60–78.
Vilhauer, Benjamin. 2017. "Kant's Mature Theory of Punishment, and a First *Critique* Ideal Abolitionist Alternative." In *The Palgrave Kant Handbook*, edited by Matthew C. Altman, 617–40. London: Palgrave Macmillan.
———. 2022. "Kantian Remorse with and without Self-Retribution." *Kantian Review* 27, no. 3 (September): 21–41.

United States Sentencing Commission. 2021. "About—Mission." https://www.ussc.gov/about-page.
Walker, Nigel. 1999. "Even More Varieties of Retribution." *Philosophy* 74, no. 4 (October): 595–605.
Waller, Bruce N. 2018. *The Injustice of Punishment*. New York: Routledge.
Zaibert, Leo. 2018. *Rethinking Punishment*. Cambridge: Cambridge University Press.

10

Rethinking Mixed Justifications

Leo Zaibert

H. L. A. Hart—arguably the most important philosopher of law in the last hundred years—famously reacted against "the view that there is just one supreme value or objective (e.g., Deterrence, Retribution or Reform) in terms of which *all* questions about the justification of punishment are to be answered" (2008, 2). The view Hart criticizes is, however, quintessential to the traditional justifications of punishment: eschewing the pluralism toward which Hart gestures, they are proudly monistic, or non-mixed. That Hart was onto something, and that there is indeed something "somehow wrong" (2) with monistic approaches explains why we have witnessed such an explosion of mixed justifications of punishment during the last few decades.[1] Mixed justifications have become the overwhelmingly dominant position. A reaction against monism explains also my own embrace of a decidedly pluralistic justification of punishment (Zaibert 2018). Since I am terribly sympathetic to what I think motivates most mixed justifications, writing against them is a most peculiar exercise.

[1] "Mixed justifications" is better than "mixed theories"—for reasons, see Zaibert (2006, 1). In order to avoid terminological diatribes, I shall (unless otherwise noted) use here "justifications" and "theories" interchangeably.

L. Zaibert (✉)
Andreas von Hirsch Professor of Penal Theory and Ethics,
University of Cambridge, Cambridge, UK
e-mail: lz465@cam.ac.uk

© The Author(s), under exclusive license to Springer Nature Switzerland AG 2023

M. C. Altman (ed.), *The Palgrave Handbook on the Philosophy of Punishment*, Palgrave Handbooks in the Philosophy of Law, https://doi.org/10.1007/978-3-031-11874-6_10

Still, I believe that extant mixed justifications of punishment are inadequate. Despite the laudable motivation that animates them, despite the high degree of sophistication of some of them, and despite their lofty advertised goals, these mixed theories do not take pluralism seriously enough. This eschewing of the right type of pluralism was already discernible in Hart's seminal views, and it continues essentially unabated to our day in the various and popular mixed justifications currently on offer. Proponents of mixed justifications have vastly underestimated the difficulty of the problem that they face, and they have vastly overestimated the tools they utilize. As a result, they often caricaturize the relevant positions, end up not really mixing nearly enough, and—most importantly—not mixing the right things.

I shall proceed as follows. I will first present a survey of the territory, trying to explain what exactly the two classical justifications that are supposed to be mixed are, why the debate between them does invite syncretism, and what the main mixed justifications on offer are. In section 2, I will attempt to show ways in which insufficient attention to the *suffering* (or hard treatment) that is conceptually inseparable from punishment has impoverished the debate. Participants to this debate have downplayed the depth of the essentially axiological problem here: whether the moral valence of suffering is variable or fixed. This discussion will highlight an important sense in which the classical debate is not really the more fundamental debate that can be had about the justification of punishment. So, in the third and last section 3, I will explore the importance of this other debate, and explore different varieties of pluralism and the promising tools that some developments in moral philosophy offer to deal with the justification of punishment.

In the last two sections, Hart will play a prominent role. So will John Gardner, whose untimely death robbed us of a truly prodigious intellect. Commemorating the fiftieth anniversary of Hart's *Punishment and Responsibility*, Gardner wrote a long and ambitious "Introduction." I do not think I have ever encountered a harder-hitting introduction to any book. While Gardner is relentlessly—almost brutally—critical of Hart, he manages to brilliantly showcase the immense quality and depth of Hart's thought. I hope that I can here emulate Gardner's accomplishment—for while I will below disagree with him in some important respects, I hope to also highlight how Gardner's introduction to Hart's classic is among the best things written on the justification of punishment in the last fifty years, and how it deserves much more attention than it has received.

1 The Classical Debate and Its Superficiality

The famous classical debate concerning the justification of punishment confronts two radically distinct positions: consequentialism and retributivism. The first of these is itself composed of a wide variety of justifications, whereas the second is more unitary. Among consequentialist justifications we regularly encounter approaches that justify punishment based above all on prevention, which could in turn be attained via deterrence, rehabilitation, incapacitation, education, and so on, or on appeasement, reconciliation, and even social reintegration and community-building. Despite this variety of rationales, consequentialist thinkers all share the conviction that what justifies punishment is some good consequence(s) that punishment is supposed to cause.

Consequentialists thus see punishment as itself inherently bad—a badness that can perhaps be somehow canceled out, countered, or compensated by the goodness of this or that ensuing consequence. So, assuming that crimes are, in principle, bad things, punishment may be revealed as all-things-considered justified insofar as it seeks to prevent crime. (The "in principle" hedge is unfortunately necessary, in light of the regrettable over-criminalizing ethos of our times: some "crimes" are not genuine bad things [Husak 2008].) Fundamentally, consequentialists are wedded to the Benthamite credo: "all punishment in itself is evil"; and the only way in which it could be admitted (i.e., *justified*) is "in as far as it promises to exclude some greater evil" (Bentham 1970, ch. XIII, §2 [p. 158]). The Benthamite influence is twofold: first (and most obviously) regarding the intrinsic badness of punishment just sketched; second, regarding a certain mechanistic view whereby some evils "exclude" (rather than *defeat*) other evils—the sort of view that Bernard Williams (1973), above all, has compellingly criticized, and to which I will return.

Retributivist thinkers, in contrast, do not invoke any of the consequences that consequentialists suggest justify punishment, but instead they turn to the notion of desert (or merit). Just as the best poem deserves the first prize at the poetry competition, and my friend who has helped me so much deserves my gratitude, wrongdoing deserves to be punished—and that is what the justification of punishment is about. This does not mean that retributivists oppose, or that they do not value, some of those consequences so dear to consequentialists—but it does mean that they do not think that those consequences, good as they may be, are what justifies the infliction of punishment. To put it in the pithy words of a famous retributivist, these admittedly good consequences of punishment are best seen merely as a "happy surplus" (Moore

1997, 89, 153). To think that these consequences—again, good as they may be—have justificatory force is to miss the point of a justification: to give the poetry award not to the most deserving poem but to the one that will, say, better promote the potential growth of one of the competitors, is to miss the point of judging the quality of competing poems.

For the sake of conceptual clarity, however, it needs to be recognized that this classical debate is *not*, strictly speaking, the most fundamental. For there are thinkers (often called abolitionists) who take the reality of the suffering that is conceptually inseparable from punishment so seriously that they conclude that its badness is so extreme that punishment simply cannot be justified. The classical debate is really an in-house debate among people who all agree that punishment can (albeit for radically different reasons) be justified. The most fundamental debate is between those who believe that punishment *cannot* be justified (abolitionists) on the one hand, and those who believe that it *can* (consequentialists, retributivists, mixed theorists, etc.) on the other. I will return to this point later, because many consequentialist thinkers can, in a way, be seen as crypto-abolitionists, and also because something *related* to abolitionism is in fact quite important. But, for now, we do well to focus on the classical debate.

Just as retributivists are skeptical about the justificatory efficacy of consequentialist rationales, consequentialists are skeptical of the justificatory efficacy of desert. And in many ways, the consequentialists' skepticism is more radical. Many consequentialists believe that the very supposition that desert *could* justify punishment is either woefully empty or confused (Cottingham 1979) or mere "magical thinking" (Nussbaum 2016, 24, 25, 29, 33, 36, 38, 54, 127, 136, 161, 184, 185, 187).[2] Some consequentialists doubt the very existence of desert globally—no one can *really* deserve anything;[3] but at least one influential author seems to believe that, although we can deserve all sorts of things, we can never deserve to suffer (Parfit 2011).[4] Others believe that even if suffering can be deserved, it is always wrong to inflict it absent other (consequentialist) justifications.[5] But all these skeptics speak in one voice when it comes to opposing retributivism. As, Jeffrie Murphy tersely summed

---

[2] For criticisms of Cottingham's list of "retributivisms," see Moore (1997, 88–91). For criticisms of Nussbaum's (repetitious) charge that retributivism is "magical thinking," see Zaibert (2018, 177–88).

[3] This is of course another foundational tenet of classical utilitarianism (Smart 1973). Some free will skeptics, such as Derk Pereboom, deny both that anyone could "deserve to be blamed or praised just because she has performed [an] action, given an understanding of its moral statues [*sic*]" and that this denial is necessarily utilitarian (2014, 127).

[4] For criticisms, see Zaibert (2017).

[5] A particularly illuminating discussion is that between Scanlon (2013) and Strawson (1962).

it, they all think that retributivism is "primitive, unenlightened and barbaric" (1973, 227).

Enter, then, the mixed justifications of punishment. It is easy to see why the goal of combining these rationales (thus abandoning the reliance on the "one supreme value" of which Hart spoke) is attractive. But it is not at all easy to see how this is supposed to be accomplished, particularly when those on one side of the debate think that their opponents are engaged in magical thinking or worse, and those on the other side think that their opponents just miss the point. More worryingly: it is hard to see why any of the adherents to the traditional justifications would *want* to accomplish any combining at all: why combine your view with something that you see as so bad? Adding bad elements to one's account, just so that one's account has more variety, cannot be an attractive strategy. A look at the recent history of the mixed justifications shall prove useful in better understanding the state of the debate.

Mixed justifications became all the rage in the late 1950s, with the publication of highly influential (and, for our purposes, remarkably similar) articles by Hart (2008), Anthony Quinton (1954), and John Rawls (1955). The *idée mère* of this push is that retributivism and consequentialism are, despite appearances, less opposed to each other than typically assumed, since they attempt to answer different questions. In Quinton's words: one question is eminently logical, and its answer "does not provide a moral justification of the infliction of punishment but an elucidation of the use of the word." This logical question calls for a retributivist answer. By the lights of defenders of mixed justifications à la Quinton, retributivism is then revealed as "not a moral but a logical doctrine" (1954, 134). The other question concerns the consequences of punishment, and this (somehow) renders it a properly "moral" question. The answer to this other question is consequentialist.

A remarkable—and remarkably obvious—weakness of this approach is that no retributivist has ever understood the position as merely a logical or semantic thesis. Were Quinton right, it would be extraordinarily hard to understand how a merely logical or semantic thesis can be seen as being "barbaric," as retributivism has so often been. So, at best, this element of mixed justifications thrusts upon us a caricature of retributivism. But there is more that is wrong with Quinton's grotesque strawman: the position unceremoniously assumes that properly ethical matters necessarily call for consequentialist solutions. In so doing, Quinton and other mixed theorists who share his stance simply beg the question. They smuggle utilitarianism assumptions into what was supposed to be at stake, gratuitously excluding retributivism from the realm of morality, and thus confusing matters. As Murphy insightfully points out, "you cannot refute a retributive theory merely by noting that it is a retributive theory and not an utilitarian theory" (1973, 227).

Rawls's position is very similar to Quinton's—a point that Rawls explicitly concedes (1955, 4n4). But Rawls connects Quinton's two questions to two branches of government in a way that Quinton did not pursue as conspicuously. The first question, which Rawls, just like Quinton, believes has an unproblematically retributive answer, belongs in the judicial branch. This is the question that judges need to ask themselves—in the words of a son asking his father in Rawls's example: "Why was J put in jail yesterday?" (1955, 5). The answer is not only "retributive," but also a matter of semantics or logic (à la Quinton): J was put in jail because they were found guilty by a jury of their peers, in a properly constituted court of law, with their rights to due process fully protected, and so on. Jail, then, is what *logically* follows from the constitutive rules of those institutions. That is simply what (state) punishment *means*. The second question, which Rawls, again like Quinton, believes has a wholly and unproblematically consequentialist answer, is the question that legislators need to ask themselves—in the words of Rawls's imagined son: "Why do people put other people in jail?" (1955, 5; see also Gardner 2008, li).[6] To answer this second question by saying something along the lines of "because they deserve it" is *verboten*: it is to miss the point of the question. The question directs us to the (allegedly good) effects that prisons have.

While Hart talks about "a number of different questions," and while he explicitly mentions three questions (one of which is subdivided into two more), he emphasizes just two: the question of punishment's "distribution" and the question of punishment's "general justifying aims" (2008, 3–4). Hart's two main questions largely correspond to Rawls's two questions (and, perhaps slightly more indirectly, to Quinton's two questions) (Hart 2008, 3–13, esp. 9).[7] I have dubbed this Quintonian, Rawlsian, and Hartian strategy "the two-question strategy"—and I have thoroughly criticized it elsewhere (Zaibert 2006, 10–24, 140–44).[8]

The main problem facing the two-question strategy is that it operates with a rather odd (and thin) sense of mixing. The mixing of which it is capable (such as it is) happens to be a mere emergent property of the entire system (of

[6] Although Gardner and I largely agree on the nature and role of these questions in these thinkers, he (unlike me) believes that this is only a "selling point" for Rawls's "defense" of punishment, and not for Hart's. For further valuable historical background, see Altman (2021, 6–7).

[7] I reverse Hart's order of presentation to underscore the parallelism with Rawls and Quinton.

[8] Recently, Altman (2021) has undertaken a systematic defense of the two-question strategy. Despite its many virtues, and despite his view that his theory "avoids the two biggest criticisms of mixed theories" (9), I think that my misgivings about mixed justifications here apply to his efforts too.

government, in this case—a crucially important point to which I will return in due course). Within the context of each of the questions themselves, there is scarcely any mixing at all. In other words, and following Rawls's ingenious and influential elaboration of the strategy, if you are a judge, you are not supposed to be mixing any rationales at all: you are supposed to be a straight-up retributivist, and that is that. Similarly, if you are a legislator, then you are not supposed to be alive to the pull of different rationales at all: you are supposed to be a straight-up consequentialist, and that is that. This is, I think, a scandalously humble victory (if a victory at all) for the "mixed" justifications of punishment.

Another type of mixed justification deserves attention, particularly in that it helps set the stage for what really is at stake in this debate. While aspects of these "expressivist" or "communicative" justifications of punishment extend at least as far back as the heyday of the other mixed justifications we have considered (Hart 1958; Feinberg 1965), they have become very popular in more recent times, thanks chiefly to the work of R. A. Duff (2001). But these communicative approaches deserve attention not only due to their popularity. Particularly within the context of state punishment, it seems hard to deny that there is significant value in "communicating" society's condemnation of certain actions; moreover, privileging this condemnation (rather than suffering as such) may promote more humane criminal justice systems. Still, and while communicative justifications do not exhibit the weakness inherent to two-question strategy, they do share (and help highlight) other problems facing mixed justifications generally.

Duff believes that state punishment

> should communicate to offenders the censure they deserve for their crimes and should aim through that communicative process to persuade them to repent those crimes, to try to reform themselves, and thus to reconcile themselves with those whom they wronged. (2001, xvii)

Duff's communicative justification is then even more ambitious than the traditional mixed justifications we have discussed, for he wishes punishment to accomplish *reconciliation*, something rarely mentioned in the classical mixed justifications. (Repentance as such is seldom mentioned either, but perhaps one could see repentance as part of rehabilitation or of reform.) This ambitiousness aggravates our problems.

Imagine, for example, that reconciliation is best achieved by *not* giving wrongdoers what they deserve (whether censure or hard treatment or whatnot), or, conversely, that giving them what they deserve is *not* conducive to reform or to reconciliation, and so on. What is to be done? This puts the foundational problem facing the mixed justifications we have sketched above back into focus: how are we supposed to mix these disparate goals? If reform, say, could be promoted (or assured) at the expense of deserved censure (and particularly if this deserved censure is in any way suffering-inducing) then, from the consequentialist perspective, it is absurd (or perverse) to insist on censuring. Similarly, if there is a sense in which censure really is deserved, then this retributive rationale (if that is what it is) will not cede (or even share) the stage too easily. In either case, and despite how laudable these disparate goals may be in themselves, the communicative approach does not really fare better than mixed justifications based on the two-question strategy in helping us understand how to resolve potential conflicts between all these sundry goals that they pursue.

Perhaps the most obvious peculiarity of the emphasis on communication is that what is deserved turns out to be "censure," and it is not clear that, as a conceptual matter, censure needs to involve the sort of hard treatment that has been rightly seen as one essential aspect of punishment—not only crucial for the discussion of its justification, but for its very definition (as I will discuss further below). Williams tackles this problem with his usual eloquence:

> The idea that traditional, painful, punishments are simply denunciations is incoherent, because it does not explain, without begging the question, why denunciations have to take the form of what Nietzsche identified as the constant of punishment, "the ceremony of pain." (1997, 100)[9]

If, by way of avoiding the suspicion of incoherence of which Williams speaks, one were to insist that inflicting suffering is somehow necessary to communicate condemnation (deserved or otherwise), then one needs to deal with the fact that, as Gardner (inter alia) has nicely brought up:

> one can … communicate the guilt of the guilty by announcing it, or by reproaching it in strong language. [But] if one is to express or communicate the guilt of the guilty instead by visiting suffering upon them, one needs further and weighty considerations in favour of choosing this singularly brutal way of making one's point. (2008, xxix–xxx)

Of course, it is possible that the appropriate sort of censure that wrongdoers deserve constitutes hard treatment in and of itself. But it is also possible that

[9] For the unclear provenance of this passage, see Zaibert (2018, 7n15).

censure is either not feasible or not advisable, and that a wrongdoer nonetheless deserves hard treatment; or it could be that censure, in and of itself, is not all that is deserved.

Despite differences, two general points apply to both traditional mixed justifications (based on the two-question strategy) and to communicative justifications. First, Gardner's plea for weighty considerations applies to all of them. After all, prevention, rehabilitation, education, and other typical consequentialist rationales need not be punitive; not even incapacitation need be punitive (as public health quarantines may show). So, we need an explanation as to why we should pursue these consequentialist goals in punitive ways. Second, although perhaps Duff is most explicit about his narrow focus on criminal punishment,[10] all these mixed justifications are largely (or completely) circumscribed to criminal punishment. And we also need an explanation for why we theorists should restrict our focus in this way.

2 The Value of Suffering and the Nature of Justification

It is generally a good idea to distinguish purely conceptual (or descriptive) questions from normative (or, in our particular case, justificatory) questions. It is one thing to ask what a promise, or an apology, or anything else—including punishment—*is*, and quite another to ask when and why we are justified in keeping or breaking a promise, or in apologizing, or in punishing. This is not always easy to do. Consider defining, for example, a "white lie" without dealing with normative matters. Punishment is one of those difficult cases. And thus, while we are concerned here with the justification of punishment, it is important to highlight the ways this justificatory discussion is linked to punishment's very definition. The main reason for this, and sidestepping the many thorny debates concerning that fraught definition, is that whatever else punishment seeks to do, it seeks to make wrongdoers suffer (by somehow diminishing their well-being or by visiting upon them something they do not want). The use of the term "suffering" here need not conjure up images of extreme torture in order to highlight the fact that this essential *definitional* aspect of punishment immediately begs for a justification. After all, and to understate it, to make people suffer is not a nice thing to do.

[10] Tellingly, however, Duff often turns to non-criminal scenarios to illustrate his points. See Zaibert (2018, 126–30).

Retributivists, however, claim that some actions are so bad that, *as a matter of justice*, those who carry them out *deserve* to be punished—that these agents *deserve* to suffer. And it is the opposition between this particular retributive answer (centered around desert) and those centered around some good consequences of punishment that breathes life into the classical debate. The problem facing any real prospect of mixing the classical justifications is that the influence of the view that suffering is an *irremediably* bad thing is enormous; many, including many allegedly mixed theorists, are under the spell of what at bottom is the quintessential tenet of utilitarianism: that suffering is irremediably and invariantly bad, and thus to be minimized at all costs. The mixing worth pursuing is that which combines the retributivist view that deserved suffering is intrinsically good with the consequentialist (utilitarian) view that it is not. But achieving such mixing *is* a tall order indeed, and mixed theorists have not been up to the task, despite trumpeted claims of success.

As we have seen, Quinton explicitly privileges the diminution of suffering over any appeal to justice: morality seems to him wholly a matter of consequences, as he downgrades the talk of justice inherent to retributivism to a mere logical or semantic matter. It may appear that matters are slightly different in Rawls's case, since although he flatly excludes retributive rationales from the legislative branch—that is, from the very task of designing our government—he at least gives retributive ideas primordial relevance within the judicial branch. But, again, this is insufficient: Rawls's retributivism of the judicial branch does reduce, like in Quinton's case, to a matter strictly circumscribed to the logic of institutions. Given the institutions that we have—which, importantly, are themselves devised in a consequentialist fashion[11]—then it is simply a logical consequence of the fact that someone was found guilty in a court of law that they (logically) must be punished now.

Perhaps Hart is different. In fact, so it has appeared to Gardner, one of his most brilliant interpreters. Gardner sees a significant difference between Hart and Rawls; he suggests that those of us who think that "Rawls also [i.e., like Hart] had a 'mixed theory' of punishment" are "confused," and he points out that "Hart's quarrel with Rawls is precisely that Rawls's [theory] is a single value one" (2008, xxviii, note 24). Gardner dislikes what he detects (and what he thinks Hart detected) in the Rawlsian position: "retributive rule, but no underlying retributive value" (2008, xxvii). So do I. But there are two crucial disagreements between Gardner and me. First, I am much more unsure as to the allegedly retributive nature of even Rawls "retributive rule" than is

[11] Admittedly, Rawls's stance vis-à-vis utilitarianism in this early piece underwent changes, although that stance remained complicated throughout his career. See Scheffler (2002) and Geuss (2005).

Gardner. As pointed out above, Rawls is only "retributivist" in the overly logistical sense that he shares with Quinton. Second, and even more importantly, I do not think that in the end Hart fares much better than Rawls. Thus, while I largely agree with Gardner that Rawls's retributivism is but a "veneer" (simply ratcheting Gardner's verdict up by insisting that it is *at best* a thin veneer), Hart's retributivism strikes me as much as a thin veneer as does Rawls's. In my view, *all* these "mixed" theorists are under the spell of the foundational utilitarian tenet regarding the irremediable badness of suffering. Hence, in my view, what they offer are not really mixed justifications, at least not in any interesting or promising sense.

Oddly, at times Gardner admits this much. There is of course Gardner's piercing description of Hart's "wishful thinking" regarding an alleged demise of retributivism (2008, xxvi), and his assessment that, with respect to the "appeal and prospects" of retributivism, "Hart could scarcely have been more wrong" (xxviii). But there is also the very detailed and pointed way in which Gardner dismantles Hart's mixed justification, chiding Hart for its "incompleteness" (though Gardner believes that, oddly, this "incompleteness" saves Hart's view from "incoherence"). Crucially, Gardner finds Hart's position incomplete because, in his view, Hart "needs to stir a more authentically retributive element into his mix" (xxix). And Gardner further concedes that Hart's "retributivism" is essentially inauthentic (i.e., at best a *veneer*) precisely because Hart could never shake off the spell of the badness of suffering: for Hart suffering is "an intrinsically obnoxious aim" (xxii); after all, "Hart agrees with Bentham about suffering," in that suffering "is in no way intrinsically good" (xiv). I cannot help concluding that Gardner is inconsistent here. But I will postpone the discussion of our disagreement until the next section, after I address the other type of "mixed" justification I have mentioned above.

The problem facing communicative approaches is different. They neither openly adhere to the view that suffering is irremediably bad (though they *may* adhere to it), nor obviously reduce retributivism to a logico-semantic thesis. Duff explicitly cares about desert—albeit, as we have seen, his concern is deserved *censure*, and we do not know what the relation between censure and suffering is supposed to be. Even leaving that crucial relationship aside, the problem they face is that, absent an account for reconciling conflicts between the many different values they seek to realize, we simply cannot ascertain how seriously the communicative approach takes this potentially authentic retributive element. Bandying about the word "desert" is not enough.

Whether or not suffering is indeed irremediably a bad thing requires a systematic engagement with axiology (or value theory). For our purposes here, a brief definition of axiology should suffice: axiology is the study of value. Thus, axiology investigates which things are good and which things are bad, and to what extent, and on what basis, they are good or bad. The crucial contrast to keep in mind is between axiological considerations and deontic considerations. Deontic considerations relate to the question of what to do (or forbear); they concern human *action*. Obviously, there must be some connection between axiological matters and deontic matters: the fact that something is good gives us reasons to do it; the fact that something is bad gives us reasons to refrain from doing it. Almost as obviously, I think, the connection is loose: those reasons need not be dispositive—some things may be good and yet they should not be done; some things may be bad and yet should be done.[12]

The debate between consequentialists and retributivists is best understood as an offshoot of a more fundamental axiological disagreement. Whatever differences may exist among consequentialist theories and their axiological brethren (utilitarianism), they all share the foundational axiological view that there is only one good thing: the minimization of suffering. In our context, the maximization of utility (however it is defined) and the minimization of suffering are simply two different formulations of the same axiological ethos. The consequentialist simply has no theoretical space for more goods. The retributivist, in contrast, has theoretical space for various goods. Moreover, the retributivist has theoretical space for actions being right—or, in our context, *justified*—without them necessarily maximizing the good. Thus, the retributivist can, *ultima facie*, justify inflicting deserved suffering *either* because it is good, or because even if it is not good it may still be the right thing to do. The consequentialist cannot do that.

These axiological considerations reveal a problem for mixed justifications that has not received sufficient attention. What each of the opposing camps in the classical debate over the justification of punishment understands by "justification" is different, and this difference renders any prospect of mixing even more elusive than it has traditionally been assumed. The suffering punishment inherently causes is, for consequentialists, supposed to prevent greater suffering. Nothing else is sought by it, and nothing else could possibly justify its infliction. As we have seen, this greater suffering may be prevented because the wrongdoer (and/or others) will learn important lessons and not inflict suffering on others; because the wrongdoers will be afraid of having this suffering

[12] Despite their etymological proximity, "deontic" and "deontological" ought to be distinguished. "Deontic" picks out an *area* of moral philosophy, just like axiology picks another such area. "Deontology," on the other hand, is not an area of moral philosophy, but a type of comprehensive moral theory. Deontological ethical theories (say, Kant's) are typically (and profitably) contrasted with teleological ethical theories (say, Aristotle's or, more importantly for current purposes, Bentham's), not against "axiological" theories.

inflicted on them (the etymological root of "deterrence" is after all *terror*) and thus not inflict it on others; or because the type of suffering inflicted on the wrongdoer incapacitates her, rendering her unable to inflict suffering on others, and so on. It does not really matter why or how prevention is achieved, provided it is achieved. Crucially, however, if there is a way of preventing suffering without the suffering of punishment, the consequentialists' axiology *requires* them to prefer it.

I have recently resurrected an illuminating way of referring to consequentialist justifications. Leibniz referred to this family of justifications as "medicinal" (1952; see also Zaibert 2018, 7–12). On the consequentialist view, punishment is indeed very much like a medicine which may be unpleasant or painful but which we take because the disease it prevents would be even worse. Evidently—and on pain of masochism—if we can avoid (or cure) the disease without the medicine (or without any of its unwanted side effects) we would prefer that. It would be as *absurd* (or as pathological) not to see the little bit of suffering needed to prevent the serious disease as justified as it would be not to recognize the preferability of the situation in which the serious disease is prevented without even having to put up with the little bit of suffering. *Mutatis mutandis*, consequentialist assume, for punishment.

Matters are different when it comes to retributivism. Since retributivists believe that what justifies punishment is the fact that it is deserved (and not any of its potential consequences, and no matter how beneficial or otherwise defensible these consequences may be), they do not merely *tolerate* punishment. Retributivists believe that, when deserved, punishment is no longer a bad or obnoxious thing. No one need deny that the world would have been a better place had, say, the Nazi Holocaust not occurred; but once it occurred, the retributivist insists that the world *is* a better place if perpetrators are punished than if they enjoy impunity—even though that may mean adding suffering to the world. Again, the retributivist need not at all shun the usual goals that the consequentialist has in mind—it would be very good indeed if something like the Holocaust never happens again—but, independently of those potential consequences, the retributivist would see value in the infliction of deserved punishment in and of itself. Why? Because justified punishment realizes *justice*—and justice is precisely what the medicinal model necessarily leaves out, and why retributivism is not medicinal.

The contrast then is crisp. For the consequentialist to say that punishment is justified is to say that it is to be *tolerated* because, although in itself a bad thing (an infliction of suffering), it prevents worse things. For the retributivist to say that punishment is justified is to say that it is *just*—and justice is valuable in and of itself, not a bad or obnoxious thing (regardless of what it may prevent or bring about down the road). Extant mixed justifications have (unwittingly?) inherited a consequentialist worldview: to justify punishment is to render it tolerable. The problem is that that is not the sense of justification for retributivists. For the latter, to justify punishment is to show why (deserved) punishment is *good*—and to say that the *good* is to be "tolerated" is to be seriously confused. This instability at the heart of mixed justifications highlights the profundity and magnitude of the difficulties inherent to the effort to combine retributive and consequentialist rationales.

As it emphasizes *justice*, retributivism evidently shatters the analogy between medicine and morality, so popular among abolitionists, utilitarians, and mixed theorists of all stripes (Zaibert 2013). These thinkers are all in a certain ideological proximity because, given their foundational axiological commitments, they all endorse the view that if it were possible to achieve the admittedly commendable goals of preventing crime (or wrongdoing in general) without having to inflict suffering in any way, this would be preferable. Of course, there are differences—some of them important—between the thinkers I have just grouped together in this paragraph. Consequentialists think that since it is not possible to completely eradicate crime (or wrongdoing in general), they are not in favor of getting rid of punishment entirely either, and in this they differ from more thoroughgoing abolitionists. Also unlike abolitionists, mixed theorists at least have *some* room for (something resembling) the notion of desert, even if this room is reductive, mysterious, or otherwise inadequate. Still, for all of these thinkers the evil of punishment is, in itself, essentially irremediable.

This axiological view has generated a crypto-abolitionist literature of sorts that recommends the end of punishment and its replacement with treatments, quarantines, restitutive schemes, and the like (see, for example, Boonin 2008; Tadros 2011; Caruso 2021). Often, however, these efforts amount to little more than word games in which putative "restitution" or "treatment," for example, do look rather punitive: they are forced upon "wrongdoers," and these are things wrongdoers do not want done unto them, that they find unpleasant, and that are inflicted upon them against their will (and as a response to a "wrong"). Even in cases in which these approaches are not mere euphemistic exercises, they reveal a remarkable lack of concern with the notion of justice. In fact, the notion of justice is sometimes explicitly jettisoned by these types of consequentialists and by abolitionists—even if this is done inconsistently, sometimes scandalously so.[13] To talk about "justification" without caring about justice strikes some of us as a terribly uninspiring and misguided exercise: "to justify" better be closely related to "rendering just."

This is not to thereby concede the game to the retributivists. They still need to explain how it is that the fact that suffering is deserved (if it is a fact) renders the infliction of punishment just and good. But that is not my goal here.[14] My goal here is to highlight the deep difficulty that confronts mixed justifications, namely, the contrast between the at best emaciated sense of "justification" of consequentialist approaches and the much more robust sense of "justification" (tied, via desert, to a robust sense of justice) of retributivism. When mixed theorists claim that they are mixing two distinct types of justifications, they fail to realize that the very term "justification" *means* something different in each of those two schools of thought. Mixed theorists are not, as it turns out, merely supposed to mix different values but different theoretical endeavors altogether. This of course renders their task all the more difficult—and in ways that have not been sufficiently recognized.

These two different theoretical endeavors, I cannot stress enough, are the direct consequence of two underlying, opposing axiological positions. What mixed justifications are supposedly mixing is an axiological view that asserts that suffering is intrinsically bad, irremediably and invariantly so, and an axiological view that asserts that it is not. If I am correct in putting it like this, the task ahead for mixed theorists is nothing short of explaining away a contradiction. If this looks like a huge problem, that is because *it is*. Again, it is a much harder problem to solve than mixed theorists have realized. Not that I will be able to solve this problem here either, but below I will offer some general suggestions that should help us engage with it in more promising and mature ways.

3 Varieties of Pluralism

We are now in a position to return to my disagreement with Gardner as to the differences between Hart and Rawls. Gardner claims that Hart "misses Rawls's main point" because Hart fails to realize that Rawls is perfectly aware that he is operating with one single value (Gardner 2008, xxi). By Gardner's lights, Rawls's famous article is to be read very narrowly, as *exclusively* connected to

[13] See Menninger (1968), and for criticism, see Moore (1997, 112–14). For a recent reprise of this mistake, see Caruso (2021). For a reminder of Moore's seminal criticism (and other criticisms), see Zaibert (2021).

[14] See, however, Zaibert (2018), where such explanation is attempted.

an analysis of different senses of rules. Regarding punishment, Hart rejects "the Rawlsian strategy," for the Rawlsian strategy is, if not committed, at least consistent with the existence of one single value, "e.g. the value of avoiding suffering," whereas Gardner's Hart is much more seriously invested in pluralism (Gardner 2008, xxi). For the reasons I presented in the previous section, I doubt that the gap separating Rawls and Hart (and Quinton) is very significant (or as significant as Gardner takes it to be). These at most slightly different paths share enough (based as they are on the two-question strategy) so as to recommend treating them together. Still, Gardner's take on Hart's pluralism is useful for my purposes here.

Very creatively—partly given his recognition that Hart fails to take retributivism seriously and to shake off Benthamite intuitions—Gardner endeavors to show that, unlike Rawls (and Quinton), Hart actually cares about values other than those on the humdrum consequentialist list (all related to suffering-reduction). Gardner suggests that the other (non-consequentialist) value Hart sees in punishing the guilty relates to *freedom*—to a *mens rea*-mediated sense of freedom, and even to a *mens rea*-mediated sense of the rule of law itself. Gardner's efforts are dazzling, and this is not the place to do them full justice. But there are two reasons why they do not really save Hart's mixed justification. First, if Gardner is right about this, then he has in fact given the game away, for Hart has not really mixed consequentialism and *retributivism* at all. At best, Gardner would have succeeded in showing that Hart combined some traditional consequentialist rationales with other less traditional but *a fortiori also* consequentialist rationales. Interesting as this may be, it is hardly the sort of mixing that we wanted—or, importantly, that Hart himself advertised. If Gardner is right about this, then it is hard to see why Hart even bothered talking about retributivism *at all.*

In other words, that a justification of punishment is pluralistic does not entail that it is a mixed justification of punishment in the required (or interesting) sense.[15] The required sense is, again, to resolve the deep axiological impasse between consequentialism and retributivism concerning suffering. Consider, for example, a "pluralistic" justification of punishment that values both incapacitation and deterrence. My scare quotes around "pluralistic" here of course seek to highlight how uninteresting (in our context) such pluralism would be. Gardner's Hart—committed to both suffering-diminution and freedom-maximization—is admittedly more interesting than the example I have just presented. But it is still not what we need. The pluralism of Gardner's

[15] For more on the different forms of pluralism regarding the justification of punishment, see Zaibert (2018, 15–20; 2019, 1023–29).

Hart is, by Gardner's own lights, *not* of the right sort. For, just like Rawls and Quinton, Gardner's Hart fails to seriously incorporate retributivism's main rationale. (As we saw above, communicative accounts may perhaps succeed here, but we just do not know enough as to how they may solve conflicts of values.)

The second reason why I find Gardner's reading of Hart inert packs even more potential for advancing the thorny problem of the justification of punishment. After uncovering the peculiar type of pluralism he detects in Hart, Gardner concludes his tour de force with a section titled "A Political Morality of Punishment?" in which he echoes some of my views. We both find it odd that these views are even contentious. The central point about which Gardner and I wholeheartedly agree is that state punishment is but one manifestation of punishment, among many. Granted, state punishment deserves "special attention mainly because it raises additional questions on top of those raised by the practice of punishment in general," as Gardner correctly puts it (2008, l). But such special attention is responsive to *political* (or at any rate *practical*) considerations—not responsive to *theoretical* needs. Thus, reflecting on Hart's failure to take non-state punishment seriously, Gardner explicitly claims not to share Hart's "conceptual intuition," and he further confesses that he does not even see "where it gets its appeal" (2008, xlix). Like me, Gardner understands that the *theoretical* discussion of punishment's justification is best carried outside the legal context, where the admittedly pressing and unavoidable issues requiring (artificially) bright lines and (artificially) non-vague distinctions concomitant to the practicalities of state punishment need not arise. This reveals, however, that the sort of pluralism that Gardner identifies in Hart is, by Gardner's own lights, exactly of the wrong kind in yet another way—for it only obtains in the context of the state.

As we broaden our conceptual horizons, the failure of extant mixed justifications becomes increasingly prominent. Imagine that someone has done you some wrong, and you are reflecting on whether or not to punish them. How is learning about the two-question strategy (whether in Quinton's semantic reduction of retributivism, in Rawls's distinction between the legislative and judicial branches, or even in Gardner's reconstruction of Hart's pluralism) supposed to help you? Alas, very little—if at all. Perhaps communicative approaches fare better. They certainly have the potential to do better. Whether or not we wish to communicate something to someone is clearly a question we may ask ourselves outside of the legal context. But then again, the typical communicative approach—and explicitly so in Duff's case, as we have seen—limits itself to criminal punishment. Taking pluralism seriously entails engaging with values in general—"with and without the state."[16]

Upon being wronged by someone, your *first* dilemma is not whether to punish them on retributive or consequentialist grounds or on grounds that may "mix" these two, but much more fundamentally, whether to punish them or not. In some cases, you will conclude that the most valuable state of affairs you could help bring about involves punishing them, and *then* you may face the further dilemma as to what would justify such punishment. But in other cases, you may conclude that the most valuable state of affairs you could help realize involves *forgiving* this person. This is obviously not the place to undertake the analysis of such a complex notion as forgiveness. Suffice it to say that elsewhere I define forgiveness as the "deliberate refusal to punish" (Zaibert 2009).

Forgiveness and abolitionism differ in many ways, chiefly among them two. First, abolitionists tend to think that punishment is simply never justified. Forgivers do not think that. They instead think that, although punishment could sometimes be fully justified, other times refraining from inflicting it is in fact more valuable. Second, abolitionists just want no punishment at all: whatever reason we invoke to not punish is good enough. In contrast, forgivers care very much about reasons: only some reasons can render a given refusal to punish an instance of forgiveness. But there is a similarity between these thinkers worth our attention. Both abolitionists and forgivers care a lot about suffering, in ways that others—including consequentialists, retributivists, and mixed theorists—tend not to care. Once a certain infliction of suffering is seen as justified by thinkers in the latter groups (whatever it is that does the justification), the reality of suffering somehow is swept under the rug. Once justification obtains, these thinkers tend to assume, problems are over.

This way of seeing things offers rather uninspiring views of human beings and human lives. Consider another example of a justification, perfectly familiar to punishment theorists: acting in self-defense. Imagine that you are the victim of unprovoked attack that threatens your life, that you have no way of escaping or otherwise frustrating this attack, and that your only way of repelling it is to respond to the attack with deadly force (imagine, that is, that all the conditions that are necessary for self-defense—whatever they are—obtain), and that you indeed succeed in killing your attacker. *Ex hypothesi*, you are justified in doing this. It would nonetheless be chilling if, after deliberately killing a human being, you went on your merry way, light as a breeze, comforted by the fact that you were after all justified. The same, I submit,

[16] To quote from the title of a relevant section in Zaibert (2006, 16).

holds for punishment. If, after deliberately inflicting suffering upon someone else, you went on your merry way, light as a breeze, because you were justified, your behavior would be chilling, and this would be so regardless of whatever particular justification—retributivist, consequentialist, or mixed—you happen to endorse.

Forgiveness theorists thus are much more alive to the complex axiological dynamic at play here. Whenever we punish, we fail to realize the value that forgiveness would have generated; whenever we forgive we fail to realize the value that punishment would have generated. Forgiveness theorists, that is, are much less *simpleminded* than punishment theorists,[17] for they realize that forgiveness forces upon us a deep conflict of values. Although punishment theorists face essentially the same conflict of values, they tend to dismiss it. Despite the extraordinary conceptual proximity between punishment and forgiveness, punishment theorists tend to look askance (if not dismissively or condescendingly) at that other specialized literature.[18] Yet, it is in the discussion of the axiological debate between punishment and forgiveness that we are most likely to find illumination concerning the problem that mixed theorists facilely think they have solved.

This brings us back to the point flagged at the outset regarding the inadequacy of the language of "exclusion," "canceling out," and so on that pervades so much of the specialized literature on the justification of punishment. The suffering we inflict when we punish is not "canceled out" or otherwise *erased* by the fact that we may be justified in inflicting it (whatever that justification may turn out to be). It is merely *defeated* by other considerations. The crucial point here is that the normative force of both the defeated and the prevailing considerations remains. Expecting otherwise is to be simpleminded. Punishment is a deeply dilemmatic phenomenon—and not all of this dilemmatic complexity vanishes into thin air the moment it is seen as justified. We are justified in doing all sorts of things whose moral implications transcend their justification. In other words, the fact that we may have been justified in having done something does not eliminate all the effects—including unsavory, disagreeable, and even deeply painful and life-changing effects—of having had to do it. Real morality—the morality of real human beings—is not supposed to work in as neat and clean a way as punishment theorists have assumed. Proponents of mixed justifications, of all people (given their

[17] "Simplemindedness," in Williams's useful sense of "having too few thoughts and feelings to match the world as it really is," is a condition that entails neither "lack of intellectual sophistication" nor "simple-heartedness" (1973, 149).

[18] A remarkable exception is John Tasioulas. See, e.g., Tasioulas (2003, 2006).

ecumenical goals), would do well to abandon this traditional (and flat) way of approaching the extremely difficult problem of punishment's justification.

References

Altman, Matthew C. 2021. *A Theory of Legal Punishment: Deterrence, Retribution, and the Aims of the State*. London: Routledge.

Bentham, Jeremy. 1970. *An Introduction to the Principles of Morals and Legislation*. Edited by J. H. Burns and H. L. A. Hart. Oxford: Clarendon.

Boonin, David. 2008. *The Problem of Punishment*. Cambridge: Cambridge University Press.

Caruso, Gregg D. 2021. *Rejecting Retributivism: Free Will, Punishment, and Criminal Justice*. Cambridge: Cambridge University Press.

Cottingham, John. 1979. "Varieties of Retribution." *Philosophical Quarterly* 29, no. 116 (July): 238–46.

Duff, R. A. 2001. *Punishment, Communication, and Community*, Oxford: Oxford University Press.

Feinberg, Joel. 1965. "The Expressivist Function of Punishment." *Monist* 49, no. 3 (July 1): 397–423.

Gardner, John. 2008. Introduction to *Punishment and Responsibility: Essays in the Philosophy of Law*, by H. L. A. Hart, 2nd ed., xiii–liii. Oxford: Oxford University Press.

Geuss, Raymond. 2005. *Outside Ethics*. Princeton, NJ: Princeton University Press.

Hart, Henry M., Jr. 1958. "The Aims of the Criminal Law." *Law and Contemporary Problems* 23, no. 3 (Summer): 401–41.

Hart, H. L. A. 2008. *Punishment and Responsibility: Essays in the Philosophy of Law*. 2nd ed. Oxford: Oxford University Press.

Husak, Douglas. 2008. *Overcriminalization: The Limits of the Criminal Law*. Oxford: Oxford University Press.

Leibniz, Gottfried Wilhelm von. 1952. *Theodicy: Essays on the Goodness of God, the Freedom of Man and the Origin of Evil*. Edited by Austin Farrer. Translated by E. M. Huggard. New Haven, CT: Yale University Press.

Menninger, Karl. 1968. *The Crime of Punishment*. New York: Viking.

Moore, Michael S. 1997. *Placing Blame: A General Theory of the Criminal Law*. Oxford: Oxford University Press.

Murphy, Jeffrie G. 1973. "Marxism and Retribution." *Philosophy & Public Affairs* 2, no. 3 (Spring): 217–43.

Nussbaum, Martha C. 2016. *Anger and Forgiveness: Resentment, Generosity, Justice*. Oxford: Oxford University Press.

Parfit, Derek. 2011. *On What Matters*. 2 vols. Oxford: Oxford University Press.

Pereboom, Derk. 2014. *Free Will, Agency, and Meaning in Life*. Oxford: Oxford University Press.
Quinton, A. M. 1954. "On Punishment." *Analysis* 14, no. 6 (June): 133–42.
Rawls, John. 1955. "Two Concepts of Rules." *Philosophical Review* 64, no. 1 (January): 3–32.
Scanlon, Thomas M. 2013. "Giving Desert Its Due." *Philosophical Explorations* 16, no. 2: 101–16.
Scheffler, Samuel. 2002. *Boundaries and Allegiances: Problems of Justice and Responsibility in Liberal Thought*. Oxford: Oxford University Press.
Smart, J. J. C. 1973. "An Outline of a System of Utilitarian Ethics." In *Utilitarianism: For and Against*, by J. J. C. Smart and Bernard Williams, 1–74. Cambridge: Cambridge University Press.
Strawson, P. F. 1962. "Freedom and Resentment." *Proceedings of the British Academy* 48: 1–25.
Tadros, Victor. 2011. *The Ends of Harm: The Moral Foundations of Criminal Law*. Oxford: Oxford University Press.
Tasioulas, John. 2003. "Mercy." *Proceedings of the Aristotelian Society* 103: 101–32.
———. 2006. "Punishment and Repentance." *Philosophy* 81, no. 2 (April): 279–322.
Williams, Bernard. 1973. "A Critique of Utilitarianism." In *Utilitarianism: For and Against*, by J. J. C. Smart and Bernard Williams, 75–150. Cambridge: Cambridge University Press.
———. 1997. "Moral Responsibility and Political Freedom." *Cambridge Law Journal* 56, no. 1 (March): 96–102.
Zaibert, Leo. 2006. *Punishment and Retribution*. Aldershot, UK: Ashgate.
———. 2009. "The Paradox of Forgiveness." *Journal of Moral Philosophy* 6, no. 3 (January): 365–93.
———. 2013. "The Instruments of Abolition, or Why Retributivism Is the Only Real Justification of Punishment." *Law and Philosophy* 32, no. 1 (January): 33–58.
———. 2017. "On the Matter of Suffering: Derek Parfit and the Possibility of Deserved Punishment." *Criminal Law and Philosophy* 11, no. 1 (March): 1–18.
———. 2018. *Rethinking Punishment*. Cambridge: Cambridge University Press.
———. 2019. "Responses to Critics." *Rutgers University Law Review* 71, no. 4 (Summer): 1021–66.
———. 2021. "Embracing Retributivism." Review of *Rejecting Retributivism: Free Will, Punishment, and Criminal Justice*, by Gregg D. Caruso. *Philosopher* 109, no. 4 (Autumn): 105–17.

Part III

Beyond the Traditional Approaches

11

Expressive Theories of Punishment

Bill Wringe

1 Introduction

Expressive actions are those that convey a message from one agent or group of agents to another agent or group of agents, or that express an emotional response to some state of affairs. According to expressive theorists of punishment, some forms of hard treatment meted out by an appropriate authority to those who have transgressed a norm are expressive actions. Definitional expressivists take this fact to play an important role in explaining what punishment is; justificatory expressivists take it to play a part in explaining how our penal practices can be justified. As we shall see, expressivists of both kinds have defended a range of views about what exactly punishment expresses and who, if anyone, it expresses it to (Hampton 1988, 1992; Metz 2000, 2007; Duff 2001; Bennett 2008; Glasgow 2015; Wringe 2016, 2017). But a central element in the accounts I shall be discussing here is that what is expressed includes some kind of censure, disapproval, or repudiation of the act being punished.

Some elements of an expressive theory of punishment can be found in Hegel's *Philosophy of Right* and in other nineteenth-century works on punishment (Hegel 1942; Stephen 1967). Contemporary philosophical writing on expressive aspects of punishment can be traced back to Joel Feinberg's

B. Wringe (✉)
Bilkent University, Ankara, Turkey
e-mail: wringe@bilkent.edu.tr

© The Author(s), under exclusive license to Springer Nature Switzerland AG 2023

M. C. Altman (ed.), *The Palgrave Handbook on the Philosophy of Punishment*, Palgrave Handbooks in the Philosophy of Law, https://doi.org/10.1007/978-3-031-11874-6_11

influential paper “The Expressive Function of Punishment” (1965). Feinberg argued for a version of definitional expressivism. However, unlike many of those who have discussed the expressive dimension of punishment in recent years, Feinberg was not a justificatory expressivist. In fact, he seems to have held that the expressive aspects of punishment make it harder rather than easier to justify our penal practices.

In this chapter, I shall review some arguments in favor of definitional expressivism, focusing on considerations put forward by both Feinberg (1965) and by David Boonin (2008), and I shall consider two particularly influential accounts of the way in which the expressive dimension of punishment might play a role in justifying punitive institutions. I shall argue that neither of these accounts avoid a problem that Feinberg identified in his initial discussion of punishment’s expressive function, and I shall suggest a way forward that may be more promising.

2 Expressive Definitions of Punishment: Extensional Adequacy

As we have seen, Feinberg was not the first to notice that punishment often has an expressive or symbolic dimension. However, one innovative feature of his 1965 paper is his claim that a definition of punishment should incorporate some reference to the expressive dimension. In taking this position, Feinberg was responding to a well-known account of punishment put forward in slightly different forms by Hart (1960), Benn (1958), and Flew (1954). I shall call this the HBF account. According to this account, punishment consists in the inflicting of hard treatment in response to specifiable wrongdoing by an appropriate authority.[1] Feinberg (1965), by contrast, argues that punishment must, in addition, incorporate a reprobative element, and that any attempt at justifying punishment must explain not only why hard treatment is justified but also account for its reprobative dimension.

One kind of argument for incorporating a reprobative element into definitions of punishment concerns extensional adequacy. It is sometimes suggested that the HBF account of punishment classifies some things as punishment which should not be so classified. Some writers, including Ambrose Lee (2019), interpret Feinberg himself as having appealed to considerations of

[1] There is some controversy about whether hard treatment must merely be treatment, which is likely to burden the recipient, or whether it must be intended to harm the recipient (Wringe 2013, 2019; Hanna 2017, 2020). This will be important later.

extensional adequacy, in making the case for an expressive definition of punishment. In the introduction to his paper, Feinberg draws attention to a distinction between "punishment in the emphatic sense," or as he later labels it "punishment in the strict and narrow sense"—of which he presents imprisonment at hard labor as a clear example—from "penalties (merely)," under which he includes "parking tickets, offside penalties, sackings, flunkings and disqualifications" (1965, 398). He suggests that items in the latter category differ from instances of punishment "in the emphatic sense" insofar as they do not involve any element of reprobation.

As Lee notes, this is not a persuasive argument for an expressive *definition* of punishment (2019, 381–84). Some of the items on Feinberg's list, such as parking fines, seem to be examples of things which—without further theoretical motivation—many people would be inclined to count as examples of punishment; and others, such as disqualifications, only seem to be clear examples of things that are not punishments in cases where they also fail to meet the conditions in the HBF definition. Consider, for example, the case of someone who is disqualified from driving because they suffer from a medical condition such as epilepsy. On the other hand, these examples do not seem to provide a clear case against an expressive definition either. This is because one might think that (say) parking tickets and sackings can count as punishments when and because they are capable of bearing the kind of reprobative significance that Feinberg accords to "punishment in the strict and narrow sense."

It is not clear that Feinberg is best understood as appealing to considerations of extensional adequacy in arguing for definitional expressivism. But David Boonin (2008) has argued in this way. Boonin invites us to consider the following example. Consider a criminal gang that has a painful initiation rite, such as branding new members. In order to become a member of the gang, one must commit a crime (Boonin's example is stealing a car) (2008, 22–23). Boonin suggests that the HBF account of punishment entails—wrongly—that the branding inflicted on a new recruit constitutes punishment, whereas an account which requires that punishment has a reprobative element does not. The requirement that punishment have a reprobative element does more than simply correct the misclassification that the HBF account entails. It explains, illuminatingly, why we should not count this as a case of punishment: the branding is a mark of approbation rather than condemnation.

How convincing is this? Some might deny that those inflicting the punishment satisfy the HBF account's "appropriate authority" condition, insisting either that "authority" must be state authority or that "appropriate" must mean something like "morally justifiable." Neither response seems compelling. Non-state institutions such as clubs, schools, families, and religious communities can punish their members; and there is nothing incoherent about the idea that fundamentally illegitimate states such as Nazi Germany or Apartheid-era South Africa punished their subjects. Whether such punishments could have been justified is, of course, another matter. The appropriate authority condition seems intended to rule out revenge and vigilante action as cases of punishment. If so, we should take "appropriate" in this context to refer to a relationship between the wrongdoing and the response: those meting out the hard treatment must be acknowledged to have the standing to do so. If we think, as seems plausible, that acknowledgement in question is the acknowledgment by a community of which the wrongdoer is a member, then the appropriate authority condition is met in Boonin's example.

Lee claims that, on a proper understanding of the "response to wrongdoing" condition, the branding of the gang member should not be counted as a response to wrongdoing (2019, 376–77). He suggests that, on a plausible understanding of Boonin's example, the gang members do not take the stealing of cars to be wrong. If so, the branding is not inflicted because a wrong has been done. Instead, the branding occurs because the intending recruit to the gang has done something that is conventionally perceived as wrong. On Lee's view, the "response to wrongdoing" condition should be understood as requiring that the notion of wrongness should figure in the reasons that those inflicting hard treatment have for inflicting the hard treatment. Lee contrasts Boonin's case with an alternative case where a group of former criminals who now regret their criminal pasts get together and brand one another so that they can recognize one another. Here we have hard treatment inflicted in a way that does involve a response to wrongdoing (on Lee's understanding of that notion), and Lee counts this as punishment.

This is unconvincing. For one thing, it seems possible to imagine a case parallel to Boonin's where the branding does constitute a response to wrongdoing even on Lee's understanding of that notion. Suppose that the gang members are all devout Catholics, and the requirement for membership involves some kind of blasphemous action, such as stealing the consecrated host from a church and spitting on it. There does not seem to be any reason for denying the possibility of a scenario where what gains one entry into the gang is performing an action that all the gang members, including the leader, regard as wrong. (Perhaps this gives the gang leader a hold over the gang members.) If so, it seems that the wrongness of the action committed by the new recruit figures in the reasons of those inflicting the branding in a way that means that, even on Lee's interpretation, the "response" condition is fulfilled.

It is also unclear whether the "response" condition, interpreted as Lee suggests, needs to be satisfied in cases that we would normally count as punishment. Lee notes that, on his account, hard treatment imposed in response to the commission of strict liability offences will sometimes not meet the "response to wrongdoing" condition (since the point of such offences is that individuals can be penalized in the absence of culpability, and hence of wrongdoing) (2019, 379–80). Lee takes this to be an advantage of his view, suggesting that in order to justify the imposition of hard treatment in these cases we need to appeal to considerations (typically consequentialist considerations) that are independent of the way in which punishment might otherwise be justified. But it is not at all clear whether even straightforward cases of punishment need satisfy Lee's version of the response condition.

It is not obvious whose reasons the notion of wrongness needs to figure in on Lee's view. Perhaps it is the judge's. Consider a case where a judge thinks that the law criminalizes behavior that is not morally wrong, but nevertheless takes it to be important to issue judgments that accord with the law. On Lee's view, criminals sentenced by the judge are not punished. This seems wrong. We might think that, as in the case of penalties imposed in response to strict liability offences, these are not really punishments. But this seems implausible: whether or not someone has been punished for an offence ought to be a matter discernible from facts that are available as part of the public record, rather than depending on the judge's private convictions. We should, for example, avoid an account of punishment on which an individual's appeal against their wrongful punishment could be defeated on the grounds that the judge had not thought that there was anything wrong with their behavior, and therefore that they had not been punished at all, still less wrongfully punished.

Perhaps the reasons we should be considering here are the reasons of the state, considered as a collective agent, rather than the judge's reasons. However, this suggestion is problematic. Some hold that the state can only legitimately criminalize actions that are wrongful. This view, known as legal moralism, is controversial (though it may be correct). Lee's view does not commit us to legal moralism. But it does seem to commit us to the view that, in order to punish, the state must subscribe to legal moralism: it must regard actions that it makes criminal as morally wrong. It is not obvious that states must hold this view. We should not adopt a view that says they must.

3 The Hard Treatment Condition

On some interpretations of the HBF account of punishment, hard treatment is to be understood as treatment that is *intended* to harm or burden the individual on whom it is inflicted. An alternative view is that hard treatment should be understood as treatment that is *liable* to harm or burden that individual, irrespective of the intentions with which it is inflicted. Elsewhere, I have argued for an expressive definition of punishment on the grounds that it enables us to give an extensionally adequate account of punishment that does not rely on an intention-based understanding of hard treatment (Wringe 2013). In particular, expressive considerations enable us to explain why standard cases of quarantine, pre-trial arrest, psychiatric hospitalization, and lawful self-defense should not count as instances of punishment without appealing to considerations about the intentions of those inflicting these measures.

Quarantine, psychiatric hospitalization, pre-trial arrest, and lawful self-defense all involve treatment that is liable to harm or burden the individual on whom they are inflicted. On a version of the HBF account that does not rely on an intention-based conception of hard treatment, they will count as punishment. Intuitively this seems wrong. So, we need to add something to this version of the HBF account in order to explain this intuition. Incorporating a reference to intentions in the hard treatment condition is one option, since there will be no intention to harm in standard cases of these forms of treatment. However, adding an expressive condition to the definition of punishment achieves the same result. For none of the non-punishment cases of hard treatment listed here need involve expression of the kinds of attitudes that, the expressive theorist claims, are characteristic of punishment.

One might object that, on this account, some non-standard cases of these forms of hard treatment—for example, involuntary psychiatric detention imposed after a court process and imposed in such a way as to stigmatize the individual on whom they are inflicted, or pre-trial arrest processes such as the "perp walk," which can be understood as having similar purposes, will count as instances of punishment. But this seems to be a strength rather than a weakness of the view: perhaps these practices should be recognized as instances of punishment. Doing so would be a reason for ensuring that individuals who are subjected to them are afforded the same kinds of institutional protection as are standard in paradigmatic instances of punishment.

This suggests that we should see the debate between advocates of definitional expressivism and defenders of the HBF account as turning on the question of whether we should prefer an expressive condition or an intention-based condition in a definition of punishment. The advocate of expressivism can appeal to three kinds of consideration here. First, there are problem cases: Consider, for example, a situation in which a judge, Careless, is faced by two unusual offenders, Indigent and Shameless, both of whom have been duly convicted by a jury. Indigent is homeless, and a short spell in jail over hard winter months means they are more likely to survive the winter; Shameless would hate to go prison but will not object to doing community service (and would in fact have donated their time to a scheme that has some voluntary and some involuntary participants). Careless thinks that both Indigent and Shameless have been unfairly treated by the legal system and intends to punish neither of them. Careless therefore intends to sentence Indigent to a short spell of imprisonment and Shameless to a period of community service. Unfortunately, Careless has confused two files in his memory and sentences Shameless to prison and Indigent to community service. Since Careless does not intend that either should suffer, it seems as though an advocate of a version of the HBF account that incorporates an intention to cause suffering into the hard treatment condition will have to say that neither Shameless nor Indigent is punished. This seems counterintuitive.

Can a proponent of the expressive conception do any better? One might think not. After all, if Careless does not intend to harm either Shameless or Indigent, they need not intend to express any form of condemnation in sentencing them either. But this is too quick. For the expressivist may say that, regardless of the Careless's intentions, both imprisonment and community service carry socially understood meanings and that both can, for this reason, express censure.[2] If so, the expressive account may do better than the HBF account here.

However, a defender of the intention condition might suggest that it is not Careless's intentions that matter here but some other agent or agents. Perhaps it is the intentions of legislators that matter. However, this seems implausible. It may be quite difficult to discern what the intentions of individual legislators might have been in passing a piece of legislation, and it would be strange to make the question of whether an individual is being punished turn on pieces of legislative history that may have little to do with how the law currently functions.[3]

---

[2] One might here appeal to the distinction that philosophers of language draw between speaker meaning and utterance meaning, and suggest that when we are looking at what punishment expresses we should be looking at something analogous to utterance meaning rather than speaker meaning.

[3] On some theories of the American constitution, facts about the intentions of legislators may cast a long shadow over subsequent interpretation of the law, but we should not assume that what is true in the U.S. is true everywhere in the world.

An alternative might be to take the relevant intentions to be the intentions of the state, considered as a collective agent. The definitional expressivist might object that it may be as hard to read the intentions of this collective agent from its behavior as it is to read the intentions of individual legislators from the legislative record. However, it may be difficult for the advocate of an expressive view to deploy this response in a dialectically effective manner. This is because a plausible account of how punishment expresses anything at all may need to appeal to the intentions of the state considered as a collective agent as well. This will be true if one holds, as some expressive theorists have, that what punishment expresses depends on the intentions of the punishing agent (Nozick 1981; Wringe 2016, 2021).

4 Considerations of Abolitionism

Considerations of extensional adequacy do not seem to give us compelling reasons for preferring an expressive definition of punishment over a version of the HBF definition that incorporates a reference to intentions to harm. We might instead consider the consequences of each view, in particular their consequences for debates over the abolition of punishment.

Some philosophers who argue for the abolition of punishment, such as David Boonin (2008) and Nathan Hanna (2008), claim that punishment as standardly conceived is impermissible. Furthermore, they take this impermissibility to derive from the intention to harm that is, in their view, constitutively involved in punishment. On the expressive view, arguments of this sort will not succeed as arguments for the abolition of punishment as such, since punishment need not involve an intention to harm.[4]

The fact that definitional expressivism blocks this kind of argument for abolitionism might be regarded as a point in favor of definitional expressivism. It might seem unclear how one could think this without assuming that our existing penal institutions must be justifiable. Those who do so are sometimes accused of "begging the institution." However, we should distinguish between two versions of that charge. One way of begging the institution is to assume that something approximating our existing institutions, practices, and methods of punishment must be justifiable. A second way of doing so is to

[4] They may nonetheless succeed in showing that many instances of punishment and many existing penal institutions are unjustified. The question at issue here is whether there could be permissible instances of punishment.

assume that *some* practices of punishment—perhaps very different from our own—must be justifiable.

It seems obvious that the first kind of begging the institution is objectionable. However, it is less clear that the second must be. To think that it is requires us to regard it as an open possibility that no form of punishment could be (morally) justified. But we might think that claims about moral justifiability are constrained by the principle that "ought implies can." If so, then objecting to the second kind of begging the institution seems to commit us to the idea that there could be a complex society in which there was nothing corresponding in any way to our current punitive institutions. And it is far from clear that there could. An argument in favor of the expressive definition based on the fact that it blocks arguments for penal abolitionism seems only to beg the institution in this second sense.

The debate between expressivists and advocates of an intention-based version of the HBF definition bears on abolitionism in a second way. Since expressivists and advocates of the intention-based conception disagree on what counts as punishment, they will also disagree on what counts as abolishing punishment. In particular, some of the practices and institutions that abolitionist advocates of the intention-based definition of punishment propose as alternatives to punishment may count as alternative forms of punishment on the expressivist account. So, for example, the state-enforced restitution that Boonin envisages as an alternative to punishment is in fact a form of punishment (Cholbi 2010; Wringe 2013).

In particular, the abolitionist who relies on the intention-based definition seems to leave open the possibility that a system of mass incarceration with many of the features of the U.S. prison system that horrify outside observers might fail to constitute a form of *punishment*, as the abolitionist understands it, and thus be untouched by the kinds of abolitionist argument they put forward. For it is unclear that a system of mass incarceration need involve an intention to harm (even though there can be little doubt that intentions to harm play a central role in the system of mass incarceration that we actually have). Paradoxically, abolitionists of this sort may be in more danger of succumbing to the charge of begging the institution in the first, objectionable sense than expressivists who take it to be an advantage of their view that it circumvents arguments for abolition of this sort.

5 Back to Feinberg

As I noted earlier, Feinberg does not appeal to considerations of extensional adequacy in arguing for an expressive definition of punishment. Instead, he appeals to explanatory considerations, commenting that "some of the jobs that punishment does and some of the problems it raises cannot intelligibly be described" unless some version of the expressive theory is true. Feinberg mentions four such jobs: "authoritative disavowal," "symbolic non-acquiescence," "vindication of the law," and "absolution of others" (1965, 404–8).[5]

There are at least two ways in which one might resist the argument that Feinberg puts forward here. First, one might deny that punishment does do these jobs. Second, one might claim that we can explain how punishment does these jobs without incorporating an expressive element into our definition of punishment. I shall consider each in turn. However, it is worth noting at the beginning that the kinds of examples that Feinberg gives are all examples of jobs that punishment does when imposed by a state. While it might be possible to find examples of punishments imposed by other kinds of punishing authorities that do similar kinds of jobs, skeptics about definitional expressivism could suggest that punishment's capacity to do this job does not depend on the nature of punishment but on the nature of states and the ways in which they deploy punishment.

Feinberg provides some vivid examples of cases where punishment fulfills the roles he suggests. For example, he suggests that one way in which a state might disavow the actions of a rogue member of the military would be by punishing them (Feinberg 1965, 404–5). But cases of this sort cannot be typical. The only reason for thinking that punishment expresses non-acquiescence here is that, in a case of this sort, failure to punish would constitute acquiescence. And this is because a member of the military, performing military activities, is acting on behalf their state. His actions are, in a sense, the state's actions. Most crimes are not like this. Most murders and burglaries are not carried out by state officials. There is no obvious reason to think of them as actions of the state, and thus no reason why failure to punish should count as acquiescence. One might reply that "citizenship" is a kind of office, and that courses of action which states permit can be seen as ways in which individuals are permitted to exercise this office, and thus as courses of conduct in which

[5] I ignore a fifth function that Feinberg mentions—namely that of "condemnation"—since Feinberg's argument for the claim that punishment serves this function seems to depend primarily on an appeal to the authority of other writers on American criminal law, and because what he says about it seems to constitute a restatement of the expressive view rather than an independent argument for it.

the state acquiesces. But it is not clear that we should conceive of citizenship as an office in this sense; and even if we do, the account will not cover the punishment of crimes by non-citizens.

Feinberg's suggestion that punishment plays a role in absolving the innocent also seems hard to sustain. We can understand the suggestion in two ways. First, we might think that when one individual is found guilty of a crime, others are thereby absolved of guilt in that crime. Second, we might think that when an individual is tried for a crime, acquitted, and, as a result, not punished, they are absolved of that crime. On the second point, Feinberg seems mistaken. Someone who is acquitted is absolved—to the extent that they are—by the acquittal, rather than the substantial failure to punish. This can be seen by considering the Scottish legal system, which permits a verdict of "not proven," after which an individual is not punished, but also not absolved. Nor is it true that when one individual is punished, others are absolved. One individual's being found guilty of a crime does not in any way preclude a judgment that others share in their guilt. Consider a case where two individuals are suspected of having acted in concert, but only one is prosecuted because of a lack of evidence sufficient to convict the second, or a case where two individuals are convicted but one escapes punishment on some public policy-related grounds—for example, an amnesty targeted at certain kinds of individual.

Feinberg is on stronger ground when he suggests that the practice of punishment can play a role in vindicating a law. I understand the notion of vindication in the following way: an expressive act is vindicated when a state of affairs that might otherwise lead someone to doubt its supposed significance is addressed in such a way as to reaffirm the significance of the original expressive act. If we understand criminal statutes to be prohibitions on certain courses of conduct, then crimes will be actions that, by contravening those prohibitions, give reasons for doubting that the prohibition exists. Punishment can then be seen as a way of reaffirming the status of the initial prohibition.

Some have held that criminal laws are simply prohibitions backed by threats (Austin 1995; for a dissenting view, see Hart 1961). A view of this sort might seem incompatible with the point Feinberg makes here. For if a prohibition only constitutes a law when backed by the threat of punishment, then it is hard to see how punishment could vindicate a law. Without the punishment, the threat would be an empty one: there would be no law to vindicate. However, whatever the status of this as a view about either the law as a whole or the criminal law in particular, the most it shows is that the expressivist needs to be careful how they express their view. They should say, if this view of law is correct, not that punishment vindicates the law, but that it vindicates the prohibition contained in the law.

One might also worry that this view does not provide an argument in favor of an expressive conception of punishment, but instead presupposes it. For something can only be vindicated if it has some expressive significance. But this is a mistake. Strictly speaking, what punishment vindicates on this view are the actions (other than punishment) by which the law gains its standing as law. There is nothing question-begging about assuming that these actions are expressive actions. Of course they are: this is precisely their point.

Feinberg seems correct, then, in arguing that some of the jobs that punishment does require it to have a symbolic significance. It is less clear whether this job requires us to incorporate the expressive role of punishment into a *definition* of punishment. We might think that punishment's having capacity to vindicate the law, in the way I have described, requires only that it typically and predictably has a symbolic role, not that it always does. But perhaps this is to think of the task of definition in the wrong way. For we might think of the task of definition, as undertaken by philosophers, not as that of capturing all the cases that we typically classify as punishment, but as that of enabling us to identify the features of a kind of action that make it morally distinctive. If expressive considerations play an important role either in showing that punishment is morally problematic or in showing that it is morally legitimate, then we will still have good reason to incorporate reference to expressive considerations into our definition of punishment.

6 Feinberg's Critique of Penal Expression

I noted earlier than Feinberg differed from more recent advocates of expressive conceptions of punishment insofar as he sees the expressive aspects of punishment as making our punitive practices harder rather than easier to justify. Feinberg's expressivist critique of punishment has two elements. First, the expressive dimension of punishment gives rise to a distinctive category of harms that go beyond those involved in the hard treatment that punishment entails. Second, the functions that the expressive dimension of punishment enables it to perform could be achieved in other ways, ways that involve neither hard treatment nor the kinds of additional harm that Feinberg takes to be distinctive of punishment.

To assess this critique, it is important to have some idea of the functions that punishment's expressive dimension could have. We have seen reason to question Feinberg's own account of these purposes. So, in what follows I shall consider a range of alternative suggestions as to what the expressive dimension of punishment enables it to achieve. These include Hampton's (1988) view that punishment reaffirms the status of victims; Duff's (2001) view that it communicates a message from the state to the criminal, inviting remorse and allowing for the possibility of reintegration; Bennett's (2008) suggestion that it is a formalized communication of repentance from an offender to their community; Glasgow's (2015) pure expressive view; and my own view that what is expressed is a denunciatory message from the state to the political community (Wringe 2016).

7 Expressive Justifications of Punishment (1) —Hampton

Hampton's expressive justification of punishment starts from a broader account of expressive action, which incorporates an expressive view of crime. On her view, paradigmatic examples of crimes do not simply harm their victims; they express disrespect for the agency of the victims. The message that crimes convey is that the victims have a degraded status: they are the kind of beings who *can* be treated this way. Punishment—and in particular state punishment—is a way of setting the record straight (though Hampton concedes that it may not be the only way of setting the record straight).

Hampton's view is puzzling in a number of respects. In arguing for an expressive view of crime, she gives examples of crimes that seem clearly intended by their perpetrators to degrade their victims. However, crimes that are deliberately intended to degrade seem atypical. In many cases, perpetrators of crimes will be indifferent to their victims. There may even be cases where criminals show some kind of respect for their victims—for example, by avoiding violence against them.

Hampton responds to this line of argument by appealing to Grice's (1957) account of meaning, and in particular to his account of natural meaning. This seems like a misstep. Natural meaning is Grice's name for the kind of meaning that is at stake when we say, for example, "those spots mean measles." What something means in this sense can, as Hampton says, be independent of what it is intended to mean. But as Grice notes, when used in this sense, the verb "to mean" is factive. If S means that p in this sense, then p must be true. If a particular crime "means" that the victim is worthless, then it must be the case that the victim is worthless. It seems unlikely that Hampton would endorse this suggestion. Doing so would make her theory untenable: if a particular crime means (in this sense) that a victim is worthless, then nothing the state (or anyone else) can do can mean that the victim is not worthless.

There are some possible ways out for Hampton here. One would be to argue for a counterfactualized version of the view that crime has an expressive dimension. The idea here would be that crimes do not, in societies like ours where crimes are punished, mean that victims are valueless, but that in a society where perpetrators could harm victims with impunity, this would be true, and crimes would mean this (in Grice's sense of natural meaning). Whatever the merits of this view, it does not seem to be one on which punishment itself expresses anything at all; it merely prevents crimes from having the natural meaning that they would otherwise have.[6] Compare a situation where I prevent you from spraying offensive graffiti on a fence by replacing the paint in your spray can with water. In doing so, I deprive you of the means to express a message that you might otherwise have expressed, but my own actions need not be seen as expressive of anything at all.

We might instead opt for a notion of natural meaning on which "S means p" is not factive, but defeasible. The idea here would be that "S means that p" gives one a strong reason for believing p in the absence of further evidence. By punishing a perpetrator, the state would be providing the necessary countervailing evidence. Again, though, this does not seem to be a genuinely expressive account of punishment. The evidence that the state's punishing of a perpetrator would provide against the claim that the punishment supposedly expresses does not seem to depend on punishment's having expressive properties. Furthermore, it would presumably also be true that, even if punishment meant that the victim was not worthless, this would only provide defeasible evidence of the victim's worth. (And why not treat the perpetrator's actions as undermining this message?)

The idea that the kind of meaning that crime and punishment have is Gricean natural meaning seems unfruitful. A more plausible suggestion is that we need to appeal to a Gricean distinction between two aspects of what he calls "non-natural" meaning—namely, that between utterance meaning and speaker meaning. That there is a distinction here seems fairly intuitive: if I am ignorant or simply careless about certain facts of linguistic usage, my utterance may convey a message very different from the one I intended. If so, we

[6] One might wonder whether, on this view, punishment could be said to express, in the natural meaning sense, that victims have value. But I do not think it could. The factivity of non-natural meaning seems to raise a problem here too. We could presumably punish someone who harmed something that does not have the kind of value that persons have, such as a statue. Punishing that individual could not mean (in the natural meaning sense) that the statue had this value, since it does not. So, it is not clear how punishing an individual who harms a victim—someone who does have this kind of value—could mean this either.

might think that a crime might express something independent of what the perpetrator intended to convey; and, indeed, something that it would make sense for the state to contradict.

However, once Hampton's view is expressed in these terms, it seems vulnerable to both of Feinberg's lines of critique. Let us start with the idea that the expressive dimension of punishment gives rise to a range of distinctive harms. It is natural to think that Feinberg had in mind distinctive harms against those who are punished, and to think that the kinds of harm he had in mind are connected with particular emotions—specifically, the emotion of contempt that is expressed here. We might think that Hampton has a plausible rejoinder here: punishment need not inflict these kinds of dignitary harms on the perpetrators of crimes.

However, we might also worry about a different kind of harm. As Gert et al. (2004) have noted, the view that the way in which crime expresses disrespect involves non-natural meaning is naturally understood as one on which the connection between harm and disrespect is conventional. However, it is also natural to think that the force of a convention depends on its being endorsed authoritatively. The worry is then that, by punishing perpetrators as a way of bringing them low, the state endorses a conventional connection between being on the receiving end of violence and being degraded, and that this is a convention that we should be seeking to undermine rather than reinforce.

So much for the idea that the expressive dimension of punishment gives rise to a distinctive range of harms. We might have good reason to tolerate those harms if they were an unavoidable corollary of some kind of benefit that could only be brought about by punishment. But on the version of Hampton's view we are considering, it is hard to see why this should be the case. There are two points to note here. First, the state might find other ways of affirming the value of victims of crime than by inflicting harm on the perpetrators of crime. (Feinberg suggests several.) Second, if the connection between harming and the affirmation of value is indeed conventional, as we are currently supposing, then it is hard to see why it should not be possible to find alternatives.

8 Expressive Justifications of Punishment (2) —Duff

As we have seen, Feinberg saw two reasons for being concerned about the expressive dimension of punishment: first, that it is insufficient to justify punishment, because the expressive goals of punishment could be achieved in other, less harmful ways; and second that it produces a range of distinctive harms, going beyond those involved in the hard treatment of the punished. I have argued that Hampton's version of the expressive theory is vulnerable to both lines of criticism. But if I am correct, this is true because of the kind of expressive goal that Hampton takes punishment to have. So, it is worth considering an alternative account.

Antony Duff's version of an expressive justification of punishment might seem to fit the bill here. Duff's view is distinctive in a number of respects. He holds that we have a duty to punish and that this duty is a relational or directed duty, and more specifically a duty we owe to the criminal rather than to the victim (as we might think Hampton's view suggests) or to society at large. We owe this duty to those who we share a society with because we owe it to them to treat them as persons with who we are in community rather than mere threats, and our being in community with them entails a duty to hold them to account for wrongdoing rather than merely taking evasive or preemptive action against them (Duff 2001, 75–79).

Duff's view of our duty to punish provides for one kind of response to one of Feinberg's lines of critique. Even if it is true that the expressive dimension of punishment gives rise to a range of distinctive harms, the fact that we have a duty to punish may mean that we must simply accept that we will bring about those harms (just as in other cases where fulfilling a duty may require me to cause harm to individuals to whom I have no countervailing duty).

Duff's account of our duty to punish also puts constraints on the form that punishment can take. The kind of punishment we have a duty to inflict expresses a particular kind of message (condemnation of the crime rather than, say, contempt for the criminal); to a particular audience (in the first instance, the criminal themselves, rather than, say, society at large or the world in general); and with a particular goal (inducing remorse and reintegrating the criminal into society). Punishments that do not fit this description are punishments that we do not have a duty to inflict—and presumably many countervailing duties not to inflict. Furthermore, Duff is explicit about the fact that many of our punitive practices may be unacceptable when judged in light of these considerations. So, it may well be that the kinds of punishment Duff would regard us as having a duty to inflict would not bring about the range of expressive harms that our current punitive practices cause.

However, Duff does regard hard treatment as an essential constituent in punishment. So, he faces a second line of critique from Feinberg: namely, whether the kinds of communicative goal which he takes to be essential to punishment can only be achieved by inflicting hard treatment. Duff has two lines of response here, neither of which seems entirely satisfactory. The first is that since the kind of punishment we have a duty to inflict is aimed at bringing about remorse, and since remorse is by its nature unpleasant for the individual who suffers remorse, the kind of punishment we have a duty to inflict must aim at being unpleasant for the person who suffers punishment (Duff 2001). Christopher Bennet (2006) has objected that the state (or at least, liberal states) have no proper interest in whether an individual offender is genuinely remorseful. But whether or not this is true, Hanna (2008) has raised a more powerful objection: namely, that even if Duff has made a case for thinking that we have a duty to try to make offenders experience remorse, he has not made a case for thinking that the characteristic harms of paradigmatic forms of punishment such as incarceration and the deprivation of liberty are necessary for achieving this goal.

A second line of response may be more helpful here. This is to suggest that hard treatment may be a particularly effective way of communicating condemnation in a way that is likely to elicit remorse. However, this line of argument has two weaknesses: one empirical, the other conceptual. The conceptual weakness is that even if hard treatment is the most effective way of communicating a message that we have a duty to convey, it does not follow from the fact that we have a duty to communicate a message that we have a duty to communicate in it the most effective way. The most effective way to do something that I have a duty to do may be ruled out by other moral considerations. For example, I may have promised to give you a birthday gift that you will love. Even if the most effective way of doing so is to steal a particularly desirable gift, my duty to give you a gift does not license me—still less require me—to steal the item in question.

Leaving this aside, it seems far from obvious that hard treatment is the most effective way of inducing remorse in criminals. There is little evidence that existing methods of punishment are effective in this respect. Admittedly, we might respond on Duff's behalf that he is not interested in defending existing forms of punishment (Duff 2001, xv–xvi). But if a defense of Duff's view is instead based on the idea that some imaginable forms of punishment might be an effective way of promoting remorse, then it is even less clear what kind of evidence we might have here.

9 Expressive Justifications of Punishment—Further Variants

The kinds of expressive justification of punishment that I have discussed in the previous two sections share some common features. Both of them see punishment as involving the state's expressing something (whether condemnation of a crime or reaffirmation of the status of a victim), and both of them see the value of punishment as deriving from the possibility of successfully communicating what is expressed to the right kind of audience. However, some accounts of the justification of punishment that fall within this general family do not share these features.

Bennett (2008) has defended a form of expressivism in which punishment—or the undergoing of punishment—constitutes a form of ritualized penance on the part of the individual undergoing punishment to society as a whole. On Bennett's account, the offender's state of mind is irrelevant to the message expressed. What we have here is a kind of formalized gesture. We might compare the way in which (in pre-COVID times), a handshake might be a gesture of welcome even when offered by someone who does not in fact welcome the individual to whom the handshake is offered.

On Bennett's account, punishment offers a distinctive benefit to the individual punished: the opportunity to be seen as having atoned for their wrongdoing, and hence to be a candidate for reintegration into society. This benefit is so significant that individuals have a right to be punished, and this right is so significant that it cannot be waived (Bennett 2008). This view is compatible with the idea that punishment also involves distinctive harms. Someone who believes this may nonetheless believe that the existence of these harms is outweighed by the benefit that punishment provides to the punished person (provided, of course, that there is no other way of producing that benefit).

This claim sits ill with the idea that the expressive content of punishment is fixed purely conventionally. If it was, then individuals could presumably do their penance in ways that did not involve the imposition of hard treatment. But Bennett rejects the idea that the kind of expression typical of emotions is purely conventional. He suggests rather that some physical expressions of emotion are symbolically adequate to particular kinds of emotion. Thus, for example, slow movement is appropriate for the expression of grief, loud noise for the expression of joy, and so on. Similarly, one might take various kinds of self-abasement to be symbolically appropriate to the expression of remorse. If so, one might think, nothing could achieve symbolically what punishment achieves without involving hard treatment. And perhaps more obviously, nothing could do that job without exposing one to expressive harms such as stigmatization.

The idea that forms of emotional expression are not infinitely malleable plays an important role in another recent defense of expressivism put forward by Joshua Glasgow (2015). Glasgow's view differs from some standard versions of expressivism in finding no role for the idea that punishment expresses something to an *audience*. On his view, a punishment is justifiable insofar as it involves the punishing authority's giving appropriate expression of the right kind of emotional response to an offender's wrongdoing. Like Bennett, Glasgow responds to Feinberg's worry about hard treatment based on the idea that the way in which we express such emotions is not so malleable as to allow for the possibility of appropriate expression without the inflicting of hard treatment.

While it might be tempting to respond to Feinberg's worry by insisting that the expressive goals of punishment can only be achieved by hard treatment, Bennett and Glasgow seem to be on the wrong track when they appeal to a lack of plasticity in the ways in which we express our emotions to justify this claim. For even if it is true that many emotions have natural forms of expression, it is also true that these natural forms of expression can be elaborated in a variety of ways. Consider here the vast range of mourning practices that can be found around the world.

One striking fact about these practices is that they seem remarkably adaptable to changing material and cultural circumstances. Once, it might have seemed impossible adequately to mourn a spouse without wearing black for a year, but that no longer seems to be the case. If it now seems that punishment has to involve hard treatment in order to symbolize the humbling of an offender, we might look to adjust our symbolic practices—not, perhaps, as Feinberg suggests, by throwing a ticker-tape parade for offenders, but, for example, by symbolically destroying them in effigy.

If we wish to appeal to the non-malleability of forms of expression in order to respond to Feinberg's concern about hard treatment, it may be better to return to a version of the idea common to both Hampton and Duff (but not shared by the authors I have discussed in this section) that punishment involves the state communicating a message to a particular audience. Doing so opens up a new possibility: that of appealing to the non-malleability of the interpretative resources of the audience rather than that of the expressive resources of the agent conveying the message.

The view I have in mind is a view that I have elsewhere labelled a "denunciatory" view of punishment (Wringe 2016, 2017; following Narayan 1993). On this view, punishment expresses a condemnatory message to society at large, not to the offender. Someone who holds this view is in a position to argue that hard treatment is necessary for the intended audience of the message it expresses—namely, the society whose laws have been broken—to understand the condemnation as condemnation. Indeed, it may not simply be that punishment must involve hard treatment of some sort. It may even be the case that particular forms of hard treatment, such as incarceration, may be called for in certain times and places. It would not follow from this that there is no possibility of introducing forms of punishment that, while involving hard treatment, do not bring with them the collateral harms typical of these paradigmatic forms of hard treatment. Doing so is, however, likely to have as a prerequisite the success of a significant campaign of public education rather than simply depending on legislative or judicial fiat.

The denunciatory view, then, seems to be the version of expressivism that is best equipped to meet the challenges identified by Feinberg more than fifty years ago. This is not to deny that it faces difficulties of its own. A full exploration of them must await another occasion.

References

Austin, John. 1995. *The Province of Jurisprudence Determined.* Edited by Wilfrid E. Rumble. Cambridge: Cambridge University Press.

Benn, S. I. 1958. "An Approach to the Problems of Punishment." *Philosophy* 33, no. 127 (October): 325–41.

Bennett, Christopher. 2006. "Taking the Sincerity Out of Saying Sorry: Restorative Justice as Ritual." *Journal of Applied Philosophy* 23, no. 2 (May): 127–43.

———. 2008. *The Apology Ritual: A Philosophical Theory of Punishment.* Cambridge: Cambridge University Press.

Boonin, David. 2008. *The Problem of Punishment.* Cambridge: Cambridge University Press.

Cholbi, Michael. 2010. "Compulsory Victim Restitution Is Punishment: A Reply to Boonin." *Public Reason* 2, no. 1 (June): 85–93.

Duff, R. A. 2001. *Punishment, Communication, and Community.* Oxford: Oxford University Press.

Feinberg, Joel. 1965. "The Expressive Function of Punishment." *Monist* 49, no. 3 (July): 397–423.

Flew, Antony. 1954. "The Justification of Punishment." *Philosophy* 29, no. 111 (October): 291–307.

Gert, Heather J., Linda Radzik, and Michael Hand. 2004. "Hampton on the Expressive Power of Punishment." *Journal of Social Philosophy* 35, no. 1 (March): 79–90.

Glasgow, Joshua. 2015. "The Expressive Theory of Punishment Defended." *Law and Philosophy* 34, no. 6 (November): 601–31.
Grice, H. P. 1957. "Meaning." *Philosophical Review* 66, no. 3 (July): 377–88.
Hampton, Jean. 1988. "The Retributive Idea." In *Forgiveness and Mercy*, edited by Jeffrie G. Murphy and Jean Hampton, 111–61. Cambridge: Cambridge University Press.
———. 1992. "Correcting Harms versus Righting Wrongs: The Goal of Retribution." *UCLA Law Review* 39, no. 6 (August): 1659–702.
Hanna, Nathan. 2008. "Say What? A Critique of Expressive Retributivism." *Law and Philosophy* 27, no. 2 (March): 123–50.
———. 2017. "The Nature of Punishment: Reply to Wringe." *Ethical Theory and Moral Practice* 20, no. 5 (November): 969–76.
———. 2020. "The Nature of Punishment Revisited: Reply to Wringe." *Ethical Theory and Moral Practice* 23, no. 1 (February): 89–100.
Hart, H. L. A. 1960. "Prolegomenon to the Principles of Punishment." *Proceedings of the Aristotelian Society* 60, no. 1 (June): 1–26.
———. 1961. *The Concept of Law*. Oxford: Oxford University Press.
Hegel, Georg Wilhelm Friedrich. 1942. *Hegel's Philosophy of Right*. Translated by T. M. Knox. Oxford: Clarendon.
Lee, Ambrose Y. K. 2019. "Arguing against the Expressive Function of Punishment: Is the Standard Account That Insufficient?" *Law and Philosophy* 38, no. 4 (August): 359–85.
Metz, Thaddeus. 2000. "Censure Theory and Intuitions about Punishment." *Law and Philosophy* 19, no. 4 (July): 491–512.
———. 2007. "How to Reconcile Liberal Politics with Retributive Punishment." *Oxford Journal of Legal Studies* 27, no. 4 (Winter): 683–705.
Narayan, Uma. 1993. "Appropriate Responses and Preventive Benefits: Justifying Censure and Hard Treatment in Legal Punishment." *Oxford Journal of Legal Studies* 13, no. 2 (Summer): 166–82.
Nozick, Robert. 1981. *Philosophical Explanations*. Cambridge, MA: Belknap.
Stephen, James Fitzjames. 1967. *Liberty, Equality, Fraternity*. Edited by R. J. White. Cambridge: Cambridge University Press.
Wringe, Bill. 2013. "Must Punishment Be Intended to Cause Suffering?" *Ethical Theory and Moral Practice* 16, no. 4 (August): 863–77.
———. 2016. *An Expressive Theory of Punishment*. Basingstoke, UK: Palgrave Macmillan.
———. 2017. "Rethinking Expressive Theories of Punishment: Why Denunciation Is a Better Bet Than Communication or Pure Expression." *Philosophical Studies* 174, no. 3 (March): 681–708.
———. 2019. "Punishment, Jesters and Judges: A Response to Nathan Hanna." *Ethical Theory and Moral Practice* 22, no. 1 (February): 3–12.
———. 2021. "Expressive Theories of Punishment: Who Says What to Whom?" In *Collective Action, Philosophy and Law*, edited by Teresa Marques and Chiara Valentini, 229–46. London: Routledge.

12

Justifying Criminal Punishment as Societal-Defense

Phillip Montague

The broad philosophical context within which theories of punishment are developed is the very basic moral presumption against doing harm to other people. The concept of harm is relevant in two ways: criminal punishments are commonly imposed on those convicted of harming others, and yet punishment is itself harmful by its very nature. We suppose that there is a difference—that is, a moral difference—between the two types of harming, yet the precise nature of this difference is not at all obvious. Of course, various explanations of its nature appear in the literature on punishment; references to deterrence and retribution commonly occur in this context. Some comments on both of these explanations will be offered later, but right now I want to ask this more general question about the morality of harming: In what sorts of situations are people most obviously morally justified in harming others? And here, intuitively speaking, is the answer: these are situations involving self-defense against culpable aggression.

This intuition provides a point of departure for the discussion that follows. I propose to explain how criminal punishment is morally justifiable as an

P. Montague (✉)
Western Washington University, Bellingham, WA, USA
e-mail: montague@wwu.edu; phillip.montague@wwu.edu

© The Author(s), under exclusive license to Springer Nature Switzerland AG 2023
M. C. Altman (ed.), *The Palgrave Handbook on the Philosophy of Punishment*, Palgrave Handbooks in the Philosophy of Law, https://doi.org/10.1007/978-3-031-11874-6_12

instrument of societal-defense[1]—and this notwithstanding its being imposed on people for past harms they have done, whereas in justified self-defense, individuals harm others to prevent themselves from being harmed.[2] Developing this account of the justifiability of criminal punishment will require first identifying the principle that justifies harming others in self-defense, and then applying that principle to societal-defense. As will be explained in due course, this principle locates the justification of punishment squarely within the realm of justice, although the relevant form of justice is not retributive, as is commonly claimed.[3]

1 Justifying Individual Self-Defense

We will begin by focusing on situations with individuals who pose threats of harm and individuals who are under threat of being harmed. And in the situations of particular interest to us here, the former are culpable aggressors and the latter are their innocent intended victims. The severity of harm that might be done by culpable aggressors or by their intended victims can obviously vary, but we will simplify matters initially by restricting our attention to "kill-or-be-killed" situations. These are situations in which a culpable aggressor poses a deadly threat to some innocent person, and where the latter can avoid being killed by—and only by—using deadly defensive force against the aggressor. We will simplify matters further—again, initially—by considering cases in which there are no innocent bystanders who would be harmed by defensive actions on the part of the intended victims.

Although there are those who maintain that taking a human life is always immoral, we will assume that this view is mistaken: that using deadly defensive force under the conditions described above is morally justified. What we need is a principled basis for this assumption, and there are two very general

[1] I first presented this theory in Montague (1983). The theory is more fully developed in Montague (1995).

[2] A moral justification can take either of two forms: a mere permission, where being permitted to act is compatible with being permitted to refrain; or a requirement, where being required to act is not compatible with being permitted to refrain. It seems to me clear that an acceptable theory of criminal punishment should not imply that those authorized to impose punishments have moral discretion either to punish or to refrain from doing so. In other words, the task of justifying criminal punishment consists in explaining how it can be morally required. The distinction between permissions and requirements will come into play at several stages of the discussion that follows.

[3] In claiming that punishment is necessarily harmful, I am not equating punishment with *corporal* punishment. I am construing "harmful" very broadly—along the lines suggested by Joel Feinberg—who interprets harm as the invasion of an interest. See Feinberg's (1987) insightful and thorough investigation of the moral and legal status of harming.

approaches to developing such a basis. One of these approaches centers on the concept of defense, and the other on the concept of culpability.

On the former approach, self-defense against culpable aggression is seen as having to fall within a general theory of morally justified defensive harming. Such a theory would presumably include explanations of justified self-defense not only against culpable aggression, but also against innocent aggressors and "innocent threats." Within this approach, the key concept is defense. I believe, however, that we should proceed according to the second of the two approaches referred to above: we should focus not on defense, but on culpability. That is, explaining justified self-defense against culpable aggressors should not occur within a comprehensive theory of self-defense. Rather, it should occur within a theory that focuses on individuals who are culpable for performing actions that are not aggressive but are nevertheless similar in appropriate respects to the actions of culpable aggressors.[4] A look at some cases will be useful in explaining how this works, beginning with two variations on the "runaway-trolley" theme.

The first case is somewhat reminiscent of those usually discussed:

> Alice is driving a trolley down a steep hill when the brakes fail. The tracks ahead curve sharply. If Alice continues on the current route, then—at the speed Alice is traveling—the trolley will derail and Alice will be killed. Fortunately for Alice, there is a spur onto which the trolley can be steered, but—unfortunately for Al—Al is walking in the middle of that spur. If Alice does turn, the trolley will hit and kill Al.

In turning the trolley, Alice would clearly not be fending off an attack, and hence—although acting in self-protection—Alice would not be acting in self-defense. In this vein, the question that is usually addressed in discussions of such cases is whether someone in Alice's circumstances is morally justified in causing another person's death in order to preserve the first person's own life. And although numerous philosophers have proposed various answers to this question, it is fair to say, I think, that none of them are unquestionably correct.

But now suppose that Al has deliberately disabled the brakes of Alice's trolley in the hope that the trolley will crash and Alice will be killed. Then answering the question of what Alice is morally justified in doing is quite

[4] Two theories of self-defense that center on the concept of defense are developed in Thomson (1977, 1991) and McMahan (2005). For a variety of other ways in which theories of self-defense can be categorized, see Doggett (2011). I believe that the distinction I have drawn between two fundamentally different approaches to justifying self-defense cuts across those drawn by Doggett and is, in any case, essential for my purposes.

straightforward: Alice is justified in saving Alice's own life even though that results in Al's death.

The reason Alice is justified in acting in this way is that Al is culpable for creating a situation in which Alice faces a "forced choice" between lives—a situation in which, no matter what Alice does, either Alice's life or Al's will be lost. And, in these circumstances, Alice is justified in choosing in Alice's own favor. Analogously, the intended victim of culpable aggression in a kill-or-be-killed situation is morally justified in killing the aggressor in self-defense.[5] The justifications in both the latter situations and in the "Alice" case are permissions, not requirements. Alice is permitted to turn the trolley, but also permitted to go straight ahead and allow Alice to be killed. Similarly, the intended victims in self-defense situations of the sort considered above are permitted to kill their attackers but are also permitted to refrain, allowing themselves to be killed. This interpretation of the justifiability of self-defense is implicit in the idea of a *right* of self-defense: having a right to act implies being permitted either to act or to refrain.

There is a principle implicit in what has been said about the case of Al and Alice, and about the analogous self-defense cases—a principle that applies to two-party kill-or-be-killed self-defense and self-protection situations. A more general principle would apply to harm-or-be-harmed situations that might include innocent bystanders, and it would apply not only to the prevention of harm to oneself but also to the prevention of harm to others. The more general principle would apply to cases like these:

> Bob will be harmed by Bo, a culpable attacker, unless Brenda harms Bo in other-defense.
>
> Cal is responsible for vaccinating the members of a group of people against a serious disease; there is not enough of the vaccine to go around, and those who are not vaccinated will become ill; some potential recipients of the vaccine culpably caused this scarcity.

We cannot conclude straightaway that Brenda is justified in defending Bob until we know how severely Bob would be harmed if Brenda did not do so, and how much harm Brenda would need to inflict on Bo to defend Bob. We would also need to know whether Brenda's acting other-defensively would

[5] Note that the above characterization of one's facing a forced-choice situation makes no mention of what the person reasonably believes, or what a reasonable person would believe, or what is probable, and so on. While such (primarily epistemic) considerations commonly play prominent roles in formulations of laws relating to self-defense, and while they might be relevant to matters of moral exculpation, they play no role in my explanation of the moral justifiability of using defensive force.

harm any innocent bystanders. Similarly, determining whether Cal is justified in withholding the vaccine from those responsible for its scarcity would require knowing how seriously ill they would become if not vaccinated as compared with the effects of withholding it from the other potential recipients. And we would also need to know whether different vaccine distributions within the group would affect the spread of the illness to people outside the group.

So, we can say this: Brenda is justified in harming Bo, and Cal is justified in withholding the vaccine from those who caused the shortfall—but only if other things are equal. Moreover, the justifications in these cases of, respectively, other-defense and other-protection are requirements, not mere permissions. If Brenda is indeed justified in defending Bob against Bo's attack, then Brenda is required to do so. And if Cal is justified in withholding the vaccine from the culpable parties, then this is a requirement, not a mere permission.

We are now in a position to formulate the principle that underlies the various cases that we have considered:

> JUSTICE: If someone culpably creates a situation in which harm is unavoidable from others' standpoints and *ceteris paribus*, then harming the culpable person is permissible or required (depending on the circumstances)—and this as a matter of justice in the distribution of burdens.[6]

The *ceteris paribus* conditions for JUSTICE concern the minimization of proportional harm to culpable individuals, to the presence of what will be referred to as graded culpability, and to effects on innocent bystanders. These conditions require some explanation. For although they have been introduced in connection with the actions of individuals, they have analogues that will later be applied to acts of societal-defense.

According to the proportionality condition, the distribution of unavoidable harm among those who are culpable for the existence of that harm must not exceed that which is proportional to the harm that would be suffered by innocent persons under a different distribution. It is important to recognize that this condition concerns individual rather than collective harm. If a choice must be made between distributing harm to one person or to several, and if the several are jointly culpable for the existence of that harm; then the innocent person must be favored even if the total harm resulting from such a distribution is much greater than that which would result from a distribution favoring those who are culpable. But the harm suffered by each culpable

[6] For an early formulation of this principle (although with a different name), see Montague (1981).

individual under a given distribution must not be out of proportion to that which would be suffered by an innocent person under a different distribution.

Returning to our other-defense example of Brenda, Bob, and Bo, the proportionality condition would prevent JUSTICE from being used to justify doing major harm to Bo (or to any number of jointly culpable attackers) in order to save Bob from suffering minor harm. If the only harm possible in a given situation is the loss of life, then the proportionality condition is automatically satisfied, and questions about the quantity of harm done do not arise unless innocent persons are affected differently by different distributions.

The proportionality condition places a maximum on the amount of unavoidable harm that may be done to individuals according to JUSTICE. There is also a minimization condition according to which those culpable for the existence of unavoidable harm may not themselves be harmed more than is necessary in order to protect innocent persons. Turning again to our other-defense example, JUSTICE with this minimization condition cannot be used to justify a distribution of harm that results in Bo's death if another distribution is possible that, although somewhat harmful to Bo, preserves his life as well as Bob's.

The graded culpability condition for JUSTICE can come into play in forced-choice situations that are culpably created by multiple individuals. Suppose we have such a situation that is culpably created by two people, where the culpability of one individual is greater than that of the other. Then, if possible, the burdens in those situations should be distributed accordingly. Thus, consider the following case:

> Dora raises cattle on a farm that is downwind from a chemical factory owned and operated by Ed and Edith. Edith dislikes Dora and deliberately releases fumes from the factory that the wind carries to the farm, killing Dora's cattle. If Ed had been paying proper attention to the factory's machinery, he could have—and would have—prevented the fumes from escaping; but Ed was watching a TV game show instead. A county official can decide whether to (a) require Edith and Ed to compensate Dora for her losses; or (b) compensate Dora from county funds; or (c) do nothing.

In this forced-choice situation culpably created by Edith and Ed, JUSTICE requires the county official to pursue option (a). Although the situation is culpably created by both Edith and Ed, Edith's level of culpability is greater than Ed's, so Edith should be required to bear the greater compensatory burden.

A fourth *ceteris paribus* condition for JUSTICE concerns the harmful side effects for innocent persons that might result from distributions of harm aimed at protecting other innocent persons. The need for this condition can be illustrated by "innocent-bystander" cases. Thus, Brenda might be able to prevent Bob from being killed by Bo only at the expense of other innocent lives. Then JUSTICE would not straightforwardly imply that Brenda should defend Bob.

The idea, then, is that the justified killing of culpable aggressors in self-defense can be explained by appealing to JUSTICE. It is worth emphasizing, though, that JUSTICE might have been developed without any consideration of self-defense situations—by focusing exclusively on non-defensive, culpably created, forced-choice situations. And because JUSTICE provides plausible explanations of morally justified harming in these latter situations, it could then have been applied to situations involving self-defense against culpable aggression. This fact about JUSTICE helps explain why I suggested above that, in formulating a theory of self-defense against culpable aggression, the key concept is culpability, not defense.

Although JUSTICE does apply to situations having nothing to do with actions that are strictly speaking defensive, we will henceforth focus exclusively on defense situations. Moreover, we will move from forced-choices and defensive actions by individuals to corresponding choices and actions by societies. We will do this because we need to know whether imposing criminal punishments on individuals is justified; and, although JUSTICE provides a principled basis for justifying criminal punishment, the principle cannot be applied directly to the punishment of individuals. For situations in which the punishment of individuals is being contemplated do not typically involve forced-choices. As was emphasized at the very outset of this inquiry, unlike acts of self- or other-defense, say, which are aimed at preventing harm, punishment is imposed after the fact of harm's being done. Punishing people after they have harmed others would inflict additional harm that is avoidable simply by refraining from punishment. In other words, those who are contemplating punishing others are not faced with forced choices in the distribution of harm that is unavoidable from their standpoints, and JUSTICE is therefore not directly applicable to their situations.

In order to explain the justifiability of imposing criminal punishment on individuals, we must first explain why societal decisions to establish systems of punishment can be morally justified. The former explanation grows out of the latter with the aid of some extremely plausible empirical propositions. In combination, these explanations constitute the theory of punishment as societal-defense. But, as I will now explain, the theory faces a problem associated with its references to societal choices and actions. These references cannot be taken at face value; they require interpretation and explanation if they are not to be seriously problematic.

2 The Problem of Societal Action

At first glance, the applicability of JUSTICE to societal-defense may seem straightforwardly analogous to the principle's application to individual defense. That is, if a society can be faced with a forced-choice in distributing unavoidable harms, and if some potential recipients of the harms are aggressors who culpably created the forced-choice situation, then (other things being equal) it would seem that the society is justified in distributing the harms to the aggressors. However, while this explanation of how JUSTICE applies to societal-defense is essentially correct, it also sidesteps a problem that I now propose to address. Doing so will have the added benefit of shedding light on what exactly is meant by punishment as societal-defense.

The problem to which I allude arises from references to defensive actions by societies. Such references seem to presuppose the possibility of collective actions—actions by collections per se. We attribute apparently collective actions to teams, legislative bodies, theater companies, corporations, armies, nations, and so on. For example, we might say that the Kansas City Chiefs played in the Super Bowl, Congress passed the Affordable Care Act, the Royal Shakespeare Company performed *Romeo and Juliet*, Delta merged with Northeastern, or Pickett's division attacked the Union lines. Such statements appear to attribute actions to collections of individuals, which actions are related to but are distinct from actions performed by members of those collections.

Thus, consider Pickett's charge at Gettysburg. That action did not consist simply in an attack by this Confederate soldier, and an attack by that Confederate soldier, and an attack by this other Confederate soldier, and so on. Similarly, the Union response did not consist simply in a defensive action by this Union soldier, and so on. Over and above these individual aggressive and defensive actions, there was an organized charge and an organized defense, each of which appears to be a kind of collective action. In other words, in attributing actions of a certain type to a collection, we are not simply aggregating actions of that kind performed by everyone in that collection. Rather, we seem to be attributing actions to the collections themselves.

Yet collections of individuals can reasonably be regarded as abstract entities, and it is at least unclear that such entities are capable of performing actions. An action is, after all, a piece of behavior that is intentional under some description—is therefore essentially related to beliefs and desires—and it is very hard to see how abstract entities can possibly possess such mental properties. The problem here obviously extends to the idea of collective choices—to collective forced-choices in particular. If societies, like other abstract entities, are incapable of making genuine choices, and therefore cannot possibly face forced-choices, then it would appear that JUSTICE cannot be used to justify punishment as societal-defense. And of course, the problem here is not solved by eliminating references to societal choices in favor of references to choices by states, governments, legislatures, and so on.[7]

Although there is good reason to question the existence of genuinely collective actions, however, statements seeming to attribute actions to collections are not only common in ordinary discourse but are also often true. For example, it is undeniably true that the Kansas City Chiefs played in Super Bowl LIV, and that the Royal Shakespeare Company performed *Romeo and Juliet* in 2018. It is also undeniably true that Belgium defended itself against a German invasion in 1914.

So, we have something of a dilemma here: collections per se cannot possibly perform actions, but some sentences apparently attributing actions to collections express true propositions. To resolve this dilemma, I suggest that we do two things: we distinguish collective actions from what I shall call "joint actions"; and we investigate the truth conditions of propositions apparently attributing actions to collections. Let us examine these two suggestions, beginning with a look at the notion of a joint action.

Whereas collective actions—if they existed—would have abstract entities as agents, joint actions have multiple concrete individuals as agents. Here is a homely example that illustrates this distinction:

> Sally's car has a dead battery. Harry offers to help with Sally's problem by connecting the battery to Harry's by means of jumper cables, and Sally accepts the offer. When Harry completes the connection, Harry signals Sally, who is at the controls. Sally engages the starter and the car starts.

So, who started Sally's car? Why, Sally and Harry, of course. However, while the proposition that Sally and Harry started the car is true, the proposition

[7] For a very useful collection of essays on this topic, see May and Hoffman (1992).

that Sally started the car and Harry started the car is false. We might interpret the former proposition as implying that a pair of people started Sally's car. That is, we might say that a collection—an abstract entity—containing Sally and Harry as members performed a collective action. However, a more perspicuous interpretation would refer to the joint action—the starting of Sally's car—whose agents are the concrete individuals, Sally and Harry.

We now consider the truth conditions of the proposition that Sally and Harry started Sally's car: we ask, "What are the conditions in virtue of which this proposition is true?" We ask this because, if we want to know what a sentence says in a given context, then we must determine the truth conditions of the proposition expressed by the sentence in that context. And it turns out that these questions can be answered without any references to abstract entities. A statement of these truth-conditions in our current example would refer to certain individual actions performed by Sally and Harry respectively, and to ways in which these actions are connected with each other. It is in virtue of the nature of the individual actions that are performed by Sally and Harry, and of how these actions are interconnected, that it is true that they started the car. In other words, over and above the individual actions respectively performed by Sally and Harry, there is a joint action that consists in the starting of Sally's car, and whose agents are both Sally and Harry.[8]

What has been said here about joint actions in the Sally/Harry example can be extended to situations containing more than just two agents. Moreover, joint actions can be composed not only of individual actions, but also of other joint actions. If, in our example, some friend of Harry's helps Harry connect the cables and does so with appropriate beliefs and desires, then their joint

---

[8] Here is a statement of the truth conditions for the proposition that Sally and Harry started Sally's car:

> Sally wants the car to be started. Sally believes that, if Sally engages the starter and Harry does Harry's part, then the car will start. Harry wants Sally's car to be started. Harry believes that, if Harry connects Sally's battery to Harry's and Sally does Sally's part, then the car will start. Sally's desires and beliefs lead Sally to engage the starter (call this action A). Harry's desires and beliefs lead Harry to connect the two batteries (call this action B). Assuming that the car is otherwise in working order and the cables are properly connected, Sally's performing A initiates a sequence of events that merges with the sequence of events initiated by Harry's performing B, forming a sequence of events that results in the starting of Sally's car.

While it is not true that Sally started the car, and it is not true that Harry started the car, each of them performs an action (A and B respectively) that is a component of the joint action that consists in starting Sally's car. They exercise joint agency in doing so, in virtue of the common contents of the beliefs and desires that lead them to perform the individual components of their joint action. Although Sally and Harry's joint action and joint agency are distinct from their individual actions and exercises of agency, the former are explicable in terms of the latter. For other discussions of actions with multiple agents, see Bratman (1993) and Kutz (2000).

action is a component of a larger joint action performed by Sally, Harry, and the friend.

Because joint actions admit of this sort of structuring, they can be quite complex and involve large numbers of agents. Plays and games provide contexts within which complex joint actions are commonly performed. For example, the proposition that Kansas City played in Super Bowl LIV is true because individuals who were members of the Kansas City Chiefs on February 8th, 2020, individually and jointly performed actions of certain sorts on that date. And if it is true that the Royal Shakespeare Company performed *Romeo and Juliet* on August 23rd, 2018, then this is because of certain individual and joint actions performed by members of the Company on that date.[9] We have here partial statements of the truth conditions for the two original propositions. And it should be clear enough that a complete statement of these conditions would contain no references to abstract entities.

The upshot here is that we can correctly use the language of action in connection with collections—we can apparently attribute actions to collections—without thereby committing ourselves to the idea that collections per se are literally capable of performing actions. In particular, sentences of the form "Society S created a system of punishment" can express true propositions without attributing actions to abstract entities. Stating the truth conditions for such propositions would doubtless be a complex business, but would be no more difficult than stating truth conditions for the proposition that Germany invaded Belgium in 1914, or the proposition that Delta Airlines merged with Northeastern Airlines in 1972. Each of these propositions refers to a complex joint action that is composed of many other joint actions; and the agents of all these joint actions are concrete individuals.

3 Punishment as Societal-Defense

Imagine a society S that is organized as a political community, with provisions and mechanisms for creating necessary laws and institutions that conform to applicable moral principles. Suppose that S contains a subclass S′ of

[9] In many—perhaps most—cases, a sentence of the form "Group G performed A" can express a true proposition even though not every member of G is an agent of the joint action A. For example, not every member of the Chiefs played in the Super Bowl, and not every German invaded Belgium. In such cases, the agents of the joint actions "represent" the overall group membership, where the "represents" relation would be explained in a complete theory of joint action.

individuals who are both strongly inclined and quite able wrongfully to kill or injure innocent members of S, and who will do so unless they are directly prevented from acting. Assume for now that S can protect innocent members of S by, and only by, establishing a police force with powers of direct intervention in cases where those in S′ attempt to injure or kill innocent persons. Assume finally that self- and other-defensive actions by the police will inevitably result in harm to some members of S′.

If we focus on the choice facing S, then we have a situation exactly analogous to the cases of individual other-defense described earlier. That is, there are harms that are unavoidable from S's standpoint, but they can be distributed by S in different ways. Moreover, certain members of S (i.e., those in S′) are culpable for creating this situation in which S faces a forced-choice regarding how to distribute unavoidable harms. Thus, according to JUSTICE, S is justified in distributing the harm among those in S′, and hence in establishing a police force. Moreover, since S's action would fall within the realm of other-defense, the justification here is a requirement, not a mere permission.

Note that the choice facing S (as opposed to the choices facing members of the police force) is not whether to defend individuals against wrongful aggression. Rather, it is a choice whether to establish a police force—a mechanism by which S justly distributes harms that it is not in a position simply to prevent.

Let us now modify our example somewhat. Suppose that those in S′ cannot be prevented from harming innocent persons no matter how large and diligent a police force S establishes, but that some members of S′ can be deterred from harming innocent people by real and credible threats to their own well-being. Assume too that S can pose such threats by establishing and effectively implementing a system of criminal punishment. For the threats embodied in this system to be real and credible, they would need actually to be carried out. That is, members of S′ who harm innocent people would themselves need to be harmed by being punished. Otherwise, the threats would have—or certainly come to have—little deterrent value. Now assume that some members of S′ will ignore the threats and be punished as a result. Then harm is again unavoidable from S's standpoint, although S does have some control over how this harm is distributed. A distribution involving real and credible threats of punishment will favor innocent members of S over those in S′, while a distribution not involving such threats will have the opposite result. And since those in S′ are culpable for the fact that there is unavoidable harm to be distributed, then—other things being equal—JUSTICE requires S to establish a system of criminal punishment.[10]

The foregoing account explains the justifiability of *establishing and implementing* systems of criminal punishment, where implementation includes punishing individuals who ignore the threats implicit in the prohibitions of the systems' criminal laws. Hence, as was maintained above, punishment as societal-defense contains an explanation of the justifiability of individual punishment that grows out of its account of how establishing systems of punishment can be morally justified.[11]

Two points are worth emphasizing before we proceed. One is analogous to that made above in connection with S's establishment of a police force—namely, that the forced choice faced by S is not whether to punish individuals; it is rather a choice whether to establish a system of punishment in the face of risks to innocent members of S created by those in S′. Hence, the problem noted above as associated with applying JUSTICE to individual punishment—namely, that punishment is after the fact of harm's being done to innocent persons—does not arise.

A second point to bear in mind is that S's choice is not simply between establishing a system of punishment and not establishing any such system.

---

[10] According to Deirdre Golash,

> In practice, there is of course no such neat division between those who are prone to commit crimes and those who are likely to be victimized. None of us can claim not to be a potential wrongdoer, any more than we can claim not to be a potential victim. … we would not be justified in shifting harms from the innocent members of S to the members of S′ simply on the ground of the moral superiority of the innocent. (2005, 111)

But Golash's critique is off-target in two respects. First of all, she ignores the fact that members of S′ are not merely inclined to harm innocent people; they will do so if not prevented. And we surely can distinguish people who will harm innocents from those who will not. I suspect that Golash has relied on epistemic considerations that—as was noted above—are irrelevant in the present context. Golash's second mistake consists in assuming without reason that I treat "moral superiority" as relevant to just distributions of harms. I do not—and nothing I say suggests that I do.

[11] According to David Alm,

> On the one hand we have the *self-defense view*. It tries to derive the right (meaning the moral justification) to punish from the relatively uncontroversial right of self-defense. In other words, it claims that the right to defend oneself against potential attacks by threatening retaliation is primary to and gives rise to a right to punish attacks that have already taken place. (2013, 92)

However, Alm's "self-defense" view differs from the theory of punishment as societal-defense in two significant respects. First of all, while the former is concerned with a right of self-defense, the latter centers on a requirement of other-defense. Secondly, while there is a sense in which the requirement to impose criminal punishment arises from a requirement to create systems of punishment that embody threats, both requirements rest ultimately on JUSTICE, which concerns conditions under which harms are justly distributed.

Rather, S must decide what sort of system of punishment would best conform to applicable moral principles; and the available options are varied because of how systems of punishment can be structured. They typically consist (at least partly) of sets of rules of certain sorts. These sets can include rules specifying the types of acts that count as offenses; rules that group offenses into categories (misdemeanors, felonies, and so on); rules that correlate offenses with punishments; procedural rules for determining candidates for punishment; and rules governing the imposition of punishments. Systems of punishment can therefore differ from each other in significant ways: with respect to whether they incorporate the death penalty, with respect to whether their punishments fit their offenses, with respect to whether they divide offenses into many distinct categories or only into a few such categories, and so on.

Now, some of these choices among systems of punishment are constrained by the *ceteris paribus* conditions for JUSTICE. For example, the proportionality condition requires that harm done to offenders within a given system of punishment not exceed that which is proportional to the harm that would be done to innocent people if no system of punishment were established. At the level of systems, this captures part of the requirement that punishments must fit crimes—a requirement that can now be seen to arise from basic and very general considerations of distributive justice that are embodied in JUSTICE. Punishments must be proportional to crimes for some of the same reasons that any distribution of unavoidable harm satisfying the conditions mentioned in JUSTICE must meet proportionality requirements.

However, proportionality for punishments does have a distinctive and complicating feature: namely, the existence of two very different interpretations of the idea of proportional punishments. On the one hand, we have the requirement that the severity of particular forms of punishment corresponds appropriately to the seriousness or gravity of the specific types of wrongdoing to which they are assigned. And, on the other hand, we have the notion that equally severe punishments must be correlated with equally grave categories of wrongdoing, while more/less severe punishments must be assigned to more/less serious types of wrongdoing. Call these "absolute proportionality" and "relative proportionality," respectively.

So, for example, since murder is more harmful than theft, relative proportionality requires that murder be punished more severely than theft. But this requirement implies nothing about the specific punishments that must be assigned to either category of wrongdoing. Relative proportionality would presumably accommodate systems of punishment in which murderers were executed and thieves imprisoned for five years, as well as systems in which murderers received ten-year prison sentences and thieves one-year sentences.

This kind of flexibility is evidently precluded by absolute proportionality, however, since the latter presupposes that murder, say, is a certain degree of seriousness and that it must be matched by punishments that have the same degree of severity. A system of punishment is morally acceptable only if, in that system, the two types of proportionality for punishment are reconciled and function together.

Let us now turn from the proportionality condition for JUSTICE to its graded culpability condition. Recall that society S contains members S′ who are disposed to harm innocent members of S, and who will do so if not prevented or deterred. If S is assumed to be a modern, heavily populated urban society, then the kinds of wrongful harm that those in S′ are disposed to do might well include intentional and premeditated homicide, as well as homicide that is intentional but not premeditated, and homicide that is neither premeditated nor intentional but is due to negligence or recklessness. The perpetrators of homicides of each of these types are culpable to varying degrees, and graded culpability requires that this is reflected in differences in the severity of their punishments. Thus, first-degree murder must be punished more severely than second-degree murder, and both more severely than manslaughter. Graded culpability is not the same as relative proportionality, since the latter is concerned with kinds of harm rather than with levels of culpability.

Along with the proportionality and graded culpability conditions for JUSTICE, its minimization and side-effect conditions must also be satisfied when the principle is applied to the choices facing S. Thus, S must select a system that results in the minimum harm to those in S′ that is necessary to protect innocent persons. If, therefore, it is possible to deter those in S′ from engaging in some category of wrongdoing by correlating with that class of wrongdoings a punishment less than proportionality permits, then the minimization condition of JUSTICE requires that the lesser punishment be selected. S must also be concerned with the harm that may be distributed to some innocent persons as side effects of protecting others. If threats of punishment for given offenses will have harmful side effects for innocent persons, then this must be taken into account when assessing the moral acceptability of that system.

In this way, limits are placed on the kinds of punishments that may be correlated with different kinds of wrongdoing in a system of punishment. A system that stipulates the death penalty for burglary surely violates any acceptable interpretation of the proportionality requirement; a system according to which premeditated murder is punishable by death might satisfy an acceptable interpretation of the proportionality requirement, but it might fail to meet the minimization requirement. And a system of punishment that prescribes the death penalty for certain offenses might have unacceptably harmful side effects for innocent persons.

Determinations of whether a given system of punishment satisfies the minimization or side-effects conditions are empirical matters. As was noted above, however, certain conceptual considerations would need to be taken into account in determining whether proportionality is satisfied. Whether empirical or conceptual, these problems are relevant to how JUSTICE applies to particular systems of punishment rather than to the principle's acceptability, and can therefore be ignored here. However, there is a problem that cuts across this conceptual/empirical divide, and that does warrant some consideration at this point. I refer to the problem of capital punishment.

The conceptual aspect of this problem is a special instance of the general problem that is the topic of this chapter, namely, that of morally justifying harming people through criminal punishment. Thus, a common objection to capital punishment is that it is as morally impermissible as the actions for which it is imposed—that it amounts to "murdering murderers." Now, punishment as societal-defense explains how harms can justly be distributed by establishing systems of criminal punishment, and there are no restrictions on the sorts of harms to which the theory applies. This is because punishment as societal-defense is based on JUSTICE, a principle that explains the conditions under which harms in general are justly distributed in culpably created forced-choice situations. Establishing systems of punishment that include the death penalty is no more theoretically objectionable than is the use of deadly force in situations involving individual self- or other-defense.

So, punishment as societal-defense explains how establishing systems of punishment that contain the death penalty can be morally justified in theory. However, whether establishing a particular system containing the death penalty is justified in practice is a question that can be answered only by examining the actual circumstances surrounding that case.

4 Matters of Justice

According to John Rawls, "the purpose of the criminal law is to uphold basic natural duties, those which forbid us to injure other persons in their life and limb, or to deprive them of their liberty and property, and punishments are to serve this end." Rawls goes on to say:

> It is clear that the distribution of economic and social advantages is entirely different. These arrangements are not the converse, so to speak, of the criminal law, so that just as the one punishes certain offenses, the other rewards moral worth. The function of unequal distributive shares is to cover the costs of training and education, to attract individuals to places and associations where they are most needed from a social point of view, and so on. ... To think of distributive and retributive justice as converses of one another is completely misleading and suggests a different justification for distributive shares than the one they in fact have. (1971, 314–15)

Rawls is distinguishing between what might be called "social justice" on the one hand, and retributive justice on the other. The implication is that these two forms of justice are concerned, respectively, with the equitable distribution of benefits and burdens, and with the punishment of criminal offenders. This distinction is familiar, as is the idea that, if criminal punishment is a requirement of justice, then it is a requirement of *retributive* justice. Let me now explain why I believe that the latter idea is mistaken—why I do not believe that retributive justice can play a role in the moral justification of criminal punishment. If I am right, then the door is at least left open to regarding the justification of criminal punishment as a matter of distributive justice—as has been suggested here.

To gain a clear picture of the nature of retributive justice, it must first be distinguished from retributivism—that is, from retributivist theories of criminal punishment. The importance of this distinction becomes evident on recognizing that, like all theories of punishment, retributivist theories require principled bases, and the most plausible basis for retributivism, in its most recognizable form, would be a principle of retributive justice. This form of retributivism is commonly referred to as "desert-based," and the requisite principle of retributive justice would be desert-centered.[12]

We need a principle whose role in retributive theory parallels that of a consequentialist principle in deterrence theories, and of JUSTICE in punishment

[12] According to Larry Alexander, "Retributivism, of whatever stripe, depends on the existence of desert" (2013, 161). In contrast, David Boonin (2008) discusses a number of theories that he characterizes as retributivist but have nothing to do with desert. If there are indeed theories of punishment that are unrelated to desert but nevertheless qualify as retributive, they will play no role in the discussion in this section.

Unfortunately, the necessary distinction between retributivism and retributive justice is almost invariably ignored in the literature. Indeed, it is very difficult to find a philosophical discussion of retributive justice *per se*. For example, Richard Lippke (2019) employs the expressions "retributive justice" and "retributivism" interchangeably. And the entry on "retributive justice" in the *Stanford Encyclopedia of Philosophy* (Walen 2020) characterizes retributive justice in a manner strikingly similar to H. L. A. Hart's characterization of retributivism (1968, 231).

as societal-defense. When conjoined with appropriate subsidiary premises, consequentialism would imply conclusions about the morally justified imposition of criminal punishment. And the same is true of JUSTICE and suitable conjoined premises. In both cases, the conclusions are normative, which underscores the normative character of both JUSTICE and consequentialism. Note too that both JUSTICE and consequentialism possess a level of generality that renders them applicable to actions and practices having nothing to do with punishment. This sort of generality enhances the plausibility of the two: the more general and fundamental is a principle that is aimed at justifying theories of punishment, the less likely is the account to be *ad hoc*—to contain components specifically designed to avoid problems that would otherwise arise.

So, our desired principle of retributive justice must apply outside the realm of punishment, but it must be capable of supporting normative conclusions about criminal punishment. Here, it seems to me, is a principle of justice that is at least consistent with those implicit in discussions that are nominally concerned with retributive justice:

> Justice requires that people receive the treatments they deserve, and this irrespective of any good or ill that might result from their being so treated.

And here is how retributivism might be stated:

> Those who engage in criminal wrongdoing deserve to suffer for their actions in proportion to the degree of their wrongdoing, and criminal punishment is therefore a means by which retributive justice is done.

As it is stated here, retributivism clearly presupposes something much like the suggested principle of justice. In any case, my concern here is with the latter, and with retributivist theories of criminal punishment only as potentially based on retributive justice. Because the suggested principle is not restricted to undesirable treatments, it does not appear to be a principle of *retributive* justice: there seems to be nothing retributive about according people deserved rewards, for example. To avoid confusion here, let us distinguish retributive justice—which concerns only deserved treatments that are undesirable—from what I will call "retrospective justice," which concerns all deserved treatments.[13] The general principle stated above will be referred to

[13] Some writers equate something much like what I am calling retrospective justice with justice *simpliciter*. According to John Hospers, for example, justice consists in "treating each person in accordance with his or her deserts" (1978, 73). See also John Stuart Mill's remarks on the relation of desert to justice in *Utilitarianism* (2011, ch. 5).

as RETROSPECTIVE, and the result of restricting the latter to undesirable treatments will be referred to as RETRIBUTIVE.

Although the concept of requirement and the concept of value both appear in the RETROSPECTIVE principle (and, by implication, the RETRIBUTIVE principle), there is no indication of whether the requirement is meant to be *based on* the value of deserts—whether there is a requirement to accord people their deserts *because* doing so is a good thing in and of itself. Sorting this out (something I will not attempt to do here) would generate two different interpretations of retributive justice. Regardless of how this is done, however, the bottom line in both cases will be a flat assertion that according deserts is good in itself, and in one case a flat assertion that according deserts is a requirement of justice. When these assertions are applied to the problem of justifying criminal punishment, they lead to a solution that is entirely backward-looking. What we will now see is that, regardless of whether according deserts is good in itself, the concept of desert cannot be the basis of a requirement of justice. If the argument succeeds, then desert-based retributivist theories of criminal punishment must be rejected.

The question before us is whether deserts of all types can, in and of themselves, generate moral requirements. Does the proposition that P deserves treatment T entail the proposition that there is a moral requirement of justice to accord P treatment T for any values of T?

At first glance, the answer to this question is emphatically "no"! After all, people can deserve credit or criticism, praise or blame for behaving in various ways, and yet—typically, at least—no others are required to accord those treatments. According to George Sher, however, deserts (or "desert-claims") have "normative force," which includes

> any significant implication that something ought, or ought not to be the case. Given this stipulation, a desert-claim will … have normative force if a specific person (or arm of society) is obligated to provide the deserving party with what he deserves. But a claim will also have normative force if the deserving party's having what he deserves would, for reasons connected with the basis of the desert, be an especially good thing. (1987, xi)

Sher is maintaining that a desert-claim has normative force if someone or some "arm of society" is obligated to accord the deserve treatment. But explaining the normative force of deserts as a mere coincidence of desert and obligation could not exhaust the content of acceptable principles of either retrospective or retributive justice. Obligations would need to be not only coincident with deserts but also generated by them. This point can be illustrated by an example:

> Suppose that you offer a reward for the return of your lost cat Sophia, and that Cleo finds and returns her to you. You are then obligated to give Cleo the offered reward because Cleo has a right to it, and rights imply corresponding obligations. The obligation and right here are "special," in that the former is incurred by you in offering the reward, and the latter is conferred on whoever returns Sophia.

So far, however, deserts have not entered the picture: whether Cleo deserves the offered reward depends on the circumstances surrounding Sophia's return. Suppose that Cleo devotes considerable time and effort to finding and returning Sophia, because Cleo knows how you love your cat. Then Cleo not only has a right to the offered reward, but Cleo also deserves it. On the other hand, suppose that Cleo happens to be walking by your house and, noticing Sophia sitting by your door, rings the doorbell and points to her. Then, while Cleo has a right to the reward—and you are obligated to give it to Cleo—Cleo does not deserve it.

Similar remarks apply to punishment. While it may be true that an "arm of society" is obligated to impose some deserved punishment, it does not follow that the obligation is generated by the desert.

In the absence of good reasons for believing deserts can generate moral requirements, desert-based retributivist theories cannot justify criminal punishment. To be sure, there are backward-looking considerations other than desert—blame, fault, or culpability, for example—to which a theory of punishment might attribute necessary moral significance, as in the case of the theory of punishment as societal-defense. Even in the latter case, however, the backward-looking consideration does not in itself generate a requirement to punish.

5 Concluding Remarks

The discussion here has been guided by two methodological assumptions: that morally justifying criminal punishment requires an explicitly formulated moral principle; and that this principle must be general enough to apply outside the realm of criminal punishment. The theory of punishment as societal-defense satisfies these conditions. It is based on JUSTICE, a principle that applies not only to criminal punishment, but also to culpably created forced-choice situations having nothing to do with punishment. The conditions are satisfied as well by consequentialist-based deterrence theories, since consequentialism is a general moral theory. And desert-based retributivism would satisfy the conditions if something like RETROSPECTIVE rather than RETRIBUTIVE is assumed to be its underlying principle. But consequentialism is famously problematic, and I argued above that deserts lack intrinsic normativity, and hence cannot by themselves generate moral requirements—requirements to punish in particular.

Whether other theories of punishment incorporate explicitly formulated principles with appropriate generality depends on how those theories are formulated. For example, consider forfeiture-based and fairness-based theories. A theory of the former sort would need a general account of rights-forfeiture. And an adequate account of rights-forfeiture would identify the rights-violations that lead to the forfeiture of rights, would explain how the forfeited rights are related to the violated rights, and would answer the question of how, if at all, forfeited rights can be regained.

Fairness-based theories need an explanation of the conditions under which it is permissible to harm those who change distributions of benefits and burdens, as well as an explanation of why the immorality of a rights-violation should be equated with creating distributive unfairness rather than as a wrong to the person whose right is violated. It is implausible to suggest that the wrong-making feature of a murder, say, is that it creates a general maldistribution of benefits and burdens.[14]

Both fairness theories and forfeiture theories commonly depict criminal punishment as a collective response to criminal wrongdoing, and expressivists build collective expressions of attitudes into their theories. Yet, as was pointed out in the second part of this chapter, the idea of actions or expressions of attitudes by collections *per se* is fraught with difficulties. I proposed the notion of a joint action as a possible way to avoid these difficulties. But the important point is that there are difficulties to be dealt with, and they are invariably overlooked by punishment theorists.

One final point. If criminal punishment is morally justified, then it must be justified as a requirement—not as a mere permission. And certain theories cannot readily accommodate this feature of justified punishment. Consider expressivism, for example, according to which expressions of condemnatory attitudes toward lawbreakers is, in and of itself, relevant to whether

[14] It is perhaps tempting to regard fairness theories of punishment as related in some important way to Rawls's theory of distributive justice. However, any attempt to connect the two would need to proceed very cautiously, and contend with Rawls's explicit denial that his theory has anything to do with punishment.

punishment is morally justified. What needs to be argued, however, is that such expressions have sufficient normative force to play more than a minor role in creating moral requirements to punish criminal wrongdoing. Forfeiture theorists have a different sort of problem, stemming from their view that punishing people is justified when they forfeit rights not to be harmed by violating the rights of others. The problem here is that forfeiture of a right by someone *at most* permits the person to be treated in ways that would otherwise be impermissible; rights-forfeiture does not by itself generate requirements. Moreover, the absence of a right need not even imply a permission. After all, we can recognize that cruelty to nonhuman animals is immoral without having to assume that the animals have moral rights.

This section's critiques of fairness-based, forfeiture, and expressivist theories are by no means intended to be the final word on these views. Rather, they raise questions that I believe need to be addressed by proponents of the theories. And, of course, there are theories of punishment about which I have had nothing at all to say—not because these theories are not interesting and important, but because a comprehensive examination of theories of criminal punishment would have been far beyond the scope of this chapter. My central purpose here has been to advance the theory of punishment as societal-defense, which I believe explains how criminal punishment is morally justifiable and does answer the questions raised above in connection with alternatives to that theory.

References

Alexander, Larry. 2013. "Can Self-Defense Justify Punishment?" *Law and Philosophy* 32, nos. 2–3 (March): 159–75.

Alm, David. 2013. "Self-Defense, Punishment and Forfeiture." *Criminal Justice Ethics* 32, no. 2: 91–107.

Boonin, David. 2008. *The Problem of Punishment.* Cambridge: Cambridge University Press.

Bratman, Michael E. 1993. "Shared Intention." *Ethics* 104, no. 1 (October): 97–113.

Doggett, Tyler. 2011. "Recent Work on the Ethics of Self-Defense." *Philosophy Compass* 6, no. 4 (April): 220–33.

Feinberg, Joel. 1987. *Harm to Others*. Vol. 1 of *The Moral Limits of the Criminal Law.* New York: Oxford University Press.

Golash, Deirdre. 2005. *The Case against Punishment: Retribution, Crime Prevention, and the Law.* New York: NYU Press.

Hart, H. L. A. 1968. *Punishment and Responsibility: Essays in the Philosophy of Law.* Oxford: Oxford University Press.

Hospers, John. 1978. "Free Enterprise as the Embodiment of Justice." In *Ethics, Free Enterprise, and Public Policy: Original Essays on Moral Issues in Business*, edited by Richard T. De George and Joseph A. Pichler, 70–96. New York: Oxford University Press.

Kutz, Christopher. 2000. "Acting Together." *Philosophy and Phenomenological Research* 61, no. 1 (July): 1–31.

Lippke, Richard L. 2019. "The Nature of Retributive Justice and Its Demands on the State." *Law and Philosophy* 38, no. 1 (February): 53–77.

May, Larry, and Stacey Hoffman, eds. 1992. *Collective Responsibility: Five Decades of Debate in Theoretical and Applied Ethics*. Lanham, MD: Rowman & Littlefield.

McMahan, Jeff. 2005. "The Basis of Moral Liability to Defensive Killing." *Philosophical Issues* 15, no. 1 (October): 386–405.

Mill, John Stuart. 2011. *Utilitarianism*. 2nd ed. Edited by George Sher. Indianapolis, IN: Hackett.

Montague, Phillip. 1981. "Self-Defense and Choosing between Lives." *Philosophical Studies* 40, no. 2 (September): 207–19.

———. 1983. "Punishment and Societal Defense." *Criminal Justice Ethics* 2, no. 1: 30–36.

———. 1995. *Punishment as Societal-Defense*. Latham, MD: Rowman & Littlefield.

Rawls, John. 1971. *A Theory of Justice*. Cambridge, MA: Harvard University Press.

Sher, George. 1987. *Desert*. Princeton, NJ: Princeton University Press.

Thomson, Judith Jarvis. 1977. "Self-Defense and Rights." *The Lindley Lecture*. Lawrence, KS: University of Kansas Press.

———. 1991. "Self-Defense." *Philosophy & Public Affairs* 20, no. 4 (Autumn): 283–310.

Walen, Alec. 2020. "Retributive Justice." *Stanford Encyclopedia of Philosophy* (Summer 2021 edition), edited by Edward N. Zalta. https://plato.stanford.edu/archives/sum2021/entries/justice-retributive/.

13

Fair Play Theories of Punishment

Göran Duus-Otterström

1 Introduction

Fair play theories of punishment locate the permissibility or desirability of legal punishment in its ability to restore relations of fairness between lawbreakers and other members of society. They are a family of views whose lineage traces back to Herbert Morris's seminal 1968 essay "Persons and Punishment." In this essay, Morris applied the fair play theory of political obligation—itself a relatively recent invention—to the topic of punishment.[1] Construing the criminal law as a system of mutually beneficial restraints on behavior, Morris argued that those who break the law gain an unfair advantage over others insofar as they release themselves from the restraints upon which the system depends. What justifies punishment, Morris claimed, is that it corrects that unfairness.

The aim of this chapter is not to offer a comprehensive overview of the, by now, large literature on fair play theories of punishment. Rather, it is to discuss one particular objection to these theories, which I refer to as the

[1] The fair play theory of political obligation holds that the moral duty of citizens to obey the law stems from the expectation that mutually beneficial compliance be repaid in kind. The theory was set out in systematic form by Hart (1955) and Rawls (1999). Its contemporary defenders include Klosko (2004, 2005) and Dagger (2018). For criticism, see, e.g., Simmons (2001, chs. 1–2) and Wellman (2001).

G. Duus-Otterström (✉)
University of Gothenburg, Gothenburg, Sweden
e-mail: goran.duus-otterstrom@pol.gu.se

© The Author(s), under exclusive license to Springer Nature Switzerland AG 2023

M. C. Altman (ed.), *The Palgrave Handbook on the Philosophy of Punishment*, Palgrave Handbooks in the Philosophy of Law, https://doi.org/10.1007/978-3-031-11874-6_13

no-benefit objection. According to this objection, many crimes simply do not produce any kind of benefit to the offender and thus cannot put them at the sort of unfair advantage that punishment is supposed to correct. The objection is pivotal because it suggests that fair play theories can at best provide an incomplete justification of punishment. The bulk of the chapter, therefore, is devoted to evaluating responses to the no-benefit objection.

I begin by introducing Morris's original account and by distinguishing among different views that this account admits. Focusing on a comprehensively retributivist version of the fair play theory, I then proceed, in section 3, to present the no-benefit objection and assess the responses defenders of the fair play theory have historically offered to counter it. Finding these responses wanting, in sections 4 and 5, I discuss two recent attempts to respond to the objection, one emphasizing that crime may inflict unfair losses on others and one emphasizing that crime renders it unfair that offenders retain the benefits of social cooperation. I argue that both attempts are promising. Section 6 concludes that it is time for philosophers of punishment to move on from the no-benefit objection and address other problems that deserve more attention.

2 The House Herbert Morris Built (in Passing)

The fountainhead of fair play theories is, as noted, Herbert Morris's "Persons and Punishment."[2] This is in one sense surprising, considering that the bulk of Morris's paper is actually devoted to other issues.[3] Indeed, given how quickly Morris presents the idea of justifying legal punishment based on fair play, it is remarkable that it ended up inspiring so many legal and political philosophers. Clearly, Morris struck on an intuitively appealing idea, which subsequent generations of scholars have sought to develop and improve.

Morris's account begins by noting that the core rules of the criminal law provide benefits to everyone insofar as they guarantee "noninterference by others with what each person values." However, these benefits will only be secured if people generally comply with the rules. For Morris, this means that the benefits depend on people's willingness to shoulder a burden, namely "the exercise of self-restraint by individuals over inclinations that would, if satisfied, directly interfere or create a substantial risk of interference with others in

[2] Another prominent early defender of the fair play theory was Jeffrie Murphy (1971, 1973).

[3] The main aim of Morris's (1968) essay is to defend punishment over the "therapy model" as an institution of social control. Morris's argument is that punishment, unlike the therapy model, respects persons as autonomous agents.

proscribed ways." This paves the way for Morris's justification of punishment. His thought is that breaking the law is inherently unfair, since it is tantamount to refusing to contribute to a collective good from which one benefits. As he puts it, a lawbreaker eschews "a burden which others have voluntarily assumed and thus gains an advantage which others, who have restrained themselves, do not possess" (1968, 477). What justifies punishment is that it counters this state of affairs. Punishment ensures that offenders gain no unfair advantage in virtue of having broken the law.[4]

It is interesting to note that, while the fair play theory is overwhelmingly interpreted as a retributivist position—that is, one that deems that the permissibility or desirability of punishment depends on the offender's negative moral desert—it can also be seen as a forward-looking theory that justifies punishment based on good consequences. This is because one could argue that removing unfair advantage is only important because it incentivizes future compliance with legal rules. However, while several fair play theorists stress forward-looking considerations in their accounts, none of them, to the best of my knowledge, does so exclusively.[5] They all reserve some role for justice and desert in their justification of punishment.[6]

Morris himself seems to have thought of his theory as a mixed one. He suggested that one reason that speaks in favor of removing lawbreakers' unfair advantage is that people's "disposition to comply voluntarily will diminish as they learn that others are with impunity renouncing burdens they are assuming" and that legal punishment will "induce compliance with the ... rules among those who may disinclined to obey" (1968, 477). Thus, Morris seems to have thought of the justification of punishment partly in terms of preventing crime through assurance and deterrence. Nevertheless, he clearly also thought that his theory was retributivist in central respects, and the enduring fame of his paper lies in how it construes the offender's negative desert in terms of a failure to play fair:

---

[4] A corollary of this is that, if all people were to break a law, then it would not be justified to punish someone for breaking it. This is because breaking the law would not produce an unfair advantage.

[5] In the social sciences, however, it is common to argue that "punishment" (here understood as the imposition of a cost) is essential for solving public goods problems since it assures people that they will not be rendered "suckers" by contributing to collective action. For a classical statement of this kind of view, see Runge (1984).

[6] There are some doubts about whether fair play retributivism is about desert as much as it is about paying debts (Boonin 2008, 122). I shall not delve into this debate here, but since the fair play theory holds that lawbreakers commit a moral wrong, it has no apparent problem in saying that lawbreakers deserve punishment in a familiar sense of "deserves" (e.g., that it would be impersonally and non-instrumentally good or just to punish them).

> A person who violates the rules has something others have—the benefits of the system—but by renouncing what others have assumed, the burdens of self-restraint, he has acquired an unfair advantage. Matters are not even until this advantage is in some way erased. Another way of putting it is that he owes something to others, for he has something that does not rightfully belong to him. Justice—that is punishing such individuals—restores the equilibrium of benefits and burdens by taking from the individual what he owes, that is, exacting the debt. (478)

The focus in this chapter will be on this retributivist reading of the fair play theory, since this is what offers a normatively distinctive position in the philosophy of punishment. However, even when we understand the fair play theory in this way, we can further distinguish between different types of theory. This is because different theorists disagree as to which questions the fair play theory is supposed to answer. We can distinguish three basic normative questions of legal punishment:

1. The *permissibility* question: what gives the state a right to punish?
2. The *desirability* question: why should the state punish?
3. The *sentencing* question: how (and how much) should the state punish?

As people like H. L. A. Hart (2008) taught us, there is no reason why the three questions must be answered by the same theory or normative consideration. One can think, for example, that negative desert plays an essential role in explaining why the state is permitted to punish an offender (question 1) without thinking that desert is weighty reason, if a reason at all, to *act* on that permission (question 2). Philosophers accordingly can, and do, take different positions as to which role the fair play theory is supposed to play. Here, however, I consider it as a comprehensively retributivist position, that is, one that is supposed to supply at least partial answers to all three questions. This is how defenders and critics tend to understand the view. In what follows, when I refer to "the fair play theory," it is the comprehensively retributivist position I have in mind.

The fair play theory has been the subject of severe criticism ever since its conception. Before we turn to the critical discussion, however, we should first explain why theorists have been attracted to it. One reason is that it promises to supply the basic retributivist intuition—that the justification of punishment depends on the intrinsic justice of punishment rather than on its instrumental effects—with a more appealing basis than other forms of retributivism.

Some retributivists locate the justification of punishment simply in the non-instrumental value of deserved suffering. Michael Moore (1997), for example, defends his brand of retributivism based on the intuition that it is intrinsically good that wrongdoers suffer. But this defense seems to put retributivism on shaky ground, not only because the intuitions in question may be less prevalent than Moore thinks (Bauer and Poama 2020), but also because they can seem beside the point. Even if most people would have the intuition that it would be good to make offenders suffer, we may feel that this is a *private* belief which has no bearing on how the institution of state punishment should be organized. Political liberals, for example, may argue that retributivism of the Moorean stripe is simply outside the realm of public reason (Flanders 2017; see also Husak 2008, 196–206).[7] The fair play theory fares much better in this respect, since there is little doubt that fairness is an important public value that the state is supposed to protect and promote (Duus-Otterström 2017).

Related to this, the fair play theory also comes with a pleasing connection to wider issues in political philosophy. Since the theory construes law and order as a public good, it offers a familiar and compelling account of punishment as a method for responding to free riding. The point is that, if each of us has a duty to contribute to the provision of the public good, then those who breach this duty are liable to sanctions, just as shirkers are generally liable to ill treatment within cooperative schemes. Richard Dagger (2018) devotes a whole monograph to arguing that fair play offers an integrated account of both political obligation and punishment, that is, one that justifies punishment against the backdrop of a general theory about the moral relationship between members of a polity regulated by laws. This is attractive for anyone who thinks that punishment cannot be properly justified unless it is understood as a species of coercion requiring political legitimacy.[8]

3 The No-Benefit Objection

The most obvious problem for the fair play theory is that many crimes do not seem to produce a benefit for the offender. Consider, for example, a pointless brawl in a bar. The suggestion that an assault committed because of an

[7] Moore is alive to the political questions (1997, 739–95).

[8] That political legitimacy might be a precondition for justified punishment has been explored with particular clarity in the debate about moral standing. See Duff (2001, 179–96) and Tadros (2009) for influential treatments. For examples of penal theories that do not vest any fundamental importance in political legitimacy, see Thorburn (2012) and Duus-Otterström and Kelly (2019).

alcohol-fueled perception of a slight generates some kind of "benefit" to the perpetrator appears strange. Such crimes do not render the offender better off in any standard sense of the word. If anything, they seem merely harmful. Call this the *no-benefit objection.*[9]

The no-benefit objection is potentially devastating for the fair play theory since, if committing a crime does not make offenders better off, then it seems that offenders cannot gain an unfair advantage by doing so, which in turn would prevent the idea of justifying punishment based on the removal of unfair advantage from getting off the ground. It could of course be argued that the fair play theory might still apply to crimes where unfair advantage uncontroversially *does* seem to be the case. Tax evasion, for example, is a crime whose wrongness seems best explained by the idea of free riding, so we might think that the fair play theory is needed properly to account for the punishment of this crime.[10] But most proponents of the fair play theory do not believe that their view only applies in the margins of criminal law. The challenge is to explain how it could apply more generally.

The traditional answer to this challenge is to stress that, while crimes may not produce what we normally think of as benefits (such as economic gain), they nevertheless involve something of value for the offender, since they represent a refusal to restrain one's actions in accordance with legal commands. Morris captured this by saying that lawbreakers cast off the "burdens of self-restraint" that others shoulder. But this idea is famously problematic since it is far from always the case that people experience legal compliance as burdensome. Consider, for example, murder. For most of us, it is completely effortless to follow the law against murder for the simple reason that we have no desire to murder anyone, so it is unclear why murderers would gain an unfair

[9] The no-benefit objection is my way of crystallizing a worry many people have had about the fair play theory (e.g., Burgh 1982; Dolinko 1991; Hampton 1991; Duff 2008). I state it more fully in Duus-Otterström (2017); see also Falls (1987). Note that "benefit" is vague between "being better off than before" and "being better off than otherwise." I stay neutral between these two uses here. Note also that "benefit" and "better off" can come apart insofar as a person can be rendered better off *than others* (i.e., gain a relative advantage) despite having gained no absolute benefit. I return to this below when I discuss loss-based versions of the fair play theory. Critics of the fair play theory have generally been unclear about whether their point is that lawbreakers have not benefited in an absolute sense or have not been rendered better off than others.

[10] For a discussion of whether we need fair play to account for the wrongness of a crime like tax evasion, see Dagger (2018, 150–55).

advantage over us in virtue of breaking this law.[11] The claim "it is unfair that A did not resist the temptation to X" is unconvincing if uttered by people who have no desire to X in the first place. Moreover, if one were to take the idea of self-restraint seriously and draw up a sentencing scheme based on how tempting crimes are, one would get absurd results. For example, it seems plausible that property or welfare crimes are more tempting to the average person than violent crimes. Yet we would for obvious reasons want to avoid saying that the former crimes are therefore more serious than the latter (see, e.g., Burgh 1982; Dolinko 1991).

Conscious of these difficulties, proponents of the fair play theory have sought to respond to the no-benefit objection in other ways. Some have settled for what David Boonin refers to as the *general compliance response* (2008, 124–26). According to this response, which is primarily associated with Dagger, the burden that each offender casts off is the burden of complying with the law in general. The thought is that, since each of us find it burdensome to comply with the *system* of laws, offenders do take unfair advantage of others, not because they indulge particular criminal desires that the rest of us also have, but because they do not accept the burdens of living in a society in which people's actions are constrained by the law in a general sense.

The problem with the general compliance response is that it makes the fair play theory unable to account for differences between crimes. If crimes are unfair because they involve casting off the general burden of obeying the law, then it looks as though all crimes are equally unfair and thus equally serious (Burgh 1982). Proponents of the general compliance response have methods for dealing with this problem, however. Zachary Hoskins (2011), for example, argues that the role of fair play is strictly to explain why punishment of crime is permissible. On Hoskins's view, questions about whether and how much punishment should be inflicted are answered by other normative considerations than fair play, such as the need to deter future lawbreaking. The general compliance response involves, then, a scaling back of the ambition of the fair play theory. This is not a problem in itself. However, since most

[11] This objection can also be raised in a moralized way. The objection would then be that it would be *inappropriate* to locate an offender's desert in others' grudging compliance with moral duties (Duff 2008, 279). The non-moralized version of this objection is clearly better, as it is plausible that morally abhorrent crimes *would* be unfair, in the sense of free riding on a mutually beneficial system of cooperation, if most people were tempted to commit such crimes. For a defense of treating fair play obligations in a non-moralized way, see Simmons (2001, 6–11) and Duus-Otterström (2021).

defenders of fair play theory understand it as a comprehensive retributivist view, it is unlikely to be satisfactory to most participants in the debate.[12]

Others have sought to respond to the no-benefit objection by way of the *particular compliance response* (Boonin 2008, 126–35). The idea here is to explain why offenders gain variable unfair advantages from breaking particular laws, but to do so in a way that avoids treating either material gains or giving in to temptation as the metric of benefiting. If successful, this would enable the fair play theory to account for our intuitions about proportionate sentencing. The problem is that, precisely because many crimes do not produce any tangible benefits for the offender, the accounts one must offer to ground the response are abstract and quite strained. George Sher, for example, argues that the benefit inherent in crime is freedom, but that the freedom in question varies depending on the strength of the prohibition broken (1987, 82; see also Finnis 1980, 263–64). Sher's thought is that, since the prohibition against murder is morally more forceful than the prohibition against cheating on one's tax returns, a violation of the former must involve more freedom—it casts off a more morally pressing burden. But it is doubtful that this idea succeeds. One problem is that it is unclear whether offenders really do gain more freedom than others by violating moral prohibitions, since other people could just as well have violated the prohibitions in question (Dolinko 1991). Another problem is that more freedom does not seem to matter in this context. Even if offenders were to gain a substantial amount of freedom by releasing themselves from the prohibition against murder, why would this be unfair, considering that most people are uninterested in having that freedom (Boonin 2008, 128)?

---

[12] Dagger offers two reasons why different crimes can be differently unfair even though one embraces the general compliance response. First, crimes can leave victims unequally able to participate in social cooperation. As he writes,

> the tax evader takes unfair advantage of many people, but her offense typically does not make it difficult for them to continue doing their part in the cooperative practice. With the rapist, the murderer, and the batterer, however, the offender has done something that makes it difficult or even impossible for his victim to contribute further to the ongoing cooperative endeavour. (2018, 192)

Second, the need to preserve social cooperation requires tracking the members' opinions about which crimes are worse than others (194). Dagger is here arguably guilty of equivocating between the unfairness *of* a crime and the extent to which the crime is a threat to a society guided by the principle of fair play, but even if we let this slide, the reasons he offers raise questions. For example, it seems strained to say that murdering someone is an especially flagrant violation of fair play because it means that the victim cannot contribute at all to social cooperation moving forward. I generally doubt that our intuitive sense of criminal seriousness will track how unable people would be to participate in reciprocal exchanges. As for the idea that social cooperation requires empirical legitimacy to sustain it, this is no doubt true, but this is an indirect and contingent way of connecting fair-play considerations and sentencing.

Other philosophers have tried less conceptual approaches to defend the particular compliance response. Michael Davis, for example, famously argues that we should think about the benefits drawn from crime in terms of what price a one-off license to commit a particular crime would fetch at a hypothetical auction (1993; see also Kramer 2013). Davis's idea is that there is no need to consider how tempting a crime is in general to gauge the size of the unfair advantage it yields. Instead, we should focus on how valuable it would be for someone to commit that crime with impunity, which is what the auction is supposed to model. Thinking about the issue this way, Davis argues, it is quite clear that a license to commit murder would fetch a higher price than tax evasion, and this in turn explains why murder yields a greater unfair advantage than tax evasion.

The problem with this argument is that, even if we accept the premise that unfair advantages can be measured in market prices, it does not offer a response to the no-benefit objection. This is because the prices would be a function of how beneficial the crime would be to prospective perpetrators. Suppose that the auction would sell licenses to commit serious but merely harmful crimes. Presumably, no one would pay anything for those licenses precisely because they produce no benefits. Yet we would clearly not want to say that these crimes are therefore minor. It is worth noting that Davis also "cheats" a bit because a lot of work in his argument is done by the number of licenses sold (1993, 146). Part of the reason a license to commit murder would fetch an unusually high price is that society would make few such licenses up for sale. Davis's account here assumes that murder is worse than tax evasion rather than explaining it.

4 Loss-Based Accounts

Having noted the inadequacy of the traditional responses to the no-benefit objection, let us now consider a pair of recent responses that fare better. I start by considering what I term loss-based accounts in this section, before turning to entitlement-based accounts in the next section. What unites these accounts is that they reject the idea that offenders must benefit from the crime in order to deserve punishment. Both require, as we shall see, that we stop thinking about crimes in terms of giving in to desires that others resist. Instead, we should make the misallocation of legal benefits and burdens the central idea.

Loss-based accounts respond to the no-benefit objection by pointing out that benefitting, whether in the sense of becoming better off than before or otherwise, is not necessary to gain an unfair advantage. This is because unfair advantages are comparative in nature and can be created simply by *reducing* someone else's position. This seemingly allows the fair play theory to justify punishment even when we are dealing with merely harmful crime. The idea is that, if an offender gains an unfair advantage over others merely by making them worse off, then fairness dictates that the offender also be made worse off.[13]

A successful loss-based account would completely take the sting out of the no-benefit objection. It would do so by rejecting as false the assumption that offenders can only gain an unfair advantage if they benefit from their crimes. Yet taking a loss-based approach raises several questions. Before we get to the criticisms, however, we should first note that, while emphasizing losses would require us to reinterpret the nature of the fair play theory in some respects, there is textual support for doing so even in Morris's original account. Morris notes, for example, that "fairness dictates that a system in which benefits and burdens are equally distributed have a mechanism designed to prevent a *maldistribution* in the benefits and burdens" (1968, 477, emphasis added). Since those who have been victimized by crime do not possess the benefits that legal rules are designed to deliver, such people clearly face a "maldistribution." After all, they have not enjoyed the protections that are supposed to accompany their legal compliance. In this way, one could argue that, if punishment were to reduce the legal benefits enjoyed by the offenders, then this would be another way in which the maldistribution would be corrected. What is more, since the size of the unfair advantage would be measured by how much worse off victims have been rendered with regard to legally protected interests, one would generally speaking face no problem in pairing the theory with an intuitive ranking of criminal seriousness. Taking a loss-based approach would also allow the fair play theory to respond to another traditional charge, which is that it misrepresents what is wrong about crime. Critics have argued that it is inaccurate to the point of being obscene to suggest that crimes against persons are wrong because they are unfair (see, e.g., Duff 2008). This objection is less powerful once we associate the relevant unfairness with invading other people's legally protected interests rather than with giving in to temptation.

Some of the questions raised against loss-based accounts are not especially weighty. For example, while such accounts clearly admit a "leveling down"-type justification of punishment, they are hardly unique in doing so, and leveling down is only a problem if we assume that punishment must be good *for* someone to be justified (cf. Murphy 1973, 227).[14] Other objections, how-

[13] For loss-based versions of the fair play theory, see McDermott (2001) and Duus-Otterström (2017).

[14] "Leveling down" refers to the idea of making an outcome or distribution equal merely by reducing the position of the better off. For a valuable discussion, see Temkin (2003).

ever, deserve to be taken more seriously. Perhaps the most obvious worry is that loss-based accounts only seem convincing if they operate, implausibly, with a dyadic account of the relevant unfairness (Chau 2017, 624). To visualize this objection, suppose that Adam and Bert face the same burdens related to upholding the legal order (e.g., constraining their actions, paying taxes, supporting authorities) but enjoy the same legally protected interests as a result (e.g., to life, liberty, property). To make the point maximally clear, let us stipulate that both receive ten benefits and that this distribution of benefits and burdens is fair or just. Now suppose that Adam sets back one of Bert's legally protected interests—say, by assaulting him. As illustrated by Table 13.1, the resulting distribution would be unfair, and there is a sense in which fairness dictates that Adam, too, should have his benefits reduced to nine.

However, a problem emerges once we consider that the unfairness is not restricted to the relationship between Adam and Bert. As illustrated by Table 13.2, even after Adam is punished, Bert is unfairly disadvantaged compared to all other members of society. This seems to suggest that the fair play theory must endorse that the rest should also have their legally protected interests reduced, which is clearly unacceptable.

But the crucial difference between Adam and the rest is that the rest have not committed a criminally wrongful act. They have done what they are supposed to under the system of cooperation codified by the laws and can thus rightfully lay claim to all its benefits. This enables defenders of the fair play theory to say that, while the inequality between Bert and the rest is indeed unfair, it is not an unfairness that may or should be corrected, since doing so would require treating people in ways they do not deserve. Put differently, Adam is the only one who stands in a *culpable* position of unfair advantage over Bert.

Table 13.1 Unfairness between Adam and Bert

	Legal benefits before the crime	Legal benefits after the crime	Legal benefits after punishment
Adam	10	10	9
Bert	10	9	9

Table 13.2 Unfairness between Bert and the rest

	Legal benefits before the crime	Legal benefits after the crime	Legal benefits after punishment
Adam	10	10	9
Bert	10	9	9
The rest	10	10	10

To my mind, this offers a conclusive response to the objection that loss-based accounts require a general leveling down of legally protected benefits. It might be thought, though, that the response turns the fair play theory into a simpler form of retributivism according to which wrongdoers deserve to suffer. But the reason it is permissible and desirable to punish Bert remains that he stands in a position of unfair advantage over Adam; the difference is just that, for the purposes of justifying punishment, we need not worry about the fact that Adam is also disadvantaged compared to the law-abiding, who have done nothing to upset the distribution of benefits and burdens. Since the fair play theory is a species of retributivism, it is unsurprising that it treats the difference between offenders and the innocent as morally significant in this way.

Peter Chau (2017) has raised further objections against loss-based accounts. One is that such accounts are unable to explain why attempted crimes may be punished. Chau's thought is that, since criminal attempts often cause no losses to anyone, they often involve no unfair advantage. If correct, this would reveal a significant flaw of loss-based accounts, because there is little doubt that attempted crimes should be punished. But notice that Chau assumes that unsuccessful criminal attempts do not invade anyone's legally protected interests. This is implausible, since being protected from criminal risks of harm is an interest a legal order is supposed to protect. Thus, attempts produce "losses" in the relevant sense.

Chau's objection is instructive because it illustrates how important it is that fair play theorists restrict the loss metric to legally protected interests. The reason he thinks that attempted crimes inflict no losses is that he adopts something like well-being, or even subjective well-being, as the relevant standard. That is why Chau ends up arguing that potential murder victims face no loss when someone secretly attempts to shoot at them but (unbeknownst to the shooter) there is no bullet in the gun (2017, 630). But if legally protected interests are the metric and we have a legally protected interest in not being subjected to assassination attempts (which seems plausible enough), then it is impossible to be subjected to an assassination attempt without facing a loss. There is *necessarily* a loss since there is a setback to an interest that the legal system is supposed to protect. The focus on legally protected interests also means that it is irrelevant if, say, someone is made happier because they are subjected to a crime. As long as a legally protected interest has been violated, there is a loss in the relevant sense regardless of how a violation affects well-being in the individual case.[15]

[15] This is the same as saying that acts can wrong us even though they do not harm us (and may even benefit us). For a defense, see, e.g., McDermott (2001, 412), Kumar (2003), and Slavny and Parr (2015).

A better explanation of why some crimes cause no losses is that they are *victimless*. Suppose, for example, that some people cheat on their taxes, but that there are so few tax cheats that it makes no difference whatsoever to the public services that the state offers. It would then arguably be incorrect to say that anyone's legally protected interests have been set back by the tax cheats. But this is not a serious problem for the fair play theory because the theory may rely on a loss-based *and* a benefit-based component to explain why crimes create unfair advantage (Duus-Otterström 2017). There is no need to choose between the two components, and keeping both would make the fair play theory more powerful as it would allow it to account for crimes where the primary unfairness consists in the offender benefiting (e.g., tax evasion) as well as crimes where the primary unfairness consists in making the victim worse off (e.g., violent crime). The result would not be *ad hoc* since the overarching aim in both types of case would be to ensure that benefits and burdens are fairly distributed.

Another objection is that loss-based accounts are unable to explain why specifically *punishment* should be forthcoming (Chau 2017; see also Boonin 2008, 213–24). The thought here is that if we are concerned with unfair inequalities between offenders and victims, then it will always be an open question whether we remove the inequality by punishing the offender or by compensating the victim. To illustrate the objection, consider again the case of Adam and Bert, but now suppose that (as shown by Table 13.3) there is an opportunity to compensate Bert instead of punishing Adam. The objection is that the fair play theory will then be unable to explain why punishment should be inflicted.

This objection raises a real issue for loss-based versions of the fair play theory, but different responses are available. One option is to stress that Adam deserves to fare worse in virtue of his criminal wrongdoing. The idea here is that merely compensating Bert would be unjust since Adam would then enjoy the same interest-satisfaction as everyone else, despite having invaded other people's interests. If anything, it seems just that Adam's benefits are reduced *and* that Bert is restored to his former level, so that Adam would have nine and Bert have ten. It is not obvious how the loss-based account is able to

Table 13.3 Punishment or compensation

	Legal benefits before the crime	Legal benefits after the crime	Legal benefits after remedy	
			Punishment	Compensation
Adam	10	10	9	10
Bert	10	9	9	10

explain this intuitive view, however. The idea must be that, in causing criminal losses to others, one should no longer enjoy the full suite of benefits, making pure victim compensation inadequate. To forestall the discussion below, this seems like a point the entitlement-based interpretation of the theory explains better since this interpretation will say that punishment-plus-compensation is the solution which ensures that each person has the benefits they are entitled to.

A second option is simply to concede that compensation sometimes *would* remove unfair advantage just as well as punishment, but add that punishment will still be called for in those cases where full compensation, for some reason or another, is infeasible. While this may seem tantamount to giving up on the notion of a loss-based theory of punishment, whether this would be so depends on how common it is that punishment is the feasible remedy. We would still have a theory of punishment as long as compensation is rarely an adequate remedy, though it would not be a theory that is committed to punishment in a deep sense. It is worth noting that compensation probably *is* an inadequate remedy in many cases. If compensation requires that victims be restored to a previous level of advantage, it is not difficult to see that many crimes are difficult if not impossible to compensate (Goodin 1989). A further worry about compensation is that it introduces problematic inequalities in the way different crimes are responded to (e.g., it allows rich offenders, but only rich offenders, to pay their way out of punishment). This worry, however, would be mitigated by making compensation come from a state institution as opposed to from individual offenders.

A third option is to argue that compensation is *never* an adequate response since it fails to respond to the distinctive losses inflicted by crime. Daniel McDermott (2001) has defended this option. In McDermott's view, the distinctive loss inherent in crimes, at least when we are dealing with crimes against persons, is that victims had their moral rights disrespected. For example, in being assaulted by someone else, we are treated as though we are not rights-holding persons worthy of bodily integrity and security. Correcting this kind of loss requires punishment, McDermott argues, because whereas material harms can be corrected by restitutionary remedies—maybe the assailant must cover income that the victim lost while recuperating, for instance—the loss of having one's rights disrespected cannot be corrected simply by transferring money or resources. The loss also cannot be corrected by transferring the moral good that the crime undermined, because we cannot "take" the respect for rights normally accorded to the wrongdoer and give it to the victims. If Adam is imprisoned for assaulting Bert, for example, then Adam's loss of liberty could not be given to Bert for the simple reason that liberty is not a transferrable good. What we are left with to respond to the loss, McDermott argues, is to inflict comparable losses on offenders, namely punishment.[16]

As this shows, there are several ways to respond to the compensation objection. In light of these, it is unlikely that the compensation objection would be impossible to overcome for loss-based versions of the fair play theory.

5 Entitlement-Based Accounts

Entitlement-based accounts also stress that unfairness can emerge even though the offender does not benefit from committing a crime. However, whereas loss-based accounts focus on the fact that offenders may make others worse off, entitlement-based accounts instead stress that it is unfair for offenders to retain the benefits of the legal order. I call such approaches "entitlement-based" since they focus on the fact that offenders are not entitled to possess the full benefits of social cooperation.

Peter Westen (2016) has provided a defense of the entitlement-based approach. Westen calls attention to Morris's claim that "a person who violates the rules has something … that does not *rightfully belong to him*" (Morris 1968, 478, emphasis added). Westen argues that this claim is not directed at the benefits associated with offending. Instead, it speaks about the benefits made possible by living under a legal order. As Westen explains:

> All persons who continue to live in … an organized society, even those who are occasionally victimized, reap enormous benefits in well-being vis-à-vis the fate they would suffer in alternative, predatory societies in which … moral and legally declared rights are lacking. An actor in such a society who fails to show others the respect that morality and law rightly expect of him should be officially condemned for it. In addition, because he has benefitted enormously from the existence and general recognition of moral and legal rights that he has not

[16] McDermott (2001) arguably goes too far, though, since he comes perilously close to saying that material goods (being "categorically" different from the moral good of respectful treatment) can *never* correct the distinctive loss inflicted by crime. This would be too strong considering that fines can be punishments even though they go after the perpetrator's money. However, this does not change the crucial point that compensation via rights-respecting treatment is often impossible, for if the distinctive loss of crime is that one is not treated as a person, then it seems that the only way this loss could be compensated would be for the victim to be treated as *more* than a person for a period. But the idea of treating someone as more than a person, if it is even desirable, is incoherent insofar as our rights are satiable. For example, once a person's right to bodily integrity is respected, no more bodily integrity can be gained; there is no "extra" bodily integrity to dole out.

> respected in others, it is just that he forfeit, and that the society compel him to forfeit, a portion of those benefits—namely the portion that his lack of reciprocal respect renders it unfair for him to retain—and that society do so by inflicting suffering commensurate with that portion. (2016, 69–70)

Westen's idea is that, since all people generally benefit greatly from living under rights-protecting legal orders, fair play dictates that each person contribute their fair share to the production of these benefits. This contribution takes the form of showing reciprocal respects for rights. When someone fails to offer such respect and breaks the law, then it is no longer fair for them to retain all the benefits provided by the legal order. Punishment is justified because it takes away some of these benefits.

Westen's view stakes out an interesting middle ground in the debate. On the one hand, it retains an intuitive and ordinary conception of benefits. Westen is essentially speaking of things like security of person and property. On the other hand, by focusing on whether it is fair to keep benefits someone already enjoys, it avoids the problems associated with linking the benefits to the criminal act. As Westen puts it, his account focuses on benefits that "malefactors gain not *by* wrongdoing but *prior to* wrongdoing" (2016, 67; cf. Burgh 1982, 203).[17]

The idea that justice requires stripping offenders of welfare to which they are not entitled enables Westen to explain why punishment, and not compensation, should be forthcoming. If it is unfair for offenders to retain the full range of benefits associated with living under a legal order, then punishment is essential in order for fairness to be restored. The fact that Westen's view offers a robust explanation of why compensation and punishment are not substitutable is one of its strengths. The view is also able, at least in the abstract, to ground proportionality in punishment. Westen argues that "wrongdoers forfeit only as much of their unfairly retained welfare as is commensurate with the lack of respect that they have manifested toward others" (2016, 70). The thought is that, when people commit a serious crime, they deserve to lose more welfare than if they commit a minor crime.

Westen's account is arguably too loose, though, on the nature of the benefits. It is no doubt correct that virtually everyone benefits enormously from living under a legal order, especially when this order aims to protect moral rights. But the risk is that references to "welfare" make the account overly inclusive. Consider, for example, Steve Jobs. It is obvious that a precondition

[17] Westen (2016) also claims that this is the point Morris had in mind, although Westen admits that Morris stated his view so vaguely that the door was opened to other interpretations.

for Jobs's extremely high welfare was that he did not live in a Hobbesian state of nature.[18] However, the mere fact that the legal order helped explain his quality of life surely does not mean that the state would have had a right to attack the part of his welfare that stemmed from running Apple. This part of his welfare was too far removed from the reciprocal respect for rights the criminal law codifies to count as the relevant kind of benefit. Put more generally, if some people are able to convert the stability offered by the legal order into high-welfare lives, then it is unclear why they would thereby deserve greater punishment for breaking the law.

My sense is that entitlement-based approaches would do well to abandon the idea of welfare in favor of a thinner account of the relevant benefits. The benefits should be (in line with my references to "legally protected interests" above) restricted to the content of the rights protected by criminal law. A proponent of an entitlement-based version of the fair play theory would then say that it would be unfair if people who violated the rights of other members of society would themselves have intact rights. This would explain why fairness demands that offenders face, say, fines or imprisonment.

6 Conclusion: Time for Other Questions

The no-benefit objection has plagued the fair play theory ever since the start, but I have argued that it can be avoided by interpreting the theory in a loss-based or an entitlement-based way. Once we acknowledge that unfair advantage can be created merely by reducing someone else's position or that it can be unfair to possess legal benefits, it ceases to be a problem that some crimes do not render the perpetrator better off.

Which account is better: the loss-based or the entitlement-based one? This is an open question, but the loss-based account certainly raises more puzzling questions than the entitlement-based account. The entitlement-based account is also more general than its loss-based counterpart in that it can explain why punishment is due even in cases where no losses are inflicted. The unfairness on which the entitlement-based account focuses is the unfairness of enjoying the benefits of the legal order without contributing one's fair share to the maintenance of that order. This makes the entitlement-based account able to handle any kind of crime, regardless of whether it is primarily harmful,

[18] Thomas Hobbes famously argued that life in the state of nature (a pre-societal condition without overarching political authorities) would be plagued by war and be "solitary, poor, nasty, brutish, and short" (1996, 89).

primarily beneficial, or neither harmful nor beneficial. Hence, if one had to choose between the two accounts, the case for the entitlement-based account is more compelling.

I do not think, however, that choosing between the accounts is necessary, and keeping both would allow fair play retributivists to give a more robust set of tools to explain why breaking the law justifies punishment. In particular, the loss-based account can fill out the somewhat "bloodless" image offered by the entitlement-based account. It highlights that committing crimes against others results in a loss of entitlements because the failure to contribute takes the form of violating rights. Once maldistribution of benefits and burdens is made the central concern, the fair play theory will naturally go in a pluralist direction, where committing crimes causes a loss of entitlement to legally protected benefits, but the reason the crime leads to a maldistribution differs.

My ambition here, however, is not to explore the content of this pluralist version of the fair play theory. The key point I want to make is that there is an adequate response (and possibly several adequate responses) to the no-benefit objection. This means that it is time for philosophers of punishment to move on from that objection, at least as the dominant focus of the debate. Doing so would free up intellectual resources for other questions. Let me end this chapter by flagging two issues that, in my estimation, stand out as especially pressing.

The first issue is proportionality. As previously noted, most fair play theorists want their view to guide sentencing, and it is essential that the guidance be in line with intuitive understandings about which crimes are worse. However, almost without exception, they have stayed away from getting into the details about how their view would translate into a proportionate scheme of punishment (but see Davis 1983). This may reflect a general pessimism about whether proportionality is a topic on which penologists could make much progress (Tonry 2020; Chiao 2022). It may also be a side effect of what has so far been a largely defensive debate. Regardless, it is high time that fair play theorists think more closely and constructively about which factors go into ranking crimes in terms of seriousness as well as what punishments would be needed to correct them. While there are limits to how detailed theories of punishment can be when it comes to such questions, in the absence of work exploring them, the risk is that the theory's talk about removing unfair advantage comes across as merely an evocative metaphor without much practical substance.

A second issue concerns punishment in less-than-just societies. This issue was raised already by Jeffrie Murphy (1973), and it has received a fair amount of attention (see, e.g., Anderson 1997; Westen 2016; Duus-Otterström 2017; Dagger 2018, 286–96; Duus-Otterström 2021). However, much more needs to be said about it. The general problem is that the fair play theory seems to struggle when applied to less-than-just societies since punishment will not necessarily correct unfairness if the prior distribution of benefits and burdens was unfair. For example, if an offender does not have their legally recognized interests protected by the state because of racist patterns in law enforcement, then it seems that such an offender would not deserve a punishment, or as harsh a punishment, compared to people whose interests the state does secure. If the fair play theorist is to avoid becoming an abolitionist who thinks that punishment is justified only in principle (and not in practice), it is essential to explain why the theory is compatible with some (although surely not *any*) degree of injustice. But here more thought is needed. Westen (2016, 75–76) stresses the fact that almost everyone is vastly better off by living in organized societies than they would be in a Hobbesian state of nature. His suggestion is that fair play duties obtain in less-than-just societies because people draw sufficiently large benefits from the existence of criminal law.

However, it is not obvious that this is the correct standard to use, because the critics do not deny that an unjust society can be better for each person than the state of nature. Their point is that we should compare unjust societies with *just* ones rather than with no society at all. Now this kind of view is arguably guilty of equivocating between the benefits of criminal law and the benefits of social cooperation more generally. It is much easier to see why everyone might in fact have what they are entitled to when it comes to protection from crime than when it comes to, say, society's income and wealth. Nevertheless, it is not clear how to assess whether a legal order is capable of generating fair play obligations. In virtue of which standard or point of comparison can we say that a person has a fairness-based obligation to obey the law? Must they benefit the same or do they only have to benefit "enough"? From particular laws or from the criminal law as a whole? What happens to the right to punish when someone does not benefit in the required way?[19] These are also questions that fair play theorists ought to explore further.[20]

[19] For discussion of these issues, see Shelby (2016) and Duus-Otterström (2021).

[20] I am grateful for written feedback from Peter Chau, William Bülow, Peter Westen, and Zachary Hoskins.

References

Anderson, Jami L. 1997. "Reciprocity as a Justification for Retributivism." *Criminal Justice Ethics* 16, no. 1: 13–25.

Bauer, Paul, and Andrei Poama. 2020. "Does Suffering Suffice? An Experimental Assessment of Desert Retributivism." *PLOS ONE* 15, no. 4 (April 20): e0230304.

Boonin, David. 2008. *The Problem of Punishment*. Cambridge: Cambridge University Press.

Burgh, Richard W. 1982. "Do the Guilty Deserve Punishment?" *Journal of Philosophy* 79, no. 4 (April): 193–210.

Chau, Peter. 2017. "Loss-Based Retributive Justifications of Punishment." *Oxford Journal of Legal Studies* 37, no. 3 (Autumn): 618–35.

Chiao, Vincent. 2022. "Proportionality and Its Discontents." *Law and Philosophy* 41, nos. 2–3 (June): 193–217.

Dagger, Richard. 2018. *Playing Fair: Political Obligation and the Problems of Punishment*. Oxford: Oxford University Press.

Davis, Michael. 1983. "How to Make the Punishment Fit the Crime." *Ethics* 93, no. 4 (July): 726–52.

———. 1993. "Criminal Desert and Unfair Advantage: What's the Connection?" *Law and Philosophy* 12, no. 2 (May): 133–56.

Dolinko, David. 1991. "Some Thoughts about Retributivism." *Ethics* 101, no. 3 (April): 537–59.

Duff, R. A. 2001. *Punishment, Communication, and Community*. Oxford: Oxford University Press.

———. 2008. "The Incompleteness of 'Punishment as Fair Play': A Response to Dagger." *Res Publica* 14, no. 4 (December): 277–81.

Duus-Otterström, Göran. 2017. "Fairness-Based Retributivism Reconsidered." *Criminal Law and Philosophy* 11, no. 3 (September): 481–98.

———. 2021. "Fair-Play Obligations and Distributive Injustice." *European Journal of Political Theory* 20, no. 2 (April): 167–86.

Duus-Otterström, Göran, and Erin I. Kelly. 2019. "Injustice and the Right to Punish." *Philosophy Compass* 14, no. 2 (February): e12565.

Falls, M. Margaret. 1987. "Retribution, Reciprocity, and Respect for Persons." *Law and Philosophy* 6, no. 1 (April): 25–51.

Finnis, John. 1980. *Natural Law and Natural Rights*. Oxford: Oxford University Press.

Flanders, Chad. 2017. "Punishment, Liberalism, and Public Reason." *Criminal Justice Ethics* 36, no. 1: 61–77.

Goodin, Robert E. 1989. "Theories of Compensation." *Oxford Journal of Legal Studies* 9, no. 1 (Spring): 56–75.

Hampton, Jean. 1991. "Correction Harms versus Righting Wrongs: The Goal of Retribution." *UCLA Law Review* 39, no. 6 (August): 1659–702.

Hart, H. L. A. 1955. "Are There Any Natural Rights?" *Philosophical Review* 64, no. 2 (April): 175–91.

———. 2008. *Punishment and Responsibility: Essays in the Philosophy of Law*. 2nd ed. Oxford University Press.
Hobbes, Thomas. 1996. *Leviathan*. Edited by Richard Tuck. Cambridge: Cambridge University Press.
Hoskins, Zachary. 2011. "Fair Play, Political Obligation, and Punishment." *Criminal Law and Philosophy* 5, no. 1 (January): 53–71.
Husak, Douglas. 2008. *Overcriminalization: The Limits of the Criminal Law*. Oxford: Oxford University Press.
Klosko, George. 2004. *The Principle of Fairness and Political Obligation*. Lanham, MD: Rowman & Littlefield.
———. 2005. *Political Obligations*. Oxford: Oxford University Press.
Kramer, Matthew. 2013. "Retributivism in the Spirit of Finnis." In *Reason, Morality, and Law: The Philosophy of John Finnis*, edited by John Keown and Robert P. George, 167–85. Oxford: Oxford University Press.
Kumar, Rahul. 2003. "Who Can Be Wronged?" *Philosophy & Public Affairs* 31, no. 2 (April): 99–118.
McDermott, Daniel. 2001. "The Permissibility of Punishment." *Law and Philosophy* 20, no. 4 (July): 403–32.
Moore, Michael S. 1997. *Placing Blame: A General Theory of the Criminal Law*. Oxford: Oxford University Press.
Morris, Herbert. 1968. "Persons and Punishment." *Monist* 52, no. 4 (October): 475–501.
Murphy, Jeffrie G. 1971. "Three Mistakes about Retributivism." *Analysis* 31, no. 5 (April): 166–69.
———. 1973. "Marxism and Retribution." *Philosophy & Public Affairs* 2, no. 3 (Spring): 217–43.
Rawls, John. 1999. "Legal Obligation and the Duty of Fair Play." In *John Rawls: Collected Papers*, edited by Samuel Freeman, 117–29. Cambridge, MA: Harvard University Press.
Runge, Carlisle Ford. 1984. "Institutions and the Free Rider: The Assurance Problem in Collective Action." *Journal of Politics* 46, no. 1 (February): 154–81.
Shelby, Tommie. 2016. *Dark Ghettos: Injustice, Dissent, and Reform*. Cambridge, MA: Belknap.
Sher, George. 1987. *Desert*. Princeton, NJ: Princeton University Press.
Simmons, A. John. 2001. *Justification and Legitimacy: Essays on Rights and Obligations*. Cambridge: Cambridge University Press.
Slavny, Adam, and Tom Parr. 2015. "Harmless Discrimination." *Legal Theory* 21, no. 2 (June): 100–114.
Tadros, Victor. 2009. "Poverty and Criminal Responsibility." *Journal of Value Inquiry* 43, no. 3 (September): 391–413.
Temkin, Larry S. 2003. "Equality, Priority or What?" *Economics and Philosophy* 19, no. 1 (April): 61–87.

Thorburn, Malcolm. 2012. "Proportionate Sentencing and the Rule of Law." In *Principles and Values in Criminal Law and Criminal Justice: Essays in Honour of Andrew Ashworth*, edited by Lucia Zedner and Julian V. Roberts, 269–84. Oxford: Oxford University Press.

Tonry, Michael. 2020. "Is Proportionality in Punishment Possible, and Achievable?" In *Of One-Eyed and Toothless Miscreants. Making the Punishment Fit the Crime*, edited by Michael Tonry, 1–29. New York: Oxford University Press.

Wellman, Christopher Heath. 2001. "Toward a Liberal Theory of Political Obligation." *Ethics* 111, no. 4 (July): 735–59.

Westen, Peter. 2016. "Retributive Desert as Fair Play." In *Legal, Moral, and Metaphysical Truths: The Philosophy of Michael S. Moore*, edited by Kimberly Kessler Ferzan and Stephen J. Morse, 63–78. Oxford: Oxford University Press.

14

The Rights-Forfeiture Theory of Punishment

Whitley Kaufman

The justification of punishment, that is, of the deliberate infliction of suffering on a person in response to their having done wrong, remains arguably the most perplexing and profound moral problem today.[1] We inflict severe suffering on convicted criminals on a massive scale, claiming that it is demanded by justice, and yet we lack a clear idea of just why or even whether this practice is justified. Indeed, *prima facie* punishment would seem not only morally unjustified but obviously so. There is an overwhelming moral presumption against the intentional infliction of harm, yet punishment is deemed not merely permissible but obligatory and even praiseworthy.[2] Punishment also seems to clearly violate the widely-accepted Kantian principle that one may not use people as mere means to a further end, whether that end be retribution

[1] For more details, see my discussion of this problem in Kaufman (2013, ch. 1). The present essay focuses on legal punishment administered by the state, though the question of why the state is the legitimate and exclusive administrator of punishment is itself of course a further challenging problem, in addition to the question of why anyone at all is justified in administering punishment.

[2] One arguable exception to the prohibition of intentional harm is self-defense, though the traditional double effect theory of self-defense claims that the harm inflicted on the attacker is not fully intentional (Kaufman 2009). In any case, self-defense presents similar problems of moral justification, and indeed rights-forfeiture proponents usually defend self-defense along the very same lines, in that an unjustified attacker has forfeited the right not to be harmed. I criticize the rights-forfeiture theory of self-defense in Kaufman (2004).

W. Kaufman (✉)
University of Massachusetts Lowell, Lowell, MA, USA
e-mail: whitley_kaufman@uml.edu

© The Author(s), under exclusive license to Springer Nature Switzerland AG 2023

M. C. Altman (ed.), *The Palgrave Handbook on the Philosophy of Punishment*, Palgrave Handbooks in the Philosophy of Law, https://doi.org/10.1007/978-3-031-11874-6_14

or deterrence.[3] It is true that consequentialism permits the infliction of harm on some in order to produce greater overall good, and it presents this as a sufficient justification for punishment. However, it is just this feature of the theory that has caused most moral philosophers to reject consequentialism as a plausible moral theory. Hence the dilemma: we inflict enormous suffering on people in the name of punishment, yet our intuitive assumption that punishment is justified lacks a plausible moral explanation.

One attempt to explain and justify punishment is the *rights-forfeiture theory* of punishment. It agrees that the deliberate infliction of harm on a person is *prima facie* wrong, a violation of that person's rights. However, the theory claims that, by committing a wrong (moral or legal), the wrongdoer forfeits their right against being harmed, and therefore society may inflict suffering on them in the name of punishment. Further, the extent of the forfeiture is relative to the extent of the wrongdoing; a minor infraction justifies only a minor punishment while a major wrong justifies severe punishment. The theory thus gives us a simple, clear explanation of why punishment is justified, why punishment must be proportionate to the wrongdoing, and why innocent people may not be "punished." It is of course an incomplete theory of punishment, for it does not address the question of the purpose for which punishment is inflicted; hence, it does not resolve the debate between retributivists and deterrence advocates. Nonetheless, if correct it resolves arguably the most fundamental problem in the debate over the legitimacy of punishment: how it can ever be morally justified to intentionally inflict harm on people.

Despite its attractions, the rights-forfeiture theory of punishment has never been accepted by more than a small minority of moral and political philosophers. Traces of it can be found, so its proponents claim, in Hobbes, Hume, and Locke, but none of these present a systematic development or defense of the theory.[4] W. D. Ross is the most prominent explicit defender of rights-forfeiture, but he does so only briefly in an appendix to *The Right and the Good.* Christopher Wellman's recent monograph, *Rights Forfeiture and Punishment*, is (to my knowledge) the only book-length defense of the theory. Wellman expresses frustration that there are "so few advocates" of the rights-forfeiture theory, since to him the theory is "obvious" and "self-evident" (2017, 29). Nonetheless, the critical response to this theory has been overwhelmingly negative (see, e.g., Lippke 2001; Boonin 2008; Rosebury 2015; Renzo 2017). In this essay, I address the reasons that critics have overwhelmingly

[3] To be sure, Kant himself did not think so (see Kant 1996, 6:331–35 [pp. 473–76]). But Kant's defense of punishment is almost universally rejected today as implausible and barely even coherent.

[4] For discussion of Locke, see Simmons (1991, 239–44).

rejected the theory. I argue that the attraction of the rights-forfeiture theory is that it affirms the near-universal intuition that punishment is justified, but that the central flaw of the theory is that it fails to go beyond that intuition, not providing either an explanation of our intuitive beliefs or a moral justification of them.

1 Intuitions about Punishment

The rights-forfeiture theory holds that wrongdoers cannot complain about their rights being violated by punishment, since they have failed to respect the rights of others. The theory claims to explicate and justify this intuition, to make it explicit and to present it within the context of a moral framework. The danger of relying on unaided intuitions is of course that they can be badly misguided. For example, the United States Supreme Court in 1873 upheld a state law prohibiting women from becoming lawyers, on grounds of what they claimed was the obvious natural incapacity of women for the workplace: "The natural and proper timidity and delicacy which belongs to the female sex evidently unfits it for many of the occupations of civil life" (*Bradwell v. Illinois*, 83 U.S. 130 [1873], 141 [Bradley, concurring]).[5] More recently, we have seen the power of the intuition that marriage and sex is only legitimate between men and women. Thus moral intuitions need to be carefully examined to see if they are based on mere bias in favor of the status quo. In particular, they need to be tested against general moral principles by the method of "reflective equilibrium" to see if they have a moral foundation.

Unfortunately, the intuition that punishment is legitimate is *prima facie* deeply suspect on just these grounds. As a practice that has existed since time immemorial, there is the worry that our intuitions are biased in favor of an age-old traditional practice. There is further the problem that punishment does not seem to fit at all with our moral principles; as I noted, punishment is unique in that it involves deliberate infliction of harm on persons. Finally, there is the possibility that this intuition is not grounded in morality but has a nonmoral origin: specifically, it might be an instinct or impulse implanted in us by evolution.[6] Indeed, it is very hard to distinguish retributive punishment from revenge, yet the latter instinct is widely taken as morally suspect. If so, the impulse, no matter how powerful, cannot be taken as a reliable

[5] The word "evidently" in this opinion means it is taken as self-evident, and no further evidentiary support is needed or given.

[6] The position that the desire for retributive punishment is the product of evolution is defended by McCullough (2008, 11) and Daly and Wilson (1988, 251).

moral intuition but must be evaluated as to whether it is morally legitimate by showing how it coheres with accepted moral principles.

Critics have charged that this is just where the rights-forfeiture theory fails: it fails to show how our intuition is grounded in moral principles. The worry is that the rights-forfeiture theory, rather than explicating our intuitions, merely restates them in the pseudo-technical jargon of "rights" and "forfeiture." In Molière's 1673 comedy, *Le Malade imaginaire*, the pedantic physician "explains" how opium induces sleep by saying that it is due to its "dormitive virtue": that is, it causes sleep because of its power to cause sleep. Molière satirizes the doctor's attempt to hide his ignorance behind learned-sounding phrases, masking what is a circular explanation. For critics, explaining the legitimacy of punishment on the grounds that the wrongdoer has forfeited his rights commits the same fallacy. Brian Rosebury, for example, raises the concern that, "if all we mean by saying that a criminal 'has an altered moral status,' or 'has forfeited a right,' is that it is now permissible for us to grapple with him or punish him," then we have merely created a "tautology" (2015, 264). Massimo Renzo suggests that the notion of forfeiture does no work in itself, but serves merely as a "placeholder" for other moral arguments (2017, 335). It will not do therefore simply to assert that wrongdoers forfeit their right not to be punished. The rights-forfeiture theory will have to provide detailed and substantive arguments as to why wrongdoers can be taken as having forfeited their right against hard treatment.

Unfortunately, the arguments that have been presented as yet in favor of the idea of rights-forfeiture have been largely rejected as unconvincing, as we will see below. It is somewhat disconcerting therefore that Wellman in his recent defense of rights-forfeiture simply gives up on the need for presenting arguments to support his view. He begins his book by conceding, "for the sake of argument," that critics have made a convincing case against all previous defenses of rights-forfeiture. He admits that he has no new argument in favor of the theory, but that his strategy will be instead merely to "assert" and to "assume" its truth, on the grounds that it is a "considered conviction" of his, and that "all arguments have to start somewhere" (2017, 24). His fundamental premise is that "violating the rights of others alters the moral standing of the wrongdoers." As for those who reject this premise, "we simply agree to disagree." Wellman insists that "very few will actually deny this particular premise" (27). But this approach only magnifies the worry that rights-forfeiture theory is merely reaffirming our intuition that punishment is legitimate. The question at stake is whether the idea of forfeiture of rights is a useful way to analyze or justify this intuition. Wellman draws on the former intuition (that wrongdoers deserve punishment) and purports to explain it on the grounds that wrongdoers forfeit their rights. Few people will deny the former "premise," but the problem is that there is little reason to accept the latter one. Unless the rights-forfeiture claim can be systematically developed, and shown to cohere better with accepted moral principles or to explain our punitive practices, then it is hard to see how the rights-forfeiture theory can even claim to be a theory at all, rather than merely another way of asserting that punishment is permissible. We need then to examine the two central claims of the theory: that people have some sort of right that punishment would ordinarily violate, and that they "forfeit" this right by committing a moral wrong.

2 Rights and Forfeiture

The central assumption of the rights-forfeiture theory is that the problem of punishment can be analyzed through the idea of rights. But it is far from obvious that it is either helpful or necessary to analyze moral or political problems in terms of rights. Critics have charged that "rights" claims are rhetorically effective but of little intellectual substance, at least with respect to moral or natural rights; communitarians have challenged rights theories as embodying a one-sided atomistic individualism that neglects responsibilities to the society (see, e.g., Glendon 1991).[7] We can all agree that punishment is permissible only if there is a moral basis for it; however, it does not follow that the morality of punishment must be addressed in terms of whether anyone's rights are violated. Indeed, the notion of rights plays essentially no role in the two most important ethical theories, Kantian deontology and consequentialism, and in their respective approaches to justifying punishment (retribution and deterrence). The retributivist, for example, would say that it suffices morally to establish that the wrongdoer deserves punishment; the notion of rights is otiose. The deterrence theorist would go even further, claiming that the notion of "rights" only obfuscates the issue; following Bentham, he might say that the notion of natural rights is "nonsense upon stilts."

Wellman's defense of the rights-based approach, unfortunately, is blatantly circular: "Only a rights-based analysis will suffice here, because the type of justification we seek for punishment must demonstrate that punishment is permissible, and it would be permissible only if it violated no one's

[7] The present discussion involves of course moral rights rather than legal or positive rights (such as the right to a speedy trial), which are concrete and precise legal guarantees that are binding on the state. There is no doubt a legal right to punish; the question is whether there is a moral right to do so.

rights" (2017, 2). That is, Wellman simply assumes that punishment must be shown not to violate rights. Other defenders of the rights-forfeiture theory do little better. David Alm tells us that it is a "background assumption" of his approach that people "have a right not to suffer the kind of hard treatment involved in punishment, and that to offer a moral justification of punishment is to show that it does not *infringe* that right" (2013, 91–92).[8] Alan Goldman writes:

> If we are to justify punishment of particular wrongdoers, … we must argue that they have forfeited those rights of which we are depriving them. … It seems clear that this is the only way we could convince criminals themselves that they are not being treated unjustly in being punished. (1979, 43)[9]

Christopher Morris argues that punishment is "not unjust" if "wrongdoers do not possess moral rights that stand in the way of their being punished" and there are "compelling reasons" for punishment (1991, 55). Stephen Kershnar begins his essay by asserting that "Violence, whether performed by the state or private individuals, is ordinarily thought to be wrong because people have rights protecting them against it" (2010, 224).

The substantive position of the rights-forfeiture theory is the far from obvious one that the only theoretically sound way to understand why punishment could be justified is in terms of the possession of rights. This claim cannot merely be assumed or taken to be intuitively obvious, yet it is hard to find any actual arguments for this key idea. It is unclear why Goldman thinks that we could convince criminals of the justice of their punishment "only" in terms of rights forfeiture, or that any criminals would be convinced by this explanation. As popular as it is, especially in the United States, to assert one's grievances in terms of "rights,"[10] there is little reason to believe that a moral theory must be constructed in terms of rights, or even must incorporate moral rights into its structure. To hold that punishment must be analyzed in terms of rights is a very strong claim requiring a substantial argument; however, none seems to be forthcoming from the rights-forfeiture theorists.

[8] Note the ambiguity between the claim that people *ought* not to suffer, versus that they have a "right" not to.

[9] The claim that it "seems clear" is another version of the self-evidence claim.

[10] It was, for example, common during the COVID pandemic to hear people insist that they had a "right" not to wear a mask. This assertion functioned in effect to relieve the claimant of having to make a moral argument for this dubious position.

3 What Rights Are Forfeited?

A systematic defense of the rights-forfeiture theory would require at the very least addressing the initial and crucial question: just what right (or rights) is forfeited by the wrongdoer? Surprisingly, however, there is little agreement on the answer to this question, or even much of an effort to address it, or even how one would go about determining what rights people have that are relevant to punishment. In fact, defenders of the theory frequently leave it undetermined just what right or rights are at stake. For example, Morris says that wrongdoers lose "certain rights" and that they are deprived of "some part of their moral standing" (1991, 65); Wellman insists that rights-forfeiture theory "need take no stand on which particular rights are forfeited" (2017, 40); and John Simmons indicates only that wrongdoers forfeit "certain of" their rights (1991, 330, 337).

There is a natural temptation to provide a seemingly simple answer: the wrongdoer forfeits exactly those rights that he violated against others. For example, Goldman writes: "if we ask which rights are forfeited in violating rights of others, it is plausible to answer just those rights that one violates (or an equivalent set)" (1979, 33). Ross holds that "the offender, by violating the life or liberty or property of another, has lost his own right to have his life or liberty or property respected" (2002, 60). Morris suggests: "It may be thought that loss of the rights that wrongdoers violate is actually a most appropriate punishment for individuals unwilling to respect the requirements of justice" (1991, 70). Kershnar holds that the offender loses the right they have violated, or an "equivalent right" (2010, 322). The intuitive appeal here is similar to that of the *lex talionis* in retributive theories (Morris 1991, 70): people should be punished in the same way they harmed others.

However, this seductive symmetry lacks any convincing rational basis. The *lex talionis* principle is today all but universally rejected (e.g., Zimmerman 2011, 65–66). It would lead to morally absurd results: Should we blind those who have blinded another? Torture the torturers? Rape the rapists? Steal from the thieves? Hammurabi's Code declared that if a homebuilder builds a home badly and it falls and kills the owner's son, then the son of the homebuilder shall be put to death. And does one punish an attempted murder by "attempting" to kill the wrongdoer? Exact retribution is not even logically possible: you cannot take away multiple lives from a serial killer. Indeed, nothing close to this principle is followed in practice; the dominant form of punishment is imprisonment, but logically that should be applied only to those who violate the *freedom* of others (e.g., kidnappers). Finally, this invocation of *lex talionis* suggests that the rights-forfeiture theory is merely another name for retributivism, rather than an independent theory. Ironically, of course, the *lex talionis* principle is an example of an intuition that is *not* reliable, making us wonder whether the rights-forfeiture intuition is any less problematic.

Even the advocates of the idea that one forfeits exactly the rights one violates in others have backed off from the *lex talionis* principle, using the "equivalence principle" as an escape clause. That is, one need not forfeit the exact rights one violates, for obvious practical reasons, but one can be said to forfeit "equivalent" rights (Goldman 1979; Kershnar 2010, 322). Goldman, for example, says we can measure what counts as "equivalent" in terms of some suitable "preference scale" (1979, 45), so that the wrongdoer suffers harm equivalent to that suffered by the victim (47). This version of the theory is more intuitively plausible and matches our actual punitive practices: we impose imprisonment not because the wrongdoer has forfeited the right to freedom, but because imprisonment is deemed a form of punishment that is an appropriate level of suffering given the suffering he has imposed. However, the problem is that now the notion of rights (and forfeiture) seems to play no role anymore.[11] The equivalence principle is just another name for the intuitively plausible Proportionality Principle: punishment should be proportionate to the crime. Thus Wellman rejects the *lex talionis* view in favor of the idea that a wrongdoer "forfeits her right against a *fitting* or *proportionate* punishment" (2017, 34). Simmons attributes to Locke the position that one forfeits "that portion of one's own rights against others that will make an interference in one's own life, proportionate to one's interference in others' lives, morally permissible" (1991, 331). The notion of rights-forfeiture does not explain or justify that principle, and it provides no useful guidance as to how to apply it in terms of rights. So again the rights-forfeiture theory seems to merely restate the intuitive proportionality principle but not to provide an independent justification for it.

A further problem is that by intentionally harming others, one does not in general forfeit the right not to be harmed proportionately. This is the Problem of Relatedness (see, e.g., Wellman 2017, 120–30). Otherwise, a convicted murderer sentenced to execution could be killed by anyone at any time for any reason prior to his execution: by a sadistic guard, by a fellow prisoner, or by someone else. But this cannot be correct. Rather, the wrongdoer can only

[11] Indeed, it is implausible that there exists an indefinitely long list of natural rights corresponding to every possible type of harm: a right not to have one's pinky scratched, one's nose punched, one's shin kicked, one's eye removed (as well as a separate right not to have both eyes removed), one's hand burned by a cigarette, and so on.

be harmed for the right reason: for punitive reasons.[12] So then the rights-forfeiture theorist must retreat to a narrower notion: that the right that is forfeited is not the right to be harmed (proportionately), but the right to be harmed for punitive purposes or motives. That is, the right that is forfeited by a wrongdoer is the right not to be *punished.*

Thus some defenders of the rights-forfeiture theory have taken this position. Wellman supports the idea that "a wrongdoer does not forfeit her right against hard treatment; more specifically, she forfeits her right against *being punished*" (2017, 142).[13] Patrick Tomlin too declares that there is a "right against being punished" that is forfeited by wrongdoing (2017, 253). But is there really a right not to be punished? To be sure, there is a right not to be punished unjustly (i.e., if one is innocent, or punished disproportionately).[14] But it seems quite implausible that there is a natural right not to be punished proportionately for wrongdoing; indeed, the very intuition that we are examining here is that punishing a wrongdoer is legitimate. And even if there were such a right, it makes little sense to say one forfeits that right by engaging in wrongdoing. If one has a right not to be punished for committing a wrong, then one can hardly be said to forfeit that right by committing that very same wrong—for that would render the right not to be punished meaningless! It would be simpler and far more intuitive to hold that there is to begin with no right not to be punished for committing a wrong.[15] If so, then rights-forfeiture plays no explanatory or justificatory role.[16]

4 What Is Forfeiture?

Even if we knew just what right was at stake, still there would be a question as to what it means to say the right is forfeited by wrongdoing. Although "forfeiture" sounds like a technical term, it is anything but precise, nor is the term consistently utilized. Ross refers to the "loss" of rights; Goldman says they are

[12] And also, only by the appropriate authority. But I leave aside this complication.

[13] Wellman ends up endorsing this idea, though tentatively (2017, 146).

[14] Equally puzzling is that Simmons (1991) argues that victims have a "right to punish." But it seems unlikely that there is a right to punish persons who have done wrong, and also a general right not to be punished for having done wrong, the latter of which must be forfeited for the former right to be actionable.

[15] Indeed, it only seems to lead to a regress. For if there is a right not to be punished for a wrongdoing, then why is there not also a right not to forfeit one's right not to be punished for that wrongdoing?

[16] Note also how different this version of the theory is from the *lex talionis* version, which tries to ground forfeiture in the principle of tit-for-tat. This again suggests that rights-forfeiture is not a substantive theory, but an intuition in search of a reason.

"alienated" or "cease to exist" (1979, 43); Morris wavers between saying they are forfeited versus saying the wrongdoer does not have them in the first place (he writes that contract killers, war criminals and other such people "no longer have, or never had," the right to life or liberty [1991, 70]). Moreover, whatever rights are forfeited for the purposes of punishment, they are apparently forfeited only for a certain time, only with respect to certain rights, only to a certain degree, only as against certain persons, and only for certain reasons. Thus, once the wrongdoer has completed his punishment, shall we say their rights have been "unforfeited"? Returned? Restored? Even so, such restoration is usually only partial; ex-felons for example are often denied the right to vote, or to hold certain jobs. People in prison have forfeited their freedom, but only in part: they still have the right not to be held in shackles, not to be subjected to solitary confinement except for good reasons, as well as numerous other forms of freedom (freedom as to whom to associate with, freedom of religion, and so on). The concept of "forfeiture" gives us no guidance on any of these problems; it functions merely as an empty shell into which we can put whatever we want.

Even more fundamentally, the rights-forfeiture theory merely asserts rather than explains why rights are forfeited. Morris tells us that "the act, insofar as it manifests an unwillingness to abide by the constraints of justice, will bring about this loss [of rights]" (1991, 69), but this is not an explanation. As Simmons explains, we need to be told

> *why* the violation of another's rights causes us to lose our own (to the extent deserved). The answer is surely not obvious, as defenders of the doctrine of forfeiture seems to assume. It is the "mystery" or apparent emptiness of the idea of forfeiture that has led critics in this century to reject it (e.g. critics of W. D. Ross and other intuitionists). When asked why the punishment is justified, defenders of forfeiture say: because the criminal has forfeited his rights. But no account is forthcoming of *why* the criminal loses his rights on this occasion. As a result, it appears that saying the criminal forfeits his rights is saying nothing *more* than that punishing him is justified. (1991, 334).

Simmons suggests an argument from natural fairness: "Protection under the rules is contingent on our obeying them; any rights the rules may define are guaranteed only to those who refrain from violating them" (335). But fairness or "unfair advantage" theories have long been rejected, among other things for implying that rapists and murders are getting an unfair benefit while not sharing the burden of restraint from these crimes. Moreover, why should we assume that the right not to have harm inflicted on oneself is merely a "contingent" right? The fairness account seems simply to assume that punishment is justified. Finally, fairness theories do not seem to require the notion of rights-forfeiture. If fairness dictates that punishment is justified, then that is sufficient to justify punishment; there is no need for a further theory of rights-forfeiture (see Wellman 2017, 164).[17]

Indeed, the very assumption that rights can be forfeited is problematic even among rights theorists. An alternative tradition holds that fundamental rights, such as life and liberty, are "inalienable." This issue involves a fundamental question in rights theory: do people have rights in virtue of being persons (i.e., rational, autonomous beings), or do they have rights only conditionally, in virtue of their being morally abiding and respecting the rights of others? If the former, then the rights of virtually all wrongdoers cannot be forfeited, for they remain autonomous persons. It is not obvious why we should accept the latter view; indeed, the former seems more plausible. The rights-forfeiture theory depends essentially on the conditional rights view (itself often dependent on a social contract theory), so it owes us a strong argument in favor of it. Wellman address the argument that human rights can never be lost, claiming that

> This argument cannot be sound, because it implausibly implies that all countries that incarcerate criminals are illegitimate. This is because imprisoning someone who has done nothing wrong would also violate her human rights, so unless one can forfeit one's human right against being imprisoned, all existing countries would be illegitimate. (2017, 172)

But again, the argument is patently circular. Wellman assumes that punishment is only valid if one's rights are forfeited. But one who rejects rights-forfeiture theory or one who believes in inalienable rights can hold that there is no right to begin with not to be punished for wrongdoing, so there is no need for forfeiture. Or consider Simmons' (1991) defense of the Lockean view that victims have a natural right to punish wrongdoers. If there is such a right, does that not justify punishment by itself, without need for any further doctrine of forfeiture? Again, this points to the lack of a systematic development of the theory: How many rights are there? How do we ascertain what they are? How do we balance conflicting rights against each other? It will not do simply to hold that wrongdoers forfeit their rights against being punished.[18]

[17] Wellman takes fairness theories as a form of theory distinct from rights-forfeiture theories, arguing that the latter are superior (2017, 165).

[18] Simmons even claims that an "unruly dog … lacks the right not to be harmed" (1991, 343). Are we to take it that well-behaved animals have the right not to be harmed? (Does a mouse being in one's house count as misbehaving?) And that misbehaving results in forfeiture, even there is no autonomous moral choice involved? The skeptic will have doubts that there is anything like a systematic theory of who has rights and how they are forfeited.

In the end, the doctrine of rights-forfeiture seems only to restate our prior intuitions without constraining or guiding them. If Jack thinks the death penalty is permissible, he says that wrongdoers have forfeited their right to life. If Jill thinks the death penalty is wrong, she says that wrongdoers do *not* forfeit their right to life. There is no independent means or procedure to determine whether the right to life has been forfeited, other than to consult our existing intuitions about what punishment is appropriate. Wellman's book seems implicitly to admit this point; he repeatedly concedes that there is no way to rationally establish what rights are forfeited: "There is," he writes, "unquestionably a moral right to human life, but it is not clear why this right cannot be forfeited" (2017, 172). Indeed, Wellman even leaves open the question of whether torturing someone to death might be legitimate: "It is not clear," he writes, "how one could establish the unreasonableness of the claim that Hitler forfeited his right not to be tortured to death."[19] He then "conced[es] the difficulty (if not the impossibility) of defeating these claims," but he assures us, "I am not insisting that there are no limits on which rights these wrongdoers forfeited" (2017, 32). Then he leaves it undecided whether there are any such limits, or how to determine what they are. Morris too leaves it an open question whether torture is permissible (1991, 74–75). But if there are no procedures or rational methods to settle crucial issues like this, then it is hard to see how the rights-forfeiture account can be called a theory at all.[20] It gives us no help to settle disputes about the appropriate punishment, but sends us back to our intuitions (especially the proportionality principle) to decide all such questions.[21] Such questions will be decided by our intuitions about what the offender deserves, or what counts as a proportionate punishment. The theory of rights-forfeiture seems to do no work.[22]

[19] Note that here Wellman suggests there is a specific right "not to be tortured to death." Surely this is a dubious claim. Is there also a right not to be tortured almost to death? Not to be tortured halfway to death? Etc.

[20] Wellman raises this concern, writing that "rights forfeiture does so little—it answers so few of our questions—that it hardly qualifies as a *theory* of punishment." Wellman's response only seems to concede the point: he claims that the theory is a "family of views" with "plenty of room for vigorous debate" among its members (2017, 41). He also suggests there is a "double standard" operating, since other theories also seem to have the same indeterminacy. Even if this is true (and I have presented reasons to believe that rights-forfeiture theory is uniquely indeterminate and unprovable), then the very best that can be said for rights-forfeiture theory is that it presents yet another unhelpful theory of punishment.

[21] One of Wellman's favorite phrases in the book is that "reasonable people can disagree" on various matters (2017, 27, 32, 44, 78, 93, 125, 147, etc.). It is hard to find any examples in his book of issues that the rights-forfeiture account *can* settle, even among proponents of the account.

[22] Wellman notes that Douglas Husak reaches the same conclusion he does (that our current punitive system is excessive) but without using the framework of rights-forfeiture, though Wellman says that "I would express it in terms of rights forfeiture" (2017, 174). Strikingly, Wellman does not claim that Douglas Husak's analysis is in any way deficient, nor does he indicate how the rights-forfeiture theory is preferable.

5 Defenses of the Rights-Forfeiture Theory

As we have seen, Wellman insists that the rights-forfeiture theory is "obvious and self-evident" and hence needs no controversial assumptions or arguments to defend it (2017, 29). However, he adopts this strategy in response to the history of failure of rights-forfeiture theorists to come up with a convincing defense of their position.[23] This fallback position is hardly convincing, and indeed it is notable that previous defenders of the theory assumed that it was *not* self-evident but needed a substantive defense. Nor is this a strategy that has any serious chance of success. Given that critics have overwhelmingly rejected rights-forfeiture theory to date, there is little likelihood that Wellman's claim that it is simply self-evident will convince any of them. At this late stage in the debate, the defender of the theory will need to provide concrete arguments on all the key points: that people have a natural right against being punished, that committing wrongs forfeits that right, and even that the question of punishment needs to be framed in terms of rights. However, the substantive arguments provided by rights-forfeiture theorists are themselves deeply problematic—which is the very reason why Wellman avoids them.

The most natural foundation for the rights-forfeiture account is the social contract theory. If one's moral rights arise by dint of a contractual agreement, then by failing to abide by the contract, one loses any claim to those rights. Robert Nozick writes: "One might take a contract-like view of moral prohibitions and hold that those who themselves violate another's boundaries forfeit the right to have certain of their own boundaries respected" (1974, 137). Morris defends a contractarian account of rights, under which justice is an "artificial" virtue and rights are conditional upon compliance with principles of justice (1991, 66). He also cites Rachels in support of the view that the social contract theory justifies punishment on the grounds that, "by violating the rule with respect to us, criminals release us from our obligation toward them" (Rachels 2007, 130; cited in Morris 1991, 63n21). But such an account is, to say the least, highly controversial. Indeed, Morris fails to observe that Rachels presents an extremely clear and cogent explanation of the reasons why the vast majority of philosophers have rejected social contract theory (see Rachels 2007, 155–59). It is for this reason that Wellman specifically disclaims any reliance on social contract theory, noting that there never was any such voluntary transaction between state and citizens (2017, 47; see also 196n22). But if one rejects social contract theory, there is little reason to think

[23] Wellman explains that he is deliberately avoiding "taking a stand on many of these controversial issues" (2017, 42).

that moral rights are "artificial" or conditional upon one's behavior, or indeed to think that justified punishment violates a right in the first place. Indeed, even a defender of social contract theory need not accept the idea that punishment requires the forfeiture of rights, or that rights are involved at all; the notion of consent to punishment for wrongdoing is sufficient.

Rights-forfeiture theory also typically draws on another highly controversial account of punishment, the "mixed theory" of punishment promulgated by H. L. A. Hart and others. Hart's theory was an attempt to escape the impasse between retributive and utilitarian theories by separating the justification of punishment into two separate issues or "questions": the "general justifying aim" of punishment (which for Hart was utilitarian) versus the "distribution" of punishment (which for Hart was retributive, ensuring that only the guilty are punished and only proportionately) (Hart 1960). However, the mixed theory is implausible, among other things in its basic assumption that there are two distinct forms of justification, one of the "aim" and the other of the "distribution" (why can retributivism not be an aim as well? why do utilitarian principles not apply to the "distribution" of punishment?).[24] Nonetheless, Hart's dualism functions as a starting point in several rights-forfeiture theories. Wellman, for example, begins his book by invoking a version of Hart's distinction, in this case between the "general justifying aim" of punishment versus "side constraints" (2017, 1). This distinction underlies the general strategy of his book, which argues that traditional theories of punishment have focused excessively on the general aim or purpose of punishment and neglected the question of its "permissibility," where "permissibility" means that it violates no one's rights (2). Hence Wellman defends his focus on the question of forfeiture (i.e., the permissibility question) as distinct from the aims of punishment, such as deterrence or retribution (4).[25]

One understands Wellman's desire to get beyond traditional theories of punishment and try a new approach. However, the distinction between "justification" and "permissibility" is ultimately untenable. If an action (such as punishment) is justified as a general matter, it cannot also be morally impermissible.[26] Similarly, if an action is not morally permissible, then it cannot be

[24] For a detailed critique of the mixed theory, see Kaufman (2008).

[25] In this way, he departs radically from Hart's dualism. For Wellman, retributivism and deterrence belong together as distinct sort of "aims"; whereas for Hart, deterrence provides the general aim while retribution provides a principle of "distribution." The fact that this "mixed" strategy of dividing a problem into different "questions" can be used to such radically different ends is even more reason to be skeptical of it.

[26] Cf. Zimmerman, who presents the standard view (though not in response to rights-forfeiture theory): "To say that an act is morally justified is to say that it is not morally wrong, that it is at least morally permissible and perhaps even morally required" (2011, 25). Of course, to say that an action (e.g., punishing) is in general justified is not to say that it is justified (or permissible) in every case, nor is it to say that its being justified shows that it is morally ideal in every case.

justified either.[27] The problem for retributivists, for example, is *not* that they have demonstrated a justified purpose for punishment but lack a basis for its permissibility; rather, the problem is that it has proven difficult to show how retributivism can be justified in the first place. Further, Wellman cannot of course assume that "permissibility" simply means no rights are violated; this is to build into one's interpretive framework the assumption that all actions must be evaluated both as to their morality and also as to whether they violate rights.[28] In short, the adoption of this dualistic framework seems to be a way of begging the question in favor of a rights-forfeiture account. It simply assumes that in any moral debate there is always a further, separate question to be asked: does an action violate rights?

Wellman in fact suggests the possibility of rejecting the dualistic framework—though not by rejecting permissibility as a separate question, but by making permissibility and rights the *only* question. That is, he suggests a "strong" and "more radical" version of the rights-forfeiture theory, one in which the forfeiture of rights is both necessary and sufficient for inflicting harm on wrongdoers: "one may permissibly punish anyone who has forfeited her rights *even if this hard treatment will not serve any important purpose*" (Wellman 2017, 4). That is, stated more clearly, once a person has forfeited their rights, one can inflict harm on them for any reason whatever—even for mere sadistic pleasure (18). Wellman admits that this view "seems barbarous" (12), but he declares that he "favors" the strong view nonetheless, because it follows from the theory of rights-forfeiture: once a right is forfeited, it ceases to exist (4). However, Wellman seems to recognize that this strategy constitutes a *reductio ad absurdum* of his theory, and he builds into his theory two major qualifications that renders the strong view irrelevant: first, that there may be "aretaic" moral reasons not to gratuitously inflict harm on others, such that in fact morality does require the weak view;[29] and second, that punishment as a state institution requires a strong moral reason (a "general justifying aim") in order to be legitimate, so endorsing strong rights-forfeiture theory "has no

[27] Wellman is grossly mistaken to think that that traditional theories about the justifiability of punishment simply aim to describe why we should "want" a system of punishment, as distinct from why a system of punishment is morally permissible (2017, 2). All of these theories are about why punishment is justified, not merely why we "want" it.

[28] Compare also Alm's (2013) Hart-inspired dualism between "rational justification" and "moral justification," where "rational" seems to mean whatever produces the results one desires, regardless of the morality of the means, and "moral" means that no rights have been violated. Again, this seems to be simply a way of critiquing consequentialism and (falsely) assuming that any such moral critique must be in terms of rights.

[29] Wellman suggests that inflicting such gratuitous harm on a person simply because one can may indicate a "character flaw" (2017, 18) and that there may be "aretaic" moral reasons rather than deontic ones to "refrain from gratuitously harming someone" (22).

implications for criminal legal institutions in a legitimate state" (22). This maneuver will strike some readers as taking away with one hand what one gives with the other; the strong theory turns out in practice to be equivalent to the weak theory, and hence has no problematic practical implications.[30]

Nonetheless, the argument is revealing as to the morally implausible implications of the rights-forfeiture theory. Wellman ends up rejecting one of the most fundamental principles of justified punishment, the Necessity Principle: that wrongdoers should not be harmed unless necessary to achieve one's aim (whether that be retribution, deterrence, or something else). One who has committed a wrong does not become a nonperson, a mere thing who may be used for any purposes we like, even tortured for pleasure. As we saw, Wellman implicitly admits the untenability of his views by avoiding the practical implications of his view through two maneuvers (the idea of "aretaic" requirements and the limits of state punishment). But it would be far more straightforward simply to admit that the "strong" view is morally implausible—and that it calls into question even the "weak" rights-forfeiture position, since the strong view seems simply to carry to its logical implications the idea that wrongdoers have forfeited their rights. In any case, it can hardly be plausibly claimed that the rights-forfeiture is obvious and self-evident.

6 Conclusion

The undeniable attraction of the idea of rights-forfeiture is its attempt to articulate the intuition that wrongdoers have acted in such a way that they deserve to be punished. Intuitively, the fact that wrongdoers have knowingly chosen to act badly allows us to "use" them for the purpose of deterrence. But the weakness of the theory, as we have seen, is that it does not seem to get beyond merely redescribing that intuition in the language of rights. And this is doubly problematic: first, it is a mere redescription rather than a substantive

[30] The strong theory is also quite unconvincing. If it is legitimate for an individual to inflict gratuitous harm because the offender has forfeited their rights, then why is it not legitimate for the state to do so too? If one person can kill an offender for fun, why can the entire society not gather and burn the person at the stake for entertainment? Indeed, Wellman gives as one of the values served by state punishment that it "provides an effective outlet for what would otherwise be socially disruptive tensions" (2017, 47). This reason would seem to provide ample justification for throwing offenders to the lions, if that is what the people want. Wellman is correct that the establishment of a state-based criminal legal system as a whole requires strong moral reasons (that it "secured vitally important goods that would be unavailable in its absence" [23]); however, it does not follow that therefore the state needs a strong moral reason for each individual act of punishment. If offenders have forfeited their rights, then the state does no wrong in harming them, even if just for the entertainment of the people. And what if the goal is a morally important one, like harvesting the internal organs of those who have lost their rights, in order to save lives?

explanation or justification of our intuitions, and second, it is far from obvious that moral problems can or should be addressed in terms of rights. There is little to say to skeptics of this theory to persuade them that rights-forfeiture is a useful way to analyze the permissibility of punishment.

Defenders of the theory like to claim that it is merely common sense, but as we have seen the arguments in favor of it are extremely controversial, both in its substantive foundations (social contract theory, *lex talionis*, fairness) and in its purported results (e.g., that torturing someone to death is in principle morally permissible). The traditional arguments made for the theory if anything make it less plausible, and Wellman's strategy of giving up trying to provide arguments for it is less than reassuring. The theory is claimed to be self-evident at the cost of being vacuous. Wellman's own defense of the theory oscillates between defending it as self-evidently true and arguing for a wildly implausible version of the theory.[31] Moreover, without a full and adequate account of just what rights we have (or how we go about deciding this question), one can have little confidence that the rights-forfeiture theory is more than a merely verbal solution to the problem of punishment. It lacks a theoretical structure or method to guide or constrain our intuitions, and thus it answers no questions about when and how punishment is permissible. Wellman is forced to repeatedly defend himself against the claim that the theory is entirely "ad hoc" (2017, e.g., 20, 27, 34, 35, 123, 142).[32] Similarly, we lack even a clear explanation—or any explanation at all—of why rights are forfeited by wrongdoing that is any more helpful than the retributive claim that wrongdoers "deserve" punishment. Renzo's observation seems accurate: that the role of rights-forfeiture theory is not to justify punishment but "ultimately to avoid talking about controversial aspects of their justification" (2017, 341).

The "abolitionist" challenge to the very institution of punishment argues that it is morally without foundation and must be either eliminated or drastically scaled back (e.g., Golash 2005; Boonin 2008; Zimmerman 2011). This movement calls us to inquire deeply into the practice to determine whether it can be morally justified. I do not believe that the abolitionist case is convincing (see Kaufman 2013). Still, it will not suffice to refute the abolitionist case

[31] Even rights-forfeiture theorists admit that the implications of their theory appear "barbarous" (Wellman 2017, 12), "absurd" (Wellman 2017, 30), or "preposterous" (Simmons 1991, 339), the response to which is to add a new ad hoc qualification on rights-forfeiture.

[32] Simmons insists that his account is "not unbearably awkward or ad hoc" (1991, 340), setting a rather low bar for the theory!

simply by asserting that wrongdoers have forfeited their rights.[33] How do we know that this intuition is not merely a reflection of an existing prejudice? Renzo (2017) may be right that the idea of rights-forfeiture can serve as a useful "placeholder" while we seek to develop a plausible account of why and when punishment is justified. But the danger is that it will become more than merely a placeholder, and that it will provide an excuse for avoiding the urgent need to find a plausible moral justification for the practice of punishment—or else to end the practice.

Of course, nothing in this essay is meant to discourage further inquiry into the rights-forfeiture theory. It is possible that its defenders will in the future come up with a systematic, coherent account with real explanatory and justificatory force. And, as I said, the rights-forfeiture theory does seem to respond to a genuine intuition that by knowingly engaging in wrong, the wrongdoer cannot complain about being punished. But it is unclear how describing this intuition in terms of the forfeiture of rights helps elucidate or explicate this intuition. It seems no more than a merely verbal solution to the paradox of punishment: we cannot live without it, but we do not know why or even whether it is morally justified.

References

Alm, David. 2013. "Self-Defense, Punishment, and Forfeiture." *Criminal Justice Ethics* 32, no. 2: 91–107.

Boonin, David. 2008. *The Problem of Punishment.* Cambridge: Cambridge University Press.

Daly, Martin, and Margo Wilson. 1988. *Homicide.* New Brunswick, NJ: Transaction.

Glendon, Mary Ann. 1991. *Rights Talk: The Impoverishment of Political Discourse.* New York: Free Press.

Golash, Deirdre. 2005. *The Case against Punishment: Retribution, Crime Prevention, and the Law.* New York: New York University Press.

Goldman, Alan H. 1979. "The Paradox of Punishment." *Philosophy & Public Affairs* 9, no. 1 (Autumn): 42–58.

Hart, H. L. A. 1960. "Prolegomenon to the Principles of Punishment." *Proceedings of the Aristotelian Society* 60, no. 1 (June): 1–26.

Kant, Immanuel. 1996. *The Metaphysics of Morals.* In *Practical Philosophy,* translated and edited by Mary J. Gregor, 363–602. Cambridge: Cambridge University Press.

[33] As noted above, Wellman simply concedes the abolitionist refutation of the arguments in favor of rights-forfeiture theory, but retreats to defending the theory as self-evidently true, thus insulating it from criticism (and evading the need to provide arguments for it).

Kaufman, Whitley R. P. 2004. "Is There a 'Right' to Self-Defense?" *Criminal Justice Ethics* 23, no. 1: 20–32.

———. 2008. "The Rise and Fall of the Mixed Theory of Punishment." *International Journal of Applied Philosophy* 22, no. 1 (Spring): 37–57.

———. 2009. *Justified Killing: The Paradox of Self-Defense*. Lanham, MD: Lexington.

———. 2013. *Honor and Revenge: A Theory of Punishment*. Dordrecht: Springer.

Kershnar, Stephen. 2010. "The Forfeiture Theory of Punishment: Surviving Boonin's Objections." *Public Affairs Quarterly* 24, no. 4 (October): 319–34.

Lippke, Richard L. 2001. "Criminal Offenders and Rights Forfeiture." *Journal of Social Philosophy* 32, no. 1 (Spring): 78–89.

McCullough, Michael E. 2008. *Beyond Revenge: The Evolution of the Forgiveness Instinct*. San Francisco: Jossey-Bass.

Morris, Christopher W. 1991. "Punishment and Loss of Moral Standing." *Canadian Journal of Philosophy* 21, no. 1 (March): 53–77.

Nozick, Robert. 1974. *Anarchy, State, and Utopia*. New York: Basic.

Rachels, James. 2007. *The Elements of Moral Philosophy*. 5th ed. New York: McGraw Hill.

Renzo, Massimo. 2017. "Rights Forfeiture and Liability to Harm." *Journal of Political Philosophy* 25, no. 3 (September): 324–42.

Rosebury, Brian. 2015. "The Theory of the Offender's Forfeited Right." *Criminal Justice Ethics* 34, no. 3: 259–83.

Ross, W. D. 2002. *The Right and the Good*. Edited by Philip Stratton-Lake. Oxford: Clarendon.

Simmons, A. John. 1991. "Locke and the Right to Punish." *Philosophy & Public Affairs* 20, no. 4 (Autumn): 311–49.

Tomlin, Patrick. 2017. "Innocence Lost: A Problem for Punishment as Duty." *Law and Philosophy* 36, no. 3 (June): 225–54.

Wellman, Christopher Heath. 2017. *Rights Forfeiture and Punishment*. New York: Oxford University Press.

Zimmerman, Michael J. 2011. *The Immorality of Punishment*. Toronto: Broadview.

Part IV

Punishment in the Political Context

15

Criminal Justice and the Liberal State

Matt Matravers

Any student or scholar surveying much of the Anglophone literature on the justification of punishment of the last half century or so would be forgiven for thinking they had stumbled into what Vincent Chiao characterizes as "an exercise in applied moral philosophy" (2019, vii). On the one hand, there are consequentialists who argue that punishment is justified only if, and when, its expected benefits outweigh its expected detriments. On the other, there are retributivists for whom punishment is justified by the "desert" that arises from the offender's prior moral wrongdoing.

This chapter begins by briefly surveying the debate described above and its relation to questions of political theory. It argues that both sides present arguments that are inappropriate when it comes to state punishment. The chapter next turns to punishment theory's "political turn"[1] in the form of arguments that locate criminal law and punishment in public law. Putting aside differences between them, such arguments are of the right kind. The final parts of the chapter develop an account of criminal laws, and the sanctions that flow

[1] I am not sure where the phrase "political turn" first emerged. It was used for a conference in 2019 and has since appeared in the literature, including in papers that emerged from that conference (Burchard and Duff 2021) and in Brown Coverdale and Wringe (2022) and Thorburn (2022).

M. Matravers (✉)
University of York, York, UK
e-mail: matt.matravers@york.ac.uk

© The Author(s), under exclusive license to Springer Nature Switzerland AG 2023

M. C. Altman (ed.), *The Palgrave Handbook on the Philosophy of Punishment*, Palgrave Handbooks in the Philosophy of Law, https://doi.org/10.1007/978-3-031-11874-6_15

from them, as best understood as *constitutive* elements of a liberal political community. One account of such a community—a liberal society based on cooperation for mutual advantage—is sketched, and it is argued that in such a community criminal law and punishment are necessary to ensure stability, to reinforce the commitment of the members to the rules as regulative of their plans of life, and to communicate and censure the offender for the wrong that has been done. The chapter does not consider international criminal law or crimes against humanity, but focuses only on domestic law.

1 The Traditional Debate

As noted above, much recent Anglophone work in the philosophy of punishment has revolved around a debate between retributivists, consequentialists, and those who would mix the two in some form of hybrid theory (for an excellent overview, see Hoskins and Duff 2021). As others have noted, these labels can be misleading in that there are many and various theories in each group, but it is nevertheless possible to say something about the ways in which the key claims of each relate—or do not relate—to the state. To do this, consider each in turn.

1.1 Retributivism

In a recent survey of retributive theories, Alec Walen (2020) argues that retributivism is best understood as "committed to the following three principles":

1. that those who commit certain kinds of wrongful acts, paradigmatically serious crimes, morally deserve to suffer a proportionate punishment;
2. that it is intrinsically morally good—good without reference to any other goods that might arise—if some legitimate punisher gives them the punishment they deserve; and
3. that it is morally impermissible intentionally to punish the innocent or to inflict disproportionately large punishments on wrongdoers.

Like others, Walen goes on to distinguish between "positive" and "negative" retributivists. The former hold that moral desert just by itself provides a strong positive reason to inflict the deserved punishment (that is, roughly principles 1 and 2 above). The latter hold only that moral desert makes inflicting the deserved punishment permissible, but that further consequentialist reasons are needed to justify actual punishment (that is, their focus is on principle 3).

Even on this brief sketch, the challenges for retributive theory should be clear. It needs to explain what kinds of wrongful acts give rise to moral desert, what moral desert is, and how moral desert is related to punishment. Different answers to these questions give rise to different retributive theories. For simplicity's sake, I am going to take one particularly strong exemplar—the retributive theory expounded by Michael S. Moore (1997)—as the basis for the argument in this section. Other, more nuanced and more plausible retributive theories will be considered in later parts of the chapter.

According to Moore,

> We are justified in punishing because and only because offenders deserve it. Moral responsibility ("desert") in such a view is not only necessary for justified punishment, it is also sufficient. Such sufficiency of justification gives society more than merely a *right* to punish culpable offenders. ... For a retributivist, the moral responsibility of an offender also gives society the *duty* to punish. (1997, 91)

Moore's arguments in favor of his desert account need not detain us.[2] Rather, what is worth noting is that, as Douglas Husak puts it, the account "is problematic because it offers no principled reason to believe that the *state* should punish persons who break its criminal laws" (2008, 203).[3]

For Moore, this is not an omission. Punishment—and criminalization—are about moral wrongs and moral desert, and if deserved punishment could be better delivered by ordinary people, other institutions, or indeed God,[4] then there would be no reason to favor the state. As it happens, Moore does not think it could be better delivered by these others and so argues for "the state being the exclusive exacter of retributive justice." This is for three contingent reasons: "institutionalized punishment can reduce the opportunities for sadism, abuse, and the pleasure of giving pain that can corrupt our virtue"; the state is more likely than ordinary people to achieve "comparative propor-

[2] For details, see Moore (1997); for criticisms, see Dolinko (1991, 555–59), Matravers (2000, 81–87), and Hoskins and Duff (2021, §4).

[3] A similar criticism is made by Malcolm Thorburn: "Moore has no tools available to explain why it *must be* the state and *only* the state that delivers criminal justice" (2012, 86–87). One of the more remarkable features of the very long first chapter of Moore's book is that, despite its length and its focus on being "a theory of criminal law theories," it does not mention the state once in its seventy-eight pages.

[4] In *Punishment and the Moral Emotions*, Jeffrie Murphy writes of Moore that, "if he believed in God he probably would not favor this [retributive] account of secular, state punishment" (2012, 29).

tionality" because it "can better coordinate its decisions, both at a time and over time"; and "in the achieving of substantive proportionality—making the punishment fit the crime—a state less blinded by the passions of vengeance and revenge [than private citizens] has a better chance of accurately gauging just deserts" (Moore 2009, 42).

Whatever else one might think of such an account, it is inapt as a theory of legal punishment for at least two reasons. First, it misdescribes the scope and content of actual systems of criminal law.[5] Some moral offenses—for example, gratuitously and intentionally being rude to one's aunt—are not candidates for criminalization by the state. At the same time, actual criminal codes extend far beyond moral wrongdoing. As Chiao notes in a vigorous attack on the idea that the criminal law has a "core":

> By any measure, American criminal law is concerned with enforcing manifest wrongdoing to only a very limited extent. One way of assessing this is to note that only a very small number of offenses—the various forms of assault, sexual assault, homicide, reckless endangerment, perhaps robbery and a few others—are plausibly construed as manifestly wrong. In comparison, federal law has been estimated to recognize approximately 4,000 distinct offenses carrying criminal sanctions. This number represents only the provisions contained in the United States Code, and does not include the regulations promulgated by myriad federal regulatory agencies that formally rely on the threat of criminal sanctions to enforce their rules. Taking those into account, there may be "more than 10,000 regulatory requirements or proscriptions carrying criminal sanctions." … Looking beyond the United States, Chalmers and Leverick have reported that of 3,155 new crimes created by legislation in the UK in the years 1997–1998 and 2010–2011, a grand total of 31—or about 1 percent—were categorized as traditional criminal law offenses. In contrast, there were nearly 1,000 new agriculture-related offenses, 400 health- and safety-related offenses and about 200 new offenses related to environmental protection and food production. (2019, 150–52, footnotes omitted)

[5] It also misrepresents the origins and development of the criminal law. On the ways in which the criminal law was, and is, centrally concerned with order, see Farmer (2016).

Second, and more importantly, criminal law is inexplicable other than as part of the state (or in the case of international criminal law, a system of states).[6] As Antony Duff puts it,

> the criminal law is not simply the moral law given institutional form. It is a part of the political structure of the state—a part of our political or civic lives rather than of our more personal moral lives; its proper aims and role must be understood in that context, in terms of the contribution it makes, or should make, to that dimension of our lives. (2014, 223)

As we shall see, this insight changes the way in which we should understand—and go about—thinking about the justifications of punishment, but before we move to that we need to consider the other party in the traditional debate: consequentialism.

1.2 Consequentialism

Consequentialists hold that if there is a justification of punishment, it must lie in punishment realizing better expected consequences—usually crime reduction and rehabilitation—than could be achieved by some other policy or by simply doing nothing. As such, consequentialist justifications of punishment belong to a general teleological tradition of moral theorizing, and they have in turn contributed to the sense noted at the start of the chapter of punishment theory as applied moral philosophy.

That said, consequentialist arguments have, from their inception, also been associated with institutions. Its "founding fathers"—Jeremy Bentham and John Stuart Mill—were as much, if not more, concerned with what we would now call questions of governance and public policy as they were with matters of individual ethics.[7] Moreover, this concern can be seen in one of the most important developments in consequentialist thinking itself, well-illustrated by a debate in the theory of punishment.

In an influential paper, H. J. McCloskey (1968) argued that if the "unit" of consequentialist evaluation was individual *acts*, then there are plausible

[6] It is important to distinguish this claim from the claim that all punishment is state punishment or that theorists of state punishment have nothing to learn from other instances of punishment. Legal punishment—which follows criminal lawbreaking, which in turn presupposes criminalization—is distinct in that very sense. However, that is not to say that non-legal punishments have nothing to teach us or that we should always focus on "paradigmatic punishments" such as imprisonment. For a useful survey, see Brown Coverdale and Wringe (2022); for a recent monograph, Radzik (2020).

[7] For an interesting account of how utilitarianism is particularly suited to public policy—often for precisely the same reasons as it is not suited to ordinary interpersonal morality—see Goodin (1995).

circumstances in which a consequentialist—more specifically, a utilitarian—sheriff would be morally obliged to punish an innocent. The circumstances McCloskey described were of a small town with two antagonistic racial communities. Following the rape of a woman, the members of the community to which she belongs are threatening to riot, causing widespread damage and potential fatalities. To avert the riot, the sheriff considers framing an innocent member of the other community who happened to have been near the scene of the crime.

If the overall consequences of framing the innocent man are better than of allowing the riot, then the sheriff would seem to be morally obliged to do the former. However, no adequate theory of punishment—or moral theory—should endorse that conclusion. Fortunately for consequentialism, there is an alternative, which is to move the unit of evaluation from the act to the *rule* under which the act falls. That is, rule-consequentialists hold that we should ask what rule the sheriff should follow, and of course when we do so it matters that he is *the sheriff*. In brief, a set of rules that allowed—indeed, mandated—sheriffs to frame innocents in such circumstances would not lead to as good consequences as an alternative set that prohibited such actions, provided procedural protections from the use of state power, and so on.

This move—from act to rule—fails in rescuing consequentialism from its critics. In part, this is because it seems as if rules can, and should, be broken if that can be kept a secret. In part, it is because, if one accepts that circumstances may sometimes be such that there are warranted exceptions to the rule, then the rule, once fully specified with all its exceptions, would be equivalent to act-consequentialism. However, the main reason is that even were it to deliver the right outcome—the sheriff does not frame the innocent man—it does so for the wrong reasons. He should not frame the innocent because it would be wrong to do so—it would wrong the person framed—not because doing so falls under a rule the general application of which would not yield maximal net good consequences.[8]

Nevertheless, the example points again to Duff's insight that the criminal law is "part of the political structure of the state," and needs to be thought of as such (2014, 223). To understand how and why that matters, it is time to turn more directly to the relation between the justification of punishment and the justification of the state.

---

[8] For critical discussions of utilitarianism (both act and rule), see Mabbott (1955), Lyons (1965), and Williams (1973). For a more detailed account of the argument above with respect to punishment, see Matravers (2000, ch. 1).

2 Criminal Law as "Public Law"

Section 1 of this chapter highlighted the difficulties, and inappropriateness, of thinking of the question of state punishment as an extension of interpersonal morality, as if we decide the answer to the question, "how ought I to act?" and then apply that answer to questions of criminal law and punishment.[9] In this section and the next, I focus on a different approach that makes central the ways in which criminal law and punishment are integrated with the state. The argument progresses from those for whom criminal law and punishment are merely instruments of state power—and are to be evaluated as such—to those for whom the relation is constitutive. What all of them share is a commitment to the idea that the right way to begin to think about criminal law and punishment is to think about how they fit in an account of how we live together in a political society.

One way to think of criminal law and punishment is that they are simply tools that the state deploys in much the same way as it uses other instruments of public policy. In this sense, there is nothing "special" or "distinctive" about criminal law and punishment, and they are to be justified and evaluated in the same ways as other public institutions and policies. In an important recent book, Chiao (2019) defends this view. For Chiao, punishment is "a means of fostering social cooperation … by assuring those who are willing to cooperate that they will not be taken advantage of by those who defect" (2019, viii). Of course, not all forms of social cooperation are equally good, so the account of criminal law and punishment must be embedded in a general normative political theory, which in Chiao's case takes the form of a defense of a particular kind of "anti-deference" democratic egalitarianism.

On this account, criminal law and punishment are instruments of government policy to be used and evaluated along with policies that, for example, govern public health, education, and financial markets. Criminal law and punishment might be distinctive in that they threaten and use harms deliberately inflicted by a state on (characteristically) its own citizens, but that simply means that they must be closely examined to see if other, less intrusive and harmful policies might achieve the same (or better) ends. In this sense, the account resembles that given by the rule-consequentialist in that the relationship between the institutions of criminal law, punishment, and the purposes of the state is straightforwardly *instrumental.* Were we able to achieve stable

[9] In addition to the authors discussed below, others who have criticized the suitability of "interpersonal morality" as a basis for discussing state punishment, and who have offered alternative accounts of the latter, include Lindsay Farmer (2016) and Nicola Lacey (2004, 2016a, 2016b).

social cooperation and advance democratic egalitarianism more effectively in other ways, then we should adopt those other ways and dispense with criminal law and punishment.

One advantage of such an instrumental account is that it invites us to think about the "costs"—both economic and in terms of human misery—of criminal law and punishment, and when and why those costs are worth paying.[10] However, the disadvantage is that, in reducing criminal law and punishment to just another instrument of state policy, it seems to miss what is distinctive about these institutions and their relation to state authority.

In a series of papers, Malcolm Thorburn (2011, 2012, 2017, 2020) has argued that the mistake that is common to retributivists, consequentialists, and the instrumental account given above is that they all "look to some good that can be identified without reference to the law or legal institutions" (2020, 45)—the goods they look to being, respectively, giving what is deserved, reducing future harms, and securing cooperation. This mistake, Thorburn argues, not only means that these theories do a poor job of tracking existing practices of criminal law and punishment but also that they miss what he describes as the "conceptually prior" question of "what is required by the state's claim of practical authority over its subjects in the first place" (46).[11]

According to Thorburn, one of the things so required is the possibility of legal punishment. The argument is complex and spread over several papers, but in summary Thorburn argues that states claim *authority*—that is, the right to rule—and that the idea of authority contains three elements: the normative power to create obligations, the exclusive right to determine the content of the law, and the possibility of a remedy when that exclusive right is violated. In committing a criminal offense, a person "usurps" the state's role in determining the content of the law, and "the appropriate remedy through which to vindicate the state's right to rule is available only where the state threatens punishment for disobedience" (Thorburn 2020, 57).

Thorburn's account is attractive in that it not only locates criminal law and punishment in the structures of the state but argues that the two are non-contingently related. That said, it is not obvious why the (only) appropriate remedy to vindicate the state's right to rule is the threat of punishment. Given

[10] For an interesting discussion of these costs in relation to whether the achieving of retributive justice is "worth" the price, see Husak (2008, 203–6). As Husak puts it, "the expense of our system of criminal justice is astronomical. … Persons might reasonably prefer to use their tax dollars for any number of other worthy purposes" (203–4).

[11] Thus, Thorburn joins with Chiao and Farmer in arguing that "criminal wrongs and justifications in the common law world do not even approximately follow the contours of moral wrongdoing and justification" (Thorburn 2011, 23).

that punishment does not always follow the commission of a crime, it cannot be the fact of punishment that vindicates the state's right to rule. Rather, the argument must hinge on criminalization: that when the state sets the rules for its citizens, it must add the threat of punishment as an expression of its *right* to rule. However, quite why that is the case is not clear.

In addition, Thorburn's right-to-rule account has the implication that all crimes are attempts at usurpation. As he puts it,

> the wrong [in an attempted or completed criminal offense] in question is simply the wrong of usurpation. … Where someone takes it upon himself to act contrary to the demands of the state's laws because he is acting instead upon his own view of his rights and duties, powers, and liabilities, he is directly challenging the state's claim to have the exclusive right to make the law around here. (2020, 57)

However, this does not seem correctly to capture all instances of criminal behavior or the appropriate wrong when it comes to some such instances. On the one hand, is it really the case that *all* criminal behaviors—for example, deliberately avoiding paying one's television license fee in England—are instances of challenging the state's right to rule? On the other, in many cases of criminal behavior, we should surely be concerned with the wrong done to the particular victim and not only with the wrong done to the state.

With respect to the first issue, Thorburn might reply that it is simply a conceptual truth: insofar as the state claims authority, and lays down the rules to be followed, then the breaking of any one of those rules *just is* a challenge to that authority. But if he takes that approach, then in many cases that conceptual truth will not matter very much once translated into real-world criminality. With respect to the second issue, Thorburn argues that "the right-to-rule account does not deny the moral significance of the underlying interpersonal wrong that the offender might have committed" (2020, 63). Yet, his account captures this moral significance not in its response to the criminal act, but only through criminalization. That is, a crime of, for example, murder instantiates the wrong of usurpation. When the family of the victim demands that the state punish the murderer for the wrong done to the victim, the answer that they are given by the right-to-rule account is that the state has recognized that wrong in criminalizing murder. However, that seems to miss the point of the family's demand. What they are—correctly—demanding is a recognition of the particular wrong that has been done to a particular person, not a recognition of the general wrongness of murder.

Chiao and, particularly, Thorburn often present their "public law" theories explicitly in opposition to the legal moralism of Moore and Duff. As should be clear, I am sympathetic to this approach with respect to Moore (and, indeed, this chapter has adopted a similar structure). With respect to Duff—and whether, and if so to what degree, he previously endorsed a form of legal moralism similar to Moore's—the situation is less clear,[12] but in any case Duff has embraced aspects of the public law approach in his latest work (2018, 2020), so it is to that that we next turn.

That Duff (now) believes an account of criminal law and punishment must begin with the state is something he makes clear:

> we must theorize criminal law as part of the institutional, legal structure of the state—a theorization that belongs to political philosophy rather than to moral philosophy, if we understand 'moral philosophy' as concerned with 'inter-personal morality' rather than with political structures. We must therefore theorize criminal law as part of the institutional structure of a political community: for a state is or should be the institutional mechanism through which a polity governs itself; its institutions must be theorized in terms of their contribution to the polity's existence and its good. (2018, 149)

This has three implications for the arguments of this chapter. The first picks up the promise to explain the implications of rejecting Moore's ambitious moralism made at the end of the section on retributivism. Theorizing the criminal law as part of the state means that, when it comes to criminalization, we should not begin with moral wrongdoing generally and then try to establish what subset of those wrongs ought to be criminalized—in "a kind of moral witch hunt" (Duff 2014, 222). Instead, we should begin with political theory—that is, with the political community—and we should try to work out how such a community—*our* community—should identify and respond to those wrongs that in some sense matter to it. Second, and connectedly, those wrongs will be what Duff calls "public" in the sense that they "fall within or bear on" the political community (2018, 7).[13] Third, the focus is on the community rather than, as might be thought to be the case in Thorburn's work, on an abstract sovereign. As Findlay Stark puts it in a review of Duff's book, for Duff "the criminal law speaks not with the detached voice of a sovereign, but instead in the voice *of* citizens *to* other citizens" (2019, 454).

A political community for Duff is characterized by a "civil order," which is

[12] For a clear statement of his differences with Moore, see Duff (2014).

[13] For a detailed discussion of Duff's account public wrongs, see Dempsey (2011).

> in part legal order: that is to say, it is structured by law, and consists in important part in legally constituted institutions and legal practices. … That is not to say, however, that civil order consists *only* in legal order. A polity's civil order includes a social order—a set of social practices and expectations that, although they exist and are sustained within the framework of law, are not themselves legal practices, and are not directly regulated by law. (Duff 2018, 152)

Criminal law is part of this civil order.[14] Its function is to define and declare "public wrongs" and to provide a process—paradigmatically, a criminal trial—"through which those accused of committing such wrongs are called formally to answer to those accusations, and to answer for those wrongs if their guilt is proved" (Duff 2018, 7). The punishment that typically follows provides a mechanism for the polity to censure the wrongdoer and for the wrongdoer to express appropriate remorse. It can only be intended for that purpose and must not, according to Duff, be inflicted for crime reduction reasons, as that would not be to respect the moral agency of the offender. This leaves Duff with a difficulty in justifying burdensome hard treatment.[15]

On Duff's account, criminal law is necessarily part of the structure of the state; indeed, a constitutive part. It is through the criminal law that citizens are called to account for their alleged (public) wrongdoing and, if appropriate, it is through conviction and punishment that they are censured (Duff 2001, 2007). But it is important to note that Duff insists that the criminal law merely declares and defines public wrongs. It does not create them (that is, the criminal law marks out what is already prohibited; it does not itself prohibit). The conduct picked out is (pre-legally) wrong because it violates the ways in which members of the community ought to treat one another, and it is public because it belongs to that set of pre-legal wrongs that "fall within or bear on" the concerns of the political community (Duff 2018, 7).

Thus, although criminal offenders are answerable to their fellow citizens only through the state—it is the state that prosecutes and calls to account for wrongs that are identified as part of the civil order—Duff's account is not vulnerable to the charge that it mislocates the wrong done. This is because the wrong for which the offender is convicted is, for example, the wrong done to the individual murdered victim. However, what makes the offender *liable*—answerable to a particular court—is that murder is a crime identified by a

[14] In addition to Farmer (2016), the relationship of civil society, liberalism, and punishment is examined in Jonathan Jacobs's important recent book, *The Liberal State and Criminal Sanction* (2020).

[15] For discussion of the place of punishment in Duff's theory, see Matravers (2011). For Duff's response, see Duff (2011, 374–75).

particular jurisdiction because it threatens or violates the civil order of that jurisdiction:

> The wrong for which he [the criminal defendant] is convicted is, in the case of victimizing crimes such as rape, the wrong that is done to the individual victim: but a legal condition of his being properly convicted is that that wrong constitutes a crime under English law (if he is in England); and a normative condition of its being criminalizable by English law is that it threatens or violates the civil order of England. That is not what makes rape, or this rape, wrong; nor would its wrongful character differ if it was committed somewhere else: but that is what makes it the business of, brings it properly within the ambit of, English criminal law, and thus within the jurisdiction of English courts. (Duff 2018, 217)

The claim that the wrongful character of rape does not change depending on where it is committed suggests a Moorean-style moral realism to Duff's "pre-legal" wrongs. However, that is not at all clear.[16]

In earlier work, Duff situates his philosophy of criminal law in a "liberal communitarian" vision of the political community, one that recognizes "individual freedom and autonomy as crucial values" (2001, 47). Although that provides the context and clearly expresses Duff's normative commitments, it is not clear whether such a context is a necessary part of his theory of criminal law and punishment. The worry is that without some independent account of pre-legal wrongs—for example, one grounded in the values of freedom and autonomy—Duff's account would allow political communities whose civil order is racist or sexist to have systems of criminal law that instantiate racism or sexism. In short, the allegation is that pre-legal public wrongs are merely conventional.[17]

In one sense, Duff invites this response in describing his account of public wrongs as "context-dependent," by which is meant that "both the identity of that public, and the scope of its legitimate interests, depend on the practice or form of life in which the distinction is being drawn" (2018, 83). However, we should not be too quick. In the same section, Duff argues that the account is also "normative" in that "the question of whether something is a public or a

---

[16] I am indebted in what follows to Hanafy (2021, 54–64).

[17] This criticism has been made by several people. For example, Michael Moore alleges that the account of public wrongs is "in danger of returning us to the conventionalist and relativist ethics that made Devlin's brand of legal moralism so distasteful" (2014, 199). Victor Tadros claims that "any wrongdoing could become the state's business by the public binding itself together by the values that underpin the wrong" (2016, 126). And Patrick Tomlin says, "'public wrongs' seems so permissive as to provide hardly any brakes on the criminalization process at all—if we think something is 'our' business, we can criminalize it" (2020, 320).

private matter is the question whether it is something that *properly* concerns a specifiable 'public,' something in which they have a *legitimate* interest" (2018, 83).

The importance of this becomes clear when Duff (writing together with Sandra Marshall) directly confronts the charge of relativism (Duff and Marshall 2019). There it becomes clear that we need to think separately about the proper purposes of political community and the ways in which a particular political community might reflect its civil order in its criminal law. With respect to the latter, it is possible that a racist or sexist civil order might reflect those values in its criminal law. However, in doing so it would be mistaken because racism and sexism are not part of a justified *political* theory of the state. In other words, Duff and Marshall "can argue forcefully against such an illiberal conception of civil order" (2019, 38), but that argument goes to the appropriate account of the state, not to the morality of racism or sexism or to the aptness or otherwise of the criminal law of racist or sexist civil orders. What is needed, of course, is a liberal political theory with which to mount the argument.

Duff's argument not only locates criminal law and punishment in the civil order of the state but makes it in part constitutive of that order. However, his account diverges from the standard understanding of the criminal law as (in large part) laying down prohibitions, and it struggles to find a place for the burdens of punishment (Matravers 2011). Moreover, the justifications of the state and that of criminal law can come apart, as when an illiberal state properly reflects its illiberal values in its criminal law. The next section retains the idea of the criminal law as in part constitutive of civil order while addressing those other issues.

3 The Justification of Punishment and the Justification of the Liberal State

Two tensions arise in Duff's account. First, he seems to draw on specific pre-legal wrongs (the moral wrongs in assault, rape, theft, and so on) to limit the scope of the criminal law while insisting that criminal law and punishment are embedded within, and reflective of, particular communities' civil orders. Second, his concern that the criminal law should not "resort to the language of threats" (Duff 2011, 375) makes it difficult for him to explain why the state's communication of censure can justifiably take the form of burdensome hard treatment. What follows sketches an account, and justification of, the liberal state that avoids these tensions.[18] It makes no appeal to prior moral rights and wrongs, and it explains how "the language of threats" can appropriately respect the agency of members of the community.

In taking up the question of the justification of the liberal state, I do not mean to explain how such a state might have developed. Rather, I take it that many people live in political communities characterized by certain commitments and practices that reflect values of freedom and equality. Following Duff, we might say that liberal societies exist with a variety of civil orders and that those orders are both legal and social. The question of justification arises because each of us can stand back from the "rules"—both legal and social—and ask what reasons we have to endorse them as regulative of our lives.

One answer might appeal to the intrinsic worth of each individual (as "made in the image of God" or as a bearer of Kantian rational will), in which case we can endorse the rules as reflecting the free and equal nature of humanity. However, such an answer is inappropriate in what the philosopher David Gauthier calls our "post-anthropomorphic, post-theocentric, post-Nietzschean world" (1988, 385). Instead, we must think of each person considering the question from their own point of view: "what reason do I have to endorse these (or some alternative) sets of rules as regulative of my life?" While that question is rightly proposed at an individual level, it is also inherently social in that the answer depends on others in the political community also reflecting on, and endorsing (or not), the rules. That is not to say that the reflective citizen should ask, "what reasons do *we* have?" but rather, "what reasons do I, together with these others, have to endorse these rules as regulative of our political community?"

The reasons each of us has stem from our interest in living together with others as social beings and realizing the benefits of social cooperation. As John Rawls put it, "social cooperation makes possible a better life for all than any would have if each were to live solely by his own efforts" (1971, 4). However, social cooperation can be fragile, and cooperating can leave one vulnerable to being taken advantage of by others. It is here that the accounts of the liberal state and of criminal law and punishment intersect.

The argument is that the reasons each of us has to endorse certain sets of rules as regulative of our lives depend on others being willing to endorse those same rules as regulative of theirs. Those rules—legal and social—are constitutive of the political community. As John Charvet puts it, describing the situation from the third person: "the collectivity to which they are to subject themselves is just themselves committing to pursuing their fundamental

[18] In developing this account, I have drawn on Charvet (1995, 2013, 2019) and Matravers (2000).

interests together through binding common rules and institutions" (2019, 197). Why should these rules include criminal law and punishment? The answer relates to the fragility of the political community as constituted by nothing more than a reciprocal agreement for mutual advantage.[19] First, it is only reasonable for persons to endorse the set of rules as regulative of their plans of life if others do so, too. To do this, they need assurance that others will not only endorse the rules but will generally live in accordance with them. Unsurprisingly, this is known as the assurance problem:

> The assurance problem ... is to assure the cooperating parties that the common agreement is being carried out. Each person's willingness to contribute is contingent upon the contribution of the others. Therefore to maintain public confidence in the scheme that is superior from everyone's point of view, or better anyway than the situation that would obtain in its absence, some device for administering fines and penalties must be established. (Rawls 1971, 270)

In other words, criminal law and punishment—including the threat of burdensome hard treatment—are necessary to ensure that it makes sense for members of the political community to endorse their membership, and given that such mutual endorsement is constitutive of the political community, they are intrinsically connected to the very possibility of living together in stable conditions of mutual advantage.

Second, conviction and punishment express censure for breaking the rules that constitute the political community and so "remind" offenders of their reciprocal commitment to those rules and reinforce in them that commitment.[20] In that sense, punishment thus has an educative purpose in that it communicates to offenders the wrong that they have done in not respecting the rules of a political community that is constituted by their commitment to it.

Third, those who break the rules and in so doing victimize their fellow citizens commit a wrong that goes beyond the mere failure to respect the rules. They, for example, commit the wrongs of rape and murder. Such actions are not to be understood as violating pre-political rights, such that the criminal law merely picks out the preexisting wrong. Rather, while of course such actions set back the interests of victims, it is only through the commitment

[19] What follows draws on Matravers (2000, chs. 8–9).

[20] This raises the issue of what to do with those offenders who do not endorse, but reject, the entirety of the rules and thus their membership of the political community. It may be that a political community has no other option at that point other than what Andrew von Hirsch calls "tiger control" (1993, 6)—that is preventative control—while, if possible, engaging with the offender to convince them of the value of the civil order.

that each makes in the reciprocal agreement for mutual advantage that those interests are turned into rights. Thus, conviction and punishment condemn the offender both for the wrong done to the community and for that done to the victim.

The account shares something with most of those described as adhering to a public law conception of criminal law and punishment. Like Chiao, I think of criminal law and punishment as purposive institutions that belong to, and should be evaluated as, elements of public policy. However, unlike him and in common with Thorburn, I also think they are distinctive in being constitutive of the political community. Unlike Thorburn, but in common with Duff, I think punishment expresses censure, both for the wrong done to the community and for the wrong done to the victim. However, unlike Duff, I think criminal law and punishment are (in part) coercive institutions that issue and carry out threats as a mechanism of providing assurance.[21]

I have said very little about the content of the rules, including the rules of the criminal law. With respect to the latter, this is not the place to try to offer an account of criminalization. What can be said is that, given the coercive nature of the criminal law, we have reason to endorse its use only as a last resort and in ways that instantiate penal parsimony (Tonry 2020). With respect to the former, I have said very little partly to emphasize the *structural* connection between the conception of the grounds of political community and criminal law and punishment. However, that will not do because we need to consider the implications of the sets of rules being such as to undermine the reasons for reciprocal agreement. That is, and finally, the problem of injustice.

4 Injustice and the Justification of Punishment

If those involved in a liberal political community, and who reflect on its rules, are to endorse those rules as regulative of their plan of life, then the rules must reflect liberal commitments to the freedom and equality of its members. This can be done in a number of ways, which is why liberal states vary in kind from social democracies with strong welfare states (such as Norway and Sweden) to liberal democracies with a more limited commitment to welfare (such as the U.K.). However, at a minimum the rules must include equal political rights.

[21] Cf. Simester and von Hirsch: "Rational coercion operates via, and appeals to, the subject's responsible agency; it offers her reasons for action, reasons she may choose to ignore. It does not make the decision for her" (2011, 6–7).

This rules out, for example, arrangements such as those found in Apartheid South Africa, but also societies that are so profoundly unjust as to incorporate substantive inequalities in political rights despite their commitment to formal equality.

Of course, non-liberal arrangements also exist, and members of non-liberal political communities can similarly stand back from the rules under which they live and ask if they have reasons to endorse those arrangements. The assumption of this chapter is that we are concerned with liberal states, so I am not going to pursue this, although I believe and have argued elsewhere (2000, chs. 7–9; see also Charvet 2019) that there are no such good reasons and that, therefore, liberal rules are the only ones that can be justified. Nevertheless, that still leaves the issue of how we should respond to societies that profess liberal principles but fail to instantiate those principles in practice.

The model of justification offered in this chapter involves there being positive reasons for citizens to endorse the rules under which they live as regulative of their lives. It follows that there may not be such reasons, that a society may fail to provide equal rights to some. In one sense, this is simply a conceptual point. A theory such as the one offered above must recognize the possibility of the ties of reciprocity not holding. In another, it is (sadly) a substantive point about countries such as the U.S.A. and U.K. in which inequalities are profound. Moreover, one way in which that might be true is in its use of its criminal justice system. The criminal law binds and protects, but what happens when it binds some but fails to protect them while protecting others whom it does not bind?

The traditional contractualist answer given by someone like Thomas Hobbes (1994) is that the failure of the contract returns us to the state of nature. However, in reality, that some person or group of persons does not have reason to endorse the rules under which they live does not mean that those rules or the society to which they belong evaporate. What, then, does it mean?

One answer is provided in a recent book by Tommie Shelby (2016), who argues that, in circumstances of profound injustice, those who are disadvantaged may permissibly engage in resistance or dissent, including criminality. Shelby presupposes a background of natural duties to constrain what is permissible. As he puts it,

> Taking the lives of others, except in self-defense or in defense of others, is almost never justified. However, taking the possessions of others, especially when these others are reasonably well off, may be permissible. Mugging someone at gunpoint does not show sufficient respect for the victim's claim to be free from

> threats against their person. But shoplifting and other forms of theft might be permissible. In light of the hazards of participating in gang culture, recruiting children into gangs shows insufficient concern for the weak and vulnerable. Yet given the advantages of concerted group action, participating in gangs may be a defensible and effective means to secure needed income. Something similar can be said in favor of prostitution, welfare fraud, tax evasion, selling stolen goods, and other off-the-books transactions in the underground economy. (2016, 220)

Invoking natural duties is a move that is not available on the account developed above, which eschews what J. L. Mackie (1977) called "queer" metaphysical properties. However, that need not mean that "anything goes." Rather, we might think of the social contract as not fully dissolved, but rather as partially suspended while the injustices are corrected. That said, it is not clear what follows beyond recourse to mere individual prudential reason—that is, the self-interested reasons people have to do or not do certain things—if those injustices are left uncorrected.

5 Conclusion

The argument of this chapter supports those who think that the justification of criminal law and punishment needs to be addressed by asking what they are for and how they fit into our collective organization of ourselves in political communities. More than that, the argument is that criminal law and punishment are integral to, and partly constitutive of, those communities. Thus, justifying the state and justifying criminal law and punishment is one task, not two.

One implication of that is, if the justification of the state fails, then so too does the justification of criminal law and punishment. The chapter presents a particular version of the argument grounded in the idea of a political community as nothing other than the community constituted by its members. However, as the quotation from Shelby above makes clear, one can reject that argument and still accept the implication that profound injustice dissolves the reciprocal obligations that tie us together.[22]

[22] I am grateful to the Leverhulme Trust for a Major Research Fellowship (award MRF-2020-090) that enabled me to work on this chapter.

References

Brown Coverdale, Helen, and Bill Wringe. 2022. "Non-Paradigmatic Punishments." *Philosophy Compass* 17, no. 5 (May): e12824.

Burchard, Christopher, and Antony Duff. 2021. "Criminal Law Exceptionalism: Introduction." *Criminal Law and Philosophy*. https://doi.org/10.1007/s11572-021-09612-6.

Charvet, John. 1995. *The Idea of an Ethical Community*. Ithaca, NY: Cornell University Press.

———. 2013. *The Nature and Limits of Human Equality*. Basingstoke, UK: Palgrave Macmillan.

———. 2019. *Liberalism: The Basics*. Abingdon, UK: Routledge.

Chiao, Vincent. 2019. *Criminal Law in the Age of the Administrative State*. New York: Oxford University Press.

Dempsey, Michelle Madden. 2011. "Public Wrongs and the 'Criminal Law's Business': When Victims Won't Share." In *Crime, Punishment, and Responsibility: The Jurisprudence of Antony Duff*, edited by Rowan Cruft, Matthew H. Kramer, and Mark R. Reiff, 254–72. Oxford: Oxford University Press.

Dolinko, David. 1991. "Some Thoughts about Retributivism." *Ethics* 101, no. 3 (April): 537–59.

Duff, R. A. 2001. *Punishment, Communication, and Community*. Oxford: Oxford University Press.

———. 2007. *Answering for Crime: Responsibility and Liability in the Criminal Law*. Oxford: Hart.

———. 2011. "In Response." In *Crime, Punishment, and Responsibility: The Jurisprudence of Antony Duff*, edited by Rowan Cruft, Matthew H. Kramer, and Mark R. Reiff, 351–79. Oxford: Oxford University Press.

———. 2014. "Towards a Modest Legal Moralism." *Criminal Law and Philosophy* 8, no. 1 (January): 217–35.

———. 2018. *The Realm of Criminal Law*. Oxford: Oxford University Press.

———. 2020. "Criminal Law and the Constitution of Civil Order." *University of Toronto Law Journal* 70, no. suppl. 1: 4–26.

Duff, R. A., and S. E. Marshall. 2019. "Crimes, Public Wrongs, and Civil Order." *Criminal Law and Philosophy* 13, no. 1 (March): 27–48.

Farmer, Lindsay. 2016. *Making the Modern Criminal Law: Criminalization and Civil Order*. Oxford: Oxford University Press.

Gauthier, David. 1988. "Moral Artifice." *Canadian Journal of Philosophy* 18, no. 2: 385–418.

Goodin, Robert E. 1995. *Utilitarianism as a Public Philosophy*. Cambridge: Cambridge University Press.

Hanafy, Hend. 2021. *The Justification of Punishment in Authoritarian States*. Ph.D. thesis, University of Cambridge. https://doi.org/10.17863/CAM.81813.

Hobbes, Thomas. 1994. *Leviathan*. Edited by Edwin Curley. Indianapolis, IN: Hackett.

Hoskins, Zachary, and Antony Duff. 2021. "Legal Punishment." *Stanford Encyclopedia of Philosophy* (Winter 2021 edition), edited by Edward N. Zalta. https://plato.stanford.edu/entries/legal-punishment/.

Husak, Douglas. 2008. *Overcriminalization: The Limits of the Criminal Law*. Oxford: Oxford University Press.

Jacobs, Jonathan A. 2020. *The Liberal State and Criminal Sanction: Seeking Justice and Civility*. Oxford: Oxford University Press.

Lacey, Nicola. 2004. "Criminalization as Regulation: The Role of Criminal Law." In *Regulating Law*, edited by Christine Parker, Colin Scott, Nicola Lacey, and John Braithwaite, 144–68. Oxford: Oxford University Press.

———. 2016a. *In Search of Criminal Responsibility: Ideas, Interests, and Institutions*. Oxford: Oxford University Press.

———. 2016b. "Socializing the Subject of Criminal Law? Criminal Responsibility and the Purposes of Criminalization." *Marquette Law Review* 99, no. 3 (Spring): 541–57.

Lyons, David. 1965. *Forms and Limits of Utilitarianism*. Oxford: Clarendon.

Mabbott, J. D. 1955. "Professor Flew on Punishment." *Philosophy* 30, no. 114 (July): 256–65.

Mackie, J. L. 1977. *Ethics: Inventing Right and Wrong*. New York: Penguin.

Matravers, Matt. 2000. *Justice and Punishment: The Rationale of Coercion*. Oxford: Oxford University Press.

———. 2011. "Duff on Hard Treatment." In *Crime, Punishment, and Responsibility: The Jurisprudence of Antony Duff*, edited by Rowan Cruft, Matthew H. Kramer, and Mark R. Reiff, 68–84. Oxford: Oxford University Press.

McCloskey, H. J. 1968. "A Non-Utilitarian Approach to Punishment." In *Contemporary Utilitarianism*, edited by Michael D. Bayles, 239–59. Garden City, NY: Anchor.

Moore, Michael S. 1997. *Placing Blame: A General Theory of the Criminal Law*. Oxford: Oxford University Press.

———. 2009. "A Tale of Two Theories." *Criminal Justice Ethics* 28, no. 1: 27–48.

———. 2014. "Liberty's Constraints on What Should be Made Criminal." In *Criminalization: The Political Morality of the Criminal Law*, edited by R. A. Duff, Lindsay Farmer, S. E. Marshall, Massimo Renzo, and Victor Tadros, 182–212. Oxford: Oxford University Press.

Murphy, Jeffrie G. 2012. *Punishment and the Moral Emotions: Essays in Law, Morality, and Religion*. Oxford: Oxford University Press.

Radzik, Linda. 2020. *The Ethics of Social Punishment: The Enforcement of Morality in Everyday Life*. Cambridge: Cambridge University Press.

Rawls, John. 1971. *A Theory of Justice*. Cambridge, MA: Harvard University Press.

Shelby, Tommie. 2016. *Dark Ghettos: Injustice, Dissent, and Reform*. Cambridge, MA: Belknap.

Simester, A. P., and Andreas von Hirsch. 2011. *Crimes, Harms, and Wrongs: On the Principles of Criminalisation*. Oxford: Hart.
Stark, Findlay. 2019. Review of *The Realm of Criminal Law*, by R. A. Duff. *Cambridge Law Journal* 78, no. 2 (July): 453–56.
Tadros, Victor. 2016. *Wrongs and Crimes*. Oxford: Oxford University Press.
Thorburn, Malcolm. 2011. "Criminal Law as Public Law." In *Philosophical Foundations of Criminal Law*, edited by R. A. Duff and Stuart P. Green, 21–43. Oxford: Oxford University Press.
———. 2012. "Constitutionalism and the Limits of the Criminal Law." In *The Structures of the Criminal Law*, edited by R. A. Duff, Lindsay Farmer, S. E. Marshall, Massimo Renzo, and Victor Tadros, 85–105. Oxford: Oxford University Press.
———. 2017. "Punishment and Public Authority." In *Criminal Law and the Authority of the State*, edited by Antje du Bois-Pedain, Magnus Ulväng, and Petter Asp, 7–32. Oxford: Hart.
———. 2020. "Criminal Punishment and the Right to Rule." *University of Toronto Law Journal* 70, no. suppl. 1: 44–63.
———. 2022. "In Search of Criminal Law's Person." In *The Criminal Law's Person*, edited by Claes Lernestedt and Matt Matravers, 99–118. Oxford: Hart.
Tomlin, Patrick. 2020. "Duffing Up the Criminal Law?" *Criminal Law and Philosophy* 14, no. 3 (October): 319–33.
Tonry, Michael. 2020. *Doing Justice, Preventing Crime*. Oxford: Oxford University Press.
von Hirsch, Andrew. 1993. *Censure and Sanctions*. Oxford: Oxford University Press.
Walen, Alec. 2020. "Retributive Justice." *Stanford Encyclopedia of Philosophy* (Summer 2021 edition), edited by Edward N. Zalta. https://plato.stanford.edu/entries/justice-retributive/.
Williams, Bernard. 1973. "A Critique of Utilitarianism." In *Utilitarianism: For and Against*, by J. J. C. Smart and Bernard Williams, 75–150. Cambridge: Cambridge University Press.

16

From the Philosophy of Punishment to the Philosophy of Criminal Justice

Javier Wilenmann and Vincent Chiao

Why have philosophers devoted a great deal of care and attention to examining the moral bases for punishment, but almost none to examining the moral bases of policing? While the police, in the sense of a public institution devoted to responding to emergencies, preventing crime, and maintaining order, have existed in England and North America for nearly two hundred years, and longer in Europe, they are notably absent from political philosophy. This might appear surprising. Moral and political philosophers write extensively about a wide range of applied topics, from abortion to tax policy to criminal justice. In addition to theories of punishment in criminal justice, legal philosophers have devoted considerable attention to the examination of criminal law's basic concepts, as well as proposing "moral limits" to its reach. Nevertheless, historically few philosophers have had much to say about policing.[1] What explains this curious silence about an institution as salient,

[1] Kleinig (1996) is one of the earlier book-length treatments of the subject.

J. Wilenmann
Universidad Adolfo Ibáñez, Santiago, Chile
e-mail: javier.wilenmann@uai.cl

V. Chiao (✉)
University of Richmond, Richmond, VA, USA
e-mail: vchiao@richmond.edu

© The Author(s), under exclusive license to Springer Nature Switzerland AG 2023

M. C. Altman (ed.), *The Palgrave Handbook on the Philosophy of Punishment*, Palgrave Handbooks in the Philosophy of Law, https://doi.org/10.1007/978-3-031-11874-6_16

controversial, and consequential as the police? And, more constructively, what would a philosophy of policing contribute to our understanding of criminal justice?

This paper represents our attempt to think through how to answer these questions. In the first part, we argue, somewhat speculatively, that philosophers have had little to say about policing for two reasons: First, that while order and the exclusion of violence was a major theme in post-Enlightenment political philosophy, they did not specifically discuss policing because the concept of the police as a distinct institution engaged in a distinctive type of activity only clearly emerged after the canon had largely solidified. Second, we argue that in more recent years the predominance of retributivism has encouraged a narrow focus on the morality of punishment, rather than a broader view of the morality of criminal justice more generally.

The second part of the paper is more constructive, sketching a positive agenda for a philosophy of criminal justice that includes the police. In our view, one of—if not *the*—central question for a philosophy of criminal justice is choosing between different ways of encouraging people to obey the law, whether through punishment, policing, and/or social welfare. In the third and final part of the paper, we turn to application, and show how recent calls to "defund the police" presuppose—contrary to what their proponents sometimes suggest—an overarching, if sometimes implicit, philosophy of criminal justice.

1 Why Have Philosophers Ignored Policing?

Histories of the police in the Anglo-American tradition conventionally date the advent of the police, in the sense of a permanently staffed public institution, to the creation of the Metropolitan Police in London in 1829. Obviously, it is not that societies only realized they needed a way of keeping order in 1829; rather, the creation of the Metropolitan Police is taken to mark a qualitative shift in how what we now think of as policing services were provided, from more communitarian, private, and ad hoc practices—often connected to courts—to a more bureaucratic, public, and professional institution. The concept of "the police" as a public institution charged with deterring criminal acts, as well as investigating and pursuing those who commit such acts, arguably only really comes into focus in the late nineteenth century with the creation of urban police forces that engaged in regular patrols, and staffed by permanent, full-time officers (Monkkonen 1981; Emsley 2021, chs. 4–5). Although constables and citizen watches may have deterred some, their primary aims were peacekeeping and order maintenance.[2] When it comes to investigating crimes, the state was mostly involved in cases of perceived threats to the government, with European states practicing what Clive Emsley refers to as "political policing," that is, censoring the press, as well as spying on (and encouraging others to inform on) dissidents, radicals, and revolutionaries (2021, 84–88, 121). Investigating ordinary crime and bringing the wrongdoer to justice was mostly a private matter. In England, "thief takers"—that is, individuals privately retained to identify wrongdoers and resolve disputes, such as the return of stolen property—predate the creation of public police forces (113–21).[3]

Some form of what we would recognize as policing existed on the Continent well before 1829, with historians commonly referring to the 1667 establishment of the Lieutenant Générale of Paris as a key event. The French *gendarmerie* were an outgrowth of the military, focused on pacification, and were responsible for a multitude of order-maintenance functions as well as governing the city more generally.[4] In the Anglo-American context, wariness about permanently installing soldiers as urban peacekeepers meant that "police" had to be sharply distinguished from the military, a tendency that went so far as to generate serious controversy in the United States as to whether police should be expected to wear uniforms (Monkkonen 1981, Appendix A). This sensitivity was predicated on a sense of English liberty, and different norms applied when others were being policed. For instance, when Robert Peel established the precursor to London's Metropolitan Police, the Irish "Peace Preservation Force," he privately acknowledged its paramilitary character even as he emphasized that it needed a less "startling" name (Emsley 2021, 98). In the United States, organized police institutions on the London model spread throughout the mid-nineteenth century, although "slave patrols" intended to control the slave population have existed since the early eighteenth century (Monkkonen 1981, ch. 1; Akbar 2020, 1817–18; Emsley 2021, 142).

Given the relatively late emergence of organized policing, perhaps it is unremarkable that Hobbes, Locke, Kant, and Hegel would have more to say

[2] Constables and city officials were responsible for tasks as diverse as managing markets and slaughterhouses; enforcing rules designed to prevent fires, keeping waterways clean and streets clear; and breaking up fights and resolving disputes. For example, medieval officials in Ghent were responsible for "keeping the streets clear of prostitutes, vagabonds, waste and family pigs" (Emsley 2021, 47).

[3] London's Bow Street Runners were quasi-publicly funded, relying on both government grants and rewards. See Beattie (2012, ch. 3). Somewhat later, the exploits of Eugène-François Vidocq, a notorious French criminal informant who used his network to criminals to identify wrongdoers, helped popularize the idea of police as investigators of crime. See Emsley (2021, 127–28).

[4] The term itself appears to derive from *gens d'armes*, or men at arms. See Oxford English Dictionary, "gendarme." See also Neocleus (1998, 44) and Emsley (2021).

about the judicial administration of punishment than about the police.[5] Neither the institution of the police, nor even the concept of policing as an active organizational effort by government to prevent crime, was clearly established prior to the early nineteenth century. In contrast, a system of law and punishment *did* exist and was widely appreciated as a key marker of political sovereignty. Although it was primarily a private person's responsibility to protect themselves, and, failing that, to bring a wrongdoer to justice if they were able to do so, the King's courts were open to dispense justice and mete out punishment for the offence. Hence, it may not be entirely surprising that punishment would figure more substantially than policing in modern political philosophy's foundational texts. Cesare Beccaria's (1995) observation that education is preferable to punishment as a means of reducing crime stands out in the philosophical tradition both for its brevity and its singularity.

Of course, pointing out that the concept and institution of police did not crystallize until relatively recently does not prove that pre-nineteenth century political philosophers would have regarded policing as equally worthy of attention as punishment. We cannot rule out that perhaps they would have disregarded policing, and continued to focus solely on punishment, even had organized policing emerged earlier than it did. That said, Hobbes, Locke, Bentham, and Kant were largely interested in understanding punishment's role in securing peace, safeguarding rights, and upholding the law. The existence, or not, of socially organized efforts to prevent and investigate crime is, on its face, intimately related to all three of these aims, which suggests that, had policing been a salient part of governmental power at the time, it would merit philosophical attention on the same terms as a system of public punishment.

Why did philosophers not take a greater interest in policing in the many decades since organized police forces became entrenched? A greater proportion of criminal justice spending is devoted to policing than to punishment, and far more people have experience interacting with police than being incarcerated. In the United States, the Bureau of Justice Statistics estimates about sixty-one million contacts with the police in 2018 (Harrell and Davis 2020), whereas about two million felonies and 13 million misdemeanors go through criminal courts each year (Stevenson and Mayson 2018). Nonetheless, while philosophers have written scores of volumes over the last fifty years examining the morality of punishment, we are aware of only one monograph devoted to

[5] Bentham, however, was clearly aware of the significance of crime detection in preventing "mischief," although he regarded the concept of police as both "multifarious" and, still worse, "foreign" (1970, ch. XVI, §17, esp. notes u-v [pp. 196–201]).

the philosophy of policing (namely, Kleinig 1996). While we do not attempt to provide a comprehensive answer, two factors are worth mentioning. First, the revival of interest in political philosophy after the publication of John Rawls's *A Theory of Justice* in 1971 mostly did not extend to criminal justice, and focused instead largely on questions of distributive justice and the welfare state (Flanders 2016). Second, for a wide range of reasons—some internal to philosophy as an academic discipline, and some germane to American political culture at the time—retributivism became a widely accepted framework among the philosophers who were working on punishment.[6] Retributivism, especially when detached from part of an overarching political philosophy, lends itself to the view that punishment is morally *sui generis*, in the sense that the moral value of retribution is analyzed purely on its own terms, rather than in terms of other values, such as its contribution to preventing crimes or even protecting people from the harm that flows from crime (Moore 2010).

The resurgence of interest in retributivism over the last generation may partially explain why policing has remained a minor concern in legal philosophy. Retributivism is uniquely focused on the *ex post* perspective of punishment. Consequently, from the retributivist's point of view, policing is either a mere adjunct to retribution (helping to solve crimes) or a completely different undertaking (helping to prevent crimes). Either way, retributivists can safely ignore the police as they are not major players in the judicial administration of punishment.

The success of the retributivist research paradigm has three further implications. First, retributivism suggests that punishment instantiates a morally distinctive value—retribution for realized wrongs—and hence cannot simply be traded out for other modes of crime prevention. It is focused on the resentment you feel after you have been wronged, and how that resentment should manifest in negative attitudes and actions toward the person responsible for the wrong. From that perspective, even if we have reason to prevent crime,

[6] Why has the retributivist research paradigm been so successful? While this obviously has something to do with the quality of the work produced by contemporary retributivists, it may also be associated with the rise of anti-government sentiment from the 1960s onwards, both on the right and the left. Moralistic strands of retributivism speak to natural rights—rights that individuals or communities have independent of government. Retributivism thus serves as a natural vehicle for embodying both libertarian and communitarian opposition to the many missteps of criminal justice policy by liberal democratic governments in the last fifty years, especially although not exclusively in the United States. On the left, despair at the perceived failures of rehabilitation made retribution—which at least held out the promise of principled limits on punishment—appealing in comparison. As Flanders puts it, there is something "simpler and clearer, if not more ennobling, about saying that one was being punished because one deserved it (it was a matter of justice) or that society needed to lock you up to protect itself. These theories did not carry with them the implication that you were somehow diseased or sick and in need of a doctor's care" (2015, 391). See also Green (2014) for further discussion of the rise of retribution in the second half of the twentieth century.

that cannot be a substitute for retribution; that would be like telling a victim, "We don't care about what happened to you, although we will see that it doesn't happen again." Retributivism thus tends to focus on the narrower question of what justifies punishing someone who has culpably wronged another while ignoring the broader question of justifying our chosen means of protecting people from being wronged in the first place.[7]

Second, retributively minded philosophers have tended to operate with what one of us has elsewhere characterized as the "desert island" approach to normative theory (Chiao 2015). This approach to moral theory operates by eliciting intuitions on the basis of highly stylized hypotheticals involving a small number of individuals: for instance, supposing that it would be wrong for A to do X to B, what would A deserve by way of punishment? The desert island approach is individualistic in that it appeals to intuitions about the rights that people have quite apart from their status as rights-holders under a set of public institutions governed by law. It is also moralistic, in that it privileges the philosopher's personal moral convictions—or at least that subset which they expect their readers to share—thereby downplaying disagreement, power, and politics in shaping norms and values.

This approach works better for thinking about punishment than for policing. Policing is too closely identified with concrete institutions to be plausibly abstracted into a context-free practice suitable to form the subject of armchair philosophizing. The philosophically salient dimensions of policing are unabashedly political and institutional. They have more to do with the value of maintaining social order, the fair distribution of costs and benefits, political legitimacy, and equality than with natural rights, desert, and proportionality. Compared to the conceptual analysis of punishment, policing is simply too empirical, too contingent, too institutional, and too political. Indeed, some have argued that retributivism cannot be squared with criminal procedure's constitutive commitment to due process (Galoob 2017).

Finally, perhaps because many of the most prominent retributivists of the last fifty years are law professors, retributivists have tended to share the lawyer's fascination with formal concepts of legal responsibility, as exemplified in the so-called "general part" of criminal law. There is an alliance between the success of the retributivist research agenda and a tendency to focus on doctrinal issues in criminal law, as opposed to a broader concern with criminal justice. Thus, retributivists have tended to be more interested in linking moral ideas about punishment with concepts of *mens rea*, *actus reus*, insanity, excuses,

[7] This tendency is exacerbated by the popularity of "rational reconstruction." See Kleinfeld (2016) and Duff (2018).

justifications, attempts, and their Continental equivalents. In American law schools, policing is relegated to a different course—criminal procedure—and that topic, particularly in North America, is generally regarded as focused on increasingly baroque questions of constitutional law. Similar trends can be observed elsewhere, with police law subsumed under constitutional criminal procedure or a narrow area of administrative law. As a result, the *general* question, "What should we do about crime?" is not really raised in any direct way in law schools. That is perceived as a question of pure social policy rather than law, even for the ostensibly "realist" culture of American law schools (Harmon 2016).

2 From the Philosophy of Punishment to the Theory of Criminal Justice

In recent years, philosophers and legal theorists have increasingly been interested in examining the political dimensions of criminal justice, broadening their focus from the philosophy of punishment to more comprehensive theories of criminal justice. The motivation for broadening the scope of philosophical inquiry is that the invention of the police, and subsequently of the modern welfare state, greatly expands state capacity to actively manage the risk of crime as compared to a pre-police, pre-welfare state world. In such a world, the retributive instinct—wait for crime to happen, and then punish it (assuming someone happens to catch the criminal)—is sensible, as state capacity is extremely limited. But the invention of the police, and then the welfare state, markedly changes the equation, as both provide means for intervening more directly to better protect people from the risk of victimization. In an institutional context that is dense with large, complex, and powerful bureaucracies, as well as armies of social scientists and policy analysts bristling with ideas about nonpunitive means for reducing crime, it does not seem unreasonable to hold out for a crime policy that goes beyond "punish it." (Admittedly, our patchy understanding of which interventions are effective at reducing crime, and at scale, cautions against exaggerating our level of state capacity.)

In contrast to the philosopher's traditional focus on punishment, a philosophy of criminal justice aspires to provide an account of how the various parts of the justice system relate to each other, as well as to society's other major institutions, norms, and policies. A theory of criminal justice is, as Chad Flanders and Zachary Hoskins put it, "holistic" (2016, 8). In addition, a theory of criminal justice cannot but be thoroughly interdisciplinary (Flanders and Hoskins 2016, 9). Understanding the normative demands, uncertainties, and tradeoffs that inevitably arise with anything as complex as the justice system requires leaving the philosopher's proverbial armchair. A theory of criminal justice cannot operate purely at the level of conceptual analysis and must take political and institutional realities into account (Wilenmann 2021). Nonetheless, we think that philosophers can make a significant contribution to a conversation that has so far largely been dominated by social scientists, lawyers, and activists.

We do not propose to sketch a full-fledged theory of criminal justice in this chapter. Instead, we briefly highlight three points. First, given that criminal justice is a frequent proving ground for controversies over a society's values, a theory of criminal justice should be sensitive to the significance of power, social conflict, and disagreement, including the role of democratic norms and institutions in channeling those phenomena. Second, as a theory of the justice system, it stands to reason that it should be less concerned with the moral story told by individual transactions than with the institutions that comprise the justice system—police, prosecutors, legal aid, courts, prisons, probation officers, and so forth. And third, it should explain how criminal justice relates to social policy more generally, since the bottom line is not to justify punishment as a self-standing enterprise, but to evaluate different means of encouraging people to respect each other's rights and comply with law.

As we have noted, the motivation for a turn to a broader theory of criminal justice is a desire to incorporate both policing and the welfare state within the parameters of an overarching theory of justice. The police are a public institution that claims exclusive authority to use force in responding to a wide array of social crises and problems in a manner that can sometimes be violent or even deadly.[8] Because of this, police have a significant impact on life chances, particularly for racial minorities and the poor, and are arguably crucial to maintaining attitudes of trust and tolerance, as well as, in other contexts, attitudes of distrust and exclusion. Thus, insofar as freedom from criminal victimization is centrally about safeguarding basic rights to bodily integrity, sexual autonomy, and property, then policing occupies a similar place in the theory of justice as the welfare state. After all, not being the victim of a serious crime is plausibly a primary good, essential to the exercise of central capabilities, and a major component of human welfare.

[8] The egalitarian account we sketch stands in contrast to those Brennan-Marquez (2021) canvasses, namely the sovereign pedigree, precursor-to-punishment, and line of fire theories.

An important feature of both public policing and social welfare provision is that they *socialize* the costs of crime prevention, in something like the way that disability insurance socializes the risk of injury or old age insurance socializes the foreseeable costs of supporting the elderly. The public police spread the cost of purchasing a given amount of security from victimization. Some of those costs remain private (people still lock up their bikes and watch where they walk at night), but some of it—the increment attributable to having a police force as opposed to none—is publicly borne. Insofar as the police are paid for out of the public coffers, rather than being financed on a fee-for-service model, policing is in effect redistributive social policy. The establishment of shared means of preventing victimization institutionalizes what Rawls referred to as the sense, in liberal democratic societies, of a "shared fate" (1972, 102). The polity as a whole steps up to provide a certain modicum of security, including for those who would be unable to purchase security on the private market, for instance by hiring private security guards, alarm systems, and the like. This parallels the way in which disability insurance, for example, links the fate of those who become injured and unable to work to that of those who do not.

For this reason, we regard the normative heart of a theory of criminal justice as a matter of understanding whether linking people's fates in this way—or, more prosaically, spreading the costs of crime prevention—is a good or bad idea. This chapter is not the occasion to make that case in any complete manner. Nevertheless, we briefly note several reasons to think that it might be a good idea on balance.

First, in comparison to a world without police, public investment in policing not only spreads the costs of crime prevention but may also raise the level of expected punishment, on the assumption that many or most victims of crime lack the resources, opportunity, and/or risk tolerance to pursue, detain, and prosecute those they suspect of wronging them. Since it is well established that the probability of detection has a significantly greater effect on deterrence than the severity of the punishment, this provides an argument in favor of absorbing the expense of creating and staffing a police force. Doing so may be a necessary condition for transitioning from a low-probability, high-severity enforcement regime to a high-probability, low-severity one. We think egalitarians should prefer a high-probability, low-severity policy regime to a low-probability, high-severity one. This is because the former is fairer than the latter, since both fiscal and human costs are spread more broadly. Making punishment more likely means the punishments actually imposed can become milder without impacting deterrence.

Second, both crime and punishment come with significant human costs. While not everyone who commits a crime serves time in prison, many do, with severe consequences for the prisoners as well as their families and communities. Almost everyone who goes to prison eventually comes out, but reintegration is difficult and uncertain. Fines, which in theory amount to reallocation of resources rather than their destruction (as with incarceration), in practice have a significant impact on the poor. And for everyone who is convicted, the stigma of a criminal record is long-lasting and pervasive, with negative effects on housing, employment, education, mobility, and family formation (Western 2007). These costs suggest that, along with easing reintegration, encouraging people not to commit crimes in the first place—whether through social welfare provision or through making deterrence more effective—is likely to come with significant welfare gains as compared to a policy that focuses solely on punishing the guilty, at least on the assumption that organized public policing and social welfare provision are more effective at discouraging crime than realistic non-state alternatives.

Third, a highly salient difference between crime prevention through social welfare policy and policing is that social welfare policy—both in terms of its intended beneficiaries, and in terms of those who are asked to fund it—is not limited to those who are, or are suspected of being, guilty of committing crimes. Libertarians in particular are likely to object to asking the innocent to, in effect, pay off those who would otherwise go on to commit crimes by funding social welfare policies. However, prioritizing nonpunitive means of managing crime can be defended on egalitarian principles. Consider an egalitarian commitment to take *each* person's basic interests seriously, including the interests of those who commit crimes. This commitment, in turn, can be defended on the basis that while most people are law-abiding most of the time, most people also have moments of weakness, impulsiveness, and poor judgment. Those who do not may owe their good fortune largely to factors outside their control, such as their upbringing, their life circumstances at youth, or sheer lack of opportunity—features that no one can claim moral credit for. The same goes, of course, for those who simply happen to not get caught. Consequently, even though people may be culpable for committing crimes, egalitarian principles suggest that we regard criminals as ordinary people who got caught during moments of weakness, or exhibiting moral failures that many people share to some degree. Egalitarian principles thus favor going beyond the retributivist's insistence on guilt and proportionality and actively seeking out less harsh and stigmatizing means of preventing crimes. The egalitarian commitment to protecting each person's basic interests as fully as possible thus gives us reason to prefer nonpunitive means of crime prevention when they are available and to create them when they are not.[9]

For a contrasting perspective, consider a libertarian framework focused on the rights of individuals. On this approach, the basic question is whether A is culpably invading B's rights. If so, then B or his agent would be entitled to use defensive force to stop A (Nozick 1974, ch. 2). If, having already invaded B's rights, A is subsequently punished for doing so, then A has no legitimate complaint, at least so long as the process is fair and the punishment is proportionate. A libertarian framework along these lines would thus reject the utilitarian and egalitarian arguments canvassed above. The utilitarian argues that earlier interventions, from early childhood education to hiring more police to enhance deterrence, are more cost-effective ways of protecting people from crime, but to a libertarian that is beside the point, since it does not deny what the libertarian framework asserts, namely that criminals are responsible for the crimes they choose to commit. The egalitarian argument that criminals are our moral equals is met by the response that they are *not* our equals, as they have forfeited some of their moral rights in virtue of their decision to invade someone else's rights. That does not necessarily mean we *must* punish them for their crimes, but if we choose to prioritize social welfare programs over punishment, that is our charity, not their right (Wellman 2017). From a libertarian point of view, criminals, insofar as they are responsible agents, do not have a claim right that others—their potential victims—expend resources to prevent them (e.g., through policing or social welfare provision) from making the regrettable decisions they are otherwise prone to make. A libertarian framework thus suggests *not* spreading the costs of crime prevention, regards policing as essentially outsourced self-defense, and views punishment as just retribution for a wrong.

Note that there is a consilience between a libertarian attitude toward criminal justice and the common law world's historical suspicion of full-time, professional police. In a political context deeply suspicious of government power, where the presence of a permanent corps of uniformed, quasi-military police officers are regarded as a step toward authoritarianism, it would be natural to insist that the police should have no inherent normative powers beyond those held by ordinary people: they are citizens in uniform, and nothing more

[9] We recognize that it may seem counterintuitive to defend policing on egalitarian grounds, given their persistent association with harassing the poor and lower status groups. We note, however, that social welfare has its own history of humiliating and patronizing those whom it was meant to serve. See, e.g., Tani (2016). Needless to say, we do not seek to defend those aspects of either policing or social welfare policy. Nevertheless, our sense is that egalitarian commitments are ultimately better served by prioritizing less punitive modes of preventing crime over more punitive ones (Lewis and Usmani 2022).

(Gardner 2010; for a contrasting view, see Thorburn 2008). This type of view is reminiscent of libertarianism, as it grounds the normative powers of the police in preventing crime in the natural right of private citizens to defend themselves from attack. The police are something like the bodyguards of the citizenry: our agents, exercising our rights by our delegation and on our behalf. Just as this view of policing differs sharply from one that derives the authority of the police from the authority of the paternalistic state, so too it differs sharply from one that emphasizes the role of the police in minimizing the social costs of crime prevention, whether on utilitarian or egalitarian grounds.

There is a lot to recommend the libertarian framework. It is undeniably elegant, is grounded in familiar moral intuitions about rights, and appears to dispense with complicated, messy, and uncertain "policy" questions, such as whether we might be better off if we spent less on punishment and more on schools and police. On the other hand, it fails to appreciate that every dollar spent on *ex post* punishment is a dollar not spent on *ex ante* prevention, and hence that a preference for punishment does not avoid policy questions so much as ignore them. Because it is oblivious to the social conditions that explain the distribution of deviance and policing among social groups, it minimizes shared responsibility for crime prevention, preferring instead to lay those costs entirely at the feet of criminals. Among other things, this makes it very hard to explain what is wrong with mass incarceration (Chiao 2018).

Ultimately, how you feel about the libertarian framework will probably depend on how you evaluate libertarian principles against utilitarian or egalitarian ones. Our aim in this chapter is not to engage in those fundamental questions, but rather to show that how philosophers think about the police—or, indeed, whether they think about them at all—is influenced by these underlying commitments. We have illustrated the point by arguing that the invention of both the police and the social welfare state can be rationalized on utilitarian and egalitarian grounds, both of which emphasize the benefits of a partially shared responsibility for crime prevention. In contrast, the individualistic and deontological character of much retributive theorizing suggests conceptualizing the moral powers of the police as grounded in the moral right to self-defense, while disregarding the crime prevention aspects of social welfare policy.

3 The Case of Police Abolition

As we noted, policing has been ignored both in criminal law as a legal discipline and in the philosophy of punishment. This situation has radically changed in recent years, at least on the side of legal scholarship. From Paris to São Paulo, from Ferguson to Santiago, from Minneapolis to Seattle, and many more places, the legitimacy of state policing has rapidly become one of the dominant questions in today's politics of criminal justice. Although police abolitionist movements predate the summer of 2020 by several years, it became a movement with international attention following the murder of George Floyd and the cycle of protests that it ignited. What do the intellectual underpinnings of police abolitionism say about the challenges of criminal justice theory and policing? What type of philosophy underlies its tenets?

In this section, we explore these questions. We claim that police abolitionism reflects a concern with structure and structural distribution rather than with agency and allocation based on individual desert. This is a pattern that fits the transition from a philosophy of punishment to a theory of criminal justice. At the same time, the lack of a coherent theoretical framework for thinking about the police has stymied both abolitionists and retentionists, as neither side has been able to make a case grounded on first principles. Indeed, some abolitionists claim to reject reasoning from first principles, even as their very position is premised on them (McLeod 2019).

Contemporary scholarly police abolitionism was born out of opposition to purely instrumental accounts of policing. Its intellectual adversaries are associated with instrumental thinking, not philosophical retributivism.[10] Engaging with the dominance of instrumental accounts of what organizational decisions foster police efficacy, abolitionists focus on the concentrated harm on marginalized and racialized communities that emerge from police action. That object of concern is certainly not new. For more than twenty years, it has been the main concern of dominant progressive reformist movements such as community policing and procedural justice.[11] The difference lies in the approach. Although both community policing and procedural justice take police violence as a starting point, they focus on how to decrease violence to improve efficacy through increasing trust and cooperation with local

[10] But see Ristroph (2018) for critical theory focused on retributivism and the philosophy of punishment.

[11] For a recent review of the development of research on harm emanating from policing, see Kramer and Remster (2022).

communities.[12] For abolitionists, that frame is inadequate. They argue that the concentration of harm emanating from policing embodies a form of structural domination, a problem that requires basic institutional change rather than adjustments to existing policies (Bell 2017).

Jocelyn Simonson (2021) has characterized this development as a shift from an instrumental understanding of legitimacy to a conception of legitimacy focused on power. This follows partly from traditional tenets of critical theory, which encourage revealing an institution to be something different from what it seems to be. Policing poses as a neutral force meant to improve overall welfare, but in practice it incarnates a mode of domination based on race and class hegemony. In the words of Dorothy Roberts, "The expanding criminal punishment system functions to oppress black people and other marginalized groups in order to maintain a racialized capitalist regime" (2019, 7). On this account, policing and criminal justice were never about keeping those communities safe but rather were always aimed at segregating Black and poor communities and keeping them on the leash (Akbar 2020). Police abolition thus stands as a correction to that form of domination. All reforms seeking to improve the outcomes connected to the structural position of policing suffer from ignoring the distribution of power that it serves.

There are of course several questions connected with police abolitionism that we cannot tackle here. Most notably, the abolitionists' skepticism about the harm-reducing power of police is empirically dubious. Increases in policing are often associated with reductions in crime and, more importantly, discrete reductions of police activity tend to connect to increases in violence that concentrate on marginalized communities (Sharkey 2018; Kramer and Remster 2022). What is central for our purposes, however, is the fact that, unlike community policing or procedural justice, police abolitionism rests on a challenge to what we earlier described as a libertarian theory of criminal justice, especially its individualistic elements.

Recall that the libertarian framework rests on the idea that those who wrongly invade the rights of others have no complaint if they are made to bear the burdens of crime prevention and punishment. The abolitionist challenge is at its most plausible when formulated as a question about the *distribution* of burdens and benefits. Abolitionists are surely right to point to the fact that the burdens connected to policing concentrate on marginalized neighborhoods

---

[12] On the history and politics of community policing development, see Skogan and Harnett (1997). On the general ideas of community policing, see Skogan (2006). On procedural justice, see Tyler and Fagan (2008), Trinkner and Tyler (2016), and Jackson et al. (2021).

and follow racial distribution lines, even while those communities also suffer higher rates of victimization. This poses a legitimacy challenge.

A libertarian framework obscures the aggregate distributional impact of policing by focusing solely on individual wrongdoing. An exclusive focus on individual actions and wrongdoing is blind to the fact that crime concentrates in deprived communities because of structural socioeconomic conditions (Western and Pettit 2010; Braga et al. 2019). By responding to crime, policing will track patterns of background injustice that affect the prevalence of crime. It is not an accident that police are far more present in poor and disadvantaged communities than they are in wealthy and privileged ones. The kinds of crimes that garner police attention are more prevalent in the former. However, abolitionists rightly point out that this cannot be chalked up entirely to culpable decisions by poorly motivated individuals, and they call attention to structural and criminogenic inequities (Akbar 2020).

As we noted above, a central feature of the turn to a theory of criminal justice is its focus on assessing the systemic impact of criminal justice institutions. The abolitionist's arguments about the structural problems with policing are one example of the kind of analysis we have in mind (Akbar 2020). Their insistence on the social dimensions of policing mirror the egalitarian argument we canvassed above, which similarly stresses that the line separating those who commit (or are suspected of committing) crimes and those who do not is to a large degree arbitrary from a moral point of view. This is not because people who commit crimes do not voluntarily choose to do so, but because the choice to commit crime is usually subject to substantial causal influences, including those emanating from background injustices, that could easily have affected any of us. These influences can unjustly limit people's options even when they do not render the resulting choice 'involuntary.'

The challenge posed by abolitionism to the libertarian framework illustrates the need for a theory of criminal justice in yet another way. Police abolitionists typically shy away from defending their abolitionism by appealing to an explicit political philosophy; in fact, in some cases they deny they have any political philosophy at all (McLeod 2019). As we have seen, that is not plausible. Their arguments are squarely grounded in egalitarian political thought and a rejection of a libertarian theory of criminal justice. More importantly, abolitionists' inattention to political philosophy sometimes leads them to odd places. For instance, abolitionists who insist that informal social arrangements and voluntary civil society organizations can stand in for full-time, professional police not only hearken back to the common law world's longstanding skepticism about the police, but also reanimate the libertarian framework that motivated that skepticism in the first place (Wertheimer 1975; Duran and

Simon 2019). Simply empowering communities to regulate themselves is, after all, a recognizably libertarian and anti-statist principle. Indeed, one might argue that police abolitionism is libertarianism on steroids. For instance, Roger Wertheimer, an early police abolitionist, defended his abolitionism in part on the ground that "government is continuously tempted to increase its power and the extent of its interference in people's lives," and "whether well-intentioned or not, any extension of state activity is by its nature problematic" (1975, 56–57). Clearly, the case for replacing policing with the institutionally more demanding requirements of social welfare policy would sit uneasily with such anti-government sentiment. Consequently, abolitionists who espouse replacing policing with social welfare require a less libertarian political philosophy.

As we have not sought to defend any particular theory of criminal justice here, we also do not seek to defend any particular conclusion about the merits of police abolition. Our aim, rather, has been to show how the debate about abolition both presupposes and would be enriched by a more explicit theoretical framework for thinking about policing, social welfare, and punishment. With that caveat, we offer three general remarks in regard to the call for abolition.

Abolitionists are correct to argue that a single-minded focus on crime control is a limited measure of legitimacy because it neglects harms connected to crime prevention, such as those stemming from aggressive policing. However, this does not mean crime control is unimportant. Crime control is a central justification for having a justice system. A more balanced assessment of crime control considers both benefits and burdens associated with a given modality of crime control. A policy that decreases crime is not automatically welfare maximizing, much less rights respecting.

Second, abolitionists have a point that a focus on individual wrongdoing has major shortcomings. It is blind to the fact that the direction of causality between where law enforcement agencies direct their attention and where people are found committing crimes is not always obvious. As a system of full enforcement is simply out of the question in our contemporary world, the question of who is controlled or sanctioned depends on where police and prosecutors use their resources. Concentration of policing resources in one community or population will likely expose it to more control than other communities and, depending on the approach employed by the police, it may (or may not) offer more protection to its residents. Conscious decisions on territorial allocation of resources, policing and prosecutorial tactics, as well as bias, are thus central to the distribution of criminal justice burdens and benefits. Individual wrongdoing certainly stands as a necessary condition to impose those measures, but it is not a sufficient moral principle.

Finally, abolitionists are right to stress the ways in which criminal justice interacts with and compounds other forms of disadvantage. What it means to "control crime" is to encourage people to obey the law. But people may legitimately feel less inclined to obey the law if they do not regard the law and the state system in general as treating them fairly to begin with. If people perceive that the lions' share of the benefits of social cooperation flow to others, while they are left bearing most of its burdens, they may perceive a breakdown in civic reciprocity (Shelby 2016). Simply arguing about whether police do or do not make people safer does not address this more fundamental question. Doing that requires, we have suggested, a theory of how criminal justice relates to the broader institutions, norms, and policies that set out a society's basic terms of social cooperation—in other words, a theory of criminal justice as part of a broader theory of justice.

4 Conclusion

In this chapter, we have claimed that legal philosophy's lack of engagement with policing points to a disconnect with the challenges of contemporary governance. The focus on punishment stems from a pre-policing, pre-welfare state configuration of state power. This has kept philosophical engagement with criminal justice limited to narrow questions that neglect central challenges in contemporary criminal justice. Taking a broader view, in this chapter we have sought to sketch the basic parameters of a theory of criminal justice that takes seriously its systematic insertion in a bureaucratic system devoted to crime prevention and punishment. We have illustrated our argument by pointing out that contemporary debates on police abolitionism often rest on a latent political philosophy, although the lack of an explicit theoretical framework limits the coherence of the abolitionist project.

We acknowledge that our arguments in this chapter are sketchy, both in terms of accounting for the shortcomings of the dominant philosophical approaches to punishment, as well as in providing a more fully worked out theory of criminal justice that accounts for the relative place of social welfare policy, the police, and punishment. Nonetheless, we are hopeful that the political turn in criminal justice scholarship will ultimately provide more substantive answers to these challenges.[13]

References

Akbar, Amna A. 2020. "An Abolitionist Horizon for (Police) Reform." *California Law Review* 108, no. 6 (December): 1781–844.

Beattie, John M. 2012. *The First English Detectives: The Bow Street Runners and the Policing of London*. Oxford: Oxford University Press.

Beccaria, Cesare. 1995. *On Crimes and Punishments and Other Writings*. Translated by Richard Davies, Virginia Cox, and Richard Bellamy. Edited by Richard Bellamy. Cambridge: Cambridge University Press.

Bell, Monica C. 2017. "Police Reform and the Dismantling of Legal Estrangement." *Yale Law Journal* 126. no. 7 (May): 2054–150.

Bentham, Jeremy. 1970. *An Introduction to the Principles of Morals and Legislation*. Edited by J. H. Burns and H. L. A. Hart. Oxford: Clarendon.

Braga, Anthony A., Rod K. Brunson, and Kevin M. Drakulich. 2019. "Race, Place, and Effective Policing." *Annual Review of Sociology* 45, no. 1 (July 30): 535–55.

Brennan-Marquez, Kiel. 2021. "Toward a Political Theory of Police Violence." *Connecticut Law Review* 53, no. 3: 697–702.

Chiao, Vincent. 2015. "Two Conceptions of the Criminal Law." In *The New Philosophy of Criminal Law*, edited Chad Flanders and Zachary Hoskins, 20–36. London: Rowman & Littlefield.

———. 2018. *Criminal Law in the Age of the Administrative State*. Oxford: Oxford University Press.

Duff, R. A. 2018. *The Realm of Criminal Law*. Oxford: Oxford University Press.

Duran, Eduardo Bautista, and Jonathan Simon. 2019. "Police Abolitionist Discourse? Why It Has Been Missing (and Why It Matters)." In *The Cambridge Handbook of Policing in the United States*, edited by Tamara Rice Lave and Eric J. Miller, 85–103. Cambridge: Cambridge University Press.

Emsley, Clive. 2021. *A Short History of Police and Policing*. Oxford: Oxford University Press.

Flanders, Chad. 2015. "The Supreme Court and the Rehabilitative Ideal." *Georgia Law Review* 49, no. 2: 383–432.

———. 2016. "Criminals behind the Veil: Political Philosophy and Punishment." *Brigham Young University Journal of Public Law* 31, no. 1: 83–109.

Flanders, Chad, and Zachary Hoskins, eds. 2016. *The New Philosophy of Criminal Law*. London: Rowman & Littlefield.

[13] We are grateful to Chad Flanders for feedback on an earlier draft, and to Aaqib Mahmood and Rose Ma for research assistance. Research for this chapter was supported in part by an SSHRC Insight Development Grant.

Galoob, Stephen R. 2017. "Retributivism and Criminal Procedure." *New Criminal Law Review* 20, no. 3 (Summer): 465–505.

Gardner, John. 2010. "Justification under Authority." *Canadian Journal of Law & Jurisprudence* 23, no. 1 (January): 71-98.

Green, Thomas Andrew. 2014. *Freedom and Responsibility in American Legal Thought.* New York: Cambridge University Press.

Harrell, Erika, and Elizabeth Davis. 2020. "Contacts between the Police and the Public, 2018." *Bureau of Justice Statistics Report.* https://bjs.ojp.gov/content/pub/pdf/cbpp18st.pdf.

Harmon, Rachel. 2016. "Reconsidering Criminal Procedure: Teaching the Law of the Police." *Saint Louis University Law Journal* 60, no. 3 (Spring): 391–411.

Jackson, Jonathan, Tasseli McKay, Leonidas Cheliotis, Ben Bradford, Adam Fine, and Rick Trinkner. 2021. "Centering Race in Procedural Justice Theory: Systemic Racism and the Under-Policing and Over-Policing of Black Communities." *SocArXiv Papers* (Preprint, April 1). https://doi.org/10.31235/osf.io/kgwhc.

Kleinfeld, Joshua. 2016. "Reconstructivism: The Place of Criminal Law in Ethical Life." *Harvard Law Review* 129, no. 6 (April): 1485–565.

Kleinig, John. 1996. *The Ethics of Policing.* Cambridge: Cambridge University Press.

Kohler-Hausmann, Issa. 2018. *Misdemeanorland: Criminal Courts and Social Control in an Age of Broken Windows Policing.* Princeton, NJ: Princeton University Press.

Kramer, Rory, and Brianna Remster. 2022. "The Slow Violence of Contemporary Policing." *Annual Review of Criminology* 5: 43–66.

Lewis, Christopher, and Adaner Usmani. 2022. "The Injustice of Under-Policing in America." *American Journal of Law and Equality* 2: 85–106.

McLeod, Allegra. 2019. "Envisioning Abolition Democracy." *Harvard Law Review* 132: 1632–1649.

Monkkonen, Eric H. 1981. *Police in Urban America, 1860–1920.* Cambridge: Cambridge University Press.

Moore, Michael. 2010. "The Moral Worth of Retribution." In *Responsibility, Character, and the Emotions: New Essays in Moral Psychology*, edited by Ferdinand Schoeman, 179–219. Cambridge: Cambridge University Press.

Neocleus, Mark. 1998. "Policing the System of Needs: Hegel, Political Economy, and the Police of the Market." *History of European Ideas* 24, no. 1: 43–58.

Nozick, Robert. 1974. *Anarchy, State, and Utopia.* New York: Basic.

Rawls, John. 1972. *A Theory of Justice.* Cambridge: Harvard University Press.

Ristroph, Alice. 2018. "The Thin Blue Line from Crime to Punishment." *Journal of Criminal Law & Criminology* 108, no. 2: 305–34.

Roberts, Dorothy E. 2019. "Abolition Constitutionalism." *Harvard Law Review* 133, no. 1 (November): 1–122.

Sharkey, Patrick. 2018. *Uneasy Peace: The Great Crime Decline, the Renewal of City Life, and the Next War on Violence.* New York: Norton.

Shelby, Tommie. 2016. *Dark Ghettos: Injustice, Dissent, and Reform.* Cambridge, MA: Harvard University Press.

Simonson, Jocelyn. 2021. "Police Reform through a Power Lens." *Yale Law Journal* 130, no. 4 (February): 778–860.

Skogan, Wesley G. 2006. "Advocate: The Promise of Community Policing." In *Police Innovation*, edited by David Weisburd and Anthony A. Braga, 27–43. Cambridge: Cambridge University Press.

Skogan, Wesley G., and Susan M. Harnett. 1997. *Community Policing, Chicago Style*. New York: Oxford University Press.

Stevenson, Megan, and Sandra Mayson. 2018. "The Scale of Misdemeanor Justice." *Boston University Law Review* 98, no. 3 (May): 731–77.

Tani, Karen M. 2016. *States of Dependency: Welfare, Rights, and American Governance, 1935–1972*. Cambridge: Cambridge University Press.

Thorburn, Michael. 2008. "Justification, Powers, and Authority." *Yale Law Journal* 117, no. 6 (April): 1070–130.

Trinkner, Rick, and Tom R. Tyler. 2016. "Legal Socialization: Coercion versus Consent in an Era of Mistrust." *Annual Review of Law and Social Science* 12: 417–39.

Tyler, Tom R., and Jeffrey Fagan. 2008. "Legitimacy and Cooperation: Why Do People Help the Police Fight Crime in Their Communities?" *Ohio State Journal of Criminal Law* 6, no. 1 (Fall): 233–75.

Wellman, Christopher Heath. 2017. *Rights Forfeiture and Punishment*. New York: Oxford University Press.

Wertheimer, Roger. 1975. "Are Police Necessary?" In *The Police in Society*, edited by Emilio C. Viano and Jeffrey Reiman, 49–60. Lexington, MA: Lexington.

Western, Bruce. 2007. *Punishment and Inequality in America*. New York: Russell Sage.

Western, Bruce, and Becky Pettit. 2010. "Incarceration and Social Inequality." *Dædalus* 139, no. 3 (Summer): 8–19.

Wilenmann, Javier. 2021. "It Is the Interaction, Not a Specific Feature! A Pluralistic Theory of the Distinctiveness of Criminal Law." *Criminal Law and Philosophy*. https://doi.org/10.1007/s11572-021-09616-2.

17

Beware of Prosecutors Bearing Gifts: How the Ancient Greeks Can Help Cure Our Addiction to Excessive Punishment

Clark M. Neily III and Chris W. Surprenant

Much of the dysfunction in the U.S. criminal justice system is connected to the process of punishment. In theory, the police arrest someone who they believe has broken a law based on the evidence; that person is then charged with breaking that law; a judge or jury then examines the evidence to determine if, in fact, this person did what he is accused of doing; and, if so, the person is then punished appropriately for what he did. In practice, however, the process is not as straightforward.

More than 97 percent of federal criminal convictions (Pew Research Center 2019) and 94 percent of state criminal convictions (Yoffe 2017) are obtained through plea bargains, meaning that for the vast majority of cases people are waiving their right to have a judge or jury determine their guilt or innocence. And many of these people are admitting to crimes that they did not commit. Since 1987, 21 percent of people exonerated of state and federal crimes actually pled guilty to those offenses (National Registry of Exonerations 2021). Countless others plead guilty on a daily basis to lesser offenses—including crimes they did not commit—when faced with a long list of charges and the prospect of significant fines or jailtime.

C. M. Neily III
Cato Institute, Washington, DC, USA
e-mail: cneily@cato.org

C. W. Surprenant (✉)
University of New Orleans, New Orleans, LA, USA
e-mail: csurpren@uno.edu

© The Author(s), under exclusive license to Springer Nature Switzerland AG 2023

M. C. Altman (ed.), *The Palgrave Handbook on the Philosophy of Punishment*, Palgrave Handbooks in the Philosophy of Law, https://doi.org/10.1007/978-3-031-11874-6_17

So why do so many people in the U.S. who have been accused of crimes plead guilty, especially to crimes they did not commit, foregoing the opportunity to take their case to a judge or jury? The answer is *risk*. In what is referred to frequently as the "trial penalty," defendants who are offered but turned down plea deals, opting to go to trial instead, almost always receive significantly harsher punishments when convicted (National Association of Criminal Defense Lawyers 2018; Bhatt et al. 2019; Joseph 2021). Why this happens is not just a function of prosecutorial incentives and human psychology, but how we approach punishment in our legal system.

This chapter argues that the approach to punishment in the U.S.—in particular, how it is determined what punishments are appropriate for which crimes—not only fails to achieve justice, but also drives much of the dysfunction in the U.S. criminal justice system. We then compare this system of punishment to the approach to trial and punishment used in ancient Athens and explain why this approach to punishment would lead to more trials and more just outcomes. The concern, however, is that using this—or any—approach to punishment that leads to more trials seems as if it might cripple the U.S. justice system. We argue that this concern is unfounded and should not stand in the way of procedures that would likely produce more just results.

1 Plea Bargains and Punishment in the U.S.

Two key questions a criminal justice system must answer are (1) what conduct should we punish, and (2) how severely we should punish that conduct? In a well-functioning system, the emotional desire for vengeance and the impulse to inflict disproportionately severe sentences to make an example of transgressors are tempered by various procedural constraints designed to ensure that the decision is made dispassionately, deliberatively, and with due regard to the often dire consequences of state-sanctioned punishment, both for the recipient and for society at large.

Much of the pathology in our criminal justice system flows from the government's remarkable success in subverting those constraints, including particularly the process by which criminal charges are adjudicated. Rather than the speedy and public jury trials the Constitution contemplates, most criminal cases today are resolved through plea bargaining—a quick and efficient, but often extraordinarily coercive, method of resolving charges that vastly increases the number of prosecutions the government may pursue while effectively removing ordinary citizens from the administration of criminal justice. As explained in this chapter, the quality of our system's decisions about when and how to inflict punishment would be substantially improved by a sharp reduction in the use of plea bargaining and a return to constitutionally prescribed jury trials as the default mechanism for adjudicating criminal charges in America.

The story of how the American government replaced constitutionally prescribed jury trials with the ad hoc, extra-constitutional and legally fraught practice of plea bargaining is a cautionary tale about the hazards of good intentions. Starting in the mid-nineteenth century, judges and prosecutors increasingly came to believe that it was both infeasible and unnecessary to take most criminal cases to trial because courts were being overwhelmed with a rapidly increasing volume of litigation and because there was rarely any real doubt about the defendant's guilt. Thus, the reasoning went, not only would individual defendants be better off confessing their guilt in exchange for a reduction in punishment for saving the state the expense of a trial, but society too would benefit by avoiding the pointless expenditure of resources on a labor-intensive adjudicative process the outcome of which was essentially preordained.

The problem from the government's standpoint is that the right to take one's case to trial is extremely valuable, particularly in a system that is strongly optimized to prefer false acquittals to false convictions, as ours is. Even a factually guilty defendant may reasonably hope for acquittal (or a hung jury) in a system that saddles the government with multiple asymmetric burdens, including particularly proving guilt beyond a reasonable doubt to the satisfaction of a unanimous jury. Thus, the question for a government seeking to obviate jury trials in a system that guarantees a right to them is whether there is some way to induce most defendants to relinquish that right. Supplying an affirmative answer to that question involved two different moves: first, devalue the right itself and thus diminish the "cost" to defendants of waiving it; and second, figure out how to exert coercive pressure on defendants without arousing the protective impulses of an ostensibly neutral judiciary.

Diminishing the value of jury trials turned out to be easier than one might suppose and simply entailed systematically misleading jurors about their role in the process of adjudicating criminal charges. In essence, there are two distinct views about the proper role of criminal juries. The one that holds sway in common-law countries today is that the only legitimate role of a jury is to find facts: Did the defendant pay those two witnesses to perpetrate a fake hate-crime against him? Was the defendant acting in self-defense when he shot that person? Did the defendant intend to deceive investors when she claimed her invention could run hundreds of blood tests that in fact it could not? And so on.

But the Founding-era conception of the jury was much different. Consistent with centuries of Anglo-Saxon custom and practice predating the Magna Carta, criminal juries were understood to play both a fact-finding role and an injustice-preventing role by refusing to convict when they felt that the charges or the proposed punishment were unwarranted. Thus, for example, colonial jurors in New York famously acquitted the publisher John Peter Zenger of seditious libel for his criticisms of royal governor William Cosby, even though Zenger had plainly committed that crime. An even more common basis back then for acquitting against the evidence was when the jury felt the punishment—often capital—was vastly disproportionate to the nature of the defendant's wrongdoing (Kemmitt 2006).

The prospect of being acquitted even if factually guilty doubtless has strong appeal to at least some defendants, including particularly those who have arguably been the target of unsavory government tactics in the investigation or prosecution of their case. But the government developed a straightfoward process for minimizing the chances of so-called jury nullification: first, falsely represent to jurors that they are bound to apply the law as it is given to them by the judge, which is widely understood as shorthand for agreeing not to acquit against the evidence (Craven 2021); second, purge from the jury pool anyone who expresses an understanding of and belief in the legitimacy of so-called jury nullification; and third, deny jurors sentencing information so they will be unaware of the consequences for the defendant if they convict (Epps and Ortman 2022).

With the value of the criminal jury trial thus debased, all that remains is for prosecutors to apply enough pressure to induce defendants to waive their constitutional right to bring their case before an institution that the government has rendered a "shadow of its former self" (Amar 1991). Prosecutors have a panoply of extraordinarily coercive levers that they can bring to bear on defendants to elicit a guilty plea (Neily 2020). These levers include: (1) pretrial detention; (2) increasing the defendant's exposure to punishment through creative charge-stacking and mandatory-minimum sentences; (3) threatening savage trial penalties such as the life sentence imposed on a check-fraud defendant who refused a five-year plea offer (upheld by the Supreme Court in *Bordenkircher v. Hayes*, 434 U.S. 357 [1978]); and even (4) threatening to indict (or refrain from indicting) a defendant's family members simply to exert plea leverage (*United States. v. Yong*, 926 F.3d 582, 591 [2019]). As palpably coercive as those tactics are, the judiciary has consistently upheld them even as their ruthless application has created an environment in which almost no rational defendant—even ones about whose guilt there is real doubt—can afford the risk of exercising their right to a jury trial.

2 Overcriminalization and Prosecutorial Incentives

If you believe that the current—seemingly excessive and coercive—use of plea bargains undermines the U.S. justice system, one solution would be to eliminate them entirely. But this solution has its practical challenges, and where it has been tried—such as in Alaska and El Paso, Texas—it was unsuccessful (Hessick 2021, 219–20). Even when formally prohibited, it is simply too tempting for prosecutors and defense counsel to work around this formal prohibition—prosecutors want convictions and overburdened public defenders, who represent 80 percent of defendants in our system, are stretched far too thin to take more than a small fraction of cases to trial—and for judges to turn a blind eye when they do. Given that we have created a system in which *de jure* or *de facto* plea bargaining is possible, it does not seem possible to eliminate it.

The philosophical argument in favor of somehow eliminating plea bargains is straightforward: Justice demands that people are punished for the crimes they commit, not the crimes that they are willing to say that they committed, either to avoid being convicted of more serious crimes that they committed, or because they fear being convicted of more serious crimes that they did not commit. But this either/or does not capture all plea bargains, even if it captures most of them. Often, people plead guilty to crimes they did in fact commit, agreeing to a lesser punishment than the maximum allowed under the law so that the state can avoid a costly trial. It is not unreasonable to believe that allowing plea bargains in these cases is both reasonable and just: the state has an interest in avoiding the cost of trials (financial, additional harm to victims, etc.), and less severe punishments may be appropriate for people who acknowledge their wrongdoing.

The issue, therefore, may not be that plea bargains in principle undermine the aims of justice, but rather that, in practice in the U.S., plea bargaining has been abused and the justice system now depends on it to function. This abuse is connected to, among other things, prosecutorial incentives and how punishments get determined for people who are found guilty. While one way to solve the problems connected to plea bargaining is to target the front end (e.g., eliminate plea bargains), this strategy has the same effect of treating symptoms of a disease instead of the disease itself. Here, the problems stem from the back end, that is, the sheer volume of laws and how punishments are determined for people who break those laws.

Plea bargaining plays such a significant role in the system because we have a problem with overcriminalization and overcharging for criminal offenses, the literature on which is voluminous and largely uncontested (Healy 2004; Kozinksi and Tseytlin 2009; Silverglate 2011; Reynolds 2013; Surprenant and Brennan 2019). The result is that most adults in our society have committed a criminal offense for which they could in theory be prosecuted. To take just a few examples, the simple possession of marijuana remains a misdemeanor under federal law, while cultivation and distribution are serious felonies; laws restricting people's ability to possess and carry firearms are both widespread and routinely ignored, as is the government's attempt to prevent people from driving by suspending their license for a variety of often unrelated transgressions, such as failing to pay court costs. Simply put, we have become a nation of lawbreakers because so many of our criminal laws proscribe peaceful, morally permissible behavior that many people wish to engage in and will continue engaging in despite the fact that it is illegal to do so. Thus, even if it were feasible for the government to discover and prosecute every single criminal act—which it plainly is not—the social and economic cost of incarcerating everyone who committed a jailable offense would be incalculable.

And this presents an extraordinarily important question to which our society has no good answer: given that it is neither possible nor desirable to go after everyone who commits a criminal offense, precisely what subset of "offenders" *should* we prosecute and why? Again, this is a profound and inherently fraught question that most people would agree our system does an appallingly bad job of answering. Among other things, America is the world's leading jailer, with an incarceration rate three to six times that of other liberal democracies like Canada and the United Kingdom, despite having some of the lowest clearance rates for homicide in the developed world and failing to solve more than 50 percent of all reported violent crimes and more than 80 percent of all reported property crimes. Of the ten to thirteen million arrests American police make every year, more than 80 percent are for misdemeanors such as traffic offenses, underage drinking, and low-level drug possession.

Some scholars argue, in effect, that because we catch only a fraction of those who commit criminal offenses, it is axiomatic that we do not have a mass-incarceration problem; if anything, they suggest, we have an under-incarceration problem (Latzer 2020). But this ignores the fact that, as suggested above, it would be socially suboptimal—even disastrous—to attempt to identify, convict, and punish every single person who committed a jailable offense. Again, assuming this is true, we must necessarily decide which *subset* of offenders to go after. The answer to that question is neither easy nor obvious, and while the Constitution certainly does not tell us which offenders the government should go after, it does provide an elegant mechanism for determining which ones the government should *not* pursue—namely, anyone whose alleged crime does not merit the trouble of a criminal jury trial.

Think of it this way: How would you feel about being forced to take anywhere from several days to a month or more away from your work or your family in order to serve as a juror in a case involving the alleged possession or sale of marijuana—crimes that accounted for more than a third of a million arrests last year despite overwhelming popular support for decriminalization (Phox 2021)? In some jurisdictions, both grand and petit jurors have staged what amounts to a revolt against such charges, refusing to return indictments (Steller 2018) or render guilty verdicts (Sledge 2019) in cases involving low-level marijuana crimes. The takeaway is simple, yet profound: if a given criminal offense is not worth the expense and inconvenience of a jury trial, then it does not merit putting a human being in cage either.

Again, there is (or, more precisely, is meant to be) an elegant internal control mechanism here. Public choice dynamics may inevitably impel policymakers to enact far more criminal laws than they should (Larkin 2013), but when the only way for the government to obtain a criminal conviction is to persuade twelve people that the gravity of the offense justifies both their own expenditure of time and effort participating in the adjudication of the case *and* the imposition of significant punishment, the government will be far more selective in deciding which cases to pursue.

But it is the nature of government to expand its powers beyond prescribed limits and to neutralize restrictions on its ability to pursue various ends, including here the ability to convict people it has accused of breaking the law. As suggested above, the government's success in transforming an adjudicative process that was carefully designed to be transparent, deliberative, and relatively inefficient into an essentially transactional process that is cheap, swift, and certain is among the unheralded tragedies of American history. From an historical and constitutional perspective, the criminal sanction was meant to be imposed sparingly, as a policy of last resort; today, however, it has become a tool of first resort, wielded essentially indiscriminately by government to address a host of social ills such as drug abuse, mental illness, and the challenges of poverty.

3 The Consequences of More Trials

In America today, jury trials in criminal cases are vanishingly rare. An interesting thought experiment is to try to imagine what our criminal justice system would look like if it became impossible—or at least substantially more difficult—for the government to obtain convictions from guilty pleas. In trying to envision what our system might look like with less plea bargaining, it is necessary to first determine *why* it would become less prevalent. This matters because the reaction of actors in the system—including particularly judges and prosecutors, but also legislators and criminal defense lawyers—might well vary depending on precisely what happened to make it harder to obtain convictions via guilty pleas.

At least in theory, there are a variety of ways we could see a sharp reduction in the use of plea bargaining. For instance, judges could simply decide, en masse, to stop accepting guilty pleas, as Judge Joseph Goodwin, of the U.S. District Court for the Southern District of West Virginia, did in a series of opinions he wrote in the spring of 2017 (see, for example, *United States v. Walker*, 423 F. Supp.3d 281 [S.D. W. Va. 2017]). Or a state supreme court could decide that the state constitution, properly interpreted, categorically proscribes guilty pleas by designating jury trials as the only valid mechanism for obtaining a criminal conviction. That is precisely how one appellate court judge in Houston has interpreted section 10 of the Texas Constitution's Bill of Rights, which provides that "In all criminal prosecutions the accused shall have a speedy public trial by an impartial jury" (*Farris v. State*, 581 S.W.3d 920 [Tex. App.—Houston (1st Dist.)] [2019]). Alternatively, a legislative body or executive branch official could prohibit plea bargaining as a matter of policy, as the attorney general of Alaska did in 1975 (Rubenstein and White 1979). Finally, one or more of the systemic dynamics that make it irrational for most defendants to insist on their right to trial could change in a way that makes trials relatively more attractive compared to plea bargaining than they are now—examples include a significant reduction in the number of crimes carrying a mandatory-minimum sentence, a cap on the amount of the sentencing discount prosecutors may offer in exchange for guilty pleas, and an inability to purge juries of people who believe in so-called jury nullification.

The response of system actors to a sudden reduction in the availability of plea bargaining may include everything from informal efforts to sidestep the new policy to a lobbying campaign seeking a return to the status quo ante, to the discovery and deployment of new coercive levers designed to reset the plea calculus to its former steady state. But putting aside the question of countermeasures for purposes of this inquiry, let us imagine a reality in which plea bargaining has either been eliminated altogether or marginalized to the point where it is used only sporadically in truly exceptional cases, such as one involving allegations of child abuse where the victim and the accused would each strongly prefer to avoid reliving the trauma of the underlying events through their respective trial testimony.

So, what would a system look like in which plea bargaining is largely off limits to judges, prosecutors, and defendants as a mechanism for resolving criminal charges? First, the system certainly would not "grind to a halt," as many proponents of the status quo self-servingly contend. Think about it: Would we really stop prosecuting murder, sexual assault, and armed robbery if it suddenly became necessary to take every one of those cases to trial? Certainly not. Prosecutors would pursue those charges with the same (if not more) zeal as they do now, and the idea that we would start giving free passes to accused murders and rapists simply because we had to provide a jury trial in each of those cases is not credible. Instead, prosecutors would simply decline to pursue cases involving lesser offenses, just as they do today, while ensuring that necessarily scarce law-enforcement resources are devoted to taking genuinely dangerous people off the street.

One could even foresee a virtuous cycle in which citizens, who are suddenly being called for jury duty far more often than they are now, exert pressure on prosecutors not to waste their time with cases involving transgressions that do not merit the expense and inconvenience of jury service. The subtext might well be something like this: "Look, Madame Prosecutor—I'm willing to take time off from my job and away from my family in order to make our community safer by helping to put a genuinely bad actor behind bars, but don't even think about making me come down here for some stupid drug deal or a drunken brawl in which everyone got what they deserved."

Second, it does not follow that, simply because prosecutors would have to decline a much larger percentage of cases than they do now, the underlying conduct would necessarily go unaddressed. To the contrary, there are plenty of other ways society can respond to antisocial behavior besides a criminal prosecution, and it is quite likely that the government would make greater—and perhaps also more effective—use of less punitive alternatives such as monetary fines, community service, rehabilitation programs, and civil commitment. The judiciary might even help streamline the procedures for invoking those and other non-criminal responses as more cases come sloshing out of a punishment-oriented criminal justice system that can no longer avail itself of the efficiencies provided by plea-driven mass adjudication.

At the same time, it is possible—perhaps even likely—that the government would simply decide to leave more people alone altogether for engaging in conduct that frequently prompts an arrest in the current system. Likely examples include low-level drug possession and distribution, driving without a license, public intoxication, disorderly conduct, and ambiguous property crimes such as unauthorized use of a motor vehicle.

Another way the system could respond is by allowing defendants to opt into special courts where the maximum punishment is capped at some statutory amount (e.g., two or three years beyond which most experts agree that the net utility of incarceration starts to plummet) but the procedures are highly simplified and streamlined—for example, bench trials only, no discovery, limited motion practice, appeals for plain-error only, and so on. This may superficially resemble plea bargaining, but in fact there is no "bargaining" as such—instead, there is simply a one-size-fits-all opportunity for certain defendants to cap their exposure to punishment in return for opting into a less resource-intensive adjudicative process.

Finally, it seems likely that police, prosecutors, and prison officials (perhaps joined by some judges) would use their considerable political muscle to challenge whatever legal or practical impediment was preventing them from relying on plea bargaining as the default mechanism for resolving cases the way they do today. The law-enforcement lobby is among the strongest interest groups in the country, and legislators on both sides of the aisle have historically shown an almost servile devotion to the policy preferences of that demographic on such diverse issues as propping up the failed campaign of drug prohibition, lavishly equipping civilian law-enforcement agencies with unnecessary military hardware such as grenade launchers and bayonets, and maintaining our policy of near-zero accountability for police and prosecutors. Thus, as difficult as it would be to supplant plea bargaining with constitutionally prescribed jury trials, maintaining that framework against the near-certain backlash from the law-enforcement community might be harder still. Simply put, once the serpent of coercive plea bargaining has entered the garden of criminal adjudication, the challenge of removing it altogether cannot be overstated.

That said, while it is impossible to predict with any precision just how the system would respond to a sudden reduction in the availability of plea bargaining, we can be confident that there would be far fewer criminal prosecutions and correspondingly fewer convictions, incarcerations, and prisoners. America's criminal justice system would become vastly less punitive than it is now.

4 A Different Model for Jury Trials

While regular citizens do not have much say in what laws are implemented or how lawbreakers are prosecuted, they do have a say in the legal process via the jury. At the end of the day, if you are accused of committing a serious crime, you can demand that a group of regular people determine your fate. As a result, one solution to these abuses is to think through how the jury process can better serve the interests of justice. In the U.S. right now, juries in criminal cases determine guilt or innocence, but they are generally left out of the sentencing phase of the trial, with some exceptions. In capital murder cases with death penalties, juries determine whether a convicted defendant should be sentenced to death or life in prison. Beyond capital cases, six states (Arkansas, Kentucky, Missouri, Oklahoma, Texas, and Virginia) allow for jury sentencing in certain circumstances. Otherwise, sentencing is up to the judge, who, in most states and for most offenses, must follow strict guidelines. Even though these guidelines permit judges some discretion, it is rare that they make significant deviations from whatever is perceived to be the normal sentence for similar offenses. On the rare occasions when they do, they put themselves at significant risk for public backlash, especially in cases where they show leniency due to the circumstances.

A recent high-profile example is Judge Aaron Persky, the California judge who presided over the trial of former Stanford student Brock Turner. After Turner was found guilty of sexually assaulting a twenty-two-year-old woman, Persky sentenced him to six months in jail and three years of probation, near the bottom of what was allowed per the sentencing guidelines. At sentencing, Persky justified this seemingly low jail sentence by referencing the circumstances of the assault made it unlikely that Turner would reoffend, Turner's personal and family background, and that his actions have caused him permanent reputational damage. There was significant and widespread public outrage to this decision, which, ultimately, led to a successful recall effort to remove Persky from his position.

But it does not have to be this way. Juries could be responsible for determining not just if someone has broken a law, but also what the punishment should be for that behavior. The advantage of having juries make this decision is that they are relatively anonymous and are not subject to the same incentives and career concerns as judges. Further, it gives the people, represented through the jury, an additional check on laws passed and enforced by state agents. When a regular person is asked if someone has violated a law beyond a reasonable doubt, they are not being asked if that law should be in place.

Putting the jury in charge of sentencing, especially if mandatory minimums and other sentencing guidelines are removed, would at least allow for the possibility of reasonable people to say, "Yes, this person did what the state has accused him of doing, but we don't think it's appropriate to punish him for that behavior."

Without sentencing guidelines, a reasonable concern is that the task faced by a jury at sentencing would be overwhelming and they would have little guidance on what the range of just punishments might look like. But this problem can be remedied by rethinking how we approach the sentencing phase of trial. Here, we may be able to look to the procedure used in ancient Athens for some assistance.

Almost every student who has taken an introduction to philosophy class has read Plato's *Apology*, Plato's semi-historical account of Socrates's trial in ancient Athens where Socrates was accused of impiety and corrupting the youth, found guilty of these charges, and then sentenced to death. While most attention is normally given to Socrates's defense of "philosophy," almost no one spends much time thinking about the process through which Socrates was ultimately sentenced to death. While some laws in ancient Athens prescribed specific punishments when they were broken, in many cases the punishment was not defined, and it was up to the jury to determine what the appropriate punishment should be.

What made this process unique was that, in these cases, the jury did not have a full range of possible punishments to choose from, but rather it had to select between two options: one offered by the prosecution, and one offered by the defense (MacDowell 2014). When a majority of the jury found Socrates guilty of two charges that did not have prescribed punishments, he and his accusers each provided an option for the jury to select from. His accusers suggested death as the appropriate punishment (Plato 1961, 35d-e [p. 21]). Socrates, at first, suggested that his "punishment" should be receiving the highest honors in the city if he was, in fact, guilty of what he had been accused of doing (36c-e [pp. 21–22]). But then after his friends offered to pay a significant fine of thirty minae on his behalf (equivalent to just under three pounds of silver), Socrates then formally proposed this fine to be his punishment (37b [p. 22]). When a majority of the jury voted for the accusers' punishment, Socrates was sentenced to death.

Most relevant for our discussion about this procedure was the process by which the jury received the punishment options to select from. In the relatively rare cases in the U.S. when juries assign punishments, the juries are choosing either between very specific options prescribed by law (e.g., death or life in prison), or from within a narrow range of punishments also prescribed by law. In this example from ancient Athens, there was no predetermined range of possible punishments—both sides got to propose a punishment and the jury had to choose between these two possible options. This was not like a U.S. civil case where both the plaintiff and defense make suggestions for how much they should pay in damages and then the jury ultimately decides, and it may or may not take these suggestions into account. Two options were presented, the jury had to pick between only those two options, and a simple majority determined the punishment.

Imagine how the criminal process in the U.S. would change—all the way down—if we adopted a similar approach to punishment, especially if the prosecutor's proposed punishment had to be selected by a supermajority of jurors, otherwise the defendant's proposed punishment would be selected. On the downside, trials would take longer, especially for members of the jury, as the punishment phase would operate almost as a second trial. Another potential downside is that we would almost never see the same punishment for the "same crime." While no two crimes are really the same, most people think that similar crimes should receive similar punishments. One reasonable concern about moving away from sentencing guidelines is that people who are members of historically disadvantaged groups are likely to receive harsher punishments, and, in the other direction, people who have personal connections to the prosecutor or who otherwise have political influence likely will receive significantly lighter punishments. But these things are happening now. Black Americans routinely receive harsher sentences for similar crimes at both the federal and state level (Rehavi and Starr 2014; United States Sentencing Commission 2017; Durante 2021), and people with political connections or who are members of advantaged groups (e.g., wealthy Americans) often receive preferential treatment and more lenient punishments. This may well be a classic case of not letting the perfect be the enemy of the good—or at least substantially better.

While the idea of reaching back to ancient times for solutions to modern challenges like the severe pathologies of the U.S. criminal justice system may strike some as impractical or even naïve, it bears considering how many of those pathologies stem from our own failure to heed the accumulated wisdom of centuries of experience—of trial and error, as it were—about better and worse ways to for society to decide when to let government inflict upon a particular citizen the often life-destroying violence of the criminal sanction. At the risk of oversimplifying, the distilled essence of that experience was to never allow the government to make that decision unilaterally. And yet, that is precisely what we have done by allowing mass plea bargaining to transform what was meant to be a transparent and adversarial process into an opaque and transactional one in which citizens not only do not make the ultimate decision about who deserves punishment—today they have scarcely any role in the process at all.

Thus, it comes as no surprise that a growing number of scholars have, like us, begun thinking about whether there is some way to resurrect the criminal jury trial—to rescue participatory adjudication, as it were, from it near-total extinction at the hands of plea-driven mass adjudication. And while this is not the place for a comprehensive review, a brief overview is both worthwhile and encouraging.

One category of reforms involves giving jurors more information than they customarily receive now. This includes fairly modest proposals, like that from Daniel Epps and William Ortman (2022), to give jurors sentencing information so they will have a clear understanding of the stakes for the defendant and do a better job of holding the government to its various burdens. A more radical approach involves an aggressive social-media campaign designed to educate jurors about their right to ask questions during the trial—such as what the punishment will be along with any collateral consequences if they convict; whether the defendant was threatened with a trial penalty; and what the substance of any plea offer was—along with information about jurors' unquestioned authority to acquit against the evidence if the answers to those questions leave doubts in their mind about the fairness of the potential punishment or the process itself.

A reform proposed by one of the authors is the creation of a "plea integrity unit" that would scrutinize cases in which a provisional plea agreement has been reached in order to independently scrutinize the strength of the government's case, determine whether potentially coercive pressure has been applied to the defendant during the plea process, and ensure that all material that would be discoverable at trial has been produced. In a similar vein, Kiel Brennan-Marquez, Darryl Brown, and Stephen Henderson (2021) have suggested a "trial lottery" that would randomly select a number of cases in which a plea agreement has been reached and send them to trial in order to see what the outcome would have been. If the defendant is convicted, they get the agreed-upon plea deal; if the jury acquits, they go free. Besides helping to avoid improper convictions in particular cases, the trial lottery would serve an audit function, helping us better understand how often—and why—false guilty pleas occur.

Concerns about practicality aside, the upside could be enormous in terms of limiting prosecutorial overreach. The prevalent strategy among prosecutors right now is to overcharge defendants, threatening them with the maximum amount of time the law allows to coerce a plea. But if defendants knew that there were no predetermined punishments under the law if they are found guilty (or admit to guilt), they would likely be less willing to negotiate a plea, especially for drug crimes and other offenses where most regular people think current punishments are too harsh. As a result, prosecutors would approach the plea process much differently than they do now. Instead of approaching it like a hostage negotiation, where they are the ones holding the gun to the head of the hostage, they would likely approach these discussions with an aim to finding a truly just resolution. If not, we would likely see more jury trials with ordinary citizens being able to decide not just if someone committed a crime, but how that person should be punished for breaking that law, including if they should be punished at all.

References

Amar, Akhil Reed. 1991. "The Bill of Rights as a Constitution." *Yale Law Journal* 100, no. 5 (March): 1131–210.

Bhatt, Shruti, Angela Roberts, and Nora Eckert. 2019. "System Favoring Plea Deals Penalizes Defendants Who Go to Trial." *Capital News Service*, January 3. https://marylandreporter.com/2019/01/03/system-favoring-plea-deals-penalizes-defendants-who-go-to-trial/.

Brennan-Marquez, Kiel, Darryl K. Brown, and Stephen E. Henderson. 2021. "The Trial Lottery." *Wake Forest Law Review* 56, no. 1: 1–46.

Craven, James. 2021. "Don't Let Judges Lie to Juries about Conscientious Acquittal." *Cato at Liberty*, February 9. https://www.cato.org/blog/dont-let-judges-lie-juries-about-conscientious-acquittal.

Durante, Katherine A. 2021. "Courts in More Republican-Leaning Counties Sentence Black Individuals to Longer Prison Terms Than White Individuals." *London School of Economics United States Politics and Policy Blog*, August 10. https://blogs.lse.ac.uk/usappblog/2021/08/10/courts-in-more-republican-leaning-counties-sentence-black-individuals-to-longer-prison-terms-than-white-individuals/.

Epps, Daniel, and William Ortman. 2022. "The Informed Jury." *Vanderbilt Law Review* 75, no. 3: 823-90.

Healy, Gene, ed. 2004. *Go Directly to Jail: The Criminalization of Almost Everything.* Washington, DC: Cato Institute.

Hessick, Carissa Byrne. 2021. *Punishment without Trial: Why Plea Bargaining Is a Bad Deal.* New York: Abrams.

Joseph, George. 2021. "Defendants Who Refuse Plea Deals Often Get Tougher Sentences: Will the Next Manhattan DA End That?" *Gothamist*, March 26. https://gothamist.com/news/defendants-who-refuse-plea-deals-often-get-tougher-sentences-will-next-manhattan-da-end.

Kemmitt, Chris. 2006. "Function over Form: Reviving the Criminal Jury's Historical Role as a Sentencing Body." *University of Michigan Journal of Law Reform* 40, no. 1: 93–148.

Kozinksi, Alex, and Misha Tseytlin. 2009. "You're (Probably) a Federal Criminal." In *In the Name of Justice: Leading Experts Reexamine the Classic Article "The Aims of the Criminal Law,"* edited by Timothy Lynch, 43–56. Washington, DC: Cato Institute.

Larkin, Paul J., Jr. 2013. "Public Choice Theory and Overcriminalization." *Harvard Journal of Law and Public Policy* 36, no. 2 (Spring): 715–93.

Latzer, Barry. 2020. "An Incarceration Nation?" *Law & Liberty*, March 2. https://lawliberty.org/forum/an-incarceration-nation/.

MacDowell, Douglas Maurice. 2014. "Law and Procedure, Athenian." In *The Oxford Companion to Classical Civilization*, 2nd ed., edited by Simon Hornblower and Antony Spawforth, 437. Oxford: Oxford University Press.

National Association of Criminal Defense Lawyers. 2018. *The Trial Penalty: The Sixth Amendment Right to Trial on the Verge of Extinction and How to Save It*. Washington, DC: National Association of Criminal Defense Lawyers. https://www.nacdl.org/getattachment/95b7f0f5-90df-4f9f-9115-520b3f58036a/the-trial-penalty-the-sixth-amendment-right-to-trial-on-the-verge-of-extinction-and-how-to-save-it.pdf.

National Registry of Exonerations. 2021. "Exonerations in the United States, 10/25/21 Data." https://www.law.umich.edu/special/exoneration/Pages/Exonerations-in-the-United-States-Map.aspx.

Neily, Clark. 2020. "A Distant Mirror: American-Style Plea Bargaining through the Eyes of a Foreign Tribunal." *George Mason Law Review* 27, no. 3: 719–47.

Pew Research Center. 2019. "The Number of Federal Criminal Defendants Opting for a Trial Has Fallen 60% in Two Decades." June 10. https://www.pewresearch.org/fact-tank/2019/06/11/only-2-of-federal-criminal-defendants-go-to-trial-and-most-who-do-are-found-guilty/ft_19-06-11_trialsandguiltypleas-2/.

Phox, Jason. 2021. "Marijuana-Related Arrests Decreased Sharply Nationwide in 2020, but Not in Pa., FBI Data Shows." *Pennsylvania Capital Star*, October 10. https://www.penncapital-star.com/criminal-justice/marijuana-related-arrests-decreased-sharply-nationwide-in-2020-but-not-in-pa-fbi-data-shows/.

Plato. 1961. *Socrates' Defense (Apology)*. Translated by Hugh Tredennick. In *The Collected Dialogues of Plato*, edited by Edith Hamilton and Huntington Cairns, 3–26. Princeton, NJ: Princeton University Press.

Rehavi, M. Marit, and Sonja B. Starr. 2014. "Racial Disparity in Federal Criminal Sentences." *Journal of Political Economy* 122, no. 6 (December): 1320–54.

Reynolds, Glenn Harlan. 2013. "Ham Sandwich Nation: Due Process When Everything Is a Crime." *Columbia Law Review Sidebar* 113 (July 8): 102–8.

Rubenstein, Michael L., and Teresa J. White. 1979. "Alaska's Ban on Plea Bargaining." *Law & Society Review* 13, no. 2 (Winter): 367–83.

Silverglate, Harvey A. 2011. *Three Felonies a Day: How the Feds Target the Innocent.* New York: Encounter.

Sledge, Matt. 2019. "A New Orleans Man Faced a Felony Marijuana Charge; Too Many Potential Jurors Wouldn't Consider It." *Nola.com*, October 9. https://www.nola.com/news/courts/article_b01d0794-eade-11e9-8114-0f789d4d4ccc.html.

Steller, Tim. 2018. "Steller Column: Tucson Grand Jurors Rebel against Drug Prosecutions." *Tucson.com*, February 8, updated December 1. https://tucson.com/news/local/steller-column-tucson-grand-jurors-rebel-against-drug-prosecutions/article_76c3af81-5832-52c2-b0ca-3cff04dfef05.html.

Surprenant, Chris W., and Jason Brennan. 2019. *Injustice for All: How Financial Incentives Corrupted and Can Fix the US Criminal Justice System.* London: Routledge.

United States Sentencing Commission. 2017. "Demographic Differences in Sentencing: An Update to the 2012 *Booker* Report." https://www.ussc.gov/sites/default/files/pdf/research-and-publications/research-publications/2017/20171114_Demographics.pdf.

Yoffe, Emily. 2017. "Innocence Is Irrelevant." *Atlantic*, September. https://www.theatlantic.com/magazine/archive/2017/09/innocence-is-irrelevant/534171/.

Part V

Proportionality and Sentencing

18

Proportionality Collapses: The Search for an Adequate Equation for Proportionality

Stephen Kershnar

1 Thesis

In the context of various negative treatments—for example, compensation, defensive violence, or punishment—proportionality is a systematic relation between what a wrongdoer does and what a person responding to the wrongdoer is permitted to do. More specifically, proportionality is the systematic mathematical relationship between the significance of the wrongdoing and severity of coercion, force, or violence permitted.

In state punishment, proportionality limits the amount of punishment that the state may impose on a wrongdoer. The focus here is on a wrongdoer rather than an offender because an act that justifies punishment might not be criminalized, and vice versa. On different theories, proportionality is justified by what the wrongdoer deserves, the wrongdoer's rights (for example, what rights the wrongdoer forfeits), or some other side-constraint based on something other than desert or rights.[1]

Proportionality is a backward-looking requirement. It makes the correct amount of punishment depend on what the wrongdoers did in the past rather than the good consequences of giving them a punishment of particular

[1] For desert-based retributivism, see Moore (1997). For a classic statement of retributivism, see Kant (1996).

S. Kershnar (✉)
State University of New York at Fredonia, Fredonia, NY, USA
e-mail: stephen.kershnar@fredonia.edu

© The Author(s), under exclusive license to Springer Nature Switzerland AG 2023
M. C. Altman (ed.), *The Palgrave Handbook on the Philosophy of Punishment*, Palgrave Handbooks in the Philosophy of Law, https://doi.org/10.1007/978-3-031-11874-6_18

severity. As a side note, the backward-looking justification includes the present if the present is viewed as the limit of the past. A forward-looking account of proportionality would likely be strongly counterintuitive because it would not track our intuitions regarding proportionality. This is because punishment efficiency can diverge from proportionality based on factors such as the deterrability, efficiency, and amenability to reform of various classes of wrongdoers. None of these factors invariably tracks the significance of past wrongdoing.

My thesis is that there is no property of proportionality. A property here is a relation because it relates punishment and wrongdoing. That is, proportionality is not part of moral reality. That is, I argue for the following:

1	No Proportionality	There is no proportionality in punishment.

The failure to satisfy our intuitions evidences this claim. If this thesis is correct, then either there is no just punishment or just punishment does not require proportionality.

In the next part, I set out the requirements a theory of proportionality must satisfy. In the third part, I argue that no theory meets these requirements. In the fourth part, I consider objections.

This result is problematic for several reasons. First, consider the plausibility of non-consequentialism. Consequentialism asserts that the right always maximizes the good. Non-consequentialism asserts that there are right actions, but that consequentialism is false. Non-consequentialism tries to explain how people should act when one person aggresses on a second—that is, trespasses on her moral boundary—and when one person consents or makes a promise—that is, changes or eliminates a moral boundary. Because responding to aggression lies at the heart of morality, non-consequentialism must provide a plausible theory of how people may respond to aggression (see Sher 2021). This includes preventing it (for example, self-defense) and responding to it after the fact (punishment or compensation). If non-consequentialism cannot provide a convincing account of how we ought to respond to aggression, it fails. While I will not defend the claim here, many of the same problems that plague proportional punishment also plague proportional defensive violence.

Second, consider practical problems in the context of punishment. Judges, legislators, and bureaucrats (for example, wardens) must provide just sentences. As a result, they must know how proportionality works. For instance, they must know how to classify crimes and how much punishment is warranted for each class of crime. They must also apply these classifications.

There are proportionality-related practical issues. Consider, for example, who is best placed to discover what a proportional punishment is: legislature, judge, or jury. Consider, also, whether parole boards, probation boards, and prosecutors should consider proportionality. Consider, also, when wardens should implement their own proportionality-based treatment when assigning prisoners to different parts of the prison, jobs, or solitary confinement. Last, consider how proportional punishments should be applied in non-criminal contexts, such as parenting, schools, and sports.

2 Assumptions

In this part, I set out the requirements that a plausible theory of proportionality must satisfy. Here I assume that just punishment requires proportionality. On this account, a disproportionate punishment is unjust, perhaps as unjust as punishment of the innocent. We now turn to specific assumptions.

First, a mere thought does not merit punishment. For example, a brain in a vat would not merit punishment even if the brain planned and willed shocking acts of violence without knowing that its thoughts did not affect the world.

Second, just punishment entails blame (see Nozick 1974). That is, just punishment requires that the wrongdoer was blameworthy for the act. If punishment necessarily involves condemnation, then this assumption follows. This is because an individual should be condemned for, and only for, a blameworthy decision or act. If a decision is a type of act—specifically, a mental act—then a person should be only condemned for acts. On this assumption, blame is necessary for punishment. Because brains in vats can be blameworthy for trying to do—or, perhaps, merely willing—wrongdoing, blameworthiness by itself is not sufficient for punishment.

On my account, praiseworthiness is positive moral responsibility and blameworthiness is negative moral responsibility. The underlying idea is that a person is basically responsible for, and only for, an act.[2] The basic responsibility merits credit (praiseworthiness) or discredit (blameworthiness). Discredit is the focus of condemnation. On this account, a person can have a zero-level of moral responsibility because the person does a neutral act. Other purported grounds of responsibility—for example, capacities that constitute one of the following: libertarian free will, meshed desires, or reason-responsiveness—are merely capacities that enable a person to be morally responsible.

[2] For a defense of this notion, see Kershnar (2018).

Also, on my account, blameworthiness occurs in an amount (+46 units) rather than a degree (0.6). This can be seen in that blameworthiness is negative praiseworthiness and praiseworthiness occurs in an amount rather than a degree. Here a degree is understood as a percentage. Intuitively, for example, God has infinite moral responsibility for his acts. Blame is thus similar to utility or virtue in that what matters is an amount, not a percentage.[3]

If blameworthiness were a percentage of what the individual is capable of, then the percentage would be for an individual or a population. If the percentage is of an individual, then this would result in two people having an equal degree of blame (for example, 0.6) even though one is far more blameworthy than the second. This is because one (for example, a smart and well-adjusted wrongdoer) has much greater capacities than the second (for example, a dumb and poorly adjusted wrongdoer).

If, instead, the degree depends on some feature of a population (for example, the average capacity of people currently living in Ithaca, New York), then an actor's blameworthiness would depend on facts about others. Intuitively, how blameworthy someone is does not depend on facts about others. Worse, blameworthiness would depend on arbitrary facts about the reference class. If this is correct, then the degree of responsibility is an amount, not a percentage.

There is a further problem in that if, as I believe, people are not directly blameworthy for negligence, then a person who does not know that the act is wrong, but should know this, would not be blameworthy for the act. This results in true believers not warranting punishment. This reduces the number of wrongdoers who merit punishment, perhaps significantly. It also reduces the severity of punishment that wrongdoers warrant if the wrongdoers see themselves as doing only a minor wrong. Consider, for example, a member of the mafia family who sees killing soldiers in an opposing family as permissible violence between combatants. Such a member would not be blameworthy.[4]

Third, a just punishment entails a moral-right infringement. The general intuition here is that punishment is justified only if one person wrongs a second, and one person wrongs a second only if the first fails to satisfy a duty owed to the second. Because a duty owed to someone is a right (specifically, a claim-right), a person may be justly punished only if that person infringed someone's right. The underlying picture here is that people have moral

[3] For the idea that blameworthiness can be ranked or perhaps even quantified, see Coates and Swensen (2013) and Vargas (2013). For the notion that it cannot be quantified, see Ryberg (2020) and Kershnar and Kelly (n.d.).

[4] A further problem arises if no one is blameworthy because no one is morally responsible. For arguments in support of this, see Strawson (1994), Pereboom (1995), and Kershnar (2018).

boundaries, moral rights constitute those boundaries, and punishment is the proper response to a boundary invasion.

This assumption is controversial. On this account, state punishment for non-right-infringing acts is unjust and impermissible. Consider, for example, offenses in which no one's right is directly infringed such as the sale of drugs, guns, or sex.

A problem arises regarding attempted crimes. Consider, for example, a shooter who fires at someone and misses, and in which the intended victim never finds out about the attempt. The shooter neither harms nor wrongs the intended victim. A mere attempt does not harm intended victims if they are no worse off than they would have been had the attempted wrongdoing not occurred. The intended victims do not have less pleasure, fewer fulfilled-desires, or fewer objective list goods (for example, autonomy and love) than they would have had if the missed shots were not fired.

A mere attempt does not wrong the intended victim if the intended victim does not have a right infringed. The intended victim does not have a right infringed because what justifies a right—autonomy or interest—is not set back. An attempt might risk harm (or injustice), but a risk of harm is not itself a harm. If the third assumption is correct—an injustice is necessary for just punishment—this contradicts the notion that a mere attempt warrants punishment. For now, let us merely note the conflict.

An assumption here is that injustice comes in amounts rather than degrees (understood as a percentage). This is in part because it is unclear what the percentage of justice would be a percentage of. This is also in part because, intuitively, an injustice is a function of the stringency of a right and the extent to which an act infringes it, and these can be represented as a cardinal number. In addition, if some consequentialist gains are so large that they override an individual's rights, then we have to compare the amount of injustice—on the scale of badness or wrongness—with the avoidance of a catastrophe.

Fourth, consider harm. Harm is neither necessary nor sufficient for punishment. Harm is not necessary for just punishment because, in some cases, punishment is warranted even when the wrongdoer does not harm anyone. Consider, for example, a high school football player who digitally rapes a drunk and passed-out girl in a case in which she never finds out about it.[5] Intuitively, justice requires that the player should be punished even though he does not harm anyone.

In the original case, the young woman was digitally raped, and it was recorded. One might think that there was a harm in that case—both a

[5] The idea for this case comes from Almasy (2013).

physical violation and a digital record of it. Alternatively, one might cite other harms here, including social stigma, humiliation, and so on. I am using "harm" to mean "setback to an interest." In the above hypothetical case, if a digital rape of a passed out young woman did not to set back her interest, perhaps because she never finds out about it and it does not affect how others treat her, then it would not harm her. In the hypothetical scenario, the digital rape does not set back her interest because it does not make her have less pleasure, fewer desires fulfilled, fewer objective-list goods (consider goods such as autonomy, knowledge, love, and virtue), or have objective-list goods to a lesser degree than she would have had were the rape not to have occurred.

A simpler case is when one person leaves a rusty hammer in his field and does not care about it. A second person steals the hammer. The second person merits punishment even though the second did not harm the first.

In addition, harm is not sufficient for punishment because merely causing harm does not warrant punishment. Consider a person who blamelessly transmits the flu to another and thereby causes them to die. Intuitively, the state should not punish them.

The harm- and wrongdoing-factors face another problem. A harm is a setback to an interest. There is an issue as to whether the relevant harm is an all-things-considered harm or other-things-being-equal harm (that is, a pro tanto harm). The problem with all-things-considered harm is that there is no way to limit harm to screen out far-reaching effects—such as tipping-point effects—without sneaking in blameworthiness as a way of setting a boundary on the relevant effects. Limiting effects to those effects that are proximately caused—assuming proximate cause elliptically refers to foreseeability—sneaks in blameworthiness. The all-things-considered harm has another counterintuitive result because horrific crimes might benefit the victim overall. For example, crime victims sometimes state that being victimized forced them to look at who they are and make needed changes in their lives. If so, the lack of all-things-considered harm would undermine a harm-based justification for punishment.

Other-things-being-equal harm escapes these problems. However, it requires an account of which effects are within the other-things-being-equal boundary. Consider the case when a battery victim is brought to the hospital where doctors discover that the person has a heart blockage that will kill them if not promptly removed. Ordinarily, medical treatment—including accompanying embarrassment, price, and time—are within the boundary of the relevant effects of a wrongdoing. Yet despite the other-things-being-equal benefit, it does not prevent the wrongdoer from meriting punishment.

Right-infringement faces a similar problem. Insofar as the stringency of a right depends on the amount or importance of an interest it protects, the above problems reoccur with regard to all-things-considered and other-things-being-equal setbacks to interests. The same is true for autonomy.

Fifth, in a completed crime, a wrongdoer does not merit punishment that exceeds the harm or right-infringement the wrongdoer imposed on the victim. For example, a wrongdoer who commits a minor battery (such as pinching a victim) does not warrant twenty years imprisonment. The latter is more harmful and would infringe a far more significant right or, perhaps, infringe a similar right but to a far greater extent.

Sixth, our ordinary intuitions are correct. A proportionate punishment for murder is greater than that for rape. A proportionate punishment for rape is greater than that for battery. A proportionate punishment for battery is greater than that for petty theft. An exception to this might occur when the wrongdoer has an excuse or justification. This is because an excuse undermines blameworthiness, and a justification undermines an act's wrongfulness. As a result, excused and justified acts are not exceptions to the overall pattern of intuitions.

This intuitive ordering does not always track harm because a person might inadvertently benefit a victim through their wrongdoing. For example, a battery might do more damage than a rape if it is the tipping point in a vulnerable woman's life and causes her to kill herself. Perhaps this result can be avoided if there were a principled way to identify the relevant other-things-being-equal harm.

Here are the above assumptions:

	Requirement	Content
1	Thought	A thought does not merit punishment.
2	Blame	Just punishment entails blame.
3	Injustice	Just punishment entails a right-infringement.
3′	Attempt	Attempts merit punishment.
4	Harm	Harm is neither necessary nor sufficient for just punishment.
5	Ceiling	A wrongdoer does not merit punishment that exceeds the harm or injustice the wrongdoer imposed on the victim.
6	Intuition	Our intuitive ordering of punishment is correct.

There is another metaphysical assumption here: *If there is a proportionate punishment, then it depends on, and only on, facts about the wrongdoer, the victim, and the relation between them.* It does not depend on facts about other people. Intuitively, justice does not permit or require one person to be punished for what a second does.

If there is proportionate punishment, then an equation captures it. Two assumptions underlie this notion. First, if proportionality is a feature of moral reality, then it fits into a comprehensible pattern. Second, if proportionality fits into a comprehensible pattern, then an equation captures this pattern.

An issue here is what kinds of equations there might be. For example, we might think that attempts merit less punishment than actual unjust harms. So, we might have an account of proportionality that has a disjunctive form: P = such-and-such, if the act is an attempt, and P = so-and-so, if the act is an unjust harm. Would we call this an equation? On another view, we might have one clause if there is injustice with no harm, and another if there is injustice and harm. Requiring one equation might be unreasonable, even if a complete theory will have equations in it.

There is good reason to think that there are not multiple equations. This is true even if the justification has multiple justifiers. Consider, for example, a theory of punishment in which desert and consequentialist gain are individually necessary and jointly sufficient for punishment. A single equation can express this account. Even if the justifiers are individually sufficient—for example, desert and consequentialist gain are each sufficient for punishment—again, a single equation can express this account. Intuitively, it seems unlikely that there are different justifications for punishing different sorts of acts such that the different justifications cannot be captured by a single equation, albeit one with disjunctive conditions. The wide range of candidate-equations makes it unlikely that different equations capture what justifies punishment and, thus also, justifies the proportionality constraint.

3 Argument

In this part, I argue that there is no adequate equation for proportionality. That is, there is no equation that satisfies the six assumptions. An equation tries to track the mathematical relation between punishment severity and some aspect of the wrongdoer or the act. The most plausible features are blame, harm, or injustice. Consider the candidate-equations below for the value of a proportional punishment: P. These equations set forth necessary and sufficient conditions for punishment.

The variables are as follows: 'P' means "proportional punishment," 'B' means "blame," 'I' means "injustice," and 'H' means "harm." Thus, the full equation might be $P = B$, $P = B \times I$, $P = B \times I \times H$, or something else.

#	Factor
1	B
2	I
3	H
4	B × I
5	B + I
6	B × H
7	B + H
8	I × H
9	I + H
10	B × I × H
11	B + I + H

This list contains the most plausible candidate-equations. There are other possibilities—for example, B × (I + H)—and, also, other factors (for example, virtue). They are less plausible than the above candidates. In any case, they are false if the above candidate-equations are false.

3.1 Argument #1: Necessary and Sufficient Conditions

Consider Assumption #1 (a thought does not merit punishment). If this is correct and people are blameworthy for thoughts—such as a decision or willing—then blame alone does not warrant punishment. The notion that a person is basically blameworthy for a thought is plausible because a person is basically responsible for a decision and indirectly responsible for anything else for which that person is responsible. A person is basically responsible for a decision because that person basically controls it and because of its close connection to their psychology.

Consider a minister who refuses to baptize his wife's adulterous lover because he wants the man to go to hell and believes that this will bring it about. He believes that what he is doing is very wrong but hates the man. If P = B, the minister should be severely punished, even though he did not perform a wrongdoing, at least if we reject the notion that hell exists or that baptism prevents someone from going there. Here a wrongdoing is a right-infringement.

If B alone does not merit punishment, then P ≠ B. In addition, any equation in which B by itself adds to the punishment that someone merits is also false. As a result, B + I, B + H, and B + I + H are false.

Consider Assumption #2 (blame is necessary for just punishment). If this is correct, then any equation that does not have B in isolation (B) or in a multiplicative function (B × H, B × I, or B × I × H) is mistaken.

Consider Assumption #3 (injustice is necessary for just punishment). If this is correct, then any equation that does not have I in isolation (I) or in a multiplicative function (B × I, I × H, or B × I × H) is mistaken.

By itself, I is not sufficient for just punishment. Consider, for example, a psychotic attacker who kills someone. If we assume that the attacker is not blameworthy for the onset of psychoticism or its aftermath, the attacker is not blameworthy. Intuitively, the state should not punish them. Because I is not sufficient for punishment, I, B + I, H + I, B + H + I are mistaken. In these equations, injustice by itself—that is, I—justifies punishment. This is because in these equations, it is an independent basis for punishment. This can be seen in that it justifies punishment even when the other potential bases for punishment have zero value.

Consider, instead, Assumption #3′ (an attempt merits punishment). As argued above, an attempt need not involve harm or injustice. If 3′ were to be true, then any equation involving I and H in isolation or in a multiplicative function would be incorrect. Still, the conflict between 3 and 3′ might be seen as a reason to reject the latter.

Consider Assumption #4 (harm is neither necessary nor sufficient for just punishment). Because harm is not necessary, H, B × H, I × H, and B × I × H are mistaken. Because harm is not sufficient, H, B + H, I + H, and B + I + H are mistaken. Each of these entails that by itself, harm merits punishment. These assumptions regarding harm also falsify complex theories such as (B + I) × H, B + (I × H), B × (I + H), and so on, which are not listed among the candidate theories.

Consider Assumption #5 (a wrongdoer does not merit punishment that exceeds the harm and injustice—separately—imposed on someone). This assumption rules out equations that make just punishment exceed both of these. Consider I + H and B + I + H. If B is greater than one—because it comes in amounts—this also rules out theories that make just punishment a product that exceeds the injustice or harm the wrongdoer imposes on the victim. Consider B × I and B × H.

Consider Assumption #6 (our intuitive ordering of punishment is correct). This assumption contradicts any equation other than I. This is because it is the injustice that tracks our intuitive ordering of wrongdoings. Other factors do not always track this ordering. This is true for equations that include B and H as the single punishment determinant or include one or both as multipliers and thus cause the equation to deviate from proportionality.

It might seem that what tracks our intuitions is unjust harmfulness rather than injustice or harm. However, this reintroduces the issue of all-things-considered and other-things-being-equal harm and, also, the issue of harmless injustice.

Here, again, are the assumptions:

	Requirement	Content
1	Thought	A thought does not merit punishment.
2	Blame	Just punishment entails blame.
3	Injustice	Just punishment entails a right-infringement.
3′	Attempt	Attempts merit punishment.
4	Harm	Harm is neither necessary nor sufficient for just punishment.
5	Ceiling	A wrongdoer does not merit punishment that exceeds the harm or injustice imposed on the victim.
6	Intuition	Our intuitive ordering of punishment is correct.

Here is a table specifying which assumptions falsify which equation. An 'X' indicates that the assumption contradicts the equation. Again, note that 3 and 3′ conflict.

Factor	1	2	3	3′	4	5	6
B	X		X				X
I		X		X			
H		X	X	X	X	X	X
B × I				X		X	X
B + I	X	X	X			X	X
B × H			X	X	X	X	X
B + H	X	X	X		X	X	X
I × H		X		X	X	X	X
I + H		X	X		X	X	X
B × I × H				X	X	X	X
B + I + H	X	X	X		X	X	X

An objector might wonder if there are other variables—perhaps condemnation, desert, or virtue—that should be part of the equation. At the very least, the objector might argue, I have not ruled them out. The problem with this objection is that these things are either indirectly tied to wrongdoing or depend on the above variables. For instance, a person's overall desert-level and performance of a particular wrongdoing are independent of one another. If a person's act makes it such that they deserve some specific treatment, this is most likely because that person was blameworthy for doing it, or it was unjust or harmful. That is, a person's desert—if relevant to just punishment—depends on the above variables.[6] The same is true for just condemnation or virtue.

[6] There are still other problems with desert-justified punishment. First, there is the issue of whether anyone deserves anything. For an argument against this, see Kershnar (2021). Second, there is an issue of the time frame of punishment-justifying desert. For an exploration of this problem, see Husak (1990), Tadros (2011), and Kolber (2019).

A second objector may claim that this account is more promising: P = B × I if there is no H, and P = (B × I) × H if there is H. The objector claims that this equation satisfies the assumptions, especially if we reject 3′. On this account, blame sets a threshold. If the agent is sufficiently blameworthy, this merits a punishment; but it is not as if more blame merits more punishment. By analogy, in the context of corrective justice, if the thief who stole a bike was blameworthy, the thief owes the victim a bike. But is not as if the thief owes the victim two bikes if the thief were really evil-minded. This would make P = I if the agent is blameworthy and there is no H, and P = I × H if the agent is blameworthy and there is H.

One problem with this objection is that it makes harm a punishment-justifier only when it occurs. This makes it mysterious why harm is sometimes a punishment multiplier and sometimes not. This is odd in that harm would intuitively seem to justify punishment simpliciter, or it does not. Also problematic is Assumption 5 (a wrongdoer does not merit punishment that exceeds the harm or injustice imposed on the victim). On this proposed equation, the proportionality ceiling would exceed the harm or injustice imposed when they both are present and, in some cases, significantly do so. In some cases, then, this equation would produce significantly disproportionate punishment.

3.2 Argument #2: The No-Shared-Unit Argument

In addition to the problems in satisfying our intuitive sense of proportionality, the lack of shared units makes these equations mysterious. Consider, for example, if punishment is set out in terms of "utils." Neither blameworthiness nor injustice is set out in terms of utils. Nor is there a function that intuitively seems capable of converting their product into utils. Other than a very rough sense of equivalence between a wrongdoing and a punishment, we do not even have workable intuitions regarding how different degrees of blame should enhance or diminish a punishment. Adding harm to the mix makes the product or sum even harder to convert to an amount of utils rather than easier because it adds yet another unit to the equation.

This is unlike equations in chemistry or physics where the units of both sides of the equations are the same. Consider Boyle's Law, Newton's Second Law, or the law of momentum:

Name	Equation	Variables
Boyle's Law	$v_1 \times p_1 = v_2 \times p_2$	v = volume, p =pressure
Newton's Second Law	f = m × a	f = force, m = mass, a = acceleration
Law of momentum	n = m × v	n = momentum, m = mass, v = velocity

Perhaps a proportionality-defender might claim that morality is different from the natural sciences and so does not need the same units on both sides of an equation. This approach is unsatisfying because we are trying to find a mathematical relation between punishment and wrongdoing, and the failure to have a shared value involves a refusal to do this rather than a different take on it. After all, it leaves us nothing to equalize. It does not even leave us two things to stand in a fixed mathematical relation.[7]

Alternatively, the proponent might claim that the units on the left side of the equation are stipulated to be the same as those on the right side of the equation. Perhaps "momentum" is defined in terms of "the product of mass and velocity." The problem is that the left side of the equation is not stipulated. Rather, severity of punishment is a function of the degree to which an individual's interest is set back. This might depend on a theory of interest—consider, for example, hedonic, desire-fulfillment, and objective-list theories—but it is not simply defined in terms of the product or sum of what is on the right side of the equation. As a result, there is no stipulation-solution to the amount-of-punishment problem.

3.3 Argument #3: The Condemnation Argument

On some accounts, condemnation is essential to punishment and, as a result, proportional punishment should take condemnation into account. On one version of the theory, punishment expresses this condemnation. Condemnation can be understood in terms of whether people condemn a wrongdoer for his act (subjective interpretation) or should condemn the wrongdoer (objective interpretation). Both are implausible.

The subjective interpretation is implausible because it makes just punishment depend on what people *think* about what the wrongdoer did as opposed to what the wrongdoer actually did. However, people can be, and often are, mistaken about what acts warrant punishment and, also, how much punishment an act warrants.

The objective interpretation is implausible because what matters is what justifies condemnation. This will be the usual suspects: blame, harm, injustice, or closely related properties (most likely, desert). The equation should

[7] One underlying assumption here is that punishments can be cardinally ranked. Such a ranking satisfies reflexivity, symmetry, transitivity, and completeness. Completeness asserts that any two punishments can be ranked. There is an issue as to whether comparability requires commensurability, but it need not be addressed here. For a discussion of the relation between them, see Chang (2002).

thus include what justifies condemnation rather than including condemnation itself.

Moreover, if condemnation were a distinct determiner of how much punishment someone merits, the no-shared-unit problem worsens.[8] We would need another variable 'C' to add to the mix of B-, H-, or I-units. This would make balancing the equations harder, not easier.

3.4 Still More Counterintuitive Consequences

There are still other problems with the equation. Consider, for example, Adam Kolber's arguments regarding how similar punishments might vary greatly in terms of how much harm they cause to the wrongdoer (see Kolber 2009, 2013; see also Tonry 2011). This is because people have different responses to punishment depending on their different psychological and physical features. The upshot of this is that, in some cases, two wrongdoers who merit the same punishment will warrant facially different punishments. For example, a rich man who batters a junkie prostitute might be given one-fourth the incarceration of a junkie prostitute who batters a rich man because prison costs the rich man more—perhaps because he misses out on more—than the prostitute. Still, this is not a problem with proportionality so much as a counterintuitive implication of it.

Intuitively, though, punishment should track type of wrongdoing. Consider, for example, theft, battery, rape, and murder. This can even be true if wrongdoing-types are viewed in more fine-grained terms. Consider, for example, first degree rape, second degree rape, third degree rape, and so on.

3.5 Conclusion

Here is a summary of the argument against proportionality:

(P1)	There is no equation for proportionality.	**Assumption #1a: Necessary and Sufficient Conditions**. Proportionality-assumptions rule out every plausible equation. **Assumption #1b: Unit**. There is no metric by which to equalize punishment and the punishment-determinant.

[8] For a similar point, see Husak (2020). For the notion that punishment should censure criminals, see von Hirsch (1993), Duff (2001), and Matravers (2014).

(P2)	If there is no equation for proportionality, then there is no proportionality.	**Assumption #2a: Justification.** If there is no equation for proportionality, then there is no general justification for proportionality. **Assumption #2b: Proportionality.** If there is no general justification for proportionality, then there is no proportionality (as a moral demand).
(C1)	Hence, there is no proportionality.	[(P1), (P2)]

It is worth noting that proportionality in defensive violence faces similar problems to that of punishment. Here blame and harm intuitively seem not to be part of the equation. This is because blameless aggression—for example, by a psychotic attacker—still seems to justify defensive violence. This is also because blameworthy thoughts unaccompanied by aggression do not justify defensive violence. Also, again, non-wrongful harm does not justify defensive violence. See, for example, economic competition. Once again, the problem is that an attempt that is unsuccessful—perhaps due to defensive violence—does not involve an injustice. In addition, the no-shared-unit problem also arises.

4 Objections

One objection is that punishment should be proportional to blame alone or, perhaps, the product of blame and injustice, but the proportionality-requirement is sometimes overridden by other moral considerations. The overriding factors might be a forward-looking consideration such as deterrence, efficiency, incapacitation, moral reform, or perhaps overall consequences. It might also be a backward-looking factor such as compensatory justice, distributive justice, or equality. This objection, however, does not defuse the no-equation problem because the problem arises even when there are no competing factors.

A second objection is that we know, roughly, what punishments are proportional without an equation. The objector argues that by analogy, the lack of a satisfactory equation is no reason—or, at least, not a strong reason—to think that desert, equality, and moral rights are not moral properties that affect the right or the good. Nor is the lack of an equation a reason to think that we lack sufficient knowledge to act based on them when deciding how to punish criminals. For instance, the objector might note that there is no adequate equation for desert whether in general (for example, lifetime desert) or in particular (for example, deserved income), and yet we know when people do not get what they deserve. If proportionality is a feature of deserved punishment, the absence of an equation is neither surprising nor significant.

Jesper Ryberg (2020) points out that, by analogy, theoretical problems with grading papers do not prevent us from correctly grading them.

One response to this objection is that proportionality in punishment addresses a precise issue: *How much punishment should a wrongdoer be given?* This requires a ratio scale. A ratio scale is one that has a true zero point and equal intervals (that is, equal-sized units). The true zero point and equal-sized units in wrongdoing and punishment and a fixed mathematical relation between them allows for a scale that generates correct sums and products and, in so doing, tracks actual quantities.

An ordinal scale—correct ranking but no equal sized intervals or true zero point—fails because a ranking of wrongdoings and punishments can satisfy the scale when we have a wide range of wrongdoings (for example, minor theft, battery, rape, and murder) and when every punishment is a different intensity wet-noodle slap on the wrist. An interval scale fails because it does not have a true zero-point (that is, a no-punishment point). For proportionality, it matters how severe punishments are when compared to no punishment, and this depends on the differences between different punishments and the zero-point having the correct mathematical relations.[9]

In addition, the lack of an equation to track desert indicates that we do not have sufficient knowledge to use it in deciding how to treat specific people or forming policies. Consider deserved income. The lack of an equation indicates that we do not know what grounds such desert—for example, contribution, effort, or sacrifice—or how to convert these things into either a specific dollar amount or percentage of an employer's payroll. The same is true for a woman deciding how to distribute her time and energy between two people who deserve her love, for example, her husband and mother. Similarly, the lack of an equation for right-stringency is one of the reasons we so poorly understand when an interest or autonomy becomes weighty enough to justify a right, when rights are overridden, and how to adjudicate between conflicting rights.

In summary, proportionality requires an equation in order for us to know whether morality demands it and, if so, what proportionality demands. This is true in other areas, such as desert and rights. An equation is required if we are to know what, if anything, makes someone deserving, have rights, be justly punished, and so on, and also if we are to correctly act on these considerations. The idea here is that the left side of the equation—amount of justified punishment—has the same units as the right side of the equation—amount of wrongdoing—perhaps, though, with a negated value. This is similar to how

[9] An ordinal scale lacks an anchor. For a discussion of proportionality anchors, see Ryberg (2004) and von Hirsch and Ashworth (2005).

under corrective justice, just compensation, expressed in dollars, equals unjust harm, also expressed in dollars.

A third objection is that proportionality depends on some feature of a population. For example, it might depend on what schedule of punishments is most efficient (see Becker 1968; Cooter and Ulen 2012). Alternatively, it might depend on the political role of punishment. On one account, the political role of punishment is to express censure. As a result, the state expresses censure through proportionate punishment (see Matravers 2020). By analogy, the purpose of academic grading determines its ranking. If it were to have information- and incentive-purposes, then grading-proportionality would reflect these purposes.[10]

If proportionality were to depend on facts about populations—for example, efficiency or a political role—then the punishment someone warrants based on what that person did to a second person would depend on facts about a third person.[11] This is an incorrect basis for punishment. This is because the justification—efficiency or systematic censure—would be for a collection of rules rather than a justification based on what the particular wrongdoer did or what happened to the particular victim. In addition, wrongdoings can be framed more narrowly or broadly depending on how finely grained one considers things such as intention, injustice, harm, or motive. The same is true with regard to populations. They can be grouped more narrowly or broadly. Worse, if the relevant reference class includes past people, then a proportional punishment today depends on facts about ancient Egyptian wrongdoing. Surely, this is irrelevant. If the relevant class includes future people, a proportional punishment today depends on facts about thirtieth-century Egyptian wrongdoing. Again, this is irrelevant. These problems—Egyptology and Reverse Egyptology—are just as problematic here as they are in population ethics (see Parfit 1984).

A fourth objection is that non-consequentialism is true only if it can explain what people may do when they come into conflict. Consider, for example, issues of coerced compensation, defensive violence, and punishment. The objector continues that non-consequentialism explains what people may do when they come into conflict only if proportionality is a feature of the good or

[10] The example comes from Ryberg (2020).

[11] If desert justifies punishment and desert is in part comparative—the relation between people getting what they individually deserve—then facts about third parties might determine what punishment a wrongdoer ought to receive. However, this assumes that punitive desert is not purely non-comparative. For an exploration of comparative desert, see Miller (2003) and Kagan (2012). On a different version, proportionality depends on a population's negative valuation of a crime. This also makes a proportional punishment depend on the facts about third parties. See Davis (1992).

the right. As a result, the denial of proportionality undermines non-consequentialism. The objector notes that we should be wary of accepting such an extreme result. This Moorean-shift argument purports to show that there is a correct equation for proportionality, even if we do not know what it is.

The problem with this objection is that proportionality is something with which we are quite familiar. We think about it in the context of events we see happen in clubs, criminal sentences, families, marriages, schools, universities, and so on. Thus, we are familiar with the assumptions listed above and the candidate-equations. The assumptions and the candidate-equations are inconsistent with one another. This is so even after many years of talented scholars trying to discover the equation. This is strong evidence that there is no proportionality-relation. Perhaps this tells us that non-consequentialism does not entail proportionality. Perhaps, instead, it tells us that non-consequentialism is silent regarding conflict. In any case, we should not assume proportionality exists when, despite all the personal experience regarding it and the professional energy put into thinking about it, we still have no idea how it might work. The case for skepticism regarding proportionality strengthens when we consider the growing case for skepticism regarding moral responsibility in general, moral responsibility for negligence, retributivism, and right-forfeiture.

Here is a summary of these objections and responses:

Objection #1: Overridden. Punishment should be proportional to blame alone or the product of blame and injustice, but the proportionality-requirement is sometimes overridden by other moral considerations.	**Response #1: Irrelevant.** This objection does not defuse the no-equation problem because the problem arises even when there are no competing factors.
Objection #2: No Equation Needed. We know what punishments are proportional without an equation.	**Response #2: Equation Needed.** Proportionality requires an equation in order for us to know whether morality demands it and, if so, what proportionality demands.
Objection #3: System-Wide Justification. Some general value—for example, efficiency or censure—justifies a system of proportional punishment.	**Response #3: Incorrect Ground.** If proportionality were to depend on facts about populations, then the punishment someone warrants based on what that person did to a second would depend on facts about a third person. This is an incorrect basis for punishment.
Objection #4: Non-Consequentialism. We have more evidence that non-consequentialism is true than that the above argument is sound. Hence, it is likely unsound.	**Response #4: Evidence.** We have strong evidence—personal and professional—that the above argument is sound. This evidence is stronger than the claim that non-consequentialism entails proportionality.

5 Implications

If this argument succeeds, then a punishment is neither proportionate nor disproportionate to a wrongdoing. This is a problem for nearly every non-consequentialist theory of punishment. Theories that address the justification of punishment—consider, for example, forfeiture and retributivist theories of punishment—presuppose proportionality. They do so by filling out what rights wrongdoers lose and, also, what they deserve. The same is true for split-level theories and mixed theories of punishment. An example of a split-level theory is one that asserts that utilitarianism justifies a system of punishment and retributivism justifies a particular punishment within that system (see Rawls 1955). An example of a mixed-level theory is one that asserts that forfeiture and good consequences are individually necessary and jointly sufficient for punishment.

The theories that do not presuppose proportionality fall into two categories. First, a (non-justicized) consequentialist justification of punishment does not require proportionality because proportionality is contingently related to maximizing the good. Even then, an appearance of proportionality is likely all that is necessary for the consequentialist gain. There is no further gain for actually satisfying proportionality. Second, a consent justification of punishment does not require proportionality because what a wrongdoer consents to is contingently related to proportionality. This is true whether the wrongdoer consents to a system of punishment or a particular punishment.

Both theories face devastating objections. Consequentialism treats guilt—whether moral or legal—as neither necessary nor sufficient for punishment. Nor does it require proportionality. Consent theory treats moral guilt as neither necessary nor sufficient for punishment and, also, does not require proportionality. These aspects of the theories are counterintuitive.

There are also standard objections to a consent-based justifications of government that undermine it as a justification for legitimate state authority. The best objection—aimed at the view that people tacitly consent to the government by residing within its borders—is that this begs the question by presupposing that the government has the standing by which to make residing within its borders an act of consent. It begs the question because it must already have legitimate authority to—as a moral matter—make residence have this consequence. There are also objections based on the absence of actual consent—as opposed to counterfactual or hypothetical consent—and on the involuntariness of such consent were it given. I am less impressed by these last two objections, but this is a discussion for another day.

Versions of consequentialism that give weight to desert also require proportionality.[12] This is because those who wrong others or are vicious deserve less happiness or, perhaps, unhappiness, and an equation is necessary to convert a person's wrongdoing or viciousness into a devaluing or negative valuing of their happiness. This relation is systematic only if there is an equation for it. Such an equation, then, must include proportionality.

In summary, the most plausible non-consequentialist theories of punishment presuppose proportionality, and proportionality presupposes an equation. The same is true for desert-adjusted consequentialism. Because one of the main functions of morality is to address how we should respond to wrongdoing, this endangers non-consequentialism itself.

6 Conclusion

In punishment, proportionality is the systematic mathematical relationship between the significance of the wrongdoing and the amount of punishment that may be imposed on the wrongdoer. I have argued that there is no adequate equation for proportionality. The lack of an adequate equation rests on intuitions and the absence of a shared metric. If there is no equation for proportionality, then there is no proportionality. This is because if there is no equation for proportionality, then there is no general justification for proportionality. Purported justifications of punishment that lack proportionality—specifically, consequentialism and consent theory—are implausible. The lack of proportionality, then, is a threat to the notion that some punishment is justified, and that non-consequentialism is true.[13]

References

Almasy, Steve. 2013. "Two Teens Found Guilty in Steubenville Rape Case." *CNN*, March 17. https://www.cnn.com/2013/03/17/justice/ohio-steubenville-case/index.html.

Becker, Gary S. 1968. "Crime and Punishment: An Economic Approach." *Journal of Political Economy* 76, no. 2 (March-April): 169–217.

Chang, Ruth. 2002. *Making Comparisons Count*. Abingdon, UK: Routledge.

[12] For theories that treat desert as a feature of the good, see Hurka (2001), Feldman (2012), and Kagan (2012).

[13] I am grateful to Neil Feit and Travis Timmerman for their extremely helpful comments and criticisms of this chapter.

Coates, D. Justin, and Philip Swensen. 2013. "Reasons-Responsiveness and Degrees of Responsibility." *Philosophical Studies* 165, no. 2 (September): 629–45.
Cooter, Robert, and Thomas Ulen. 2012. *Law and Economics*. 6th ed. Boston: Addison-Wesley.
Davis, Michael. 1992. *To Make the Punishment Fit the Crime: Essays in the Theory of Criminal Justice*. Boulder, CO: Westview.
Duff, R. A. 2001. *Punishment, Communication, and Community*. Oxford: Oxford University Press.
Feldman, Fred. 2012. *Utilitarianism, Hedonism, and Desert: Essays in Moral Philosophy*. Cambridge: Cambridge University Press.
Hurka, Thomas. 2001. *Virtue, Vice, and Value*. New York: Oxford University Press.
Husak, Douglas N. 1990. "'Already Punished Enough.'" *Philosophical Topics* 18, no. 1 (Spring): 79–99.
———. 2020. "The Metric of Punishment Severity: A Puzzle about the Principle of Proportionality." In *Of One-Eyed and Toothless Miscreants: Making Punishment Fit the Crime?* edited by Michael Tonry, 76–96. New York: Oxford University Press.
Kagan, Shelly. 2012. *The Geometry of Desert*. Oxford: Oxford University Press.
Kant, Immanuel. 1996. *The Metaphysics of Morals*. In *Practical Philosophy*, translated and edited by Mary J. Gregor, 363–602. Cambridge: Cambridge University Press.
Kershnar, Stephen. 2018. *Total Collapse: The Case Against Morality and Responsibility*. Cham, Switzerland: Springer.
———. 2021. *Desert Collapses: Why No One Deserves Anything*. New York: Routledge.
Kershnar, Stephen, and Robert M. Kelly. n.d. *Zero Shades of Grey: A Rejection of Degrees of Responsibility*. Unpublished manuscript.
Kolber, Adam J. 2009. "The Subjective Experience of Punishment." *Columbia Law Review* 109, no. 1 (January): 182–236.
———. 2013. "Against Proportional Punishment." *Vanderbilt Law Review* 66, no. 4 (May): 1141–79.
———. 2019. "The Time Frame Challenge to Retributivism." In *Of One-Eyed and Toothless Miscreants: Making the Punishment Fit the Crime?* edited by Michael Tonry, 183–208. New York: Oxford University Press.
Matravers, Matt. 2014. "Proportionality Theory and Popular Opinion." In *Popular Punishment: On the Normative Significance of Public Opinion*, edited by Jesper Ryberg and Julian V. Roberts, 33–53. Oxford: Oxford University Press.
———. 2020. "The Place of Proportionality in Penal Theory: Or Rethinking Thinking about Punishment." In *Of One-Eyed and Toothless Miscreants: Making the Punishment Fit the Crime?* edited by Michael Tonry, 76–96. New York: Oxford University Press.
Miller, David. 2003. "Comparative and Non-Comparative Desert." In *Desert and Justice*, edited by Serena Olsaretti, 25–44. Oxford: Oxford University Press.
Moore, Michael S. 1997. *Placing Blame: A General Theory of the Criminal Law*. Oxford: Oxford University Press.
Nozick, Robert. 1974. *Anarchy, State, and Utopia*. New York: Basic.

Parfit, Derek. 1984. *Reasons and Persons*. Oxford: Clarendon.

Pereboom, Derk. 1995. "Determinism al Dente." *Nous* 29, no. 1 (March): 21–45.

Rawls, John. 1955. "Two Concepts of Rules." *Philosophical Review* 64, no. 1 (January): 3–32.

Ryberg, Jesper. 2004. *The Ethics of Proportionate Punishment: A Critical Investigation*. Dordrecht: Kluwer.

———. 2020. "Proportionality and the Seriousness of Crimes." In *Of One-Eyed and Toothless Miscreants: Making the Punishment Fit the Crime?* edited by Michael Tonry, 51–75. New York: Oxford University Press.

Sher, George. 2021. *A Wild West of the Mind*. New York: Oxford University Press.

Strawson, Galen. 1994. "The Impossibility of Moral Responsibility." *Philosophical Studies* 75, nos. 1–2 (August): 5–24.

Tadros, Victor. 2011. *The Ends of Harm: The Moral Foundations of Criminal Law*. Oxford: Oxford University Press.

Tonry, Michael. 2011. "Can Twenty-First Century Punishment Policies Be Justified in Principle?" In *Retributivism Has a Past: Has It a Future?* edited by Michael Tonry, 3–29. Oxford: Oxford University Press.

Vargas, Manuel. 2013. *Building Better Beings: A Theory of Moral Responsibility*. Oxford: Oxford University Press.

von Hirsch, Andrew. 1993. *Censure and Sanctions*. Oxford: Oxford University Press.

von Hirsch, Andrew, and Andrew Ashworth. 2005. *Proportionate Sentencing: Exploring the Principles*. Oxford: Oxford University Press.

19

Sentencing Pluralism

Douglas Husak

1 Disciplinary Pluralism

In what follows I make a number of theoretical observations in favor of a general conception of sentencing I call *sentencing pluralism.* The sum total of these observations hardly amounts to a *theory* of sentencing. At most, they provide a partial framework in which a particular theory must be situated. Still less do they qualify as an *adequate* theory. Unfortunately, no wholly adequate theory of sentencing exists; nothing approximating an algorithm can specify unique sentences. To be sure, several candidates for a theory have been advanced, but none of them is altogether satisfactory. Each of them fails to satisfy one or more of the several desiderata it seems reasonable to believe a theory of sentencing should meet. These desiderata, to be listed below, are not *logically* contradictory, but they are in such tension with one another that no coherent theory can expect to satisfy them all. Thus any theory of sentencing must compromise between competing considerations, and reasonable minds will strike this balance in different ways. Legal commentators who differ about which of these desiderata should enjoy priority are bound to disagree about the details of whatever theory is proposed—as well as about how defendants should be sentenced in particular cases.

D. Husak (✉)
Rutgers University—New Brunswick, New Brunswick, NJ, USA
e-mail: husak@philosophy.rutgers.edu

© The Author(s), under exclusive license to Springer Nature Switzerland AG 2023

M. C. Altman (ed.), *The Palgrave Handbook on the Philosophy of Punishment*, Palgrave Handbooks in the Philosophy of Law, https://doi.org/10.1007/978-3-031-11874-6_19

What *are* these desiderata? Obviously, any list will generate dispute. Controversy begins when we inquire how such a list might be compiled in the first place. I suggest we start by taking seriously that penal sentences are imposed *by the state*. Thus we might ask what legitimate ends the state might aspire to achieve either by constructing a system of sentencing or by pronouncing a given sentence. As a first pass, it seems plausible to suppose that an answer to this question would include the following: the state should aspire to

1) promote justice by treating offenders as they deserve;
2) increase public safety;
3) save money;
4) minimize opportunities for abuse by legal officials; and
5) gain the support of the citizens in the jurisdiction in which sentencing takes place.

As several of the items on this list make clear, sentencing is not a secular device to approximate what a god would do in meeting out divine justice. Presumably, a god need not worry about saving money, minimizing abuse, or garnering support among his flock. It is not even clear whether divine justice is concerned about how a scheme would impact compliance and public safety. In the real world in which sentencing occurs, however, a system that fails to care about these matters is deficient.

Legal philosophers need not try to identify these desiderata solely from their armchairs. Sentencing guidelines have been among the most important innovations in criminal justice over the past forty years, and the commissioners who have promulgated these guidelines in different jurisdictions generally begin by stating the objectives their scheme is designed to further. For example, the original U.S. Federal Sentencing Guidelines mandate that a "court, in determining the particular sentence to be imposed, shall consider—

(1) the nature and circumstances of the offense and the history and characteristics of the defendant;
(2) the need for the sentence imposed—

   A. to reflect the seriousness of the offense, to promote respect for the law, and to provide just punishment for the offense;
   B. to afford adequate deterrence to criminal conduct;
   C. to protect the public from further crimes of the defendant; and

D. to provide the defendant with needed educational or vocational training, medical care, or other correctional treatment in the most effective manner. (18 U.S. Code §3553)

The set of goals in this statement have been criticized because they are a hodgepodge or laundry list that fails to explain how these diverse objectives should be balanced when they inevitably come into conflict. Lucia Zedner, for example, describes "the very idea of balance" as "perilous" because "it pays too little attention to exactly which threats suffice to tip the scales" (2021, 126). How can retribution, deterrence, incapacitation, and rehabilitation *all* enjoy equal footing as legitimate aims?[1] After all, the Sentencing Guidelines were originally drafted in order to reduce disparities and impose some semblance of uniformity on judgments that had been almost wholly discretionary. But how can inequities be eliminated if authorities may appeal to such a broad menu of objectives when pronouncing a sentence (Robinson 1998)? From my perspective, however, the pluralism these statements embody is as much of a strength as a weakness. Sentencing policy *should* seek to promote a multiplicity of objectives, even though a pluralistic scheme is bound to be messy and give rise to the very inconsistencies the Guidelines sought to minimize.

I do not pretend that either of the above lists is complete. Sentencing, like the criminal law itself, should always be open to new objectives and functions (Husak 2020c). For example, many commentators have become painfully aware of the epidemic of *mass incarceration* that has plagued the United States, and they promise to take steps to eradicate it. In a place where rates of incarceration are too high, a sixth desideratum—a decrease in levels of imprisonment—may well supplement the foregoing criteria. Moreover, at the time of this writing, many citizens are more animated by racial justice than at any point in recent memory. Why should the United States have to rely on excessive amounts of punishment, especially when minorities bear the brunt of these measures? Perhaps a reduction in the racial disparities in sentencing should be added to the list as well.

In addition to controversies about whether a given factor belongs on the above list as well as uncertainty about how much weight it should be assigned, both the list itself as well as the ordering of its various components may well vary from time to time and place to place. These criteria are not ahistorical;

[1] The Model Penal Code described "the general purposes of the provisions governing the definitions of offenses" as "desert, control of the dangerous, and deterrence" (American Law Institute 1985, §1.02). In the subsequent Proposed Final Draft, desert is identified as the dominant principle, affording a lesser status to general deterrence and incapacitation (American Law Institute 2017).

material changes in the society to which they are applied are bound to alter existing priorities. Most obviously, rational taxpayers in a society with fewer resources would be expected to devote less money to sentencing than those in a country that is more affluent. In addition, increases in crime rates and the distress and anxiety that accompany them may lead citizens to value public safety more than in a jurisdiction in which offenses are relatively infrequent. Hard decisions must be made about how much effort should be expended to arrest and prosecute offenders. As a result of these variables, sentencing theory is inherently imprecise and unstable. We should no more expect an abstract set of considerations to uniquely identify a precise quantum of punishment to be inflicted than we should expect them to specify how we should be kind, virtuous, or raise our children. Here, as elsewhere in normative inquiry, *pluralism* undermines aspirations to deliver a single "right answer" for all times and places.

The above claims may seem straightforward to some readers, but it is sobering to be reminded how many theorists have resisted them (but see Berman 2021). Their reticence has at least two sources. First, uncompromising positions remain surprisingly popular in the punishment and sentencing literature composed by academics. What I have called a *pluralistic* theory of sentencing typically goes by the name of a *mixed* theory, a description usually intended as pejorative. I do not understand why the term "mixed" has caught on among legal philosophers. The pluralistic sentencing theory I have sketched is no more "mixed" than any other normative theory that is seldom criticized on this count. The Aristotelian "Golden Mean," for example, is explicitly pluralistic by design. Deontology itself is a mix between various constraints on maximization as well as the thresholds at which they give way. In the minds of many legal philosophers, however, punishment and sentencing theory stand as stark exceptions to the dominance of pluralism elsewhere in normative thought. Some small progress in combatting this phenomenon might be made if the more neutral word "pluralistic" came to replace the negative term "mixed."

Second, even those partisans in sentencing debates who accept pluralism are loath to acknowledge that their preferred approach necessitates tradeoffs between some of the above desiderata. They sometimes suppose that the United States can significantly reduce mass incarceration, for example, without jeopardizing public safety. To my mind, this combination of suppositions represents wishful thinking. It is more candid to admit that a decrease in safety can be a sensible price to pay for the many advantages that would follow if levels of incarceration were lowered. Perhaps criminologists are reluctant to concede as much because they fear a loss of public support if they openly admit that their proposals will increase crime. But offense rates are not the only measure by which to assess a proposed innovation in penal justice; a sentencing policy should be prepared to tolerate an increase in offending in order to better satisfy the remaining desiderata (Pfaff 2017). In criminal justice, we should stop pretending that we can have our cake and eat it too.

At the end of the day, it is mysterious why monist or non-pluralistic positions remain so popular among philosophers of sentencing. A theory that aims at a single desideratum faces insuperable difficulties. Since extensive criticisms of monistic visions can be found elsewhere, I will only summarize what I regard as the most powerful objections to two. Some philosophers allege that only the prevention of a greater evil can justify the deliberate infliction of the suffering inherent in punitive practices (Bentham 1970). A justifiable sentence must aim only at future goods, the most important of which is crime reduction. But this train of thought, however seductive, strains to explain why the past commission of a *crime* is needed to impose a sentence. Why suppose that only *offenders* should be sanctioned by the penal law if goods can be secured more effectively by punishing non-offenders who are reliably predicted to commit future crimes (Gardner 2008)?

Since I regard the foregoing objection as devastating, I will have nothing else to say against a monistic theory that values only consequences in its theory of punishment and sentencing. Admittedly, purely consequentialist theories are taken seriously by moral philosophers in a variety of domains. But the best indication that consequentialism is inadequate as a framework for sentencing is that *no* legal philosopher, to my knowledge, has made an extended effort to describe and defend such a position. No detailed accounts are on the table to critically examine. If consequentialism were plausible in this context, one would expect that a few legal philosophers would come to mind who have defended it. But commentators who pledge their allegiance to consequentialism seem content mostly to lodge complaints against sentencing theories that attach significance solely to desert (Kolber 2018).

Monistic theories that value only desert appear to be more popular among sentencing theorists, at least those who are trained in philosophy (Moore 1997, 83–103). In truth, however, this position is held only rarely; legal theorists who are said to embrace it typically retreat in the face of objections (Husak 2016). Philosophers who would impose punishment strictly in accordance with desert face difficulties almost as serious as that of their consequentialist counterparts. They must explain, inter alia, why a *state* should consider only desert in sentencing. In raising this worry, I do not mean to ask why the state rather than some other institution should be given the authority to levy a sentence, even though this question is important (Flanders 2019). Instead,

I mean to ask why the limited resources of the state should be expended to treat persons as they deserve even when no other goods are achieved. Is this a function rational citizens should endorse, given that a state that incurs the immense expense of funding institutions of penal justice invariably has fewer resources to devote to education, infrastructure, tax relief, or any of the other goods that compete in the real world in which money is finite? Massive state expenditures are not used elsewhere simply to treat persons as they deserve, and it is not clear why criminal justice should represent the sole exception to this generalization. Even Andrew von Hirsch (1987), the contemporary architect of a "just deserts" model, allows officials to take rates of incarceration into account when pronouncing a sentence.

Moreover, a theory that holds desert to be the only relevant factor in sentencing produces outcomes that would not be tolerated elsewhere. Suppose, for example, a defendant is terminally ill and has only a few days to live. Would anyone insist that they must be sentenced because their punishment is deserved? Or consider the reluctance to consider harms to innocent third parties when a sentence is pronounced. Most obviously, severe hardships are invariably imposed on the friends and families of individuals who are arrested, prosecuted, and convicted. Why should these harms, the existence of which is beyond dispute, not be counted in a moral evaluation of sentencing (Brown 2001–2)? Effects on other persons are taken into account in other contexts in which questions of justification are raised. Even in war, where all is said to be fair, philosophers oppose policies they would support but for the harms that would ensue to innocent third parties (McMahan 2009).

Recent history in sentencing drug offenders helps to show why desert should not be the only factor in sentencing (Husak 2011b). Since the introduction of drug courts, tens of thousands of defendants have been diverted to treatment programs while similarly situated defendants have not. The treatment program mandated by a drug court and the punishment imposed by a traditional court are almost certain to differ in their severity. How can this disparity be justifiable if sentencing is to conform solely to desert? Drug court enthusiasts have been sensitive to this difficulty and have long responded to pressure to ensure that treatment regimens are onerous so they do not deviate from desert. But a different response to this phenomenon is not to increase the severity of treatment regimes, but to acknowledge the weakness of a sentencing scheme predicated solely on past conduct. Even when two offenders have committed the same crime with the same amount of culpability, evidence that one is more likely than another to respond favorably to a different kind of sanction may suffice to warrant a deviation from desert.

If I am correct that desert plays only a partial role in all-things-considered sentencing determinations, why not punish in *excess* of desert when good consequences are attained? Does pluralism not open the door to mandatory minimums, three strikes laws, and other draconian measures that have appeared in sentencing practices? An adequate reply relies on the familiar maxim that too much punishment is far worse than too little. We would need to be supremely confident of the benefits of a punitive measure that exceeds an offender's desert. The foregoing innovations in sentencing practice fail to meet this exacting standard. A sentence that is more severe than what is deserved is extremely hard to justify; a punishment that is less severe than what is deserved is not.

I conclude that a sentencing scheme should not be monistic and aim to conform solely to desert. Still, I insist that desert must occupy an indispensable role in a theory of sentencing. It should retain this status because it is able to provide a positive reason *in favor* of punishment. In other words, if an offender *deserves* a sentence, it follows that value attaches to the state of affairs in which they receive what they deserve, and/or that someone has a *prima facie* reason to treat the offender according to their deserts. Thus desert does more than simply remove a normative barrier *against* punishment. I construe the supposition that value attaches to deserved punishments (or that desert provides a positive reason to treat persons accordingly) to be the best candidate for the defining feature of *retributivism* (Husak 2013). If this supposition is accepted, and a sentencing scheme should (inter alia) aspire to do justice by treating offenders as they deserve, I conclude that an adequate theory of punishment must include a retributive component.

But retributivists get less mileage than meets the eye from concluding that value attaches to deserved punishments, and/or that desert provides a positive reason to punish. For desert to do a great deal of work in a theory of sentencing, not only must value be added when offenders are given the sentences they deserve, but also *enough* value must be added to offset the many reasons *not* to punish. As elsewhere in normative inquiry, it is hard to be precise in specifying *how much* value results from treating persons as they deserve, or under what circumstances this value suffices to create an all-things-considered basis for punishment, despite the many countervailing reasons not to punish. But here is one important thought to indicate that desert may not be so weighty. Presumably, the weight of the value (or the strength of this reason) provided by desert is not a constant across all offenses and offenders. Only when desert is great is the reason to punish likely to be sufficiently strong to favor punishment all things considered. I suspect that many retributivists are aware of this point, even if they do not explicitly acknowledge it. My evidence for this suspicion is that the attempts of retributivists to persuade skeptics that desert can provide a sufficient reason to punish invariably involve thought-experiments in which the most heinous of criminals are imagined to have escaped their just deserts (Moore 1997, 83–103). Most respondents recoil at the prospect that a villain such as Hitler might have avoided capture and managed to live happily ever after on a beautiful desert island. But what may be true of offenders whose negative desert is enormous may not be true of offenders whose crimes are far less egregious. Fewer respondents report the intuition that a grave injustice has been done by the failure to punish if the person who escapes to the lovely island had been guilty only of garden-variety theft. My conclusion is simple. If we seek a positive all-things-considered reason to punish each and every offender, rather than only those who commit the most serious offenses, desert might turn out to deliver less than many retributivists have hoped. It might provide a sufficient reason to punish those whose crimes are monstrous without providing a comparable basis to punish the vast majority of offenders. Despite its centrality, desert does less work in a theory of sentencing than many retributivists have believed; it needs to be supplemented by non-desert considerations.

I have argued that no framework of sentencing can be adequate unless it is pluralistic and endeavors to satisfy more than a single desideratum. Neither good consequences in the future nor negative desert in the past is likely to suffice to justify the great majority of penal sentences. A theory of sentencing must invoke competing desiderata and compromise among them. Officials must draw from the empirical contributions of political science, psychology, sociology, criminology, and economics to build an adequate framework. Philosophers have less expertise than criminologists about whether and under what circumstances a sentence might deter. They have less evidence than psychologists about the conditions under which an offender might be reformed. They have less data than sociologists or political scientists about how the public would respond to a sentence or a sentencing regime. And they have less experience than economists about how to use resources efficiently. When the insights from each of these sources are consulted to somehow cobble together a sentencing policy, the end result might be called *disciplinary pluralism.*

What special expertise might a *philosopher* bring to bear in constructing a sentencing scheme? Their distinctive contribution, I believe, is to explicate the first of the desiderata mentioned above: to promote justice by sentencing in accordance with desert. Since this desideratum is indispensable, philosophers will remain important in the sentencing debate. Hence this topic will consume the remainder of my chapter. But even if a philosopher succeeds in defending a set of principles governing justice and desert in sentencing, the end result should not be mistaken for a comprehensive theory of sentencing.

It neglects the other desiderata I have mentioned and thus is only *part* of such a theory.

2 Desert Pluralism

Philosophy is among those disciplines that have a valuable role to play in constructing a viable sentencing framework. Philosophers have the most expertise to decide whether a sentence conforms to justice and desert. How might they do so? The most well-known answer, I am sure, is to implement a *principle of proportionality*. According to the thesis I will examine (and ultimately reject), offenders are treated as they deserve if and only if their sentences conform to such a principle (Duus-Otterström 2021). Although the very formulation of the principle of proportionality is controversial, my preferred version is as follows: *ceteris paribus, the severity of the punishment that is deserved should be a function of the seriousness of the offense that has been committed.*

Applications of this principle to particular defendants are notoriously problematic, requiring solutions to at least five problems, some but not all of which have spawned a massive amount of commentary (Ryberg 2004):

1) What makes one crime more serious than another? If crime seriousness is a complex function of wrongdoing, harm, and culpability, how are these ingredients to be combined? Is there a single scale along which the seriousness of all types of crimes can be ranked? Are violent crimes, for example, generally more serious than those that are nonviolent?
2) What makes one punishment more severe than another? Is the metric of punishment severity wholly objective, or are the subjective reactions of persons relevant in gauging the severity of their punishments? How is the severity of incarceration to be equated with various forms of non-custodial sanctions?
3) What is the function that relates the seriousness of a crime to the severity of a punishment? Is it linear, or does it have a more complex shape? Are some offenses so lacking in seriousness that they merit no punishment at all?
4) What issues does the *ceteris paribus* clause preclude from consideration under the scope of proportionality? How much or how little does it rule out? Can this clause be explicated in a way that does not reduce the principle to triviality or beg questions against arguments that purport to reject proportionality?

5) How should the punishment system be *anchored* to establish *cardinal* proportionality? What role, if any, do social conventions play in the answer?

Needless to say, none of these five issues has been settled, and some have barely been broached (Husak 2020b).

The uncertainties posed by the foregoing issues are potentially devastating for both the theory and practice of sentencing (Yaffe 2018). As I have indicated, the principle of proportionality is best construed as a principle of desert, and desert is integral to the retributive tradition. Justice Antonin Scalia, for example, famously remarks that proportionality is inherently tied to retributive penal theory and becomes unintelligible in the context of deterrence and rehabilitation (*Harmelin v. Michigan*, 501 U.S. 957 [1990], 989). If a principle so central to desert cannot be explicated with tolerable precision, perhaps the entire retributive framework must be jettisoned (Tonry 2020). Some theorists urge the rejection of retributivism for this reason (Lacey and Pickard 2015), and even friends of the tradition admit that "attempts to make proportionality a reasonably precise, positive guide to sentencing are doomed to failure" (Duff 2021, 31). Should sentencing schemes renounce proportionality in light of the immense difficulties in solving these problems? Even if the foregoing thesis about proportionality and desert is an exaggeration, and desert and proportionality are not exactly coextensive, abandoning proportionality seems tantamount to abandoning desert.

In my view, this radical option should be a last resort. Intuitions favoring proportionate punishments are deeply ingrained and stubbornly persistent, dating to the Magna Carta and beyond. Respondents in a variety of domains not only demand that culpable wrongdoers be punished, but also recommend that the gravity of their sentence should reflect the seriousness of their offense (Robinson and Darley 1995). Even parents and casual acquaintances who inflict deprivations on one another in interpersonal contexts tend to tailor the severity of their responses to the gravity of the infractions that have been perpetrated (Husak 2021). For my part, it is nearly unthinkable that punishment severity would be uncoupled from offense seriousness.

But even though a sentencing scheme must award a central place to desert, jurisdictions should not become obsessed with proportionality in doing so. Even if a state were to succeed in making the severity of a sentence proportionate to the seriousness of an offense, the result would not necessarily specify the sentence that is deserved. In other words, considerations in addition to those contained within the proportionality calculus must be taken into account in a determination of the punishment an offender deserves. If my claim is correct, an adequate sentencing framework must be pluralistic in yet a second sense. It must implement not only disciplinary pluralism but also what I will call *desert* pluralism. This latter type of pluralism must be incorporated into an adequate sentencing scheme because several variables other than the seriousness of the offense must be included in efforts to do justice by treating offenders as they deserve. In what follows, I briefly mention a few of these factors.

Several legal philosophers, I am sure, will resist my suggestion that these considerations bear on the defendant's desert. I speculate that their reticence reflects the spell that proportionality has cast upon them. Since many of the factors I have in mind occur after the offense has been completed, and proportionality ranges over only those aspects of the offense committed in the past, it is easy to understand why those who hold the thesis that a sentence is deserved if and only if it conforms to the principle of proportionality would be unreceptive to desert pluralism. The flawed premise in their reasoning, as I assess it, is the thesis that considerations of desert are exhausted by the factors contained within the proportionality calculus.

My point is that the considerations represented by proportionality should play only a partial or incomplete role in overall judgments of the severity of the punishment that is deserved. This point must be contrasted with the familiar claim that proportionality plays only a *limiting* role in sentencing. Because of the several problems applying proportionality introduced above, many theorists conclude that the principle establishes only a rough boundary outside of which punishments are clearly *dis*proportionate (Morris 1992). The most we can accomplish, according to this train of thought, is to invoke a principle of disproportionality in order to ensure that sentences are not manifestly *un*deserved (Frase 2012). Perhaps this familiar claim is correct. Still, our predicament is even worse than limiting retributivists have supposed. If the sentences specified by proportionality are already vague, the difficulties attaining precision can only be compounded by adding additional desert considerations into the mix. Even if proportionality *does* merely set an upper and/or a lower boundary or range within which non-desert considerations should be allowed to operate, the problems have only begun. Desert pluralism contends that even if we somehow *were* able to make accurate proportionality calculations, we still should accept a great many other grounds for departing from the resulting sentence, and several of these grounds should be included in an all-things-considered assessment of what the offender deserves. Weighing these factors in an overall balancing produces a degree of imprecision beyond what limiting retributivists have contemplated.

Some words of caution are needed before mentioning some of the considerations wrongly excluded by the thesis that a sentence is deserved if and only if it conforms to the principle of proportionality. It would be hard enough to persuade skeptics that any of the following factors should bear on sentencing *at all* (Hessick and Berman 2016). But even if these skeptics could agree that some of these extra-proportionality considerations should be incorporated into a sentence, it would be equally hard to convince them that they are relevant because they bear on the offender's desert. It is notoriously difficult to separate those features that are material to what a defendant deserves from those that are material for some other, non-desert reason (Kagan 1999). In the absence of a comprehensive theory of desert, it is nearly impossible to draw this distinction with any confidence. Still, I hope it is intuitively plausible that some of the following factors that I believe should affect a sentence are best conceptualized within the complex desert calculus.

It is clear that numerous factors that are taken into account in nearly every sentencing scheme have nothing to do with desert. The most well-known (but not the only) such example is cooperation with prosecutors. Sentencing guidelines award a downward departure from an otherwise prescribed sentence for "substantial assistance in the investigation or prosecution of another person" (United States Sentencing Commission 2018, §5K1.1 [pp. 467–68]). In what follows, I will not discuss such non-desert factors, focusing solely on those I believe to bear on the desert of the offender but are excluded from proportionality determinations because they are not germane to the seriousness of her offense.

Most (but probably not all) of these factors—those that bear on the offender's desert and serve to affect the sentence even though they are not part of the proportionality calculus—can roughly be divided into two types. The first type involves post-offense *conduct* of the offender: something the person *does* subsequent to the offense. The second type involves events that *happen* to the offender as a result of the offense. As we will see, each of these kinds of factors requires some sort of nexus or relationship between the offender and the offense, but they cannot without strain be conceptualized as features of the offense itself.

Consider a few instances of the first type. Paul Robinson and Muhammad Sarahne (2021) list several kinds of post-offense conduct that should make an offender eligible for a more lenient sentence than would otherwise be imposed. Their examples include, first, the responsible offender, who avoids further deceit and damage to others during the process leading to conviction; second, the reformed offender, who takes affirmative steps to leave criminality behind; and finally, the redeemed offender, who tries to atone for the offense out of genuine remorse. The authors are noncommittal about whether the foregoing offenders *deserve* a reduced sentence or should be punished less severely for non-desert reasons. I am less reticent. Even though each of these behaviors occurs after the commission of the offense, I believe they render a defendant less deserving of the sentence that should otherwise be inflicted.

Sincere remorse and acceptance of responsibility is probably the most obvious factor that bears on the desert of the offender but is not included within the proportionality calculus. Social scientists have concluded that whether defendants express sincere remorse, acknowledge their guilt, and apologize immediately after committing their offenses, is generally recognized as the most compelling mitigating factor by the public. In addition, people who voluntarily pay compensation to victims are also thought to qualify for a break, and the claim for mitigation is especially strong where the compensation occurred prior to the time the crimes were detected. Finally, those who lead an exemplary life, recognizing the errors of their ways and trying hard to steer clear of subsequent criminality, make a strong case for deserving a lesser sentence (Robinson et al. 2012).

Notice that none of these behaviors occurs *prior* to the offense for which the defendant is sentenced. Some factors that bear on desert take place between the time the offense is committed and the time that punishment is imposed. If I am correct, why not award some degree of mitigation for good deeds generally, even when they occur *before* the commission of the crime (Hessick 2008)? It is fair to ask why a sentencing framework does not implement a "whole-life" view of desert, according to which an exemplary life prior to the offense should be allowed to offset the sentence that would otherwise be deserved (Kolber 2018). To my mind, whole-life theories that would discount the sentence of the offender because of good conduct should generally be resisted because they sever any relationship between the offender and the offense. In the clearest cases of deserved mitigation outside the boundaries of proportionality, *some* nexus between offender and offense can be found.

The second kind of factor external to the proportionality calculus that bears on the defendant's desert does not involve conduct they subsequently perform, but rather events that *happen* to them. Two such kinds of events are as follows. Suppose a severe harm befalls a perpetrator in the course of the very criminal incident itself. Imagine, for example, that a drunk driver is seriously injured in the crash. If consigned to a wheelchair for the remainder of their life, why should the sentence be just as severe as that of a drunk driver who escapes unscathed? Part of the deprivation that would otherwise be deserved has been caused by the very offense. In addition, suppose a harm is imposed on perpetrators by a third party. Imagine, for example, that the husband of a rape victim becomes a vigilante, locates the offender, and beats him severely. If permanently disabled, why should the latter's sentence be just as harsh as that of a rapist who is undetected until he is arrested by the police? Although reasonable minds may disagree, I would take these harms into account in calculating the amount of the punishment, if any, that defendants deserve when the state calls them to account. In these kinds of cases, I am inclined to say that the sentences of defendants should be reduced or even precluded altogether because they have been "already punished" (Husak 2010a).

Notice that events that happen to defendants can bear on the sentences deserved only when they are in some sense a consequence of their offenses. They too preserve the nexus or relationship between offender and offense on which I have insisted. It is harder to contend that misfortunes wholly unrelated to his crime can be material to the desert of the defendant. The sentencing should not be affected if they are subsequently struck by lightning, for example. Perhaps states should show mercy and compassion to such an offender, but this ground for mitigation is not a matter of desert.

Let me provide a specific illustration of the kind of situation in which a reduced sentence would be deserved. At least 833 pediatric deaths have been caused by heatstroke in locked cars throughout the United States since the mid-1990s (Otterman 2019). In the scenarios I have in mind, the busy parent simply forgets the toddler is in the backseat and is subsequently horrified when they return to find the child has died. One can debate whether these cases of forgetting involve recklessness or negligence (Husak 2011a). But whatever level of culpability is involved, I believe the awful tragedy endured by the distraught parent should mitigate the sentence that would otherwise be deserved. The parent has already suffered, and probably has already suffered enough—that is, to a sufficient degree to preclude any amount of criminal punishment. Many (but not all) law enforcers apparently agree, because prosecutors in many jurisdictions elect not to bring charges in these situations. One official explained his unwillingness by stating, "There's nothing as a prosecutor you are ever going to be able to do to that parent that is going to come close to what that parent is going to have to live with for the rest of their life" (Otterman 2019). The suppressed premise in his argument is that the suffering experienced by the parent should offset or preclude the severity of whatever punishment the state inflicts. Explicit recognition of a sentence reduction in this circumstance would help to resolve any discrepancy among jurisdictions and formalize the case for partial or complete exculpation.

I do not pretend that the foregoing two types of factors exhaust the kinds of considerations that are external to the proportionality calculus but bear on the defendant's desert. Other examples can be found (Donelson 2022). For instance, suppose the victim somehow facilitates the crime, or goads the defendant in a manner or degree that does not amount to provocation. Or suppose the defendant's role in the offense is less significant or less culpable than that of others involved—as, for example, when the defendant is an accomplice, a minor participant, or induced to commit the crime by another (see United States Sentencing Commission 2018, §3B1.2[a] [pp. 352–54]). Don't these defendants deserve a less severe punishment than their counterparts?

Some examples of mitigation or aggravation are especially hard to categorize as deserved because of philosophical disagreement about their underlying rationale. An especially vexing instance that has attracted enormous attention from legal theorists is the so-called *recidivist premium*: prior offenses, even when duly punished, should increase the sentence of a defendant for their most recent crime. The U.S. Supreme Court has remarked that the "prior commission of a serious crime … is as typical a sentencing factor as one might imagine" (*Almendarez-Torres v. United States*, 523 U.S. 224 [1998], 230). Countless conferences and symposia have been convened to try to defend this widespread intuition and universal practice (Roberts and von Hirsch 2010). The recidivist premium has proved so difficult to justify within a desert framework that some penal theorists have questioned whether it is sound (Hester et al. 2018). In my judgment, von Hirsch's attempt to rationalize the significance of prior record comes closest to showing why jurisdictions pay so much attention to the earlier offenses of the defendant. According to von Hirsch (2010), it is a mistake to believe that the *presence* of a prior record should *enhance* punishment severity. Instead, the *absence* of a prior record should *mitigate* punishment severity. In light of our well-known frailty and weakness, we should empathize with those who are guilty of only a momentary and isolated lapse. Von Hirsch's explanation is especially plausible when offenses are not very serious. When crimes are egregious, however, we should be much less inclined to reduce the sentence of first offenders. Fortunately, few of us kill or commit serious crimes such as armed robbery. But we all make lesser mistakes, and it seems harsh to impose punishments for what we all do (Husak 2010b). When acts of wrongdoing are repeated, however, the case for mitigation is lessened and eventually evaporates altogether.

The plausibility of von Hirsch's rationale becomes more evident when we think about how states should respond to persons who commit low-level offenses, that is, misdemeanors rather than felonies. Issa Kohler-Hausmann (2018) painstakingly describes the process by which low-level offenders are treated more and more harshly as their contacts with police and prosecutors become more frequent. The whole point of what she describes as the *managerial model* of justice is to generate a record to determine whether and to what extent those who commit minor infractions should be monitored and eventually subjected to conventional modes of punishment if they continue to make trouble. If these criminal records are reasonably accurate, their existence forms a credible basis for determining whether a defendant has or has not engaged in whatever past behavior would justify punishing them for their current behavior (Jacobs 2015). A state sanction is deserved by minor offenders such as turnstile-jumpers or fare-evaders only when they have been warned and the state has good evidence they have committed their infraction over and over again (Husak 2020a). To apply von Hirsch's reasoning, these low-level offenders deserve a break at sentencing because of the concession that states should allow for human frailty and weakness.

Obviously, these and other examples could be (and *have been*) examined at far greater length. But my ambition has not been to provide anything that approaches a complete list of the factors that bear on desert but are not included within the proportionality calculus. Again, no such list can be generated without a comprehensive theory of desert—which I admit not to have. In the absence of such a theory, reasonable minds will differ about many of the judgments I would make. Still, I hope the plausibility of my position can be bolstered by resorting to comparative judgments. We should try to assess the quantum of desert of first offenders relative to that of offenders who, for example, commit the same infractions repeatedly despite having been warned not to do so. It seems callous to equate the desert of these two categories of defendants. If so, I conclude that an adequate theory of sentencing must accept desert pluralism as well as disciplinary pluralism.

3 Conclusion

I have argued that a theory of sentencing must be pluralistic in at least two senses: First, it must implement *disciplinary pluralism*, and not take desert to be the only consideration affecting sentencing. Factors typically examined in disciplines other than philosophy should play a role as well. Economists, sociologists, criminologists, and political scientists all have something valuable to contribute when constructing a sentencing framework. Second, a theory of sentencing should incorporate *desert pluralism*. Considerations of desert are not exhausted by a principle of proportionality, which seeks to make the severity of punishment a function of the gravity of the offense. Any number of additional factors contributes to a determination of an offender's desert as well. Unfortunately, it is impossible to specify the weight these factors should be given relative to the relevant non-desert factors, as well as to the desert factors that are not included within the principle of proportionality. Presumably, the balancing of these many considerations will change from time to time and place to place. As a result, sentencing is inherently messy and imprecise. Monists who appeal to a single consideration in sentencing can deliver greater certainty and predictability. Nonetheless, I hold that a just scheme of sentencing should embrace the foregoing kinds of pluralism and tolerate the resulting lack of precision that is bound to result.

References

American Law Institute. 1985. *Model Penal Code*. Philadelphia: American Law Institute.

———. 2017. *Model Penal Code, Proposed Final Draft*. Philadelphia: American Law Institute.

Bentham, Jeremy. 1970. *An Introduction to the Principles of Morals and Legislation*. Edited by J. H. Burns and H. L. A. Hart. Oxford: Clarendon.

Berman, Mitchell N. 2021. "Proportionality, Constraint, and Culpability." *Criminal Law and Philosophy* 15, no. 3 (October): 373–91.

Brown, Darryl K. 2001–2. "Third-Party Interests in Criminal Law." *Texas Law Review* 80: 1383–428.

Donelson, Raff. 2022. "Natural Punishment." *North Carolina Law Review* 100, no. 2 (January): 557–600.

Duff, R. A. 2021. "Proportionality and the Criminal Law: Proportionality of What to What?" In *Proportionality in Crime Control and Criminal Justice*, edited by Emmanouil Billis, Nandor Knust, and Jon Petter Rui, 29–48. Oxford: Hart.

Duus-Otterström, Göran. 2021. "Do Offenders Deserve Proportionate Punishments?" *Criminal Law and Philosophy* 15, no. 3 (October): 463–80.

Flanders, Chad. 2019. "Political Philosophy and Punishment." In *The Palgrave Handbook of Applied Ethics and the Criminal Law*, edited by Larry Alexander and Kimberly Kessler Ferzan, 521–45. Cham, Switzerland: Palgrave Macmillan.

Frase, Richard. 2012. *Just Sentencing*. Oxford: Oxford University Press.

Gardner, John. 2008. Introduction to *Punishment and Responsibility: Essays in the Philosophy of Law*, by H. L. A. Hart, 2nd ed., xiii–liii. Oxford: Oxford University Press.

Hessick, Carissa Byrne. 2008. "Why Are Only Bad Acts Good Sentencing Factors?" *Boston University Law Review* 88, no. 5 (June): 1109–63.

Hessick, Carissa Byrne, and Douglas A. Berman. 2016. "Towards a Theory of Mitigation." *Boston University Law Review* 96, no. 1 (January): 161–218.

Hester, Rhys, Richard S. Frase, Julian V. Roberts, and Kelly Lyn Mitchell. 2018. "Prior Record Enhancements at Sentencing: Unsettled Justifications and

Unsettling Consequences." In *Crime and Justice: A Review of Research*, vol. 47, edited by Michael Tonry, 209–54. Chicago: University of Chicago Press.

Husak, Douglas. 2010a. "Already Punished Enough." In *The Philosophy of Criminal Law: Selected Essays*, by Douglas Husak, 433–50. New York: Oxford University Press.

———. 2010b. "The 'But Everyone Does That!' Defense." In *The Philosophy of Criminal Law: Selected Essays*, by Douglas Husak, 338–61. New York: Oxford University Press.

———. 2011a. "Negligence, Belief, Blame and Criminal Liability: The Special Case of Forgetting." *Criminal Law and Philosophy* 5, no. 2 (June): 199–218.

———. 2011b. "Retributivism, Proportionality, and the Challenge of the Drug Court Movement." In *Retributivism Has a Past: Has It a Future?* edited by Michael Tonry, 214–33. Oxford: Oxford University Press.

———. 2013. "Retributivism *In Extremis*." *Law and Philosophy* 32, no. 1 (January): 3–31.

———. 2016. "What Do Criminals Deserve?" In *Legal, Moral, and Metaphysical Truths: The Philosophy of Michael S. Moore*, edited by Kimberly Kessler Ferzan and Stephen J. Morse, 49–62. Oxford: Oxford University Press.

———. 2020a. "Criminal Law at the Margins." *Criminal Law and Philosophy* 14, no. 3 (October): 381–93.

———. 2020b. "The Metric of Punishment Severity: A Puzzle about the Principle of Proportionality." In *Of One-Eyed and Toothless Miscreants: Making the Punishment Fit the Crime?* edited by Michael Tonry, 97–126. New York: Oxford University Press.

———. 2020c. "The Price of Criminal Law Skepticism: Ten Functions of the Criminal Law." *New Criminal Law Review* 23, no. 1 (Winter): 27–59.

———. 2021. "Proportionality in Personal Life." *Criminal Law and Philosophy* 15, no. 3 (October): 339–60.

Jacobs, James B. 2015. *The Eternal Criminal Record.* Cambridge, MA: Harvard University Press.

Kagan, Shelly. 1999. "Equality and Desert." In *What Do We Deserve? A Reader on Justice and Desert*, edited by Louis P. Pojman and Owen McLeod, 298–314. New York: Oxford University Press.

Kohler-Hausmann, Issa. 2018. *Misdemeanorland: Criminal Courts and Social Control in an Age of Broken Windows Policing.* Princeton, NJ: Princeton University Press.

Kolber, Adam J. 2018. "Punishment and Moral Risk." *University of Illinois Law Review* 2018, no. 2: 487–532.

Lacey, Nicola, and Hanna Pickard. 2015. "The Chimera of Proportionality: Institutionalising Limits on Punishment in Contemporary Social and Political Systems." *Modern Law Review* 78, no. 2 (March): 216–40.

McMahan, Jeff. 2009. *Killing in War.* Oxford: Clarendon.

Moore, Michael S. 1997. *Placing Blame: A General Theory of the Criminal Law.* Oxford: Oxford University Press.

Morris, Norval. 1992. "Desert as a Limiting Principle." In *Principled Sentencing*, edited by Andrew von Hirsch and Andrew Ashworth, 201–6. Boston: Northeastern University Press.

Otterman, Sharon. 2019. "He Left His Twins in a Hot Car and They Died: Accident or Crime?" *New York Times*, August 1. https://www.nytimes.com/2019/08/01/nyregion/children-left-to-die-in-hot-cars-accident-or-murder.html.

Pfaff, John F. 2017. *Locked In: The True Causes of Mass Incarceration—and How to Achieve Real Reform*. New York: Basic.

Roberts, Julian V., and Andrew von Hirsch, eds. 2010. *Previous Convictions at Sentencing: Theoretical and Applied Perspectives*. Oxford: Hart.

Robinson, Paul H. 1998. "Hybrid Principles for the Distribution of Criminal Sanctions." *Northwestern University Law Review* 82, no. 1 (Fall): 19–42.

Robinson, Paul H., and John M. Darley. 1995. *Justice, Liability and Blame: Community Views and the Criminal Law*. Boulder, CO: Westview.

Robinson, Paul H., Sean E. Jackowitz, and Daniel M. Bartels. 2012. "Extralegal Punishment Factors: A Study of Forgiveness, Hardship, Good Deeds, Apology, Remorse, and Other Such Discretionary Factors in Assessing Criminal Punishment." *Vanderbilt Law Review* 65, no. 3 (April): 737–826.

Robinson, Paul H., and Muhammad Sarahne. 2021. "After the Crime: Rewarding Offenders' Positive Post-Offense Conduct." *New Criminal Law Review* 24, no. 3 (Summer): 367–96.

Ryberg, Jesper. 2004. *The Ethics of Proportionate Punishment: A Critical Investigation*. Dordrecht: Kluwer.

Tonry, Michael. 2020. "Is Proportionality in Punishment Possible, and Achievable?" In *Of One-Eyed and Toothless Miscreants: Making the Punishment Fit the Crime?* edited by Michael Tonry, 1–29. New York: Oxford University Press.

United States Sentencing Commission. 2018. *Guidelines Manual 2018*. https://www.ussc.gov/sites/default/files/pdf/guidelines-manual/2018/GLMFull.pdf.

von Hirsch, Andrew. 1987. "The Sentencing Commission's Functions." In *The Sentencing Commission and Its Guidelines*, edited by Andrew von Hirsch, Kay A. Knapp, and Michael Tonry, 3–16. Boston: Northeastern University Press.

———. 2010. "Proportionality and the Progressive Loss of Mitigation: Some Further Reflections." In *Previous Convictions at Sentencing: Theoretical and Applied Perspectives*, edited by Julian V. Roberts and Andrew von Hirsch, 1–16. Oxford: Hart.

Yaffe, Gideon. 2018. *The Age of Culpability: Children and the Nature of Criminal Responsibility*. Oxford: Oxford University Press.

Zedner, Lucia. 2021. "Ends and Means: Why Effective Counter-Terrorism Requires Respect for Proportionality and Rights." In *Proportionality in Crime Control and Criminal Justice*, edited by Emmanouil Billis, Nandor Knust, and Jon Petter Rui, 125–42. Oxford: Hart.

Part VI

Neuroscience, Determinism, and Free Will Skepticism

20

The Impact of *Neuromorality* on Punishment: Retribution or Rehabilitation?

Sandy Xie, Colleen M. Berryessa, and Farah Focquaert

1 Introduction

In 1972, Cecil Clayton suffered a serious accident during which a piece of wood shot into his head and dislodged bone shards that pierced his brain, leading to around 20 percent of his frontal lobe being surgically removed. After the removal, Clayton, who had previously been a loving husband, father, and preacher, transformed into an aggressive alcoholic whose wife divorced him. Clayton spent the next twenty years after his accident trying to get psychiatric help, suffering from extreme depression, violent episodes, anxiety, and hallucinations. Eventually, Clayton killed a sheriff's deputy who responded to a domestic violence call. The deputy had not even left his car when Clayton shot him point blank. Clayton did not appear to understand the wrongness of his actions, even asking a friend who was with him at the time if he should shoot other officers that came to arrest him, to which his friend answered "no." Like the famous Phineas Gage, who suffered a similar injury, Clayton appeared to exhibit a clear personality change resulting from the incident, seemingly diminishing his capacity for moral reasoning (Litton 2018).

S. Xie • C. M. Berryessa (✉)
Rutgers University—Newark, Newark, NJ, USA
e-mail: sandy.xie@rutgers.edu; colleen.berryessa@rutgers.edu

F. Focquaert
Ghent University, Ghent, Belgium
e-mail: farah.focquaert@ugent.be

© The Author(s), under exclusive license to Springer Nature Switzerland AG 2023

M. C. Altman (ed.), *The Palgrave Handbook on the Philosophy of Punishment*, Palgrave Handbooks in the Philosophy of Law, https://doi.org/10.1007/978-3-031-11874-6_20

During sentencing for his crimes, Clayton's brain scan was introduced in court, showing a large area missing from his frontal lobe as a result of the accident. He was also found to have an IQ of 71, which is considered borderline intellectually disabled. Despite this, he was sentenced to death and executed in March 2015. For defendants like Clayton, for whom severe brain trauma appears to have influenced the exhibition of diminished moral reasoning, questions remain about what the "correct" punishment or legal response should be (Litton 2018). These issues may especially be exacerbated in cases in which the relationships between abnormal brain structure or functioning and immorality are far less clear.

Although human morality shares certain features with nonhuman primates, our commitment-driven morality, or the notion of cooperation due to commitments and feeling guilty if we do not fulfill our obligations to those commitments, is uniquely human (Tomasello 2018). Other than our erect posture and large brain, one of the main ways that we differ from primates is our judgment of human actions as either morally right or wrong, especially in terms of their consequences for others (Ayala 2010). Correspondingly, people who do not show or possess such morality are thought to be more likely to engage in antisocial or violent behavior, as they are unable to recognize the difference between what is morally right or wrong and most often do not care about their actions' consequences for others (Blair 1995).

At the same time, brain areas and networks implicated in morality have recently contributed to a notion of "neuromorality," which suggests that morality is largely neurologically influenced (Dolan 1999; Fumagalli and Priori 2012), and thus, should be understood within a biopsychosocial approach to human behavior (Berryessa and Raine 2018). Alongside recent interest in integrating neuroscience into criminal punishment, neuromorality may pose an extra challenge for questions about how and why we punish in the legal system, as well as our criminal justice response to these offenders more generally. Punishment is thought to accomplish several objectives, and determining the best way forward for sentencing and for the broader criminal justice response to offenders with moral deficits stemming from brain dysfunction is a difficult task (Greene and Cohen 2004).

This chapter explores the potential influences of neuromorality on questions about how and why we punish people under the law. First, we discuss the concept and evaluation of morality, particularly focusing on existing neuroscientific evidence that shows how numerous neural networks contribute to moral decision-making and how damage to specific brain areas can diminish the moral sense that often contributes to the exhibition of antisocial behavior. Then, we detail the ways in which neuromorality may influence traditional conceptions or theories of punishment, including how neuromorality may affect perceptions of moral responsibility in criminal sentencing. Finally, we conclude by addressing how we might integrate notions of neuromorality into modes of criminal sentencing in the future.

2 Morality

2.1 Morality, Moral Dilemmas, and Moral Responsibility

Scientists have proposed that humans have a unique "sixth sense" for morality, with our moral sense developing through human evolution (Ayala 2010). In order to ensure maximum survival in social groups, humans cooperate by engaging in behaviors that increase the social good, do not harm others, and allow for appreciating and empathizing with others' feelings (Mendez 2009). This correspondingly should lead to knowledge about which actions are considered right or wrong, as a way to specifically avoid harming others. According to Mendez (2009), human morality falls into two types: descriptive and normative. Descriptive morality stems from a certain group or society holding a code of conduct as authoritative in matters of right and wrong. This does not solely involve not harming others. It can also include loyalty and accepting authority, such as an individual's own code of conduct or a religion's set of beliefs (Gert and Gert 2020).

Yet normative morality is considered a code of "right" or "wrong" moral actions or prohibitions, independent of descriptive morality, that are thought to be held by all "rational people" who consider the potential costs and benefits of their actions to others. A key example of normative morality is the "Golden Rule," or the notion that we should do to others what we would want others to do to us. With regard to neuromorality, normative morality is typically considered since all "rational people" are expected to universally adhere to it (Mendez 2009).

Moral dilemmas, which are exercises posed to individuals in order to study moral behavior and decision-making, are often used to assess normative morality in research (Christensen et al. 2014). Dilemmas most often measure someone's reaction to witnessing direct physical harm to other people. For example, the Footbridge Dilemma has a test subject imagine that they are standing on a bridge next to a large stranger, and the only way to save five people on a train track below from an otherwise unstoppable trolley is to push the stranger off the bridge in front of it (Greene et al. 2001). The person is asked if they would be willing to throw the large stranger on the tracks to save the others. Similarly, the Trolley Dilemma examines moral responses related to indirect physical harm. In the Trolley Dilemma, a runaway trolley is headed for five people who are on the tracks and will be killed if it is not stopped. However, the person facing the dilemma is told that they can hit a switch that moves the trolley onto an alternative set of tracks where it will only kill one person, and they are asked whether they would make that choice (Nakamura 2013).

Another common type of moral dilemma involves forcing individuals to make moral judgments about moral and non-moral scenarios, as well as utilitarian and non-utilitarian decisions (Hiraishi et al. 2021). Moral scenarios involve describing harm to people, while non-moral scenarios involve describing harm to objects of personal value (Schaich Borg et al. 2006). Utilitarian versus non-utilitarian decisions include either the person involved in the dilemma causing harm to one person while others are able to escape or survive, or indirectly causing harm to several people while one person is allowed to survive (Kuehne et al. 2015). Individuals are asked to assess the utilitarian action, which is to save as many lives as possible by directly causing harm to only one person, compared to causing harm to many.

Ultimately, the concept of morality is thought to lead to the notion of moral responsibility (Applebaum 2005). Broadly speaking, making judgments about whether individuals are morally responsible for their actions, as well as judgments about holding people accountable for those actions, are key parts of morality and moral practices (Talbert 2019). According to the dominant legal approach (Morse 2008, 2011), certain capacities, such as remorse and empathy, must be present and individuals must exercise these capacities through their own agency in order for a person to be judged morally responsible (Glannon 2008).

Morally condemning or praising an individual for their actions requires that the actions come from the person in the requisite way (Smilansky 2001). To be morally judged, a person needs to have relevant control over their decisions and actions. The philosophical debate on free will focuses to a large extent on the legitimation of moral responsibility, and the conviction that we need free will in order to justify its use assumes control as a necessary condition of moral agency (Waller 2015). The crucial question, then, appears to be which kind of control is required for us to hold others morally responsible. To date, this question has led to disparate discussions on the notions of free will and moral responsibility.

For example, compatibilist philosophers such as John Martin Fischer and Mark Ravizza (1998) argue that to “have” control suggests that an individual has free will over their conduct and, thus, the capacity for moral responsibility implies that an individual can exhibit reason-responsive behavior. Reason-responsiveness generally entails that individuals who are unresponsive to rational considerations do not act of their own free will (e.g., individuals with obsessive compulsive disorder or schizophrenia), whereas agents who are responsive to rational considerations do act of their own free will and should be held morally responsible for their behavior (McKenna 2016). Thus, according to compatibilist thinkers, the most prominent conditions necessary to hold an individual morally responsible require that a person's behavior is not out of character for them, or that it resonates with their "authentic self"; that the behavior was not irresistible and conforms to a person's will; that the individual is adequately reason-responsive and able to grasp, apply, and regulate their behavior by moral reasons; and that the person has the capacity to revise and develop a moral character over time (Pereboom 2013).

However, according to free will skeptics, it is unlikely that humans have the sort of free will that would ever justify desert-based moral responsibility (Focquaert et al. 2020a). If actions are causally determined by factors beyond our control, humans cannot be held morally responsible. We cannot legitimate desert-based moral responsibility because causal determinism either precludes the ability to do otherwise or because it is inconsistent with being the source of our actions in the requisite way; having a general capacity to refrain from committing immoral acts is not sufficient. Thus, moral responsibility would only be allowable if we were able to successfully exercise that capacity at the relevant time (Focquaert 2019). Moral responsibility should also be differentiated from causal responsibility, as capacities needed for moral responsibility are not the same as causal powers. The ability to recognize and respond accurately to moral dilemmas is considered moral competence, which is a condition of moral responsibility that differentiates it from causal responsibility (Talbert 2019).

As considered in the next section, there are psychiatric conditions, as well as neurological deficits and dysfunction, that can affect the abilities needed for moral responsibility. This could significantly complicate judgments of related criminal behaviors both inside and outside the legal system.

2.2 The Neurological Basis of Morality

Using brain imaging, other techniques, and the scenarios mentioned above, a growing body of neuroscience literature has found several brain areas implicated in the exhibition of morality over the last several decades. Existing work has focused on two neural regions: the frontal lobe and the temporal lobe.

2.2.1 The Frontal Lobe

The brain's frontal lobe, more commonly known as the prefrontal cortex, is divided into subregions and makes up about 12 percent of total brain volume (McBride et al. 1999). While it is responsible for many functions, the prefrontal cortex's role in executive functioning is arguably the most important in relation to morality. Executive function underlies the ability to act with higher-level cognitive processes, such as working toward goals, recognizing future consequences of actions, determining "good" and "bad," and controlling impulses that may lead to socially unacceptable outcomes. Damage to the prefrontal cortex not only causes problems with moral reasoning, but it also increases the likelihood of antisocial behavior and punishment insensitivity (Raine and Yang 2006; Blair 2007).

Neuroimaging techniques have been commonly used to identify subareas of the prefrontal cortex implicated in morality over the last several decades. Neuroimaging measures activation in certain brain areas through blood oxygenation and flow, as areas of the brain show increased blood flow due to a higher consumption of oxygen when active (Glover 2011). If activation is shown to be increased during a task (i.e., moral dilemmas), then that brain area is implicated in related decision-making, behaviors, and processing.

When examining brain activation, the medial prefrontal cortex appears active in moral dilemmas that involve direct physical harm, including the Footbridge Dilemma. As the medial prefrontal cortex is known to be involved in both empathy and emotion regulation, Greene et al. (2001) suggest that feelings of empathy are likely involved when one chooses to avoid causing direct physical harm to another person. The medial prefrontal cortex has also been implicated in important decision-making processes, especially when they involve recalling whether previous actions were "good" or "bad," as well as connecting emotional responses from the past to specific events (Euston et al. 2012). Similarly, morality involves distinguishing right from wrong in one's own behavior, which can be determined from emotional stimuli in past actions (Young and Tsoi 2013). For example, if a person has been previously punished for doing something "wrong," they remember this past punishment and the emotional valence of that experience when they consider whether to perform the same action again.

Unsurprisingly, deficits in the medial prefrontal cortex may also lead to both immoral and antisocial behaviors. For example, psychopaths, a group of individuals who are commonly known to exhibit impairments to moral judgment and responsibility, also exhibit reduced activity in the medial prefrontal cortex, which can hamper their ability to understand how their actions affect others and how harmed individuals may feel as a result (Raine 2014). Psychopathy is considered a neuropsychiatric disorder that is characterized by a lowered sense of empathy for others, which affects moral reasoning (Glannon 2008). Indeed, the "feeling" of morality differs from rationally understanding what is normatively considered "right" or "wrong." Thus, as psychopaths have a blunted sense of empathy, they are thought to be physically unable to empathize or emotionally connect with the suffering that may result from the harm they cause (Raine 2014).

Further, individuals who lack control over their basic emotional reactions are unable to voluntarily regulate negative affect and cannot properly analyze restraint-producing cues, which can lead to violence as a solution (Davidson et al. 2000). If emotional and memory recall and their connections to decision-making are damaged via the medial prefrontal cortex, an individual can continue to perform antisocial acts without connecting the valence or experience of any previous consequences. Indeed, in one study, the medial prefrontal cortex was found to be significantly activated when subjects retaliated with reactive aggression after being provided with aversive stimuli in a moral dilemma (Lotze et al. 2007).

The ventral prefrontal cortex has also been connected to morality and antisocial behavior. Borg et al. (2006) found that individuals participating in moral scenarios involving intentional harm to other humans showed increased activation in the ventral prefrontal cortex. Similar to the medial prefrontal cortex, the ventral prefrontal cortex is responsible for many different functions, including emotional processing and decision-making (Baars and Gage 2018). As discussed above, deficits in brain areas implicated in emotions and decision-making can render individuals unable to apply moral reasoning to their own behavior (Raine and Yang 2006). For example, Saver and Damasio (1991) found that lesions in the ventromedial prefrontal cortex are related to abnormalities in moral decision-making, especially when it comes to social conduct, moral conduct, and concern for moral rules.

Individuals with damage to the ventromedial prefrontal cortex have also been found to be more willing to judge personal moral violations as acceptable behavior (Ciaramelli et al. 2007). Indeed, patients with damage to the ventromedial prefrontal cortex commonly show difficulties integrating emotion into their decision-making process (Shenhav and Greene 2014). Numerous brain imaging studies have shown reduced activation in the ventral prefrontal cortex in this population, including weakened connectivity to other neural structures in the brain responsible for emotional regulation, which may help to explain their problems with feeling empathy toward others (Motzkin et al. 2011).

More recently, using a neuroscience method called transcranial direct current stimulation, the dorsolateral prefrontal cortex has been identified as an area involved in morality. This method uses electrodes on the scalp to emit a weak electrical current, which can be used to stimulate specific parts of the brain. Kuehne et al. (2015) placed electrodes on the left dorsolateral prefrontal cortex and the right parietal cortex, with stimulation to those areas delivered before and during a moral dilemma that asked participants to react to a situation involving direct physical harm. By stimulating the left dorsolateral prefrontal cortex, participants were found to rate utilitarian actions (i.e., actions that will save as many lives as possible by directly causing harm to one person) as more inappropriate, with their preferences shifting to more non-utilitarian decisions that avoided directly harming another person regardless of the net consequences.

The dorsolateral prefrontal cortex also plays an important role in judging other people's responsibility for their behavior, as well as in situations that demand rule-based knowledge, abstract reasoning, and cognitive control (Pascual et al. 2013). These skills are often used to resolve difficult moral dilemmas that involve personal moral violations (Greene et al. 2004). Indeed, deficits in the dorsolateral prefrontal cortex have been associated with less and counterproductive regulation when making moral decisions, as individuals are less likely to possess the cognitive control needed to override emotional needs in order to avoid personal moral violations. This suggests that the dorsolateral prefrontal cortex is integral in moral and social reasoning, as well as in related personal emotional and moral beliefs, planning, judgment, and decision-making (Kuehne et al. 2015).

Interestingly, certain neurodegenerative disorders of the frontal lobe have been associated with deficits in morality as well. In the early stages, patients with behavioral variant frontotemporal dementia (bvFTD) are plagued with behavioral changes stemming from neurodegeneration of the prefrontal cortex, leading to the loss of empathy, interference with moral decision-making, and difficulty following legal and social norms (Berryessa 2016a, 2016b). Although bvFTD patients display knowledge of moral behavior, they are more likely to approve of moral violations involving direct physical harm. This suggests that their emotional morality is altered as the disease progresses (Mendez and Shapira 2009). Individuals with bvFTD are more likely to commit violent and criminal acts, as compared to other types of dementia or when compared to Alzheimer's disease (Liljegren et al. 2015). Indeed, bvFTD patients show some similar antisocial features to psychopaths, as they are unable to exercise normal emotional and care-based moral judgment because of impairments to their frontotemporal moral network (Berryessa 2016b).

2.2.2 The Temporal Lobe

The temporal lobe, which is located above both the brainstem and the cerebellum, has been found to be significantly associated with morality and related antisociality via skills associated with memory and emotional processing (Patel et al. 2021). In one study involving neuroimaging, Hiraishi et al. (2021) found that both temporal hemispheres were activated in participants during moral judgments of morally good (right hemisphere) and bad (left hemisphere) scenes. A structural neuroimaging study, focusing on temporal lobe epilepsy, also found that those with more frequent occurrences of aggression had statistically significant reductions of gray matter as compared to normal controls and non-aggressive individuals with temporal lobe epilepsy (Brower and Price 2001). Other studies have found decreased activity in the temporal lobe in patients with impulsive aggressive personality behavior (Yang et al. 2008). Damage to the temporal gyrus can also result in lack of concern for others in relation to the consequences of one's actions and difficulty following societal norms, which can lead to an increased risk of antisocial behavior (Raine and Yang 2006).

The temporal-parietal junction, which is where the temporal and parietal lobes meet, is particularly associated with Theory of Mind, a person's intuitive ability to understand other people's emotions, thoughts, beliefs, attitudes, and plans (Fumagalli and Priori 2012). Skills associated with Theory of Mind are commonly used to predict moral development and reasoning, with children developing Theory of Mind in moral dilemmas after about the age of five (Loureiro and de Hollanda 2013). Theory of Mind is thought to foster empathy and emotional reasoning, with activity at the temporal-parietal junction underlying the ability to understand others' emotions (Zaitchik et al. 2010). Indeed, Young et al. (2010) found that mental state reasoning and the ability to understand another person's state of mind when making moral decisions are both hindered when activity in the temporal-parietal junction is disrupted via transcranial magnetic stimulations (using electrical stimulation to stimulate certain areas of the brain to deactivate the polarization of neurons). This may suggest that the temporal-parietal junction is important to moral actions and decision-making by allowing individuals to take the other's perspective when they face potential harm.

The temporal poles and gyrus, which are associated with memory retrieval, are also involved in Theory of Mind. Heekeren et al. (2003) found that people use memory retrieval in order to recall past personal knowledge and experiences when making moral decisions. Theory of Mind allows individuals to know and understand other peoples' emotions and thoughts, and memory retrieval is thought to be a tool to strengthen that understanding in present and future situations involving others. Similarly, the temporal sulcus is also activated when looking at neuroimaging studies involving personal moral judgments, especially when it comes to moral decision-making regarding and emotional reactions toward events or tasks in which one is instructed to cause harm to another person in complex moral dilemmas.

The amygdala, a subcortical structure located within the temporal lobe, also contributes to emotional and behavioral control, as well as memory formation (AbuHasan et al. 2021). Fumagalli and Priori (2012) found that participants showed increased activation in the amygdala when processing moral emotions, evaluating moral judgments, and rating moral pictures. Interestingly, there is evidence that the amygdala may only be active during situations or tasks in which participants perceive the potential for salient harm, such as physical and emotional pain, and when moral emotions form during dilemmas that involve interpersonal harm (FeldmanHall and Mobbs 2015). The amygdala was also the only brain area that showed activation when detecting intentional harm, as opposed to unintentional harm, a neutral event, or personal distress in response to harmful actions toward others (Decety and Howard 2013).

Although these and other brain areas have a hand in directly influencing morality, patterns and interactions of activation between the prefrontal cortex and the temporal lobe, particularly the amygdala, comprise what is known as the moral network. The moral network includes connections between brain areas that are involved in emotional, social, and executive processes, which can include a wide scope of moral processes (FeldmanHall et al. 2014). Specifically, connections between the ventromedial prefrontal cortex and the amygdala are key in the exhibition of care-based morality, which involves moral reasoning about actions that harm others. Blair (2007) argues that the amygdala recognizes the emotional valence of harm incurred by an action or behavior, leading to activity in the ventromedial prefrontal cortex that associates the harmful action with its consequences. This creates a form of stimulus-reinforcement learning that leads individuals to shy away from committing moral transgressions.

Similarly, Shenhav and Greene (2014) found that the ventromedial prefrontal cortex is active in both emotional and utilitarian judgments in moral dilemmas, while the amygdala works to evaluate utilitarian responses as less morally appropriate in these judgments. Research suggests that psychopathic individuals have neural dysfunction to the moral network, including connections between the ventromedial prefrontal cortex and amygdala, which impairs care-based moral decision-making and often leads to a higher risk of exhibiting antisocial behavior (Shirtcliff et al. 2009).

3 Punishment

The overwhelming evidence for neuromorality, or the idea that morality is neurologically influenced, reviewed above may challenge our conceptions of how and why we punish immoral and illegal behavior. Areas of the brain that have been linked to normative morality are also connected to the commission of antisocial and criminal acts, which often leads to contact with the legal system in the form of criminal sentencing. Given this existing neuroscience evidence and the immense costs that offending incurs to our society, many have begun to consider the effect of neuromorality on different forms of punishment (Raine and Yang 2006). Indeed, Riehl (2014) estimates that atypical moral development costs over one trillion dollars annually in the United States, with the cost stemming from the consequences of antisocial and criminal behavior due to a lack of moral sense.

Thus, Raine and Yang (2006) suggest that understanding more about relationships among the brain, morality, and antisocial behavior may lead to more effective punishment alternatives for treating offenders with moral shortcomings in the criminal justice system. Indeed, issues with neuromorality may render traditional forms or goals of criminal sentencing ineffectual. In sentencing theory, there are a variety of contemporary views on potential goals of sentencing that are of relevance, such as retributivism, consequentialist or utilitarian views, mixed or hybrid deontological/utilitarian views, pure procedural justice views, forfeiture of rights views, duty views, communicative views, restorative justice approaches, and feminist views (see Focquaert et al. 2020b). For the purposes of this chapter, we will focus on two main theories, utilitarianism and retributivism, and how problems with morality can affect our understanding of their goals.

3.1 How Neuromorality May Impact Goals of Punishment

3.1.1 Utilitarianism

The goal of utilitarian punishment is to prevent future wrongdoing. Cesare Beccaria famously stated that punishment's purpose is "not that of tormenting or afflicting any sentient creature, nor of undoing a crime already committed," but that the purpose is to prevent the offender "from doing fresh harm to his fellow man and to deter others from doing likewise" (1995, 31). In a system of laws, the utilitarian function of punishment can be achieved through several different sentencing goals, including deterrence, incapacitation, rehabilitation, and restoration. Deterrence stems from the desire to prevent future wrongdoing under the utilitarian model by preventing an individual who has previously offended from committing future crimes, as well as preventing the general population from committing crimes by using an individual offender's punishment as an example (Stafford and Warr 1993). Thus, deterrence can be achieved by both stopping an individual offender from future crime commission and by using the threat of punishment to inhibit others more generally from committing similar offenses. Incapacitation, under the utilitarian model, uses punishment to physically remove offenders from society in order to prevent future offending (Lippman 2006).

Rehabilitation also falls under the utilitarian philosophy, although rehabilitation may conceptually be considered an alternative to punishment as it is currently practiced and not necessarily a punishment in itself (Caruso 2022). Rehabilitative sanctions serve to minimize an offender's likelihood of future crimes by providing treatment and tools to prevent their future offending and then to maximize reintegration back into society, such as the use of specialty courts that aim to tackle an offender's drug or mental health issues through a treatment plan (Castellano and Anderson 2013). Restoration, which takes into consideration the needs of victims and promotes individual responsibility in order for offenders to become better members of society, is often connected to communicative sentencing theories in which punishment allows victims and the community to be made "whole again" (Focquaert et al. 2020b).

When an individual has impaired morality, questions may arise regarding the ways in which they should be punished after the commission of a crime. Utilitarian punishment may ensure that an offender does not reoffend or that individuals in society do not offend, oftentimes because of fear of punishment. Yet, as discussed, there are certain brain areas that, when damaged, abnormal, or otherwise dysfunctional, can lead to pervasive and longstanding issues with morality, antisocial behavior, and the inability to associate emotional valence with potential consequences of bad behavior. For individuals with abnormal neuromorality, existing evidence suggests that they may be largely physically incapable of being deterred by previous punishments or the potential threat of punishment.

For example, psychopaths have damage to the prefrontal cortex and temporal lobe that diminishes their sense of empathy, which both affects morality and subsequent antisocial behavior (Glannon 2008; Blair 2010). However, these same abnormalities in the prefrontal cortex and temporal lobe also affect their sensitivity to, as well as their ability to learn from and fear, punishment (Umbach et al. 2015). Psychopaths are not completely unaware of punishment for violating legal and moral norms, but the significance of morality and others' feelings mean nothing to them and moral concerns are ignored during their decision-making process (Morse 2008; Berryessa and Goodspeed 2019). This combination of deficits makes it difficult to reach goals of deterrence through incapacitation. Oftentimes, morality issues contribute to a lack of consideration in antisociality and attempting to curb future crimes through incapacitation is particularly ineffective. The effects of incapacitation are also lessened through similar brain abnormalities, and this lack of understanding consequences of certain actions can make it difficult for punishment to have its intended effects (Umbach et al. 2015).

Rehabilitative sanctions also suffer from setbacks when considering issues with neuromorality. Morality issues that arise from traumatic brain injuries or other physical abnormalities have the potential for medical treatment and rehabilitation, similar to drug addiction and mental health treatment, to lower the risk of future crime commission (Berryessa 2020). For example, brain tumors and lesions in areas involved in morality and related antisociality could be removed, with affected individuals monitored to see if their moral sense and judgment return to "normal" and their antisocial behavior decreases (Darby et al. 2018).

However, this proves difficult because the full effect of the tumor on both moral and criminal behavior may be unknown. Tumors and other physical injuries can potentially diminish or remove moral reasoning, but it is unlikely that it causes the behavior by itself (Scarpazza et al. 2021). Rehabilitation proves even more questionable as a form of crime prevention when there are no distinct physical dysfunctions to observe. In the case of psychopathy, there is no well-established or known effectual treatment for it or its chief symptoms (Morse 2008; Umbach et al. 2015). Therefore, it is unclear what exactly rehabilitation might look like for those with neuromorality issues and whether there may be any "cure" to contribute to desistance under the rehabilitative model (Choy et al. 2016).

Finally, with regard to restoration, difficulties also arise from marked characteristics associated with abnormal neuromorality. Because restorative justice is centered around fixing relationships between victims and offenders, a key component of this approach involves an offender's eventual admission of responsibility for harm and making amends to "become better" in the future (Latimer et al. 2005). Yet this model may not be effective for those with neuromorality shortcomings, especially if their empathy toward others is stunted due to neural dysfunction. Particularly, psychopaths' quintessential impairments to moral judgment and moral responsibility, coupled with their inability to emotionally connect with the suffering of others, may make restorative punishment models less than ideal and potentially dangerous (Raine 2014).

Individuals with psychopathy could potentially manipulate emotions, especially of their victims, if they were to participate in restorative justice sessions, with their lack of moral responsibility unlikely to lead to any true admission of culpability (Bittick 2020).

3.1.2 Retribution

Retributive punishment can be rationalized through condemnation of an individual and their bad actions; retributivism promotes the idea that offenders need to be punished and "suffer" for their wrongdoings, echoing the notion of "just deserts" to pay for one's crimes (Gerber and Jackson 2013). Indeed, retributivism may be considered a type of societal vengeance to punish an individual for rationally choosing to harm another person. Under the retributive model, a criminal sentence is given based on a determination of what is appropriate or deserved based on a defendant's perceived moral responsibility, intent, the severity of harm incurred by an offense, and their *mens rea*, or "guilty mind" (Weiner et al. 1997). The U.S. model of punishment has traditionally been a highly retributive system, historically reflected with the implementation of long periods of incapacitation, three strikes laws, the use of capital punishment, and other policies intending to keep offenders in prison longer (Subramanian and Shames 2013). Such policies do not focus on using punishment to treat future offending, instead relying on incapacitating offenders to prevent them from contributing to future harm (Lippman 2006).

Similar to utilitarianism, neuromorality also poses several interesting dilemmas for retributivism. As public denunciation is central for retributive punishment, this condemnation demonstrates that wrongdoings will have consequences (Gerber and Jackson 2013). Although the public may be satisfied with a punishment, issues with neuromorality may complicate whether an offender with such deficits can actually understand the right or wrong of their actions, as well as consequences associated with punishment. Further, under retribution, there is the assumption that the person committing the act did so with a sense of intent, personal responsibility, and a guilty mind (Weiner et al. 1997). Neuromorality issues may affect all three of these concepts. Someone with dysfunction to brain areas associated with moral reasoning could intend to commit a certain act but be unable to understand it from the point of view of harming another (Cima et al. 2010). Indeed, personal responsibility reflects the notion that humans chose or are otherwise held accountable for their own actions based on the standards set by our commonly held morality or universally accepted moral code (Jeppsson 2021).

This is congruent with the idea of moral responsibility, which is imperative to justly administering retributive punishment (Jeppsson 2021). If individuals have trouble adhering to a society's moral code due to neural abnormalities, then it could be difficult to consider them fully personally responsible for their actions (Talbert 2019). These deficits also may impact their ability to formulate intent or a guilty mind. Individuals need knowledge that their actions constitute a crime and that committing it is a form of wrongdoing in order for there to be a true intent for those actions; again, individuals who struggle to determine the difference or "feeling" between right and wrong may struggle with having such knowledge (Berryessa 2020; Focquaert et al. 2020b). Thus, if intent or personal responsibility is not be fully present, we may question whether punishing these individuals under the retributive model is just or even "morally" correct.

These issues have been previously discussed in relation to psychopaths and offenders with bvFTD, alongside their issues with care-based morality. If moral judgment of psychopaths is flawed and they are unable to "normally" process moral responsibility for their actions, Umbach et al. (2015) suggest that we may want to reconsider their punishment under the traditional retributive model, because it assumes full intent and moral responsibility. Similarly, offenders with bvFTD develop an absence of moral understanding due to neural defects, and therefore, retributive punishment may be brought into question in terms of moral blameworthiness (Berryessa 2016b). Such questions may also extend to the consideration of retributive punishment of individuals without diagnostically labeled neuromorality issues, but who suffer from similar neural deficits to moral processing (Focquaert et al. 2020b).

The notion of retaliation in retributivism may be less affected by neuromorality. Under the "just deserts" criterion, if someone harms another person, they are punished in a manner that is proportionate to the incurred harm as a form of societal vengeance (Darley et al. 2000). If punishment of this type is predominantly based on the severity of the crime, then handing down sentences only takes the crime's consequences and harm into consideration in punishment. Under this framework, we may question whether morality is even important to such considerations, or whether every offender who commits one class of offense should receive the same punishment no matter the circumstances. If retaliation is considered the default form of retributive punishment following crime commission, then there may be no need for discretion in sentencing, with punishment being one-size-fits-all.

A factor that could further create difficulties when determining retributive punishment is if and when an offender's cognitive understanding of morality might be present, but their emotional ability to "feel" what is right and wrong is damaged. This is especially relevant for psychopaths and patients with bvFTD, since both of these groups have their neural process of empathizing with others during actions involving direct harm significantly damaged (Blair 2007; Mendez and Shapira 2009). Some offenders that have mental deficits fall under the M'Naghten standard of legal insanity, defined as suffering from a mental defect that interfered with their ability to understand the quality of the act at the time of the crime (Feuerstein et al. 2005). However, such a standard is not applicable to those with psychopathy or bvFTD and does not consider offenders who may rationally understand that their actions were wrong but lack the capacity to "feel" the immorality of their actions (Umbach et al. 2015; Berryessa 2016b). Therefore, we may question what should be done with respect to offenders with different types of defects and how this might affect retributive punishment considerations.

Finally, we also may want to reconsider the philosophical underpinnings of retributivism in light of neuromorality. Morally condemning or praising an individual for a decision or action requires that it follow from the person in the requisite way (Smilansky 2001). To count morally, the person needs to have the relevant control over their decisions and actions. The mere possibility of having free will (i.e., the requisite kind of control) is not sufficient to legitimately inflict harm on others. Further, if it is extremely unlikely, theoretically and scientifically, that we possess the kind of free will that legitimates desert-based punishment, then the rationally defensible route is to adopt a cautionary perspective that draws on non-desert related criminal justice procedures that are fair and just to all parties involved (Focquaert et al. 2020a).

However, free will skepticism does not imply that the difference between agents who are reason-responsive and those who are not is irrelevant to how we should treat offenders. On the contrary, free will skeptics most often hold that this difference is crucial for determining the right response to crime. The extent to which individuals are reason-responsive and self-governing impacts the need for and the potential effectiveness of rehabilitative and therapeutic measures, and informs us about the kind of rehabilitation and therapeutic measures that are called for in order to successfully achieve desistance. The free will skeptic's proposal that consideration of basic desert be excluded from our criminal justice approach is consistent with retaining the relevance of reason-responsiveness and self-governance. Although basic desert does not have a role to play in the criminal justice system according to free will skeptics, demanding forward-looking, "take-charge responsibility" (Waller 2015) from offenders who have rational capacities is in line with a criminal justice system that justifies punishment based on deterrence, as well as respects the rights of all parties involved. The kind of free will that is needed to justify basic desert responsibility is not needed to address an individual's capacities for reason-responsiveness and self-governance. Challenging desert-based free will does not imply that one challenges the view that individuals are faced with different degrees of freedom and that individuals differ in the extent to which they are reason-responsive and self-governing. If these capacities are in place, forms of rehabilitation that take rationality into account may be appropriate. Particularly, those offenders who suffer from neuromorality deficits that impair rationality and self-governance would be treated differently and in ways that aim to restore these capacities. Understanding the variety of causes that lead to impairment of these capacities is crucial to determining effective policies for recidivism reduction and rehabilitation (Focquaert et al. 2020b).

Both from a philosophical and biopsychosocial perspective, we suggest a much-needed debate on the desirability of a justice model that focuses on causal responsibility, one's ability to take full responsibility, and a more general forward-looking approach to moral responsibility. For example, criminal accountability for offenders with mental illness in the Netherlands utilizes a multi-point scale, instead of an all-or-nothing model, with defendants potentially considered completely, partially, or not at all accountable for criminal conduct when offending is connected to a mental disorder. A team of psychiatric and other therapeutic experts, along with criminal justice actors, conducts assessments to determine criminal accountability, with many offenders eventually sent to special clinics to receive treatment (Subramanian and Shames 2013). Such a debate may lead to future models tailored for neurological dysfunction, which would aim to achieve victim recovery, restitution, and restoration by implementing forward-looking justice mechanisms (Focquaert 2019).

4 Conclusion

Ultimately, neuromorality raises several questions with regard to determining types or goals of criminal punishment. A growing number of scholars suggest that assigning punishment should be expanded from a "one-size-fits-all" model to consider psychological, biological, and social factors that may have influenced a defendant's actions (Glenn and Raine 2014; Fondacaro and O'Toole 2015; Berryessa 2020), similar to the one described above in the Netherlands.

Although that model presently exists for mental illness, an extension to neurological deficits and issues with neuromorality could potentially be considered within such a model. At the very least, when weighing existing research on brain deficits associated with abnormal neuromorality and how affected individuals may be susceptible to antisocial behavior, we should consider whether those with such impairments truly have full moral responsibility for their actions. We do not advocate for eliminating responsibility for individuals with such brain dysfunction, but we do suggest that rethinking the goals of criminal sentencing for those with neuromorality problems may allow this evidence to be better integrated into punishment decisions that maximize public safety and future successes of offenders and society-at-large.

Future research should dive deeper into potential ways to mitigate deficits that contribute to neuromorality issues and related offending. While disorders like psychopathy still have no known effective treatments, other marked brain deficits that may contribute to problems with moral processing and decision-making, such as bvFTD or traumatic brain injuries, can be slowed or affected by pharmacological medication or forms of neurorehabilitation (Manoochehri and Huey 2012). Finally, if possible, countries with successful practices in handling and treating offenders with mental defects should be studied in order to better determine and formulate future practices in punishment that help to balance the rights and needs of offenders, victims, and society in light of neuromorality.

References

AbuHasan, Qais, Vamsi Reddy, and Waquar Siddiqui. 2021. "Neuroanatomy, Amygdala." In *StatPearls*, January. Treasure Island, FL: StatPearls. https://www.ncbi.nlm.nih.gov/books/NBK537102/.

Applebaum, Barbara. 2005. "In the Name of Morality: Moral Responsibility, Whiteness and Social Justice Education." *Journal of Moral Education* 34, no. 3: 277–90.

Ayala, Francisco J. 2010. "The Difference of Being Human: Morality." *Proceedings of the National Academy of Sciences* 107, no. 2 (May 11): 9015–22.

Baars, Bernard, and Nicole M. Gage. 2018. "Humans Are Social Beings." In *Fundamentals of Cognitive Neuroscience: A Beginner's Guide*, 2nd ed., 321–56. Waltham, MA: Academic.

Beccaria, Cesare. 1995. *On Crimes and Punishments and Other Writings*. Translated by Richard Davies, Virginia Cox, and Richard Bellamy. Edited by Richard Bellamy. Cambridge: Cambridge University Press.

Berryessa, Colleen M. 2016a. "Extralegal Punishment Factors and Judges' Normative Judgments of Moral Responsibility of BvFTD Patients." *AJOB Neuroscience* 7, no. 4: 218–19.

———. 2016b. "Behavioral and Neural Impairments of Frontotemporal Dementia: Potential Implications for Criminal Responsibility and Sentencing." *International Journal of Law and Psychiatry* 46 (June): 1–6.

———. 2020. "Brain Abnormalities Associated with Pedophilic Disorder: Implications for Retribution and Rehabilitation." In *The Routledge Handbook of the Philosophy and Science of Punishment*, edited by Farah Focquaret, Elizabeth Shaw, and Bruce N. Waller, 231–45. London: Routledge.

Berryessa, Colleen, and Taylor Goodspeed. 2019. "The Brain of Dexter Morgan: The Science of Psychopathy in Showtime's Season 8 of *Dexter*." *American Journal of Criminal Justice* 44, no. 6 (December): 962–78.

Berryessa, Colleen M., and Adrian Raine. 2018. "Neurocriminology." In *The Routledge Companion to Criminological Theory and Concepts*, edited by Avi Brisman, Eamonn Carrabine, and Nigel South, 78–82. London: Routledge.

Bittick, Jackson. 2020. "Restorative Justice and Human Nature." *Measure* 4: 37–48.

Blair, Robert J. 1995. "A Cognitive Developmental Approach to Morality: Investigating the Psychopath." *Cognition* 57, no. 1 (October): 1–29.

———. 2007. "The Amygdala and Ventromedial Prefrontal Cortex in Morality and Psychopathy." *Trends in Cognitive Sciences* 11, no. 9 (September): 387–92.

———. 2010. "Neuroimaging of Psychopathy and Antisocial Behavior: A Targeted Review." *Current Psychiatry Reports* 12, no. 1 (February): 76–82.

Brower, Montgomery C., and Bruce H. Price. 2001. "Advances in Neuropsychiatry: Neuropsychiatry of Frontal Lobe Dysfunction in Violent and Criminal Behavior: A Critical Review." *Journal of Neurology, Neurosurgery & Psychiatry* 71, no. 6 (December): 720–26.

Caruso, Gregg D. 2022. "Free Will Skepticism and Criminal Justice: The Public Health-Quarantine Model." In *The Oxford Handbook of Moral Responsibility*, edited by Dana Kay Nelkin and Derk Pereboom, 222–46. Oxford: Oxford University Press.

Castellano, Ursula, and Leon Anderson. 2013. "Mental Health Courts in America: Promise and Challenges." *American Behavioral Scientist* 57, no. 2 (February): 163–73.

Choy, Olivia, Colleen M. Berryessa, and Adrian Raine. 2016. "The Ethics of Biological Interventions on Psychopathic Prisoners." *AJOB Neuroscience* 7, no. 3: 154–56.

Christensen, Julia F., Albert Flexas, Margareta Calabrese, Nadine K. Gut, and Antoni Gomila. 2014. "Moral Judgment Reloaded: A Moral Dilemma Validation Study." *Frontiers in Psychology* 5 (July): 1–18.

Ciaramelli, Elisa, Michela Muccioli, Elisabetta Làdavas, and Giuseppe di Pellegrino. 2007. "Selective Deficit in Personal Moral Judgment Following Damage to Ventromedial Prefrontal Cortex." *Social Cognitive and Affective Neuroscience* 2, no. 2 (June): 84–92.

Cima, Maaike, Franca Tonnaer, and Marc D. Hauser. 2010. "Psychopaths Know Right from Wrong but Don't Care." *Social Cognitive and Affective Neuroscience* 5, no. 1 (January): 59–67.

Darby, R. Ryan, Andreas Horn, Fiery Cushman, and Michael D. Fox. 2018. "Lesion Network Localization of Criminal Behavior." *Proceedings of the National Academy of Sciences* 115, no. 3 (January 16): 601–6.

Darley, John M., Kevin M. Carlsmith, and Paul H. Robinson. 2000. "Incapacitation and Just Deserts as Motives for Punishment." *Law and Human Behavior* 24, no. 6 (December): 659–83.

Davidson, Richard J., Katherine M. Putnam, and Christine L. Larson. 2000. "Dysfunction in the Neural Circuitry of Emotion Regulation—A Possible Prelude to Violence." *Science* 289, no. 5479 (July 28): 591–94.

Decety, Jean, and Lauren H. Howard. 2013. "The Role of Affect in the Neurodevelopment of Morality." *Child Development Perspectives* 7, no. 1 (January): 49–54.

Dolan, Raymond J. 1999. "On the Neurology of Morals." *Nature Neuroscience* 2, no. 11 (November): 927–29.

Euston, David R., Aaron J. Gruber, and Bruce L. McNaughton. 2012. "The Role of Medial Prefrontal Cortex in Memory and Decision Making." *Neuron* 76, no. 6 (December): 1057–70.

FeldmanHall, O., and D. Mobbs. 2015. "A Neural Network for Moral Decision Making." In *Brain Mapping: An Encyclopedic Reference*, edited by Arthur W. Toga and M. D. Lieberman, 205–10. Oxford: Elsevier.

FeldmanHall, Oriel, Dean Mobbs, and Tim Dalgleish. 2014. "Deconstructing the Brain's Moral Network: Dissociable Functionality between the Temporoparietal Junction and Ventro-Medial Prefrontal Cortex." *Social Cognitive and Affective Neuroscience* 9, no. 3 (March): 297–306.

Feuerstein, Seth, Frank Fortunati, Charles A. Morgan, Vladimir Coric, Humberto Temporini, and Steven Southwick. 2005. "The Insanity Defense." *Psychiatry* 2, no. 9: (September) 24–25.

Fischer, John Martin, and Mark Ravizza. 1998. *Responsibility and Control: A Theory of Moral Responsibility*. Cambridge: Cambridge University Press.

Focquaert, Farah. 2019. "Free Will Skepticism and Criminal Punishment: A Preliminary Ethical Analysis." In *Free Will Skepticism in Law and Society: Challenging Retributive Justice*, edited by Elizabeth Shaw, Gregg D. Caruso, and Derk Pereboom, 207–36. Cambridge: Cambridge University Press.

Focquaert, Farah, Gregg Caruso, Elizabeth Shaw, and Derk Pereboom. 2020a. "Justice without Retribution: Interdisciplinary Perspectives, Stakeholder Views and Practical Implications." *Neuroethics* 13, no. 1 (April): 1–3.

Focquaert, Farah, Elizabeth Shaw, and Bruce N. Waller, eds. 2020b. *The Routledge Handbook of the Philosophy and Science of Punishment*. New York: Routledge.

Fondacaro, Mark R., and Megan J. O'Toole. 2015. "American Punitiveness and Mass Incarceration." *New Criminal Law Review* 18, no. 4 (Fall): 477–509.

Fumagalli, Manuela, and Alberto Priori. 2012. "Functional and Clinical Neuroanatomy of Morality." *Brain* 135, no. 7 (July): 2006–21.

Gerber, Monica M., and Jonathan Jackson. 2013. "Retribution as Revenge and Retribution as Just Deserts." *Social Justice Research* 26, no. 1 (January): 61–80.

Gert, Bernard, and Joshua Gert. 2020. "The Definition of Morality." *Stanford Encyclopedia of Philosophy* (Fall 2020 edition), edited by Edward N. Zalta. https://plato.stanford.edu/archives/fall2020/entries/morality-definition/.

Glannon, Walter. 2008. "Moral Responsibility and the Psychopath." *Neuroethics* 1, no. 3 (April): 158–66.

Glenn, Andrea L., and Adrian Raine. 2014. "Neurocriminology: Implications for the Punishment, Prediction and Prevention of Criminal Behaviour." *Nature Reviews Neuroscience* 15, no. 1 (January): 54–63.

Glover, Gary H. 2011. "Overview of Functional Magnetic Resonance Imaging." *Neurosurgery Clinics of North America* 22, no. 2 (April): 133–39.

Greene, Joshua, and Jonathan Cohen. 2004. "For the Law, Neuroscience Changes Nothing and Everything." *Philosophical Transactions: Biological Sciences* 359, no. 1451 (November 29): 1775–85.

Greene, Joshua D., Leigh E. Nystrom, Andrew D. Engell, John M. Darley, and Jonathan D. Cohen. 2004. "The Neural Bases of Cognitive Conflict and Control in Moral Judgment." *Neuron* 44, no. 2 (October): 389–400.

Greene, Joshua D., R. Brian Sommerville, Leigh E. Nystrom, John M. Darley, and Jonathan D. Cohen. 2001. "An FMRI Investigation of Emotional Engagement in Moral Judgment." *Science* 293, no. 5537 (September 14): 2105–8.

Heekeren, Hauke R., Isabell Wartenburger, Helge Schmidt, Hans-Peter Schwintowski, and Arno Villringer. 2003. "An FMRI Study of Simple Ethical Decision-Making." *NeuroReport* 14, no. 9 (July): 1215–19.

Hiraishi, Hirotoshi, Takashi Ikeda, Daisuke N. Saito, Chiaki Hasegawa, Sachiko Kitagawa, Tetsuya Takahashi, Mitsuru Kikuchi, and Yasuomi Ouchi. 2021. "Regional and Temporal Differences in Brain Activity with Morally Good or Bad Judgments in Men: A Magnetoencephalography Study." *Frontiers in Neuroscience* 15 (April). https://www.frontiersin.org/articles/10.3389/fnins.2021.596711/full.

Jeppsson, Sofia M. I. 2021. "Retributivism, Justification and Credence: The Epistemic Argument Revisited." *Neuroethics* 14, no. 2 (July): 177–90.

Kuehne, Maria, Kai Heimrath, Hans-Jochen Heinze, and Tino Zaehle. 2015. "Transcranial Direct Current Stimulation of the Left Dorsolateral Prefrontal Cortex Shifts Preference of Moral Judgments." *PLOS ONE* 10, no. 5 (May): e0127061.

Latimer, Jeff, Craig Dowden, and Danielle Muise. 2005. "The Effectiveness of Restorative Justice Practices: A Meta-Analysis." *Prison Journal* 85, no. 2 (June): 127–44.

Liljegren, Madeleine, Georges Naasan, Julia Temlett, David C. Perry, Katherine P. Rankin, Jennifer Merrilees, Lea T. Grinberg, William W. Seeley, Elisabet Englund, and Bruce L. Miller. 2015. "Criminal Behavior in Frontotemporal Dementia and Alzheimer Disease." *JAMA Neurology* 72, no. 3 (March): 295–300.

Lippman, Matthew. 2006. "Punishment and Sentencing." In *Contemporary Criminal Law: Concepts, Cases, and Controversies*, edited by Matthew Lippman, 2nd ed., 55–86. Thousand Oaks, CA: Sage.

Litton, Paul. 2018. "Traumatic Brain Injury and a Divergence between Moral and Criminal Responsibility." *Duquesne Law Review* 56, no. 1 (Winter): 35–55.

Lotze, M., R. Veit, S. Anders, and N. Birbaumer. 2007. "Evidence for a Different Role of the Ventral and Dorsal Medial Prefrontal Cortex for Social Reactive Aggression: An Interactive FMRI Study." *NeuroImage* 34, no. 1 (January): 470–78.

Loureiro, Carolina Piazzarollo, and Debora de Hollanda Souza. 2013. "The Relationship between Theory of Mind and Moral Development in Preschool Children." *Paidéia* 23, no. 54 (April): 93–101.

Manoochehri, Masood, and Edward D. Huey. 2012. "Diagnosis and Management of Behavioral Issues in Frontotemporal Dementia." *Current Neurology and Neuroscience Reports* 12, no. 5 (October): 528–36.

McBride, Thomas, Steve E. Arnold, and Ruben C. Gur. 1999. "A Comparative Volumetric Analysis of the Prefrontal Cortex in Human and Baboon MRI." *Brain, Behavior and Evolution* 54, no. 3 (September): 159–66.

McKenna, Michael. 2016. "Reasons-Responsive Theories of Freedom." In *The Routledge Companion to Free Will*, edited by Kevin Timpe, Meghan Griffith, and Neil Levy, 27–40. London: Routledge.

Mendez, Mario F. 2009. "The Neurobiology of Moral Behavior: Review and Neuropsychiatric Implications." *CNS Spectrums* 14, no. 11 (November): 608–20.

Mendez, Mario F., and Jill S. Shapira. 2009. "Altered Emotional Morality in Frontotemporal Dementia." *Cognitive Neuropsychiatry* 14, no. 3 (May): 165–79.

Morse, Stephen J. 2008. "Psychopathy and Criminal Responsibility." *Neuroethics* 1, no. 3 (July): 205–12.

———. 2011. "Mental Disorder and Criminal Law." *Journal of Criminal Law and Criminology* 101, no. 3 (Summer): 885–968.

Motzkin, Julian C., Joseph P. Newman, Kent A. Kiehl, and Michael Koenigs. 2011. "Reduced Prefrontal Connectivity in Psychopathy." *Journal of Neuroscience* 31, no. 48 (November 30): 17348–57.

Nakamura, Kuninori. 2013. "A Closer Look at Moral Dilemmas: Latent Dimensions of Morality and the Difference between Trolley and Footbridge Dilemmas." *Thinking and Reasoning* 19, no. 2 (May): 178–204.

Pascual, Leo, David Gallardo-Pujol, and Paulo Rodrigues. 2013. "How Does Morality Work in the Brain? A Functional and Structural Perspective of Moral Behavior." *Frontiers in Integrative Neuroscience* 7 (September). https://www.frontiersin.org/articles/10.3389/fnint.2013.00065/full.

Patel, Anand, Grace Marie Nicole R. Biso, and James B. Fowler. 2021. "Neuroanatomy, Temporal Lobe." In *StatPearls*, January. Treasure Island, FL: StatPearls. https://www.ncbi.nlm.nih.gov/books/NBK519512/.

Pereboom, Derk. 2013. "Free Will Skepticism and Criminal Punishment." In *The Future of Punishment*, edited by Thomas A. Nadelhoffer, 49–78. Oxford: Oxford University Press.

Raine, Adrian. 2014. *The Anatomy of Violence: The Biological Roots of Crime*. New York: Vintage.

Raine, Adrian, and Yaling Yang. 2006. "Neural Foundations to Moral Reasoning and Antisocial Behavior." *Social Cognitive and Affective Neuroscience* 1, no. 3 (December): 203–13.

Riehl, John. 2014. "Arrested Development: How Brain Damage Impairs Moral Judgment." *Iowa Now*, March 28. https://now.uiowa.edu/2014/03/arrested-development-how-brain-damage-impairs-moral-judgment.

Saver, Jeffrey L., and Antonio R. Damasio. 1991. "Preserved Access and Processing of Social Knowledge in a Patient with Acquired Sociopathy Due to Ventromedial Frontal Damage." *Neuropsychologia* 29, no. 12 (December): 1241–49.

Scarpazza, Cristina, Colleen M. Berryessa, and Farah Focquaert. 2021. "A Biopsychosocial Approach to Idiopathic versus Acquired Pedophilia: What Do We Know and How Do We Proceed Legally and Ethically?" In *Neurolaw: Advances in Neuroscience, Justice & Security*, edited by Sjors Ligthart, Dave van Toor, Tijs Kooijmans, Thomas Douglas, and Gerben Meynen, 145–78. Cham, Switzerland: Palgrave Macmillan.

Schaich Borg, Jana, Catherine Hynes, John Van Horn, Scott Grafton, and Walter Sinnott-Armstrong. 2006. "Consequences, Action, and Intention as Factors in Moral Judgments: An FMRI Investigation." *Journal of Cognitive Neuroscience* 18, no. 5 (May): 803–17.

Shenhav, Amitai, and Joshua D. Greene. 2014. "Integrative Moral Judgment: Dissociating the Roles of the Amygdala and Ventromedial Prefrontal Cortex." *Journal of Neuroscience* 34, no. 13 (March 26): 4741–49.

Shirtcliff, Elizabeth A., Michael J. Vitacco, Alexander R. Graf, Andrew J. Gostisha, Jenna L. Merz, and Carolyn Zahn-Waxler. 2009. "Neurobiology of Empathy and Callousness: Implications for the Development of Antisocial Behavior." *Behavioral Sciences & the Law* 27, no. 2 (March-April): 137–71.

Smilansky, Saul. 2001. "Free Will: From Nature to Illusion." *Proceedings of the Aristotelian Society* 101, no. 1 (June): 71–95.

Stafford, Mark C., and Mark Warr. 1993. "A Reconceptualization of General and Specific Deterrence." *Journal of Research in Crime and Delinquency* 30, no. 2 (May): 123–35.

Subramanian, Ram, and Alison Shames. 2013. *Sentencing and Prison Practices in Germany and the Netherlands: Implications for the United States*. Vera Institute of Justice, October. https://www.vera.org/downloads/Publications/sentencing-and-prison-practices-in-germany-and-the-netherlands-implications-for-the-united-states/legacy_downloads/european-american-prison-report-v3.pdf.

Talbert, Matthew. 2019. "Moral Responsibility." *Stanford Encyclopedia of Philosophy* (Winter 2019 edition), edited by Edward N. Zalta. https://plato.stanford.edu/entries/moral-responsibility/.

Tomasello, Michael. 2018. "Precís of a Natural History of Human Morality." *Philosophical Psychology* 31, no. 5 (August): 661–68.

Umbach, Rebecca, Colleen M. Berryessa, and Adrian Raine. 2015. "Brain Imaging Research on Psychopathy: Implications for Punishment, Prediction, and Treatment in Youth and Adults." *Journal of Criminal Justice* 43, no. 4 (July–August): 295–306.

Waller, Bruce N. 2015. *The Stubborn System of Moral Responsibility*. Cambridge, MA: MIT Press.

Weiner, Bernard, Sandra Graham, and Christine Reyna. 1997. "An Attributional Examination of Retributive versus Utilitarian Philosophies of Punishment." *Social Justice Research* 10, no. 4 (December): 431–52.

Yang, Yaling, Andrea L. Glenn, and Adrian Raine. 2008. "Brain Abnormalities in Antisocial Individuals: Implications for the Law." *Behavioral Sciences & the Law* 26, no. 1 (January): 65–83.

Young, Liane, Joan Albert Camprodon, Marc Hauser, Alvaro Pascual-Leone, and Rebecca Saxe. 2010. "Disruption of the Right Temporoparietal Junction with Transcranial Magnetic Stimulation Reduces the Role of Beliefs in Moral Judgments." *Proceedings of the National Academy of Sciences* 107, no. 15 (April 13): 6753–58.

Young, Liane, and Lily Tsoi. 2013. "When Mental States Matter, When They Don't, and What That Means for Morality." *Social and Personality Psychology Compass* 7, no. 8 (August): 585–604.

Zaitchik, Deborah, Caren Walker, Saul Miller, Pete LaViolette, Eric Feczko, and Bradford C. Dickerson. 2010. "Mental State Attribution and the Temporoparietal Junction: An FMRI Study Comparing Belief, Emotion, and Perception." *Neuropsychologia* 48, no. 9 (July): 2528–36.

21

Punishment without Blame, Shame, or Just Deserts

Bruce N. Waller

Punishment is fundamentally unfair, never justly deserved, and cannot be eliminated. That disturbing claim violates two powerful convictions: a deep but largely nonconscious *belief in a just world*, and the cherished philosophical principle that *ought implies can*. Both convictions are false and destructive, and—borrowing a line from T. S. Eliot—both are "believed in as the most reliable—and therefore the fittest for renunciation."

No one is ever morally responsible (Waller 2011) and no one justly deserves punishment. But in our unjust world punishment cannot be eliminated. It can and should be minimized, but it is sometimes required as a deterrent, and some people must be coercively isolated to prevent them from inflicting greater harm. But it is essential that we recognize that the punishment we must inflict is an injustice rather than an exercise of virtue.

Unjust punishment is wrong, though unavoidable; but like many wrongs, the harm is exacerbated by the attempt to cover it up. That cover-up is especially injurious when it is designed to hide the truth from ourselves. Two powerful and mutually supportive beliefs are the chief instruments for obscuring the troubling necessity of unjust punishment: Belief in a Just World (BJW) commonly exerts its subtle influence without our awareness, while belief in moral responsibility operates consciously—even obsessively—in support of belief in a just world.

B. N. Waller (✉)
Youngstown State University, Youngstown, OH, USA
e-mail: bnwaller@ysu.edu

© The Author(s), under exclusive license to Springer Nature Switzerland AG 2023

M. C. Altman (ed.), *The Palgrave Handbook on the Philosophy of Punishment*, Palgrave Handbooks in the Philosophy of Law, https://doi.org/10.1007/978-3-031-11874-6_21

1 Belief in a Just World

We must sometimes inflict punishment, and punishment is always unjust. Our immediate reaction to that claim is that it *cannot* be true. We *ought* to avoid acting unjustly, and therefore we *can* avoid unjust acts. "Ought implies can" is a comforting philosophical shibboleth backed by the authority of Kant and the nonconscious conviction that we live in a just world. Its authority and intuitive appeal notwithstanding, it is false. Why is it so difficult to acknowledge that—in our imperfect world—there are times when we cannot avoid participating in unjust acts? Because Belief in a Just World shapes our view of the world. Studied in many contexts and cultures, BJW typically flies under our conscious scrutiny and is protected by its central role in a sophisticated and pervasive belief *system* (Waller 2015b). BJW is difficult to confront and even harder to reject.

Adrian Furnham supplies this brief description of belief in a just world: "The BJW asserts that, quite justly, good things tend to happen to good people and bad things to bad people despite the fact that this is patently not the case" (2003, 795). A leading researcher into belief in a just world, Melvin Lerner (1980), characterizes the belief as a "fundamental delusion" that operates nonconsciously and exerts a subtle but powerful influence on our beliefs and judgments. BJW is not a belief that survives close examination. We do not live in a just world. Slaves suffered cruel exploitation while their "masters" enjoyed wealth, privilege, and respect: in the U.S., five of the first six Presidents were slaveholders and champions of the brutal system of slavery, including the venerated "Father of our country." The world is full of innocent refugees fleeing wars, "ethnic cleansing," drought, and poverty. Innocent children die from starvation and excruciating diseases while other children suffer horrible abuse. Wrongly convicted people are imprisoned for years and even lifetimes. Innocent women are the victims of brutal assaults and rapes. Despised poor people suffer the effects of environmental toxins while the elite who profit from environmental degradation bask in luxury and acclaim.

The power and resilience of our nonconscious belief in a just world can be measured by the desperate efforts to preserve it. How can the suffering of innocent children be reconciled with belief in a just world? The children are not really innocent: they are infected with original sin and therefore are receiving their just deserts in the just world created by a just God. Innocent women are brutally raped, injured, traumatized; how can innocent people suffer such injustice in our just world? The rape victims must not have been so innocent: as extensively studied by BJW researchers (Wagstaff 1983; Furnham and

Gunter 1984; Harper and Manasse 1992; Dalbert and Yamauchi 1994; Montada 1998), often victims of rape are further victimized by judgments (in protection of BJW) that they were promiscuous, drank too much, "led him on," and brought their suffering on themselves by their own bad acts. The impoverished "have only themselves to blame," for they live in a "land of opportunity" and their poverty is the result of their own indolence, while the wealthy are receiving their just deserts for their hard work and creative efforts.

It is not only the "folk" and the theologians who cling to belief in a just world: philosophers have struggled for centuries to fashion a just world in the face of injustice and unfairness. As Bernard Williams describes this central theme in the history of philosophy: "Plato, Aristotle, Kant, Hegel are all on the same side, all believing in one way or another that the universe or history or the structure of human reason can, when properly understood, yield a pattern that makes sense of human life and human aspirations" (1993, 163), a pattern that makes the world *just*. Moral responsibility is a powerful philosophical tool for constructing a just world, and it forms the nucleus of the pervasive philosophical system constructed for that purpose. Both the suffering and the privileged are receiving their just deserts, and—when seen through the lens of moral responsibility—the world is truly just.

2 Moral Responsibility

Moral responsibility is the essential guardian of BJW. While belief in the sinfulness of children and the wickedness of rape victims is a painful illustration of the power of belief in a just world, it is the tenacious devotion to moral responsibility that manifests the resilience and strength of BJW. The most intuitive and popular foundation for moral responsibility is appeal to a first cause or *causa sui* power, and it is no accident that in the United States—a culture with an exceptionally strong commitment to individual moral responsibility (Cavadino and Dignan 2006a, 51)—the implausible belief in the "self-made man" is an article of common faith. But *causa sui* self-making powers have a long history. In 1486 Pico della Mirandola proposed that God grants to humans a special unique power to *make themselves*: "Thou, constrained by no limits, in accordance with thine own free will, in whose hand We have placed thee, shalt ordain for thyself the limits of thy nature" (1948, 225). Five centuries later C. A. Campbell proposed a similar "contra-causal" free choice as the basis for moral responsibility: a free "*creative activity*, in which … nothing determines the act save the agent's doing of it" (1957, 177). Roderick Chisholm based moral responsibility on our possession of "a prerogative which some would attribute only to God: each of us, when we really act, is a prime mover unmoved" (1982, 32). For Jean-Paul Sartre the special power of free will that makes us morally responsible for ourselves and all our choices is the power of self-created "being for itself": a godlike first cause that "escapes contingency by being its own foundation, the *Ens causa sui*, which religions call God" (1958, 615). Even if we allow miraculous powers, there remains the fundamental problem of *who* is making these absolutely unqualified, self-determining, "make yourself out of nothing" choices, and on what basis that ethereal pre-existent being is making "choices." Friedrich Nietzsche laid bare the absurdity—even the incoherence—of the *causa sui* model: "The *causa sui* is the best self-contradiction that has been conceived so far, it is a sort of rape and perversion of logic," requiring that one "pull oneself up into existence by the hair, out of the swamps of nothingness" (1966, §21 [p. 28]).

Robert Kane (2007) constructs a heroic version of self-making that eschews miracles while drawing on chaos theory to amplify the effects of quantum indeterminacy. Adina Roskies proposes a more modest account of self-making: "It is not necessary to create oneself out of whole cloth. Continual shaping of the given over time establishes sufficient control of the agent to suffice as a grounding kind of self-causation" (2012, 338). Even Daniel Dennett—with his rich understanding of the complex and subtle causes of our character and behavior—is beguiled by the self-making model:

> I take responsibility for any thing I make and then inflict upon the general public; if my soup causes food poisoning … I, the manufacturer, am to blame. … Common wisdom has it that much the same rationale grounds personal responsibility; I have created and unleashed an agent who is myself; if its acts produce harm, the manufacturer is held responsible. I think this common wisdom is indeed wisdom. (1984, 85)

Self-making may seem like wisdom when under the influence of belief in a just world. But as appealing as self-making in its various guises may be, it runs aground on the problem of *who* is doing the self-making and what strengths and weaknesses various self-makers bring to their distinctly different "raw materials" in their radically divergent self-making "workshops" (some affluent workshops with wonderful support, others with few resources and many perils).

Causa sui miracles are out of fashion among contemporary philosophers, but the commitment to moral responsibility endures. Appeals to a near-miraculous power of conscious reason is championed by Christine Korsgaard, a contemporary Kantian: "When you deliberate, when you determine your own causality, it is as if there is something over and above all your incentives, something which is *you*, and which chooses which incentive to act on" (2009, 72). Harry Frankfurt's higher-order reflection unites an exalted account of reason with a special *willed* "resounding commitment" (1971, 16). Appeal to super powers of reason remains philosophically popular, notwithstanding the psychological evidence demonstrating the limits and frailties of human reason (Cacioppo and Petty 1982; Cacioppo et al. 1996; Haidt 2001; Wilson 2002; Kahneman 2011; Haidt 2012; Davies 2013; Davies 2020).

P. F. Strawson's (1982) question-begging model *assumes* moral responsibility as the default position (and "exempts" only the severely demented and incompetent). The result is the *reductio ad absurdum* that the universal denial of moral responsibility implies universal derangement—and consequently, a rejection of all "participant reactive attitudes" (such as resentment and love). *Within* the moral responsibility system everyone is morally responsible *unless* they have some special excuse of exemption. But those who reject the moral responsibility system do not start from the assumption of moral responsibility and then extend and enlarge the range of excuses until it covers everyone. They argue that moral responsibility requires conditions that can never be met (in the absence of miracles) and that rigorous examination of the deep causes of our behavior makes claims of moral responsibility implausible if not incoherent. When one starts with the assumption of moral responsibility, it is not surprising that denial of moral responsibility results in absurdity (Waller 2020, 95–97).

A variety of approaches "redefine" moral responsibility into something that no one doubts. Some claim we are morally responsible when we can give an *account* of our acts; but as Jonathan Haidt (2012, 46) notes, our System 2 deliberative thought functions as a "press agent" that readily contrives socially acceptable "explanations" for whatever we do. Or we are morally responsible when we can place our choices in a narrative (Fischer 2009, 157). But we are all charmed by "promiscuous teleology" (Kelemen 2003; Kelemen and Rosset 2009; Kelemen et al. 2013), and making up purposeful narrative explanations is easy: the challenge is resisting the siren song of teleological explanation. "Instrumentalists" (such as Vargas 2013; Jefferson 2019; McGeer 2019) count all who can be influenced or shaped by the instruments of blame and moral evaluation as morally responsible; but the unfortunate fact that many people have been shaped (and misshapen) by blame and guilt is not grounds for believing they are morally responsible.

Other champions of moral responsibility simply assume moral responsibility as something indubitable. Peter Van Inwagen provides a clear example of such absolute commitment to moral responsibility: "If incompatibilism is true, then either determinism or the free-will thesis is false. To deny the free-will thesis is to deny the existence of moral responsibility, which would be absurd" (1983, 223). Adina Roskies takes a similar line, appealing to "the most vivid of our intuitions": "We ought to explore the possibility that freedom is a concept derivative on more robust intuitions about responsibility rather than vice versa. … Doing so preserves perhaps the most vivid of our intuitions about human behavior: that, given certain circumstances, we are responsible for our choices and actions" (2014, 121). Justin Coates and Neal Tognazzini pursue a similar path: "Blame is not only the natural human response to actions that display a kind of interpersonally significant ill will or disregard, but it is also the lens through which we can even know what counts as a free action in the first place" (2013, 6).

Free will was the traditional foundation for moral responsibility, but there are daunting difficulties in finding a *nonmiraculous* account of free will that can carry that weight. It is "absurd" to deny moral responsibility, so philosophers conclude that, because we *must* be morally responsible, therefore we *must* (somehow) meet the conditions for free will (whatever they are). The splendid free will steed that propelled the moral responsibility wagon has foundered, so now philosophers load the worn out free will horse aboard the broken-down moral responsibility wagon and insist it has become a horseless carriage.

When we look deeper into the causes of behavior, that inquiry destroys the basis for moral responsibility: we soon discover critical causal factors that were not under our control and were basically a matter of good or bad fortune (Levy 2011; Waller 2011). Preserving belief in moral responsibility requires blocking inquiry (Waller 2015b, 233–51). In his desperate but creative effort to save moral responsibility, John Martin Fischer makes a virtue of that necessity. Rather than seeking to understand the deeper causes of behavior, we should reject the "metaphysical megalomania" that insists on "ultimate" responsibility (2012, 171), and instead embrace the "middle way" (Fischer likens it to the wisdom of the Buddhist Middle Path of moderation):

> I believe that our moral responsibility requires that we play the cards that are dealt us; but surely this does not require that we deal ourselves the cards, or that we own the factory that made the cards (as well as all of the inputs into the manufacturing process), and so forth. (21)

But "the cards that are dealt us" include our self-control, our reflective powers, and the many conditions that shaped our values and abilities. If we refuse to consider those, then moral responsibility may seem to make sense; indeed, we may even convince ourselves that we are self-made.

Some of the futile arguments for moral responsibility would make Leibniz blush, and such efforts would have been abandoned long ago were it not that the nonconscious belief in a just world requires the support of moral responsibility. But one current trend takes a different approach, claiming that we should believe in moral responsibility because "it works" (Dennett 1984); or we should *pretend* to believe in moral responsibility because the *illusion* is valuable (Smilansky 2000); or—the "neoretributivist" (Green 2014, 347) line favored by Herbert Morris (1968), C. S. Lewis (1971), and Michael Moore (1997)—commitment to moral responsibility protects dignity and liberty. In short, moral responsibility should be believed because of its practical social and psychological benefits, including benefits for those blamed: they develop more "responsible" behavior (Dennett 1984, 163–64), strengthen their skills of moral rule-following (McGeer 2019), maintain their self-respect (Smilansky 2011, 228), and preserve their godlike status (Lewis 1971).

3 Moral Responsibility and Criminal Justice

The moral responsibility system provides three "benefits": it preserves BJW, makes us feel good about our privileges, and assuages our concern with the injustice of punishment. The price for such benefits is paid in promoting and maintaining moral wrongs. The U.S. system of criminal justice—like the larger U.S. culture—is saturated with belief in moral responsibility (*Steward Machine Company v. Davis*, 301 U.S. 548 [1937], 590; *Morissette v. United States*, 342 U.S. 246 [1952], 250; *United States v. Grayson*, 438 U.S. 41 [1978], 52; Kadish 1987, 198; Scalia 2002, 19), and the wrongs of moral responsibility are writ large in that system.

When we *look hard* at the actual American criminal justice system—not as we imagine it to be, blinded by the myth of America as an exemplary society with liberty and justice for all—then the gross unfairness is obvious. The U.S. *adversarial system* is a crude instrument for seeking justice, even at its best on a level playing field; at its worst—the more common situation, when one adversary has disproportionate power—it is an instrument of injustice. It heavily favors the wealthy and powerful and is stacked against the poor and powerless—which explains why this unjust system has endured for so long. The prosecution has a legal and forensic and investigative team, while many criminal defendants have only a public defender balancing an enormous caseload who has neither the time nor the resources to prepare an adequate defense. As William Stuntz notes: "In an adversarial justice system, the government can more easily convict a poor and innocent defendant than a rich and innocent one—perhaps more easily than a rich and guilty one" (2008, 47; see also Menkel-Meadow 1996; Findley 2011, 912; Slobogin 2014). In medieval trial by combat, a just God intervened to guarantee victory to the side of truth and justice. In the American trial by combat, we are eager to believe that in our just world—and in our exceptionally just and virtuous country—the adversarial contest will be won by the side of truth and justice. The two beliefs are equally implausible. This unfair adversarial contest is not confined to the courtroom, but also operates in the setting in which some 95 percent of criminal charges are settled: in plea bargaining between the defendant (and his or her overworked public defender) and the prosecutor. The prosecutor offers a take-it-or-leave-it plea deal. The reckless defendant who rejects the deal and demands a trial must pay the notorious "trial tax": the prosecution will tack on more charges, including even the draconian "three strikes" law that places the defendant at risk for life imprisonment. That is the price for claiming the "right" to a trial by jury, and also the reason many innocent defendants make the practical choice to plead guilty.

The unfairness of the "adversarial" contest between grossly uneven contestants is only one of many problems. The U.S. cash bail system—dominated by commercial bail bondsmen—is an almost uniquely American injustice (the only other country using that system is the Philippines, installed when it was a U.S. colony during the first half of the twentieth century). Thousands of people who have been arrested but *not* convicted of any crime are currently incarcerated because they lack the funds to post a cash bail. The poor are held in jail, while the affluent post bail and go free (Olderman 2021). On a typical day in 2013 (Drug Policy Alliance 2014), there were more than ten thousand people in New Jersey jails who were awaiting trial, and their average wait was ten months. 40 percent of these lacked the funds to post bail, and a majority were charged with nonviolent offenses.

The U.S. bail system jails people for the crime of being poor. But that is only the first step in a process that wrongly convicts thousands of innocent people, with little concern about the level of injustice. One major source of wrongful convictions is flawed forensic evidence. False forensic evidence has been generated by city crime labs in Chicago, Cleveland, Detroit, Houston, Oklahoma City, Omaha, San Francisco, and Washington; state crime labs in California, Illinois, Maryland, Mississippi, North Carolina, Virginia, and West Virginia; the FBI crime lab; and the crime lab of the U.S. Army (Balko 2011). And these are only the extreme cases that could not be covered up, the tiny tip of an enormous system of distorted "evidence." In the adversarial system, too many prosecutors knowingly present flawed evidence in an effort to "win" a conviction. As Bennett Gershman points out, "Documented cases of open and notorious misconduct by forensic laboratories and of rogue experts giving fraudulent testimony strongly suggest that many prosecutors are fully aware that the laboratory and the expert have been engaging in a long-standing practice and pattern of misconduct" (2003, 26–27).

Of all the unjust practices in the U.S. moral responsibility system of criminal justice, the most blatantly abusive is the common use of *jailhouse informants* to secure convictions: the use of perjured *purchased* testimony. An inmate awaiting trial or sentencing contacts the District Attorney's office and offers to testify against someone suspected of a crime: the jailhouse informant will testify that the accused person bragged or confessed that he committed the crime *if* the District Attorney will drop or reduce the charges against the informant. The informant gets a huge break, the prosecutor gets powerful perjured testimony to shore up a weak case, and the informant's unfortunate victim gets convicted. Ninth Circuit Court Justice Stephen Trott offers a clear description of the corrupt and widely known practice: "Defendants or suspects with nothing to sell sometimes embark on a methodical journey to manufacture evidence and to create something of value, setting up and betraying friends, relatives, and cellmates alike" (quoted in Raeder 2007, 1419). One polished jailhouse informant heard so many "confessions" that he was nicknamed "The Monsignor." Myrna Raeder poses a painful rhetorical question: "Is it really arguable that prosecutors do not know that jailhouse informants who repeatedly claim they obtained confessions are likely to be fabricating?" (2007, 1438).

The U.S. criminal justice system, grounded in moral responsibility, convicts thousands of innocent criminal defendants and deprives almost all defendants of basic rights; the corresponding system of criminal punishment is its iniquitous partner. Other than Belarus, no European nation allows capital punishment; in 2020 the U.S. executed 17 people, and there are currently some 2500 on death row. As William Stuntz points out, the U.S. incarceration rate for Blacks is 80 percent higher than the rate at which Russians were sent to the Gulag by Stalin (2011, 48). The current imprisonment rate in the U.S. is 639 for every 100,000 of population (the highest rate in the world), while in most European countries the number is well under 100 (World Prison Brief 2021). The U.S. imprisons more people for longer sentences in harsher conditions.

The European Court of Human Rights (2021) condemns solitary confinement as a form of torture and a violation of human rights, yet long-term solitary confinement is a common practice in U.S. prisons. Amnesty International

(2012) characterized the notorious U.S. "supermax" prisons—where many prisoners live in extreme isolation for years on end, suffering severe psychological damage that is often irreversible (Grassian 2006; Arrigo and Bullock 2008; Casella and Ridgeway 2016)—as institutions that violate human rights. Consider the stark contrast between the U.S. prison system and the prison system of Norway, a country with much weaker commitment to moral responsibility (Cavadino and Dignan 2006b, 448). When James Conway, the former superintendent of Attica Correctional Facility in New York, visited Halden prison (a maximum security prison in Norway), he was dismayed to observe prisoners treated with respect and made as comfortable as possible in a prison setting that looked more like a college campus. A prison where inmates were treated well and rehabilitated and lived in relative comfort violated Conway's powerful retributive beliefs about what prison should be:

> Prison is not supposed to be comfortable. Prison is not a comfortable situation. Society is supposed to be comfortable, the inmate has given up his right to be in society by violating laws, by violent crimes, by committing murder, by committing rape. That person shouldn't be coddled, shouldn't be given a situation where we're concerned about how they should feel if someone should walk by their cell and see them on the toilet. Who cares how they feel? (quoted in Francis 2017)

The American attachment to harsh punitive measures—packaged as "righteous retribution" and extolled as an exercise of virtue—is nurtured by strong belief in a just world and devotion to moral responsibility, and that toxic combination is worse than the sum of its parts.

4 BJW and American Culture

Punishment is *never* just. The belief that it is just—a belief supported by BJW that is especially strong in the U.S.—causes terrible harms. The special American attachment to BJW stems from several sources. A virtuous and God-fearing America won its independence against all odds because it trusted in a just God who remains firmly on our side. This central doctrine of the American myth is celebrated in the second stanza of the national anthem: "Then conquer we must, for our cause it is just, and this be our motto, in God is our trust." We are one nation, under God, and uniquely blessed by that just God. America is not only God's favored country; the other half of that equation is that America is favored by God *because* America is preeminently the nation of justice for all: the nation in which "all men are created equal" and enjoy their unalienable rights to life and liberty. All countries promote a myth of virtue and goodness, but few take it to such heroic lengths as does the United States.

Alongside this glorious myth is an egregious reality. The man who wrote the inspiring words that "all men are created equal" and are endowed with an "unalienable right to liberty" was a slaveholder. Slavery continued in the U.S. long after almost all other Western countries had outlawed it—and continued in a different form in the prison labor camps and sharecropping and lynching during the Jim Crow era, with its effects still obvious in housing and employment discrimination, mass imprisonment of minorities, voter suppression, and harsh "targeted enforcement" by police forces. How can we reconcile belief in a just country with these blatant and longstanding practices of fundamental injustice? The great protector and preserver of belief in a just world—from Augustine's doctrine of original sin to the present—is belief in moral responsibility. In the U.S., the combination of glorious myth and vile practice requires an exceptionally robust belief in moral responsibility. America *is* the land of justice for all: slaves were *justly* enslaved, perhaps because they had been condemned by the Hebrew God in some distant era, or because of their inherent faults of laziness and instability (and in any case they were treated with paternal care by their virtuous masters); indigenous peoples were bloodthirsty savages who without provocation attacked peaceful American settlers; mistreated immigrants lacked the basic American virtues of hard work and honesty; the massive numbers of poor and homeless—in the midst of plenty—are indolent, improvident, and probably drug abusers; the many imprisoned persons made free choices to commit criminal acts and justly deserve their brutal ignominious treatment; and those who were wrongfully convicted were certainly guilty of *some* crime. Moral responsibility, in league with belief in a just world, has a remarkable capacity to transform victims into villains.

The uniquely strong American devotion to moral responsibility was also nurtured by the powerful and enduring experience of the American *frontier*, and its special support for "rugged individualism." The self-sufficient, self-made individual who needs no help from anyone and "takes full responsibility" for his life and actions is the iconic hero of Western movies and a persistent element of American culture. According to historian Frederick Jackson Turner's (1893) "frontier thesis," American culture was shaped by its open frontier and the opportunities that offered. Recent empirical studies, inspired by Turner's thesis, have confirmed the frontier contribution to American rugged individualism:

> The frontier fostered the development of distinctive cultural traits, including individualism and opposition to government intervention. The combination of these two traits characterizes "rugged individualism." … The significance of the frontier can be explained by three factors. First, frontier locations attracted individualists able to thrive in harsh conditions. Second, frontier conditions—isolation and low population density—further cultivated self-reliance, and they offered favorable prospects for upward mobility through effort, nurturing hostility to redistribution. Finally, frontier conditions shaped local culture at a critical juncture, thus generating persistent effects. (Bazzi et al. 2017, 1)

That research discovered a strong link between counties that had long periods of "total frontier experience" between 1790 and 1890 and an enduring positive contemporary attitude toward rugged individualism. Counties that (by measures of population density) remained frontier rather than becoming settled continue to have stronger cultures of conservative rugged individualism.

The authors conclude that "over the process of westward expansion, the frontier imbued a culture of rugged individualism throughout the U.S." that remains strong (Bazzi et al. 2017, 4). The researchers note:

> Once frontier culture put down roots, it may have persisted through various mechanisms, even if the distinctive features of frontier settlement were long gone. Initial conditions can determine the long-run equilibrium through the dynamics of intergenerational cultural transmission. Moreover, since the frontier shaped culture at the earliest stages, it was bound to influence the formation of local institutions and social identity, which likely affected the subsequent evolution of cultural traits. (Bazzi et al. 2017, 25; see also Kitayama et al. 2006)

Michael Cavadino and James Dignan make clear the influence of individualism on American culture:

> A highly *individualistic* social ethos … fosters the social belief that individuals are solely responsible for looking after themselves. In neo-liberal society, economic failure is seen as being the fault of the atomized, free-willed individual, not any responsibility of society—hence the minimal, safety-net welfare state. Crime is likewise seen as entirely the responsibility of the offending individual. The social soil is fertile ground for a harsh "law and order ideology." (Cavadino and Dignan 2006a, 448)

Ronald Reagan was the cowboy symbol of hardline, law-and-order individualism: "Our forebears were never concerned about why a person misbehaves. We are straying from the principle of holding the individual responsible for his actions" (quoted in Beckett 1997, 66). British Prime Minister John Major championed the same radical individualism in his speech to the 1992 Conservative Party Conference: "Crime wrecks lives, spreads fear, corrupts society. It is the fault of the individual, and no one else" (Major 1992). The individual bears total responsibility, and larger social factors—bad schools, malnutrition, childhood abuse, poor health care, lead poisoning—are irrelevant.

5 Facing Our Unjust World

The moral responsibility/just deserts system is so deeply entrenched that efforts to replace it seem absurd. In "Hard Determinism and Punishment: A Practical *Reductio*" (2011), Saul Smilansky provides a brilliant account of the inevitable *injustice* of incarcerating wrongdoers who (according to those who reject moral responsibility) do *not* justly deserve incarceration. Smilansky argues that:

> Murderers, rapists, violent bullies, thieves, and other miscreants need to be kept apart from lawful society. … Hard determinists [who reject moral responsibility and just deserts] cannot, however, permit incarceration in institutions of punishment such as those that currently prevail. Instead of punishment, they must opt for funishment. Funishment would resemble punishment in that criminals would be incarcerated apart from lawful society; and institutions of funishment would also need to be as secure as current prisons. … But here the similarity ends. For institutions of funishment would also need to be as delightful as possible. They would need to resemble five-star hotels, where the residents are given every opportunity to enjoy life. … Since hard determinism holds that no one deserves the hardship of being separated from regular society, this hardship needs to be *compensated* for. Hence no effort and no expense should be spared. … The hard determinist equivalent of punishment will be horrendously expensive. (355–56)

So expensive that it would soon bankrupt the country. And that's not the only problem. Delightful funishment institutions would encourage some to commit crimes in order to gain entry, making funishment an anti-deterrent for crime: "following hard determinism would lead to a flood of crime" (360). In sum: "A hard determinist order would be nightmarish, even for hard determinism, if *correctly* implemented [with funishment replacing punishment]. … Hard determinism is, in practice, self-defeating" (361). This is an insightful and provocative *reductio* argument. But it does not show the absurdity of rejecting moral responsibility; instead, it shows the absurdity of *rejecting* moral responsibility while simultaneously *embracing* the foundation of the moral responsibility *system*: Belief in a Just World.

Smilansky is correct on three important points. First, we cannot—at least for the imaginable future—forgo incarceration of some violent criminals. We can and should minimize the practice and make enormous reductions in and improvements of the horrific U.S. prison system; but incarceration for the worst offenders cannot be eliminated. Second, for those who deny moral responsibility, incarceration of criminals is profoundly *unjust*. Third, there is no way to eliminate that injustice: funishment would be counterproductive and would bankrupt the country; and prisoners restrained in gilded cages are still *unjustly* deprived of their liberty. Deprivation of liberty remains a severe punishment, even if the surroundings are pleasant. The moral of this account is not that denying moral responsibility is wrong, but that Belief in a Just World—the belief that requires *moral responsibility* to sustain it—is a destructive mistake. Belief in moral responsibility does not make punishment just; it makes punishment *seem* just, at the price of blocking inquiry and making us comfortable with injustice. We cannot provide funishment, but we can minimize incarceration, treat prisoners with respect, offer effective rehabilitation, and make the secure setting reasonably comfortable—achievable goals that are already met in the Norwegian prisons of Halden and Bastoy Island, in a country that has a much weaker commitment to individual moral responsibility and "a stronger sense that 'there but for the grace of God go I'—in terms of both economic failure and criminal activity" (Cavadino and Dignan 2006a, 448). But even the best prisons will still involve the *unjust* treatment of those who are incarcerated. We cannot make imprisonment just: no one is ever morally responsible, and therefore no one justly deserves punishment. We should not pretend—by means of moral responsibility and just deserts—that we can make punishment just.

Suppose we could demonstrate that coercive confinement is unavoidable if society is to survive and flourish. That would be a strong *justification* of the coercive practice, but it would *not* show that the coercive detention of an individual avoids treating that individual *unjustly*. However *justified* such a practice might be, it remains fundamentally *unjust* to individuals who are deprived of liberty and do *not* (in the absence of moral responsibility) *justly deserve* such deprivation. That disturbing result conflicts with our nonconscious *belief in a just world*: we *ought* to avoid treating any individual unjustly, therefore we *can* avoid treating any individual unjustly. "Ought implies can" is true in Kant's ideal, just world. In our actual world, bereft of any deity that imposes a just order, there is no reason to think it is true; the reasons to think it false are legion.

If we embrace the common assumption that any legitimate system of criminal justice must not knowingly and purposefully inflict unjust treatment, then we have surrendered the field to the proponents of moral responsibility, just deserts, and righteous retribution. The advocates of moral responsibility and retributive punishment are solidly entrenched on the heights of just deserts, and no system that rejects moral responsibility can compete on those grounds. Making punishment—as well as privilege—*just* was precisely what moral responsibility was designed to do. Both the wealthy and the destitute, the suffering prisoner and the prospering judge, are all receiving their *just deserts* for their self-made and self-chosen vice or virtue. If we demand a model that claims to establish *just deserts* in a *just world*, then the moral responsibility system promises fulfillment. It fails to deliver on that promise: it distorts human powers of reason and will, fails again and again to establish a plausible basis for moral responsibility, and is the source of enormous injustice (ranging from inequitable economic policies to needlessly cruel penal programs). But its *ideal* of justice in a just world sets an impossibly high bar—a bar we can never clear in our *unjust* world—and alternative proposals are condemned for failing to achieve that impossible standard.

When we reject the system of moral responsibility, we will *not* discover a system that avoids injustice; worse, we will not find a system that avoids knowing acquiescence in the unjust treatment of many individuals. But if we reject the moral responsibility system and deal honestly and zealously with the problem of *unavoidable injustice* even in the best possible system of criminal justice, then we can greatly reduce injustice. Instead of the massive injustice in the actual functioning of the moral responsibility system, we can labor to build a system that minimizes injustice in our unjust world. The key to *minimizing* injustice is the clear recognition that injustice cannot be *eliminated.*

6 Reducing Injustice in Our Unjust World

We live in an unjust world in which there are injustices that cannot be eliminated. There are two important reasons to remain acutely aware of the unavoidable injustice in even the optimum system of criminal justice. First, such painful awareness prevents the *cover-up* of the injustice, and the cover-up exacerbates the injustice. Second, the painful awareness of injustice can be a powerful motivating source for improving our system and *minimizing* the inevitable injustice. Consider first the harms caused by injustice cover-up, a cover-up designed to preserve belief in a just world. There are basically two methods of cover-up, and both cause severe problems. First, deny that the injustice actually happened. Witness the furious denial of systemic racism in the U.S. The cruel history of slavery, the savagery of the Jim Crow era, the extreme segregation and denial of voting rights, the harsh discriminatory treatment of minorities—from police stops to sentencing—by the criminal justice system: all are denied. If there is no injustice, why struggle to fix a system that isn't broken? The essential first step in fixing a profoundly flawed criminal justice system and a grossly inequitable economic system is the painful recognition of the injustice. The second means of cover-up is blaming the victim. The poor justly deserve to suffer for their indolence; rape victims "brought it on themselves"; the wrongly convicted "must have been guilty of something." Moral responsibility is the powerful destructive tool used to justify wrongs: those suffering the dignity-destroying brutality of Attica or the psychological harm of supermax solitary confinement are receiving their just deserts, and all is right with the world. It is righteous retribution, not unjust punishment.

Rejecting the cover-up and facing the disturbing fact that we live in an unjust world has positive motivational force. The *desire* for justice is demonstrated by the extraordinary efforts—blaming the victim, original sin—employed to preserve the *illusion* of justice. We *want* our world to be just, and that can motivate us to work toward that goal. Research shows that people are disturbed by injustice and are eager to fix it (Lerner and Simmons 1966); however, if removing the injustice is too difficult, they "restore justice" by blaming the victim and condemning the victim's character. If we block the "easy fix" of moral responsibility, then that energy can be channeled into positive efforts to reduce injustice.

The desire for justice and fairness is powerful, but that powerful desire can be either a destructive or a constructive force. If—using the ready resources of moral responsibility—we cling to belief in a just world, then the powerful desire for justice convinces us that all is right with the world, privilege is the just reward of virtue, poverty results from the vice of indolence and is justly deserved, and harsh punishment is righteous retribution. But if we recognize and confront the injustice in our world (and reject the addictive analgesic of moral responsibility) then the powerful desire for justice and fairness becomes an energizing motive to combat injustice and *fix* the wrongs: rather than justifying the suffering of infants by blaming them for their sinful natures, we strive to find cures and effective means of prevention; rather than blaming rape victims for their moral turpitude, we study the causes—including deep cultural causes—that lead to rape, and work to change them; rather than blaming individual criminals for crime and applying harsh just deserts, we probe the causes of criminal behavior (Raine 2013) and undertake the hard work of fixing those problems. We will not eliminate injustice, nor will we eliminate the necessity of inflicting unjust punishment. But we can greatly reduce the injustice. Imprisoning in Halden is unjust, but much *less* unjust than imprisoning in Attica. The harms of preserving BJW through the myopia of moral responsibility are great; the benefits of harnessing the desire for justice to effect real changes that reduce injustice are greater.

Because the "unjust punishment model" recognizes that "punishment" (or coerced isolation) and other criminal penalties are unavoidable, it takes seriously the need to carefully restrict and regulate all punitive practices. The potential dangers and ongoing harms of the moral responsibility/retributive model have already been described, and many more destructive consequences of that model could be added. But as Micheal Corrado (2015, 2021) emphasizes, we can recognize the profound failure and destructiveness of the retributive model while also recognizing that we need a clear system of laws and procedures and penalties as a way of protecting liberty. The effective exercise of liberty requires that we know the limits of our freedom: the specific acts that the state will punish, and the extent and severity of such punishment. There is real danger of a profoundly biased and unprincipled and opportunistic government making terrible use of a program based on a vague standard of "dangerousness." As Corrado notes, a law against homosexual behavior is terrible; but a policy in which one could be confined and "treated" for "dangerous homosexual inclinations" is horrifying. Corrado appeals to the basic "principle of legality" as a way of restricting the powers of the state to interfere in the lives and liberties of citizens: citizens may be punished *only in accordance with the statutory requirements* (only for the violation of specific statutes) and *only within the statutory limits* (no punishment in excess of those set down by law) (Corrado 2015, 4). The justification he offers is clear: "the simple fact that a society organized around the institution of personal liberty … is preferable to any society without it" (Corrado 2021, 368).

Recognizing the reality of unjust punishment is consistent with recognizing the value of personal liberty, and it enriches our understanding and appreciation of genuine free will and substantive liberty. Moral responsibility is the essential guardian of belief in a just world, while free will and liberty have traditionally been the essential grounds for moral responsibility. Since almost everyone is assumed to be morally responsible, it follows that almost everyone enjoys adequate resources of free will and liberty. Our free will is sturdy and secure, and we need not worry about strengthening or sustaining or protecting it; and our liberty is also strong and the only danger to liberty is that it will be infringed. It is not surprising that the neoretributivists and neoliberals celebrate the *negative* liberty—basically, the liberty to be left alone in the enjoyment of one's property and freedom—that Isaiah Berlin (1969) praises, in contrast to the *positive* liberty they despise as compromising valuable negative liberty: providing the essential resources to strengthen positive liberty (through education, health care, housing, and genuine opportunities for choice and control) will require "infringing" on the "justly deserved" wealth of the privileged. Negative liberty is important; positive liberty is vital. When we reject moral responsibility and look deeper and harder at the real free will that human animals need and value—the power to have and make choices, and the power to exercise effective control (Waller 2015a)—it is obvious that many people do *not* have rich resources of free will, and that far from being a godlike power enjoyed by almost all humans it is instead comprised of natural powers that are often limited or damaged, that require support and effective exercise, and that can be and often are severely compromised by social, environmental, and psychological factors. In addition, many people enjoy very little in the way of liberty—in their jobs, homes, communities, cultures, opportunities—and leaving them "free to enjoy their negative liberties" is harsh neglect. By eliminating the myopia of moral responsibility, we can examine the deprivations and problems that weaken free will, destroy liberty, and contribute to crime.

Recognizing that the world (and the punishment we cannot avoid inflicting) is *unjust* is painful and difficult but ultimately beneficial. Believing that the world is *just* (and that moral responsibility makes it so) is pleasant and easy (especially for the privileged) but ultimately it exacerbates injustice (especially for the less fortunate). Rejecting justly deserved retribution and acknowledging the necessity of unjust punishment will not result in a just world, but it opens the way to a world with much less injustice.

References

Amnesty International. 2012. *Cruel Isolation: Amnesty International's Concerns about Conditions in Arizona Maximum Security Prisons.* www.amnestyusa.org/research/reports/cruel-isolation-amnesty.

Arrigo, Bruce A., and Jennifer Leslie Bullock. 2008. "The Psychological Effects of Solitary Confinement on Prisoners in Supermax Units: Reviewing What We Know and Recommending What Should Change." *International Journal of Offender Therapy and Comparative Criminology* 52 no. 6 (December): 622–40.

Balko, Radley. 2011. "Private Crime Labs Could Prevent Errors, Analyst Bias: Report." *Huffington Post*, June 14, updated August 14. https://www.huffpost.com/entry/the-case-for-private-crime-labs_n_876963.

Bazzi, Samuel, Martin Fiszbein, and Mesay Gebresilasse. 2017. "Frontier Culture: The Roots and Persistence of 'Rugged Individualism' in the United States." NBER Working Paper No. 23997, June. https://www.bu.edu/econ/files/2018/08/BFG_Frontier.pdf.

Beckett, Katherine. 1997. *Making Crime Pay: Law and Order in Contemporary American Politics*. New York: Oxford University Press.

Berlin, Isaiah. 1969. "Two Concepts of Liberty." In *Four Essays on Liberty*, 118–72. Oxford: Oxford University Press.

Cacioppo, John T., and Richard E. Petty. 1982. "The Need for Cognition." *Journal of Personality and Social Psychology* 42, no. 1 (January): 116–31.

Cacioppo, John T., Richard E. Petty, Jeffrey A. Feinstein, and W. Blair G. Jarvis. 1996. "Dispositional Differences in Cognitive Motivation: The Life and Times of Individuals Varying in Need for Cognition." *Psychological Bulletin* 119, no. 2 (March): 197–253.

Campbell, C. A. 1957. *On Selfhood and Godhood*. London: George Allen & Unwin.

Casella, Jean, and James Ridgeway. 2016. Introduction to *Hell is a Very Small Place*, edited by Jean Casella, James Ridgeway, and Sarah Shourd, 16–24. New York: New Press.

Cavadino, Michael, and James Dignan. 2006a. "Penal Policy and Political Economy." *Criminology & Criminal Justice* 6, no. 4 (November): 435–56.

———. 2006b. *Penal Systems: A Comparative Approach*. London: Sage.

Chisholm, Roderick M. 1982. "Human Freedom and the Self." In *Free Will*, edited by Gary Watson, 24–35. New York: Oxford University Press.

Coates, D. Justin, and Neal A. Tognazzini. 2013. "The Contours of Blame." In *Blame: Its Nature and Norms*, edited by D. Justin Coates and Neal A. Tognazzini, 3–26. New York: Oxford University Press.

Corrado, Michael Louis. 2015. "Fichte and the Psychopath: Criminal Justice Turned Upside Down." Social Science Research Network, March 14. https://papers.ssrn.com/sol3/papers.cfm?abstract_id=2585077.

———. 2021. "The Takings Doctrine and the Principle of Legality." In *The Routledge Handbook of the Philosophy and Science of Punishment*, edited by Farah Focquaert, Elizabeth Shaw, and Bruce N. Waller, 366–76. New York: Routledge.

Dalbert, Claudia, and Lois A. Yamauchi. 1994. "Belief in a Just World and Attitudes toward Immigrants and Foreign Workers: A Cultural Comparison between Hawaii and Germany." *Journal of Applied Social Psychology* 24, no. 18 (September): 1612–26.

Davies, Paul Sheldon. 2013. "Skepticism concerning Human Agency: Sciences of the Self versus 'Voluntariness' in the Law." In *Neuroscience and Legal Responsibility*, edited by Nicole A. Vincent, 113–34. New York: Oxford University Press.

———. 2020. "Foundational Facts for Legal Responsibility: Human Agency and the Aims of Restorative Interventions." In *Neurointerventions and the Law*, edited by

Nicole A. Vincent, Thomas Nadelhoffer, and Allan McCay, 319–49. New York: Oxford University Press.

Dennett, Daniel C. 1984. *Elbow Room: The Varieties of Free Will Worth Wanting*. Cambridge, MA: MIT Press.

Drug Policy Alliance. 2014. *New Jersey State Commission of Investigation Releases Damning Report on Commercial Bail Industry Practices*, May 20. https://drugpolicy.org/news/2014/05/new-jersey-state-commission-investigation-releases-damning-report-commercial-bail-indus.

European Court of Human Rights, Council of Europe. 2021. *Guide on the Case-Law of the European Convention of Human Rights: Prisoners' Rights*, April 30. https://www.echr.coe.int/Documents/Guide_Prisoners_rights_ENG.pdf.

Findley, Keith A. 2011. "Adversarial Inquisitions: Rethinking the Search for the Truth." *New York Law School Law Review* 56, no. 3: 911–43.

Fischer, John Martin. 2009. *Our Stories: Essays on Life, Death, and Free Will*. New York: Oxford University Press.

———. 2012. *Deep Control: Essays on Free Will and Value*. New York: Oxford University Press.

Francis, Nathan. 2017. "A Look at Life inside Norway's Halden Prison, Where There Are No Bars and Inmates Have Flat-Screen TVs inside Their Cells." *Inquisitr*, November 8. https://www.inquisitr.com/1550875/a-look-at-life-inside-norways-halden-prison-where-there-are-no-bars-and-inmates-have-flat-screen-tvs-inside-their-cells/.

Frankfurt, Harry G. 1971. "Freedom of the Will and the Concept of a Person." *Journal of Philosophy* 68, no. 1 (January 14): 5–20.

Furnham, Adrian. 2003. "Belief in a Just World: Research Progress over the Past Decade." *Personality and Individual Differences* 34, no. 5 (April): 795–817.

Furnham, Adrian, and Barrie Gunter. 1984. "Just World Beliefs and Attitudes towards the Poor." *British Journal of Social Psychology* 23, no. 3 (September): 265–69.

Gershman, Bennett L. 2003. "Misuse of Scientific Evidence by Prosecutors." *Oklahoma City University Law Review* 28, no. 1 (Spring): 17–42.

Grassian, Stuart. 2006. "Psychiatric Effects of Solitary Confinement." *Washington University Journal of Law and Policy* 22: 325–83.

Green, Thomas Andrew. 2014. *Freedom and Criminal Responsibility in American Legal Thought*. New York: Cambridge University Press.

Haidt, Jonathan. 2001. "The Emotional Dog and Its Rational Tail: A Social Intuitionist Approach to Moral Judgment." *Psychological Review* 108, no. 4 (October): 814–34.

———. 2012. *The Righteous Mind: Why Good People Are Divided by Politics and Religion*. New York: Pantheon.

Harper, David J., and Paul R. Manasse. 1992. "The Just World and the Third World: British Explanations for Poverty Abroad." *Journal of Social Psychology* 132, no. 6: 783–85.

Jefferson, Anneli. 2019. "Instrumentalism about Moral Responsibility Revisited." *Philosophical Quarterly* 69, no. 276 (July): 555–73.

Kadish, Sanford H. 1987. *Blame and Punishment: Essays in Criminal Law.* New York: Collier Macmillan.

Kahneman, Daniel. 2011. *Thinking, Fast and Slow.* New York: Farrar, Straus and Giroux.

Kane, Robert. 2007. "Libertarianism." In *Four Views on Free Will*, edited by Robert Kane, John Martin Fischer, Derk Pereboom, and Manuel Vargas, 5–43. Malden, MA: Blackwell.

Kelemen, Deborah. 2003. "British and American Children's Preferences for Teleo-Functional Explanations of the Natural World." *Cognition* 88, no. 2 (June): 201–21.

Kelemen, Deborah, and Evelyn Rosset. 2009. "The Human Function Compunction: Teleological Explanation in Adults." *Cognition* 111, no. 1 (April): 138–43.

Kelemen, Deborah, Joshua Rottman, and Rebecca Seston. 2013. "Professional Physical Scientists Display Tenacious Teleological Tendencies: Purpose-Based Reasoning as a Cognitive Default." *Journal of Experimental Psychology: General* 142, no. 4 (November): 1074–83.

Kitayama, Shinobu, Keiko Ishii, Toshie Imada, Kosuke Takemura, and Jenny Ramaswamy. 2006. "Voluntary Settlement and the Spirit of Independence: Evidence from Japan's 'Northern Frontier.'" *Journal of Personality and Social Psychology* 91, no. 3 (September): 369–84.

Korsgaard, Christine M. 2009. *Self-Constitution: Agency, Identity, and Integrity.* New York: Oxford University Press.

Lerner, Melvin J. 1980. *The Belief in a Just World: A Fundamental Delusion.* New York: Plenum.

Lerner, Melvin J., and Carolyn H. Simmons. 1966. "Observer's Reaction to the 'Innocent Victim': Compassion or Rejection?" *Journal of Personality and Social Psychology* 4, no. 2 (August): 203–10.

Levy, Neil. 2011. *Hard Luck: How Luck Undermines Free Will and Moral Responsibility.* New York: Oxford University Press.

Lewis, Clive S. 1971. "The Humanitarian Theory of Punishment." In *Undeceptions: Essays on Theology and Ethics*, 238–49. London: Curtis Brown.

Major, John. 1992. "Leader's Speech, Brighton 1992." *British Political Speech.* http://britishpoliticalspeech.org/speech-archive.htm?speech=138.

McGeer, Victoria. 2019. "Scaffolding Agency: A Proleptic Account of the Reactive Attitudes." *European Journal of Philosophy* 27, no. 2 (June): 301–23.

Menkel-Meadow, Carrie. 1996. "The Trouble with the Adversary System in a Postmodern, Multicultural World." *William & Mary Law Review* 38, no. 1: 5–44.

Montada, Leo. 1998. "Belief in a Just World: A Hybrid of Justice Motive and Self-Interest." In *Responses to Victimizations and Belief in a Just World*, edited by Leo Montada and Melvin Lerner, 217–45. New York: Plenum.

Moore, Michael S. 1997. *Placing Blame: A General Theory of the Criminal Law.* Oxford: Oxford University Press.

Morris, Herbert. 1968. "Persons and Punishment." *Monist* 52, no. 4 (October): 475–501.
Nietzsche, Friedrich. 1966. *Beyond Good and Evil: Prelude to a Philosophy of the Future.* Translated by Walter Kaufmann. New York: Vintage.
Olderman, Justine. 2021 "Pre-Trial Detention and the Supplanting of Our Adversarial System." In *The Routledge Handbook of the Philosophy and Science of Punishment,* edited by Farah Focquaert, Elizabeth Shaw, and Bruce N. Waller, 344–54. New York: Routledge.
Pico della Mirandola, Giovanni. 1948. *Oration on the Dignity of Man.* Translated by Elizabeth Livermore Forbes. In *The Renaissance Philosophy of Man,* edited by Ernst Cassirer, Paul Oskar Kristeller, and John Herman Randall Jr., 223–54. Chicago: University of Chicago Press.
Raeder, Myrna S. 2007. "See No Evil: Wrongful Convictions and the Prosecutorial Ethics of Offering Testimony by Jailhouse Informants and Dishonest Experts." *Fordham Law Review* 76, no. 3 (December): 1413–52.
Raine, Adrian. 2013. *The Anatomy of Violence: The Biological Roots of Crime.* New York: Pantheon.
Roskies, Adina L. 2012. "Don't Panic: Self-Authorship without Obscure Metaphysics." *Philosophical Perspectives* 26, no. 1: 323–42.
———. 2014. "Can Neuroscience Resolve Issues about Free Will?" In *Moral Psychology,* vol. 4: *Free Will and Moral Responsibility,* edited by Walter Sinnott-Armstrong, 103–26. Cambridge, MA: MIT Press.
Sartre, Jean-Paul. 1958. *Being and Nothingness: An Essay on Phenomenological Ontology.* Translated by Hazel Barnes. London: Routledge.
Scalia, Antonin. 2002. "God's Justice and Ours." *First Things* 123 (May): 17–21.
Slobogin, Christopher. 2014. "Lessons from Inquisitorialism." *Southern California Law Review* 87, no. 3 (March): 699–731.
Smilansky, Saul. 2000. *Free Will and Illusion.* New York: Oxford University Press.
———. 2011. "Hard Determinism and Punishment: A Practical *Reductio.*" *Law and Philosophy* 30, no. 3 (May): 353–67.
Strawson, Peter F. 1982. "Freedom and Resentment." In *Free Will,* edited by Gary Watson, 59–80. New York: Oxford University Press.
Stuntz, William J. 2008. "Inequality and Adversarial Criminal Procedure." *Journal of Institutional and Theoretical Economics* 164, no. 1 (March): 47–51.
———. 2011. *The Collapse of American Justice.* Cambridge, MA: Harvard University Press.
Turner, Frederick Jackson. 1893. "The Significance of the Frontier in American History." *Annual Report of the American Historical Association*: 197–227.
Van Inwagen, Peter. 1983. *An Essay on Free Will.* Oxford: Oxford University Press.
Vargas, Manuel. 2013. *Building Better Beings.* New York: Oxford University Press.
Wagstaff, Graham F. 1983. "Correlates of the Just World in Britain." *Journal of Social Psychology* 121, no. 1: 145–46.
Waller, Bruce N. 2011. *Against Moral Responsibility.* Cambridge, MA: MIT Press.

———. 2015a. *Restorative Free Will: Back to the Biological Base*. Lanham, MD: Lexington.

———. 2015b. *The Stubborn System of Moral Responsibility*. Cambridge, MA: MIT Press.

———. 2020. *Free Will, Moral Responsibility, and the Desire to Be a God*. Lanham, MD: Lexington.

Williams, Bernard. 1993. *Shame and Necessity*. Berkeley, CA: University of California Press.

Wilson, Timothy D. 2002. *Strangers to Ourselves: Discovering the Adaptive Unconscious*. Cambridge, MA: Harvard University Press.

World Prison Brief. 2021. "Highest to Lowest—Prison Population Total." Institute for Crime & Justice Policy Research, University of London. Accessed August 27. https://www.prisonstudies.org/highest-to-lowest/prison-population-total.

22

Retributivism, Free Will, and the Public Health-Quarantine Model

Gregg D. Caruso

Within the criminal justice system one of the most prominent justifications for legal punishment, both historically and currently, is *retributivism*. The retributive justification of legal punishment maintains that, absent any excusing conditions, wrongdoers are morally responsible for their actions and *deserve* to be punished in proportion to their wrongdoing. Unlike theories of punishment that aim at deterrence, rehabilitation, or incapacitation, retributivism grounds punishment in the *blameworthiness* and *desert* of offenders. It holds that punishing wrongdoers is intrinsically good. For the retributivist, wrongdoers deserve a punitive response proportional to their wrongdoing, even if their punishment serves no further purpose. This means that the retributivist position is not reducible to consequentialist considerations nor in justifying punishment does it appeal to wider goods such as the safety of society or the moral improvement of those being punished.

In this chapter, I outline six distinct reasons for rejecting retributivism, not the least of which is that it is unclear that agents possess the kind of free will and moral responsibility needed to justify it. I then sketch my novel non-retributive alternative, which I call the *public health-quarantine model*. As we will see, the model draws on the public health framework and prioritizes prevention and social justice. I contend that it not only offers a stark contrast to retributivism, but it also provides a more humane, holistic, and effective

G. D. Caruso (✉)
State University of New York at Corning, Corning, NY, USA
e-mail: gcaruso@corning-cc.edu

© The Author(s), under exclusive license to Springer Nature Switzerland AG 2023

M. C. Altman (ed.), *The Palgrave Handbook on the Philosophy of Punishment*, Palgrave Handbooks in the Philosophy of Law, https://doi.org/10.1007/978-3-031-11874-6_22

approach to dealing with criminal behavior, one that is superior to both retributivism and other leading non-retributive alternatives. I begin by taking a closer look at the retributive justification of punishment.

1 Retributivism

According to the retributivist justification of legal punishment, wrongdoers deserve the imposition of a penalty solely for the backward-looking reason that they have knowingly done wrong. Michael S. Moore, a leading retributivist, highlights this purely backward-looking nature of retributivism when he writes:

> retributivism is the view that we ought to punish offenders because, and only because, they deserve to be punished. Punishment is justified, for a retributivist, solely by the fact that those receiving it deserve it. Punishment may deter future crime, incapacitate dangerous persons, educate citizens in the behaviour required for a civilized society, reinforce social cohesion, prevent vigilante behaviour, make victims of crime feel better, or satisfy the vengeful desires of citizens who are not themselves crime victims. Yet for the retributivist these are a happy surplus that punishment produces and form no part of what makes punishment just: for a retributivist, deserving offenders should be punished even if the punishment produces none of these other, surplus good effects. (1997, 153; see also Moore 1987, 1993)

This backward-looking focus on desert is a central feature of all traditional retributive accounts of punishment (see, e.g., Kant 1996; von Hirsch 1976, 1981, 2007, 2017; Husak 2000; Kershnar 2000, 2001; Berman 2008, 2011, 2013, 2016; Walen 2020). And it is important to emphasize that the desert invoked in retributivism (in the classical or strict sense) is *basic* in the sense that it is not in turn grounded in forward-looking reasons such as securing the safety of society or the moral improvement of criminals. Thus, for the retributivist, the claim that persons are morally responsible for their actions in the *basic desert* sense is crucial to the state's justification for giving them their just deserts in the form of punishment for violations of the state's laws.[1]

[1] Retributivists typically also hold, in addition, that just punishments must be *proportional* to wrongdoing. Both the justificatory thesis and the proportionality requirement for punishments are reflected in Mitchell Berman's statement of retributivism: "A person who unjustifiably and inexcusably causes or risks harm to others or to significant social interests deserves to suffer for that choice, and he deserves to suffer in proportion to the extent to which his regard or concern for others falls short of what is properly demanded of him" (2008, 269).

In the U.S. criminal justice system, the retributivist justification of legal punishment and the attendant proportionality requirement are widely embraced. In fact, a number of sentencing guidelines in the United States have adopted the retributivist conception of desert as their core principle,[2] and it is increasingly given deference in the "Purposes" section of state criminal codes,[3] where it can be the guiding principle in the interpretation and application of the code's provisions.[4] Indeed, the American Law Institute recently revised the Model Penal Code so as to set desert as the official dominant principle for sentencing.[5] And courts have identified desert as the guiding principle in a variety of contexts,[6] as with the Supreme Court's enthroning of retributivism as the "primary justification for the death penalty"[7] (Robinson 2008, 145–46). Additional examples can be found in legislation, judicial decisions, sentencing guidelines, and criminal codes in England, Wales, Scotland, Australia, Canada, New Zealand, and Israel (see, e.g., Dingwall 2008; von Hirsch 2017).

Depending on how retributivists view the relationship between desert and punishment, we can identify three different varieties of the view—*weak*, *moderate*, and *strong* (see, e.g., Alexander et al. 2009; Walen 2020). *Weak retributivism* maintains that negative desert, which is what the criminal law is concerned with when it holds wrongdoers accountable,[8] is merely necessary but not sufficient for punishment. That is, weak retributivism maintains that while desert is a necessary condition for punishment, it is not enough on its

---

[2] E.g., 204 Pa. Code Sect. 303.11 (2005); see also Tonry (2004).

[3] E.g., Cal. Penal Code Sect. 1170(a)(1) (2010): "The legislature finds and declares that the purpose of imprisonment for crime is punishment."

[4] E.g., Model Penal Code Sect. 1.02(2) (Official Draft 1962).

[5] American Law Institute, Model Penal Code Sect. 1.02(2), adopted May 24, 2017.

[6] See, e.g., the U.S. cases *Spaziano v. Florida*, 468 U.S. 447 (1984), 462; and *Gregg v. Georgia*, 428 U.S. 153 (1976), 183–84. See also Cotton (2000).

[7] *Spaziano v. Florida*, 468 U.S. 447 (1984), 461.

[8] *Negative desert* can be contrasted with *positive desert*, which has to do with an agent deserving praise or reward for good actions. It is important to note that there is another conception of "negative desert" that is widespread in the literature. This latter notion refers to the negative component of the retributivist thesis. For example, Walen writes, "retributivism … involves both positive and negative desert claims. The positive desert claim holds that wrongdoers morally deserve punishment for their wrongful acts." On the other hand,

> this positive desert claim is complemented by a negative deontic claim: Those who have done no wrong may not be punished. This prohibits both punishing those not guilty of wrongdoing (who deserve no punishment), and punishing the guilty more than they deserve (i.e., inflicting disproportional punishment). (2020, §3.2)

Having two different notions of negative desert can potentially be confusing, but I will try my best to make clear which conception is at play in different contexts.

own to justify punishment—other conditions must also be met. As Alec Walen describes it, weak retributivism is the view that "wrongdoers forfeit their right not to suffer proportional punishment, but that the positive reasons for punishment must appeal to some other goods that punishment achieves, such as deterrence or incapacitation." Wrongdoing, on this view, is merely a necessary condition for punishment: "The desert of the wrongdoer provides neither a sufficient condition for nor even a positive reason to punish" (2020, §3.3; see also Mabbott 1939; Quinton 1954).

Moderate retributivism, on the other hand, maintains that negative desert is necessary and sufficient for punishment but that desert does not mandate punishment or provide an obligation to punish in all circumstances—that is, there may be other goods that outweigh punishing the deserving or giving them their just deserts (Robinson and Cahill 2006). Leo Zaibert, while eschewing the taxonomy offered here, defends a kind of moderate retributivism when he argues:

> There are many reasons why sometimes refraining from punishing a deserving wrongdoer is more valuable than punishing him—even if one believes that there is [intrinsic] value in inflicting deserved punishment. Perhaps the most conspicuous cases are those in which the refraining is related to resource-allocation and opportunity costs. … To acknowledge the existence of these cases is not to thereby *deny* the value of deserved punishment: it is simply to recognize that this value, like any value, can be—and often is—lesser than other values. (2018, 20)

Mitchell Berman (2016) also defends a form of moderate retributivism, which he calls "modest retributivism," since he maintains that negative desert grounds a justified reason to punish, but not a duty. For moderate retributivists, negative desert is sufficient to justify punishment but other values and considerations may outweigh inflicting the deserved punishment.

Lastly, *strong retributivism* maintains that desert is necessary and sufficient for punishment but it also grounds a duty to punish wrongdoers. Immanuel Kant is perhaps the most famous representative of this latter view, since he argued that the death penalty was not only deserved but also obligatory in cases of murder:

> If … he has committed murder he must *die*. Here there is no substitute that will satisfy justice. There is no *similarity* between life, however wretched it may be, and death, hence no likeness between the crime and the retribution unless death is judicially carried out upon the wrongdoer. (1996, 6:333 [p. 474])

He goes on to write:

> Even if a civil society were to be dissolved by the consent of all its members (e.g., if a people inhabiting an island decided to separate and disperse throughout the world), the last murderer remaining in prison would first have to be executed, so that each has done to him what his deeds deserve and blood guilt does not cling to the people for not having insisted upon this punishment; for otherwise the people can be regarded as collaborators in this public violation of justice. (1996, 6:333 [p. 474])

Of course, not all retributivists support the death penalty—in fact, many contemporary retributivists do not—but in the above quote, Kant is embodying the strong retributivist view that we are not only justified in giving offenders their just deserts by punishing them, but we also have a duty to do so. Moore also defends a form of strong retributivism and argues, like Kant, that society has a duty to punish culpable offenders:

> We are justified in punishing because and only because offenders deserve it. Moral responsibility ("desert") in such a view is not only necessary for justified punishment, it is also sufficient. Such sufficiency of justification gives society more than merely a right to punish culpable offenders. It does this, making it not unfair to punish them, but retributivism justifies more than this. For a retributivist, the moral responsibility of an offender also gives society the duty to punish. Retributivism, in other words, is truly a theory of justice such that, if it is true, we have an obligation to set up institutions so that retribution is achieved. (1997, 91)

Strong retributivists therefore defend two distinct claims: (1) that negative desert is sufficient to justify punishing wrongdoers on the grounds that they deserve it, and (2) that we have a duty to do so. Moderate retributivists, on the other hand, seek only to defend the first claim.

In what follows, I will limit my discussion to moderate and strong varieties of retributivism and leave weak retributivism aside. I will do so because, first, most leading retributivists defend one of these stronger forms of retributivism—see, for example, Moore (1987, 1993, 1997); Kershnar (2000, 2001); Husak (2000); Berman (2008, 2011); von Hirsch (1976, 2007, 2017); Alexander (2013); and Alexander et al. (2009)—and it is my desire to address the dominant view, not a subordinate view held by few. Second, weak retributivism is considered by many retributivists to be "too weak to guide the criminal law" and as amounting to nothing more than "desert-free consequentialism side constrained by negative desert" (Alexander et al. 2009, 7). In fact, some theorists simply define retributivism in a way that excludes *weak retributivism* from consideration altogether. David Boonin, for example, defines retributivism as the claim that “committing an offense in the past is *sufficient* to justify punishment now, whether or not this will produce any beneficial consequences in the future” (2008, 86, emphasis added). Berman maintains that the “core retributivist thesis” is that

> the goodness or rightness of satisfying a wrongdoer’s negative desert morally justifies [i.e., is sufficient for] the infliction of criminal punishment, without regard for any further good consequences that might be realized as a contingent result of satisfying the wrongdoer’s desert. (2016, 37)

And Walen, in his *Stanford Encyclopedia of Philosophy* entry on “Retributive Justice,” defines retributivism as committed to the following three principles:

1. that those who commit certain kinds of wrongful acts, paradigmatically serious crimes, morally deserve a proportionate punishment;
2. that it is intrinsically morally good—good without reference to any other goods that might arise—if some legitimate punisher gives them the punishment they deserve; and
3. that it is morally impermissible to intentionally punish the innocent or to inflict disproportionately large punishments on wrongdoers. (2020)

Lastly, the weight the criminal law gives desert and the way retributivism is practically implemented in the law (especially in the United States) indicate that the desert of offenders is typically seen as sufficient for punishment. The revised Model Penal Code makes this point rather clear.

For these reasons, I will take as my target the claim that the desert of offenders provides sufficient grounds for punishment and that we are therefore justified in sometimes punishing wrongdoers for no purpose other than to see the guilty get what they deserve. Since this core claim is held in common among all moderate and strong varieties of retributivism, I will henceforth drop the moderate/strong distinction and focus instead on this shared feature.

2 Rejecting Retributivism

While retributivism provides one of the main sources of justification for punishment within criminal justice systems, there are good philosophical and practical reasons for rejecting it. One such reason is that it is unclear that agents *truly deserve* to suffer for the wrongs they have done in the sense required by retributivism. This is because, for an agent to *deserve* to suffer for the wrongs they have done in the purely backward-looking sense required for retributivism, they would need to possess the kind of control in action—namely, free will—required for basic desert moral responsibility (see Caruso 2021a). Yet there are good philosophical reasons for thinking agents are never free and morally responsible in this sense. *Hard determinists*, for example, have long argued that determinism is true and incompatible with free will and basic desert moral responsibility—either because determinism precludes the *ability to do otherwise* (leeway incompatibilism) or because it is inconsistent with one's being the "ultimate source" of action (source incompatibilism). More recently, a number of contemporary philosophers have presented additional arguments against basic desert moral responsibility that are agnostic about determinism (e.g., Strawson 1986; Pereboom 2001, 2014; Levy 2011; Waller 2011; Caruso 2012, 2021a; Caruso in Dennett and Caruso 2021).

In my own work, I have offered two distinct sets of arguments in support of *free will skepticism.* The first features distinct arguments that target the three leading rival views—event-causal libertarianism, agent-causal libertarianism, and compatibilism—and then claims that the skeptical position is the only defensible position that remains standing. It is a form of *hard incompatibilism*, which maintains that free will is incompatible with *both* causal determination by factors beyond the agent's control *and* with the kind of indeterminacy in action required by the most plausible versions of libertarianism. Against the view that free will is compatible with the causal determination of our actions by natural factors beyond our control, I argue that there is no relevant difference between this prospect and our actions being causally determined by manipulators (see Pereboom 2001, 2014; Caruso 2012, 2021a). Against event-causal libertarianism, I object (among other things) that on such accounts agents are left unable to settle whether a decision occurs and hence cannot have the control required for moral responsibility (see Pereboom 2001, 2014; Caruso 2012, 2021a). I further maintain that non-causal accounts of free will suffer from the same problem (see Pereboom 2001, 2014). While agent-causal libertarianism could, in theory, supply this sort of control, I argue that it cannot be reconciled with our best philosophical and scientific theories about the world (see Pereboom 2001, 2014; Caruso 2012, 2021a) and faces additional problems accounting for mental causation (Caruso 2012, 2021a). Since this exhausts the options for views on which we have the sort of free will at issue, I conclude that free will skepticism is the only remaining position.

In addition to hard incompatibilism, I also defend a second, independent argument against free will which maintains that regardless of the causal structure of the universe, free will and basic desert moral responsibility are incompatible with the pervasiveness of *luck*—a view sometimes called *hard luck.* This argument is intended not only as an objection to libertarianism but extends to compatibilism as well. At the heart of the argument is the following dilemma, which Neil Levy (2011) calls the *luck pincer*: Either actions are subject to *present luck* (luck around the time of action), or they are subject to *constitutive luck* (luck in who one is and what character traits and predispositions one has), or both. Either way, luck undermines free will and basic desert moral responsibility since it undermines responsibility-level control.

Consider, for instance, the problem constitutive luck raises for the compatibilist. Since our genes, parents, peers, and other environmental influences all contribute to making us who we are, and since we have no control over these, it seems that who we are is largely a matter of luck. And since how we act is partly a function of who we are, the existence of constitutive luck entails that what actions we perform depends on luck. A compatibilist could respond, as they often do, that as long as an agent *takes responsibility* for her endowments, dispositions, and values, over time she will *become* morally responsible for them. The problem with this reply, however, is that the series of actions through which agents shape and modify their endowments, dispositions, and values are *themselves* subject to luck—and as Levy puts it, "we cannot undo the freedom-undermining effects of luck by virtue of more luck" (2011, 96). Hence, the very actions to which compatibilists point, the actions whereby agents take responsibility for their endowments, either *express* that endowment (when they are explained by constitutive luck) or reflect the agent's present luck, or both. Hence, the luck pincer.

What these and other arguments for free will skepticism have in common, and what they share with classical hard determinism, is the thesis that what we do and the way we are is ultimately the result of factors beyond our control, and because of this we are never morally responsible for our actions in the basic desert sense—the sense required for retributive punishment. This is not to say, of course, that other conceptions of responsibility cannot be reconciled with determinism, chance, or luck. Nor is it to deny that there may be good reasons to maintain certain systems of moral protest in the face of bad behavior (see Pereboom 2014, 2021; Caruso and Pereboom 2022). Rather, it is to insist that to hold people *truly* or *ultimately* morally responsible for their actions—that is, to hold them responsible in a non-consequentialist desert-based sense—would be to hold them responsible for the results of morally arbitrary features of their characters and actions, for what is ultimately beyond their control, which is fundamentally unfair and unjust.

My first argument, then, against retributivism—i.e., the *Skeptical Argument*—maintains that free will skepticism undermines the retributive justification for punishment since it does away with the idea of *basic desert.* The justification of retributivism depends on the assumption that criminals are (or at least can be) deserving of blame in the basic desert sense for their criminal behavior. But, if free will skepticism is true, then *no one* is ever deserving of blame in the basic desert sense for any of their actions. So, the truth of free will skepticism entails that retributive punishment cannot be justified, and thus retributivism should be rejected.

But what if one is not totally convinced by the arguments for free will skepticism? Well, I maintain that *even in the face of uncertainty about the existence of free will*, it remains unclear whether retributive punishment is justified. This is because the burden of proof lies on those who want to inflict harm on others to provide good justification for such harm. This means that retributivists who want to justify legal punishment on the assumption that agents are free and morally responsible (and hence *justly deserve* to suffer for the wrongs they have done) must justify that assumption. And they must justify that assumption in a way that meets a high epistemic standard of proof, since the harms caused in the case of legal punishment are often quite severe. It is not enough to simply point to the mere possibility that agents possess libertarian or compatibilist free will. Nor is it enough to say that the skeptical arguments against free will and basic desert moral responsibility fail to be conclusive. Rather, a positive and convincing case must be made that agents are in fact morally responsible in the basic desert sense, since it is the backward-looking desert of agents that retributivists take to justify the harm caused by legal punishment.

This brings me to my second argument against retributivism, the so-called *Epistemic Argument* (Caruso 2020, 2021a). Versions of this argument have also been developed by Derk Pereboom (2001), Benjamin Vilhauer (2009, 2012, 2015), Elizabeth Shaw (2014, 2021), Michael Corrado (2017), and Sofia Jeppsson (2021). My version of the argument can be summarized as follows:

1. Legal punishment intentionally inflicts harms on individuals, and the justification for such harms must meet a high epistemic standard. If it is significantly probable that one's justification for harming another is unsound, then, *prima facie*, that behavior is seriously wrong.
2. The retributive justification for legal punishment assumes that agents are morally responsible in the basic desert sense and hence justly deserve to suffer for the wrongs they have done in a backward-looking, non-

consequentialist sense (appropriately qualified and under the constraint of proportionality).

3. If the justification for the assumption that agents are morally responsible in the basic desert sense and hence justly deserve to suffer for the wrongs they have done does not meet the high epistemic standard specified in (1), then retributive legal punishment is *prima facie* seriously wrong.
4. The justification for the claim that agents are morally responsible in the basic desert sense provided by both libertarians and compatibilists face powerful and unresolved objections and as a result fall far short of the high epistemic bar needed to justify such harms.
5. Hence, retributive legal punishment is unjustified and the harms it causes are *prima facie* seriously wrong.

Note that the Epistemic Argument requires only a weaker notion of skepticism than the one defended in the Skeptical Argument, namely one that holds that the justification for believing that agents are morally responsible in the basic desert sense, and hence justly deserve to suffer for the wrongs they have done, is too weak to justify the intentional suffering caused by retributive legal punishment.

Premise (1) places the burden of proof on those who want to justify legal punishment, since the harms caused in this case are often quite severe—including the loss of liberty, deprivation, and in some cases even death. Victor Tadros spells out these harms:

> Punishment is probably the most awful thing modern democratic states systematically do to their own citizens. Every modern democratic state imprisons thousands of offenders every year, depriving them of their liberty, causing them a great deal of psychological and sometimes physical harm. Relationships are destroyed, jobs are lost, the risk of the offender being harmed by other offenders is increased, and all at great expense to the state. (2011, 1)

Given the gravity of these harms, the justification for legal punishment must meet a high epistemic standard. If it is significantly probable that one's justification for harming another is unsound, then, *prima facie*, that behavior is seriously wrong (Pereboom 2001, 199; see also Vilhauer 2009).

Support for premise (1) can be found both in the law and everyday practice. As Corrado writes:

> The notion of a burden of proof comes to us from the adversarial courtroom, where it guides the presentation of evidence. In both criminal and civil cases the defendant is presumed not guilty or not liable, and it is up to the accuser to

> persuade the finder of fact. The only difference between the two cases lies in the measure of the burden that must be carried, which depends upon the seriousness of the outcome. When all that is at issue is the allocation of a loss that can be measured in financial terms, the accuser needs only to prove the defendant's fault by a preponderance of the evidence, but where the defendant's very life or freedom is at stake the burden is considerably higher: the prosecutor must prove beyond a reasonable doubt. (2017, 1)

Our ordinary everyday practices also place the burden of proof on those who knowingly and intentionally cause harm to others. In fact, even in cases where harm is *foreseeable* but not intended, we often demand a high level of justification. Let us say a newspaper receives a tip on a story that will likely cause great harm to a public figure, potentially sinking their career. In such circumstances, good journalistic standards demand that the story be independently verified and properly vetted before it is run. If the newspaper were to run the story without properly vetting it, and later discover that the tip came from an organization that seeks to undermine the public's trust in the media, we would rightly condemn the newspaper for not applying a higher epistemic standard. Things are even clearer when the harm caused is intentional, like in the case of a just war or when a nation decides to use deadly force.

In the case of legal punishment where the severity of harm is beyond question, I maintain that we should place the highest burden possible upon the state. If the state is going to punish someone for first-degree murder, say, then the epistemic bar that needs to be reached is guilt beyond a reasonable doubt. But does this burden of proof carry over to theoretical debates—for example, the debate over free will and moral responsibility? Here I follow Massimo Pigliucci and Maarten Boudry (2014) as well as Michael Corrado (2017, 3) in distinguishing between *evidential* burden of proof, which comes into play only when there is no costs associated with a wrong answer, and *prudential* burden of proof, which comes into play precisely when there are significant costs associated with a wrong answer. As Corrado applies the distinction to theoretical matters:

> in a purely philosophical contest where nothing of a practical nature hangs on the outcome it is the evidential burden of proof that is required, and the standard of proof must be "by a preponderance of the evidence": whoever simply has the better evidence must win. On the other hand, if something practical does depend on the outcome of the philosophical debate, then what would matter is the prudential burden. The costs on either side would determine the allocation of the burden and the standard by which satisfaction of the burden is to be measured. (2017, 3)

I contend that given the practical importance of moral responsibility to legal punishment, and given the gravity of harm caused by legal punishment (to the individuals punished as well as those family and friends who depend upon the imprisoned for income, love, support, and/or parenting), the proper epistemic standard to adopt is the prudential burden of proof beyond a reasonable doubt.

Vilhauer, for instance, has persuasively argued that "if it can be reasonably doubted that someone had free will with respect to some action, then it is a requirement of justice to refrain from doing serious retributive harm to him in response to that action" (2009, 131). Pereboom has also proposed applying the reasonable doubt standard:

> Punishment—in particular, punishment designed to satisfy the retributive goals—harms people. If one aims to harm another, the justification must meet a high epistemic standard. If it not beyond reasonable doubt that retributivist justifications are disguised vengeful justification, and vengeful justification are illegitimate, then there is reason to believe that it is immoral to justify punishment policy retributivistically. More generally, where there is a substantial likelihood that one's justification for harming someone is illegitimate, then harming that person on the basis of that justification could well be morally wrong. (2001, 161)

The proof-beyond-a-reasonable-doubt standard is the appropriate epistemic standard to apply when we are talking about intentional harm and institutional punishment. When the stakes are high, as they are with legal punishment, both the law and everyday practice demand that we set the epistemic bar accordingly. As Vilhauer notes, the prudential burden of proof beyond a reasonable doubt has a close kinship to another "reasonable doubt" principle, which is widely recognized to be a requirement of justice: "that is the requirement in Anglo-American criminal legal proceedings that the accused can only be convicted of a crime if it is proven beyond reasonable doubt that he acted criminally" (2009, 133). The grounds for accepting this high epistemic standard for criminal conviction are the same as the grounds for accepting it with regard to premise (1).

When premise (1) is combined with (2), which is simply a statement of the retributivist justification for legal punishment, we get the requirement that retributivists must justify their core assumption—that is, that agents are free and morally responsible in the basic desert sense and hence justly deserve to suffer for the wrongs they have done. As Vilhauer puts it:

> When the claim that someone has free will plays a role in a retributive justification of serious harm, that claim must be held to the same standard [as criminal conviction], for the same reason. That is, in this context, the claim that someone has free will plays a role in an argument for seriously harming someone, just as the claim that someone has committed a crime typically does. For this reason, it must be held to the "reasonable doubt" standard, just as the claim that someone has committed a crime must be. (2009, 134)

While this demand for justification is reasonable given the strength of (1), many retributivists simply deny or ignore it (see Caruso 2021a for a discussion of such views). And those libertarian and compatibilist accounts that do try to justify the assumption of free will fail to overcome the high epistemic burden of proof needed to justify retributive harm. This is because they tend to be either scientifically implausible (as in the case of agent causation), empirically unwarranted (as in the case of event-causal libertarianism), beg the question (as in the case of Strawson and other forms of compatibilism), or end up "changing the subject" (as in the case of Dennett and others).[9] Furthermore, the debate over free will has been waging for over two thousand years, and reasonable people still disagree. In the face of such professional disagreement and uncertainty, I maintain that we should refrain from intentionally harming wrongdoers on the philosophically questionable assumption that they deserve it and that such punishment is intrinsically good.

In *Rejecting Retributivism* (2021a), I also develop four additional arguments against retributivism that are independent of worries over free will and basic desert moral responsibility. They include the *Misalignment Argument*, which maintains that it is philosophically problematic to impart to the state the function of intentionally harming wrongdoers in accordance with desert since it is not at all clear that the state is capable of properly tracking the desert and blameworthiness of individuals in any reliable way. This is because criminal law is not properly designed to account for all the various factors that affect blameworthiness, and as a result the *moral criteria of blameworthiness* are often misaligned with the *legal criteria of guilt* (see also Kelly 2018). I also present a closely related argument, which I call *Poor Epistemic Position Argument (PEPA)*. It argues that for the state to be able to justly distribute legal punishment in accordance with desert, it needs to be in the proper epistemic position to know what an agent basically deserves, but since the state is (almost) never in the proper epistemic position to know what an agent basically

[9] See Caruso (2020, 2021a) for further details.

deserves, it follows that the state is not able to justly distribute legal punishment in accordance with desert.

My final two arguments against retributivism are the *Indeterminacy in Judgment Argument* and the *Limited Effectiveness Argument*. The former maintains that how the state goes about judging the gravity of wrong done, on the one hand, and what counts as proportional punishment for that wrong, on the other, is wide open to subjective and cultural biases and prejudices, and as a result, the principle of proportionality in *actual practice* does not provide the kind of protections against abuse it promises. The latter argues that there are good additional pragmatic reasons for rejecting retributivism since it has limited effectiveness in promoting important social goals such as rehabilitation and reforming offenders (see Caruso 2021a for more details).

I maintain that these six arguments—the Skeptical Argument, Epistemic Argument, Misalignment Argument, Poor Epistemic Position Argument, Indeterminacy in Judgment Argument, and Limited Effectiveness Argument—give us more than ample reason to reject retributivism.

3 The Public Health-Quarantine Model

If, then, we come to doubt or deny the existence of free will, or reject retributivism for other reasons, where does that leave us with regard to criminal justice? Many worry that without the justification of retributivism and the putative protection afforded by the principle of proportionality, we would be unable to successfully deal with criminal behavior. I contend, however, that this is not the case and that there is an ethically defensible and practically workable alternative to retributive legal punishment, one that is consistent with free will skepticism and preferable to other non-retributive alternatives. I call it the *public health-quarantine model* (see Caruso 2016, 2021a, 2021b; Pereboom and Caruso 2018; Caruso and Pereboom 2020).[10] The model not only provides a justification for the incapacitation of dangerous criminals consistent with free will skepticism, but it also provides a broader and more comprehensive approach to criminal behavior generally, since it draws on the public health framework and prioritizes prevention and social justice.

[10] I should note that there are other alternatives to classical retributivism that are consistent with the rejection of retributivism—such as consequentialist deterrence theories, educational theories, communicative theories, and mixed accounts. But I have elsewhere argued that these approaches have ethical problems of their own that are difficult to overcome and make them less desirable than my non-retributive and non-punitive alternative (see Caruso 2021a).

The public health-quarantine model is based on an analogy with quarantine and draws on a comparison between treatment of dangerous criminals and treatment of carriers of dangerous diseases. It takes as its starting point Pereboom's famous account (2001, 2013, 2014). In its simplest form, it can be stated as follows:

> The free will skeptic claims that criminals are not morally responsible for their actions in the basic desert sense. Plainly, many carriers of dangerous diseases are not responsible in this or in any sense for hav[ing] contracted these diseases. We generally agree that it is sometimes permissible to quarantine them nevertheless. (Pereboom 2014, 156)

The justification for doing so is the right to self-protection and the prevention of harm to others.

> But then, even if a dangerous criminal is not morally responsible for his crimes in the basic desert sense (perhaps because no one is ever in this way morally responsible) it could be as legitimate to preventatively detain him as to quarantine the non-responsible carrier of a serious communicable disease. (156)

The first thing to note about the theory is that, although one may justify quarantine (in the case of disease) and incapacitation (in the case of dangerous criminals) on purely utilitarian or consequentialist grounds, both Pereboom and I want to resist this strategy (see Pereboom and Caruso 2018; see also Caruso 2021a). Instead, on our view incapacitation of dangerous criminals is justified on the ground of the right to harm in self-defense and defense of others. That we have this right has broad appeal, much broader than utilitarianism or consequentialism has. In addition, this makes the view more resilient in the face of objections (see Pereboom and Caruso 2018; Caruso 2021a).

Second, the quarantine model places several constraints on the treatment of criminals (see Pereboom 2001, 2014; Pereboom and Caruso 2018; Caruso 2021a). For one thing, "as less dangerous diseases justify only preventative measures less restrictive than quarantine, so less dangerous criminal tendencies justify only more moderate restraints" (Pereboom 2014, 156). We do not, for instance, quarantine people for the common cold even though it has the potential to cause some harm. Rather, we restrict the use of quarantine to a narrowly prescribed set of cases. Analogously, on the public health-quarantine model, the use of incapacitation should be limited to only those cases where offenders are a serious threat to public safety and no less restrictive measures are available. In fact, for certain minor crimes, perhaps only some degree of monitoring could be defended. Furthermore, the incapacitation account that results from this analogy demands a degree of concern for the rehabilitation and well-being of the criminal that would alter much of current practice: "Just as fairness recommends that we seek to cure the diseased we quarantine, so fairness would counsel that we attempt to rehabilitate the criminals we detain" (Pereboom 2014, 156). Rehabilitation and reintegration would therefore replace punishment as the focus of the criminal justice system. Lastly, "If a criminal cannot be rehabilitated, and our safety requires his indefinite confinement, this account provides no justification for making his life more miserable than would be required to guard against the danger he poses" (Pereboom 2014, 156).

Third, this account also provides a more resilient proposal for justifying criminal sanctions than other non-retributive options. One advantage it has, say, over consequentialist deterrence theories is that it has more restrictions placed on it with regard to using people merely as means. For instance, as it is illegitimate to treat carriers of a disease more harmfully than is necessary to neutralize the danger they pose, treating offenders with violent criminal tendencies more harshly than is required to protect society will be illegitimate as well. In fact, in all our writings on the subject, Pereboom and I have always maintained the *principle of least infringement*, which holds that the least restrictive measures should be taken to protect public health and safety (Caruso 2016, 2017, 2021a; Pereboom and Caruso 2018). This ensures that criminal sanctions will be proportionate to the danger posed by an individual, and any sanctions that exceed this upper bound will be unjustified.

In addition to these restrictions on harsh and unnecessary treatment, the model also advocates for a broader approach to criminal behavior that moves beyond the narrow focus on sanctions. On the model I have developed, the quarantine analogy is placed within the broader justificatory framework of *public health ethics* (Caruso 2016, 2017, 2021a). Public health ethics not only justifies quarantining carriers of infectious diseases on the grounds that it is necessary to protect public health. It also requires that we take active steps to *prevent* such outbreaks from occurring in the first place. Quarantine is only needed when the public health system fails in its primary function. Since no system is perfect, quarantine will likely be needed for the foreseeable future, but it should *not* be the primary means of dealing with public health. The analogous claim holds for incapacitation. Taking a public health approach to criminal behavior would allow us to justify the incapacitation of dangerous criminals when needed, but it would also make prevention a *primary function* of the criminal justice system. So, instead of myopically focusing on punishment, the public health-quarantine model shifts the focus to identifying and addressing the systemic causes of crime, such as poverty, low socioeconomic status, systematic disadvantage, mental illness, homelessness, educational inequity, abuse, and addiction (see Caruso 2021a).

In *Rejecting Retributivism* (2021a), I argue that the social determinants of health (SDH) and the social determinants of criminal behavior (SDCB) are broadly similar, and that we should adopt a broad public health approach for identifying and taking action on these shared social determinants. I focus on how social inequities and systemic injustices affect health outcomes and criminal behavior, how poverty affects brain development, how offenders often have preexisting medical conditions (especially mental health issues), how homelessness and education affect health and safety outcomes, how environmental health is important to both public health and safety, how involvement in the criminal justice system itself can lead to or worsen health and cognitive problems, and how a public health approach can be successfully applied within the criminal justice system. I argue that, just as it is important to identify and take action on the SDH if we want to improve health outcomes, it is equally important to identify and address the SDCB. And I conclude by offering eight broad public policy proposals for implementing a public health approach aimed at addressing the SDH and SDCB.

Furthermore, the public health framework I adopt sees *social justice* as a foundational cornerstone to public health and safety (Caruso 2016, 2021a). In public health ethics, a failure on the part of public health institutions to ensure the social conditions necessary to achieve a sufficient level of health is considered a grave injustice. An important task of public health ethics, then, is to identify which inequalities in health are the most egregious and thus which should be given the highest priority in public health policy and practice. The public health approach to criminal behavior likewise maintains that a core moral function of the criminal justice system is to identify and remedy social and economic inequalities responsible for crime. Just as public health is negatively affected by poverty, racism, and systematic inequality, so too is public safety. This broader approach to criminal justice therefore places issues of social justice at the forefront. It sees racism, sexism, poverty, and systemic disadvantage as serious threats to public safety, and it prioritizes the reduction of such inequalities (see Caruso 2021a).

While there are different ways of understanding *social justice* and different philosophical accounts of what a theory of justice aims to achieve, I favor a *capability approach* according to which the development of capabilities—what each individual is able to do or be—is essential to human well-being (e.g., Sen 1985, 1999; Power and Faden 2006; Nussbaum 2011). For capability theorists, human well-being is the proper end of a theory of justice. And on the particular capability approach I favor, social justice is grounded in six key features of human well-being: *health*, *reasoning*, *self-determination*, *attachment*, *personal security*, and *respect* (Caruso 2021a).[11] Following Powers and Faden (2006), I maintain that each of these six dimensions is an essential feature of well-being such that "a life substantially lacking in any one is a life seriously deficient in what it is reasonable for anyone to want, whatever else they want" (Powers and Faden 2006, 8). The job of justice is therefore to achieve a sufficiency of these six essential dimensions of human well-being, since each is a separate indicator of a decent life.

The key idea of capability approaches is that social arrangements should aim to expand people's capabilities—their freedom to promote or achieve *functionings* that are important to them. *Functionings* are defined as the valuable activities and states that make up human well-being, such as having a healthy body, being safe, or having a job. While they are related to goods and income, they are instead described in terms of what a person is able to do or be as a result. For example, when a person's need for food (a commodity) is met, they enjoy the functioning of being well-nourished. Examples of functionings include being mobile, being healthy, being adequately nourished, and being educated. The genuine opportunity to achieve a particular functioning is called a *capability*. *Capabilities* are "the alternative combination of functionings that are feasible for [a person] to achieve"—they are "the substantive freedom" a person has "to lead the kind of life he or she has reason to value" (Sen 1999, 87).

As Tabandeh, Gardoni, and Murphy describe:

> Genuine opportunities and actual achievements are influenced by what individuals have and what they can do with what they have. What they can do with what they have is a function of the structure of social, legal, economic, and political institutions and of the characteristics of the built environment (i.e., infrastructure). For example, consider the functioning of being mobile. The number of times an individual travels per week can be an indicator of mobility achievement. When explaining a given individual's achievement or lack of achievement, a capability approach takes into consideration the conditions that must be in place for the individual to be mobile. For instance, the possession of certain resources, like a bike, may influence mobility. However, possessing a bike may not be sufficient to guarantee mobility. If the individual has physical disabilities, then the bike will be of no help to travel. Similarly, if there are no paved roads or if societal culture imposes a norm that women are not allowed to

[11] Note that this is a pared down list from the ones offered by Martha Nussbaum (2011) and other capability theorists.

> ride a bike, then it will become difficult or even impossible to travel by means of a bike. As this example makes clear, different factors will influence the number of times the individual travels. (2018, 411)

Thinking in terms of capabilities therefore raises a wider range of issues than simply looking at the amount of resources or commodities people have, because people have different needs. In the example given above, just providing bicycles to people will not be enough to increase the functioning of being mobile if you are disabled or prohibited from riding because of sexist social norms. A capabilities approach to social justice therefore requires that we consider and address a larger set of social issues.

Bringing everything together, my public health-quarantine model characterizes the moral foundation of public health as social justice, not just the advancement of good health outcomes. That is, while promoting social goods (like health) is one area of concern, public health ethics as I conceive it is embedded within a broader commitment to secure a sufficient level of health and safety for all and to narrow unjust inequalities (see Powers and Faden 2006). More specifically, I see the capability approach to social justice as the proper moral foundation of public health ethics. This means that the broader commitment of public health should be the achievement of those capabilities needed to secure a sufficient level of human well-being—including, but not limited to, health, reasoning, self-determination, attachment, personal security, and respect. By placing social justice at the foundation of the public health approach, the realms of criminal justice and social justice are brought closer together. I see this as a virtue of the theory since it is hard to see how we can adequately deal with criminal justice without simultaneously addressing issues of social justice.

Retributivists tend to disagree since they approach criminal justice as an issue of individual responsibility and desert, not as an issue of prevention and public safety. I believe it is a mistake to hold that the criteria of individual accountability can be settled apart from considerations of social justice and the social determinants of criminal behavior. Making social justice foundational, as my public health-quarantine model does, places on us a collective responsibility—which is forward-looking and perfectly consistent with free will skepticism—to redress unjust inequalities and to advance collective aims and priorities such as public health and safety. The capability approach and the public health approach therefore fit nicely together. Both maintain that poor health and safety are often the byproducts of social inequities, and both attempt to identify and address these social inequities in order to achieve a sufficient level of health and safety.

Summarizing the public health-quarantine model, then, the core idea is that the right to harm in self-defense and defense of others justifies incapacitating the criminally dangerous with the minimum harm required for adequate protection. The resulting account would not justify the sort of criminal punishment whose legitimacy is most dubious, such as death or confinement in the most common kinds of prisons in our society. The model also specifies attention to the well-being of criminals, which would change much of current policy. Furthermore, the public health component of the theory prioritizes prevention and social justice, and it aims at identifying and taking action on the social determinants of health and criminal behavior. This combined approach to dealing with criminal behavior, I maintain, is sufficient for dealing with dangerous criminals, leads to a more humane and effective social policy, and is actually preferable to the harsh and often excessive forms of punishment that typically come with retributivism.[12]

References

Alexander, Larry. 2013. "You Got What You Deserved." *Criminal Law and Philosophy* 7, no. 2 (June): 309-19.

Alexander, Larry, Kimberly Kessler Ferzan, and Stephen Morse. 2009. *Crime and Culpability: A Theory of Criminal Law*. New York: Cambridge University Press.

Berman, Mitchell N. 2008. "Punishment and Justification." *Ethics* 118, no. 2 (January): 258–90.

———. 2011. "Two Kinds of Retributivism." In *Philosophical Foundations of Criminal Law*, edited by R. A. Duff and Stuart P. Green, 433–57. New York: Oxford University Press.

———. 2013. "Rehabilitating Retributivism." *Law and Philosophy* 32, no. 1 (January): 83–108.

———. 2016. "Modest Retributivism." In *Legal, Moral, and Metaphysical Truths: The Philosophy of Michael S. Moore*, edited by Kimberly Kessler Ferzan and Stephen J. Morse, 35–48. New York: Oxford University Press.

Boonin, David. 2008. *The Problem of Punishment*. Cambridge: Cambridge University Press.

Caruso, Gregg D. 2012. *Free Will and Consciousness: A Determinist Account of the Illusion of the Free Will*. Lanham, MD: Lexington.

———. 2016. "Free Will Skepticism and Criminal Behavior: A Public Health-Quarantine Model." *Southwest Philosophical Review* 32, no. 1 (January): 25–48.

[12] For my replies to various objections to the public health-quarantine model, see Pereboom and Caruso (2018) and Caruso (2021a, 2021b, 2021c).

———. 2017. *Public Health and Safety: The Social Determinants of Health and Criminal Behavior*. UK: ResearchLinks Books.
———. 2020. "Justice without Retribution: An Epistemic Argument against Retributive Criminal Punishment." *Neuroethics* 13, no. 1 (April): 13–28.
———. 2021a. *Rejecting Retributivism: Free Will, Punishment, and Criminal Justice*. Cambridge: Cambridge University Press.
———. 2021b. "Retributivism, Free Will Skepticism, and the Public Health-Quarantine Model: Replies to Corrado, Kennedy, Sifferd, Walen, Pereboom and Shaw." *Journal of Legal Philosophy* 46, no. 2 (October): 161–215.
———. 2021c. "Rejecting Retributivism: Reply to Leo Zaibert." *Philosopher* 109, no. 4 (Autumn): 118–26.
Caruso, Gregg D., and Derk Pereboom. 2020. "A Non-Punitive Alternative to Retributive Punishment." In *The Routledge Handbook of the Philosophy and Science of Punishment*, edited by Farah Focquaert, Elizabeth Shaw, and Bruce N. Waller, 355–65. New York: Routledge.
———. 2022. *Moral Responsibility Reconsidered*. Cambridge: Cambridge University Press.
Corrado, Michael Louis. 2017. "Punishment and the Burden of Proof." UNC Legal Studies Research Paper, March 3. https://papers.ssrn.com/sol3/papers.cfm?abstract_id=2997654.
Cotton, Michele. 2000. "Back with a Vengeance: The Resilience of Retribution as an Articulated Purpose of Criminal Punishment." *American Criminal Law Review* 37, no. 4 (Fall): 1313–57.
Dennett, Daniel C., and Gregg D. Caruso. 2021. *Just Deserts: Debating Free Will*. New York: Polity.
Dingwall, Gavin. 2008. "Deserting Desert? Locating the Present Role of Retributivism in the Sentencing of Adult Offenders." *Howard Journal of Crime and Justice* 47, no. 4 (September): 400–410.
Husak, Douglas. 2000. "Holistic Retributivism." *California Law Review* 88, no. 3 (May): 991–1000.
Jeppsson, Sofia M. I. 2021. "Retributivism, Justification and Credence: The Epistemic Argument Revisited." *Neuroethics* 14, no. 2 (July): 177–90.
Kant, Immanuel. 1996. *The Metaphysics of Morals*. In *Practical Philosophy*, translated and edited by Mary J. Gregor, 363–602. Cambridge: Cambridge University Press.
Kelly, Erin I. 2018. *The Limits of Blame: Rethinking Punishment and Responsibility*. Cambridge, MA: Harvard University Press.
Kershnar, Stephen. 2000. "A Defense of Retributivism." *International Journal of Applied Philosophy* 14, no. 1 (Spring): 97–117.
———. 2001. *Desert, Retribution, and Torture*. Lanham, MD: University Press of America.
Levy, Neil. 2011. *Hard Luck: How Luck Undermines Free Will and Moral Responsibility*. New York: Oxford University Press.
Mabbott, J. D. 1939. "Punishment." *Mind* 48, no. 190 (April): 152–67.

Moore, Michael S. 1987. "The Moral Worth of Retribution." In *Punishment and Rehabilitation*, edited by Jeffrie G. Murphy, 3rd ed., 94–130. New York: Wadsworth.

———. 1993. *Act and Crime: The Philosophy of Action and Its Implications for Criminal Law*. Oxford: Oxford University Press.

———. 1997. *Placing Blame: A General Theory of the Criminal Law*. Oxford: Oxford University Press.

Nussbaum, Martha C. 2011. *Creating Capabilities: The Human Development Approach*. Cambridge, MA: Belknap.

Pereboom, Derk. 2001. *Living without Free Will*. Cambridge: Cambridge University Press.

———. 2013. "Free Will Skepticism and Criminal Punishment." In *The Future of Punishment*, edited by Thomas A. Nadelhoffer, 49–78. Oxford: Oxford University Press.

———. 2014. *Free Will, Agency, and Meaning in Life*. Oxford: Oxford University Press.

———. 2021. *Wrongdoing and the Moral Emotions*. Oxford: Oxford University Press.

Pereboom, Derk, and Gregg D. Caruso. 2018. "Hard-Incompatibilist Existentialism: Neuroscience, Punishment, and Meaning in Life." In *Neuroexistentialism: Meaning, Morals, and Purpose in the Age of Neuroscience*, edited by Gregg D. Caruso and Owen Flanagan, 193–222. Oxford: Oxford University Press.

Pigliucci, Massimo, and Maarten Boudry. 2014. "Prove It! The Burden of Proof Game in Science vs. Pseudoscience Disputes." *Philosophia* 42, no. 2 (June): 487–502.

Powers, Madison, and Ruth Faden. 2006. *Social Justice: The Moral Foundations of Public Health and Health Policy*. Oxford: Oxford University Press.

Quinton, A. M. 1954. "On Punishment." *Analysis* 14, no. 6 (June): 133–42.

Robinson, Paul H. 2008. *Distributive Principles of Criminal Law: Who Should Be Punished How Much*. Oxford: Oxford University Press.

Robinson, Paul H, and Michael T. Cahill. 2006. *Law without Justice: Why Criminal Law Doesn't Give People What They Deserve*. Oxford: Oxford University Press.

Sen, Amartya. 1985. *Commodities and Capabilities*. Oxford: Oxford University Press.

———. 1999. *Development as Freedom*. New York: Anchor.

Shaw, Elizabeth. 2014. "Free Will, Punishment, and Criminal Responsibility." Ph.D. diss., Edinburgh University.

———. 2021. "The Epistemic Argument against Retributivism." *Journal of Legal Philosophy* 46, no. 2 (October): 155–60.

Strawson, Galen. 1986. *Freedom and Belief*. Oxford: Oxford University Press.

Tabandeh, Armin, Paolo Gardoni, and Colleen Murphy. 2018. "A Reliability-Based Capability Approach." *Risk Analysis* 38, no. 2 (February): 410–24.

Tadros, Victor. 2011. *The Ends of Harm: The Moral Foundations of Criminal Law*. Oxford: Oxford University Press.

Tonry, Michael. 2004. "U.S. Sentencing Systems Fragmenting." In *Panel Reform in Overcrowded Times*, edited by Michael Tonry, 21–28. Oxford: Oxford University Press.

Vilhauer, Benjamin. 2009. "Free Will and Reasonable Doubt." *American Philosophical Quarterly* 46, no. 2 (April): 131–40.
———. 2012. "Taking Free Will Skepticism Seriously." *Philosophical Quarterly* 62, no. 249 (October): 833–52.
———. 2015. "Free Will and the Asymmetrical Justifiability of Holding Morally Responsible." *Philosophical Quarterly* 65, no. 261 (October): 772–89.
von Hirsch, Andrew. 1976. *Doing Justice: The Choice of Punishments*. New York: Hill & Wang.
———. 1981. "Desert and Previous Convictions in Sentencing." *Minnesota Law Review* 65, no. 4 (April): 591–634.
———. 2007. "The 'Desert' Model for Sentencing: Its Influence, Prospects, and Alternatives." *Social Research* 74, no. 2 (Summer): 413–34.
———. 2017. *Deserving Criminal Sentences: An Overview*. Portland, OR: Hart.
Walen, Alec. 2020. "Retributive Justice." *Stanford Encyclopedia of Philosophy* (Summer 2021 edition), edited by Edward N. Zalta. https://plato.stanford.edu/archives/sum2021/entries/justice-retributive/.
Waller, Bruce N. 2011. *Against Moral Responsibility*. Cambridge, MA: MIT Press.
Zaibert, Leo. 2018. *Rethinking Punishment*. Cambridge: Cambridge University Press.

23

Do Rapists Deserve Criminal Treatment?

Katrina L. Sifferd

In this chapter I will argue that persons who commit rape deserve criminal blame, and in some cases, criminal punishment. Those who are not in academic philosophy may be surprised that criminal blame of serious criminal actors like rapists is even in question, for surely rapists deserve criminal blame and punishment. Who is labeled a rapist, what sort of punishment rapists deserve, and how severely they ought to be punished are interesting questions that deserve careful treatment. However, that rapists (fairly labeled) deserve to be found guilty of a crime and in some cases punished would seem to be something we can agree upon.

But it isn't. Smart philosophers in this volume claim rapists do not deserve criminal treatment. This is because such treatment is grounded in a blaming response, and they claim nobody ever deserves praise or blame for anything they do, including discovering a vaccine for COVID-19 or committing a rape or murder (see Caruso's chapter in this volume). Typically, desert claims operate in this way: someone (the "deserver") deserves something (the "desert") in virtue of their possession of some feature (the "desert base") (Feldman and Skow 2020). The feature humans are thought to have to make them deserving is typically some cognitive capacities—for example, guidance control over one's actions. Many desert skeptics argue that the desert base responsibility

K. L. Sifferd (✉)
Elmhurst University, Elmhurst, IL, USA
e-mail: sifferdk@elmhurst.edu

© The Author(s), under exclusive license to Springer Nature Switzerland AG 2023

M. C. Altman (ed.), *The Palgrave Handbook on the Philosophy of Punishment*, Palgrave Handbooks in the Philosophy of Law, https://doi.org/10.1007/978-3-031-11874-6_23

theorists identify does not exist. For this reason, they claim desert claims are baseless and unjust.

There is a long history of desert skepticism in philosophy. However, arguments that human beings lack "ultimate" control over their actions and thus are not responsible have become more popular in the past decade or so (see, e.g., Pereboom 2013; Pereboom and Caruso 2018; Caruso 2021). This may be due to data from neuroscience and other scientific disciplines that depict our cognitive processes as mechanistic, operating in response to our environments in deterministic, probabilistic, or indeterministic ways. If our actions are largely outside of "our" control, say the desert skeptics, then it does not seem fair to hold us accountable for them.[1]

In this chapter, I expand upon a familiar compatibilist account of the features some humans possess that ground claims of desert. A primary aim of the chapter is to try to bridge the gap between moral and legal accounts of the features that make us responsible. My capacitarian view of responsible agency can support robust mental causation, which I claim is a key requirement for criminal culpability. I will also note the ways in which the capacity for reasons-responsiveness is developed and maintained over time, and claim that diachronic agency can instantiate meaningful self-control and self-formation with moral and legal rules in mind. I believe that this desert base can ground a desert response in the form of a criminal verdict, which in turn may qualify the deserver for criminal punishment depending on other aims (besides delivering "just deserts").

This chapter thus focuses on trying to ground desert claims in some feature of human agency. Of course, even if one is convinced that we are the sorts of things that deserve blame, there is further work to do explaining whether the harm of blame and punishment, especially criminal blame and punishment, can be justified (and how it can be justified). The account I provide here attempts to lay the foundations for an argument that, when a person with certain capacities commits the wrong of committing a crime, the harm of a criminal verdict can be justified because this expressive form of blame can be understood as either intrinsically or extrinsically (but not only

[1] I often wonder who this "we" is that ought not to be held responsible on the desert skeptical view. Except for the few philosophers who believe there is some immaterial aspect of human existence (e.g., souls), most think we are lumps of physical stuff with very complex functional organization and thus phenomenal experiences. The physical stuff most important to complex human behavior are our embodied (and yes, mechanistic) cognitive processes. If a real and robust "we" or "I" can emerge from these physical processes, why not a responsible self?

instrumentally) good.[2] If I am correct, no appeal to instrumental goods, such as public safety or deterrent effect, will be necessary to justify criminal verdicts, although I think they are relevant to criminal punishment. I am a "weak retributivist" about criminal punishment, which means that I think desert is necessary but not sufficient for criminal sanctions. When a criminal offender deserves the blame of a criminal verdict, I believe this opens up the possibility that the further harm of criminal punishment may be justified given both retributive and instrumental concerns (namely, that moral and legal agency are supported by the application of that sort of criminal punishment to that sort of crime). In philosophical speak, this means that backward-looking desert is necessary but not sufficient for criminal punishment.

This short overview of some the issues surrounding desert ought to make it clear that it is a complicated and thorny topic. Again, my primary aim here is to articulate an account of legal agency (directly related to an account of moral agency) that can ground desert claims, where what is deserved is a guilty verdict. I will offer the example of rape offenders as worthy of criminal blame. I focus on trying to articulate the grounds for a desert claim not just because it seems like the right place to start when one is interested in justifying criminal punishment—which I see as contingent on desert—but also because many desert skeptics think this hurdle to punishment cannot be cleared (Caruso 2016, 2021; Pereboom and Caruso 2018).

1 What Does It Mean to Be a Criminally Culpable Agent?

It is easiest, I think, to begin with the structure of criminal responsibility, and then to drill down to the mental or cognitive capacities that make us criminally culpable. (It is here that traditional compatibilist accounts will become important.) The criminal law places mental states in a privileged role in the explanation of human action, where such states are seen as the source or cause of behavior (Morse 2003, 2007, 2011; Sifferd 2006). This means that the criminal law trades in, and has codified, the psychological theory that most human beings naturally utilize to attribute psychological states to themselves and others when they attempt to understand or explain human behavior

[2] See McKenna (2019) for excellent arguments that desert claims may be justifiable if moral blame is extrinsically (and not just intrinsically) good. McKenna leaves open the possibility that instrumental goods may also flow from moral blame.

(Sifferd 2006).[3] For example, imagine Sally and Quayshawn work together at the university and are both in the faculty lounge. Quayshawn sees Sally glance outside and frown at the rain pouring down; and then watches her grab a raincoat before heading for the door. It would be typical for Quayshawn to attribute to Sally the mental states of *believing it is raining* and *desiring not to get wet*, and to assume she put the raincoat on with the *belief that it would help keep her dry*. Quayshawn makes these mental state attributions to explain and predict Sally's behavior. Many have called this process of making mental state attributes our "theory of mind." Humans tend to develop theory of mind around two to three years of age, although there are exceptions, and as is the case with many of our cognitive capacities, some people are better than others at exercising it.[4]

To be found guilty of a crime, a defendant must possess certain folk psychological mental states at the time the crime was committed. Further, these mental states must be causally related to criminal harm for which the defendant has been arrested. So, for example, to be guilty of murder, a defendant must have caused the unlawful death of a person by committing a voluntary action—for example, by aiming and pulling the trigger of the gun—where that action is also causally related to certain mental states held at the time (e.g., the intent to cause a death, or knowledge that a death was likely to occur). An aggravated rape conviction requires that a person threaten or restrain his victim with the intent of getting them to submit to nonconsensual sex (MPC 2.13[1]).

In general, the tighter the relationship between the mental states of the defendant and the criminal harm they cause, the higher the level of criminal culpability is assigned to the defendant. The U.S. Model Penal Code sorts defendant mental states into four categories: (1) purposeful, (2) knowing, (3) reckless, and (4) negligent.[5] A defendant is more culpable for an act of pulling the trigger with the *purpose* of killing another than for the act of pulling the trigger in a way that exhibits recklessness regarding the fact that a bullet might hit and kill someone. This is the case even if the criminal harm is the same in

---

[3] Prominent legal scholar Stephen Morse claims that our ordinary understanding of human behavior posits that "virtually all actions for which agents deserve to be praised, blamed, rewarded, or punished are the product of mental causation" (2011, 530).

[4] One group of persons who may not have this commonsense "theory of mind" necessary to attribute mental states to others is autistics (Baron-Cohen 1995). For more information on folk psychology, see Fodor (1987), Jackson and Pettit (1990), and Morse (2008).

[5] The Model Penal Code is a model act designed by the American Law Institute to assist U.S. state legislatures in updating and standardizing the penal law. It was published in 1962 and has undergone several revisions, including recent revisions to the sexual assault provisions. See A.L.I. (August 18, 2020), Model Penal Code: Sexual Assault and Related Offenses, tentative draft no. 4.

both scenarios (e.g., a person is dead). Another example is the case of simple rape (sex without consent) versus aggravated rape (mentioned above). In the first case, the rapist might be aware of, but *recklessly disregard* a risk that the person does not consent to intercourse (MPC 213.6). In the second case, the rapist must act with the *purpose* of securing submission to nonconsensual sex. More severe penalties are attached to the latter aggravated rape (say, a ten- to-fifteen-year term of incarceration as compared to a three-to-five-year term of incarceration for simple rape).

Why do mental states matter to criminal punishment when the criminal harm done is the same? One might explain this in a few different ways. A person interested in justifying criminal punishment via backward-looking desert might argue that acting for the purpose of causing criminal harm is a more serious form of moral wrongdoing than acting with reckless disregard for the fact that one might cause that harm, and thus persons who commit purposeful criminal harm deserve a more severe response. In addition, where criminal harm is the aim of an action, it is generally the case that the moral reasons against the action are obvious to the actor, although they may be ignored or overridden by other considerations. This often means the actor has a fair opportunity to engage with such moral reasons and to avoid the action based upon these reasons (more on this below, but see Brink and Nelkin 2013; Brink 2021). These features of the act would again seem to increase the level of moral wrongdoing committed by the actor when compared to a case of recklessness or negligence, where the actor may have quickly dismissed moral reasons against the act—"without thinking"—or did not consciously engage with such reasons, although they should have. In these cases, a person would seem less morally blameworthy.

A consequentialist or instrumentalist who wishes to justify the existing gradations in blame and punishment based upon mental states must do so by looking to the criminal law's forward-looking effects. For example, one might claim that a person who acts for the *purpose of causing criminal harm* is more dangerous or likely to recidivate than a person who acts recklessly or negligently, and thus are more likely to need more serious punishments to incapacitate or rehabilitate them. Consequentialists might also claim that lesser punishments are associated with less serious offenses because such lesser punishments are sufficient to deter at least some offenders from committing reckless or negligent acts. On the other hand, a very serious punishment may be necessary to deter a person who has the aim or intent to commit a rape or murder (for example).

These consequentialist explanations face serious difficulties, so much so that an account based upon moral desert seems to emerge as a better explanation of the criminal law's gradations in culpability and punishment.[6] First, how intentional an act is, and how well the criminal harm was known to the actor, do not seem to be very good predictors of whether or not the actor is "dangerous"—e.g., likely to act in a criminally harmful way in the future. A more intentional criminal actor is not necessarily more likely to recidivate. Many reckless and negligent persons may be likely to act recklessly and negligently in the future; one might imagine a date rapist who is serially reckless about securing consent, or a person who very often drives recklessly because they are texting. Second, there are offenders who commit serious, intentional harm—say, they kill a partner or a parent who was abusive—who are unlikely to recidivate. And offenders who commit less serious property crimes, such as auto theft, may be more likely to recidivate. There also seems to be no reliable relationship between the type or seriousness of the offense a person commits and their likelihood of recidivism.

If the gradations in culpability essential to the structure of the criminal law cannot be justified in a forward-looking way, to retain this basic structure we must look to persons' relationship to moral reasons and moral blameworthiness. I posit that the relative categories of criminal verdicts may reflect institutionalized gradations in blaming responses related to features of the actor and the act that track degree of moral wrongdoing. Persons who act with the aim of causing criminal harm, and persons who cause more serious criminal harm, are generally more deserving of blame (and harsher blame), all things being equal. Such people were likely aware of and engaged with moral and legal reasons not to perform the act but performed the act anyway.

A moral desert justification for the imposition of graded criminal verdicts (and related punishments) also requires that mental states can be *accurately* attributed to defendants by law enforcement, prosecutors, defense attorneys, judges, and jurors; and it must be true that such mental states are *causally related* to the criminal harm for which the defendant is arrested. That is, mental causation must be true. If this is not the case, then the criminal law sends attorneys, judges, and jurors on a fool's errand when they are trying to determine if a defendant is guilty of a particular crime; and defendants are assigned very serious penalties, including execution and life in prison in the U.S., based upon them having fictional causal entities in their heads.

We might note at this point some specific features of the mental causation required for criminal verdicts to be justified. The law does not require that

[6] In Sifferd (2021), I claim this is partly because utilitarianism works as a justification for the criminal law only at the institutional level—that is, criminal law and punishment serve to make legal and moral norms more salient to persons, thereby enhancing their moral agency.

defendants are "uncaused causers." That is, the law's commitment to mental causation is compatible with the idea that a defendant's culpable mental states are themselves causally related to other mental/physical states, such as perceptual states and emotional states (as they surely are). Given what we know from neuroscience, it seems likely that mental causes work in probabilistic and, to some extent, determinist ways. Indeed, if mental causes often operated in indeterminist or random ways, our theory of mind would fail and we would not be able to understand and predict human behavior by attributing mental states.[7] For all these reasons, legal scholars tend to agree with Stephen Morse that "criminal responsibility doctrines and practices are fully compatible with the truth of determinism (or causal closure)" (2015, 253). If the criminal law is correct in its identification of those who deserve guilty verdicts (and in some cases, punishment), what must be the case is that we are sensitive to moral and legal reasons. This is true even if our capacity to be reasons-responsive operates in lawlike or probabilistic ways. To be responsible, says Morse, we must be responsive to and guided by reasons. Until science conclusively demonstrates that that this is not the case, "the folk-psychological model of responsibility will endure as fully justified" (253).

To conclude this section: The structure of criminal offenses is best explained by appeal to backward-looking desert, and from the perspective of legal responsibility practices, the sort of control that matters to desert is the capacity to act in accordance with our own reasons for action, which we can understand as our beliefs and desires. Let us again look to rape as an example. Another way of saying that Tony held down Belinda for the purpose of having nonconsensual sex is to say he held Belinda down *for that reason*. All things being equal, we expect Tony to know that physically dominating someone to secure nonconsensual sex is to act for *immoral and illegal reasons*. If Tony has the capacity to act because of his reasons, and if he has the capacity to know his reasons for acting were immoral/illegal, Tony deserves criminal blame.

Of course, there are cases where a person may possess the requisite mental states required to be found guilty of a crime, and these mental states are causally related to criminal harm, but the person still does not deserve blame for the harm caused (blame is not fitting). This may be true in cases of legal excuse. For example, if a person is very young or legally insane, they may be exempt from legal liability and punishment even if they intended and caused

[7] Christian List (2019) seems to disagree in his recent book, arguing that, although the brain may operate in deterministic ways, mental states can supervene on the brain in such a way that it does not co-opt these determined casual properties. This argument seems broadly similar to the supervenience argument originally made by Donald Davidson (1970). In Sifferd (2014), I argue that this brand of supervenience is too weak to support the full-bodied mental causation required by the criminal law.

very serious criminal harm such as a rape. In this case, the person does not have the capacities necessary for a blaming response. In other cases, extreme circumstances may render a blaming response inappropriate even where the person does possess these capacities and caused criminal harm. Such harm can be justified, for example, in cases of self-defense. Possessing the appropriate capacities—and even exhibiting poor quality of will—and thereby causing harm only create *pro tonto* reasons to blame (McKenna 2019), and these considerations seem built into the criminal law.

2 Acting for Reasons

In this section, I further explore the mental capacities necessary to recognizing, forming, deliberating about, inhibiting, and acting for reasons, and why many philosophers argue in favor of the criminal law's supposition that these capacities are crucial to a person's moral and legal responsibility. I offer a positive account of responsible agency predicated primarily on reasons-responsiveness and mental capacity, or what legal scholar H. L. A. Hart (1968) calls "capacity-responsibility." Some of the claims will expand upon arguments I have offered elsewhere (Hirstein et al. 2018; Sifferd 2021).

Above I argued that backward-looking desert provides a better account of the structure of criminal offenses and penalties than forward-looking consequentialist justifications. For those, like me, who claim that persons found guilty of a crime and punishment ought to be morally deserving, the requirements for moral agency will be directly relevant to assessments of criminal culpability. According to John Martin Fischer and Mark Ravizza (1998), persons must have the mental capacity to be "reasons-responsive" in order to be held responsible for their acts. More specifically, Fischer and Ravizza claim we are morally responsible for an action when the action is issued by a cognitive mechanism or system that is *moderately* reasons-responsive. One is moderately reasons-responsive if and only if: (1) they are regularly receptive to a range of reasons, including moral reasons, such that they manifest an intelligible pattern of responsiveness over time; (2) they would react to at least one sufficient reason to do otherwise than they actually did (however, this being a compatibilist theory, it does not follow that the agent could have responded differently to the actual reasons); and (3) they own the cognitive processes or mechanism such that they take responsibility for it giving rise to their actions (Fischer and Ravizza 1998, 207–39).

Fischer and Ravizza's criteria for moral responsibility overlap considerably with criteria that Hart identified as necessary to be considered a legal agent, or a person to whom legal demands fairly apply. Hart (1968) claimed that legal responsibility actually refers to two different types of responsibility. The first type, which he calls "capacity-responsibility," consists of the general qualifying conditions for criminal responsibility. This is the type of responsibility that I think requires very similar capacities to those necessary for moral responsibility and reasons-responsiveness. The second type of legal responsibility, "legal liability-responsibility," requires specific mental state attributions such as those discussed above. Such mental states are assigned to a defendant in the process of finding them guilty of a particular criminal act. Hart was clear that capacity-responsibility is necessary for legal liability—if one lacks capacity-responsibility, they are disqualified for legal/criminal liability.

Hart claims that capacity-responsibility consists in the following abilities: to understand, reason, and control conduct; to understand what conduct legal and moral rules require and to deliberate and reach decisions concerning these requirements; and to conform behavior to decisions made (1968, 227). As Antony Duff notes, Hart's capacity-responsibility

> specifies a minimal condition of liability, which is satisfied alike by a willful murderer and by one who negligently causes death … a person has the capacity to obey the law, we can say, only if she would obey the law if she chose to do so, and has a fair opportunity to obey only if she has a real choice of whether to obey or not. (1993, 347)

Hopefully the similarity between the criteria for reasons-responsiveness and Hart's capacity-responsibility is obvious. On Fischer and Ravizza's theory, to be morally responsible one must have the cognitive capacity to (1) recognize reasons, including moral and legal reasons; (2) be able to understand these reasons and use them in deliberation and decision-making; and (3) be able to act in accordance with those reasons. In his conception of capacity-responsibility, Hart includes the capacities to understand what conduct legal and moral rules require and to reach decisions and take actions given these requirements. Thus, reasons-responsiveness tracks very similar cognitive and volitional capacities to those described by Hart as providing persons with a "fair opportunity" to be law-abiding. At the risk of redundancy, a person who is reasons-responsive, and a person with capacity-responsibility, can understand moral and legal rules and behave so as to avoid breaking such rules. In this case, the law's demands apply to them, and they are legally responsible for their actions, because they have a fair opportunity to be law-abiding (Brink and Nelkin 2013; Brink 2021).

I embrace this sort of capacitarian account of legal agency despite some "classical" compatibilist's misgivings.[8] However, for such an account to provide us with a robust understanding of agency, we must consider the way in which these capacities work *diachronically*. Persons who are reasons-responsive and have capacity-responsibility not only have the ability to identify, understand, deliberate about, and act in accordance with reasons during a particular moment in time. They can also work to elicit and support valued dispositions to act and suppress or even recalibrate disvalued dispositions. That is, they can support (and also undermine) the moral and legal agency of their future selves. Often this is done, at least initially, via manipulation of one's environment. A few examples: Tomas might make sure to avoid committing a DUI by refusing to drive to parties or bars; Jean, a former car thief, might move to a new town to avoid the pressure from her old crew to continue to steal; Bert might avoid forgetting that it is his weekend to come home straight after work to care for his children by setting a reminder in his phone; and Juanita, a cop, might wear a body camera to encourage her to think hard about the way she treats minority citizens during traffic stops. (This last example might be a case of Juanita voluntarily supporting her future moral agency, or of Juanita's supervisors taking actions to try to support her future moral and legal decision-making.) Not only do we all use these "tricks" that manipulate our future actions and selves—we are *expected* to use them. If dad Bert were to commit an immoral and illegal action like neglecting his child due to forgetfulness, others would rightfully ask why he did not use the many tools available to ensure he remembered his responsibilities.[9]

There are also more direct ways that we can strengthen our capacities for moral and legal rule recognition, deliberation, and self-control, and thereby affect our future moral agency. One of these is via practice. One might practice following ethical decision-making protocols until they become second nature. For example, I teach students such protocols in my Business Ethics and Biomedical Ethics courses and make them apply them repeatedly to different fact patterns with the hope the protocols will become ingrained.[10] Anger management lessons can help people learn to create space between feeling, thinking, and action. We can also become better moral agents—say, more

[8] Michael S. Moore, for example, argues that capacitarian compatibilism does not provide a sufficient account of the abilities that ground responsible action. "Classical" compatibilism, he says, can better account for these abilities using counterfactuals (2020, 286–98).

[9] For a full discussion of Bert's case, see Sifferd (2016).

[10] These protocols include things such as considering who the stakeholders impacted by the decision may be, using moral imagination to consider the possible harm caused by the decision, and applying multiple ethical theories to evaluate this possible harm (deontological and consequentialist).

honest—by repeatedly paying attention to the features of moral situations related to the moral norm of honesty, and by making consistently honest decisions. This process may look somewhat similar to using practical reason to make good decisions, termed habituation by Aristotle (1985), and involves making future moral choices easier by establishing and managing our dispositions.

We can enhance our sensitivity to certain reasons, including moral and legal reasons, by framing decisions in a certain way. This is something our parents are likely to teach us to do quite early: e.g., "How would you feel if Jonah did that to you?" People also can train themselves to be more sensitive to moral reasons by assigning negative emotions to harmful outcomes, and by habitually focusing on the moral features of a situation, such as the way in which their actions might affect others. This may involve specific skill acquisition and even the development of something like moral expertise. According to Merim Bilalić (2017), the essence of expertise is attention, where attention is quickly and automatically drawn to the important aspects of a situation. This reduces the complexity of the environment and ensures that limited cognitive resources are focused upon the important features of a situation (8). There is very good evidence that our brain's plasticity allows it to undergo functional reorganization in response to repeated physical and cognitive tasks. This functional reorganization is particularly typical of expertise (19). It seems likely that learned and repeated attentional focus on morally significant properties would sharpen skills and even develop moral expertise, especially within particular realms, as Aristotle (1985) indicates.[11]

All of this means that recognizing moral and legal reasons to act or refrain from acting in situations where they are relevant, deliberation about reasons, choice-making, and self-control can be understood as abilities that can be developed with practice. Such practice can involve long stretches of time and effort whereby abilities and dispositions are established and trained. It is of course true that we are often not on an even playing field when it comes to developing and practicing the abilities necessary for moral and legal agency: legal and moral agency can be made easier or harder by environmental and cognitive factors over which we have little control. For example, certain moral and legal reasons may be more or less salient to those within certain social or economic groups, or to those with greater cognitive skills (e.g., a greater ability for theory of mind). For persons who do not have their basic needs met or

[11] There is some evidence that persons with deficits relevant to moral agency, such as certain persons with autism spectrum disorder (ASD), can learn to accommodate or even overcome these deficits (Jefferson and Sifferd 2018).

who are not safe, moral and legal rules may conflict with the desire to meet these needs or to become safe; and persons with certain cognitive deficits may struggle to access information relevant to certain moral decisions. Given all of this, it may be the case that we have an obligation to support people's moral agency via social and governmental institutions. That is, as a society, we may have a moral obligation to provide persons with things they need to have a fair opportunity to be law-abiding. This might include free public schooling, social and economic support, and acknowledgement and support for cognitive differences.[12] It might also include a fair and just system of criminal law. And we may need to excuse persons who find being law-abiding so extraordinarily difficult that they lacked a fair opportunity to avoid a criminal act. (Again, we can see here that in some cases the pro tanto reasons to blame may be, and should be, overridden.)

Many of us do indeed possess the capacities listed by Hart and those constitutive of reasons-responsiveness, and over time these capacities can provide the means to shape our lives and choices such that we have a fair opportunity to abide by moral and legal rules. Possession of these diachronic capacities, I claim, is the feature that many of us possess that make us appropriate targets for a blaming response, including criminal blame in the form of a verdict. In the next section, I will provide an example to show that, where a person causes criminal harm, these capacities may qualify them for institutional criminal blame.

3 Case Study: Rape

Let us return to the primary question of this chapter: Do (some) rapists deserve criminal blame, which I claim is necessary (but not sufficient) for criminal punishment? I will use the material above to address this primary question by way of a real-life example.

Anthony Westerman was convicted in 2021 of two counts of second-degree rape and two counts of second-degree assault for incidents from 2017 and 2019 with two separate women (Cohen 2021). The first incident, which I will focus on here, happened in 2017. Westerman, then twenty-four, and a twenty-two-year-old woman were among a group drinking at a bar. According to the arrest warrant, the victim consumed a large amount of alcohol and passed out in her car outside the bar. Westerman and a friend of the victim woke her up,

[12] See my argument that a decent K-12 education may be necessary to acquire the moral knowledge to have a fair opportunity to follow moral and legal rules in Sifferd (2022).

and Westerman offered to order an Uber to take them back to the friend's home. The warrant states that the victim and her friend fell asleep during the Uber ride, and when they woke up, they were at Westerman's residence. While inside, the victim fell asleep on Westerman's couch. Eventually the victim woke up alone on the couch with Westerman, with Westerman on top of her and her pants removed. Westerman then raped her, and the victim claimed that in the process he "liked it when she pushed at him and when she told him to stop and get off." Afterwards the victim fell asleep on the couch, and she and her friend left when she awoke (Stelloh 2021).

Westerman was arrested and brought to trial for second-degree rape in Maryland. Despite the Model Penal Code's attempt to inspire a uniform criminal structure across U.S. jurisdictions, almost every U.S. state has a somewhat different statute defining sexual assault (Sifferd 2023).[13] Under Section 3-304(a) of the Maryland penal code, an offender commits second-degree rape if they have vaginal intercourse[14] under one of three different sets of circumstances. One such circumstance is that the act occurred without the consent of the victim through the perpetrator's use of force or threat of force.[15] Although the Model Penal Code was recently revised to remove the force requirement from basic rape, Maryland retains such a requirement.

The court found Westerman guilty of second-degree rape. I will assume that the court performed its appropriate duties as factfinder and was correct in its application of the facts to the law in this case. Westerman was found deserving of a blaming response in the form of a guilty verdict beyond a reasonable doubt. But let us now examine the case as philosophers and explore whether Westerman is an apt target for a blaming response in the form of a criminal verdict. We will primarily be interested in whether he possessed the mental capacities necessary for him to be a responsible agent, and whether he possessed them for a reasonable amount of time such that he had a fair opportunity to be law-abiding. First, was Westerman reasons-responsive and did he have capacity-responsibility in Hart's sense? There is no information in the

---

[13] Above I hinted that the structure of criminal offenses—and their corresponding penalties—can be understood as institutionalized categories of blame, based upon features of the actor and act relevant to the level of wrongdoing and blameworthiness. If this is the case, one might wonder why jurisdictions cannot seem to agree on what level of blame rapists deserve. I offer some initial thoughts about this in Sifferd (2023).

[14] Yes, this means that men cannot be a victim of second-degree rape in Maryland. Men can only be first-degree rape victims, where serious force and threats are used. These ethically problematic sex-differences in sexual assault statutes will be eliminated if states choose to adopt the MPC's new structure of sexual assault offenses.

[15] The other two have to do with features of the victim—namely, that they are "mentally defective" or younger than fourteen. See Maryland Penal Code 3-304(a).

arrest or court record indicating that Westerman lacked the cognitive skills necessary to identify, understand, and act in accordance with moral and legal norms; there is no evidence that he lacked skills such as attentional focus, planning, deliberation, and inhibitory ability required for voluntary and culpable action. Indeed, these skills seem very important to the job Westerman held right up until his arrest. Westerman was a police officer, which means that he ought to have been skilled in understanding moral and legal rules and applying them to behavior. Police officers are generally expected to know the law and be capable of law-abiding behavior.

It is thus exceedingly likely that Westerman knew that using force to secure nonconsensual sex was both immoral and illegal—in this case, we need not wade into the thorny debate about whether persons are responsible for behavior that they *should have known* was immoral/illegal. It also seems likely given his age, and as he had no history of mental disorders, that Westerman had the capacity to manage his dispositions to act in accordance with moral and legal rules over some period of time—for example, he had diachronic capacity-responsibility.[16] Persons who desire to be law-abiding specifically with regard to their sexual activity have many opportunities to identify and commit to behavioral rules to make this more likely. This might include a self-imposed habituated rule that one does not have sexual encounters with persons who are very intoxicated, or to explicitly ask a new or casual partner if specific sexual acts are consensual. One might also learn to avoid casual sexual encounters with persons who appear very young, have mental impairments, or are otherwise less likely to be capable of consent. Finally, one might pay special attention to moral reasons related to sexual encounters and thereby focus one's attention in such situations on monitoring one's partner's behavior to make sure they are not missing signals to stop.

Despite having the capacity to act in accordance with moral and legal norms in a diachronic sense (over a significant time frame leading up to his crime) and synchronic sense (at the time of the crime), Westerman violated such norms and thereby caused the serious criminal harm of rape.[17]

[16] Although my colleagues and I disagree with the law's current assessment that persons are full moral and legal agents at eighteen (and sometimes younger, if they commit a violent crime), we feel it is safe to assume full agency by the age of twenty-one (which should be a rebuttable presumption) (Fagan et al. 2016). If this is true in Westerman's case, he had several years to hone his moral and legal agency in a way that made him more likely to be law-abiding.

[17] Although no *mens rea* has been stipulated by statute with regard to rape in Maryland, courts seem to apply the highest levels to rape charges—purposely or knowingly. In *State v. Rusk*, the Maryland Court of Appeals indicated that the force requirement could be satisfied "without violence" if "the acts and threats of the defendant were reasonably calculated to create in the mind of the victim … a real apprehension … of imminent bodily harm" (Kinports 2001, citing *State v. Rusk*, 424 A.2d 720, 726 [Md. 1981]).

Westerman's victim indicated in court that the incident was the "most traumatic of her life." Upon hearing the facts of this case, a reaction of moral blame and anger, especially on the part of the victim and her loved ones, seems fitting. After an investigation and process whereby certain facts regarding features of the actor and the act relevant to Westerman's blameworthiness was established, institutionalized blame by the state in the form of a guilty verdict also seems fitting.

This last claim needs more explanation than I can provide here—but I will offer a quick sketch. Blaming responses in the form of reactive attitudes like moral anger and blame may be deserved and fitting when a person with certain cognitive capacities commits a wrongful act. Many, including me, think these responses are expressive: they express moral concerns, and these concerns relate to the fact that a person is a part of the moral community, and this community is let down and disappointed when its moral rules have been broken. Blame, even when aimed at an apt target, causes harm, but this harm may be justified by the good of a desert response. This good is not (only) instrumental but intrinsic (good in itself) and/or extrinsic (good in the larger context of the moral community).[18] It is *good* for a person who deserves censure due to harm related to their poor quality of will toward others to receive this expression of censure.

One of the overarching aims of the criminal law, I think, is to serve as an institutional stand-in for individualized blame and punishment. Guilty verdicts can be seen as institutional representations of the reactive attitudes that are the natural response persons have when serious moral and legal expectations are not met (Sifferd 2021). Violations of moral and legal rules reflect poor quality of will toward members of the moral community. Individuals are in very different positions regarding their ability to voice censure of others, and they face very different risks in expressing this censure. Plus, there are many reasons for society to discourage individual attempts to punish others. It is reasonable to think that the criminal law institutionalizes the process of deserved censure and punishment, and that the law can do this is a better and more just way than individuals.

The institutionalized blaming of qualified persons for wrongful acts in the form of verdicts can be justified as delivering deserved desert responses. That an offender is deserving of such a response means they may also be appropriate targets for punishment. As I have said above, I think being deserving of moral blame in the form of a verdict is necessary but not sufficient for punishment. This is because punishments must also meet instrumental requirements

[18] Again, see McKenna (2019) for an argument that blaming may secure extrinsic goods.

to be justified, including the requirement that the categories and types of punishment stipulated in law ought to have the overall effect of supporting moral and legal agency. One way that criminal punishment supports agency is by making the moral and legal norms of society more salient, thereby enhancing sensitivity to these norms (Sifferd 2021).

If the rough sketch above is correct, in some cases where institutional blame is justified, punishment will also be justified, and in other cases, punishment will not be appropriate. Further, some forms of punishment may be unjustifiable because they do not have the effect of enhancing moral and legal agency. One might argue, for example, that incarceration, at least as it is practiced in the U.S., has the overall effect of undermining moral and legal agency, and thus is not justified as a criminal punishment. In this case, even offenders deserving of a blaming response in the form of criminal verdict related to serious crimes such as rape ought not to be incarcerated.

Turning back to Westerman, my aim here is only to convince readers that, because of his capacities to recognize moral and legal norms and abide by them (over time), *Westerman is deserving of an institutional blaming response in the form of a criminal verdict.* This is what many desert skeptics deny. Westerman's deservingness may then qualify him for punishment. It is a further step to consider whether and what form of punishment might be justified.

Readers may be interested to know what sentence Officer Westerman was actually assigned. In the state of Maryland, the statutory sentence for Westerman's crime is zero to twenty years of incarceration, which is a very wide range that provides a lot of judicial discretion. Westerman was sentenced not just for the rape described above, but for two second-degree rapes, a third-degree sexual offense, a fourth-degree sexual offense, and two counts of second-degree assault. For these crimes, Baltimore County Circuit Court Judge Keith Truffer sentenced Anthony Westerman to fifteen years in prison, a hefty sentence. However, the judge then suspended the sentence except for four years in home detention. This is a light sentence in comparison. The judge's reason for being lenient seemed related to a misunderstanding about the harm of rape. Judge Truffer claimed there was no evidence of any psychological injury to the victim, despite her own testimony indicating the event was traumatic, and her claim that she needed therapy following the incident.[19]

[19] Cases where judges apply very light sentences for rape—compared to the typical sentence in the U.S. for other violent crimes—are common where the offenders are white and/or privileged. For example, Christopher Belter, a twenty-year-old New York man who recently pleaded guilty to rape and sexual abuse for assaulting four teenage girls during parties at his parents' home, also did not face prison time for his crimes. Instead, the judge sentenced him to eight years' probation. Although Belter could have been assigned a maximum sentence of eight years in prison, Judge Matthew J. Murphy III concluded that time behind bars for "a promising man" like Christopher would be inappropriate.

If you feel Westerman's sentence was too lenient, I may have convinced you that some rapists, including Westerman, deserve a blaming response in the form of a guilty verdict. If you feel his sentence was appropriate or even too severe, I may have also convinced you. I have only failed if, after all you have read about the grounds for moral and legal desert, you think Westerman is undeserving of any blaming response at all.

4 Conclusions: The View That No One Deserves Praise or Blame

Thomas Nagel famously said this about moral blame:

> Moral judgment of a person is judgment not of what happens to him, but of him. It does not say merely that a certain event or state of affairs is fortunate or unfortunate or even terrible. … We are judging him, rather than his existence or characteristics. (1979, 36)

However, Nagel also noted that concentrating on what is not under an agent's control can have the effect of "mak[ing] this responsible self seem to disappear, swallowed up by the order of mere events" (36). Responsible agency can seem to disappear and then reappear (poof!) depending on whether one is positioned within, or outside of, our blaming practices.

The position of desert skepticism is an external critique—a position one can only take from outside the subjective experience of agency; from a position where actions seem like mere events. From this external perspective, it may seem that no one deserves praise or blame, so the state ought not to be applying institutionalized blame and punishment. What to do with persons who harm others, then? Gregg Caruso (2016, 2021) advocates for a Public Health Model and says that dangerous actors should be quarantined like persons carrying serious contagious diseases until they can be deemed safe to society (see also Caruso's chapter in this volume).

As I indicated in my introduction, I do not think there is a compatibilist response that will convince the skeptics. The arguments above are offered from an internal perspective. But I have two short observations regarding the skeptical view to offer here.

First, desert skepticism does not seem to parse persons regarding mental and behavioral capacities in the right way. Three-year-olds, persons suffering from active symptoms of a serious mental illness like schizophrenia, and a twenty-four-year-old police officer with no cognitive challenges are equally non-agents on this view, unable to exhibit "ultimate control" such that they deserve praise or blame. However, one cannot deny that the twenty-four-year-old police officer is, generally speaking, better able than three-year-olds and persons with active schizophrenic symptoms to understand moral and legal norms, and to deliberate, plan, and execute behavior in light to those rules. We reasonably expect a police officer to know and follow legal rules, but one does not reasonably expect a three-year-old to do so. The criminal law can have an effect on the reasoning and action of regular actors. Codified moral and legal norms are considered reasons, whereas such norms are not likely to be identified as a reason for action (certainly not in the same way) by the three-year-old or a person who is seriously mentally ill. If it is correct to expect moral and legal norms to influence a group of agents, why is it not just to blame them when they fail to take sure reasons into account—especially when this process of blame (and related punishment) can strengthen the salience of reasons to be law-abiding?

Second, it is not clear to me that desert skepticism is a position human beings can hold in a meaningful way. This does not prove it is false, but it does say something about desert skepticism's utility. We *necessarily* praise and blame ourselves and others. To see others as the cause of their actions and to experience reactive attitudes and desert responses regarding those actions is just how we experience we world. We cannot talk ourselves out of it. Even proponents of desert skepticism like Caruso note that they embrace agency, praise, and blame in their everyday lives. In this way, the call to throw out praise and blaming practices seems similar to the Churchlands' call in the 1980s and 1990s for us to throw out mental state concepts (Churchland 1981; Churchland and Churchland 1998). While it is clearly possible to write a book discussing this theoretical possibility, it is impossible for neuroscientists and cognitive scientists, much less philosophers and social scientists, to work without concepts such as facial recognition, long-term memory, and attention, which at bottom all rest upon folk notions of mental states (e.g., "the belief that there is a face there"). Talk of neural states is essentially meaningless unless they are tied to folk psychological concepts, and speaking of behavior as just events and not actions we perform for reasons is similarly meaningless.

As Nagel notes, "We cannot simply take an external evaluative view of ourselves—of what we most essentially are and what we do" (1979, 37). Arguing to revise a crucial human institution such as the criminal law by taking a perspective we are unable to occupy in any extended or substantive sense seems unwise. Even if a smart philosopher like Caruso can occupy this imaginative position long enough to redesign a system for handling dangerous persons, those asked to approve, implement, staff, and support this system are still likely to see the dangerous persons handled by the system as blameworthy. If a Public Health system like the one Caruso advocates for were ever adopted—which it will not be, due to the dearness and essential nature of our views of agency—its implementation would be terribly hampered by our moral psychologies.

In the end, what we need to justify criminal verdicts and punishment is to identify the grounding for claims that some persons deserve criminal blame, and possibly punishment. I have argued here that our diachronic capacities to recognize and abide by moral and legal rules provide such grounds. Some rapists deserve criminal blame, and Anthony Westerman is one of them.[20]

References

Aristotle. 1985. *Nicomachean Ethics*. Translated by Terence Irwin. Indianapolis, IN: Hackett.

Baron-Cohen, Simon. 1995. *Mindblindness: An Essay on Autism and Theory of Mind*. Cambridge, MA: MIT Press.

Bilalić, Merim. 2017. *The Neuroscience of Expertise*. Cambridge: Cambridge University Press.

Brink, David O. 2021. *Fair Opportunity and Responsibility*. Oxford: Oxford University Press.

Brink, David O., and Dana K. Nelkin. 2013. "Fairness and the Architecture of Responsibility." In *Oxford Studies in Agency and Responsibility*, edited by David Shoemaker, vol. 1, 284–313. Oxford: Oxford University Press.

Caruso, Gregg D. 2016. "Free Will Skepticism and Criminal Behavior: A Public Health-Quarantine Model." *Southwest Philosophy Review* 32, no. 1 (January): 25–48.

———. 2021. *Rejecting Retributivism: Free Will, Punishment, and Criminal Justice*. Cambridge: Cambridge University Press.

Churchland, Paul M. 1981. "Eliminative Materialism and the Propositional Attitudes." *Journal of Philosophy* 78, no. 2 (February): 67–90.

Churchland, Paul M., and Patricia S. Churchland. 1998. *On the Contrary: Critical Essays, 1987–1997*. Cambridge, MA: MIT Press.

Cohen, Li. 2021. "Former Baltimore County Police Officer Convicted of Raping 22-Year-Old Woman Sentenced to Home Detention." *CBS News*, November 24. https://www.cbsnews.com/news/anthony-westerman-rape-baltimore-county-police-officer-home-prison-suspended-sentence/.

[20] The author gratefully acknowledges the research and editorial assistance of Elmhurst University student Lillian Armentrout.

Davidson, Donald. 1970. "Mental Events." In *Experience and Theory*, edited by Lawrence Foster and J. W. Swanson, 79–101. Amherst, MA: University of Massachusetts Press.

Duff, R. A. 1993. "Choice, Character, and Criminal Liability." *Law and Philosophy* 12, no. 4 (November): 345–83.

Fagan, Tyler, William Hirstein, and Katrina Sifferd. 2016. "Innocent Minds: Child Soldiers, Executive Functions, and Culpability." *International Criminal Law Review* 16, no. 2 (February): 258–86.

Feldman, Fred, and Brad Skow. 2020. "Desert." *Stanford Encyclopedia of Philosophy* (Winter 2020 edition), edited by Edward N. Zalta. https://plato.stanford.edu/archives/win2020/entries/desert/.

Fischer, John Martin, and Mark Ravizza. 1998. *Responsibility and Control: A Theory of Moral Responsibility*. Cambridge: Cambridge University Press.

Fodor, Jerry A. 1987. *Psychosemantics: The Problem of Meaning in the Philosophy of Mind*. Cambridge, MA: MIT Press.

Hart, H. L. A. 1968. *Punishment and Responsibility: Essays in the Philosophy of Law*. Oxford: Clarendon.

Hirstein, William, Katrina L. Sifferd, and Tyler K. Fagan. 2018. *Responsible Brains: Neuroscience, Law, and Human Culpability*. Cambridge, MA: MIT Press.

Jackson, Frank, and Philip Pettit. 1990. "In Defense of Folk Psychology." *Philosophical Studies* 59, no. 1 (May): 31–54.

Jefferson, Anneli, and Katrina Sifferd. 2018. "Are Psychopaths Legally Insane?" *European Journal of Analytic Philosophy* 14, no. 1: 79–96.

List, Christian. 2019. *Why Free Will Is Real*. Cambridge, MA: Harvard University Press.

McKenna, Michael. 2019. "Basically Deserved Blame and Its Value." *Journal of Ethics and Social Philosophy* 15, no. 3: 255–82.

Moore, Michael S. 2020. *Mechanical Choices: The Responsibility of the Human Machine*. Oxford: Oxford University Press.

Morse, Stephen J. 2003. "Inevitable Mens Rea." *Harvard Journal of Law & Public Policy* 27, no. 1 (Fall): 51–64.

———. 2007. "Criminal Responsibility and the Disappearing Person." *Cardozo Law Review* 28, no. 6: 2545–75.

———. 2008. "Determinism and the Death of Folk Psychology: Two Challenges to Responsibility from Neuroscience." *Minnesota Journal of Law, Science & Technology* 9, no. 1: 1–36.

———. 2011. "Neuroscience and the Future of Personhood and Responsibility." In *Constitution 3.0: Freedom and Technological Change*, edited by Jeffrey Rosen and Benjamin Wittes, 113–29. Washington, DC: Brookings Institution.

———. 2015. "Neuroscience, Free Will, and Criminal Responsibility." In *Free Will and the Brain: Neuroscientific, Philosophical, and Legal Perspectives*, edited by Walter Glannon, 251–86. Cambridge: Cambridge University Press.

Nagel, Thomas. 1979. "Moral Luck." In *Mortal Questions*, 24–38. Cambridge: Cambridge University Press.

Pereboom, Derk. 2013. "Free Will Skepticism and Criminal Punishment." In *The Future of Punishment*, edited by Thomas A. Nadelhoffer, 49-78. Oxford: Oxford University Press.

Pereboom, Derk, and Gregg D. Caruso. 2018. "Hard-Incompatibilist Existentialism: Neuroscience, Punishment, and Meaning in Life." In *Neuroexistentialism: Meaning, Morals, and Purpose in the Age of Neuroscience*, edited by Gregg D. Caruso and Owen Flanagan, 193-222. Oxford: Oxford University Press.

Sifferd, Katrina L. 2006. "In Defense of the Use of Commonsense Psychology in the Criminal Law." *Law and Philosophy* 25, no. 6 (November): 571–612.

———. 2014. "What Does It Mean to Be a Mechanism? Stephen Morse, Non-Reductivism, and Mental Causation." *Criminal Law and Philosophy* 11, no. 1 (March): 143–59.

———. 2016. "Unconscious *Mens Rea*: Lapses, Negligence, and Criminal Responsibility." In *Philosophical Foundations of Law and Neuroscience*, edited by Dennis Patterson and Michael S. Pardo, 161–78. Oxford: Oxford University Press.

———. 2021. "How Is Criminal Punishment Forward-Looking?" *Monist* 104, no. 4 (October): 540–53.

———. 2022. "Legal Insanity and Moral Knowledge: Why Is a Lack of Moral Knowledge Related to Mental Illness Exculpatory?" In Agency in Mental Disorder: Philosophical Dimensions, edited by Matt King and Joshua May, 113-35. Oxford: Oxford University Press.

———. 2023. "Do Rape Cases Sit in a Moral Blindspot? The Dual Process Theory of Moral Judgment and Rape." In *Advances in Experimental Philosophy of Action*, edited by Paul Henne and Samuel Murray. London: Bloomsbury.

Stelloh, Tim. 2021. "Maryland Police Officer Convicted of Rape Is Sentenced to Home Detention." *NBC News*, November 22. https://www.nbcnews.com/news/us-news/maryland-police-officer-convicted-rape-sentenced-home-detention-rcna6416.

24

Free Will Skepticism and Criminals as Ends in Themselves

Benjamin Vilhauer

1 Introduction

Free will skepticism undermines retributivism, which plays a crucial role in many justifications of punishment and remorse. Free will skeptics often think that retributivism is cruel and undermining it is a victory. But they must confront difficult questions about developing a non-retributive ethics for criminal wrongdoing. It is perfectly coherent for free will skeptics to hold that no form of punishment is justified and that we should never feel remorse. However, it is natural to worry that a society which ceased to punish altogether would revert to the state of nature, and that advocating remorselessness is too much like advocating psychopathy. If free will skeptics seek to justify punishment and remorse, their most obvious option is consequentialism, which has its own problems. It is plausible that punishment and remorse have good consequences—that punishment deters, and remorse improves behavior. But if these are our only justifications, we use criminals as mere means to ends, and remorse is a mere means rather than an experience that "fits" our wrongs.

This chapter offers non-retributive, broadly Kantian justifications that resolve these problems and can be endorsed by free will skeptics. The justification of punishment draws on non-retributive original position deliberation: we consent to humane punishment if we assume we are equally likely to be

B. Vilhauer (✉)
City College of New York, New York, NY, USA
e-mail: bvilhauer@ccny.cuny.edu

© The Author(s), under exclusive license to Springer Nature Switzerland AG 2023

M. C. Altman (ed.), *The Palgrave Handbook on the Philosophy of Punishment*, Palgrave Handbooks in the Philosophy of Law, https://doi.org/10.1007/978-3-031-11874-6_24

among the punished and among those protected by punishment when the veil is raised. It has consequentialist features but is deontologically founded in the duty to avoid using others as mere means. The justification of remorse is care-based. It draws on the value of sympathizing with people we have wronged, which has a Kantian ground in the duty to take others' ends as our own.

These accounts of punishment and remorse are Kantian in that they emphasize the idea that people are ends in themselves. As understood in this chapter, to be an end in oneself (which I will typically abbreviate as "to be an end") is to have a moral status with four key features:

(1) One ought never to be coerced or deceived into serving as a *mere means* to ends to which one would not rationally take as one's own. This element grounds a *perfect* duty: we must *never* treat others as mere means. We need not avoid treating each other as means in all cases, since it is sometimes rational to consent to serving as a means to another's end, for example, when they are reciprocally serving as a means to one's own end. If I have the end of teaching, then my students are among my means, and if they have the end of learning, then I am among their means. Such reciprocity is central for the account of punishment below.

(2) One's own permissible ends are valuable in a way that gives others reasons to take those ends as their own. This feature grounds an *imperfect* duty that grants us latitude—we must *sometimes* take others' ends as our own. It is because of this latitude that Kantianism is often thought to be less demanding than utilitarianism. But even for Kant, this duty becomes more demanding, in a way that brings it closer to perfect duty, when we have relationships with morally salient others such as friends and family. This point figures in the account of remorse to be presented here. Adopting others' ends requires sympathy, and sympathy sometimes involves pain. It is intuitive to think that relationships with one's victims are as morally salient as relationships with family and friends.

(3) One ought to treat others in conformity with (1) and (2).

(4) The fact that something is an end does not imply that we have reasons to make *more* things like it. To be an end is to be a normative node in the practical reasoning of rational agents such that (1), (2), and (3) constrain their reasoning. This is a key feature of Kant's non-consequentialist moral teleology. So, recognizing criminals as ends does not give us a reason to make more criminals.

The accounts of punishment and remorse are only *broadly* Kantian, however, since they modify his views in (at least) three important ways:

1. Kant's mature ethics adds a fifth key feature to the list of four above: we can only regard ourselves as ends if we know we have free will of a libertarian kind, which he calls "transcendental freedom." But the kind of autonomy we have when we are treated as ends is not conceptually dependent upon free will. Agents who are treated as ends are independent of others' undue control. Agents who have transcendental freedom are independent from their causal histories. We can have the former without the latter.
2. Retributivism plays an essential role in Kant's account of punishment, though he offers little in the way of argument for retributivism. He appears to see it as the only way to avoid endorsing punishing people as mere means (1996b, 6:331 [p. 473]).
3. Retributivism plays an essential role in Kant's account of remorse (1996b, 6:394 [p. 524]) and he does not consider a sympathy-based alternative, but he has an account of rational sympathy that provides a basis for this alternative.

Readers may wonder: if Kant has to be revised so much to be useful to free will skeptics, then why bother with Kant in the first place? The reason is that it has long been thought, not just by Kant but by many philosophers working on free will and moral responsibility, that free will skepticism inevitably pushes us away from Kantian ethics and toward consequentialism. For example, one of P. F. Strawson's main arguments in his influential paper "Freedom and Resentment" (1962) is that free will skepticism requires us to adopt a depersonalizing "objective attitude" in which our only moral reasons are utilitarian. Strawson and his many followers see this as a reason to endorse free will so that we can retain broadly Kantian ethical views. Saul Smilansky (2000) thinks that we lack free will, but he also thinks that free will denial pushes us away from broadly Kantian commitments which are so important that we should cultivate the illusion that we have free will. On the other hand, some theorists think that Kant's influence has been largely inimical, so moving away from him is valuable progress (e.g., Waller 2015a, 2015b, and his chapter in this volume). If it can be shown that key Kantian ideas can be usefully retained by free will skeptics, this gives skeptics a more resourceful moral theory, especially when they respond to criminal wrongdoing.[1]

[1] To my knowledge, Pereboom (2001, 150–52) is the first contemporary free will denier to argue that Kantian ideas can be preserved by skeptics, but Kantianism plays only a limited role in his response to criminal wrongdoing (see below).

2 Defining and Motivating Free Will Skepticism

As understood here, *free will* is the control condition for moral responsibility, and *moral responsibility* is the relationship to our actions that would legitimize *action-based desert claims*, such as claims that people deserve praise, blame, reward, or punishment for their actions. *Retributivism* is the view that action-based desert claims play a necessary role in justifying punishment.

Free will skepticism is the view that we do not know whether we have free will.[2] Kant is a skeptic about free will from the perspective of theoretical rationality, but he claims practical knowledge that we have free will (1996a, 5:30–31 [p. 163]). Free will skepticism as understood in this chapter accepts Kant's theoretical skepticism but rejects his practical knowledge claim.

Free will skepticism is different from *free will denial*, which is the view that we do not have free will. Free will skepticism is more epistemically modest and theoretically conservative than free will denial. This makes it more plausible than free will denial in important ways. Free will skeptics need not prove that compatibilist accounts of free will are inadequate or that there are no libertarian metaphysical sources for free will. They need only introduce reasonable doubts that suffice to undermine knowledge claims. The raging controversies about the viability of compatibilism and the plausibility of libertarian metaphysics suggest that such reasonable doubts are readily available, so this chapter will not provide an inventory. Free will skepticism is also more theoretically conservative with respect to widely accepted features of moral theory. I argue that the possibility that we have free will is sufficient to ground "cans" corresponding to "oughts" in the "ought implies can" principle (Vilhauer 2012, 2015). I also argue for an asymmetry in the standards of justification we must meet to hold people morally responsible in the contexts of "positive" and "negative" responsibility-attribution practices, such that the possibility of free will suffices for some forms of praise—for example, praise that helps people understand themselves as valuable moral agents (Vilhauer 2012, 2015).

However, the possibility that we have free will is not sufficient to support retributivism about criminal wrongdoing. As explained above, action-based desert entails moral responsibility, and moral responsibility entails free will. This means that free will denial entails the denial of retributivism. But it also

[2] Some writers in this literature use "free will skepticism" to refer to the view I call "free will denial." But these are importantly different positions that should be distinguished appropriately. "Skepticism" traditionally refers to claims about what we can know about things, not claims about how things are. Skeptics about other minds rarely hold that there are no other minds. So we ought not refer to the view that there is no free will as "free will skepticism." (I must confess, however, that I too used the term in this problematic way in some earlier papers.)

means that free will skeptics' reasonable doubts about free will entail reasonable doubts about retributivism. Reasonable doubts about retributivism are enough to undermine retributivism, at least in the context of the ethics of criminal wrongdoing, where retributivists rely on the claim that we have free will to justify profound suffering. It is obvious that criminal punishment often involves profound suffering. The suffering of remorse can also be profound. People sometimes choose suicide over continuing to live with remorse. The remorseful suffering typically expected in response to serious crimes is especially profound. It is widely acknowledged that justifications for inflicting the suffering involved in criminal punishment must meet an extremely high justificatory standard. This is why so many people find it intuitive that arguments in the criminal court must be proven beyond reasonable doubt. A similarly high standard should be met for remorse. Retributive justifications of such suffering cannot meet these standards in light of free will skeptics' reasonable doubts (Pereboom 2001; Vilhauer 2009a, 2012; Caruso 2021; Jeppson 2021). So, it is not only the radical position of free will denial that undermines retributivism—a modest and comparatively conservative free will skepticism undermines it too.

3 The Variety of Desert Bases

As mentioned earlier, consequentialism is the most obvious option for skeptics seeking non-retributive justifications of punishment and remorse. The discussion in this chapter primarily addresses utilitarianism, because it is a simple and clear form of consequentialism. Skeptics may be troubled by utilitarianism's implications for criminal wrongdoing. Objectors may protest that it is disingenuous for skeptics to claim to be troubled by utilitarianism, because if nobody really deserves anything, intellectual honesty demands that we bite the bullet and accept that the only moral reasons still standing are utilitarian. But neither skeptics nor deniers should hold that nobody deserves anything.[3] Skepticism undermines action-based desert. But it is plausible that action is not the only desert base (that is, the thing that grounds legitimate claims about desert).

Personhood is a desert base that is plausibly distinct from action (Vilhauer 2009b, 2013). For example, we deserve to be treated as innocent until proven

[3] Pereboom holds that free will is required for what he calls "basic desert," but he endorses "forward-looking" moral responsibility, which makes room for non-basic desert (2014, 2, 126–52). However, his view seems to be that without free will nobody *fundamentally* deserves anything.

guilty just because we are people, and there is a special kind of kind of respect we deserve just because we are people.[4] We do not deserve these things because we have *acted* in a way that makes us deserve them, and there is no way we could act that would make us *cease* to deserve them. Even if we felt confident that somebody was a murderer, they would not cease to deserve the presumption of innocence, and even if they were convicted, they would deserve protection from punishment that disrespects their humanity. Universal human rights that cannot be alienated or forfeited are plausibly grounded in personhood as a desert base.

Need is another desert base that is plausibly distinct from both action and personhood. We respond to need with forms of care. Children deserve love from their parents even when they are too young to have done anything to *earn* their love.[5] People lying bleeding on the sidewalk deserve a call for an ambulance from passersby even if they *did* play a role in the circumstances that led to their injuries. Need is a more complex desert base than personhood, as the obligations it confers do not always universalize. Children deserve love from their parents in a way they do not deserve it from others, while people who lie bleeding on the sidewalk deserve an ambulance call from anyone passing by.

The independence of action, personhood, and need as desert bases makes it sensible for skeptics and deniers to acknowledge desert claims based on personhood and need despite doubting or rejecting desert claims based on action. Multiple approaches to moral theory may allow this, but the focus here is on non-retributive Kantianism. From this perspective, the most fundamental way to understand what we deserve based on our personhood is to be treated as we would rationally consent to be treated if we had only our personhood in view, and the most fundamental way to understand what others deserve from us based on their need is in terms of our duty to adopt others' ends as our own. The accounts of punishment and remorse below aim to unpack these ideas in the context of criminal wrongdoing.

---

[4] By contrast, Smilansky holds that "the idea of respect for persons … is control related, and not personhood related as for Vilhauer. And the concern with 'being used merely as a means' … is also firmly embedded in control-related ideas" (2019, 31). However, as mentioned in the introduction, while there is a kind of voluntariness at issue in treating people as ends, it is conceptually independent of free will.

[5] McLeod (2013) makes a similar argument.

4 Non-retributive Kantian Punishment for Skeptics

As already noted, utilitarianism is a ready option for skeptics seeking to justify punishment. Utilitarians think criminals' pain is as bad as anybody else's, and they see the pain involved in punishment as justified only insofar as it diminishes overall suffering in society, for example, by incapacitating criminals and deterring potential criminals. So utilitarianism can seem less cruel than retributivism. However, if our only reason to punish criminals is to reduce suffering elsewhere in society, then we are using criminals as mere means. Further, suppose we get the best ratio of pain inflicted to pain prevented with practices that violate moral intuitions most ethicists want to preserve, such as framing people and weakening due process. Utilitarians have to endorse these practices if they cannot find a way to rule them out.[6] Some philosophers adopt a hybrid view according to which punishment must increase utility *and* be deserved based on actions. Skeptics do not have this option.

Kantian skeptics can point out that, while the action-based desert claims favored by retributivists are undermined by skepticism, personhood-based desert claims are not, and we have a personhood-based desert claim not to be used as mere means. So, they can propose an institution of punishment to which we could rationally consent. The notion of consent to punishment can seem bizarre. Few criminals *actually* consent to punishment—coercion is in the nature of punishment, and it is in the nature of coercion that we do not consent to it. Thus any plausible account of consent to punishment must rest on hypothetical consent, consent we *would* give under appropriate hypothetical conditions. We can model this with social contract theories based on hypothetical consent. John Rawls's approach is a natural fit for free will skeptics who want to model personhood-based but not action-based desert, since Rawls himself recommends original position deliberation (OPD) in part because it screens out undeserved inequalities (1999, 86–89).

In OPD, deliberators use maximin reasoning to select basic social principles that make the circumstances of the worst-off as good as possible. Rawls argues for OPD as risk-averse in a way that is rational under uncertainty, and this has been disputed (e.g., Harsanyi 1975). However, he also defends OPD as conforming to moral facts that are normatively prior to the social contract: OPD procedurally specifies an underlying Kantian conception of fairness and equality among rational beings. This chapter draws on the latter approach.

[6] Perhaps there is a rule-utilitarianism that can adequately explain why we should follow rules like "do not frame" when breaking them would maximize utility. It seems unlikely to me. But even if there is, we should also know whether a non-retributive Kantian option is available.

Rawls applies OPD to distributive justice, not punishment. Although OPD can be extended to punishment,[7] a disanalogy between distributive justice and punishment complicates maximin reasoning. There is only one worst-off social position in distributive justice—the poorest. In punishment, crime victims and the people punished compete for the worst-off position (though later it will be argued that this competition is not fundamental). If punishment deters, then adjusting punishment to improve things for one party worsens things for the other. Perhaps technological and social innovations can someday eliminate this competition in a morally attractive way. Someday speedy AI ticklebot police may overwhelm all would-be criminals with incapacitating but harmless giggles before they complete crimes, eliminating the need for punishment and the position of the punished in the competition equation. But yet-unimagined social innovations would be required to prevent ticklebots from becoming tools of authoritarian repression. We could of course eliminate the position of the punished by ceasing to punish criminals, but we would worry that crime might explode and cast us into the state of nature.

If criminals and victims will compete for the foreseeable future, how should OPD weigh their interests? To be fair to both, we must assume that we have an equal chance of ending up in each position—that we are just as likely to be harmed by punishment as we are to benefit. The relevant harmed parties are obviously the people punished. The beneficiaries upon whom we should focus are potential victims rather than actual victims, because victims have already suffered the harm OPD deliberators would hope to avoid by instituting punishment.

What principles of punishment would we choose under this assumption? Fear of punishment would make OPD deliberators initially prefer a society that did not punish. They would invest in research on technologies and practices (like authoritarian-proof ticklebots) that would yield a just but crime-free society with no need for punishment. Since such innovations are not yet on hand, they would also invest in attractive crime-prevention measures already available: more jobs, education, public services, and voluntary therapy for those most at risk of committing crimes. But they would endorse some

[7] For previous justifications of punishment drawing on OPD, see Murphy (1973), Sterba (1977), Clark (2004), and Dolovich (2004). The justification provided in this chapter is novel in its claim to use OPD to unpack what we deserve based on personhood but not action. The other justifications import retributivist premises and cannot be endorsed by skeptics. Clark aims to provide a non-retributive Kantian approach to punishment, but he allows a "negative retributivism" that explains why we should punish the guilty rather than the innocent. Skeptics cannot allow this. The justification provided in this chapter shares more features with Dolovich's account than the others, despite the fact that I developed this justification before I became aware of her paper.

form of punishment in order to avoid the state of nature. This motivation for endorsing punishment is consequentialist, but it only has normative significance because it unfolds from rational consent. Thus, this justification of punishment is fundamentally deontological despite the consequentialist motivation.[8]

What particular form of punishment would OPD deliberators choose based on these general principles? Punishment imposes significant harm on the punished to confer what may be a very modest benefit on the potential victim. Even radically reformed prisons would cause significant harm by blocking prisoners' freedom of movement and damaging their social relations. A reduction in someone's odds of becoming a victim does not confer a similarly tangible benefit. If I was confident that OPD adoption of some particular form of punishment would ensure that I did not find myself an actual victim when the veil is lifted, I might think the benefit of punishment to potential victims was equal to the harm to the punished. But I cannot be confident about this in OPD. The aggregate benefit of punishment to society as a whole may be much greater than the harm it imposes: even if we cannot know which individuals will be saved from victimization, we may confident that victimization will dramatically decline overall. But this is not relevant in OPD, since it requires us to consider social outcomes one person at a time, thereby avoiding the utilitarian deletion of the boundaries between persons. This is part of why it is a deontological justification.

In OPD, we would be unwilling to risk imprisonment to protect ourselves against nonviolent crime. We would choose less-intrusive alternatives such as fines and ankle monitors. On the other hand, we would risk imprisonment to protect ourselves against crimes of violence. But we would insist on humane prisons that offered education, meaningful work, voluntary therapy, regular visits from friends and loved ones, very frequent parole review to determine whether prisoners could be released without undue risk of repeated violence, and radically enhanced post-release support to help people avoid new violence. The main function of such prisons would be incapacitation rather than deterrence. But we could not ignore deterrence, since a primary reason to want punishment in OPD would be maintenance of enough order to avoid the state of nature. Prison would provide a substantial deterrent even if prison conditions were comfortable, since we prefer not to be controlled and separated from loved ones. But if conditions were *too* comfortable, they would

[8] Kant's own justification of punishment has consequentialist elements (1997, 27:286 [p. 79]), so this feature of the OPD approach is compatible with its Kantian foundations. See Vilhauer (2017) for discussion.

become an incentive to commit violent crime, and prison would work against its intended purposes. We would therefore choose a policy of calibrating prison conditions at a level of unpleasantness high enough to maintain deterrence, but no higher. Conditions would not have to be intrinsically unpleasant to deter, just unpleasant relative to life outside prison. As discussed earlier, OPD deliberators' fear of punishment would prompt them to diminish incentives for crime by funding jobs, education, and social services. When life gets better outside prison, it can get better inside while still deterring.

According to the OPD approach, both special and general deterrence are justified because we would rationally consent to them. Rational consent means that general deterrence uses criminals as *means*, but not *mere* means. But it is easiest to be satisfied with contract-based claims about rational consent when we identify ends of people burdened by the contract that are achieved despite their burdens. Any plausible social contract theory acknowledges that it is not rational to consent unless the contract gives us lives better than the state of nature. If life inside prison is no better than the state of nature, then we can only justify it through contract if we represent criminals as contract-breakers who have forfeited their contractual claims. But this move turns on an implicit retributivism, and skeptics must reject it. They must instead make life in prison better than the state of nature. This is achievable in the humane prisons endorsed in OPD, since we make prison conditions as good as possible without undermining deterrence. It seems reasonable to think that life in prison could be quite a lot better than the state of nature when it is designed this way. Further, the punished and the protected *use each other reciprocally*. Both parties pursue the end of a life better than the state of nature. The protected pursue this end by using the punished to generate deterrence. The punished pursue this end by using the protected to generate the social resources necessary to provide the best prison conditions possible. If deterrence is necessary to avoid the state of nature, then it is only possible for the punished to have lives better than the state of nature if they consent to serve as means to deterrence. It is in this sense that the competition between the punished and the protected is not fundamental.

What if future research shows that we do not need prison conditions to deter after all, perhaps because the prospect of unpleasant imprisonment does not play a significant role in potential criminals' decision-making, or because the mere fact of imprisoning violent offenders for a time prompts enough behavior improvement? The OPD justification is sensitive to this possibility, since such research would prompt deliberators to imprison only to incapacitate. But the OPD justification is equally sensitive to the possibility that future research will reinforce the need for deterrence, and it has the resources to justify it.

On this point, it may be useful to compare the OPD justification and another justification based on the concept of *quarantine*, which Smilansky has called the "two most developed denialist attempts to defend deontological constraints concerning punishment" (2019, 30). The quarantine justification is defended by Derk Pereboom and Gregg Caruso in a number of joint papers, and independent papers and books (e.g., Pereboom 2001, 2014, 2021; Pereboom and Caruso 2018; Caruso and Pereboom 2020; Caruso 2021; Caruso's chapter in this volume). They hold that our right to *self-defense* makes it permissible to quarantine carriers of dangerous diseases even though they do not deserve to be sick, and they draw an analogy between quarantine and imprisoning violent criminals, arguing that we have as much right to imprison violent people as we do to quarantine carriers of dangerous diseases, even if violent people do not deserve to be incarcerated. As I understand their overall ethical theory, it is fundamentally consequentialist (Smilansky [2019] interprets it the same way). However, they think the quarantine justification is not consequentialist because they think (1) the right to self-defense need not be construed consequentially, and (2) their theory adequately protects criminals' rights not to be treated as mere means. (1) seems plausible, though simply positing non-consequentialist rights within a basically consequentialist view raises questions. (2) raises similar questions, but there are further puzzles about how their theory interprets the right not to be used as a mere means.

Pereboom's position on this point seems to have evolved. In *Free Will, Agency, and Meaning in Life* (2014), he holds that people who I "harm in self-defense" are "being used merely as a means," and while this is a concern, it is "outweighed by the right to harm in self-defense," so long as "the harm inflicted is the minimal amount reasonably required" (167). But Kantian perfect duties are absolute and cannot be outweighed—instead we need to show why people would rationally consent to be used, as the OPD approach endeavors to do. In more recent work, Pereboom and Caruso hold that using people without their consent is only problematic if we use them *manipulatively* toward ends other than self-defense, such as general deterrence (Caruso 2021; Pereboom 2021; see also Shaw 2019). Similar Kantian objections should be made to this move.

Having made this move, Pereboom and Caruso claim to justify quarantine based on self-defense without licensing illegitimate use, and to justify imprisonment via analogy with quarantine. They then claim that the quarantine analogy yields "free general deterrence," that is, general deterrence we can rely on without having to justify using people as means to general deterrence. The idea is that hardly anyone wants to be quarantined, so quarantine inevitably produces deterrence as a *side effect*, and the same is true for imprisonment. However, as John Lemos (2016) and I (2019) have argued in different ways, quarantine does *not* inevitably deter.[9] The COVID-19 era has shown that many of us are not unduly distressed by being required to stay at home. Many would not be distressed at all if the state sent checks to everybody required to quarantine. Presumably the state would have a *moral reason* to send such checks, to compensate the quarantined for the undeserved restriction of their freedom. But we would want to ensure the checks were not too big, because then people at low risk of dying might intentionally expose themselves to the coronavirus to get the checks, and our quarantine practices would work against their intended purposes. So, we need quarantine practices calibrated to make life as good as possible in quarantine while still *deterring* people from intentional exposure. We need a justification of general deterrence to justify such calibration. This means that general deterrence does not come as a "free" byproduct—we cannot justify *effective* quarantine without justifying general deterrence, and the discussion earlier in the paper has shown how the same considerations apply to imprisonment.

Here is another way of seeing the same point. Suppose that my aim in setting up a prison is merely to incapacitate violent offenders in comfortable conditions, because I think I am not entitled to aim at general deterrence, since I think calibrating conditions for general deterrence would nonconsensually and impermissibly use the imprisoned. And suppose I discover that the conditions are producing general deterrence as a side effect. Perhaps general deterrence comes for free until I discover this, since I meant well in setting up the prison. But upon discovery, it is no longer free: my belief about the impermissibility of calibrating conditions for general deterrence gives me a reason to improve conditions. If I wish to preserve general deterrence, I need a justification of general deterrence. I could appeal to consequentialism and argue that it is not impermissible to nonconsensually use people for general deterrence after all, or I could appeal to a Kantian contractualism to show why people would rationally consent to such use.

Perhaps in response to arguments like this, Pereboom now offers a theory that supplements free deterrence with a straightforwardly consequentialist argument for general deterrence (2021, 101), and he holds that even nonconsensual, manipulative use is consistent with treating someone as an end (95) so long as they are not treated too severely (85). This takes us far from Kantian foundations. Caruso remains committed to the view that the only general

[9] Both Lemos and I draw on arguments from Smilansky (2011).

deterrence we should seek is free general deterrence (2021, 312). But if the argument above is correct, there is no free deterrence, so relying on it obscures a demand for justification that punishment theorists should confront. The OPD approach confronts this demand.

Let me now turn to two other problems for utilitarian punishment mentioned earlier: framing and weakening due process. Imagine that we could strengthen general deterrence by occasionally framing and punishing celebrities, because of all the media attention it provides. To rule this out, we have to be a bit creative with OPD as Rawls understands it, so that we can use it to capture Kant's notion that *deception* is a way of using people as mere means. A practice that aims to deter by penalizing anybody other than actual criminals can only succeed by deception: punishing a framed celebrity is only effective if almost everyone is deceived about the framing. If the framing becomes widely known, we get less deterrence, not more. In OPD, I must assume that I may be among the deceived, so I would be volunteering to be deceived and thereby using myself as a mere means to increase deterrence.[10]

How do we rule out weakening due process? The guiding principle in applying OPD to criminal wrongdoing is to be fair, by assuming equal odds of being harmed and benefited when the veil is lifted. When we choose principles for due process, the competing parties are no longer potential victims and the punished—now they are potential victims and the *accused.* The accused have more to lose by weakening due process than potential victims have to gain. If we lower the conviction standard from "reasonable doubt" to (say) "preponderance of the evidence," we make things worse for the accused by increasing their odds of conviction. Some additional convicts will have been correctly accused, and getting the violent ones off the street will improve things for potential victims. However, the lowered standard will also facilitate sloppy or politicized prosecutions that convict non-criminals, worsening things for the accused *without* improving things for potential victims. Since this would harm the accused more than it would benefit potential victims, OPD deliberators would not choose to weaken due process. As explained earlier, this holds even if weakening due process yields an aggregate reduction in victimization, because aggregate effects are irrelevant in OPD, since it makes us focus on one person at a time, and this is part of what makes it a deontological alternative to utilitarianism.

---

[10] See Kant (1996c, 8:381 [p. 347]) for a related argument and Vilhauer (2017) for discussion.

5 Non-retributive Kantian Remorse for Skeptics

It is intuitive to think that remorse plays an important role in the moral experience of anyone who is not perfect, and it has a special importance for philosophy of punishment, as it is often a mitigating factor in sentencing (see, e.g., Maslen 2015). This is a problem for skeptics, because it is not obvious how we could have a reason for remorse if we do not deserve to suffer, and without a reason for remorse we have no reason to treat it as a mitigating factor in sentencing. The very frequent parole review chosen in OPD would transform sentencing practices, but intuitively remorse would still be helpful in gauging the dangerousness of people we imprison, which is important for imprisoning them safely. So, it is worth exploring whether skeptics can justify remorse.

It would be perfectly consistent with the basic principles of skepticism to advocate remorse-elimination therapy, but this sounds uncomfortably like therapy for inducing psychopathy. The most obvious strategy for skeptics who want to justify remorse is (once again) utilitarianism: it seems reasonable to suppose that the pain of remorse may improve behavior, if only as a sort of self-administered aversion therapy, and that the pain of remorse is outweighed by the pain it prevents. But if this is my *only* reason for feeling remorse, then I am using remorse as a mere means: I experience remorse not because there is anything *fitting* (morally appropriate) about this experience, but merely because it improves behavior. Clearly remorse is not the kind of thing I can *wrong* by using it as mere means. So, it might seem that feeling remorse as a mere means to behavior improvement is no more problematic than enduring painful physical therapy as a mere means to mobility improvement in my knee after an injury. However, it would be perverse to choose painful knee therapy if technicians offer me a device I can strap to my knee that makes me feel a soothing warmth but improves mobility just as well. It does not seem perverse to experience remorse after I commit a murder instead of strapping a device to my head that causes soothing warmth and improves my behavior just as well. This is because of an intuition that remorse is morally important not only as a means to improved behavior, but also because it is fitting.

Retributivists can explain the fittingness of remorse in terms of action-based desert, but skeptics must reject this explanation. They can instead explain the fittingness of remorse in terms of the value of care. As understood here, sympathy is part of care.[11] When I care about someone, I sympathetically share their joy but also their pain. The value of care is not grounded in action-based desert. Even if we are not skeptics but instead believe firmly in free will, it would be absurd to think that, in befriending someone, I have acted in some way that entails that I deserve to suffer when my friend suffers. Care *is* quite plausibly grounded in need-based desert, but as explained earlier, need is a distinct desert base from action and is not undermined by skepticism.

According to the care justification of remorse, we should have this sort of sympathetic connection not just to friends but to a broader range of morally salient others, including people we have wronged. Wronging someone thus gives us a reason to care about them that parallels our reason to care about a friend. All forms of sympathy give us a reason to alleviate the pain of those with whom we sympathize by removing the causes of their pain. When we sympathize with people we have wronged, the cause is *our own actions*, and this gives us reasons to be pained *by* our actions, to alleviate their pain by making amends, and to improve our behavior toward others in general.

Human nature seems to contain deeply embedded desires about wrongdoer's responses to their wrongs. When people violate moral norms and hurt us, we desire not only that they make amends and improve their behavior, but also that they *understand* their wrong, in a way that involves not only cognition but also painful feeling. The idea that painful feeling is part of understanding one's wrongs helps explain the idea that painful feeling can be fitting. Some philosophers may wish to model this desire for wrongdoers to suffer in terms of Strawson's (1962) "reactive attitudes," which can be understood as essentially involving desires for the wrongdoer to experience deserved suffering. But to assume this model is to over-theorize our experience. Wrongdoers' sympathetic pain sometimes satisfies victims' desires. Since the value of sympathy is not grounded in action-based desert, victims' desires need not always be understood as retributive.

Since the care-based justification includes reasons to make amends and improve our behavior, it has a consequentialist dimension. But it is not fundamentally consequentialist, because care is valuable even when it does not have good consequences. Care requires sympathizing even when there is

[11] As I will discuss below, the emotional orientation called "sympathy" here could just as well be called "empathy," and "empathy" might in some ways be a better fit for the contemporary literature. However, Kant calls it "sympathy" (*Sympathie* in Kant's German), and given the present chapter's goal of providing a Kantian ethics for skeptics, Kant's term will be used here. Since there is no generally accepted account of how we might usefully distinguish sympathy and empathy (Stueber 2006, 27), this poses no conceptual problem.

nothing we can do to help.[12] If I am marooned on a desert island and receive a message in a bottle informing me that my friend is in pain, and I feel no sympathetic pain just because I cannot help, my claim to care is undermined. This is also true for people we have wronged: care motivates us to make amends if we can, but if we cannot, we still sympathize, because we care. In this way, the care-based justification of remorse can explain why remorse is fitting, rather than a mere means to the end of good consequences. The care-based justification of remorse can be included within any moral theory that recognizes sympathetic pain as fitting. This includes varieties of care ethics and virtue ethics, and Kantian ethics as well.[13]

The claim that Kantian ethics can value sympathetic pain probably sounds strange to philosophers with limited familiarity with Kant, and even to some with considerable familiarity. So let me discuss Kant in a bit more detail than I did in the justification of punishment, which drew on more familiar Kantian ideas. Kant makes dismissive-sounding remarks about sympathy in his most famous moral works, the *Groundwork for the Metaphysics of Morals* and the *Critique of Practical Reason*, which can easily seem to imply that the sort of sympathy just discussed does not count as a moral emotion. But those remarks elide a distinction that is important in his ethics between two ways of sympathizing.[14] One is what we might call *natural sympathy*—an instinctive, pre-reflective reactivity to others' feelings that we share with many other animal species, which can overwhelm us and make it difficult to act prudently or morally. The other is what we might call *rational sympathy*—it is what we experience when we reflectively regulate that animal capacity according to moral reasons. In the context of Kant's corpus as a whole, it is clear that Kant denies natural sympathy a role in moral feeling, but not rational sympathy. Rational sympathy is an intentional activity of the imagination that puts us "in the other's place" (Kant 2012, 25:476 [p. 52]): we imagine what it is like to be in the other's situation, and this prompts sympathetic feelings.[15] Kant's distinction between natural sympathy and rational sympathy corresponds

[12] Kantian "sages" can appear to reject sympathy when they cannot help (Kant 1996b, 6:457 [p. 575]), but what they reject is natural sympathy, not rational sympathy. This distinction is explained below. See Vilhauer (2021b) for discussion.

[13] See Vilhauer (2004) for a virtue ethics approach.

[14] For passages that illustrate this distinction, see Kant (1996b, 6:457 [p. 575]; 1997, 27:677–78 [pp. 408–9]; 2007, 7:235–38 [pp. 338–40]; 2012, 25:606–7, 1320–21 [pp. 156–57, 429]). See Vilhauer (2021a) for commentary.

[15] For passages that illustrate the connection between sympathy and imagination, see Kant (1996b, 6:321, 456–57 [pp. 464, 575]; 1997, 27:58, 65 [pp. 25, 30]; 2007, 7:179, 238 [pp. 288, 341]; 2012, 25:476, 574–76, 606–7 [pp. 52, 130, 156]).

(and in fact appears identical) to a distinction in contemporary psychology between *empathic distress* and *empathic concern.*[16]

Kant clearly thinks sympathy is related to the duty to take others' ends as one's own, but the nature of the relationship is a matter of controversy.[17] I have argued that sympathy is necessary for taking others' ends as one's own, based on a distinction between *adopting* and *promoting* others' ends (Vilhauer 2022b). Many of others' permissible ends are ends they have because of the particular things that make them happy, due to features of their personality that are contingent relative to the more abstract perspective of Kantian rational agency. Rational sympathy lets me imagine my way into others' perspectives and call up feelings like theirs. This gives me sympathetic joy when they achieve their ends and sympathetic pain when they do not. In this way, I not only promote but also adopt their ends. I can *promote* others' ends without sympathy as means to *different* ends that others do *not* have. If somebody wants their bleeding stopped, I may bandage their wound because the sight of blood disgusts me, because I think it will help my reputation, or because I think it will help fulfill my duty. I promote their end in all these ways, and there may be no difference at all in the consequences I produce, but I do it as means to ends they do not have.

The Kantian idea that we should universalize our maxims may seem to require us to sympathize equally with everyone, and this may prohibit us from cultivating especially strong sympathy for particular others. But Kant does not advocate this. We have a duty of friendship (Kant 1996b, 6:469 [p. 585]), and while we ought to have "general good-will toward everyone," "to be everybody's friend will not do, for he who is a friend to all has no particular friend; but friendship is a particular bond" (Kant 1997, 27:430 [p. 190]). Friendship is an "ideal of each sympathizing and communicating about the other's well-being," which guides us toward a "maximum" (Kant 1996b, 6:469 [p. 585], translation modified) in which "each mutually sympathizes [*teilnehmen*] with every situation of the other, as if it were encountered by himself" (Kant 1997, 27:677 [p. 408], translation modified).

Kant himself does not propose a sympathy-based account of remorse. His own account relies on retributivism (Kant 1996b, 6:394 [p. 524]; see Vilhauer [2022a] for commentary). But it is just as intuitively plausible to think that we ought to sympathize in a special way with people we have wronged as it is to think this about friends. So, it is a natural extension of Kant's view to hold

[16] Empathic concern is an "intentional capacity" that involves "emotion-regulation"—it "involves an explicit representation of the subjectivity of the other" rather than "a simple resonance of affect between the self and other," while empathic distress involves "emotional contagion" (Decety et al. 2007, 254).

[17] See Fahmy (2009) for an influential alternative.

that we ought to extend such sympathy to our victims. In fact, Kant nearly suggests this account himself in a discussion of why oppressors should sympathize with the oppressed (Kant 2012, 25:606 [p. 156]).

Objectors may argue that self-retribution is part of the nature of remorse, so it misdescribes the sympathetic pain discussed here to call it a kind of remorse. I think this is wrong, but even if it is right, I am not sure it matters if sympathetic pain can play the roles described above in a skeptical moral psychology. Objectors may claim that sympathetic pain cannot play these roles because some wrongs that ought to prompt remorse do not cause pain. Suppose I murder someone instantly and painlessly. Where is the pain with which I ought to sympathize? On Kant's account of sympathy, we can imagine our way into the perspectives of not just actual but possible others. We do this when we read fiction (Kant 2012, 25:476 [p. 53]). So, I can imagine my way into the perspective of a fictional version of the person I murdered and their profound sorrow over the life I have stolen from them. This should not seem *ad hoc*, as the foundation of sympathy in imagination is fundamental to Kant's account.

In conversation, Smilansky has claimed that sympathetic pain is too *weak* relative to the pain of self-retribution to be a powerful enough motivator to improve behavior. If we take this claim as empirical, then it requires empirical evidence, and while the respective roles of sympathy and self-retributive pain in moral psychology are a contested matter in empirical psychology, it is clear that sympathy plays a crucial role.[18] Even if, as an empirical matter, sympathetic pain is on average a weaker motivator than self-retributive pain, it seems plausible to think it can be a *strong enough* motivator to be valuable. If we take the claim that sympathetic pain is too weak as a claim about the *concept* of sympathy, then it is clearly false, at least as Kant construes sympathy. As we saw above, Kant's ideal of friendship is an ideal of *maximal* sympathy: I should imagine myself in my friend's place and try to feel their feelings as vividly as if they were my own. If we think victims are as morally salient as friends, and merit the same kind of sympathetic attachment, then Kant's ideal suggests that wrongdoers should imaginatively undergo everything they have done to their victims with equal vividity. The imaginations found among human beings at this point in our history typically present us with imaginings less vivid than immediate sensations. However, Maysa Khedr points out that the progress of technology may give us more vivid imaginations.[19] Virtual reality may be contributing to this already, and direct brain interfaces may

[18] As noted earlier, this is often under the label of "empathy" (e.g., Decety et al. 2007).

[19] Class discussion, "Philosophy of Law," City College of New York, Fall 2021.

contribute more. If we have moral reasons to harness such tools to put us in the place of people with whom we ought to sympathize more vividly, then perhaps criminals ought to use them to experience what they have done to their victims just as vividly as the victims. This would yield an emotional proportionality of equality, in a kind of non-retributive parallel with the *lex talionis*. My point here is not to endorse this equal proportionality, only to show that it follows from a natural line of thought about Kant's ideal, to show that the concept of sympathy does not imply that sympathy is a weak emotional experience. Skeptics might be reluctant to endorse equal proportionality. It might seem to prescribe more pain than necessary for a fitting response to wrongs. This would give us a reason to constrain Kant's ideal when it prescribes pain. But skeptics could endorse equal proportionality without importing retributivist premises.

6 Conclusion

To conclude, let me comment on what readers may feel is a dissonance between these justifications of punishment and remorse. The former aims at making criminals' imprisonment as painless as possible, while the latter says that criminals should suffer along with their victims. The latter view may seem inhumane relative to the former. But care is typically understood as an essential feature of humaneness, and sometimes it hurts to care. Here is another point that may diminish dissonance. Principles of punishment chosen in OPD correspond to what Kant calls *principles of right* in that they justify coercion, while care-based reasons for remorse correspond to what Kant calls *duties of virtue*, with which we cannot legitimately coerce compliance. It is up to each of us, on our own, to fulfill our duties of virtue. Thus, measures such as coercively strapping sympathy helmets onto criminals would violate Kantian ethics. Further, the value of wrongdoers' sympathy for their victims may be reciprocal, such that victims have a duty of virtue to sympathize with wrongdoers too.[20] Victims' sympathy for wrongdoers' sympathetic pain can prompt them to offer wrongdoers opportunities to make amends, which can in turn promote reunification of moral communities. Adopting this attitude may seem to be a lot to ask of victims. But skepticism about action-based

[20] I read Kant (1996b, 6:459–61 [pp. 577–78]) as supporting this view.

desert may make it easier to adopt. This concluding thought may be a first step toward an account of forgiveness for free will skeptics.[21]

References

Caruso, Gregg D. 2021. *Rejecting Retributivism: Free Will, Punishment, and Criminal Justice*. Cambridge: Cambridge University Press.

Caruso, Gregg D., and Derk Pereboom. 2020. "A Non-Punitive Alternative to Punishment." In *The Routledge Handbook on the Philosophy and Science of Punishment*, edited by Farah Focquaert, Elizabeth Shaw, and Bruce N. Waller, 355–65. New York: Routledge.

Clark, Michael. 2004. "A Non-Retributive Kantian Approach to Punishment." *Ratio* 17, no. 1 (February): 12–27.

Decety, Jean, Philip L. Jackson, and Eric Brunet. 2007. "The Cognitive Neuropsychology of Empathy." In *Empathy in Mental Illness*, edited by Tom F. D. Farrow and Peter W. R. Woodruff, 240–60. Cambridge: Cambridge University Press.

Dolovich, Sharon. 2004. "Legitimate Punishment in Liberal Democracy." *Buffalo Law Review* 7, no. 2 (January): 307–442.

Fahmy, Melissa Seymour. 2009. "Active Sympathetic Participation: Reconsidering Kant's Duty of Sympathy." *Kantian Review* 14, no. 1 (March): 31–52.

Harsanyi, John. 1975. "Can the Maximin Principle Serve as a Basis for Morality? A Critique of John Rawls's Theory." *American Political Science Review* 69, no. 2 (June): 594–606.

Jeppson, Sofia. 2021. "Retributivism, Justification and Credence: The Epistemic Argument Revisited." *Neuroethics* 14, no. 2 (July): 177–90.

Kant, Immanuel. 1996a. *Critique of Practical Reason*. In *Practical Philosophy*, translated and edited by Mary J. Gregor, 137–271. Cambridge: Cambridge University Press.

———. 1996b. *The Metaphysics of Morals*. In *Practical Philosophy*, translated and edited by Mary J. Gregor, 363–602. Cambridge: Cambridge University Press.

———. 1996c. *Toward Perpetual Peace*. In *Practical Philosophy*, translated and edited by Mary J. Gregor, 315–51. Cambridge: Cambridge University Press.

———. 1997. *Lectures on Ethics*. Translated by Peter Heath. Edited by Peter Heath and J. B. Schneewind. Cambridge: Cambridge University Press.

———. 2007. *Anthropology from a Pragmatic Point of View*. Translated by Robert B. Louden. In *Anthropology, History, and Education*, translated and edited by

[21] Thanks to Jeffrey Blustein, Gregg Caruso, John Lemos, Neil Levy, Derk Pereboom, Saul Smilansky, Jens Timmermann, Bruce Waller, and Allen Wood for helpful advice at various points in the history of this project.

Günther Zöller and Robert B. Louden, 231–429. Cambridge: Cambridge University Press.
———. 2012. *Lectures on Anthropology*. Translated by Robert R. Clewis, Robert B. Louden, G. Felicitas Munzel, and Allen W. Wood. Edited by Allen W. Wood and Robert B. Louden. Cambridge: Cambridge University Press.
Lemos, John. 2016. "Moral Concerns about Responsibility Denial and the Quarantine of Violent Criminals." *Law and Philosophy* 35, no. 5 (October): 461–83.
Maslen, Hannah. 2015. *Remorse, Penal Theory, and Sentencing*. Oxford: Hart.
McLeod, Owen. 2013. "Desert." *Stanford Encyclopedia of Philosophy* (Winter 2013 edition), edited by Edward N. Zalta. https://stanford.library.sydney.edu.au/archives/spr2013/entries/desert/.
Murphy, Jeffrie G. 1973. "Marxism and Retribution." *Philosophy & Public Affairs* 2, no. 3 (Spring): 217–43.
Pereboom, Derk. 2001. *Living without Free Will*. Cambridge: Cambridge University Press.
———. 2014. *Free Will, Agency, and Meaning in Life*. Oxford: Oxford University Press.
———. 2021. *Wrongdoing and the Moral Emotions*. Oxford: Oxford University Press.
Pereboom, Derk, and Gregg D. Caruso. 2018. "Hard-Incompatibilist Existentialism: Neuroscience, Punishment, and Meaning in Life." In *Neuroexistentialism: Meaning, Morals, and Purpose in the Age of Neuroscience*, edited by Gregg D. Caruso and Owen Flanagan, 193–222. Oxford: Oxford University Press.
Rawls, John. 1999. *A Theory of Justice*. Rev. ed. Cambridge, MA: Harvard University Press.
Shaw, Elizabeth. 2019. "Justice without Moral Responsibility?" *Journal of Information Ethics* 28, no. 1 (Spring): 95–130.
Smilansky, Saul. 2000. *Free Will and Illusion*. Oxford: Clarendon.
———. 2011. "Hard Determinism and Punishment: A Practical *Reductio*." *Law and Philosophy* 30, no. 3 (May): 353–67.
———. 2019. "Free Will Skepticism and Deontological Constraints." In *Free Will Skepticism in Law and Society: Challenging Retributive Justice*, edited by Elizabeth Shaw, Derk Pereboom, and Gregg D. Caruso, 29–42. Cambridge: Cambridge University Press.
Sterba, James P. 1977. "Retributive Justice." *Political Theory* 5, no. 3 (August): 349–62.
Strawson, P. F. 1962. "Freedom and Resentment." *Proceedings of the British Academy* 48: 1–25.
Stueber, Karsten. 2006. *Rediscovering Empathy: Agency, Folk Psychology, and the Human Sciences*. Cambridge, MA: MIT Press.
Vilhauer, Benjamin. 2004. "Hard Determinism, Remorse, and Virtue Ethics." *Southern Journal of Philosophy* 42, no. 4 (Winter): 547–64.
———. 2009a. "Free Will and Reasonable Doubt." *American Philosophical Quarterly* 46, no. 2 (April): 131–40.
———. 2009b. "Free Will Skepticism and Personhood as a Desert Base." *Canadian Journal of Philosophy* 39, no. 3 (September): 489–511.

———. 2012. "Taking Free Will Skepticism Seriously." *Philosophical Quarterly* 62, no. 249 (October): 833–52.
———. 2013. "Persons, Punishment, and Free Will Skepticism." *Philosophical Studies* 162, no. 2 (January): 143–63.
———. 2015. "Free Will and the Asymmetrical Justifiability of Holding Morally Responsible." *Philosophical Quarterly* 65, no. 261 (October): 772–89.
———. 2017. "Kant's Mature Theory of Punishment and a First *Critique* Ideal Abolitionist Alternative." In *The Palgrave Kant Handbook*, edited by Matthew C. Altman, 617–42. London: Palgrave Macmillan.
———. 2019. "Deontology and Deterrence for Free Will Deniers." In *Free Will Skepticism in Law and Society: Challenging Retributive Justice*, edited by Elizabeth Shaw, Derk Pereboom, and Gregg D. Caruso, 116–38. Cambridge: Cambridge University Press.
———. 2021a. "'Reason's Sympathy' and Its Foundations in Productive Imagination." *Kantian Review* 26, no. 3 (September): 455–74.
———. 2021b. "Sages, Sympathy, and Suffering in Kant's Theory of Friendship." *Canadian Journal of Philosophy* 51, no. 6 (August): 452–67.
———. 2022a. "Kantian Remorse with and without Self-Retribution." *Kantian Review* 27, no. 3 (September): 421-41.
———. 2022b. "'Reason's Sympathy' and Others' Ends in Kant." *European Journal of Philosophy* 30, no. 1 (March): 96-112.
Waller, Bruce N. 2015a. *The Stubborn System of Moral Responsibility*. Cambridge, MA: MIT Press.
———. 2015b. *Restorative Free Will: Back to the Biological Base*. New York: Lexington.

Part VII

Abolitionism

25

Against Legal Punishment

Nathan Hanna

1 Introduction

Here is a preliminary statement of my thesis: legal punishment is morally wrong because it is too morally risky. I will revise the preliminary statement later in response to objections, but for now it gives a good sense of the position that I will defend on the morality of punishment.[1] In this introductory section, I will briefly explain how my argument differs from similar ones in the philosophical literature on punishment. Then, in the rest of the chapter, I will explain why punishment is morally risky, argue that it is too morally risky, and discuss objections.

I am not the only one who thinks that punishment is morally risky or that it is wrong. The former view is increasingly popular and the latter—called *abolitionism*—has a few defenders. Those who share my worry about moral risk are rarely abolitionists, though. They typically argue that we should reform how we punish or reject certain justifications for punishment (e.g., Pereboom 2001, 161; Vilhauer 2009; Gross 2012, 9–14; Tomlin 2013, 2014; Huemer 2018,15-16; Kolber 2018; Caruso 2020; Caruso and Pereboom

[1] For ease of exposition, I will use *punishment* to mean *legal punishment* throughout.

N. Hanna (✉)
Drexel University, Philadelphia, PA, USA
e-mail: nth34@drexel.edu

© The Author(s), under exclusive license to Springer Nature Switzerland AG 2023

M. C. Altman (ed.), *The Palgrave Handbook on the Philosophy of Punishment*, Palgrave Handbooks in the Philosophy of Law, https://doi.org/10.1007/978-3-031-11874-6_25

2020; Jeppsson 2021).[2] And most abolitionists do not appeal to moral risk. The few who do focus on just a single source of it (e.g., Roebuck and Wood 2011). By contrast, I will argue that punishment is morally risky in a variety of ways that combine to make a good case for abolitionism. Most abolitionists try to show that extant justifications for punishment all fail or that a necessary condition for its permissibility cannot be satisfied (e.g., Sayre-McCord 2001; Golash 2005; Boonin 2008; Zimmerman 2011). These strategies have important limitations. The first does not show that better justifications cannot be developed. And the second invariably relies on controversial claims about why the relevant condition cannot be satisfied. By contrast, I will argue that there cannot be a successful justification for punishment. And I will do it by appealing to fairly uncontroversial claims about our epistemic fallibility, the badness of wrongful punishment, and what the necessary conditions for punishment's moral permissibility might be.

2 Punishment Is Morally Risky

In this section, I will argue that punishment is morally risky in a variety of ways. That is, I will argue that the moral risk involved in punishment has multiple sources. I will not say anything about *how* morally risky punishment is until the next section.

We can start to get a sense of punishment's moral risks if we think about what the necessary conditions for its moral permissibility are. Here are some plausible candidate conditions:

- The punishee [P] must have broken the law.
- P must have acted freely.
- P must have acted wrongly.
- P must have acted culpably.
- P must be liable to punishment.

With the possible exception of the liability condition, which I will clarify later, I expect that readers will have a good intuitive grasp of what these conditions mean.[3] The conditions are also fairly uncontroversial and consistent

[2] Tomlin (2014, 444–46) and Kolber (2018, 491) do anticipate arguments like mine, though.

[3] The key concepts in conditions 2–5 typically have both legal and nonlegal senses. I am using the nonlegal senses. So, to take an example, P may not have acted freely in my sense even if the law counts her as having acted freely. Ditto for conditions 3–5. It is uncontroversial that there are nonlegal necessary conditions for punishment's permissibility and that the law can be mistaken about whether they are satisfied.

with many different theoretical commitments, including different moral theories and different justifications for punishment. Of course, some theorists will want to reject or even add some conditions. I will discuss the significance of this later. But for now, I will just assume that the list is a good enough approximation of the truth. To start: the list highlights the fact that there are multiple conditions that must be satisfied for punishment to be permissible. This is important because more conditions tend to increase the likelihood that we will be mistaken whenever we think that all of the necessary conditions are satisfied.[4] This risk of epistemic error makes punishment morally risky because the relevant errors can lead to wrongful punishment. Each condition on my list is associated with specific risks of error. I will illustrate by discussing each condition, starting with the ones that involve the most familiar risks of error: the lawbreaking and wrongdoing conditions.

We sometimes falsely believe that someone broke the law. This can be due to false beliefs about what they did or about what the law forbids. The causes of these errors are familiar, such as misleading evidence and ignorance of the law. Similarly, we sometimes falsely believe that certain acts are wrong. This can be due to false beliefs about what makes acts wrong in general or false beliefs about whether the things that do so are present in a given case. The causes of these errors are also familiar, for example, bias and bad moral education. These specific errors can and do lead us to punish wrongfully. Many punishments are morally risky partly because we inflict them despite the risk that we are making these errors.

That said, it is plausible to think that we do not always risk making these errors when punishing. Sometimes there is just no denying that someone wrongfully broke the law—or so I will assume. To keep my argument simple, I will focus on risks of error that we run whenever we punish. I mention the above risks for two reasons. First, their familiarity makes pointing to them the clearest way to show that punishment can be morally risky. Second, their similarities to the risks of error that I will focus on will support my claims about the latter. Both the familiar and the unfamiliar risks of error stem from our epistemic fallibility in the face of what are often complex matters of fact and value. And both generate moral risk. The free will, culpability, and liability conditions are all associated with risks of error that we run whenever we punish. I will discuss these conditions in turn.

[4] Note that each condition on my list can fail to be satisfied when the ones preceding it are satisfied. To illustrate, someone can break the law freely and wrongly but non-culpably, e.g., because they were non-culpably ignorant of morally relevant facts. Or someone might not be liable despite satisfying the other conditions, e.g., because they freely and culpably committed a crime that is really just a private or minor wrong that should not have been criminalized.

Consider the free will condition: P must have acted freely. Most of us believe that free will is real. But what it takes to have free will and whether we have it at all are hard questions that are subjects of longstanding philosophical debate.[5] This is not the place to rehearse these debates. What matters for my purposes is that they are complex and the best arguments on each side are sophisticated and hard to evaluate. Given our epistemic fallibility, we should not be completely confident in our views here. Even those of us who are confident that we have free will should admit that there is a possibility that the free will deniers are correct. (I will say more about the sense of *possibility* that I am using later.) This possibility makes punishment morally risky to at least some extent. Whenever we punish people, it is possible that we are punishing people who lack free will and so punishing wrongly.[6] Similar points apply to the other conditions.

Take the culpability condition: P must have acted culpably. Most of us believe that people are typically culpable for their wrongdoing. But again, what it takes to be culpable and whether we ever are culpable are hard questions that are subjects of longstanding philosophical debate. These debates are also complex and the best arguments on each side are sophisticated and hard to evaluate. Some philosophers worry that exculpating factors such as non-culpable ignorance and the absence of relevant kinds of control are ubiquitous (e.g., Nagel 1979, 35–38; Strawson 1994; Zimmerman 1997, 2002, 2011; Rosen 2003, 2004; Levy 2011).[7] It is possible that our belief in culpability is mistaken and that the skeptics' doubts are correct. This possibility also makes punishment morally risky: whenever we punish people, it is possible that we are punishing non-culpable people and so punishing wrongly.

Finally, consider the liability condition: P must be liable to punishment. Before getting to the moral risks here, some clarifications are in order because it may not be obvious what this condition means. I take the claim that P is liable to punishment to mean that certain facts that used to be moral reasons not to punish P either no longer hold or are no longer reasons not to punish

[5] Prominent contemporary free will deniers include Pereboom (2001) and Levy (2011). For an overview of arguments against free will, see O'Connor and Franklin (2021).

[6] One might object that, if we lack free will, punishment is never wrong because none of our acts are ever wrong. I will reply to this objection later.

[7] Levy (2011) equates these kinds of control with free will, but I think that free will is a distinct kind of control and not the only kind that might be necessary for moral responsibility. Zimmerman (2011, 144–50) argues that we can be both culpable and *inculpable* (his term) for our acts and that punishing us for our acts is permissible only if we are culpable for them and not inculpable for them. For my purposes, we do not need to worry about what inculpability is. Instead, we can take Zimmerman to be endorsing an additional necessary condition on punishment's permissibility. I will discuss the significance of possible additional conditions below. For an overview of arguments against moral responsibility, see Caruso (2021).

P. Such facts include the fact that punishing people is normally a violation of their rights and the fact that it intentionally harms them. Some theorists argue that people can forfeit their rights and that, when they do, punishment does not violate their rights. And some argue that people can deserve to be harmed or punished and that, when they do, the fact that punishment will harm them is not a reason not to punish them and may even be a reason to punish them.[8] For convenience, I will understand liability in terms of rights forfeiture and desert. But what I say about it will generalize to many other ways of understanding it.

Here is why the liability condition, so understood, makes punishment morally risky: As with the other conditions, whether this condition is ever satisfied turns on the answers to hard questions that are subjects of longstanding philosophical debate. These questions include questions about what rights people have, what the basis of our rights are, what people deserve, and what the normative significance of desert is. The debates over these sorts of questions are complex and the best arguments on each side are sophisticated and hard to evaluate. Some philosophers question whether people can forfeit their rights against punishment, some question whether people can deserve to be harmed or punished, and some question whether deserving to be harmed or punished can eliminate reasons not to harm or punish.[9] It is possible that the skeptics' doubts about these things are correct. This possibility makes punishment morally risky: whenever we punish people, it is possible that we are punishing people who are not liable to punishment and so punishing wrongly.

I started this section by listing some fairly uncontroversial candidate conditions for punishment's permissibility. I have argued that each of them makes punishment morally risky. But when I listed the conditions, I said that some theorists will want to reject some of them or even add to them. I will conclude this section by briefly discussing the significance of these reactions.

First, consider the position of those who want to reject some of the conditions on my list. I am willing to grant for argument's sake that such critics might be right and that any given condition on my list might not be a genuine condition, even approximately. But this is not a problem for me because I do not need to insist that these conditions are genuine to establish my claims about moral risk. The mere possibility that they are genuine and never satisfied suffices for moral risk. To illustrate, it is possible that the following claim

[8] Wellman (2012) defends the first claim. Berman (2008) defends both claims. For an interestingly different take on liability, see Tadros (2011).

[9] Boonin (2008, 103–19) and Hanna (2012, 609–16) question the first position. Hanna (2019, 111n6) gives several examples of philosophers who question the second. Hanna (2013, 2019) and Nelkin (2019) question the third.

is true: punishing people is permissible only if they acted culpably and no one ever acts culpably. The mere possibility that this is true makes punishment morally risky to at least some extent.

Next, consider the position of those who want to add to my list. Potential additions include: punishing P is the only way to achieve goods like deterrence and is the only way to express adequate disapproval of wrongdoing. For my purposes, there is nothing special about these conditions. Everything that I have said about the ones on my list applies to these new ones. It is possible that these are—or at least that they approximate—genuine conditions and that the theorists who think that they are never satisfied are correct.[10] My point here is not just to identify more necessary conditions that are sources of moral risk, though. My point is more general: no matter how confident we are in our views about what it takes for punishment to be permissible, it is always possible that we have overlooked some necessary conditions that may not be satisfiable. This adds to punishment's moral risks.[11]

I have argued that punishment is morally risky in a variety of ways. But I have not yet said anything about how morally risky it is. For all that I have said, the risks might be minimal. In the next section, I will argue that they are not and that punishment is morally wrong because it is too morally risky.

3 Punishment Is Too Morally Risky

Here is my main argument. Call it the *Risk Argument.*

1. Punishment is permissible only when we have shown the following beyond reasonable doubt: all of the conditions that are necessary for its permissibility are satisfied.
2. We can never do that.
3. So, punishment is wrong.

Before I defend the premises, I should emphasize that this argument is about a *conjunction* of claims, specifically the conjunction of all of the conditions (whatever they may be) that are necessary for punishment's permissibility. The argument says that this conjunction—*not* its individual conjuncts—must be demonstrated beyond reasonable doubt and cannot be demonstrated beyond

[10] For arguments that punishment is not the only way to do such things, see, e.g., Sayre-McCord (2001, 514–16), Golash (2005, 22–48, 153–72), Boonin (2008, 264–67), and Hanna (2008, 2014).

[11] Another upshot is that particular justifications for punishment are often committed to conditions that would make punishment morally risky. This makes such justifications vulnerable to distinctive moral risk-based objections. For an argument that this is true of retributive justifications, see Kolber (2018).

reasonable doubt. The argument does not say that we must demonstrate beyond reasonable doubt that someone acted freely (or that someone acted culpably, or that someone is liable to punishment) and that we cannot demonstrate this beyond reasonable doubt.[12] The argument is consistent with the view that these claims often cannot be reasonably doubted. The argument exploits the fact that a conjunction of claims can sometimes be reasonably doubted even if its individual conjuncts cannot be. This is true because the probability that a conjunction is true can be much lower than the probability of each conjunct. I will illustrate.

Suppose that I can reasonably doubt a claim only if I judge that it is less than 99 percent likely to be true. And suppose that I judge six claims to each be 99 percent likely to be true. Even though I cannot reasonably doubt them individually, I can still reasonably doubt their conjunction because I am rationally committed to judging it to be 94.1 percent likely to be true.[13] This illustration is artificial, partly because the numbers are made up and partly because reasonable doubt is arguably a qualitative rather than quantitative concept. But none of this affects my point, which is that a conjunction of claims can sometimes be reasonably doubted even if its individual conjuncts cannot be. Premise 2, which I will defend below, says that the conjunction of all the conditions that are necessary for punishment's permissibility can always be reasonably doubted.

Now I will defend the Risk Argument's premises. Here is my argument for 1:

4. Punishment is permissible only when we have shown the following beyond reasonable doubt: the punishee broke the law.
5. If premise 4 is true, then punishment is permissible only when we have shown the following beyond reasonable doubt: all of the conditions that are necessary for its permissibility are satisfied.
6. So, punishment is permissible only when we have shown the following beyond reasonable doubt: all of the conditions that are necessary for its permissibility are satisfied.

Premise 4 is widely accepted. Here is a paraphrase of the standard rationale for it (Tomlin 2013, 48–52; Tomlin 2014, 434–35; Huemer 2018, 16):[14]

[12] In this respect, the argument differs from those of Vilhauer (2009), Caruso (2020), and Caruso and Pereboom (2020), among others. They argue that the claim that we have free will can be reasonably doubted and that this undermines retributive justifications for punishment specifically.

[13] Assuming that the probabilities for the six claims are independent of each other, the calculation is straightforward: 0.99^6 = 0.941 (Kolber 2018, 490).

[14] For arguments against the rationale, see Laudan (2006, 2011, 2012). For a critique of Laudan's arguments, see Gardiner (2017).

> Punishing people who have not broken the law is wrong, and our beliefs about whether people broke the law are fallible. This makes punishment morally risky. And this risk is a comparatively serious one: other things equal, wrongful punishment is much worse than wrongful non-punishment. 4 is true because using the reasonable doubt standard is necessary to appropriately balance these risks.

I will assume that this rationale for premise 4 is correct. Premise 5 is true because there is no relevant difference between the claim that the punishee broke the law and the claim that all of the conditions that are necessary for punishment's permissibility are satisfied. As others have observed, the rationale for premise 4 generalizes. It applies to any claim that is like the lawbreaking condition in relevant respects. That is, it applies to claims that state necessary conditions on punishment's permissibility and about which we are fallible.[15] The conjunction of all of the necessary conditions is like the lawbreaking condition in these respects, so the same rationale applies to it.

Before moving on, I should pause to address a potential misunderstanding. I have argued that punishment is permissible only when we have shown beyond reasonable doubt that all of the conditions that are necessary for its permissibility are satisfied. This appeal to reasonable doubt is liable to be misunderstood. The concept of reasonable doubt is most popularly associated with a legal rule of evidence that is applied by juries or judges in criminal trials. Because of this, some readers might think that I am arguing that punishment is permissible only if we have shown the above during a criminal trial. And these readers might complain that it is unreasonable to expect juries and judges to grapple with all the difficult philosophical issues on which, I have argued, punishment's permissibility depends.

In response, I am not sure that it would be unreasonable to expect juries and judges—or anyone with the power to decide whether someone will be punished—to grapple with these issues before deciding whether someone will be punished. But I do not have to insist on this. When I talk about reasonable doubt, I am not talking about a legal rule of evidence. I am talking about *an epistemic standard* that can be applied in any context. So understood, my claim that punishment's permissibility requires showing certain things beyond reasonable doubt does not entail that this must be done by juries or judges

[15] Huemer (2016, 16) applies the reasoning to the wrongdoing condition. Tomlin applies it to the claim that some conduct is worthy of punishment (2013, 45, 52) and to the claim that a given punishment is not disproportionately harmful (2014, 432, 445).

specifically. One can accept my claim and think that much of this work would have to be done by others, such as legislators or academics.[16]

Moving on, here is my argument for premise 2 of the Risk Argument:

7. Many of the conditions that are or might be necessary for punishment's permissibility are such that they are satisfied only if certain controversial philosophical claims are true.
8. Premise 2 of the Risk Argument is true if the following can be reasonably doubted: for every such condition, either the condition is not actually necessary or the controversial philosophical claims associated with it are true.
9. That can be reasonably doubted.
10. So, premise 2 of the Risk Argument is true; we can never show the following beyond reasonable doubt: all of the conditions that are necessary for punishment's permissibility are satisfied.

My discussion in the previous section shows that premise 7 is true. And premise 8 is obviously true. So, I will focus on defending premise 9. It is true because there are just too many conditions of the sort mentioned in premises 7 and 8 to preclude reasonable doubt about the claim that *all* of the conditions that are necessary for punishment's permissibility are satisfied. Consider just the ones from the last section. I discussed three at some length: the free will, culpability, and liability conditions. And I mentioned two more in passing: the good consequences and expression conditions. Given the complexity of the issues here and our fallibility, it seems reasonable to doubt the claim that each condition is either not genuine or that the controversial philosophical claims associated with it are true. Moreover, given the possibility that we may have overlooked some relevantly similar conditions, it seems even more reasonable to doubt the claim that all of the necessary conditions are satisfied. In short, rejecting 9 requires endorsing an overly optimistic view about our epistemic situation.

4 Objections

In this section, I will discuss a variety of objections. Along the way, I will revise my thesis in a couple of important ways.

[16] Compare Tomlin (2013), who argues that conduct should not be criminalized in the first place unless the conduct has been shown beyond reasonable doubt to be worthy of punishment. I have not put my arguments in terms of criminalization because, unlike Tomlin, I do not think that punishment is essential to the criminal law (Tomlin 2013, 45n1).

4.1 The Terrible Consequences Objection

Objection: The Risk Argument must have gone wrong somewhere because its conclusion is obviously absurd. Not punishing would have terrible consequences. At worst, it would result in social collapse and anarchy. At best, it would result in massive injustice because most if not all criminals would be able to get away with their crimes.

Reply: This objection assumes that punishment is necessary to maintain social order and hold criminals to account. But that is not obviously true. Though I do not have the space to go into the details here, abolitionists and their sympathizers have plausibly argued that there are non-punitive responses to crime that can do these things. To take just two examples, David Boonin (2008, 213–75) defends what he calls the theory of pure restitution, and Geoffrey Sayre-McCord (2001) defends what he calls legal reparations. Both argue that forcing criminals to compensate their victims is a genuine and viable alternative to punishment. Importantly, they also both argue that especially dangerous criminals can be non-punitively incapacitated or even confined to protect others (Sayre-McCord 2001, 508–9; Boonin 2008, 231–35).[17]

Advocates of the terrible consequences objection typically find it plausible because they mistakenly equate punishment with any coercive or harmful response to crime. It is plausible to think that refraining from such responses would have terrible consequences. But abolitionists are not committed to refraining from such responses.

4.2 The Overgeneralization Objection

Objection: The preceding reply fails. The arguments of this chapter generalize to every harmful act or practice, including the abolitionist alternatives to punishment just mentioned. This is because punishment's harmfulness is what makes it especially morally risky. Any harmful act or practice will be comparably morally risky.

Reply: The claim that harm is what makes punishment especially morally risky is false. To take just one set of counterexamples, civil courts often inflict harm without punishing. And this harm is sometimes comparable to the punitive harms inflicted by criminal courts. Yet the standard view seems to be

[17] Boonin's work on restitution significantly expands on the work of others. For references, see Boonin (2008, 216). Golash (2005, 22–48, 153–72) also discusses a variety of non-punitive responses to crime. For responses to the objection that abolitionist alternatives are actually punishments, see Sayre-McCord (2001, 506–7), Boonin (2008, 233–35), and Hanna (2022).

that the moral risk involved in harmful applications of the civil law are less serious—hence, the lower standards of evidence applied in civil courts. I will not defend this view or an account of what makes punishment's moral risks especially serious. But it is plausible to think that these risks stem from a variety of features. Among them: punishment is harmful, it is intended to be harmful, and it stigmatizes the punishee in a distinctive and especially serious way.[18] The abolitionist alternatives mentioned above do not have all these features. So, the Risk Argument does not obviously generalize to them.

To be clear, I am not saying that harm can never make an act especially morally risky, only that this is not necessarily the case. Harm comes in degrees. It can be slight or severe. Acts that inflict severe harm may be especially morally risky because of the severity of the harm. I think that considerations of moral risk generate a presumption against harming and that the strength of this presumption gets stronger as the harm becomes more severe. I am inclined to think that some harms are so severe that the presumption against inflicting them is for all practical purposes insurmountable, regardless of whether the harms are punitive or non-punitive. In short, I think that considerations of moral risk exert strong downward pressure on the severity of harm that we can permissibly inflict (Tomlin 2014). To repeat, though: there are good reasons to think that harmful acts are not necessarily especially morally risky simply because they are harmful.

4.3 The Countervailing Moral Risks Objection

Objection: The arguments of this chapter entail a contradiction. They assume that morally risky acts are wrong if their permissibility can be reasonably doubted. But not punishing can also be morally risky and its permissibility can also be reasonably doubted. So, the arguments of this chapter entail that punishing and not punishing are sometimes both wrong.

Reply: My arguments do not assume that morally risky acts are wrong if their permissibility can be reasonably doubted, just that this is true of *punishment*. Punishment is special in ways that require the use of the reasonable doubt standard. This view is widely accepted, partly because of something captured in my paraphrase of the standard rationale for premise 4: wrongful

[18] On my view, punishment stigmatizes the punishee in such a way largely because it is intended to harm the punishee, and this sends a highly stigmatizing message about the punishee's moral status. Abolitionists typically think that the intent to harm is morally significant. They argue that it makes punishment especially hard to morally justify and that non-punitive alternatives to punishment that do not intend harm are easier to morally justify, other things equal. See, e.g., Sayre-McCord (2001, 506–7), Boonin (2008, 15–16, 28–9, 234), Zimmerman (2011, 159–65), and Hanna (2021).

punishment is much worse than wrongful non-punishment, other things equal. That is to say, there is a significant asymmetry in terms of the seriousness of the moral risks here. So, my arguments do not entail a contradiction. At most, they entail that an act is wrong if it has a similar moral risk profile and if its permissibility turns on a comparably complex set of philosophical issues about which we are fallible. But that is a plausible result (Guerrero 2007, 92–94).

4.4 The Counterexamples Objection

Objection: There are counterexamples to the arguments of this paper. That is, there are acts or practices that are obviously permissible, and the arguments of this paper generalize in a way that entails that these acts or practices are impermissible.

Reply: I do not have the space to consider every such alleged counterexample here. But I will outline my strategy for dealing with them. In response to an alleged counterexample like this, I would say one of two things: (1) My arguments do not generalize to the act or practice. This is because (a) the act or practice does not have a similar moral risk profile or (b) its permissibility does not turn on a comparably complex set of philosophical issues about which we are fallible. (2) My arguments do generalize in the alleged way and do entail that the act or practice is impermissible, but that is the correct result (Guerrero 2007, 92–94).

4.5 The My-Favorite-Theory Objection

Objection: The arguments of this paper rely on highly controversial claims. These claims are highly controversial because they are inconsistent with certain moral theories. For example, premise 4 seems inconsistent with certain versions of consequentialism.[19]

Reply: I have appealed to what I take to be relatively uncontroversial and widespread commonsense moral intuitions. I grant that some moral theories are inconsistent with some of these intuitions. But that is a problem for the theories, not the intuitions. Or at least, I will take it to be a problem for the theories until I hear arguments for them that are more plausible than the

[19] Compare Kolber (2018, 520–22) and Laudan (2006, 2011, 2012). Kolber argues that moral risk is a serious problem for retributivists, but not as serious of a problem for consequentialists. And Laudan challenges, along partly consequentialist lines, many of the ways that the reasonable doubt standard is used.

intuitions to which I have appealed. I do not think that good enough arguments have been given in defense of any moral theory to make any of them a reliable basis for moral reasoning (Huemer 2010, 430–31).

4.6 The Magical Doubts Objection

Objection: Premises 1 and 4 are false. They basically say that doubting the morality of an act can make it wrong. But there are good objections to that view (Weatherson 2014; Harman 2015).

Reply: This objection misunderstands the premises. It takes them to be saying that a certain subjective psychological state can make an act wrong, namely doubt about the act's permissibility. But that is not what the premises say. Basically, they say that punishment is wrong if its permissibility *can be reasonably doubted*. Punishment's permissibility can be reasonably doubted only if there are objective facts that make such doubt reasonable. My arguments should be taken to be saying that there are such objective facts and that they are what make punishment wrong—not any subjective psychological states that they might justify. Those objective facts include the fact that punishment's permissibility depends on a set of complex philosophical issues about which we are fallible and the fact that wrongful punishment is far worse than wrongful non-punishment.

4.7 The Low Stakes Objection

Objection: Premise 4 says that punishment is permissible only when we have shown beyond reasonable doubt that the punishee broke the law. But this is false, at least when the punishment and the crime are minor. For example, a small fine seems like a permissible punishment for a minor traffic violation. And it seems permissible even if we have not shown beyond reasonable doubt that the punishee broke the law.

Reply: Assuming that these really are cases of punishment, I am not so sure that it is permissible to inflict them without having shown beyond reasonable doubt that the punishee broke the law.[20] But I will not defend that view here. Instead, I will revise my thesis in a way that does not require me to take a stand on this issue. Here is my revised thesis: punishment is wrong because it is too morally risky, at least when its permissibility requires showing beyond

[20] Some philosophers seem willing to say that these are not punishments, though, e.g., Feinberg (1965, 398).

reasonable doubt that the punishee broke the law. This is still an important thesis that, if true, requires radical criminal justice reform. Punishment's advocates should find little comfort in the fact—if it is a fact—that my arguments do not apply to the sorts of cases to which the objection appeals.

4.8 The Epistemic Possibility Objection

Objection: The argument for premises 7 and 9 rely on certain claims about what is possible, for example, that we have no free will and that no one is ever culpable. But there is no obviously good sense of possibility on which it is uncontroversial to say that these claims are possibly true. The most natural way to understand the possibility claims is in terms of epistemic possibility, which is typically defined as follows: a proposition p is epistemically possible for a subject S if p could be true for all that S knows. But it would be highly controversial to say that the above claims are possible in this sense because that would entail, among other things, that we do not know that we have free will or that people are sometimes culpable.

Reply: I do not want to say that the above claims are possible in this sense. For one thing, the objection is right that this would be highly controversial. For another thing, I happen to believe that some people, including myself, know that people have free will and that people are sometimes culpable. But none of this means that there is no good sense of possibility on which the above claims are possibly true. Here is one such sense of possibility: the claims are true *for all that we know for certain* (Chalmers 2011, 60).

4.9 The No Necessary Conditions Objection

Objection: The arguments of this chapter assume that there are necessary conditions for punishment's permissibility. But there are not—there are only conditions that are usually necessary for its permissibility. For any allegedly necessary condition, we can imagine a case where punishment is permissible even though the condition is not satisfied. Showing this is trivial for the conditions discussed in this chapter. If, for example, not punishing someone who satisfies none of these conditions will have catastrophically bad consequences, it would be permissible to punish the person (Wellman 2012, 375n7).

Reply: At best, all that this shows is that the conditions that I have discussed must be qualified in certain ways. For purposes of illustration, let us focus on just one of them: the culpability condition. To accommodate the above considerations, the condition can be restated as follows: P must be culpable or there must be an outweighing factor present that makes punishing the non-culpable permissible. Other conditions can be modified in similar ways. And everything that I have said about the conditions as I originally stated them applies to their modified versions.

4.10 The Moral Fetishism Objection

Objection: The rationale for premise 4 is implausible because the claim that it can be wrong to risk doing wrong is false. It treats the fact that an act might be wrong as a reason not to perform the act. But the fact that an act might be wrong is not a reason not to perform the act. This is because wrongness does not in itself matter morally. What matters morally are the facts that can make acts wrong. Concerns about moral risk fetishize wrongness (Weatherson 2014).

Reply: Nothing that I have said commits me to the claim that wrongness itself matters morally. What matters is the risk of doing things like punishing people who did not act freely, who did not act culpably, and who are not liable to punishment. More broadly, what matters are things like not treating people in deeply disrespectful ways and not intentionally harming them without sufficient reason (Sepielli 2016, 2959–60; MacAskill et al. 2020, 27). Anything that I have said about the risk of doing wrong is just a convenient way of talking about the risk of doing these sorts of things.

4.11 The Incompatibility Objection

Objection: The Risk Argument must have gone wrong somewhere because it is inconsistent with certain reasonable beliefs.[21] To see this, consider the following summation of the argument:

> Punishment is wrong because its permissibility can be reasonably doubted.

And consider the following belief:

> Punishment might not be wrong.

Anyone who accepts the former claim cannot reasonably believe the latter. But believing the latter is obviously reasonable. Considerations of moral risk

[21] The following objection is adapted from Weatherson (2014, 146), who deploys a similar objection against the following principle: if an agent has a choice between two options, and one might be wrong, while the other is definitely permissible, then it is wrong to choose the first option. For present purposes, I am agnostic about this principle. But I suspect that my reply to the above objection can be adapted to defend the principle from Weatherson's objection.

might give us some reason to doubt punishment's permissibility, but they cannot show that there is simply no possibility that it is permissible.

Reply: There are two different ways that punishment might be wrong: for reasons related to moral risk or for reasons unrelated to moral risk. For argument's sake, I grant that the belief that punishment might not be wrong in the second way is reasonable. But that belief is consistent with my arguments. The belief that punishment might not be wrong in the first way is inconsistent with my arguments. But it is also not obviously reasonable to believe, at least for people who understand my arguments. Insisting otherwise just begs the question.

4.12 The Subjectivism Objection

Objection: Premises 1 and 4 are false or at least highly controversial. They entail that wrongness is subjective in the sense that it depends on our evidence. And there are good objections to that view (Zimmerman 2008; Graham 2010).

Reply: First, we must distinguish the claim that wrongness depends only on our evidence from the claim that it can be affected by our evidence. Critics of subjectivism typically attack the former claim, but I am not committed to it. Maybe I am committed to a version of the latter claim, but I am not obviously committed to an unacceptable version of it. It is plausible to think that excessive moral risk can sometimes make acts wrong. Here is an example: if it is reasonable to worry that an act will kill an innocent person, it is plausible to think that this can make the act wrong even if it will not in fact kill an innocent person. Or at least, it is plausible to think that this risk can make the act wrong if one has not sufficiently investigated whether the act will do this.

Second, to the extent that subjectivism seems implausible, it seems implausible as a view about individual action. It seems more plausible as a view about collective political action, such as laws and legal practices. If, as many philosophers think, laws and legal practices are morally acceptable only if they are in some sense justifiable to everyone affected, then it is plausible to think that moral risk can make certain laws and legal practices—e.g., punishment—wrong.[22]

Third, even if my previous replies fail, my thesis can be revised to sidestep the objection. I discuss this revision in response to the next objection.

[22] The idea that laws and legal practices must in some sense be justifiable to everyone affected is a core tenet of public reason liberalism. For discussion, see Quong (2018).

4.13 The Irrelevance Objection

Objection: Premises 2 and 9 are partly motivated by the possibility that we lack free will. But that possibility does not support the Risk Argument's conclusion. If we lack free will, punishment would not be wrong because all of our acts would be unfree and unfree acts are not wrong. Appealing to the possibility that we lack free will therefore exaggerates punishment's moral risks.

Reply: I am not so sure that unfree acts cannot be wrong (Kelly 2018, 83–84). But I will set that issue aside. Instead, I will revise my thesis again to sidestep the issue. Here is my modified thesis: punishment is morally *unjustified* because it is too morally risky, at least when its justifiability requires showing beyond reasonable doubt that the punishee broke the law. To say that an act is morally unjustified is to say that it is morally wrong or overall morally bad or morally vicious.[23] Punishing people for their unfree acts is presumptively very morally bad even if the act of punishment is not wrong because it is not free. And to take an excessive risk of doing this is overall morally bad as well as morally vicious (e.g., morally reckless), even if the act of punishment is not wrong because it is not free.

5 Conclusion

Here is the definitive statement of my thesis: legal punishment is morally unjustified because it is too morally risky, at least when its moral justifiability requires showing beyond reasonable doubt that the punishee broke the law. Unlike some prominent defenses of abolitionism, I have not individually criticized every justification of punishment in the literature. Instead, I have sidestepped the lengthy debates about these justifications and have tried to argue that no such justification can possibly work because there is no way to show beyond reasonable doubt that punishment is justified. And unlike many other theorists who discuss punishment's moral risks, I have not emphasized any one source of moral risk. Instead, I have argued that punishment is morally risky in a variety of ways that combine to make a good case for abolitionism.[24]

[23] See Hanna (2021) for further discussion of this sense of justification and its moral significance.

[24] Thanks to Marcus Hedahl and Adam Kolber for extensive comments on earlier versions of this chapter. Thanks also to audiences at CU Boulder, the 2021 Rocky Mountain Ethics Congress, and the 2019 meetings of the Alabama Philosophical Society, the North American Society for Social Philosophy, and the North Carolina Philosophical Society.

References

Berman, Mitchell. 2008. "Punishment and Justification." *Ethics* 118, no. 2 (January): 258–90.

Boonin, David. 2008. *The Problem of Punishment*. Cambridge: Cambridge University Press.

Caruso, Gregg D. 2020. "Justice without Retribution: An Epistemic Argument against Retributive Criminal Punishment." *Neuroethics* 13, no. 1 (April): 13–28.

———. 2021. "Skepticism about Moral Responsibility." *Stanford Encyclopedia of Philosophy* (Summer 2021 edition), edited by Edward N. Zalta. https://plato.stanford.edu/archives/sum2021/entries/skepticism-moral-responsibility/.

Caruso, Gregg D., and Derk Pereboom. 2020. "A Non-Punitive Alternative to Retributive Punishment." In *The Routledge Handbook of the Philosophy and Science of Punishment*, edited by Farah Focquaert, Elizabeth Shaw, and Bruce N. Waller, 355–65. New York: Routledge.

Chalmers, David. 2011. "The Nature of Epistemic Space." In *Epistemic Modality*, edited by Andy Egan and Brian Weatherson, 60–107. New York: Oxford University Press.

Feinberg, Joel. 1965. "The Expressive Function of Punishment." *Monist* 49, no. 3 (July): 397–423.

Gardiner, Georgi. 2017. "In Defence of Reasonable Doubt." *Journal of Applied Philosophy* 34, no. 2 (February): 221–41.

Golash, Deirdre. 2005. *The Case against Punishment*. New York: New York University Press.

Graham, Peter A. 2010. "In Defense of Objectivism about Moral Obligation." *Ethics* 121, no. 1 (October): 88–115.

Gross, Hyman. 2012. *Crime and Punishment: A Concise Moral Critique*. New York: Oxford University Press.

Guerrero, Alexander A. 2007. "Don't Know, Don't Kill: Moral Ignorance, Culpability, and Caution." *Philosophical Studies* 136, no. 1 (October): 59–97.

Hanna, Nathan. 2008. "Say What? A Critique of Expressive Retributivism." *Law and Philosophy* 27, no. 2 (March): 123–50.

———. 2012. "It's Only Natural: Legal Punishment and the Natural Right to Punish." *Social Theory and Practice* 38, no. 4 (October): 598–616.

———. 2013. "Two Claims about Desert." *Pacific Philosophical Quarterly* 94, no. 1 (March): 41–56.

———. 2014. "Facing the Consequences." *Criminal Law and Philosophy* 8, no. 3 (October): 589–604.

———. 2019. "Hitting Retributivism Where It Hurts." *Criminal Law and Philosophy* 13, no. 1 (March): 109–27.

———. 2021. "Why Punitive Intent Matters." *Analysis* 81, no. 3 (July): 426–35.

———. 2022. "Punitive Intent." *Philosophical Studies* 179, no. 2 (February): 655–69.

Harman, Elizabeth. 2015. "The Irrelevance of Moral Uncertainty." In *Oxford Studies in Metaethics*, vol. 10, edited by Rudd Shafer-Landau, 53–79. New York: Oxford University Press.
Huemer, Michael. 2010. "Is There a Right to Immigrate?" *Social Theory and Practice* 36, no. 3 (July): 429–61.
———. 2018. "The Duty to Disregard the Law." *Criminal Law and Philosophy* 12, no. 1 (March): 1–18.
Jeppsson, Sofia M. I. 2021. "Retributivism, Justification, and Credence: The Epistemic Argument Revisited." *Neuroethics* 14, no. 2 (July): 177–90.
Kelly, Erin I. 2018. *The Limits of Blame: Rethinking Punishment and Responsibility*. Cambridge, MA: Harvard University Press.
Kolber, Adam J. 2018. "Punishment and Moral Risk." *University of Illinois Law Review* 2018, no. 2 (March): 487–532.
Laudan, Larry. 2006. *Truth, Error, and Criminal Law: An Essay in Legal Epistemology*. New York: Cambridge University Press.
———. 2011. "The Rules of Trial, Political Morality, and the Costs of Error: Or, Is Proof beyond a Reasonable Doubt Doing More Harm Than Good?" In *Oxford Studies in Philosophy of Law*, vol. 1, edited by Leslie Green and Brian Leiter, 195–227. New York: Oxford University Press.
———. 2012. "Is It Finally Time to Put 'Proof beyond a Reasonable Doubt' Out to Pasture?" In *The Routledge Companion to Philosophy of Law*, edited by Andrei Marmor, 317–32. New York: Routledge.
Levy, Neil. 2011. *Hard Luck: How Luck Undermine Free Will and Moral Responsibility*. New York: Oxford University Press.
MacAskill, William, Krister Bykvist, and Toby Ord. 2020. *Moral Uncertainty*. New York: Oxford University Press.
Nagel, Thomas. 1979. "Moral Luck." In *Mortal Questions*, 24–38. New York: Cambridge University Press.
Nelkin, Dana Kay. 2019. "Guilt, Grief, and the Good." *Social Philosophy and Policy* 36, no. 1 (Summer): 173–91.
O'Connor, Timothy, and Christopher Franklin. 2021. "Free Will." *Stanford Encyclopedia of Philosophy* (Spring 2021 edition), edited by Edward N. Zalta. https://plato.stanford.edu/archives/spr2021/entries/freewill/.
Pereboom, Derk. 2001. *Living without Free Will*. Cambridge: Cambridge University Press.
Quong, Jonathan. 2018. "Public Reason." *Stanford Encyclopedia of Philosophy* (Spring 2018 edition), edited by Edward N. Zalta. https://plato.stanford.edu/archives/spr2018/entries/public-reason/.
Roebuck, Greg, and David Wood. 2011. "A Retributive Argument against Punishment." *Criminal Law and Philosophy* 5, no. 1 (January): 73–86.
Rosen, Gideon. 2003. "Culpability and Ignorance." *Proceedings of the Aristotelian Society* 103, no. 1 (June): 61–84.

———. 2004. "Skepticism about Moral Responsibility." *Philosophical Perspectives* 18, no. 1 (December): 295–313.

Sayre-McCord, Geoffrey. 2001. "Criminal Justice and Legal Reparations as an Alternative to Punishment." *Philosophical Issues* 11, no. 1 (October): 502–29.

Sepielli, Andrew. 2016. "Moral Uncertainty and Fetishistic Motivation." *Philosophical Studies* 173, no. 11 (November): 2951–68.

Strawson, Galen. 1994. "The Impossibility of Moral Responsibility." *Philosophical Studies* 75, nos. 1/2 (August): 5–24.

Tadros, Victor. 2011. *The Ends of Harm: The Moral Foundations of Criminal Law*. New York: Oxford University Press.

Tomlin, Patrick. 2013. "Extending the Golden Thread? Criminalisation and the Presumption of Innocence." *Journal of Political Philosophy* 21, no. 1 (March): 44–66.

———. 2014. "Could the Presumption of Innocence Protect the Guilty?" *Criminal Law and Philosophy* 8, no. 2 (June): 431–47.

Vilhauer, Benjamin. 2009. "Free Will and Reasonable Doubt." *American Philosophical Quarterly* 46, no. 2 (April): 131–40.

Weatherson, Brian. 2014. "Running Risks Morally." *Philosophical Studies* 167, no. 1 (January): 141–63.

Wellman, Christopher Heath. 2012. "The Rights Forfeiture Theory of Punishment." *Ethics* 122, no. 2 (January): 371–93.

Zimmerman, Michael J. 1997. "Moral Responsibility and Ignorance." *Ethics* 107, no. 3 (April): 410–26.

———. 2002. "Controlling Ignorance: A Bitter Truth," *Journal of Social Philosophy* 33, no. 3 (Fall): 483–90.

———. 2008. *Living with Uncertainty: The Moral Significance of Ignorance*. Cambridge: Cambridge University Press.

———. 2011. *The Immorality of Punishment*. Peterborough, ON: Broadview.

26

The Abolition of Punishment

Michael Davis

The summer of 2021 recorded many street demonstrations in the United States, South America, Europe, and Asia calling for "abolition of the police." These calls joined similar calls for abolition of bail, imprisonment, solitary confinement, and torture. Some calls, such as the call to abolish the death penalty, have succeeded in many legal systems, from Austria to Uzbekistan, from Mexico to Australia. Others, such as the call to abolish the police, seem unlikely to succeed in their present form in part at least because advocates do not seem sure whether they are calling for modest reform or revolutionary transformation. What, for example, is the difference between a police department and a department of public safety (see Kaepernick 2021; Purnell 2021; Vitale 2021)?

The subject of this paper, the abolition of *punishment*, is related to these other "abolitionist movements." Like most of them, the chief difficulty in this one seems to be understanding one or more of the terms in the arguments that the proponents or opponents rely on rather than on gathering more evidence in favor of or against the conclusion that abolition "works," that it is efficient, that it is morally required, and so on.

Punishment is a means of social control. Among other means are walls, locks, traffic signals, customs, cameras, detectives, armed guards, textbooks, professional journals, audits, the military, and mental hospitals. Those

M. Davis (✉)
Illinois Institute of Technology, Chicago, IL, USA
e-mail: davism@iit.edu

© The Author(s), under exclusive license to Springer Nature Switzerland AG 2023

M. C. Altman (ed.), *The Palgrave Handbook on the Philosophy of Punishment*, Palgrave Handbooks in the Philosophy of Law, https://doi.org/10.1007/978-3-031-11874-6_26

proposing abolition of punishment seem to understand themselves as at least proposing to abandon an entire category of social control, a change in society much more dramatic than abolishing the death penalty or imprisonment. Such a radical change would seem to require a very strong argument. More attractive are proposals to moderate punishments (for example, by reducing the maximum statutory penalty for any crime from death to a term of imprisonment) or to limit punishment to certain persons (for example, to competent adults, repeat offenders, or violent criminals). I shall hereafter ignore the less radical proposals, considering first, what it would be for a society to abandon punishment entirely; and second, what arguments, if any, can be made in favor of entirely abandoning punishment in that sense.

1 Preliminary Distinctions

The call for abolition of punishment has only three terms. Since the genitive ("of") can be eliminated by talking about "abolishing punishment" rather than "abolition *of* punishment," there are only two terms for analysis: "abolishing" and "punishment." "Abolishing" seems to be relatively precise. It means (something like) ending, stopping, eliminating, terminating, or doing away with the practice in question. We abolish slavery by doing away with the practice of slavery; and by doing away with that practice, we do away with all the acts that constitute the practice: slave owning, slave catching, slave buying, slave using, and so on. So, it seems, we abolish punishment by ending, stopping, or otherwise doing away with the practice of punishment, whatever that practice is.

What is the practice of punishment that is to be ended by its "abolition"? Consider the variety of uses that the term "punishment" (or its transforms) has in the following sentences:

1. The frigate struggled against a punishing sea.
2. Xerxes had his soldiers flog the sea to punish it for destroying the pontoon bridge by which he had just connected Asia to Europe.
3. The owner kicked the dog as punishment for dragging the holiday turkey from the table.
4. Higher prescription prices punish the poor.
5. The boxer punished his opponent with many quick punches to the face.
6. The toddler was sent to bed as punishment for throwing food during lunch.
7. God will punish you for working on the Sabbath.
8. Nature punishes those who do evil.
9. Illinois punishes speeders with a large fine.

These nine sentences use "punishment" in a variety of ways. In some (1, 4, and 8) the punishment is unintended. Neither the sea, nor higher prices, nor nature intends to punish (or has any intention at all). In others (3, 5, and 6), the "punishment" (or, at least, the harm it does) is intended, but not as part of a practice. In some (4, 5, 7, 8, and 9), the subject of punishment is (probably) a reasonable agent, but in others (1, 2, 3, and 6), the agent is not reasonable. The "punishing sea" in 1 is just a rough sea—though the frigate, as a corporate entity that includes its crew, does seem reasonable enough to be punished. Much the same is true in 2, except that this time the sea (the Dardanelles) does not seem reasonable enough to be punished. In contrast, the dog in 3 and the toddler in 6 seem not to be clearly reasonable enough to be punished or clearly unreasonable enough to be entirely excused from punishment. They are more reasonable than the Dardanelles even though not reasonable enough to count as reasonable agents without qualification.

These nine uses are so varied that they can only support a very thin definition of "punishment," for example, *punishment as an undesirable outcome delivered by one entity to another*. Definitions like that seem too thin for the arguments that abolitionists make. Much that a dictionary might call punishment seems to include more than what those favoring abolition of punishment seem to want to abolish. For example, what abolitionist wants nature to stop punishing evil (8)—assuming that nature can punish evil? Even when abolitionists want to abolish a certain practice, such as the non-state punishment of children or animals (3 and 6), the arguments they typically make are quite different from those they make for abolishing *state* punishment (9).

If, instead, we consider the context in which abolition of punishment is in fact being called for (typically, state punishment), we can develop a thicker definition, one designed primarily for use in that context (the context from which example 9 comes). Such a definition may allow us to treat many of the common uses of "punishment" (all but 9) as mere analogs or even metaphorical uses of punishment-strictly-so-called.

The subject of this paper is the abolition of *state* punishment. Even close analogues of state punishment, such as the formal discipline of elementary schools or professions, can be ignored. They are (for our purposes) not instances of punishment-strictly-so-called. The call to abolish punishment does not, it seems, call for abolishing punishment in schools, professions, or other domains in which the term "punishment," but not "state punishment," seems to find an uncontroversial use.

Any call for abolition of punishment-strictly-so-called should distinguish *legal* abolition from *factual* abolition. If the practice of punishment-strictly-so-called exists in law, but not in practice, punishment has not in fact been abolished. If punishment exists in practice but not in law, punishment has also not in fact been abolished. The call for abolition of punishment should therefore be understood as a call for abolition of punishment both in law and in practice.

Consider this historical analogue: In 1865, the Thirteenth Amendment to the U.S. Constitution legally abolished slavery in the United States. Yet so many of the practices characteristic of slavery survived or revived during the fifty years after slavery's legal abolition that the former "slave states" could be said to have developed a new slavery ("Jim Crow"), a practice primarily enforced not by law but by such extra-legal practices as assassination, lynching, cross burning, assault, false imprisonment, and discrimination in employment.

What, then, is it to abolish state punishment strictly speaking (in law and in fact)? The current discussion seems to concern the abolition of *criminal* punishment. But scattered through many legal systems are other kinds of harm for misconduct, such as "punitive damages" and "civil penalties," that seem to be forgotten by both sides when debating the merits of abolition. Should we consider such special (non-criminal) legal punishments to be punishments-strictly-so-called and therefore part of what abolitionists must (by parity of reasoning) also seek to abolish—or only analogues or metaphors ("punishments-in-a-sense")? How we answer that question should depend in part at least on the arguments needed to justify their abolition. If the arguments are much the same for abolition of "punitive damages," "civil penalties," and the like as for criminal punishment, counting them as criminal punishment would be convenient. Otherwise, counting them as criminal punishment would be a distraction.

2 Criminal Punishment

What then is criminal punishment (for the purposes of abolition)? Given something like the thin definition identified above (the one covering "entities"), criminal punishment must consist of all those acts imposing "harm"[1] as part of a practice having the following features:

---

[1] A "harm" is a significant setback to a person's or other entity's interests. "Harm" includes death, pain, disability, shame, and confinement. A harm is a substantial (non-trivial) reason. If all else is equal, a harm is (or at least should be) decisive. I prefer "harm" (in this sense) to other terms commonly used in definitions of punishment—such as "evil," "pain," "rough treatment," or "suffering"—because some punishments-strictly-so-called (such as a fine, probation, parole, or suspended sentence) do not seem to be pains, rough treatments, suffering, or the like.

1. A body of rules (and principles for interpreting them) capable of guiding ordinary conduct—what we may call "primary rules."
2. Reasonable agents, that is, beings capable of following primary rules or not as they choose, capable of choosing based on reasons, and capable of treating the prospect of harm, even harm distant in time or space, as a reason against doing an act to be weighed with other reasons for and against.
3. "Secondary rules" (conventions) designed to connect (and generally succeeding in connecting) failure to follow primary rules with substantial specified harms ("penalties").
4. Conventional (non-natural) procedures imposing penalties upon reasonable agents in accordance with secondary rules. Fining or imprisonment is a conventional procedure; aging or hunting a deer is not.
5. A justified presumption that both primary and secondary rules, especially rules setting penalties for violation of primary rules, are generally known to reasonable agents subject to them.
6. A practice of justifying imposition of penalties (in part at least) by the fact that the reasonable agent upon whom a penalty is to be imposed, though (more or less) reasonable, failed to follow the primary rule (or rules) in question.
7. The practice consists of acts generally morally justified or at least presumptively just.

The first six of these features together constitute what used to be called the "Flew-Benn-Hart definition of law" because Anthony Flew (1954), Stanley Benn (1958), and H. L. A. Hart (1960) all defended (something like) it at about the same time.[2]

The Flew-Benn-Hart definition is entirely formal. Like other "positivist" definitions of law, it allows any system of rules meeting certain conditions (1–6), however immoral, to count as a *system of law*. According to this definition, a system of rules need not be morally defensible, attractive, or valuable to count as a system of law strictly so called.

I have added feature 7 to acknowledge the widespread intuition (which I share) that any rule-governed practice that does not at least try to be substantively moral or just is not a system of *law*. Those with a different intuition (such as legal positivists) are free to delete feature 7. I shall hereafter call this combination of seven features "the standard definition of law," both for

[2] For a sustained critique of this definition, see McCloskey (1962), which denies, among other things, that the standard definition identifies a central "problem of punishment," the solution to which is likely to be independent of the solution of any corresponding problem where "punishment" has one of its other senses; and also McPherson (1967), which denies, among other things, that "punishment" can usefully be defined except within a specific theory of punishment.

brevity and because it (or something like it) seems to have become the most likely choice when theorists require a definition of law.

Note, however, that this definition is also a definition of *criminal* law insofar as its secondary rules provide penalties for violating primary rules. Primary rules typically prohibit unjustified infliction of such substantial harms as killing, maiming, involuntary confinement, robbery (taking property by force), and vandalism (unjustified destruction of property). The secondary rules typically provide procedures for imposing fines, forced labor, suspended sentences, probation, corporal punishment, imprisonment, death, or other substantial harms for violating primary rules. Insofar as secondary rules also establish just procedures for finding facts, interpreting rules (adjudication), enforcing those rules (police, detectives, magistrates, prison guards, parole officers, and so on), and setting penalties, the practice will count as a system of criminal *justice*.

3 Some Ways to Abolish Criminal Punishment

Given the complexity of this definition, there should be many ways to abolish criminal punishment. Some may be unreasonable; others, at least *prima facie* reasonable. But reason does not seem to require any (interesting) form of abolition, that is, totally doing away with all criminal punishment. Chief among the *unreasonable* ways to abolish criminal punishment are:

1. *Repealing all primary rules*. Repealing all primary rules would abolish the practice of legal punishment by doing away with punishable acts. What would remain of the legal system are its secondary rules (including rules for identifying disputes, gathering facts, reaching decisions, and enforcing decisions). Moral rules (similar in content to primary rules) can also exist—outside the legal system—as morality; but inside the legal system, moral rules can exist only as the possibility of legal rules. Once that possibility is realized as statute or common law, the moral rules simply become (morally attractive) primary rules of the legal system. For example, the moral prohibition of killing becomes the legal prohibition of homicide. The legal system as such would be radically incomplete without any primary rules drawn from morality. It would even be radically incomplete without just those primary rules which, like traffic laws, go beyond morality to serve the public health, safety, and welfare. Hence, repealing all primary rules cannot be a reasonable way to abolish punishment (though it would abolish it).

2. *Repealing all secondary rules related to punishment*. Repealing all secondary rules related to punishment would do away with punishment by doing away with the *procedures* by which a legal system identifies its primary rules, the disputes about them worth deciding, the standards of decision, and the

means of enforcement (including penalties). A legal system without such secondary rules would be radically incomplete, too incomplete to compensate for whatever advantages this sort of abolition of punishment promises. There can be no "system" of punishment without secondary rules that identify its primary rules, the disputes about them worth deciding, the standards of decision, and the means of enforcement.

3. *Adopting a system of rules that* (like the rules of a classic concentration camp) *are radically unjust.* A system of rules, however unjust, remains a system of rules. But adopting a radically unjust system of rules achieves abolition of punishment, when it does, only by changing the subject from doing justice to keeping order. Legal positivists seem to become confused when their defense of abolition assumes that radically unjust penalties can be morally justified, for example, by efficiency or efficacy (see, for example, Bentham 1970). If a system of rules must seek justice to be a legal system, then punishment cannot be abolished by repealing primary or secondary rules; punishment has already been abolished by the positivist's unreasonable assumption that the legal system need not seek justice.

4. *Combining two or more of these.* The first two ways to abolish punishment are unreasonable insofar as they abolish more of the legal system than necessary. They abolish the system of justice when the objective is merely to abolish punishment within the system of justice. There are ways to abolish punishment without abolishing the system of justice. For example, consider amending feature 3 above to read:

3′. "Secondary rules" trying to connect (and generally connecting) failure to follow primary rules with *benefits* designed to encourage everyone to follow those rules.

The idea underlying proposal 3′ is that it is morally permissible, all else equal, for the state to benefit its subjects, just as it is morally permissible, all else equal, for its subjects to benefit each other. When the law calls for a certain benefit in response to crime, the benefit can often be justified merely by the fact that it is a benefit, while punishment is never justified merely by the fact that it is a harm. Like penalties, benefits can be structured to improve social order, incentives replacing disincentives. For example, the more serious the crime, the greater should be the incentive to avoid it.

Among benefits commonly proposed to encourage following primary rules, some are *individual*, such as training, education, or therapy *for the convict*, while others are *social*, such as better street lighting (to make avoiding criminals on the street easier), more accurate tracking of crime (for better allocation of preventive resources), or free meals in school (to reduce the need to steal or rob). Individual benefits are assigned to individuals (much as penalties are); social benefits are intended to benefit some group (such as a neighborhood, an occupation, or the poor). What justifies assigning benefits to individuals in response to their violation of one or more primary rules is the assumption that most such violations result from one or more flaws in the character of the convict that the benefit in question can correct or undo.

A training regime might identify the failure of character in a particular convict as, for example, poor work habits: "If you had good work habits, you would have a good job and no need to rob, steal, or defraud." Training might impart good work habits by a quasi-military regime in which the convict is made to awake at a set time each day, to dress in a uniform, to march off to breakfast, and so on. As Aristotle might say, convicts will develop good work habits by repeatedly acting as if they already had them. The duration of training (the sentence) would depend on how quickly convicts "learn their lesson." Since good work habits, all else equal, typically benefit the person who has them (as well as benefiting society as a whole), the training that teaches good work habits is not punishment even if it otherwise resembles punishment.

To constitute punishment, the judicial sentence must both harm the convict overall and be administered with that intention. Training, as such, does not harm. Even the forced confinement that typically goes with training is not punishment, however much it resembles it, so long as it is imposed to benefit convicts, for example, to assure that they do not escape the training they need for a better life. So, training as such cannot be punishment.

Depending on context, education may differ from training in many ways, but for our purposes, we may make the distinction this way. Training depends on repetition to teach good habits. Education, in contrast, works through reason and imparts understanding rather than habits. Its justification relies on some such argument as this: "If you better understood the justification of law in this reasonably just society, you would be less inclined to rob, steal, or defraud others." Since understanding benefits the person who has it much as good work habits benefit those who have good work habits, improving a convict's understanding cannot, all else equal, be punishment. The title of Jean Hampton's classic, "The Moral Education Theory of Punishment" (1984), is, therefore, paradoxical: Insofar as moral education seeks to benefit the convict, it cannot be punishment; and, insofar as moral education is punishment, it must seek to harm the convict. There can, therefore, be no moral education theory of punishment.

Therapy is to education what a hospital is to a college. Therapy seeks to "cure" flaws in character that lead to crime. The tools of therapy are the medication, surgery, and counseling typically used to restore mental health.[3] The

---

[3] I am inclined to count Duff's (2003) "penance" as an early form of therapy ("a cure of souls") rather than as a form of training or education. But nothing significant turns on which category we assign it to.

assumption relied on to justify therapy in response to crime is that crime is the product of mental illness (or mental disability) that cannot be trained or educated away but can be cured. Insofar as mental health is good for those who have it, therapy cannot be punishment. A "hospital for the criminally insane" is not a prison.[4]

Until the end of the eighteenth century, a prison was still "a cage" or "jail," primarily a place of confinement for a brief time before trial or after sentencing. The typical sentence was a fine, shaming (stocks), maiming, whipping, branding, forced labor, hanging, or exile, not long-term confinement. Among typical places of punishment were public squares, galleys, mines, plantations, and other domains of (temporary or permanent) enslavement. Only in the nineteenth century did mere long-term confinement (imprisonment, incarceration) become a common penalty. Prisons were no longer places for detention until punishment. They were instead places of "punishment"—whether the punishment was to be penance, training, correction, reform, or the like.

This new understanding led to radical changes in prisons, beginning with a new name. Consider, for example, the first "penitentiary" realized in practice: the Eastern State Penitentiary in Philadelphia, opened in 1821. It seems to have intended both its buildings and its practices humanely to encourage prisoners to repent their crimes and prepare themselves to live better lives. Each prisoner had his or her own cell, much larger than the double cells of today's prisons, with solid walls and doors. Each cell also had its own sink, flush toilet, and running water. The cells were not cages but, in effect, private rooms where prisoners took their meals, worked on useful projects, read the Bible, meditated, and slept (Manion 2005).

If the nineteenth century may be called "the age of penitence," the twentieth century is "the age of correction." Prisons built (or rebuilt) starting in the twentieth century typically ceased to have "penitentiary" in their official names and became instead "correctional institutions," "reformatories," or the like. The difference between "penitence" and "correction" (or "reform") is not easy to state briefly but is obvious if one tours a modern prison after touring the Eastern State Penitentiary (now a museum). If, for our purpose, penitence is the process by which wrongdoers come to understand that they have done wrong, correction is improvement in the conduct of prisoners because of how penal institutions treat them. A correctional center will typically have "cages" (rooms with one or more walls consisting of bars), especially when dedicated to maximum security. But a correctional center will also provide health care, a library, educational programs, weight rooms, social workers to help prepare prisoners for a return to society, and so on.

[4] See, for example, Morris's (1968) classic critique of the therapy model of punishment.

If the state's "right to punish" is only a right to benefit those it "punishes," justifying that right is much easier than justifying a right to punish strictly speaking. More difficult than justifying a right to punish strictly speaking is justifying that right to punish while also seeking to render punishment more humane (without abolishing it). The theory must find a way to reform punishment that preserves the state's intention to harm. Unless the harm can be integral to the benefit as, for example, amputating a foot might be integral to preventing the foot from gangrening, the right to punish-strictly-so-called will have to include a right to harm, a right considerably harder to justify than a right to benefit (3′).

The moral education theory of punishment is, therefore, not the only theory of punishment that does not fit well with the "practice of punishment" during the last two or three centuries. Deterrent theories of punishment typically propose to reduce crime by threatening harm to those who break the law. They are undoubtedly theories of punishment-strictly-so-called. Deterrent theorists therefore have a reason to condemn penitentiaries and correctional centers for "coddling" prisoners. Anything that improves the life of a prisoner reduces the deterrent effect of the prisoner's sentence. The only way to compensate for the loss of deterrence that coddling produces is to lengthen the sentence.

Standard retribution theories have a similar problem. So long as they seek to do justice by harming criminals as much as they harm their victims, their justification of punishment must rely on a right to punish-strictly-so-called. They must therefore condemn prisons which, like Pennsylvania's Eastern State Penitentiary, seek to benefit the prisoners while the prisoners serve their sentences. Insofar as punishment should be harm proportioned to the harm the convict caused, retribution has no room for abolishing punishment.

Incapacitation theories escape this criticism. Incapacitation, whether in a slave galley, penitentiary, correctional institution, or the like will prevent crime, whatever the intention of the judge or legislature, provided the institution holds its prisoners under conditions making crime difficult. For example, the solitary confinement of all prisoners in Pennsylvania's Eastern State Penitentiary made crimes against the outside world difficult; made crimes against cellmates impossible (all confinement being solitary); and made crimes against staff or other prisoners rare because the prison's regime allowed prisoners little contact with staff or other prisoners. Today's prisons typically have gangs because they allow prisoners to meet in the mess hall, exercise yard, weight room, library, and the like where they can organize gangs. The Eastern State Penitentiary's solitary confinement had different harmful effects, though unintended. For example, its solitary confinement was so complete that long-confined prisoners commonly lost much of their hearing and ability to speak.

4 Social Change Instead of Punishment?

Alongside these individualistic alternatives to punishment, there are some that seek to prevent crime by changing *social* arrangements. The assumption is that the convict's crime is a symptom of a larger social problem. Change society in the appropriate way and crime of that sort will become less frequent. For example, society might respond to public transit-riders boarding buses without paying the fare by making public transit rides free and raising taxes to pay for the change. Making the transit rides free would make the theft of rides impossible without harming the would-be thieves. Indeed, free transit rides would benefit the would-be thieves insofar as their free rides are legal and the tax supporting free transit did not burden them unfairly. The former transit thieves would no longer risk the embarrassment of arrest or the burden of a fine. Society would benefit insofar as the cost of law enforcement would be reduced, ridership increased, and so on.

This example of changing social arrangements to reduce crime relies on (harmless) incapacitation. Abolition of bus fares makes theft of bus rides impossible. Of course, not all changes in social arrangements that reduce crime depend on incapacitation. Consider, for example, this change in social arrangements: A transit system might try to reduce theft of rides by placing a large digital camera beside the farebox with a sign just above that reads, "We see you!" followed by a large red arrow pointing to a camera. The camera and sign may reduce theft of rides by reminding riders that failing to pay a bus fare is a crime punishable by a small fine (a harm). That is simple deterrence. But the presence of the camera and sign may also reduce crime by what has recently been called "a nudge" (a form of "choice architecture" that alters people's behavior in a predictable way without restricting options or significantly changing their economic incentives) (Thaler and Sunstein 2008).

5 Conclusions

We may draw at least two conclusions from this investigation of abolition of punishment. First, some "theories of punishment" are theories of punishment strictly speaking, that is, they are concerned with justifying the ways a state may *harm* lawbreakers for breaking the law. The most popular of these are deterrence and retribution. A deterrent is a threat of harm that the state announces to discourage lawbreaking. A deterrent is justified (according to the theory) if the society in question is better off, all else equal, with that deterrent than without it. Typically, deterrent theories require that penalties be set to reduce crime in the most efficient way, that is, taking into account the harm that the crimes do, the difficulty of detecting the crime, the cost of administering the penalty (police, courts, prisons, parole officers), and so on. Deterrent theories require substantial benefits to compensate for the harm punishment does.

Retributive theories treat penalties as reestablishing a just order of society by imposing a harm on lawbreakers proportionate to the unjustified harm they did. One important difference between deterrent theories and retributivism is that, while both are concerned with proportioning punishment to crime, only the retributivist explicitly seeks to achieve a *just* distribution of harms and benefits. So (according to retributive theory), any proposal to abolish punishment strictly speaking must, all else equal, be proposing to abandon a *just* distribution of harms and benefits for a social order that is less just.

Most other theories of punishment, such as incapacitation or reform, are *not* about punishment strictly speaking. Incapacitation is an incomplete theory of punishment since some punishments, such as a fine or suspended sentence, do not incapacitate while some forms of incapacitation are not forms of punishment because they do not harm the convict. Consider, for an example, a city responding to theft of transit rides by making all rides free. Since no one can any longer steal transit rides, punishment for *this* crime has been abolished. There is also a limit to what crimes incapacitation can prevent. For example, five years imprisonment for armed robbery will prevent convicts from committing armed robbery for five years, but five years imprisonment for battery or murder will not prevent criminals from committing battery or murder within the prison.

Reform theories are concerned with reducing crime by benefiting criminals, not harming them. Those theories are, in effect, proposals for abolishing punishment rather than theories of punishment. This conclusion is a direct consequence of the definition of punishment with which we began. Those who want to categorize reform as a theory of punishment should defend another definition of punishment, one that distinguishes punishment-strictly-so-called from its analogues in a way at least as close to common sense as the standard definition.

A second conclusion we may draw from this investigation is that there is a large gap between all the classic theories of punishment, including those that are theories of punishment strictly speaking, and the practice of punishment for at least the last three centuries. All the classic theories of punishment are monistic. They rely on just one principle or standard (utility, justice, or the like) to justify punishment. Each succeeds in justifying much punishment but not all. For example, reform seems just the theory for the original practices of

Pennsylvania's Eastern State Penitentiary, but not for today's "supermax." The supermax has many partial justifications: as a means of isolating prisoners awaiting execution or in danger in the general population (child molesters, former police officers, and so on); as a means of incapacitating prisoners who are extreme threats to the prison's order (gang leaders, drug dealers, the mentally ill, and so on); as the appropriate place for prisoners serving a life sentence without parole; and as a prison within a prison helping to maintain order in the general population by threatening those frequently violating important prison rules with an unusually severe regime of incarceration. While a few convicts may come out of a supermax morally better than they were when they went in, reform is seldom offered as a justification for a prison having a supermax or a warden placing a prisoner in one.

Like many contemporary philosophers, I have adopted a pluralistic theory: punishment has many overlapping justifications (Davis 2009). I therefore doubt that there can be a single argument for abolishing punishment. An argument that seems to justify abolishing some punishments (such as the death penalty or life without parole) does not seem to justify abolishing others, for example, long prison terms for mass murder or embezzlement of many billion dollars. Abolishing punishment seems much more plausible for minor crimes than major ones.

References

Benn, S. I. 1958. "An Approach to the Problems of Punishment." *Philosophy* 33, no. 127 (October): 325–41.

Bentham, Jeremy. 1970. *An Introduction to the Principles of Morals and Legislation.* Edited by J. H. Burns and H. L. A. Hart. Oxford: Clarendon.

Davis, Michael. 2009. "Punishment Theory's Golden Half Century: A Survey of Developments from (about) 1957 to 2007." *Journal of Ethics* 13, no. 1 (January): 73–100.

Duff, R. A. 2003. "Penance, Punishment and the Limits of Community." *Punishment & Society* 5, no. 3 (July): 295–312.

Flew, Antony. 1954. "The Justification of Punishment." *Philosophy* 29, no. 111 (October): 291–307.

Hampton, Jean. 1984. "The Moral Education Theory of Punishment." *Philosophy & Public Affairs* 13, no. 3 (Summer): 208–38.

Hart, H. L. A. 1960. "Prolegomenon to the Principles of Punishment." *Proceedings of the Aristotelian Society* 60, no. 1 (June): 1–26.

Kaepernick, Colin, ed. 2021. *Abolition for the People: The Movement for a Future without Policing & Prisons.* New York: Kaepernick.

Manion, Jen. 2005. *Liberty's Prisoners: Carceral Culture in Early America*. Philadelphia: University of Pennsylvania Press.
McCloskey, H. J. 1962. "The Complexity of the Concepts of Punishment." *Philosophy* 37, no. 142 (October): 307–25.
McPherson, Thomas. 1967. "Punishment: Definition and Justification." *Analysis* 28, no. 1 (October): 21–27.
Morris, Herbert. 1968. "Persons and Punishment." *Monist* 52, no. 4 (October): 475–501.
Purnell, Derecka. 2021. *Becoming Abolitionists: Police, Protests, and the Pursuit of Freedom*. New York: Astra House.
Thaler, Richard H., and Cass R. Sunstein. 2008. *Nudge: Improving Decisions about Health, Wealth, and Happiness*. New Haven, CT: Yale University Press.
Vitale, Alex S. 2021. *The End of Policing*. New York: Verso.

Part VIII

Forgiveness and Restoration

27

Punishment and Forgiveness

John Kleinig

It is generally considered that if punishment is justified, it is justified in part because the person to be punished is guilty of wrongdoing of some kind—ordinarily, what we also see as moral wrongdoing. So, even though the crime of murder is defined in legal terms, we ordinarily see it as involving a moral transgression (Feinberg 1964). If the wrong is of a different kind, we are more likely to see the imposition as a mere penalty. It is often said that, when justified, punishment must be deserved, though whether desert is sufficient to justify punishment is another matter. The question of sufficiency arises whether the punishment is informal, as in the case of a communal setting (a family or group), or a more formalized context is envisaged, such as that of an institution or, most commonly, the state. Desert, insofar as it is articulable, may be only one among other factors relevant to justified punishment.

Other—though not always incompatible—options are available to those confronted with others' wrongdoing. We may ignore or condone it or simply level blame at those who perpetrate it. We may sometimes rebuke, berate, or even censure without punishing. A conciliatory (restorative) process may be initiated. Whether and to what extent these alternative responses to wrongdoing are permissible/justified/required are matters for debate, ones that I will not enter upon here.

J. Kleinig (✉)
John Jay College of Criminal Justice, New York, NY, USA
e-mail: jkleinig@jjay.cuny.edu

© The Author(s), under exclusive license to Springer Nature Switzerland AG 2023

M. C. Altman (ed.), *The Palgrave Handbook on the Philosophy of Punishment*, Palgrave Handbooks in the Philosophy of Law, https://doi.org/10.1007/978-3-031-11874-6_27

In this chapter, I propose to explore the place of forgiveness in a social environment that justifiably countenances punishment. Unlike some other responses to wrongdoing, forgiveness is sometimes seen as compatible with punishment, and sometimes as incompatible with it.[1] My task here will be to explore and evaluate the rationales for these different responses, and, insofar as each has some claim, to determine the appropriate place of each. Briefly, I argue that forgiveness is compatible with punishment, though the circumstances in which forgiveness is sought or given may sometimes justify punishment's moderation or even revocation.

In section 1, I make some preliminary comments about an issue that complicates the discussion, that of the *standing* to forgive or punish. In section 2, I outline some of the relevant contours of *forgiveness*. In section 3—perhaps the central section—I review arguments that see *forgiveness as incompatible with punishment*, and in section 4, I give an overview of arguments that see *forgiveness as compatible with punishment*. In the final section (section 5), I endeavor to provide a more *unified account* of the relations between forgiveness and punishment.

1 Standing

Who may punish, and who may forgive? There has been an ongoing debate about each, and rather less about their coordination. The issue is of some significance, because forgiveness is often construed as an interpersonal matter,[2] whereas punishment is largely treated as an institutional phenomenon, and having standing to forgive and standing to punish are differentiated. Crudely, those with standing to forgive are those who have been wronged and those with standing to punish are authorized by some institutional arrangement, most commonly the state (though differentiated punishment within familial contexts is also quite common). It could appear that the two practices operate on different levels, with little connection.

Though there is something to be said for this bifurcation of standing, it is, as is the case with a lot of bifurcations, oversimplified. If we start with something like a state-of-nature theory, in which people live in informal communities, it is wholly conceivable that forgiveness and punishment will be

[1] For some of that discussion, see Kleinig (1973, 90–92), North (1987), Corlett (2006), Griswold (2007, 32–33), Zaibert (2009, 2010, 2012), Warmke (2011, 2013), Pettigrove (2012, 117–21), Russell (2016), Tosi and Warmke (2017), and Lenta (2020). I leave to one side a number of studies dealing with divine forgiveness and punishment.

[2] I leave aside political forgiveness. See, e.g., Griswold (2007, chs. 4–5) and MacLachlan (2012).

coordinated and the matter of standing will be simplified. Those who wrong others, and thereby become eligible for punishment, may or will be punished and/or forgiven by those who are wronged. If Ben wrongs Alice, Alice will be morally positioned to forgive or punish Ben—maybe both. Those who have standing to forgive will also have standing to punish. Social contract theorists have traditionally argued that there are deficiencies to the state of nature that have led—by consent—to a separation of powers. Disputes about the character of wrongdoing have necessitated the formation of legislatures to standardize social understandings of wrongdoing (lawmaking); disputes over the interpretation and application of laws that determine wrongdoing have necessitated an adjudicatory system (a judicial system); and problems associated with enforcement have necessitated executive organizations (policing and penal institutions).[3] In this way, although the standing to forgive has remained with the wronged individual, the standing to punish has been (provisionally) ceded to public authorities.

We can leave aside the huge literature (and legitimate controversy) that surrounds social contract theory. It nevertheless remains an illuminating theoretical conceit. And it also helps to cast light on ways in which the bifurcation of standing is fuzzy as well as instructive. Social contract theory is centrally a theory about public wrongs (most saliently, crimes): it addresses issues that have come to have societal significance and ignores many wrongs of a more intimate or parochial kind. The state, therefore, as an agent of punishment, is not the sole repository of punishment, even though it imposes some broad limits on extra-judicial punishments. Parents may punish their children, and organizations may punish their members, but imprisonment and execution are not permitted to them. They can spank, ground, ostracize, ban, fire, and countenance the infliction of some other impositions or deprivations. In the latter cases, those with standing to forgive may also have standing to punish.

Even where the state has standing to punish and the individual has standing to forgive, the issue of punishment may arise. If Ben commits a crime in which Alice is the victim, Alice may still have a range of punishments available to her over which the state will not exercise a veto. Alice may terminate various connections she has with Ben—for example, by divorcing or firing him, by changing her will or severing all relations with him. And, saliently, she may withhold these responses as part of forgiveness or even impose them and then forgive. There is a complexity to the forgiveness-punishment nexus.

---

[3] A classic formulation is found in Locke (1980, ch. 9). For present purposes, I leave to one side Charles Mills's (1997) important argument that contract theory has traditionally been white supremacist.

Although we have, in the case of state punishment, differentiated those with standing to forgive from those with standing to punish, the theory provides avenues for one to influence the other. So, for example, people who have been victims of public wrongs or crimes may indicate to a court that they have forgiven the wrongdoers and plead for mercy to be shown. There is, of course, no guarantee of that, because the adjudicating agency has chosen to concern itself with wrongdoing that has public significance and may choose to give that priority in its decision-making. It may, however, choose to discount the penalty if the reasons for forgiveness are of a particular kind.

It should be noted that the standing to forgive is also fuzzily, even if paradigmatically, restricted to those who have been the direct victims of wrongdoing. Ordinarily, it is the victim of that wrongdoing who has standing to forgive. But there are circumstances under which we might want to extend that standing, especially when the wrong has injured others or has displayed some form of group animus. Black people, for example, may be thought to have standing to forgive or refuse to forgive white people for slavery and Jim Crow.[4] Not anyone may forgive, but insofar as wrongdoing has wider communal ripples, we may see others as also having a legitimate standing to forgive.

So, although there is something of a mismatch between the standing to forgive and the standing to punish, they are not so incongruous as to make the current project a pointless one.

2 Forgiveness

Most commonly, we see forgiveness, unlike pardon or clemency, as an interpersonal response to wrongdoing. That may not be a strict requirement, as institutions (such as a church) may sometimes offer forgiveness to those who transgress their requirements.[5] I shall focus mainly on interpersonal forgiveness as the more paradigmatic context.

When Alice forgives Ben, what is she doing or conveying? If it is forgiveness for wrongdoing on Ben's part, must Alice have been the or a victim of Ben's wrongdoing? Does Ben need to be present to be forgiven, or is Alice's forgiveness something she may privately determine? Is forgiveness a change of

[4] On expanding the standing to forgive, see Pettigrove (2009), Zaragoza (2012), and Chaplin (2019). On the standing to punish, see Kleinig (1973, 72–77), Beade (2019), and Duus-Otterström and Kelly (2019). Debates about the standing to forgive frequently arise in the context of responses to the Holocaust.

[5] In section 3, I consider economic forgiveness, such as the forgiveness of student debt, and the analogical use made of it.

attitude or a communicative act? And when Alice forgives Ben, should this forgiveness be conditioned in some way on Ben's behavior—say, an apology, remorse, or reparation—or might it be extended without such conditions? Each of these questions has garnered a diversity of sometimes competing responses, and we should at least be open to the possibility that there is no single or simple response.[6]

One time-honored response has been to claim that forgiveness is an act of "forswearing resentment."[7] That is—though I pick up on only one of the possibilities here—forswearing resentment amounts to the victim's resolute determination to cease *continued indignation* at the wrongdoer whose act appropriately generated the resentment. Indignation is a somewhat narrower and broader moral emotion than resentment (which may involve anger, malice, and other hard feelings[8]), but it picks up on what might be seen as the opprobrium fittingly experienced when one is wronged. And in forswearing it, the forgiver may confront a moral and psychological challenge. There is more to forswearing than turning off a psychological switch. It has consequences for action, and if those actions are not present, the genuineness of proffered forgiveness can be questioned. Once forgiven, the wrongdoing no longer figures as a moralized barrier to relations between the wronged person and the wrongdoer.

In some contexts, at least, forgiveness represents not simply a determination to cease feelings of indignation or resentment, but also a decision to move on—*to put the past behind one*—a determination not to allow it to continue to occupy or consume one. Forgiveness here has a social utility that is not inherent to the forswearing of resentment. In other contexts, forgiveness may be seen as a *reconciliatory* gesture—a desire to patch up a relationship (or presumptive human connection) broken by the wrongdoing—a desire no longer to allow the wrongdoing to poison the moral connection one had with the wrongdoer. Such reconciliatory gestures will sometimes presume what is not always the case, namely a preexisting relationship between the wrongdoer and the person wronged. Reconciliation, however, is ambiguous, with stronger and weaker understandings. Sometimes, even if there was a preexisting relationship, forgiveness need not presage reconciliation in the sense of

[6] Perhaps the major contemporary contributor has been Griswold (2007), though my own views differ from his in a number of ways.

[7] The phrasing is usually associated with Butler (2017), Sermons 8 and 9 ("Upon Resentment" and "Upon Forgiveness of Injuries," respectively), though whether Butler was himself committed to that formulation has been questioned. See Griswold (2007, 20) and Garcia (2011).

[8] A wider range of possibilities is canvassed by Warmke (2017a, 3). Also, one forswears attitudes such as vindictiveness, hatred, bitterness, and rancor (see, e.g., Garrard and McNaughton 2003).

restoring a relational status quo ante. An abused partner may forgive the other without any intention or desire to resume the relationship. It seeks merely to put the wrongdoing behind oneself as one moves on.[9] At other times, something even weaker is implied—accepting the wrongdoer back into the world of social agency, a moralized version of prisoner reentry.

The foregoing account focuses on conditions associated with the forgiver—whether the forgiveness involves the overcoming of indignation, a determination to move on, or a gesture toward reconciliation of some kind. On some accounts, that is all that forgiveness requires. But insofar as forgiveness is usually seen as virtuous or required, it is often argued that forgiveness requires more—it is a transactional relation, requiring remorse, repentance, apology, or reparation on the part of the offender. This debate—about "conditionality"—is sometimes conducted as one concerning the conditions of forgiveness. That is, forgiveness is viewed as a normative concept—positively evaluated—and therefore as one requiring the fulfillment of certain conditions by the wrongdoer. At other times, however, such conditionality is not seen as a condition either for viewing an act as one of forgiveness or as essential to its valuation. Although the latter is most often associated with a particular normative tradition (most commonly, Christianity), it is not exclusive to that.

The association of unconditionality with the Christian tradition reflects, albeit not exclusively, the influence of Bishop Butler, who uses "love your enemies" (Matthew 5:44) as the epigraph of his sermons on forgiveness (2017, 68, 75).[10] For others, unconditionality may reflect the recognition that we are all human, prone to moral failure—perhaps a secular version of "there but for the grace of God go I." It may not be intended to exempt a person from punishment, but it exemplifies a way of interpreting the view that "to understand all is to forgive all," and it is consonant with the withdrawal of emotions that often express condescension or a "holier than thou" attitude. Such forgiveness is not totally unconditional, but the conditions are those associated with generosity, love, charitableness, mercy, grace, and gifting.

For some writers, so-called conditional forgiveness is paradigmatic forgiveness, and unconditional forgiveness is seen as parasitic on it; for others, the reverse is true. Even conditional forgiveness is seen as a discretionary gift, an

[9] There is a large sociological and psychological literature on forgiveness and reconciliation. See Worthington (2006). On its philosophical dimensions, see Warmke (2017b). A problem with the view that forgiveness primarily expresses a desire to move on or to patch up differences is that it is reduced to a self-help mechanism rather than a moral revamping.

[10] The passage may or may not advocate unconditional forgiveness, though Butler probably understands it that way.

act of non-required (even if warranted) generosity on the part of a person who has been wronged.[11] Although I favor the latter (Kleinig 2021a, 2021b), we do not have to resolve this debate, as the question of punishment may arise in either view.

3 Arguments for the Incompatibility of Forgiveness and Punishment

To a considerable extent, my discussion of the arguments against the compatibility of forgiveness with punishment prefigure those in section 4.

(1) As noted at the beginning of this chapter, forgiveness is variously understood. Moral wrongdoing is sometimes viewed as analogous to incurring a moral debt (Aristotle 1984, 1163a24–b27 [pp. 1838–39]), and forgiveness seen as the cancellation of that debt. Although that understanding continues to have a strong representation in economic circles ("the forgiveness of student debt"), it has also—for historical reasons—continued to have a broader resonance. A New Testament parable recounts the story of a master who is owed money by one of his servants. Unable to repay his debt, the servant begs for the master's mercy. The subsequent forgiveness of the economic debt is used as a metaphor for divine forgiveness: the master's forgiveness of the servant's indebtedness is seen as analogous to God's forgiveness of those who are unable to repay the debt accumulated by virtue of their moral shortfalls (Matthew 18:21–35).[12]

Brandon Warmke (2016) seeks to show the explanatory advantages of comparing economic debt cancellation and moral forgiveness. Although he does not claim a one-to-one correspondence between economic and moral forgiveness, Warmke believes that they have a similar conceptual structure, namely, one in which one person's act incurs a debt with respect to another, a debt from which the other can release the first. The attraction of this model is that it offers an explanation of how the wrongdoer's obligation to the victim arises and may be erased: wronging another creates indebtedness to that other, even though that indebtedness may be canceled. This is important, as it shows how having or overcoming resentment provides an explanation of how

[11] To watch this played out, see, for example, Fricker (2019) and Allais (2019).

[12] Although this initially appears to be a case of unconditional forgiveness, the unfolding of the parable indicates that, although the servant is not required to repay the master, he is expected to display a similar forgiving spirit to another who owes him. The biblical parable presents its own challenges: see De Boer (1988).

forgiveness alters the wrongdoer's normative situation vis-à-vis the victim (Warmke 2017a, 7–8).

Might forgiveness construed as debt cancellation be taken to imply cancellation of punishment that would be due as a result of wrongdoing? It is tempting to think so. However, as Warmke warns, formal structural similarity—helpful though it may be to explain the normative character of moral forgiveness—does not indicate a one-to-one correspondence of normative content. For example, economic debts may be partially forgiven (e.g., forgiving the first $10,000 of student debt), and economic debt may usually be paid by others. That is not so obvious in the case of moral forgiveness—though it is plausible to think that, even if resentment may be forsworn, a punishment associated with the wrongdoing may be allowed to stand. There are also various unclarities involved in the analogy—concerning, for example, the kinds of acts that are debt-incurring (acts performed in ignorance of their moral qualities, accidents, etc.), the nature of the debts in question (liability to punishment, recompense, etc.), which debts may be canceled (are some unforgiveable?), the consequences of debt cancellation (forsworn resentment, reconciliation, etc.), and the moral expectations of debt cancellation (gratitude? adopting a similar spirit toward others? etc.). On its own, the debt-cancellation theory does not answer these questions.

Should we therefore take the debt-cancellation theory to eschew punishment? Not obviously so. As my remarks in the previous paragraph presage—why should that be the case? Might forgiveness relieve the indebted person of the continued ire of the person wronged, but not of the obligation to apologize? Cancellation of a debt might seem to require nothing of the forgiven person, but perhaps the forgiver believes that (some) legal punishment continues to be an appropriate response to the wrongdoing while deciding to forswear resentment and demand no apology. When members of the Emanuel African Methodist Episcopal Church forgave the white supremacist Dylann Roof for the massacre of nine of their number, they made clear to the court that they forgave Roof, but they made no attempt to seek pardon or clemency. Forgiveness reflected a personal decision not to nurse resentment; the state was left to fulfill its retributive (or other) purposes. It is highly likely that, in the moral case, debt cancellation will involve a determination to withdraw continued resentment, but there is little in the theory that demands much more than that.

This is not to deny that debt cancellation and the cancellation of punishment may come together when the forgiver is also the punisher. Thus, a parent, in forgiving, may choose not to punish the child who has stolen money from the change jar. Cancellation (or reduction) of punishment is an understandable option when the forgiver also determines what is to be done to the wrongdoer. There does not seem, however, to be any necessity about linking forgiveness to non-punishment in such cases. I am aware of a case in which the owner of a business forgave his accountant for cooking the books (to cover gambling losses) and showed forgiveness by not reporting the accountant to the authorities. Nevertheless, the accountant was fired—punished—but not in one of the standard ways available to the business owner.

Wrongdoing may deserve punishment, but deservingness may not make punishment justified or, if justified, obligatory. In the case of the accountant, he was deeply ashamed by his behavior and shaken out of his gambling habit, and the business owner could determine how to show both forgiveness and the importance of not letting the wrongdoing go unpunished. The business in question was able to swallow the losses and also cancel the economic debt that the accountant had incurred (though I understand that the accountant gradually repaid some portion of what was lost).

(2) Leo Zaibert has argued that "to forgive is to deliberately refuse to punish" (2009, 368).[13] It is Zaibert's contention that when Ben blameworthily wrongs Alice, Ben does something that leaves the world in a worse place than it would have been. Ben's doing this also tends to create a negative emotion (such as indignation) on the part of Alice. Under the circumstances, Zaibert contends, the world would be a better place were something to happen to Ben to offset his wrongdoing. If Alice forgives Ben, she refuses to try to offset Ben's wrongdoing because she believes that her imposing something on Ben to offset it would make the world worse. If, however, Alice offsets Ben's wrongdoing by imposing something painful on Ben, what she does amounts to punishment. It is Zaibert's contention that the last two sentences are "mutually synchronically exclusive" (2009, 387), and therefore that Alice's forgiving Ben amounts to her refusing to punish him.

Zaibert points out that his analysis does not require conditionality on Alice's part: she may forgive Ben without his sorrow or repentance. Zaibert sees this as a strength of his account, as it does not take a stand on an issue that strongly divides forgiveness theorists (Kleinig 2021b). He also claims, *contra* the mainstream, that his account does not require that Alice withdraw her negative emotions (Zaibert 2009, 388)—a far more contentious consequence.

[13] Zaibert's account builds on conceptions that he developed at greater length in Zaibert (2006). In a later paper (Zaibert 2012), he responds to criticisms. The idea of forgiveness as the withholding of punishment is also common in much of the burgeoning social work and psychological literature. See, for example, Enright et al., where, in their account of forgiveness, they see "the casting off of deserved punishments" as "a consistency between ancient writings and modern philosophies," along with "the abandonment of negative reactions, the imparting of love toward the other person, the self-sacrificial nature of forgiveness, the potential for restoration of relationship, and the positive benefits for the forgiver" (1991, 88).

It is not plausible for Alice to say to Ben: "The world would be a better place were I to punish you, but, although I remain indignant at what you did, I am forgiving you." She is letting Ben off rather than forgiving him. It is true that the withdrawal of resentment may not provide a clear account of why forgiveness might be a good thing (something that the debt-cancellation account attempts to provide), but there is a counterintuitiveness to Zaibert's analysis that he does not alleviate. Zaibert also tends to run blame and resentment together, partly because of ambiguities in "blame." Forgiving someone need not involve a withholding of blame (holding someone responsible); it does not amount to condonation. It is, however, likely to involve a decision to cease resentment. What is withheld is ongoing indignation and upbraiding—or blaming in a different sense.

One feature of Zaibert's position that may make it attractive is that, in cases in which Alice can be both victim and punisher, forgiveness may encompass a decision not to punish. Should Ben apologize profusely to Alice, offering to recompense her for losses and harms, Alice may choose to acknowledge Ben's remorse and his desire to make amends by determining, inter alia, not to punish him. But this does not strictly need to be the case. As noted earlier, whatever is encompassed by forgiveness—if anything beyond the "forswearing of indignation"—it may not always include the (complete) remission of punishment. A lesser punishment may be imposed lest the wrongdoer be tempted to discount the seriousness of what was done. And, in some cases, the forgiveness may be subsequent to punishment.

For Alice's decision to forgive Ben to be morally acceptable, whether or not some punishment is administered, it may not require some change of heart on Ben's part, but it may need to appeal to other kinds of reasons that carry moral weight. What such reasons could be is a matter of continuing contention, but they could include Ben's persistent and reasoned belief that he does not think that what he was doing was wrong (he was just asking questions that he thought were legitimate) or that he thought he was doing the right thing (say, acting as a Good Samaritan). These reasons have some claim to legitimacy, unlike those that are self-serving (fear of retaliation, a desire for future favors). It is true that different reasons may make for different moral outcomes: some might be thought to make forgiveness obligatory (though I question that), others morally desirable, others merely permissible, others supererogatory, and so forth.

(3) To disengage punishment from forgiveness, one need not accept Zaibert's claim that to forgive is to refuse to punish, as though one excludes the other. The argument may instead be expressed as a moral one, namely, that if Alice forgives Ben for what he did, then *ceteris paribus* she *ought* to

refrain from either punishing Ben or, for that matter, supporting his punishment by others (Tosi and Warmke 2017).[14] One reason to think this may be embedded in the contention that certain key elements of forgiveness, namely, the forswearing of indignation or resentment, are concretized in acts of certain kinds, viz., that if Ben deserves to be punished because of what he did to Alice, and Alice still seeks Ben's punishment after forgiving him, she would, in effect, be reneging on that commitment. In forswearing resentment of Ben, she gives up her moral claim to his punishment.[15]

The point here is that Alice's resentment at what Ben has done is expressive of her belief that Ben has acted toward her in a way that warrants his punishment. A fairly tight moral connection is assumed between wrongdoing and punishment. As John Stuart Mill famously puts it (albeit more generally): "We do not call anything wrong unless we mean to imply that a person ought to be punished in some way or other for doing it—if not by law, by the opinion of his fellow creatures; if not by opinion, by the reproaches of his own conscience" (2001, 48). Thus, forgiveness, insofar as it involves a decision to cease resentment at another's wrongdoing, is also a decision to pull back from the view that the wrongdoer ought (*pro tanto* if not *tout court*) to be punished.

How well does this work? One way of taking it is that, in forgiving Ben, Alice indicates only that she has chosen not to pursue Ben's punishment. What Ben did may deserve punishment independently of Alice's sense of her own victimhood. So, although she has chosen not to facilitate Ben's punishment, others may—and not because of any personal resentment on their part, but because what Ben did was wrong and therefore deserving of punishment. This will most obviously be the case where the wrong that Ben perpetrated on Alice was also a public wrong, or crime.

We might, however, press the initial contention harder. In being wronged, and appropriately experiencing resentment, does one *ipso facto* believe that the wrongdoer deserves punishment? And does forgiveness, as a forswearing of resentment, constitute a withdrawal of that moral understanding or commitment? It *may*, but Alice could also say (in effect) to Ben: "Ben, I'm going to forgive you in that I am determined not to continue feeling resentful at what you did, and I want to move on with my life. However, we can't wind the clock back. You violated me horribly and although I will not pursue any further action against you, I want you out of my house and life." The point is not

[14] Tosi and Warmke (2017) offer three versions of this argument. I believe, however, that they can be effectively considered together.

[15] On this view, presumably, forgiveness is most likely to be seen as morally permissible or supererogatory, though stronger versions are possible. Where the forgiveness is tied to subsequent actions of the wrongdoer, the forgiveness is sometimes seen as obligatory.

that her forgiveness lacks moral bite, but that it need not involve some restoration of the status quo ante. Some form of punishment may be imposed, along with a significant change in moral disposition.

There is a somewhat deeper problem. Even if, to be justified, punishment needs to be deserved, and, for it to be deserved, some wrong must have been committed, it does not clearly follow that, if Ben does some wrong to Alice, he deserves punishment. It is one thing to say that justified punishment must be deserved; it is another to say that what wrongdoing deserves is punishment. Perhaps Ben should feel bad about what he did and perhaps he should be sorry for what he did, but punishment, as a specific kind of deserved imposition for wrongdoing, may not follow without further argument. Alice's forgiveness, therefore, may not amount to a morally sanctioned withdrawal of punishment. No doubt forgiveness expects something of Alice, some change on her part, but what it implies for Ben may be less obvious.

Might the moral calculus work out differently if we think of forgiveness not merely as the forswearing of resentment, but as the forswearing of resentment by virtue of some responsiveness on the part of the wrongdoer—remorse, apology, reparation, or something of that kind? Does it become morally inappropriate for Alice to punish Ben or to support Ben's punishment if Ben sincerely apologizes to Alice for what he has done to her and even compensates her for what he did? Suppose Ben took Alice's car without permission and then totaled it. He is remorseful and apologetic and offers to replace it with a new one. Alice forgives him. Should that include a withdrawal of punishment on Alice's part? It certainly may if Ben and Alice are siblings; Alice may think it contributes to their reconciliation if she refuses to press charges against Ben. There is a relational connection to be healed.

It is not so clear, however, that conditional forgiveness morally requires a decision not to punish, particularly if there is no preexisting relationship between Alice and Ben that she is determined to restore. Here of course we have a case in which Ben's stealing Alice's car is not a private offense but has public significance. Ben has committed a crime. That is also true of the previous case, but there Alice may simply refuse to press charges. In this second case, Alice may say to the authorities that she appreciates Ben's remorse and compensation, but then asks that they be taken into account when he is dealt with by the appropriate authorities. What is contemplated is not so much a moral withdrawal of punishment but a moral discounting that goes with her conditional forgiveness. Without Ben's remorse and compensation, Alice may not have been willing to forgive him, but even with it, it may not follow that Alice should be opposed to all punishment.

Note that I am not arguing for the impropriety of a decision to withhold punishment, only that forgiveness encompasses a range of possible moral alterations in the relation between wrongdoer and victim, the withholding of punishment being only one of them.

(4) In certain contexts, as dictionaries allow, forgiveness may be equated with pardon (or even mercy). This might be thought to indicate the incompatibility of forgiveness with punishment. It is true, historically, that some writers have treated forgiveness and pardon as the same. Thomas Hobbes, for example, says of his sixth law of nature that, "*upon caution of the Future time, a man ought to pardon the offences past of them that, repenting, desire it*" (1996, 106). Although this—along with the other laws of nature—can, according to Hobbes, be secured only through the coercive powers of government, a fact that may lead Hobbes to conflate them, it is clear from its place in the Hobbesian scheme that this precept is intended to characterize forgiveness. As it is generally used, however, pardon is a formal, institutionally backed device, whereas forgiveness is normally interpersonal. When the president (or judge) pardons a felon, it is not forgiveness that is proffered, but a type of remission: the slate is formally wiped clean. Neither the president nor the judge have been wronged. Mercy might also be shown either personally or institutionally. Usually it is based on the personal circumstances of the wrongdoer—say, an inability to bear some punishment or, maybe, remorse. But it need not involve any forswearing of resentment on the part of the wronged person. Nor need it involve the remission of punishment—though mercy may sometimes be shown in the moderation of punishment. Mercy does not have as its condition some wrong done that stands in need of forgiveness.[16]

(5) One common—and perhaps unexpected—set of circumstances might be appealed to in defense of the view that forgiveness and punishment are not compatible. Suppose that, as a result of what Ben has done to her, Alice punishes him informally by cutting off all contact and depriving him of things he valued, such as hearth and home. Somewhere down the road, however, whether because Ben has changed or repented. because Alice wants to get on with her life without the shadow of Ben's ongoing punishment, or, perhaps, because she has had a change of heart, she generously offers him her forgiveness and, along with the forgiveness, ceases the punishment that she originally intended to be in perpetuity. Here we have a case in which Alice's forgiveness is correlated with a cessation of the punishment to which he has been subject.

[16] See, for example, Murphy (2011). I think, however, that Murphy draws the boundaries of mercy too narrowly, See also Hughes and Warmke (2017, §2.4).

But what does this show? I do not believe that circumstances such as these can be used to show the incompatibility of punishment with forgiveness. True, Alice's forgiveness may involve a cessation of punishment, but it carries with it no implication that, along with the forgiveness, Alice now regrets the punishment she has imposed to this point. True, Alice is manifesting her forgiveness by ceasing her ongoing punishment of Ben. That is an option she has chosen. But without the punishment so far imposed Alice may not have come to the point of wanting or being prepared to forgive.

4 Arguments for the Compatibility of Forgiveness and Punishment

To some extent, the critiques offered in the preceding section also presage arguments for the compatibility of forgiveness with punishment.

(1) One argument for their compatibility may draw on the differences in standing that I noted earlier (see Mabbott 1939, 158). Many wrongs are public as well as private, and even though Alice may forgive Ben for what he did specifically to her, what Ben did also fell into the category of a public wrong (most commonly, a misdemeanor or crime). True, Alice may also, in choosing to forgive Ben (say, for an act of domestic violence), refuse to cooperate with prosecutors wishing to indict Ben, thus upending the legal process; but if prosecutors have sufficient alternative evidence, indictment and punishment may proceed despite Alice's refusal to cooperate.

However, as my earlier arguments indicated, standing for each may coincide and, as part of the forgiveness, punishment may be forsaken, withdrawn, or diminished. Forgiveness and punishment may be compatible without being hard-wired. Even if we accept Mill's claim that moral wrong *ipso facto* implies punishment-worthy, it may be open to the wronged person to determine whether other factors might take precedence.

(2) A second argument focuses on the character of forgiveness as the forswearing of resentment—an attitudinal determination that may either precede or (continue to) follow punishment. Even if we think of wrongdoing as rendering one eligible for punishment, the resentment that is experienced by the wronged person need not carry with it the implication that its withdrawal (because of forgiveness) requires the cancellation of punishment. Punishment may be canceled, but that is no requirement of forgiveness. Consider a situation in which Ben assaults Alice. Ben may be punished by Alice and/or some authority, and still not be forgiven. Or, after Ben has been punished, Alice

may forgive him. Perhaps in the first case we may think it appropriate that Alice forgive him; but whether appropriate or not, forgiveness is one thing and punishment (or its cancellation) another.

(3) A further argument focuses on the discretionary character of forgiveness. Those who are wronged are not required to forgive those who wrong them, and if they are forgiven, the terms of their forgiveness—apart from the determination to forswear resentment—are also discretionary. If Alice chooses to forgive Ben, it is for her to determine what that forgiveness may encompass—simply a determination to forswear resentment that is a natural to the wrongdoing that Ben has perpetrated against her, a determination to lessen or perhaps seek to have lessened any punishment that may be due, a reestablishment of relations with Ben after punishment has been served, and so on. If we think of forgiveness as a statement of the moral terms, going forward, of Alice's relationship with Ben, anything more than choosing to remove the moral barrier that Ben has created by his wrongdoing lies with Alice. Of course, she cannot both forgive and continue to resent what Ben does, though she need not (and presumably will not) see Ben as anything less than blameworthy for what he did.

Given what has been said in sections 3 and 4, it is fairly clear that forgiveness, insofar as it involves the forswearing of resentment, does not also require withdrawal of or resistance to the punishment of the wrongdoer.

5 Theorizing the Connection

If most of the foregoing arguments and considerations are accepted, the relation of forgiveness to punishment has something of the following form. Although in some cases—particularly those in which wrongdoing is deemed to be exclusively private—the choice not to punish may be an option, there are many cases in which forgiveness of wrongdoing has few implications for justified punishment. True, it may lead to a cessation of punishment already instituted or a desire to diminish punishment otherwise justified. The circumstances may vary and that decision may be variously evaluated. Forgiveness may be cheapened if too readily given; unforgivingness may manifest a vengeful heart. Forgiveness that involves the cancellation of punishment may sometimes express a lack of self-respect on the part of the wrongdoer or a devaluing of the wrong that was involved. At other times it may express an admirable generosity on the part of the forgiver, to the extent that punishment of the wrongdoing lies within the power of the wrongdoer. Although mercy—displayed as a determination not to punish—is a somewhat broader notion and can intersect with forgiveness, it may not always be called for or appropriate. Like forgiveness, it has moral constraints, albeit not necessarily as narrowly drawn as those associated with advocates of conditional forgiveness.

References

Allais, Lucy. 2019. "The Priority of Gifted Forgiveness: A Response to Fricker." *Australasian Philosophical Review* 3, no. 3: 261–73.

Aristotle. 1984. *Nicomachean Ethics*. Translated by W. D. Ross; revised by J. O. Urmson. In *The Complete Works of Aristotle*, edited by Jonathan Barnes, vol. 2, 1729–1867. Princeton, NJ: Princeton University Press.

Beade, Gustavo A. 2019. "Who Can Blame Whom? Moral Standing to Blame and Punish Deprived Citizens." *Criminal Law and Philosophy* 13, no. 2 (June): 271–81.

Butler, Joseph. 2017. *Fifteen Sermons Preached at the Rolls Chapel and Other Writings on Ethics*. Edited by David McNaughton. Oxford: Oxford University Press.

Chaplin, Rosalind. 2019. "Taking It Personally: Third-Party Forgiveness, Close Relationships, and the Standing to Forgive." In *Oxford Studies in Normative Ethics*, edited by Mark Timmons, vol. 9, 73–94. Oxford: Oxford University Press.

Corlett, J. Angelo. 2006. "Forgiveness, Apology, and Retributive Punishment." *American Philosophical Quarterly* 43, no. 1 (January): 25–42.

De Boer, Martinus C. 1988. "Ten Thousand Talents? Matthew's Interpretation and Redaction of the Parable of the Unforgiving Servant (Matt 18:23–35)." *Catholic Biblical Quarterly* 50, no. 2 (April): 214–32.

Duus-Otterström, Göran, and Erin I. Kelly. 2019. "Injustice and the Right to Punish." *Philosophy Compass* 14, no. 2 (February): e12565.

Enright, Robert, David L. Eastin, Sandra Golden, Issidoros Sarinopoulos, and Suzanne Freedman. 1991. "Interpersonal Forgiveness within the Helping Professions: An Attempt to Resolve Differences of Opinion." *Counseling and Values* 36, no. 2 (October): 84–103.

Feinberg, Joel. 1964. "On Being 'Morally Speaking a Murderer.'" *Journal of Philosophy* 61, no. 5 (February 27): 158–71.

Fricker, Miranda. 2019. "Forgiveness—An Ordered Pluralism." *Australasian Philosophical Review* 3, no. 3: 241–60.

Garcia, Ernesto V. 2011. "Bishop Butler on Forgiveness and Resentment." *Philosophers' Imprint* 11, no. 10 (August): 1–19.

Garrard, Eve, and David McNaughton. 2003. "In Defence of Unconditional Forgiveness." *Proceedings of the Aristotelian Society* 103: 39–60.

Griswold, Charles L. 2007. *Forgiveness: A Philosophical Exploration*. Cambridge: Cambridge University Press.

Hobbes, Thomas. 1996. *Leviathan*. Edited by Richard Tuck. Cambridge: Cambridge University Press.

Hughes, Paul M., and Brandon Warmke. 2017. "Forgiveness." *Stanford Encyclopedia of Philosophy* (Summer 2017 edition), edited by Edward N. Zalta. https://plato.stanford.edu/entries/forgiveness/.

Kleinig, John. 1973. *Punishment and Desert*. The Hague: Nijhoff.

———. 2021a. "Defending Unconditional Forgiveness: A Reply to Brookes." *International Journal of Applied Philosophy* 35, no. 1 (Spring): 109–15.

———. 2021b. "Forgiveness and Unconditionality." *International Journal of Applied Philosophy* 35, no. 1 (Spring): 83–96.

Lenta, Patrick. 2020. "Forgiving and Forbearing Punishment." *International Journal of Applied Philosophy* 34, no. 2 (Fall): 201–14.

Locke, John. 1980. *Second Treatise of Government*. Edited by C. B. Macpherson. Indianapolis, IN: Hackett

Mabbott, J. D. 1939. "Punishment." *Mind* 48, no. 190 (April): 152–67.

MacLachlan, Alice. 2012. "The Philosophical Controversy over Political Forgiveness." In *Public Forgiveness in Post-Conflict Contexts*, edited by Bas van Stokkom, Neelke Doorn, and Paul Van Tongeren, 37–64. Cambridge: Intersentia.

Mill, John Stuart. 2001. *Utilitarianism*. 2nd ed. Edited by George Sher. Indianapolis, IN: Hackett.

Mills, Charles W. 1997. *The Racial Contract*. Ithaca, NY: Cornell University Press.

Murphy, Jeffrie G. 2011. "Forgiveness and Mercy." In *Routledge Encyclopedia of Philosophy Online*. London: Routledge. https://www.rep.routledge.com/articles/thematic/forgiveness-and-mercy/v-2.

North, Joanna. 1987. "Wrongdoing and Forgiveness." *Philosophy* 62, no. 242 (October): 499–508.

Pettigrove, Glen. 2009. "The Standing to Forgive." *Monist* 92, no. 4 (October): 583–603.

———. 2012. *Forgiveness and Love*. Oxford: Oxford University Press.

Russell, Luke. 2016. "Forgiving while Punishing." *Australasian Journal of Philosophy* 94, no. 4: 704–18.

Tosi, Justin, and Brandon Warmke. 2017. "Punishment and Forgiveness." In *The Routledge Handbook of Criminal Justice Ethics*, edited by Jonathan Jacobs and Jonathan Jackson, 203–16. Abingdon, UK: Routledge.

Warmke, Brandon. 2011. "Is Forgiveness the Deliberate Refusal to Punish?" *Journal of Moral Philosophy* 8, no. 4 (January): 613–20.

———. 2013. "Two Arguments against the Punishment-Forbearance Account of Forgiveness." *Philosophical Studies* 165, no. 3 (September): 915–20.

———. 2016. "The Economic Model of Forgiveness." *Pacific Philosophical Quarterly* 97, no. 4 (December): 570–89.

———. 2017a. "Divine Forgiveness I: Emotion and Punishment-Forbearance Theories." *Philosophy Compass* 12, no. 9 (September): e12440.

———. 2017b. "Divine Forgiveness II: Reconciliation and Debt-Cancellation Theories." *Philosophy Compass* 12, no. 9 (September): e12439.

Worthington, Everett L., Jr. 2006. *Forgiveness and Reconciliation: Theory and Application*. New York: Routledge.
Zaibert, Leo. 2006. *Punishment and Retribution*. Aldershot, UK: Ashgate.
———. 2009. "The Paradox of Forgiveness." *Journal of Moral Philosophy* 6, no. 3 (January): 365–93.
———. 2010. "Punishment and Forgiveness." In *Punishment and Ethics: New Perspectives*, edited by Jesper Ryberg and J. Angelo Corlett, 92–110. Basingstoke, UK: Palgrave Macmillan.
———. 2012. "On Forgiveness and the Deliberate Refusal to Punish: Reiterating the Differences." *Journal of Moral Philosophy* 9, no. 1 (January): 103–13.
Zaragoza, Kevin. 2012. "Forgiveness and Standing." *Philosophy and Phenomenological Research* 84, no. 3 (May): 604–21.

28

Restorative Justice, Punishment, and the Law

Lode Walgrave

Restorative justice is deeply rooted in history, but it reappeared in modern Western debates by the end of the 1970s, based on several trends and movements, such as communitarianism, critical criminology, and victims' movements (Weitekamp 1999).

It is crucial to recall briefly that restorative justice is inspired primarily by socio-ethical intuition. Restorative justice is focused on restoring/repairing crime-caused harm and suffering, instead of on punishing the actor of the crime; it gives priority to inclusive deliberation among the most direct stakeholders, instead of submitting them to authoritative top-down sentencing. Both characteristics presuppose a different conception of human relations and how to govern them. This wider and deeper social-ethical approach to social life and relations also inspires other areas of criminology, such as the prevention or treatment of offenders (Walgrave et al. 2021). It is believed that all policy regarding crime, justice and (in)security must rest upon a foundation of respect, solidarity, equity, and inclusion. The deep conviction that the quality of social life depends on how we relate to each other is the inspiration to opt for restorative justice. The focus on repairing what has been damaged individually and collectively; the respect and trust in fellow citizens, including in those who have committed offenses; the attempt to involve the direct stakeholders in the search for a constructive solution and the confidence in their

L. Walgrave (✉)
Katholieke Universiteit Leuven, Leuven, Belgium
e-mail: lode.walgrave@kuleuven.be

© The Author(s), under exclusive license to Springer Nature Switzerland AG 2023

M. C. Altman (ed.), *The Palgrave Handbook on the Philosophy of Punishment*, Palgrave Handbooks in the Philosophy of Law, https://doi.org/10.1007/978-3-031-11874-6_28

capacity to do so—all this expresses, more than formalized punitive responses do, the concern for quality of social life based on respect, participation, and inclusion.

Currently, the positive potential of restorative justice is generally recognized. Less evident, however, is its relation to traditional criminal justice. Many consider it a path for diversion. For some, it is a kind of alternative punishment. Other scholars are more ambitious and see restorative justice as a direction for a fundamental change in the way justice is done after the occurrence of an offense.

This chapter takes the latter position. It describes the essentials of what I call a "consequential" approach to restorative justice and argues why this option is desirable. My interpretation of restorative justice is based on critical observations of current criminal justice and on the positive argument that aiming at reparation of crime-caused damage and suffering is more constructive for social life.[1]

1 Consequential Restorative Justice

Restorative justice as a term was first coined in the 1950s by Albert Eglash (Van Ness and Heetderks Strong 2002; Maruna 2014), but the real breakthrough came in the 1990s. Since then, restorative justice gradually became a "widening river" of innovative practices, theoretical debates, and empirical evaluations (Zehr 2002, 62). It is also currently an inescapable theme in reforms of youth justice and criminal justice.

1.1 Two Starting Points

A commitment to restorative justice rests upon two fundamental beliefs:

1. Social wrongs equal causing harm to social life, and
2. The intervention against social wrongs must prioritize repairing or mitigating the harms to social life they have caused.

[1] This chapter is not the place to discuss empirical evaluations of restorative justice practices. However, despite methodological issues, it is safe to draw the provisional conclusion that victims are generally more satisfied after participating in a restorative process, that offenders' recidivism tends to be lower, and that no additional threats to public safety are observed. Among the many surveys, see especially Bonta et al. (2006), Sherman and Strang (2007), Ward et al. (2014), and Suzuki and Yuan (2021).

By criminalizing certain conduct, the political community declares that it rejects this conduct and may provoke a coercive public intervention limiting the liberties of the citizen who has performed such conduct. After an offense, the state can act proactively, in the absence of a complaint by a citizen. In case of a tort, on the contrary, the state can only intervene as a reaction to a complaint. Hence, enforcement of criminal law appears to be more important for society than other laws and rules.

Some authors, such as Antony Duff (2002), distinguish public wrongs from harm. For him, criminal punishments do not sanction the causation of a harm to social life, but the commitment of a public wrong. This position supposes the existence of a dogmatic system of *mala in se*, conduct that is intrinsically wrong regardless of its impact. In my view, such systems may exist in strict moral or religious contexts, but it would be dubious to use them as frames for public law enforcement. It would risk throwing our societies back to a kind of Talibanization, where the religious convictions of the rulers are forced upon the entire population.

It is difficult to imagine harmless wrongs or, inversely, harm causation, intentional or by neglect, that is morally right. The godfathers of the social sciences have stripped moral rules of their dogmatic appearance. Sigmund Freud considered morality as a psychodynamic construct to keep our libido within socially acceptable channels. For Émile Durkheim, its function is to preserve cohesion in society. And Norbert Elias ([1939] 2000) links the emergence of moral rules to the increasing complexity and mutual interdependencies of social life. Therefore, one cannot but conclude that there is no such thing as abstract "public wrongs." Rejection of wrong appears to be inspired by a pragmatic aversion to what our community sees as a threat to our personal and social lives and comfort.

For example, the public prohibition on burglary or on private violence is not simply because these acts are morally wrong. It is because, if they are not forbidden and if the prohibition is not enforced, private counteractions would follow, gradually dragging down public life into a climate of mutual distrust, fear, violence, and counterviolence. It is the potential harm to public life that inspires the selection of conduct to be criminalized: "Crime hurts our feelings in a secondary and derived way only. Basically, it hurts our interests" (quoted in Debuyst 1990, 357).[2] Public institutions should not concern themselves with actions that do not pose threats to public life, even if the actions are morally reprehensible.

---

[2] "Le crime ne blesse les sentiments que d'une façon secondaire et dérivée. Primitivement, ce sont les intérêts qu'il lèse" (Maxwell 1914, 35).

Many other authors also consider the harm principle as the main criterion for criminalizing behavior. Andrew von Hirsch and Nils Jareborg (1991) distinguish four types of "damage to standards of living" to decide on the blameworthiness of a crime. John Braithwaite and Philip Pettit (1990) speak in terms of "intrusion upon dominion." And Hans Boutellier (2000) advances "victimalization" as the "moral minimum" to underpin a commonly acceptable criminal justice system. They all consider harm or damage to others or to collective life as the reason to criminalize behavior. Of course, behavior may be harmful by accident, whereas the wrongfulness lies in the *intention* to cause harm. But still, wrongfulness depends on *the harm* intended.[3]

The second belief follows logically from the first one. If public harm is the reason for criminalizing certain behavior, then the intervention following a transgression should logically aim at repairing as much as possible the harm caused by it. It is illogical to advance social harm as the reason to prohibit conduct and then to respond to it by punishing the offender, making reparation of the harm done more difficult.

Clearly, this statement is inspired by instrumental concerns. In this chapter, I will argue that criminal justice, an expensive and grievous system, must earn its right to exist through what it achieves, and that a restorative approach has better chances of achieving socially constructive results than the punitive premise does.

1.2 An "Espresso-Definition" of Restorative Justice

Initially, restorative justice was developed in the field of criminal justice as an attempt to find more constructive responses to offending by involving more directly the immediate stakeholders in the handling of "their" case.[4] Meanwhile, the field has been extended toward dealing with disciplinary problems, conflicts, and injustices in other areas of social life such as schools, neighborhoods, and workplaces. Several scholars still widen the extension and involve restorative justice as the innovative drive for a broad transformation of social relations and their governing (Sullivan and Tifft 2006; Llewellyn 2021).

In my view, this is an unfortunate development (Walgrave 2021). Extending a concept too widely decreases its accuracy, which is detrimental for good research. Putting too much in a concept makes it empty of significance, which

[3] … and criminal punishment does not address people with "bad intentions," but their actual conduct.

[4] An iconic quotation from Nils Christie (1977) is that the state had "stolen" the conflict from their owners.

causes great losses in credibility. Moreover, dealing with the aftermath of an offense is a particular matter, characterized by the possibility of institutional coercion. Constitutional democracies must use coercive power parsimoniously and in accordance with stringent rules. That is why it must be confined to a unique specialized institution, clearly distinguished from other social fields and institutions. It helps to preserve specific labels for it. It is therefore better to restrict "restorative justice" to the field where it started, as a response to what has been classified as an offense, under the direct or indirect mandate of criminal justice.[5]

The relation of restorative justice to criminal justice is a subject of discussion, opposing the so-called "diversionist" to the "maximalist" or "consequential" vision (McCold 2000).[6] The mainstream holds a process-based view of restorative justice and characterizes it by the deliberative process among the direct stakeholders. These "diversionists" try to expand the implementation of such processes by diverting as many cases as possible from criminal justice institutions to para- or extrajudicial agencies that specialize in facilitating restorative encounters. In this view, restorative justice stops when the more or less voluntary process among the stakeholders appears to be impossible.[7] They leave the criminal justice system as such out of their concern.

The other perspective is consequential, advancing an outcome-based perspective of restorative justice. Consequential restorative justice pursues the objective of restoration/reparation.[8] Deliberative processes are the most vital tool to achieve it. Well-conducted encounters may indeed open the pathway toward a powerful sequence of moral emotions and exchanges, leading to a common understanding of the harm and suffering caused and to an agreement on how to make amends (Harris et al. 2004; Suzuki and Yuan 2021). In both victim and offender, the chances for a sense of procedural justice (Tyler

[5] Not including other practices into the restorative justice concept does not deny their often huge value for constructive social relations.

[6] In earlier publications, I used to refer to it as the "maximalist" view of restorative justice (Walgrave 2008). But I have recently switched to calling it "consequential," because the term maximalist appeared to provoke misunderstandings, suggesting that this view would argue for a restorative response to all offending in all cases, in all circumstances, and that the restoration should erase all negative consequences of the crime. That is not possible and is also not what I defend (Walgrave 2021).

[7] A restorative encounter after an offense is never completely free. There is at least the pressure of possible judicial prosecution, but most offenders are also pressured by their informal social environment (Johnstone 2020).

[8] The nuances in the meaning of "restoration" versus "reparation" are sometimes difficult to understand to me, as a non-native English speaker. I use "reparation" as a partial, often material restitution or compensation of what is damaged in the past, while "restoration" is understood in a more holistic, more relational meaning, oriented to the future.

2006), satisfaction, and compliance with the agreements are much higher than after a traditional judicial procedure.

But, contrary to the diversionist view, consequential restorative justice goes beyond the process. If a direct dialogue is not desirable or is refused by the victim or the offender, the reparative orientation is consequentially pursued in the coercive criminal justice intervention. It should also prioritize the possible reparative effects of its action. The consequential option does not ignore the problems existing with the punitive criminal justice system, but it tries to answer them by curbing the current punitive premise toward a priority for reparative interventions.

The main argument for the consequential position is that the reasons for the restorative option, which I will develop later in this chapter, do not vanish after severe crimes or when a dialogue between victim and offender appears to be unsatisfying, undesirable, or impossible. The need for reparation remains following serious crimes provoking severe victimization, heavy public indignation, and feelings that we are unsafe. And the punitive response to such acts still is exclusionary, destructive, and mostly ineffective.[9] Moreover, the impossibility of organizing a satisfying dialogue between the direct stakeholders does not exclude the victim's profound yearning for vindication and reparation, and the offender's possible regret and wish for a second chance through reparative gestures.

Consequentialism is not monopolism, though. Restoration/reparation is not always possible or sometimes only partially possible. Basically, two kinds of limits exist:

1. Concerns for public safety. Risks of serious reoffending or risks of revenge by the victims or their family may reduce the space for restorative actions.
2. The mental capacities of the stakeholders. It is, for example, difficult to include very young children in a restorative encounter. Victims may be too shocked by the event to be involved constructively in such encounter. Or some offenders may be in a state of mind that excludes them from having a meaningful dialogue or making reparative gestures.

But even such cases do not completely exclude any possibility for reparative actions. Dialogues may become possible in the longer term. The priority for dialogue and concertation may be released in favor of imposed sanctions,

[9] Matthew Altman, for example, is sensitive to the benefits restorative justice can offer, but he alleges: "For many crimes, especially the most serious, there is still a need for more traditional punishments, including hard treatment" (2021, 251). In my view, the priority of reparative dimensions in the judicial sanction should still prevail.

which then also can be imposed with an eye to the possible reparative impact. An imprisoned offender may be encouraged to undertake reparative gestures, even if direct contact with the victim is not possible.

Both the narrower focus on responding to crime and the characterization of restorative justice through the objective to restore/repair lead to the following definition of restorative justice:

> an option for doing justice after the occurrence of an offence that is primarily oriented towards repairing the individual, relational and social harm caused by that offence. (Walgrave 2008, 21)

I have called it an "espresso-definition" (Walgrave 2008, 2021). Like an espresso, it is at once short, because it is strictly limited to its core of doing justice after the occurrence of a crime, and strong, because it pushes the restorative way consequentially through to penetrate the judicial procedures and sanctions. All options and actions that aim at putting right (as far as possible) crime-caused harm are included in restorative justice. Options and actions that do not address these harms are excluded from being restorative justice, though they may be respectable and worthwhile.

1.3 Emerging Contours of a Restorative Criminal Justice System

Criminal justice is the ultimate line of defense for social institutions to preserve the quality of social life. Currently, it seeks to ensure safety by trying to enforce conformity through fear and obedience, provoked by deterrence and punishment. Consequential restorative justice switches this up. It seeks commitment through inclusion and peace, pursued by persuasion and an attempt to repair to the greatest extent possible the losses caused by offending. The long-term objective is to modify current penal criminal justice practices into a restorative criminal justice system.

Some legislation, especially in youth justice, is now already heading in a restorative justice direction. However, even on an optimistic account, the achievement of a consequential restorative criminal justice system lies far in the future. It is a long-term goal based on growing experience, inspired by continuous socio-ethical and juridical reflection, oriented by social scientific research, driven by out-of-the-box thinking and experimenting.

Restorative justice law enforcement has often been positioned in a pyramid (Braithwaite 2002; Dignan 2002; Walgrave 2008). The broad bottom provides wide opportunities for deliberation on resolving conflicts and injustices in the community, offered in schools, neighborhoods, workplaces, and so on. At the narrow top is a reduced possibility for judicial incapacitation of dangerous and recalcitrant offenders, where traditional judicial procedures lead to proportionate sentences and reparative gestures are subsidiary to security needs.

Between the bottom and the top of this pyramid is the work area for a restorative criminal justice system in the strict sense. It has modalities to increase or decrease pressure and coercion, depending on possibilities and the willingness of stakeholders; it is always primarily oriented to achieving reparation. In the pyramid, "the rights/procedural justice discourse percolates down into restorative justice conferences," and restorative justice concerns "bubble up the pyramid into legal discourse and procedures" (Braithwaite and Parker 1999, 116).

Coercion is also implicitly present at the bottom. The stakeholders know that the victim, the community of care, the wider community, and, finally, the criminal justice system may expect, demand and, if necessary, enforce a gesture of reparation. This knowledge has an influence on even the most freely accepted deliberative level. For the victim, it is reassuring that victimization is never tolerated and must be repaired. For the offender, it makes clear that they will not escape taking responsibility. For both, it is reassuring to know that the legal framework keeps the response within limits. For the community at large, it confirms that the authorities take offending seriously.

If deliberation between the main stakeholders is not possible or is unsatisfactory, judicial intervention is considered, which must also primarily serve the reparative objective. When it is favorable for restoration and possible in terms of public security, the cases should be left with, or given back to, the less coercive levels. This presupposes a moderated and reserved attitude in the coercive justice system. The criminal justice system must transform its premise and procedures in view of proportionate punishments into a coherent priority for restoration in processing and in sanctioning.

What such a restorative criminal justice system would look like is a matter of ongoing reflection. Recognizing similarities with the current criminal justice system, I have suggested some crucial differences (Walgrave 2008):

1. A restorative criminal justice system emphasizes the harm criterion in the selection of conduct to be criminalized.
2. Victim support moves from the margins of the system to the first line of the response to crime.
3. Criminal investigation not only focuses on establishing the facts and the guilt, but also on the harm suffered and on the willingness of the stakeholders for deliberation with the other party.

4. Procedures prioritize deliberation among the main stakeholders, if possible.
5. All stages of the criminal justice procedures provide exits toward deliberation among the main stakeholders and/or space for such deliberation under more direct judicial mandate.
6. Sanctions primarily address the possible reparative impact for all kinds of harms at the individual, relational, and collective levels.[10]

Consequential restorative justice, including also reparative judicial sanctions, faces three challenges. First, protagonists of a process-based view of restorative justice fear that judicial sanctions will lose their reparative character and turn into being punishments, including all the negative implications they have. Second, penal theorists state that punishing crime is needed as a moral imperative or as an indispensable instrument to safeguard social life. Third, penal theorists also fear that replacing punishment as the mainstream response to offending will lose the ground for developing legal safeguards. I will now deal with these three challenges.

2 Essential Differences between Consequential Restorative Justice and Punishment

For those who have committed an offense, participation in a restorative justice encounter can be a hard experience. Contrary to traditional procedures and court sessions, such encounters include direct personal confrontations, often provoking sequences of intense, unpleasant emotions such as shame, guilt, embarrassment, and humiliation (Harris et al. 2004). Carrying out the agreements may also require serious and unpleasant commitments. Therefore, several scholars consider restorative justice as an alternative punishment, not an alternative to punishment (Duff 1992; Daly 2002). From an opposite standpoint, Paul McCold (2000) criticizes the "maximalist" version of restorative justice (currently the "consequential" version), because he alleges that accepting coercive judicial sanctions as potentially reparative reintroduces punishment into restorative justice.

[10] It would go beyond the scope of this chapter to discuss other scholars who also explore possible tracks to switch criminal justice from being primarily oriented at inflicting the correct proportionate punishment on the offender toward seeking a reasonable reparation/restoration to benefit the victim, the community, and the offender. See, for example, Dignan (2002), Mazzucato (2017), Rossner (2019), and Claessen (2020).

2.1 Punishment

The literature offers many definitions of criminal punishment.[11] In a recent article, Christian Gade (2021) distinguishes nine dimensions considered differently in the many definitions of punishment. Inspired by some of the most quoted views (Benn 1958; Hart 1960; von Hirsch 1993), I consider criminal punishment as *the intentional infliction of suffering by a person or an institution with legal power to do so, on somebody, as a response to a behavior that is considered undesirable by the inflictor*. Painfulness is essential in punishment. Looking for painless punishments, as a few scholars do, is like looking for dry water.

The pain is intended by the punisher. It is not the pain experienced by the punished. If a juvenile, for example, feels his punishment by a court mainly as a source of prestige among his peers, it is still a punishment. Inversely, if an offender finds a rehabilitative or reparative sanction hard to comply with and calls it "a punishment," it is not necessarily a punishment.

The pain is inflicted because the punished individual has committed an undesirable behavior. The undesirability is judged by the one who inflicts the pain. It is the punisher who judges a behavior to be undesirable and who wants the offender to suffer for it.

Only persons or institutions with legal power to do so can inflict punishment. The power is given according to strict legal procedures. If this legal power is lacking, the judgment and the response can be considered a kind of revenge and/or abuse of power.

Several scholars also include the blaming dimension in their definition of punishment (as, for example, von Hirsch 1993).[12] For some, the blame could even be the most painful element of the punishment. While punishment may indeed be imbued with a moral dimension, I do not believe it is essential. Many criminal punishments are just settlements. Malcolm Feeley and Jonathan Simon (1992), for example, describe "actuarial justice" as a kind of risk management. Punished offenders then do not experience any moral communication but only feel a painful price to pay.

[11] I speak of criminal punishment only here. Punishment in informal settings such as in family or school, for example, are of a different kind. The relation between the punisher and the punished is more informal and often imbued with a dimension of affection. That makes the potential impact of punishment also completely different (Walgrave 2001).

[12] For Erin Kelly (2018), morally blaming the act is the most important basis for retributive punishment. But according to her, offenders' social circumstances and/or psychological capacities may reduce seriously the blameworthiness of their acts, which undermines the moral ground for retributive punishment. As an alternative, Kelly looks for a justice-oriented approach aimed at harm reduction.

2.2 Restorative Justice Does Not Include Punishment

Considering all painful obligations imposed after a censured behavior as punishments rests upon a double confusion. Contrary to punishments, reparative sanctions do not intentionally inflict pain. Obliging someone to repair or compensate for the damage caused by their conduct is not the same as intentionally imposing pain as a kind of "streamlined revenge." For example, having an offender serve in the kitchen of a community house as a form of compensation for the commotion caused in the community is a symbolic compensation, understandable for all stakeholders and for the community. That is not the case with serving jail time or paying a fine. Moreover, it should be noted that the distinction between punishment and compensation is also included in conventional criminal justice. On top of a punishment, the judge can instruct an offender to compensate the victim. This payment is painful, but it is formally not a punishment.

Although the painfulness of an obligation to repair is not intended, reparative sanctions must also reckon with their painfulness, but only as a secondary consideration. The painfulness can only be an argument to decrease the sanction, and never to increase it, so as to prevent it from placing an unreasonably heavy burden on the one who must repair. In punishment, on the contrary, painfulness is explicitly pursued. The degree of painfulness is the primary standard to increase or decrease the punishment in the pursuit of what is considered proportionality.

A second distinction is that punishment and restoration are at different levels. Punishment is a means, while restoration/reparation is a goal. Punishment in conventional criminal justice is the *a priori* tool. It is an act of power to express disapproval, possibly to enforce compliance. In contrast, restoration/reparation is not a tool, but a pursued outcome. Restoring a broad range of harm and suffering is the objective, for which a variety of social and legal tools may be chosen, such as dialogue, persuasion, social pressure, and reparative sanctions. Theoretically, punishment can also be a tool for reparation, but, as we shall see, it is not the most effective tool for achieving it.

Whether we consider restorative justice sanctions as punishments has important socio-ethical implications. It is part of life that having to comply with social obligations may be painful. But all ethical systems reject willfully inflicting pain on another person, unless it is necessary for some higher purpose. The Golden Rule, "do not do to others that which you would not want others to do to you" (Claessen 2010; London 2011), is applicable also in judging about how to respond to criminal behavior. If punishment as the intentional infliction of pain can be avoided, it is ethically imperative to do so.

Anger and revenge may be psychologically understandable emotions, but the consequent inclination to inflict pain on the offender is ineffective and unethical (Nussbaum 2016).

Therefore, calling restorative sanctions alternative punishments ignores the distinction between the intentional infliction of pain and the painfulness of social obligations, while this distinction draws a crucial socio-ethical line (see also Christie 1981). "Given that punishment harms both offenders and non-offenders, and given that it is very costly, there is every reason to seek alternatives" (Tadros 2013, 40). That is exactly what restorative justice is seeking.[13]

3 Is Punishment Needed?

For penal theorists, restorative justice misses an indispensable element in the governing of social life: punishment. Traditionally, retributivists argue that punishing crime is morally imperative; instrumentalists consider punishment a crucial tool to safeguard social life.[14] The many variations and complications of these basic statements seem to lead to a growing awareness that they cannot be maintained as opposites (Davis 2009; Tadros 2013; Wall 2018; Altman 2021). Pure retributivism leads to the absurd situation that an expensive and grievous criminal justice system would be kept in place without any controlling objective. Mere instrumentalism risks yielding loss of reasonable safeguards and draconian punishments. That is why it may be better to speak of retributivist arguments and instrumentalist expectations.[15]

3.1 Retributivist Arguments

Retributivist arguments follow Kant's position that punishing crime is a categorical imperative. Several moralistic and/or legalistic constructs are presented, such as, for example, those highlighting the expressive function of

[13] Distinguishing clearly between restorative sanctions and punishment also has strategic implications. Certainly, in the current era of punitive populism, accepting restorative justice as alternative punishment leads to accepting punishment *tout court*. The adjective "restorative" in "restorative punishment" would fade quickly, leading to the gradual "domestication" of restorative justice's fundamentally innovative appeal (Walgrave 2021).

[14] The literature offers other terms, speaking of retributivist, conceptual, deontological, internal versus instrumentalist, consequentialist, utilitarian, and external theories, among others. Because the nuances are not always clear and terms are often used interchangeably, I stick in this contribution to the two traditional approaches.

[15] I cannot extrapolate here on the variations and nuances in the rich field of penal theories but must confine myself to the basics needed to position restorative justice in relation to the penal premise.

criminal punishment (seeing it as a public moral denunciation of the act, as in von Hirsch 1993) or those advancing the fairness argument (seeing punishment as a way to rebalance benefits and burdens, as in Morris 1968).

Retributivism is backward-looking. Punishment is inflicted because of an act committed in the past. All criteria for punishing—the commitment of the legally forbidden act, the seriousness of the act, the guilt of the actor—are situated in the past and are available for the necessary checks and balances at the moment of sentencing. The retrospective dimension of retributivism offers the grounds for constructing legal safeguards.

It is, however, strange that the retributivist arguments, based on a moral vision, remain vague about the social morals criminal punishment is supposed to defend. It does not argue why, for example, criminal justice focuses on preserving individual possession and physical integrity, and focuses less on preserving social justice. This obscurity about the values it safeguards makes retributivist punishment vulnerable to being misused as an act of power to enforce discipline in any type of regime, in constitutional democracies but also in the most severe dictatorships (Walgrave 2005).

Still, the public censure of socially harmful behavior is necessary. By declaring conduct legally punishable, authorities proclaim publicly that such acts are not acceptable in their political community. Criminal justice is a beacon of social disapproval. By investigating a crime and prosecuting the alleged offender, authorities express that they take seriously the transgression of norms. The political community enforces legal norms.

The question is whether the intentional infliction of pain is indispensable to publicly disapprove of an offense. While the public receives the disapproving message, it also observes "the dark side" of social institutions (Mazzucato 2017, 243). If punishment is inflicted without obvious necessity, it is destructive for social trust in those institutions. As we will see, the rise of restorative justice is a challenge in that respect. Consequential restorative justice also displays a clearly disapproving message. It leaves space for deliberation among the stakeholders about possible restoration, but if such deliberation cannot take place, state institutions can intervene to enforce reparative sanctions. Restorative justice also takes law transgression seriously and it does not let it pass without consequences. I shall come back to this issue later in the chapter.

In sum, while Michael Davis rightly observes that "punishment has an important place in every substantial legal system" (2009, 79), that does not answer the fundamental ethical problem mentioned earlier in this chapter. Willfully inflicting pain on one another is to be avoided as much as possible if other responses are feasible. No retributivist theory offers convincing arguments as to why responding to offending would be an exception to this fundamental ethical rule. Inflicting pain on another is an evil that does not miraculously turn into something good simply by calling it a response to lawbreaking.

3.2 Instrumental Expectations

The principal expectation is that the threat of punishment will deter potential offenders from committing criminal acts. Some also believe that punishment may keep an offender from reoffending, by provoking repentance or by inflicting a bad experience that they do not want to suffer again. Punishing an offender would also satisfy vindicative needs in the victim and channel public emotional indignation into rational, proportionate responses.[16]

Ample empirical research is available to check the reality of these expectations, but it is impossible here to extend on it. A short comment must suffice. All in all, empirical evidence does not support the assumptions. In a review of available investigations of deterrence, Daniel Nagin (2013) concludes that it is low. The perceived risk of being caught has some deterrent strength, but not the severity of punishments. Paradoxically, threatening with criminal punishment appears to be more effective to deter white collar crime, even though it is implemented less to prevent such offenses.

Deterrence theory supposes that an individual balances possible benefits and costs before deciding rationally to commit a crime. But most crimes are not the result of cool, intelligent considerations. Moreover, the risks of being caught are low and potential offenders mostly underestimate the risk. The general statement that penal law is needed to deter potential offenders is a doctrinal myth rather than an empirically sustainable theory.

Possible rehabilitative effects of punishing offenders are not empirically confirmed either, despite some nuances in findings linked to the age of the offenders and their previous crime involvement (Andrews and Bonta 2003). In fact, some data suggest that incarceration *increases* the risk of reoffending (Nagin et al. 2009).[17] Results of more recent research[18] also reveal that punishment may be an obstacle in the path toward desistance rather than a support

[16] Incapacitation is often mentioned as a possible effect of criminal punishment, while it is in fact not a punishment in the strict sense. In punishment, pain is inflicted on a person because *they* have committed a punishable act. In incapacitation, a person is incapacitated because *we* are afraid of their conduct. The main question, then, is not whether *they* have committed the act but whether *our* fear is justified.

[17] Comparison with rehabilitative results obtained by restorative processes show better results for the latter (see note 1).

[18] Desistance is a wider concept than reoffending. It also includes the personal motivation and life choices of the (former) offender.

for it (Wright 2017). This is not surprising. Judicial punishment reduces the social prospects of those who undergo it, while having positive social prospects is the most important element for social conformity.

The need for punishment is also located in public perception. As Mark Reiff (2005) argues, the public[19] wants to see the law enforced so that it can rely on it. Indeed, surveys find that most of the population wants offenders to be punished. This is not surprising. Punishing crime is presented by the (judicial) authorities and by the media as evidence, as if it were only natural. The public is scarcely informed about other possible responses to crime. More complex investigations deliver more nuanced results. They show that degrees of punitiveness depend on personal, social demographic, and other variables (Adriaenssen and Aertsen 2015), and that there is considerable support for non-carceral alternatives (Roberts et al. 2003). Recent data indicate that more public awareness of restorative justice tends to increase support for it (Karp and Frank 2016; Ekos Research Associates 2017).

The so-called public opinion is thus not bluntly punitive. Data reveal a more complicated picture. Reiff (2005) is probably right that the population considers law enforcement crucial, but it is not evident that punishment is the only possible way to enforce the law. There is great openness for alternative ways, as long as the risks of reoffending are minimized and attention is paid to the victims' losses.

Understandably, victims feel indignation and anger about their victimization, which may provoke a desire for revenge. Victim surveys thus show high degrees of punitive demands among the victims. But not all victims want the same thing. For some, the victimization is a "threefold attack on herself" (Pemberton 2019, 456), while it is for others just an unpleasant event without an enduring impact. That depends on the kind and seriousness of the victimization but also on individual differences in punitive attitudes (Okimoto et al. 2012). Research that also includes offers of restorative/reparative responses shows that most victims do want offenders to be "held accountable and reprimanded by a formal body," but they do not demand harsh punishment (De Mesmaecker 2011, 325).

Pending more differentiated research, my supposition is that victims mostly want:

1. a public recognition of the injustice done to them,
2. the opportunity to fully express their emotional indignation about the event,

[19] Speaking of "the public" is always risky. Many surveys show great diversity within a population in information, opinions, and options on almost all relevant subjects of life. Statistical majorities may be volatile and hide wiser minorities; mediatized opinions often hide silent majorities.

3. the assurance that everything is done to avoid further victimization, and
4. a decent emotional, relational, and material reparation/compensation.

The punitive demands mentioned in most victim surveys are in fact demands for a formal response to victimization, which most surveys mistakenly identify with a punitive response, due to a lack of information. The zero-sum logic (the more the offender suffers, the more satisfactory for the victim, and vice versa) does not exist in reality (van Stokkom 2013).

There is no doubt that every society needs clear norms and effective norm enforcement. But retributivist arguments or empirical assessments of instrumentalist expectations do not offer convincing arguments as to why punishment should the *a priori* response to achieve that. On the contrary. The arguments are not convincing as to why criminal punishment would be an exception to the rule not to inflict pain on people. The effectiveness of systematic punishment is weak. The expensive and ethically dubious system provokes more defiance among offenders than compliance (Sherman 1993), the priority for punishment puts up obstacles for a decent treatment of the victims, and the system sends a negative exclusionary message to the public at large.

Restorative justice scholarship seeks a fundamental alternative. It explores the possibility of a restorative criminal justice system that would guarantee law enforcement and public safety while giving priority to repairing the harm, suffering, and social commotion caused by crime, and to restoring relations in social life.

4 Restorative Justice and the Law

Because a restorative criminal justice system prioritizes restorative encounters and departs from the punitive premise, it faces serious challenges regarding its legal status (von Hirsch 1998; Feld 1999; Ashworth 2002). Current criminal justice is guided by a series of principles, such as equality, presumption of innocence, due process, right to a defense, proportionality, and so on. These social constructs are meant to safeguard the legal rights of defendants and other players in a procedure that usually ends in the imposition of punishment.

Restorative justice is inspired by another philosophy. It conceptualizes the essentials of crime differently, aims at different goals, involves other key actors, uses dissimilar means, and operates in a distinct social and juridical context.[20]

[20] Restorative justice has been called another paradigm, in analogy with Kuhn's concept applicable to scientific revolutions.

Hence, the principles for a punitive system cannot just be transferred unchanged to a restorative justice system. One cannot play rugby on a soccer pitch. The principles need to be reconsidered and possibly revised, focused at safeguarding the rights of the participants in a procedure with ample space for restorative deliberation among the stakeholders pursuing reparative outcomes.

In both conventional criminal justice and restorative criminal justice, two axioms are to be respected:

1. equivalence of all citizens before the law, and
2. protection of all citizens against abuse of power by social institutions and by co-citizens.

The equality principle, as stated in legal philosophy, needs some nuance. If an illiterate person is subject to the same complicated judicial rules as a defendant with a law degree, if one citizen can afford an expensive and smart lawyer and the other has to do with the cheapest lawyer they can get, and if the rich pay the same fine as the poor, it is "a travesty of equal justice" (Braithwaite 2002, 160). It is like an "equal" tree-climbing contest between a cat and a dog. Equality should better be understood as equivalence (Claes 2004), guaranteeing equal access and equal possibilities before the judiciary, which means that differences in individual capacities are taken into account.

The second axiom, protection against abuse of power, is the very reason for the existence of law. Legal dispositions accord power to the authorities and their institutions to intervene coercively in our lives, but the same dispositions also confine the exertion of power through procedural and other conditions. The most important condition is parsimony (or subsidiarity): wherever and whenever possible, the least coercive intervention must be given priority.

4.1 Restorative Justice as Inversed Constructive Retributivism

The platform on which to erect the legal construct for restorative justice is the conception of restorative justice as inversed retribution (Walgrave 2008). Punitive retribution rejects the breaking of the law, indicates the responsibility (guilt) of the actor, and tries to reestablish a balance. The same three components subsist in restorative justice but in an inverted and more constructive way.

Restorative justice unambiguously disapproves of the criminal act. But contrary to conventional censuring in criminal justice, restorative justice includes the reasons for the disapproval in its intervention. The offender is explicitly confronted with the kind and amount of relational, material, and social harm their conduct has caused. Restorative censuring thus refers to the obligation to respect the quality of social life, rather than making the simple observation that a blameworthy offense has been committed.

Restorative justice also addresses the responsibility of the actor. Conventional justice submits the offender to passive responsibility only. The offender must submit to the punitive consequences imposed by the system. Restorative justice relies on active responsibility. The offender is invited (under pressure) to take active responsibility by making gestures of restoration. Eventually, an imposed sanction may require an active contribution to (symbolic) reparation. The active responsibility is retrospectively invoked because of an offense committed in the past, but the restorative/reparative response is prospectively taken with a view on the quality of social relations in the future.

In punitive retributivism, it is considered fair to take away the illegitimate advantages by imposing on the offender a proportionate amount of suffering (Morris 1968). As a result, the amount of suffering is doubled, but equally spread. Restorative justice, on the contrary, aims to reduce or compensate for the suffering and damage: "Because crime hurts, justice should heal" (Braithwaite 2005, 296). Hence, the idea of restorative justice as reversed retribution. Instead of "just deserts," one could speak now of "just due." Restorative justice asks what debt the offender has taken on by the criminal act and what they can reasonably do to redeem it.

In sum, restorative justice is clear in its censuring and in the indication of the offender's responsibility. But its objective is to reduce the amount of suffering instead of increasing it. It recalls the original meaning of the Latin *retribuere*, a contraction of *re-attribuere*: to give back.

4.2 Constructing Legal Safeguards in Restorative Justice

Recognizing the retributive character of restorative justice connects it to its retrospective dimension. It is the platform on which to construct legal safeguards. Restorative justice looks back to assess whether the facts have been validated, to investigate the guilt of the presumed offender, and to gauge the relation of the kind and intensity of the restorative/reparative response with the seriousness of the crime and the harm caused, and the degree of guilt. These steps are partly taken informally by the participants in a restorative encounter, and they are executed formally in a judicial procedure aiming toward a reparative sanction.

Building legal safeguards on this platform is an ongoing undertaking. More and more countries include fragments of restorative justice in their legislations. An increasing number of innovative practices are carried out by creative practitioners, supported by open-minded judges and lawyers. Ideas and theoretical constructs are designed by enlightened jurists and philosophers. An emerging tradition of empirical research examines the conditions needed to fulfill the promises of restorative justice. All this is contributing to the emergence of a "new architecture of criminal law and criminal justice" (Mazzucato 2017, 243) in which restorative encounters are penetrated by an awareness of justice and judicial coercion is carried out with an eye on possible reparation.

Yet, legal safeguards can never be complete or perfect. Much of the current penal justice rhetoric upholds the illusion of offering a watertight system of checks and balances, but it hides many leaks and stoppages. For example, so-called equality is an illusion in a society where inequality is endemic, the assumed proportionality between an offense and doing time in prison is a dubious social construct, due process is a technical concept that is often not experienced as such by the victims and/or the offenders. Many of the current legal safeguards offered in conventional penal justice are theoretical constructs that do not hold their own in confrontation with reality.

Essentially, crime is an emotional event. Doing justice is a human affair, not an affair of a punishing machine. It may be better to recognize this and to include the emotional dimension in the handling of crime, and keep it into a constructive orientation by promoting, as far as possible, participation of the immediate stakeholders in the attempt to find a constructive solution to the problems created by the crime. Emotions should be given a place to favor the expression of anger and indignation, but also of respect and mutual understanding. It may yield more chances for a sense of procedural justice (Tyler 2006)[21] and mercy (Nussbaum 2016). Not only must justice be done formally, but the stakeholders must also feel that justice is done, which enhances the chances for recovery and compliance.

The judicial frame for these processes is meant to guarantee equivalence for all citizens and to protect them against abuses of power by other citizens or by social institutions. The widening river of restorative practice, juridical and philosophical reflection, and empirical research on restorative justice show increasing credibility and interest in this approach. Making a full-fledged restorative justice system is a long undertaking, in which the contribution by

[21] With "procedural justice," Tyler (2006) refers to the sense "clients" of police and/or the judiciary have that they have been dealt with fairly. This appreciation of the procedure appears to be more decisive for compliance than the outcome of the procedure.

open-minded and creative jurists is indispensable. Good legislation is crucial for the quality of our living together. But good legislation does not rest upon rigid dogmatism. It is based upon a vision of how law and the judiciary can best serve the quality of social life.

5 Conclusion: Restorative Justice as a Step in the Civilization Process?

Elias ([1939] 2000) describes the civilization process as a pathway toward societies and communities with constructive relations among its citizens, avoiding as much as possible the use of violence and coercion. In a civilized society, violence is increasingly concentrated in the hands of the state. Private violence is reduced or even eliminated. David Garland (1990) has focused this view on developments in criminal punishment. Gradually, central states have become more capable of imposing a decent level of law in an orderly way. The death penalty has disappeared in most civilized countries. Torture and other physical violence has been excluded (in principle), and penal regimes have been rationalized and professionalized. Welfare and rehabilitation concerns have penetrated the criminal justice system, its sanctions and regimes. The system has become a "penal welfare complex" (Garland 2001).

Such a description of advancing civilization may seem to be unworldly in the current hardening of social and economic life, where penal populism leads to increasing trends for exclusion and drives political authorities, police, and judicial agencies to more and harsher punishment. Under the circumstances, John Pratt (1998) fears the "decivilizing of punishment."

That may be a too pessimistic view. Cultural developments occur over centuries, with ups and downs. The civilization process is not a deterministic process that unrolls automatically. One could say that "civilization is a verb." It is to be activated by being aware of our options and making conscious choices, bringing civilization under the umbrella of social ethics. Civilizing forces must navigate through the wildly surging waters of social life, oriented by material facts and events, but also by social, ideological, and socio-ethical movements, aiming at communities and societies based on mutual respect and solidarity, driven by actively responsible citizens in the pursuit of this respect and solidarity.

As argued in the very first paragraphs of this chapter, restorative justice rests upon a socio-ethical choice. It is in fact the choice to promote further civilization in criminal justice. There is no reason to believe that the civilization process of criminal punishment, as described originally by Elias ([1939] 2000) and Garland (1990, 2001), has reached its finish. It can continue. After giving the state a monopoly on violence, and after making the use of violence more rational and more moderate, the next step is to reduce as much as possible the use of violence itself in the response to offending. That means giving priority to solutions based on bottom-up deliberation rather than top-down imposed reactions, while keeping clear norm enforcement. Consequential restorative justice is a paradigm that explores consequentially the potential of dealing with the aftermath of crime in such a way. Perhaps a restorative criminal justice system represents another step in civilizing criminal justice (Walgrave 2013).

References

Adriaenssen, An, and Ivo Aertsen. 2015. "Punitive Attitudes: Towards an Operationalisation to Measure Individual Punitivity in a Multidimensional Way." *European Journal of Criminology* 12, no. 1 (January): 92–112.

Altman, Matthew C. 2021. *A Theory of Legal Punishment: Deterrence, Retribution, and the Aims of the State.* London: Routledge.

Andrews, D. A., and James Bonta. 2003. *The Psychology of Criminal Conduct.* 3rd ed. Cincinnati, OH: Anderson.

Ashworth, Andrew. 2002. "Responsibilities, Rights and Restorative Justice." *British Journal of Criminology* 42, no. 3 (Summer): 578–95.

Benn, S. I. 1958. "An Approach to the Problems of Punishment." *Philosophy* 33, no. 127 (October): 325–41.

Bonta, James, Rebecca Jesseman, Tanya Rugge, and Robert Cormier. 2006. "Restorative Justice and Recidivism: Promises Made, Promises Kept?" In *Handbook of Restorative Justice: A Global Perspective*, edited by Dennis Sullivan and Larry Tifft, 108–20. Abingdon, UK: Routledge.

Boutellier, Hans. 2000. *Crime and Morality: The Significance of Criminal Justice in Post-Modern Culture.* Dordrecht: Kluwer.

Braithwaite, John. 2002. *Restorative Justice and Responsive Regulation.* Oxford: Oxford University Press.

———. 2005. "Between Proportionality and Impunity: Confrontation → Truth → Prevention." *Criminology* 43, no. 2 (May): 283–306.

Braithwaite, John, and Christine Parker. 1999. "Restorative Justice Is Republican Justice." In *Restorative Justice for Juveniles: Repairing the Harm by Youth Crime*, edited by Gordon Bazemore and Lode Walgrave, 103–26. Monsey, NY: Criminal Justice.

Braithwaite, John, and Philip Pettit. 1990. *Not Just Deserts: A Republican Theory of Criminal Justice.* Oxford: Oxford University Press.

Christie, Nils. 1977. "Conflicts as Property." *British Journal of Criminology* 17, no. 1 (January): 1–15.

———. 1981. *Limits to Pain: The Role of Punishment in Penal Policy.* Oxford: Martin Robertson.

Claes, Erik. 2004. "Punitieve rechtshandhaving, herstelrecht en menselijke gelijkwaardigheid." In *Straf en herstel: Ethische reflecties over strafdoeleinden*, edited by Bas van Stokkom, 229–53. The Hague: Boom.

Claessen, Jacques. 2010. *Misdaad en straf: Een herbezinning op het strafrecht van mystiek perspectief.* Nijmegen, NL: Wolf Legal Publishers.

———. 2020. "Pleidooi voor en uitwerking van een maximalistisch herstelrecht." *Tijdschrift voor Herstelrecht* 20, no. 4: 18–30.

Cornwell, David. 2009. *The Penal Crisis and the Clapham Omnibus: Questions and Answers in Restorative Justice.* Sherfield on Loddon, UK: Waterside.

Daly, Kathleen. 2002. "Restorative Justice: The Real Story." *Punishment & Society* 4, no. 1 (January): 55–79.

Davis, Michael. 2009. "Punishment Theory's Golden Half Century: A Survey of Developments from (about) 1957 to 2007." *Journal of Ethics* 13, no. 1 (January): 73–100.

Debuyst, Christian. 1990. "Pour introduire une histoire de la criminologie: Les problématiques du départ." *Déviance et Société* 14, no. 4: 347–76.

De Mesmaecker, Vicky. 2011. "Perceptions of Justice and Fairness in Criminal Proceedings and Restorative Encounters: Extending Theories of Procedural Justice." Ph.D. thesis, Katholieke Universiteit (KU) Leuven. https://core.ac.uk/download/pdf/34510494.pdf.

Dignan, Jim. 2002. "Restorative Justice and the Law: The Case for an Integrated, Systemic Approach." In *Restorative Justice and the Law*, edited by Lode Walgrave, 168–90. Cullompton, UK: Willan.

Duff, R. A. 1992. "Alternatives to Punishment – or Alternative Punishments?" In *Retributivism and Its Critics*, edited by Wesley Cragg, 43–68. Stuttgart: Steiner.

———. 2002. "Restorative Punishment and Punitive Restoration." In *Restorative Justice and the Law*, edited by Lode Walgrave, 82–100. Cullompton, UK: Willan.

Ekos Research Associates. 2017. *National Justice Survey: Canada's Criminal Justice System.* Ottawa: Department of Justice Canada. http://publications.gc.ca/site/eng/9.850310/publication.html.

Elias, Norbert. (1939) 2000. *The Civilising Process: Sociogenetic and Psychogenetic Investigations.* Rev. ed. Edited by Eric Dunning, Johan Goudsbloem, and Stephen Mennel. Oxford: Blackwell.

Feeley, Malcolm M., and Jonathan Simon. 1992. "The New Penology: Notes on the Emerging Strategy of Corrections and Its Implications." *Criminology* 30, no. 4 (November): 449–74.

Feld, Barry. 1999. "Rehabilitation, Retribution and Restorative Justice." In *Restorative Justice for Juveniles: Repairing the Harm by Youth Crime*, edited by Gordon Bazemore and Lode Walgrave, 17–44. Monsey, NY: Criminal Justice.

Gade, Christian B. N. 2021. "Is Restorative Justice Punishment?" *Conflict Resolution Quarterly* 38, no. 3 (Spring): 127–55.
Garland, David. 1990. *Punishment and Modern Society: A Study in Social Theory*. Chicago: University of Chicago Press.
———. 2001. *The Culture of Control: Crime and Social Order in Contemporary Society*. Oxford: Oxford University Press.
Harris, Nathan, Lode Walgrave, and John Braithwaite. 2004. "Emotional Dynamics in Restorative Conferences." *Theoretical Criminology* 8, no. 2 (May): 191–210.
Hart, H. L. A. 1960. "Prolegomenon to the Principles of Punishment." *Proceedings of the Aristotelian Society* 60, no. 1 (June): 1–26.
Johnstone, Gerry. 2020. "Voluntariness, Coercion and Restorative Justice: Questioning the Orthodoxy." *International Journal of Restorative Justice* 3, no. 2: 157–67.
Karp, David, and Olivia Frank. 2016. "Anxiously Awaiting the Future of Restorative Justice in the United States." *Victims and Offenders* 11, no. 1: 1–21.
Kelly, Erin I. 2018. *The Limits of Blame: Rethinking Punishment and Responsibility*. Cambridge, MA: Harvard University Press.
Llewelyn, Jennifer. 2021. "A Restorative Approach for Social and System Transformation." *International Journal of Restorative Justice* 4, no. 3: 374–95.
London, Ross. 2011. *Crime, Punishment, and Restorative Justice: From the Margins to the Mainstream*. Boulder, CO: First Forum.
Maruna, Shadd. 2014. "The Role of Wounded Healing in Restorative Justice: An Appreciation of Albert Eglash." *Restorative Justice: An International Journal* 2, no. 1: 9–23.
Maxwell, Joseph. 1914. *Le concept social du crime: Son évolution*. Paris: Alcan.
Mazzucato, Claudia. 2017. "Restorative Justice and the Potential of 'Exemplarity': In Search of a 'Persuasive' Coherence within Criminal Justice." In *Critical Restorative Justice*, edited by Ivo Aertsen and Brunilda Pali, 241–58. Oxford: Hart.
McCold, Paul. 2000. "Toward a Holistic Vision of Restorative Justice: A Reply to the Maximalist Model." *Contemporary Justice Review* 3, no. 4 (December): 357–414.
Morris, Herbert. 1968. "Persons and Punishment." *Monist* 52, no. 4 (October): 475–501.
Nagin, Daniel S. 2013. "Deterrence in the Twenty-First Century." In *Crime and Justice – A Review of Research*, vol. 42: *Crime and Justice in America: 1975–2025*, edited by Michael Tonry, 199–263. Chicago: University of Chicago Press.
Nagin, Daniel S., Francis T. Cullen, and Cheryl Lero Jonson. 2009. "Imprisonment and Reoffending." In *Crime and Justice – A Review of Research*, vol. 38, edited by Michael Tonry, 115–200. Chicago: University of Chicago Press.
Nussbaum, Martha C. 2016. *Anger and Forgiveness: Resentment, Generosity, Justice*. New York: Oxford University Press.
Okimoto, Tyler G., Michael Wenzel, and N. T. Feather. 2012. "Retribution and Restoration as General Orientations towards Justice." *European Journal of Personality* 26, no. 3 (May/June): 255–75.

O'Mahoney, David, and Jonathan Doak. 2017. *Reimagining Restorative Justice: Agency and Accountability in the Criminal Process.* Oxford: Hart.
Pemberton, Antony. 2019. "Time for a Rethink: Victims and Restorative Justice." *International Journal of Restorative Justice* 2, no. 1: 13–33.
Pratt, John. 1998. "Towards the 'Decivilizing' of Punishment?" *Social & Legal Studies* 7, no. 4 (December): 487–515.
Reiff, Mark R. 2005. *Punishment, Compensation, and Law: A Theory of Enforceability.* Cambridge: Cambridge University Press.
Roberts, Julian V., Loretta J. Stalans, David Indermaur, and Mike Hough. 2003. *Penal Populism and Public Opinion: Lessons from Five Countries.* Oxford: Oxford University Press.
Rossner, Meredith. 2019. "Restorative Justice, Anger, and the Transformative Energy of Forgiveness." *International Journal of Restorative Justice* 2, no. 3: 368–84.
Sherman, Lawrence W. 1993. "Defiance, Deterrence, and Irrelevance: A Theory of the Criminal Sanction." *Journal of Research in Crime and Delinquency* 30, no. 4 (November): 445–73.
Sherman, Lawrence W., and Heather Strang. 2007. *Restorative Justice: The Evidence.* London: Smith Institute. https://www.iirp.edu/pdf/RJ_full_report.pdf.
Sullivan, Dennis, and Larry Tifft. 2006. "Introduction: The Healing Dimension of Restorative Justice: A One-World Body." In *Handbook of Restorative Justice: A Global Perspective*, edited by Dennis Sullivan and Larry Tifft, 1–16. Abingdon, UK: Routledge.
Suzuki, Masahiro, and Xiaoyu Yuan. 2021. "How Does Restorative Justice Work? A Qualitative Metasynthesis." *Criminal Justice and Behavior* 48, no. 10 (October): 1347–65.
Tadros, Victor. 2013. *The Ends of Harm: The Moral Foundations of Criminal Law.* Oxford: Oxford University Press.
Tyler, Tom R. 2006. "Restorative Justice and Procedural Justice: Dealing with Rule Breaking." *Journal of Social Issues* 62, no. 2 (June): 307–26.
Van Ness, Daniel W., and Karen Heetderks Strong. 2002. *Restoring Justice: An Introduction to Restorative Justice.* 2nd ed. Cincinnati, OH: Anderson.
van Stokkom, Bas. 2013. "Victims' Needs and Participation in Justice: Is There a Role for Vengeance?" *Restorative Justice: An International Journal* 1, no. 2: 168–89.
von Hirsch, Andrew. 1993. *Censure and Sanctions.* Oxford: Oxford University Press.
———. 1998. "Penal Theories." In *The Handbook of Crime and Punishment,* edited by Michael Tonry, 659–82. Oxford: Oxford University Press.
von Hirsch, Andrew, and Nils Jareborg. 1991. "Gauging Criminal Harm: A Living-Standard Analysis." *Oxford Journal of Legal Studies* 11, no. 1 (Spring): 1–38.
Walgrave, Lode. 2001. "On Restoration and Punishment: Favourable Similarities and Fortunate Differences." In *Restorative Justice for Juveniles: Conferencing, Mediation and Circles*, edited by Allison Morris and Gabriele Maxwell, 17–37. Oxford: Hart.

———. 2005. "Retributivism and the Quality of Social Life: A Reply to Duff." In *Punishment, Restorative Justice and the Morality of Law*, edited by Erik Claes, René Foqué, and Tony Peters, 145–56. Antwerp: Intersentia.

———. 2008. *Restorative Justice, Self-Interest and Responsible Citizenship*. Abingdon, UK: Routledge.

———. 2013. "From Civilising Punishment to Civilising Criminal Justice: From Punishment to Restoration." In *Civilising Criminal Justice: An International Restorative Agenda for Penal Reform*, edited by David J. Cornwell, John Blad, and Martin Wright, 347–77. Hook, UK: Waterside.

———. 2021. *Being Consequential about Restorative Justice*. The Hague: Eleven.

Walgrave, Lode, Tony Ward, and Estelle Zinsstag. 2021. "When Restorative Justice Meets the Good Lives Model: Contributing to a Criminology of Trust." *European Journal of Criminology* 18, no. 3 (May): 444–60.

Wall, Jesse. 2018. "Public Wrongs and Private Wrongs." *Canadian Journal of Law & Jurisprudence* 31, no. 1 (February): 177–96.

Ward, Tony, Kathryn J. Fox, and Melissa Garber. 2014. "Restorative Justice, Offender Rehabilitation and Desistance." *Restorative Justice: An International Journal* 2, no. 1: 24–42.

Weitekamp, Elmar G. M. 1999. "History of Restorative Justice." In *Restorative Juvenile Justice: Repairing the Harm by Youth Crime*, edited by Gordon Bazemore and Lode Walgrave, 75–102. Monsey, NY: Criminal Justice.

Wright, Serena. 2017. "Narratives of Punishment and Frustrated Desistance in the Life of Repeatedly Criminalized Women." In *New Perspectives on Desistance: Theoretical and Empirical Developments*, edited by Emily Luise Hart and Esther F. J. C. van Ginneken, 11–35. London: Palgrave Macmillan.

Zehr, Howard. 2002. "Journey to Belonging." In *Restorative Justice: Theoretical Foundations*, edited by Elmar G. M. Weitekamp and Hans-Jürgen. Kerner, 21–31. Cullompton, UK: Willan.

29

Punitive Restoration

Thom Brooks

1 Introduction

Restorative justice is a large tent of diverse practices where the main aim is to restore, or heal, wrongdoing and its effects. It is practiced in various contexts ranging from schools to Truth and Reconciliation Mediation. One especially promising application of restorative justice is in criminal justice as an alternative to using formal trials, which this chapter will focus on. The appeal is in the evidence that restorative justice can deliver up to one-quarter less reoffending and higher victim satisfaction at significant cost savings in comparison to using formal trials.

The problem for restorative justice approaches is they face several difficulties in being used more widely in criminal justice, and so embedding its many positives further. Restorative justice is usually limited to only less serious offenses and mostly those by youth offenders—its use is then primarily for minors doing minor crimes.

The probable reason for this limitation is the concern that going further would not have public confidence This is because *traditional* restorative justice approaches rule out any use of imprisonment and other forms of hard treatment. The concern is that, while restorative practices might be more effective

T. Brooks (✉)
Durham University, Durham, UK
e-mail: thom.brooks@durham.ac.uk

© The Author(s), under exclusive license to Springer Nature Switzerland AG 2023

M. C. Altman (ed.), *The Palgrave Handbook on the Philosophy of Punishment*, Palgrave Handbooks in the Philosophy of Law, https://doi.org/10.1007/978-3-031-11874-6_29

and much less costly than the alternative, it might be viewed as too soft an option and fail to attract sufficient popular support.

This chapter will provide a brief survey of restorative justice's wide tent, the diversity of approaches within it, and the evidence for its success. It will then turn to the limitations of these approaches, both theoretical and practical. The chapter then considers a way forward that I call *punitive restoration*, a form of restorative justice that allows for more ways of providing support for offenders, including where hard treatment might be effective, and tougher sanctions where restorative arrangements are breached. Punitive restoration rejects the view of other mainstream restorative approaches that hard treatment can never provide rehabilitative or other support to offenders. At the same time, punitive restoration shows a way of embedding restorative justice that is true to its foundational principles, fulfills the many benefits, commands wider public support for its use, and, in so doing, provides a more viable form of restoration that can achieve the overall restorative aim of reducing punitiveness in the criminal justice system while improving effectiveness.

2 Restorative Justice's Promise

Restorative justice is a term that refers to a variety of approaches rather than a single practice (Braithwaite 2002; Brooks 2021, 76–101). Generally speaking, all such approaches favor informal dialogues over a formal process, ensuring that those involved have a voice, whether victim or offender. However, the different restorative formats have varying views on how to achieve their aims, disagreeing on what is "restored" and the desired goals (Johnstone and Van Ness 2007, 5). This diversity of what restorative justice "is" and seeks to achieve can make it difficult to speak of restorative justice as a singular approach. Joanna Shapland, Gwen Robinson, and Angela Sorsby claim that the "very broad range of practices and approaches" makes "a definitive definition ... elusive" (2011, 4; see also Cunneen and Hoyle 2010). For example, restorative approaches are used in schools (Morrison 2007), prison interventions (Van Ness 2007), and South Africa's Truth and Reconciliation Commission (Llewellyn and Howse 1999). Restorative justice approaches are also found in applications that are the focus of this essay: restorative justice as an *alternative* to traditional sentencing, including victim-offender mediation and restorative conferencing. Most of my attention will be directed to its uses in England and Wales, but the points raised are intended to apply more widely to other jurisdictions.

The golden thread, or "conceptual umbrella," that all restorative approaches share is their aim at bringing closure to conflicts through informal, but not unstructured, deliberation (Shapland et al. 2011, 4). This is believed to enable understanding that contributes to healing. The best-known working definition is by T. F. Marshall in his report for the U.K.'s Home Office: "*Restorative justice is a process whereby all parties with a stake in a particular offence come together to resolve collectively how to deal with the aftermath of the offence and its implications for the future*" (1999, 5). Marshall signals the sharp difference between restorative justice approaches and traditional sentencing. The latter is a formal process where judges decide sentencing outcomes from their courtrooms following official procedures, whereas restorative justice is an informal process that is more inclusive and collective.

Restorative justice approaches provide an alternative process where victims can regain their voice, such as in victim-offender mediation or restorative conferences. These approaches are led by a trained facilitator rather than a judge or magistrate. The meetings are held in a space like an informal office conference room, not a court. These meetings require the consent of offenders and victims to take part—and, critically, they require the offender to admit guilt for the meeting to take place. While legal representation is permitted, they are not normally present, and offenders are expected to engage directly with those present rather than through a lawyer.

Each meeting begins with the facilitator making clear the parameters and purposes of the gathering. There is guidance and training available via a recognized national body, the Restorative Justice Council (2020). The victim speaks next, addressing the offender with an opportunity to explain the impact of the crime. In a conference setting, members of the victim's support network, such as friends and family, typically follow next, alongside any attending members of the local community. Each discusses the impact of the crime on them. The offender speaks last and is expected to apologize to the victim and account for the crimes committed.

After each has spoken, the meetings conclude with participants agreeing to a "restorative contract" that the offender is also asked to accept. The contract's contents are tailored to the needs of the specific individual, but typically they include some combination of community service hours, paid restitution, and, where appropriate, required meetings for cognitive behavioral therapy and/or drug and alcohol treatment, among other outcomes.

There are consequences for non-compliance. If the offender does not fulfill the contract in full, then either the offender is sent to attend court and undergo the traditional formal process to address crimes or, on occasion, a second restorative meeting may be held to try again with a new restorative contract. The differences are that going to court is more likely to lead to more punitive outcomes, including the possibility of time in prison. By agreeing to the restorative process, the offender has the opportunity to definitely avoid prison if a restorative contract can be agreed to and fulfilled in full. It is noteworthy that an offender who admits guilt in accepting a restorative contract, but does not fulfill its terms in the allotted time and so breaches it, is able to plead not guilty in court without prejudice—which is a concern discussed further in the next section.

Restorative justice has become an increasingly popular process because of the evidence in its beneficial results. First, most restorative meetings end successfully, with up to 98 percent ending in a restorative contract accepted by all participants (Shapland et al. 2007, 27; see also Shapland et al. 2006). Second, such contracts reduce reoffending up to 25 percent better than alternatives (Shapland et al. 2008; Restorative Justice Council 2011). This success is achieved by targeting offenders' specific needs through greater flexibility in determining outcomes. These outcomes may include requirements that offenders attend treatment to overcome their substance abuse or problems with anger management, participate in training to improve employability and general life skills, compensate the victim, and often receive some element of community sentencing. Third, restorative justice is cheaper than traditional trials. One study found that using restorative justice could save £9 for every £1 spent (Shapland et al. 2008; Restorative Justice Council 2011).

Restorative approaches significantly improve outcomes associated with victim displacement. It has been a growing concern that the formal trial process exacerbates victim displacement from the system, with most cases closed through a plea deal and few opportunities for victims to share their voice, if they wanted to (Brooks, forthcoming). John Gardner says:

> we seem to have lost sight of the origins of the criminal law as a response to the activities of *victims*, together with their families, associates and supporters. The blood feud, the vendetta, the duel, the revenge, the lynching: for the elimination of these modes of retaliation, more than anything else, the criminal law as we know it today came into existence. (1998, 31)

Gardner correctly notes how much of the development of criminal justice has moved victims from being at the center of a dispute to the periphery. This shift was aimed at ensuring that criminal justice was more consistent and transparent. But, for some, this shift has gone too far, to the point where victims are mostly silent bystanders. Nils Christie argues:

> The victim is a particularly heavy loser in this situation. Not only has he suffered, lost materially or become hurt, physically or otherwise. And not only does the state take the compensation. But above all he has lost participation in his own case. It is the [state] that comes into the spotlight, not the victim. It is the [state] that describes the losses, not the victim. (1998, 314)

Restorative justice approaches attempt to address this shift by bringing the victim back into the criminal justice system and giving them a voice. Unsurprisingly, victims report high satisfaction when participating in restorative meetings, as do offenders (Shapland et al. 2008, 25–26). This is in marked contrast with reported experiences of alienation and general frustration from victims for cases heard in courtrooms. Whereas victims rarely get any opportunity to participate in our courts, they are encouraged to take part in restorative meetings—and this has helped many more victims find closure in a safe and constructive environment. Their dialogue with offenders in restorative meetings facilitates this—and tackling reoffending by offenders is served, in part, from their hearing directly from victims about how the crimes have impacted them.

3 Restorative Limitations

Restorative justice appears to deliver significant benefits for victim satisfaction, reducing reoffending and saving public money. This naturally raises the issue of why restorative justice is not used more widely so these benefits could have greater impact on the criminal justice system overall. This section will identify some of the key limitations that have restricted the use of restorative justice.

Restorative justice's use is limited to mostly minor crimes by youth offenders, and it is only rarely used for adults (Brooks 2021, 76–101). This means that restorative justice does not represent a full-scale alternative to punishment like retributivism or deterrence, as the former is only applied to a relatively small number of offenders (79–80). The restricted ambit of restorative justice is likely related to the fact that its use prohibits the possibility of hard treatment. This restriction is likely why it is not used for more serious offenses or more adult offenders, as it might be seen as too "soft" an option for those offenses and offenders. So, even if restorative justice *could* bring wider benefits to the criminal justice system, the problem is that it is not seen as a viable option for more than minor offenses by minors.

The concern about what is (or is not) politically palatable lurks in the background. There are too many examples of penal policies that have enjoyed popular support but are ineffective or counterproductive—hence highlighting that popularity may not align with effectiveness, especially in criminal justice matters. Perhaps the most prominent examine is California's so-called "Three Strikes and You're Out" laws. These require any offender convicted of a third eligible criminal offense to face a minimum of twenty-five years imprisonment (Cullen et al. 2000; Zimring et al. 2001).

The major problem with these populist penal policies is that they have led to an explosion not in crime, but in a fast-growing prison population. "Three Strikes" filled California's prisons to capacity but had no more than a 2 percent deterrent effect (*Brown v. Plata*, 563 U.S. 493 [2011]; Durlauf and Nagin 2011, 28). Of course, the main thrust of the popular appeal for such punitive policies is the mistaken belief that this will translate into better effects, such as crime reduction at an affordable cost—neither of which is true (Williams 2012).

Restorative justice takes a very different tack. With its roots in the abolitionist movement against the use of prisons generally, restorative justice approaches all reject the use of hard treatment, including imprisonment. As a result, prison is not an option for restorative contracts, nor suspended sentences in the event that the contract is breached (see Ashworth 1994, 833).

The reason for this is that the use of prison is held to be counterproductive to reducing reoffending and enabling any sort of restoration to take place. Imprisonment is so often not the start of someone's legal (and other) difficulties, but a confirmation of them—where bad situations can become even worse. The common risk factors for reoffending include such things as economic insecurity, employment insecurity, financial insecurity, and housing insecurity, to name only a few (Brooks 2021, 72, 96, 163–67, 220–22). These serious problems can often become exacerbated through even brief time spent in prison. Some studies suggest prison is "criminogenic," as it might contribute to a greater, not lower, likelihood of an offender reoffending post-release (Durlauf and Nagin 2011, 14, 21–23; see also Lippke 2007; Tony 2011, 138, 140–41).

While imprisonment can often make it more difficult to combat reoffending in the future, hard treatment need not always make matters worse. The problem is not *that* prison is used at all, but *how* it is used—and its use can and should be improved to better achieve desired outcomes such as reducing future reoffending. Restorative justice advocates are right to highlight the many compelling reasons for using an alternative criminal justice process that tailors outcomes better to the particular needs of specific individuals while avoiding costly and often ineffective hard treatment. Indeed, its "abolitionist" position is often viewed as a strength of these approaches (Braithwaite 2002). Moreover, the deprivation of individual liberty is a most serious matter, so we should think carefully about ways to avoid prison where appropriate. Nonetheless, the issue remains that there will be cases, especially of serious violent offenders, for whom public safety—as well as public opinion—will direct us to support some use of incarceration. To use prison as sparingly as possible to improve outcomes generally is a noble aim of restorative justice, but the failure to include *any* form of hard treatment limits the applicability of restorative justice to more kinds of offenses and offenders—and it denies the use of hard treatment even where it might, in fact, enable restorative justice to flourish in specific cases—thereby undermining the general aim of restorative justice in those instances.

A final issue is the question of what is "restored" through restorative justice. This concern is important because, strictly speaking, restorative justice rejects the use of prison, as it is claimed to be a barrier to "restoration"—and, thus, we must have some understanding of what this means (Johnstone and Van Ness 2007). In my view, this is a contestable empirical claim.

For example, restorative justice aims to restore a damaged relationship between an offender and the wider community. This raises several questions, such as: which community, and who are its members? Many have argued that this claim "remains shrouded in mystery" (Ashworth 2010, 94). Andrew Ashworth says:

> If the broad aim is to restore the 'communities affected by the crime' ..., as well as the victim and the victim's family, this will usually mean a geographical community; but where an offence targets a victim because of race, religion, sexual orientation etc., that will point to a different community that needs to be restored. (2002, 583)

Ashworth insightfully raises two important concerns. The first is the problem that restorative justice approaches have in identifying the relevant community to be "restored," and the second is the problem of how to select representative individuals from whatever community this is to participate in the restorative meeting. This first problem is significant. Restorative justice requires a restoration of the members within that community, but we each identify with multiple and sometimes overlapping communities, so it is unclear how we should choose among them. These communities are rarely static and our identities are not created in a vacuum, suggesting that, even if we could identify "the community," this may be of limited practical benefit for the purposes of achieving restorative justice (see Parekh 2008, 21–26).

A further issue concerns the idea of "restoration" itself. The aim is the restoration of an offender with their community. This aim presupposes that there is some wrong to be made right and that this injustice between affected persons needs closure. If this is true, then it may be unclear why restorative justice demands we limit such restoration to only those instances of crime—as it might be argued that there may be many injustices requiring repair and that restoration could bring benefits even if no crime had taken place. One clear example is the case of restorative approaches used in schools for children to resolve conflicts and promote healing. If this is our goal, then crimes can be incidental to whether restoration is required.

Restorative justice approaches bring several potential benefits that include higher victim satisfaction, more effective crime reduction, and lower costs. These benefits are not without their own costs. Restorative justice approaches are difficult to pinpoint and offer broad comparisons given their diversity, they have limited applicability, they suffer from limited public confidence, they operate with limited options by excluding prison, and they are subject to a serious problem concerning what is "restored" and by which community.[1]

Restorative justice approaches may be worth defending, but we require a new approach to yield the potential benefits while avoiding these obstacles. Otherwise, restorative justice approaches might remain an underutilized resource at the margins of mainstream criminal justice policy. This situation might change if there is a new formulation of restorative justice that could address these challenges.

4 Punitive Restoration: An Alternative Form of Restorative Justice

Let us now consider an alternative, distinctive form of restorative justice called *punitive restoration* (Brooks 2014b; 2021, 83–97). This is a practice taking the form of a restorative conference-like setting where the victim, offender, their support networks, and members of the local community come together. The meeting is *restorative* insofar as its aim is to achieve the restoration of rights infringed or threatened by crime. This is achieved through facilitated dialogue and the making of a tailored restorative contract in the way restorative justice conferencing normally works. But this form of restorative justice is also *punitive* because there is a wider available range of options for this restorative

[1] There is a further concern that there is a gap between the rhetoric of restorative justice approaches and their practical achievements that will not be considered here (Daly 2003, 219).

contract, specifically including forms of hard treatment, such as intensive drug and alcohol treatment in custody, the use of suspended sentences, or brief imprisonment.

The idea of punitive restoration can be sharpened in how it differs from other forms of restorative justice. For example, restorative justice approaches are often criticized for lacking clarity about *what* is restored and *how* it is achieved. Andrew von Hirsch and Andrew Ashworth argue that restorative justice "suffers from unduly sweeping definition of aims and insufficient specifications of limits" with a conceptually incoherent model (2005, 110–11). When bringing "restoration" to a community, most uses of restorative justice leave the community out, because the majority of meetings are conducted as victim-offender mediation.

Punitive restoration has a more specific understanding of "restoration" and how it can be achieved (Brooks 2015). Punitive restoration always includes the community in a conference meeting, as community involvement is key to restoring offenders to their local surroundings. This is justified on grounds of stakeholding: those who have a stake in penal outcomes should have a say in decisions about them (Brooks 2016b). Stakeholders are individuals who have a stake, or interest, in penal outcomes, including the victims (if any), those who support them, and the local community.

This view of stakeholding is embedded in restorative justice's origins. As noted earlier, in the most cited definition of restorative justice from his report for the U.K.'s Home Office, Marshall said: "*Restorative justice is a process whereby parties with a stake in a specific offence collectively resolve how to deal with the aftermath of the offence and its implications for the future*" (1999, 5). Restorative justice has often been understood as a process that brings "stakeholders" together (Braithwaite 2002, 11, 50, 55). Its distinctive form as punitive restoration better guarantees this understanding by promoting the conference meeting instead of victim-offender mediation, as the latter leaves out the important stakeholder of the community.

Relevant stakeholders become more easily identifiable as persons immediately involved or connected with a crime. This does not require *all* such persons to participate, but rather that some opportunities exist for persons beyond the victim and offender to take part. This working idea of a conference setting is without any specific recommendation on capping the number of persons included, although feasibility may render groups of ten or more impractical, as has been found with restorative conferencing generally. The idea is that restoration is not a private affair, but the restoration of a public wrong that impacts the community, too.[2] Moreover, studies have shown that including the community in restorative conferencing contributes to higher participant satisfaction for victims and offenders than victim-offender mediation alone (Shapland et al. 2007, 20). We should take the idea of stakeholding central to restorative justice approaches more seriously and ensure that any restoration of offenders with their community is enabled by including the community—as this is too often not the case.

So, one benefit of punitive restoration is its specifying the restorative process. Restoration is aimed at stakeholders through a conference setting. Furthermore, we should recall that our focus is on alternatives to sentencing: punitive restoration is conceived as an alternative to the formal procedures of the criminal trial and sentencing guidelines. Punitive restoration can then overcome the obstacle of the diversity of restorative approaches. This is because our speaking of "punitive restoration" is linked with a particular informal use of restorative justice as an alternative to the trial and sentencing. We can then better compare the dynamics and outcomes from punitive restoration given the more specified content.

Another benefit is that punitive restoration can better address the needs of the community than alternative restorative approaches. This is because punitive restoration endorses the principle of stakeholding, where those who have a stake should have a say (Brooks 2016c). There is no need to engage in the more difficult task of discerning which type of community is most relevant for "restoration"; rather, we should identify the primary stakeholders and engage them.

Punitive restoration works within several safeguards common to restorative justice practices (Restorative Justice Council 2020). For example, offenders have a right to legal representation throughout the process. All participation by offenders, victims, and others is voluntary. Meetings are chaired and administered by trained facilitators following national guidelines to maintain consistency.

But there is a crucial difference between punitive restoration and other restorative justice approaches in terms of their applicability. The latter are used primarily for minor crimes and are often restricted to youth offenders. This is likely due to their perceived lack of public support for use in more serious offenses, especially violent crimes, as all forms of hard treatment are off the table.

---

[2] One study found that restorative conferences often include friends and family of the victim and of the offender, respectively, in 73 and 78 percent of cases examined. Parents were far more likely to attend restorative conferences (50 percent of offenders and 23 percent of victims) than partners (3 percent of offenders and 5 percent of victims) (Shapland et al. 2007, 20).

However, punitive restoration allows for more penal options, including the use of hard treatment, as it does not assume restoration could never require it. While incarceration often makes successful crime reduction efforts more difficult, it is also clear that prisons can, and should, be transformed to improve their disappointing results (Liebling 2006). For example, restorative contracts regularly include an obligation for offenders to have treatment for any drug or alcohol abuse as well as to participate in programs designed to develop their employability and life skills (Towl 2006). While restorative justice approaches rightly seek to reduce the use of prisons, hard treatment can prove the best environment for some offenders in specific circumstances (Pérez and Jennings 2012).

Prisons can and should be transformed so incarceration does not undermine offender rehabilitation. Short-term imprisonment is associated with high rates of reoffending. This is a significant problem because most offenders receive short-term sentences of less than twelve months and about 60 percent will reoffend within weeks of their release (Brunton-Smith and Hopkins 2013). Most offenders receiving short-term imprisonment do not receive any rehabilitative treatment. This is a major contributing factor to the likelihood that these offenders will reoffend when released from prison.

This problem may be overcome by providing more effective treatment. For example, brief intensive interventions have been employed to address problems associated with drug use, and offenders were found to benefit from "significant gains in knowledge, attitudes and psychosocial functioning" (Joe et al. 2012). These interventions are corrections-based treatment of moderate (thirty outpatient group sessions, three days per week) or high intensity (six-month residential treatment) and found to produce cost savings of 1.8 to 5.7 times the cost of their implementation (Daly et al. 2004). Policies like these suggest that reforming the way prisons are used can support improved offender rehabilitation and post-release crime reduction efforts, but without sacrificing cost savings.

This has importance for punitive restoration because offenders who have more serious needs may require more punitive outcomes than currently available under other restorative approaches, such as intensive interventions in correctional facilities. Hard treatment might play a further role, such as a backup to broken restorative contracts. In England and Wales, an offender who admits guilt and apologizes to victims can then breach their restorative contract without penalty—the alternative is typically starting afresh in the formal trial process. Offenders can even plead "not guilty" without prejudice, despite having had admitted guilt at a restorative meeting. A punitive restoration approach might disallow a not guilty plea for offenders who had agreed to a restorative contract because this undermines the sincerity of their apology to victims and their desire to seek amends. Moreover, contracts might include a suspended sentence for cases of noncompliance. This option would extend the flexibility of punitive restoration to more varieties of offense-types and offenders, bypassing the need for a trial in cases of noncompliance and further reducing potential sentencing costs. Nor should this be problematic: offenders receiving a suspended sentence in a punitive restoration conference meeting would retain access to legal representation throughout, must confirm any guilt without coercion, and must agree to all terms presented to him or her at the conclusion of this meeting for committing offenses, *where the alternative—through the traditional formal procedures of the courtroom—would include options that are at least as punitive*. Note that one major difference is that only with punitive restoration would the *possibility* of hard treatment be an issue that must be agreed to by the offender prior to its use.

Punitive restoration might justify hard treatment in two other circumstances. The first is the use of *less* time in prison, but with *more* intensity. At present, most offenders serve relatively shorter sentences of less than a year and without any rehabilitative support. The problem is that this support can be somewhat costly, and prison wardens usually reserve it for offenders serving more than a year, which provides more time for these programs to be effective. Yet, these programs are only rarely intensive. As noted above, more high intensity programs have been found to be more effective at reducing drug and alcohol abuse, for example (Daly et al. 2004; Joe et al. 2012). While intensive treatment comes at a higher price tag, these greater costs can be accounted for by both the reduced time required in prison and the reduction in subsequent reoffending. We can use prisons less while achieving better restorative results.

A second way that punitive restoration might justify hard treatment is as a form of "cooling off." Prison is rarely the start of an offender's economic or legal troubles, but rather its confirmation and escalation. Prison can play a potentially restorative role in *disrupting* an offender's everyday situation. Some offenders might have fragile or negative support networks to support their reintegration to society that can make their future journey to prosperity tenuous at best. While not relevant to all, some offenders might benefit from the disruption—and separation—from these negative influences. In these specific circumstances, prison can provide a welcome opportunity for offenders to be separated from their networks where they might become more amenable to personal transformation because they are in a prison-like environment. This might be assessed by probation officers in pre-sentencing reports prior to any such decision being made to ensure this would be suitable for an offender.

5 Possible Objections

It might be argued that punitive restoration should be rejected because hard treatment, even if for only a few days, is a major curtailment of an offender's liberty. This requires special safeguards against abuse that only the formal procedures of the courtroom could satisfy.

There are two possible responses. The first is that very few cases ever go to trial, as most are the result of guilty plea sentencing discounts (Ashworth and Redmayne 2005, 6–7). Guilty pleas are routinely accepted as both sides in our adversarial system come to agreement. There remain safeguards in place to avoid pleas accepted only at face value, although judicial scrutiny could be more robust (Brooks, forthcoming). Nonetheless, punitive restoration is also more stringent than merely accepting a guilty plea and apology at face value, as each side engages with the other in dialogue to better understand why the crime happened and the impact it had on others.

A second response is that, in the majority of courtroom scenarios, the victim and others affected by crime lack any opportunity to express their voice and gain closure. It is no wonder that there is such widespread dissatisfaction by victims of the criminal justice system when they often play little or no role in courtrooms concerning cases involving them. In contrast, punitive restoration brings victims back into the criminal justice system where they have a voice. But it is not anything goes. All meetings are chaired and administered by a trained facilitator following national guidelines with all present able to have legal counsel. If anything, the safeguards are no less in a restorative context, as the crime is not a matter of dispute while all present have greater control in setting out the terms of a restorative contract. Unsurprisingly, victims show far higher satisfaction in a process like this—and so do offenders.

Another possible objection to punitive restoration is its lack of any stated purpose beyond endorsing the principle of stakeholding: this may help identify relevant participants, but which penal purpose should inform their sentencing outcomes? Punitive restoration is more than an improvement over alternative approaches to restorative justice, but an illustration of a compelling perspective on penal purposes in practice. Punishment is often justified in reference to a justifying aim or purpose, such as retribution, deterrence, or rehabilitation. Philosophers disagree about which among these is most preferable despite general agreement that hybrid combinations of two or more purposes often suffer from inconsistency. This is illustrated well in Britain by section 142 of the Criminal Justice Act 2003, which states that punishment must satisfy at least one of five penal purposes. This claim is restated in more recent sentencing guidelines (Sentencing Council 2022). However, there has been no attempt to claim how two or more such purposes can be brought together in a coherent, unified account. This "penal pluralism" may be legally possible, but its practicality remains questionable.[3]

Punitive restoration is one form that a *unified theory of punishment* might take. This is because it is able to bring together multiple penal purposes within a coherent, unified framework.[4] For example, desert is satisfied because offenders must admit guilt without coercion prior to participation in a conference meeting. The penal goals of crime reduction, including the protection of the public and enabling offender rehabilitation, are achieved through targeting stakeholder needs arising from the meeting. The satisfaction of these goals is confirmed through the high satisfaction all participants report, which suggests a general unanimity that the appropriate set of contractual stipulations have been agreed to by all. The improvements in reducing reoffending suggest success in crime reduction and treatment consistent with deterrence and rehabilitation. The argument here is not that any such unified theory is best or preferable to alternative theories. Instead, punitive restoration is an example of how multiple penal principles might be addressed within a coherent, unified account (Brooks 2011, 2012).

6 Conclusion

Restorative justice is an approach that shows enormous potential for transforming the criminal justice system. Its use has shown high satisfaction by victims, lower reoffending by offenders, and significant cost savings. The problem is that it has been restricted to minor offenses by minors. Restorative justice's restricted use is likely linked to limited public support for widely rolling out an approach—while successful and less costly where it has been used—that expressly forbids the use of hard treatment for offenders.

Punitive restoration is a new and distinctive idea about restorative justice. It is modelled on an important principle of stakeholding, which states that those who have a stake in penal outcomes should have a say about them.

[3] On penal pluralism, see Brooks (2014a, 2016a).

[4] A unified theory of punishment may be constructed in different ways. The construction favored here is to view crime as a harm to individual rights and punishment as a response to crime with the purpose of protecting and maintaining individual rights. This model rejects the view that penalties and hard treatment have different justificatory foundations; rather, they share a common justificatory source: the protection and maintenance of rights. The model of a unified theory can then better address the fact that penal outcomes are often multidimensional and include both financial and punitive elements (Brooks 2021).

Punitive restoration brings relevant stakeholders together, including victims, offenders, and members from the local community, to consider together the appropriate penal outcomes. Punitive restoration is *restorative* insofar as it aims to achieve the restoration of rights infringed or threatened by criminal offenses. This is accomplished through recognition of the crime as a public wrong leading to a contractual arrangement agreed to by stakeholders. Punitive restoration is *punitive* insofar as the available options for this agreement are more punitive than most restorative justice approaches, such as the option of some form of hard treatment. This expansion of options within a restorative framework overcomes the many obstacles that limit the application, flexibility, and public confidence of restorative alternatives.

Punitive restoration offers a new form of restorative justice that might be able to extend the use of restoration to more kinds of offenses, and so more offenses. While having more penal options, the wider use of punitive restoration—as an alternative to traditional sentencing—would reduce the punitiveness of the overall criminal justice system while improving satisfaction, enabling better outcomes and at lower costs. We can better embed the use of restorative justice to promote greater restoration, but we must become more open-minded about the limited ways in which hard treatment can, in specific circumstances, support restoration. The road ahead to some form of restorative justice for more offenders is through punitive restoration.

References

Ashworth, Andrew. 1994. "Sentencing." In *The Oxford Handbook of Criminology*, edited by Mike Maguire, Rod Morgan, and Robert Reiner, 819–60. Oxford: Oxford University Press.

———. 2002. "Responsibilities, Rights and Restorative Justice." *British Journal of Criminology* 42, no. 3 (Summer): 578–95.

———. 2010. *Sentencing and Criminal Justice*. 5th ed. Cambridge: Cambridge University Press.

Ashworth, Andrew, and Mike Redmayne. 2005. *The Criminal Process*. 3rd ed. Oxford: Oxford University Press.

Braithwaite, John. 2002. *Restorative Justice and Responsive Regulation*. Oxford: Oxford University Press.

Brooks, Thom. 2011. "Punishment: Political, Not Moral." *New Criminal Law Review* 14, no. 3 (July): 427–38.

———. 2012. "Hegel and the Unified Theory of Punishment." In *Hegel's Philosophy of Right*, edited by Thom Brooks, 103–23. Oxford: Blackwell.

———. 2014a. "On F. H. Bradley's 'Some Remarks on Punishment.'" *Ethics* 125, no. 1 (October): 223–25.
———. 2014b. "Stakeholder Sentencing." In *Popular Punishment: On the Normative Significance of Public Opinion*, edited by Jesper Ryberg and Julian V. Roberts, 183–203. Oxford: Oxford University Press.
———. 2015. "Punitive Restoration: Rehabilitating Restorative Justice." *Raisons Politiques* 59, no. 3: 73–89.
———. 2016a. "In Defence of *Punishment* and the Unified Theory of Punishment: A Reply." *Criminal Law and Philosophy* 10, no. 3 (September): 629–38.
———. 2016b. "Justice as Stakeholding." In *Theorizing Justice: Critical Insights and Future Directions*, edited by Krushil Watene and Jay Drydyk, 111–27. New York: Rowman & Littlefield.
———. 2016c. "Punitive Restoration: Giving the Public a Say on Sentencing." In *Democratic Theory and Mass Incarceration*, edited by Albert Dzur, Ian Loader, and Richard Sparks, 140–61. Oxford: Oxford University Press.
———. 2021. *Punishment*. 2nd ed. New York: Routledge.
———. Forthcoming. "Why Should Guilty Pleas Matter?" In *Sentencing the Self-Convicted: The Ethics of Pleading Guilty*, edited by Julian V. Roberts and Jesper Ryberg. Oxford: Hart.
Brunton-Smith, Ian, and Kathryn Hopkins. 2013. *The Factors Associated with Proven Re-offending Following Release from Prison: Findings from Waves 1 to 3 of SPCR*. London: Ministry of Justice.
Christie, Nils. 1998. "Conflicts as Property." In *Principled Sentencing: Readings on Theory and Policy*, edited by Andrew Ashworth, Andrew von Hirsch, and Julian Roberts, 312–16. Oxford: Hart.
Cullen, Francis T., Bonnie S. Fischer, and Brandon K. Applegate. 2000. "Public Opinion about Punishment and Corrections." *Crime and Justice* 27: 1–79.
Cunneen, Chris, and Carolyn Hoyle. 2010. *Debating Restorative Justice*. Oxford: Hart.
Daly, Kathleen. 2003. "Mind the Gap: Restorative Justice in Theory and Practice." In *Restorative Justice and Criminal Justice: Competing or Reconcilable Paradigms*, edited by Andrew von Hirsch, Julian V. Roberts, Anthony E. Bottoms, Kent Roach, and Mara Schiff, 219–36. Oxford: Hart.
Daly, Marilyn, Craig T. Love, Donald S. Shepard, Cheryl B. Petersen, Karen L. White, and Frank B. Hall. 2004. "Cost-Effectiveness of Connecticut's In-Prison Substance Abuse Treatment." *Journal of Offender Rehabilitation* 39, no. 3: 69–92.
Durlauf, Steven N., and Daniel S. Nagin. 2011. "Overview of 'Imprisonment and Crime: Can Both Be Reduced?'" *Criminology & Public Policy* 10, no. 1 (February): 13–54.
Gardner, John. 1998. "Crime: In Proportion and in Perspective." In *Fundamentals of Sentencing Theory: Essays in Honour of Andrew von Hirsch*, edited by Andrew Ashworth and Martin Wasik, 31–52. Oxford: Clarendon.
Joe, George W., Kevin Knight, D. Dwayne Simpson, Patrick M. Flynn, Janis T. Morey, Norma G. Bartholomew, Michele Staton Tindall, et al. 2012. "An

Evaluation of Six Brief Interventions That Target Drug-Related Problems in Correctional Populations." *Journal of Offender Rehabilitation* 51, nos. 1–2: 9–33.

Johnstone, Gerry, and Daniel W. Van Ness. 2007. "The Meaning of Restorative Justice." In *Handbook of Restorative Justice*, edited by Gerry Johnstone and Daniel W. Van Ness, 5–23. New York: Routledge.

Liebling, Alison. 2006. *Prisons and Their Moral Performance: A Study of Values, Quality, and Prison Life*. Oxford: Clarendon.

Lippke, Richard L. 2007. *Rethinking Imprisonment*. Oxford: Oxford University Press.

Llewellyn, Jennifer J., and Robert Howse. 1999. "Institutions for Restorative Justice: The South African Truth and Reconciliation Commission." *University of Toronto Law Journal* 49, no. 3 (Summer): 355–88.

Marshall, Tony F. 1999. *Restorative Justice: An Overview*. Home Office Occasional Paper. London: Home Office.

Morrison, Brenda. 2007. "Schools and Restorative Justice." In *Handbook of Restorative Justice*, edited by Gerry Johnstone and Daniel W. Van Ness, 325–50. New York: Routledge.

Parekh, Bhikhu. 2008. *A New Politics of Identity: Political Principles for an Interdependent World*. Basingstoke, UK: Palgrave Macmillan.

Pérez, Deanna M., and Wesley G. Jennings. 2012. "Treatment behind Bars: The Effectiveness of Prison-Based Therapy for Sex Offenders." *Journal of Crime and Justice* 35, no. 3: 435–50.

Restorative Justice Council. 2011. *What Does the Ministry of Justice RJ Research Tell Us?* London: Restorative Justice Council.

———. 2020. *Restorative Practice Guidance 2020*. https://restorativejustice.org.uk/sites/default/files/resources/files/Restorative%20Practice%20Guidance%202020_April%2020_0.pdf.

Sentencing Council. 2022. *About Sentencing Guidelines*. https://www.sentencing-council.org.uk/sentencing-and-the-council/about-sentencing-guidelines/.

Shapland, Joanna, Anne Atkinson, Helen Atkinson, Becca Chapman, Emily Colledge, James Dignan, Marie Howes, Jennifer Johnstone, Gwen Robinson, and Angela Sorsby. 2006. *Restorative Justice in Practice: The Second Report from the Evaluation of Three Schemes*, July. Sheffield, UK: Centre for Criminological Research, University of Sheffield.

Shapland, Joanna, Anne Atkinson, Helen Atkinson, Becca Chapman, James Dignan, Marie Howes, Jennifer Johnstone, Gwen Robinson, and Angela Sorsby. 2007. *Restorative Justice: The Views of Victims and Offenders*. London: Ministry of Justice.

Shapland, Joanna, Anne Atkinson, Helen Atkinson, James Dignan, Lucy Edwards, Jeremy Hibbert, Marie Howes, Jennifer Johnstone, Gwen Robinson, and Angela Sorsby. 2008. *Does Restorative Justice Affect Reconviction? The Fourth Report from the Evaluation of Three Schemes*. London: Ministry of Justice.

Shapland, Joanna, Gwen Robinson, and Angela Sorsby. 2011. *Restorative Justice in Practice: Evaluating What Works for Victims and Offenders*. New York: Routledge.

Tonry, Michael. 2011. "Less Imprisonment Is No Doubt a Good Thing: More Policing Is Not." *Criminology & Public Policy* 10, no. 1 (February): 137–52.

Towl, Graham J. 2006. "Drug-Misuse Intervention Work." In *Psychological Research in Prisons*, edited by Graham J. Towl, 116–27. Oxford: Blackwell.

Van Ness, Daniel W. 2007. "Prisons and Restorative Justice." In *Handbook of Restorative Justice*, edited by Gerry Johnstone and Daniel W. Van Ness, 312–24. New York: Routledge.

von Hirsch, Andrew, and Andrew Ashworth. 2005. *Proportionate Sentencing: Exploring the Principles*. Oxford: Oxford University Press.

Williams, Monica. 2012. "Beyond the Retributive Public: Governance and Public Opinion on Penal Policy." *Journal of Crime and Justice* 35, no. 1: 93–113.

Zimring, Franklin E., Gordon Hawkins, and Sam Kamin. 2001. *Punishment and Democracy: Three Strikes and You're Out in California*. Oxford: Oxford University Press.

Part IX

Applications

30

Mass Incarceration as Distributive Injustice

Benjamin Ewing

The concept of "mass incarceration"—which has spawned an enormous amount of academic and public commentary in the past ten years especially—is typically traced back twenty years to the work of sociologist David Garland (2001). He coined the term "mass imprisonment," in a symposium bearing witness to the unprecedented rise in the number of people incarcerated in America from about 500,000 in 1980 to nearly two million at the start of the new century.[1] In Garland's view, for the concept of "mass" imprisonment to apply, not only must the prison population be large, but there must be a "social concentration of [its] effects" such that "it ceases to be the incarceration of individual offenders and becomes the systematic imprisonment of whole groups of the population" (2001, 5–6).

By the time Michelle Alexander published her influential book, *The New Jim Crow: Mass Incarceration in the Age of Colorblindness*, in 2010, the total incarcerated population in the United States had plateaued at approximately 2.3 million in 2008. The new decade would see it slowly decline to roughly

[1] A reason to favor the term "mass incarceration" over "mass imprisonment"—which may also help explain why the former appears to have overtaken the latter in usage—is that the total population of those who are confined behind bars in connection with criminal charges includes both those who are in "prison" serving relatively long sentences and those who are in "jail" either for shorter sentences or in pretrial detention.

B. Ewing (✉)
Queen's University, Kingston, ON, Canada
e-mail: benjamin.ewing@queensu.ca

© The Author(s), under exclusive license to Springer Nature Switzerland AG 2023

M. C. Altman (ed.), *The Palgrave Handbook on the Philosophy of Punishment*, Palgrave Handbooks in the Philosophy of Law, https://doi.org/10.1007/978-3-031-11874-6_30

2.1 million in 2019 before quickly dipping to around 1.8 million in 2020 amid the COVID-19 pandemic (Kang-Brown et al. 2021). Alexander is credited with popularizing what John Pfaff (2017) calls the "standard story" of mass incarceration. In her "New Jim Crow" telling of it, mass incarceration is the product of a conscious effort by white Americans to lash back at the racial progress made by the Civil Rights Movement, targeting Black Americans to be discriminatorily policed and disproportionately punished, predominantly for nonviolent offenses, especially drug crimes.

That narrative has been extremely important in directing the attention of activists and academics to mass incarceration. Yet it has also come to seem misleading to a coterie of scholars, who have recently highlighted ways in which it oversimplifies and distorts mass incarceration from historical, sociological, and criminological standpoints. As critics of the "standard story" have emphasized, in response to a substantial rise in both violent and nonviolent crime, many Black Americans as well as white ones supported the War on Drugs and the tough-on-crime politics of the last three decades of the twentieth century (Fortner 2015; Forman 2017; Clegg and Usmani 2019). At least half of Americans in state prison appear to be serving time for violent crimes (Forman 2012, 47; Pfaff 2017, 32–33), and many of those incarcerated for nonviolent offenses have committed otherwise serious crimes, have criminal histories, or were suspected of violence but faced drug charges because of the ease of proving them (Gottschalk 2015, 168–69). There is also evidence that what drove the unprecedented growth in the U.S. incarceration rate was not increases in time served for any given category of crime but, rather, increases in the number of felony charges brought by prosecutors (Pfaff 2017, 51–77). Finally, as Jill Leovy (2015) and others have emphasized, Black Americans are under-protected against criminal victimization even as they are over-policed. It is no wonder that they have often taken strong stands against crime given that they have long been disproportionately the victims of it—particularly of homicide, which takes the lives of young men in America who are poor and Black with appalling frequency.[2]

[2] In response to her critics, Alexander has argued that nonviolent offenders serving shorter sentences flow in and out of the prison system more frequently than violent offenders serving longer sentences; hence, a snapshot of who is incarcerated at any given time does not necessarily provide an accurate reflection of the overall composition of those who are ever incarcerated (2020, xxiv–xxvi). She has also emphasized the significance of other forms of correctional control besides incarceration—such as parole and probation—which may well apply to many more nonviolent offenders than violent ones (xxvi–xxix). These are fair and important points. But they do not insulate the New Jim Crow narrative from many remaining charges against it, such as, for example, that it: understates the role of increased crime (including violent crime) in the emergence of mass incarceration; overlooks the extent to which supposedly "nonviolent" drug offenders are often involved in violence; fails to recognize the extent to which racial disparities in incarceration reflect racial disparities in rates of offending; and downplays both Black Americans' special vulnerability to criminal victimization and the moral culpability of typical incarcerated individuals.

Mass incarceration is a large and complex problem, the causes and consequences of which historians, criminologists, and sociologists are still only beginning to understand. Still, it is a testament to the depth and progress of empirical inquiry into the subject that it has already yielded and transcended a "standard story." By contrast, the study of mass incarceration from the standpoint of normative theory is only just beginning to emerge in embryonic form. It is now taken for granted by many Americans that mass incarceration is among the most pressing moral crises of the twenty-first century. Yet surprisingly little work in the philosophy of punishment has sought to give that reflexive belief a rigorous theoretical foundation.

Undoubtedly, part of the problem is that the injustice of mass incarceration may appear overdetermined and all too obvious. The U.S. incarceration rate continued to rise steadily even as crime fell across the 1990s and into the twenty-first century (Pfaff 2017, 2–3). It is now virtually unrivaled globally (Fair and Walmsley 2021). And because of economic, educational, racial, geographic, and age- and gender-based disparities in incarceration rates within the U.S., the outsized overall incarceration rate understates greatly the extent to which incarceration has been a routine experience for millions of poor, undereducated young men—especially ones who are Black—living in areas of concentrated poverty. That poor Black men's share of the U.S. population is dwarfed by their share of the prison population is strong evidence that they face a potent combination of (a) bias, discrimination, and disadvantage in the enforcement of the criminal law and (b) unfair criminogenic social disadvantages making it harder to avoid crime in the first place.

However, empirical thorns in the side of the "standard story" of mass incarceration should cause us to question whether it is an injustice that is as extreme, or as obvious, as many have come reflexively to assume. The data challenge the idea that mass incarceration is primarily the result of disproportionate sentences for low-level offenses, such as so-called nonviolent drug offenses and other supposedly minor crimes. And they caution that the gap between the Black and white incarceration rates in America appears to be explained at least as much by greater rates of offending by Black Americans as by race-based inequalities in treatment of equally serious offenders (see, e.g., Western 2006, 50; Gottschalk 2015, 125–26; Western 2018, 171). They thus raise the specter that mass incarceration may be, to a significant extent, simply a result of more reliably prosecuting and punishing the perpetrators of (often serious) crimes.

Partly in response to those and similar concerns, a handful of criminal law theorists (e.g., Chiao 2017; Stewart 2018; Yankah 2020; Flanders 2021) have recently taken up a pair of related questions. First, what if anything is wrong with mass incarceration over and above specific wrongs that contingently contribute to it (e.g., unequally harsh sentences for offenders from discriminated-against groups) or arise from it (e.g., negative impacts on innocent members of incarcerated persons' families and communities)? Second, can familiar justifications and principles of punishment explain the intuition that there is something distinctively unjust about mass incarceration, apart from individual, independently identifiable injustices that are contingent causes and consequences of it? Fused into a single two-pronged inquiry: is there a wrong in mass incarceration for which existing theories cannot account, such that mass incarceration has something important to teach us about the normative theory of punishment?[3]

In the next part of this chapter, I offer a critical review of answers to that question that have thus far emerged in a small but burgeoning literature, which promises to sprout new growths in the years to come. As I show, mass incarceration has already served as fodder for critics of "strictly deontological" theories of punishment (including but not limited to certain variants of retributivism) and for defenders of the centrality of *political* philosophy to the justification of punishment. In my view, however, what unifies and best explains skepticism that traditional normative theories of criminal justice can account for the injustice of mass incarceration is that such theories tend to view the justification of punishment as an individualistic relationship between a crime and culpable offender, on the one hand, and a punishment, on the other. Mass incarceration by contrast is an aggregate, structural problem. To understand mass incarceration as a failure of criminal justice, it may therefore be necessary to adopt a more holistic understanding of criminal justice. One salient, too-often-overlooked way of doing so is by treating it as a fundamentally distributive problem: how to promote and fairly allocate security against both crime and punishment. Hence, in the final part of the chapter, I

[3] Irrespective of whether they can explain the injustice of mass incarceration in theory, there is a further question one can ask about traditional normative theories of punishment, from the standpoint of the sociology of knowledge: in practice, do such theories legitimize mass incarceration, whether because they are frequently degraded or imbued with biases, or because they serve covert ideological functions? Whitman (2003b) once argued powerfully that whatever its most attractive construal might in theory prescribe, retributivism seemed in practice to have helped legitimate the harshness of American criminal justice. In more recent reflections on mass incarceration, Altman and Coe (2022) charge the ideas both of retribution and deterrence with functioning in practice to rationalize unjust racial inequalities in American criminal justice. I am interested primarily in the explanatory power of familiar justifications and principles of punishment when they are considered on their own terms and construed charitably. How such theories may be abused or instrumentalized, and whether some are better fortified against misuse than others, are questions peripheral to this chapter. Nevertheless, my analysis may aid us in beginning to answer those questions, because if traditional justifications of punishment struggle even in theory to explain the injustice of mass incarceration, this surely makes them vulnerable in practice to being used to rationalize and legitimize mass incarceration.

motivate such a perspective by reflecting on distributive dimensions of the problem that criminal justice seeks to solve. And I begin to reflect on how a distributive view of criminal justice might illuminate the injustice of mass incarceration.

1 Mass Incarceration as Theoretical Challenge

Strictly deontological theories. In his incisive article "Mass Incarceration and the Theory of Punishment" (2017), Vincent Chiao argues that mass incarceration poses a particular challenge for any "strictly deontological theory of punishment," which he defines as "any theory that (a) purports to provide an explanation of when it is permissible to punish those who commit crimes, and that (b) does so in terms that exclude the consideration of the expected costs and benefits of punishment" (433). The problem, in his view, is that mass incarceration seems intuitively to be a great injustice, yet one that cannot be adequately explained by strictly deontological theories of punishment.

Why, in Chiao's view, are strictly deontological theories of punishment (which include some forms of retributivism, but need not be retributive) incapable of explaining the injustice of American mass incarceration? Because "the current American incarceration rate is not the result of systematic violation of deontological constraints" (Chiao 2017, 437). More specifically:

> The paradigmatic deontological constraints on punishment are that punishment be restricted to people who are actually guilty of true crimes, and be administered in proportion to their culpability. ... So a strictly deontological theory must seek to explain American incarceration rates via systematic punishment of the innocent, overcriminalization and/or disproportionately harsh punishment. ... [However,] there is reason to believe that the United States could actually incarcerate many *more* people than it currently does while still fully respecting all of these constraints. (438–39)

Here, Chiao's argument dovetails with criticisms of the "standard story" of mass incarceration. For he deploys revealing criminal justice statistics to challenge the idea that mass incarceration is the product of systemic violations of familiar deontological constraints on just punishment.

First, as Chiao suggests, as high as America's incarceration rate is, it is much lower than it would be were all perpetrators of serious crimes to be identified and punished. Even a substantial minority of culpable homicides go unsolved, to say nothing of such crimes as rape, robbery, burglary, and auto theft—the perpetrators of which will more often than not escape criminal accountability altogether (Chiao 2017, 439–40). So the need to restrict punishment to the factually guilty cannot explain why the percentage of people incarcerated in America is too high.

Second, although some people may be serving prison sentences for conduct that it was wrong to criminalize in the first place, drug offenders constitute the one large, salient group of offenders commonly thought to fit that description. And in line with critics of the "standard story" of mass incarceration, Chiao emphasizes that because only about 20 percent of prisoners have been incarcerated for drug offenses, the U.S. incarceration rate would still be at a level warranting the term mass incarceration even if it were not for drug prisoners (2017, 441).[4]

Third, surprisingly, disproportionately harsh sentences may have played much less of a role in creating mass incarceration than one might naturally assume. Chiao cites the work of criminologist John Pfaff, who has found evidence that mass incarceration has been driven not by increases in sentence lengths (which for some offenses actually declined over periods of growth in the incarceration rate),[5] but rather the frequency with which prosecutors have brought felony charges, which has in turn increased the rate of prison admissions.[6] Prison terms in the federal and state systems *are* conspicuously longer than in many developed western liberal democracies.[7] But as the late criminal procedure scholar William Stuntz (2001) stressed, the practical impact of tougher available prison terms has often been simply to give prosecutors greater leverage to extract quick guilty pleas in exchange for lenience.

Even if penal sentences have (counterintuitively) remained more consistent over time than one would suspect, there remain strong moral arguments for thinking they are systematically too harsh. And even if Pfaff is correct that longer prison terms for particular crimes were not what caused mass incarceration in the first place, shorter prison terms going forward could still be an

[4] As Chiao rightly notices, when we insist that the percentage of prisoners serving time for drug offenses not be overstated, we must also remember that many offenses besides possession and trafficking—including many murders and other acts of violence—are themselves direct or indirect products of the War on Drugs (2017, 442). At the same time, however, we must not forget the insight of William Stuntz (2001) and others that, because of the ease of proving drug offenses and the stiff sentences attached to them, prosecutors have often used them as an expedient way to throw the book at individuals strongly suspected of violent crime that is more difficult to prove.

[5] Pfaff recognizes that, if and when the net of imprisonment is extended to more marginal offenders, all else equal we should *expect* average time served to decline, not because of lighter punishment of any given offender but because of the introduction of higher numbers of lower-level offenders (2017, 59–61).

[6] Chiao (2017) cites Pfaff (2011, 2012). Pfaff's landmark book on mass incarceration, *Locked In* (2017), which compiles and extends insights of his prior work, postdates Chiao's essay.

[7] On that point, Chiao (2017, 442) cites the excellent comparative work of James Whitman (2003a).

important way of reducing the prison population. However, neither observation challenges what I take to be Chiao's fundamental claim: a rate of incarceration comparable to (or even greater than) America's is compatible with respect for familiar deontological constraints on punishment; hence, we cannot rely upon systematic violation of such constraints to explain what makes mass incarceration as such a failure of criminal justice.[8]

Yet I have made it a point to refer just now to "familiar" deontological constraints on justified punishment. For in critiquing the inability of deontological constraints to account for the wrong of mass incarceration, Chiao focuses on such traditional, individualistic constraints as the prohibitions on punishing the innocent and punishing the guilty out of proportion to their culpability. Indeed, Chiao ultimately implies that the reason strictly deontological theories of punishment are unable to explain the characteristic wrong of mass incarceration is precisely that there is a mismatch between the individualistic character of the former and the aggregative nature of the latter:

> And, hence, the source of the problem: the judgment that the United States now incarcerates too many people is, like the judgment that income inequality is too high, a judgment about an aggregate pattern of outcomes. It is not a judgment about the quality of the individual transactions that lead to that result. (2017, 448)

I wonder, therefore, whether the inability of various justifications of punishment to account for the injustice of mass incarceration is best described as a function of their strict deontology or, instead, their individualistic characters. Later in the chapter, I explore the possibility that a more holistic—and in particular *distributive*—view of criminal justice might be precisely what is needed in order to explain what makes mass incarceration a failure of criminal justice.

Insufficiently political (applied moral) theories. Chiao concludes his article with a claim distinct from, but closely related to, his point about strictly deontological theories: "a theory of punishment should start with a conception of criminal punishment as the subject matter of a political theory of justice, not simply private morality writ large" (2017, 452). This is an important theme

[8] One might suppose that mass incarceration is a failure of *criminal* justice only to the extent that it is made up of injustices to particular punished persons that familiar theories of punishment can explain. And one could argue that, insofar as it reflects or reinforces social or political inequality, it is merely a contingent consequence and cause of broader *social* or *political* injustice—and, not, strictly speaking, a failure of *criminal* justice. But like Chiao, I take it many informed observers will share the intuition that mass incarceration constitutes a distinctive failure of *criminal* justice—over and above recognizably disproportionate punishments for specific individuals that have contributed to it.

also stressed by others who have written about the implications of mass incarceration for normative penal theory. Because Chad Flanders (2021) takes the theme to be the central lesson of mass incarceration for the philosophy of punishment, we may treat his discussion of the matter as a convenient focal point.

In his book chapter "What Is Wrong with Mass Incarceration?" Flanders makes it clear that he has no desire to downplay the many potential injustices that are contingent *causes* and *symptoms* of mass incarceration—whether overcriminalization, mandatory minimums, and racism (potential causes), or prison overcrowding, community harms, and large numbers of people facing barriers to reentering society after serving penal sentences (potential symptoms). His theoretical interest in the chapter, however, is in what if anything is wrong with mass incarceration as such—which he, like Chiao, takes many traditional justifications of punishment to be unable to explain.

Flanders contends that what is non-contingently wrong with mass incarceration cannot be explained by the philosophy of punishment itself, but only by political theory (2021, 165–68). In his preliminary sketch of what makes it a political injustice, Flanders ventures that even if everyone incarcerated is serving a sentence that cannot be directly impugned as itself unjust, if the aggregate result is something we would classify as "mass" incarceration, then the society has failed to achieve what John Rawls called stability "for the right reasons" or widespread principled obedience to the law owing to its perceived legitimacy rather than fear of sanctions (168–71). Relatedly, Flanders suggests that, in a state experiencing mass incarceration, too many people are unable to flourish, and it is inadequate to say that this is simply their (not unjust) misfortune.

However, if the punishments themselves are individually just, then should we not say that those subject to them have had a fair opportunity to avoid them, and thus that their prison terms are *not* unfair obstacles to their flourishing?[9] And if the concern is what mass incarceration says about the ability of a state and its laws to garner principled allegiance for the right reasons, then is the problem mass incarceration, or the level of crime giving rise

[9] I agree wholeheartedly with Flanders's passing suggestion that mass incarceration may be evidence that "in Rawls's terms, we have not given citizens enough of an opportunity to develop 'a sense of justice'" (2021, 170). Indeed, I have elsewhere argued in detail that if people are to have a fully fair opportunity to avoid punishment, not only must punishment be restricted to culpable conduct prescribed in advance, but background social conditions must be such as to secure for all people "fair moral opportunity" to develop and exercise their capacities to act in accordance with the moral reasons to refrain from crime (Ewing 2021). Yet I consider an individual's lack of fair moral opportunity to be an appropriate ground for sentence mitigation (Ewing 2019, 432–34), such that a failure to account for it may give rise to individual injustices or wrongs to specific offenders.

to it? Finally, if the problem is partly the frequency of serious criminal wrongdoing, then we will not fully solve it by simply tolerating more crime by punishing people less often and harshly—as Flanders proposes a state experiencing mass incarceration may be morally required to do (2017, 170).

Setting aside the merits of Flanders's specific sketch of the political problems with mass incarceration, what should we make of his broader thesis, also endorsed by Chiao (2017) and Ekow Yankah (2020), among others, that we need resources from normative *political* theory—too frequently ignored by philosophers of punishment—in order to explain what is wrong with mass incarceration?

I am certainly disposed to be sympathetic to that position, having previously argued that retributivism is vulnerable to a political critique—namely, that it prioritizes a sectarian conception of the good (which is an inappropriate basis for the justification of punishment in a politically liberal society) over basic individual rights not subject to reasonable disagreement (Ewing 2015). A theory of the justification of punishment that abstracts from political theory risks foundering on a failure to incorporate normative political constraints on justified punishment—such as, for example, that it be consistent with requirements on public justification among the free and equal citizens of a liberal democracy, and that it take the accurate measure of special claims that unjustly disadvantaged members of society may have against hard treatment or condemnation by the state (Ewing 2018, 2021).

That said, in order to grapple adequately with mass incarceration, it appears necessary but not sufficient to embed one's philosophy of punishment within a broader political theory. Those who situate criminal justice within political theories of liberal perfectionism or illiberalism, for instance, will not have the same reasons as political liberals to think there are special constraints on how punishment can be justified by a state to its citizens and other legal subjects. Furthermore, in articulating why familiar theories of justified punishment are unable to reckon with mass incarceration, Chiao (2017, 448) and Flanders (2021, 167) both suggest that the former have an individualistic character that makes them unable to capture the latter, given its aggregative nature. And both compare the individualistic character of traditional theories of the justification of punishment with libertarian political views that reject a distributive conception of social justice in favor of the view that what matters is justice in individual transactions (Chiao 2017, 432, 448; Flanders 2021, 167). What that shows is that adopting a political perspective on criminal justice is no guarantee one will endorse the kind of structural view of it that Chiao and Flanders each see as required for understanding what is wrong with mass incarceration.

Perhaps unsurprisingly, therefore, I take the most compelling insight of both authors' reflections on the implications of mass incarceration for the philosophy of punishment to be the same: widely shared intuitions about the injustice of mass incarceration put theoretical pressure on us to give aggregative or structural—especially distributive—theories of the justification of punishment more serious consideration than they have historically received. In the next section, let us pursue that thought further by beginning to reflect upon what a plausible distributive perspective on criminal justice might look like and what new insights it might give us into the problem of mass incarceration.

2 Mass Incarceration as Distributive Injustice

Criminal justice as a problem of distribution. There is no better discussion of the "individualistic" character of familiar approaches to criminal justice—and how it contrasts with the "holistic" character of distributive justice—than Samuel Scheffler's essay "Justice and Desert in Liberal Theory" (2000). In it, Scheffler seeks to defend the coherence of simultaneously (a) endorsing a distributive conception of social justice that rejects individual desert as an input shaping the content of justice, while still (b) maintaining that there is a form of retributive desert that appropriately shapes (and is not merely a label for the conclusions of) what criminal justice requires. Scheffler's apparent motivation for defending such an "asymmetry" between distributive social justice and retributive criminal justice is to help fortify a Rawlsian liberal view of social justice against the criticism that it would force us to discount individual desert in criminal justice.

Scheffler argues that the problem to which distributive justice is a solution is "the problem of how to allocate scarce goods [or social advantages] among moral equals" when the goods or social advantages that will exist, and which people will benefit from them, are matters "heavily dependent on social institutions" (2000, 986). The nature of the problem thus helps explain why the form of justice meant to solve it should not be shaped by a notion of individual personal desert *prior to that form of justice itself.* It is difficult to believe that individuals' desert of some level of wealth or position of employment can shape social justice (rather than be an upshot of it), because the production and consumption decisions people make and their perceived value and expense, respectively, are inextricably linked—not only to each other but also to the background rules, principles, and practices that determine who has control over what, and on what terms. We first need a system of just rules, principles, and practices. Only when we have one in view can we determine individual entitlements, in concrete terms, by examining what people would come reasonably to expect if the rules, principles, and practices of a just system were followed—or so the argument goes.

"By contrast," Scheffler writes:

> the problem of retributive justice ... is not the problem of how to allocate a limited supply of benefits among equally worthy citizens but rather the problem of how society can ever be justified in imposing the special burden of punishment on a particular human being. (2000, 986)

Here Scheffler is channeling the conventional wisdom of lay people and philosophers of punishment alike. While there may be limits to the amount of punishment a society can impose or forgo, Scheffler is obviously correct that criminal justice is not familiarly or intuitively modeled as a problem of how to allocate scarce resources. It is no surprise, therefore, that even as many criminal law theorists have become increasingly cognizant that criminal justice implicates *political* morality and not merely applied moral theory, they have seldom applied to it a lens that is distributive in anything like the sense in which Rawls-inspired theories of social justice are distributive.[10]

Scheffler may be correct that there are principled grounds for rejecting a role for individual desert in the determination of social justice while embracing one in the context of criminal justice. There are no doubt other important asymmetries between social justice and criminal justice. Yet an approach to criminal justice broadly modeled after distributive justice holds great untapped

[10] A theory of criminal justice is not yet distributive, in anything like that sense, merely because it follows H. L. A. Hart (2008) in using the term "distributive principles" of punishment to refer to the principles governing whom to punish and how much (as distinct from what Hart called the "general justifying aims" of punishment) (see, e.g., Robinson 2008). For the "principles of distribution" of punishment in a Hartian theory need not have anything to do with the overall incidence and distribution of crime and punishment across society; they may instead simply be individualistic principles—such as, for example, that only crimes proscribed in advance should be punished, that intentional wrongdoing should be punished more harshly than accidental wrongdoing, and that extreme constraints on a specific choice (such as necessity or duress) should excuse. Nor is a theory necessarily distributive, in the sense of interest to us here, simply because it conceives of punishment as a means of redistributing a risk or harm from an actual or potential victim onto an actual or potential offender (see, e.g., Gruber 2010, 11). Theories of punishment based on principles of defensive harm are often concerned about the distribution of risks or harms, but in an individualistic way. For example, they may treat the punishment of a specific offender as made permissible by a right to threaten that offender with it (Quinn 1985), or by a duty such offender incurred to bolster the security of the victim as a next best alternative to having not offended in the first place (Tadros 2011, 265–92). Only if and when additional layers are added to such theories' core may they become concerned about the overall distribution across society of the benefits and burdens of crime and punishment. This occurs in Victor Tadros's theory, for instance, when he seeks to extend his initial argument that offenders have a duty to bolster the security of their victims to a broader argument for the permissibility of punishing for the sake of general deterrence (2011, 275–92).

potential for the philosophy of punishment—and not merely because of the light it may shed on what is wrong with mass incarceration. Ironically, Scheffler's stylized contrast between the holism of social justice and the individualism of criminal justice may be the closest thing we have to a treasure map of the path toward a distributive theory of criminal justice. A natural first step toward developing such a theory is to reflect on salient ways in which the problem that criminal justice is meant to solve is—initial appearances to the contrary—analogous to the question that a distributive theory of social justice seeks to answer.

First, in each context, we are seeking rules, principles, and practices that will facilitate social cooperation to increase the supply of not-unlimited social advantages: roughly, goods and services, in the context of social justice, and security against force and fraud, in the context of criminal justice. Although there are clear limits to our ability to shape human behavior, it is undeniable that incentives play a significant role in encouraging productivity and discouraging wrongdoing.

Second, in both the social and penal spheres, we aim to promote a dimension of aggregate well-being (whether meaningful work and sustainable consumption, or liberty and security) while attending to the rights and interests of each and every individual, and not allowing them to be sacrificed to the collective good. In each case we therefore confront something broadly similar to a constrained maximization problem: the search for a system that will yield both the vigorous production and fair allocation of fruits of social cooperation.

Third, in social and criminal justice alike, the allocation of both benefits and burdens is at stake. Theories of the justification of punishment sometimes oddly downplay the benefits of security against crime as a key justifying aim of criminal justice. And theories of social justice even more often overlook the burdens of laboring to produce goods and services—and the question of who shall be made to bear them (but see Stanczyk 2012). But in both contexts, people must bear burdens in order that society shall flourish, so a question of fairness in allocation arises with respect to not only consumer benefits but also producer burdens, and not only the harm of punishment but also the good of security against crime.

Fourth, in assessing acceptable social rewards and penal deterrents, and who shall bear which burdens of producing goods and services or security against crime and punishment, individual *choice* is a crucial mediating hinge that can link and balance the pursuit of our competing goals. By allowing people's choices to affect the benefits and burdens we require or allow to lie with them, we can simultaneously leverage incentives to promote the collective good and protect people against non-preferred fates by giving people good options by which to avoid those negative outcomes if they so choose.

Fifth, although the intuitive force of individual "desert" claims may appear stronger in criminal justice than social justice, such claims are embraced by some people and rejected by others in both contexts. Many of the same people who insist on the primacy of individual retributive desert also cling to the idea that individual effort or talent deserves to be rewarded (notwithstanding the structural interdependence of social and economic activity). And many of those who follow Rawls in rejecting a role for prejusticial desert in social justice also reject the idea that there is such a thing as "desert" of punishment which is prior to, and an input into, criminal justice (rather than a mere label for the conclusion that punishment is justified).

Sixth, neither in social justice nor in criminal justice does a distributive perspective require rejecting altogether a role for prejusticial desert claims. Criminal justice need not be as radically holistic as Rawlsian social justice in order for it to be usefully modeled as a problem of how fairly to allocate the benefits and burdens of cooperation and conflict around the creation of a not-unlimited social good. Even in its quintessential Rawlsian form, distributive justice hardly constitutes the entirety of social justice—so it should not be thought odd that it might be just a part, and not the whole, of criminal justice.

To be sure, there are obvious disanalogies between what the state does when it proscribes, polices, and punishes crime, and when it guides the "invisible hand" of the marketplace by creating rules of property, contract, and taxation. But we are here on an exploratory, imaginative journey. It began with the observation that the individualistic character of familiar theories of criminal justice inhibits their ability to grapple with the aggregate phenomenon of mass incarceration. That insight led us to consider overlooked ways in which the problem that criminal justice seeks to solve is, in fact, a problem with distributive contours. So having sketched half-a-dozen reasons for seeing criminal justice as a distributive problem, rather than turn to potential counterarguments, let us close instead by reflecting on the promise of a distributive approach to criminal justice as a way of better understanding what is wrong with mass incarceration.

Mass incarceration as a problem of distribution. The idea that there is something wrong with mass incarceration implies that when punishment becomes "mass," there is too much of it—in an aggregate sense or as concentrated on particular groups or communities. But we are interested in the wrong of mass incarceration over and above the extent to which it is made up of already recognizable wrongs to individuals that traditional theories of criminal justice are perfectly capable of explaining. For instance, what could make "mass" incarceration "too much," from the standpoint of criminal justice, if it arises simply because there is more crime, or because a much greater percentage of the guilty start to receive the punishments to which they were already previously liable?

To answer that question, it may help first to draw on distributive ideas from the context in which they are most familiar and intuitive: social justice. Though the analogy is obviously imperfect, it is worth asking: what would make "mass" (i.e., systemic) *unemployment* "too much" even if it were to arise simply from fewer jobs being necessary or fewer people having the qualifications or appetite for the work society needs and wants?

One obvious concern is that a high level of structural unemployment may not be necessary for economic efficiency but instead deeply wasteful of human potential—which mass incarceration also seems to be, insofar as it involves punishment well past the point of diminishing marginal returns to crime control. But beyond that, even if systemic unemployment could be explained by a large percentage of the population lacking (or being unwilling to use) the talents or skills required for necessary labor, we would still have to ask ourselves: might that not in turn be a manifestation of society's failure to secure for everyone a fair opportunity *to develop* the talents, skills, and willingness to use them, required for gainful, meaningful work? Likewise, even to the extent that American mass incarceration simply reflects more crime and more of the guilty receiving punishments to which they were already previously liable, it casts serious doubt on whether society has secured for everyone a fair opportunity to flourish without resorting to crime.

Many traditional theories of the justification of punishment take its fairness to depend on offenders having had a fair opportunity to avoid their crimes. But the standard idea is merely that criminal offenders have lacked a fair opportunity to avoid their crimes when, and to the extent that, crimes of general applicability fail to capture their true culpability because of (at least partially) exculpatory circumstances (see, e.g., Brink 2021). For example, a man who aids another in a bank robbery under gun-to-the-head duress is said to be non-culpable, or a woman who kills her husband in a rage upon finding him sexually abusing their child is said to be less culpable—in each case because the circumstances have deprived him or her (at least to some extent) of a fair opportunity to avoid wrongdoing. In the most compelling cases of full or partial exculpation, we do not need to appeal to the agent's lack of fair opportunity to perform well, morally speaking. For the circumstances will have altered the moral reasons for or against the agent's conduct, such that in those circumstances, the agent's conduct simply was not a moral failure, or not as extreme a moral failure in the case of partial excuse (see Ewing 2021).

In my view, the idea that wrongdoers have lacked a fair opportunity to avoid their offenses just in case special circumstances made them less culpable is analogous to the thought that job applicants have lacked a fair opportunity to secure sought-after positions only to the extent that standardized measures of qualification (e.g., prestigious degrees, good grades, high test scores) have failed to capture their true merit (because, e.g., poverty made them choose a low-cost university, work and study at the same time, or forgo expensive test-prep). In each context, our effort to individualize standardized measures (whether the commission of the *actus reus* with the required *mens rea*, or the attainment of some degree, GPA, or test score) need not even be motivated by a concern for "fair opportunity" as such. Quite apart from fairness to individuals, there are good reasons for criminal justice systems to condemn and deter more forcefully any given crime when its perpetrator is more culpable, and for employers to hire the truly (rather than superficially) most qualified candidates.

And in the context of social justice, the following is a familiar thought: even if we were both to eradicate invidious discrimination in hiring and to control for bias in our metrics of qualification, such that jobs would be allocated only on the basis of candidates' active capacity and willingness to perform them, many individuals would still lack a fair opportunity to secure them. Why? Because of unfair inequalities in their background opportunities *to develop* their latent capacities into active ones, by cultivating their knowledge, skills, ambitions, and dispositions to use them.

It is easier and more comfortable to argue that systemic unemployment and incarceration concentrated on disadvantaged communities arise from employers and the state engaging in invidious discrimination by treating candidates equally qualified for employment or punishment differently, based on their race and class backgrounds. For one thing, this enables us to avoid confronting real tradeoffs between fairness and the other aims of employers and the criminal justice system. But a singular focus on whether the equally meritorious are treated equally pushes us to play up the extent to which we misperceive qualification and play down the extent to which inequalities in people's background opportunities can make it unfairly challenging for some people to develop and exercise their capacities (whether economic or moral). And if we do so, we risk obscuring a deeper injustice likely to lie beneath the surface injustices of systemic unemployment and incarceration alike. Mass unemployment and incarceration are bad enough, but arguably worse are social conditions that lead to large, concentrated groups of people being unable or unwilling to perform meaningful work, or culpable for criminal wrongdoing and thus liable to punishment.

In addition, we are interested in what is wrong with mass incarceration even to the extent that it is a product not of readily identifiable injustices to particular punished persons but, rather, of greater crime or more reliable accountability for it. Insofar as that is the case, and crime is a predominantly local phenomenon, the communities that bear the concentrated costs of mass incarceration are likely to be the same communities in which people are the most exposed to the regular threat of violence and other crime. If mass incarceration constitutes a failure of criminal justice over and above the sum of individual failures to punish only the guilty or only in proportion to their culpability, it is likely because it is enabled by a Janus-faced injustice at its roots: large and concentrated groups of people lack a fair opportunity to avoid succumbing to culpable crime (such that they lack a fully fair opportunity to avoid punishment) and, for precisely that reason, they and other members of their communities are unfairly vulnerable to criminal victimization, and their basic rights are insecure. Taking a distributive view of criminal justice enables us to see both sides of the problem.

As common as it has become for them to decry the simultaneous "over-policing" and "under-protection" of Black Americans, critics of mass incarceration often appear reluctant to acknowledge the full social costs of crime,[11] the critical role of the criminal justice system in protecting people against crime, and the way this complicates an honest appraisal of the problem of mass incarceration and how to solve it. To the extent that this arises from a failure to conceive of protection against crime as a good that may be distributed unfairly across society, a distributive perspective on the injustice of mass incarceration offers a salutary corrective. But there are also other important reasons—about which something must be said—why critics of mass incarceration may be reluctant to accept that taking the measure of mass incarceration as a moral evil requires putting at center stage not only punishment but also crime.

[11] Patrick Sharkey has shown in powerful research that the psychological weight of a recent homicide in a local community can substantially reduce a young person's performance on a cognitive task (2018, 76–95). The cumulative trauma of growing up in a community with a high level of violent crime can hardly be overstated.

First, mass incarceration may seem detached from crime control imperatives given that incarceration continued to rise sharply through the end of the 1990s and into the 2000s, even as crime had been declining for years (Pfaff 2017, 2–3). Yet this observation actually underscores that we cannot adequately understand mass incarceration or what makes it wrong unless we put the extent and concentration of incarceration in the context of the extent and concentration of crime. Indeed, our sense of when incarceration in America became "mass" incarceration may depend on whether we focus only on the incarceration rate or the incarceration rate relative to the crime rate. In Pfaff's view: "when we scale by crime, not population, incarceration doesn't turn 'mass' until sometime in the late 1990s or 2000s, well into the crime drop that began in 1991" (2017, 9). Quite rightly, in my view, a distributive perspective on criminal justice invites us to think not only about the incidence and distribution of punishment, but also how they compare with the incidence and distribution of crime.

Second, the significance of crime control as an aim of criminal justice is often dismissed on account of accumulated empirical evidence that marginal changes to sentence severity are unlikely to increase deterrence (see, e.g., Doob and Webster 2003). But as we have seen, if Pfaff (2017) is correct, then mass incarceration is more a product of an expanding net of felony prosecutions than of longer sentences served. And the proposition that security against crime depends upon reliable accountability for its perpetrators has considerable backing: from the conventional wisdom of criminology that the swiftness and certainty of sanctions trump their severity in importance (see, e.g., Kleiman 2009, 74); from the emerging social-scientific consensus that putting more police on the streets does tend to reduce crime (see, e.g., Sharkey 2018, 47); from the devasting cycles of violence that can accompany systemic deficits of accountability for it (see, e.g., Leovy 2015); and from America's two most salient social movements of the day, #MeToo and Black Lives Matter. From a distributive perspective, low rates of accountability may lead to higher rates of crime, and both may in turn put pressure on the criminal justice system to impose unfairly harsh sentences as poor compensation. Conversely, high rates of accountability may lead to lower rates of crime, and both may in turn facilitate the luxury of lenience toward those who still offend.

Third and finally, critics of mass incarceration may be reluctant to accept that the criminal justice system plays a central role in securing people against crime because, even if it is capable of playing that role, in a society like America it may be asked to shoulder more of that burden than it should. In particular, it may be relied upon as a cheap substitute for robust redistributive taxation and social spending, which may ultimately reduce crime more effectively and fairly (Clegg and Usmani 2019). Indeed, one suspects that a big part of what is wrong with American mass incarceration is precisely that it is a tawdry substitute for transforming America into a society of equals in which far fewer people need the heavy hand of the state to prevent them from engaging in crime. That is a deep and important point, but one that we see all the more clearly by taking seriously the magnitude and distribution not only of punishment but also of crime. It is also a reminder of a vexing problem in which mass incarceration is bound up: the problem of criminal justice amid social injustice (see generally Ewing 2018).

That a society is plagued by a high level of serious crime is far from a guarantee that it will experience anything approaching American mass incarceration. Even a decades-long spike in crime need not necessarily be met with a commensurate or greater increase in prosecutions and punishments. Instead, a society may use tools other than law enforcement to address the problem and allow rates of arrest and punishment for crime to fall as the incidence of offending rises. We need not have mass incarceration in order to confront grave injustice in the frequency, magnitude, and distribution of crime. Nevertheless, when a society does experience something that merits the label mass incarceration, and this is not due predominantly to systematic violations of familiar deontological constraints on just punishment, it is a manifestation of excess and concentrated vulnerability not only to punishment, but also to crime.

3 Conclusion

As novel as a distributive perspective on criminal justice may seem, there have already been scattered contributions to the philosophy of punishment that have explicitly attempted, or implicitly gestured toward, precisely the sort of paradigm shift this chapter envisions. Alon Harel and Gideon Parchomovsky (1999) have argued for the need for a fair distribution of protection against crime. Sharon Dolovich (2004) has attempted to work out principles of criminal justice that would be chosen for society behind a Rawlsian veil of ignorance, and has argued that they would seek to maximize the expectations of those who would be worst off in their combined expected exposure to crime and punishment. And others have sketched accounts of criminal justice that might be characterized as either incipiently distributive or at least amenable to a distributive reconstruction, such that they might be further illuminated by teasing out or filling in their distributive dimensions (see, e.g., Braithwaite and Pettit 1990; Scanlon 1998, 263–67; Kelly 2009, 2018).[12] Such admirable steps toward reimagining criminal justice in distributive terms have not gone unnoticed. But they merit more attention than they have received—particularly by theorists interested in explaining what is wrong with mass incarceration.

To take up a distributive view of criminal justice and mass incarceration is not yet to answer the many challenging questions it raises. It is one thing to argue that our understanding of the problem of mass incarceration—and of criminal justice more broadly—might be illuminated by viewing security against crime and punishment as important social goods, the distribution of which is subject to norms of fairness. It is another thing to work out a compelling theory of what would constitute a fair distribution of security against crime,[13] or a fair opportunity to avoid not merely formal "wrongdoing" but also the criminal culpability that makes a person liable to punishment.[14] Yet if the philosophy of punishment is to move forward in answering such questions, we will first need to convince more theorists to ask them. In this chapter, I have contended that the challenge of explaining the distinctive wrong of mass incarceration gives us good reason to reconsider a distributive approach to crime and punishment. Rather than try to shoehorn the problem of mass incarceration into well-worn, premade theories of punishment, perhaps we can learn from mass incarceration new lessons about our age-old subject of criminal justice.[15]

---

[12] Even "fair play" theories of retributivism might be characterized as "distributive," insofar as they are grounded in the putative need to disgorge offenders of some unfair advantage over society that they have supposedly reaped by their crimes (see, e.g., Sher 1987; Westen 2016). Proponents of such theories have often formulated them in ways designed to explain and justify traditional, individualistic intuitions about deserved punishment. But they have also long had to fight off the contention of Jeffrie Murphy (1973) that fair play retributivism might end up a Trojan horse for a radical critique of retributive justice amid social injustice. For as he suggested, it seems daft to tell typical offenders—whose poverty and lack of education place them among society's most disadvantaged members—that they owe a debt to society because of an unfair advantage they have taken of it. "Fair play" retributivists have accused Murphy of running together incommensurable benefits and burdens from different spheres of justice (see, e.g., Sher 1987, 84–85) or of wrongly taking duties to refrain from serious crime to be contingent on background social justice (Westen 2016, 75–76). Yet as our discussion of distributive theories of punishment has revealed, in a society experiencing mass incarceration, those at greatest risk of criminally offending are likely also to be among those most disadvantaged *in their vulnerability to being victims of crime, specifically.* And even if that insecurity does not relieve them of their natural duty to refrain from serious crime (see, e.g., Shelby 2007), it may still be relevant to what they are owed as a matter of criminal justice. So it remains less than clear that fair play retributivism can so easily escape appropriation by those who might wish to leverage it in critique of mass incarceration.

[13] For preliminary thoughts, see Harel and Parchomovsky (1999, 523–29).

[14] For a first attempt to work through that problem, see Ewing (2021).

[15] I am grateful to Lisa Kerr for helpful conversations related to this chapter, and to Nick Morrow for useful editorial suggestions.

References

Alexander, Michelle. 2020. *The New Jim Crow: Mass Incarceration in the Age of Colorblindness*. 10th anniversary ed. New York: New Press.

Altman, Matthew C., and Cynthia D. Coe. 2022. "Punishment Theory, Mass Incarceration, and the Overdetermination of Racialized Justice." *Criminal Law and Philosophy* 16, no. 3 (October): 631–49.

Braithwaite, John, and Philip Pettit. 1990. *Not Just Deserts: A Republican Theory of Criminal Justice*. Oxford: Oxford University Press.

Brink, David O. 2021. *Fair Opportunity and Responsibility*. Oxford: Oxford University Press.

Chiao, Vincent. 2017. "Mass Incarceration and the Theory of Punishment." *Criminal Law and Philosophy* 11, no. 3 (September): 431–52.

Clegg, John, and Adaner Usmani. 2019. "The Economic Origins of Mass Incarceration." *Catalyst* 3, no. 3 (Fall): 9–53.

Dolovich, Sharon. 2004. "Legitimate Punishment in Liberal Democracy." *Buffalo Criminal Law Review* 7, no. 2 (January): 307–442.

Doob, Anthony N., and Cheryl Marie Webster. 2003. "Sentence Severity and Crime: Accepting the Null Hypothesis." *Crime and Justice* 30: 143–95.

Ewing, Benjamin. 2015. "The Political Legitimacy of Retribution: Two Reasons for Skepticism." *Law and Philosophy* 34, no. 4 (July): 369–96.

———. 2018. "Recent Work on Punishment and Criminogenic Disadvantage." *Law and Philosophy* 37, no. 1 (February): 29–68.

———. 2019. "Mitigating Factors: A Typology." In *The Palgrave Handbook of Applied Ethics and the Criminal Law*, edited by Larry Alexander and Kimberly Kessler Ferzan, 423–42. Cham, Switzerland: Palgrave Macmillan.

———. 2021. "Criminal Responsibility and Fair Moral Opportunity." *Criminal Law and Philosophy*. https://doi.org/10.1007/s11572-021-09621-5.

Fair, Helen, and Roy Walmsley. 2021. *World Prison Population List*. 13th ed. London: Institute for Crime & Justice Policy Research.

Flanders, Chad. 2021. "What Is Wrong with Mass Incarceration?" In *The Routledge Handbook of the Philosophy and Science of Punishment*, edited by Farah Focquaert, Elizabeth Shaw, and Bruce N. Waller, 161–72. New York: Routledge.

Forman, James, Jr. 2012. "Racial Critiques of Mass Incarceration: Beyond the New Jim Crow." *New York University Law Review* 87, no. 1 (April): 21–69.

———. 2017. *Locking Up Our Own: Crime and Punishment in Black America*. New York: Farrar, Straus and Giroux.

Fortner, Michael Javen. 2015. *Black Silent Majority: The Rockefeller Drug Laws and the Politics of Punishment*. Cambridge, MA: Harvard University Press.

Garland, David. 2001. "Introduction: The Meaning of Mass Imprisonment." *Punishment and Society* 3, no. 1 (January): 5–7.

Gottschalk, Marie. 2015. *Caught: The Prison State and the Lockdown of American Politics*. Princeton, NJ: Princeton University Press.

Gruber, Aya. 2010. "A Distributive Theory of Criminal Law." *William and Mary Law Review* 52, no. 1 (October): 1–73.
Harel, Alon, and Gideon Parchomovsky. 1999. "On Hate and Equality." *Yale Law Journal* 109, no. 3 (December): 507–39.
Hart, H. L. A. 2008. *Punishment and Responsibility: Essays in the Philosophy of Law*. 2nd ed. Oxford: Oxford University Press.
Kang-Brown, Jacob, Chase Montagnet, and Jasmine Heiss. 2021. *People in Jail and Prison in Spring 2021*. New York: Vera Institute of Justice.
Kelly, Erin I. 2009. "Criminal Justice without Retribution." *Journal of Philosophy* 106, no. 8 (August): 440–62.
———. 2018. *The Limits of Blame: Rethinking Punishment and Responsibility*. Cambridge, MA: Harvard University Press.
Kleiman, Mark A. R. 2009. *When Brute Force Fails: How to Have Less Crime and Less Punishment*. Princeton, NJ: Princeton University Press.
Leovy, Jill. 2015. *Ghettoside: A True Story of Murder in America*. New York: Spiegel & Grau.
Murphy, Jeffrie G. 1973. "Marxism and Retribution." *Philosophy & Public Affairs* 2, no. 3 (Spring): 217–43.
Pfaff, John F. 2011. "The Myths and Realities of Correctional Severity: Evidence from the National Corrections Reporting Program on Sentencing Practices." *American Law and Economics Review* 13, no. 2 (Fall): 491–531.
———. 2012. "The Causes of Growth in Prison Admissions and Populations." Social Science Research Network, January 23. https://papers.ssrn.com/sol3/papers.cfm?abstract_id=1990508.
———. 2017. *Locked In: The True Causes of Mass Incarceration—and How to Achieve Real Reform*. New York: Basic.
Quinn, Warren. 1985. "The Right to Threaten and the Right to Punish." *Philosophy & Public Affairs* 14, no. 4 (Autumn): 327–73.
Robinson, Paul. 2008. *Distributive Principles of Criminal Law: Who Should Be Punished How Much?* Oxford: Oxford University Press.
Scanlon, T. M. 1998. *What We Owe To Each Other*. Cambridge, MA: Harvard University Press.
Scheffler, Samuel. 2000. "Justice and Desert in Liberal Theory." *California Law Review* 88, no. 3 (May): 965–90.
Sharkey, Patrick. 2018. *Uneasy Peace: The Great Crime Decline, the Renewal of City Life, and the Next War on Violence*. New York: Norton.
Shelby, Tommie. 2007. "Justice, Deviance, and the Dark Ghetto." *Philosophy & Public Affairs* 35, no. 2 (Spring): 126–60.
Sher, George. 1987. *Desert*. Princeton, NJ: Princeton University Press.
Stanczyk, Lucas. 2012. "Productive Justice." *Philosophy & Public Affairs* 40, no. 2 (Spring): 144–64.
Stewart, Hamish. 2018. "The Wrong of Mass Punishment." *Criminal Law and Philosophy* 12, no. 1 (March): 45–57.

Stuntz, William J. 2001. "The Pathological Politics of Criminal Law." *Michigan Law Review* 100, no. 3 (December): 505–600.

Tadros, Victor. 2011. *The Ends of Harm: The Moral Foundations of Criminal Law*. Oxford: Oxford University Press.

Westen, Peter. 2016. "Retributive Desert as Fair Play." In *Legal, Moral, and Metaphysical Truths: The Philosophy of Michael S. Moore*, edited by Kimberly Kessler Ferzan and Stephen J. Morse, 63–78. Oxford: Oxford University Press.

Western, Bruce. 2006. *Punishment and Inequality in America*. New York: Russell Sage Foundation.

———. 2018. *Homeward: Life in the Year after Prison*. New York: Russell Sage Foundation.

Whitman, James Q. 2003a. *Harsh Justice: Criminal Punishment and the Widening Divide between America and Europe*. Oxford: Oxford University Press.

———. 2003b. "A Plea against Retributivism." *Buffalo Criminal Law Review* 7, no. 1 (April): 85–107.

Yankah, Ekow. 2020. "Punishing Them All: How Criminal Justice Should Account for Mass Incarceration." *Res Philosophica* 97, no. 2 (April): 185–218.

31

Blaming Kids

Craig K. Agule

1 Introduction

We should give kid wrongdoers a break.[1] We should not bring the full force of our blame upon them, nor should the criminal justice system treat them as harshly as it treats adult wrongdoers. This break is familiar, it is intuitively attractive, and moral and legal philosophy offers a ready explanation for it. Kids are less mature, so they are less responsible; thus, when they act wrongly, they are less culpable. Because blame and punishment should track culpability, kids' reduced culpability is good grounds for giving them a break. This explanation of the break kids should receive connects an attractive story about moral and legal responsibility to something intrinsic to childhood: immaturity.

But this is not the whole story. In this chapter, I argue that we can enrich the explanation of how we should treat kid wrongdoers by recognizing that it matters who does the blaming and punishing. That we should think about who does the blaming and punishing is perhaps unsurprising, but it is

[1] Why 'kids'? Why not the less-informal 'children,' the more precise 'those under eighteen years old,' or some other term? I prefer 'kids' to 'children' because, to my ear, 'kids' better points to the relatively older group that is more likely to be ensnared by the criminal justice system. Second, 'kids' is both vague and informal, and given the social commitments in the arguments to follow, I want to avoid committing myself to any firm metaphysics regarding the people under discussion. For similar thoughts, see Yaffe (2018, 1–2) and Schapiro (1999, esp. 717).

C. K. Agule (✉)
Rutgers University—Camden, Camden, NJ, USA
e-mail: craig.agule@rutgers.edu

© The Author(s), under exclusive license to Springer Nature Switzerland AG 2023

M. C. Altman (ed.), *The Palgrave Handbook on the Philosophy of Punishment*, Palgrave Handbooks in the Philosophy of Law, https://doi.org/10.1007/978-3-031-11874-6_31

nonetheless often underappreciated. Here, I offer two lessons about blame and punishment by thinking about who judges kids. First, the right account of moral and legal responsibility should allow that kids may rightly blame each other, and I argue that we can best accommodate this by relativizing the threshold of competence needed for responsibility. Second, although each kid is an individual and, as a result, the implications of immaturity vary significantly from kid to kid, we should give kids a break as kids, that is, based on our categorizing them as kids. That we should and do categorize in that way reflects the nature of the criminal justice system as an institution and the nature of us as social beings.

Both arguments suggest that we cannot have a complete understanding of why we should give kid wrongdoers a break if we think only about kids, the nature of being a kid, and what kids deserve in the abstract. We must also think about who does the blaming. This is just the tip of the iceberg. Much of our theorizing about blame and criminal punishment has focused almost exclusively on the wrongdoers we blame and punish. I suspect that we will learn much about how we should react to each other when we think about us, across all the ways that we react to wrongdoing.

2 The Standard Story: Kids Are Immature and Thus Less Culpable

The standard story of the break given to kids in blame and punishment appeals to their diminished culpability.[2] In briefest form: Culpability is a product of wrongdoing and responsibility, and responsibility is a matter of the fair opportunity to avoid wrongdoing. Because kids are immature, kids generally have a diminished opportunity to avoid wrongdoing. Accordingly, kids are generally less responsible and thus less culpable for their wrongs. I begin by surveying this standard explanation of why we give kids a break in criminal punishment.

This explanation of the break owed to kids in accounting for their wrongdoing is grounded in a compatibilist, normative-competence account of

[2] For examples, see Marshall (1972), Tiboris (2014), Hirstein et al. (2018, ch. 8), Kessler (2019), and Brink (2004, 2020, 2021). The standard story is familiar in the law; we see it for example in both the Model Penal Code (MPC) §6.14(1) and the United Nation's Standard Minimum Rules for the Administration of Juvenile Justice §4. (The Model Penal Code is an idealized criminal law framework crafted by the American Law Institute in 1961 and revised several times since then.)

This story about reduced culpability is the standard story, but it is not the only story. A complementary story points out that blame and punishment might compete with important tasks like educating and nurturing kids. Yet a further complementary story urges us to see that, because kids are immature, impulsive, and the like, the criminal law's deterrence penalties are less efficacious for them.

responsibility.[3] Rather than appealing to a metaphysically inscrutable notion of openness, this account of responsibility turns to the familiar features of our ordinary moral psychology that allow us to work with normative reasons. To respond to normative reasons, we must both detect those reasons and act on our detection of them. Accordingly, we are responsible for our actions only if we possess two normative capacities: the capacity to receive reasons and the capacity to react to reasons. These conditions of moral psychology are necessary but not sufficient for responsibility, as outside conditions can interfere with or occlude the working of our mental capacities.[4] For example, it is easier to sort out reasons in times of quiet than in times of interfering chaos. Thus, an agent is responsible for their behavior in the way needed to render blame and punishment permissible if and only if the agent had a fair opportunity to act permissibly when the agent acted, and an agent has a fair opportunity to act permissibly if and only if the agent has both adequate moral-psychological capacities and adequate external circumstances.

This account of responsibility is incomplete. First, more must be said about the nature of the psychological capacities at issue, about the sorts of external circumstances that are relevant, and about how these two prongs of the responsibility framework interact. Nonetheless, the account already provides an attractive and promising framework for thinking about responsibility. For example, it nicely captures a wide range of factors that familiarly and intuitively undermine responsibility.[5] Why do certain forms of mental illness and distress excuse? Because they compromise our normative mental faculties. Why does duress excuse? At least sometimes, it is because duress denies us the adequate social circumstances needed for responsibility.[6] Accordingly, while challenges remain for fully detailing and defending a normative-competence account of responsibility, it is not out of place to use the account to frame our ongoing applied philosophy.

There is a second aspect to the incompleteness of this account. Just as the moral and legal account of responsibility is incomplete, the relevant empirical

[3] For normative-competence accounts of moral and legal responsibility, see especially Wallace (1994), Fischer and Ravizza (1998), Hart (2008), Nelkin (2011), Brink and Nelkin (2013), and Brink (2021).

[4] Some deny that reasons-responsiveness is necessary, arguing that we can be responsible for wrongdoing even if we are not reasons-responsive at the time if our lack of reasons-responsiveness can be traced to our own prior self-incapacitating action. See, most prominently, Fischer and Ravizza (1998, 49–51). I am skeptical of tracing (see Agule 2016), but we can set that dispute aside here.

[5] As Moore explains (1997, 548), quoting Freud, thinking about the cases of non-responsibility provides the royal road to a theory of responsibility.

[6] See for example Aristotle (1998, Bk. III) and Brink (2021, §68), although I argue (2020a) that, at least sometimes, duress combines elements of both excuse and justification.

sciences are themselves relatively immature.[7] A fully informed and fully grounded assessment of juvenile culpability is still in the promissory distance. Instead, my argument here is conservative. I draw from my own familiarity with childhood (a familiarity hopefully shared to a significant degree with my readers) and from the existing literature on the culpability of children to tell a story consistent with early reports from the developing science and with the account of moral responsibility. Thus, the goal of my argument here is showing how the received account of the significance of immaturity is plausible, not to provide anything like a deductive proof.

The normative-competence account of responsibility allows us to identify three aspects of immaturity that can explain why immaturity excuses.[8] First, children have immature cognitive faculties. A significant part of maturation is developing the capacities to know what morality demands, to understand why morality makes the demands it makes, to identify the descriptive circumstances that alert us to a moral issue, and to learn the strategies and habits that are tools for behaving morally. For example, we learn that it is important to share, that it is important to share because our behavior affects others' happiness and because others have moral claims similar to our own, that the moral significance of sharing is important to consider when there are limited goods and other agents about, and that we can use both voluntary action and social arrangements to help fulfill our moral obligations to share. There is much to know for acting rightly! It is in part because kids lack enough background knowledge and moral reasoning skill that we often find ourselves saying things like "Because I said so" or "You'll understand when you're older."

Second, kids have immature volitional faculties. As Justice Elena Kagan wrote in *Miller v. Alabama* (567 U.S. 460 [2012]), "children have a 'lack of maturity and an underdeveloped sense of responsibility,' leading to recklessness, impulsivity, and heedless risk-taking" (471). Children experience intense, urgent impulses, they lack the tools to regulate those impulses, and they lack the ability to reliably focus on distant or delayed rewards. These limits on kids' volitional faculties mean that, even in cases where kids

---

[7] For example, the field of Childhood Studies is barely thirty years old, though of course thinkers have wrestled with childhood, immaturity, and the like since antiquity. And I am sympathetic to Morse's (2005, 2013) persistent diagnosis of Brain Overclaim Syndrome, i.e., that it is too tempting to treat the findings of contemporary cognitive neuroscience as far more final, unequivocal, and probative than a careful consideration of the science supports. You can find earlier evidence of Morse's call for humility in Morse (1997). For discussions of the particular implications of contemporary science for the responsibility of kids, see esp. Tiboris (2014), Hirstein et al. (2018, ch. 8), Kessler (2019), and Brink (2021, ch. 12).

[8] Although immaturity surely bears on how we should treat kid wrongdoers, I do not think this means we should see childhood, or even immaturity, solely as a deficiency or a predicament. For a discussion of positive accounts of childhood, see Gheaus (2021).

recognize what they ought to do, they are not always reliably able to act accordingly. Sometimes they cannot resist the marshmallow in front of them, often because the marshmallow in front of them makes it exceedingly hard for them to think of anything else, including the reasons they have to leave the marshmallow alone.[9]

Finally, kids often find themselves in circumstances that make it harder to act appropriately. Kids are surrounded by kids, and peer pressure and peer temptations are constant. It is easier to act in accordance with moral reasons when you have time to reflect, when you are surrounded by role models who have done so and are doing so in similar situations, and when your peers are cajoling you into acting well. By contrast, it is relatively harder to act in accord with moral reasons when your peers are both themselves transgressing and leaning on you to transgress.

Although these three aspects of juvenile immaturity are familiar and plausible, their relevance in any particular case is likely to be complicated. First, maturation is a process, so immaturity is a matter of degree. Even very young children have some capacity to respond to moral reasons, and even fully mature adults are imperfect at responding to moral reasons. Accordingly, the question is not whether a given kid is immature but just how immature that kid is. Second, the different elements of moral responsibility develop at varying rates. We should not expect a perfectly linear slope across the cognitive, volitional, and circumstantial aspects of moral responsibility, showing similar growth in each element, year after year, nor should we expect each kid's growth to follow the same pattern. Third, not only will there be variance within an individual, but different kids will mature at different paces and in different patterns. Thus, the responsibility of a particular kid is going to depend upon how developed their particular capacities are, rather than upon what would be typical for kids generally. Finally, different elements will bear on different wrongs.[10] Kids' susceptibility to peer pressure matters more for wrongs involving peers than for solo wrongs, kids' impulsiveness matters more for wrongs committed on the spur of the moment than long-planned wrongs, and kids' cognitive limitations matter much more in cases where the harms are harder to understand than in cases where the harms are obvious.

Still, the standard story captures something correct. Kids are characteristically immature, that immaturity extends to their developing cognitive and volitional capacities, and they often face distinctive social pressures and

[9] Here, I appeal to intuitive familiarity with kids' behavior, and I do not mean to endorse any of the particulars of Mischel and Ebbesen (1970) or the sprawling subsequent literature.

[10] Ryberg (2014) makes this argument particularly well.

circumstances. Because of these matters, kids are characteristically less responsible for their behavior than otherwise similar adult wrongdoers. This is a matter of degree, so kids are less culpable but not ordinarily wholly excused. This is the heart of the intuitive explanation of the break owed kids in responding to their wrongs.

3 Kids Blaming Kids

On this standard story, whether someone is culpable has to do with them: what did they do, and what was their condition when they did it? It is not particularly surprising that culpability should be focused on the culpable in this way. But notice: the standard story yields the suggestion that kids cannot rightly blame each other. If kids deserve a break because they are less than fully responsible, then kids deserve a break from everyone, including each other. But this suggestion is, to my mind, counterintuitive: kids *can* rightly blame each other. That requires us to complicate the standard story, as I argue in this section.[11] In particular, I suggest that the quality of the opportunity to avoid wrongdoing required for blame to be appropriate is relative to the blamer. Exploring that relativity can give us space to accommodate kids blaming kids.[12] Thus, in this section, I will outline how the standard story of moral and legal responsibility can be augmented in a way that captures the intuition that kids may rightly blame each other.

To begin, I rehearse two related and standard claims: first, competence is a matter of degree, and second, responsibility requires a threshold level of competence. That the elements of competence are matters of degree is intuitive and widely accepted. I may be okay at solving crossword puzzles, whereas my colleague may be great at them and my friend abysmal. We should not be

[11] My intuition may be challenged. Perhaps while it is impermissible for kids to blame kids, that wrongful behavior is either excused or valuable. Even if kids who blame kids thereby do wrong, they are not themselves fully culpable, for they too are kids. Moreover, there is value in kids blaming each other, even if mistakenly. Moral maturation requires learning how to participate in a moral community, including learning how to correctly participate in the shared practice of holding responsible. Consider, for example, Fischer and Ravizza's (1998, ch. 8) argument that we are fully responsible only after we have been adequately socialized. Although I raise these possibilities to acknowledge a limitation of my argument, I rely on my initial intuition here.

[12] For an important related puzzle, see Thomason (2016). Thomason considers whether coerced child soldiers can appropriately feel guilt for their acts of violence. In those cases, the kids-blaming-kids blame is self-directed, not other-directed (although I suspect that often the guilt is actually past-self-directed, so it may not be kids-blaming-kids). Thomason urges us to see the moral value of guilt in such cases, and I suspect that her comments there could be borrowed with modification for the case of other-blame. Also, although Thomason worries primarily about the implications of coercion for guilt, her arguments are illuminating for other constraints on full responsibility.

surprised to find that elements of moral and legal responsibility are likewise matters of degree. Thus, for example, we should not be surprised to find that some people struggle to act in accord with moral reasons and that others readily and reliably act in accord with moral reasons.

Philosophers have recognized that the elements of moral and legal responsibility come in degrees.[13] John Martin Fischer and Mark Ravizza, for example, consider weak, moderate, and strong reasons-responsiveness. An agent (or, more accurately, their relevant agential mechanism) is weakly reasons-responsive if "there exist[s] *some* possible scenario (or possible world)—with the same laws as the actual world—in which there is a sufficient reason to do otherwise, the agent recognizes this reason, and the agent does otherwise" (1998, 63). An agent is moderately reasons-responsive if the agent "act[s] on a mechanism that is regularly receptive to reasons, some of which are moral reasons, and at least weakly reactive to reason" (82).[14] And, finally, an agent is strongly reasons-responsive if, in cases where there is sufficient reason to do otherwise, "the agent would *recognize* the sufficient reason to do otherwise and thus *choose* to do otherwise and *do* otherwise" (63). Likewise, David Brink recognizes that reasons-responsiveness is a matter of degree:

> Reasons-responsiveness is clearly a modal notion and admits of degrees—one might be more or less responsive. … An agent is more or less responsive to reason depending on how well her judgments about what she ought to do and her choices track her reasons for action in different possible circumstances. (2021, 60–61)[15]

Here we see again that we can make sense of different degrees of competence, and we can see that greater degrees of competence should correspond to wider and more reliable behavioral success in tracking moral reasons.

---

[13] Here, I am primarily concerned with one way that the elements of moral competence can come in degrees, namely that the elements can be more or less powerful or reliable. There are other potential ways that the elements may come in degrees, namely in terms of scope. For example, Fischer and Ravizza argue that there is a "gradually expanding range of responsiveness that indicates the class of actions for which the child is properly held accountable" (1998, 80).

[14] Fischer and Ravizza argue for an asymmetry in their account of moral responsibility, in that moderate reasons-responsiveness requires a greater degree of reasons-receptivity (the capacity to perceive the reasons) than it requires of reasons-reactivity (the capacity to act on the reasons) (1998, 81). I am skeptical of the argument for this asymmetry, but I set that aside here.

[15] These comments echo similar points made by Brink and Nelkin (2013).

Although the underlying capacities are scalar in this fashion, our responsibility practices are more granular, often to the point of being binary.[16] Either you have an excuse or not, for instance. We see this in the Model Penal Code's insanity framework. According to §4.01(1) of the MPC,

> A person is not responsible for criminal conduct if at the time of such conduct as a result of mental disease or defect he lacks substantial capacity either to appreciate the criminality [wrongfulness] of his conduct or to conform his conduct to the requirements of law.

It is not the case that the insanity defense is available to the extent that the person lacks the relevant capacities; instead, the defense is available, in its entirety, to someone who lacks the relevant capacities to a substantial degree, and not otherwise.

However, the standards offered by leading theorists of moral and legal responsibility are not especially demanding. Fischer and Ravizza argue that only moderate reasons-responsiveness "requires an understandable pattern of reasons-recognition, minimally grounded in reality" (1998, 73). Children, even young children, are not incomprehensible, and they are minimally grounded in reality (or, at least, not categorically less grounded in reality than many adults often are). Likewise, Brink offers a moderate Goldilocks standard: "Where there is sufficient reason for the agent to act, she regularly recognizes the reason and conforms her behavior to it" (2021, 62). Here, too, it should be familiar that children regularly respond to moral reasons. *Lord of the Flies* is a warning, not a report. We should see these two accounts as calling for a moderate threshold without giving us a sense of where to place it.[17]

Let me make the moderate threshold more precise. I suspect that, when agents take their own basic condition to be the stuff of capable agency, they have reasons of consistency to see others' similar basic conditions as the stuff of capable agency. Ordinarily, blaming agents take themselves to be normatively competent, both particular to the act of blaming and more generally. To

[16] Although many endorse some form of threshold thinking, that position is not uncontroversial. Brink argues that, while our actual, non-ideal responses will display thresholds, the ideal reactions may be scalar (2021, ch. 15). Similarly, Ryberg offers a sustained skepticism regarding thresholds: "Being *fully responsible* is a threshold concept that should be abandoned" (though Ryberg allows that we could have pragmatic reasons for maintaining the concept in practice) (2014, 330–32).

[17] Brink also offers a pragmatic account of a threshold of application. Given that any threshold will result in false positives (holding agents to account beyond their culpability) and false negatives (granting excuses to agents who are in fact culpable), we should pick the threshold that best balances those, taking into account the relative importance of each (2021, 261–63). I do not doubt that we should engage in this sort of balancing when considering the best practices for our non-ideal circumstances. However, here I offer a complementary if more fundamental story.

blame is to respond to reasons, so someone who blames (and appreciates that they blame) is someone who is responding to reasons, both the reasons that the wrongdoer ran afoul of and the further reasons to engage in the social practice of blaming. Thus, blaming agents ordinarily take their own moral psychology and circumstances to be the moral psychology and circumstances of a competent agent. Something has gone awry if an agent extends an excuse to someone who is, in the relevant particulars, similar to the blaming agent. This gives us a helpful input on how we set the threshold of responsibility within the broad middle swath identified by Fischer, Ravizza, and Brink. The threshold for competence is at least in part relative to the blamer: insofar as a blamer also takes themselves to be a competent agent, then the blamer does not take their basic condition to be excuse-grounding, so the threshold should be no higher than the blamer's basic condition.

This helps explain why kids may fully blame kid wrongdoers even if we adults cannot. Kids occupy a first-person perspective on their own agency. Of course, kids have a sense of themselves as kids, and they have a sense of childhood. Still, it is not implausible that kids experience their own agency as more stable, sensitive, and robust than we adults, in charge of raising and shepherding the same kids, experience their agency. Kids have projects and make efforts to engage in many of the other behaviors of stable agency. And, when kids blame each other, they recognize the particular moral reasons at stake and react to them. Kids can take themselves to be agents. They can take themselves to be the sorts of beings who take on projects, interact with the world, rightly feel pride in their accomplishments, and rightly feel guilt when they act inappropriately. Thus, a kid blamer does not take their nature as a kid (including their degree of development) to be excuse-grounding. Accordingly, given that kids regularly take themselves to be competent, kids are under pressure of consistency not to take their basic condition to be excuse-grounding. Thus, in addition to whatever else goes into setting the threshold of responsible agency, kids have reason to treat kids as competent, reason that we adults lack. Accordingly, for a kid, the mere fact of immaturity is not excuse-grounding.[18]

What implications do my conclusions here have for the criminal justice system? One implication goes beyond juvenile justice. Many criminal justice systems are staffed in significant part by white-collar professionals. Advanced

[18] What does this mean for how kids might treat adults? Perhaps it is reasonable to treat everyone above the threshold as fully responsible, without further distinctions between them, such that kids treat adults like kids treat kids. Or perhaps holding responsible is variable above some minimal threshold, such that kids hold adults to a higher standard. I am inclined toward this second possibility, although I am here agnostic.

degrees are common—law degrees, social work degrees, and the like. Many of the staff members, especially the counsel and the judges, are financially secure, at least relatively so. By contrast, many within the criminal justice system have been shortchanged in the ways that matter for having robust opportunities for living alternative lives. Thus, my argument here leads to a broad suspicion about the ordinary operation of the criminal justice system. There is something amiss in a system where those with hugely robust opportunities to avoid wrongdoing are in the business of constantly chastising those with greatly diminished opportunities to avoid wrongdoing.

And what about the implications for juvenile justice in particular? First, we should recognize that there are many systems that respond to kid wrongdoers. Consider, for example, two contrasting academic-integrity disciplinary systems, one run by faculty and one run by students (in fact and not just in name). My argument here tells us that the former should be more lenient and understanding of excuse than the latter.[19] Second, insofar as the criminal justice system involves adults blaming kids and doing so on behalf of a generally adult population, there is little tension in those adults extending a break to kid wrongdoers. This point should be qualified, however. Kid wrongdoings often involve kid victims, and insofar as the court proceedings are also supposed to legitimate the voices of the victims of wrongs, courts must be careful not to undermine the agency of the kid victims in blaming the kid wrongdoers. Finally, I worry about the interaction between the criminal justice system and other disciplinary systems, especially systems that are kid-focused. Often, we defer too much to court adjudications, as in when we rely upon "innocent until proven guilty" in our social interactions. This is worrisome if forums for kids to grapple with wrongdoing (such as those student-run academic integrity systems) defer to criminal court evaluations, in that the kid forums might unreflectively endorse the diminished view of kid agency or the resulting punishments that the criminal courts explicitly endorse. We should be cautious about treating criminal adjudications as a starting point for other ways that we respond to wrongdoing.

[19] Or consider New York's Youth Court system. The Youth Court system is an alternative sentencing forum for young offenders where the court officials—the advocates, judges, bailiffs, jurors, and the like—are the offenders' young peers. Although the system itself may be designed with rehabilitation, education, and integration in mind, from within the system, the young administrators aim to hold the offenders before them responsible for their wrongdoing. As New York's Wyoming County Youth Court describes itself, the Youth Court "is designed to help the respondent become accountable to the community for their unlawful behavior, by accepting responsibility for their behavior, and to help them repair the harm caused" (Wyoming County Youth Bureau 2022). I thank the philosophy students of SUNY–Geneseo for this example.

4 Age as a Proxy for Immaturity

On the story so far, whether we should give someone a break depends on the person being blamed and the person who would blame them. We should ask about the nature of the agency of the wrongdoer, and we should ask about the nature of the agency of the would-be blamer. In both cases, the particulars of the agents involved are what matter. However, I think that in fact we blame kids *as kids*, both interpersonally and institutionally. That is, we give kids a break not just because of their particular development but also because we classify them as kids. As with my argument in the prior section, my argument here requires us to think about the nature of the agents who do the blaming.

4.1 The Institutional Proxy

I begin with an institutional-design element of the standard story of the break extended to kids in the criminal justice system.[20] In light of kids' immaturity, criminal courts might engage in particularized psychological and agential evaluations of individual kids. However, that is not (in the main) what American courts do. Instead, American courts often give kids more lenient sentences or otherwise give them a break in criminal adjudication on the basis of age.[21] That is, American courts (in the main) treat age as a proxy for immaturity.

Treating age as a proxy for immaturity is an imperfect strategy. Some kids are precocious, and some kids are, even for their age, immature. Thus, treating age as a proxy for immaturity will result in some kids getting a break greater than they deserve, and it will result in some kids being denied as great a break as they deserve. It will also deny an immaturity break to immature young adults, if consideration of immaturity is entirely or even only predominantly exhausted by the proxy. These are not insignificant errors, given the high stakes of the criminal justice system.

Nonetheless, we can make out a *prima facie* case for an age proxy for culpability within the criminal justice system where the proxy would be expected to produce a more attractive combination of due convictions, under-convictions,

[20] The best sustained defense of this strategy is Brink (2004; 2020; 2021, ch. 12).

[21] Although particular jurisdictions vary a great deal in how they handle juvenile wrongdoers, the MPC provides a not-atypical framework. According to MPC §4.10(a), whether a case is routed to specialized juvenile courts tracks the offender's age at the time of offense, rather than the particulars of their maturation process. The MPC also provides juvenile-specific limits on punishment, providing relief to kids not available to adults, in §6.14, especially (6), (7), and (8).

and over-convictions than an alternative practice. Because kids are generally immature, there are many kid wrongdoers who are not fully responsible. Accordingly, treating age as a proxy for immaturity and thus exculpation will result in roughly due verdicts in many cases. Moreover, because kids are generally immature, we should not expect there to be very many cases of significant under-conviction. Although some kids are more mature than the average, I am skeptical that many kids are tremendously more mature than the average, and I am further skeptical that many kid wrongdoers are tremendously more mature than average. And, in our criminal justice system, we are significantly less concerned with errors of under-conviction than with errors of over-conviction.[22] So, not only are there likely to be few cases of under-conviction, but also such cases are not likely to be particularly worrisome.

What of cases of over-conviction? We might worry that deploying this proxy will result in overly punishing immature young adults. This worry should push us to think about the right threshold. If there are many sufficiently immature eighteen-year-olds, then eighteen-year-olds plausibly should count as kids. And the same for nineteen-year-olds, twenty-year-olds, and so on. Accordingly, while I here support a kids defense grounded in generalities about kids, this defense is consistent with thinking that the age of those to whom this defense is available might be raised.[23] Moreover, relying on the proxy defense does not preclude considering immaturity as a mitigating factor for particular adults.

Any policy option should be evaluated in light of its potential alternatives. Here are two chief reasons to favor the kids proxy over individuated evaluations. First, the kids proxy is very cheap to deploy. The criminal justice system, like all elements of our practical lives, has only so much time and so many resources. Applying the kids proxy is, in most cases, relatively straightforward, and it requires no particular expertise. By contrast, individuated evaluations could be very expensive and cumbersome. Imagine the evidence needed to assess all the relevant elements of moral and agential psychology. Plausibly, this could include surveys of a wrongdoer's history, school records, interviews with neighbors, and psychological evaluations. The resources needed for all

[22] Perhaps the most famous statement of this difference in concern is from eighteenth-century commentator William Blackstone: "It is better that ten guilty persons escape than that one innocent suffer."

[23] Raising the age of the culpability defense would potentially mean separating the age of defense in the criminal law from the age of adulthood for other things, such as the right to vote. That's not obviously a problem, as our concerns about over- and under-inclusion presumably are different in the different cases. It is much more worrisome to convict someone innocent than to allow someone a bit too young one vote, for example. For an example of separating the proxy ages for criminal liability and voting, see Nelkin (2020). For an even greater separation, see Wall (2021), who argues that all children who want to vote should be permitted to vote.

those investigations must come from somewhere, and the material must be evaluated by skilled and often highly educated professionals.

These are the material costs. Individuated evaluations would also impose harms. These investigations would be quite invasive. A young defendant might be forced to choose between defending themselves adequately and subjecting themselves to quite personal psychological and psychiatric inquiries, permitting their family members, teachers, and friends to testify about normally private matters, and the like. We should not lightly underestimate the emotional and personal burdens of litigation, and I suspect having to prove your own immaturity to a courtroom of strangers may be a case where those burdens could be significant.

Second, individuated evaluations are themselves imperfect because we are imperfect evaluators. For example, I suspect that individuated evaluations are likely to result in denying defenses to some kids who should deserve them. Our evaluations of harm and potential wrongdoing often influence our assessments of the separate matters of maturity. The same kid, with the same psychology, could appear more responsible (and thus culpable) in the context of a wrongdoing than the kid would appear in other contexts. If the facts of wrongdoing influence our particular assessments of the agent's psychology, then the kids proxy will be immune to a flaw that afflicts individuated evaluations. Likewise, our individuated evaluations are likely be sensitive to the personal expectations and stereotypes that evaluators bring to the case. For example, as I discuss in the next section, we should expect that individuated evaluations may comparatively disfavor children of color. It is important not to assume that individuated evaluations will be more likely to get individual cases right nor to assume that the resulting errors will be minor or distributed in a fair fashion. A proxy may be, in these regards, preferrable.

Thus, while the devil is in the details, there is good reason to think that the criminal justice system can rightly use age as a proxy for immaturity. Doing so is likely to produce outcomes that track the underlying degree of culpability, its mistakes are unlikely to be particularly worrisome, and its deployment will be cheaper and less invasive than individuated evaluations, which are themselves imperfect. Thus, even though a proxy like this is imperfect, we likely have good reason to adopt it as a practical guide. Moreover, to return to my overarching theme, we neither properly appreciate that we should have a proxy nor rightly pick out the particular the proxy that we should have if we focus only on the apparent offenders who face criminal charges. We also need to think about us, our systems, the limitations we and our systems face, and the characteristics of the set of cases that we and our systems are likely to confront.

4.2 The Individual Proxy

It is not surprising that the criminal justice system relies upon proxies: it has practical aims and is a finite system, with limited epistemic capacities and limited resources. However, the criminal justice system is not the only place in our practical lives where we find practical aims constrained by finite capacities and resources. We should expect proxies to be nearly omnipresent in our practical lives. Here, I consider proxies we rely upon individually; in particular, I consider the role of social generics and how they might affect our interpersonal reactions to kid wrongdoers. Because of the epistemic and framing effects of social generics, when we recognize someone as a kid, we will be disposed to see them as immature.

Consider this claim: "dogs have tails." This is a claim that relates a type, dogs, to a property, having tails. But this is not a universal claim, as some dogs certainly lack tails, for one reason or another. Nor is this even a statistical claim. Of course, it is also true that most dogs have tails. But that is a different matter. After all, most people are right-handed, and yet "people are right-handed" is false. Instead, "dogs have tails" is a generic generalization. A generic generalization is a proposition connecting a type to a property by way of the essence of the type. To know "dogs have tails," you do not need to do a survey; you just need to be familiar with what it is to be a dog.[24]

Generics are an important part of our lives, and they are deeply natural features of our cognitive psychology. As Sarah-Jane Leslie (2014) explains, research on young children shows that generics are quite easy to learn and to process and that children often treat universals as generics. This should not be surprising, once we recognize that generics are cognitively fundamental, as Leslie urges us to accept, and once we understand that generics are less cognitively taxing than more precise, quantified statements. The natural inclination we have toward generics and the efficiency with which we learn, process, and deploy generics show that they are an important cognitive tool for us.

Of particular importance for my arguments here is that social generics have epistemic and perceptual effects. Accepting a social generic means recognizing an essentialized kind. This recognition has evidentiary and interpretive implications. Someone who accepts generics about teachers will be especially sensitive to evidence and interpretations that warrant the perception of someone as a teacher. Moreover, accepting a social generic also means recognizing a

[24] I have especially benefitted from Wodak et al. (2015), Leslie (2008, 2013, 2014, 2017), and Ritchie (2019). I have also found Murphy's (2006) account of natural law helpful in thinking about essences and normativity in the law.

connection between that essentialized kind and the property referenced in the generic sentence. We expect things to have their essential properties, so we are sensitive to evidence of their presence or their absence.[25]

I speculatively claim that we should and do learn social generics connecting kids to immaturity.[26] The exact nature of the generics that we accept is, of course, a matter of descriptive, empirical study. Nevertheless, we should expect a number of social generics involving kids, given the pervasiveness of kids in our lives and the many overlapping interests we have in their lives. Given these interests and the goods commonly associated with childhood, we should expect to perceive "kids" as an essentialized kind, relating being a kid to characteristic properties such as immaturity, impulsiveness, and openness to joy.

Because of the epistemic and framing effects of social generics, when we recognize someone as a kid, we will be inclined to see them as immature. We will be especially sensitive to evidence of their immaturity, evidence of opportunities to teach them and to help them develop, and evidence of innocence and joy. We will also be inclined to interpret the evidence we perceive about kids in ways consistent with their being a kid, with their being still in development, with their being joyous, and so on. Thus, our understandings and perceptions of the moral and agential development of any particular kid is driven by our perception of them as a kid, even if it is also driven by particularized evidence of their underlying moral and agential faculties.

Finally, the epistemic and perceptual effects of social generics have implications for how we should treat kids. We should rely upon social generics, given how cognitively and socially valuable they can be. An appropriate set of social generics plausibly includes social generics regarding kids. Therefore, it is appropriate for us to sometimes perceive young people as immature, perhaps more than we would were we not to recognize the juvenile offender as a kid. Insofar as we should treat people in accord with how we should perceive them (a key subjectivist assumption that I do not defend here), we should

---

[25] This helps explain the danger of some social generics. For example, many vicious stereotypes are social generics. Someone who accepts the stereotype "Americans are loud" thinks that there is an American essence that includes a disposition to be loud. It is not hard to see how social stereotypes like this (and others far more vicious) can be harmful. Moreover, that such harmful social stereotypes are grounded in generics makes them resistant to correction, as contrary evidence is likely to be overlooked or interpreted away.

[26] "Kids" is not the only essentialized kind in the area. As with most social generics, there are a range of related kinds, and these related kinds are both overlapping and vague at the boundaries. Accordingly, "children," "teenagers," "adolescents," and the like presumably play similar roles. Here, "kids" stands in for all the members of that set, with minor variations over the members of the set.

sometimes give young people a break on grounds of immaturity that is a function of more than the available, particularized evidence.

Recognizing the importance of social generics for how we react to kid wrongdoers points to a perhaps underappreciated problem in our blaming practices. The set of those whom we perceive as kids has an imperfect relationship with the set of actual kids. I assume optimistically that our epistemic dispositions to see and understand kids as kids are fairly sensitive to whether the person we are considering is, in fact, a kid, but surely these dispositions are not perfectly sensitive. Accordingly, there will be some adults we perceive as kids, and there will be some kids we fail to perceive as kids. Thus, there will be some adults we give breaks to as if they were kids, and there will be some kids whom we fail to give breaks to. These mismatches are worrisome, and my worry is compounded given that some of these mismatches may be systematic. Plausibly, children of color are disproportionately denied being seen as a kid.[27] Given the importance of social generics for our background processing of the world around us, we should then expect that a seemingly neutral and principled application of ostensibly fair principles of culpability would result in systemic injustice, a concern highlighted by appreciating the role of social generics in our blaming practices.

4.3 The Interaction of These Proxies and Yaffe's Objection

These framing effects of our social generics have implications for our experience with the criminal law's institutional age proxy for partial competence. Here, I argue that recognizing these social generics should affect how we rely upon casuistry and intuition in considering our criminal justice institutions.[28]

There is significant overlap between the institutional proxies and our social generics. Many of the same people the institutional proxy categorizes as kids will be categorized as kids by our social generics. This significant overlap will

[27] For examples among a significant empirical literature, see Tatum (2003), Shook (2005), and Espinoza et al. (2011).

[28] Although here I focus on an important objection from Yaffe, social generics have other important implications for our criminal law practice. For instance, recognizing that courts still exercise discretion (e.g., in considering whether to transfer a juvenile defendant to an adult court), social generics can explain a significant part of what goes wrong with racist disparities in blaming and punishing children of color. Children of color are going to be more likely to have their cases transferred to adult courts, where they are more likely to receive harsher sentences, and they are less likely to be the beneficiaries of leniency in sentencing discretion. I leave this other implication aside not because it is unimportant but rather because it warrants more sustained attention than I can give it here. For more on this worry, see Jackson and Pabon (2000), discussing race, juvenile transfer, and "the fear of other people's children."

tend to increase our confidence in the institutional proxy. That is because the social generics' framing will lead us to perceive individual kids as more immature than we otherwise would perceive them. Imagine, for example, a precocious seventeen-year-old who in fact deserves less of a culpability break than the institutional proxy would give them. When we consider the case, however, we cannot immediately and perfectly access the underlying psychological and agential facts. Accordingly, we should expect our assessment of this person to track our own personal epistemic tools and framings—including those of the social generics we accept. If we have internalized a kids generic and if we perceive this person as a kid, we will therefore perceive them as immature, and we will be less likely to see this as a case where the institutional proxy is imperfect.

This helps to address a concern about the institutional proxy raised by Gideon Yaffe (2018, 30–39). Yaffe's worry is that our intuitions about appropriate criminal punishment are not empirically sensitive in the way that we would expect proxies to be. He has us consider a number of competitor proxies that could be available. He argues that if kids are given a break in criminal adjudication as a proxy, then we should feel the intuitive pull toward other proxies if we imagine various factual circumstances (or, at least, we should feel the intuitive discomfort when we imagine relying upon an ill-fitting proxy). Consider, for example, the plausible claim that girls mature faster than boys. Imagining that to be true, perhaps a better proxy for tracking immaturity would be gender-sensitive, such that girls get less of a break in the criminal law than boys. Or perhaps careful attention to the facts would reveal that height is a better predictor of normative maturity than age. Should we then measure each defendant on their way into courtroom? Yaffe argues that we would not be tempted by these competitor proxies even if the facts supported them and that the recognition that we would not be tempted gives us evidence that the breaks we actually give kids are not grounded in a proxy for immaturity.[29]

One response to Yaffe's objection denies his data; that is, it rejects his claim that we would not be attracted to the competitor proxies. Yaffe has his intuitions, but we may not share them. For instance, it is plausible to me that,

[29] Yaffe uses this objection to spur his search for an alternative account of the break owed to kids in the criminal law. He argues that being a kid entails not having the right to vote and that not having the right to vote (at least in the case of kids) entails reduced culpability for violating the law. Yaffe's political argument is interesting and provocative, but (1) the reduced culpability for kids in cases of *mala in se* crimes like battery or homicide does not track additional culpability grounded in political obligation, and (2) his political explanation would create a stark divide in practice between interpersonal and institutional obligation that does not track my intuitions. Kelly (2020) is sympathetic to aspects of Yaffe's argument; for skeptical responses to Yaffe, see Husak (2018), Agule (2020b), Brink (2020), Guerrero (2020), Morse (2020), and Nelkin (2020).

were some alternative proxy to be significantly more accurate than an age proxy, and were I to carefully consider the data, my intuitive responses may well shift. Indeed, I suspect that recent changes in juvenile justice reflect changes in beliefs regarding the very sorts of empirical matters Yaffe has in mind.

But we may accept Yaffe's data. I would be suspicious of a policy of granting a break based on a combination of age and gender, especially if that break penalized young women. Does that give me reason to think that the break we give kids is not in fact a proxy? Even if Yaffe's alternatives are more accurate, they might run afoul of constraints like fairness. For example, we may reasonably have equal protection concerns about a gender-sensitive proxy in the criminal law, concerns heightened when we recognize our history of mistreating people on the basis of gender (in large part a history of erroneously and wrongly treating gender as a proxy for other matters). Given those concerns, an intuitive resistance to a gender proxy is consistent with thinking that greater accuracy is, *ceteris paribus*, preferable. Although I think this response to Yaffe is both charitable and substantive, notice that we should nonetheless experience our proxies with a wince. If we know that there is an alternative proxy, and if we know that we are setting it aside based on a constraint like fairness, then we should feel that compromise.

Here, however, I offer a response to Yaffe that both accepts his data and provides a partial explanation of our comfort with the proxy. When we consider his alternative proxies, we should not imagine that we are evaluating things from some detached perspective. Rather, we remain as socialized as ever. Accordingly, we bring the framing effects of our social generics to our consideration of alternative proxies. Thus, because we are socially conditioned to see kids as immature, and because that conditioning is deep, hard to change, and often working below the level of our awareness, we should expect that our intuitions will be resistant to abstract data about juvenile brains and the like. Stereotypes are hard to dislodge! Accordingly, even if the institutional proxy for kids is justified by empirical data about fit and cost, and even if data from the social sciences may seem the sort of thing to dislodge our confidence in matters of fit, we are not well-positioned to easily evaluate the underlying facts of the matter. We should expect our intuitions to be sticky in just the way Yaffe reports that his intuitions are sticky. But this is not because our institutional break is not a proxy; rather, it is because there are both institutional and social-generic proxies at work.

This is good news for defenders of the proxy, especially those worried by Yaffe's objection. However, the news is not entirely good. As I argued earlier, I suspect that an age-grounded proxy for giving kids a break in the criminal law is at least a sufficiently good strategy, justified by how well it sorts cases and its ease of application. However, my evaluation of individual cases, both real and hypothetical, is sure to be affected by the potential coincidence between the institutional proxy and social generics. My confidence in the fitness of the age-grounded proxy is tempered by this recognition. Given that the case for any particular proxy is of necessity incomplete (at least for the foreseeable future), I recognize that I will be particularly tempted to those proxies that ring intuitively true because they coincide with the social generics I already accept. This does not mean that we should not adopt an age-grounded proxy, but it does mean that my confidence in the proxy is qualified.

5 Conclusion

It is widely accepted that the reason why kid wrongdoers should be treated less harshly than otherwise-similar adult wrongdoers is because kids are immature. This explanation is a significant part of the truth: the most attractive accounts of moral and legal responsibility ground responsibility partially in the possession of mature moral-psychological capacities, capacities that are still developing in kids. However, as I have argued here, this explanation is only part of the story. In order to fully theorize how we should treat kid wrongdoers, we must think about those of us who would do the treating. First, sometimes kids appropriately blame each other, and we can best explain why we should not blame kids, even though kids may rightly blame kids, by seeing that the degree of normative competence needed for moral responsibility can vary depending upon who is doing the blaming. Second, although normative competence is what matters for desert, neither we nor our legal systems have perfect, direct access to the relevant underlying psychological details. Although we can consider the particulars, we often rely upon personal and institutional proxies, epistemic and otherwise, proxies that reflect our limitations and the limitations of our systems. Given these two lessons, our theories of moral and legal responsibility will be oversimplified if we think only about who does wrong and not also about who responds to the wrong.

These lessons apply beyond the cases of kid wrongdoers, and they extend to matters beyond the relevant threshold for responsibility and our epistemic and perceptual faculties.[30] For instance, much of our theorizing about responding to wrongdoing moves too quickly from the belief that someone is culpable to the belief that we have substantial reason to blame or punish them; examining the gap in that inferences requires us to think about our own priorities. How we should respond to wrongdoers turns significantly upon facts about us, going beyond the wrongdoer's culpability and how our responses can shape a wrongdoer's future life and behavior. Hopefully the arguments here help encourage us to see criminal law theory in those broader lights.[31]

References

Agule, Craig K. 2016. "Resisting Tracing's Siren Song." *Journal of Ethics and Social Philosophy* 10, no. 1: 1–24.

———. 2020a. "Distinctive Duress." *Philosophical Studies* 177, no. 4 (April): 1007–26.

———. 2020b. Review of *The Age of Culpability: Children and the Nature of Criminal Responsibility*, by Gideon Yaffe. *Ethics* 130, no. 2 (January): 271–76.

Aristotle. 1998. *The Nicomachean Ethics*. Translated by W. D. Ross. Oxford: Oxford University Press.

Brink, David O. 2004. "Immaturity, Normative Competence, and Juvenile Transfer: How (Not) to Punish Minors for Major Crimes." *Texas Law Review* 82, no. 6 (May): 1555–85.

———. 2020. "The Moral Asymmetry of Juvenile and Adult Offenders." *Criminal Law and Philosophy* 14, no. 2 (July): 223–39.

———. 2021. *Fair Opportunity and Responsibility*. Oxford: Clarendon.

Brink, David O., and Dana Kay Nelkin. 2013. "Fairness and the Architecture of Responsibility." In *Oxford Studies in Agency and Responsibility*, edited by David Shoemaker, vol. 1, 284–313. Oxford: Oxford University Press.

[30] Thus, I am sympathetic to Larisa Svirsky's claim that "it matters significantly what one's relationship is to a given marginal agent whether or not one should hold her responsible" (2020, 249). I believe my two arguments here are in deep sympathy with her arguments that the ways that it is appropriate to hold someone responsible depend upon your relationship with that person and that we better understand the broader practice of holding responsible if we treat these cases as ordinary and not marginal. Here, for example, thinking about kids holding kids responsible helps us understand the competence threshold, a threshold that matters for all of us, not just kids.

[31] This paper has traveled a winding road, and I have many people to thank for comments and insights along the way. I thank audiences at the APA Committee on Philosophy and Law session at the American Philosophical Association–Eastern Division; the Blame, Punishment, and Health Workshop at Rutgers University-Camden; and the Annual Congress of the Canadian Philosophical Association. Each of those discussions was both deeply enjoyable and intellectually productive. I also thank Amy Berg, Brian Berkey, David Boonin, Eric Chwang, and Allison Page for their feedback on prior versions of these arguments. Their time, energy, and thoughtfulness are greatly appreciated.

Espinoza, Russ K. E., Beth Joanne Ek, and Herbert Alexander Espinoza. 2011. "An Examination of Juveniles Being Tried as Adults: Influences of Ethnicity, Socioeconomic Status and Age of Defendant." *National Social Science Journal* 37, no. 1: 30–37.

Fischer, John Martin, and Mark Ravizza. 1998. *Responsibility and Control: A Theory of Moral Responsibility*. Cambridge: Cambridge University Press.

Gheaus, Anca. 2021. "Childhood: Value and Duties." *Philosophy Compass* 16, no. 12 (December): e12793.

Guerrero, Alexander. 2020. "Children, Political Power, and Punishment." *Journal of Ethics* 24, no. 3 (September): 269–80.

Hart, H. L. A. 2008. *Punishment and Responsibility: Essays in the Philosophy of Law*. 2nd ed. Oxford: Oxford University Press.

Hirstein, William, Katrina L. Sifferd, and Tyler K. Fagan. 2018. *Responsible Brains: Neuroscience, Law, and Human Culpability*. Cambridge, MA: MIT Press.

Husak, Douglas. 2018. Review of *The Age of Culpability: Children and the Nature of Criminal Responsibility*, by Gideon Yaffe. *Notre Dame Philosophical Reviews*, June 4. https://ndpr.nd.edu/reviews/the-age-of-culpability-children-and-the-nature-of-criminal-responsibility/.

Jackson, Rodger, and Edward Pabon. 2000. "Race and Treating Other People's Children as Adults." *Journal of Criminal Justice* 28, no. 6 (November-December): 507–15.

Kelly, Erin I. 2020. "Comments on Gideon Yaffe, *The Age of Culpability: Children and the Nature of Criminal Responsibility*." *Journal of Ethics* 24, no. 3 (September): 281–86.

Kessler, Michael Joel. 2019. "Childhood, Impairment, and Criminal Responsibility." *Journal of Global Ethics* 15, no. 3: 306–24.

Leslie, Sarah-Jane. 2008. "Generics: Cognition and Acquisition." *Philosophical Review* 117, no. 1 (January): 1–47.

———. 2013. "Essence and Natural Kinds: When Science Meets Preschooler Intuition." In *Oxford Studies in Epistemology*, edited by Tamar Szabo Gendler and John Hawthorne, vol. 4, 108–66. Oxford: Oxford University Press.

———. 2014. "Carving Up the Social World with Generics." In *Oxford Studies in Experimental Philosophy*, edited by Joshua Knobe, Tania Lombrozo, and Shaun Nichols, vol. 1, 208–31. Oxford: Oxford University Press.

———. 2017. "The Original Sin of Cognition: Fear, Prejudice, and Generalization." *Journal of Philosophy* 114, no. 8 (August): 393–421

Marshall, J. D. 1972. "On Why We Don't Punish Children." *Educational Philosophy and Theory* 4, no. 2: 57–68.

Mischel, Walter, and Ebbe B. Ebbesen. 1970. "Attention in Delay of Gratification." *Journal of Personality and Social Psychology* 16, no. 2 (October): 329–37.

Moore, Michael S. 1997. *Placing Blame: A General Theory of the Criminal Law*. Oxford: Oxford University Press.

Morse, Stephen J. 1997. "Immaturity and Irresponsibility." *Journal of Criminal Law and Criminology* 88, no. 1 (Autumn): 15–67.
———. 2005. "Brain Overclaim Syndrome and Criminal Responsibility: A Diagnostic Note." *Ohio State Journal of Criminal Law* 3, no. 2 (Spring): 397–412.
———. 2013. "Brain Overclaim Redux." *Minnesota Journal of Law & Inequality* 31, no. 2: 509–34.
———. 2020. "Against the Received Wisdom: Why the Criminal Justice System Should Give Kids a Break." *Criminal Law and Philosophy* 14, no. 2 (July): 257–71.
Murphy, Mark C. 2006. *Natural Law in Jurisprudence and Politics*. Cambridge: Cambridge University Press.
Nelkin, Dana Kay. 2011. *Making Sense of Freedom and Responsibility*. Oxford: Oxford University Press.
———. 2020. "What Should the Voting Age Be?" *Journal of Practical Ethics* 8, no. 2 (December): 1–29.
Ritchie, Katherine. 2019. "Should We Use Racial and Gender Generics?" *Thought* 8, no. 1 (March): 33–41.
Ryberg, Jesper. 2014. "Punishing Adolescents—on Immaturity and Diminished Responsibility." *Neuroethics* 7, no. 3 (December): 327–36.
Schapiro, Tamar. 1999. "What Is a Child?" *Ethics* 109, no. 4 (July): 715–38.
Shook, Jeffrey J. 2005. "Contesting Childhood in the US Justice System: The Transfer of Juveniles to Adult Criminal Court." *Childhood* 12, no. 4 (November): 461–78.
Svirsky, Larisa. 2020. "Responsibility and the Problem of So-Called Marginal Agents." *Journal of the American Philosophical Association* 6, no. 2 (Summer): 246–63.
Tatum, Becky. 2003. "Trying Juveniles as Adults: A Case of Racial and Ethnic Bias." In *Racial Issues in Criminal Justice: The Case of African Americans*, edited by Marvin D. Free Jr., 159–75. Boulder, CO: Rienner.
Thomason, Krista K. 2016. "Guilt and Child Soldiers." *Ethical Theory and Moral Practice* 19, no. 1 (February): 115–27.
Tiboris, Michael. 2014. "Blaming the Kids: Children's Agency and Diminished Responsibility." *Journal of Applied Philosophy* 31, no. 1 (February): 77–90.
Wall, John. 2021. *Give Children the Vote: On Democratizing Democracy*. London: Bloomsbury.
Wallace, R. Jay. 1994. *Responsibility and the Moral Sentiments*. Cambridge, MA: Harvard University Press.
Wodak, Daniel, Sarah-Jane Leslie, and Marjorie Rhodes. 2015. "What a Loaded Generalization: Generics and Social Cognition." *Philosophy Compass* 10, no. 9 (September): 625–35.
Wyoming County Youth Bureau. 2022. "What Is the Wyoming County Youth Court?" Accessed April 29. https://www.wyomingco.net/DocumentCenter/View/285/Youth-Court-Pamphlet-PDF.
Yaffe, Gideon. 2018. *The Age of Culpability: Children and the Nature of Criminal Responsibility*. Oxford: Oxford University Press.

32

Punitive Torture

Peter Brian Barry

The United Nations 1984 Convention against Torture and Other Cruel, Inhuman and Degrading Treatment or Punishment identifies four different possible purposes of torture: to obtain a confession, to obtain information, to punish, and to coerce the sufferer or others to act in certain ways. These four functions are probably not exhaustive of torture's potential purposes (Davis 1985), but the U.N. Convention is enough to remind us that torture has historically been used as a mechanism of punishment even if contemporary torturers tend to use it mostly to interrogate or intimidate (Miller 2017). No surprise then that contemporary philosophers have had much to say about the ethics of interrogational torture, especially in the familiar ticking-bomb scenario, and comparatively less to say about punitive torture. Perhaps the thought has been that, however often punitive torture *was* practiced, punitive torture is so obviously unjust and widely regarded as such that it is not even worth discussing it. Thus, philosophers who have found at least some conceptual justification for capital punishment quickly dismiss punitive torture as "morally illegitimate" (Kramer 2011, 58n21) and, along with the punishment of the innocent, among the "clearly immoral punishments" (Yost 2019, 76). That said, torturous methods are almost certainly used more frequently than many of us are comfortable acknowledging, and at least some arguments

P. B. Barry (✉)
Saginaw Valley State University, University Center, MI, USA
e-mail: pbbarry@svsu.edu

© The Author(s), under exclusive license to Springer Nature Switzerland AG 2023

M. C. Altman (ed.), *The Palgrave Handbook on the Philosophy of Punishment*, Palgrave Handbooks in the Philosophy of Law, https://doi.org/10.1007/978-3-031-11874-6_32

purporting to justify punitive torture are available in the extant literature (Machan 1990; Kershnar 1999, 2001).

Independent of other reasons to focus on the topic, philosophers have an interest in considering punitive torture because what torture *is* is a matter of some controversy. For example, any conception of punitive torture must begin with rejecting the suggestion that, of necessity, torture aims at breaking the will (Davis 1985; Sussman 2005). Punitive torturers might aim to do many things without aiming to break anyone's will: they might intend to give someone their just deserts, to deter future crime, or simply to do their job. Some persons tasked with using torture to punish might have rather complicated aims or intentions. Jeremy Wisnewski suggests that the aim of punitive torture is "to *demonstrate* the already-known truth of the power of the sovereign by inscribing this power, in horrific and awe-inspiring splendor, on the limp and frail body of the accused" (2010, 35).[1] But punitive torturers need have no such aim; again, they might simply aim to mete out just deserts. Wisnewski's conception also has the problematic implication that non-sovereigns cannot engage in punitive torture: absent an empowered sovereign, there could be no power of the sovereign to inscribe. But just as parents can punish their children and owners can punish their pets, non-sovereigns can surely punitively torture their victims. Let a single example illustrate: a roving band of vigilantes might punitively torture their subject by tarring and feathering them, as was the case in feudal Europe and the American frontier where state-like actors were largely absent. So, I do not assume that punitive torture must have an aim beyond the aim of punishing nor that it must be administered by anyone in particular. All this matters for determining whether punitive torture is ever morally permissible: if a punitive torturer must intend to inflict horrific and awesome suffering on the helpless accused, punitive torture is going to be all but impossible to justify; if punitive torturers can operate with simpler, more familiar intentions, their task may be easier to justify.

In what follows, I give punitive torture a fair hearing. First, I first consider various justifications of punishment to assess their plausibility as part of an argument in defense of punitive torture. I conclude that, except for a particular kind of consequentialist argument, only retributivism has much of a chance. Next, I articulate a parsimonious conception of retributivism that invokes only the most basic retributivist commitments to generate an argument that punitive torture is sometimes morally permissible. If sound, this

[1] This may historically have been the case, as Wisnewski suggests (2010, 48). But this assertion must be inconsistent with his later claim that "all forms of torture (be it punitive, interrogational, terroristic, or judicial)—has [*sic*] one aim: the breaking of the agent" (73).

argument shows that a parsimonious retributivist is probably going to have to allow that the retributive desert of some culpable wrongdoers guilty of especially heinous crimes supplies pro tanto reasons that tend to justify punitive torture. However, I argue, those basic retributivist commitments also supply powerful reasons to conclude that punitive torture is probably not morally permissible all-things-considered. And, I conclude, since the most promising argument for punitive torture fails, there is good reason to doubt that punitive torture is morally permissible, a result that should lead us to refrain from institutionalizing or legalizing punitive torture.[2]

1 Why Punitive Torture?

In this section, I consider some familiar theories of punishment, many of which receive extended attention in this collection, and consider whether they might justify punitive torture. Some are nonstarters; some are more plausible.

Fritz Allhoff suggests that "the only way that punitive torture could be justified would be in terms of the deterrent value that such punishment would have for future crime (by *other* would-be criminals)" (2012, 72–73). But, Allhoff thinks, appealing to the deterrent effect of punitive torture does not offer "much moral promise" given that such an appeal "just wades into many of the stock criticisms of utilitarian theories of punishment," most notably that the torture of the innocent would also be justified if torturing them would adequately deter (77). Allhoff's dismissal is surprising given that he endorses some version of consequentialism—he explains repeatedly that, other things being equal, lesser harms are preferable to greater ones (114, 116, 130)—which allows that the torture of innocent persons might sometimes be morally permissible if their torture could be reasonably thought to be the only way to prevent a still greater harm (201). I am uncertain why punitive torture could never be reasonably thought to be the only way to prevent a still greater harm, especially given its putative deterrent effect; at least, I can see no reason to rule out the possibility that punishing some miscreant with torture would yield better consequences overall than any alternative response. In that case, Allhoff's consequentialism would also have to justify at least some instances of punitive torture.

I am only so interested in trying to resurrect a consequentialist justification of punitive torture that an avowed consequentialist is unwilling to defend, so let me bracket consequentialist arguments for punitive torture presently with

[2] For the relevance of this distinction, see Steinhoff (2013, 48).

the promise to return to them later. Allhoff's discussion of punitive torture remains surprising: Why can punitive torture *only* be justified on consequentialist grounds? Are there no other justifications of punishment that could be marshalled in its defense? True, some familiar justifications of punishment are probably nonstarters in this context, including rehabilitation-orientated justifications of punishment. The conditional claim that "if torture turns out to be an effective way … to get culpable wrongdoers to understand the fear, degradation, and frustration felt by crime victims and to sympathize with these victims, then torture would be a useful way in which to improve the wrongdoer's moral character" rests on a dubious antecedent (Kershnar 2001, 169–72). It is not at all clear how serious painful physical assaults and their resulting trauma make anyone more responsive to reasons to act better. Equally dubious are communication-orientated justifications of punishment that suggest that punishment is justified because it communicates to wrongdoers, in their capacity as rational agents, just how wrong their conduct was (see, e.g., Duff 2001). After all, if only especially hard treatment gets wrongdoers to understand why their conduct was wrong, then punitive torture might be justified. But just as torture is unlikely to rehabilitate, it is unlikely to be effective as a means of communication. Successful communication demands not only that a speaker delivers some message but that an audience is able to receive and understand it, and no audience is well primed to receive and understand a message during or in the wake of electrotorture, beating, whipping, exhaustion, sleep and sensory deprivation, and so forth. A persistent objection to the use of interrogational torture is that torturers will have great difficulty distinguishing between truthful revelations and desperate pleas for relief (Shue 1978, 135). So with punitive torture: even experienced torturers are going to have great difficulty distinguishing between responses that indicate that the message has been received and those simply intended to bring agony to an end.

Arguably more plausible are expressive-orientated justifications that understand punishment as an authoritative expression that what a wrongdoer did was wrong and merits a response (see, e.g., Feinberg 1970; Hampton 1984). To be sure, punitive torture is surely not justified *simply* because it expresses condemnation, since other, less brutal ways of expressing that a wrongdoer did wrong are surely available: Couldn't we publish a notice in a local paper condemning what they did? Couldn't we just hold up a sign with words to that effect? And if other, less brutal ways of expressing that a wrongdoer did wrong are always available, why *ever* resort to the hard treatment of punishment (Boonin 2008, 176–77)? To handle this objection, the typical expressivist about punishment will make clear that not just any expression of condemnation will do. On this line of thought, to succeed in expressing condemnation, a punishment must be proportionate, in some sense, to the object of condemnation. Here, Jean Hampton offers the relevant thought:

> By victimizing me, the wrongdoer has declared himself elevated with respect to me, acting as a superior who is permitted to use me for his purposes. A false moral claim has been made. The retributivist demands that the false claim be corrected. The lord must be humbled to show that he isn't the lord of the victim. If I cause the wrongdoer to suffer in proportion to my suffering at his hands, his elevation over me is denied, and moral reality is reaffirmed. I master the purported master, showing that he is my peer. (1988, 125)

If a wrongdoer is not made to suffer "in proportion" to adequately express just how wrong their conduct was and they are, then an expressive-orientated justification holds that their proffered punishment is not justified just because it fails to adequately condemn.

Hampton's response, I am willing to allow, makes clear why an expressive-orientated justification of punishment needs a proportionality requirement lest holding up signs would suffice as punishment for the evildoing of evil persons, but it also suggests an argument for punitive torture. If only especially hard treatment could adequately condemn some evildoer, then, if punitive torture is the best or only means to deliver that hard treatment, punitive torture would be morally permissible on an expressive-orientated justification of punishment.

Classificatory boundaries might be getting a bit blurred. Some defenders of expressive-orientated justifications make it clear that their "core position" is that punishment is justified "at least in part because it is the only, or best, way for society to express condemnation" (Glasgow 2015, 602–3), a formulation that allows that punishment might *also* be justified by retributivist concerns. Some taxonomies of justifications of punishment count expressive-orientated justifications as versions of retributivism (Tonry 2011, 109). But since it seems possible to exact retribution without condemning (say, by punishing in secret) and to condemn without exacting retribution (say, by holding up a sign), there is probably conceptual space between the two. Still, for my part, any plausible expressive-orientated justification will be retributivist, lest holding up signs should suffice as punishment. But now it might feel like retributivist concerns, especially concerns about proportionality, are really driving the argument for punitive torture sketched above: if what makes punishing an evildoer morally permissible is that the proffered punishment is proportional, then retributivist concerns are at least doing a lot of the justificatory work. So, it is probably prudent to simply consider what sort of conception of retributivism could justify punitive torture. I turn to that task in the next section.

2 Parsimonious Retributivism and Punitive Torture

By most accounts, retributivism makes a substantive claim about desert: that wrongdoers deserve punishment just because of their wrongdoing. Stronger and weaker versions of this appeal to desert are available. On a strong version, "we are justified in punishing because and only because offenders deserve it" (Moore 1987, 181), thus ruling out any other justification of punishment. On a weaker version, "the primary justification for punishing a criminal is that the criminal deserves it" (Murphy 2007, 11), leaving open the possibility of other reasons to punish. Still, any retributivist worth their salt will insist that the moral permissibility of just punishment is, at least partly, a function of desert. It follows quickly that those who have done no wrong deserve no punishment and cannot be permissibly punished.

These pithy remarks about desert paired with the above concern about proportionality suggest a parsimonious retributivism committed only to the following three principles:

(1) Those who commit certain kinds of wrongful acts, paradigmatically serious crimes, morally deserve to suffer a proportionate punishment.
(2) It is intrinsically morally good—good without reference to any other goods that might arise—if some legitimate punisher gives them the punishment they deserve.
(3) It is morally impermissible intentionally to punish the innocent or to inflict disproportionately large punishments on wrongdoers.[3]

I do not mean to suggest that a retributivist need only affirm these three propositions. A full-blown conception of retributivism will have to explain, among other things, whether a relational or non-relational conception of retributive justice is preferable—see Leora Dahan Katz's chapter in this volume. Even parsimonious retributivists will have to respond to H. L. A. Hart's charge that only via "moral alchemy" could one derive intrinsic goodness from the dual evils of the offender's wickedness and their subsequent suffering (1968, 234). So the parsimonious retributivist is going to have work to do. Still, these three principles represent what I understand to be the core of

[3] I borrow this way of putting the core commitments of retributivism from Walen (2020).

retributivism, however a fully defensible retributivism is ultimately amended and adorned. And, I contend, parsimonious retributivism, the core of retributivist thought, is enough to demonstrate that some arguments that purport to justify punitive torture on retributivist grounds are fatally flawed.

For example, consider the following argument offered by Tibor Machan:

> [Torture] may indeed be morally justified at times but only if some measure of moral guilt is present or highly probable on the part of the party about to experience violence. ... accordingly, I should not torture someone I knew to be entirely innocent of the relevant evils even if his or her torture would secure some great good; I *may*, however, use torture if some probable or demonstrable guilt is present in the party to experience the torture and the end of the torture is itself worthy. (1990, 94)

Machan's appeal to guilt suggests sympathy with retributivism, but the parsimonious retributivist should abhor this argument for at least three reasons. First, that someone is very probably guilty might suffice as a legal standard for punishment—someone whose guilt has been demonstrated beyond a reasonable doubt is very probably guilty even if guilt is not certain—but insufficient to justify punitive torture given the retributivist's commitment to (3): someone who is probably, but not actually, guilty merits no punishment in virtue of that odd fact. Second, Machan is silent about just what the guilty person is guilty *of.* Given the retributivist's commitment to (1), someone certainly guilty of a minor moral transgression does not deserve punitive torture because such punishment is disproportionate. Guilt, per se, justifies nothing. Third, Machan moves too quickly from the guilt of the offender to the conclusion that punishment is justified all-things-considered; (2) above only affirms that deserved punishment is intrinsically good, not that it is good all-things-considered. That there are pro tanto reasons for torturing some deserving miscreant is implied by (2); that torturing them is all-things-considered justified in virtue of that fact is not, since the intrinsic goodness of deserved punishment might be outweighed by other, weightier reasons demanding that we abstain (Katz 2021, 608).

To secure this last point, which will be important below, it will help to consider a debate about distributive justice. Some egalitarians insist that equality is intrinsically good and inequality intrinsically bad, a position imperiled by the familiar levelling-down objection that is supposed to suggest that such egalitarians are weirdly indifferent between bringing everyone down to the level of well-being of the worst off rather than raising everyone to the level of well-being of the best off, since either response results in intrinsically good equality (Parfit 2000, 84). But egalitarians need not be indifferent so long as they care about other things relevant to justice that favor levelling up. For egalitarians, that a distribution promotes equality is a pro tanto reason to think that it is good, but not to conclude that it is good all-things-considered: the egalitarian's response should be that "equality is not all that matters. But it matters some" (Temkin 2002, 155). A retributivist should offer an analogous pluralist response: giving people what they deserve is good, but it is not all that is good (Husak 2021, 340), a response that allows that pro tanto reasons favoring punishment do not yield an undefeatable moral obligation to punish.

There are two conclusions to take away from this discussion of parsimonious retributivism. First, it is not committed to supposing that retributive desert always suffices to answer questions about just punishment. Second, parsimonious retributivism has teeth insofar as it is substantive enough to deflect some seemingly retributivist arguments for punitive torture. What might a more plausible argument for punitive torture consistent with the principles of parsimonious retributivism look like? We need not wonder.

3 A Parsimonious Argument for Punitive Torture

Retributivists can chide consequentialists for having no principled basis for rejecting torture and other inhumane punishments that have a serious deterrent effect. But torture can be a part of an attack directed at retributivists who defend capital punishment: if the seriousness of murder sometimes warrants capital punishment, as the argument goes, why doesn't the seriousness of torture sometimes warrant punitive torture (Finkelstein 2002)?[4] Some retributivists are happy to bite the bullet and reply: "It does."

Stephen Kershnar defends punitive torture on retributivist grounds in the following argument:

P1) A particular punishment is deserved if and only if it is proportional to the agent's culpable wrongdoing.
P2) For some culpable wrongdoings, a particular punishment is proportional if and only if it involves torture.
C1) Hence, in some cases torture is deserved as punishment.
P3) If a particular punishment is deserved, then if it is not overridden by other moral reasons then it is all-things-considered morally justified.

---

[4] The argument is noted in Yost (2019, 57).

P4) In some cases [including some of the cases mentioned in (P2)] deserved punishment that includes torture is not overridden by other moral reasons.

C2) Hence, torture as punishment is sometimes all-things-considered morally justified. (2001, 169–70; see also Kershnar 1999)

Kershnar's argument is retributivist by design and demands nothing more than parsimonious retributivism, a result that helps to block some objections that have been levelled against it.

Jeremy Wisnewski complains that Kershnar's argument depends upon a problematic reading of *lex talionis*—he calls it "the lynch pin of Kershnar's entire argument"—that offenders "must be punished strictly according to the crime he has committed" in lieu of a reading of the *lex* as a limiting principle that specifies the maximum degree of punishment that may be inflicted on a wrongdoer but does not require punishment (2010, 116–17). Why prefer the limited reading of the *lex*? Wisnewski prefers the limited reading because it "seems to be much more in line with what justice requires" since, unlike the literal reading, it does not demand eye for eye, rape for rape, and torture for torture (117). Aside from the fact that some legal philosophers deny that raping rapists and torturing torturers must be unjust,[5] it is not clear why such a preference must be a problem for Kershnar's argument. He only demands that punishment be "equal to the harm that typically results from the acts of the type that the fully culpable wrongdoer has performed" (1999, 55), not that punishments be identical in kind and degree to the harm inflicted by the wrongdoer. Wisnewski also prefers the limited reading of the *lex* insofar as it makes room for mercy, whereas a literal reading makes any showing of mercy a "violation of the dictates of justice," an absurd result (2010, 118). But here too, Kershnar can dodge the charge: his argument allows that there can be overriding reasons to refrain from punishing that would thereby justify showing mercy and render otherwise deserved punishment unjust.

The parsimonious retributivist should agree with Kershnar that punishment need be proportional if not literally identical in kind and degree to the wrongdoing of the offender and that retributivist reasons favoring punishment are pro tanto reasons and might be overridden. Yet the parsimonious

[5] Jeremy Waldron (1992) insists that the *lex talionis* implies that punishments must reproduce relevant wrong-making features of the offense and thus denies that there is anything morally objectionable about raping rapists or torturing torturers, but he still condemns such punishments for other reasons: those persons tasked with carrying out the punishment have a tendency to become sadistic or sexually corrupted. To meet the demands of the *lex*, those tasked with punishment will have to reproduce the wrong-making features of crimes like rape and torture in a more abstract sense.

retributivist should still reject Kershnar's argument, stated above, as unsound. Kershnar regards P2 as one of the especially controversial premises (2001, 174),[6] but the parsimonious retributivist will have a hard time rejecting it. A commitment to proportionality is widely endorsed among retributivists,[7] and it arguably constitutes the bedrock of retributivism (von Hirsch and Ashworth 2005, 143), even as there is real disagreement about how proportionality should be understood. A punishment is ordinally proportionate when it is less severe than punishments imposed for more serious crimes and more severe than punishments imposed for less serious crimes, and it is cardinally proportionate when it matches the seriousness of the crime that merited punishment.[8] Proportionality, in the sense that should interest the parsimonious retributivist, might be a function of both. Apparently, most retributivists think that an anchored sentencing scheme—say, one where punishments are rank ordered from less to more severe, corresponding to crimes similarly ranked in terms of their seriousness, but the relationship between the most grievous crime and the most severe range of punishments satisfies cardinal proportionality—is perfectly suitable for the retributivist's task.[9] That still leaves us with questions about how to measure the seriousness of a wrongdoer's crime. Ought we appeal to the amount of harm caused? To the level of culpability of the offender (see, e.g., Alexander 2021)? Both? Tricky questions, but for present purposes, it probably does not matter: some evildoers are going to be so very culpable and have caused so much harm that, however seriousness is determined, no punishment matches the seriousness of their offense except punitive torture. At least sometimes, however proportionality is understood, only punitive torture will be proportional to the object of retributivist concern. And if that's right, the parsimonious retributivist is stuck with P2.

The parsimonious retributivist should be less sanguine about P4. In the next section, I contend that there are probably always overriding reasons that defeat whatever pro tanto reasons favor meting out deserved torturous punishments. These overriding reasons follow from the commitments of parsimonious retributivism.

[6] Given Kershnar's argument in this volume, I am uncertain if he now rejects this premise altogether.
[7] For a recent exception, see Ryberg (2021).
[8] For discussion, among others, see von Hirsch (1993, 2017).
[9] My authority here is Yost (2019, 46–47). Kershnar seems on board: see Kershnar (2001, 174).

4 The Parsimonious Retributivist Case against Punitive Torture

If there are probably always going to be overriding reasons that defeat pro tanto reasons favoring punitive torture, what reasons are they? Elsewhere I have tried to articulate what I understand to be the Kantian case against torture (Barry 2015), and Kant, for his part, clearly rejects some kinds of punitive torture as morally impermissible:

> There can be disgraceful punishments that dishonor humanity itself (such as quartering a man, having him torn by dogs, cutting off his nose and ears). Not only are such punishments more painful than loss of possessions and life to one who loves honor …; they also make a spectator blush with shame at belonging to a species that can be treated that way. (Kant 1996, 6:463 [p. 580]).

Yet even if drawing and quartering are out on Kantian grounds, other torturous acts might escape Kant's analysis. A whole range of "clean" torture techniques—that is, painful physical techniques that leave few marks, in contrast to scarring torture techniques that do (Rejali 2007, 406)—including electrotorture and beatings (when properly done), water tortures, exhaustion exercises, restraints, sleep deprivation, noise, and still more are not clearly wrong for the reasons Kant identifies above. It is an open question whether all these techniques are more painful than loss of possessions or have any tendency to make spectators blush. That some kinds of clean punitive torture are still widely practiced is some reason to question whether they could be wrong for the Kantian reasons that apparently make drawing and quartering wrong.

Consider, for example, the fairly widespread use of prolonged solitary confinement in prisons. This happens despite the adoption of the "Mandela Rules" by the United Nations that prohibit the use of prolonged solitary confinement—that is, solitary confinement in excess of fifteen consecutive days—and condemn such practices as torture (Gregg and Lieberman 2021). Very many persons are still punished by prolonged solitary confinement, especially in the United States where, even prior to a global pandemic, tens of thousands of prisoners were housed in long-term solitary confinement (Manson 2019). Extended solitary confinement is not a scarring torture technique that tends to create discernable wounds. But it does tend to deprive prisoners of free movement and human interaction as well as disrupting sleep and normal sensation in a way that can have profound physical and psychological consequences. Some jurisdictions in the United States have outlawed prolonged solitary confinement, but not many, and enforcing prohibitions proves difficult. Is prolonged solitary confinement more painful than loss of possessions? Would an honorable person find it more painful than loss of life? I have no empirical evidence to support my suspicions, but surely some self-identified tough guys would willingly undergo prolonged solitary confinement for the promise of a handsome reward, and many of us would prefer a month of solitary confinement to being shot in the head. That there is not more public support for outlawing prolonged solitary confinement suggests that it does not make spectators feel shame, embarrassment, or any other emotion expressed by blushing. So it is far from clear that all torturous punitive techniques, especially clean ones, must be regarded by the Kantian as morally impermissible. And in any case, making too many Kantian assumptions goes beyond the borders of parsimonious retributivism.

Perhaps we could appeal instead to the rights of prospective victims of torture, say, the right asserted in the United Nations 1984 Convention affirming that all human beings have a right to be free from torture and other inhumane treatment. Establishing that all human beings have such a right could not settle the question unless that right was both inviolable and inalienable. Even our most ardent libertarians have declined to affirm an absolutism about our rights generally (Brennan 2012, 40–41), leaving open the possibility that a right to be free from torture could be defeated, and since rights that would otherwise make punishment wrongful can be forfeited by culpable wrongdoers (Wellman 2017), there has to be some question as to whether the right to be free from torture could also be forfeited by some culpable wrongdoer. And once again, invoking a supposed right as the source of an overriding reason goes well beyond the borders of parsimonious retributivism.

For all that, I suspect that those overriding reasons that defeat pro tanto reasons favoring punitive torture can be mined from the commitments of parsimonious retributivism itself. Indeed, I contend that two different kinds of overriding reasons will tend to defeat whatever pro tanto retributive reasons might otherwise justify punitive torture, and I offer two arguments appealing to those reasons in this section. One argument suggests that the actual practice of meting out torturous punishments will run afoul of parsimonious retributivism's commitment to proportionality as captured in (1). Another argument suggests that the actual practice of meting out torturous punishments will run afoul of parsimonious retributivism's commitment to refraining from punishing the innocent as captured in (3).

(1) **Portia and punitive torture**

Famously, in *The Merchant of Venice*, Portia responds to Shylock's demand for a pound of flesh by turning his argument on its head: Shylock is promised, she notes, a pound of flesh, "nor more, no less," but "if the scale do turn," she reminds him, "in the estimation of a hair, Thou diest and all thy goods are confiscate" (4.1.325, 330–32). Portia's quibble is a matter of substance and wins the day given that even Shylock's sincere attempts to extract what is owed him, no more and no less, are bound to fail. Justice demands that he take something else as compensation.

My suspicion is that those persons tasked with carrying out punitive torture are situated rather like Shylock and that justice demands that they administer lesser punishments than what is otherwise deserved. They will be confronted, as if by Portia, with the reality that even sincere attempts at executing a deserved torturous punishment will be nigh impossible given the demands of justice—in this case, the parsimonious retributivist's commitment to proportionality—such that they must settle for something else, some lesser punishment, even for those who deserve torture. The challenge in *The Merchant of Venice* was to take only flesh, not blood or bone or sinew; the challenge faced by punitive torturers is to inflict a proportional degree of harm, no more and no less.

There has been some lip service given to the notion that we can administer pain in a precise, scientific manner. Lt. Col. Roger Trinquier, the French Army officer who developed and defended the use of torture techniques in the Algerian War, explained that:

> If the prisoner gives the information requested, the examination is quickly terminated; if not, specialists must force his secret from him. Then, as a soldier, he must face the suffering, and perhaps the death, he has heretofore managed to avoid. ... Science can easily place at the army's disposition the means for obtaining what is sought. (1964, 21–22, 23)

Dan Mitrione, an American who instructed the use of torture in Uruguay, explained that "you must cause only the damage that is strictly necessary, not a bit more," adding that "you have to act with the efficiency and cleanliness of a surgeon and with the perfection of an artist" (quoted in Rejali 2007, 447). The conviction, expressed here, that interrogational torture can be administered efficiently, cleanly, and scientifically has not been borne out in actual practice, as evidenced by decades of research into the use of torture and the study of pain. Indeed, "there is little empirical evidence of a science of torture, only misleading folklore about pain" (Rejali 2007, 448).

Here, I borrow from Darius Rejali, the author of *Torture and Democracy*, one of the most comprehensive studies of torture and its contemporary practice, who explained that:

> There is reason to think that a science of torture is a utopian idea. A science of torture requires at least this: general rules, fixed in advance, that identify the correct choice in particular situations. It also requires a unit that is commensurable regardless of its source. When I boil water, I have a common measure for heat whether it comes from a fire, a stove, or an electric burner. All I need to know are the laws that govern that particular liquid, and I can choose correctly in advance how much heat to apply. (2007, 449)

But there are no such general rules about torture, and "pain, unlike heat, is not a single commensurable unit" (450). There is simply no way to quantify the agony of torture, no means to measure its awfulness. The problem does not arise out of any dualist conceptions of qualia that make the experience of pain a mystery to everyone but the person feeling it. Rather, the problem arises because the experience of pain is a function of any number of factors that cannot realistically be anticipated or quantified themselves: pain endurance thresholds vary among persons and change given experience, circumstances, context, motivations, and more. A classic work in the study of pain concludes that "the word 'pain' represents a category of experiences, signifying a multitude of different unique experiences having different causes and characterized by different qualities varying along a number of sensory and affective dimensions" (Melzack and Wall 1982, 71),[10] a result that is not terribly promising for anyone interested in quantifying the experience of pain. Even rough-and-ready good faith estimates about just how much a victim of torture is suffering and can take before they crack must be suspect.

Things are actually worse. While we lack the means to measure the experience of pain, we also lack good predictive measures with respect to recovery from the pain of torture. Seemingly minor damage may yield great trauma later; substantial damage may have surprisingly few consequences. The parsimonious retributivist committed to refraining from punishing persons more than what they deserve has to not only consider the harm imposed as they are torturing but that imposed as a consequence of torturing. If there is little reason to think that we can only inflict proportionate harm during punitive torture, there is no better reason to think that we can anticipate and factor

[10] For a related argument directed at interrogational torture, but relevant here, see O'Mara (2015).

into our deliberations those harms that accumulate in the months and years that follow.

I do not mean to set up a straw man here. My worry is not that retributivists who contend that punitive torture is sometimes morally permissible must produce a precise metric for purposes of punishment, that they must make literal use of phraseology like "The defendant is sentenced to an experience of twenty sadons"[11] or whatever. But retributivists who endorse the first commitment of parsimonious retributivism, the principle that wrongdoers deserve proportional punishment, have got to be skeptical that we can administer a proportional degree of punishment via punitive torture if our ability to measure and quantify pain is largely a fiction. If we simply cannot track the suffering of a victim of torture, we are especially likely to punish disproportionately. My argument is not that punishing via torture within the constraints of proportionality is impossible, but rather that it is *risky*: since we know that we lack reliable mechanisms for measuring and predicting responses to pain, adopting punitive torture increases greatly the risk that we will punish excessively and disproportionately. Parsimonious retributivists, given their commitment to delivering proportionate punishment, should be unwilling to take the risk. Even if there are pro tanto retributivist reasons to torture punitively, those reasons are swamped by the core retributivist commitment to refrain from punishing excessively.

(2) **Torrents of torture**

Parsimonious retributivists should be risk-averse to punitive torture out of a concern for punishing disproportionately, but they should be risk-averse for other reasons too.

In a now-classic paper, Henry Shue mounts an attack on supposed justifications for torture but seemingly allows that some cases of interrogational torture are morally permissible. Here, Shue offers his own "standard philosopher's example" of a ticking-bomb scenario:

> Suppose a fanatic, perfectly willing to die rather than collaborate in the thwarting of his own scheme, has set a hidden nuclear device to explode in the heart of Paris. There is no time to evacuate the innocent people or even the movable art treasures—the only hope of preventing tragedy is to torture the perpetrator, find the device, and deactivate it. (1978, 141)

[11] A sadon is a fictional unit to measure pain, the counterpart of a hedon. I owe the term to Alastair Norcross.

Shue's assessment comes quick: "I can see no way to deny the permissibility of torture in a case *just like this*" (141), although this allowance promises rather less than might be thought. Shue is clear that

> there are imaginable cases in which the harm that could be prevented by a rare instance of pure interrogational torture would be so enormous as to outweigh the cruelty of the torture itself and, possibly, the enormous potential harm which would result if what was intended to be a rare instance was actually the breaching of the dam which would lead to a torrent of torture. (141)

In the fictional example he proffers, the use of interrogational torture on one occasion does not result in a torrent of torture that outweighs that harm thereby prevented. Prospective cases of morally permissible torture must be *just like that*: they too must not result in a torrent of torture that swamps the harm thereby prevented. In retrospect, it should have been clear that Shue doubts that there are very many actual cases *just like that* given that he notes torture's "metastatic tendency" (143)—that is, the tendency of states to practice torture more frequently once the initial rare case occurs—but he is certainly clear in later work when he explains that "the exceptional case" in which torture lacks any metastatic tendency "is probably in fact impossible" (Shue 2006, 235).

There is room to quibble here: if scenarios in which torture lacks any metastatic tendency are imaginable, then, if conceivability (of some sort) implies possibility, non-metastasizing torture is possible. Perhaps for that reason some absolutist opponents of torture have tried to argue that coherent ticking-bomb scenarios are not even conceivable (for discussion, see Barry 2013). But the mere conceivability of morally permissible, metastasis-free torture should not cure the parsimonious retributivist's risk aversion to the use of punitive torture. If there is good empirical evidence to think that torture *will* metastasize, then the parsimonious retributivist should worry that the actual practice of punitive torture will result in a torrent of torture such that innocents and those who do not deserve punitive torture will be imperiled (insofar as they are more likely to be tortured unjustly). That result is intolerable for parsimonious retributivists who endorse (3), the principle that it is morally impermissible intentionally to punish the innocent and the undeserving.

The relevant questions, then, are whether practicing punitive torture risks unleashing a torrent of torture and how likely that torrent will be unleashed if it does. Shue worried in 1978 that "torture is widespread and growing" (124) and that "there *is* considerable evidence of all torture's metastatic tendency"

(143),[12] citing a report from Amnesty International suggesting the same (1973, 21–33). True, that report is now more than forty years old, but in 1999 a representative of Amnesty International suggested that torture was as widespread then as it was in 1978,[13] and between January 2009 and May 2013, Amnesty International (2022) received reports of torture in 141 countries from every region of the world. Increased scrutiny has perhaps mitigated the practice but—and this is one of Rejali's central theses—public monitoring has perversely led democratic institutions to use clean torture techniques rather than scarring ones to avoid detection, not to refrain from torturing altogether; public monitoring of human rights violations has not so much led democracies to abandon torturing but to torture more stealthily (Rejali 2007, 8). Indeed, Rejali identifies multiple ways that torture can metastasize:

> Torture generates not one, but three slippery slopes. Torturers expand the range of victims that they are authorized to interrogate. They use greater variety of techniques than they are authorized to use. And they increasingly pursue their own interests, constituting themselves as a separate professional class and heightening bureaucratic devolution. (2007, 576)

The empirical evidence strongly suggests that there are scant few cases *just like* Shue's morally permissible ones, that the initial rare use of torture is more likely to unleash a torrent than remain rare. As such, retributivists have good reason to conclude that the actual practice of meting out torturous punishments will run afoul of the third commitment of parsimonious retributivism: persons tasked with meting out punitive torture are likely to punish more often, utilize more torturous techniques, and operate free from accountability, all of which increases the likelihood that the undeserving will be tortured unjustly. Here too, my argument is not that just punitive torture is impossible, but that its practice is *risky*: given empirically founded worries about unleashing torrents of torture, the parsimonious retributivist committed to regarding the punitive torture of the undeserving as unjust should decline the use punitive torture.

It is not just the parsimonious retributivist who should be risk averse to the practice of punitive torture; consequentialists should also be risk-averse. As I noted above, there is little reason to rule out the possibility that some token

[12] In a footnote, Kershnar notes that "one might also argue against torture on the basis of its likely misuse" and notes Shue as having raised that point (2001, 200n46). Kershnar's response suggests that Shue objects specifically to the use of torture as an interrogational procedure and leaves open whether torture would be misused as punishment. Shue's concern about torture's metastatic tendency is perfectly general, as noted here.

[13] As reported by Rejali (2007, 22).

case of punitive torture would yield better consequences overall than any alternative response. But if even the rare use of torture unleashes a torrent in which more persons suffer in more garish ways, then the consequentialist calculus is less clear. Certainly, those consequentialists contemplating the institutionalization or legalization of punitive torture must be more skeptical that such measures can be warranted on consequentialist grounds. I doubt that there is a plausible argument that punitive torture could never be justified on consequentialist grounds; at least, it is hard to make the case that there are no conceivable cases in which using punishment to torture will yield more utility than any alternative. Still, given the concerns noted above for any token instance in which punitive torture is being contemplated, act-consequentialists should be extremely skeptical that they are able to reliably determine the harm inflicted and thus equally skeptical that the token instance of punitive torture will maximize overall happiness. So, and I take this to be the strongest argument against consequentialist attempts to justify punitive torture, consequentialists too ought to worry that the actual practice of punitive torture is too risky to warrant its adoption.

5 Conclusion

I allow that there is a powerful argument that punitive torture is sometimes morally permissible, one grounded in a parsimonious version of retributivism that only demands assent to fairly minimal retributivist commitments. I regard this argument as the most plausible argument that punitive torture is sometimes morally permissible, the sort of argument that will succeed if any such argument is going to. But that retributivist argument ultimately fails given the existence of overriding reasons that defeat pro tanto reasons that otherwise justify punitive torture, reasons that a parsimonious retributivist should be especially responsive to. The parsimonious retributivist should be especially risk-averse to the practice of punitive torture since there is good empirical reason to think that the actual practice of punitive torture will tend to result in the infliction of disproportionate punishments and unleash a torrent of torture that will result in the punishment of the undeserving, states of affairs that clearly run afoul of the commitments of even the most parsimonious of retributivisms. Accordingly, I conclude that the prospects of morally permissible punitive torture are quite dim.

I will mention two caveats in closing. First, parsimonious retributivism is rivaled by other, fancier conceptions that I do not consider here. For all I know, some self-identified retributivists may produce a justification of punishment that allows that punitive torture is sometimes morally permissible on retributivist grounds. I cannot rule out that possibility. But I am deeply skeptical that any such supposed retributivism will be able to deliver the goods. The commitments of parsimonious retributivism are pretty core commitments, and whatever accoutrements might adorn fancier versions of retributivism, punitive torture is going to conflict with these core commitments. If that is right, then deep skepticism about the prospects of justifying punitive torture on retributivist grounds is warranted.

Second, my argument depends upon various empirical facts. For that, I make no apology. For my own part, that an argument is beholden to empirical facts is not a bug but a feature of applied ethics and applied political philosophy: our ethical obligations and duties are partly a function of facts about the world that may change or fail to obtain in other possible worlds. Such is life. Perhaps I can be convinced by some sound argument free from empirical assumptions about pain or the tendency of torturers to torture more. Perhaps someone can show that punitive torture is wrong whatever the contingencies of the world as we find it. While I wait for that argument, I rest content with the conclusion that punitive torture is probably not morally permissible in our actual world because of facts about it, the actual world.

Some years ago, Hart averred that "some punishments are ruled out as too barbarous or horrible to be used whatever their social utility" (1968, 80). I agree, even as I allow that some miscreants deserve the especially hard treatment of punitive torture. Punitive torture is unjust even by the standards of parsimonious retributivism.

References

Alexander, Larry. 2021. "Proportionality's Function." *Criminal Law and Philosophy* 15, no. 3 (October): 361–72.

Allhoff, Fritz. 2012. *Terrorism, Ticking Time-Bombs, and Torture: A Philosophical Analysis*. Chicago: University of Chicago Press.

Amnesty International. 1973. *Report on Torture*. New York: Farrar, Straus, and Giroux.

———. 2022. "Torture." Accessed April 29. https://www.amnesty.org/en/what-we-do/torture/#:~:text=Between%20January%202009%20and%20May,when%20governments%20allow%20its%20use.

Barry, Peter Brian. 2013. "Fantasy, Conceivability, and Ticking Bombs." *Public Affairs Quarterly* 27, no. 2, (April): 87–110.

———. 2015. "The Kantian Case against Torture." *Philosophy* 90, no. 4 (October): 593–621.

Boonin, David. 2008. *The Problem of Punishment*. Cambridge: Cambridge University Press.

Brennan, Jason. 2012. *Libertarianism: What Everyone Needs to Know*. Oxford: Oxford University Press.

Davis, Michael. 1985. "The Moral Justifiability of Torture and Other Cruel, Inhuman, or Degrading Treatment." *International Journal of Applied Philosophy* 19, no. 2 (Fall): 161–78.

Duff, R. A. 2001. *Punishment, Communication, and Community*. Oxford: Oxford University Press.

Feinberg, Joel. 1970. "The Expressive Function of Punishment." In *Doing & Deserving: Essays in the Theory of Responsibility*, 95–118. Princeton, NJ: Princeton University Press

Finkelstein, Claire. 2002. "Death and Retribution." *Criminal Justice Ethics* 21, no. 2: 12–21.

Glasgow, Joshua. 2015. "The Expressivist Theory of Punishment Defended." *Law and Philosophy* 34, no. 6 (November): 601–31.

Gregg, Tammie, and Donna Lieberman. 2021. "Prolonged Solitary Confinement Is Torture. It's Time for All States to Ban It." *Washington Post*, April 28. https://www.washingtonpost.com/opinions/2021/04/28/ban-prolonged-solitary-confinement/.

Hampton, Jean. 1984. "The Moral Education Theory of Punishment." *Philosophy & Public Affairs* 13, no. 3 (Summer): 208–38.

———. 1988. "The Retributive Idea." In *Forgiveness and Mercy*, by Jeffrie G. Murphy and Jean Hampton, 111–61. Cambridge: Cambridge University Press.

Hart, H. L. A. 1968. *Punishment and Responsibility: Essays in the Philosophy of Law*. Oxford: Oxford University Press.

Husak, Douglas. 2021. "Proportionality in Personal Life." *Criminal Law and Philosophy* 15, no. 3 (October): 339–60.

Kant, Immanuel. 1996. *The Metaphysics of Morals*. In *Practical Philosophy*, translated and edited by Mary J. Gregor, 363–602. Cambridge: Cambridge University Press.

Katz, Leora Dahan. 2021. "Response Retributivism: Defending the Duty to Punish." *Law and Philosophy* 40, no. 6 (December): 585–615.

Kershnar, Stephen. 1999. "Objections to the Systematic Imposition of Punitive Torture." *International Journal of Applied Philosophy* 13, no. 1 (Spring): 47–56.

———. 2001. *Desert, Retribution, and Torture*. Lanham, MD: University Press of America.

Kramer, Matthew H. 2011. *The Ethics of Capital Punishment: A Philosophical Investigation of Evil and Its Consequences*. Oxford: Oxford University Press.

Machan, Tibor R. 1990. "Exploring Extreme Violence (Torture)." *Journal of Social Philosophy* 21, no. 1 (March): 92–97.

Manson, Joshua. 2019. "How Many People Are in Solitary Confinement Today?" *Solitary Watch*, January 4. https://solitarywatch.org/2019/01/04/how-many-people-are-in-solitary-today/.

Melzack, Ronald, and Patrick D. Wall. 1982. *The Challenge of Pain*. Harmondsworth, UK: Penguin.
Miller, Seumas. 2017. "Torture." *Stanford Encyclopedia of Philosophy* (Summer 2017 edition), edited by Edward N. Zalta. https://plato.stanford.edu/archives/sum2017/entries/torture/.
Moore, Michael S. 1987. "The Moral Worth of Retribution." In *Responsibility, Character, and the Emotions: New Essays in Moral Psychology*, edited by Ferdinand Schoeman, 179–219. Cambridge: Cambridge University Press.
Murphy, Jeffrie G. 2007. "Legal Moralism and Retribution Revisited." *Criminal Law and Philosophy* 1, no. 1 (January): 5–20.
O'Mara, Shane. 2015. *Why Torture Doesn't Work: The Neuroscience of Interrogation*. Cambridge, MA: Harvard University Press.
Parfit, Derek. 2000. "Equality or Priority?" In *The Ideal of Equality*, edited by Matthew Clayton and Andrew Williams, 81–125. Basingstoke, UK: Palgrave Macmillan.
Rejali, Darius. 2007. *Torture and Democracy*. Princeton, NJ: Princeton University Press.
Ryberg, Jesper. 2021. "Retributivism and the (Lack of) Justification of Proportionality." *Criminal Law and Philosophy* 15, no. 3 (October): 447–62.
Shue, Henry. 1978. "Torture." *Philosophy & Public Affairs* 7, no. 2 (Winter): 124–43.
———. 2006. "Torture in Dreamland: Disposing of the Ticking Bomb." *Case Western Reserve Journal of International Law* 37, no. 2: 231–39.
Steinhoff, Uwe. 2013. *On the Ethics of Torture*. Albany, NY: State University of New York Press.
Sussman, David. 2005. "What's Wrong with Torture?" *Philosophy & Public Affairs* 33, no. 1 (Winter): 1–33.
Temkin, Larry. 2002. "Equality, Priority, and the Levelling Down Objection." In *The Ideal of Equality*, edited by Matthew Clayton and Andrew Williams, 126–61. Basingstoke, UK: Palgrave Macmillan.
Tonry, Michael. 2011. *Why Punish? How Much? A Reader on Punishment*. Oxford: Oxford University Press.
Trinquier, Roger. 1964. *Modern Warfare: A French View of Counterinsurgency*. Translated by Daniel Lee. Westport, CT: Praeger.
von Hirsch, Andreas. 1993. *Censure and Sanctions*. Oxford: Oxford University Press.
———. 2017. *Deserved Criminal Sentences*. Oxford: Bloomsbury.
von Hirsch, Andrew, and Andrew Ashworth. 2005. *Proportionate Sentencing: Exploring the Principles*. Oxford: Oxford University Press.
Waldron, Jeremy. 1992. "Lex Talionis." *Arizona Law Review* 34: 25–51.
Walen, Alec. 2020. "Retributive Justice." *Stanford Encyclopedia of Philosophy* (Summer 2021 edition), edited by Edward N. Zalta. https://plato.stanford.edu/archives/sum2021/entries/justice-retributive/.

Wellman, Christopher Heath. 2017. *Rights Forfeiture and Punishment*. New York: Oxford University Press.
Wisnewski, J. Jeremy. 2010. *Understanding Torture*. Edinburgh: Edinburgh University Press.
Yost, Benjamin S. 2019. *Against Capital Punishment*. Oxford: Oxford University Press.

33

The Justice of Capital Punishment

Edward Feser

In this chapter, I will defend the traditional view that the death penalty can be a just punishment for certain extremely serious crimes. The basic argument is straightforward and goes like this:

1. Wrongdoers deserve punishment as a matter of retributive justice.
2. The more grave the wrongdoing, the more severe is the punishment deserved.
3. Some crimes are so grave that no punishment less than death would be proportionate in its severity.
4. Therefore, wrongdoers guilty of such crimes deserve death.
5. Governmental authorities have the right to inflict on wrongdoers the punishments they deserve.
6. Therefore, governmental authorities have the right to inflict the death penalty on those guilty of the gravest offenses.

The premises here are 1, 2, 3, and 5, and the conclusions 4 and 6 clearly follow from them. The premises can be, and are, accepted by philosophers of diverse general moral and metaphysical commitments. However, they are nevertheless controversial, and therefore they stand in need of defense themselves.

I agree with critics of capital punishment who judge some of the standard defenses of these premises to be weak. For example, in defense of premise 1,

E. Feser (✉)
Pasadena City College, Pasadena, CA, USA
e-mail: ecfeser@pasadena.edu

© The Author(s), under exclusive license to Springer Nature Switzerland AG 2023

M. C. Altman (ed.), *The Palgrave Handbook on the Philosophy of Punishment*, Palgrave Handbooks in the Philosophy of Law, https://doi.org/10.1007/978-3-031-11874-6_33

some would appeal to our moral intuitions, or would argue that the notion of retributive justice provides a better justification of punishment in general than alternative views such as consequentialism do. The problem with the first argument is that not everyone shares the intuitions in question, and even if they did, the intuitions might be mistaken. The problem with the second is that it presupposes that punishment as a general practice is indeed justifiable, which not all critics would concede. In both cases, the defender of capital punishment is essentially simply appealing to what most people have believed historically and what many people still believe, and the problem is that whether the beliefs in question are true is, for the critic of capital punishment, precisely what is at issue (see Walen 2020).

A satisfying argument for the justice of the death penalty thus has to offer a deeper philosophical defense of the premises in question. And the most plausible way to defend them is, in my opinion, to ground them in the metaphysical and moral foundations provided by Aristotelian-Thomistic (A-T) natural law theory—which is, needless to say, itself highly controversial. Hence, I must confess at the outset that, though much better than a mere appeal to intuitions or the like, the deepest philosophical foundations of the justification of capital punishment are bound to be no less controversial than capital punishment itself is.

I think the exercise is nevertheless worthwhile, not least because the overall position I will be describing is, in my view, correct. But even those who disagree with me about that should find of interest an exposition of the natural law justification of the death penalty. It is fashionable to suppose that capital punishment and other components of traditional morality rest on little more than religious dogma or prejudice (where appeals to intuition and the like only reinforce that suspicion). But that is not the case. In fact, they are perfectly justifiable given certain (broadly Aristotelian) metaphysical premises. And, though these premises are more controversial today than they were in previous centuries, they are still defensible, and indeed increasingly being defended in contemporary philosophy even by thinkers who have no interest in the moral uses to which they may be put. Meanwhile, nontraditional views about the death penalty and other moral issues presuppose challengeable metaphysical assumptions no less than traditional views do (in particular, naturalistic assumptions). But those assumptions, reflecting as they do the current conventional wisdom in philosophy, are usually simply taken for granted by nontraditional ethicists rather than argued for in any depth.

Accordingly, such ethicists might find it a useful philosophical exercise to "think outside the box" of this conventional wisdom, at least for the sake of argument, and see how traditional views on issues such as capital punishment can be made intelligible given a different but rationally defensible general moral and metaphysical worldview. If agreement is not likely to result, at least understanding might be.

In what follows, I will first give an exposition of the metaphysical and moral aspects of traditional natural law theory most relevant to the defense of the justice of capital punishment. Then I will explain how the necessity and goodness of retribution follow from that theoretical picture, in a way that justifies premises 1, 2, and 3 above. The next step will be to show how the general natural law framework also entails a conception of social and political order that justifies premise 5. In the final section, I will respond to what some regard as a devastating objection to any defense of the death penalty on grounds of retributive justice.[1]

1 Foundations of Natural Law

Natural law theory in the A-T tradition is grounded in a metaphysics of *teleological essentialism*. The jargon may seem forbidding, but the basic idea is simply a philosophical articulation of common sense. It holds, first, that each of the substances that make up the natural world has a *nature* or *essence* that makes it a thing of the kind that it is, and that this is an objective fact rather than an artifact of human linguistic or classificatory practices or the like. Hence, there is an objective fact of the matter about what it is to be water or stone, an objective fact of the matter about what it is to be a tree or a squirrel, an objective fact of the matter about what it is to be a human being, and so on. That is the "essentialism" part of teleological essentialism.

The view holds, second, that among the things that are true of a natural substance by virtue of its essence is that it is *directed* or *aimed toward* the realization of certain ends. For example, it is of the nature of water that it is directed toward freezing at thirty-two degrees Fahrenheit, it is of the nature of a tree that it is directed toward sinking roots into the soil and carrying out photosynthesis, it is of the nature of a squirrel that it is directed toward gathering acorns and scampering up trees, and so on. Such directedness too is an objective feature of reality rather than an artifact of human convention. This is the "teleological" part of teleological essentialism.

[1] See Feser and Bessette (2017) for a book-length treatment of these issues. Despite the book's subtitle, much of its argumentation will be of interest to non-Catholics, being purely philosophical and social scientific in character.

Needless to say, both elements of the view are controversial and raise metaphysical questions that go well beyond anything that can be canvassed in a chapter on the death penalty. Suffice it for present purposes to note that both can be, and in fact are, defended on general metaphysical grounds by writers having no axe to grind vis-à-vis capital punishment or natural law theory. In contemporary metaphysics, the objective reality of teleological properties in nature is defended by some causal powers theorists, who argue that powers or dispositions are *aimed* or *directed toward* their characteristic manifestations. The objective reality of essences or natures is also defended by many writers working in contemporary metaphysics, philosophy of biology, philosophy of chemistry, and philosophy of science more generally. Though a minority to be sure, the number of mainstream academic philosophers now defending views of this sort is sizable enough that "neo-Aristotelianism" has become an option on the menu of views, and it is well represented in several monographs and anthologies.[2]

The thing to emphasize for present purposes is the way that teleological essentialism underwrites goodness and badness as objective features of the natural world. Consider, for example, that given its nature or essence, an oak tree is directed or aimed toward sinking long and deep roots into the ground, and that a lioness, given its nature or essence, is directed or aimed toward nurturing its young. There is an obvious sense in which an oak that sinks such roots is, accordingly, to that extent a *good* oak, and a lioness that nurtures its young is a *good* lioness. By the same token, an oak with weak or sickly roots is to that extent a *bad* oak, and a lioness that fails to nurture her cubs is to that extent a *bad* lioness. The senses of "good" and "bad" operative here are those operative when we speak of a good or bad *specimen* of a certain kind of thing. Philippa Foot (2001), from whom I borrow the examples, characterizes this as the notion of "natural goodness"—goodness defined in terms of what fulfills the functions or realizes the ends that follow upon the nature of a thing. Natural badness is to be understood in terms of *dys*function, a thing's failure to realize some end toward which it is by nature directed.

So far I am not describing specifically moral goodness or badness, but rather more general notions of which moral goodness and badness are species. Morality enters the picture with rational creatures such as ourselves, who can come to *know* the ends toward which our nature directs us, and *choose* to act in a way that either facilitates or frustrates the realization of those ends.

[2] For a survey of the relevant contemporary literature, see Feser (2019b). I defend A-T metaphysics in depth in Feser (2014b, 2019a).

Morally good actions are those which facilitate those ends and morally bad actions are those which frustrate them.

For A-T natural law theory, our nature or essence is to be *rational social animals*, specifically. This entails a variety of ends the realization of which is essential to our flourishing, with these ends ordered in a hierarchy. Most fundamentally, there are the ends we share with all living things, such as preserving ourselves in existence and acquiring what is necessary in order to do so (food, shelter, and the like). Second, there are those ends we share with other animals of the social kind, such as sexual intercourse and rearing of the children that follow from it. The third and highest of our ends are those unique to us as social animals of the rational kind, such as acquiring knowledge and participating in a social order governed by law.

The intellect, on this picture, has as its natural end knowledge of what is true and good, and the will has as its natural end the pursuit of what the intellect knows to be true and good. Hence an intellect clouded by error and a will directed at what is in fact bad for us are as dysfunctional as an oak tree with sickly roots or a lioness that fails to nurture her cubs. For natural law theory, pursuing what is true and good is therefore constitutive of rationality, so that skeptical doubts about whether we should care about what is true or about doing what is good are ultimately incoherent. The very entertaining of such skepticism involves taking skepticism itself to be true and adherence to it to be good. The skeptic who tries to use reason to cast doubt on the imperative to pursue the true and the good is like someone who tries to play chess without following the rules constitutive of chess.

Needless to say, this exposition of A-T natural law theory is truncated. I am not trying here to provide a complete exposition or to answer every question or objection that might be raised about what has been said so far.[3] The point is simply to give a general idea of those aspects of the theory, and especially of its metaphysical foundations, relevant to the natural law defense of capital punishment.

2 The Metaphysics of Retribution

Punishment involves the infliction of something unpleasant on the person being punished, and ordinarily this would, of course, be a bad thing to do. So, how can punishment be justified? To understand natural law theory's answer,

[3] For more detailed exposition and defense of A-T natural law theory, see Feser (2009, ch. 5; 2014a) and Feser and Bessette (2017, 20–37).

it is necessary to understand the role that pleasure and pain play in human life according to the theory. For natural law theorists like Saint Thomas Aquinas, it is an error to *identify* happiness with pleasure or unhappiness with pain. Instead, happiness has essentially to do with the realization of the ends toward which we are directed by nature—the pursuit of truth, fellowship with others, bodily health, and so on—and unhappiness with the failure to realize those ends. Nevertheless, pleasure and pain have a key role to play in our happiness or unhappiness. It would, after all, be absurd to suggest that, having realized the ends that follow upon our nature, we would be perfectly happy even if we were in constant pain; or that having failed to realize those ends, we would be perfectly unhappy, even if we felt nothing but pleasure.

For the A-T natural law theorist, nature has attached pleasure to certain goods precisely so that we will pursue them, and it has attached pain to certain evils precisely so that we will avoid them. That is why vicious behavior (such as immoderate indulgence of our appetites) so often results in "unhappiness" in the popular sense that associates it with mental and physical pain, and why virtuous behavior (such as moderation in indulgence of the appetites) results in "happiness" in the popular sense that associates it with a feeling of mental and physical well-being. Of course, the match is by no means always perfect, and particular vicious acts may bring pleasure while particular virtuous acts may be painful. This is in part a consequence of the fact that what is good for human beings is to be understood in terms of their overall character and the realization of their natural ends in the *long* term, and what brings pain at the moment may be part of a larger pattern of actions that will bring pleasure in the long run. It is also in part a consequence of the fact that, here as elsewhere, there are defects and aberrations in nature. Human beings who take pleasure in what is bad are in this sense like tree roots that grow in deformed patterns, or the lioness who kills rather than nurtures her cubs. But in general and in the long run, and when things are functioning properly, the realization of the ends toward which nature has directed us results in pleasure and the failure to realize them brings pain.

Hence, though happiness is not the same as pleasure, pleasure is nevertheless what Aquinas calls a "proper accident" of happiness (1948, I-II.2.6 [p. 593]). A "proper accident" of a thing is neither its essence nor part of its essence but nevertheless flows or follows from its essence. For example, the capacity for humor is not our essence—our essence, for the A-T natural law theorist, is to be rational animals—but this capacity follows *from* our essence as rational animals. Similarly, pleasure is not the same thing as happiness, but it naturally flows from happiness (that is, from the realization of the ends our nature directs us toward), not in the sense that it always in fact follows from it, but that it tends in the long run to follow from it and will do so unless prevented. As Aquinas says, "delight … is nothing else than the appetite's rest in good" (1948, I–II.2.6 [p. 593]). Or as one commentator more colorfully puts it, for Aquinas "pleasure is the whip cream on a sundae, the 'something added' to a recognized possessed good" (Reutemann 1953, 4). Happiness consists in the realization of the good, and delight or pleasure is a natural byproduct of this.

We might say, then, that just as a fully healthy specimen of a tree will grow thick roots and a fully healthy specimen of a lioness will nurture her cubs, so too will human happiness in the sense of the realization of the ends nature has set for us be associated with pleasure. And just as a tree with weak roots or a lion disinclined to hunt will typically grow sickly, so too will a failure to realize the ends nature has set for us be associated with pain. There is in the order of the world a *natural teleological association* between, on the one hand, pleasure and the realization of the ends that follow from our essence, and on the other hand, pain and the failure to realize these ends. The connection is not without exceptions, any more than every single tree has healthy roots or every single lioness nurtures her cubs. But like these latter examples, it is the *norm*, the way things tend to go when everything is functioning as it should.

The relevance to punishment may be obvious. Evildoers have deliberately acted in a way contrary to the ends toward which their nature has directed them. And they have done so in order to secure some pleasure that such action will afford them (even if, when considered from the point of view of the big picture, the action is detrimental to their happiness). Punishment is a matter of restoring the natural connection between pain and acting contrary to nature's ends—somewhat, you might say, as the gardener or horticulturalist who treats a disease of the roots or leaves is restoring a tree to its natural state. As one Thomistic natural law theorist puts it:

> That is what crime and sin are—the inordinate indulging of our own will or the inordinate securing of pleasure at the expense of the law or of the order required by reason. The restoration of the right order of pleasures by the infliction of a proportionate pain is what we mean by retributive punishment. (Cronin 1939, 588)

As this passage indicates, the moral evil of wrongdoing is a consequence of its following from the *will*—something the tree or the lion does not have, which is why their failures to realize the ends their natures have set for them do not count as moral failures. The offender, Aquinas says, "has been too indulgent to his will," and thus rightly "suffers, either willingly or unwillingly, something contrary to what he would wish" for the sake of the "restoration of the equality of justice" (1948, I–II.87.6 [p. 977]). The "equality of justice" in this context has to do with the proper balance of wrongdoing and pain, like two sides of a scale at equal levels. Evildoers put the scale out of balance, increasing wrongdoing in a way that avoids the pain that ought to go along with it. Restoring the equality of justice is thus a matter of inflicting pain so that the two sides are level again. Hence, on Aquinas's view, punishment should involve "depriving a man of what he loves most," which includes "life, bodily safety, his own freedom, and external goods such as riches, his country and his good name" (II-II.108.3 [p. 1652]). Which of these punishments is appropriate will depend on the nature of the crime, but the "equality of justice" will be restored by answering offenders' overindulgence of their wills with the infliction of something that is contrary to their wills.

So, punishment is *inherently* good or fitting on the A-T natural law theorist's view—good in itself and not just for the sake of practical benefits like deterrence and rehabilitation (though those ends are good too)—since it restores a natural balance that has been disrupted by the offender's overindulgent will. And no less good, in Aquinas's view, is our *inclination to inflict* punishment on wrongdoers, for this is natural to us, just as sinking roots is natural to an oak and nurturing her cubs is natural to a lioness.[4] Aquinas writes:

> Wherefore we find that the natural inclination of man is to repress those who rise up against him. … Consequently, whatever rises up against an order, is put down by that order or by the principle thereof. And because sin is an inordinate act, it is evident that whoever sins, commits an offense against an order: wherefore he is put down, in consequence, by that same order, which repression is punishment. (1948, I-II.87.1 [p. 973])

What Aquinas means by a "natural inclination" here is an inherent tendency toward some end the realization of which is necessary to our flourishing, given our nature. Since it arises from a natural inclination in this sense, the tendency to punish is a virtue, so long as it is motivated by justice, say, rather than hatred. Aquinas writes:

> Wherefore to every definite natural inclination there corresponds a special virtue. Now there is a special inclination of nature to remove harm, for which reason animals have the irascible power distinct from the concupiscible. Man resists harm by defending himself against wrongs, lest they be inflicted on him,

[4] See chapter 3 of Koritansky (2012) for an extended treatment of this theme in Aquinas.

> or he avenges those which have already been inflicted on him, with the intention, not of harming, but of removing the harm done. And this belongs to vengeance. … Therefore vengeance is a special virtue. (1948, II–II.108.2 [p. 1651])

It might sound odd to contemporary ears to call vengeance a "virtue," given that words like "vengeance," "revenge," and "vindictiveness" have an entirely negative connotation these days. But from the A-T natural law theorist's point of view, this reflects a tendency to confuse the *abuse* of vengeance with vengeance itself. As Aquinas writes:

> Vengeance consists in the infliction of a penal evil on one who has sinned. Accordingly, in the matter of vengeance, we must consider the mind of the avenger. For if his intention is directed chiefly to the evil of the person on whom he takes vengeance and rests there, then his vengeance is altogether unlawful. …
>
> If, however, the avenger's intention be directed chiefly to some good, to be obtained by means of the punishment of the person who has sinned (for instance that the sinner may amend, or at least that he may be restrained and others be not disturbed, that justice may be upheld, and God honored), then vengeance may be lawful, provided other due circumstances be observed. (1948, II–II.108.1 [p. 1650])

However we use words like "vengeance," the substantive point is that A-T natural law theory entails not only the goodness of punishment in itself, but also the virtuousness of following our natural inclination to inflict it. This entails a twofold teleological foundation for punishment. Evildoing aims or is directed toward pain as its natural consequence, and punishment restores this connection where the evildoer has tried to sever it; and human beings by nature aim or are directed toward inflicting punishment on evildoers. Since securing the realization of natural ends is constitutive of the good, punishment is good.

But what sorts of punishments ought to be inflicted? Traditional natural law theorists like Aquinas appeal to the *principle of proportionality*, according to which a punishment ought to be *proportionate* to the offense. Aquinas writes:

> Since divine justice requires, for the preservation of equality in things, that punishments be assigned for faults and rewards for good acts, then, if there are degrees in virtuous acts and in sins … there must also be degrees among rewards and punishments. Otherwise, equality would not be preserved, that is, if a greater punishment were not given to one who sins more, or a greater reward to one who acts better. Indeed, the same reasoning seems to require different retri-

> bution on the basis of the diversity of good and evil, and on the basis of the difference between the good and the better, or between the bad and the worse. (1975, III.142.1 [p. 210])

And again:

> Punishment should proportionally correspond to the fault, as we said above. …
>
> Besides, if a man makes inordinate use of a means to the end, he may not only be deprived of the end, but may also incur some other injury. …
>
> As good things are owed to those who act rightly, so bad things are due to those who act perversely. But those who act rightly, at the end intended by them, receive perfection and joy. So, on the contrary, this punishment is due to sinners, that from those things in which they set their end they receive affliction and injury. (1975, III.145.1, 3–4 [pp. 218–19])

Notice that, in the first of these two passages from *Summa Contra Gentiles*, Aquinas says that "the same reasoning seems to require *different* retribution on the basis of the *diversity* of good and evil." This indicates that proportionality in punishment is not merely a *quantitative* but also a *qualitative* matter. That is to say, to satisfy Aquinas's principle of proportionality, it is not necessarily sufficient to inflict more of a certain sort of punishment on worse crimes than on lesser ones—for instance, larger fines for bank robbery than for petty theft, and larger fines still for murder, but where the punishment consists in each case of a fine.[5] The *character* of the punishment should somehow fit the character of the offense. Notice also that, in the second passage, Aquinas says that it is in the nature of some offenses that their punishment can merit not merely the loss of a good that the offender should have pursued, but a positive injury as well. Hence with some offenses it is not sufficient that offenders merely be deprived of some pleasure or benefit that they otherwise would have gotten. The active infliction of some pain or harm is called for. "Punishment," Aquinas writes, "is proportionate to sin in point of *severity*" (1948, I–II.87.3 [p. 975], emphasis added).

This principle of proportionality is essentially just an extension of the idea that there is—in the long run and when things are functioning properly—a natural correlation between goodness and pleasure on the one hand and evil and pain on the other. The natural correlation is, specifically, between *degrees* of goodness and pleasure on the one hand and *degrees* of evil and pain on the other. Hence the natural order of things is—again, in the long run and when

[5] This *might* be sufficient on the very different notion of proportionality criticized in Nathanson (2001, 76–77).

things are functioning properly—for greater goodness to be associated with greater pleasure and less goodness with less pleasure, and for greater evil to be associated with greater pain and less evil with less pain. This seems to be the force of Aquinas's argument that "*since* divine justice requires, *for the preservation of equality in things*, that punishments be assigned for faults and rewards for good acts, *then*, if there are *degrees* in virtuous acts and in sins, as we showed, there must also be *degrees* among rewards and punishments" (1975, III.142.1 [p. 210], emphasis added). And the correlation is, again, *qualitative* as well as quantitative.

This natural correlation, made intelligible by A-T essentialism and teleology, is for the traditional natural law theorist the deep metaphysical reality that we grasp in an intuitive way when we judge that people have received or failed to receive their "just deserts." We cannot help but regard it as *fitting* when things go well for good people and badly for bad people, and as *unfair* when the reverse occurs. For the traditional natural law theorist, this is not the mere expression of some noncognitive affective state but rather the inchoate apprehension of the objective order of things—of the fact that, given our nature, our good acts inherently "point to" or are "directed toward" happiness and our bad acts inherently "point to" or are "directed toward" unhappiness. When things do not work out this way, we rightly perceive this as a kind of disorder, just as we rightly perceive bodily or psychological abnormalities as instances of disorder. Rewards and punishments are, like medical and psychological treatment, essentially attempts to restore the proper order of things.

It must be emphasized, though, that while the A-T natural law theorist's position is *consistent with* and indeed *explains* our moral intuitions about punishment, it is not *grounded in* an appeal to intuition. Natural law theory is not saying: "This metaphysical account of punishment fits our intuitions; therefore it is true." Rather, it is saying: "We know on grounds independent of our intuitions that this metaphysical account of punishment is true, and it also happens to account for why we have the intuitions we have." Because they have abandoned the metaphysics that underlies traditional natural law theory, contemporary philosophers who defend aspects of commonsense morality often ground their arguments in an appeal to intuition, and that is as true with regard to punishment as it is with regard to other moral issues. Unsurprisingly, their critics have little difficulty exposing the weaknesses in such appeals.[6] The A-T natural law account, whatever else one thinks of it, is not open to such criticism.

[6] See Boonin (2008, ch. 3) for criticism of attempts to justify retribution by appeal to intuitions.

The restoration of what Aquinas calls "the equality of justice" by inflicting on offenders harms proportionate to their offenses is for A-T natural law theory the essence of *retribution*, and it is one of three traditional purposes of punishment, the others being *correction* or rehabilitation of the offender and the *deterrence* of those tempted to commit the same crimes as the offender (see Oderberg 2000, 146–56). Yet other purposes identified by writers on the subject are the *incapacitation* of offenders lest they commit further crimes, and *restitution* or compensation to the victims of their crimes.

In modern society, retribution is the most controversial of these ends of punishment, and sometimes it is thought to be something we not only may dispense with but ought to dispense with. However, as our discussion to this point indicates, for the A-T natural law theorist, retribution is not only *a* legitimate end of punishment, but it is the *fundamental* end. Indeed, the other functions of punishment become problematic in the absence of retribution. If we need not give people their just deserts, then there can be no objection *in principle* to realizing the corrective and deterrent functions of punishment by meting out extremely mild punishments for major crimes or extremely harsh punishments for minor crimes. Perhaps certain murderers could be deterred or persuaded to change their ways by a moderate fine, and perhaps minor thefts could be virtually eliminated by the threat of summary execution. There might be *practical* problems implementing such policies, but there could be no *moral* objection if there were no objective fact of the matter about whether offenders deserve punishments proportionate to their offenses. But if we *do* object morally to such disproportionate punishments, then we need rationally to justify this objection, and this cannot plausibly be done unless we acknowledge that there is such a thing as desert.

In any event, the arguments for the teleological connection between wrongdoing and pain, and for there being a teleological connection between the specific *nature* of the wrongdoing and a pain proportionate to it, give us a foundation for the first two premises of the argument for capital punishment set out at the beginning of this chapter. These are, again:

1. Wrongdoers deserve punishment as a matter of retributive justice.
2. The more grave the wrongdoing, the more severe is the punishment deserved.

3 The Social Organism

Given that a wrongdoer merits a punishment proportionate to the offense, there is still the question of who is to inflict this punishment. Aquinas answers as follows:

> Now it is evident that all things contained in an order, are, in a manner, one, in relation to the principle of that order. Consequently, whatever rises up against an order, is put down by that order or by the principle thereof. And because sin is an inordinate act, it is evident that whoever sins, commits an offense against an order: wherefore he is put down, in consequence, by that same order, which repression is punishment.
>
> Accordingly, man can be punished with a threefold punishment corresponding to the three orders to which the human will is subject. In the first place a man's nature is subjected to the order of his own reason; secondly, it is subjected to the order of another man who governs him either in spiritual or in temporal matters, as a member either of the state or of the household; thirdly, it is subjected to the universal order of the Divine government. Now each of these orders is disturbed by sin, for the sinner acts against his reason, and against human and Divine law. Wherefore he incurs a threefold punishment; one, inflicted by himself, viz. remorse of conscience; another, inflicted by man; and a third, inflicted by God. (1948, I–II.87.1 [p. 973])

So, since an offense is an offense against an order of things, it is the head of that order who has the primary responsibility for repairing that order by inflicting punishment. In the case of immoral actions that affect only offenders themselves, their intellects, which govern the rest of their nature, will punish them via a troubled conscience. In the case of offences against divine law, God will punish them. Writes Aquinas, "if man were by nature a solitary animal, this twofold order would suffice. But since man is naturally a civic and social animal … a third order is necessary, whereby man is directed in relation to other men among whom he has to dwell" (1948, I–II.72.4 [p. 905]). Hence it is the head of this third, social sort of order who has the primary responsibility for punishing offenses against it and thereby restoring the proper connection between evildoing and pain.

In the family, the responsibility lies with parents. In the political order, "the care of the common good is entrusted to persons of rank having public authority" (Aquinas 1948, II–II.64.3 [p. 1461]). Of the need for these governmental authorities, Aquinas writes:

> Since some people pay little attention to the punishments inflicted by God, because they are devoted to the objects of sense and care only for the things that are seen, it has been ordered accordingly by divine providence that there be men in various countries whose duty it is to compel these people, by means of sensible and present punishments, to respect justice. … Now, it is just for the wicked to be punished, since by punishment the fault is restored to order. (1975, III.146.1 [pp. 219–20])

I will put aside for present purposes the issue of divine providence, since it is tangential to our main topic. The relevant theme to which Aquinas gives expression in these passages is the idea that social order is organic, and that this follows from our nature as social animals. To be sure, society is not an organism in the same sense in which a tree, a lion, or a human being is an organism, because those things possess a substantial unity that society does not have. But neither is society either a mere aggregate (as a pile of stones is) or an artifact (as a table or a sports fan club is), because the elements that make up such things lack any *intrinsic* or built-in teleological relation to the whole of which they are parts. Natural human social orders like the family and the state *do* have such an intrinsic teleological basis, which makes them an intermediate sort of thing standing between true substances on the one hand and mere aggregates and artifacts on the other. For example, we are made in such a way that we need the family for our completion and flourishing qua rational animals, whereas we do not need to be members of sports fan clubs for that. As Aristotle famously argued in the *Politics*, we also need the larger social order of the state for our completion and flourishing. Moreover, the parts of a family or a state are functionally related to one another in a manner that is analogous to the way the parts of an organic whole like the body are, each doing its part for the sustenance of the order of the whole. Most relevant for present purposes, the governing authorities in a social order relate to the rest of it in something analogous to the way the human intellect relates to the rest of the human organism.

Part of what is involved in governing an order is making sure that its elements do their part in contributing to its proper functioning, and especially that they do not act in a way that positively subverts its proper functioning. When those elements are below the level of rationality (as, for example, the parts of the human body are), this may involve healing them when that is possible (as medicine, surgery, and the like can heal a damaged body part), but it may involve removing and destroying them instead (as with a gangrenous limb or cancer-ridden organ). When the elements are rational creatures like ourselves, as they are in a social order like the state, questions of moral praise and blame, and thus of rewards and punishments, arise in a way that they do not in the case of body parts and the like. Might there in the case of such a social order be punishments that are analogous to the removal and destruction of a diseased body part?

Let us approach this question by first addressing the grounds for affirming premise 3 of the argument for capital punishment set out at the beginning of this chapter. Recall that the premise states:

3. Some crimes are so grave that no punishment less than death would be proportionate in its severity.

This is, I think, obviously true, but perhaps further comment is appropriate. If wrongdoers deserve punishment, and if punishment ought to be proportionate to the gravity of the crime, then it seems absurd to deny that there is *some* level of criminality for which nothing less than capital punishment would be proportionate. For on the principle of proportionality, there is no such thing as deserving a punishment merely *of some severity or other*, any more than there is such a thing as being of *some height or other*. It makes no sense to say that it is an objective fact that rape (for example) merits punishment but that there is no fact of the matter about whether it merits a punishment as mild as a fifty-cent fine or as harsh as scourging, any more than it makes sense to say that it is an objective fact that Joe Biden has height but no fact of the matter about whether he is five feet tall, or six feet tall, or any other particular height. To have height is to have *some specific* height, and to deserve punishment is to deserve a punishment of *some specific severity*. It is to deserve a punishment *as severe as the offense is grave*. Proportionality, then, is built into the notion of desert, and thus is built into the notion of punishment. (To be sure, we might not always be able, in *practice*, to determine exactly how severe is the punishment some offense merits, but that does not mean that there is no such specific severity, any more than the fact that some object might be too small or too large for us to measure entails that it does not have a specific height.)

Since there are crimes as grave as death or even more grave, so too must there be crimes for which nothing less than death would be a sufficiently severe penalty.[7] Even if it were claimed that a single murder would not be such a crime, it is not difficult to imagine a crime that would be. Mass murder? Genocide? Genocide coupled with the rape and torture of the victims? To claim that there is *no* crime for which death would be a proportionate punishment—to claim, for instance, that a cold-blooded, genocidal rapist can never *even in principle* merit a greater punishment than the lifelong imprisonment that might be inflicted on, say, a recidivist bank robber—is implicitly to give up the principle of proportionality. For to agree that genocide is a far worse offense than bank robbery while maintaining that genocide cannot in principle merit a punishment worse than the punishment for bank robbery is implicitly to deny that a punishment ought to be proportionate to the offense.

[7] David Oderberg (2000, ch. 4) defends capital punishment on the grounds that there is such a thing as the worst possible crime and the worst possible punishment, and that the former merits the latter. But it seems to me that this is a stronger claim than one needs in order to provide a defense of capital punishment based on the principle of proportionality.

If, as I have argued, the legitimacy of punishment entails desert, and desert in turn entails proportionality, then to deny proportionality is implicitly to deny desert, and thus implicitly to deny the legitimacy of punishment. But proportionality entails the legitimacy in principle of capital punishment. Hence to deny the legitimacy in principle of capital punishment is implicitly to deny proportionality, and thus desert, and thus the legitimacy of punishment itself. In short, the legitimacy of *punishment in general* and the legitimacy in principle of *capital* punishment in particular *stand or fall together.*

To be sure, sometimes inflicting a proportionate punishment is impossible—for example, a mass murderer cannot be executed multiple times—but the practical difficulties involved in implementing a principle do not *per se* cast doubt on a principle itself. After all, restitution is also often practically impossible, but that does not entail that we should not at least try to approximate it. Furthermore, when the other aims of punishment (correction, deterrence, etc.) are taken into account, we may have reason to give some offenders a punishment other than what they strictly deserve. And of course there are cases where considerations of mercy might lead us to inflict a much lesser punishment or no punishment at all. Then there is the fact that moral hazards entailed by certain punishments ought to make us wary of inflicting them. For instance, murderers whose preferred method is to stab their victims multiple times may deserve the same treatment; but given the psychological damage the infliction of such grisly punishments would do to executioners, we ought to confine ourselves to the more antiseptic methods of execution typical of modern times. In short, the principle of proportionality does not require that we *must* always in fact inflict on wrongdoers punishments that are exactly proportionate to their offenses. Rather, it provides us with a presumption that can be overridden, a baseline from which we will often have practical and moral reasons to deviate.

So, we have good reason to affirm premise 3. But more must be said before concluding that the state might legitimately inflict a punishment analogous to removing and destroying a diseased body part, even given that some offenders deserve it. True, as we have seen, according to A-T natural law theory, retribution is the *primary* aim of punishment insofar as we must always have retribution in view when punishing, even if we have other aims in view as well. Purposes of correction, deterrence, and the like are never *by themselves* sufficient to justify punishment, since it is never legitimate to inflict a punishment on someone unless it is *deserved.* But if retribution is a necessary aim of punishment, is it also sufficient? Can we inflict a punishment *merely* to secure retributive justice? Aquinas and other Thomists have thought not. Aquinas writes:

> The punishments of this life are more medicinal than retributive, since retribution against sinners is reserved to God's righteous judgment. And so judgment in this life inflicts the punishment of death only for mortal sins that cause irreparable harm or have a terrible deformity, not for every mortal sin. (2002, II–II.66.6 [p. 139])

As this passage indicates, Aquinas thinks that recourse to the death penalty can be called for when the other aims of punishment are considered alongside the retributive end. For example, it is in his view justifiable for purposes of deterrence:

> The punishment that is inflicted according to human laws, is not always intended as a medicine for the one who is punished, but sometimes only for others: thus when a thief is hanged, this is not for his own amendment, but for the sake of others, that at least they may be deterred from crime through fear of the punishment. (1948, I–II.87.3 [p. 975])[8]

Emphasizing our social nature, Aquinas stresses especially the value of capital punishment in incapacitating those members of society who pose a danger to the whole. He writes:

> Now every part is directed to the whole, as imperfect to perfect, wherefore every part is naturally for the sake of the whole. For this reason we observe that if the health of the whole body demands the excision of a member, through its being decayed or infectious to the other members, it will be both praiseworthy and advantageous to have it cut away. Now every individual person is compared to the whole community, as part to whole. Therefore if a man be dangerous and infectious to the community, on account of some sin, it is praiseworthy and advantageous that he be killed in order to safeguard the common good. (1948, II–II.64.2 [p. 1461])

In a similar passage in the *Summa Contra Gentiles*, Aquinas says:

> The common good is better than the particular good of one person. So, the particular good should be removed in order to preserve the common good. But the life of certain pestiferous men is an impediment to the common good which

[8] Punishing theft with death certainly seems disproportionate by modern standards, but Aquinas presumably had in mind premodern circumstances in which, for example, bandits might raid villages more or less with impunity without police to deter them or prisons to restrain them, so that execution seemed the only realistic remedy.

> is the concord of human society. Therefore, certain men must be removed by death from the society of men. …
>
> Now, the physician quite properly and beneficially cuts off a diseased organ if the corruption of the body is threatened because of it. … [Similarly] the ruler of a state executes pestiferous men justly and sinlessly in order that the peace of the state may not be disrupted. (1975, III.146.4–5 [pp. 220–21])

It is important to emphasize that, contrary to the impression given by some commentators, there is nothing in these passages that implies that Aquinas regards deterrence, protection of the community, and the like as sufficient *in themselves* to justify capital punishment, independent of retributive justice. Indeed, that cannot be what Aquinas thinks, given that, as we have seen above, he is committed to the principle that a punishment should be proportionate to the offense. Obviously, Aquinas would not say that we might justly execute someone to deter others even if such a punishment were out of proportion to what the person actually deserves. Indeed, in the very passage in which he says that "the punishments of this life are more medicinal than retributive," he nevertheless emphasizes that capital punishment is called for when the offenses involve "*irreparable* harm or have a *terrible* deformity"—thus indicating the *proportionality* of the death penalty to such offenses. Rather, in these passages, it is simply taken for granted that the offenders in question already deserve death as a matter of retributive justice. What Aquinas is addressing is the question of why we should sometimes actually inflict on them what they deserve *given that* "the punishments of this life are more medicinal than retributive."

So, given what has been said about the function of governmental authorities together with the supposition that an offender deserves a certain punishment *and* that that punishment serves the common good of those who make up the social organism (say, by protecting society against that offender or deterring other offenders), we have a justification of premise 5 of the argument I gave at the beginning of this chapter:

5. Governmental authorities have the right to inflict on wrongdoers the punishments they deserve.

This includes capital punishment, in cases where that is both deserved and conducive to protecting society against the one executed or deterring others, so our premises do indeed support our overall conclusion:

6. Therefore, governmental authorities have the right to inflict the death penalty on those guilty of the gravest offenses.

4 Does the Argument Prove Too Much?

As I have indicated, like other rights, the state's right to inflict the death penalty is presumptive and can be overridden. Some would argue that in modern Western societies there are no cases where the death penalty is strictly necessary in order to protect society from an offender. Some argue that there is a significant risk of executing an innocent person, or at least that the deterrence value of capital punishment is not high enough to outweigh that risk. Some argue that capital punishment has no significant deterrence value in the first place. Some argue that it is applied in a way that is racially discriminatory, or in a way that discriminates against the poor. If such claims were true, then one could make a case that the state ought not to exercise its right to execute those guilty of the worst offenses. That these claims are *not* in fact true is something Joseph Bessette and I try to show in our book on capital punishment (2017, esp. 70–73, 77–78, 312–35, 338–74).

In another chapter in this volume, Benjamin Yost argues that, because there is always enough uncertainty in capital cases about whether an offender really merits the death penalty, we ought never to inflict that penalty. For even when we are certain of an offender's guilt and the gravity of the offense, there will not be sufficient certainty about whether the offender is of sound mind and thus merits execution. Why would this not rule out lesser punishments too, such as imprisonment? Because, Yost argues, the state can always remedy unjust punishments of a lesser sort, including even the years that an innocently imprisoned person has lost.

But it seems to me that Yost's argument faces a dilemma. Both Yost's argument that we cannot be sufficiently certain that an offender is of sound mind, and his argument that the state can sufficiently remedy an unjust punishment of many years imprisonment, rest on assumptions and arguments of a philosophical and psychological sort. If Yost's standards of certainty are so high that they rule out our ever being certain that an offender is of sound mind, then why would they not also rule out our ever being certain that the state really can remedy unjust imprisonment? And in that case, his argument would rule out even imprisonment, and not just capital punishment.

If instead Yost's standards of certainty are low enough that we can be certain that the state really can remedy unjust imprisonment, then why would they not also be low enough that we can be certain in at least some cases that an offender in a capital case is of sound mind? And in that case, Yost's argument would not only allow for imprisonment, but it would also allow for capital punishment in at least some cases.

Some may think that the position I have been defending faces a fatal dilemma of its own. Christopher Tollefsen (2011) rightly notes that rape is "intrinsically wrong" and thus "not available as an option for punishment, regardless of its feasibility or the proportion of goods to bads it might bring about" (see also Nathanson 2001, 74; Boonin 2008, 110). So, if A-T natural law theory claimed, on the basis of the principle of proportionality, that a rapist could at least *in principle* be punished with rape, it would entail a falsehood. Yet if it acknowledges instead (as I certainly do) that the principle of proportionality cannot justify rape, even in principle, as a legitimate punishment, then (Tollefsen seems to conclude) I should agree that it also cannot, by itself, justify capital punishment, even in principle.

This argument breaks down, however, because there is a crucial disanalogy between rape and the taking of someone's life. To take a life is, essentially, to inflict a single harm, namely the taking of the life. (Of course, other harms might follow from this—one's children might be orphaned, one's spouse widowed, etc.—but the taking of a life would still be a harm, even if such other harms did not follow.) Rape, however, essentially involves *several* harms. There are the humiliation and bodily harm inflicted on the victim, but there is also the sexual perversion and sadism by which rapists harm their own character. To indulge in such sexual perversion and sadism is intrinsically immoral; and therefore rape is intrinsically immoral, even if carried out as a punishment. Nor does the principle of proportionality imply otherwise. Rather, it implies, at most, only that rapists deserve the humiliation and bodily harm they have inflicted on others—just as it implies that murderers deserve to suffer the same harm *they* have inflicted on others—but it does not imply that anyone, including those with authority to punish wrongdoers, can even in principle legitimately indulge in the sexual perversion and sadism that are also involved in rape.

A more general objection along these lines is that the retributivist defense of the death penalty, if applied consistently, would require the infliction on offenders of all kinds of gruesome punishments—torturing torturers, chopping off the limbs of those who have maimed others, and so on. The answer to this objection is that we need to distinguish the question of whether offenders deserve a certain punishment from the question of whether in a particular case it is, all things considered, a good idea to give them what they deserve. Did Lawrence Singleton, who raped a girl and chopped off her arms, deserve to have his own arms chopped off? Retributivists would say (or should say) that he did deserve this, and that a government that inflicted this punishment on him would not have been doing an injustice. But it does not follow that governments should in fact inflict such punishments, and various considerations—moral considerations no less than pragmatic ones—might tell against doing so.

The same thing is true in the case of capital punishment. The A-T natural law position is not that of Kant, who argued that murderers *must* be executed (1996, 6:333 [p. 474]). I have been concerned to argue here only that the death penalty can be *just*. Whether it ought to be inflicted in any particular case is a question that must take that into account, but it ought also to take into account considerations other than justice. I have not addressed those here.[9]

References

Aquinas, Thomas. 1948. *Summa Theologica*. 5 vols. Translated by the Fathers of the English Dominican Province. New York: Benziger.

———. 1975. *Summa Contra Gentiles*. Vol. 3: *Providence*, pt. 2. Translated by Vernon J. Bourke. South Bend, IN: University of Notre Dame Press.

———. 2002. *On Law, Morality, and Politics*. Translated by Richard J. Regan. Edited by William P. Baumgarth and Richard J. Regan. 2nd ed. Indianapolis, IN: Hackett.

Boonin, David. 2008. *The Problem of Punishment*. Cambridge: Cambridge University Press.

Cronin, Michael. 1939. *The Science of Ethics*. Vol. 1: *General Ethics*. Dublin: Gill.

Feser, Edward. 2009. *Aquinas*. Oxford: Oneworld.

———. 2014a. "Being, the Good, and the Guise of the Good." In *Neo-Aristotelian Perspectives in Metaphysics*, edited by Daniel D. Novotny and Lukas Novak, 84-103. London: Routledge.

———. 2014b. *Scholastic Metaphysics: A Contemporary Introduction*. Heusenstamm, DE: Editiones Scholasticae.

———. 2019a. *Aristotle's Revenge: The Metaphysical Foundations of Physical and Biological Science*. Neunkirchen-Seelscheid, DE: Editiones Scholasticae.

———. 2019b. "Natural Law Ethics and the Revival of Aristotelian Metaphysics." In *The Cambridge Companion to Natural Law Ethics*, edited by Tom Angier, 276–96. Cambridge: Cambridge University Press.

Feser, Edward, and Joseph M. Bessette. 2017. *By Man Shall His Blood Be Shed: A Catholic Defense of Capital Punishment*. San Francisco: Ignatius.

Foot, Philippa. 2001. *Natural Goodness*. Oxford: Clarendon.

Kant, Immanuel. 1996. *The Metaphysics of Morals*. In *Practical Philosophy*, translated and edited by Mary J. Gregor, 363–602. Cambridge: Cambridge University Press.

Koritansky, Peter Karl. 2012. *Thomas Aquinas and the Philosophy of Punishment*. Washington, DC: Catholic University of America Press.

[9] I thank Benjamin Yost for helpful comments on an earlier version of this chapter.

Nathanson, Stephen. 2001. *An Eye for An Eye? The Immorality of Punishing by Death*. 2nd ed. New York: Rowman & Littlefield.

Oderberg, David S. 2000. *Applied Ethics: A Non-Consequentialist Approach*. Oxford: Blackwell.

Reutemann, Charles. 1953. *The Thomistic Concept of Pleasure as Compared with Hedonistic and Rigoristic Philosophies*. Washington, DC: Catholic University of America Press.

Tollefsen, Christopher O. 2011. "Capital Punishment, Dignity, and Authority: A Response to Ed Feser." *Public Discourse*, September 30. http://www.thepublicdiscourse.com/2011/09/4045/.

Walen, Alec. 2020. "Retributive Justice." *Stanford Encyclopedia of Philosophy* (Summer 2021 edition), edited by Edward N. Zalta. https://plato.stanford.edu/archives/sum2021/entries/justice-retributive/.

34

The Impermissibility of Execution

Benjamin S. Yost

I will start with a confession. Although I am revolted and outraged by the death penalty, I am not entirely sold on arguments for its intrinsic immorality. I find it hard to draw any firm conclusions one way or the other, as so much depends on one's core intuitions, preferred balancing of competing moral values, and the like. I also suspect that some retributivist arguments in favor of capital punishment are stronger than many of my abolitionist comrades appreciate.[1] But while I demur on whether executions violate some fundamental principle of morality, my reticence does not alter my conviction that the death penalty contravenes important principles of political morality. In my view, the death penalty is wrong because it violates mid-level moral principles that flow from liberal norms governing the criminal justice system—one important example being the principle of remedy, which states that legal institutions must fix their mistakes. This chapter will show how these principles of political morality ground an argument for death penalty abolition.

Here is my argument in a nutshell. When sentencers have, or should have, some uncertainty about which penalty is precisely proportionate to an offense,

[1] I have reconstructed one of these in Yost (2010) and analyzed others in Yost (2019).

B. S. Yost (✉)
Cornell University, Ithaca, NY, USA
e-mail: benjamin.yost@cornell.edu

© The Author(s), under exclusive license to Springer Nature Switzerland AG 2023

M. C. Altman (ed.), *The Palgrave Handbook on the Philosophy of Punishment*, Palgrave Handbooks in the Philosophy of Law, https://doi.org/10.1007/978-3-031-11874-6_34

they have a duty to err on the side of leniency. This is especially the case when the punishment in question is irrevocable, or incapable of remedy. Because unjust custodial sanctions can be compensated for, they are subject to a less stringent demand for leniency: the possibility of revoking wrongful punishment counterbalances some of the risk of wrongful overpunishment. Execution, on the other hand, is irrevocable—the dead cannot be compensated. In capital cases, the risk of overpunishment goes unmitigated. Because all capital cases are characterized by uncertainty, or so I will argue, capital sentencers must always err on the side of leniency. Sentencers are thus barred from choosing execution as a punishment. For this reason, capital punishment is impermissible.

1 Preliminaries

Before elaborating and defending these claims, I want to make some preliminary clarifications. First, my strategy is a procedural one. It is procedural in that it takes no stand on the intrinsic morality of execution. Although I invoke substantive moral principles, these apply to institutional practices and individuals in their official capacities. Many friends of the death penalty believe that if they can show execution to be morally permissible *in principle*, they have succeeded, even if they must concede that the death penalty is permissible only in jurisdictions with just penal institutions (and so might not pass muster in the U.S.). But this belief is mistaken. The death penalty's putative intrinsic moral permissibility does not entail permissibility all things considered, even in the context of reasonably just legal regimes. Indeed, I will argue that capital punishment is morally forbidden for reasons pertaining to its implementation. I am not hanging my hat on the familiar assertion that execution is prohibited in careless or discriminatory legal systems. I defend a stronger claim: *even in legal institutions that are as fair and rigorous as can be expected*, capital punishment violates principles of political morality.

Second, I assume that states are permitted to punish criminal offenders. I am aiming at an argument for the abolition of capital punishment that does not entail the abolition of legal punishment whole cloth.[2] I have doubts about the morality of punishment, but I do not want my criticisms of capital punishment to depend on them. This is because I want to immunize my proposal against the common objection that anti-death penalty arguments require the

[2] An example of such an argument is the hard determinist claim that people lack free will and thus cannot deserve execution, or any other punishment.

rejection of punishment as such. For many, this consequence would be a bridge too far, and I have no need to court such controversy.

Third, I endorse a sentencing framework with at least some important retributivist commitments. While I take no stand on the best justification of the institution of punishment, I am committed to the idea that sentencing ought to aim for proportionality.

2 A Proceduralist Argument against Capital Punishment

Stated a bit more formally, my argument runs as follows:

1. Sentencers must risk underpunishment by *n* units rather than risk overpunishment by *n* units and the failure to remedy said overpunishment.
2. Wrongful execution cannot be remedied.
3. Jurisdictions with the death penalty preclude the possibility of revocation in capital cases.
4. The death penalty must be abolished in all jurisdictions.

The rest of this section will be devoted to defending the first two premises, which is where all the excitement happens. I will start with the second, because it is the least complicated.

2.1 The Irrevocability of Execution

Most people I have queried agree that death penalty is irrevocable. The common intuition seems to be that revocation involves compensation, and that wrongfully executed people cannot be compensated because they are dead. But some philosophers dissent from this position, so I want to explain why we should endorse it. First, I need to clarify the notion of irrevocability. Confusion here can lead one to think that no *custodial* punishment is revocable. After all, we cannot return the days stolen from the wrongly imprisoned person any more than we can revive the dead. If punishment as such is irrevocable, and if irrevocability is a reason to discard a punishment, then we have a problem: *all* punishments need to be foresworn. Irrevocability abolitionist arguments would thus be hitched to wholesale abolitionism.

But this overlooks the crucial distinction between what Michael Davis calls absolute and substantial revocability (1984, 145). Absolute revocation would return the wrongly punished person back to the very same conditions they were in before their punishment. If we understand revocability to be absolute revocability, all serious punishments are irrevocable, small fines excepted. However, there is ample reason to reject this conception. No moral wrong is absolutely revocable, yet we frequently, sincerely, and intelligibly talk about fixing our mistakes or undoing the wrongs we have committed. We believe many wrongs to be revocable, even though they are not absolutely so. The absolute conception thus should be discarded as objectionably revisionary.

Substantial revocability counts compensation of the wrongly punished person as a (potentially) sufficient remedy. On this conception, a state can fix its mistakes by financially compensating an injured party or otherwise advancing their interests. Clearly, appropriate compensation must be roughly commensurate to the wrong incurred; an innocent person imprisoned for ten years would *not* be compensated by a payment of $25,000.[3] I will borrow Davis's criterion for substantial revocation, which is that "we do all in our power to compensate the convict (and what we do is far from negligible) or that we do enough so that he would say, 'that would make [the wrongful punishment] worth it'" (1984, 150).[4] Because wrongful custodial sentences are substantially revocable, rejecting irrevocable punishments does not imply the total abolition of punishment.

The question before us now is whether the death penalty is substantially irrevocable. (The following discussion will be brief; interested readers can find a more detailed account in Yost [2019, ch. 3]). As I noted earlier, execution appears to be substantially irrevocable in that the wrongly executed person cannot receive compensation. However, if sufficient compensation can be *posthumously* granted, the death penalty is revocable.

The prospect of compensating the dead might sound absurd. So consider the following scenario: a single parent has devoted his life to one purpose, ensuring that his daughter enjoys something better than his meagre financial prospects. He works two menial jobs in the doomed hope that she can afford to attend college. Unfortunately, he is diagnosed with an incurable disease, and he scrubs dishes knowing he will die in a few years' time. Then the man is convicted of, and executed for, a crime he did not commit. After his execution, his innocence is discovered. The state exonerates him and publicly clears his reputation. The state also deposits $1,000,000 into his estate, which his daughter inherits. Here the father's most important goals are posthumously advanced. Had he been offered a choice between living the rest of his life or

[3] This is the statutory cap on compensation for wrongful imprisonment in Wisconsin.

[4] Davis adopts the substantial conception of revocability but denies the irrevocability of execution.

being executed and richly compensated, choosing execution would not be irrational. Even if he decided to live, he would certainly consider the alternative of execution "worth it" in some important sense. This is because the money posthumously advances his interests to a significant degree, far more than he could achieve himself. Examples like this suggest that one's interests can be posthumously advanced, one can be the recipient of posthumous benefits, and a wrongly executed person can be compensated after his demise. So, there are grounds for denying the irrevocability of capital punishment.

Now that we see why execution might be revocable, let us see why it is not. My main contention is that the conception of revocation as compensation is incomplete.[5] While compensation might be necessary for revocation, it is not sufficient. Another necessary component is that the state return to the wrongly punished person control over their life. I do not mean anything extravagant by this. Someone has control over their life to the extent that they can self-reflectively guide their actions in light of their aims and desires. So long as we have a generous set of desires, we do not normally lack the ability to direct our lives. This metaphysical modesty should not obscure the phenomenon's importance. Control over one's life is an intrinsic good: we give meaning to our existence, in part, by striving for goals that emerge from our notion of the good life. It is also a basic good: it is good for someone regardless of their particular conception of the good life. Because control over one's life is a basic, intrinsic good, any plausible political morality will bar states from unjust dispossessions thereof. It follows that when the state divests citizens of such goods for no reason, as in cases of wrongful punishment, it must immediately return or restore them.[6]

So, returning the wrongfully punished person's control over their life is a nonnegotiable part of revocation. Penalties that foreclose this possibility are irrevocable. Clearly, legal authorities *cannot* return control to the wrongfully executed, even if they can somehow issue posthumous compensation. The death penalty is irrevocable, despite claims to the contrary.

[5] The preference theory of well-being that secures claims about the possibility of posthumous compensation is fairly controversial, but I will set that issue aside.

[6] We can arrive at this duty from a different route. For mainstream liberal political thought, one of the central aims of legitimate legal and political institutions is to ensure that citizens have the maximum amount of control compatible with other citizens' control over their lives. This aim is shared by a variety of normative political philosophies, including Nozickian libertarianism, which interprets control as sovereignty over one's personal moral sphere; Pettitian non-domination theory, which construes control as thoroughgoing freedom from arbitrary interference; as well as a Rawlsian egalitarianism, which conceives of control as a positive capacity to accomplish one's ends regardless of one's draw in the natural lottery. On all these views, states must protect and enhance individuals' ability to control their lives. Accordingly, unjust state interference with that ability must be immediately discontinued and remedied.

2.2 The Principle of Remedy

Unfortunately for abolitionists, one cannot repudiate capital punishment by gesturing toward the irrevocability of execution and calling it a day. This is because it is eminently reasonable to demand an explanation of *why* irrevocable punishments must be abjured. Irrevocability is just one of the moral considerations bearing on the legitimacy of capital punishment, so the abolitionist owes an argument establishing its priority. Only then will irrevocability ground death penalty abolitionism.

The most important execution-friendly consideration issues from the retributivist commitment to proportionality. This commitment generates a pro tanto reason to inflict the full amount of deserved punishment: when punishment p is proportionate to a crime, selecting a sanction lighter than p violates proportionality. Abolishing capital punishment thus seems to create retributive injustice, insofar as it causes the underpunishment of all those for whom execution is proportionate.[7] This line of reasoning, which I will call the "retributivist challenge," poses a challenge to any irrevocability argument for abolition.

My first step in meeting this challenge develops a point made previously. It is a fundamental principle of political morality that legal institutions must remedy their mistakes. In the criminal justice context, this means that legal authorities must furnish a remedy to those who are improperly punished, a class that includes both those innocent of wrongdoing and those punished more harshly than their offense merits (e.g., someone convicted of, and executed for, first-degree murder who is actually guilty only of manslaughter).

To defend the principle of remedy, I will first register the uncontroversial claim that liberal states are committed to refraining from unjustly coercing their citizens. Roughly speaking, an unjust exercise of coercion is one that violates citizens' basic rights, is more injurious than necessary, or unduly burdens citizens without providing a counterbalancing benefit. The bar on unjust coercion correlates with a requirement to try to *alleviate* the illicit burdens the state imposes. A commitment to averting unjust coercion is meaningless unless it is accompanied by a state's attempt to rectify its unjust coercive acts. To fail to try to put things right evinces an objectionable insensitivity to injustice. In liberal societies, then, government actors must endeavor to undo wrongful interferences in citizens' lives.

Support for the principle of remedy comes from other quarters. Some philosophers contend that conformity to the principle is a constitutive condition

[7] I am assuming that execution might be proportionate to some murders. For more on this point, see §3.2.

of legal legitimacy (Fuller 1969, 81). And legal scholars are virtually unanimous in the view that error correction is one of the essential functions of appellate courts (Shapiro 1980; Resnick 1984; Dalton 1985; Shavell 1995; Oldfather 2010; Primus 2010). The principle of remedy is also embedded in retributivist theories of punishment. If the central aim of sentencing is to tailor penalties to offenses, a good retributivist system will institute legal mechanisms geared toward discovering and correcting error (Davis 1984, 149; Berman 2008, 282; Schedler 2011, 254; Simons 2012, 70).

The principle of remedy explains why legal systems should look upon irrevocable punishments with deep suspicion—irrevocable punishments cannot be remedied. But it does not yet demonstrate the priority of irrevocability. Two additional steps are key to this effort. The first is to show that all capital cases are shot through with uncertainty. The second is to argue that, for retributivism, broadly construed, sentencing under uncertainty is governed by a rule stating that it is better to risk underpunishment than to risk overpunishment and the impossibility of revoking the unjust punishment. As a result, we see that in all capital cases, it is better to opt for a life sentence (risking underpunishment) than execution (risking overpunishment).

2.3 Sentencing Uncertainty

Uncertainty and certainty name different levels of confidence one has in one's beliefs. Sentencing uncertainty occurs when judges distrust their ability to proportionately sentence wrongdoers. (In what follows, I will employ an idealization whereby judges are rational, and admit uncertainty whenever they ought to. This is just to simplify the exposition; a token judge's irrational confidence poses no problem for my view.) I will stipulate that certainty involves a degree of belief of 0.9 or greater; anything less is uncertainty.[8] So, sentencing uncertainty occurs when a judge is not certain that a sentence is proportionate to an offense, or when they have a < 0.9 credence in the sentence's proportionality. Sentencing uncertainty has both evidential and moral sources. An example of the former can be found in a judge who doubts that

[8] Certainty is not a legal concept, although it does have a kinship with the beyond-a-reasonable-doubt standard of proof, the standard of proof that imposes the greatest epistemic burden on the prosecution. Standards of proof are supposed to provide practical guidelines that inform judges and jurors when their confidence in a legal proposition is sufficiently likely to meet whatever epistemic standard (from mere belief to justification to full-blown knowledge) renders the proposition in question valid, such that acting on the basis of this confidence is permissible and blameless (see Walen 2015; see also Laudan 2006). U.S. courts have not specified the degree of belief needed to place a legal proposition beyond reasonable doubt, though scholars usually venture 0.9 or 0.95.

the evidence offered at trial properly establishes the elements of an offense. Even if a judge finds the evidence sufficient, they might still harbor moral uncertainty, or uncertainty about how to establish the duration of incarceration appropriate to the offense.

To move forward, we must distinguish between first-order uncertainty and what I call higher-order uncertainty. First-order uncertainty involves moral or epistemic misgivings about the reasons supporting the conviction or sentencing of the accused. Are murderers like Robert Alton Harris, who suffered from horrific child abuse and was then thrown into a hellish juvenile criminal justice system where he was repeatedly raped and beaten, fully culpable for their crimes? Should someone accused of murder be convicted solely on the basis of eyewitness testimony, in the absence of any corroborating evidence or plausible motive? If you are skeptical, it is because you think such cases are marred by first-order uncertainty. But it seems likely that not all trials are marked by first-order uncertainty. Sentencers would not have been subject to any first-order reasons for doubt had Hitler, Goebbels, Mengele, and Heydrich been tried at Nuremburg (Kramer 2011, v).[9] Procedural abolitionism thus cannot be built on this brand of uncertainty. If uncertainty is to play a role in an anti-death penalty argument, it has to be present in all capital cases.

Higher-order uncertainty, unlike first-order uncertainty, is universal. Higher-order uncertainty is constituted by our inability to distinguish between cases in which first-order uncertainty is warranted and those in which it is not. My claim is that all capital trials feature higher-order uncertainty, even when sentencers are, with good reason, utterly confident in their determination. This is owing to the lack of any secure way to draw the line, at the time of sentencing, between instances in which judges' and juries' findings track the truth and instances in which their decision to convict is epistemically justified, given the factual and normative information available to them, but wrong all the same. Notably, asserting the pervasiveness of higher-order uncertainty is consistent with acknowledging that some trials are free from first-order uncertainty. The only problem is that we have no criteria for identifying which they are!

Let me say a bit more about the universality of higher-order uncertainty. Higher-order uncertainty is the product of what epistemologists call uneliminated error possibilities. These are potential grounds for error that have not

[9] I will consider one objection to this claim below.

been satisfactorily ruled out; some examples are false or coerced confessions,[10] judicial misconduct,[11] and tainted laboratory data.[12] Another prominent source is jurors who misapply the beyond a reasonable doubt standard of proof.[13] Higher-order uncertainty is pervasive because some legally salient possibilities cannot be eliminated at trial, at least given the economic and human resources we are willing to spend. One obvious reason for this is that technicians who tamper with lab results, detectives who coerce confessions, and judges on the take try hard to hide their misdeeds. And jurors who misapply the beyond a reasonable doubt standard are unaware of their mistakes. Because judges, jurors, and defense counsel cannot know what they cannot know, cases in which uneliminated error possibilities undermine the verdict cannot, at the time of the proceeding, be reliably distinguished from those in which they do not.

Probably the most significant cause of higher-order uncertainty is the combination of forensic technological limitations and the potential for progress. Since 1989, 375 wrongly convicted persons in the U.S. have been exonerated by DNA evidence, twenty-one of whom were on death row (Innocence Project 2022). Notably, more than half of those wrongly convicted of murder confessed! In fact, the first DNA analysis employed at law was used to exclude the testimony of an English teenager who falsely confessed to rape (Innocence Project 2018). But exoneration statistics drastically understate the importance of forensic DNA. In the U.S., tens of thousands of people suspected of, or charged with, serious criminal offenses have been shown to be innocent through DNA evidence presented prior to conviction. Because DNA fingerprinting did not exist until 1984, all criminal proceedings concluded prior to 1984 are saturated with higher-order uncertainty. But this source of

[10] Confessions are surprisingly easy to coerce; detectives have well-known ways of persuading the accused that they are guilty, even when they are innocent (Davis and Leo 2012). Basically, investigators present the accused with fabricated evidence of their guilt, induce a dissonance between their belief in their innocence and their belief in the investigators' truthfulness, then suggest to them that they suffered momentary unconsciousness or are repressing the memory.

[11] In 2011, Mark Ciavarella and Michael Conahan were convicted of taking kickbacks from a private prison developer in repayment for sending minors to the developer's for-profit juvenile detention center.

[12] Annie Dookhan, a chemist for a Massachusetts state drug lab, was sentenced to three years in prison for tampering with more than 60,000 drug tests, skewing them in favor of the prosecution. Another Massachusetts lab employee performed thousands of tests while under the influence of cocaine, ecstasy, and LSD (Lithwick 2015).

[13] In a criminal trial, jurors are supposed to convict only if they believe beyond a reasonable doubt that the defendant displays the *mens rea* and *actus reus* belonging to the offense. Mock jury studies suggest that this standard is rarely met. Jurors often interpret the beyond a reasonable doubt standard as permitting conviction when there is, objectively speaking, only a preponderance of the evidence for the defendant's guilt (Walen 2015, 375). That is, they misunderstand, and thus misapply, the basic epistemic criteria governing their deliberation. They thus render verdicts that fail to meet those criteria.

higher-order uncertainty persists into the present. Many states restrict access to DNA testing, and only in the past few years have all fifty states even authorized post-conviction DNA analysis. Although these institutional problems could be remedied immediately, there are also deficiencies in the technology itself. DNA samples degrade over time, and small samples are inhospitable to accurate analysis, if not downright useless. Researchers are working to overcome these issues, as well as develop new forensic applications, like DNA phenotyping, which will predict donor appearance. Importantly, the inevitability of such forensic advances means that some offenders who are not currently exonerated by DNA analysis will be exonerated in the future. But we have no idea who these people are, or what totally novel technology might come on the scene. Criminal trials are thus saturated with higher-order uncertainty.

The epistemic optimist might push back on this insistence, doubling down on the existence of legal proceedings that appear to lack any uncertainty. Here is a fictional example of such a case. A school shooter's slaughter of thirty children is recorded on security camera in grisly detail. Investigators uncover a video the shooter posted to social media detailing his plan. He voluntarily confesses, and appears to be of sound mind and responsible for his deed. Do such examples undermine assertions of universal uncertainty? No. Presenting scenarios with a baked-in absence of first-order uncertainty does not mean that such scenarios can be identified in practice, or that legislators can write statutes that reliably guide jurors to identify them.

Consider how we would generalize from this specific example to a legal rule defining death-eligible offenses. We would say that the only death-eligible offenses are those where (a) thirty or more people are murdered, (b) the murders are captured on video and corroborated by a multitude of reliable witnesses, (c) the murderer confesses, and (d) the murderer is of sound mind. The first and fourth criteria might seem to dispose of moral uncertainty, the second and third its epistemic variant.

The problem for the optimist lies with (d), or more precisely, with its application. Moral responsibility is a nonnegotiable feature of death eligibility for most theorists, because responsibility is a condition of moral desert and criminal liability. However, the more severe the crime, the more we are warranted in doubting that the criminal is of sound mind and believing that they suffer from psychopathy. As recent empirical work suggests, psychopathic offenders are not culpable for their misdeeds (Levy 2007), so the properties of heinousness and egregiousness that place an offender's crime in the ranks of the execution-worthy also suggest their inculpability, or at least hinder juries from ruling it out. There are other epistemic problems here, having to do with vigorous disagreement among psychological experts regarding the impact of mental illness, cognitive disability, and childhood abuse on moral responsibility, that will also often come into play.[14] Expert dissensus indicates that accurately assigning moral culpability is a confounding task, at least in the case of extraordinarily heinous offenses. And if *experts* disagree, how can jurors be confident in their assessments of culpability? And even if the jurors themselves are confident, how can a judge share that confidence? (The two juries that tried Andrea Yates, who drowned her five children to deliver them from Satan, reached opposite verdicts on her sanity.) To sum up, the more clearly an offense escapes moral uncertainty, the murkier attributions of responsibility become. And uncertainty returns.

2.4 The Principle of Expanded Asymmetry and the Retributivist Challenge

The final part of my argument aims to show that, when sentencers are confronted with uncertainty, they must err on the side of leniency. This leads to my abolitionist conclusion: because capital sentences are pervaded by uncertainty, sentencers may not impose the death penalty and must settle on a lesser sanction.

The demand for leniency in the context of uncertainty issues from what I call the *principle of expanded asymmetry*:

> **Principle of expanded asymmetry (EA)**: It is better to underpunish P by *n* units than to overpunish P by *n* units.

Obviously, EA does not apply when the precisely proportionate sentence is known. A commitment to proportionality precludes intentionally overpunishing or underpunishing. But when a sentencer is *uncertain* about the proper punishment for an offender, EA says to risk underpunishment rather than overpunishment. Owing to the uncertainty in capital trials, sentencers must thus risk underpunishment (a custodial sanction) instead of risking overpunishment (execution).

---

[14] Steiker (2015) discusses these points more carefully than I can do here. One might wonder if I am letting Nazis off the hook by raising questions about their mental fitness. This is a difficult question, but my sense is that people do not care if Nazis and other genocidaires are of sound mind, and are happy to execute them regardless. In other words, I suspect there is a threshold of evil above which the retributivist insistence on culpability is no longer thought to apply. But if this is so, whatever justification vindicates the execution of horrible but inculpable evildoers will not support the death penalty as practiced today.

Expanded asymmetry is a modified version of the *asymmetry principle*. In its canonical form, the asymmetry principle holds that punishing an innocent person for crime *c* is worse than letting someone guilty of *c*-ing go free. The best-known expression of the principle is William Blackstone's estimation that "the law holds it better that ten guilty persons escape, than that one innocent party suffer." Some might quibble with this ratio—especially the stinginess of the antecedent term—but the underlying idea is virtually undisputed.

The basic commitments of canonical asymmetry can be used to support an expanded version of the principle. Consider the beyond a reasonable doubt standard of criminal conviction and the legal presumption of innocence. Both express the view that trial procedures should lower the risk of punishing the innocent even if it increases the risk of letting the guilty off the hook. This judgment implies that we should reduce the chances of punishing too harshly (i.e., punishing the innocent) at the cost of punishing some offenders too leniently (i.e., failing to punish the guilty). Expanded asymmetry seems to follow from asymmetry.

Because expanded asymmetry is more controversial than asymmetry, a more robust defense might be in order. My brief for EA relies on an uncontroversial principle of liberal political morality.

> **Minimal invasion principle (MIP)**: When faced with alternative means of achieving a legitimate political or legal aim, and when one alternative is clearly less invasive than the other, authorities must choose the less invasive means.[15]

I characterize a liberal state as one in which interferences in, or domination over, citizens' lives must be justified. This justificatory burden will be high, regardless of whether one prefers a libertarian, neo-republican, or egalitarian framework. When fundamental rights are at stake, discharging the burden will be almost impossible. We thus find within liberalism a second-order principle mandating minimal invasion of citizens' liberties. Because freedom is a value of paramount importance, officials cannot justify infringing on citizens' liberty any more than they must. Of course, abrogations of freedom are sometimes necessary to achieve a sufficiently important political purpose. In such cases, authorities have a duty to adopt the least invasive policy available. In other words, if the state is faced with two different policies that (legitimately) infringe on freedom, both of which target the same end, only the least invasive can be permissibly pursued. MIP thus applies to all instances of political

[15] I borrow this moniker from Bedau (2002), although my formulation of the principle differs slightly from his.

coercion, including policing, trials, and legislative deliberation regarding criminalization and sentencing.

Here is the argument for EA:

1. Overpunishing P by *n* units for *c* is wrong.
2. Underpunishing P by *n* units for *c* is wrong.
3. The wrong of overpunishing P by *n* units for *c* = the wrong of underpunishing P by *n* units for *c*.

These three premises simply state the importance of proportionality. Now let's put MIP on the table.

4. When faced with alternative means of achieving a legitimate political or legal aim (here, retributive justice), and when one alternative is clearly less invasive than the other, authorities must choose the less invasive means.
5. Underpunishing P by *n* units is less invasive than overpunishing P by *n* units.
6. Overpunishing P by *n* units violates MIP.

From (1) and (6) an intermediate conclusion can be drawn:

7. Overpunishing P by *n* units is a retributive wrong and a violation of MIP.

(7) expresses the key insight that overpunishment encompasses two wrongs, the violation of MIP and the wrong of disproportionate punishment.

8. The cumulative wrongs of overpunishing P by *n* units for *c* > the cumulative wrongs of underpunishing P by *n* units for *c*.

The principle of expanded asymmetry follows.

9. It is better to underpunish P by *n* units than to overpunish by *n* units.

Therefore, it is better to risk underpunishment than overpunishment.

It is important to reiterate that EA applies only under conditions of uncertainty. If offenders' just deserts are known, they must be punished to that extent. Punishing them any less would violate proportionality. However, in conditions of uncertainty, *two (or more) sanctions of different severity count as alternate means to the end of proportionality.*[16] If, despite their best efforts,

[16] For a detailed explanation of how this works, see Yost (2021).

judges cannot determine which of two or more sanctions is more proportionate, the sanctions must be deemed equally choiceworthy. In such circumstances, MIP requires judges to risk underpunishment rather than overpunishment. Notice that the retributivist challenge is now met. Because the less severe punishment cannot be characterized as less proportionate, imposing it does not count as a retributive injustice.

But now we have ourselves a problem: this argument for leniency can be reiterated. If it is better to sentence a carjacker to ten years than twelve on the basis of higher-order uncertainty, it seems to be better to sentence them to eight rather than ten, and then six rather than eight, and then five rather than six, and so on. It thus seems impossible to keep the consequences of higher-order uncertainty in check and to satiate the demand for leniency. Accordingly, EA under higher-order uncertainty appears to mandate that all offenders go free. This conclusion is implausibly strong and might seem to revive the retributivist challenge, insofar as the offender is not to be punished at all.

Worries along these lines can be disposed of rather easily. The conclusion of the argument for EA does not express the full range of considerations relevant to sentencing. Earlier, I explained that reasonably just legal institutions adhere to the principle of remedy. Sentencers can thus anticipate the possibility of compensating overpunished offenders. To capture the principle of remedy's normative impact on the criminal justice system, we need a new premise.

10. It is better to risk underpunishment of P by *n* units than to risk overpunishment of P by *n* units and potential remedy for said overpunishment.

With this amendment, the threat recedes. The inclusion of the possibility of remedy blocks a total abolitionist conclusion. Under higher-order uncertainty, it is *not* obviously better to refrain from punishing an offender than to risk overpunishment. This is because officials can undo errors that come to light. Accordingly, there is far less downward pressure on sentencing than there would be if there were no possibility of remedy. In a manner of speaking, the principle of remedy serves as a release valve enabling a legal system to honor proportionality's demand to punish as much as deserved. It keeps the downward normative pressure of EA from overwhelming proportionality and instigating a slide to wholesale abolition.[17]

[17] Calculating the consequences of EA is easier in capital cases than in noncapital ones. For some discussion of the impact of EA on noncapital sentencing, see Yost (2021).

2.5 The Argument for Abolition

Although accounting for higher-order uncertainty does not entail eschewing punishment altogether, it does bear striking consequences for the legitimacy of capital punishment. Because no remedy for a wrongful execution exists, capital sentencers may not risk terminal overpunishment. They must instead risk underpunishment by selecting a custodial sanction.

Here, again, is my procedural abolitionist argument in all its glory:

1. Sentencers must risk underpunishment by *n* units rather than risk overpunishment by *n* units and the failure to remedy said overpunishment.
2. Wrongful execution cannot be remedied.
3. Jurisdictions with the death penalty preclude the possibility of revocation in capital cases.
4. The death penalty must be abolished in all jurisdictions.

We can now see how all the pieces fit together. The higher-order uncertainty endemic to capital trials subjects capital sentencers to the expanded asymmetry principle. The irrevocability of execution makes capital sentencing especially sensitive to EA's demand for leniency. Because legal institutions must ensure that wrongful penalties can be remedied, and because it is impossible to remedy wrongful executions, the countervailing upward pressure exerted by proportionality is overcome. Although the value of giving offenders their just deserts may count as a reason to refuse leniency in noncapital proceedings marked by uncertainty, this is so only because the punishments in question are revocable. If financial or custodial punishments turn out to be wrongful, the victims of injustice can be compensated and returned control over their lives. This remedial option is not available in capital contexts. So even if a sentencer is confident in their proportionality analysis, the sentencer must choose to (potentially) underpunish a convicted murderer rather than foreclose the possibility of revocation. Because execution is never choiceworthy, the death penalty must be discarded.

3 Substantive Objections to Capital Punishment

Although my strategy is a procedural one and is designed to succeed regardless of the merits of pro-death penalty arguments, I want to say a few words about the substantive defects of the latter. The main consequentialist justifications can be disposed of rather easily, while retributivist justifications are a harder nut to crack. Regarding the latter, I will limit myself to a criticism of Edward Feser's efforts, as it will likely be most interesting for readers of this volume.

3.1 Consequentialist Justifications

Consequentialism is a big tent, but the most common consequentialist justifications of punishment are utilitarian. These state that the harms and costs associated with punishment are permissibly imposed because they are outweighed by the positive social benefits of deterring crime or incapacitating dangerous malefactors.[18] I doubt that utilitarian justifications of punishment succeed. My misgivings center on the implications of these theories for conviction and sentencing: utilitarianism appears to promote the punishment of the innocent and the disproportionate punishment of the guilty.[19] But let us imagine that these worries can be ameliorated. Does utilitarian sentencing theory license the death penalty?

It does not. Utilitarian sentencing deliberations are governed by the principle of parsimony, which requires sentencers to impose the least costly sanction (in terms of money or well-being) that will serve the purposes of punishment (Morris 1974, 59).[20] Parsimony bars sentencers from using a more costly punishment than is needed to achieve the aims of the penal system. This means that the death penalty cannot be employed unless its benefits outweigh its costs, which, in economic terms, are far higher than life in prison. The social goods that are thought to outweigh execution's significant costs are its deterrent and incapacitive effects. But neither suffices to vindicate capital punishment. Execution cannot be justified in terms of incapacitation, because in contemporary supermax prisons like ADX-Florence (home to El Chapo, Ted Kaczynski, and others), murderers are incapacitated to a similar degree as they would be were they to be executed. The case for deterrence is also quite frail. Note that the point to be established is not just that the death penalty deters, but that it deters *more* than life in prison, and that it deters *so much more* that it is worth the additional cost. There is no reason to believe in a

[18] Specific deterrence aims at deterring an offender from committing a more serious offense or from reoffending. General deterrence aims at deterring the general public from committing crime.

[19] For a lucid overview of these problems, see Boonin (2008). Two-level theories justify the institution of punishment in consequentialist terms and sentencing in retributivist terms (see, e.g., Rawls 1955; Hart 1968). These proposals fare somewhat better, insofar as they are specifically aimed at countering the innocence and disproportionality objections. Ultimately, though, two-level theories turn out to exhibit serious shortcomings of their own, as clearly explicated in Primoratz (1989).

[20] Richard Frase develops the principle of parsimony into what he calls the "alternative means" principle of proportionality (2020, 105–6). Both are straightforward applications of a utilitarian efficiency principle.

marginal deterrent effect. The National Research Council assembled a Committee on Deterrence and the Death Penalty to examine four decades of studies on deterrence and capital punishment. The Committee's report concluded that the research "is not informative about whether capital punishment decreases, increases, or has no effect on homicide rates" (Nagin and Pepper 2012, 2). One of the major problems identified by the Committee is that no study identifies or accounts for the deterrent level of carceral sanctions for murder. Clearly, the marginal deterrent effect of execution can be measured only after identifying the baseline effect of a custodial sanction. Absent such a baseline, any measured deterrent effect could just as well derive from the prospect of life in prison. Since all studies fail to establish the baseline, their estimations of the deterrent effect of capital punishment (which are all over the map in any case) are simply guesswork. Given the available research, deterrence theorists must conclude that the death penalty may not be utilized.

In short, the principle of parsimony commits the consequentialist to justifying costlier courses of action in terms of their counterbalancing contribution to the social welfare. But there is no evidence that execution comes with incapacitive or deterrent benefits. Because there are no benefits, as far as we can tell, we do not need to take the next step and weigh the benefits of execution against the costs. The consequentialist justification of the death penalty fails to get out of the gate.

3.2 Retributivist Justifications

There are a wide variety of retributivist attempts to vindicate capital punishment (van den Haag 1986; Sorell 1987; Pojman and Reiman 1998; Yost 2010). Space precludes even a cursory examination of these efforts.[21] I will instead briefly assess the retributivist views of Edward Feser, author of the companion chapter in this volume.

At the heart of Feser's project is an argument that is quite popular among friends of the death penalty (including all those just cited), one which can be stated without recourse to Aristotelian or Thomistic premises. The basic contention is that the permissibility of execution is baked into the notion of proportionality. If you value proportionality, the argument goes, you must admit that death is a proportionate punishment for some offense or other. As Feser puts it:

[21] For a comprehensive overview of retributivist justifications, see Kramer (2011).

1. Wrongdoers deserve punishment as a matter of retributive justice.
2. The more grave the wrongdoing, the more severe is the punishment deserved.
3. Some crimes are so grave that no punishment less than death would be proportionate in its severity.
4. Therefore, wrongdoers guilty of such crimes deserve death (725).[22]

(1) indicates an allegiance to a desert-based retributivist theory of punishment. (2) expresses the uncontroversial requirement of ordinal proportionality. An ordinally proportionate sentencing scheme is one in which crimes and punishments are properly ranked: the most trivial crimes are attached to the most trifling punishments—fines, probation, and so on—and the gravest crimes are attached to the most severe punishments. Intermediate crimes are then ranked in order of seriousness and attached to intermediate penalties that are likewise ranked. I am happy to accept (2); in fact, I think it is more or less conceptually contained within retributivism. (3) and (4) are where the rubber hits the road, and those will be the focus of my remarks.

(3) is a dense and complex premise, so I will spend some time unpacking it. As Feser notes, (3) assumes that that severity of punishment should fit the gravity of the crime. This assumption is utterly anodyne within the context of desert-based retributivism, and I am happy to accept it. To hold that the amount of hard treatment inflicted on an offender must fit the gravity of the offense is to insist on cardinal proportionality (sometimes dubbed "commensurability"). To illustrate the distinction between ordinal and cardinal proportionality, consider a sentencing scheme that assigned ten days in jail to murder, five days to sexual assault, and no penalty at all to a variety of lesser offenses. This scheme would be ordinally, but not cardinally, proportionate. A murderer deserves more than ten days in jail, so this sanction would be disproportionately lenient in a cardinal sense. (Feser does not distinguish between ordinal and cardinal proportionality, but as we shall see, this conflation obscures a problem with his argument.)

So far, so good. But (3) also makes a substantive judgment of cardinal proportionality. It claims that execution is the sole cardinally proportionate punishment for some crimes.[23] For these crimes, a sentence less that death is said to be disproportionately lenient. Determining the absolute amount of pun-

[22] Page numbers for Edward Feser's "The Justice of Capital Punishment" refer to page numbers in this volume.

[23] Some believe that life in prison is just as severe as execution, if not more so, but I will set this debate aside. John Stuart Mill's 1868 speech contends that life in prison is worse than death (1988), but most proponents of the death penalty claim the opposite (van den Haag 1986, 1662; Pojman and Reiman 1998, 30–31; Oderberg 2000, 161–62; Feser 2011). A few retentionists, like Sorrel, claim the two types of harm are equivalent (1993, 209).

ishment deserved is certainly within the purview of cardinal proportionality. However, to simply assert that some criminal acts merit *execution* is to beg the entire question at issue. The retributivist controversy over the permissibility of the death penalty is in large part a controversy about whether any offender in fact deserves death, and there are plenty of philosophers who answer in the negative.[24] So this part of (3) is massively controversial.

Feser's chapter contains a couple strategies for defending his key premise. To my mind, the strongest one occurs in the following passage:

> To claim that there is *no* crime for which death would be a proportionate punishment—to claim, for instance, that a cold-blooded, genocidal rapist can never *even in principle* merit a greater punishment than the lifelong imprisonment that might be inflicted on, say, a recidivist bank robber—is implicitly to give up the principle of proportionality. For to agree that genocide is a far worse offense than bank robbery while maintaining that genocide cannot in principle merit a punishment worse than the punishment for bank robbery is implicitly to deny that a punishment ought to be proportionate to the offense. (739)

Feser emphasizes that without the death penalty, a state cannot punish the worst of the worst (the genocidal rapist) more than the very bad (the recidivist bank robber). Given our intuitions about ordinal proportionality, we are meant to find this intolerable—the worst of the worst surely *should* be punished more than the very bad. Accordingly, if the very bad are punished with life in prison, as they tend to be, honoring ordinal proportionality means that we must punish the worst of the worst more harshly by executing them. As Feser puts it, the idea is to derive (3) from the concept of proportionality: "if punishment ought to be proportionate to the gravity of the crime, then it seems absurd to deny that there is *some* level of criminality for which nothing less than capital punishment would be proportionate" (739). More specifically, the goal is to squeeze substantive judgments of cardinal proportionality out of our intuitions about ordinal proportionality.

To show how this attempt falls short, consider the following thought experiment. Let us assume that some wrongdoers deserve death, and let us set the threshold of death eligibility at the murder of ten people. Accordingly, Alabamian Michael Kenneth McClendon would have gotten his just deserts had be been executed (he committed suicide before he could be apprehended). But a decade later, Patrick Wood Crusius murdered twenty-three people in an El Paso Walmart. Crusius's crime was clearly more heinous, so in a strict sense,

[24] A partial list of objectors includes Dolinko (1986), Nathanson (2001), Bedau (2002), Finkelstein (2002), Roberts-Cady (2010), and Kramer (2011).

ordinal proportionality would have been violated had both been executed. Ordinal proportionality would have been violated because crimes of different moral gravity would have been sanctioned almost identically.

Should we have spared McClendon and only executed Crusius? This would be an odd result for the desert-based retributivist. And it would only displace the problem, because no matter how bad a crime, someone can commit one that is worse. It looks like the attempt to respect ordinal proportionality requires that we never execute anyone.

Here is the takeaway: ordinal proportionality is always imprecise at the top (and bottom) of a sentencing scheme. The fact that our penal techniques are not infinitely gradated means that the class of death-worthy crimes will be internally differentiated in terms of desert: some members of this class will be significantly morally worse than others. At the same time, all of those who commit the crimes contained in this set will be punished exactly the same—with death. When architects of genocide and first-degree murderers are executed, they are punished almost identically, even though the former is guilty of a more heinous offense. And so ordinal proportionality is *guaranteed* to be imperfectly realized, unless one maintains that only the absolute worst possible crime, whatever it is, deserves punishment by death. But this latter proposal is not Feser's, and if it were, it would not justify executing anyone, much less any existing capital sentencing scheme. Ultimately, then, the death penalty does not fulfill Feser's promise and secure ordinal proportionality. Because it does not do so, the key premise in Feser's argument goes unsupported.

I have argued that both noncapital and capital schemes display the same defect of ordinal proportionality, so they are on a par in this respect. Feser might reply that a death penalty regime boasts a *comparative* superiority. Here the claim would be that a schedule of sanctions omitting execution is more homogenous and suffers from ordinal imprecision to a greater degree. Even if no scheme perfectly reflects ordinal proportionality, it might be thought that a capital scheme does so better than a noncapital one. But this response does Feser no favors. Imagine a jurisdiction that executes the most deserving first-degree murderers. During an official review of sentencing policy, authorities grow concerned about the prospect of a domestic terrorist killing hundreds of innocents. And they worry that such an offender would be punished no more than first-degree murderers. So they entertain a new penalty: torture followed by execution.[25] (The torture will be inflicted by a machine, so that no person

[25] In medieval England, those convicted of high treason were dragged to a gallows, hanged almost to the point of death, revived, then emasculated, eviscerated, beheaded, and posthumously quartered. A slightly relaxed version of this practice continued into the early 1800s.

bears the moral and psychological cost of carrying out the sentence.) Clearly, this torture-execution scheme is more finely differentiated than an orthodox capital punishment regime, and it better respects ordinal proportionality. Feser's line of argument suggests that the torture-execution system is more just. But should we draw this conclusion?

Many retributivists would refuse to do so for the following reason: torture-executions violate moral constraints on the types of punishment that may be employed. So, torture-executions may not be used, even if they better accomplish ordinal proportionality. The lesson here should be clear: if there are retributive prohibitions against torture, there may be retributive prohibitions against execution! To assert that execution does not run afoul of any such restrictions again begs the question at issue. And death penalty proponents bear the burden of proof here, on the same moral ground that generates the initial need to justify punishment: the intentional infliction of harm is wrong, unless there are reasons that render the type of harm permissible. To justify legal punishment, one must supply such reasons. A parallel burden applies in disputes about the kinds and amounts of punishment that may be imposed. A successful justification of punishment does not permit a state to impose any punishment for any offense. Retributivists are thus tasked with sorting out which types of punishment are permissible and which are not. So, retributivist friends of capital punishment must affirmatively demonstrate the permissibility of executing a wrongdoer.[26]

In sum, Feser fails to establish that proportionality requires execution. This should not be surprising, given that many other retributivist justifications of the death penalty have tumbled over the same hurdle. Of course, even if Feser's retributivist argument were unimpeachable, his conclusion would still fall prey to my proceduralist argument.

References

Bedau, Hugo Adam. 2002. "The Minimal Invasion Argument against the Death Penalty." *Criminal Justice Ethics* 21, no. 2: 3–8.

[26] The easiest way to do this is to endorse a literal "eye for an eye" version of the *lex talionis*, which prescribes that the punishment be exactly the same as the offense. But this view has many fatal flaws. A salient one is that some literally fitting penal techniques (e.g., torture or rape) are morally impermissible, either owing to their intrinsic wrongfulness or the wrongfulness of their extrinsic effects, such as the brutalization inflicted on the agent of punishment (Waldron 1992, 38). Few retributivists subscribe to this atavistic view, much less defend it, and Feser is not one of them. If he did endorse a strict interpretation of the *talion*, he would not need the argument I have been analyzing, but he would be in even hotter water.

Berman, Mitchell N. 2008. "Punishment and Justification." *Ethics* 118, no. 2 (January): 258–90.

Boonin, David. 2008. *The Problem of Punishment*. Cambridge: Cambridge University Press.

Dalton, Harlon Leigh. 1985. "Taking the Right to Appeal (More or Less) Seriously." *Yale Law Journal* 95, no. 1 (November): 62–107.

Davis, Deborah, and Richard A. Leo. 2012. "Interrogation-Related Regulatory Decline: Ego Depletion, Failures of Self-Regulation, and the Decision to Confess." *Psychology, Public Policy, and Law* 18, no. 4 (November): 673–704.

Davis, Michael. 1984. "Is the Death Penalty Irrevocable?" *Social Theory and Practice* 10, no. 2 (Summer): 143–56.

Dolinko, David. 1986. "How to Criticize the Death Penalty." *Journal of Criminal Law and Criminology* 77, no. 3 (Autumn): 546–601.

Feser, Edward. 2011. "In Defense of Capital Punishment." *Public Discourse*, September 29. https://www.thepublicdiscourse.com/2011/09/4033/.

Finkelstein, Claire. 2002. "Death and Retribution." *Criminal Justice Ethics* 21, no. 2: 12–21.

Frase, Richard. 2020. "Punishment Purposes and Eighth Amendment Disproportionality." In *The Eighth Amendment and Its Future in a New Age of Punishment*, edited by Meghan J. Ryan and William W. Berry III, 101–17. Cambridge: Cambridge University Press.

Fuller, Lon. 1969. *The Morality of Law*. 2nd ed. New Haven, CT: Yale University Press.

Hart, H. L. A. 1968. *Punishment and Responsibility: Essays in the Philosophy of Law*. Oxford: Oxford University Press.

Innocence Project. 2018. "DNA's Revolutionary Role in Freeing the Innocent." April 18. https://innocenceproject.org/dna-revolutionary-role-freedom/.

———. 2022. "DNA Exonerations in the United States." Accessed January 8. https://innocenceproject.org/dna-exonerations-in-the-united-states/.

Kramer, Matthew. 2011. *The Ethics of Capital Punishment: A Philosophical Investigation of Evil and Its Consequences*. Oxford: Oxford University Press.

Laudan, Larry. 2006. *Truth, Error, and Criminal Law: An Essay in Legal Epistemology*. Cambridge: Cambridge University Press.

Levy, Neil. 2007. "The Responsibility of the Psychopath Revisited." *Philosophy, Psychiatry, & Psychology* 14, no. 2 (June): 129–38.

Lithwick, Dahlia. 2015. "Crime Lab Scandals Just Keep Getting Worse." *Slate*, October 29. https://slate.com/news-and-politics/2015/10/massachusetts-crime-lab-scandal-worsens-dookhan-and-farak.html.

Mill, John Stuart. 1988. "Speech in Favor of Capital Punishment 1868." In *The Collected Works of John Stuart Mill*, edited by John M. Robson and Bruce Kinzer, vol. 28: *Public and Parliamentary Speeches*, 266–73. Toronto: University of Toronto Press.

Morris, Norval. 1974. *The Future of Imprisonment*. Chicago: University of Chicago Press.

Nagin, Daniel S., and John V. Pepper, eds. 2012. *Deterrence and the Death Penalty.* Washington, DC: National Academies Press.

Nathanson, Stephen. 2001. *An Eye for an Eye : The Immorality of Punishing by Death.* 2nd ed. Lanham, MD: Rowman & Littlefield.

Oderberg, David S. 2000. "Capital Punishment." In *Applied Ethics: A Non-Consequentialist Approach*, 144–81. Oxford: Blackwell.

Oldfather, Chad M. 2010. "Error Correction." *Indiana Law Journal* 85, no. 1 (Winter): 49–85.

Pojman, Louis, and Jeffrey Reiman. 1998. *The Death Penalty: For and Against.* Lanham, MD: Rowman & Littlefield.

Primoratz, Igor. 1989. *Justifying Legal Punishment.* Amherst, NY: Humanity.

Primus, Eve Brensike. 2010. "A Structural Vision of Habeas Corpus." *California Law Review* 98, no. 1 (February): 1–57.

Rawls, John. 1955. "Two Concepts of Rules." *Philosophical Review* 64, no. 1 (January): 3–32.

Resnick, Judith. 1984. "Tiers." *Southern California Law Review* 57, no. 6 (September): 837–1038.

Roberts-Cady, Sarah. 2010. "Against Retributive Justifications of the Death Penalty." *Journal of Social Philosophy* 41, no. 2 (Summer): 185–93.

Schedler, George. 2011. "Retributivism and Fallible Systems of Punishment." *Criminal Justice Ethics* 30, no. 3: 240–66.

Shapiro, Martin. 1980. "Appeal." *Law & Society Review* 14, no. 3 (Spring): 629–61.

Shavell, Steven. 1995. "The Appeals Process as a Means of Error Correction." *Journal of Legal Studies* 24, no. 2 (June): 379–426.

Simons, Kenneth W. 2012. "Statistical Knowledge Deconstructed." *Boston University Law Review* 92, no. 1 (January): 1–86.

Sorell, Tom. 1987. *Moral Theory and Capital Punishment.* Oxford: Blackwell.

———. 1993. "Aggravated Murder and Capital Punishment." *Journal of Applied Philosophy* 10, no. 2 (October): 201–13.

Steiker, Carol S. 2015. "Can/Should We Purge Evil through Capital Punishment?" *Criminal Law and Philosophy* 9, no. 2 (June): 367–78.

van den Haag, Ernest. 1986. "The Ultimate Punishment: A Defense." *Harvard Law Review* 99, no. 7 (May): 1662–69.

Waldron, Jeremy. 1992. "Lex Talionis." *Arizona Law Review* 34, no. 1: 25–51.

Walen, Alec. 2015. "Proof Beyond a Reasonable Doubt: A Balanced Retributive Account." *Louisiana Law Review* 76, no. 2 (Winter): 355–445.

Yost, Benjamin S. 2010. "Kant's Justification of the Death Penalty Reconsidered." *Kantian Review* 15, no. 2 (July): 1–27.

———. 2019. *Against Capital Punishment.* New York: Oxford University Press.

———. 2021. "Lowering the Boom: A Brief for Penal Leniency." *Criminal Law and Philosophy.* https://doi.org/10.1007/s11572-021-09609-1.

35

Cruel and Unusual Punishment

Chad Flanders

Those familiar with the United States Constitution and the Bill of Rights probably know, even if vaguely, the text of the Eighth Amendment, which prohibits (in part) the imposition of "cruel and unusual punishment."[1] Two features of the phrase have been the subject of constant puzzlement, if not fascination, among scholars. The first feature is that, by using the word "cruel," the drafters of the Constitution practically seemed to invite a sort of moral philosophizing, given the seemingly obvious "thickness" of the concept of cruelty (Stinneford 2017, 449).[2] Indeed, among the other provisions in the Bill of Rights, the Eighth Amendment stands out as at least seeming to promote an overtly substantive norm, as opposed to a merely formal (e.g., "equality") or procedural (e.g., "due process") one. The burden would seem to be on those who would read "cruel" in a non-normative or positivist way, draining the phrase of its substance and moral weight. The second feature—somewhat tied to the first feature—is the addition of the word "unusual' to the phrase.

[1] The amendment also prohibits excessive bail and excessive fines.

[2] A "thick" moral term, like being "cruel" or "wicked" or "kind," is to be contrasted with "thin" moral terms like "right" or "wrong" and "good" and "bad"—the former being richer in content and more intricate than the latter (Väyrynen 2021).

C. Flanders (✉)
Saint Louis University, St. Louis, MO, USA
e-mail: chad.flanders@slu.edu

© The Author(s), under exclusive license to Springer Nature Switzerland AG 2023

M. C. Altman (ed.), *The Palgrave Handbook on the Philosophy of Punishment*, Palgrave Handbooks in the Philosophy of Law, https://doi.org/10.1007/978-3-031-11874-6_35

The puzzle here is not so much what "unusual" means (although it does include that), but also what point it could possibly serve: if a punishment is cruel, why is that not enough to ban it (Hershenov 2002)? The idea that cruelty is made somehow okay by doing it regularly seems bizarre. The deeper worry here may be—especially for those who want to give a strong moral reading to "cruel"—that adding "unusual" as a qualifier gives the ban on cruelty much less force.

No short chapter can capture all of what has happened, philosophically and especially jurisprudentially, in the centuries since the passage of the Bill of Rights and its prohibition on punishments that are cruel and unusual. It may also seem foolish to try to find much in the way of philosophical insight in what is, at the end of the day, only a legal text. Looking at a provision of a law (in this case, a provision of the Eighth Amendment to the Constitution) can be a strange enterprise. On the one hand, we might wonder: why we should suppose that the language in the law embodies any deep insight or even comes close to getting it right? On the other hand, we might also wonder why it should matter what morality has to say about the provision—the law is the law, no matter what morality would say. There are deep debates here, and I cannot wade into them too much. But the Eighth Amendment offers us an interesting and promising way to address, if not answer, both sides. Here, the law itself seems to invite us into moral philosophy by using a normatively thick moral term (i.e., cruelty). In addition, the limits the law puts on applying moral concepts can give us insight into how (or how not) to reconcile the competing demands of law and morality.

My chapter proceeds in three parts. In the first part, I examine competing methodologies as to how to interpret the Eighth Amendment. In the second part, I briefly survey contemporary constitutional doctrine regarding cruel and unusual punishment, according to the relevant U.S. Supreme Court precedent. In the last part, I examine some broader questions about the idea of cruelty and punishment, as applied both to imprisonment and to the practice of punishment itself.

1 Reading the Eighth Amendment: Two Methods

1.1 Moralism

In an essay collected in his first book, *Retribution, Justice, and Therapy* (1979), Jeffrie Murphy gives a perfect example of an aggressively philosophical and aggressively *moral* reading of the Eighth Amendment's prohibition on cruel and unusual punishments. Taking his starting point from Ronald Dworkin, Murphy all but assumes that the ban on cruel and unusual punishments must involve something like a principle of political morality that is placed in the middle of the Bill of Rights. The Eighth Amendment is a (textual) location, Murphy writes, quoting Dworkin, where political morality has been "inject[ed]" by the Constitution into American law (1979, 33). In what nowadays would seem a rather extraordinary statement of interpretive method,[3] Murphy, again drawing from Dworkin, holds that it follows from this idea of Constitutional morality that if "one can mount a good argument that to treat a person in a certain way is gravely unjust or would violate some basic human rights" then "this is *also a necessarily* a good argument that it is unconstitutional to treat him that way" (Murphy 1979, 233, emphasis added). This is rather resolute moralizing as a method of constitutional interpretation. The political morality tail wags the textual dog. In other words, one starts with moral philosophy out of the blue and then, if one finds a good, philosophical argument that something is unjust or a violation of human rights, we *ipso facto* have a good argument not just about the wrongness but about the unconstitutionality of the practice.

In the rest of the essay, this is what Murphy proceeds to do. Murphy very briefly canvasses some ways of looking at the constitutional text that are inconsistent with his interpretive methodology, and then he summarily rejects them. Should we interpret the Eighth Amendment in a (crudely) literal way, so that only punishments that cause "great physical suffering and which happen with statistical infrequency" are "cruel and unusual" (Murphy 1979, 224)? To do so would be "absurd" (224). It could not be the case, morally, that making a punishment *frequent* would somehow insulate it from moral objection. So too is the idea that we should ban only those punishments that the Founders regarded as cruel and unusual at the time of the Constitution's enactment. This also "will not do," says Murphy (225).

Murphy's explanation for this latter point is worth examining at greater length, for it provides more substance to his methodology. In Murphy's view, what the Founders were intending to do was not to institute some *policy* of punishment, but rather some *principle*. The principle that they were intending to formulate generally in the Constitution was a set of "reasonable deontological side constraints or restrictions of principle on the pursuit of majoritarian utilitarianism" (Murphy 1979, 225). This, according to Murphy, should inform what we take to be good guesses as to what they (the Founders) meant

[3] This is especially so, given the rise in so-called "textualist" theories of interpretation discussed *infra*.

when they wrote that while some punishments are permissible, those that are cruel and unusual are not.

After going through and rejecting two other ways of interpreting the Eighth Amendment (one founded on consensus and one based in utilitarianism), Murphy goes on to spell out what he takes to be at the core of the ban on cruel and unusual punishments, which is founded in a type of Kantianism.[4] A punishment that violates human dignity, that debases or demeans human beings, is one that is unjust and is *therefore* (again, given that the Constitution instantiates not just policy choices but moral principle) unconstitutional. Although everybody should be interested in the restrictions demanded by justice, these restrictions should be of interest to those with a "particular concern for constitutional law" (Murphy 1979, 228). Spelling out his Kantian theory a little further, Murphy says that a punishment should be banned in principle if it is (1) a direct assault on the dignity of persons, or (2) it is grossly disproportionate to the seriousness of the conduct punished.

Murphy goes on to say that these conclusions have a "secure place" in Eighth Amendment jurisprudence, either as a matter of its original meaning or as a matter of interpretations that the United States Supreme Court has given it (1979, 235). Murphy also spends considerable time showing (on his theory) that the death penalty is at the very least extremely problematic under the Eighth Amendment and requires—and here again he refers to U.S. Supreme Court decisions—either placing extreme restrictions on the imposition of the death penalty or its outright ban. But one gets the sense that, had the Supreme Court *not* reached decisions consistent with Murphy's deontological moral theory, this would be grounds (for Murphy) for criticizing the Court, namely, for saying that the Court would have gotten it wrong if it did not find in the Eighth Amendment a ban on intrinsically heinous punishments or strong (even impossible to satisfy) limitations on the application of the death penalty. The Court—and even the Founders—would be unfaithful to what Murphy calls the retributive and deontological "core" of the Eighth Amendment's ban on cruel and unusual punishments if they interpreted it as permitting punishments that degraded the dignity of human beings or that were grossly disproportionate to the offense criminalized (1979, 224).

In Murphy's picture, it is the morality of just punishment that drives the interpretation of the text, not what the text (or even the text's authors) may imply about punishment. Dworkin (1997) would later make the same point in a brief exchange with Justice Antonin Scalia (1997) on the Eighth Amendment. On Dworkin's reading, in setting out the text of the Eighth

[4] This is unsurprising, given the Kantian flavor of much of Murphy's work around this time.

Amendment, the Framers were not just stipulating that the punishments *they* thought were cruel and unusual should be banned but were "laying down a principle forbidding *whatever* punishments are cruel and unusual" (1997, 120). To use Murphy's terms (which were, in fact, borrowed from Dworkin), the Framers were not just making a policy declaration; they were making a statement of general principle about those things that were actually, morally unacceptable. We would do the Framers wrong if we only held them to be referring to what they thought was cruel (treating "cruel" as shorthand for "what we now think cruel") as opposed to what is, in principle, really cruel (Dworkin 1997, 121).

Both Murphy and Dworkin do not ignore the text—Dworkin is a little better at this than Murphy—but the text is not doing the real work in deciding what is cruel and unusual. Rather, what does the work is the underlying "political morality" implicit in the Constitution. We have to determine what that political morality is in order to get at what content "cruel and unusual" *should* have. The text of the amendment is useful only insofar as it signals that there is a moral principle regarding punishment in the text. The harder work comes in determining the content of that principle.

1.2 Textualism

To see the other major way of reading the Eighth Amendment, we can start by leaning into what Murphy and Dworkin see themselves as *against*: a literal, wooden, interpretation of "cruel and unusual" that takes it to mean only what the Founders thought was cruel and unusual. On this understanding, what the Eighth Amendment bans is those things that were cruel and unusual at the time, or (more accurately) what those in the Founding generation would have taken to be cruel and unusual punishments. When we look at the phrase "cruel and unusual," we are not doing moral philosophy; we are doing history. We are trying to figure out what those words meant *in their historical context*. To the extent that morality matters, it is the morality of the time of the Founding, not some abstract moral principle that can (in principle) change over time as we get a better and better understanding of what "cruelty" really is. As Scalia makes clear in his response to Dworkin, the furthest we can abstract from the Eighth Amendment is only to "the moral perceptions *of the time*" (1997, 145). And again, to do this means not doing first-order philosophy but doing research into history.

The benefit of the history, to be fair, is that it does a much better job of capturing both of the key terms in the phrase "cruel and unusual." The moral reading of the phrase tends to downplay or ignore the "unusual" part. It treats it as eliminable, or at best something that is redundant (as banning punishments that are unusual *because* cruel, perhaps). According to the historical story, or at least how the best accounts have it, "cruel and unusual" was a phrase meant to capture a ban on *new* and strange punishments that did not have a sufficiently long historical pedigree. The thought is, in other words, that the Founders wanted to prevent the revival of some barbarous punishments that had existed in England but had been given up in the American colonies. In the past, those might have been acceptable, but we do not think that anymore, and so we do not want to bring those types of punishments back. The Eighth Amendment, then, speaks to those types of cruel punishment *methods* that had existed at one point in the shared Anglo-American history, but they are forever prohibited.

So put, we can see the Founders as themselves giving us a (somewhat) abstract moral principle, but not of the type that Murphy and Dworkin wanted to find in the Eighth Amendment. *Contra* Murphy and Dworkin, the Eighth Amendment does not empower judges to continually update and adapt our understanding of cruelty and apply it to punishments that we have been imposing all along. Murphy and Dworkin see, or want to see, the Eighth Amendment as an engine of moral progress. But this is not what the textual view sees as the morality of the Eighth Amendment. Rather, the Eighth Amendment only gives judges the power to prevent legislatures from *bringing back* punishments that were properly lost to history, or from *inventing* new, more horrible punishments. The Eighth Amendment exists, as Scalia puts it, to stop us from *backsliding* to some worse moral state, and not to bring us into some better and less cruel future, according to our newer understanding of what "cruelty" is. The Founders were worried about us becoming *more* brutal, not about making us less brutal—with the Eighth Amendment, we at least had the guarantee that we would not be regressing (Scalia 1997, 145; Bray 2016, 714–15).

Still, however we might see this as a moral principle, it is a very limited one, applying its ban to a very limited set of punishments: to old ones made new, or to new modes of punishment. Again, it is not what *we* would find cruel, but what *they* would have found cruel, and not merely what *they* would have found cruel, but what they would have found as *cruel and unusual*—namely, those (cruel) punishments that might be brought back after a long period of disuse, or brand new (cruel) punishments that the Framers would have recoiled from, given what they took cruelty to be. Far from a freestanding moral principle that can change, what the Eighth Amendment amounts to is basically a set of specific prohibitions on particular *methods* of punishments (we cannot bring back drawing and quartering, the thumbscrew, etc.). It looks more and more like what Murphy derided as a kind of "policy" or set of policies against certain types of punishment.

Recently, John Stinneford has tried to interpret the principle in the text of the Eighth Amendment a little more abstractly, loosening it from the idea that it is only particular historical methods of punishment that can be thrown out, but still hanging on to the idea of a sort of originalism (2008, 1745). Stinneford says that the Framers meant to embody a broader principle than just "holding the line on punishments that were given up by the time of the Founding." They meant to adopt the principle that, *in general*, using punishments that do not have a long history and that are unduly harsh can be "cruel and unusual." Stinneford thus takes "unusual" to mean not only "unusual" to the Framers, but "unusual to us" or, better yet, "contrary to our traditional practices of punishment." For Stinneford, the historical meaning of the Eighth Amendment does not give us the type of moral principle that Murphy and Dworkin want, but it does give us a standard by which we can call punishments "cruel" that may not have been considered cruel at the Founding: punishments that were "previously tried, and then rejected" (Stinneford 2008, 1745). When a punishment—even a punishment widely used at the Founding (Stinneford offers flogging as an example)—falls out of use, it loses its presumption of constitutional validity (2008, 1746).

I return to Stinneford's important and pathbreaking work in section 3 of this chapter. Here I only want to highlight the gap between Scalia and Stinneford, as well as Murphy and Dworkin. For Scalia, the proper baseline for determining whether something is unusual is the baseline *at the Founding*. We look to see what they thought would have been cruel and unusual had it been used, and *that* is what the Eighth Amendment bans. For Stinneford, that does not get the principle at the right level of abstraction. For the Founders, what matters is the idea of instituting new punishments that we have not used before, even if that "we" is "America of the last 50 years" rather than "America at the Founding." History matters for Stinneford, but in a rolling sort of way, not in a static sort of way. With Scalia, it is more about the actual "cruel and unusual" punishments that the Founders did not approve of; Stinneford puts things more abstractly, aiming at the broader *meaning* of "cruel and unusual" the Founders intended. For Murphy and Dworkin, by contrast, history matters practically not at all—the only history that matters is the fact that, in history, the Founders put a moral principle in the Constitution. What matters after that is moral philosophy, and getting the morality right, and not the history. We want to get at what *cruelty* really is in the end, not what the Founders may have believed about what cruelty really is.[5]

2 The Supreme Court and the Death Penalty: Proportionality and "Evolving Standards"

2.1 Proportionality

When we turn from theories of interpreting the Eighth Amendment to what the Supreme Court has done in actually interpreting that amendment, we get a profoundly variable doctrine, on multiple levels. For one, the Court has basically gone on two largely parallel lines in applying the amendment. Cases that involve sentences to years in prison get analyzed one way; but cases that implicate the death penalty get looked at another way. And it is almost an understatement to say that the Court looks at them in different ways—the Court has applied almost entirely distinct interpretive *doctrines* in analyzing the two sets of cases (imprisonment cases and death cases). But even within each of these two tracks, the doctrine is divided. There is a constant push and pull between the two modes of interpretation discussed in the previous part, although the textualist strand seems to dominate the Court's discussions of imprisonment as a punishment, while the moralistic strand is mostly limited to the Court's death penalty cases.

I begin with the Court's treatment of sentences of imprisonment (or "term of years" sentences). In an early, important case, the Supreme Court held that the prohibition on cruel and unusual punishments extended to punishments that were grossly disproportionate to the offense the defendant was convicted of. In *Solem v. Helm* (463 U.S. 277 [1983]), the defendant was convicted of passing a bad check. Because it was his seventh nonviolent criminal conviction, under the law in South Dakota at the time Solem was sentenced to life in prison without the possibility of parole. The Court reversed Solem's conviction as unconstitutional under the Eighth Amendment. In doing so, it articulated, if in only a hazy and cursory way, a principle of proportionality, or the idea that some punishments might be so grossly disproportionate or excessive that they could be held unconstitutional. Although the Court gestured weakly in the direction of English and American history, Justice William O. Douglas

[5] Dworkin does also say that judges must "keep faith with past decisions," i.e., precedent, but it is unclear at times how Dworkin reconciles this with his insistence that "political morality is the strongest force in jurisprudence" (1997, 123, 127).

was clear that it was fundamentally a "matter of principle" that "a criminal sentence must be proportionate to the crime for which the defendant has been convicted" (290). In applying the principle to Solem's case, Douglas found it an easy call that he had been punished excessively for this crime: Solem was not a murderer, but he was being punished like one.

Solem was a 5–4 opinion, and now, in retrospect, it looks like the high-water mark of the Court's morality-based proportionality jurisprudence—where sentences could get struck down for being grossly disproportionate, whatever precise content could be given to the idea of disproportionality. In his dissent to the *Solem* case, Chief Justice Warren Burger referred to a hypothetical case of a person who was punished by life imprisonment for a parking violation (310n2). Burger seemed to hold out that, with a case such as *that*, it might be right to strike it down as unconstitutional, but Solem's case was not like that: Solem had many prior convictions and in fact was chargeable in South Dakota as a "habitual criminal." Burger, in his dissent, had hit on what would become the default, compromise position of the Supreme Court: supply the promise of a doctrine of proportionality-based review of prison sentences, but in practice, almost never grant relief on that basis.

This had become basically the Court's position by the time the case of *Harmelin v. Michigan* (501 U.S. 957 [1991]) was decided. Harmelin was convicted of possessing 672 grams of cocaine and, like Solem before him, sentenced to life in prison without the possibility of parole. Like Solem, Harmelin argued that his sentence was disproportionate to the crime he committed. He lost. Scalia, in his opinion, tried to get *Solem* overturned as bad law because, based on his reading of the history, "the Eighth Amendment contains no proportionality guarantee" (965). For Scalia, the prohibition contained in the Eighth Amendment "only outlawed certain *modes* of punishment," but did not contain any independent proportionality principle, against which punishments could be measured (982). Accordingly, as the Constitution did not prohibit disproportionate sentences, Harmelin's argument was a nonstarter. There was no moral principle of proportionality contained in the Eighth Amendment.

But Scalia's broadside against the very idea of a proportionality constraint in the Eighth Amendment only won him one vote from the other members of the Court. The binding part of the Court's decision in *Harmelin* on the precise issue of proportionality was written by Justice Anthony Kennedy. He agreed with Scalia on the bottom line: Harmelin's sentence of life in prison was constitutional. But Kennedy—along with the three Justices who joined his opinion—did not want to give up on the idea of proportionality *tout court*. At the same time, the opinion held out very little hope that the Court would be regularly reviewing sentences to see if they were "proportional" or not. Case in point was *Harmelin* itself. Harmelin was convicted of a nonviolent crime, namely drug possession. He was sentenced to life in prison without parole, the most severe sentence short of the death penalty. Kennedy, and the Justices joining his opinion, found no problem. The proportionality demanded by the Constitution was not one that should be applied to every case, to test whether the punishment "fit" the crime, along some measurement of "fit." It was to be applied only in select cases, where it was obvious that the punishment was "grossly" disproportionate, whatever that might mean.

Ever since *Harmelin*, the Court has gone down the path laid by Kennedy—not giving up on the idea of a proportionality constraint (Scalia never got the votes to overturn *Solem*), but not finding any examples of sentences of years in prison that were "grossly disproportionate" to the offense. So, Scalia may have lost the battle, but he won the war. Famously, many obviously disproportionate sentences—life in prison for stealing videotapes or golf clubs—have been upheld. To revert again to Murphy's helpful distinction, although this time in a different register: if legislatures want to make rules about which punishments are too much for a crime, they are free to—but the Court is not going to get in their way and second guess those legislative judgments. It is a policy question left to legislatures, not a question of principle that the Court will take up, even if asked to. The "rare" case of disproportionality seems to have pretty much resolved itself into a class of only one: namely, *Solem v. Helm*.

2.2 Decency

Compared to the now very limited role of proportionality in the Supreme Court's decisions on term-of-years sentences, the use of moral principle in the Court's death penalty cases seems practically florid. In assessing the death penalty in general, or as applied to certain offenses or certain offenders, the Court has looked to what it has termed "the evolving standards of decency that mark the progress of a maturing society" (*Trop v. Dulles*, 356 U.S. 86 [1958], 101). Although the standard was first invoked in a case that did not deal with the death penalty as a punishment, it has since been almost wholly confined to the use of that punishment, with one exception.[6] Nor is the Court's assessment of "evolving standards of decency" the only way that the Court has heavily relied on moral intuitions when it comes to the death penalty. The Court has said that the last word on the constitutionality of the

[6] Recently, the Supreme Court has applied its "evolving standards of decency" jurisprudence to juvenile life in prison without parole sentences.

death penalty depends on the Court's exercise of its own "independent judgment" about the appropriateness of the death penalty. That "last word" involves the Court's own *moral* assessment of whether the penalty can be justified by reference to traditional rationales for punishment, namely, retribution, deterrence, rehabilitation, and incapacitation. The Court seems more willing, especially as compared to its review of prison sentences, to intervene on grounds of moral principle when the punishment is death.

What, then, are evolving standards of decency that the Court has appealed to in deciding death penalty cases? It is hard to say. To a first approximation, it means a consensus of states as to the appropriateness of the death penalty. The "appropriateness" question typically runs along one of three dimensions: whether the death penalty is appropriate for this type of *crime* (rape, murder, etc.), whether the death penalty is appropriate for this type of *offender* (the intellectually disabled, juveniles), and whether a particular manner of imposing the death penalty is appropriate (electrocution, lethal injection, etc.). What the Court does, or at least *says* it does, is to survey what states are doing when a particular application of the death penalty is being challenged. If most states do not have the death penalty for, e.g., juveniles, then this is good *prima facie* evidence that the punishment is not considered to be "decent," as applied to that class of offenders. If we were seeking a textual hook for this surveying move, we could peg it to the idea of "unusualness." If few states have the death penalty for this crime, or for this offense, or in this way, or if the states that have the death penalty for those things rarely use it, or even if the *trend* is away from states having the death penalty for those things, this might show that the death penalty in those cases is "unusual" enough for it to run afoul of the Eighth Amendment.

But what of cruelty? This is where the Court seems to apply its own "independent judgment." A cruel punishment, according to the Court's precedents, is one that does not fulfill the *purpose* of punishment. A cruel punishment, in short, is one that serves no legitimate "penological purpose." Of course, this has to be somewhat exaggerated. A punishment that executes someone will guarantee that the person will not commit any future crimes—the incapacitation rationale for punishment thus will always seem to apply in death penalty cases (cf. Stinneford 2008, 1824). What seems to interest the Court most, however, is whether the death penalty is retributively appropriate and whether it deters *in a given case*. Thus it is very relevant for the Court and its independent evaluation of the death penalty whether, for example, a juvenile has the same culpability as an adult when they commit a crime, or would be deterred in the same way as an adult would. If the answers to these questions are "no," the case that executing a juvenile for the crime is "cruel" punishment is made that much stronger.

The moralistic approach the Court has taken to the death penalty has its limits, though. The Court seems reluctant to say that the death penalty *itself* may someday be unconstitutional—even if a majority of states stopped using it, and even if the Court found that it served no real penological purpose. This is because the text of the Constitution itself seems to allow it: the Fifth Amendment to the Constitution explicitly speaks about the deprivation of life, so long as it is done with adequate procedural protections. The Court has also been reluctant to find any particular method of execution unconstitutional, although a number of challenges have been made over the years. Indeed, the Court has said on more than one occasion that, because the death penalty is constitutional, there must be *some* constitutional way of applying it—a move that has puzzled many. Even so, the Court does not seem to be ready to abandon its relatively moralizing way of looking at the death penalty, both in assessing the "evolving standards of decency" among the states, or in using its own independent moral assessment of whether the death penalty serves a purpose when imposed in a certain way, or against certain groups of people for certain crimes. At the same time, we might predict—as with the evolution of the Court on proportionality—that the Supreme Court will probably have fewer occasions to pronounce the death penalty "cruel and unusual" in the coming years, as the composition of the Court now includes more Scalia-types who are skeptical of any importation of an "Enlightened" political morality into the Constitution.

3 Is Imprisonment Cruel and Unusual? Is Punishment?

3.1 The Morality of Imprisonment

Imprisonment is nowadays the default mode of punishment for those convicted of serious crimes.[7] People are sentenced to a jail term or to a prison term, and they spend their time mostly cut off from the outside world (this is even more so during the COVID-19 pandemic [Carroll 2020, 62]). What is more, the conditions in most prisons and jails are not very good—they are crowded, unsanitary, and there is often violence between inmates and other

[7] For lesser offenses, usually the sentence is probation—some form of community supervision—but with incarceration as a "backup" if probation conditions are violated.

inmates, and brutality from correctional officials. And we can add to this that sometimes inmates are put into not just confinement but *solitary* confinement, either as a result of prison design or because of disciplinary measures taken against the offender. In other words, prisons can be places where it is not just unpleasant to be, but positively degrading and inhumane. If we were to take Murphy's moralizing interpretation of "cruelty" in the Eighth Amendment, there seems no *prima facie* reason why imprisonment could not (in many cases, perhaps all) be an example of "cruel and unusual" punishment.

Moreover, although it is standard that people are incarcerated upon conviction of a criminal offense, this was not the norm at the Founding. Far from it. Prisons only came into widespread use after the period of the Founding. They were, if we take the Founding period as the baseline, "novel," and in that sense, unusual. In his reading of the cruel and unusual punishments clause, Stinneford raises the prospect that it is not just relatively recent technological changes in methods of punishment—for example, chemical castration—that might be unusual, but even the very existence of prison itself.[8] The fact that sentences of imprisonment are commonplace now does not cut against their novelty *then*. Even if we are Scalia-type originalists—indeed, especially if we are Scalia-type originalists—this may give us good reasons to consider the possibility that our now-usual mode of punishment may have been considered "cruel and unusual" at the Founding. This seems *a fortiori* the case if we add to the fact of imprisonment the many things that seem almost inevitably to accompany it, namely, violence within prison walls, unsanitary conditions, solitary confinement, the lack of transparency, even the sheer massiveness of it, and so on. All these things make imprisonment especially cruel and seem to make it uniquely cruel—that is, cruel in ways that other physical punishments could not be. The growth of "mass incarceration" may also be the growth in cruel and unusual punishment. This may seem strange only if we take our present mode of punishing people (putting them in prison) as somehow natural or inevitable.

---

[8] It is worth quoting Stinneford at length in this regard:

> In the eighteenth century, crimes were typically punished with fines, corporal punishment, public humiliation, banishment, or execution. Imprisonment was rarely used and sentences of more than a few years were almost never imposed. Moreover, the modern prison, in which prisoners are completely segregated from society and sometimes subjected to coercive "treatment" for their criminogenic characteristics, was not born until 1790 and did not achieve anything like its current form until the end of the nineteenth century. (2008, 1818)

In the first few arresting chapters of his *Discipline and Punish* (1977), Michel Foucault juxtaposed extreme physical punishments and the regimented, deadening experience of being incarcerated in a Benthamite prison. Part of Foucault's point, I take it, is that there could be many varieties of cruelty, and the fact that we seem to have gotten rid of one type of cruelty does not mean that we cannot invent other, perhaps even more insidious ways of harming people. The implications of Foucault's comparison can be taken too far, of course. There are ways we can make prisons more humane, and Foucault should not be taken (or at least I do not take him) as pining for a return to the days when punishment, while awful and bloody, was at least open to the public and gave the accused a chance at some sort of sympathy or even vindication. Foucault presses us to think about whether *even in the ideal case* prison can be a sort of cruelty toward the offender. Imprisonment, no less than flogging or boiling in oil or other punishments, may be a kind of torture. The contemporary abolitionist rhetoric of calling imprisonment "caging" serves to call attention to this fact: caging humans like animals seems to be a degrading and cruel thing to do to them.

Far from considering the possibility that imprisonment might be *intrinsically* cruel, contemporary courts have been reluctant even to find prisons with objectively harmful conditions to violate the Eighth Amendment.[9] Part of this has to do with the emerging doctrine that conditions that are not *intended* to be punitive cannot, as an analytical matter, count as punishment, so they cannot count as "cruel and unusual *punishment*." If one happens to get sick from a fellow inmate, even when this is based on a lack of adequate medical care or poor hygiene in the prison, this might be a bad thing that has happened to you (and may entitle you to monetary compensation or some other remedy), but it is not part of your sentence, hence not part of your punishment. Behind this analytical point also seems to be a moral one: prisons are not supposed to be comfortable, and in the absence of proof that prison officials are willfully or even deliberately ignoring your suffering, prisons—however horrible—will not be judged to be "cruel and unusual punishment." In a way, the ongoing crisis in America's prisons may prove almost the obverse of Murphy's point that it would be wrong if something becoming *usual* could make it immune to challenge under the Eighth Amendment: if something becomes usual enough, we cease to regard it as especially cruel.

---

[9] *Brown v. Plata* (563 U.S. 493 [2011]), in which the Supreme Court found the overcrowding in California prisons to violate the Eighth Amendment, is a major recent exception to this trend.

3.2 The Morality of Punishment

If we are to look at the cruelty of imprisonment—again, the default way modern society punishes people—this may cause us to wonder about going up a further level and asking: could it be the case that *punishing people at all* is cruel and unusual, no matter the method? What would it mean to analyze the very fact of punishment in this light? It would, certainly, be a hard thing to argue that punishment could be cruel and unusual under the Eighth Amendment. The syntax of the phrase does not seem to allow it: if only cruel and unusual punishments are prohibited, then there must be some set of punishments that are not cruel and unusual. But is this an inevitable result? We could imagine a society in which the only punishments authorized by the law required a sort of torture. In that society, the set of cruel and unusual punishments would be coextensive with the set of all possible punishments. In that case, and in that society, all punishments would be (unconstitutionally) cruel and unusual always and all the time.

But this is still not quite the question I want to ask. The society in which all legally authorized punishments involve torture, and for which all punishment is cruel and unusual, is not yet the same as saying that *punishment as such* could be ruled to be cruel and unusual. Again, what would it mean to hold something like that? Consider again the Supreme Court's use of its own "independent moral judgment" in assessing the constitutionality of the death penalty. When assessing whether, for example, the death penalty for juveniles is cruel and unusual, it tends to look at whether certain goals or purposes of punishment are advanced by the death penalty. In a seminal case, *Roper v. Simmons* (543 U.S. 551 [2005]), the Court said that neither retributive justice nor deterrence were advanced by executing juveniles for crimes. The death penalty was not retributive for juveniles because juveniles were not as fully culpable as adults for their crimes—the punishment of death was just too much. Nor is it the case that juveniles would be all that deterred by the death penalty: because of their lack of development, juveniles do not respond to punishment incentives in the same way as adults do. Could we analyze punishment *as such* in a similar way—so that the justifications for punishment somehow come apart from the institution of punishment?

It is a striking fact about criminal punishments that, apart from the Eighth Amendment, there is no real constraint on what the state can criminalize and, therefore, what it can punish. Punishing people by putting them in prison, for example, deprives people of their liberty, but there is no requirement that the state actually show it has a compelling interest in depriving people of their liberty—it does not have to show that its retributive interest is served, or that incarceration reduces crime rather than increasing it. The power of the state to punish *in general* is given a pass, however much it might be challenged in particular instances. And those challenges tend to be *ex post* rather than *ex ante*. That is, the state gets to punish first, and questions about the propriety of that punishment get asked later, if they get asked at all. Again, this is as a general matter; there will of course be some cases in which a criminal law will be challenged, and challenged successfully. A law that punished people for exercising their right to free speech, for example, would be struck down, unless the government could show that there is a compelling interest in having that law and there is no other less restrictive means for achieving that end. But this exception proves the general rule for criminal laws. The state does not have the burden to show, for example, that arresting people and imprisoning them for possessing drugs serves a compelling interest (Karakatsanis 2019, 866).

But maybe it is not that the state has *no* burden to show a compelling interest in punishment, but rather that the burden is presumed to be met in most cases. Is this a fair presumption? Challenging the very idea of punishment as cruel and unusual would be to show that, in fact, punishment does not serve any rational purpose. This may not be as hard as it actually sounds, at least in theory and at least in regard to some penological purposes. Suppose there was very good evidence (as there seems to be at least some evidence) that incarcerating people does not reduce crime but for various reasons increases it. This would show that the state's pursuit of punishment to deter would be irrational. The case against the retributive purpose is harder, mainly because the meaning of retribution is so hard to discern. Is retribution a matter of making the offender suffer? Of expressing the community's condemnation? Or bringing back a balance of benefits and burdens that the crime has placed out of whack? Rather than trying to show that punishment is not retributive—it could be, given the multiple meanings of retribution—we may be better off trying to suggest that retribution as such is not a valid penological purpose for a liberal state (Flanders 2016). Still, as noted before, even if we were to kick out deterrence and retribution, we would still have the fact that punishment (certainly in the form of imprisonment) does incapacitate the offender, and this is a legitimate goal for the state to pursue.

This is not nothing, and it may at least give us a stronger proportionality principle and a way to apply it. The great philosopher and penologist *avant la lettre* Cesare Beccaria famously said that any punishment that is greater than necessary to serve the good of public safety is "tyrannical" and unjustified (2008, 11). That "extra" punishment is what is cruel. To suggest such a

Beccarian principle would be to push back against the Supreme Court's rejection of the idea that proportionality could ever do real work in evaluating the constitutionality of sentences. But the idea of proportionality that the Court rejected looked at matching the offender and the punishment. More purchase might be had if we instead looked at the match between punishment and the goal of public safety—something still hard to measure, but not as hopelessly indeterminate as the idea of punitive desert. Such a limited focus on the goal of punishment as harm reduction moves it closer to the aims of the present-day abolitionist movement. Any "surplus" punishment, in excess of what is necessary for harm reduction, is cruel.

4 Conclusion

"Cruel and unusual" may seem to be of limited use as a moral principle. As noted in the introduction to this chapter, it seems to have one word too many. If a punishment is cruel, presumably that punishment is bad and should be stopped, even if it happens to be all too usual. Further, as a provision of a legal document (the U.S. Constitution), "cruel and unusual" comes with the baggage of years and years of Supreme Court and lower court cases, many of dubious soundness and consistency. It is not easy to wrench those words out of that historical and jurisprudential context, especially the Court's almost suffocating focus (bordering on obsession) on whether only the death penalty is cruel and unusual. But these limitations also have their advantages. The fact that the words do form part of a binding, and in the U.S. at least, supreme legal document gives them more bite and application than do abstract moral principles found only in philosophy texts. And even the addition of the word "unusual" may have its uses as well. It demands of us that we pick out and explain not just when the government does something cruel to those who punish it, but when that cruelty rises to a level of peculiarity, of uniqueness, so that it becomes something we cannot—and should not—ignore. In this way, we might see the phrase "cruel and unusual" as having a valence quite apart from its inclusion in the American Constitution—as giving us a new, hybrid concept, that of *unusual* cruelty, that may present itself as its own moral standard (Bray 2016).[10]

[10] My thanks to Vincent Chiao, Adam Kolber, and Danny Priel for comments on a previous draft.

References

Beccaria, Cesare. 2008. *On Crimes and Punishments and Other Writings*. Translated by Aaron Thomas and Jeremy Parzen. Edited by Aaron Thomas. Toronto: University of Toronto Press.

Bray, Samuel L. 2016. "'Necessary and Proper' and 'Cruel and Unusual': Hendiadys in the Constitution." *Virginia Law Review* 102, no. 3 (May): 687–764.

Carroll, Jenny E. 2020. "Pretrial Detention in the Time of COVID-19." *Northwestern University Law Review Online* 115: 59–87.

Dworkin, Ronald. 1997. "Comment." In *A Matter of Interpretation: Federal Courts and the Law*, by Antonin Scalia, edited by Amy Gutmann, 115–28. Princeton, NJ: Princeton University Press.

Flanders, Chad. 2016. "Time, Death, and Retribution." *University of Pennsylvania Journal of Constitutional Law* 19, no. 2: 431–84.

Foucault, Michel. 1977. *Discipline and Punish: The Birth of the Prison*. Translated by Alan Sheridan. New York: Vintage.

Hershenov, David B. 2002. "Why Must Punishment Be Unusual as Well as Cruel to Be Unconstitutional?" *Public Affairs Quarterly* 16, no. 1 (January): 77–98.

Karakatsanis, Alec. 2019. "The Punishment Bureaucracy: How to Think about 'Criminal Justice Reform.'" *Yale Law Journal Forum* 128: 848–935.

Murphy, Jeffrie G. 1979. *Retribution, Justice, and Therapy: Essays in the Philosophy of Law*. Dordrecht: Reidel.

Scalia, Antonin. 1997. "Response to Dworkin." In *A Matter of Interpretation: Federal Courts and the Law*, by Antonin Scalia, edited by Amy Gutmann, 144–49. Princeton, NJ: Princeton University Press.

Stinneford, John F. 2008. "The Original Meaning of 'Unusual': The Eighth Amendment as a Bar to Cruel Innovation." *Northwestern University Law Review* 102, no. 4 (Fall): 1739–1825.

———. 2017. "The Original Meaning of 'Cruel.'" *Georgetown Law Journal* 105: 441–506.

Väyrynen, Pekka, 2021. "Thick Ethical Concepts." *Stanford Encyclopedia of Philosophy* (Spring 2021 edition), edited by Edward N. Zalta. https://plato.stanford.edu/archives/spr2021/entries/thick-ethical-concepts/.

Index[1]

[1] Note: Page numbers followed by 'n' refer to notes.

© The Author(s), under exclusive license to Springer Nature Switzerland AG 2023
M. C. Altman (ed.), *The Palgrave Handbook on the Philosophy of Punishment*, Palgrave Handbooks in the Philosophy of Law, https://doi.org/10.1007/978-3-031-11874-6

Printed by Printforce, the Netherlands